2017 Football Preview

By: Warren Sharp

SharpFootballAnalysis.com
SharpFootballStats.com

sharp@sharpfootballanalysis.com
@SharpFootball

Written & printed in the USA

DEDICATION

TO the mute community with any variant of muteness. Whether caused by injury, autism, hearing loss, speech disorder, surgery or anything else. I gained a stronger appreciation for the gift of speech due to being without it the entire month of June (thus far) as a result of carbon monoxide exposure. I cannot imagine being permanently without the ability to speak. For those that cannot speak, I know it is amazingly difficult. For those who can speak, it's one of the basic things we take for granted daily. Be thankful. And be patient and extra kind to those who cannot

TO my Grandfather, who left us in November of 2016 - a WWII veteran and farmer, who taught me about sacrificing for others and love for family. He was as genuine a person as you could meet. I was proud to be his grandson. I loved asking him about stories of his era and he was great at telling them. He always told me "don't take any wooden nickels", so on his account, I am suspending acceptance of wooden nickels as payment for this 2017 Preview and for all future publications. I love and miss you, Pappy. I'll see you again, my friend

TO my Grandmother, who left us in September of 2016 – a mother of 5 who encouraged love, discipline and Faith in my life. Up early each morning and literally swimming laps around the other men and women of her retirement home, she taught me commitment, competitiveness and dedication. But also to enjoy and live life passionately and to laugh abundantly. She loved sports and could talk your ear off about her favorite teams. I love and miss you too, Nan. I know you're making a ton of new friends and entertaining everyone up there - we'll talk sports when I see you again

TO the decision makers in NFL front offices who exhaust every means to gain an edge because they care about winning – even when it means incorporating input from outsiders like me, armed with analytics, models and intelligence to make sound suggestions. And to the others who will inevitably will follow in their footsteps

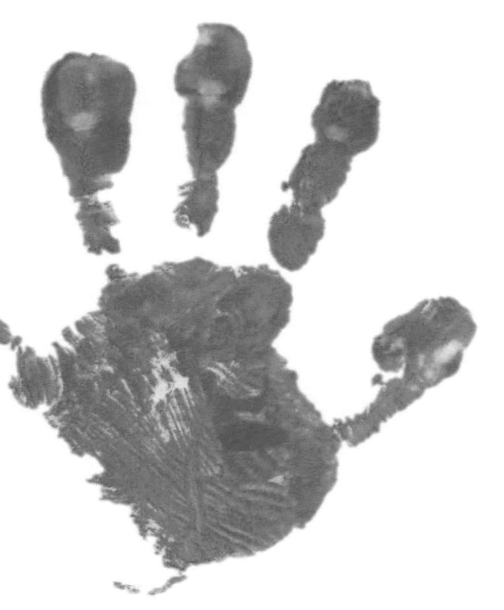

TO the good guys who daily fight in the real fights around the world to keep us free – our troops and those who support them

TO anyone who spreads the word about this book, my websites and my passion for analyzing football

TO my wife & children, who have dealt with a mute husband and father for the past month. While daddy doesn't leave his office much and works until 2am most every night, at least you know where to find me at virtually all times. I love football, but I love you guys more and all of this hard work is for you. What I've done this year for this book has been exceedingly challenging and time consuming. Thank you for your patience and understanding

THIS IS FOR YOU !!

FORWARD

COLUMNS

TEAM CHAPTERS

** Note: Ravens chapter does not factor in Jeremy Maclin, Titans chapter does not factor in Eric Decker*

Artwork courtesy of my children (and wife at end of the book). Logo designs courtesy of Addison Foote of addisonfoote.com

Irony

Irony. Look it up in the Merriam-Webster dictionary and the definition isn't even the casual definition most of us are accustomed to. We know irony when we see it. It's ironic that the definition of irony isn't well defined. It's ironic that Alanis Morissette's "Ironic" better defined irony than Merriam-Webster. It's a free ride when you've already paid.

For anyone who has ever heard me on my podcast, on my countless radio appearances or TV appearances, hearing me not talk passionately about football would be ironic, considering how passionate I am and how much I enjoy discussing it. I can't tell you the number of times during the season I'm up an on the phone for hours between the hours of midnight and 3am talking football with everyone from Evan Silva to Bill Krackomberger to other industry associates. There is very little small talk, at that hour, it's all about breaking games down. And we'll do it for hours.

I'm a licensed Professional Engineer. I'm one chain-link away from being a perfectionist. But I'm certainly an anal numbers cruncher, who focuses on detail and data and loves digesting it, processing it, and then sharing it for others to understand more directly. But a great word to describe me would be verbose. Merriam-Webster hits that definition right on the head: "given to wordiness." I might spend 2 hours researching something I can explain quite well in 10 minutes. I think that's a substantial time savings, because of how valuable an insight I've uncovered. The problem is, I need to compress those 10 minutes into 3 minutes. And that's where my verbosity (it's a word) becomes a detriment.

So it would be really ironic for someone like myself to not just be unable to talk passionately about football, but not talk at all. I don't mean "hey I can't talk now, I'm about to step into a meeting." I mean the literal definition of talk: "to express or exchange ideas by means of spoken words. To use speech." But that's exactly where I found myself almost 4 weeks ago. I opened my mouth to speak and no words would come out. Literally. I won't detail the saga too epically, even though it was certainly epic. The anal engineer inside of me wrote a 25-page report on the cause, replete with schematic diagrams and labeled photos. That was epic. But I can explain it in just a few sentences:

This book played a role, but was not the cause. The cause was a prior homeowner cutting corners and tapping into the gas hot water heater exhaust line with a line running to a bathroom fan. They tried to save money by not properly running an independent line. The inspector didn't catch them. The HVAC company who installed a brand new high-efficiency hot water heater with a high-powered blower fan didn't test to ensure that 100% of the lethal carbon monoxide and other toxic products of natural gas combustion safely left the house.

I'm lucky my wife and kids, whose artwork you'll see scattered about this preview, didn't die. I'm lucky that the exhaust, which was pouring into our basement bathroom and into the wall above the desk of my home office, didn't kill me. This book played a role, in that I've been working on it 7 days a week for several months now. And when I say "working", that doesn't mean 9-5. That means until 2 and 3am nightly. I spent a considerable amount of time near these fumes, which ultimately caused extreme swelling of my vocal chords and throat. And when your vocal cords are that swollen, you can try to talk, but not even a whisper comes out.

Here I am, trying to finish this book and record the embedded audio and video, and schedule podcast and radio appearances from a number of people who want me to discuss my findings, and I can't even talk. That's ironic. The unfortunate thing about irony is things are ironic when they happen to someone else. When they happen to you, it's beyond a pain in the ass. It's beyond highly annoying. But such is life. Life is how you live it. Are you going to look for excuses to give up or are you going to overcome obstacles and make the best out of things? With me losing my voice, I'm reminded of a quote from the movie Fight Club: "It's only after we've lost everything that we're free to do anything." Powerful. Then I'm reminded of a quote from that same movie: "This is your life, and it's ending one minute at a time."

Apart from my family, both immediate and extended, and my Faith, there is nothing I love more than football. It's difficult to explain the origin of that passion. But I view the game as a type of equation, is the best way to describe it. The line of scrimmage is the "=" sign and both teams are trying to be greater than their opponent. As any good mathematician knows, there is one right answer, but a number of ways to arrive at that answer. The problem is, most teams never arrive at the right answer. Whether in a particular game, or in the way they strategize or construct themselves. When some teams arrive there, they do so via a circuitous route. Or they simply "get lucky".

I hate inefficiency. My sin of verbosity flies in the face of that statement, but just like I can work to improve that personal weakness, teams must figure out a way to improve on their inefficiency. It's a pervasive problem. Even the smartest aren't immune from it. Obi-Wan Kenobi introduced us to the Force in 1977, and described it saying "It surrounds us and penetrates us; it binds the galaxy together." I feel inefficiency is the one thing that binds all 32 teams together.

The difference with the great teams is their approach. To solve the problem, they first fight extremely hard to understand the problem. As Sun Tzu stated in "Attack by Stratagem" from The Art of War, "If you know the enemy and know yourself, you need not fear the result of a hundred battles. If you know yourself but not the enemy, for every victory gained you will also suffer a defeat. If you know neither the enemy nor yourself, you will succumb in every battle." Step one is to understand the problem. Teams should then determine how do they measure up to the problem. Do they need to fix anything? Are they built to take advantage of the rule or the opponent? And they attack that inefficiency internally with such a vigor that it can, at times, become a strength. And then there is the final element – understanding their opponent, where they are susceptible and inefficiency, and how to properly match up to exploit that enemy.

Far too often, teams choose to focus on what they think are the important things, like teaching their players the scheme and evaluating talent on their roster to see who will make the final roster or practice squad. The reality is, those elements are no more important than understanding efficiency and allowing it to help produce results on the field. They go hand in hand. But as Sun Tzu states: "A skilled commander seeks victory from the situation and does not demand it of his subordinates." Another translation reads "The expert in battle seeks his victory from strategic advantage and does not demand it from his men." There is a reason why, throughout history, with equivalent weaponry, undermanned armies could dispatch larger armies. Strategy and planning. It's easy to overlook and get stuck in the details. Much like the cause of my present muteness, if any one person responsible for the issue had done what they were supposed to do, I'm speaking right now. If the homeowner installed the fan properly, if the inspector ensured the work was safe, or if the HVAC company tested the unit before leaving, I'm speaking right now. They all didn't have to do their job. But they all couldn't sequentially fail. All it takes is for someone internal to a team to speak up about a perceived inefficiency, support it with data and logic, and perhaps addressing and fixing that issue turns a loss into a win.

Ironically, if every team operated at optimal efficiency at all times, there wouldn't be much for me to comment on. The on-field product would be a masterful display, but the only commentary would relate to extraordinary performance, mistakes, odd bounces or fatigue. Reading that last sentence again, I wonder if it sinks in with you as it does with me that what we hear every Sunday from the commentary relates almost exclusively to those items. There is shockingly little discussion about strategy, game planning, adjustments, coaching and play calling.

This preview is as much of a defense of my thesis on efficiency as it is a 2017 preview. If you read it closely, you'll see the subtle or not so subtle findings and recommendations. My goal is to pass on everything I learned in my 5+ months of work on this preview. I started in late February. In another case of irony, I've spent more days (and nights) working on this preview of the 2017 NFL season than actually exist in the 2017 NFL season. It's been a labor of love. And now, for the final layer of irony. I created this preview in its entirety by myself, save for the Writing Contest winner's article. For all this work to create this Preview – the hours, days, nights, weeks, and months – I take home one dollar per copy. As the page count increased (last year's was 150 pages) I refused to hike up the list price and just allowed it to suck up the profits. That's the type of irony which is irony to you, but hurts me much more. So here is my plea to you, the reader: if you enjoyed this, found it useful, helpful or dare I say innovative, please share that feedback. Tweet about it, encourage others to check it out & write a positive review on Amazon. And, please purchase an electronic PDF from SharpFootballAnalysis.com, where I see 97% of the those receipts.

www.sharp football analysis.com

The Forefront of Inventing & Incorporating Custom Advanced Analytics & Metrics into Football Handicapping

Lifetime NFL Record
Totals: 455-297 (61%)
Sides (Personal Plays): 549-406 (57%)

Lifetime NFL Playoffs Record: 123-70 (64%)
Lifetime Super Bowl Record: 16-7 (70%)

Lifetime College Football Record
Totals: 647-527 (55%)

Transparent Record Keeping
All client plays publicly displayed minutes after the start of the game

NFL's Most Consistent Results
11 Years, 11 Winning Seasons
Emphasizing sound money management, +EV betting opportunities & beating the market

2016-17 Results:
NFL Totals: 28-14 (67%)
NFL ALL: 69-51 (58%)
CFB Totals: 35-29 (55%)

2015-16 Results:
NFL Totals: 34-13 (72%)
NFL ALL: 76-49 (61%)
CFB Totals: 56-40 (58%)

Respected Analysis
Numerous betting syndicates acquire recommendations & Warren's work is well known by current and former linemakers

Line Value
Using timed release system, when Warren releases a play to clients, the market reacts giving clients consistent, significant & measurable line value

"I noticed Warren was moving some lines around on Wednesdays after he put his stuff up on his site, and he was winning. Instantly, when Warren gives out his play, the books move toward his line. Very rarely will you get a better number than his. He's a consistent winner."

- Professional Bettor & Las Vegas Legend
Bill "Krackman" Krackomberger

Warren Sharp of sharpfootballanalysis.com is an industry pioneer at the forefront of incorporating advanced analytics and metrics into football handicapping after spending years constructing, testing, betting and perfecting computer models written to beat NFL and college football totals.

As currently seen in:

Hear Pro Bettor
Bill "Krackman" Krackomberger:

"Warren's synopsis on game totals is vastly superior utilizing his mathematical formulas, to any preview I have ever seen. His success is two-fold, beating the closing number by up to 3 pts and winning at a clip needed to secure a hefty profit. Getting in early ensures some fantastic middling opportunities."

- **Richie Baccellieri**, former Director of Race and Sports in Las Vegas at Caesars Palace, MGM Grand and The Palms

A licensed Professional Engineer by trade, Warren now works as a quantitative analyst for multiple professional sports betting syndicates in Las Vegas and has parlayed a long-term winning record into selections for clients which move the Vegas line and beat the closing number with regularity.

Pay NOTHING until AFTER the season:
Get all the detailed weekly analysis, write-ups and recommendations now, pay only after the 2017 season! Details at www . sharp football analysis . com

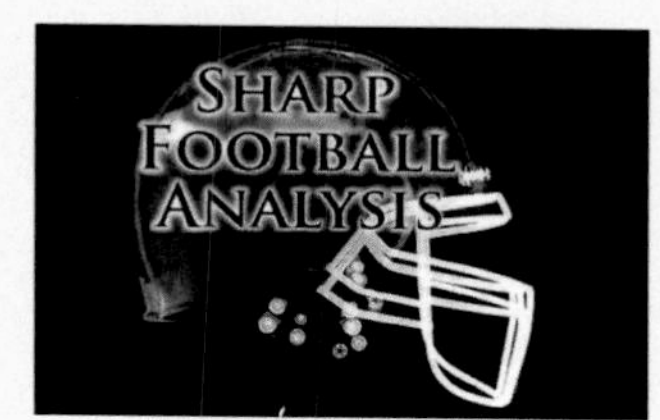

QR Code Audio and Video

One of my favorite things to do is to share as much educational information as possible. Unfortunately, every printed page in this book comes with a cost. But embedded audio is free. To quote an exchange tremendous movie about enlightenment "There is no money." "Really?" "Free to all." "Ain't that something?" "It is, actually." So here we are, with all of this free audio… but without my voice. If you read the forward, you know I lost my voice. Gone for going on four weeks as I type this. Read the Forward to learn more. At any rate, I'm not letting that stop me from providing more, free content. So as opposed to skipping the audio entirely, which I contemplated, I decided to do this: postpone the audio. I'll update the first set of division QR codes July 24th, right before training camp starts. And I'll update the August 29th links right after the 3rd preseason game. You'll get even more bang for your (free) buck this way because I'll give additional thoughts, based on what we know at those times. I'm partial to the "QR Scanner" app because it's ad-free, but download any QR Reader/Scanner app and get check back in late July & August! (Contingent upon my voice returning, of course!)

AFC North
Scan on
July 24th

AFC North
Scan on
Aug 29th

NFC North
Scan on
July 24th

NFC North
Scan on
Aug 29th

AFC East
Scan on
July 24th

AFC East
Scan on
Aug 29th

NFC East
Scan on
July 24th

NFC East
Scan on
Aug 29th

AFC South
Scan on
July 24th

AFC South
Scan on
Aug 29th

NFC South
Scan on
July 24th

NFC South
Scan on
Aug 29th

AFC West
Scan on
July 24th

AFC West
Scan on
Aug 29th

NFC West
Scan on
July 24th

NFC West
Scan on
Aug 29th

Front Office Plea: Increase Efficiency!

By Warren Sharp

I watch every NFL game. I'm not saying I watch NFL all day, every Sunday. I'm talking every, single snap of every, single game. There is a reason you won't often catch me on social media during the 1pm games. It's because I'm working, and my work involves watching every play of every game. Fortunately, I have the media setup and capability, as well as the focus to be able to do that. While that likely puts me in the minority of the total population, I know among my peers and many serious fantasy players and sports bettors, that's far from unique. However, there are distinct differences between me and the rest of the minority who watches every snap of every game as its played. I'm not rooting for a team. I'm not rooting for a fantasy player. That's not why I watch. So while those with Rob Gronkowski on their fantasy team will watch the Patriots offense and maybe tune out the Patriots defense while focusing on another offense on a different channel, I watch every snap, every game, all of the time.

The reason I watch so intently is because I want to see if what I thought would happen does happen. I want to see what decisions the coach makes, I want to see the amount of pressure the quarterback is receiving, I want to see which line is controlling the line of scrimmage, I want to see what points are scored and whether they should have been scored or not. I watch to see if there are any in-game betting edges to be had from a statistical and injury perspective. I get highly critical as I watch games. Because I work for hours every week on a single game, as I attempt to predict its outcome. I study and anticipate player matchups, offensive and defensive edges, game flow and decision making. I get to know the team, its tendencies and what it will do to attack its opponent, inside and out. I am so anal about this because I choose to bet on these games. I don't bet compulsively or habitually. I only jump on games where I see edges in the line. Where the linemakers made mistakes. And at the risk of sounding pompous, I am quite accurate with my predictions. For years, the end results have been among the best in the industry. There isn't another service out there more accurate forecasting NFL totals. But even forgetting results - and the sometimes fickle bounces of the ball - and thinking only of the matchups, angles each team will try to attack and exploit – my pre-game predictions about what I think will happen and why are batting a damn good rate.

With that said, by caring so much for predictions and for playing games out ahead of time, with what teams *should* do and then seeing what they do, I do get bent out of shape when I see inefficiency. When I see teams making terrible decisions, it bothers me. There is nothing I enjoy more than watching two teams go after each other efficiently. Each team is built differently so each team may not literally be mirroring one another's moves, but if they are being as efficient as they can be, then we get to watch beautiful football. The problem is, that's rare. More often, we see Bill Belichick completely outcoach one of his less intellectually superior opponents. Or we see two coaches make bad decisions which seemingly offset one another, as they race to see who can lose the game first.

I have tons of ideas on paper, on my computer, in my head. I'll share a few right now. Ideas for all teams to improve efficiency. Pretty much across the entire league, these items are based on the modern game and would improve efficiency leaguewide. Some teams might make more hay out of certain concepts or ideas than others. The reality is, these are the tip of the iceberg. I'm not spilling everything here, in this 2017 Preview. But as a fan watching football, even if you only watch a handful of games a week, you'd be watching a far better product if teams implemented these ideas more often. If teams started to pick up on these ideas, we'd see far better competitive balance, because the worst teams would get helped the most and the best teams are incorporating more of these already. And watching games would literally be a better experience. Of course we'd be dumbfounded by mistakes and stupid interceptions or costly turnovers. And we'd be wowed by great catches and awesome, explosive plays. But the product itself would be more easily viewed and digested because it would make more sense and would produce better efficiency for both teams. Many of these items below seem extremely obvious, but surprisingly teams do not do them enough, with a lot of these suggestions falling in the minority. And in many of these examples, I will cite from Sun Tzu "The Art of War" (SUN-TZU, & GRIFFITH, S. B. (1964). The art of war. Oxford, Clarendon Press.).

The reasons for understanding and improving the usage of these points are straightforward, but as Suz Tzu states: *"the good fighter is able to secure himself against defeat, but cannot make certain of defeating the enemy. Hence the saying: One may KNOW how to conquer without being able to DO it. Security against defeat implies defensive tactics; ability to defeat the enemy means taking the offensive. Standing on the defensive indicates insufficient strength; attacking, a superabundance of strength.... In war the victorious strategist only seeks battle after the victory has been won, whereas he who is destined to defeat first fights and afterwards looks for victory."* Teams must figure out how to improve their offensive efficiency, and they must incorporate these strategies now, in the offseason and in weekly preparation in order to win before the game. Playing the game while trying to figure out how to win is the path to defeat. Hopefully more teams will incorporate these strategies in the future:

Pass frequently against great run defenses

Far too often, teams try to "do what we do" as opposed to game plan to their opponent's weakness. Citing to Sun Tzu's The Art of War *"It is said that if you know your enemies and know yourself, you will not be imperiled in a hundred battles; if you do not know your enemies but do know yourself, you will win one and lose one; if you do not know your enemies nor yourself, you will be imperiled in every single battle."* Far too many teams fall into that second category - they know themselves but don't know their opponents well enough.

Even efficient run teams, but especially inefficient ones, should not attack at an opponent's strength. Once more, Sun Tzu's strategy makes too much sense: *"Military tactics are like unto water; for water in its natural course runs away from high places and hastens downwards. So in war, the way is to avoid what is strong and to strike at what is weak... He who can modify his tactics in relation to his opponent and thereby succeed in winning, may be called a heaven-born captain."*

An example of a team who understands this is (unsurprisingly) the Patriots. For years, the Patriots have employed a strategy against strong run teams. Surprisingly, while I've been discussing this for years, it is not well known or at least I haven't seen it broken by numbers. Against opponents with great run defenses allowing less than 3.4 yards per carry as established through at least week 8, the Patriots don't go pass heavy. When comparing pass attempts to RB runs, it's not even close: The Patriots go 73% pass in the first half and 72% pass overall. This despite the fact that they are 5-1 in these games the past 3 seasons. In 2014 and earlier, they went a bit more pass heavy from the start, such as 77%-82% pass in the first half. To see that in numbers, they are 27 first half passes to 6 first half rushes. It's that significant a margin. More recently, they've been a bit more balanced at times to start games, in the 67% pass range. But when one or two series with a bit more balance doesn't work, they just go pass heavy the rest of the way through.

What teams should take from this is, feel free to test your opponent on the first series or two. Even if you're a run heavy team with a solid run game and you want to see if you'll have success. That's fine. But when it doesn't work, forget balance. Balance means first down carries of 1 yard that immediately put a team behind schedule. The bottom line is, if you can't stay on schedule running the ball against a strong run defense, abort the pass and simply go pass heavy. Again, from Sun Tzu: "He who knows when he can fight and when he cannot will be victorious."

Pass on first down, especially with a young quarterback

This may seem counterintuitive at first, because of the archaic saying "establish the run". But the reality is, first down passes are more successful (53%) than first down runs (46%). And if you remove all those short yardage 1st down opportunities in the red zone, the situation is even more clear: First down passes average nearly 10% more success (54% vs 45%) and nearly 3 more yards per play (7.3 vs 4.4).

Far too often, teams get too predictable and conservative on first down early in games and it's a disaster. Look at the Buccaneers last year. They were the #1 most fun heavy team on first down in the first half, calling run plays 59% of the time (9% above average). They recorded a 39% success rate on their runs (31st) and averaged just 3.4 yards per carry. While their first down passing wasn't ideal, it still averaged a 43% success rate and 5.7 yards per attempt. This set them up with 2nd and much shorter. But that is just one example. Take the Miami Dolphins for a much more obvious edge:

Miami ran 57% of the time on first down in the first half, the 3rd most often. Only 46% of those runs were successful, for an average of 4.2 yards per carry. Meanwhile, 55% of their passes were successful, for an average of 6.8 yards per attempt. And outside the red zone, those numbers were even more dramatic. Rushing: 44% success rate (4.3 ypc). Passing: 56% success rate (7.0 ypa).

There is no down easier to pass on for a quarterback, especially a young one, than first down. Take a look at the data, focusing on the first half, for passing success rate (and ypa) by down. First down: 53% success, 7.0 ypa. Second down: 47% success, 6,4 ypa. Third down: 38% success, 5.8 ypa. This data is clear.

What is also clear is that first half runs on first down (46% success, 4.4 ypc) are much less efficient than runs on third down (57% success, 5.0 ypc). And why is that? The same reason why passes on first down are more efficient. You can always pass the ball on 3rd and anything. Most teams won't run the ball unless they are close to the yard to gain. [It's amazing to see how few teams have any confidence in the run anymore. On 3rd and 1, the average was 71% run. On 3rd and 2, it was 31% run. On 3rd and 3, it was just 16% run.] But when they do run, they are extremely successful (even on 3rd and 3, 4 or 5 yards to go, the success rate of 64% dwarfs that of pass success rate of 46%) . So the goal is to always stay on schedule, so you can both run or pass on any down.

As Sun Tzu shows: *"Appear at points which the enemy must hasten to defend; march swiftly to places where you are not expected... You can be sure of succeeding in your attacks if you only attack places which are undefended."*

Don't run on first down in the first half to "establish the run". Pass instead to gain more yardage and see more success, and by doing so you put yourself in 2nd and shorter which leads to a first down or a third and short. As opposed to the run first team on first down, which is faced with third and long and has no choice but to throw. Don't "establish the run". Instead, "establish the lead" by passing early, running late and staying on or ahead of schedule every down possible.

Run on 2nd and short, with tempo

Often you will hear announcers suggest that "this is the perfect time for a shot play". They most often say that on 2nd and short. At issue is the deliberation between efficiency and potency. Because while a 2nd and short run play isn't likely to produce the TD potential as a shot play might, a failed shot play sets up 3rd and short, with the opportunity for the defense to substitute in their short yardage package, presuming the pass was not intercepted.

Of any down or distance, the easiest down/distance to convert into a first down is 2nd and short. And it is significantly easier to convert when running the football as opposed to passing. All too often, teams do not understand the importance of efficiency on this particular down and distance, and waste opportunity. A huge 70% of all 2nd and short run plays gain first downs. Also, importantly only 0.7% result in a turnover. Meanwhile, only 52% of pass plays gain first downs, and a whopping 3.4% resulted in turnovers while and 2.5% result in sacks.

Referring back to Sun Tzu: *"Making no mistakes is what establishes the certainty of victory, for it means conquering an enemy that is already defeated."* NFL teams know how badly turnovers affect wins and losses. Yet far too often, they are hesitant to run the ball on 2nd and short to obtain what is a slam dunk first down, and instead favor a shot play with a low hit rate and a substantial turnover rate. There is a reason even a tremendous passing offense like the Patriots called 76% run plays on 2nd and short last year. Looking at standard down situations (1st and 10, 2nd and any measure of 10 or less, 3rd and any measure of 10 or less), the only down situation which saw a higher turnover rate than 2nd and 1-2 yards to go was 3rd and 10. That's it. All other down and distance situation (9 in total) featured a lower turnover rate.

The conversion rate on runs would be increased even more if teams simply employed tempo and cadence in auto-no-huddle situations on 2nd and short. An 8-9 yard gain and the offense runs to the line of scrimmage, keeps the 1st down package on the field (ideally one which has at least 3 pass catchers including tight ends), deploys in a spread set and runs one of a handful of variants, giving the quarterback full autonomy to audible to whatever run play (including keeping the ball) will work best, as well as utilize cadence to draw the defense offsides or do the opposite and "go" on first sound.

Throw more passes to tight ends

The NFL game has changed. For years it was about running the ball and #1 WRs. Teams still use 11 personnel (1 running back, 1 tight end, 3 wide receivers) on 60% of their plays, league wide. But the future of NFL efficiency is fewer wide receivers, not more. Take a look at the passing success rate of various grouping packages. (and here is your key: the first number is the RBs, the 2nd number is TEs, and the 3rd number [obtain by taking the number 5 and subtracting RBs and TEs] is WRs). We'll only hit those groupings run last year on at least 200 plays, and we'll start with the WR heavy packages and then transition into the TE/RB heavy formations:

- 11 personnel [3 WRs]: 49% success rate, 103 rating, 7.2 yards per attempt
- 10 personnel [4 WRs]: 41% success rate, 82 rating, 6.3 ypa
- 12 personnel [2 WRs]: 52% success rate, 122 rating, 7.6 ypa
- 21 personnel [2 WRs]: 51% success rate, 131 rating, 8.2 ypa
- 22 personnel [1 WR]: 53% success rate, 146 rating, 7.5 ypa
- 13 personnel [1 WR]: 55% success rate, 144 rating, 8.5 ypa

It's pretty obvious where the efficiency lies. Thanks to the data from Sharp Football Stats, I can tell you that targeting the TE when in 11 personnel (with 3 WRs on the field) has a higher efficiency (53% success, 93 rating) than targeting one of the WRs (48% success, 87 rating). League-wide, targeting TEs produces a higher success rate (53%) than targeting WRs (50%) or RBs (46%). There are many factors, but it starts with how they align and who is assigned coverage. From the jump, it's a benefit to the offense to target that TE.

Defensive Coordinator Jim Schwartz participated in a coaching clinic this offseason and had this to say about 13 and 22 personnel: "If you don't know exactly what you're doing on defense, 13 personnel can wear your ass out. 2 TEs, all 3 TEs lined up on one side, guy motioning across... Easy, simple stuff, like insert plays or inside zones... you can crease guys because it's hard.... guys don't practice those gap controls very much. So I'd say probably from a preparation standpoint, 22 and 13 personnel are probably the most difficult things [to prepare for] because you don't see as much of it, and it does add an extra layer to your run defense."

Last year, many of the most successful offenses in the NFL used 11 personnel well less than average, and this wasn't relegated to just run heavy teams. Offenses such as Green Bay, New England, Atlanta, Oakland, Tennessee and Kansas City used 11 personnel no more than 50% of the time, as compared to the 60% average. And this wasn't just when they winning easily, either. When the ball was snapped and the game was within one-score, these teams were still in this neighborhood with their 11 personnel usage: Green Bay (50%), New England (52%), Atlanta (47%), Oakland (24%), Tennessee (40%) and Kansas City (47%). These 6 teams ranked inside the top 10 in total offensive efficiency except for Kansas City (13th).

Once more, to Sun Tzu: *"By discovering the enemy's dispositions and remaining invisible ourselves, we can keep our forces concentrated, while the enemy's must be divided. We can form a single united body, while the enemy must split up into fractions. Hence there will be a whole pitted against separate parts of a whole, which means that we shall be many to the enemy's few. And if we are able thus to attack an inferior force with a superior one, our opponents will be in dire straits. The spot where we intend to fight must not be made known; for then the enemy will have to prepare against a possible attack at several different points; and his forces being thus distributed in many directions, the numbers we shall have to face at any given point will be proportionately few. For should the enemy strengthen his van, he will weaken his rear; should he strengthen his rear, he will weaken his van; should he strengthen his left, he will weaken his right; should he strengthen his right, he will weaken his left. If he sends reinforcements everywhere, he will everywhere be weak. Numerical weakness comes from having to prepare against possible attacks; numerical strength, from compelling our adversary to make these preparations against us."*

Using WR-light formations, such as 12, 21, 22 and 13, an offense can become highly multiple. These are extremely run-conducive formations, but as represented above, are more successful for passing than the traditional 11 personnel. The rookie tight end crop was highly skilled this year. Teams have realized riding a running back into the ground is less ideal, while rotating several into the game, along with extra blockers like TEs or RB/FBs, increases the longevity of a short life-span position (RB). My advice to all teams is to work more WR-light formations into your game plan.

Use more mortar kicks

I wrote an article last March, after the competition committee changed the rule on touchbacks, to move the ball from the 20 yard line to the 25. The title of the article? "Why Mortar Kicks Can Win Games in 2016". Fast forward from March to the start of the season in September. The biggest adopter of Mortar Kicks? The Super Bowl Champion New England Patriots.

My article hinged on the basic premise: If a team ignores the "mortar" kick, this year they essentially "give" their opponent between 0.15 and 0.24 more "points" per touchback than prior years (based on the expected point difference on 1st and 10 from the 20 to the 25 yard line). For those that don't know, a "mortar" kick is one that is executed to force a returner to catch the ball in the field of play, preferably inside their own 5 yard line. The high-arching kick puts the returner in the unenviable position of having to be extremely cognizant not only of catching the ball, but where on the field he catches it: is he on the goal line? Can he go backwards for a touchback or not? Is he near the sideline and in danger of stepping out of bounds? Instead of simply reacting, the returner must process several thoughts quickly (instead of simply focusing on the catch) and that causes mistakes.

If executed correctly, the returner gains minimal yardage after the catch, either by stepping out of bounds, getting tackled in the field of play, or worse yet, having to kneel down on a muffed catch. Examining the difference between starting at the 10 yard line following a "mortar" kick as opposed to starting at the 25 is massive:

At the 10 yard line, a team's opponent is actually more likely to score the next points than the team that has the ball on 1st and 10. The last several years, almost 55% of drives starting inside the 10 yard line ended with a punt, and 14% ended with a turnover. Both are definitively higher than if starting at the 25 yard line. Additionally, points of any kind are scored on these drives 11% less often. From an expected points perspective, the difference of starting a drive on a team's 10 yard line instead of the 25 yard line is almost 0.8 points/drive.

So what did we see in 2016? League-wide, the touchback rate was 57.6 percent, up from 56 percent last season. The percentage of kickoffs into the end zone dropped this season to 76.9 percent from 83.5 percent in 2015. Even with that approach, however, teams still lost ground in field position. The average drive start after a kickoff was the 24.8-yard line, up from the 21.6-yard line in 2015. What does this all mean?

It means knelt for touchbacks on a high rate of kickoffs which landed in the end zone. It means that even though a much higher rate of kickoffs landed outside the end zone, teams sat on a much higher rate of those which landed in the end zone. But the bottom line is, it means kickers didn't do their job very well, and coaches didn't coach their job very well. Too many teams continued to kick the ball into the end zone. Too many kickers, when trying mortar kicks, failed and either kicked the ball out of bounds or gave opponents good returns. It means there is a lot of work to do on this before the 2017 season starts.

But as to the value of the mortar kick, look to the Patriots and Bill Belichick, who said his mortar kick strategy helped the Patriots win games last season. The reason is simple (apart from the turnovers they received on fumbles, mishandled kicks). As Belichick said, "In the end, those yards showed up on the other end of the field." In other words, it forces the offense to drive the ball further, each drive, and when they don't score, those yards gained result in better starting field position for the Patriots offense. Belichick said mortar kicks helped win games last season. My article "Why Mortar Kicks Can Win Games in 2016" proved prescient. Here's a hint to the other 31 teams that still need work on this: mortar kicks can win games in 2017, too.

Kill the use of the term "3rd down back" and instead, pass to your running backs on first down

How often do we hear the term "3rd down back". The scat back who comes in on 3rd down because he's adept at catching passes out of the backfield. Why are such players used? If you answered "because they can pass block" and the team needs to pass the ball, go sit in the corner. There is little likelihood these players are the best pass blockers that could be used. Teams that use 3rd down backs inherently sacrifice pass protection, in order to achieve the main goal: because he's an outlet receiver if downfield weapons are covered or if the pass rush comes too quickly for routes to develop. The primary reason he is there is to catch the ball.

2016 Touchback Rule Change Comparison: Touchbacks vs. "Mortar" Kicks

	Yard Line	Expected Points	
NEW	25	+0.58	Team Increase of 0.24 pts/drive (vs. 2015 touchback location)
	24	+0.51	
	23	+0.46	
	22	+0.42	
	21	+0.38	
OLD	20	+0.34	
	15	+0.11	
	14	+0.04	
	13	-0.04	
	12	-0.11	
"MORTAR" KICK LANDING ZONE	7	-0.34	
	6	-0.37	
	5	-0.40	Team Decrease of 1.0 pts/drive (vs. 2016 touchback location)
	4	-0.43	
	3	-0.47	
	2	-0.50	
	1	-0.53	

@SharpFootball

The team obviously values the receiving ability of this back. But here's the problem – passes to RBs on 3rd down are garbage attempts. As a whole, passes to RBs on 3rd down gain first downs 32% of the time, which is 10% less than passes to WRs and 14% less than passes to TEs.

On 3rd and 1, as discussed earlier, most teams run. But 16% of the time they throw to RBs, and unfortunately, these are 10% less successful than passes to other positions. On 3rd and 2-4, 81% of the time teams are passing. Of the total passes, 16% go to RBs and of these, the success rate (55%) is nearly equivalent to WR passes (54%), but TE passes (61%) are still dominant. But anything 5 yards and longer and the success rate to RBs drops precipitously. At 5 yards to go, only 47% are successful. Six yards? 41%. Seven yards? 22%. Meanwhile, passes to all other positions with 7 yards to go have a 44% success rate, exactly double that of what a RB target provides.

I fully understand not all yards are created equal, so a RB target at the opponent's 30 on 3rd and 9 which gains 5 yards, while unsuccessful, makes a field goal 5 yards closer. So let's remove all targets which are inside the opponent's 40 yard line, and focus only on those outside that area. And we find the results are the same: RB targets are considerably less successful than WR or TE targets, unless inside the 2-4 yards to go range, in which case they are slightly less efficient (55% vs 56% for WRs) and they are a full 10% less successful than TE targets (65%). And we still see a precipitous drop starting at the 5 yards to go mark, where from 5-6 yards to go, RB targets are a full 10% less successful than WR targets.

RBs should not be targeted on 3rd down, unless the yards to go is 2-4 yards and then they could be used as a valve or outlet receiver in which case WRs and TEs are covered.

But there is a time that RBs should be targeted more often. And it's on first down. On first and 10, RB targets are actually 2% more successful than WR targets. Yet they are targeted just 19% of the time as opposed to 59% for WRs. In fact, RBs (58%) and TEs (60%) are more successful targets on first and 10 than WRs (55%). And one other thing 1st down passing to RBs does is reduces turnovers. Quarterbacks throw just 1 interception ever 108 pass attempts when targeting RBs in these situations (0.9%) whereas they record 1 interception every 41 pass attempts to wide receivers (2.4%).

On 3rd and short, most teams will go with their traditional RB. So why do teams use the term "3rd down back" and trot a receiving back out on 3rd and medium or long, when these targets are horrendously bad, particularly when compared to WRs or TEs? That is a great question.

My hope for the future of football is to refer to these "3rd down backs", the passing specialists, as "receiving backs". And teams should use them on first down far more frequently than they currently do.

Note that this plays on several of the other concepts mentioned above. Running on first down as frequently as teams do is highly inefficient. Passing the football on first down, where the defense is unprepared to defend everything that can be thrown at them, is ideal. It is next to impossible for the defense to adequately defend (simultaneously) on first down: RB runs, RB passes, TE targets and WR targets. After first and 10, unless a team is ahead of schedule, the defense can predict what is likely to come next, which is why the success rates drop so swiftly.

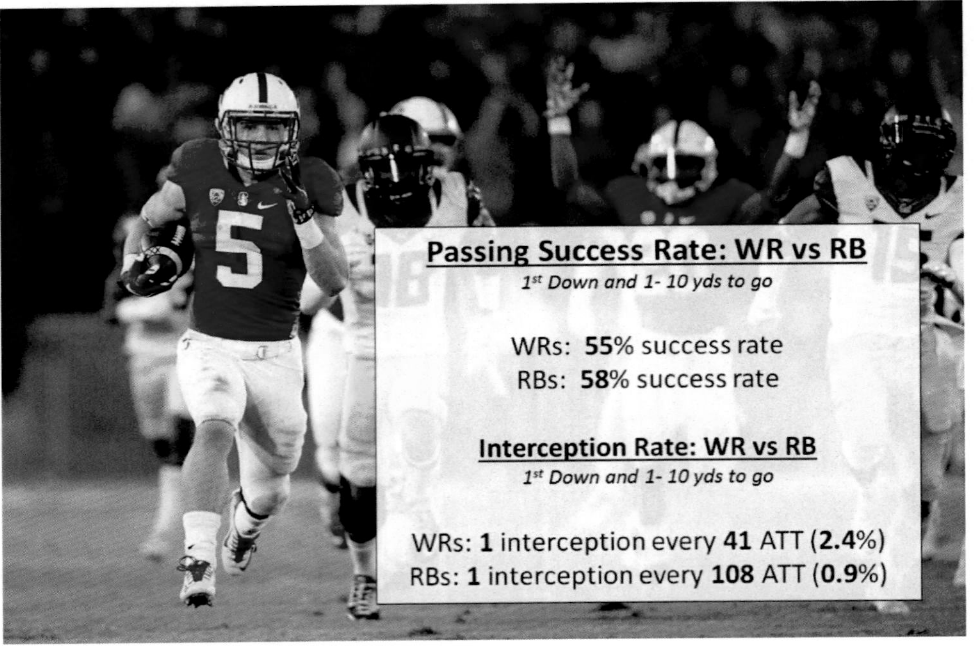

Passing Success Rate: WR vs RB
1st Down and 1- 10 yds to go
WRs: 55% success rate
RBs: 58% success rate
Interception Rate: WR vs RB
1st Down and 1- 10 yds to go
WRs: 1 interception every 41 ATT (2.4%)
RBs: 1 interception every 108 ATT (0.9%)

Early down success is the key for efficiency

The key to NFL success lies in a metric I invented several years ago, and which has been discussed by more and more people each year but has yet to be incorporated heavily enough into the NFL. Early Down Success Rate, or EDSR for short. It's an efficiency metric I created and while its proprietary in its calculation, it looks at efficiency on the early downs.

While we're peppered with 3rd down success rate in graphics packages that pop up on the TV during each game, 3rd down success pales in comparison to EDSR in terms of being predictive or correlated to winning. When the announcer says a team is converting 56% of its 3rd down attempts, that is a solid and impressive rate. But if that team is 9/16 (56%) on 3rd downs while their opponent is 3/7 (43%), guess what? The second team has attempted 9 fewer third downs and is likely having far more success in the game as a result.

I dialed back 9 years and EDSR is the most correlated statistic to winning in the postseason that exists, apart from turnovers. If you remove teams with a 2+ turnover edge (who win 88% of their games as a result), and focus on games which were lined within 9 points of a pickem (thus removing heavy, heavy favorites who may be up big and simply trying to run out the clock rather than paly efficiently), you will find that teams who have the better EDSR in these games are 36-7-1 ATS (84%) in the postseason since 2007.

Under the SAME guidelines (games lined within 9, no team with a 2+ turnover margin):

- Teams who score more points/total yards gained are 28-14 (67%)
- Teams who run for more total yards are 28-14 (67%)
- Teams who throw for more yds/attempt are 27-15 (64%)
- Teams who have the most total passing yards are 27-15 (64%)
- Teams who gain more first downs are 27-15 (64%)
- Teams who record more sacks are 22-13 (63%)
- Teams who gain more yds per play are 25-17 (60%)
- Teams who run for more yds/attempt are 24-18 (57%)
- Teams who convert a better percentage on 3rd down are 22-19 (54%)

NONE of these stats are better than 67% ATS in the postseason since 2007. None of them are close to the 88% correlation of winning the turnover battle by 2+ turnovers. But most importantly: None of them are anywhere close to the 84% correlation which EDSR shows.

The most visually stunning & artistic yet data-intensive experience available for NFL analytics...

a 100% interactive experience featuring customizable NFL information & stats, supported with data on proprietary dashboards and visualizations

- **Customize** – Every visualization is customizable and can be manipulated for efficiency in data discovery, providing the best user experience possible.
- **Visualize** – As society trends to more visual learning, Sharp Football Stats allows the user to see the stats to help better understand them.
- **Process** – The user will better make sense of these visualized metrics than most other delivery platforms. Understanding the "why" is as important as knowing the "why".
- **Retain** – A fleeting "aha" moment is worthless if not retained. Through the visual learning method, users will remember what they learned and carry it forward, opening more doors to new ideas along the way.

- Aerial Passing Distance
- Yards thrown short of sticks
- Snap rates
- Toxicity
- Explosive Play Rankings
- Personnel Grouping Frequency and Success Rates
- Strength of Schedule
- Advanced Metrics, such as Success Rate, Missed YPA, YAS% and TOARS
- Positional Target Rates
- Shotgun vs Under Center Rates
- Red Zone Metrics
- Efficiency Metrics
- Advanced Stat Box Scores for Every Game
- Highly detailed and filterable play-by-play data to find specific plays and team trends
- Updated weekly on Monday and Tuesday in-season
- And MUCH MORE

www . SharpFootballStats . com

How can teams win the EDSR battle to qualify for this extremely high correlation to winning games? It's (obviously) about being efficient on early downs. It's about avoiding third downs. It's about not being satisfied with a 3 yard gain on first down. It's about gaining enough on first and second down so as to not even need a third down. Using many of the strategies I outline in this article, teams should be able to increase their early down efficiency.

It's about passing on first down and making your playbook wide open. That means personnel wise as well as play calling. The last Super Bowl featured two defensive minded head coaches in Bill Belichick and Dan Quinn, who let young and aggressive offensive coordinators take control of the offense. Many defensive minded head coaches limit the offense, try to get them to be more conservative and avoid negative plays. Not these two coaches. Both turned their offenses over to cunning, clever and creative offensive coordinators, and have allowed these offenses to go full throttle at virtually all times. As importantly, Josh McDaniels and Kyle Shanahan were not two coordinators that "do what they do" and simply will get their team sharp for Sunday. No, these two constantly tweak and improve game plans which specifically target weaknesses of opposing defenses.

As Sun Tzu says: *"Carefully compare the opposing army with your own, so that you may know where strength is superabundant and where it is deficient. In making tactical dispositions, the highest pitch you can attain is to conceal them."* That's the essence of winning games in today's NFL. It's about attacking weak points, leverage, in all forms but starting with play calling and strategy. Avoiding predictable down/distances so that you can conceal play call. Being aggressive from the very start of the game, on first and second down, and building a lead. And that's exactly what EDSR measures.

Run more often in the red zone

Most teams get far too pass happy in the red zone, when running in the red zone is quite efficient.

On short yardage, as should be obvious, it is particularly effective. Still, on 3rd or 4th and 1-3 yards to go, teams called pass 55% and only 49% were successful in generating a first down. Meanwhile, while teams preferred calling passes, runs in the same situation were successful over 61% of the time. That is a massive efficiency edge. Additionally, there were zero turnovers and zero sacks (clearly), whereas over 8% of pass plays were negative (turnover or sack).

But even on early downs, run plays have a higher success rate than do pass plays. Inside the red zone, run plays are successful on early downs 49% of the time, whereas pass plays are successful just 43% of the time.

Balance is key, but more important is play calling. Running when the defense is playing pass is far more ideal, and that means running out of spread formations. It also means not bringing in fullbacks to block, let alone defensive tackles. Power running out of one-back formations is effective, especially when every single yard holds such value in the red zone.

Running in the red zone out of 13 or 23 personnel is ridiculously successful: such run plays produce a 58% and 60% success rate respectively, the best rate of any formation, but most of those are short yardage runs. The only time red zone pass plays are more successful than red zone run plays is in 11+ yards to go. But in standard situations (1-10 yards to go), run plays are more successful. Whether you want to look at long yardage (7-10 yards to go), mid (4-6 yards to go) or short (1-3 yards to go), rushing is more successful, to the tune of 2%, 10% or 14% respectively. Rushing obviously becomes more successful when the yardage to go is less, but the fact that even longer 7-10 yards to go situations show an efficiency edge to rushing in the red zone is something teams need to take more advantage of more frequently.

Other elements

There are many, many other edges I could write about and support with stats from Sharp Football Stats, including passing beyond the sticks on third down, fourth down aggressiveness, explosive passing, situational tempo, pre-snap motion, cadence, and much, much more. But I won't lay out all of my tricks, and this article is already long enough. If you want more, you know where to find me.

The Power of Sharp Football Stats

By Warren Sharp

Less than one year ago, I embarked on a mission to change NFL analytics via the launching of SharpFootballStats.com. The site was the first of its kind: a 100% interactive, customizable site based on providing visualized data using proprietary dashboards and visualizations. Nothing else like it publicly exists. The focus was on the user. To create more than just a better "experience" - it was a four-part educational tool:

- Customize – Every visualization is customizable and can be manipulated for efficiency in data discovery, providing the best user experience possible.
- Visualize – As society trends to more visual learning, Sharp Football Stats allows the user to see the stats to help better understand them.
- Process – The user will better make sense of these visualized metrics than most other delivery platforms. Understanding the "why" is as important as knowing the "why".
- Retain – A fleeting "aha" moment is worthless if not retained. Through the visual learning method, users will remember what they learned and carry it forward, opening more doors to new ideas along the way.

The response has been tremendous. The website and/or data produced has been cited and used in research and articles across all walks of sites, including NFL.com, Rotoworld, Pro Football Talk, The Ringer and countless others. It's also leading a change in the way many larger, more established sites attempt to project themselves publicly. The use of more infographs and tables started this past offseason (in part) after seeing the utility and success of what SharpFootballStats.com was doing.

Over the next two months, you'll see an overhaul in the site's organization to streamline visualizations better. And you'll see a substantial amount of new visualization development & improvement. By the end of the summer, you should see historical data added to the mix as well. And the craziest part is, all of these visualizations are free to access, unlike many sites out there that charge for information. It's an exciting time!

Aside from the obvious, what is one element you can gain from SharpFootballStats.com which is not present at most other sites? Context. You can visualize how each team stacks up on quality of opponent, in season, based on approximately 30 metrics. So, for instance, if you notice that Russell Wilson has been hitting Tyler Lockett with regularity the last few weeks, you may want to confirm that it's not simply a result of Seattle playing defenses who have 1) terrible pass rushes, 2) terrible pass defenses or 3) defenses which allow a tremendously high rate of explosive passes. You can do that in a visual manner, extremely quickly, at SharpFootballStats.com. You can also find context by comparing players across the league quickly using many of the league-wide advanced metrics tables. Which leads me to the next cool item:

In addition to proprietary dashboards and visualizations not found elsewhere, SharpFootballStats.com is also inventing custom, predictive, fresh and innovative NFL analytics. Early Down Success Rate was invented a few years ago. Last year, Missed YPA was created. Missed YPA takes advantage of the fact that most plays in the NFL are unsuccessful. And while success rate means far more to me than yards per play, I wanted to measure those unsuccessful plays, because each is not equal. A one yard gain on 2nd and 10 is far different than a five-yard gain, but both are graded as unsuccessful. That's where Missed YPA comes in – it tracks the yardage of unsuccessful plays that fell short of converting the play into a successful one. There are many other custom metrics, and will be more to follow.

I'm excited to announce that another chapter in the journey will start in July. In another efficiency improvement move, Sharp Football Stats is proud to announce the launch "MyStats". Researching football is time consuming. Particularly if you're an avid Fantasy/DFS player. We know what it was like – hunting around on 5-10 websites, waiting for that site to refresh their stats for the week. Then compiling them all into one stream of information upon which you can finally begin to process for intelligent decision making. MyStats takes the waiting, web surfing and frustration out of the process. MyStats users each get their own, individual page of Sharp Football Stats visualizations. And the best part is, MyStats users get to choose from an a la cart menu of what to keep, what to toss, how to lay out the page and much, much more. To check out more about the project, see page 15. MyStats will launch July, 2017!

The best way to demonstrate the power of Sharp Football Stats is to show you. So let's walk through several quick case studies to see how easy it is when stats are visualized.

The Value of Earl Thomas

Seattle's Earl Thomas was healthy weeks 1-11 and injured thereafter. Here is a visualization of his impact on the Seattle defense, in 4 images:

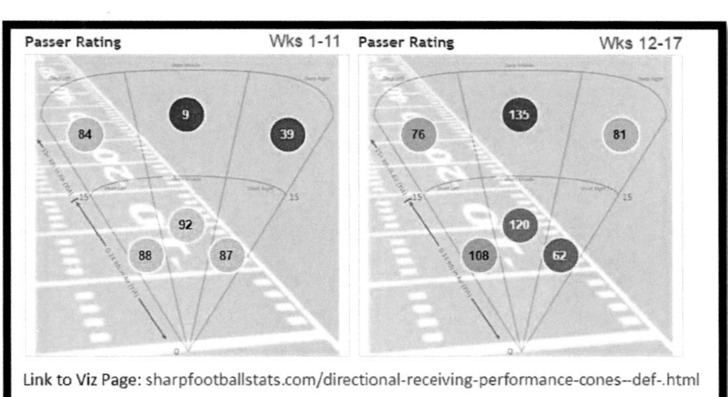

Link to Viz Page: sharpfootballstats.com/directional-receiving-performance-cones--def-.html

Above image: With Earl Thomas, the Seahawks allowed a passer rating of 9 on passes deep middle, and his presence helped the Seahawks in all areas of coverage.

Image to the right: With Earl Thomas, the Seahawks were the 8th best defense at explosive pass rates allowed, allowing an explosive pass on just 7% of all attempts. But once Thomas went out with injury, the Seahawks fell to dead last (32nd), allowing an explosive pass on 12% of attempts.

Explosive Pass Rates — Wks 1-11

Defense	Explosive Pass	Sum of Pass Play	Avg. Explosive Pass Rate	
ARI	27	356	8%	11
ATL	35	442	8%	14
BAL	26	372	7%	5
BUF	30	363	8%	17
CAR	29	410	7%	6
CHI	31	387	8%	15
CIN	33	372	9%	24
CLE	41	396	10%	29
DAL	30	400	8%	10
DEN	24	373	6%	3
DET	29	368	8%	13
GB	37	352	11%	30
HOU	26	341	8%	12
IND	35	406	9%	23
JAC	24	362	7%	4
KC	29	394	7%	9
LA	22	383	6%	1
MIA	31	368	8%	19
MIN	24	392	6%	2
NE	34	403	8%	20
NO	33	389	8%	21
NYG	36	430	8%	18
NYJ	31	380	8%	16
OAK	41	380	11%	31
PHI	37	366	10%	28
PIT	29	399	7%	7
SD	36	419	9%	22
SEA	29	397	7%	8
SF	37	370	10%	27
TB	42	367	11%	32
TEN	42	444	9%	26
WAS	36	396	9%	25

Explosive Pass Rates — Wks 12-17

Defense	Explosive Pass	Sum of Pass Play	Avg. Explosive Pass Rate	
ARI	20	239	8%	17
ATL	18	249	7%	10
BAL	24	237	10%	26
BUF	16	188	9%	19
CAR	25	250	10%	25
CHI	19	180	11%	29
CIN	13	253	5%	3
CLE	11	173	6%	7
DAL	15	268	6%	4
DEN	8	220	4%	1
DET	21	207	10%	27
GB	21	260	8%	15
HOU	12	212	6%	5
IND	20	207	10%	24
JAC	16	221	7%	11
KC	18	232	8%	13
LA	19	230	8%	16
MIA	17	258	7%	8
MIN	17	197	9%	20
NE	19	227	8%	18
NO	15	222	7%	9
NYG	22	234	9%	23
NYJ	20	191	10%	28
OAK	20	185	11%	30
PHI	20	220	9%	22
PIT	11	229	5%	2
SD	17	196	9%	21
SEA	22	181	12%	32
SF	22	185	12%	31
TB	16	219	7%	12
TEN	14	231	6%	6
WAS	18	231	8%	14

Link to Viz Page: sharpfootballstats.com/explosive-play-rankings--def-.html

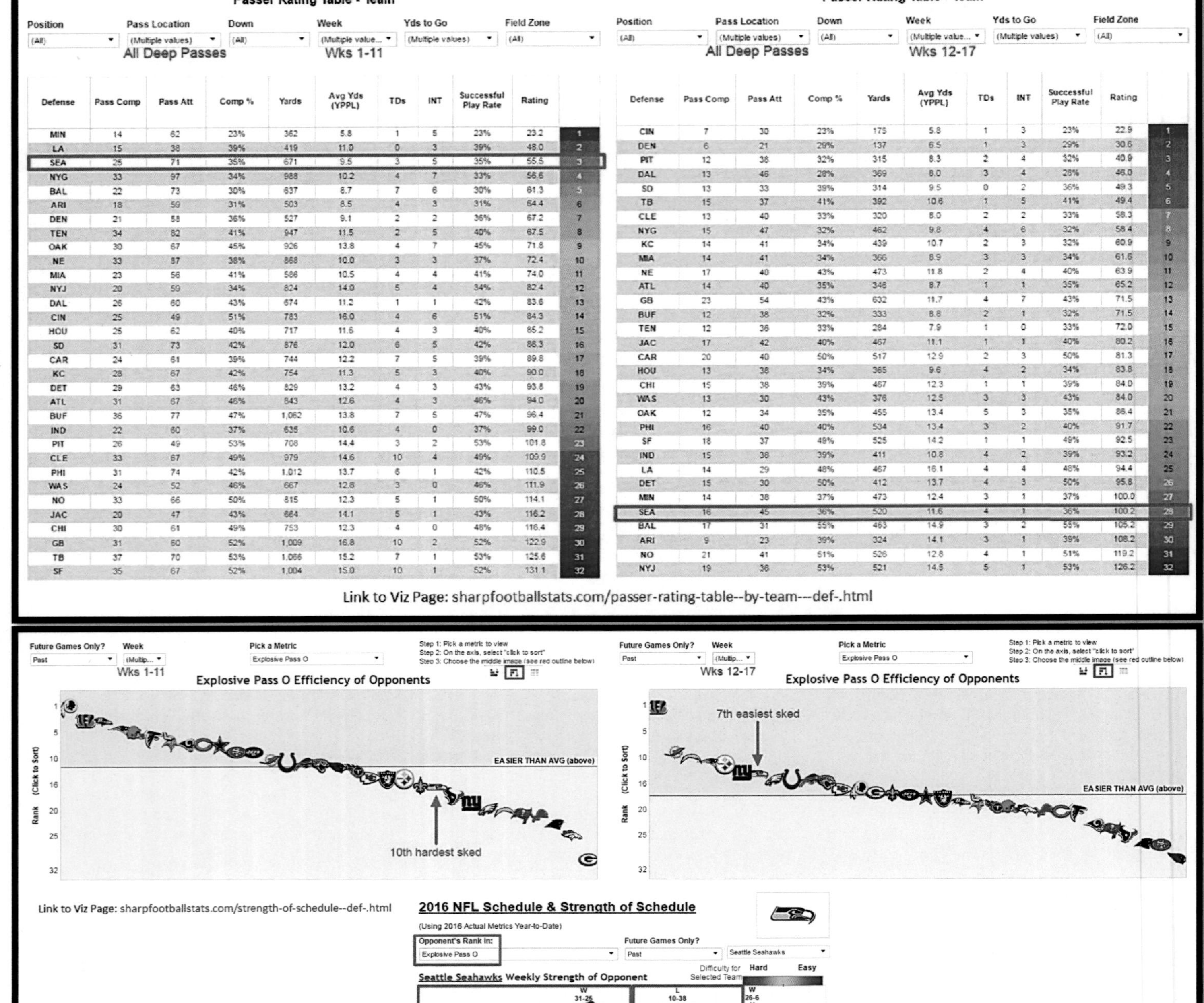

Passer Rating Table - Team — All Deep Passes, Wks 1-11

Defense	Pass Comp	Pass Att	Comp %	Yards	Avg Yds (YPPL)	TDs	INT	Successful Play Rate	Rating	
MIN	14	62	23%	362	5.8	1	5	23%	23.2	1
LA	15	38	39%	419	11.0	0	3	39%	48.0	2
SEA	25	71	35%	671	9.5	3	5	35%	55.5	3
NYG	33	97	34%	988	10.2	4	7	33%	56.6	4
BAL	22	73	30%	637	8.7	7	6	30%	61.3	5
ARI	18	59	31%	503	8.5	4	3	31%	64.4	6
DEN	21	58	36%	527	9.1	2	2	36%	67.2	7
TEN	34	82	41%	947	11.5	2	5	40%	67.5	8
OAK	30	67	45%	926	13.8	4	7	45%	71.8	9
NE	33	87	38%	868	10.0	3	3	37%	72.4	10
MIA	23	56	41%	586	10.5	4	4	41%	74.0	11
NYJ	20	59	34%	824	14.0	5	4	34%	82.4	12
DAL	26	60	43%	674	11.2	1	1	42%	83.6	13
CIN	25	49	51%	783	16.0	4	6	51%	84.3	14
HOU	25	62	40%	717	11.6	4	3	40%	85.2	15
SD	31	73	42%	876	12.0	6	5	42%	86.3	16
CAR	24	61	39%	744	12.2	7	5	39%	89.8	17
KC	28	67	42%	754	11.3	5	3	40%	90.0	18
DET	29	63	46%	829	13.2	4	3	43%	93.8	19
ATL	31	67	46%	843	12.6	4	3	46%	94.0	20
BUF	36	77	47%	1,062	13.8	7	5	47%	96.4	21
IND	22	60	37%	635	10.6	4	0	37%	99.0	22
PIT	26	49	53%	708	14.4	3	2	53%	101.8	23
CLE	33	67	49%	979	14.6	10	4	49%	109.9	24
PHI	31	74	42%	1,012	13.7	6	1	42%	110.5	25
WAS	24	52	46%	667	12.8	3	0	46%	111.9	26
NO	33	66	50%	815	12.3	5	1	50%	114.1	27
JAC	20	47	43%	664	14.1	5	1	43%	116.2	28
CHI	30	61	49%	753	12.3	4	0	48%	116.4	29
GB	31	60	52%	1,009	16.8	10	2	52%	122.9	30
TB	37	70	53%	1,066	15.2	7	1	53%	125.6	31
SF	35	67	52%	1,004	15.0	10	1	52%	131.1	32

Passer Rating Table - Team — All Deep Passes, Wks 12-17

Defense	Pass Comp	Pass Att	Comp %	Yards	Avg Yds (YPPL)	TDs	INT	Successful Play Rate	Rating	
CIN	7	30	23%	175	5.8	1	3	23%	22.9	1
DEN	6	21	29%	137	6.5	1	3	29%	30.6	2
PIT	12	38	32%	315	8.3	2	4	32%	40.9	3
DAL	13	46	28%	369	8.0	3	4	28%	46.0	4
SD	13	33	39%	314	9.5	0	2	36%	49.3	5
TB	15	37	41%	392	10.6	1	5	41%	49.4	6
CLE	13	40	33%	320	8.0	2	2	33%	58.3	7
NYG	15	47	32%	462	9.8	4	6	32%	58.4	8
KC	14	41	34%	439	10.7	2	3	32%	60.9	9
MIA	14	41	34%	366	8.9	3	3	34%	61.6	10
NE	17	40	43%	473	11.8	2	4	40%	63.9	11
ATL	14	40	35%	346	8.7	1	1	35%	65.2	12
GB	23	54	43%	632	11.7	4	7	43%	71.5	13
BUF	12	38	32%	333	8.8	2	1	32%	71.5	14
TEN	12	36	33%	284	7.9	1	0	33%	72.0	15
JAC	17	42	40%	467	11.1	1	1	40%	80.2	16
CAR	20	40	50%	517	12.9	2	3	50%	81.3	17
HOU	13	38	34%	365	9.6	4	2	34%	83.8	18
CHI	15	38	39%	467	12.3	1	1	39%	84.0	19
WAS	13	30	43%	376	12.5	3	3	43%	84.0	20
OAK	12	34	35%	455	13.4	5	3	35%	86.4	21
PHI	16	40	40%	534	13.4	3	2	40%	91.7	22
SF	18	37	49%	525	14.2	1	1	49%	92.5	23
IND	15	38	39%	411	10.8	4	2	39%	93.2	24
LA	14	29	48%	467	16.1	4	4	48%	94.4	25
DET	15	30	50%	412	13.7	4	3	50%	95.8	26
MIN	14	38	37%	473	12.4	3	1	37%	100.0	27
SEA	16	45	36%	520	11.6	4	1	36%	100.2	28
BAL	17	31	55%	463	14.9	3	2	55%	105.2	29
ARI	9	23	39%	324	14.1	3	1	39%	108.2	30
NO	21	41	51%	526	12.8	4	1	51%	119.2	31
NYJ	19	36	53%	521	14.5	5	1	53%	126.2	32

Link to Viz Page: sharpfootballstats.com/passer-rating-table--by-team---def-.html

Link to Viz Page: sharpfootballstats.com/strength-of-schedule--def-.html

Top image: Seattle moved from 3rd to 28th in deep passer rating without Thomas, going from a 55.5 rating allowed to a 100.2 rating. And from the bottom image, for the context, we can see that Seattle played the 10th hardest schedule for explosive passing offenses when Earl Thomas was active. Yet they ranked 8th best in defending explosive passes. But when Earl Thomas was out, the Seahawks played the 7th easiest schedule of explosive pass offenses, yet they ranked 32nd in explosive pass defense. We can see the Seahaks schedule alone, in a week to week basis at the far bottom, and I've highlighted the with and without Thomas games. The bar for each team relates to their rank in explosive pass offense. The red teams near were best (ranking 1st) and the green teams near the top were the worst (ranking 32nd).

Forecasting the Patriots James White's Huge Game in the Super Bowl

In my Super Bowl write-up for clients, I forecast James White's huge game based on performance, opponent and matchup. I said:

The Falcons defense is terrible defending passes to running backs. Opposing running backs have the 3rd best successful play rate against this Atlanta defense. The Patriots have thrown 130 passes to RBs this season, which is 4th most in the NFL and (obviously) well above average. That said, their YTD numbers are not tremendous because they did play the 11th toughest schedule of teams defending RB passes and they played without Dion Lewis for the bulk of the season. This will be, by far, the easiest team to use the RB pass on that NE will have faced, as you can see to the right.

In games vs the Ravens and the 49ers, the only teams even remotely close to the terrible RB-pass defense played by the Falcons, the Patriots threw 9 passes to RB James White. He caught all 9, and recorded a massive 144 yards receiving. That's an average of 16 yards/catch. In both games, there were several shorter passes followed by one that finally caught the defense and resulted in a massively huge gain. The Patriots will kill a defense with passes to the RB, particularly in the red zone. New England ranks 11th overall in passer rating to RBs in the red zone with a 115 rating. In the red zone, the Falcons defense has been abused by opponents. They have allowed a 126 rating and a 82% completion rate, both among the worst in the NFL.

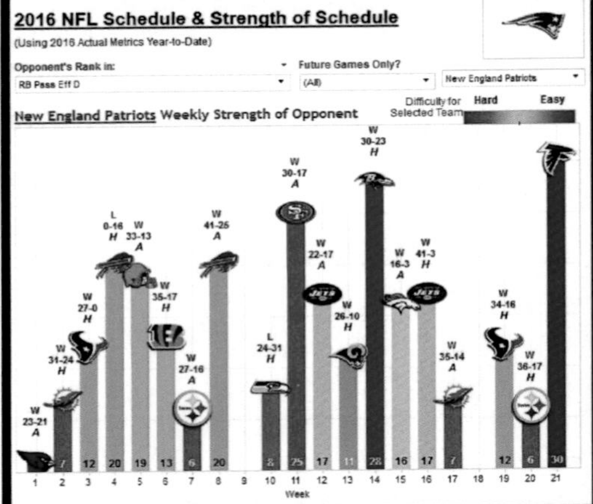

As it turned out, targeting James White was exactly what the Patriots decided to do. He was targeted a game high 16 times. He caught 14 of them, for 110 yards, a 56% success rate and a 116 passer rating. He caught 6 passes that he converted for first down, the most of any player on either team. The decision to attack the Falcons defense with James White, particularly in the second half and overtime, where White had 10 targets and caught 9, was a key reason the Patriots were able to pull off the win.

LeSean McCoy's Ridiculous 2016 Season

Not enough was made about LeSean McCoy's 2016 season. I talk more about what he did in the Bills chapter, but to keep it straightforward:

1) In 2016, the Bills faced the #1 most difficult schedule of run defenses but the #2 easiest schedule of pass defenses.

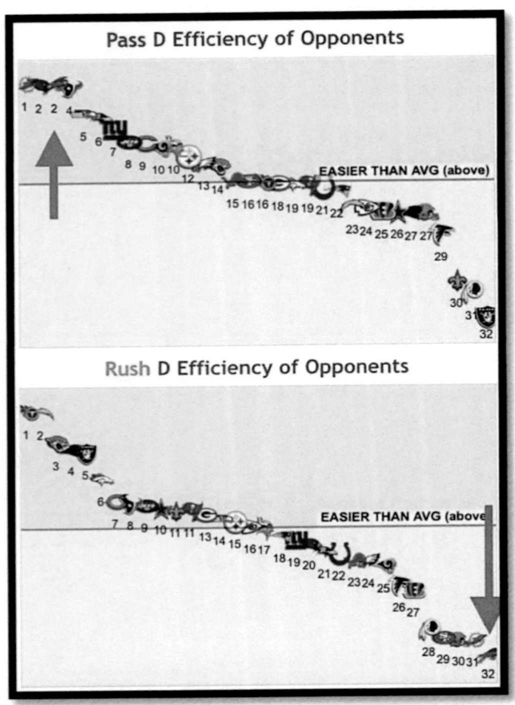

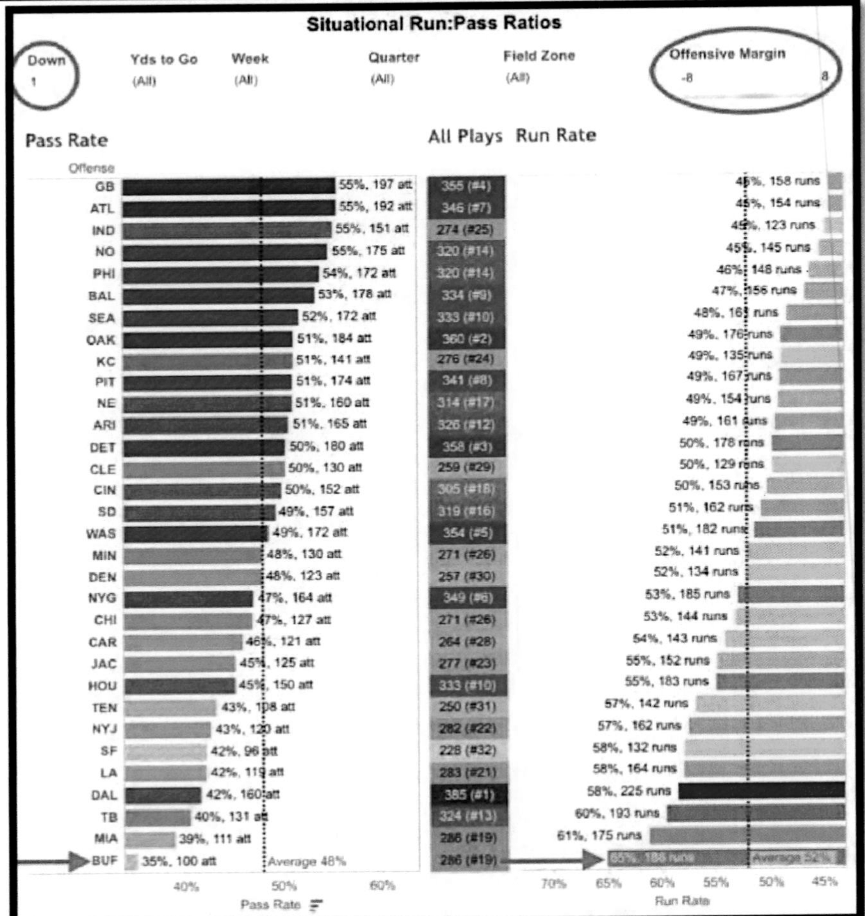

2) Despite the ease in pass defenses, the Bills decided to go extremely run heavy. It was so run heavy, it was predictable. In one-score games, from their own 20 yard-line onward, the Bills posted the #1 run rate, 10% above average. To dive even further into game theory, when a game was close (within one-score), the Bills predictably ran on first down 65% of the time! A full 13% above average.

3) Despite the predictable, run first nature of the Bills offense, and despite facing the NFL's toughest defenses, through a game's first 3 quarters, McCoy averaged 6 yards per carry, the best mark in the NFL (min 175 att).

4) On first down alone, the down where the Bills predictability put the rest of the NFL to shame, LeSean McCoy averaged a massive 6.1 yards per carry through the first 3 quarters and a 53% success rate.

5) These run numbers are not schedule adjusted in any way. Game theory would indicate there should be no way to achieve those results because of the predictable nature and the strength of the run defenses. But McCoy did. And the only reason I cut the numbers off after 3 quarters was, McCoy was worn down a bit in the 4th quarter against the stingy run defenses with such volume.

The Inevitable Quarterback Crisis

By Warren Sharp

The average NFL passer rating is approximately 90. Looking at the quarterback landscape for the last 5 years, there are clear lines of definition between great quarterbacks and average to mediocre quarterbacks. Using a minimum qualification of 10 starts in a season and a passer rating of 90 or more, here are the active quarterbacks to record 5 consecutive seasons with those results:

- Drew Brees
- Ben Roethlisberger
- Russell Wilson

Here are the quarterbacks with 4 seasons of minimum 10 starts with a 90 rating:

- Tom Brady
- Aaron Rodgers

Here are the quarterbacks with 3 seasons of minimum 10 starts with a 90 rating:

- Philip Rivers
- Matt Ryan
- Alex Smith

These top 5 quarterbacks listed are pretty much universally listed and considered great quarterbacks. Here is a problem with these quarterbacks. They won't be around all that much longer:

- Drew Brees turns 39 next January and is in his 17th season
- Ben Roethlisberger turns 36 next March and is in his 14th season, and contemplated retirement this past offseason
- Tom Brady turns 40 this August and is in his 17th season
- Aaron Rodgers turns 34 this December, and is in his 13th season

Russell Wilson is the young pup of this group (turns 29 this November). As for that lower tier with 3 season in their last 5 meeting the basic criteria, each of Rivers, Ryan and Smith are in their early to mid 30s, and Alex Smith already saw his team trade up to draft a younger quarterback to replace him.

And keep in mind, the criteria is simply to be average (90 rating) or better, and to start 10 games in a season or more. It's not very aggressive at all.

The Passing Era of the NFL

Starting in 2010, the NFL tightened hit rules on quarterbacks and defenseless receivers. It basically started the passing era of the NFL, where short to intermediate passes have a much stronger efficiency than they did in the past.

From 1990 to 1999, an average of only 2.2 quarterbacks were drafted in the first round. From 2000 – 2010, an average of 2.5 quarterbacks were drafted in the first round. But since the NFL became more pass heavy, that number has risen further: from 2011 (the first year post-rule changes) to 2017, an average of 2.9 quarterbacks were drafted in the first round. Every single year we see teams trading up to mortgage that season's draft in order to come home with what they think could be their franchise quarterback.

That is because most every team believes the only way to win in the NFL is to have a quarterback. You don't see many untalented quarterbacks win the Super Bowl.

Here are the last 14 quarterbacks to win a Super Bowl: Tom Brady, Ben Roethlisberger, Peyton Manning, Eli Manning, Drew Brees, Aaron Rodgers, Russell Wilson and Joe Flacco. That's it. The two names that stick out like sore thumbs on that list are Eli Manning and Joe Flacco, simply because their career numbers don't represent what they did in the seasons that they sparked and helped their team win Super Bowls.

But every single other quarterback who won a Super Bowl is on my list from above: Brady, Roethlisberger, Brees, Rodgers and Wilson. (The only reason Peyton Manning is not there is because he is retired.)

There is also one other similarity with all of the past 14 Super Bowl winning quarterbacks except for Drew Brees. They all won their Super Bowls with the team that drafted them. (Note that Peyton Manning won with the Colts and then with the Broncos).

Teams seem to be picking up on these facts:

1. It's a passing league;
2. Super Bowls are won (with minor exceptions) by extremely good if not great quarterbacks;
3. Rarely are such quarterbacks available via free agency, the way to obtain them is through the draft;
4. Rarely do quarterbacks outside the top 32 picks win the Super Bowl. Tom Brady and Russell Wilson are the only exceptions in the last 14 years.

A Black Hole of Quarterback Talent

And so we see teams reaching on quarterbacks, trading up, or doing anything in their power to get a quarterback into their system that meets those criteria.

The problem has been, we hit a virtual black hole in talented quarterbacks, starting (unfortunately for teams without them) the year following the new hit rules. Take a look at the quarterbacks drafted in the first round during the 4 year period from 2011-2014:

- Cam Newton
- Andrew Luck
- Robert Griffin
- Blake Bortles
- Ryan Tannehill
- Jake Locker
- Blaine Gabbert
- Christian Ponder
- Brandon Weeden
- EJ Manuel
- Johnny Manziel
- Teddy Bridgewater

Andrew Luck is the clear leader of this generation. While Cam Newton has played in a Super Bowl, he has posted a 90+ passer rating with 10+ starts just once in last 5 years. If Ryan Tannehill were to ever win a Super Bowl, it would likely be as a result of a strong defense and a truly magical season, one like we saw from Joe Flacco. The rest of those quarterbacks (if they are even starting) are no where close to the level of talent that appears capable of leading a team to the Super Bowl.

The question becomes, as our best quarterbacks are the oldest quarterbacks, what happens when we experience a span 1-2 years where multiple of these great quarterbacks walk away from the game?

Next Quarterbacks Up

Poised to fill the void, there are a handful of quarterbacks. Another very basic search of quarterbacks the last 3 seasons, who posted single seasons with a 90+ rating in at least 10 starts, while being 27 years old or younger, delivers the following results:

All 3 seasons: zero

Two seasons:

- Andrew Luck
- Russell Wilson
- Derek Carr
- Marcus Mariota

One season:

- Dak Prescott
- Kirk Cousins
- Cam Newton
- Matthew Stafford
- Ryan Tannehill
- Tyrod Taylor

I think it's safe to say that the first section of players are certainly slam dunks to step up into that void to allow us to see solid quarterback play when the greats step away. But aside from Andrew Luck (1st) and Russell Wilson (2nd) I don't know if I see any of those quarterbacks taking over records or posting clutch performances like Tom Brady, Aaron Rodgers, Drew Brees or Ben Roethlisberger.

Dak Prescott had an incredible first season, but we need to see much more from him. Kirk Cousins, while intriguing, played on a stacked offense and still needs to deliver more consistent results. And the rest of those players I don't view as talented as passers or reliable enough to step into that void.

In a few years, the tier 2 or 3 vets we currently have will become the elder generation. It's unlikely for us to see a better level of quarterbacking out of Andy Dalton, Alex Smith, Joe Flacco or even Matt Ryan than what we've seen in their careers thus far.

As those players are in their early to mid 30s, the league will become dependent on Luck, Wilson, Carr and Mariota. Because the youngest generation is what concerns me the most.

Young and Restless

Below are two quarterback tables, based on quarterback age at the end of last season, with color coding. The color coding relates to my own opinion of the long term forecast of these players, and is highly subjective. The coding I have used is as follows:

Long Term Forecast based on Current Data
Elite Career Barring Injuries
Solid Starter with Higher Ceiling
Average Starters with High Variance
Poor Starter
Backup
Not Enough Data

Take a look at the quarterbacks age 25-27 last season, sorted by starts:

QBs Age 25-27 as of December 31, 2016			
Player	Age	Tm	2016 RTG
Derek Carr	25	OAK	96.7
Andrew Luck	27	IND	96.4
Tyrod Taylor	27	BUF	89.7
Trevor Siemian	25	DEN	84.6
Cam Newton	27	CAR	75.8
Brock Osweiler	26	HOU	72.2
Matt Barkley	26	CHI	68.3
Robert Griffin	26	CLE	72.5
Blaine Gabbert	27	SFO	68.4
Bryce Petty	25	NYJ	60
Jimmy Garoppolo	25	NWE	113.3
Landry Jones	27	PIT	86.3
Tom Savage	26	HOU	80.9
Nick Foles	27	KAN	105.9
Geno Smith	26	NYJ	81.3
Matt McGloin	27	OAK	60.4
EJ Manuel	26	BUF	58.3
Mike Glennon	27	TAM	125.4
David Fales	26	CHI	53.7
A.J. McCarron	26	CIN	

There is not a lot to love here. Cam Newton possibly could have been moved up, but I don't think we can do that until we see him in 2017. He took a ton of hits last season, and I think a smart move for both his team and himself would be to run less often. If he were to do that, it would be a massive change, and needs to become more adept with his touch and accuracy on shorter routes. While he's been a solid fantasy quarterback due to his rushing, he's been a solid passer in just one year (2015) in the last 5 years, his only year with a rating of 90 or higher.

Jimmy Garoppolo is the new rage, and he could be the real deal and have a later career arc, much like Aaron Rodgers. Time will tell. I almost penciled him in as not enough data, but I've seen enough to think he can be at least an average NFL starter and obviously there is a higher ceiling which is to be determined. Thanks to his running, Tyrod Taylor can be an average NFL starter, but unlike Garoppolo, Taylor's floor and ceiling are lower. Again, I'm not talking from a fantasy perspective, from a real football perspective.

As we drop back to the youngest quarterbacks in the league, we have the following table:

QBs Age 21-24 as of December 31, 2016			
Player	Age	Tm	2016 RTG
Dak Prescott	23	DAL	104.9
Jameis Winston	22	TB	86.1
Carson Wentz	24	PHI	79.3
Blake Bortles	24	JAC	78.8
Marcus Mariota	23	TEN	95.6
Cody Kessler	23	CLE	92.3
Jared Goff	22	LAR	63.6
Jacoby Brissett	23	NE	83.9
Paxton Lynch	22	DEN	79.2
Trevone Boykin	23	SEA	91.2
Connor Cook	23	OAK	83.4
Cardale Jones	24	BUF	46
Kevin Hogan	24	CLE	31.6
Sean Mannion	24	LAR	17.4
Brett Hundley	23	GNB	0
Teddy Bridgewater	24	MIN	

I'm giving Bridgewater the benefit of the doubt that he'll return from his injury similar to how he left, but that is risky. Dak Prescott wowed us in year one, and I'm giving him the benefit of the doubt that his trajectory will continue. I'm higher on Prescott and Mariota than Winston and Wentz. I'm passing the buck on Kessler, Goff and Lynch. They are young and we don't have to rush to judgement based on limited exposure to all 3.

A Top-Heavy Organization

For any of you that have worked in corporate America for years, as an employee of a company, you know how different companies are structured. Some have a corps of younger, innovative talent. Others are led by individuals 2-4 years away from retirement, with that younger generation not yet ready to take control when they step aside.

That is the current NFL. Most of the quarterbacks who lead this league are in their mid to late 30s. While you may think this to be common, think again. Drop back to even 10 years ago. That was when the NFL was led by a 31 year old Peyton Manning, a 30 year old Tom Brady, and also had: 28 year old Drew Brees, 28 year old Carson Palmer, 27 year old Tony Romo, 26 year old Eli Manning, 26 year old Philip Rivers, 25 year old Ben Roethlisberger, and had 24 year old Aaron Rodgers about to take over in Green Bay. And it had 24 year old Vince Young and Jay Cutler. The two oldest but dominant quarterbacks were 38 year old Brett Favre and 36 year old Kurt Warner. But those were the only quarterbacks older than 32 who even meant anything in the league. Sure, there were some old guys who started games but were far from useful. Such as Jeff Garcia (37) and Jon Kitna (35). But for the most part, the 30 and under crowd ran the NFL.

In a couple of years, it will be the 40 and over crowd. Andrew Luck turns 28 this September and Russell Wilson turns 29 in November. Who will we even have in that 27 and under crowd who will compare to the young quarterbacks from 10 years ago?

The NFL is a passing league. To put a good product on the field, the NFL needs great quarterback play. In the modern passing era of the NFL, never before have we been so dependent on aging stars to carry the league's quarterback play. I'm not talking about one year of brilliance here or there. I'm talking about consistency. We have a few young talents who, perhaps one day, be in a conversation for that level of talent. But the NFL could find itself in a quarterback crisis in just a couple of years. Teams are mortgaging their draft classes in hopes of taking a young quarterback in the first round. But if those quarterbacks don't pan out, like many have not over the last 4 years, there will be a ton of quarterback-needy teams, without enough elite passers to go around. And the overall level of play will become watered down tremendously.

So to end on a softer, slightly more optimistic note, I'll say this: let's enjoy what we get this year from guys like Drew Brees, Ben Roethlisberger and Philip Rivers. These 3 quarterbacks in particular tend to get overlooked in favor of other quarterbacks. And while they each have their flaws, the way these 3 guys can spin the ball on a good day is top notch. So let's appreciate what they have and what they're doing at 35+ years old. Their level of performance didn't exist in the NFL a decade ago. The guys getting it done at that age 10 years ago are in the hall of fame (Favre, Warner). Of course, we have Tom Brady and Aaron Rodgers to pull for. But appreciate the passion and performance those 3 older quarterbacks give, because in a few years, we might look back and wish we still had guys like that again on Sunday afternoons.

Island Takes

"I might be alone on this one, but I'm not wrong"

I see many takes heading into this season on Twitter, on TV and bandied about by the throngs and I certainly don't get distracted by all of them. But every once in awhile I'll hear one that I really disagree with but is backed by many whose opinion I typically respect. Here are several of those fairly popular takes, which I genuinely disagree with:

The Patriots will be a pass heavy team in 2017

First and foremost, they should have more total pass attempts (volume) because Brady isn't suspended the first 4 games. I think anyone with any level of football understanding would agree to that. But apart from that, I don't see why they suddenly decide from a rate (or even volume) perspective to go more pass heavy than usual. Examine these factors:

1 – they face a more difficult schedule of pass defenses but a MUCH easier schedule of run defenses in 2017. The first graphic clearly shows this. Last year they played an easier schedule of pass defenses (19th hardest) than run defenses (11th hardest). This year, they move to the 12th hardest schedule of pass defenses (up from 19th) and they move to the 5th easiest schedule of run defenses (down from 11th hardest).

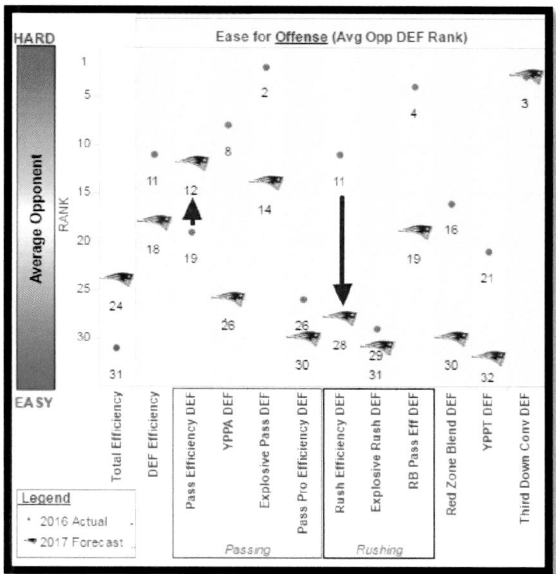

As you can see from the second graphic, those are the run defenses they are swapping out from 2016. Those teams ranked 2nd (SEA), 5th (BAL), 6th (LAR), 7th (ARI), 20th (CIN), 27th (CLE) and 31st (SF). Instead, they now get to face teams who ranked 9th (CAR), 15th (SD), 18th (OAK), 19th (NO), 24th (TB), 26th (KC) and 29th (ATL).

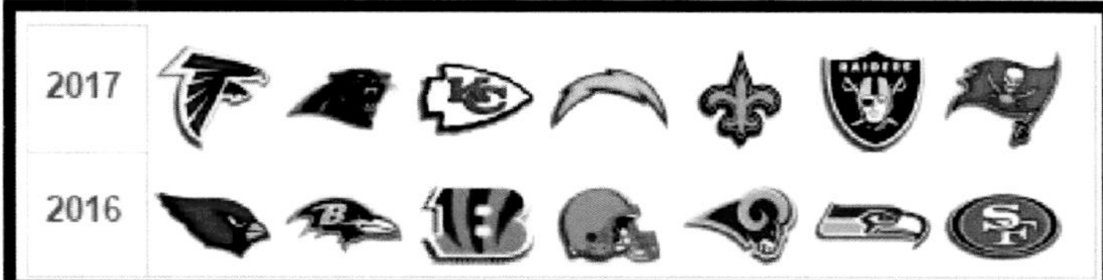

2 – what we know about Bill Belichick is he typically takes the path of least resistance. Against great run defenses, he'll abort the run entirely. But otherwise, he stays balanced. For example, last year in games projected to be closer than usual for the Patriots against good run defenses (home vs Seattle and Baltimore, away vs the Jets), Belichick ran the ball just 39% of the time when the game was within one-score (4th quarter aside). The rest of the season, that number rose to 42%. While that may not sound like much, we'll examine the 4th quarter individually below for a better understanding.

And as you can see from the below comparison, with the 2016 schedule on the left and the 2017 schedule on the right, the Patriots move from playing 6 games against top 10 run defenses to half that number in 2017. There simply aren't as many really strong run defenses that the Patriots will shy away from running on in 2016.

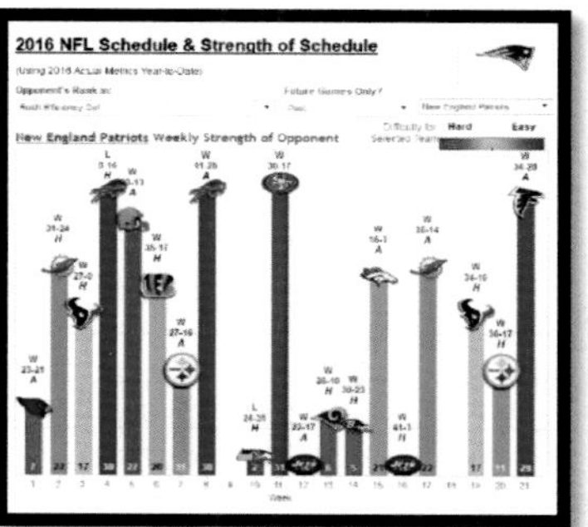

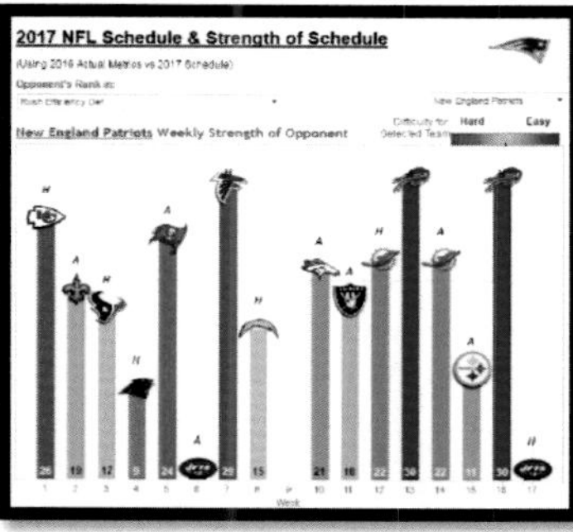

3 – A stronger team means a better game script for running the ball. Last year in Brady-run games (apart from the 3 games against solid run defenses predicted to be close games) the Patriots ran the ball on 59% of their 4th quarter offensive plays, the 3rd most run heavy rate in the NFL. In those other 3 games, they ran the ball 41% of the time in the 4th quarter, even though they won 2 of the games, simply because even late, Belichick won't go run heavy with a lead against a top 5 run defense. And again, he doesn't face as many teams like that in 2017. But back to game script:

With a lead in the 4th quarter, the Patriots run the ball (all opponents combined) on 65% of early down plays. While this was below average, their overall volume (124 total plays) was by far the most in the NFL. Thus, their 80 total runs was the most in the NFL. And against worse run defenses, expect those early down runs to be more successful, resulting in even less of a need to pass with a lead in the 4th quarter.

4 – And that transitions into what the 2017 Patriots will try to become. Recall that many thought the 2016 Patriots, once Tom Brady returned, would attempt to become the 2007 revenge tour Patriots all over again? That never materialized. The Patriots won games, but they were winning games most often by scores of 27-16, 22-17, 30-23, etc. Not so much the 41-3 beatdown they laid on the Jets. The Patriots were simply trying to win games, not set records. The Lombardi was the goal, not the highest scoring offense. I wouldn't expect 2017 to be significantly different. Of course they are trying to go 19-0 this year, as they try to do every year. But I don't envision them running up the score just for the hell of it like they did with a much younger Tom Brady and pissed off Bill Belichick back in 2007.

5 – Speaking of age, Tom Brady isn't getting any younger. Thanks to his health, the Patriots have operated at peak levels since 2009, making the conference championship in 6 straight seasons. But Brady turns 40 on August 3rd. The team wasn't willing to relinquish Jimmy Garoppolo this past offseason, despite Brady suggesting he has several more years left. There is no doubt he's on the tail end of his career, but there is also no doubt the Patriots would love for him to play well (and be paid cheaply, as he is) for years to come. Thus, the logic for him to throw more often than the last several years just because passing is more efficient than rushing isn't wise.

6 – Speaking of this efficiency, while I've been discussing it for multiple years how the passing rules made passing much more of a factor in winning games than rushing, it seems like many people are starting to discuss this relationship within the past year. While they may first have heard about it recently, it isn't new to me or those that follow my work. More important than that, it's certainly not new to the Patriots. It's not as if they thought, suddenly since last year, "you know what, I think passing might be the way to go next year because, gosh, it's just so efficient." The Patriots have known this for years, but that doesn't mean they will pass all of the time when the scoreboard and game clock is in their favor and they can beat you by running.

7 – And when it comes to running, the Patriots have a full stable of productive running backs on the roster. They just added Mike Gillislee and Rex Burkhead in the offseason. These RBs ranked #1 and #2 in rushing success rate and in missed YPA last year. While they can catch passes, like James White and Dion Lewis, they are also extremely productive on the ground. This team can cycle through these guys and they can all run and catch the ball. They have the potential to systematically play to whatever mismatches exist on a particular play. Which plays into the next point:

8 – The Patriots should be even more explosive in 2017. Rob Gronkowski was the team's top deep threat until his injury. The impetus for pass explosion shifted to Chris Hogan, and he absolutely dominated. With both Hogan and Gronkowski as proven and reliable deep threats, and Brandon Cooks capable of providing a ton of explosion in the passing game himself, there are plenty of big chunk plays likely out of this offense. While that increases passing yardage and possibly passing touchdowns, it decreases passing plays and inherently shifts the run/pass ratio over the remainder of the game. That is because explosive pass plays lead to larger leads which mean less need to pass late in the game, and more likelihood of rushing over the course of the game.

9 – Touching back on game script, let's not overlook half of the Patriots team and that is their defense. This team added Stephon Gilmore and Kony Ealey were both added. This defense is significantly stronger than 2016. And what people forget about 2016 is they were a terrible defense. The biggest fallacy entering the Super Bowl was the Patriots "#1 Scoring Defense". I burned that argument to the ground, fueled by efficiency ratings and strength of schedule faced, as you can see below.

Super Bowl Winning "Number One" Defenses (in PPG)

Year	Team	PPG	Total Eff	SOS	Pass Eff	Run Eff
2016	Patriots	1	16	32	23	4
2013	Seahawks	1	1	31	1	7
2008	Steelers	1	1	9	1	2
2003	Patriots	1	2	16	2	13
2002	Buccaneers	1	1	32	1	8
2000	Ravens	1	2	26	2	2
1996	Packers	1	1	24	1	9

One of their biggest weaknesses last year was that on early downs in the first half, the Patriots defense ranked 32nd in success rate against passes and 24th in success rate against runs inside their own 40 yard line. Overall they ranked 31st, allowing successful plays to be executed 56% of the time, which came against the easiest schedule of opposing offenses. And that can't be emphasized enough.

Hunter Henry is getting overlooked

Let me first state that I love the TE market this year and there a ton of players I think will contribute far better than WR2 numbers. But I really think Henry is getting overlooked. As I type, in PPR, he's TE10 with an ADP of 8.11 in 12 team leagues. Philip Rivers loves throwing to his TE. 26% of all attempts go to the TE, the 4th most frequent TE targeting team (HOU, KC, CAR). The key, however, is inside the red zone: last year the Chargers threw a massive 42% of all red zone passes to a TE.

Target Rate

Offense	RB	TE	WR
SD	20%	42%	38%
MIN	16%	38%	46%
DAL	7%	36%	57%
HOU	18%	33%	49%
IND	16%	33%	51%
TB	8%	32%	59%

Last year the Chargers intentionally chose to become more inefficient by playing Antonio Gates so much more than the rookie Hunter Henry. They wanted Gates to break the TD record, and he's a legend in San Diego, and the Chargers obviously were doing nothing with their season, so there were sentimental reasons why they let it happen. But when you look at virtually any advanced metric (or even basic metrics) it wasn't close. Henry averaged 9.1 yards per attempt (best on the team) while Gates averaged just 5.9. Henry delivered a 136 rating (best on the team) while Gates delivered an 86 rating.

In terms of advanced metrics, Henry ranked #1 in the entire NFL (any receiver, regardless of position, min 50 targets) for missed YPA (yards per attempt), a metric which measures how close to successful a player was on unsuccessful plays. Gates was 46th in this metric. Henry was also 16th in overall success rate while Gates was 60th. Clearly, targeting Gates 93 times to only 53 targets for Henry was not an efficient usage of these players. While Gates is back in 2017 and looking for the TD record, Henry has the ability to emerge early in the season, overtake Gates rather quickly, and become their dominant TE. And if you want to see some of Henry's stats from a site like Football Outsiders, compared to other tight ends he ranked fourth in DVOA, fifth in DYAR and fifth in YAC+, a metric that examines yards after the catch..

Gates will still see usage in an effort to get him the TD record (he has 111 receiving TDs, tied with Tony Gonzalez for most all time), but I would be exceedingly surprised if it was anything close to 2016 given his terrible production. There is simply no way a team wanting to win games in a new city with new fans should still rely on the Jurassic-aged Gates given his complete and utter lack of efficiency. I'll say it point blank: any plan designed to get Gates more targets than Henry this year is not in the team's best interest.

One final key for production this season will be how the red zone shares that went to Gates last year are divided up. In the red zone, Rivers clearly favored size. His top 3 targets were 6'5" (Hunter Henry, 17 targets), 6'4" (Antonio Gates, 20 targets) and 6'4" (Tyrell Williams, 17 targets). No other receiver saw more than 6 targets. Rookie Mike Williams is 6'4", tips the scale at 218 lbs and is the biggest WR on the roster. And Keenan Allen is healthy (for now). So we should expect some of the TE volume to shift back to WRs, but we should expect Henry to take on more of the TE load. And the TE load for the Chargers is a highly enviable volume. Henry led the Chargers with 8 receiving TDs last year despite half the receptions of several receivers. Like Rivers to Gates when Gates was in his prime, when Rivers finds a reliable guy, he will ride him. It could very well become Henry this year.

Don't Forget Jack Doyle and Kyle Rudolph, Either

There you go. How's that for verbose?

Jay Ajayi wasn't as good as you think last year

Last year Jay Ajayi totaled 1,272 rushing yards (4th most) despite missing one game, and averaged 4.9 yards per rush, 7th best in the NFL. On the surface, these numbers are great. Hell, Jay Ajayi was also Pro Football Focus' #1 graded regular season running back last year. But when you dig into the analytics, they show problems:

There are three key rushing analytics I like to use: Success Rate, Missed YPA and YAS %. Success Rate is the frequency which a player generates the required yardage (per play, based on down and distance-to-go) to grade as successful. Missed YPA measures yardage on unsuccessful plays which fell short of the required distance-to-go to grade as successful. And YAS % (Yards Above Successful) isolates only the yardage on successful plays which was in excess of required, aka measuring explosive yardage.

These are three key metrics that evaluate runs that come up short, just enough, or more than required. And they are more valuable than total or

Why the Professionals Use & Trust Warren Sharp

When I was told about and introduced to Warren Sharp I was beyond skeptical. After working with some of the most successful syndicate groups for 15+ years I knew the NFL was practically unbeatable. After all, I worked 60+ hour work weeks breaking down and analyzing lines and looked forward to my Sunday's off. Needless to say that's not the way it is anymore on Sundays due to Warren. His NFL and especially his totals are second to none. Also, nobody can break down a NFL game like Warren and I don't know how anyone bets without his analysis and selections.

I am now proud to say he is now one of my best friends and I do not fail to mention him when I am a guest on a radio or tv show. I also give him a live podcast each and every Sunday live from Las Vegas which is available free to his customers. He has proved to me and the gambling public that you CAN beat the NFL.

Warren's Football Preview is amazing. It touches on everything you could hope to find, and many things you never thought you'd find, in a preview. It's not often that a football mind like Warren lays out his thoughts as extensively, in such an organized manner for easy reading and comprehension. I don't see how anyone could afford to pass this book up if they plan to make money on football this fall. It's that good.

- Bill Krackomberger, winning professional gambler, seen on ESPN, CNN, Fox Sports and dozens of publications and newspapers around the country

Warren's dedication and acumen for analyzing football is clearly evident in the work he produces. This book is completely unlike anything I've read in a preview before, but that's what I've come to expect from Warren. His ability to approach the game logically, analytically and in a predictive manner sets him apart from the crowd. Between the narratives, articles and graphics, I have no doubt after reading this preview you will be far more prepared for your fantasy drafts and just football in general. If you're a NFL fan of any kind, I cannot recommend this preview enough.

- Evan Silva, Rotoworld.com Senior Football Editor, @evansilva

A truly indispensable resource to kick off your handicapping process for the upcoming NFL season, Warren Sharp's analytics-based Football Preview makes up for mainstream media's shortcomings by providing smart and advanced schedule analysis, insightful context to roster construction, and team and player projections, all certain to give you a leg up on both sportsbooks and your fantasy competition alike.

- Gill Alexander, Host of "A Numbers Game" - Vegas Stats & Information Network (VSiN), @beatingthebook

Been at this for 38 years in print, and have enjoyed every minute, win or lose. The NFL has given me problems forever. A few games over .500, a few games under .500, nothing exceptional, and mostly paying my guy every week. Until last season when one of the most INFLUENTIAL whales in the wagering world put me on to Warren Sharp. Read Sharp's 2016 Football Preview from cover to cover, and wound up posting a Ridiculous 137-110-8 record picking every game in the NFL. And even tastier, 12-3-1 in my weekly best bets Coincidence? NAH. It was Sharp's amazing angles and deep dives into stats I didn't even know existed. And when you see his records, it's STRAIGHT UP HONEST. How do I know? I had access to Sharp's picks every week, and his percentages tickled and exceeded the 60% range. As most know who have read my columns for the past 37 years, I have NEVER recommended any handicapper. Most are SCAMDICAPPERS that get you to pay for recycled GARBAGE. Sharp's stats, amazing graphics and advanced metrics are FREAKIN' GROUND BREAKING. Get Sharp, stay Sharp, live Sharp. You will be AMAZED!!!

- Benjamin Eckstein, AmericasLine.com, nationally syndicated sportswriter in the New York Daily News and part of Ecks & Bacon

Analytics plays a bigger role in sports betting than ever before. Information travels at a speed nobody would have thought possible a decade ago. With so many analytical options available to both the bettor and the odds maker the choices we make for analytics have never been more important. When it comes to the NFL there is no one I trust and use more than Warren Sharp. Warren has an amazing grasp of the analytics that matter in the sports betting world and how to implement those in a practical and easy to read format. I would highly recommend that anyone involved in the sports betting industry try implementing Warren's analyses into their NFL work.

- Matthew Holt, COO of CG Analytics, @MatthewHoltVP

Warren's synopsis on game totals is vastly superior utilizing his mathematical formulas, to any preview I have ever seen. His success is two-fold, beating the closing number by up to 3 pts and winning at a clip needed to secure a hefty profit. Getting in early ensures some fantastic middling opportunities.

- Richie Baccellieri, former Director of Race and Sports in Las Vegas at Caesars Palace, MGM Grand and The Palms

I can't speak highly enough about Warren to give him the credit he deserves. He's the hardest working guy I know in the business, more importantly, his attention to detail is unparalleled. I don't think we've ever had a phone conversation less than an hour due to the amazing wealth of knowledge he rolls off with ease. I hold him in great regard. I appreciate his dedication and talent.

- @lasvegascris, winning professional gambler

average yardage because those numbers lie. Take an example: A RB is used only on 1st down and has 10 rushes in a game. 9 of those 10 rushes gain exactly 2 yards. But on one play, the LB fills the wrong hole, a lineman gets to the second level and creates an even larger alley, and the RB breaks one tackle and then bulldozes a CB as he runs 82 yards for a TD. The RB totals 100 yards on the game. He averages 10 yards per carry. Sounds like a great game. But the reality was, his 2 yard gains on those other 1st downs set up 2nd and long each time, and his team was at a major disadvantage. Success rate knows that on 1st and 10, a play needs at least 4 yards to grade as successful. Therefore, only 1 of his 10 carries was successful. His missed YPA was 2.0, as on each unsuccessful run which needed 4 yards, he fell 2 yards short. And his YAS % is going to be substantial, as his lone successful play saw 82 yards gained: 4 of which were required and 78 of which were "above successful".

Jay Ajayi was not to that extreme, not by far. But while he ranked 7th best in yards per attempt and 4th best in total yards, he ranked 43rd in success rate and 49th in Missed YPA. However, his YAS % was 5th best. Much like the example above, a lot of Ajayi's yardage came on big, explosive runs.

He was bottled up an awful lot on other occasions: 23% of his total production for the entire season came on just 2.5% (7 runs) of his total runs. 57% (157 runs) of Ajayi's rushes gained 3 or fewer yards. Ajayi's success rate was not consistently bad. Without Mike Pouncey and Brandon Albert, Ajayi's success rate was 38% (on 180 carries). With both in the lineup, his success rate was 49% (on 96 carries). And over a 4-game sample size, recording a 49% success rate isn't particularly great, though it was notable how much worse he was without those key offensive linemen.

Ajayi's physical style also wore himself down by the end of the season. From week 10 onward, Ajayi averaged a 35% success rate on 168 attempts. It was the worst success rate for any RB with at least 90 carries (25 RBs). His Missed YPA was 2.5 YPA, which was also worst in the NFL. In laymen's terms, this means that on the 65% of runs which graded as unsuccessful, on average he was short of the "line to gain" to make that run successful by a full 2.5 yards each run. That's a massive amount, and it's more meaningful because of the large sample size of unsuccessful runs. It's important to note that he was substantially better in every single metric up until that point in time. Likely it was a combination of defenses keying on him, his own fatigue, and injuries to the offensive line. See the graphic for Ajayi's rushes, week 10 onward:

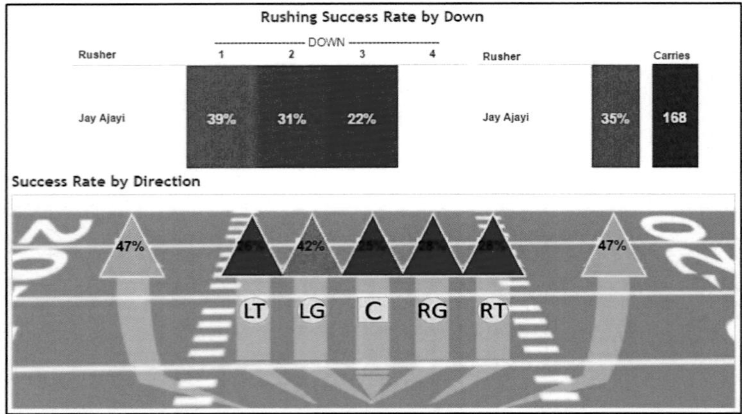

Where is room for optimism for 2017? His run schedule gets slightly easier, and his offensive line should be healthier. In OTAs, OC Clyde Christensen was quoted as gushing over Ajayi's improvement, and HC Adam Gase mentioned Ajayi could see as much as 350 attempts this year, 90 more than he received last year. While this bodes well for fantasy, I don't like it for the Dolphins from a real football perspective, particularly considering how much Ajayi wore down last season due to such a physical, punishing running style. I think it would be a big mistake, for a team which made the playoffs last year and wants to go deeper this year, to wear out Ajayi over the course of the regular season. Last season I predicted his decline, and knew for the playoff game in Pittsburgh it would be a disaster. Where other pundits were talking big about Ajayi's yards per carry average, I was talking bad about his long term and short term success rate. In that game in Pittsburgh, Ajayi posted an absolutely horrendous 19% success rate and gained just 33 yards on 16 carries (2.1 yards per attempt).

However, one positive that I heard was that Adam Gase wants Ajayi used more in the passing game. This is what gets me excited. For a couple of reasons. First, there is talk Ajayi's receiving skills are much better than they were at this time last year (as to be expected). Second, Miami was far too dependent on WR targets last year at 66% of all targets, well above average, and far less dependent on the most efficient type of targets: those to tight ends and early down RB targets. Want proof? Let's throw out garbage time in the 4th quarter for starters, and let's look at first down passes to RBs. Miami targeted RBs just 15% of all attempts on first down, which was well below average (19%). Yet a whopping 60% of those targets were successful, which was even better than the success rate to their WRs on first down (57%). And third, the Dolphins play what I'm projecting to be the easiest schedule of opposing RB-pass defenses. There could be a ton of opportunity for increased efficiency if they target Ajayi in the passing game.

And what does that allow the Dolphins? It allows them to take their bruiser, who they want to clearly ride this year (Gase loves riding RBs when his QB is less than stellar, as is Tannehill), and get him away from the defensive line and the tackle box. Getting Ajayi the ball in space means less hits on him, less of a beating. Which is why I'd prefer them to run him early in the season, and then keep using him but introduce a much heavier pass usage and a lower rush usage. This could preserve him longer into the season, reduce wear and tear on his body, and yet keep the Dolphins efficient and most of all, get the ball into his hands running downhill against safeties, corners and lighter defenders where Ajayi excels in doling out punishment.

The Chiefs Defense is Being Drafted Too High

Yes, I realize the Chiefs defense was the highest scoring fantasy defense last year. But that was last year. This year, they are being drafted as fantasy defense #3. And that's just not realistic.

Last year the Chiefs recorded 33 takeaways. They led the NFL in fumble recoveries. And as we know, stripping a fumble is one thing, recovering that bouncing football is another. They also recorded 18 interceptions, tied for the league high. But consider the competition faced:

They recorded 6 interceptions alone against Ryan Fitzpatrick, who posted 4.3 yards per attempt and an 18 passer rating. They also had the luxury of facing Trevor Siemian twice and sacked him 5 times. They faced Blake Bortles, Brock Osweiler and Andrew Luck, behind his miserable offensive line, and they sacked him 6 times. They face a much more difficult schedule this year:

While they don't have to play the Falcons or Saints, they instead must face the NFC East, which means the Cowboys, the Giants (who rarely take sacks), the Redskins and their high-powered offense, and the Eagles who should show improvement offensively. They also must take on the AFC East, which means the Patriots, the Dolphins in year 2 of Adam Gase and Tyrod Taylor's running on the ground. Bottom line, the Chiefs go from playing the 21st rated offenses to the 11th this year. They also face offenses which are 2nd in projected pass protection strength. That could mean fewer sacks and with more time, fewer interceptions and less return TDs.

Not to mention the other side of the coin, which is the more difficult road for the Chiefs offense and the absence of WR Jeremy Maclin. If the offense struggles, that means worse field position for their defense. Bottom line, there are several other defenses worthy of top-5 positioning this year, and I don't see the Chiefs repeating as the #1 scoring fantasy defense in 2017, nor living up to their DEF3 draft position.

Superior Data-Driven Measurement of 2017 Strength of Schedule

By Warren Sharp

I've attempted to pioneer a more educated analysis of strength of schedule because the current method used to analyze schedule strength is literally the least efficient possible. The established method looks only at prior year win percentage, with absolutely zero context accounted for, and measures those rates against current-year opponents. The Parcells-ism "you are what your record says you are" is true only as it relates to making the playoffs in that particular season. Apart from determining which teams make or miss the playoffs, a record is hardly the most accurate way to measure a team's strengths or weaknesses, or compare it to the rest of the NFL.

Measuring 2017 strength of schedule against 2016 record is lazy, inaccurate and inefficient. But like most things in the NFL, it was an accepted method from the past, and there is a reluctance to shift away from established thought processes, regardless of the low-intelligence level such processes reflect. I've built my foundation on questioning tradition and employing more efficient NFL decision making.

At my in-season analytical-thought website (Sharp Football Analysis.com) I attack the NFL from an analytical perspective, often using contrarian thinking to find edges, and share my ideas weekly. I also developed a free-to-use stats website (Sharp Football Stats.com) which uses advanced analytics and a visual graphical representation technique to allow users to customize, visualize, process and retain information unlike anything they've seen before.

When it comes to strength of schedule, the reality is using in-season data produces a more effective representation and measure of opponent as opposed to pre-season projections. But most NFL media don't see it that way – they will chime in a lot between now and September with strength of schedule (calculated the wrong way) but during the season, you won't hear them ever discuss strength of schedule. I've established a reputation of producing some of the most useful strength of schedule metrics for both understanding performance ("year to date") as well as predicting future capabilities based on schedule of opponents.

This article, the first of the series, will focus on 2017 Strength of Schedule using forecast win totals current as of late June from the betting market. For this article, I used one of the sharpest offshore books (Pinnacle) and two Vegas books (CG Technology & South Point). Based on the three books, I built a model to create a consensus line which factors in juice. Ignoring juice is a massive mistake. For example, ignoring juice on the Tampa Bay Buccaneers over 8 wins would be incorrect. You must lay $140 to $145 to win $100 when betting the over. That is very different than if you bet over 8 wins on the Detroit Lions, where you only need to bet $84 to win $100.

Using win totals to forecast 2017 strength of schedule is far more useful than using 2016 season results. And we now have the added benefit of these totals being crafted by the betting market for 2 months. The Titans opened at 9.5 wins, meaning to win a bet on the over, they would have to win 10 games. That plummeted and sits at 8.5 wins (-140 to the over). The Patriots opened at 11 wins, and are now up to 12.5 (-135 to the under). Whereas at open, an 11-win season was a

2017 Strength of Schedule

Based on *June* 2017 Season Win Totals

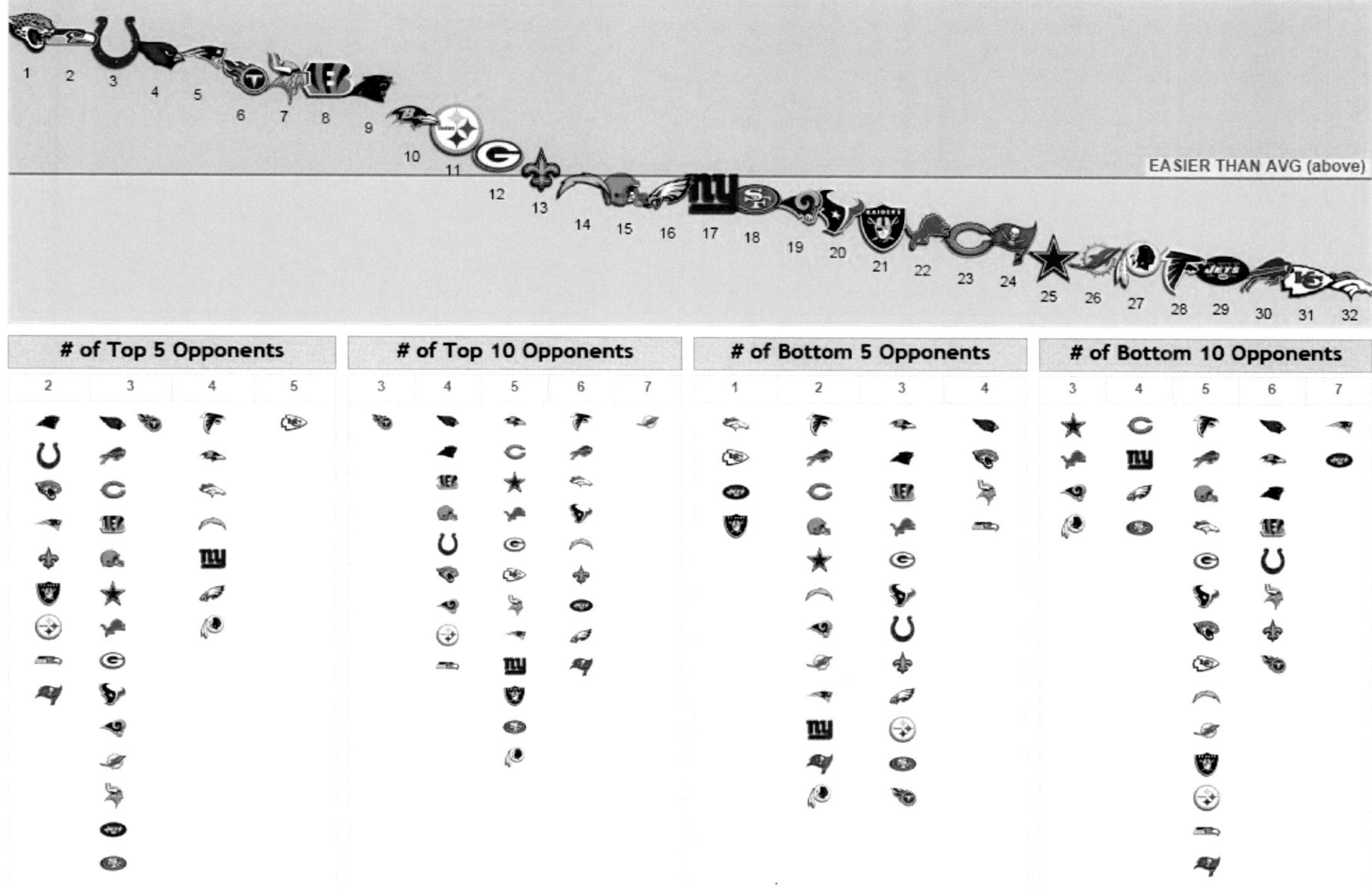

push, now a bettor needs 13 wins just to win an over bet. So, we have an even better opportunity to understand the real strength of schedule now, as opposed to in April, because we have the other side of the coin. We had the bookmaker opinion, and now we have the market's response.

And lastly, as to why strength of schedule in general is essential for fantasy as well as for the betting market, the answer is because of game script. The NFL is almost 60% pass, 40% run over the course of all teams and all 4 quarters of a game. Third down is a reactionary down, based on distance to go. So, scrapping that momentarily and looking only at the early downs: all game long early downs are 54% pass, 46% run. But across the entire game, that inverts itself for the team with the lead: they are 56% run, 44% pass. Specifically, on early downs in the second half, the team with the lead (of any size) is 64% run, 36% pass. Even with a one-score lead (one to eight points), these teams are 60% run to 40% pass. Meanwhile, the team trailing is 66% pass, 34% run. Thus, understanding which team is likely to be leading or trailing is a massive factor in fantasy production. The tougher the opponents, the less likely a team is to be leading. The below analysis should help tremendously to project fantasy fortunes in 2017.

I'll run through all 32 teams, starting with the toughest schedule (32) and moving to the easiest (1). Up at THIS page at Sharp Football Stats, I have a visualization where you can see all this data and customize for certain weeks, to see hardest/easiest starts or finishes to the season.

32. Denver Broncos

This season, Denver plays four games against top-5 opponents (teams projected to win the most games this year). Only one team plays more top-5 games (Chiefs). They play six top-10 games (only the Dolphins play more top-10 teams). The 7 games post-bye week are brutal when factoring in the travel. At least if he is passing often, Trevor Siemian will face the 2nd easiest schedule of opposing pass rushes this year.

31. Kansas City Chiefs

For the Chiefs, the 2017 season will be a study in survival. If they can survive through week 11, they have a very good chance to win 5 of their last 6 games. But getting to that point is a tall order. In total, they play five top-5 games (most in the NFL) and just one bottom-5 game (least in the NFL). Against the 5th most difficult schedule of pass defenses, Alex Smith might find himself throwing more than he (or Chiefs fans) would like to see.

30. Buffalo Bills

While the Bills only play three top-5 games, which is league-average, they play six top-10 games. Their schedule is made much less brutal by two games against the Jets, with the first at home in week 1. After week 1, they have the most difficult schedule in the NFL. While there is not a bevy of hard opponents, they don't have any non-Jets games which you would consider them to be a superior team to their opponent. This potentially could bode well for Tyrod rushing yardage.

29. NY Jets

The Jets are a terrible football team with a roller coaster schedule. They play six top-10 games, the 2nd most in the NFL) but also play seven bottom-10 games (the most in the NFL). They play teams like the Browns, Jaguars and Bills twice, but also must take on the Falcons, Raiders, Chiefs and Patriots twice. While they have the 2nd easiest schedule of run defenses, they may not have as much an opportunity to take advantage of that as they would like, due to game script.

28. Atlanta Falcons

Fresh off their great season, the Falcons and their first-place schedule must play four top-5 games and six top-10 games, both the second most in the NFL. The start of their schedule should be easy, as they play 4 of their first 5 games against bottom-10 opponents (Chicago, Detroit, Buffalo and Miami). It's the 4th easiest schedule to start the season. But from week 7 onward, they have the most difficult schedule in the NFL. I expect them to be competitive this year, balanced, and seeing a lot more ease for their passing game, facing the 8th easiest schedule (after tangling with the 4th hardest last year).

27. Washington Redskins

The Redskins overall schedule of top-10 games is league average, but their schedule trouble is they only play three bottom-10 teams, the fewest in the NFL. They play a lot of competitive teams this year, so we'll see a balanced effort. The problem for Washington is they face the #1 toughest schedule of pass defenses and the #2 schedule of run defenses. So, they'll be balanced, but nothing will be particularly easy.

26. Miami Dolphins

In the first month of the season, the Dolphins should be able to run Jay Ajayi as often as they would like, given they face the 2nd easiest schedule through week 4. But from week 5 through fantasy championship week 16, the Dolphins play the toughest schedule in the NFL. They play seven top-10 games. The NFL average is just four top-10 games. Against a potentially tough schedule of run defenses, hopefully they will turn to target Ajayi in the pass game, as they face the easiest schedule of RB-pass defenses.

25. Dallas Cowboys

From a strength of schedule perspective, I'll always pay more attention to when a bad team faces a tough schedule or a good team faces an easy schedule than I will be when a good team like the Cowboys face a tougher schedule. Dallas should be balanced even against their toughest opponents (Seahawks, Packers and Raiders). The biggest concern I have for Dallas is their start and finish. Playing a tough Giants squad followed by back to back road games in difficult environments (at Broncos, at Cardinals) isn't easy. To end the season, those same Giants kick off back to back road games, with the second being out in Oakland, followed by a home game against the Seahawks the week of fantasy championships.

24. Tampa Bay Buccaneers

The Buccaneers offense needs to be running at full potential leaving their bye, because they play the 4th most difficult schedule from weeks 12 through 17. They play four top-10 opponents in 5 weeks, and their entire schedule is filled with offensive firepower (Falcons twice, Packers, Saints, Lions and Panthers). This bodes well for late season production from Jameis Winston, who faces the 7th easiest schedule of pass defenses this year.

23. Chicago Bears

Mitch Trubisky may hope he doesn't get lucky and somehow win the starting job because the Bears schedule is brutal to start the season. It's the toughest in the NFL through week 7. They play four top-10 games (most of any team) and no team they face is ranked below 16th in projected win rankings this year. They also face zero bottom-10 games in this span. However, from week 11 onward, Chicago has by far the easiest schedule: they are the only team without a single top-10 game and play four bottom-10 games in these 7 games, making a perfect time to transition in a rookie if needed and rely on the run game assistance against beatable opponents.

22. Detroit Lions

The Lions average schedule is only 22nd, but the reality is if they didn't have 3 games against the 4 worst teams, their schedule would be significantly more difficult. They play 11 of their 16 games against top-16 opponents. If Matthew Stafford gets put into positions where he needs to win games with his arm, that could be a problem, as the Lions face the most difficult schedule of opposing pass rushes this year.

21. Oakland Raiders

For ranking 21st, the Raiders have a manageable schedule in that they play just two top-5 games, the least of any team in the league. And neither is a true road game in a hostile stadium: the Patriots week 11 in London and the Cowboys in Oakland week 15. The first 9 weeks of the season the Raiders have the 4th easiest schedule, which should allow for a lot of balance and plenty of Marshawn Lynch.

20. Houston Texans

Houston's schedule is extremely diverse. They will be in many difficult games, playing six top-10 games this year (second most). But they also play three bottom-5 games (second most). It helps their schedule playing the Jaguars twice and the Browns, Rams and 49ers. But they have three brutal non-divisional games against the Patriots, Seahawks and Steelers. The best part about their schedule is facing the 4th easiest schedule of opposing pass defenses, for whoever ends up winning the quarterback battle.

19. Los Angeles Rams

It will be hard enough for new HC Sean McVay to get Jared Goff on track when the Rams face pass defenses which rank 9th this year, up from 21st last year. But they only get three bottom-10 games this year, the fewest bad opponents this year. The good news is they only play four top-10 games, the 2nd fewest in the league. It will be imperative to stay in games, to allow for balanced play calling, as opposed to fighting from behind and into the teeth of these top pass defenses, such as (in consecutive games) the Seahawks, Jaguars, Cardinals, Giants, Texans and Vikings.

18. San Francisco 49ers

Much like the Rams, at one spot above them, the 49ers must play the NFC East and AFC South. Which means stingy defenses, strong offenses, or both. The 49ers don't play a bevy of top-5 or top-10 opponents, they fall into the NFL averages in both categories. But they play just four bottom-10 opponents, meaning they'll struggle each week to find wins. That means to keep games close, they need to be able to see success rushing early, but are facing the NFL's toughest schedule of opposing run defenses, so it won't be easy.

17. NY Giants

The Giants schedule is neatly broken into halves. The first half is weeks 1-7, where they play top-5 teams in weeks 1 and 7 (Cowboys and Seahawks) but extremely winnable games in between. The second half starts week 11 and features two more top-5 games. In between, they have a bye (week 8, and play the Rams and 49ers in back to back games), which should prove to give them a boost mentally and physically as they enter the second half of the season. While they added receiving pieces this offseason, they face a significantly more difficult schedule of pass defenses (7th hardest, up from 27th last year), so the more rushing they can do the better.

16. Philadelphia Eagles

Possibly like 2016, look for the Eagles to start better than they finish the season. From week 11 onward, the Eagles play four top-5 opponents (Cowboys twice, Seahawks and Raiders). However, until that point, they are one of only four teams to face zero top-5 opponents. This should mean competitive games and allow Doug Pederson and Frank Reich to call very balanced games, which will help Carson Wentz immensely.

15. Cleveland Browns

Unlike the Jets, who are a bad team with a difficult schedule, the Browns are a bad team with a manageable schedule. RB Isiah Crowell is a popular fantasy starlet, but if he gets drafted too high, look for him on the trade market in-season. Cleveland's schedule starts in brutal fashion, but they play plenty of defenses that can be run on, starting week 3. And many of these teams are projected as mediocre to poor, which will keep the Browns in the game longer and able to run the ball more often.

14. Los Angeles Chargers

The most difficult part of the Chargers schedule is that when they play their toughest opponents, these games are on the road. They play only three top-5 games prior to week 17, and each is on the road (Raiders, Patriots and Cowboys). However, their home schedule of opponents is extremely palatable, with just one pre-week 17 opponent ranking above 18th (the Chiefs) in forecast win total. This bodes well for the run game, but I particularly love the pass game targets, and specifically, Hunter Henry, who will face the easiest schedule of pass defenses in the league from week 10 onward. It starts out very difficult, so snatch up Henry off a competitor's roster following consecutive games against the Eagles and Giants pass defenses.

13. New Orleans Saints

While the Saints schedule overall ranks 13th, they don't play very many middle-of-the-road opponents. They play six top-10 opponents, second most of any team, and they play six bottom-10 opponents, also second most. Therefore, on a weekly basis (depending on their 2017 defense) the Saints could be more very run heavy or very pass heavy. But they play one of the easiest schedules of opposing defenses, particularly following their bye week. Which means any way it gets sliced, the Saints should be making frequent trips to the red zone, so grabbing a key red zone target could pay dividends.

12. Green Bay Packers

We're now entering the realm of what I care more about from strength of schedule and that is when a good team faces an easy schedule. The Packers are favored in 12 of their 15 lined games, however they facing the league average of top-10 and bottom-10 opponents. They face substantially easier run defenses than pass defenses, and I think Ty Montgomery (currently drafted as RB19) has significant upside potential.

11. Pittsburgh Steelers

Like the Packers, if you take a great Steelers offense and give them an easy schedule, I'm highly interested. The Steelers play just four-top 10 games this year, second least in the league. And only two top-5 games, the fewest of any team. Through week 10, they face the easiest opponents in the league and are the only team to play just one top-10 game (Chiefs). This could translate into a higher run rate and more Le'Veon Bell (especially with DeAngelo Williams no longer in Pittsburgh).

10. Baltimore Ravens

The Ravens offense is not nearly as exciting as the Steelers or Packers, so the issue won't be whether they build up quick leads in games and sit on the ball. However, the good news is that with this schedule, they should be able to run more. And that cost them in 2016, as they called 67% pass plays, the most imbalanced team in the NFL. Hopefully the Ravens will find more to like out of their run game, but in most games this year they should find them in position to be able to run if they choose to do so.

9. Carolina Panthers

Don't look now, Panthers' fans, but your team just drafted Christian McCaffrey and they play the 4th easiest schedule of opponents weeks 1 through 7, including the second most (four) bottom-10 opponents. This means an investment in McCaffrey should play immediate dividends courtesy of game script. It should also allow Cam Newton to work more on his short RB passing game, so that it's ready for when they really need it over the second half of the season. A bad 2016 allows the Panthers to get games against the 49ers and Bears, in addition to the Jets and Bills this season – which substantially lightens the load in a competitive NFC South.

8. Cincinnati Bengals

The Bengals average schedule is somewhat misleading. They face a number of very difficult and capable teams in the middle of the league, such as the Ravens twice, Texans, Colts, Vikings and Broncos. But they play very few top-10 games (just four, second fewest) and they play six bottom-10 games, second most in the NFL. Metrics wise, the Bengals play the 8th easiest schedule of run defenses, and last year they were the third most run-heavy team when leading. All of these elements bode well for a rookie I think can make a mark this year, Joe Mixon.

7. Minnesota Vikings

Through week 12, the Vikings play the 3rd easiest schedule of opponents based on forecast win totals. And with the NFL's easiest schedule of pass defenses and 4th easiest schedule of run defenses on tap, the Vikings should be in many positive game script scenarios. The other benefit for their schedule is that the only game with the potential to be impacted with winter weather is week 16 in Green Bay. This should make up for years of playing outdoors recently, and is another (hidden) value for the opportunity for passing game value late in the season.

6. Tennessee Titans

To some teams, game script matters more than others. Last year, when leading in the second half, the Titans ran the ball 64% of the time, the highest rate of any team (average was 55%). They play a very easy schedule this year, featuring a NFL low of just three top-10 games (Raiders, Seahawks and Steelers). Two of these are in the first three weeks. I expect the passing attack to be stronger early in the year, but there will be plenty of run heavy scripts later in the year, as Tennessee faces the 3rd easiest schedule in the league from week 4 onward. The Titans were the 3rd most run heavy team in the red zone last year, and should be there often in 2017.

5. New England Patriots

Giving the Patriots schedule this year, given how they retooled this offseason, seems highly unfair. At least the Patriots will be tested more through week 7, with the 16th hardest schedule until that point, featuring three top-10 games (Chiefs, Panthers and Falcons). But after that, it's remarkable how lopsided most games should be, with exceptions of the Raiders and Steelers, both on the road. The Patriots, from week 8 onward, play six bottom-10 games, the most of any team. The only question is, which running back will get all that late-lead volume this year?

4. Arizona Cardinals

Any schedule analysis for the Cardinals must consider the boos they get by playing the Rams and 49ers twice. It works wonders for any average strength of schedule. However, the Cardinals play just four top-10 games this year (Seahawks twice, Cowboys and Titans) and three of those four are at home. Look for another year full of volume for David Johnson, for as long as he can last. Arizona ran the ball more than average in the red zone, which is another reason to like Johnson this season.

3. Indianapolis Colts

The Colts schedule is as easy as this average makes it look. They play the fewest (two) top-5 games (Seahawks and Steelers) and play the second most (six) bottom-10 games. That said, the reason their schedule is easier is because they play many easy (read: bad) offenses. They literally face the easiest schedule of opposing offenses. But the defenses the Colts face won't be exactly easy (they play the 9th most difficult defenses). These potentially could depress overall game scoring to an extent. Which could work in their fantasy-owner's favor as the Colts may feel pressure to continue scoring.

2. Seattle Seahawks

Much like the Cardinals, the Seahawks get a huge boost to their average thanks to playing in the NFC West against the Rams and 49ers. Seattle plays only four top-10 games, second fewest in the league. But the Seahawks actually face a number of teams flying just outside the top-10, such as the Giants (11), Texans (13), Colts (14) and Cardinals (16) twice. The direction of Seattle's offense is largely dependent on line play. Last year they passed the ball 10% more than in 2015 when the game was within one-score, because they couldn't run block or produce a healthy enough ball carrier. They ran the ball just 38% of the time in one-score games, 5th fewest in the NFL, which should revert to more rushing if Eddie Lacy is healthy and the offensive line can open holes.

1. Jacksonville Jaguars

Unlike the other teams with top-10 easy schedules (save the Ravens), the Jaguars offense is not exciting. And their strength of schedule isn't particularly exciting either. They don't have a cakewalk schedule; they simply only play two top-5 games (least in NFL) and four top-10 games (second least). The most interesting part about this dynamic is that while the Jaguars face the easiest schedule of opponents this year, their offensive rushing strength of schedule increases from 30th in 2016 to 8th hardest in 2017. This means even in games they are faring well in, they could struggle to simply run out the clock, and even then, may need to rely on the arm of Blake Bortles to finish off games. This sounds overly pessimistic to discuss the easiest schedule in the league in this manner, so the bottom line is, the schedule couldn't be much easier for Jacksonville this year, but that doesn't guarantee positive game scripts.

Players I Might Be Higher on Than You

By Warren Sharp

After writing all the team chapters in this 2017 Football Preview, there were a number of players I felt have more upside than what is currently envisioned for them. Specifically from a fantasy perspective, I see a number of these players being drafted behind players I like less, sometimes much less. Not all of these players will likely exceed their current ADP. But hear me out, listen to the logic and reasoning, and then process your own decisions based on the added information along with your other sources. I'm organizing these based on position first, followed by which players I feel might be provide the most value:

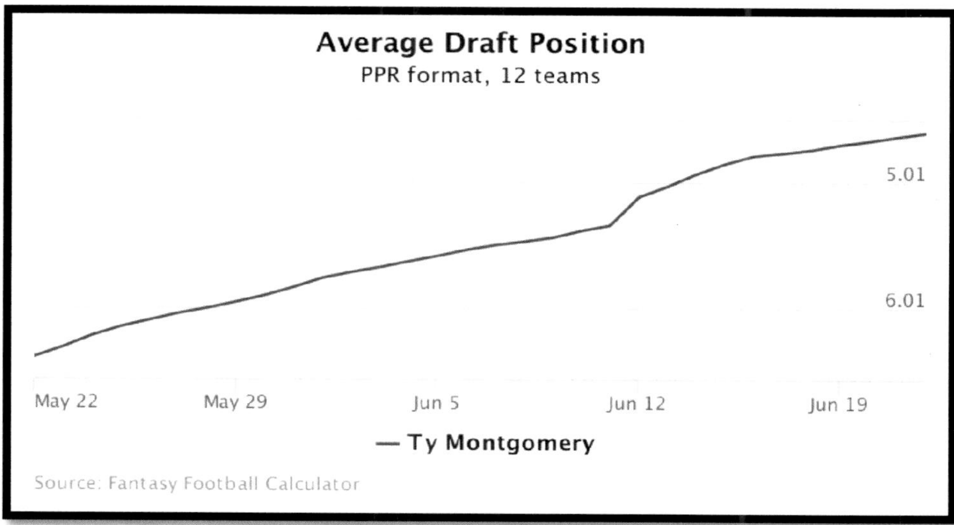

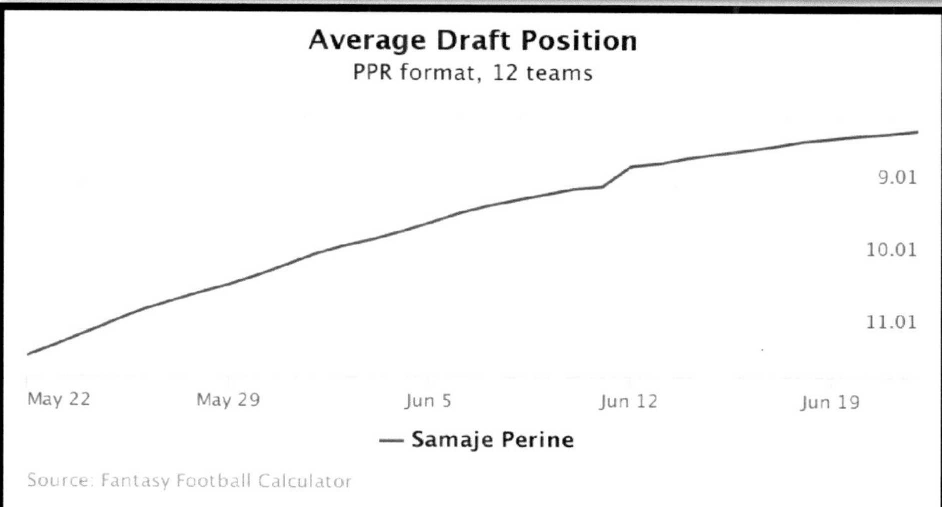

Ty Montgomery [RB19] – Montgomery's stock is on the rise, as opposed to Howard's. In March 12-team drafts, Montgomery was going in the 8th round. Right around the NFL draft, Montgomery was late 7th, early 8th. But when Mike McCarthy insisted in late April that Montgomery would be the team's starting RB, his draft stock rose immediately and hasn't stopped, and he's now a late 4th round selection. Montgomery recorded a total of 16 snaps the first 4 games of the season last year. The Packers finally moved him to RB full time starting in week 6. And he recorded 5.4 YPC, a 52% success rate, ranked 9th in missed YPA and 4th in YAS, which measures explosiveness in rushing yardage. The bottom line is, he tore it up as a RB last year. So what is the good news this year? For starters, he is the week 1 starter. He just needs to fend off a bevy of rookies, but the Packers literally purged the veteran RBs. Guys like Eddie Lacy, James Starks and Christine Michael. That means several things. First it means unlike 2016, where the Packers could pull Montgomery if he screwed up in a protection or didn't do something McCarthy liked, and put in a veteran, now McCarthy would have to throw a rookie into the mix, someone quite unfamiliar with playing alongside Aaron Rodgers. There is a greater chance Montgomery sees time. Second, those three players combined for 21 red zone rushes. And now they're all gone. Last year Montgomery led the team with 18 red zone rushes. Factor in a full season as starter, and distribute a lot of those other red zone targets his way, and suddenly you have an extremely viable red zone rushing threat. Third, it means more offseason reps at the position. He already says he has a better understanding of the position, and learned a lot of techniques and gap rules that he didn't know to start last season. Plus, you have a full offseason of Mike McCarthy dialing up plays for him. Finally, there is the schedule. The Packers play the 24th rated run defenses, but also play the 12th easiest schedule based on forecasted win totals, and are favored in 12 of their 15 lined games. There should be plenty of positive game scripts in Montgomery's future.

Samaje Perine [RB36] – Who remembers 2013? The Bengals, coming off a 10-6 season, still had their workhorse RB, BenJarvus Ellis. BGE had a somewhat lackluster 2012, however, rushing for only 3.9 YPC and scoring only 6 TDs. So, the Bengals drafted Giovani Bernard. And while BGE started the season, his performance got worse. He averaged only 3.4 YPC and while he still received 220 carries, he was phased out thanks to Bernard taking advantage of a strong start, where he averaged over 5 YPC his first 3 weeks. He earned consistent work, and ended up with over 1,100 total yards and 8 TDs on the season. And Bernard ended up as RB16 that season. I mention the Bengals because it was Gruden who ran that ship, and he runs this one as well. Last year Matt Jones ended up cast off, and Rob Kelley was thrust into the RB 1 role. He averaged 4.2 YPC and ranked 5th in Missed YPA. But really, who is Rob Kelley? He's a UDFA from Tulane who got the fortune of playing some in the preseason due to a shoulder injury to Matt Jones and impressed. Through 5 weeks in the regular season, he carried just 8 times, and after being so frustrated with Matt Jones, said Kelley is "deserving of more carries". The Redskins have no allegiance to him, other than his familiarity in the offense. He's not nearly as talented as Perine. The post-Scott McCloughan front office drafted Perine. Word immediately leaked that he would challenge Rob Kelley on early downs. Currently, Perine looks to be the favorite for that starting role. And what does that come with? Well, neither Matt Jones nor Fat Rob are particularly good RBs, and yet both averaged over 4 yards per carry and scored 9 rushing TDs between them. Between the two of them, they totaled 52 red zone touches, and that was a down year for the Redskins offense in the red zone. They play a very tough schedule this year, but they did last year as well. Last year the Redskins played the 5th most difficult schedule of run defenses, with the 10th most injured offensive line, yet ranked 4th in rushing efficiency. Bill Callahan is a tremendous line coach. The Redskins only passed the ball on 55% of plays when the game was within one score, which was the 7th fewest in the NFL. The Redskins use shotgun far less than most teams (55% vs the NFL average of 63%) and thus are more equipped to run more often. And the volume should be there as well: from week 8 onward, when Kelley first started, only 4 RBs saw more red zone rushes. Fat Rob ranked above David Johnson, Ezekiel Elliott, Le'Veon Bell and most other RBs in number of red zone rushes.

Joe Mixon [RB16] – This is the riskiest of all RBs I'll mention due to the price and the competition. Both Jeremy Hill (222 carries last year) and Giovani Bernard (91 carries, 51 targets) are on the roster. So, there are not any vacated carries from that perspective, although Rex Burkhead's 74 carries are now in New England. But Bernard is recovering from a knee issue and is questionable to be ready by week 1 and Hill has been an utter disaster the last couple of years. Hill averaged 3.8 yards per carry on 222 rushes. He ranked 44th on early down success and 44th on overall rushing success rate. Ironically, his rushing success rate on all downs was 44%. Lots of "4s" in those stats. Which naturally led to a lot of another type of "4s": 4th downs. Mixon is an established receiver out of the backfield. His PFF grade as a receiver out of the backfield was #1 in CFB last year per PFF. If I'm the Bengals, I want to recast Hill into the role of the 2nd half pounder, and let Mixon and his fresh legs start the game strong and continue to get touches all the way through. I do see the passing game usage crank back up, but the presence of a speedster like John Ross doesn't just help the pass game, it also helps spacing and lanes in the run game.

Jordan Howard [RB9] – The Bears were a remarkable run-volume team last year. Even though they won only 3 games and were in constant negative game scripts, the Bears ran the ball the 6th most often of any team. With new quarterbacks in the mix (Mitchell Trubisky and Mike Glennon) there likely will be more reliance on the second-year RB. The Bears face the 27th rated schedule of run defenses (6th easiest). The other factor here is the high pass game usage. Howard was targeted 50 times as a rookie, which is a high volume. While a couple of years ago, 25% of Glennon's completions as a starter went to his RBs. And the Bears face the 3rd easiest schedule of opposing RB-pass defenses. So, when trailing, those dumpoff passes to Howard could come in extremely valuable. Not to mention that Howard saw 39 red zone opportunities in 2016, the next closest player on the Bucs was Cameron Meredith with only 13 red zone touches. Alshon Jeffery, a more frequently targeted receiver in the red zone (with total volume cut short due to injury) is no longer in Chicago, so passing attempts to Howard could increase even more.

Adam Thielen [WR50] – While this isn't a competition against Stefon Diggs necessarily, let's go ahead and compare the two: After week 5, a game which Diggs missed and Thielen was worked into the offense in a major way (caught 7 of 8 targets for 16 yards per attempt, an 88% success rate and a perfect 158.3 passer rating with 1 TD), Thielen stayed heavily involved in the offense. Ignoring games the game where he injured his neck or the two games Diggs missed, Thielen out snapped Diggs in each of the last 5 games they played together (from weeks 10-17). On the year, Thielen recorded more TDs, a better passing rating, higher YPA (10.5) and the same 75% completion rate. Diggs had the edge in success rate and missed YPA, but both were narrow margins (Thielen still ranked 12th in the NFL in receiving success rate). And then there is the projected matchups. With Diggs commanding #1 WR coverage, Thielen will get a ton of work this year because Bradford is coached to intentionally target the open man (he broke the NFL's completion % mark last year by completing 71.6% of his passes). Which is where Thielen fits in so nicely. Not to mention the fact that the Vikings play the NFL's easiest schedule of pass defenses this season, and are able to play every single potential wind/weather game indoors except for Christmas Eve in Green Bay.

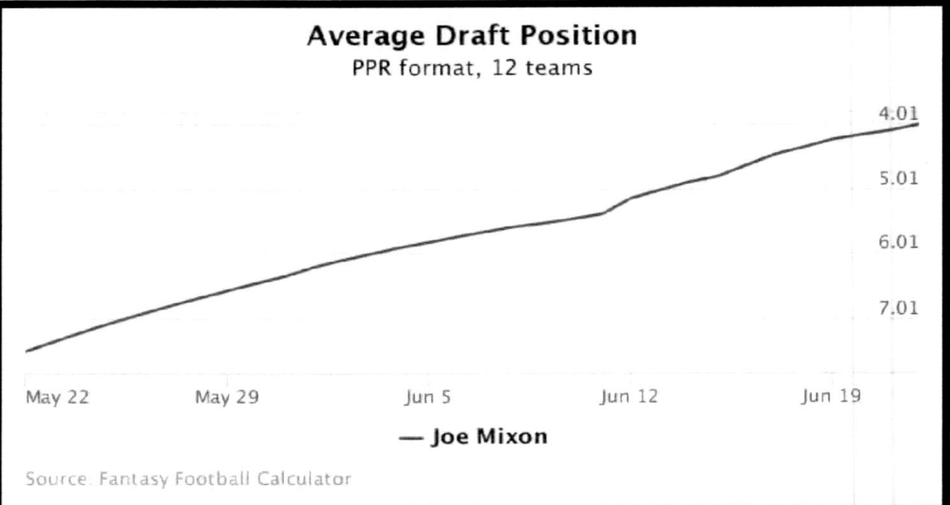

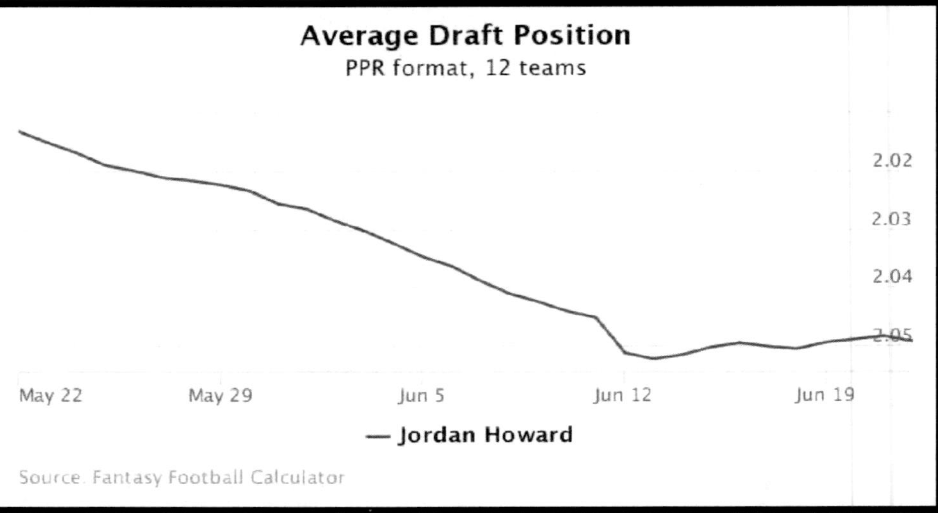

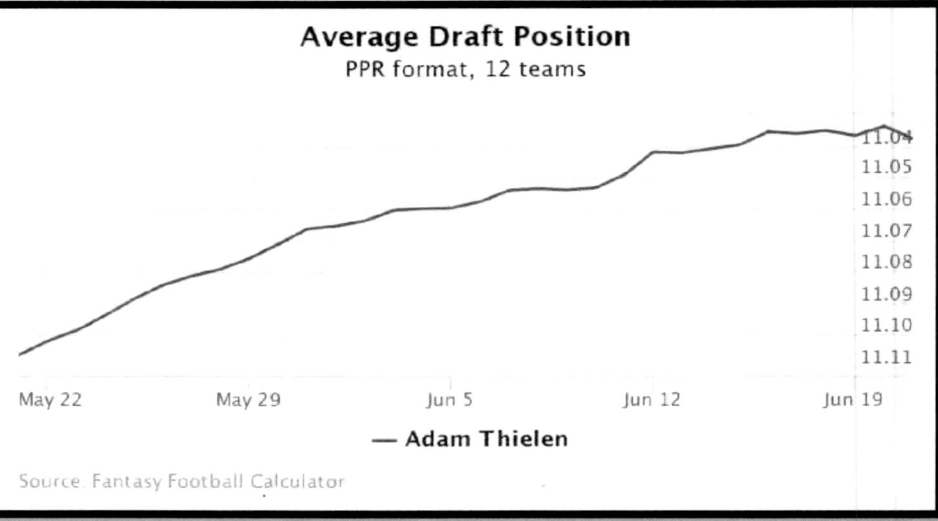

Pierre Garcon [WR38] – There is so much to like about Garcon this year. He's playing with one of the most creative offensive coordinators, who has ample experience with Garcon and intentionally signed him, rather than inherited him. The 49ers lost a ton of targets in the passing game from last year. They added Brian Hoyer as starting quarterback, who rarely goes deep due to accuracy issues, and focuses on the short to intermediate results. Which is exactly what Garcon eats up, so the meshing between the two should be extremely strong. Last year Garcon was 6th in success rate and 4th in Missed YPA, a metric that examines only the unsuccessful plays to find out how close they came to being successful. The 49ers are improving but still have a bad defense. And you can forget the run/pass ratios from 2016, where the 49ers called only 48% pass plays (fewest in the NFL) and ran the ball nearly 60% of plays, anytime they had a lead, the most in the NFL. The 49ers also are projected to face the NFL's #1 most difficult schedule of run defenses, so they will (like it or not) need to lean more on the pass game.

Ted Ginn [WR67] – I'm excited to watch Ginn operate in a Sean Payton offense with Drew Brees. He's been with Cam Newton for years, except for 26 targets in 2014 while playing a backup role in Arizona. Ginn hasn't played on a team in years which has a defense like the Saints, and which needs constant and productive offense in order to stay in and ultimately win games. First, he's in an offense with a terrible defense, so they'll have to be productive all game long. Second, this is a pass heavy offense – even when leading in games, the Saints passed the ball 67% of the time, the most frequent in the NFL. Third, they lost 882 snaps (most of the skill players) when Brandin Cooks left for the Patriots. So, there's a void. Fourth, there is a stud WR in Michael Thomas on the other side, and defense will soon have to play Thomas differently (more respect) now that Cooks is no longer in New Orleans. Fifth, the Saints play the 26th rated schedule of opposing defenses, including the 25th rated schedule of explosive pass defenses. And sixth, there is the early praise from Brees and Payton. Brees said "I could not be more impressed with him. He certainly doesn't look like he's lost a step. He can fly." While Payton said he has "an exact vision" of how to use Ginn: "I seem him playing at flanker, I see him being a guy that can take the top off the coverage. I like what this guy does...when he's playing in each game, the fastest player on the field." And he'll "do some of the same things" as Cooks for the Saints.

Kenny Golladay [WR78] – You have to expand to a 14-team league to even see his Golladay's draft history. And in the past week, he's been drafted just 8 times, which is the second lowest for any player. Only Michael Floyd, who was busted for DWI while on house arrest and blamed it on Kombucha tea, was drafted less often (3 times). That's pathetic. The only reason why this rookie is of interest to me is because Anquan Boldin isn't of interest to the Lions. That means a massive vacuum in targets (101) and specifically red zone targets (23) where he led the team. By a large margin, particularly inside the 5-yard line (9). The Lions average schedule would be far worse if they didn't have 3 games against the 4 worst teams, because they play 11 of their 16 games against top-16 opponents, including 7 in their first 8 games. And that 8th game? It's only against one of the best offenses in the league (the Saints). That means the Lions won't be able to sit around and run the air out of the ball, they will have to be productive on offense. And that means a ton of passes. While Ameer Abdullah will be back, I still envision the Lions leaning on Matthew Stafford's arm. They were the 3rd most pass heavy team in 2016. And they ran the 4th most 11 personnel (3 WRs), using it on 75% of offensive snaps. With Golden Tate locking down the slot, Marvin Jones posted a disappointing first year in Detroit, Golladay should win that 3rd role, and thus, be on the field a ton. Reports from camp are that the 6'4" WR is catching everything, and he has a massive wingspan. His catch radius is huge, he is one inch shorter than Megatron and runs a 4.5 40. I think Stafford will find a lot to like about him.

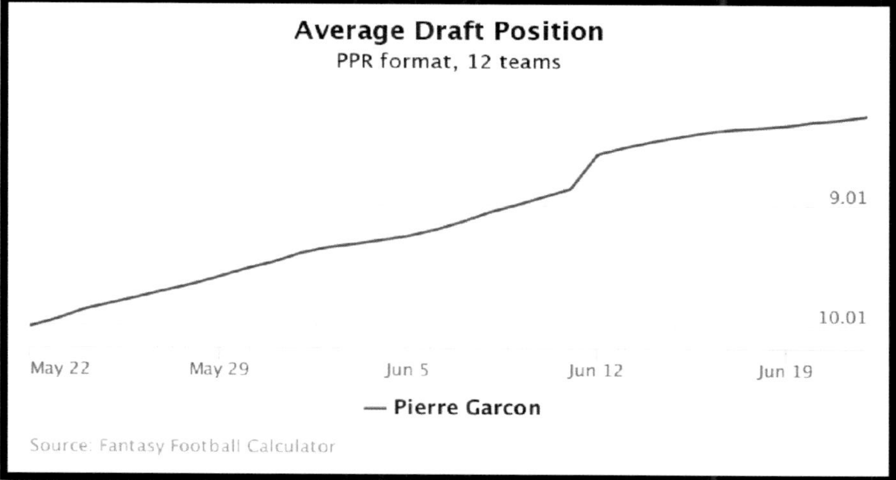

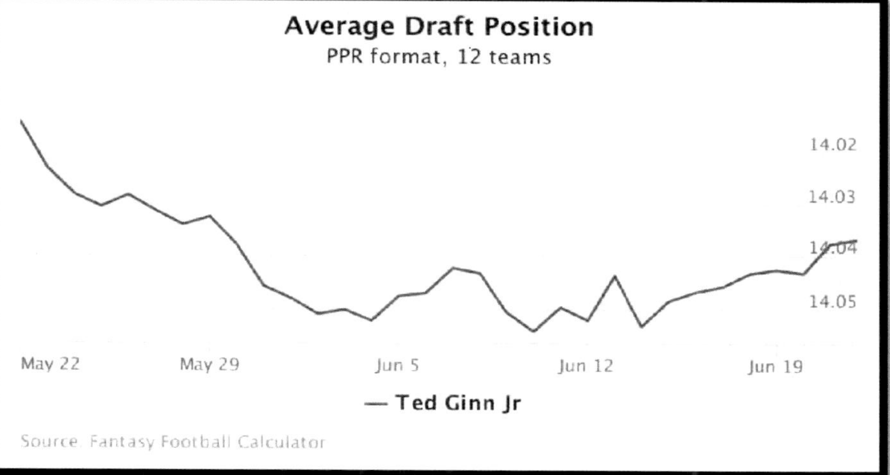

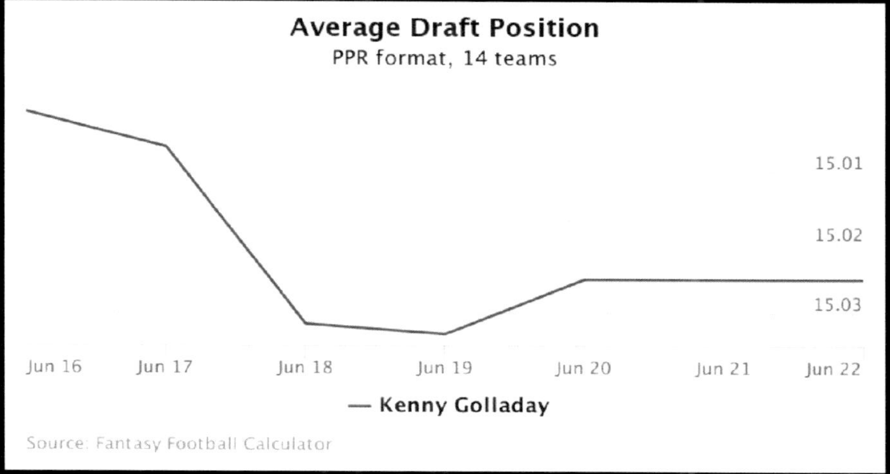

Hunter Henry [TE10] – Henry is my favorite of the TEs on this list based on his ADP and what I envision his upside. Last year Hunter Henry was the Chargers best receiver. But that's not all. Henry ranked #1 in the entire NFL for missed YPA (yards per attempt), a metric which measures how close to successful a player was on unsuccessful plays. Gates was 46th in this metric. Henry was also 16th in overall success rate while Gates was 60th. Henry averaged 9.1 yards per attempt (best on the team) while Gates averaged just 5.9. Henry delivered a 136 rating (best on the team) while Gates delivered an 86 rating. In the red zone, Rivers clearly favors size. His top 3 targets were 6'5" (Hunter Henry, 17 targets), 6'4" (Antonio Gates, 20 targets) and 6'4" (Tyrell Williams, 17 targets). No other receiver saw more than 6 targets. The Chargers face the easiest schedule of pass defenses from week 10 onward, and I imagine the Chargers will phase Gates out this season once he breaks the record, as he's a shadow of a statue of his former self. The Chargers also throw 26% of their passes to TEs, the 4th most in the NFL. The risk on Henry is if the Chargers continue to unsuccessfully ride Gates, but that approach seems so unreasonable from an efficiency perspective, it's hard to compute.

Kyle Rudolph [TE9] – Rudolph was by far the Vikings most heavily targeted player. And specifically, in the red zone, he was targeted 25 times. No other Viking had even half the target share. Inside the 5-yard line, while no other Viking had more than 2 targets, Rudolph had 8. The Vikings target their tight ends on 38% of red zone targets, the second most in the NFL (behind only the Chargers). And the Vikings face the NFL's easiest schedule of opposing pass defenses this year. Without Adrian Peterson to clutter the mind of offensive coordinators trying to appease the workload of Peterson, I believe Shurmur will continue a pass heavy approach. From week 9 onward (when Shurmur started in Minnesota last year) the Vikings were the most pass heavy team in the NFL (66% of all attempts were passes). And the score was irrelevant – even in one-score games, the Vikings were 65% pass (#1) to the NFL average of 57% pass.

Jack Doyle [TE13] – with the disappearance of Dwyane Allen and his 52 targets, including 9 in the red zone, Jack Doyle should see plenty of usage this year. Doyle had the 2nd most total targets, the 2nd most Colts' targets in the red zone last year. And his 67% success rate on targets inside the 10 was the 2nd best on the Colts. Last year in the Colts 2 favorite packages (11 and 12) Doyle delivered a 65% success rate and a 107 rating on targets. Thanks to OC Rob Chudzinski's philosophy, the Colts targeted TEs on 27% of their early down attempts, the 3rd most in the NFL, and these results posted the 2nd best success rate of any TE group in the NFL. Chud knows how to use the TE, especially in the red zone. And with the schedule of opposing offenses, the Colts offense could see a fair amount of time on the field.

Austin Hooper [TE22] – With Jacob Tamme and his 11 red zone targets gone, a larger load will fall to Hooper. The Falcons didn't utilize Hooper much at all weeks 1-7 when Tamme was healthy. But when Tamme went out, Hooper became the favored TE target and his performance took off. When targeting Hooper in their preferred 11 personnel grouping, he recorded a 121 rating, 3:0 TD:INT ratio with a 50% pass success rate. And when used in some of their more unconventional formations, such as 12 and 13, he dominated. Overall, his targets recorded a 136 rating, 4:0 TD:INT ratio, and a 61% pass success rate. That was a better passer rating, TD:INT ratio or pass success rate than when Ryan targeted his WR group or the non-Hooper TE group.

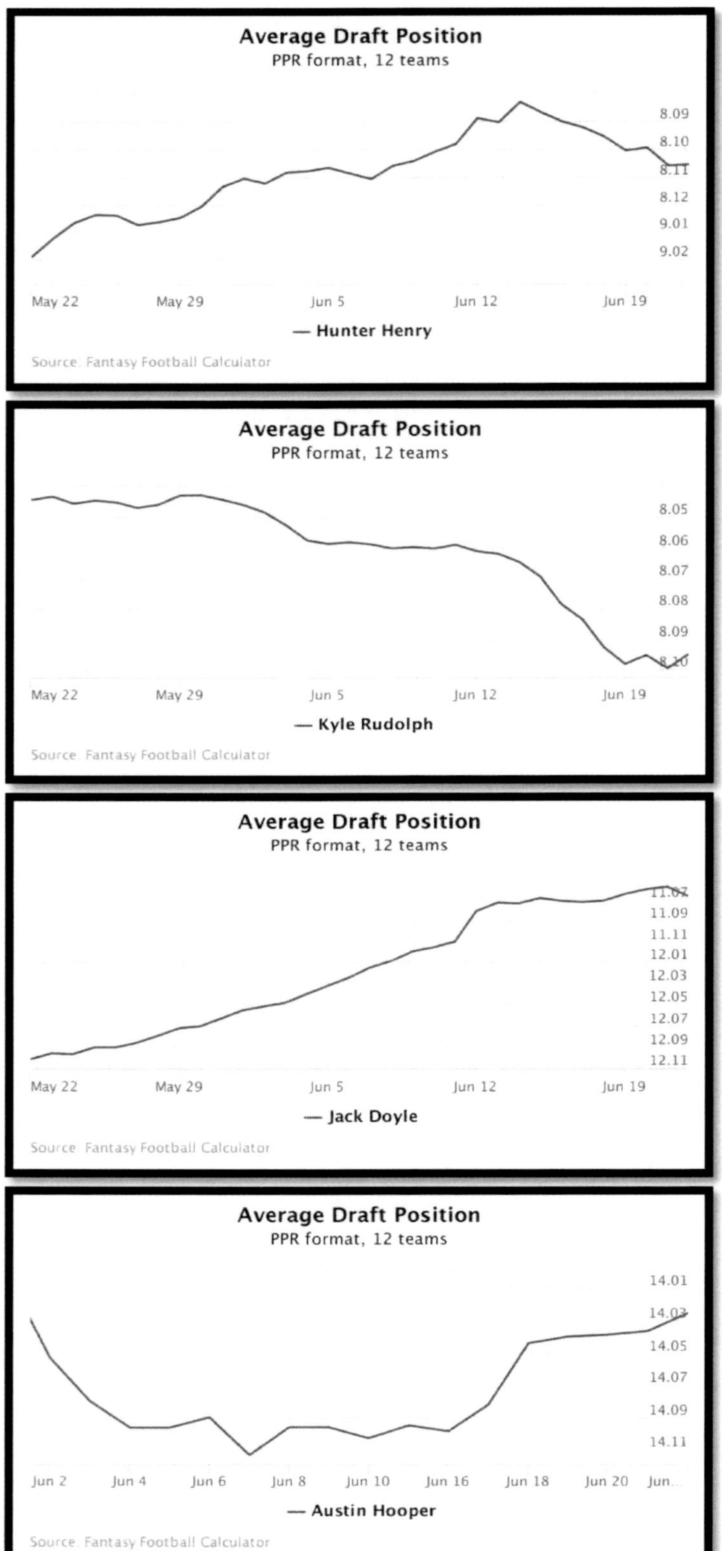

BEACH WEEK 2017
August 20-25

Efficiency Realized: Outlining the Proper Usage of Christian McCaffrey

By Warren Sharp

The first season after the NFL changed the hit rules on quarterbacks, and likewise better protected receivers over the middle of the field, was 2011. Since then, just 4 current players have recorded at least two seasons with 100+ rushes while averaging at least 4 yards per carry and 50+ receptions: LeSean McCoy, Le'Veon Bell, DeMarco Murray and Matt Forte.

Meanwhile, 35 current players recorded multiple seasons with those same rushing numbers, but without the receiving numbers. The clear majority of the non-receiving running backs are considered "3 down backs". Players big enough to carry the load and who don't need to leave the field on short yardage situations. However, the reality is many of them leave the field when it is 3rd and long, and get replaced by a "3rd down back".

There is a misconstrued concept in modern NFL of a "3rd down back". He is the "pass catching back". And he typically is more of a scat-back who isn't built to sustain pounding over 3 downs, but can be utilized as a receiving running back on 3rd down if the quarterback needs to target him. Here is the issue with that strategy: it doesn't work.

Targeting a running back out of the backfield on 3rd down and medium or longer (7+ yards to go), when most "3rd down backs" trot onto the field, results in a first down less than half as often as targeting a different position (WR/TE). The numbers are very clear: Only 17% of these 3rd down passes to running backs are successful, whereas 35% of passes to other positions are successful. Of any down and distance, the absolute worst time to throw the ball to a RB is on 3rd down and medium "+".

If a team views these "3rd down backs" as successful and elusive pass catchers, they should actually incorporate them on 1st down, potentially in place of a 1st down handoff. Last year, the league wide average for successful runs on 1st and 10 was 46%. However, 58% of passes to running backs on 1st and 10 were successful. That is a massive variance.

In fact, as the below graphic shows, targeting running backs on 1st down is more likely to result in a successful gain than targeting a WR. League-wide, success rates to running backs on 1st and 10 or less yards to go is 58%, much greater than targeting wide receivers in the same situation (55% success rate).

Pass Success Rate

Offense	RB Success Rate	RB Success % Rk	TE Success Rate	TE Success % Rk	WR Success Rate	WR Success % Rk
ARI	53%	22	60%	15	54%	18
ATL	69%	3	59%	18	65%	2
BAL	49%	27	56%	22	54%	19
BUF	50%	23	63%	12	53%	22
CAR	50%	23	61%	14	49%	27
CHI	55%	20	76%	2	60%	8
CIN	64%	8	62%	13	53%	21
CLE	57%	17	50%	28	48%	28
DAL	46%	29	64%	11	60%	7
DEN	61%	12	52%	26	57%	15
DET	57%	16	70%	4	59%	10
GB	50%	23	49%	30	57%	14
HOU	71%	2	60%	15	46%	31
IND	55%	21	66%	6	50%	26
JAC	45%	30	57%	20	50%	24
KC	56%	19	59%	18	64%	4
LA	44%	32	38%	32	47%	30
MIA	68%	4	76%	1	58%	12
MIN	45%	30	55%	23	65%	3
NE	64%	7	65%	8	54%	20
NO	60%	13	67%	5	66%	1
NYG	47%	28	66%	7	60%	9
NYJ	60%	14	60%	15	55%	17
OAK	63%	9	54%	25	50%	25
PHI	56%	18	72%	3	47%	29
PIT	67%	5	57%	21	45%	32
SD	58%	15	55%	24	56%	16
SEA	67%	5	64%	10	64%	5
SF	62%	10	44%	31	52%	23
TB	72%	1	49%	29	58%	12
TEN	50%	23	51%	27	58%	11
WAS	61%	11	65%	9	62%	6
NFL Avg	58%	1	59%	1	55%	1

The other benefit to targeting running backs on 1st and 10 does is that it reduces turnovers. Using the data from SharpFootballStats.com, passes to running backs on 1st and 10 result in interceptions 0.9% of the time (11 INTs on 1,189 ATT) whereas passes to WRs result in interceptions well over double that rate: 2.4% of the time (88 INTs on 3,636 ATT). There is no single play more likely to lose a game for an offense than a turnover. Turnover margin is the most correlated metric to wins and losses that exists. Throwing interceptions, particularly on 1st down, is a sure-fire way to lose games.

So apart from strategical edges, what does this have to do with Christian McCaffrey?

Even though becoming a legitimate receiving target has happened only to 10% of the running backs that recorded multiple seasons with 100+ rushes at 4 yards per carry (4 out of 39), McCaffrey will likely join that fraternity: the 3 down running back who is a dangerous weapon in the passing game. He'll soon join the likes of LeSean McCoy and Le'Veon Bell. McCaffrey may not be perfectly comparable to them from a body type. But McCaffrey can be an even more dangerous weapon in the passing game then the aforementioned running backs in that he can be split out more frequently and do more damage as a receiver in space. McCaffrey is an established return man and knows how to avoid hits in space.

And it is for these reasons the Panthers took McCaffrey as high as they did. It wasn't a reach. It wasn't about a position that has been devalued in the modern passing-style of the NFL. And it most certainly wasn't about running backs being fungible and interchangeable.

It was about the future of the position and the efficiency potential for running backs with McCaffrey's skillset. While many look at his 5'11", 202 pound frame and don't see a 3-down back, the reality is, they're right. He's so much more than a "back". He's a 3-down weapon:

We know that on 1st down, he'll be tremendous as a receiving running back, and can get productive carries on the ground. On 2nd and short after a nice first down gain, it will be in Carolina's best interest to get to the line of scrimmage quickly before their opponent can rotate in a short yardage package, and run McCaffrey against the base defense. On 2nd or 3rd and medium or long, McCaffrey is your prototypical "Weapon X" who can wreak havoc from any position he's lined up at. And that's one of the biggest keys for OC Mike Shula. He needs to implement McCaffrey in many different positions on the field. Every single RB position as well as line him up in the slot – he's worked with longtime reliable slot WR Brandon Stokley on releases and playing from the slot. Of course, he has the soft hands which are part of the family genes (father, WR Ed McCaffrey) and his short area quickness and acceleration make him a major threat anytime you can get him the ball in space.

Mike Shula must figure out ways to make minor tweaks as well as wholesale changes in his offense to maximize Christian McCaffrey's ability. The other thing that McCaffrey brings to the table is the return ability. And while this certainly is special, if I am Carolina I want to be careful with the frequency of how often I direct McCaffrey to do more than just fair catch the ball. There will be the temptation to rely solely on him for return duties, especially for as long as Jonathan Stewart is still in Carolina, as McCaffrey won't need to be the bellcow running back. He's no doubt a dangerous weapon anytime he has the ball in his hands. But risking injury is a big part of it as well. If I am Carolina, I use him situationally as a return man. If his fielding ability is so great that his presence on the field causes the NFL punters to change their trajectory in ways it gains field position for the Panthers regardless of a return, I may allow him to be out there more often. But every "decent" kick would be instructed to be fair caught. And I would only have him return them if the coverage or kick on a particular play was suboptimal, or if we were in a tight game.

While there are a ton of positives for McCaffrey as a player, there are several distinct concerns I have with him in Carolina, and they start and end with Cam Newton. The Carolina offense presents a unique challenge to get the most out of McCaffrey. And that is because of the style of quarterback that Cam Newton is, for a couple of reasons.

First, as we know, Newton is a running quarterback. Generally speaking, running quarterbacks are quicker to drop their eyes after downfield routes don't uncover. They use their legs as a crutch in order to try to keep the offense on track. Additionally, when a pocket collapses, the running quarterback will look to escape using his legs. Meanwhile, the traditional pocket quarterback, such as Tom Brady or Ben Roethlisberger, will not run. They will try to be evasive, but are always looking to complete a pass. And often, that comes in the form of a pass to a running back.

The NFL average for targeting running backs out of the backfield was 19% of pass attempts. Carolina targeted them 2nd least often of any team, with only 13% of attempts going to running backs. On the other end of the spectrum were pocket passing quarterbacks including Drew Brees, Tom Brady, Joe Flacco, Carson Palmer, Matt Ryan and Ben Roethlisberger, who targeted RBs over 10% more often than Carolina's 13% rate, as the below table shows.

Offense	RB	TE	WR
CLE	25%	16%	59%
NO	24%	17%	59%
NE	24%	21%	55%
BAL	24%	21%	55%
NYJ	23%	5%	72%
ARI	22%	14%	64%
ATL	22%	16%	62%
PIT	21%	21%	57%
OAK	21%	14%	65%
DET	20%	16%	64%
BUF	20%	22%	58%
PHI	19%	21%	60%
NYG	19%	19%	62%
IND	19%	26%	55%
SD	19%	26%	55%
MIA	19%	16%	66%
MIN	18%	25%	56%
CIN	18%	18%	63%
SF	18%	22%	61%
JAC	18%	20%	62%
KC	17%	29%	54%
TEN	17%	26%	57%
DEN	17%	15%	69%
DAL	16%	23%	61%
SEA	16%	23%	61%
LA	16%	22%	62%
CHI	15%	17%	68%
WAS	15%	26%	59%
TB	15%	21%	65%
HOU	14%	31%	55%
CAR	13%	27%	60%
GB	8%	17%	75%
NFL Avg	19%	20%	61%

More than just the target rate is the quality of targets. While just 13% are making its way to the Carolina running backs, many of these targets are poorly constructed. Whether last minute dump offs to running backs in precarious situations or simply bad play design, they haven't worked. Surely some of it relates to the quality of running back, and targets to McCaffrey will likely be much more successful than targets to other RBs in the past, but the fact is the success rate when targeting running backs in this offense is the same as the frequency: 2nd worst in the NFL.

Offense	RB	
	Success Rate	Success % Rk
PIT	54%	1
SEA	54%	2
NO	52%	3
HOU	51%	4
WAS	51%	5
BUF	51%	6
CIN	51%	7
ATL	50%	8
TB	49%	9
SF	49%	10
DET	49%	11
SD	48%	12
CLE	47%	13
ARI	45%	14
IND	45%	15
OAK	45%	16
CHI	45%	17
KC	44%	18
NYJ	44%	19
LA	43%	20
NE	43%	21
DAL	43%	22
PHI	43%	23
BAL	42%	24
MIA	41%	25
DEN	41%	26
MIN	40%	27
JAC	39%	28
TEN	38%	29
GB	38%	30
CAR	37%	31
NYG	36%	32
NFL Avg	46%	1

The second big concern I have for McCaffrey also relates to Cam Newton, and it is that Newton isn't adept at operating the fast-pass offense. The Panthers have built their offense to Newton's strengths, and those are deep drops and powerful, deep targets. His ball placement and short drops on timing routes is not his expertise. As Andy Benoit, from theMMQB said:

"Not only have [the Panthers] built a passing game on deep dropbacks, but they've also acquired big, methodical receivers for Newton (Kelvin Benjamin, first round in 2014; Devin Funchess, second round in 2015; Greg Olsen via trade in 2011). They haven't selected the Sproles or Cobb type players because those guys don't fit Newton or the scheme....

To maximize McCaffrey's value, the Panthers must tweak their scheme in ways it can't be tweaked. You don't just install a bunch of quick-strike throws and execute them on Sunday. Those plays must be your foundation. They must be practiced repeatedly. And they must be executed by a precise quarterback and quicker skill position players. McCaffrey is Carolina's only quick skill player."

I agree that these are concerns. However, I don't believe that it is time for doom and gloom and that McCaffrey will not work in Carolina. Far from it. But we likely won't see the ceiling for him like he would have in a variety of other offenses. However, his ceiling in Carolina is higher than it would be on a number of other offenses, as is his floor.

I love what Christian McCaffrey brings to the NFL. I love what he brings to Carolina. I love that people may underestimate the amount of efficiency he can bring to an offense. But he has to be used properly. OC Mike Shula must figure out how to target him more often than on 13% of Newton's pass attempts, as he's done in the past (2nd fewest in the NFL). In addition to more volume, Shula must design better running back pass options. Here is where they have a head start: Lance Taylor was hired from Stanford to be Carolina's wide receivers coach. His prior stint? Stanford's running backs coach where he helped design the breakout of Christian McCaffrey. Shula must rely on Taylor to help design the offense in Carolina this year. Additionally, Shula must have Carolina work in more situational tempo with McCaffrey on the field, and line him up in different positions while preventing the defense from substituting in players. McCaffrey has the potential to keep defensive coordinators up all night trying to figure out how to stop him. But if Carolina doesn't use him enough on offense, it is doing them a disservice. Much like a speedy receiver, if McCaffrey is on the field, the defense must adjust. And even if the play that is called doesn't involve McCaffrey, it still can be advantage-Carolina's offense, as the defense is shading too much to limit McCaffrey.

I'm excited to see what McCaffrey can do on the next level. I outlined a number of stats-based reasons why teams should rely on running back targets more than they do on early downs. I hope Carolina takes notice and uses him properly. More teams need to target running backs. But until other teams do, I hope at least for Carolina's sake, we see McCaffrey immediately join that still tiny fraternity of tremendous NFL dual-threat running backs.

Revisited: The Truth about Using Vegas Totals for DFS

By Warren Sharp

Vegas totals are wrong. And sports books know it. Which is why they start off the week with low limits to see which direction the money will go, and adjust accordingly. Often, they adjust quickly and at times, too much. Why? Because they are nervous and scared. They dislike risk, and they know that certain individuals are far more accurate at projecting the totals on games than they are. Those individuals end up working for betting groups or large sports bettors (who operate individually or as a collective) and bet the games they are given with a lot of money. And they win more often than they lose.

But the whole concept of "Vegas" totals is a bit silly. Hopefully, the DFS community uses the buzz word "Vegas" to describe general "betting" lines as opposed to the city itself. Because you can ask anyone from Las Vegas legendary pro bettor Bill "Krackman" Krackomberger to the grinder trying to pay his rent: totals are rarely originated in Las Vegas. Instead, most if not all totals originate at offshore books which do significantly higher volume than the books in Las Vegas. The linemakers in Las Vegas then take these lines (once posted offshore) and either copy them, or tweak their own number to closely reflect the offshore odds. There are a handful of linemakers in Las Vegas who would be capable of originating and booking action on their own lines, but if their number are set too far from the number at major offshore books, the Las Vegas linemakers will get steamrolled with sharp action. To avoid that problem, they tend to align exactly or close enough with the offshore lines. For that reason, when I use the term "Vegas" totals in this article, I (as well as you) should not confuse that to say these lines are born and bred in Las Vegas – but they are the betting line and we'll leave it at that.

I understand Vegas totals more than most, because while I am a quant and a football analyst, I got my start betting and beating the market on NFL totals. I worked to develop a model used to predict NFL totals. I spent years researching, inventing and testing the model while receiving my Engineering degree and later, my Professional license. I've been using the model for 10 years now over at SharpFootballAnalysis.com and have a long term success rate of accuracy of 60%, including recent success rates of 72% last year and 61% in 2014. Many of my recommendations move the Vegas line when I release them. What that means is, if you see a total that opened at 51 on Tuesday, and suddenly you look at the lines and the total is 50, then 49.5, then 49, there is a chance it was a game I recommended to bet under. Pro betting groups work with me and bet my recommendations and the Vegas linemakers who run the books know me. I write for ESPN Chalk where I share a couple recommendations each week, and those hit 66% last year. While perhaps superfluous, the point is: I appreciate, understand and value the attempt at setting the Vegas total more than most. It's been my primary focus both in and out of the NFL season for well over a decade now.

Trend in DFS

More and more, we see Vegas totals being incorporated into DFS. Perhaps this was because, at one point, no one playing fantasy football cared about Vegas totals. Eventually, some in the DFS community started to discuss them. They realized that some of the players that performed well played in high totaled games. And some that performed poorly played in lower totaled games. The "secret" began to get out. More and more people began discussing it. Now, it has permeated the market. DFS players want to start players with high totaled games, or high team totals.

Here is the problem: not only has it jumped the shark, the data shows it is not helpful. The reason the player with a high team total or total may perform well is NOT because the team total or game total is high. It is because he is playing on a good, offensive team which may not have the best defense, and in many cases could be playing against a weak opponent. As a result of that, the team or game total may be high. But the total is just a byproduct of the situation and matchup. You know football, so think fast – which game is likely to be higher scoring (and thus have a higher total) – the Saints at the Falcons or the Titans at the Broncos? You don't need to know the actual Vegas total to know the answer. To put it in different terms: go to a basketball court with a basketball and a beach ball. You already should know that a shot with the basketball is more likely to go in the hoop because of what it is (its weight, size and the size of the rim) as opposed to the beach ball. You don't need a physics professor who happens to be stretching out before a pick-up game to come up to you and tell you that you'll have a better chance if you don't shoot the beach ball.

So why should it matter what the total is if you already know that a certain offense (Falcons) is going up against a bad defense (Saints) and there are favorable matchups and situations for the game to be high scoring? Does it really matter if the total is 46 or 49 for DFS purposes? Absolutely not. Should you shy away from playing Mohamed Sanu if the total is 47, but play him if the total is 51? Absolutely not. But let's start discussing math, regression and correlation to explain further.

How Wrong are Vegas Totals?

Before we get into this, you should know where to find accurate Vegas totals, and by accurate I mean by real sportsbooks that take sharp action. Also by accurate, I mean the lines are "live", meaning they change as bets come in and are accurate. HERE is a great link to bookmark from my website which gives you live lines from real sportsbooks (in Vegas and offshore). It also shows you the opening line, so you can see where the line has shifted. But the cool secret about this page is if you click on any specific game's line, it will pop up and tell you exactly at what time during the week the line moved and by how much. So you can see a documented "history" of the total over time. Now that you can accurately view live Vegas totals, let's get back to the question at hand.

This question should be viewed with the lens of "...in terms of helping in DFS", but I'll discuss that momentarily. First, let's just look at the basic question. The answer is they are quite wrong.

We can examine first regression, then correlation. When you run a regression of the Vegas total to the actual points scored, you will notice that there clearly is some relationship. Inherently, there should be some type of relationship. But the key is, how weak that relationship truly is: the R^2 is just 8.7% over a 3 year sample, which is extremely small. What does it look like and what does it mean?

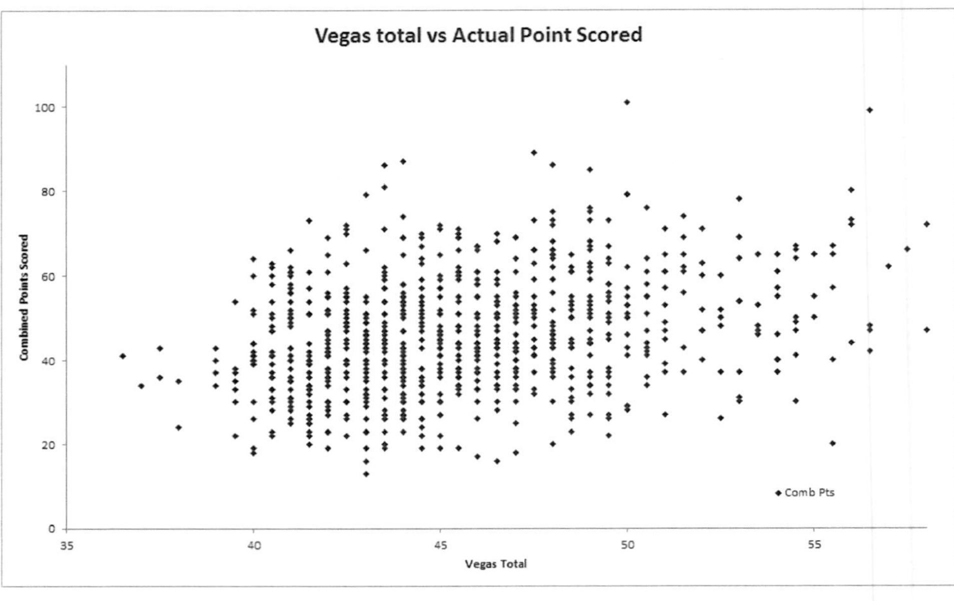

Instead of a narrow cluster of actual point scored outcomes which bunch closely together near the projected total, you see a true amalgamation of results without a dominant, definitive pattern.

When you add the linear trend line, as shown below, you can see that there does exist a relationship between the points scored and the Vegas total. But it is weak, relatively speaking. Specifically, the R^2 is 8.7%. What the R^2 means is that just 8.7% of the total points actually scored by teams are explained by the Vegas total itself. Only 8.7%.

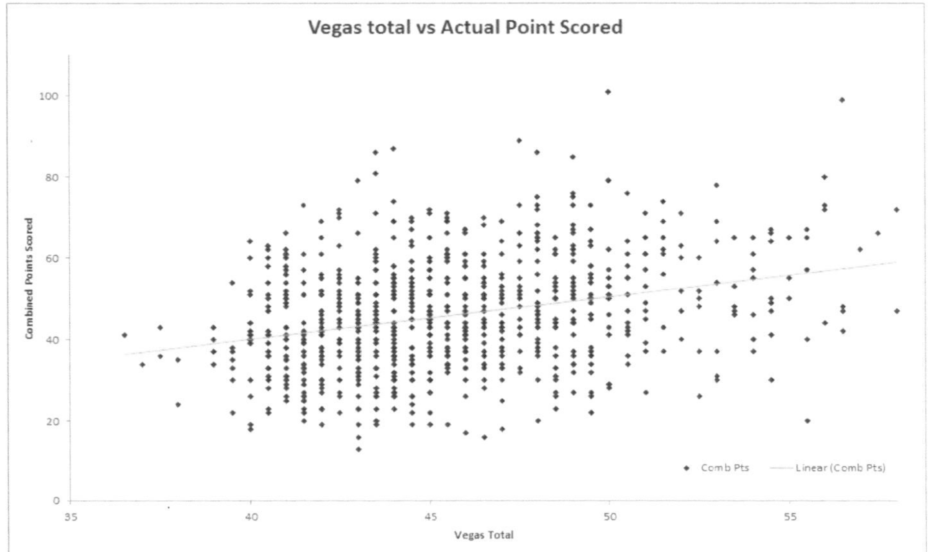

By most definitions, a low R^2 like this would fail to prove predictive. With a low (good) P value (in this case 1.62E-17), the sample size is adequate. Sometimes low R^2 values are still viewed as acceptable with acceptable P values. For instance, the number of people who eat deli meat once a week and live in cities to the number of people who develop cancer. Because so many other factors influence cancer rates, even an 8% R^2 in that sample would be large. But here is the problem with our sample. Theoretically, Vegas totals are trying to predict the combined points. There are not randomly put up against total points. We're not correlating number of TV commercials aired with combined points scored, or number of fans in the crowd with combined points scored. The Vegas total's objective is to try to predict the combined points. That is its goal. And with an 8% R^2, it fails.

Next let's move to discussing correlation using correlation itself. In this example, we are focusing only on 2015 data. The correlation coefficient between the Vegas total and actual point scored was 0.25. What does this mean? A value of exactly 1.0 means there is a perfect positive relationship. A value of -1.0 means there is a perfect negative relationship. A value of 0 means there is no linear relationship between the two variables. Values between 1 and 0 can be described from strong to weak, and in this case, a value of 0.25 means there is a very weak positive relationship between the Vegas total and actual points scored. Which is what we see after adding the trend line to the graphic.

To add context, let's compare it to something near and dear to the goal of any of this, which is to try to help you make sense of Vegas totals and (more importantly) win when playing DFS. According to TJ Hernandez of 4for4football.com, the correlation between Draft Kings player price and his actual points scored was 0.26.

This is a big issue. The player price actually has a STRONGER correlation to how many points that player will score than does the Vegas total to how many point will be scored in the game. Why is that a big issue? Ultimately, as a DFS player, you should be concerned first and foremost with how many points the player will score (when factoring in his price). Using Vegas totals to forecast game score still does not get you to your goal. If you factor in Vegas totals and assume the game sees the number of points Vegas is forecasting (a terrible idea given what was presented earlier with the regression analysis) you still need to then take the step of (hopefully) accurately distributing those points to the players themselves. It is a multi-step process. And every bit of low correlation becomes magnified with each iteration.

High Totaled Games

Hopefully we've explained why DFS players looking to Vegas totals as a secret weapon to win tournaments or cash games is not the best strategy, because the total is actually not very correlated to the actual points that will be scored. Therefore (as an example) a total of 48 is really not measurably more likely to see strong fantasy performances than a total of 44, all other factors aside.

But what about high totaled games? What if we ignore the stepwise differences between totals of 42 vs 43 vs 44, and just try to target high totaled games? Maybe those are likely to produce stronger fantasy performances?

First of all, the reality is that the last 3 years, just 49% of games totaled above 45 have gone over the total while just 48.7% of all games have gone over the total. So picking a high totaled game and assuming it will go over because of its high total is problematic. It is basically a coin flip.

Second, the research above tells us that while there is a relationship between Vegas total and total points scored, it is very weak. Over the course of many years, games with a Vegas total of 49 should see more points scored than games with a Vegas total of 45, for instance. But in the single week you're selecting your lineup, it's far from predictive. Even over the course of a couple of seasons, large sample sizes can prove the lack of use in the way DFS players use them.

As an example, over the last two full seasons, games with a Vegas total of 45 (+/- 0.5 points on the total) have actually outscored games with a Vegas total of 49 (+0.5 points on the total) across a sample of almost 150 games.

But third, we can turn to some great research done by Evan Silva of Rotoworld.com, and furthered by his colleague Sean Fakete. Evan used a three year sample to try to come up with a profile of the top overall QB on a weekly basis (what traits should DFS players look for) as well as those QBs who scored in the top 6 (Evan's article is linked in the first sentence). Sean expanded the study for WRs and RBs, and took it past just top 6 but also to top 12. And ideally, when paying DFS, particularly tournaments, this should be what you care about. You need players to not just score points, but to outscore their positional field. So you need top 6 or top 12 RBs or WRs when competing against thousands of other entrants.

What they found was insightful.

- Only 49% of top 6 QBs played in a game with a Vegas total of 47 or more.
- Only 45% of top 6 WRs played in a game with a Vegas total of 47 or more.
- Only 44% of top 6 RBs played in a game with a Vegas total of 47 or more.

The guys you should be targeting to put up top 6 performances are no more likely to be found in high totaled games than low totaled games. In fact, by a very slight majority, they are more likely found in lower totaled games. (For reference, the average total last year was ~45 points).

Now what to do? Using Vegas totals to accurately predict points scored isn't the shortcut. You can't take the work out of winning by choosing to select player A over player B just because his Vegas total is 3 points higher. And looking only at high totaled games isn't likely to help you win tournaments or other high stakes games, either. Because more often than not, the top players at each position aren't even playing in the games with the high totals. So now what?

He doesn't care about anything but the "**W**". Because it's **green**. And he's been winning every year for 25 years now.

A **real** Las Vegas "larger than live" icon. A winning professional gambler. Seen on ESPN, CNN, Fox Sports and in dozens of publications and newspapers around the country.

Coming this Summer

KrackWins.com

A sports information and lifestyle site

The next best thing to knowing Bill "Krackman" Krackomberger is getting his information. Now you can do just that.

Team Totals

Some research has turned to team totals. But like everything thus far, I've come to ruin your day. I've read several studies this offseason discussing team totals and what number are ideal for solid results.

The Rotoworld study by Sean with respect to WRs looked at a cutoff of 22.5 points for a team total, and looked at the number of times a team was lined with a team total above 22.5 points, and how often those players hit at a high rate to put them into top 1, top 6, top 12 etc. criteria for weekly performers that week. The study also modeled how often the team was favored by the linemakers. What was not discussed was how extremely similar those two sets of results were.

That is because the reality is this: last year (throwing out games that closed a pickem) there were 245 teams which closed as favorites and (therefore) 245 teams that closed as underdogs. The number of underdogs whose team total exceeded 22.5 points was just 25 (out of 245). So when looking at the teams who have a team total of at least 22.5 points, the extreme majority will be favorites.

I read another study which looked at team totals and suggested that a team with a projected team total of at least 24 is ideal. Again, while not directly measuring this, this is essentially simply targeting favorites, as last year only 8 out of 245 underdogs had a team total set at or above 24 points.

Why is it important that both studies essentially say the same thing – that teams with high team totals may produce better weekly results? Because favored teams typically produce better results. Both studies ran those correlations and found the results between favorites and top performers by position is significantly stronger than any correlation to game total. The team that is better is likely to have their way with the underdog and impose their will more often. Which is why linemakers favor them in the games. And their DFS plays perform better because they are better and win their matchups. The studies looking at high team totals are effectively doing nothing more than isolating favorites.

But there is a second brutal truth about team totals: while DFS pros try to incorporate them into the Tuesday, Wednesday and Thursday research, it is irrelevant. There is no such thing as a Vegas team total on a Wednesday. Sportsbooks will not put up lines for you to wager on team totals until (typically) the day before the game itself. Some don't even put them up until the morning of the game.

Why? Because the books understand the team total itself is basic math derived from the line and the total. And they don't like the risk involved in having to juggle the team total around so much during the week as the line could get bet one way by a few points and the total could get bet up or down by more points even than the line. You can calculate your own projected total points on Tuesday or Wednesday, but just know you must adjust as the week progresses, and the number really only becomes accurate by Sunday morning. And by that time, most lineups are already in and finalized, so it is a difficult task (and can be time consuming as well as counterproductive) to even focus on team totals.

I put together a separate analysis called Delta Points Scored. Delta Points Scored (DPS) is the team total set by linesmakers less the actual points scored. As an example: the Bengals have frequently exceeded their team total as a dog, going "over" in 11 of 14 games, 2nd best for an underdog. But as a favorite, particularly on the road, they are below average and frequently don't exceed their projection.

Meanwhile, the NFC North teams from Detroit and Green Bay have been terrible bets offensively as a home favorite. Combined, that is 15 when underdogs, failing to hit their team projection in 16 of 22 games combined. To continue the exercise, a team like the Bills, when at home, has performed tremendously against their expectations. They have exceeded the lined total in 9 of 12 games as a home dog and in 6 of 10 games of 22 games, or 68%.

When studying DPS, it's clear that blindly using team totals is a bad move. Understanding that the linesmakers are typically very wrong on a game to game basis, with some teams scoring considerably more or less than projected, but averaging out in the end. Fortunately, as bettors or DFS players, we don't have to be right about every player or game we bet. We just need to be right on the few that we target.

Trends on ATS, Totals and Team Totals

Trends have become an increasingly common part of DFS players' strategy as it relates to numbers the "pull" from Vegas.

I've seen mining on numbers where, analysts will look at game totals of 45 and higher, and then expand out to take it back to 44.5 or 44 to find a "set" which aligns with more of what they are hoping to see. The same is true with lines for favorites or team totals. They will select DFS players if favored by 4.5 or less but not 5 or above, or team totals of 26 or higher but not 25.5.

These are alarming and at the end of the day, will be proven to be a waste of time. I've seen plenty of "trend" handicappers who come, and inevitably go, because a data mined trend based on a specific yards per carry cutoff point or line on a favorite produced a very nice historical set, and may get lucky for a year or two with subtle tweaks, but is not sustainable.

Being one of the few who publicly shares totals which actually move the market, both offshore and in Vegas at release, I can tell you the "value" of a 0.5 point in totals is massive when making the bet. But what is the total from a few years ago which is being pulled into a model for use in DFS? Is it the opening line or the "closer"? If it's the "closer" (last line that existed pre-kick) who defines it as the closer? What book is that from, and is it accurate in the least? There are so many poor data points which are surely being sucked into these models to make them very inefficient.

Take this example: a leading book posts a 43.5 total on a game. Other books which opened 42 and 42.5 move to 43.5 to copy the sharper book. My model believes that line should be 45.5, and thanks to some defensive cluster injuries, even that could be short. So we move on the game. Instantly the books adjust their lines to offset our bets. Other books we didn't even hit see the movement, and once again copy the lines. Suddenly 43.5 jumped a full point to 44.5, then 45. Then come the steam players – those who bet games that quickly moved and copy the bets. So now more and more people are betting "over" 45 and even 45.5. This all happens in 30 minutes on a Tuesday. By Friday and Saturday, with players being ruled out and more public money entering the market, this game is now at 46 and 46.5 at some spots. By Sunday morning, it hits 47 and other sharp groups, some of which bet over initially, bet under at 47. And the line "closes" at 46. Over 43.5, which we bet on Tuesday, was a great bet as it closed 3 points higher. Under 47 was a good (but not great) bet as well. But the DFS model has 47 as the closing total because it's not as precise from where it pulls the closer. But 47 is a terrible number to use as the closer, and yet it will be in there at 47. If you're using this model, how do you know the closing numbers pulled are even moderately accurate?

What Next?

Some DFS players out there won't care what the real numbers show. They heard that some successful winners use Vegas totals as a key element of their analysis. Perhaps they will still use Vegas totals as a barometer or a comparison tool to help decide on a particular player ("A is in a game with a 49 point total, B is in a game with a 44 point total, so I'll ride with A"). Again, this is despite the research done by myself as well as Evan Silva and others at Rotoworld which demonstrates that high totaled games are meaningless when trying to target those players who might finish top 6 or top 12 in their position.

As mentioned earlier: the correlation between player price and his points scored is stronger than the correlation between the Vegas total and the actual real points scored in the game. And iteratively, it stands to reason that the platforms have done a better job pricing a player's actual result than you will when trying to incorporate Vegas lines into your decision making.

But what about the DFS players who incorporate the totals and swear by it? The reality is they are just getting a placebo affect from picking players on teams that ultimately score more points. It doesn't take a genius to predict that when Drew Brees plays the Jaguars, he'll likely score more than when he plays the Texans. Yes, you could look at the total on the game or the team total and find out precisely what the linemakers think of the game but it is pretty common sense to anyone without even looking at that information. Often the players targeted by DFS players factoring in team totals just so happen to be in a number of favorable categories which correlate to success more than the Vegas total itself, such as the fact the DFS player is playing at home, as a favorite (and later in the season) perhaps facing a defense with a key flaw or injury that will be exploited. You can historically look back and try to correlate this player's success that week and claim it was because of the Vegas total, but the reality is it was the other things that caused this play to be successful, and the Vegas total just came along for the ride.

1. Game totals – they are actually extremely inaccurate, inefficient and the static pricing on the DFS platforms itself is a better measure of comparative interposition strength than the lined totals.
2. Team totals – the studies done on higher team totals essentially scrap all of the underdogs and look at how often good QBs, WRs, RBs etc. play on teams that are favored. And we know that correlation (being the favorite) is stronger, so it's not the team total itself that is driving the correlation. In addition, any "team total" calculated for Sunday games which you see before Friday at the earliest, likely Saturday, is nothing more than a projection, subject to change.

In sum, the boost that some might find when layering Vegas totals into their evaluation is likely nothing more than residual impact of other factors already incorporated.

An Underappreciated Research Gem

One item from the studies I read that is helpful is so elementary it gets overlooked, but is actually far more astute than starting players based on the Vegas total: pick players from games that go over the total.

To quote Evan Silva:

"The fact that 88.2% of overall QB1s and 78.1% of top-six [weekly] fantasy passers played in games that went over the Vegas total is a reminder that identifying high-scoring contests is a critical component in forecasting high-scoring quarterback games."

Those rates are massive. And Evan is right on the money. Another Rotoworld study on other positions, such as RBs and WRs, found similar results. This should not be surprising. But, frankly, it gets totally overlooked in the modern DFS world, where the fascination is all about "Vegas totals".

From Evan and Sean's research, regarding weekly top 6 at each position:

QBs:
- 78% were from games that went over the total
- Only 49% were from games with a Vegas total of 47 or more

WRs:
- 64% were from games that went over the total
- Only 45% were from games with a Vegas total of 47 or more

RBs:
- 64% were from games that went over the total
- Only 44% were from games with a Vegas total of 47 or more

Forget trying to be "cutting edge" by trusting linemakers on their Vegas total to select DFS lineups. This has been proven to be overvalued and frankly, overused.

Zig While Everyone Else Zags

As shown above, the focus should instead be on isolating those games you believe will go over, regardless of the Vegas total. Focus on predicting games that will be higher scoring than expected. This is the key. And by selecting players from lower Vegas totaled games, you will not only be targeting lower-utilized players (another edge) but quite possibly paying less for them as well (as their game is not predicted to be high scoring).

This article should help put Vegas totals into perspective for you this season. It is certainly more than fine to talk about Vegas totals in concert with DFS. Discussing projected points is fine as well. It is useful to be aware what the total is. But don't use them to finalize your lineup decisions. Don't select players just because the game has a total of 49 points. It won't help you. Let your DFS opponents make that mistake. Instead, select the player if you believe the game will exceed expectations.

If you digest the above information, what you hopefully learned will help you immensely this season as you play DFS. Knowing what to ignore and what to focus on is critical, especially when others will be focusing in areas which may be less valuable uses of their time. So take Vegas totals with a grain of salt and instead of focusing on high totals, focus on searching for games most likely to shoot out (over whatever total was set).

Step one is realizing that Vegas totals alone won't help you win DFS tournaments. Everyone knows of them, and frankly, they are not nearly as helpful as they are cracked up to be. At this point you actually would be more likely to win tournaments (with low % lineups) to fade the common "high total" games and select (cheaper) players from lower totaled games which you believe are likely to go over the Vegas total. Frankly, most of you will do much better just given that knowledge and won't need to enlist further assistance for edges.

Step two, however, is to find a way to accurately get "on" DFS plays from games that have high odds of going over the Vegas total. Conversely (and potentially just as helpful), fading players who are in games that you believe will go under the Vegas total. You need to accurately predict games that will go over or under the Vegas total. The best way would be to build a model.

My specialty at SharpFootballAnalysis.com is predicting NFL totals more accurately than Vegas. Each week, I recommend games where the Vegas total was set too low (and we bet the over) or where it was set too high (and we bet the under). I don't share my "real" number for the total on every single game of the week (which would kill the long term edge), I simply circle and share those specific games which are likely to go over or under, along with a detailed write up explaining exactly why I think the total is wrong. My write up drills down to the specific player matchups I think will cause my recommendation to win.

Whether you take step two and build your own model that is more accurate than what is used by linemakers who set the Vegas total (and thus will give you an edge over your competition) or you obtain that information from an information service like mine or a different resource, you will do better regardless if you take away these key elements to get the next edge on the DFS community:

1) We are NOT going to focus on the Vegas total itself but instead we will predict which games will go over the total and get on those games (and stray from those we predict will go under). While quite obvious, it is vastly underutilized and will give us a major edge over DFS competitors who focus on using players from high totaled games. It will also be a far more profitable way to spend our research time. The correlation between landing a top 3, top 6, top 12 etc. player at each position is far stronger on games for games that go over (regardless of the set Vegas total) rather than playing only players in games with high Vegas totals.

2) We are going to fade what are likely to be higher utilized players in games with high Vegas totals when we don't expect the game to be as high scoring as forecasted. These players will likely be pricey, with a high ownership percentage.

3) We will identify games with average or lower Vegas totals which we believe are set too low, knowing much of our DFS competition will be focused on the higher totaled games. If we are correct and the game does shoot out, the low-ownership players we took will go a long way toward winning tournaments.

4) We will use our best judgement to predict which games are most likely to outperform or underperform expectations from a total points scored standpoint in order to accomplish the three points above. In my specific case, I'll be using the10 year track record from my NFL totals model. You're welcome to join me or you can attempt to build your own model or you can simply use your own experienced judgement in your forecast. In any case, we're focused on which games should have seen their Vegas total set higher or lower than the linemakers set them, and we'll use that to our advantage while others will blindly observe the number itself and take it as gospel.

By making smart choices like those outlined above, we will have a huge edge on the competition this year.

Football Podcast Survey Results

I host a podcast, and I also listen to several from people I respect. But much of what I do is best done by tuning outside voices down and focusing more on my own work. I need news and information to process, and I like getting the public sentiment from mainstream media (so I know what to fade) but apart from that, I work in isolation a ton, coming up with my own theories and ideas. But I've always been curious what the listeners think of my podcast, and what I can do to improve. So I paid for a survey company to allow me to host a totally anonymous survey. I asked 10 questions, which you'll see below. This survey was shared on Twitter by many, thanks to re-tweets and other link shares.

I promised to share the results, so here they are. A few things surprised and intrigued me:

First, given how prominent Fantasy is as it relates to podcasts, I was surprised that even adding DFS and season long together, people preferred general strategy football type discussions.

Second, people do consume a ton of podcasts, but to my surprise, they hated 0-30 minute (very short) podcasts. They also hated extremely long podcasts (1.5+ hours). The sweet spot was in that range of just under an hour.

I was also surprised at the number of people that preferred 3+ voices on a podcast (host, a co-host and guest(s). But even more than that, they really did not like solo podcasts. On the positive for solo pods, the question was not "which do you hate most", so when people voted, they showed their preference. And I don't know who would prefer a solo pod to multiple voices.

And finally, perhaps not too surprisingly, people might actually subscribe to your podcast if you have on a guest that the person is familiar with. Generally speaking, that guest would share the tweet/link to the podcast, a new listener would tune in, and 44% said they "might subscribe if host(s) sound interesting".

The other element of the survey was a poll to vote for your favorite top 5 football podcasts. There were over 1,300 votes, which was a pretty good number in my view. I divided it into two categories: Fantasy (DFS or Season Long) or General Strategy. Turned out most people nominated many of the same podcasts for both, which is fine. I kept the results for both separate. The biggest pain, as this was fill in the blank, was to combine all of the variants of spellings or nominations into a single podcast. For example, for Evan Silva's "Fantasy Feast", a couple nominations included: "Silva, dude" and "Evan and that former football player". So I had to combine both and file under "Fantasy Feast". I posted the top 20 podcasts for both categories on the next pages. If you're looking for new content this season, I recommend subscribing to as many of these as you can and give them all a shot.

Finally, I posted a question: "What general or specific advice would you give football podcasts to help improve their utility to you?" This was the most intriguing of all. I promised to share every, single comment because I wanted people to see what was said. Obviously, even while this question was skipped at a high rate, I still fielded nearly 200 responses and can't post them all here.

So on the next page, you'll see several of these comments plus a QR code. Scan the code and you'll see all of the comments plus a more expanded listing of voting for the favorite podcasts by name.

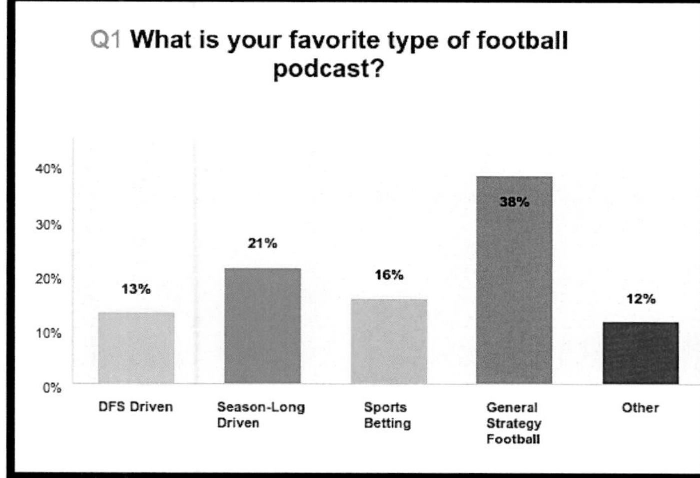

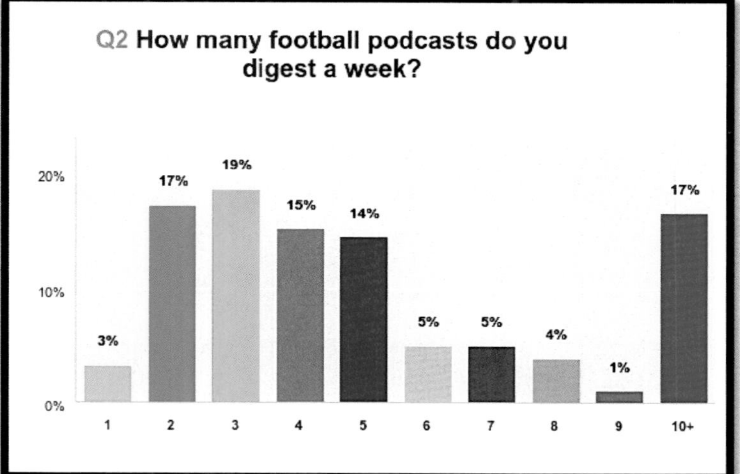

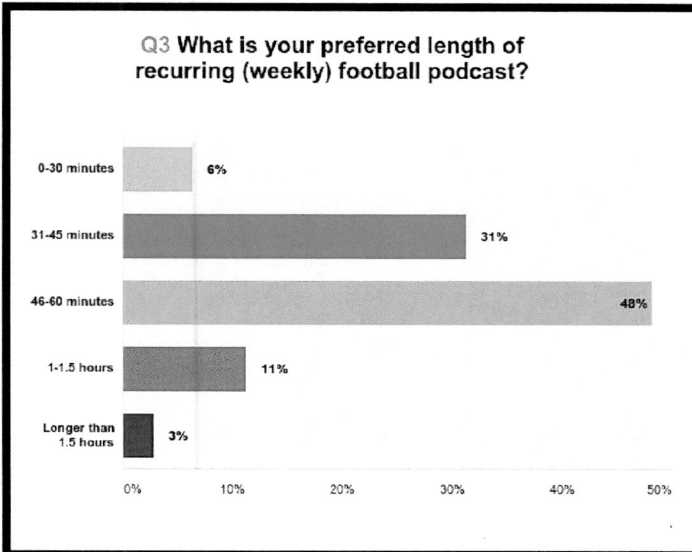

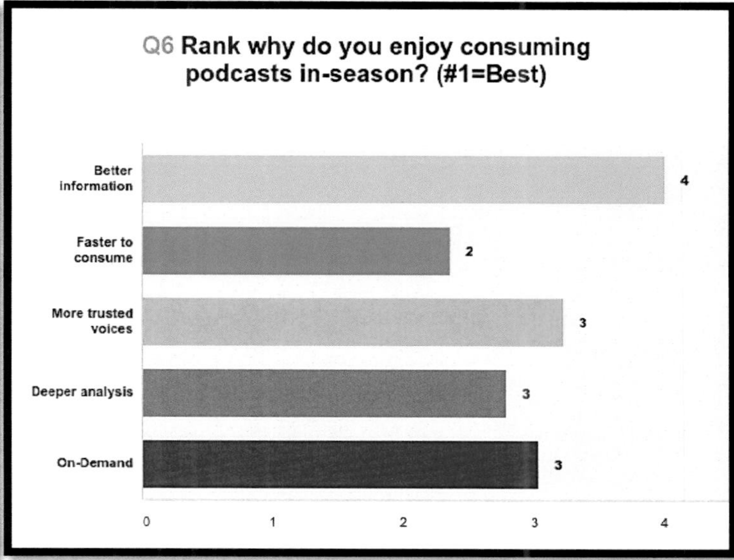

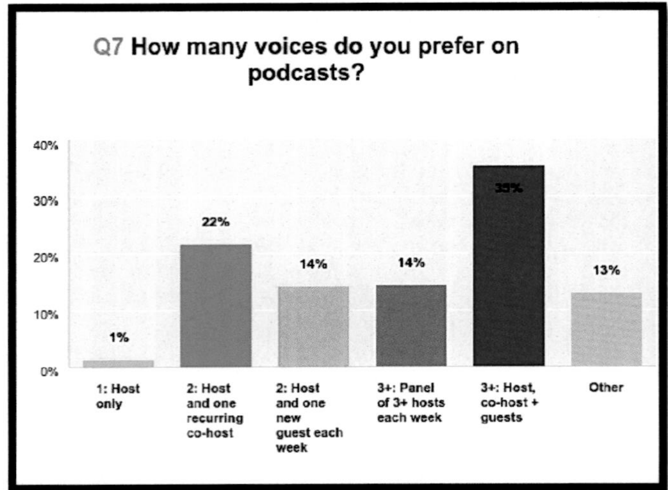

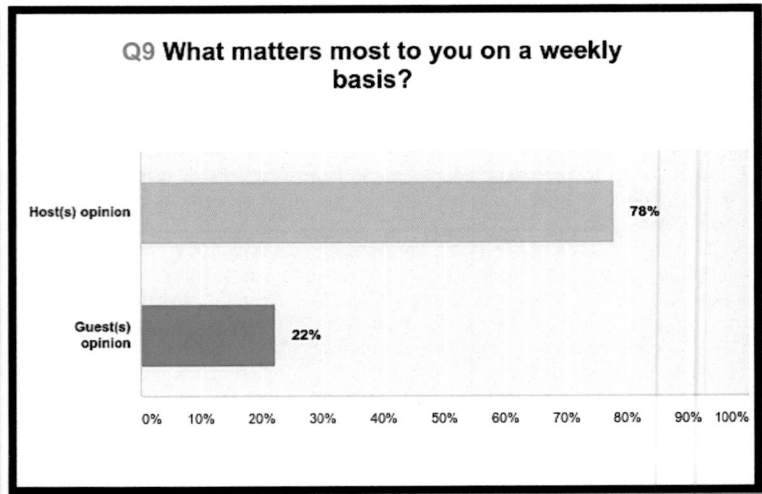

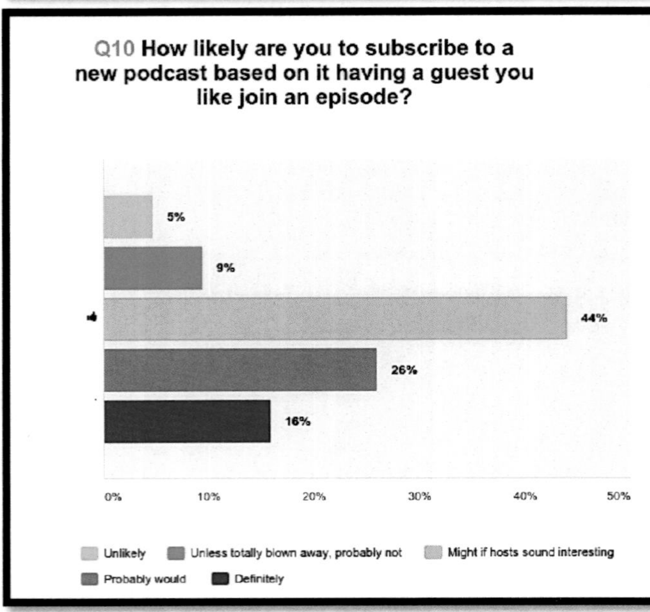

Q8 What general or specific advice would you give football podcasts to help improve their utility to you?

I'm going to summarize several of the reasons below, but will include the QR code to link to the full reasons. The only edit I made is when someone wrote a disparaging comment about a podcast by name, I'm not going to include that to call them out. Below is a sampling of some of the comments received:

- AUDIO QUALITY
- use specifics, details, reasoning to justify your opinions.
- Better audio is far & away #1. Lose the corny bumper music & lame drops. Forced laughter / humor is repulsive. Give me reasons, not just numbers
- refrain from using pronouns as often as possible when referring to players
- Stop screaming or getting overly agitated, stop saying the same thing every day/week,
- If you want to argue, make sure you don't come off as yelling because people don't want to listen to a bunch of yelling in their ears. Make sure your podcast doesn't drag. Make sure we can hear the fun in your voice.

Scan for Full Survey Results & Voting

Q4 Favorite **Fantasy** (DFS/Season-Long) Football Podcasts

Rank	Total Points	Podcast	Total Vote Rank	First Place Vote Rank
1	211	Fantasy Feast	2	1
2	207	The Audible - Football Guys	1	1
3	127	Sharp Football Analysis Podcast	3	7
4	103	Daily Fantasy Edge	7	5
5	101	RotoUnderworld	9	3
5	101	Rotoviz Radio	3	13
7	100	Fantasy Footballers	6	5
8	99	The Insiders Fantasy Football Podcast (Swolecast)	5	10
9	92	Harris Football Podcast	12	4
10	87	Living the Stream	8	8
11	77	Rotoworld	11	11
12	76	Fantasy Focus	9	11
13	58	The Fantasy Footballers	16	8
13	58	The Most Accurate Podcast	13	22
15	56	The Daily Fantasy Edge	14	16
16	48	DFS MVP	14	16
17	47	Beating the Book with Gil Alexander	18	13
18	39	The DFS Power Hour	17	19
19	38	CBS Fantasy Football Today	20	19
20	37	Dynasty Nerds	23	13

Q5 Favorite **General/Strategy** Football Podcasts

Rank	Total Points	Podcast	Total Vote Rank	First Place Vote Rank
1	154	Sharp Football Analysis Podcast	1	1
2	91	Beating the Book with Gil Alexander	2	4
3	89	The Audible - Football Guys	2	2
4	69	RotoUnderworld	7	2
5	68	Fantasy Feast	4	16
6	67	Ringer NFL Show	5	9
7	57	Bet the Board	10	6
8	55	MMQB	8	10
8	55	Rotoviz Radio	5	18
10	52	Around the NFL	11	4
11	49	Fantasy Footballers	11	6
12	45	Behind the bets	9	10
13	40	Bill Barnwell Show	14	10
14	37	Three Point Stance	17	8
15	36	Move The Sticks	16	10
16	33	Harris Football Podcast	14	10
16	33	Rotoworld	11	25
18	28	The Fantasy Footballers	20	10
19	25	Living the Stream	18	18
20	23	Dynasty Nerds	20	25

Under Pressure: Four Quarterbacks Bound to Outperform or Underperform Their 2016

By Connor Allen

Defensive pressure affects every quarterback differently. Players like Aaron Rodgers and Russell Wilson hardly break a sweat, while Ryan Tannehill becomes an entirely different player. Scott Barrett of PFF produced a chart that looked at every quarterback and their passer rating when under pressure compared to when they have a clean pocket in 2016. Combining this with Warren Sharp's projected strength of schedule tool led to finding four quarterbacks who should perform better or worse than they did in 2016.

Cam Newton had a tough 2016. After being crowned the MVP in 2015, the expectations had never been higher for the former first overall pick. He was getting his top receiver in Kelvin Benjamin back from injury and had just led the Panthers to the Super Bowl. Unfortunately as most of us know, he went on to have a career worst in completion percentage, passing touchdown percentage, yards per pass attempt, rushing yards, and rushing touchdowns. Beyond assuming a natural regression to his career average, Cam Newton should rebound closer to his MVP season than most think.

Throughout his career Cam Newton has been significantly worse when under pressure and that continued last year as he was the 5th most pressure affected quarterback in the NFL. He was under pressure a whopping 38% of the time in 2016 posting a 90.9 passer rating with a clean pocket but only a 44.4 passer rating when under pressure. However in 2017, I expect him to have a cleaner pocket much more often. Using Warren Sharp's strength of schedule tools you can see that the Panthers opposing schedule should make Cam Newton very excited.

Their schedule gets easier in terms of opposing pass rushes (17th to 24th hardest) which is big for Cam because he should be under pressure less often. It also gets easier in pass defense efficiency (6th hardest to 30th hardest), and yards per pass allowed (21st hardest to 32nd). Looking at a mixture of all these factors including explosive pass defense that Warren Sharp calls "Pass Blend", you can see not only is Carolina's schedule the easiest, but the easiest by a wide margin:

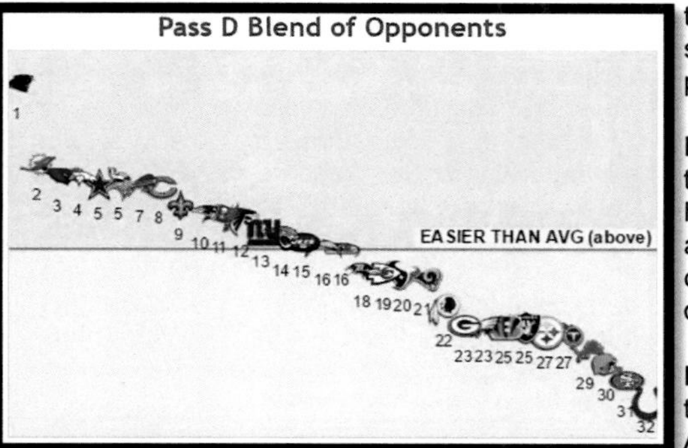

Essentially, Cam Newton should have more time to throw, have an easier time completing passes, and throw deep more often. This is also assuming the run game remains stagnant. The Panthers just drafted Christian McCaffrey 8th overall and should get him heavily involved in their game plan. McCaffrey should be a huge asset to Cam because he is a great pass-catcher and is bound to improve the Panthers running back rushing success rate which was 27th in the league last year. Beyond helping the running game, the threat of screens to McCaffrey and delayed routes out of the backfield should keep opposing linebackers from blitzing as often. The Panthers also added Curtis Samuel in the 2nd round, a slot wide receiver that will help take pressure off Cam giving him a second explosive option underneath.

Another quarterback who should rebound from a poor 2016 is Blake Bortles. Bortles is affected heavily by pressure; he had a passer rating of 90 with a clean pocket, and a 40.97 passer rating under pressure. Similarly to Cam, his schedule of opposing pass defenses also gets significantly easier in 2017. Bortles saw pressure 33% of the time in 2016 but goes from facing the 7th toughest pass rushes last year to the 21st this next year. This significant drop in strength of schedule should help him see pressure less often.

Beside pressure Bortles schedule gets easier in terms of; pass efficiency defense (17th to 24th hardest), Yards per pass attempt (16th-17th), and explosive pass defense (8th-19th). This combination gives him the 13th easiest pass defense blend in 2017.

Looking at the roster, Bortles still has a very talented receiving corps with Allen Robinson, Allen Hurns and Marquise Lee that could support his ascension. The Jaguars addressed some of their biggest needs in the draft this year as well. They drafted Leonard Fournette with the 4th overall pick which should help their 28th ranked RB rushing success rate from 2016. In the second round they drafted Cam Robinson who some made the case for as the top offensive tackle in the draft. Robinson should be able to slide into left tackle and be an improvement over Branden Albert who received a PFF grade of 42.2 last season. The Jaguars are going to try and make Bortles into more of a game manager with a run-heavy, ball-control scheme, and for Bortles that should help his efficiency immensely. While I don't expect Bortles to become a top 5 quarterback anytime soon, an emergence into the top 15 wouldn't surprise me.

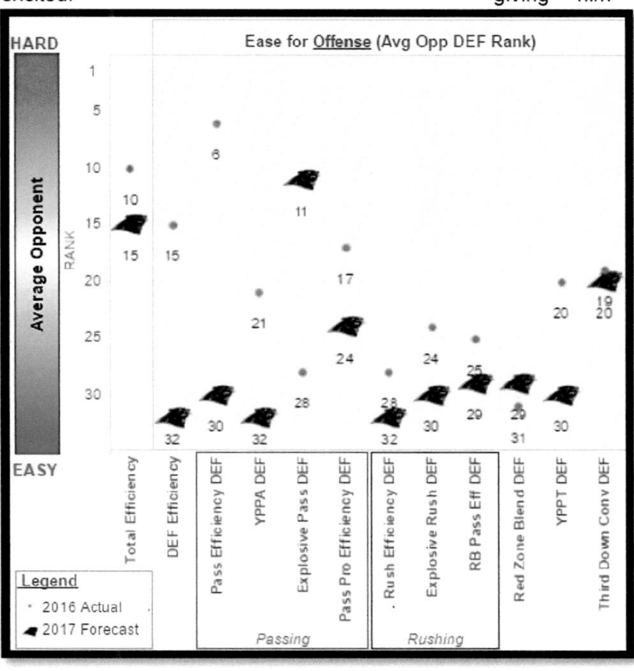

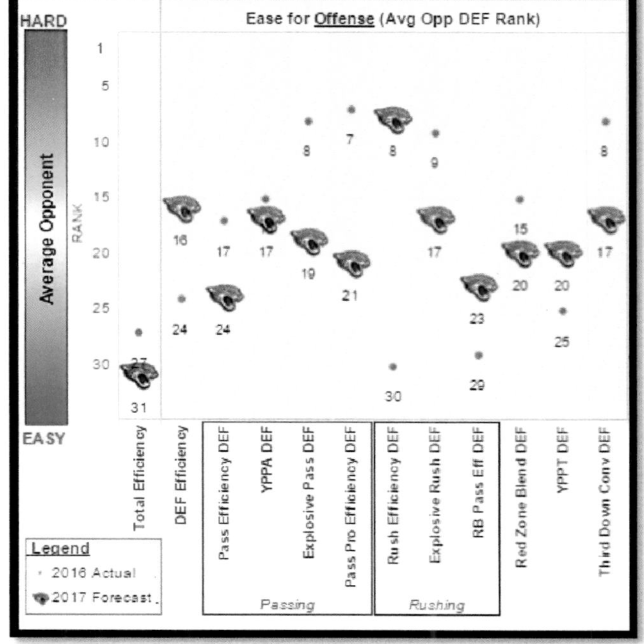

Shifting our attention to two quarterbacks who may struggle in 2017, Andy Dalton leads the way. Dalton had a passer rating of 102.5 with a clean pocket, and a 57.1 passer rating when under pressure. He was only under pressure 29% of the time last year, but I expect this to change for a lot of reasons.

For starters, the Bengals lost two elite offensive linemen. Andrew Whitworth, their starting LT, was graded as the 26th best player in the league by PFF. You read that right, PLAYER, not just offensive lineman. They also lost Kevin Zietler, PFF's 7th best guard in the NFL.

To make matters worse, the Bengals have the biggest increase in the NFL in difficulty of pass rushes they will face from 2016 to 2017 (24th to 5th hardest). To wrap up the terror that could be 2017, the Bengals also play against the 8th hardest blend of pass defenses.

Trying to find a bright spot, opposing pass defense efficiency gets easier, from 8th hardest to 19th. Unfortunately for Dalton and the Bengals offense this hasn't mattered as Dalton's splits in games against pass defenses in the bottom half of the league are relatively small. In fact, in his career he has actually thrown for more yards against teams with better pass defenses.

The Bengals drafted John Ross 9th overall which would be a great asset if Dalton had time to throw deep, but with the losses on the line and tougher strength of schedule it may not happen as often as he'd like. They continued attempting to add playmakers in Joe Mixon and Josh Reynolds in the 2nd and 4th rounds but somehow didn't address the offensive line at all. Dalton still has A.J. Green and Tyler Eifert which should help, but without time to throw Andy Dalton has shown that he will struggle.

Philly was ready to crown Carson Wentz their savior after the first three weeks of the season as the Eagles dominated the Browns, Bears, and Steelers. A media member even claimed, "(Wentz) is Peyton Manning pre-snap, he's Aaron Rodgers post-snap." After finishing the season 4-9 those kinds of comparisons aren't being thrown around anymore. Part of the reason is because Wentz was awful under pressure, posting the second biggest difference between pressure and no pressure QBR in the league. He was pressured on 30% of his pass attempts last year posting a woeful passer rating of 32.8. Comparing this to when he had a clean pocket he had a respectable passer rating of 94.4.

This is bad news for the "Wentz Wagon" as he plays the 7th hardest schedule of opposing pass-rushers, 3 spots harder than last year. But beyond being under pressure more next year, Wentz has a huge jump in the strength of opposing pass defenses. In 2016 he played against the 20th hardest opposing pass defenses, in 2017 he has to face the 6th hardest. Contrary to Andy Dalton, the toughness of opposing secondary's greatly mattered to Wentz last season.

The key to me in these splits is the touchdown and interception categories. Against teams ranked in the top 13 in pass defense he averaged 1.5 Interceptions and only half a touchdown per game. Compare this to every other team where he averaged 1.3 touchdowns per game and only half an interception.

Unfortunately for Wentz he has to play half of his games in 2017 against secondary's ranked in the top 13. The first six weeks he has to play five teams in the top 3rd of the league in defensive pass efficiency. It could be a slow start for Wentz and the Eagles in 2017 and if their passing offense loses confidence they may not be able to rebound. A key addition of Alshon Jeffery should help Wentz giving him a true #1, but one Wide Receiver may struggle to carry a pass offense.

In summary, I expect Cam Newton to have a bounce-back year. He's proven that he's a great quarterback before, especially without pressure and against bad defenses. Blake Bortles is looked at as a bust currently but the perception should change this year. With the Jaguars coaching change, team mentality, addressing their needs through the draft, and playing a much easier schedule, Bortles should play better. People will be raving about Andy Dalton's weapons all offseason and forget the Bengals lost their two star offensive lineman. Yet Dalton isn't a good quarterback under pressure, something he is bound to see more of. Carson Wentz isn't Peyton Manning or Aaron Rodgers at any point during a play and that will be definitive this year. Eagles fans may be jumping out of the "Wentz Wagon" after the first six weeks of the season.

- Connor (@Fantasy_Matrix) was crowned as a co-winner of the Sharp Football Stats 2017 Writing Contest, along with Anthony Staggs (@pyrostag). Both will contribute articles and content at Sharp Football Stats during the 2017 season. The writing contest was far more competitive than I expected, and I am going to invite multiple people who narrowly missed winning the title to contribute material during the season. So get ready to see what I expect to be thought provoking, interesting content from Connor, Anthony and others at Sharp Football Stats this year!

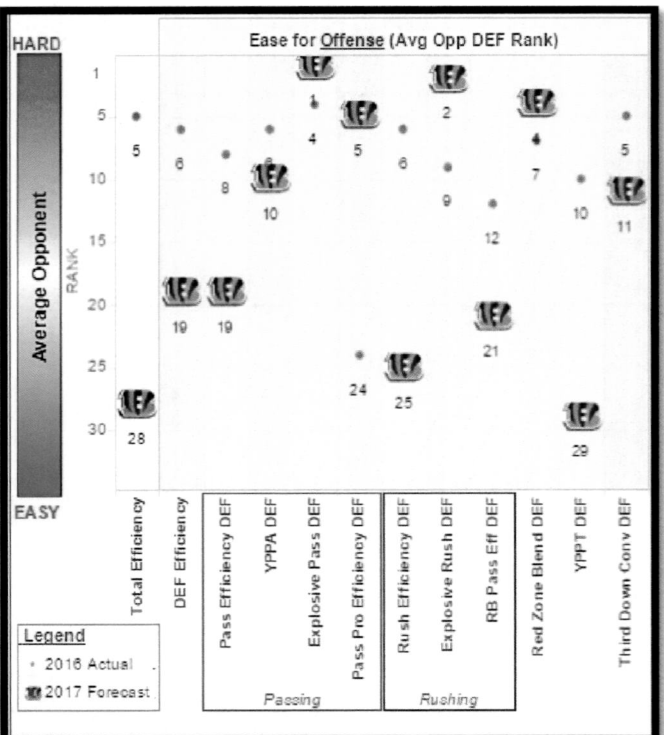

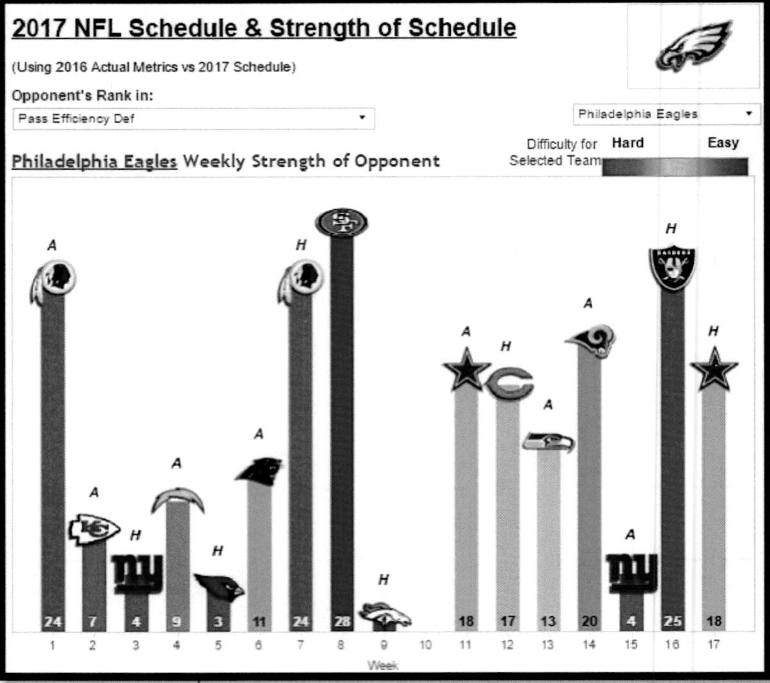

Thank you for checking out Warren Sharp's 2017 Football Preview!

If you enjoyed it or learned from it, **please** recommend it to a friend. **Please** share with your followers on Twitter or Facebook. Tag me @SharpFootball on Twitter with a photo of your copy and I'll give it a re-tweet. This took 5 full months to create, with long days and nights. To ensure there is a 2018 edition, considering my one dollar per-book profit of this Amazon printed book, please help the cause by **purchasing the PDF copy from SharpFootballAnalysis.com**, posting a kind **review on Amazon** and **telling your friends and followers**. Let's try to spread the word that analytics are educational, informative and useful. They help understanding and to improve efficiency for teams, which directly effects the quality of on-field product we watch. And if viewed the right way, they actually can make things easier to understand and retain, while saving time.

To help make that happen, I'm arranging for two giveaways. I'll announce all winners on Twitter (@SharpFootball).

1) Tweet a photo of your copy of the 2017 Football Preview and what you like about it, tagging me @SharpFootball, along with the hashtag #ILoveThisPreview. I will randomly award a .pdf copy each week in July and August.

2) Post a review on Amazon for Warren Sharp's 2017 Football Preview. Email or direct message me a copy of your review, along with a photo of your book. Multiple winners will receive a complete refund on the purchase price!

Enjoy the 2017 football season and I hope to see you around this fall, interacting on Twitter and following along on my projects **at Sharp Football Stats**. Keep up with my weekly analysis during the season on my podcast, **the Sharp Football Analysis Podcast**. And don't miss my detailed, weekly game predictions over at **SharpFootballAnalysis.com**. Have a great and safe summer – it will be football season before you know it!

Best, *Warren*

Layout and Definitions

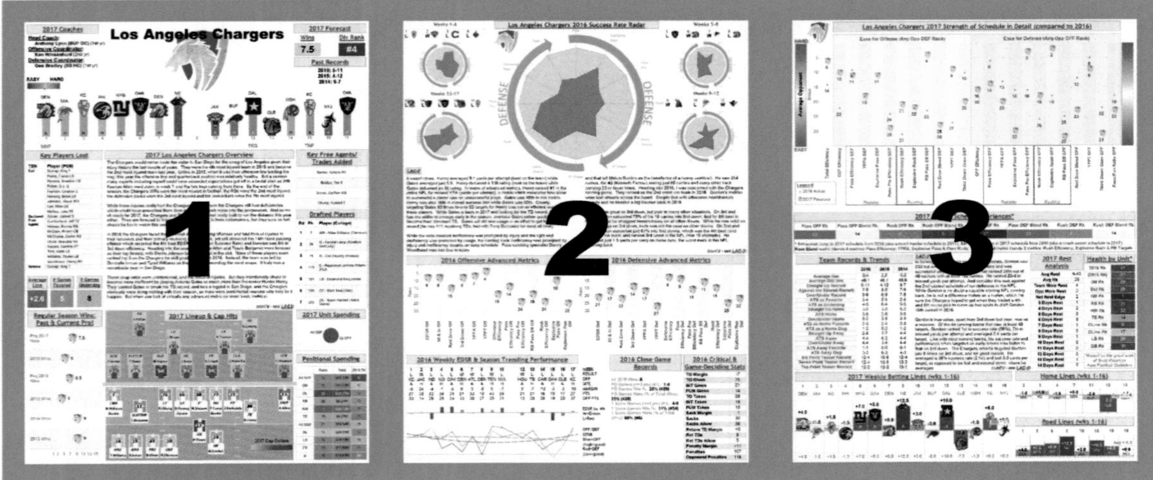

PAGE 1: Schedule listed according to strength of opponent based on win totals // Asterisk next to draft round indicates compensatory selection // Projected starting roster shaded based on current year (2017) cap hit to see where team is spending for its starters // Positional spending shows 2017 rank as "Rank" and 2016 rank as "2016 Rk" // Average line listed is based on weeks 1-16 lines which were opened by CG Technology

PAGE 2: Radars posted based on success rates only. These radars will be posted on Sharp Football Stats and updated in-season for 2017 on a weekly basis // Weekly EDSR and Season Trending Performance measures total EDSR per week, combining offense and defense together. A green vertical bar indicates the team "won" the EDSR battle that week. A red vertical bar indicates they lost. The longer the bar, the more lopsided the result. The trend chart represents offense (blue) and defense (red). When blue is high, the offense was efficient in EDSR. When the red bar is low, the defense was efficient in EDSR. EDSR stands for Early Down Success Rate, and measures efficiency on early downs only and ability to bypass 3rd down on offense, or force opponent into 3rd downs on defense.

PAGE 3: Strength of Schedule in Detail – the red "dot" is the true final result in 2016 based on the real schedule played. The logo is the 2017 forecast rank based on the real schedule the team will play // Schedule Variances indicate if the schedule became easier or harder than last year's schedule, and by how much. Extremes are most notable (a team ranking 31st or 32nd saw their schedule become much easier. A team ranking 1st or 2nd saw their schedule become much harder this year // Health by Unit are league rankings (1-32) based on Football Outsiders (Scott Kacsmar's) work.

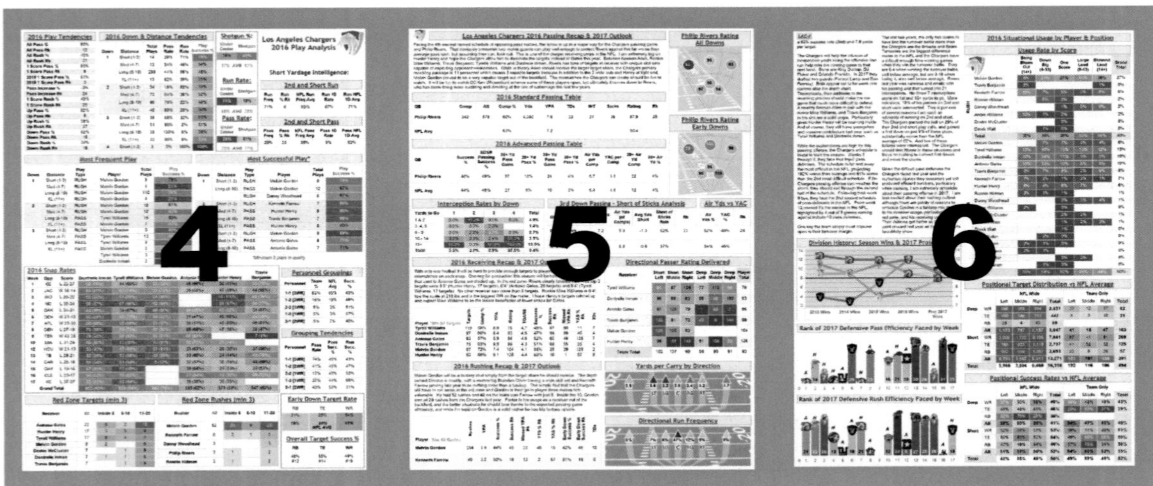

PAGE 4: Most metrics should be self explanatory // Frequent play vs successful play looks at play frequency and compares to when a team saw the most success for a particular down & distance // Snap rates include players who recorded 300+ snaps, with cutoff if too many on a certain team hit that mark // Target rates are only for early downs, target success looks at every down

PAGE 5: YPA = yards per attempt // Success rate is defined as a play which gained the minimum required yardage based on down and distance. Cutoffs are 40% of yards to go on 1st down, 60% of yards to go on 2nd down and 100% of yards to go on 3rd or 4th down // 20+ and 30+ yard pass gains are not air yards, but pass plays which totaled gains of 20 or 30 yards // Air Yds = distance ball traveled in the air per attempt // YAC = yards gained after the catch // TOARS = Target and Output-Adjusted Receiving Success – the higher the number the better the performance delivered // Missed YPA = yardage on unsuccessful plays which fell short of that required yardage cutoff. The fewer Missed YPA, the closer a player was to turning the unsuccessful play into a successful one.

PAGE 6: Usage Rate By Score examines percentage of a team's total plays in that given score margin are delivered to that player // Positional target distribution and success rates look at where a team was throwing and how successful they were, based on field location (left/mid/right) and depth (short = within 15 yards of line of scrimmage, deep = greater than that) and position // Weekly schedule for offensive players based on defensive strengths for the run and pass is found in the bottom left.

Arizona Cardinals

2017 Coaches

Head Coach:
Bruce Arians (5th yr)
Offensive Coordinator:
Harold Goodwin (5th yr)
Defensive Coordinator:
James Bettcher (3rd yr)

2017 Forecast

Wins	Div Rank
8	#2

Past Records

2016: 7-8-1
2015: 13-3
2014: 11-5

EASY HARD

Week	1	2	3	4	5	6	7	8	9	10	11	12	13	14	15	16	17
Opponent	DET	IND	DAL	SF	PHI	TB	LAR		SF	SEA	HOU	JAX	LAR	TEN	WSH	NYG	SEA
Site	A	A	H	H	A	H	A		A	H	A	H	H	H	A	H	A
			MNF				LON			TNF							

Key Players Lost

TXN	Player (POS)
Cut	Washington, Daryl LB
Declared Free Agent	Boggs, Taylor C
	Campbell, Calais DE
	Cooper, Marcus CB
	Ellington, Andre RB
	Fells, Darren TE
	Gresham, Jermaine TE
	Jefferson, Tony S
	Jenkins, Mike CB
	Johnson, Chris RB
	Mathis, Evan G
	Minter, Kevin LB
	Moore, Sio LB
	Okafor, Alex LB
	Rucker, Frostee DT
	Shipley, A.Q. C
	Swearinger, D.J. S
	Taylor, Stepfan RB
	Watford, Earl G

Average Line	# Games Favored	# Games Underdog
-1.5	8	7

Regular Season Wins: Past & Current Proj

Proj 2017 Wins  8

2016 Wins  7

Proj 2016 Wins  10

2015 Wins  13

2014 Wins  11

2013 Wins  10

1 3 5 7 9 11 13 15

2017 Arizona Cardinals Overview

After stringing together multiple double digit win seasons in consecutive order since Bruce Arians came to town, the Falcons faltered last season. It was his first losing season since becoming a head coach. Despite the NFC West being a weaker overall division last year, the Cardinals couldn't overcome their non-division record. They went 4-1-1 in division, but 3-7 outside the division. Unlike 2015, the Cardinals were +0 in overall turnover margin (+9 in 2015) and were 3-5 in one-score games (5-1 in 2015).

Was there a problem in Arizona or was it simply bad luck that drove their win total down last season? The unfortunate answer is "it's complicated". There were a number of issues for the Cardinals last season. And a lot of it boiled down to lack of talent on offense and a predictable attack. Let's begin with the issue of talent. Because it's shocking to mention this as an issue considering how loaded the 2015 Cardinals offense was.

It started with #2 WR John Brown sustaining a concussion in last year's training camp. He then had issues with his sickle-cell trait and a cyst on his spine. While Brown only missed two games, his performance was noticeably worse. He recorded just 2 TDs and his yards per attempt dropped from 9.9 in 2015 to 7.2 in 2016. The talent problems shifted to the Cardinals #3 WR last year, Michael Floyd. Off a season where he averaged 9.5 yards per attempt and pulled in 6 receiving touchdowns, Floyd entered his contract year of 2016 with high hopes. It might be impossible to have a worse contract year than Floyd. He caught just 48% of his targets and delivered a 63 passer rating when targeted. He was arrested for DUI and then waived two weeks before Christmas. When Palmer targeted Floyd on any pass longer than 14 yards in the air, Floyd delivered a 36.6 rating, catching 9 of 22 targets for 0 TDs and 3 INTs.

With the Cardinals #2 and #3 receivers virtually non-factors, Bruce Arians had to take the offense in a different direction last year. The passing game continued to focus around WR Larry Fitzgerald, but the problem with Fitzgerald is at his age, he's no longer explosive as he once was. He's more of a highly efficient tight end, who will deliver a high completion rate (72%) with an adequate yards per attempt (6.8) but he has very little explosiveness (ranked 114th in YAS %, Yards Above Successful).

(cont'd - see ARI2)

2017 Lineup & Cap Hits

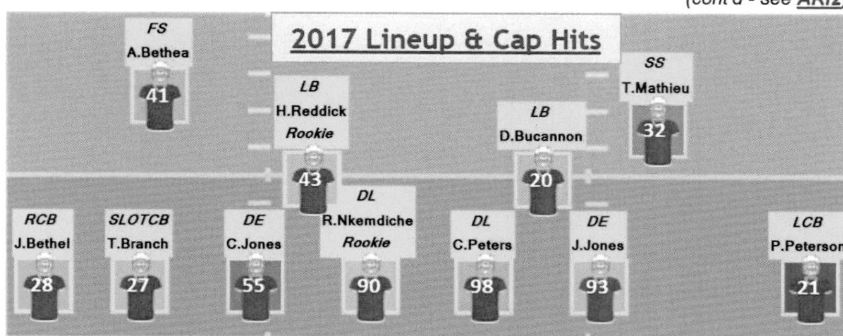

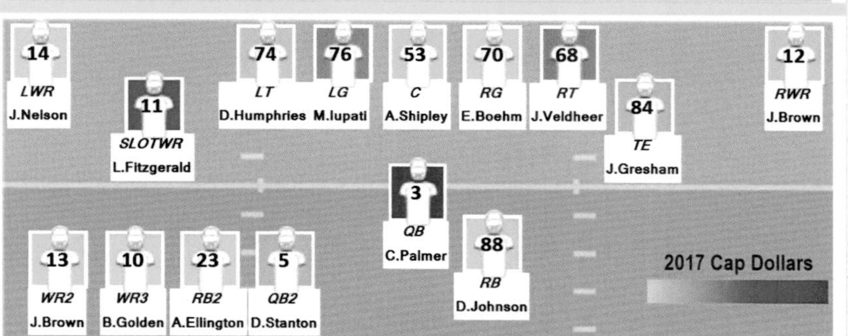

Key Free Agents/ Trades Added

Bazzie, Alex LB
Bergstrom, Tony C
Bethea, Antoine S
Binford, Harvey WR
Dansby, Karlos LB
Dobson, Aaron WR
Gabbert, Blaine QB
Jones, Jarvis LB
Rolle, Jumal CB

Drafted Players

Rd	Pk	Player (College)
1	13	LB - Haason Reddick (Temple)
2	36	S - Budda Baker (Washington)
3*	98	WR - Chad Williams (Grambling State)
4	115	G - Dorian Johnson (Pittsburgh)
5	157	OT - Will Holden (Vanderbilt)
5*	179	RB - T. J. Logan (North Carolina)
6	208	S - Rudy Ford (Auburn)

2017 Unit Spending

Positional Spending

	Rank	Total	2016 Rk
All OFF	5	$94.52M	13
QB	1	$29.36M	10
OL	11	$30.18M	23
RB	31	$3.84M	18
WR	8	$24.65M	9
TE	25	$6.50M	20
All DEF	19	$75.82M	11
DL	31	$12.30M	11
LB	11	$25.08M	13
CB	11	$22.03M	16
S	4	$16.41M	13

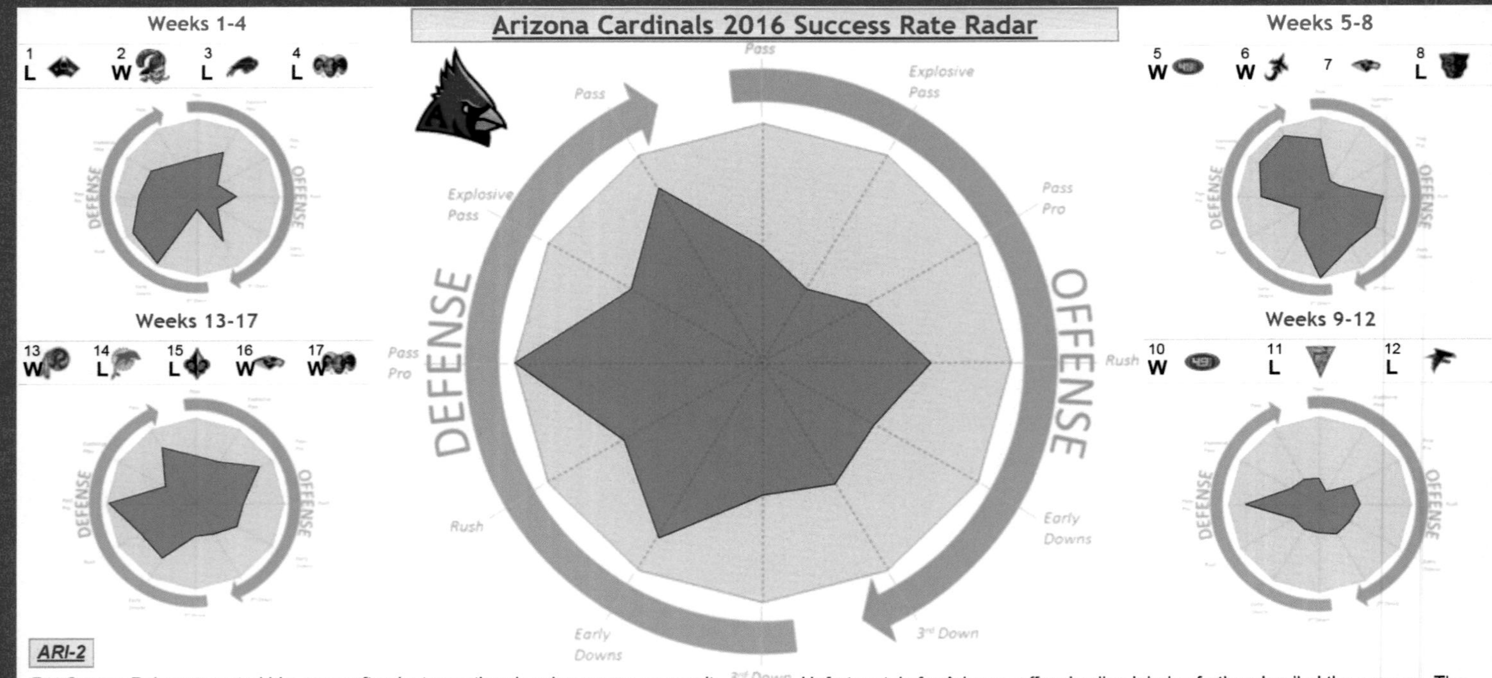

ARI-2

But Carson Palmer targeted him more often last year than in prior years as a result of the lack of talent at the position.

The second move was a ridiculous target rate to RB David Johnson. Only 4 total RBs were targeted 75+ times, and Johnson was targeted 120 times last year, the most of any RB. I've been preaching the targeting of RBs more in the passing game for some time now, and the 3 other teams who targeted RBs over 75 times were New England, Atlanta and Pittsburgh. It's shouldn't be a surprise that these 3 teams literally made it as far as you can in the postseason, as we have both AFC Championship teams and the NFC Super Bowl runner-up. These teams didn't get that far solely because they passed often to their RBs, but it does show the intelligence of the play callers. The problem for Arians was that David Johnson was far and away their best RB as well, and as such, the team needed Johnson to carry the load on the ground, which equated to 293 rushes. The combined total of 413 rushes and targets was an overwhelming volume. And eventually his rushing and receiving numbers tailed off later in the season.

Unfortunately for Arizona, offensive line injuries further derailed the season. The line was the 6th most injured in the league last season. As a result, the pass protection suffered, and without any healthy deep threats apart from JJ Nelson, the explosive passing game suffered. Explosive passing was a staple of Bruce Arians in the past. The "no risk it, no biscuit" approach was at the core of the offense. Unfortunately, last season the Cardinals risked it and still received no biscuit. They received a donut from virtually all deep receivers. The top 3 targets (JJ Nelson, Michael Floyd and John Brown) produced passer ratings of 54, 28 and 53 when targeted 15+ yards in the air. It says something when the best deep receiver on the team last year was the aged Larry Fitzgerald.

While the offense made fewer trips to the red zone, they were more successful when there because they chose to run more often, something I advocated last offseason. Arizona ran the ball on 47% of their red zone play calls, which

(cont'd - see ARI-3)

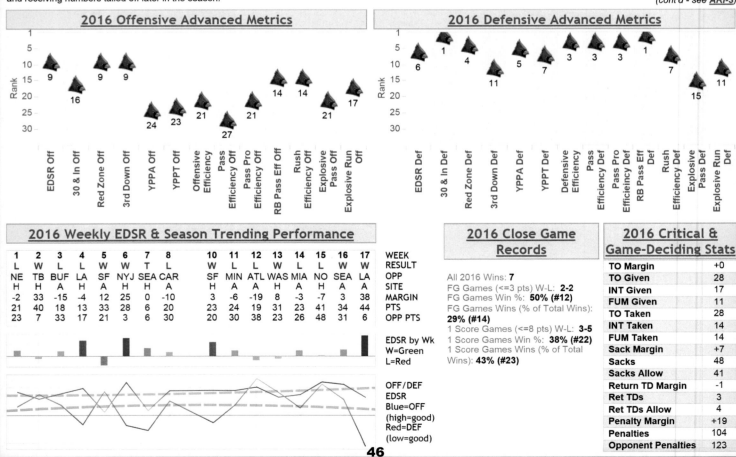

2016 Offensive Advanced Metrics

	Rank
EDSR Off	9
30 & In Off	16
Red Zone Off	9
3rd Down Off	9
YPPA Off	24
YPPT Off	23
Offensive Efficiency	21
Pass Efficiency Off	27
Pass Pro Efficiency Off	21
RB Pass Eff Off	14
Rush Efficiency Off	14
Explosive Pass Off	21
Explosive Run Off	17

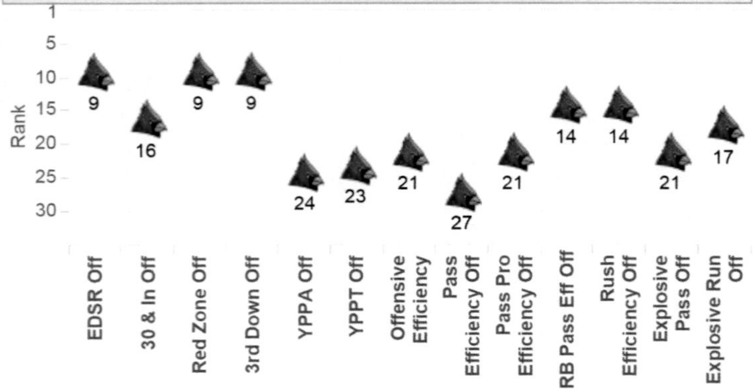

2016 Defensive Advanced Metrics

	Rank
EDSR Def	6
30 & In Def	1
Red Zone Def	4
3rd Down Def	11
YPPA Def	5
YPPT Def	7
Defensive Efficiency	3
Pass Efficiency Def	3
Pass Pro Efficiency Def	3
RB Pass Eff Def	1
Rush Efficiency Def	7
Explosive Pass Def	15
Explosive Run Def	11

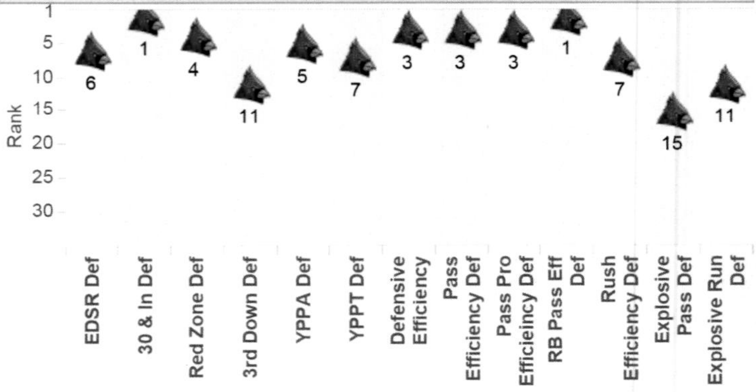

2016 Weekly EDSR & Season Trending Performance

WEEK	1	2	3	4	5	6	7	8	10	11	12	13	14	15	16	17
RESULT	L	W	L	L	W	W	T	L	W	L	L	W	L	L	W	W
OPP	NE	TB	BUF	LA	SF	NYJ	SEA	CAR	SF	MIN	ATL	WAS	MIA	NO	SEA	LA
SITE	H	H	A	H	A	H	H	A	H	A	A	H	A	H	A	A
MARGIN	-2	33	-15	-4	12	25	0	-10	3	-6	-19	8	-3	-7	3	38
PTS	21	40	18	13	33	28	6	20	23	24	19	31	23	41	34	44
OPP PTS	23	7	33	17	21	3	6	30	20	30	38	23	26	48	31	6

EDSR by Wk
W=Green
L=Red

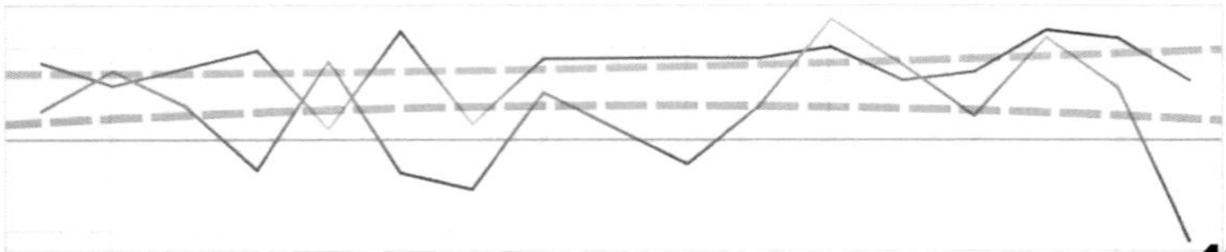

OFF/DEF
EDSR
Blue=OFF
(high=good)
Red=DEF
(low=good)

2016 Close Game Records

All 2016 Wins: **7**
FG Games (<=3 pts) W-L: **2-2**
FG Games Win %: **50% (#12)**
FG Games Wins (% of Total Wins): **29% (#14)**
1 Score Games (<=8 pts) W-L: **3-5**
1 Score Games Win %: **38% (#22)**
1 Score Games Wins (% of Total Wins): **43% (#23)**

2016 Critical & Game-Deciding Stats

TO Margin	+0
TO Given	28
INT Given	17
FUM Given	11
TO Taken	28
INT Taken	14
FUM Taken	14
Sack Margin	+7
Sacks	48
Sacks Allow	41
Return TD Margin	-1
Ret TDs	3
Ret TDs Allow	4
Penalty Margin	+19
Penalties	104
Opponent Penalties	123

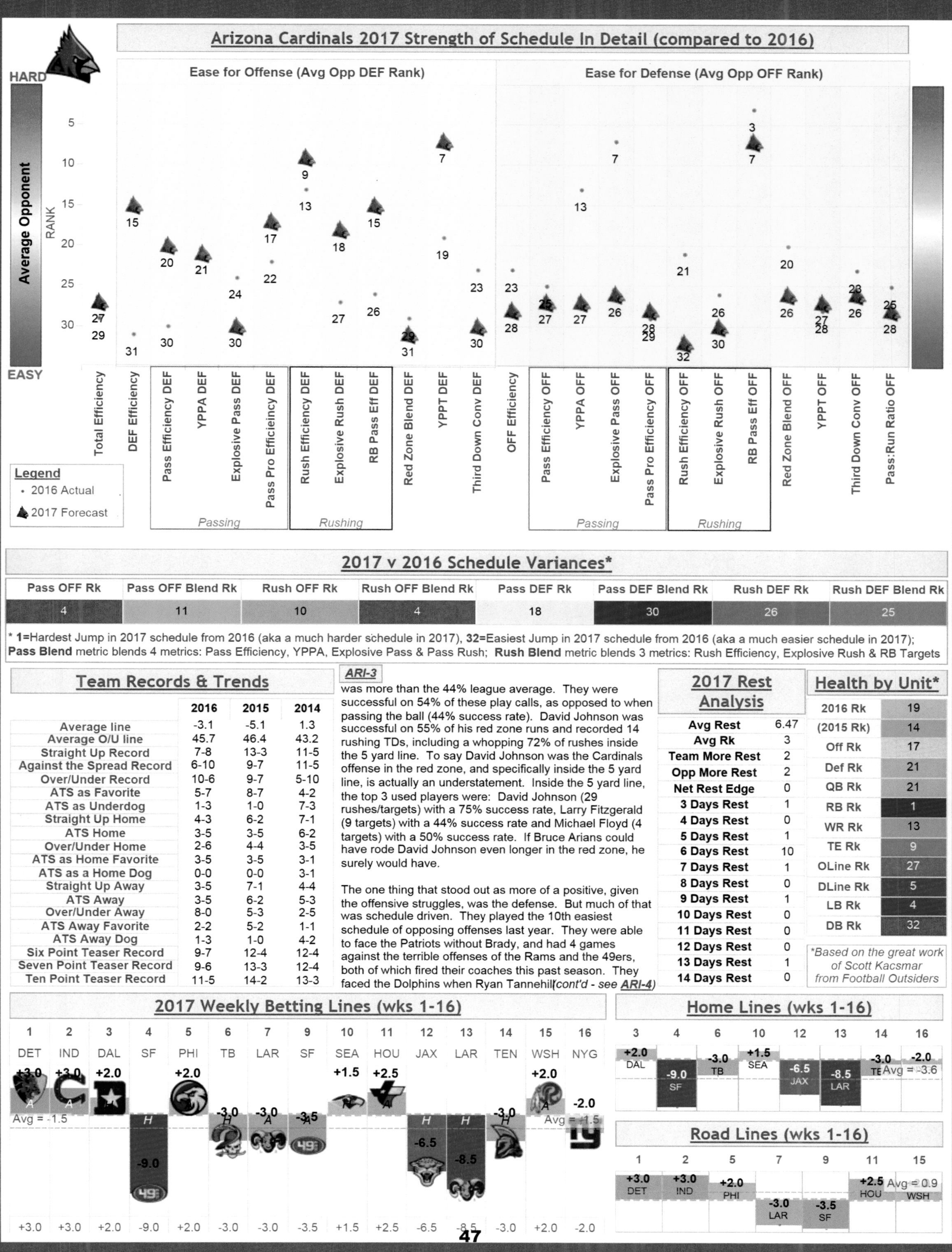

Arizona Cardinals 2017 Strength of Schedule In Detail (compared to 2016)

2017 v 2016 Schedule Variances*

Pass OFF Rk	Pass OFF Blend Rk	Rush OFF Rk	Rush OFF Blend Rk	Pass DEF Rk	Pass DEF Blend Rk	Rush DEF Rk	Rush DEF Blend Rk
4	11	10	4	18	30	26	25

* **1**=Hardest Jump in 2017 schedule from 2016 (aka a much harder schedule in 2017), **32**=Easiest Jump in 2017 schedule from 2016 (aka a much easier schedule in 2017); **Pass Blend** metric blends 4 metrics: Pass Efficiency, YPPA, Explosive Pass & Pass Rush; **Rush Blend** metric blends 3 metrics: Rush Efficiency, Explosive Rush & RB Targets

Team Records & Trends

	2016	2015	2014
Average line	-3.1	-5.1	1.3
Average O/U line	45.7	46.4	43.2
Straight Up Record	7-8	13-3	11-5
Against the Spread Record	6-10	9-7	11-5
Over/Under Record	10-6	9-7	5-10
ATS as Favorite	5-7	8-7	4-2
ATS as Underdog	1-3	1-0	7-3
Straight Up Home	4-3	6-2	7-1
ATS Home	3-5	3-5	6-2
Over/Under Home	2-6	4-4	3-5
ATS as Home Favorite	3-5	3-5	3-1
ATS as a Home Dog	0-0	0-0	3-1
Straight Up Away	3-5	7-1	4-4
ATS Away	3-5	6-2	5-3
Over/Under Away	8-0	5-3	2-5
ATS Away Favorite	2-2	5-2	1-1
ATS Away Dog	1-3	1-0	4-2
Six Point Teaser Record	9-7	12-4	12-4
Seven Point Teaser Record	9-6	13-3	12-4
Ten Point Teaser Record	11-5	14-2	13-3

ARI-3

was more than the 44% league average. They were successful on 54% of these play calls, as opposed to when passing the ball (44% success rate). David Johnson was successful on 55% of his red zone runs and recorded 14 rushing TDs, including a whopping 72% of rushes inside the 5 yard line. To say David Johnson was the Cardinals offense in the red zone, and specifically inside the 5 yard line, is actually an understatement. Inside the 5 yard line, the top 3 used players were: David Johnson (29 rushes/targets) with a 75% success rate, Larry Fitzgerald (9 targets) with a 44% success rate and Michael Floyd (4 targets) with a 50% success rate. If Bruce Arians could have rode David Johnson even longer in the red zone, he surely would have.

The one thing that stood out as more of a positive, given the offensive struggles, was the defense. But much of that was schedule driven. They played the 10th easiest schedule of opposing offenses last year. They were able to face the Patriots without Brady, and had 4 games against the terrible offenses of the Rams and the 49ers, both of which fired their coaches this past season. They faced the Dolphins when Ryan Tannehill (cont'd - see ARI-4)

2017 Rest Analysis

Avg Rest	6.47
Avg Rk	3
Team More Rest	2
Opp More Rest	2
Net Rest Edge	0
3 Days Rest	1
4 Days Rest	0
5 Days Rest	1
6 Days Rest	10
7 Days Rest	1
8 Days Rest	0
9 Days Rest	1
10 Days Rest	0
11 Days Rest	0
12 Days Rest	0
13 Days Rest	1
14 Days Rest	0

Health by Unit*

2016 Rk	19
(2015 Rk)	14
Off Rk	17
Def Rk	21
QB Rk	21
RB Rk	1
WR Rk	13
TE Rk	9
OLine Rk	27
DLine Rk	5
LB Rk	4
DB Rk	32

*Based on the great work of Scott Kacsmar from Football Outsiders

2017 Weekly Betting Lines (wks 1-16)

Week	1	2	3	4	5	6	7	9	10	11	12	13	14	15	16
Opp	DET	IND	DAL	SF	PHI	TB	LAR	SF	SEA	HOU	JAX	LAR	TEN	WSH	NYG
H/A	A	A	H	H	A	H	A	A	H	A	H	H	H	A	H
Line	+3.0	+3.0	+2.0	-9.0	+2.0	-3.0	-3.0	-3.5	+1.5	+2.5	-6.5	-8.5	-3.0	+2.0	-2.0

Avg = -1.5

Home Lines (wks 1-16)

Week	3	4	6	10	12	13	14	16
Opp	DAL	SF	TB	SEA	JAX	LAR	TEN	NYG
Line	+2.0	-9.0	-3.0	+1.5	-6.5	-8.5	-3.0	-2.0

Avg = -3.6

Road Lines (wks 1-16)

Week	1	2	5	7	9	11	15
Opp	DET	IND	PHI	LAR	SF	HOU	WSH
Line	+3.0	+3.0	+2.0	-3.0	-3.5	+2.5	+2.0

Avg = 0.9

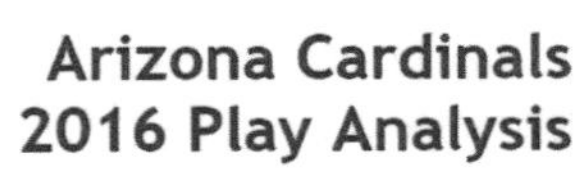

Arizona Cardinals 2016 Play Analysis

2016 Play Tendencies

All Pass %	61%
All Pass Rk	9
All Rush %	39%
All Rush Rk	24
1 Score Pass %	60%
1 Score Pass Rk	9
2015 1 Score Pass %	59%
2015 1 Score Pass Rk	16
Pass Increase %	2%
Pass Increase Rk	11
1 Score Rush %	40%
1 Score Rush Rk	24
Up Pass %	63%
Up Pass Rk	5
Up Rush %	37%
Up Rush Rk	28
Down Pass %	65%
Down Pass Rk	7
Down Rush %	35%
Down Rush Rk	26

2016 Down & Distance Tendencies

Down	Distance	Total Plays	Pass Rate	Run Rate	Play Success %
1	Short (1-3)	11	36%	64%	36%
	Med (4-7)	14	36%	64%	50%
	Long (8-10)	326	51%	49%	50%
	XL (11+)	10	50%	50%	60%
2	Short (1-3)	54	37%	63%	59%
	Med (4-7)	73	60%	40%	48%
	Long (8-10)	99	63%	37%	42%
	XL (11+)	35	94%	6%	26%
3	Short (1-3)	42	62%	38%	76%
	Med (4-7)	51	98%	2%	37%
	Long (8-10)	33	100%	0%	24%
	XL (11+)	32	84%	16%	16%
4	Short (1-3)	1	0%	100%	0%
	Med (4-7)	2	50%	50%	50%

Shotgun %:

Under Center	Shotgun
53%	47%
37%	*63%*

37% AVG 63%

Run Rate:

Under Center	Shotgun
62%	10%

68% AVG 23%

Pass Rate:

Under Center	Shotgun
38%	90%

32% AVG 77%

Short Yardage Intelligence:

2nd and Short Run

Run Freq	Run % Rk	NFL Run Freq Avg	Run 1D Rate	Run NFL 1D Avg
67%	13	65%	81%	71%

2nd and Short Pass

Pass Freq	Pass % Rk	NFL Pass Freq Avg	Pass 1D Rate	Pass NFL 1D Avg
33%	19	35%	50%	52%

Most Frequent Play

Down	Distance	Play Type	Player	Total Plays	Play Success %
1	Short (1-3)	RUSH	David Johnson	6	50%
	Med (4-7)	RUSH	David Johnson	7	57%
	Long (8-10)	RUSH	David Johnson	123	48%
	XL (11+)	RUSH	David Johnson	4	50%
2	Short (1-3)	RUSH	David Johnson	29	69%
	Med (4-7)	RUSH	David Johnson	24	42%
	Long (8-10)	RUSH	David Johnson	29	28%
	XL (11+)	PASS	David Johnson	13	31%
3	Short (1-3)	RUSH	David Johnson	12	92%
	Med (4-7)	PASS	David Johnson	9	44%
			Larry Fitzgerald	9	11%
	Long (8-10)	PASS	Larry Fitzgerald	8	38%
	XL (11+)	PASS	David Johnson	8	25%

Most Successful Play*

Down	Distance	Play Type	Player	Total Plays	Play Success %
1	Short (1-3)	RUSH	David Johnson	6	50%
	Med (4-7)	RUSH	David Johnson	7	57%
	Long (8-10)	PASS	Darren Fells	5	100%
2	Short (1-3)	RUSH	David Johnson	29	69%
	Med (4-7)	PASS	Michael Floyd	6	67%
	Long (8-10)	PASS	Jermaine Gresham	6	83%
	XL (11+)	PASS	Larry Fitzgerald	5	40%
3	Short (1-3)	PASS	Larry Fitzgerald	5	100%
	Med (4-7)	PASS	John Brown	5	60%
	Long (8-10)	PASS	John Brown	5	40%
	XL (11+)	PASS	David Johnson	8	25%

**Minimum 5 plays to qualify*

2016 Snap Rates

Week	Opp	Score	Larry Fitzgerald	David Johnson	Jermaine Gresham	J.J. Nelson	John Brown	Darren Fells	Jaron Brown
1	NE	L 23-21	59 (97%)	58 (95%)	22 (36%)	2 (3%)	17 (28%)	23 (38%)	35 (57%)
2	TB	W 40-7	59 (89%)	42 (64%)	24 (36%)		29 (44%)	45 (68%)	29 (44%)
3	BUF	L 33-18	80 (98%)	79 (96%)	18 (22%)	1 (1%)	39 (48%)	50 (61%)	47 (57%)
4	LA	L 17-13	72 (94%)	56 (73%)	35 (45%)	4 (5%)	45 (58%)	39 (51%)	70 (91%)
5	SF	W 33-21	62 (91%)	53 (78%)	57 (84%)	3 (4%)	31 (46%)		64 (94%)
6	NYJ	W 28-3	67 (87%)	67 (87%)	73 (95%)	16 (21%)	28 (36%)	31 (40%)	48 (62%)
7	SEA	T 6-6	93 (98%)	87 (92%)	82 (86%)	80 (84%)		8 (8%)	1 (1%)
8	CAR	L 30-20	56 (79%)	63 (89%)	63 (89%)	65 (92%)			38 (54%)
10	SF	W 23-20	69 (87%)	70 (89%)	68 (86%)	49 (62%)	30 (38%)	35 (44%)	
11	MIN	L 30-24	72 (97%)	63 (85%)	59 (80%)	30 (41%)	60 (81%)	11 (15%)	
12	ATL	L 38-19	64 (97%)	58 (88%)	62 (94%)	37 (56%)	26 (39%)	7 (11%)	
13	WAS	W 31-23	70 (92%)	68 (89%)	72 (95%)	34 (45%)	21 (28%)	25 (33%)	
14	MIA	L 26-23	68 (97%)	70 (100%)	55 (79%)	22 (31%)	26 (37%)	31 (44%)	
15	NO	L 48-41	59 (100%)	59 (100%)	37 (63%)	46 (78%)	35 (59%)	20 (34%)	
16	SEA	W 34-31	56 (93%)	60 (100%)	51 (85%)	42 (70%)	29 (48%)	19 (32%)	
17	LA	W 44-6	46 (66%)	15 (21%)	54 (77%)	40 (57%)	38 (54%)	27 (39%)	
	Grand Total		1,052 (91%)	968 (84%)	832 (72%)	471 (43%)	454 (46%)	371 (37%)	332 (58%)

Personnel Groupings

Personnel	Team %	NFL Avg	Succ. %
1-1 [3WR]	56%	60%	48%
1-2 [2WR]	24%	19%	47%
1-0 [4WR]	12%	3%	39%
1-3 [1WR]	4%	3%	56%
2-0 [3WR]	2%	1%	38%

Grouping Tendencies

Personnel	Pass Rate	Pass Succ. %	Run Succ. %
1-1 [3WR]	67%	47%	50%
1-2 [2WR]	46%	51%	44%
1-0 [4WR]	97%	37%	100%
1-3 [1WR]	21%	50%	58%
2-0 [3WR]	81%	43%	20%

Red Zone Targets (min 3)

Receiver	All	Inside 5	6-10	11-20
Larry Fitzgerald	20	9	3	8
David Johnson	14	4	1	9
J.J. Nelson	11	2	2	7
Jermaine Gresham	7	2	1	4
John Brown	6	1	2	3
Darren Fells	3		2	1

Red Zone Rushes (min 3)

Rusher	All	Inside 5	6-10	11-20
David Johnson	58	25	10	23
Chris Johnson	8	2	1	5
Andre Ellington	6	1	2	3
Kerwynn Williams	4	2		2

Early Down Target Rate

	RB	TE	WR
	20%	16%	64%
NFL AVG	*19%*	*20%*	*61%*

Overall Target Success %

RB	TE	WR
45% #14	52% #17	51% #14

Arizona Cardinals 2016 Passing Recap & 2017 Outlook

Carson Palmer has his work cut out for him this season. Naturally a year older and turning 38, off of his worst season since his first in Arizona in 2013, with a diminutive WR corps and a year-older Larry Fitzgerald, father time is not on Palmer's side. Although they like to use 3 and 4 WR sets more often, Arians must explore more max-2 WR formations for the flexibility in blocking schemes and matchups they present over the more traditional formations. Palmer's deep passing may be less efficient as he ages, so the more intermediate and shorter throws which involve these shorter, faster weapons could be beneficial. In either case, with Palmer's lack of mobility this offense is not going to be successful unless the offensive line stays healthy and performs better in 2017. While Palmer may still be able to go deep, it could be time for Arians to borrow a page out of Andy Reid's playbook to develop a lot of route combinations specifically designed for yards after the catch from shorter throws. Palmer was very poor throwing deep left or right last season, but recorded ratings of 94 or better to the short left, short right and short middle. Arizona must run the ball more on 2nd and short – Palmer recorded 2 interceptions on 16 "shot plays" last year.

Carson Palmer Rating All Downs

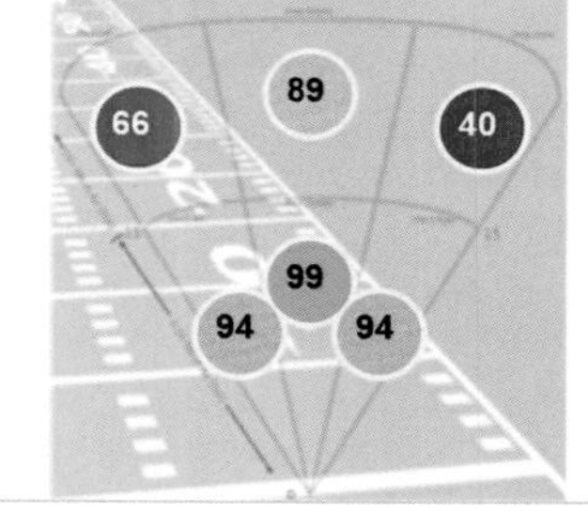

Carson Palmer Rating Early Downs

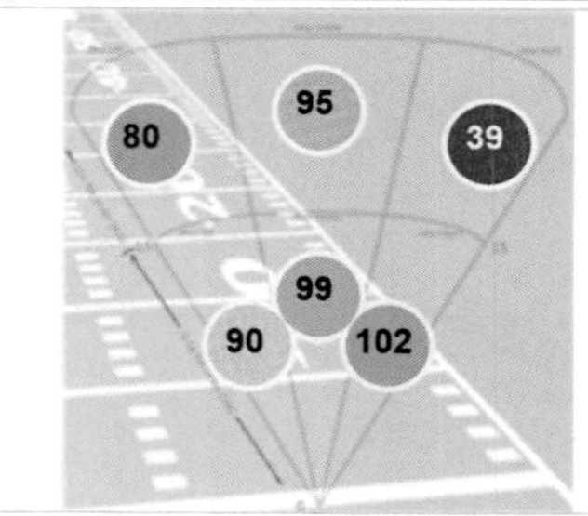

2016 Standard Passing Table

QB	Comp	Att	Comp %	Yds	YPA	TDs	INT	Sacks	Rating	Rk
Carson Palmer	365	599	61%	4,231	7.1	25	14	39	86.5	26
NFL Avg			63%		7.2				90.4	

2016 Advanced Passing Table

QB	Success %	EDSR Passing Success %	20+ Yd Pass Gains	20+ Yd Pass %	30+ Yd Pass Gains	30+ Yd Pass %	Air Yds per Comp	YAC per Comp	20+ Air Yd Comp	20+ Air Yd %
Carson Palmer	47%	50%	48	8%	13	2%	7.3	4.3	21	4%
NFL Avg	44%	48%	27	8%	10	3%	6.4	4.8	12	4%

Interception Rates by Down

Yards to Go	1	2	3	4	Total
1 & 2	0.0%	12.5%	0.0%	0.0%	5.7%
3, 4, 5	0.0%	0.0%	2.2%	0.0%	1.1%
6 - 9	0.0%	0.0%	5.8%	0.0%	2.7%
10 - 14	2.2%	1.2%	3.0%		2.0%
15+	0.0%	0.0%	4.3%		1.9%
Total	2.0%	1.4%	3.6%	0.0%	2.2%

3rd Down Passing - Short of Sticks Analysis

QB	Avg Yds to Go	Air Yds (of Comps)	Avg Yds Short	Short of Sticks Rate	Rk
Carson Palmer	7.8	7.7	-0.2	57%	18
NFL Avg	7.6	6.8	-0.8	57%	

Air Yds vs YAC

Air Yds %	YAC %	Rk
57%	43%	19
54%	46%	

2016 Receiving Recap & 2017 Outlook

Let's hope we see John "Smokey" Brown back and heathy this season, as he spent the entire year dealing with ailments, some chronic and some sustained in-season. His presence and ability to get behind the defense really opens up things underneath, and the passing attack missed that in 2016. Fitzgerald is the professor of the group – his work ethic and dedication to greatness is evident and reflects on the field. I think the overall offense would benefit from more targets to Gresham but the Cardinal also need a younger TE to step up. I'm eager to see Arians design offense for Chad Williams, who has been lauded in OTAs for his tremendous hands.

Player *Min 50 Targets*	Targets	Comp %	YPA	Rating	TOARS	Success %	Success Rk	Missed YPA Rk	YAS % Rk	TDs
Larry Fitzgerald	151	72%	6.8	95	5.4	58%	24	26	114	6
David Johnson	132	67%	7.3	92	5.1	48%	90	106	102	4
J.J. Nelson	74	46%	7.7	84	4.0	43%	121	126	4	5
John Brown	72	54%	7.2	63	3.8	51%	63	111	61	2
Michael Floyd	79	48%	6.3	63	3.9	44%	115	122	60	5
Jermaine Gresham	61	61%	6.4	83	3.8	52%	55	92	120	2

Directional Passer Rating Delivered

Receiver	Short Left	Short Middle	Short Right	Deep Left	Deep Middle	Deep Right	Player Total
Larry Fitzgerald	103	101	71	101	76	144	98
David Johnson	107	93	114	80	40	40	100
J.J. Nelson	97	108	119	49	79	9	85
John Brown	20	90	103	67	105	6	63
Michael Floyd	105	112	80	41	7	33	63
Jermaine Gresham	79	81	88	40	119	119	83
Team Total	92	97	95	53	70	52	86

2016 Rushing Recap & 2017 Outlook

As the Cardinals turn their offense over to its best player, they must be smarter in their usage rates for Johnson or they'll burn him out too quickly. If you look at the "Most Frequent Play" graphics you'll find each down is divided into 4 distances (short, medium, long and XL). That leaves 12 slots for a "most frequent play" by down and distance on 1st through 3rd down. David Johnson occupies 11 of those 12 slots, with 3rd and long being the only down/distance where plays aren't called most often to Johnson. The Cardinals need more balance. In short yardage and even 1st and 10 situations, Johnson is a monster. But 2nd and long or XL are not optimal times to target Johnson, and the team could instead have a fresher Johnson on 3rd down.

Player *Min 50 Rushes*	Rushes	YPA	Success %	Success Rk	Missed YPA Rk	YTS % Rk	YAS % Rk	Early Down Success %	Early Down Success Rk	TDs
David Johnson	293	4.2	49%	23	27	42	23	49%	32	16

Yards per Carry by Direction

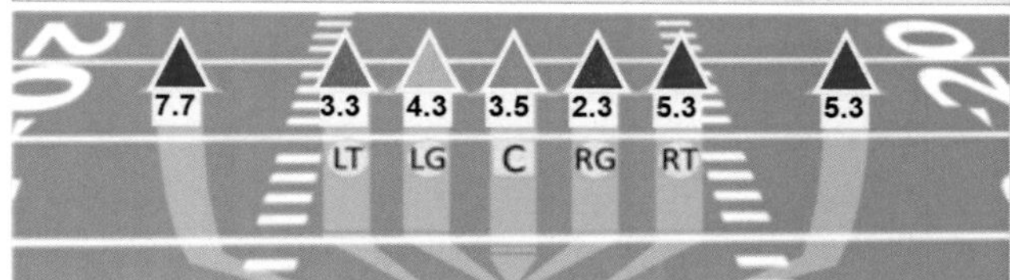

Directional Run Frequency

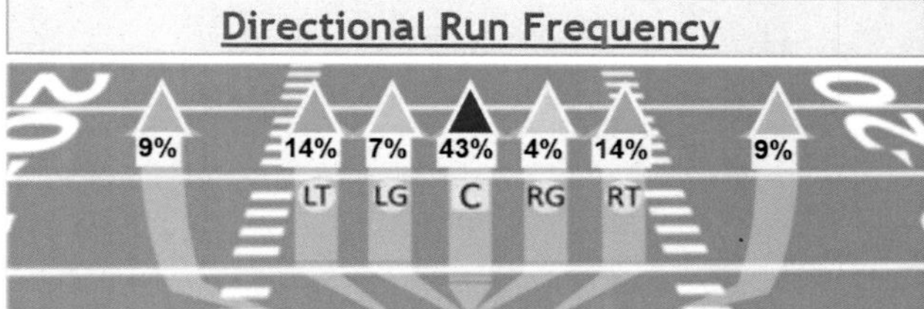

was knocked from the game and Matt Moore filled in late. Overall the schedule of offenses they faced was even easier than the strength of schedule makes it appear. And the defense performed for the most part, except when they played the NFC South. Most advanced metrics ranked the defense inside the top 5. A handful placed them squarely inside the top 10 but not far back. But it still wasn't enough to fully offset the bad offense.

In 2017, the success of this team is going to come down to the pass protection of Carson Palmer and whether he can still sling it deep. G Evan Mathis is no longer with the Cardinals, and in his place Even Boehm, a 2nd year player out of Missouri, is likely to take over. They need the line to stay healthy and play better. And it won't be easy because the team is slated to face more difficult pass rushes in 2017 than they did last year. Then the questions shift to Palmer himself. Assuming he gets adequate protection, will he be able to perform better and get the ball downfield more accurately than he did last year? It's a big question because Palmer's ratings were obviously bad last year (below average rating, completion rate and yards per attempt) but the Cardinals faced the 3rd easiest schedule of opposing pass defenses last year. This year they see a moderate increase, up to the 20th most difficult schedule. It's the 4th largest increase in passing difficult of opponent from 2016 to 2017.

If the Cardinals want to consider some of my more advanced personnel groupings for suggestions, I'll gladly tell them when they used 3+ WRs they were successful on just 45% of their passes and Palmer recorded an 85 rating with a 22:17 TD:INT ratio. But when they used 2 or fewer WRs, 51% of their passes were successful and Palmer recorded a 142 passer rating with 5 TDs and 0 INTs. When Palmer targeted his WRs out of the TE heavy groupings, he recorded a 62% success rate and a 120 rating. But when targeting WRs out of 3+ WR formations, Palmer recorded a 49% success rate and a 76 rating. Whether the extra backs or TEs were used as blockers or did a better job to flood the zones, Palmer was more comfortable and played substantially better.

The questions don't stop with the protection and Palmer, however. While Fitzgerald still should be a great inside and intermediate threat, the Cardinals need Brown to regain his health and quickness and Nelson or Chad Williams to perform as an adequate deep threat along the sideline. And then it comes down to Johnson. There is no doubt he is an absolute monster and a complete work horse, but Arizona needs to be more careful with his usage. They should run him more on 2nd and short, where they threw the ball 33% of the time but saw 31% more first downs when they ran instead of passed. They should use him less on 2nd and long, where his success rate on over 40 carries was 29%. Arizona has many unanswered questions. Arians is smart enough to coach around setbacks, and can dig into formations/play calls to help an aging Palmer. But he can't afford many if they want to return to the playoffs.

Division History: Season Wins & 2017 Projection

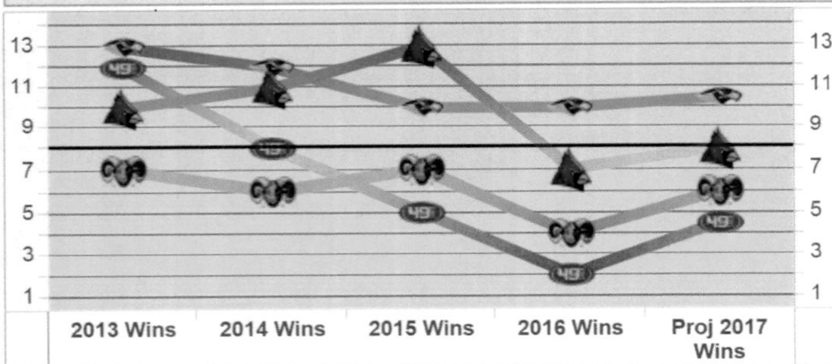

Rank of 2017 Defensive Pass Efficiency Faced by Week

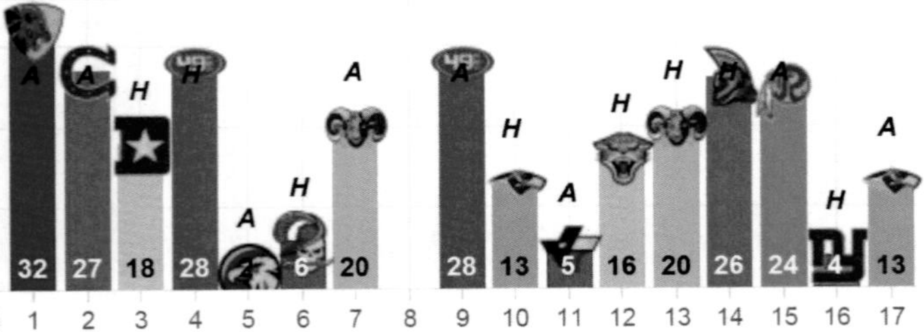

Rank of 2017 Defensive Rush Efficiency Faced by Week

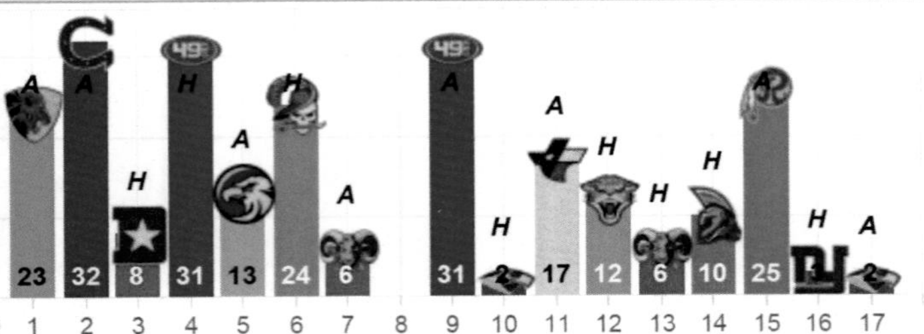

2016 Situational Usage by Player & Position

Usage Rate by Score

		Being Blown Out (14+)	Down Big (9-13)	One Score	Large Lead (9-13)	Blowout Lead (14+)	Grand Total
RUSH	David Johnson	17%	28%	33%	31%	12%	29%
	Larry Fitzgerald			0%			0%
	J.J. Nelson			0%		1%	0%
	John Brown			0%			0%
	Andre Ellington			3%	12%	11%	3%
	Chris Johnson	2%	1%	1%	3%	16%	2%
	Kerwynn Williams		1%	1%		11%	2%
	Stepfan Taylor				3%	3%	0%
	Total	19%	30%	39%	50%	55%	37%
PASS	David Johnson	16%	19%	11%	12%	5%	12%
	Larry Fitzgerald	17%	13%	16%	9%	5%	15%
	J.J. Nelson	12%	4%	8%	3%	3%	7%
	John Brown	12%	5%	6%	5%	11%	7%
	Michael Floyd	9%	6%	7%	5%	1%	7%
	Jermaine Gresham	6%	14%	5%	5%	3%	6%
	Andre Ellington	1%	3%	2%		1%	2%
	Chris Johnson			0%			0%
	Jaron Brown	4%	1%	2%	5%	3%	2%
	Kerwynn Williams			0%		1%	0%
	Darren Fells	2%	2%	1%	3%	4%	2%
	Brittan Golden	2%	1%	1%		3%	1%
	Ifeanyi Momah	1%		0%	2%		0%
	Jeremy Ross			0%		3%	0%
	Hakeem Valles			0%			0%
	Troy Niklas		1%			1%	0%
	Total	81%	70%	61%	50%	45%	63%

Positional Target Distribution vs NFL Average

		NFL Wide				Team Only			
		Left	Middle	Right	**Total**	Left	Middle	Right	**Total**
Deep	WR	994	558	965	**2,517**	37	23	36	**96**
	TE	155	146	162	**463**	3	1	1	**5**
	RB	20	3	36	**59**	5	1	4	**10**
	All	**1,169**	**707**	**1,163**	**3,039**	**45**	**25**	**41**	**111**
Short	WR	2,974	1,716	3,091	**7,781**	119	55	95	**269**
	TE	820	859	1,127	**2,806**	16	16	24	**56**
	RB	973	590	1,078	**2,641**	42	32	35	**109**
	All	**4,767**	**3,165**	**5,296**	**13,228**	**177**	**103**	**154**	**434**
Total		**5,936**	**3,872**	**6,459**	**16,267**	**222**	**128**	**195**	**545**

Positional Success Rates vs NFL Average

		NFL Wide				Team Only			
		Left	Middle	Right	**Total**	Left	Middle	Right	**Total**
Deep	WR	37%	51%	38%	**41%**	35%	30%	39%	**35%**
	TE	45%	49%	43%	**46%**	0%	100%	100%	**40%**
	RB	30%	100%	28%	**32%**	40%	0%	0%	**20%**
	All	**38%**	**51%**	**38%**	**41%**	**33%**	**32%**	**37%**	**34%**
Short	WR	52%	57%	51%	**53%**	54%	56%	62%	**57%**
	TE	50%	62%	52%	**54%**	50%	56%	54%	**54%**
	RB	46%	49%	44%	**46%**	57%	53%	43%	**51%**
	All	**50%**	**57%**	**50%**	**52%**	**54%**	**55%**	**56%**	**55%**
Total		**48%**	**56%**	**48%**	**50%**	**50%**	**51%**	**52%**	**51%**

2017 Coaches

Head Coach:
Dan Quinn (3rd yr)

Offensive Coordinator:
Steve Sarkisian (Bama QB) (1st yr)

Defensive Coordinator:
Marquand Manuel (ATL DEF Asst) (1st yr)

Atlanta Falcons

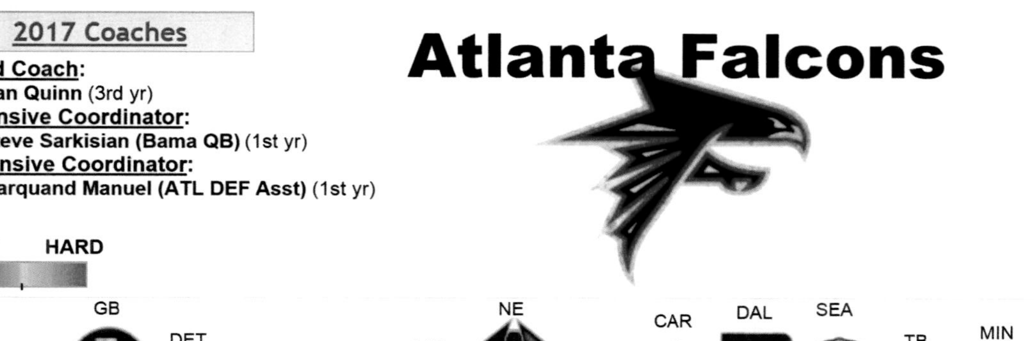

2017 Forecast

Wins	Div Rank
9.5	#1

Past Records

2016: 11-5
2015: 8-8
2014: 6-10

EASY — HARD

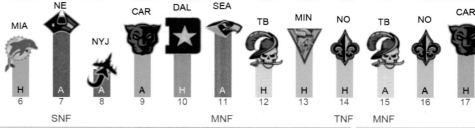

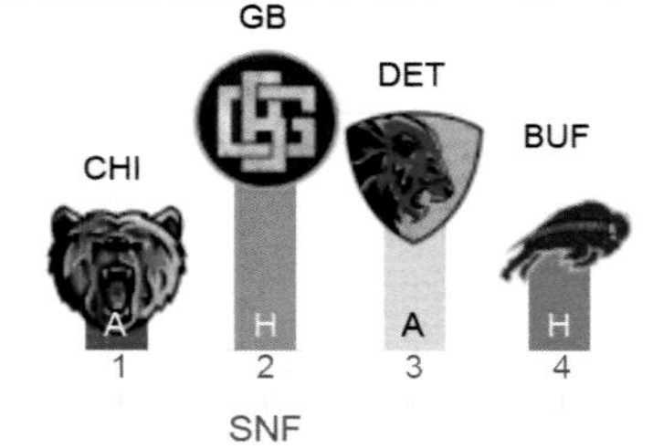

Week	Opponent	Home/Away	Game
1	CHI	A	
2	GB	H	SNF
3	DET	A	
4	BUF	H	
5			
6	MIA	H	
7	NE	A	SNF
8	NYJ	A	
9	CAR	A	
10	DAL	H	
11	SEA	A	MNF
12	TB	H	
13	MIN	H	
14	NO	H	TNF
15	TB	A	MNF
16	NO	A	
17	CAR	H	

Key Players Lost

TXN	Player (POS)
Cut	Jackson, Tyson DE
Declared Free Agent	Babineaux, Jonathan DT
	Chester, Chris G
	Compton, Tom T
	DiMarco, Patrick RB
	Freeney, Dwight DE
	Goldson, Dashon S
	Ishmael, Kemal S
	Robinson, Aldrick WR
	Tamme, Jacob TE
	Toilolo, Levine TE
	Weatherspoon, Sean LB
	Weems, Eric WR
	Wheeler, Philip LB
	Worrilow, Paul LB
	Wreh-Wilson, Blidi CB
Retired	Bykowski, Carter T
	Chester, Chris G
	Thornton, Hugh G
	White, Roddy WR

Average Line	# Games Favored	# Games Underdog
-2.9	12	2

2017 Atlanta Falcons Overview

I have to admit I loved the Atlanta Falcons last season. It was much deeper than the fact I won a lot on them during the regular season, or that I was one of the first to project their legitimate shot to win the Super Bowl and was able to earn via futures tickets which were hedged and cashed for profit. Like most of what I value in the NFL, it had to do with intelligent football. Falcons Head Coach Dan Quinn is a defensive coach. But he turned his offense over to a cunning, clever and creative Offensive Coordinator in Kyle Shanahan. Often, many defensive minded coaches will try to slow down an offense to play to do what they believes helps the defense the most. But Quinn didn't try that. He allowed Shanahan to run the offense and it resulted in a tremendous run through the regular season and to a 28-3 lead over the Patriots late in the 3rd quarter of the Super Bowl.

The Falcons strength in 2017 was clearly the offense. But it was not just the offense – it was a philosophy of play calling and style which I likened to the historical military term: Blitzkrieg (German for "lightning war"). It was a tactic used to create disorganization among enemy forces through the use of speed and surprise, with the use of short, fast and powerful attacks to pierce the line of defense. By quickly unbalancing the enemy, it was difficult for them to respond to the quickly changing front of the attackers. Interestingly, the goal was "create short military campaigns, which preserve human lives and limit the expenditure of artillery." Blitzkrieg was invented as a response to the stagnant trench warfare style that pervaded what occurred on the Western Front during WWI. Because the German forces struggled when fighting these "positional" wars, they attempted to avoid being entrenched in the first place. Enter Blitzkrieg. It was a method used to smash through enemy lines before the opponent even realized what was happening. The Germans believed the quickest way to defeat an enemy was to cut it off. To do so required speed, but it also required the ability to quickly penetrate weak points in the enemy defense. First, chaos is created along the enemy line using quick artillery strikes and air support. Weaknesses are exposed in the line and the force would immediately focus only on attacking these weak points, rather than spreading their attack thin.

While this is simply football and far from war, I couldn't think of any other way to appropriately describe the impressive style that Shanahan and the Falcons employ to start their games.

(cont'd - see ATL2)

Key Free Agents/ Trades Added

Coleman, Derrick RB
Crawford, Jack DE
Poe, Dontari DT
Roberts, Andre WR
Thornton, Hugh G
Tupou, Tani DT
Vainuku, Soma RB
Vogler, Brian TE

Drafted Players

Rd	Pk	Player (College)
1	26	OLB - Takkarist McKinley (UCLA)
3	75	LB - Duke Riley (LSU)
4	136	C - Sean Harlow (Oregon State)
	149	CB - Damontae Kazee (San Diego State)
5	156	RB - Brian Hill (Wyoming)
	174	TE - Eric Saubert (Drake)

Regular Season Wins: Past & Current Proj

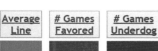

	Wins
Proj 2017 Wins	9.5
2016 Wins	11
Proj 2016 Wins	7
2015 Wins	8
2014 Wins	6
2013 Wins	4

1 3 5 7 9 11 13 15

2017 Lineup & Cap Hits

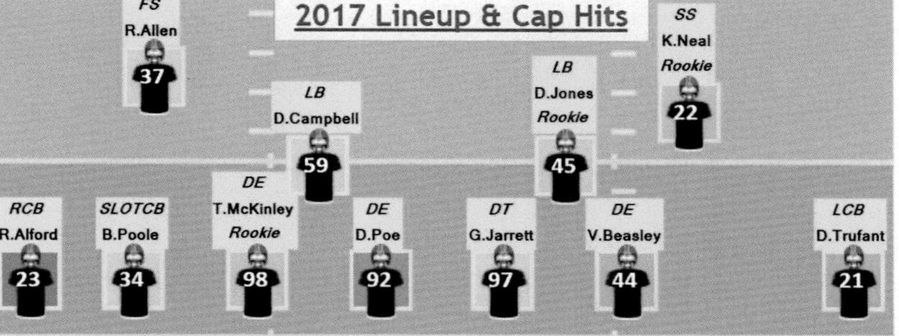

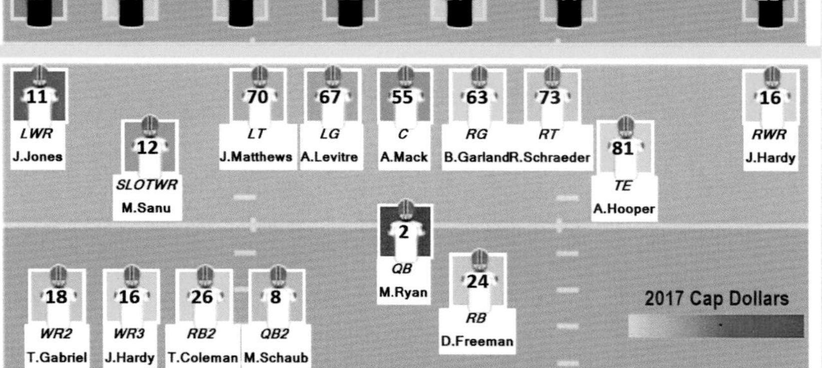

2017 Unit Spending

Positional Spending

	Rank	Total	2016 Rk
All OFF	3	$98.00M	6
QB	2	$28.95M	1
OL	14	$29.09M	17
RB	28	$4.62M	32
WR	2	$30.09M	4
TE	27	$5.25M	21
All DEF	24	$69.74M	28
DL	12	$31.69M	10
LB	30	$10.60M	28
CB	16	$19.38M	28
S	25	$8.07M	28

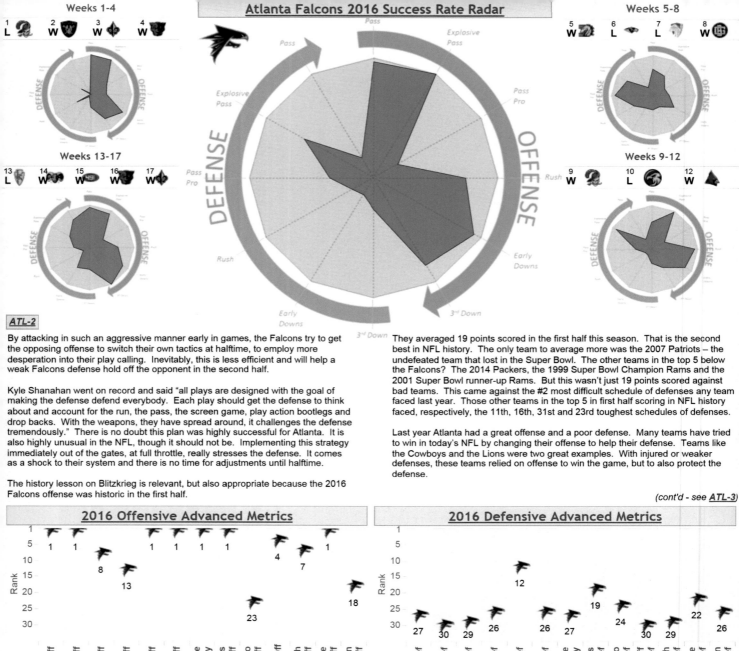

Atlanta Falcons 2016 Success Rate Radar

Weeks 1-4

1 L · 2 W · 3 W · 4 W

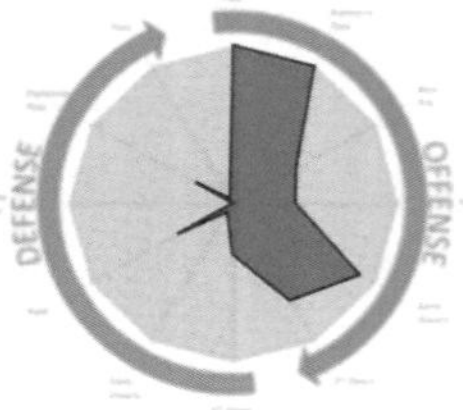

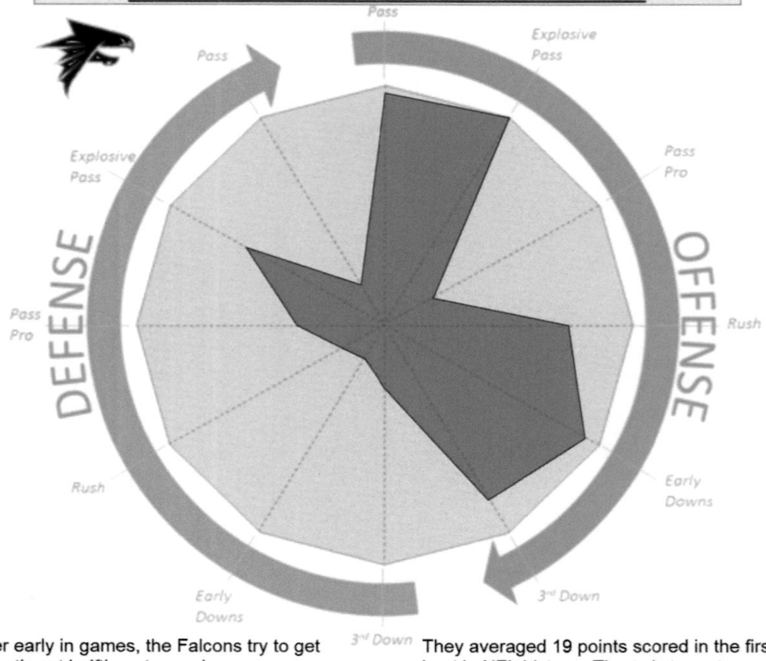

Weeks 5-8

5 W · 6 L · 7 L · 8 W

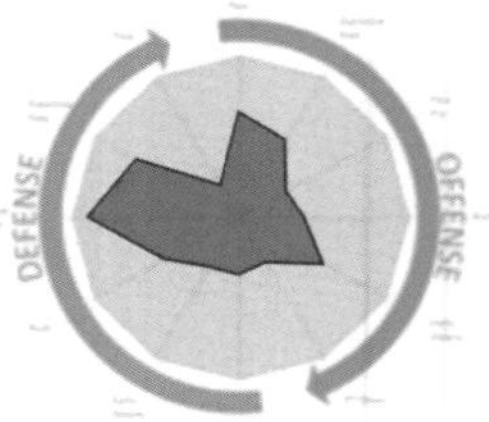

Weeks 9-12

9 W · 10 L · 12 W

Weeks 13-17

13 L · 14 W · 15 W · 16 W · 17 W

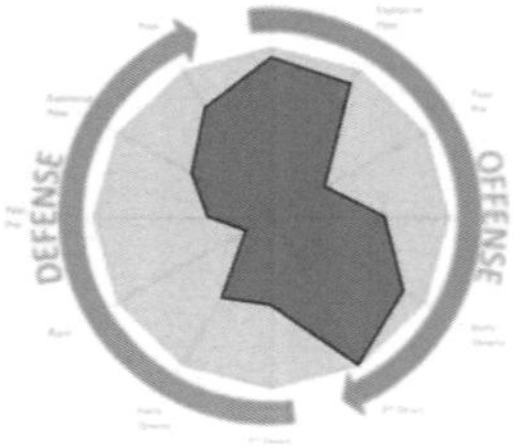

DEFENSE — OFFENSE

Pass · Explosive Pass · Pass Pro · Rush · Early Downs · 3rd Down · Early Downs · Rush · Pass Pro · Explosive Pass · Pass

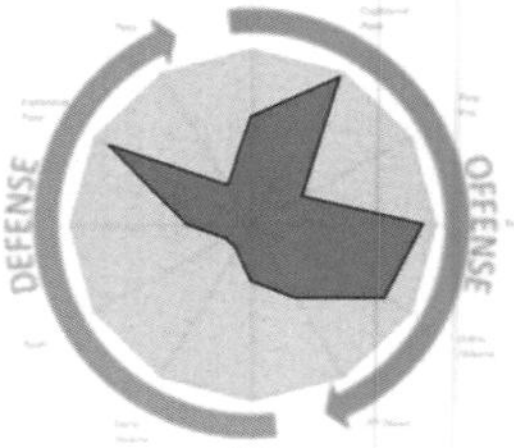

ATL-2

By attacking in such an aggressive manner early in games, the Falcons try to get the opposing offense to switch their own tactics at halftime, to employ more desperation into their play calling. Inevitably, this is less efficient and will help a weak Falcons defense hold off the opponent in the second half.

Kyle Shanahan went on record and said "all plays are designed with the goal of making the defense defend everybody. Each play should get the defense to think about and account for the run, the pass, the screen game, play action bootlegs and drop backs. With the weapons, they have spread around, it challenges the defense tremendously." There is no doubt this plan was highly successful for Atlanta. It is also highly unusual in the NFL, though it should not be. Implementing this strategy immediately out of the gates, at full throttle, really stresses the defense. It comes as a shock to their system and there is no time for adjustments until halftime.

The history lesson on Blitzkrieg is relevant, but also appropriate because the 2016 Falcons offense was historic in the first half.

They averaged 19 points scored in the first half this season. That is the second best in NFL history. The only team to average more was the 2007 Patriots – the undefeated team that lost in the Super Bowl. The other teams in the top 5 below the Falcons? The 2014 Packers, the 1999 Super Bowl Champion Rams and the 2001 Super Bowl runner-up Rams. But this wasn't just 19 points scored against bad teams. This came against the #2 most difficult schedule of defenses any team faced last year. Those other teams in the top 5 in first half scoring in NFL history faced, respectively, the 11th, 16th, 31st and 23rd toughest schedules of defenses.

Last year Atlanta had a great offense and a poor defense. Many teams have tried to win in today's NFL by changing their offense to help their defense. Teams like the Cowboys and the Lions were two great examples. With injured or weaker defenses, these teams relied on offense to win the game, but to also protect the defense.

(cont'd - see ATL-3)

2016 Offensive Advanced Metrics

2016 Defensive Advanced Metrics

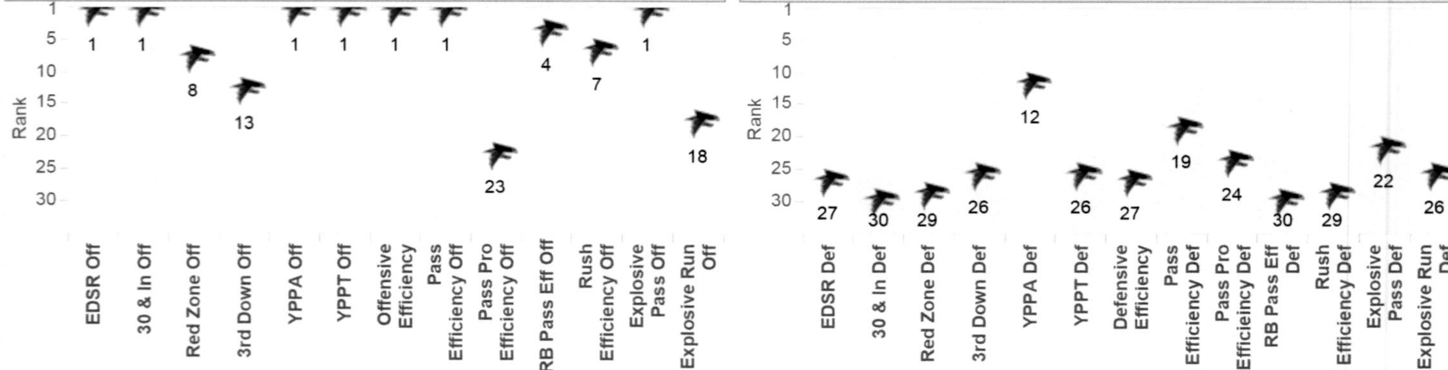

2016 Weekly EDSR & Season Trending Performance

WEEK	1	2	3	4	5	6	7	8	9	10	12	13	14	15	16	17
RESULT	L	W	W	W	W	L	L	W	W	L	W	L	W	W	W	W
OPP	TB	OAK	NO	CAR	DEN	SEA	SD	GB	TB	PHI	ARI	KC	LA	SF	CAR	NO
SITE	H	A	A	H	A	A	H	H	A	A	H	H	A	H	A	H
MARGIN	-7	7	13	15	7	-2	-3	1	15	-9	19	-1	28	28	17	6
PTS	24	35	45	48	23	24	30	33	43	15	38	28	42	41	33	38
OPP PTS	31	28	32	33	16	26	33	32	28	24	19	29	14	13	16	32

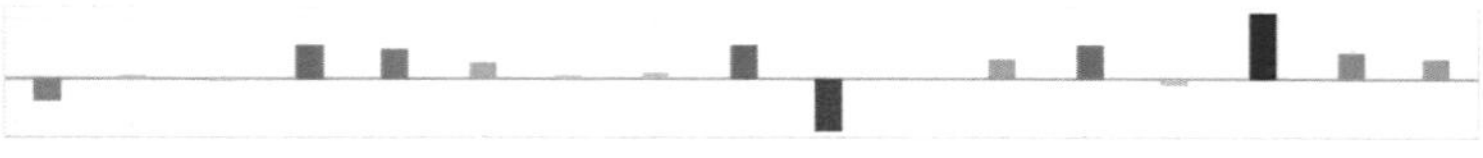

EDSR by Wk
W=Green
L=Red

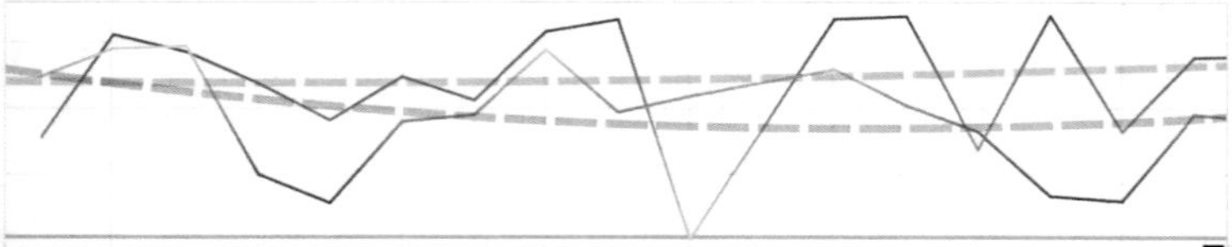

OFF/DEF
EDSR
Blue=OFF
(high=good)
Red=DEF
(low=good)

2016 Close Game Records

All 2016 Wins: **11**
FG Games (<=3 pts) W-L: **1-3**
FG Games Win %: **25% (#23)**
FG Games Wins (% of Total Wins): **9% (#26)**
1 Score Games (<=8 pts) W-L: **4-4**
1 Score Games Win %: **50% (#16)**
1 Score Games Wins (% of Total Wins): **36% (#24)**

2016 Critical & Game-Deciding Stats

TO Margin	+11
TO Given	11
INT Given	7
FUM Given	4
TO Taken	22
INT Taken	12
FUM Taken	10
Sack Margin	-2
Sacks	35
Sacks Allow	37
Return TD Margin	+3
Ret TDs	5
Ret TDs Allow	2
Penalty Margin	+9
Penalties	104
Opponent Penalties	113

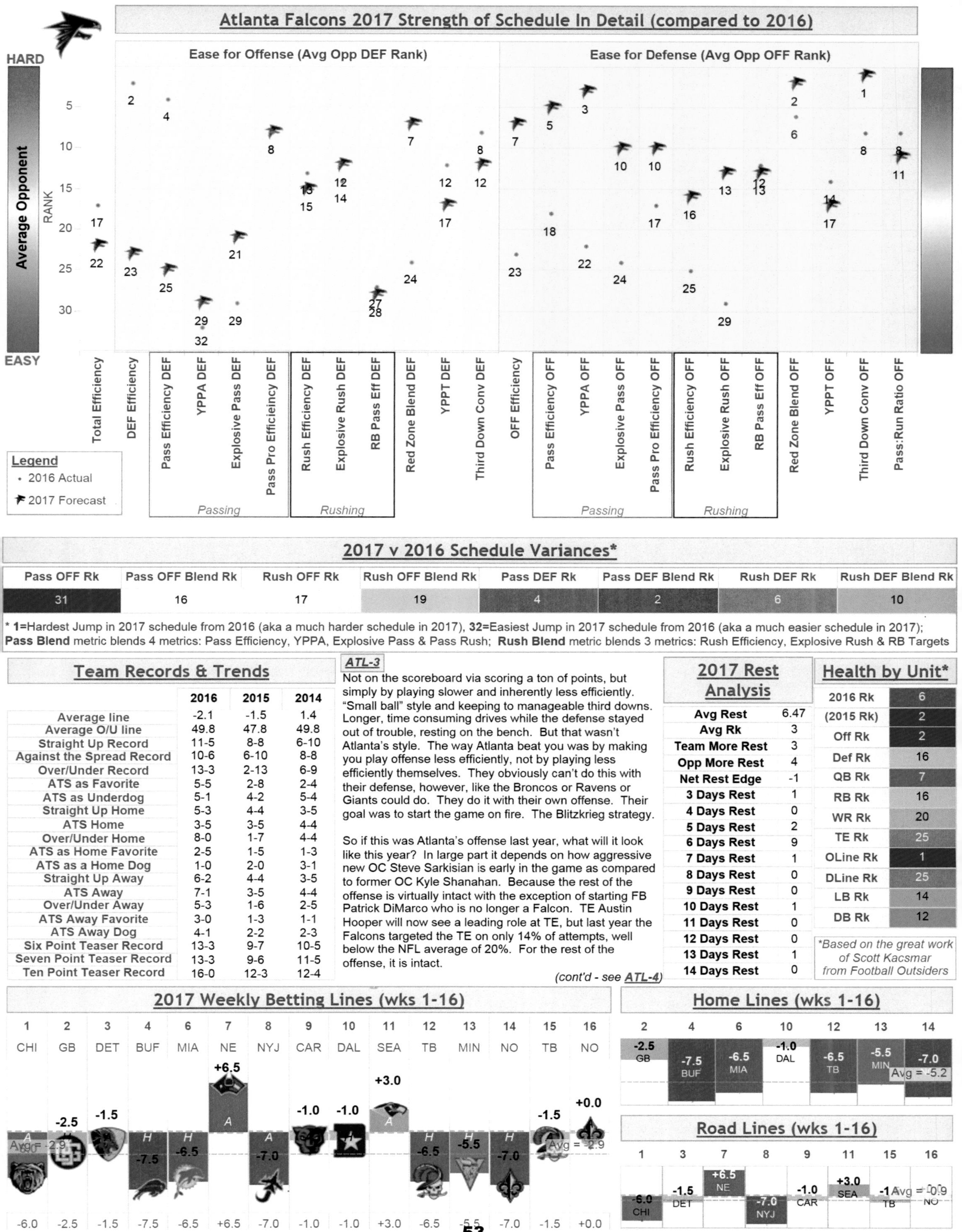

Atlanta Falcons 2017 Strength of Schedule In Detail (compared to 2016)

2017 v 2016 Schedule Variances*

Pass OFF Rk	Pass OFF Blend Rk	Rush OFF Rk	Rush OFF Blend Rk	Pass DEF Rk	Pass DEF Blend Rk	Rush DEF Rk	Rush DEF Blend Rk
31	16	17	19	4	2	6	10

* **1**=Hardest Jump in 2017 schedule from 2016 (aka a much harder schedule in 2017), **32**=Easiest Jump in 2017 schedule from 2016 (aka a much easier schedule in 2017); **Pass Blend** metric blends 4 metrics: Pass Efficiency, YPPA, Explosive Pass & Pass Rush; **Rush Blend** metric blends 3 metrics: Rush Efficiency, Explosive Rush & RB Targets

Team Records & Trends

	2016	2015	2014
Average line	-2.1	-1.5	1.4
Average O/U line	49.8	47.8	49.8
Straight Up Record	11-5	8-8	6-10
Against the Spread Record	10-6	6-10	8-8
Over/Under Record	13-3	2-13	6-9
ATS as Favorite	5-5	2-8	2-4
ATS as Underdog	5-1	4-2	5-4
Straight Up Home	5-3	4-4	3-5
ATS Home	3-5	3-5	4-4
Over/Under Home	8-0	1-7	4-4
ATS as Home Favorite	2-5	1-5	1-3
ATS as a Home Dog	1-0	2-0	3-1
Straight Up Away	6-2	4-4	3-5
ATS Away	7-1	3-5	4-4
Over/Under Away	5-3	1-6	2-5
ATS Away Favorite	3-0	1-3	1-1
ATS Away Dog	4-1	2-2	2-3
Six Point Teaser Record	13-3	9-7	10-5
Seven Point Teaser Record	13-3	9-6	11-5
Ten Point Teaser Record	16-0	12-3	12-4

ATL-3

Not on the scoreboard via scoring a ton of points, but simply by playing slower and inherently less efficiently. "Small ball" style and keeping to manageable third downs. Longer, time consuming drives while the defense stayed out of trouble, resting on the bench. But that wasn't Atlanta's style. The way Atlanta beat you was by making you play offense less efficiently, not by playing less efficiently themselves. They obviously can't do this with their defense, however, like the Broncos or Ravens or Giants could do. They do it with their own offense. Their goal was to start the game on fire. The Blitzkrieg strategy.

So if this was Atlanta's offense last year, what will it look like this year? In large part it depends on how aggressive new OC Steve Sarkisian is early in the game as compared to former OC Kyle Shanahan. Because the rest of the offense is virtually intact with the exception of starting FB Patrick DiMarco who is no longer a Falcon. TE Austin Hooper will now see a leading role at TE, but last year the Falcons targeted the TE on only 14% of attempts, well below the NFL average of 20%. For the rest of the offense, it is intact.

(cont'd - see ***ATL-4***)

2017 Rest Analysis

Avg Rest	6.47
Avg Rk	3
Team More Rest	3
Opp More Rest	4
Net Rest Edge	-1
3 Days Rest	1
4 Days Rest	0
5 Days Rest	2
6 Days Rest	9
7 Days Rest	1
8 Days Rest	0
9 Days Rest	0
10 Days Rest	1
11 Days Rest	0
12 Days Rest	0
13 Days Rest	1
14 Days Rest	0

Health by Unit*

2016 Rk	6
(2015 Rk)	2
Off Rk	2
Def Rk	16
QB Rk	7
RB Rk	16
WR Rk	20
TE Rk	25
OLine Rk	1
DLine Rk	25
LB Rk	14
DB Rk	12

*Based on the great work of Scott Kacsmar from Football Outsiders

2017 Weekly Betting Lines (wks 1-16)

1	2	3	4	6	7	8	9	10	11	12	13	14	15	16
CHI	GB	DET	BUF	MIA	NE	NYJ	CAR	DAL	SEA	TB	MIN	NO	TB	NO
A	H	A	H	H	A	A	A	H	A	H	H	H	A	A
-6.0	-2.5	-1.5	-7.5	-6.5	+6.5	-7.0	-1.0	-1.0	+3.0	-6.5	-5.5	-7.0	-1.5	+0.0

Avg = -2.9

Home Lines (wks 1-16)

2	4	6	10	12	13	14
GB	BUF	MIA	DAL	TB	MIN	NO
-2.5	-7.5	-6.5	-1.0	-6.5	-5.5	-7.0

Avg = -5.2

Road Lines (wks 1-16)

1	3	7	8	9	11	15	16
CHI	DET	NE	NYJ	CAR	SEA	TB	NO
-6.0	-1.5	+6.5	-7.0	-1.0	+3.0	-1.5	+0.0

Avg = -0.9

Atlanta Falcons 2016 Play Analysis

2016 Play Tendencies

All Pass %	60%
All Pass Rk	13
All Rush %	40%
All Rush Rk	20
1 Score Pass %	60%
1 Score Pass Rk	10
2015 1 Score Pass %	59%
2015 1 Score Pass Rk	14
Pass Increase %	1%
Pass Increase Rk	15
1 Score Rush %	40%
1 Score Rush Rk	23
Up Pass %	58%
Up Pass Rk	13
Up Rush %	42%
Up Rush Rk	20
Down Pass %	62%
Down Pass Rk	12
Down Rush %	38%
Down Rush Rk	21

2016 Down & Distance Tendencies

Down	Distance	Total Plays	Pass Rate	Run Rate	Play Success %
1	Short (1-3)	10	30%	70%	30%
	Med (4-7)	18	39%	61%	67%
	Long (8-10)	410	51%	49%	58%
	XL (11+)	21	71%	29%	38%
2	Short (1-3)	59	39%	61%	64%
	Med (4-7)	80	58%	43%	59%
	Long (8-10)	109	68%	32%	44%
	XL (11+)	42	86%	14%	36%
3	Short (1-3)	36	61%	39%	56%
	Med (4-7)	50	96%	4%	56%
	Long (8-10)	41	93%	7%	39%
	XL (11+)	24	92%	8%	17%
4	Short (1-3)	10	40%	60%	80%

Shotgun %:

Under Center	Shotgun
61%	39%
37%	*63%*

AVG row: 37% / 63%

Run Rate:

Under Center	Shotgun
60%	14%
68%	*23%*

AVG row: 68% / 23%

Pass Rate:

Under Center	Shotgun
40%	86%
32%	*77%*

AVG row: 32% / 77%

Short Yardage Intelligence:

2nd and Short Run

Run Freq	Run % Rk	NFL Run Freq Avg	Run 1D Rate	Run NFL 1D Avg
60%	25	65%	76%	71%

2nd and Short Pass

Pass Freq	Pass % Rk	NFL Pass Freq Avg	Pass 1D Rate	Pass NFL 1D Avg
40%	7	35%	69%	52%

Most Frequent Play

Down	Distance	Play Type	Player	Total Plays	Play Success %
1	Short (1-3)	RUSH	Devonta Freeman	7	29%
	Med (4-7)	RUSH	Tevin Coleman	5	60%
	Long (8-10)	RUSH	Devonta Freeman	127	49%
	XL (11+)	PASS	Julio Jones	4	75%
			Mohamed Sanu	4	50%
		RUSH	Tevin Coleman	4	50%
2	Short (1-3)	RUSH	Devonta Freeman	25	64%
	Med (4-7)	RUSH	Devonta Freeman	16	44%
	Long (8-10)	PASS	Julio Jones	21	67%
	XL (11+)	PASS	Julio Jones	8	25%
3	Short (1-3)	RUSH	Tevin Coleman	5	40%
			Matt Ryan	5	60%
	Med (4-7)	PASS	Julio Jones	10	60%
	Long (8-10)	PASS	Julio Jones	8	50%
	XL (11+)	PASS	Devonta Freeman	4	0%
			Mohamed Sanu	4	25%

Most Successful Play*

Down	Distance	Play Type	Player	Total Plays	Play Success %
1	Short (1-3)	RUSH	Devonta Freeman	7	29%
	Med (4-7)	RUSH	Tevin Coleman	5	60%
	Long (8-10)	PASS	Austin Hooper	6	83%
2	Short (1-3)	RUSH	Tevin Coleman	7	86%
	Med (4-7)	PASS	Mohamed Sanu	6	83%
			Taylor Gabriel	6	83%
	Long (8-10)	PASS	Devonta Freeman	5	80%
	XL (11+)	PASS	Julio Jones	8	25%
3	Short (1-3)	RUSH	Matt Ryan	5	60%
	Med (4-7)	PASS	Nick Williams	5	80%
	Long (8-10)	PASS	Taylor Gabriel	5	60%

**Minimum 5 plays to qualify*

2016 Snap Rates

Week	Opp	Score	Mohamed Sanu	Julio Jones	Devonta Freeman	Levine Toilolo	Austin Hooper	Tevin Coleman	Taylor Gabriel	Patrick DiMarco	Jacob Tamme
1	TB	L 31-24	56 (86%)	55 (85%)	36 (55%)	22 (34%)	9 (14%)	32 (49%)		13 (20%)	50 (77%)
2	OAK	W 35-28	46 (72%)	49 (77%)	31 (48%)	36 (56%)	21 (33%)	30 (47%)	9 (14%)	24 (38%)	44 (69%)
3	NO	W 45-32	27 (42%)	47 (73%)	38 (59%)	29 (45%)	14 (22%)	29 (45%)	36 (56%)	19 (30%)	44 (69%)
4	CAR	W 48-33	52 (78%)	47 (70%)	34 (51%)	36 (54%)	19 (28%)	29 (43%)	17 (25%)	25 (37%)	48 (72%)
5	DEN	W 23-16	46 (69%)	50 (75%)	40 (60%)	44 (66%)	21 (31%)	26 (39%)	14 (21%)	27 (40%)	45 (67%)
6	SEA	L 26-24	52 (78%)	62 (93%)	36 (54%)	42 (63%)	12 (18%)	31 (46%)	13 (19%)	21 (31%)	42 (63%)
7	SD	L 33-30	51 (78%)	57 (88%)	49 (75%)	33 (51%)	15 (23%)	14 (22%)		15 (23%)	49 (75%)
8	GB	W 33-32	55 (87%)	53 (84%)	46 (73%)	27 (43%)	46 (73%)		32 (51%)	14 (22%)	4 (6%)
9	TB	W 43-28	52 (71%)	53 (73%)	46 (63%)	39 (53%)	55 (75%)		33 (45%)	23 (32%)	
10	PHI	L 24-15	46 (92%)	41 (82%)	43 (86%)	14 (28%)	36 (72%)		34 (68%)	12 (24%)	
12	ARI	W 38-19	62 (89%)	54 (77%)	39 (56%)	40 (57%)	33 (47%)	32 (46%)	35 (50%)	20 (29%)	
13	KC	L 29-28	62 (85%)	47 (64%)	42 (58%)	41 (56%)	46 (63%)	32 (44%)	29 (40%)	27 (37%)	
14	LA	W 42-14			22 (38%)	25 (43%)	42 (72%)	21 (36%)	45 (78%)	23 (40%)	
15	SF	W 41-13	46 (68%)		30 (44%)	41 (60%)	40 (59%)	31 (46%)	24 (35%)	28 (41%)	
16	CAR	W 33-16	45 (71%)	39 (62%)	34 (54%)	48 (76%)		23 (37%)	28 (44%)	25 (40%)	
17	NO	W 38-32	46 (74%)	49 (79%)	35 (56%)	55 (89%)		25 (40%)		12 (19%)	
Grand Total			744 (76%)	703 (77%)	601 (58%)	572 (55%)	409 (45%)	355 (41%)	349 (42%)	328 (31%)	326 (62%)

Personnel Groupings

Personnel	Team %	NFL Avg	Succ. %
1-1 [3WR]	45%	60%	48%
2-1 [2WR]	24%	7%	55%
1-2 [2WR]	17%	19%	59%
1-3 [1WR]	7%	3%	56%
2-2 [1WR]	4%	3%	33%

Grouping Tendencies

Personnel	Pass Rate	Pass Succ. %	Run Succ. %
1-1 [3WR]	74%	48%	47%
2-1 [2WR]	42%	60%	51%
1-2 [2WR]	49%	64%	54%
1-3 [1WR]	54%	64%	46%
2-2 [1WR]	18%	56%	28%

Red Zone Targets (min 3)

Receiver	All	Inside 5	6-10	11-20
Devonta Freeman	19	3	5	11
Mohamed Sanu	18	8	6	4
Julio Jones	14	6	3	5
Tevin Coleman	14	1	4	9
Jacob Tamme	11	4	2	5
Justin Hardy	10	6	3	1
Austin Hooper	7	2	1	4
Taylor Gabriel	6	1	1	4
Aldrick Robinson	4	1		3

Red Zone Rushes (min 3)

Rusher	All	Inside 5	6-10	11-20
Devonta Freeman	66	22	13	31
Tevin Coleman	29	7	7	15
Matt Ryan	12	5	2	5
Terron Ward	5	2	1	2

Early Down Target Rate

	RB	TE	WR
	23%	14%	62%
NFL AVG	*19%*	*20%*	*61%*

Overall Target Success %

RB	TE	WR
52%	56%	60%
#4	#13	#1

Atlanta Falcons 2016 Passing Recap & 2017 Outlook

Matt Ryan is in a beautiful place at this point in his career. He's surrounded with highly talented receivers, a great run game with multiple RBs adept at catching the ball out of the backfield, a solid offensive line and an owner and general manager willing to make moves to acquire a Super Bowl ring. Against a far easier schedule of pass defenses this year, there is little reason to think Ryan won't see a lot of success. Ryan did a tremendous job last year of spreading the ball out in the red zone. He had 4 receivers with between 13 and 19 red zone targets. And even inside the 5, he had 5 receivers with between 3 and 8 targets. The best part is the Falcons are avid fans of using their RBs in the pass game inside the red zone. Devonta Freeman and Tevin Coleman totaled 32 red zone targets, and these highly successful plays give Matt Ryan better TD upside than if the Falcons just handed the ball off. Atlanta killed opposition with more obscure personnel groupings. Out of little used 21, 13 and 22 personnel, the Falcons passing success rates were far better than in standard 11 personnel. The only criticism for Ryan was on 3rd down he threw the ball short of the sticks too often.

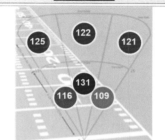

Matt Ryan Rating All Downs

125
122
121
131
116
109

2016 Standard Passing Table

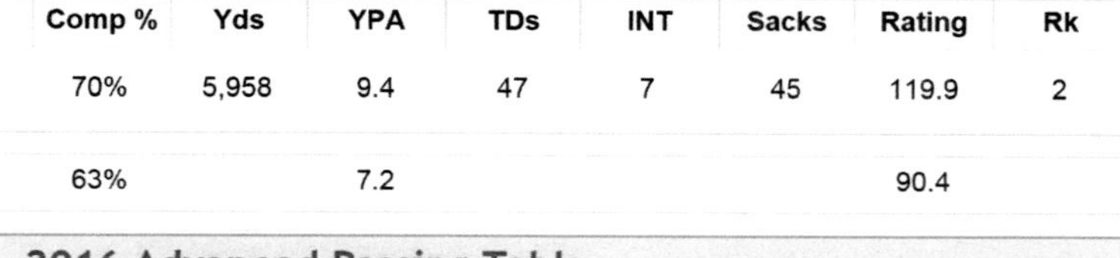

QB	Comp	Att	Comp %	Yds	YPA	TDs	INT	Sacks	Rating	Rk
Matt Ryan	443	632	70%	5,958	9.4	47	7	45	119.9	2
NFL Avg			63%		7.2				90.4	

Matt Ryan Rating Early Downs

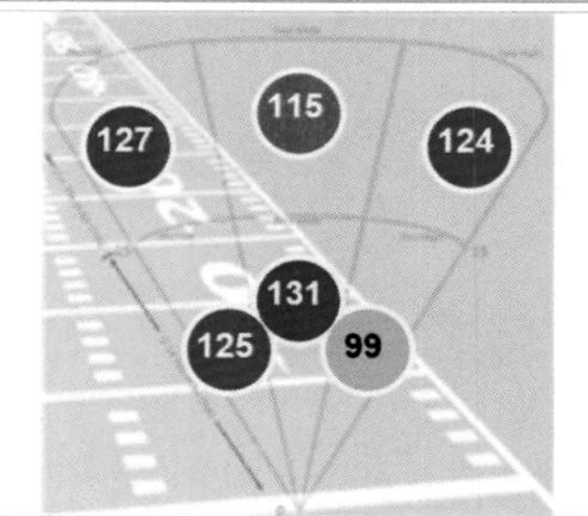

2016 Advanced Passing Table

QB	Success %	EDSR Passing Success %	20+ Yd Pass Gains	20+ Yd Pass %	30+ Yd Pass Gains	30+ Yd Pass %	Air Yds per Comp	YAC per Comp	20+ Air Yd Comp	20+ Air Yd %
Matt Ryan	53%	57%	82	13%	35	6%	7.2	6.2	39	6%
NFL Avg	44%	48%	27	8%	10	3%	6.4	4.8	12	4%

Interception Rates by Down

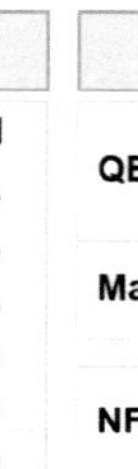

Yards to Go	1	2	3	4	Total
1 & 2	0.0%	0.0%	0.0%	0.0%	0.0%
3, 4, 5	0.0%	3.6%	0.0%	0.0%	1.2%
6 - 9	0.0%	0.0%	0.0%		0.0%
10 - 14	1.2%	2.4%	0.0%	0.0%	1.4%
15+	6.3%	0.0%	0.0%		1.9%
Total	1.5%	1.3%	0.0%	0.0%	1.0%

3rd Down Passing - Short of Sticks Analysis

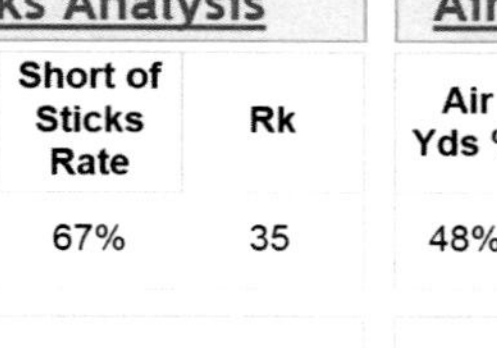

QB	Avg Yds to Go	Air Yds (of Comps)	Avg Yds Short	Short of Sticks Rate	Rk
Matt Ryan	8.0	6.3	-1.7	67%	35
NFL Avg	7.6	6.8	-0.8	57%	

Air Yds vs YAC

Air Yds %	YAC %	Rk
48%	52%	37
54%	46%	

2016 Receiving Recap & 2017 Outlook

Atlanta's receiving corps is largely the same as 2016 apart from more targets likely to go to TE Austin Hooper. Atlanta has one of each type of receiver. A clear dominant #1 stud (Julio Jones) who must be doubled and is lethal downfield, a highly efficient #2 receiver (Mohamed Sanu) whose 74% completion rate and 64% success rate (3rd best in the NFL) were tops for Atlanta, a speedy little guy capable of breaking big plays or burning deep (Taylor Gabriel), and then there are the TEs and RBs who are used well. I would like to see more targeting of the TE position, particularly on early downs.

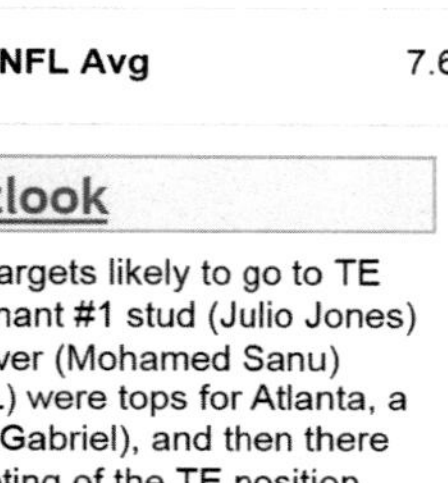

Player *Min 50 Targets*	Targets	Comp %	YPA	Rating	TOARS	Success %	Success Rk	Missed YPA Rk	YAS % Rk	TDs
Julio Jones	153	67%	11.4	114	5.7	61%	11	23	6	9
Mohamed Sanu	95	74%	8.1	118	5.1	64%	3	7	94	6
Devonta Freeman	77	83%	8.2	108	4.5	57%	30	44	115	3
Taylor Gabriel	65	69%	11.7	133	4.6	55%	38	119	13	6

Directional Passer Rating Delivered

Receiver	Short Left	Short Middle	Short Right	Deep Left	Deep Middle	Deep Right	Player Total
Julio Jones	126	146	81	71	80	110	114
Mohamed Sanu	118	117	119	84	110	117	118
Devonta Freeman	104	109	112				108
Taylor Gabriel	135	118	77	40	158	141	133
Tevin Coleman	136	99	133	119	158	82	143
Austin Hooper	90	103	117	144		110	136
Aldrick Robinson	54	158	56	144	58	110	104
Justin Hardy	127	106	133	119	119	40	128
Jacob Tamme	71	131	122		108		108
Levine Toilolo	64	106	87	158		158	131
Team Total	116	131	107	119	122	123	121

2016 Rushing Recap & 2017 Outlook

Freeman is the Falcons clear cash cow in the red zone. He received 66 rushing targets and 19 receiving targets, both were #1 on the team. Freeman last year was dominant on the second level, recording a NFL best in YAS % (Yards Above Successful). Apart from that, his bottom line results and overall ranks were nearly identical to Coleman. 49% early down success rate and overall success rate, and a similar Missed YPA ranking. While the passing game sees weaker opposition than last year, the rushing game does not. But if passes are more successful, it will inherently open up things on the ground. But much of the rushing stat line will be dependent on the Falcons taking the same Blitzkrieg approach to the 1st half and leading large at halftime.

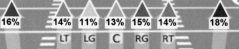

Player *Min 50 Rushes*	Rushes	YPA	Success %	Success Rk	Missed YPA Rk	YTS % Rk	YAS % Rk	Early Down Success %	Early Down Success Rk	TDs
Devonta Freeman	266	4.7	49%	27	34	59	1	49%	28	13
Tevin Coleman	147	4.3	48%	31	42	31	22	49%	31	9

Yards per Carry by Direction

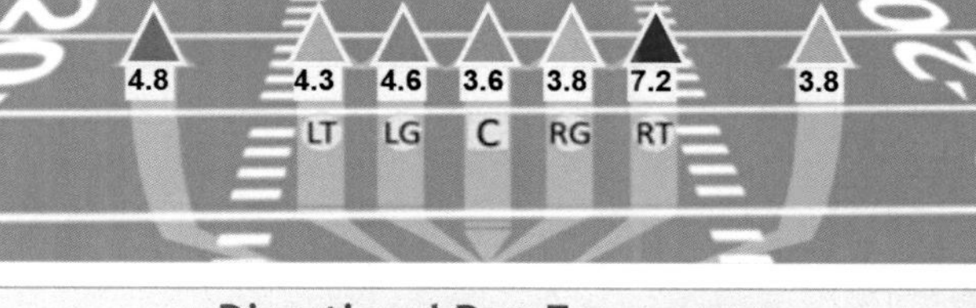

Directional Run Frequency

16%
14%
11%
13%
15%
14%
18%
LT
LG
C
RG
RT

There will be one major difference for the 2017 Falcons offense: they will face a much easier schedule of opposing defenses this season. As opposed to last year when Atlanta faced the 2nd most difficult schedule of defenses, in 2017 they will face the 23rd most difficult schedule. The pass defenses will be the 8th easiest, as opposed to last year when they were the 4th hardest. It is the 2nd easiest shift in schedule from 2016 to 2017 for any passing offense. Gone are more stout defenses like the Broncos (#1), Cardinals (#3), Eagles (#4), Chargers (#8) and Rams (#15). Inserted are defenses like the Lions (#32), Bills (#26), Bears (#22), Jets (#21) and Cowboys (#17). It is an extremely friendly schedule for this offense after dealing with an extremely difficult non-divisional schedule of defenses last year.

The other exciting thing for the Falcons this year is that last year, they didn't win games by luck or by narrow margins or by turnovers. Atlanta went just 4-4 in games decided by one-score last year. That is a far cry from the prior year's Super Bowl runner-up who fell off the next season (Carolina), as they went 7-1 in one-score games en route to their Super Bowl appearance the prior year. The Falcons did finish +11 in turnover margin last year, but they still went 5-3 in games where they lost the turnover battle, which was the 3rd best mark in the NFL. So there is nothing to say the Falcons just became super lucky in 2016. The Falcons also were not absurdly great in red zone TD rate last year, recording the 8th best (65%).

But in order to have a shot at the postseason again this year, Atlanta must improve the defense. It was astronomically bad last year, as one look at the radars or defensive advanced metrics will show. They ranked 6th worst in EDSR (Early Down Success Rate) defense and overall defensive efficiency. They were terrible at stopping the run (3rd worst) and they struggled to pressure opposing quarterbacks. The team made moves in the offseason to try and address these issues. They added DT Dontari Poe via free agency and drafted DE Tak McKinley in the first round. With their next pick they drafted LB Duke Riley, who likely will rotate in with De'Vondre Campbell. They lost LCB Desmond Trufant mid season to a torn pectoral. He is expected to be ready before training camp and signed a massive 5-year, $69M extension this offseason. Apart from Riley, those 3 players will be starters this fall who were not starting over the 2nd half of the season through the Super Bowl. The problem for the defense is the same as the reason for excitement on offense: the schedule. Atlanta's defense faces a much more difficult schedule than last year. They played the 23rd rated offenses last year, but this year they play the 7th rated offenses. Their schedule sees the 2nd most difficult increase in passing offenses faced of any team as compared to last year. That makes the job harder for Dan Quinn's squad. Likely it will take consistency on offense and improvement on defense for the Falcons to make it back to the postseason, but barring injuries it is entirely likely they do just that.

Division History: Season Wins & 2017 Projection

2013 Wins | 2014 Wins | 2015 Wins | 2016 Wins | Proj 2017 Wins

Rank of 2017 Defensive Pass Efficiency Faced by Week

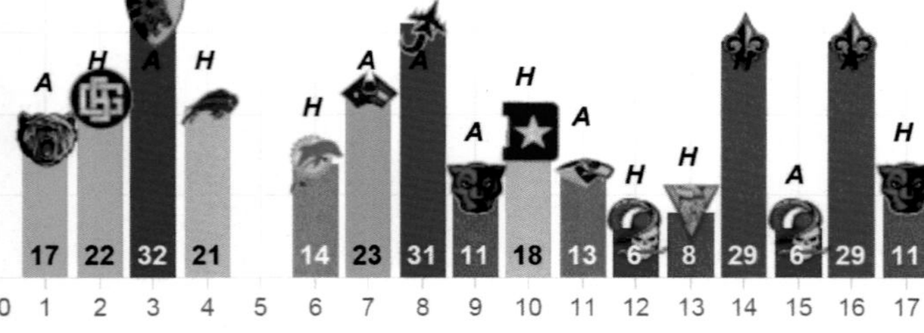

Rank of 2017 Defensive Rush Efficiency Faced by Week

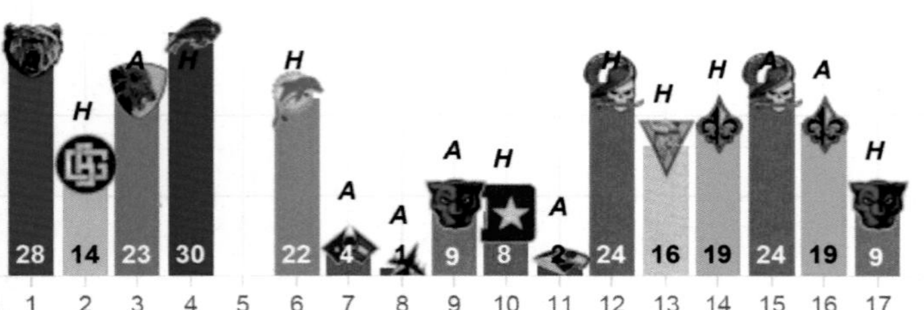

2016 Situational Usage by Player & Position

Usage Rate by Score

		Being Blown Out (14+)	Down Big (9-13)	One Score	Large Lead (9-13)	Blowout Lead (14+)	Grand Total
RUSH	Devonta Freeman	17%	30%	23%	30%	26%	25%
	Tevin Coleman	6%	13%	12%	14%	18%	14%
	Mohamed Sanu			0%			0%
	Taylor Gabriel			1%		0%	0%
	Justin Hardy			0%			0%
	Terron Ward			2%	2%	7%	3%
	Stevan Ridley					1%	0%
	Total	22%	43%	38%	45%	52%	42%
PASS	Devonta Freeman	6%	7%	7%	5%	7%	7%
	Tevin Coleman	6%	13%	4%	4%	5%	4%
	Julio Jones	17%	20%	17%	14%	7%	14%
	Mohamed Sanu	17%	4%	10%	12%	6%	9%
	Taylor Gabriel	6%	4%	6%	7%	7%	6%
	Austin Hooper	6%	2%	4%	1%	3%	3%
	Aldrick Robinson	6%		2%	5%	5%	3%
	Justin Hardy	6%		3%	1%	3%	3%
	Terron Ward			0%			0%
	Jacob Tamme	11%	7%	4%	1%		3%
	Levine Toilolo			3%	2%	2%	2%
	Patrick DiMarco			1%	2%	1%	1%
	Nick Williams			0%		2%	1%
	Josh Perkins			0%		1%	0%
	D.J. Tialavea				1%		0%
	Total	78%	57%	62%	55%	48%	58%

Positional Target Distribution vs NFL Average

		NFL Wide				Team Only			
		Left	Middle	Right	Total	Left	Middle	Right	Total
Deep	WR	990	556	968	**2,514**	41	25	33	**99**
	TE	151	144	159	**454**	7	3	4	**14**
	RB	24	3	37	**64**	1	1	3	**5**
	All	**1,165**	**703**	**1,164**	**3,032**	**49**	**29**	**40**	**118**
Short	WR	2,990	1,692	3,086	**7,768**	103	79	100	**282**
	TE	811	854	1,119	**2,784**	25	21	32	**78**
	RB	978	587	1,065	**2,630**	37	35	48	**120**
	All	**4,779**	**3,133**	**5,270**	**13,182**	**165**	**135**	**180**	**480**
Total		**5,944**	**3,836**	**6,434**	**16,214**	**214**	**164**	**220**	**598**

Positional Success Rates vs NFL Average

		NFL Wide				Team Only			
		Left	Middle	Right	Total	Left	Middle	Right	Total
Deep	WR	37%	49%	37%	**40%**	41%	68%	64%	**56%**
	TE	43%	49%	43%	**45%**	71%	67%	75%	**71%**
	RB	29%	67%	24%	**28%**	100%	100%	33%	**60%**
	All	**37%**	**50%**	**38%**	**40%**	**47%**	**69%**	**63%**	**58%**
Short	WR	52%	56%	51%	**52%**	60%	68%	58%	**62%**
	TE	50%	62%	52%	**54%**	44%	57%	56%	**53%**
	RB	47%	49%	43%	**46%**	54%	51%	54%	**53%**
	All	**50%**	**56%**	**50%**	**52%**	**56%**	**62%**	**57%**	**58%**
Total		**48%**	**55%**	**47%**	**49%**	**54%**	**63%**	**58%**	**58%**

Baltimore Ravens

2017 Coaches

Head Coach:
John Harbaugh (10th yr)
Offensive Coordinator:
Marty Morinwheg (wk 5 2016) (2nd yr)
Defensive Coordinator:
Dean Pees (6th yr)

2017 Forecast

Wins	Div Rank
9	#2

Past Records

2016: 8-8
2015: 5-11
2014: 10-6

EASY — HARD

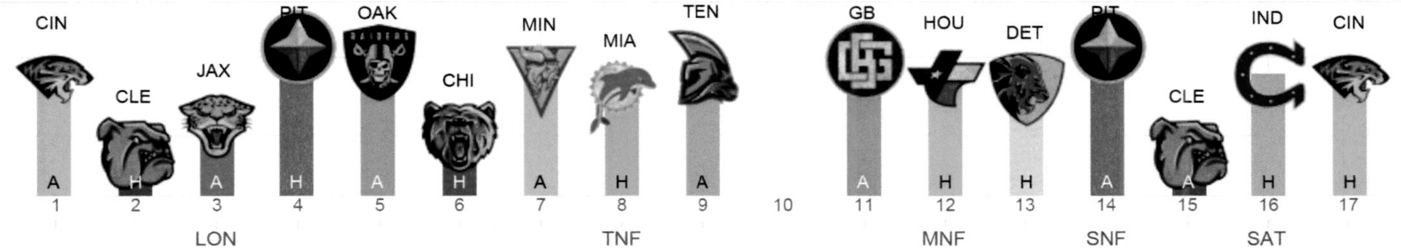

Key Players Lost

TXN	Player (POS)
Cut	Arrington, Kyle CB
	Dumervil, Elvis LB
	Lewis, Kendrick S
	Pitta, Dennis TE
	Webb, Lardarius S
	Wright, Shareece CB
	Zuttah, Jeremy G
Declared Free Agent	Aiken, Kamar WR
	Ducasse, Vladimir G
	Elam, Matt S
	Guy, Lawrence DE
	Juszczyk, Kyle RB
	Lewis-Harris, Chris CB
	Mallett, Ryan QB
	Powers, Jerraud CB
	Smith Sr., Steve WR
	Wagner, Rick T
Retired	Orr, Zachary LB
	Powers, Jerraud CB

Average Line	# Games Favored	# Games Underdog
-0.5	8	7

2017 Baltimore Ravens Overview

The Baltimore Ravens built a perfect machine for Joe Flacco to drive. This was a team that in 2006, was the #1 overall defense in the NFL and produced a 13-3 record with Steve McNair at the reins. The team drafted Joe Flacco in 2008, with a top 5 defense in every single one of his first 4 seasons as a starter. The team made annual trips to the Super Bowl, without Joe Flacco ever needing to deliver a stellar season. In fact, his passer rating in those 4 seasons was 80, 89, 94 and 81. Then, in 2012, Joe Flacco delivered a memorable run through the playoffs to the Super Bowl and broke through that door, on his last year of his 5 year rookie deal.

It was the perfect way to build a run to the Super Bowl by Ozzie Newsome. Build a tremendous team, and then slip in a talented young quarterback as the final piece to the puzzle. Don't require too much from him, except for a key throw or a key series from time to time that will win a big game for you. As long as he's not losing games for you, you'll have the ability to build your team with talented players because his rookie QB cap hit will be far smaller than most NFL teams are paying their starter. Thus, an instant advantage.

We saw it in Seattle with Russell Wilson in 2013. We saw it in New York with Eli Manning in 2007. We saw it in Pittsburgh with Ben Roethlisberger in 2005. In fact, since the 2003 season, when it wasn't Tom Brady or Peyton Manning winning multiple Super Bowls, and it wasn't two likely Hall of Famers in Aaron Rodgers or Drew Brees winning one apiece, it was a quarterback on a rookie deal winning the Super Bowl (or a repeat performance from Ben Roethlisberger or Eli Manning). It's easy to say you need a great quarterback to win a Super Bowl, so just draft a great one. It's easier to accomplish building a solid, well paid supporting cast and adding a good quarterback on a rookie deal.

Unlike Ben Roethlisberger or Eli Manning, who won a Super Bowl on their rookie deal and then won another in their first two years of their first veteran deal, Joe Flacco has produced just one winning season in his first four years of his first veteran deal, and has won just one playoff game in that span. The Ravens signed Flacco to a 6 year, $120.6M deal after his Super Bowl win, and renegoitiated prior to last season to sign him to a 3 year, $66.4M deal which included a $40M signing bonus.

(cont'd - see BAL2)

Key Free Agents/ Trades Added

Boykin, Brandon CB
Carr, Brandon CB
Jefferson, Tony S
Maclin, Jeremy WR
Malleck, Ryan TE
Shabazz, Al-Hajj CB
Williams, Brandon DT
Woodhead, Danny RB

Drafted Players

Rd	Pk	Player (College)
1	16	CB - Marlon Humphrey (Alabama)
2	47	OLB - Tyus Bowser (Houston)
3	74	DT - Chris Wormley (Michigan)
	78	DE - Tim Williams (Alabama)
4	122	G - Nico Siragusa (San Diego State)
5	159	OT - Jermaine Eluemunor (Texas A&M)
6	186	S - Chuck Clark (Virginia Tech)

Regular Season Wins: Past & Current Proj

2017 Lineup & Cap Hits

FS E.Weddle 32
SS T.Jefferson 13
LB C.Mosley 57
LB K.Correa 51
RCB J.Smith 22
SLOTCB L.Webb 21
OLB T.Suggs 55
DE B.Williams 98
DE B.Kaufusi 92
OLB Z.Smith 90
LCB B.Carr 24

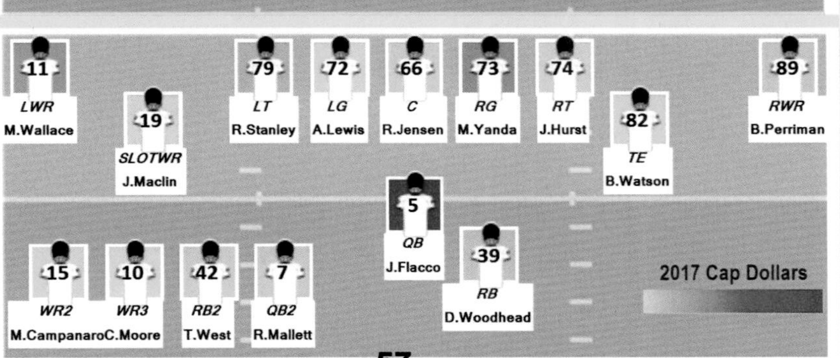

2017 Unit Spending

Positional Spending

	Rank	Total	2016 Rk
All OFF	19	$80.62M	18
QB	4	$27.09M	4
OL	28	$22.80M	26
RB	21	$6.15M	28
WR	20	$16.42M	23
TE	20	$8.15M	8
All DEF	28	$66.12M	19
DL	32	$10.70M	32
LB	16	$18.23M	9
CB	10	$22.18M	20
S	7	$15.02M	1

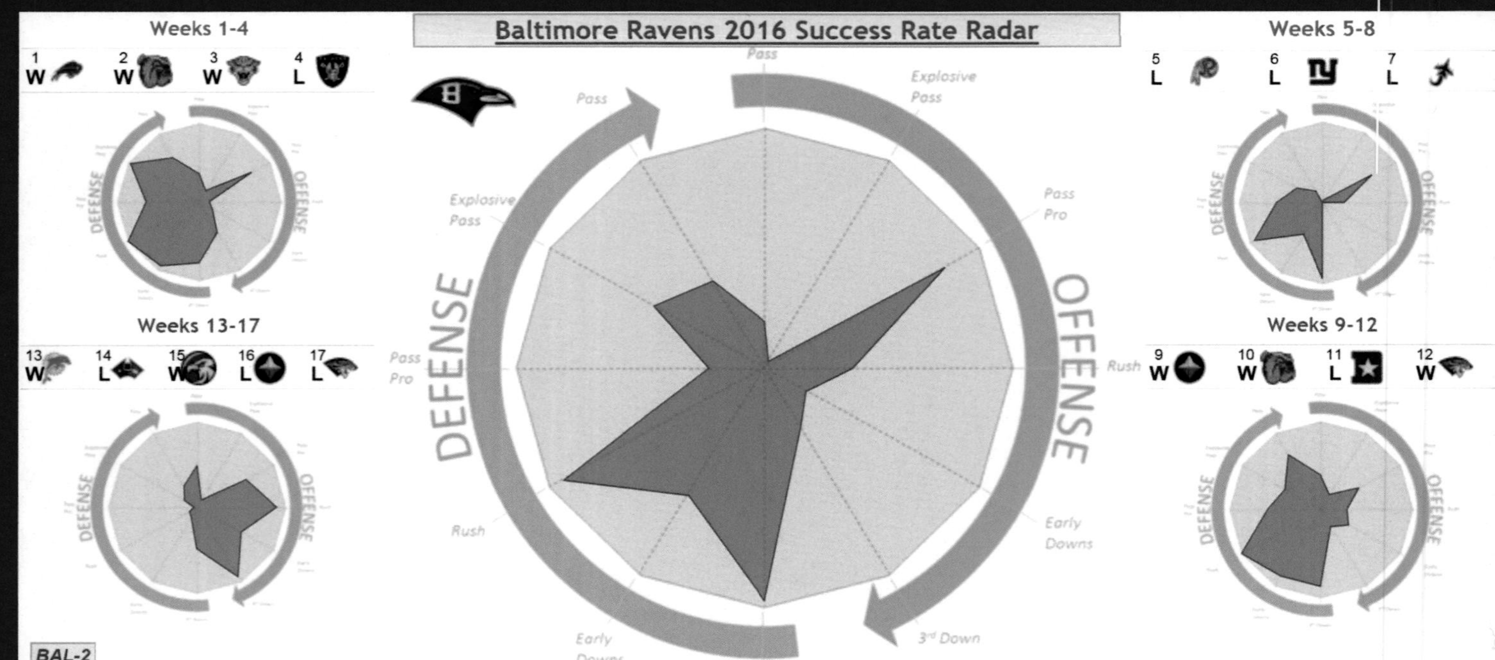

BAL-2

Flacco hits the cap this year for $24.6M, the largest cap hit for any player in the NFL this season. His cap hit in 2018 is schedule to be the second largest cap hit for any player, and the largest for any quarterback.

So the question becomes, what is Joe Flacco doing to earn that level of payment? In his 4 years since signing the $120M deal, Flacco has led the Ravens to a perfectly average .500 record (29-29), he has posted an 82.5 rating with 6.7 yds/att and 0.76 interceptions for every touchdown pass. Those are clearly not the best numbers for even an average quarterback to post, let alone the quarterback set to hit the cap for the most money in the NFL for the next two years.

Last season, Flacco ranked 33rd in passer rating, was below average in early down passing, overall passing success rate, percentage of explosive passes and air yardage of passes, and he ranked 30th in the frequency of passes thrown short of the sticks on 3rd down. Unlike 2015, we can't blame it on injuries – the Ravens offense was the 12th healthiest in 2016 (after being 30th in 2015).

We can't blame it on a tough schedule – last year the Ravens faced the 29th rated defenses, which ranked 28th against the pass and brought the 29th rated pass rushes.

And against those easy defenses, the Ravens offense ranked 27th or worse in Early Down Success Rate (EDSR), red zone efficiency, 3rd down efficiency, passing efficiency and explosive passing efficiency. In large part, the reason the 2016 Ravens even won 8 games last season was on account of the defense:

On average, an NFL team scores 23 points per game. In their 8 wins in 2016, the Ravens' defense allowed more than 20 points only one time. In half of their wins, the defense locked down the opponent such that the offense didn't even have to score more than 21 points. They won by margins of: 13-7, 19-14, 19-17 and 21-14.

*(cont'd - see **BAL-3**)*

2016 Offensive Advanced Metrics

2016 Defensive Advanced Metrics

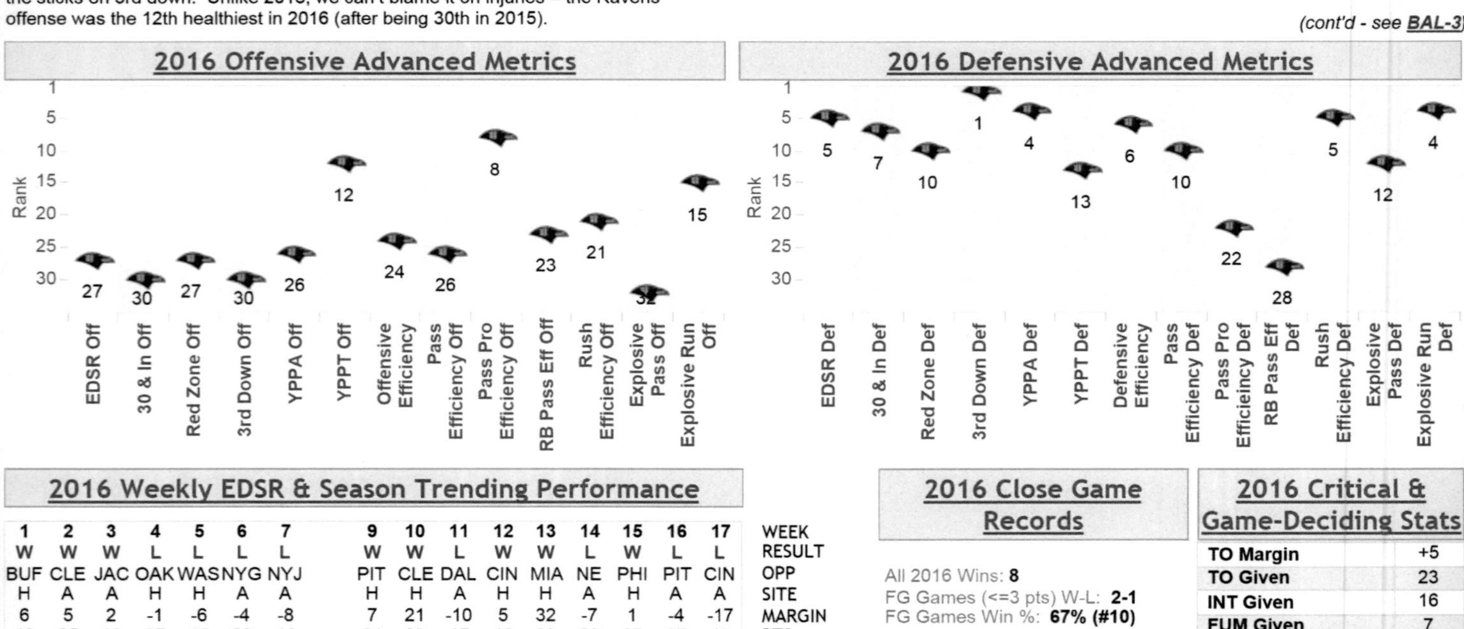

2016 Weekly EDSR & Season Trending Performance

WEEK	1	2	3	4	5	6	7	9	10	11	12	13	14	15	16	17
RESULT	W	W	W	L	L	L	L	W	W	L	W	W	L	W	L	L
OPP	BUF	CLE	JAC	OAK	WAS	NYG	NYJ	PIT	CLE	DAL	CIN	MIA	NE	PHI	PIT	CIN
SITE	H	A	A	H	H	A	A	H	H	A	H	H	A	H	A	A
MARGIN	6	5	2	-1	-6	-4	-8	7	21	-10	5	32	-7	1	-4	-17
PTS	13	25	19	27	10	23	16	21	28	17	19	38	23	27	27	10
OPP PTS	7	20	17	28	16	27	24	14	7	27	14	6	30	26	31	27

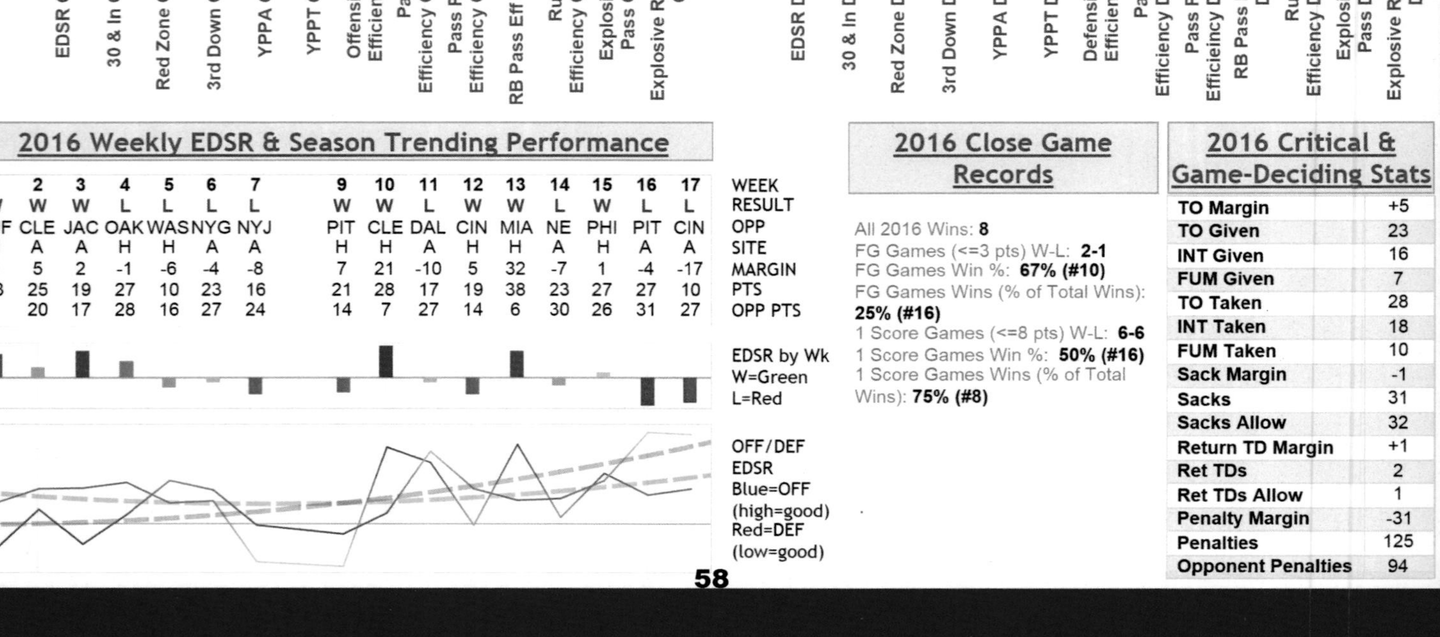

2016 Close Game Records

All 2016 Wins: **8**
FG Games (<=3 pts) W-L: **2-1**
FG Games Win %: **67% (#10)**
FG Games Wins (% of Total Wins): **25% (#16)**
1 Score Games (<=8 pts) W-L: **6-6**
1 Score Games Win %: **50% (#16)**
1 Score Games Wins (% of Total Wins): **75% (#8)**

2016 Critical & Game-Deciding Stats

TO Margin	+5
TO Given	23
INT Given	16
FUM Given	7
TO Taken	28
INT Taken	18
FUM Taken	10
Sack Margin	-1
Sacks	31
Sacks Allow	32
Return TD Margin	+1
Ret TDs	2
Ret TDs Allow	1
Penalty Margin	-31
Penalties	125
Opponent Penalties	94

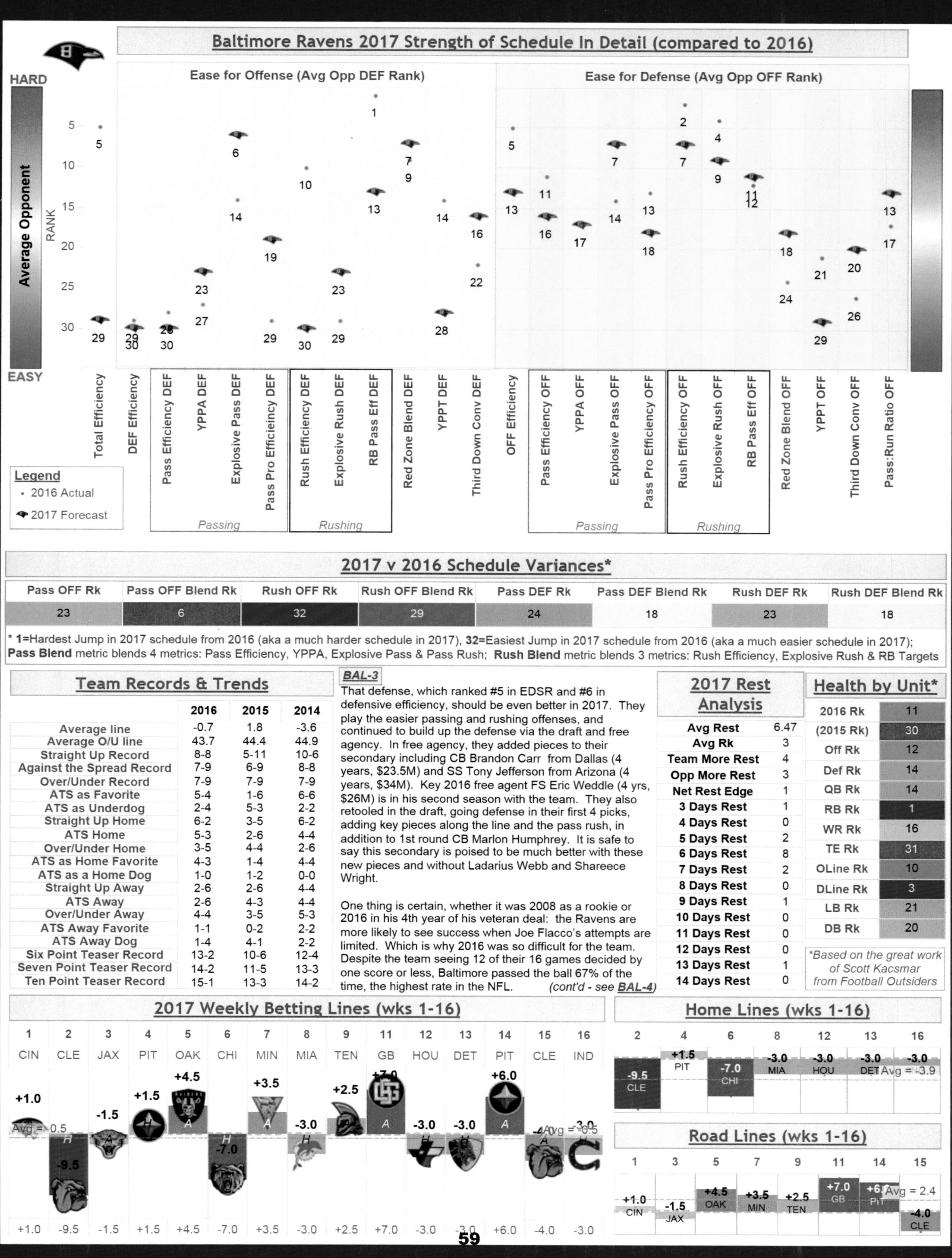

Baltimore Ravens 2017 Strength of Schedule In Detail (compared to 2016)

2017 v 2016 Schedule Variances*

Pass OFF Rk	Pass OFF Blend Rk	Rush OFF Rk	Rush OFF Blend Rk	Pass DEF Rk	Pass DEF Blend Rk	Rush DEF Rk	Rush DEF Blend Rk
23	6	32	29	24	18	23	18

* **1**=Hardest Jump in 2017 schedule from 2016 (aka a much harder schedule in 2017), **32**=Easiest Jump in 2017 schedule from 2016 (aka a much easier schedule in 2017); **Pass Blend** metric blends 4 metrics: Pass Efficiency, YPPA, Explosive Pass & Pass Rush; **Rush Blend** metric blends 3 metrics: Rush Efficiency, Explosive Rush & RB Targets

Team Records & Trends

	2016	2015	2014
Average line	-0.7	1.8	-3.6
Average O/U line	43.7	44.4	44.9
Straight Up Record	8-8	5-11	10-6
Against the Spread Record	7-9	6-9	8-8
Over/Under Record	7-9	7-9	7-9
ATS as Favorite	5-4	1-6	6-6
ATS as Underdog	2-4	5-3	2-2
Straight Up Home	6-2	3-5	6-2
ATS Home	5-3	2-6	4-4
Over/Under Home	3-5	4-4	2-6
ATS as Home Favorite	4-3	1-4	4-4
ATS as a Home Dog	1-0	1-2	0-0
Straight Up Away	2-6	2-6	4-4
ATS Away	2-6	4-3	4-4
Over/Under Away	4-4	3-5	5-3
ATS Away Favorite	1-1	0-2	2-2
ATS Away Dog	1-4	4-1	2-2
Six Point Teaser Record	13-2	10-6	12-4
Seven Point Teaser Record	14-2	11-5	13-3
Ten Point Teaser Record	15-1	13-3	14-2

BAL-3

That defense, which ranked #5 in EDSR and #6 in defensive efficiency, should be even better in 2017. They play the easier passing and rushing offenses, and continued to build up the defense via the draft and free agency. In free agency, they added pieces to their secondary including CB Brandon Carr from Dallas (4 years, $23.5M) and SS Tony Jefferson from Arizona (4 years, $34M). Key 2016 free agent FS Eric Weddle (4 yrs, $26M) is in his second season with the team. They also retooled in the draft, going defense in their first 4 picks, adding key pieces along the line and the pass rush, in addition to 1st round CB Marlon Humphrey. It is safe to say this secondary is poised to be much better with these new pieces and without Ladarius Webb and Shareece Wright.

One thing is certain, whether it was 2008 as a rookie or 2016 in his 4th year of his veteran deal: the Ravens are more likely to see success when Joe Flacco's attempts are limited. Which is why 2016 was so difficult for the team. Despite the team seeing 12 of their 16 games decided by one score or less, Baltimore passed the ball 67% of the time, the highest rate in the NFL. (cont'd - see ***BAL-4***)

2017 Rest Analysis

Avg Rest	6.47
Avg Rk	3
Team More Rest	4
Opp More Rest	3
Net Rest Edge	1
3 Days Rest	1
4 Days Rest	0
5 Days Rest	2
6 Days Rest	8
7 Days Rest	2
8 Days Rest	0
9 Days Rest	1
10 Days Rest	0
11 Days Rest	0
12 Days Rest	0
13 Days Rest	1
14 Days Rest	0

Health by Unit*

2016 Rk	11
(2015 Rk)	30
Off Rk	12
Def Rk	14
QB Rk	14
RB Rk	1
WR Rk	16
TE Rk	31
OLine Rk	10
DLine Rk	3
LB Rk	21
DB Rk	20

**Based on the great work of Scott Kacsmar from Football Outsiders*

2017 Weekly Betting Lines (wks 1-16)

1	2	3	4	5	6	7	8	9	11	12	13	14	15	16
CIN	CLE	JAX	PIT	OAK	CHI	MIN	MIA	TEN	GB	HOU	DET	PIT	CLE	IND
A	H	A	H	A	H	A	H	A	A	H	H	A	A	H
+1.0	-9.5	-1.5	+1.5	+4.5	-7.0	+3.5	-3.0	+2.5	+7.0	-3.0	-3.0	+6.0	-4.0	-3.0

Avg = -0.5

Home Lines (wks 1-16)

2	4	6	8	12	13	16
CLE	PIT	CHI	MIA	HOU	DET	
-9.5	+1.5	-7.0	-3.0	-3.0	-3.0	-3.0

Avg = -3.9

Road Lines (wks 1-16)

1	3	5	7	9	11	14	15
CIN	JAX	OAK	MIN	TEN	GB	PIT	CLE
+1.0	-1.5	+4.5	+3.5	+2.5	+7.0	+6.0	-4.0

Avg = 2.4

Baltimore Ravens 2016 Play Analysis

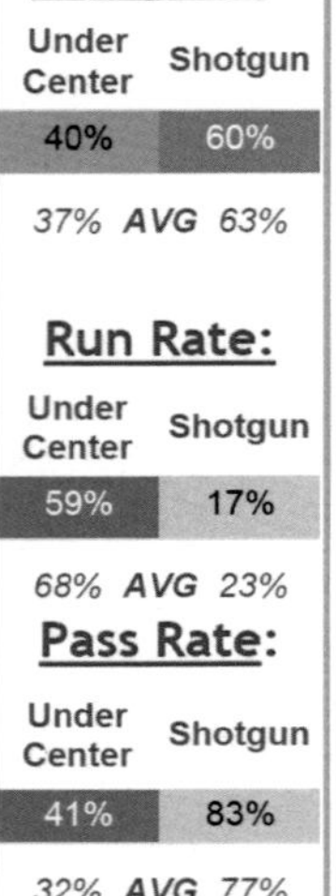

2016 Play Tendencies

All Pass %	67%
All Pass Rk	1
All Rush %	33%
All Rush Rk	32
1 Score Pass %	64%
1 Score Pass Rk	2
2015 1 Score Pass %	62%
2015 1 Score Pass Rk	5
Pass Increase %	1%
Pass Increase Rk	12
1 Score Rush %	36%
1 Score Rush Rk	31
Up Pass %	66%
Up Pass Rk	2
Up Rush %	34%
Up Rush Rk	31
Down Pass %	72%
Down Pass Rk	1
Down Rush %	28%
Down Rush Rk	32

2016 Down & Distance Tendencies

Down	Distance	Total Plays	Pass Rate	Run Rate	Play Success %
1	Short (1-3)	5	60%	40%	40%
	Med (4-7)	4	100%	0%	75%
	Long (8-10)	325	55%	45%	50%
	XL (11+)	10	80%	20%	20%
2	Short (1-3)	32	47%	53%	47%
	Med (4-7)	99	63%	37%	47%
	Long (8-10)	99	75%	25%	42%
	XL (11+)	35	83%	17%	9%
3	Short (1-3)	38	61%	39%	61%
	Med (4-7)	64	98%	2%	47%
	Long (8-10)	32	94%	6%	25%
	XL (11+)	38	92%	8%	16%
4	Short (1-3)	7	43%	57%	57%
	XL (11+)	2	50%	50%	0%

Shotgun %:

Under Center	Shotgun
40%	60%
37%	*63%*

AVG

Run Rate:

Under Center	Shotgun
59%	17%
68%	*23%*

AVG

Pass Rate:

Under Center	Shotgun
41%	83%
32%	*77%*

AVG

Short Yardage Intelligence:

2nd and Short Run

Run Freq	Run % Rk	NFL Run Freq Avg	Run 1D Rate	Run NFL 1D Avg
69%	10	65%	50%	71%

2nd and Short Pass

Pass Freq	Pass % Rk	NFL Pass Freq Avg	Pass 1D Rate	Pass NFL 1D Avg
31%	22	35%	13%	52%

Most Frequent Play

Down	Distance	Play Type	Player	Total Plays	Play Success %
1	Short (1-3)	RUSH	Terrance West	2	50%
	Long (8-10)	RUSH	Terrance West	87	51%
	XL (11+)	PASS	Mike Wallace	2	50%
			Breshad Perriman	2	0%
		RUSH	Terrance West	2	50%
2	Short (1-3)	RUSH	Kenneth Dixon	7	57%
	Med (4-7)	RUSH	Terrance West	19	26%
	Long (8-10)	PASS	Dennis Pitta	15	60%
		RUSH	Terrance West	15	27%
	XL (11+)	PASS	Mike Wallace	6	33%
3	Short (1-3)	RUSH	Terrance West	10	50%
	Med (4-7)	PASS	Mike Wallace	11	27%
	Long (8-10)	PASS	Dennis Pitta	6	17%
	XL (11+)	PASS	Dennis Pitta	9	11%

Most Successful Play*

Down	Distance	Play Type	Player	Total Plays	Play Success %
1	Long (8-10)	PASS	Kamar Aiken	12	67%
2	Short (1-3)	RUSH	Kenneth Dixon	7	57%
	Med (4-7)	PASS	Terrance West	5	80%
	Long (8-10)	PASS	Terrance West	6	67%
	XL (11+)	PASS	Mike Wallace	6	33%
3	Short (1-3)	PASS	Mike Wallace	8	75%
	Med (4-7)	PASS	Kamar Aiken	8	63%
	Long (8-10)	PASS	Dennis Pitta	6	17%
	XL (11+)	PASS	Steve Smith	5	40%

**Minimum 5 plays to qualify*

2016 Snap Rates

Week	Opp	Score	Mike Wallace	Dennis Pitta	Steve Smith	Kamar Aiken	Breshad Perriman	Kyle Juszczyk	Terrance West
1	BUF	W 13-7	44 (65%)	56 (82%)	45 (66%)	36 (53%)	21 (31%)	21 (31%)	32 (47%)
2	CLE	W 25-20	53 (71%)	45 (60%)	53 (71%)	31 (41%)	29 (39%)	15 (20%)	21 (28%)
3	JAC	W 19-17	50 (75%)	49 (73%)	40 (60%)	23 (34%)	26 (39%)	19 (28%)	17 (25%)
4	OAK	L 28-27	74 (83%)	59 (66%)	73 (82%)	23 (26%)	32 (36%)	39 (44%)	39 (44%)
5	WAS	L 16-10	59 (83%)	54 (76%)	13 (18%)	40 (56%)	35 (49%)	42 (59%)	31 (44%)
6	NYG	L 27-23	71 (86%)	64 (77%)		65 (78%)	56 (67%)	43 (52%)	50 (60%)
7	NYJ	L 24-16	54 (93%)	46 (79%)		36 (62%)	43 (74%)	30 (52%)	20 (34%)
9	PIT	W 21-14	34 (49%)	58 (83%)	58 (83%)	41 (59%)	35 (50%)	35 (50%)	29 (41%)
10	CLE	W 28-7	59 (72%)	68 (83%)	58 (71%)	48 (59%)	39 (48%)	36 (44%)	34 (41%)
11	DAL	L 27-17	47 (85%)	43 (78%)	45 (82%)	31 (56%)	23 (42%)	25 (45%)	20 (36%)
12	CIN	W 19-14	56 (82%)	41 (60%)	54 (79%)	35 (51%)	23 (34%)	25 (37%)	23 (34%)
13	MIA	W 38-6	58 (81%)	34 (47%)	49 (68%)	49 (68%)	21 (29%)	20 (28%)	37 (51%)
14	NE	L 30-23	52 (74%)	45 (64%)	63 (90%)	40 (57%)	28 (40%)	26 (37%)	14 (20%)
15	PHI	W 27-26	52 (90%)	33 (57%)	49 (84%)	34 (59%)	12 (21%)	32 (55%)	26 (45%)
16	PIT	L 31-27	63 (84%)	60 (80%)	61 (81%)	33 (44%)	27 (36%)	31 (41%)	23 (31%)
17	CIN	L 27-10	44 (60%)	54 (74%)	57 (78%)	31 (42%)	31 (42%)	25 (34%)	22 (30%)
Grand Total			870 (77%)	809 (71%)	718 (72%)	596 (53%)	481 (42%)	464 (41%)	438 (38%)

Personnel Groupings

Personnel	Team %	NFL Avg	Succ. %
1-1 [3WR]	56%	60%	45%
1-2 [2WR]	20%	19%	43%
2-1 [2WR]	11%	7%	48%
1-3 [1WR]	3%	3%	31%
2-2 [1WR]	3%	3%	27%
2-0 [3WR]	3%	1%	31%

Grouping Tendencies

Personnel	Pass Rate	Pass Succ. %	Run Succ. %
1-1 [3WR]	72%	44%	48%
1-2 [2WR]	64%	47%	35%
2-1 [2WR]	50%	37%	59%
1-3 [1WR]	41%	23%	37%
2-2 [1WR]	30%	44%	19%
2-0 [3WR]	52%	20%	43%

Red Zone Targets (min 3)

Receiver	All	Inside 5	6-10	11-20
Dennis Pitta	13	1	4	8
Steve Smith	12	2	1	9
Mike Wallace	10	1	3	6
Terrance West	9	3		6
Darren Waller	7	4		3
Kyle Juszczyk	6	2	1	3
Breshad Perriman	4			4
Kamar Aiken	4	2		2
Kenneth Dixon	3		1	2

Red Zone Rushes (min 3)

Rusher	All	Inside 5	6-10	11-20
Terrance West	30	8	2	20
Kenneth Dixon	7	2		5
Joe Flacco	5	2	1	2
Justin Forsett	2		2	

Early Down Target Rate

RB	TE	WR
27%	20%	53%
19%	*20% NFL AVG*	*61%*

Overall Target Success %

RB	TE	WR
42% #24	48% #29	46% #24

Baltimore Ravens 2016 Passing Recap & 2017 Outlook

The most expensive quarterback in the NFL (for at least the next two seasons) resides in Baltimore. Unfortunately, so does a bad 1st down turnover rate of 3.1%, which was far from ideal. Flacco was actually sacked a fair amount last year but due to the massive volume of attempts, his pressure rating was not terrible. Between the line, Flacco and the play calls, the Ravens must work the ball past the sticks on 3rd down attempts. He ranked 30th last year in this department, and while elite QBs like Tom Brady and Aaron Rodgers head the class, younger QBs such as Jameis Winston (35%) and Andrew Luck (43%) did much better than Joe Flacco (61%). Flacco's strength was middle of the field passing, which is an intelligent location for the Ravens to target with frequency, as it is the most vulnerable for a defense. But he needs improvement from his receivers and his own delivery to the perimeter of the field, for production as well as to further soften that underbelly of the defense up the seam. Last year the Ravens passed the ball significantly more under center as compared to the NFL average, but when in shotgun, the Ravens should strive to be slightly less predictable in calling pass plays.

Joe Flacco Rating All Downs

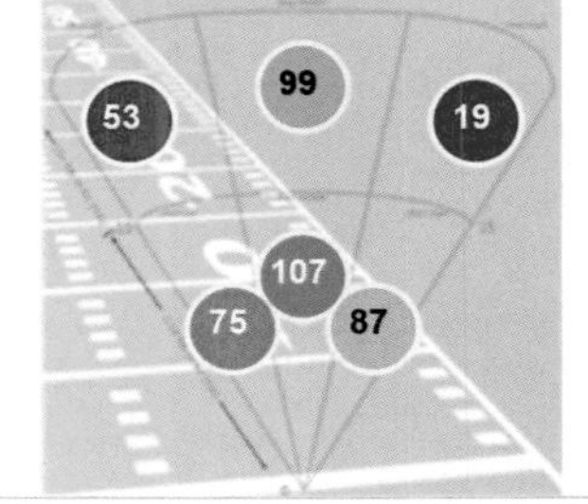

Joe Flacco Rating Early Downs

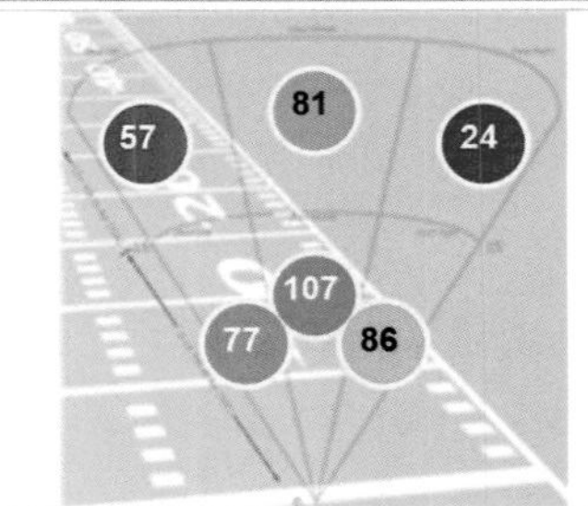

2016 Standard Passing Table

QB	Comp	Att	Comp %	Yds	YPA	TDs	INT	Sacks	Rating	Rk
Joe Flacco	437	672	65%	4,317	6.4	18	15	32	82.7	33
NFL Avg			63%		7.2				90.4	

2016 Advanced Passing Table

QB	Success %	EDSR Passing Success %	20+ Yd Pass Gains	20+ Yd Pass %	30+ Yd Pass Gains	30+ Yd Pass %	Air Yds per Comp	YAC per Comp	20+ Air Yd Comp	20+ Air Yd %
Joe Flacco	43%	47%	40	6%	18	3%	5.2	4.7	14	2%
NFL Avg	44%	48%	27	8%	10	3%	6.4	4.8	12	4%

Interception Rates by Down

Yards to Go	1	2	3	4	Total
1 & 2	100.0%	0.0%	0.0%	0.0%	3.1%
3, 4, 5	0.0%	2.6%	0.0%	0.0%	1.0%
6 - 9	0.0%	3.2%	0.0%	0.0%	1.9%
10 - 14	2.6%	2.5%	4.5%	0.0%	2.8%
15+	0.0%	0.0%	0.0%		0.0%
Total	2.7%	2.5%	1.0%	0.0%	2.1%

3rd Down Passing - Short of Sticks Analysis

QB	Avg Yds to Go	Air Yds (of Comps)	Avg Yds Short	Short of Sticks Rate	Rk
Joe Flacco	8.1	7.0	-1.1	61%	30
NFL Avg	7.6	6.8	-0.8	57%	

Air Yds vs YAC

Air Yds %	YAC %	Rk
56%	44%	23
54%	46%	

2016 Receiving Recap & 2017 Outlook

The Ravens are not at an ideal place in the receiving game, which is a problem unless they become more run heavy in 2017. Passing more frequently than any other team last year, the Ravens lost WR Kamar Aiken and Steve Smith Sr. in the offseason. Aiken was being underused and had a down year. But the Ravens did not add any new receivers yet must replace that target share (152 targets). Last year, Flacco targeted Mike Wallace a ton in close games and even when the team had a 9-13 point lead. Almost 1/3rd of all passes went to Wallace. Perriman needs to step up but last year he was used most in more garbage time situations.

Player *Min 50 Targets	Targets	Comp %	YPA	Rating	TOARS	Success %	Success Rk	Missed YPA Rk	YAS % Rk	TDs
Dennis Pitta	121	71%	6.0	78	4.7	47%	104	98	142	2
Mike Wallace	117	62%	8.7	85	4.8	49%	88	78	21	2
Steve Smith	102	69%	7.8	100	4.8	55%	39	28	63	5
Breshad Perriman	66	50%	7.6	65	3.6	36%	142	143	23	3
Kamar Aiken	50	58%	6.6	84	3.5	42%	127	134	133	1

Directional Passer Rating Delivered

Receiver	Short Left	Short Middle	Short Right	Deep Left	Deep Middle	Deep Right	Player Total
Dennis Pitta	79	85	91	40	55	0	78
Mike Wallace	83	116	73	0	138	24	85
Steve Smith	78	131	59	96	125	110	100
Breshad Perriman	60	116	104	156	33	0	73
Kamar Aiken	82	79	118	40	88	67	84
Kyle Juszczyk	81	92	88				88
Terrance West	88	90	101	40			94
Kenneth Dixon	84	89	93			0	77
Justin Forsett	79	18	79				51
Team Total	81	104	87	56	101	21	84

2016 Rushing Recap & 2017 Outlook

With Kenneth Dixon being suspended the first 4 games, the load comes down to Terrance West and newly acquired Danny Woodhead. Woodhead presents a real multi-dimensional weapon out of the backfield, and I predict Joe Flacco will enjoy what he brings to the offense, and will allow a more up-tempo look which Baltimore favors at times. Dixon was the 8th best RB in success rate last season, and West was far worse than average (52nd). So even though only 0.3 YPA separate the two, the more advanced metrics favored Dixon by a substantial margin. He was also more successful on early downs by a 10% margin. Going up against the 30th rated run defenses in 2017 (vs 10th rated in 2016) should make it easier on all Ravens' RBs.

Player *Min 50 Rushes	Rushes	YPA	Success %	Success Rk	Missed YPA Rk	YTS % Rk	YAS % Rk	Early Down Success %	Early Down Success Rk	TDs
Terrance West	193	4.0	42%	52	45	36	32	41%	53	5
Kenneth Dixon	88	4.3	56%	8	28	34	12	51%	16	2

Yards per Carry by Direction

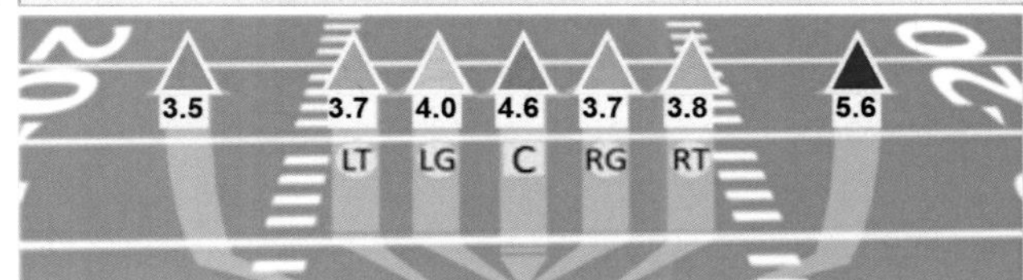

Directional Run Frequency

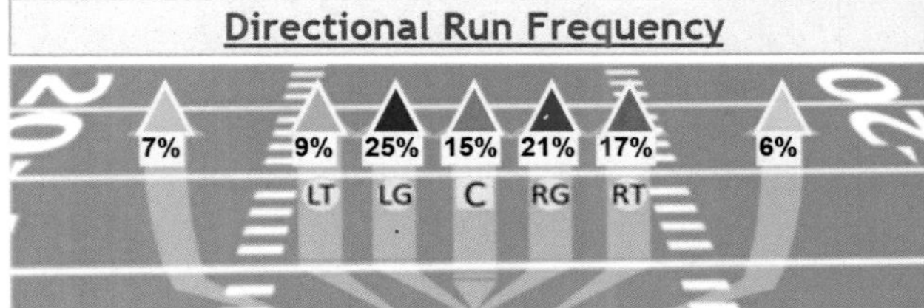

BAL-4

Thanks to a poor EDSR rate, the team faced many third downs, so they needed to pass often. And despite the season had by Joe Flacco last year, looking at their most successful plays, apart from rushes on 2nd and short, the Ravens' most successful play was a pass, which should tell you about the success of their 'run game last season.

The Ravens should be able to rely more on their defense this season, but an easy way to help a quarterback is to establish the run game. That should be something Baltimore may attempt with more success in 2017. After facing the 10th most difficult run defenses in 2016, they face the 3rd easiest schedule in 2017. It's the biggest drop-off for any team, and should allow the run game to play more of a factor. The Ravens don't have a nice stretch of bad run defenses, however, they simply don't play a single run defense better than the 10th ranked unit. And the close to the season, apart from a tough Steelers defense week 14, should be exceedingly kind, with games against the run defenses of Detroit, Cleveland and Indianapolis to close out the fantasy season.

Targeting Ravens' running backs out of the backfield should still be a focus. They targeted RBs on 27% of all pass attempts, well above the NFL average of 19%. And with Kenneth Dixon's 4 game PED suspension to start the season, look for Danny Woodhead to earn Flacco's trust as a receiving RB. If he is able to do so, Woodhead could remain in that role for much of the season.

If they can play solid defense and are more successful running the ball, it would limit the need to pass the ball most often of any team in the NFL. Oddly, the pass protection was one of the many interesting quirks for the Ravens in 2016. Baltimore ranked 8th in pass protection against a very easy schedule (29th) of pass rush units, yet Joe Flacco delivered his 2nd consecutive season with a passer rating below 85 and just 6.4 yds per attempt. The Ravens' pass offense may start slower over the first 8 weeks, as they face the 6th most difficult "pass blend" defenses (a blend of pass efficiency, yards per attempt, explosive passing and pass rush), but they close the season from weeks 9-16 with the 3rd easiest schedule of pass defenses.

While Joe Flacco was paid after the 2012 season's Super Bowl for what he did in his first 5 years in Baltimore, the annual payments far overcompensate for what he has done since. While he would surely never suggest it, I wonder if Ozzie Newsome ever had a backup plan if the team decided not to re-sign Flacco. But right now, this team is built as close to the 2008-2011 version as possible with Flacco's current salary cap. The offensive line needs some work, the run game does as well, but coupled with the defense, those parts are adequate if Joe Flacco plays to his level of compensation. One above average season surely would return Baltimore to the postseason. The Ravens hope this is the season for Flacco to regain that sparkle he delivered in the 2012 postseason.

Division History: Season Wins & 2017 Projection

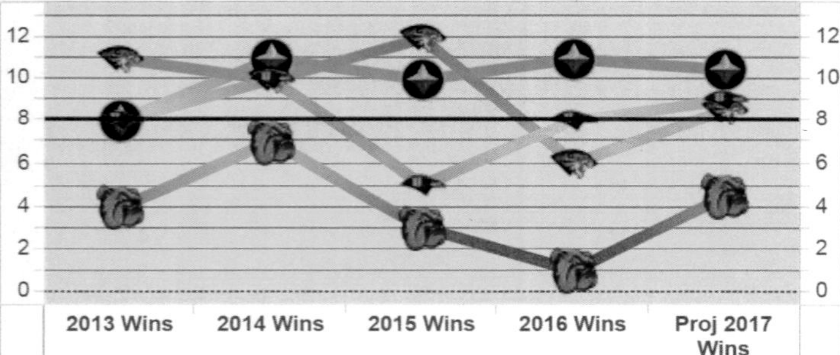

Rank of 2017 Defensive Pass Efficiency Faced by Week

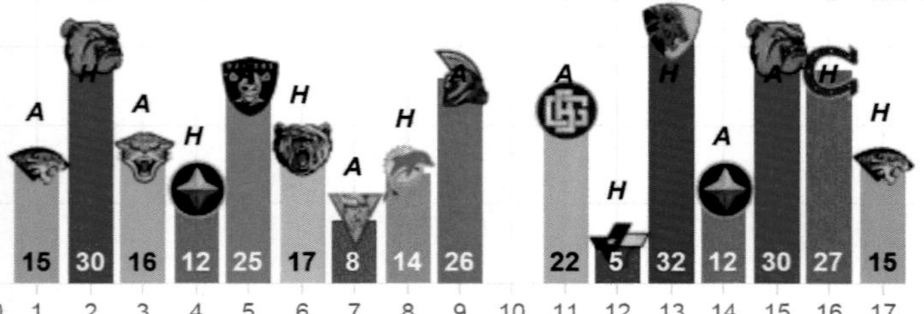

Rank of 2017 Defensive Rush Efficiency Faced by Week

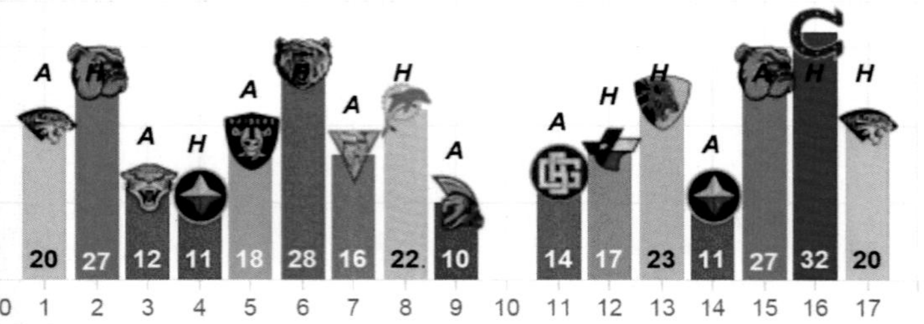

2016 Situational Usage by Player & Position

Usage Rate by Score

		Being Blown Out (14+)	Down Big (9-13)	One Score	Large Lead (9-13)	Blowout Lead (14+)	Grand Total
RUSH	Terrance West	6%	4%	21%	27%	25%	19%
	Kenneth Dixon	6%	7%	9%	10%	12%	9%
	Mike Wallace			1%			0%
	Breshad Perriman			0%			0%
	Kyle Juszczyk			1%			0%
	Justin Forsett	6%		3%			3%
	Chris Moore			0%		3%	0%
	Javorius Allen		1%	1%		3%	1%
	Lorenzo Taliaferro			0%			0%
	Michael Campanaro			0%			0%
	Total	19%	13%	36%	37%	42%	34%
PASS	Terrance West	5%	4%	5%	2%	4%	4%
	Kenneth Dixon	5%	10%	3%	4%	5%	4%
	Mike Wallace	12%	7%	12%	19%	8%	12%
	Dennis Pitta	23%	13%	11%	12%	10%	12%
	Steve Smith	11%	21%	9%	8%	10%	10%
	Breshad Perriman	8%	10%	6%	2%	8%	7%
	Kyle Juszczyk	2%	9%	5%	2%	3%	5%
	Kamar Aiken	6%	6%	5%	6%	3%	5%
	Justin Forsett	2%		2%	2%		1%
	Chris Moore	2%	3%	1%		3%	2%
	Darren Waller	2%		1%	6%	3%	2%
	Crockett Gillmore	1%		2%	2%		1%
	Javorius Allen		1%	0%			0%
	Nick Boyle	1%		1%		1%	1%
	Lorenzo Taliaferro			0%			0%
	Michael Campanaro			0%			0%
	Total	81%	87%	64%	63%	58%	66%

Positional Target Distribution vs NFL Average

		NFL Wide				Team Only			
		Left	Middle	Right	Total	Left	Middle	Right	Total
Deep	WR	1,015	553	966	**2,534**	16	28	35	**79**
	TE	156	143	160	**459**	2	4	3	**9**
	RB	24	4	39	**67**	1		1	**2**
	All	**1,195**	**700**	**1,165**	**3,060**	**19**	**32**	**39**	**90**
Short	WR	3,038	1,666	3,091	**7,795**	55	105	95	**255**
	TE	802	824	1,124	**2,750**	34	51	27	**112**
	RB	968	590	1,044	**2,602**	47	32	69	**148**
	All	**4,808**	**3,080**	**5,259**	**13,147**	**136**	**188**	**191**	**515**
Total		**6,003**	**3,780**	**6,424**	**16,207**	**155**	**220**	**230**	**605**

Positional Success Rates vs NFL Average

		NFL Wide				Team Only			
		Left	Middle	Right	Total	Left	Middle	Right	Total
Deep	WR	37%	50%	39%	**41%**	31%	50%	23%	**34%**
	TE	45%	50%	44%	**46%**	0%	25%	0%	**11%**
	RB	33%	75%	26%	**31%**	0%		0%	**0%**
	All	**38%**	**50%**	**39%**	**41%**	**26%**	**47%**	**21%**	**31%**
Short	WR	52%	56%	51%	**53%**	40%	63%	45%	**51%**
	TE	50%	62%	52%	**54%**	41%	53%	56%	**50%**
	RB	47%	49%	44%	**46%**	36%	59%	39%	**43%**
	All	**51%**	**56%**	**50%**	**52%**	**39%**	**60%**	**45%**	**49%**
Total		**48%**	**55%**	**48%**	**50%**	**37%**	**58%**	**40%**	**46%**

2017 Coaches

Head Coach:
Sean McDermott (CAR DC) (1st yr)

Offensive Coordinator:
Rick Dennison (DEN OC) (1st yr)

Defensive Coordinator:
Leslie Frazier (BAL DB) (1st yr)

Buffalo Bills

2017 Forecast

Wins	Div Rank
6.5	#3

Past Records

2016: 7-9
2015: 8-8
2014: 9-7

EASY HARD

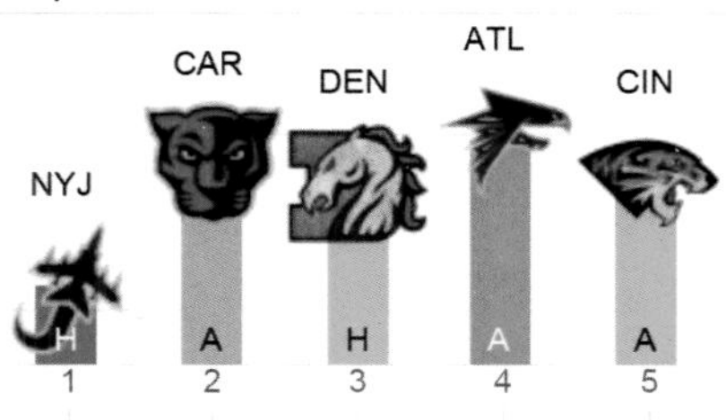
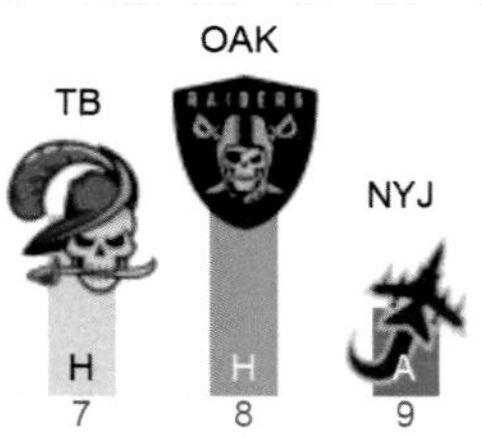

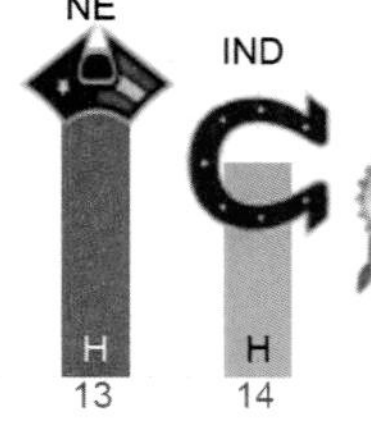

Key Players Lost

TXN	Player (POS)
Cut	Christian, Gerald TE
	Dowling, Jonathan S
	Easley, Marcus WR
	Kouandjio, Cyrus T
	Robey-Coleman, Nickell CB
	Thomas, Phillip S
	Williams, Aaron S
Declared Free Agent	Alexander, Lorenzo LB
	Brown, Sergio S
	Bush, Reggie RB
	Enemkpali, IK DE
	Felton, Jerome RB
	Gilmore, Stephon CB
	Goodwin, Marquise WR
	Ihedigbo, James S
	Manuel, EJ QB
	McCray, Lerentee LB
	Mills, Jordan T
	Spikes, Brandon LB
	Tate, Brandon WR
	Woods, Robert WR
Retired	Harvin, Percy WR

Average Line	# Games Favored	# Games Underdog
+1.8	7	8

2017 Buffalo Bills Overview

The one stat that defined the Bills the most in 2016 was that in a passing league, the #1 most targeted player on the Bills caught only 57 passes, which ranked 65th in the NFL, and averaged less than 37 yards per game, which ranked 101st in the NFL. It truly was a sad year in Buffalo. Except if you were LeSean McCoy. Then it would be simply one of the most overlooked seasons of brilliance in the modern passing era of the NFL.

Since the NFL modified rules to make it "safer" to pass the ball, with fewer hits allowed to the quarterback and wide receivers, the emphasis has been on passing the ball. In the 7 years since 2010, only 5 running backs have at least 175 rushing attempts which averaged at least 5 yards per carry, and scored at least 10 rushing TDs. Sorting by descending yards per attempt, the top season was by Adrian Peterson in 2012. He recorded 12 rushing TDs and over 2,000 total yards. He was lionized, and won the MVP that year as well as First Team All-Pro. The second best season was LeSean McCoy's season last year, where he averaged 5.4 yards per attempt and scored 13 rushing TDs. He received no MVP votes and did not make the First Team All-Pro. The 3rd best season was Ezekiel Elliott last year, where he hit 5 yards per carry and scored 15 rushing TDs. He received 9 MVP votes and won First Team All-Pro. The 4th best season was Marshawn Lynch in 2012, where he also averaged 5 yards per carry and scored 11 rushing TDs. Lynch was voted First Team All-Pro. And the 5th best season was Jamaal Charles in 2013, who averaged 4.97 yards per carry and scored 12 rushing TDs. Like everyone else on the list above him, he was voted First Team All-Pro.

Last year McCoy received no awards, no high praise and no lionization for his season. But it's much more than just gaining the 2nd most yards per carry for a back with a minimum of 175 carries and 10 TDs. It's that the chips were stacked against him. You name it, it was all set up for trouble for the Bills running back last year. Game theory helps explain why:

First, the Bills faced the #1 most difficult schedule of run defenses last year. It was far and away the most difficult. The rushing success rate for teams with the #2 and #3 most difficult schedules of run defenses were #31 and #30. These schedules made it extremely difficult to maintain consistent success. While those teams (Miami, Cleveland)

*(cont'd - see **BUF2**)*

Key Free Agents/ Trades Added

Brown, Corey WR
Crichton, Scott DE
Davis, Ryan DE
DiMarco, Patrick RB
Ducasse, Vladimir G
Hyde, Micah S
Tolbert, Mike RB
Wright, Shareece CB

Drafted Players

Rd	Pk	Player (College)
1	27	CB - Tre'Davious White (LSU)
2	37	WR - Zay Jones (East Carolina)
	63	G - Dion Dawkins (Temple)
5	163	LB - Matt Milano (Boston College)
	171	QB - Nathan Peterman (Pittsburgh)
6	195	OLB - Tanner Vallejo (Boise State)

Regular Season Wins: Past & Current Proj

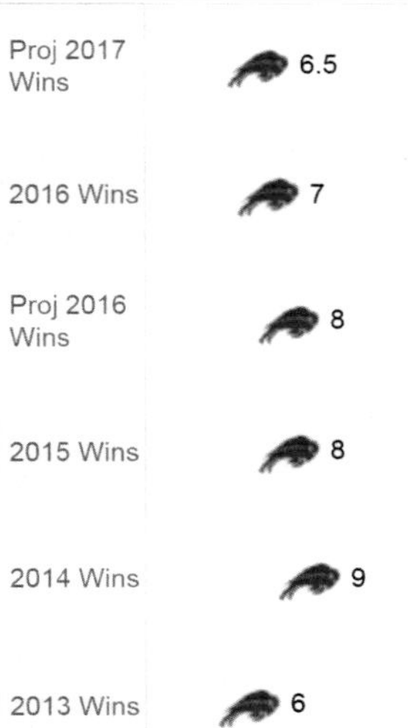

2017 Lineup & Cap Hits

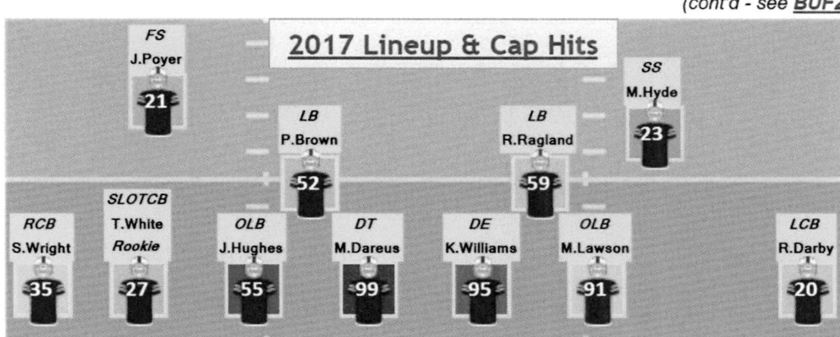

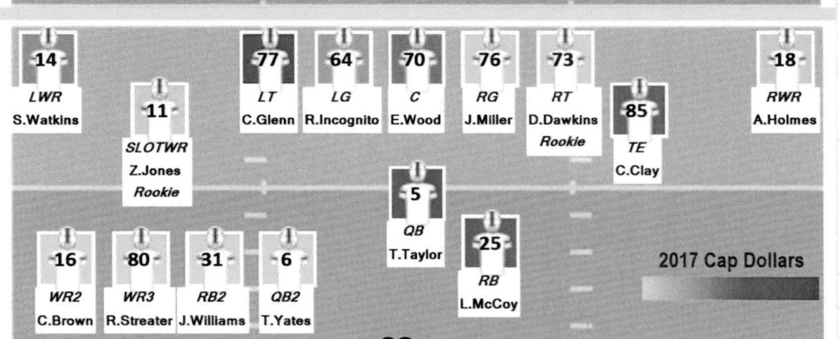

2017 Unit Spending

Positional Spending

	Rank	Total	2016 Rk
All OFF	10	$87.25M	25
QB	21	$11.53M	25
OL	5	$39.03M	22
RB	8	$11.10M	4
WR	28	$13.76M	24
TE	7	$11.84M	12
All DEF	26	$68.97M	13
DL	5	$43.41M	13
LB	32	$10.03M	17
CB	32	$6.35M	18
S	21	$9.18M	5

Buffalo Bills 2016 Success Rate Radar

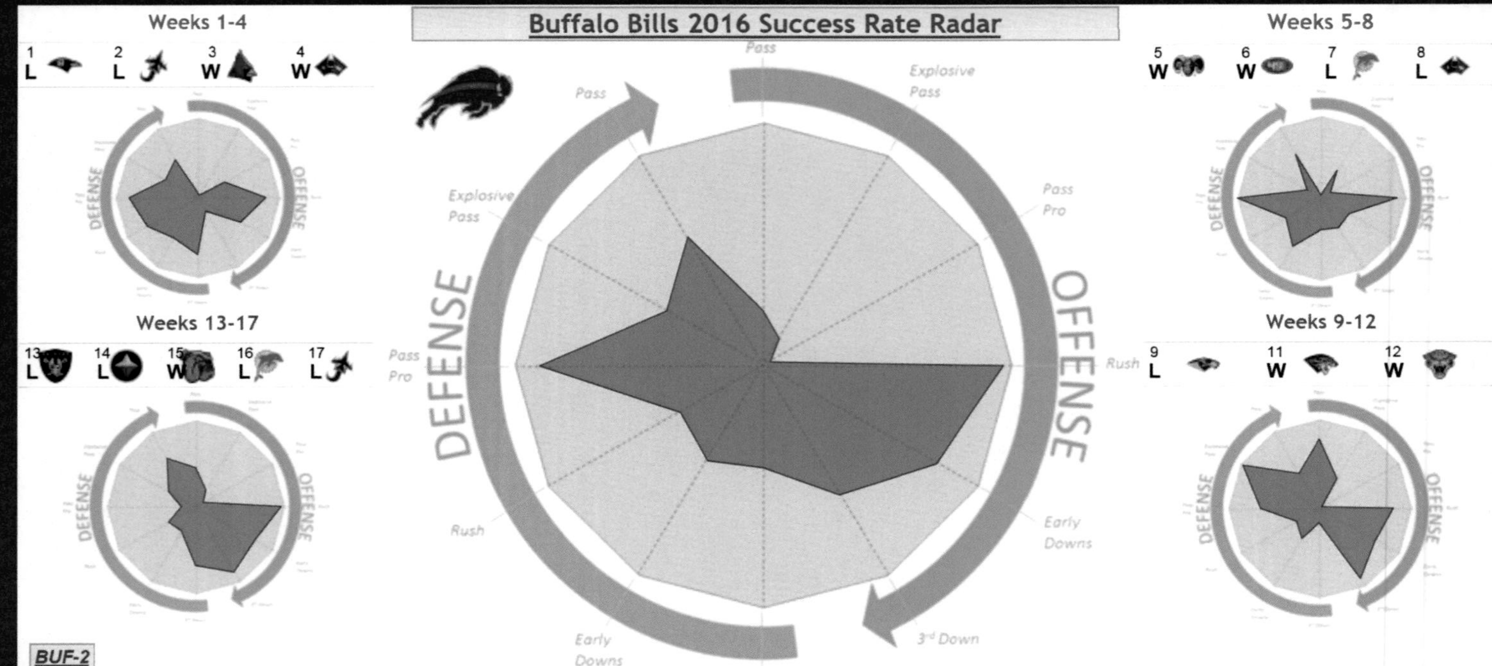

BUF-2

averaged a respectable yards per carry, they could not be successful at all. So in ranking the rushing success rate of the teams with the 3 hardest run schedules last year (from hardest to easiest) it goes: Bills: 54% (#2 best) success rate vs #1 hardest schedule, Dolphins: 40% (#31) success rate vs #2 hardest schedule, Browns: 41% (#30) success rate vs #3 hardest schedule.

Second, to say the Bills went run heavy last season was an understatement. See the very first stat at the top to appreciate the receiving corps that they had to work with. The Bills ran the ball on 49% of their offensive plays. No team ran it 50% or more. And when the game was within one score and the Bills were not backed up inside their own 20 (the other 80 yards on the field) the Bills ran it 52% of the time of their 555 offensive plays. That was the most in the NFL. It was a full 10% above the average (42%).

Third, to dive further into game theory, in one score games on first downs, the Bills were beyond predictable. They ran the ball 65% of time. That was 13% more than average, and significantly more often than any other team. Pulling it all together, versus the NFL's toughest schedule of run defenses (and despite facing the 2nd easiest schedule of pass defenses) the Bills chose to be the most run-heavy team in the NFL, and to do so by running the ball in some of the most predictable rushing situations possible. These great run defenses could key in on the run and had the extreme upper hand due to predictability of the Bills offense. Yet that didn't stop McCoy: When he was fresh, from the first quarter through the 3rd quarter, he averaged a massive 6.1 yards per carry on first down in these predictable rushing situations. This led the entire NFL. On all attempts in quarters 1 through 3, Shady averaged 6.0 yards per carry and a 52% success rate. Both were the best in the NFL.

His excellence flew under the radar and took me by surprise. I forecast the Bills to have the #2 toughest schedule of run defenses in an article I wrote for Rotoworld last summer. Success against that schedule would have been tough.

*(cont'd - see **BUF-3**)*

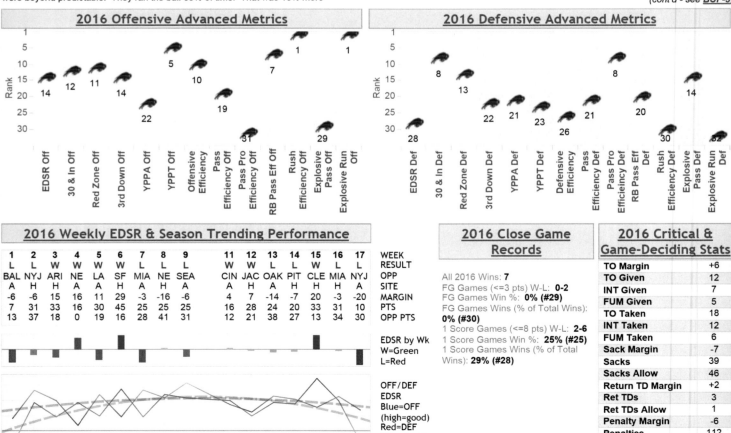

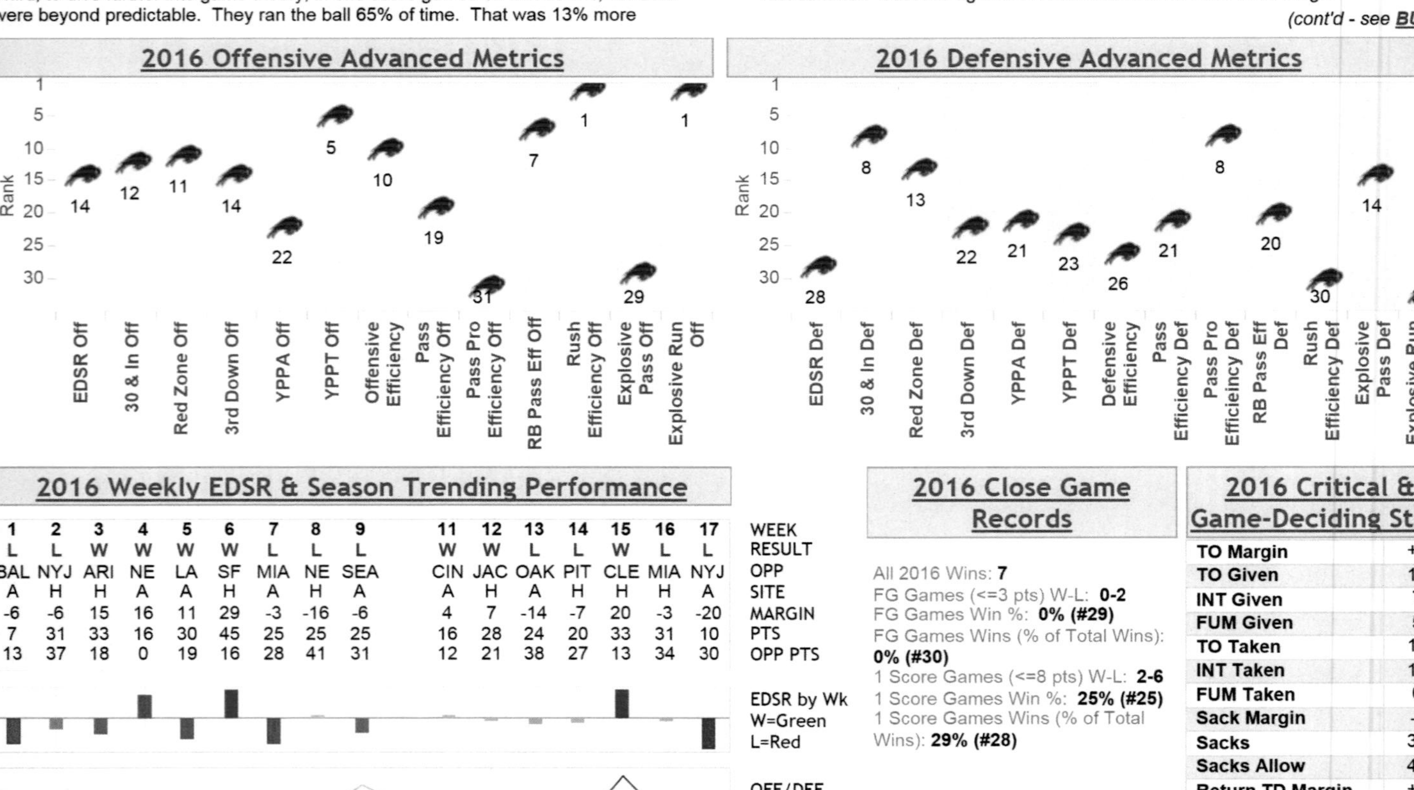

2016 Weekly EDSR & Season Trending Performance

WEEK	1	2	3	4	5	6	7	8	9	11	12	13	14	15	16	17
RESULT	L	L	W	W	W	W	L	L	L	W	W	L	L	W	L	L
OPP	BAL	NYJ	ARI	NE	LA	SF	MIA	NE	SEA	CIN	JAC	OAK	PIT	CLE	MIA	NYJ
SITE	A	H	H	A	A	H	A	H	A	A	H	A	H	H	H	A
MARGIN	-6	-6	15	16	11	29	-3	-16	-6	4	7	-14	-7	20	-3	-20
PTS	7	31	33	16	30	45	25	25	25	16	28	24	20	33	31	10
OPP PTS	13	37	18	0	19	16	28	41	31	12	21	38	27	13	34	30

2016 Close Game Records

All 2016 Wins: **7**
FG Games (<=3 pts) W-L: **0-2**
FG Games Win %: **0% (#29)**
FG Games Wins (% of Total Wins): **0% (#30)**
1 Score Games (<=8 pts) W-L: **2-6**
1 Score Games Win %: **25% (#25)**
1 Score Games Wins (% of Total Wins): **29% (#28)**

2016 Critical & Game-Deciding Stats

TO Margin	+6
TO Given	12
INT Given	7
FUM Given	5
TO Taken	18
INT Taken	12
FUM Taken	6
Sack Margin	-7
Sacks	39
Sacks Allow	46
Return TD Margin	+2
Ret TDs	3
Ret TDs Allow	1
Penalty Margin	-6
Penalties	112
Opponent Penalties	106

Buffalo Bills 2017 Strength of Schedule In Detail (compared to 2016)

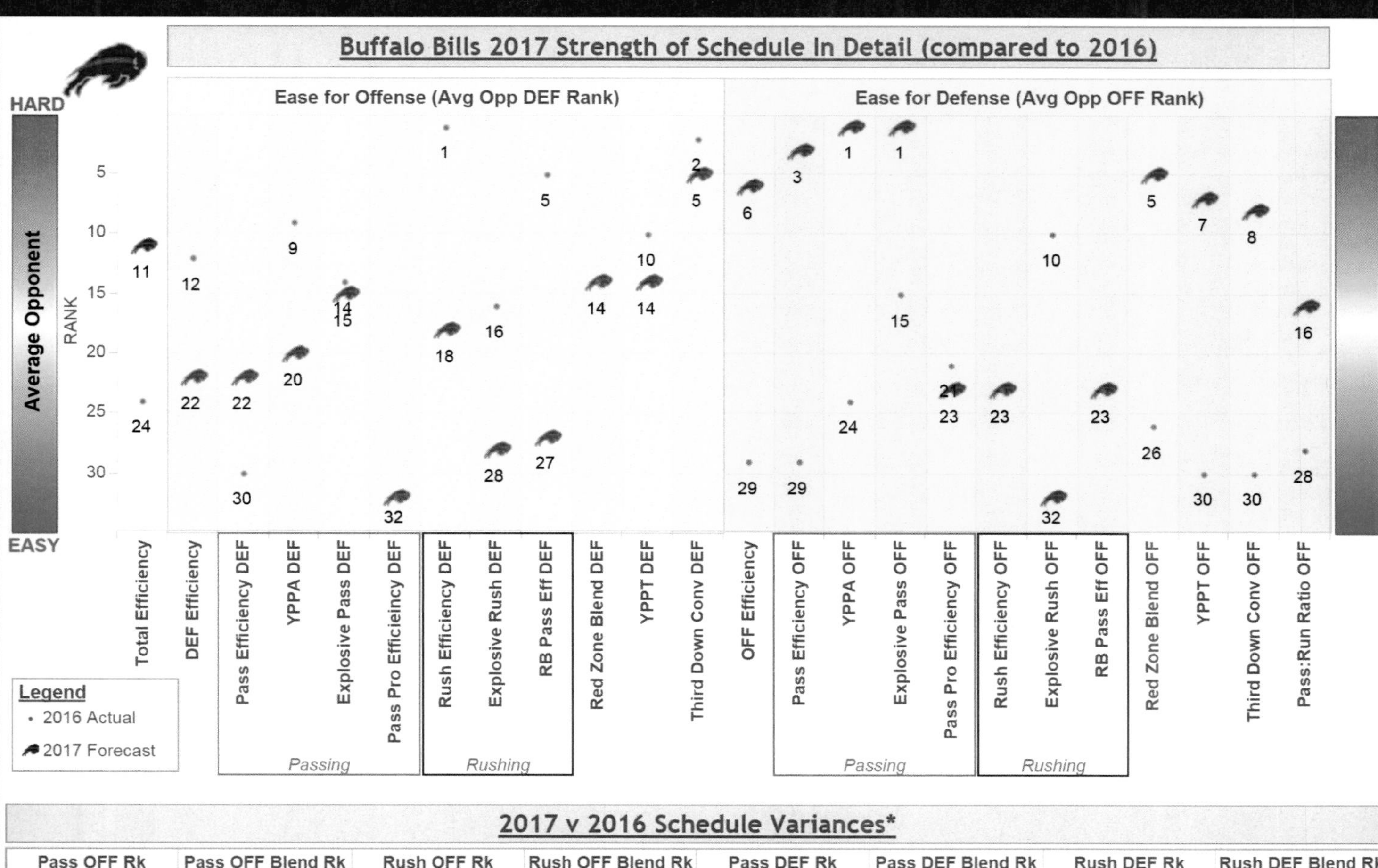

2017 v 2016 Schedule Variances*

Pass OFF Rk	Pass OFF Blend Rk	Rush OFF Rk	Rush OFF Blend Rk	Pass DEF Rk	Pass DEF Blend Rk	Rush DEF Rk	Rush DEF Blend Rk
7	27	29	32	1	1	17	17

* **1**=Hardest Jump in 2017 schedule from 2016 (aka a much harder schedule in 2017), **32**=Easiest Jump in 2017 schedule from 2016 (aka a much easier schedule in 2017); **Pass Blend** metric blends 4 metrics: Pass Efficiency, YPPA, Explosive Pass & Pass Rush; **Rush Blend** metric blends 3 metrics: Rush Efficiency, Explosive Rush & RB Targets

Team Records & Trends

	2016	2015	2014
Average line	-0.4	-0.2	1.4
Average O/U line	44.7	43.7	43.6
Straight Up Record	7-9	8-8	9-7
Against the Spread Record	6-9	7-8	9-7
Over/Under Record	12-4	8-8	3-13
ATS as Favorite	2-4	3-4	3-3
ATS as Underdog	3-4	4-3	6-3
Straight Up Home	4-4	5-3	5-3
ATS Home	3-5	5-3	4-4
Over/Under Home	8-0	4-4	1-7
ATS as Home Favorite	2-2	3-1	3-2
ATS as a Home Dog	1-2	2-1	1-1
Straight Up Away	3-5	3-5	4-4
ATS Away	3-4	2-5	5-3
Over/Under Away	4-4	4-4	2-6
ATS Away Favorite	0-2	0-3	0-1
ATS Away Dog	2-2	2-2	5-2
Six Point Teaser Record	11-4	11-5	12-4
Seven Point Teaser Record	12-4	12-4	12-4
Ten Point Teaser Record	13-3	13-2	14-2

BUF-3

I thought it would be difficult for them on the ground. In actuality my preseason prediction was extremely accurate – they faced the #1 toughest schedule of run defenses by year's end. But LeSean McCoy shattered my expectations completely.

While McCoy's season was remarkable, led by Rex Ryan the Bills recorded a 7-9 record and Rex Ryan was done in Buffalo. The team made the move to hire Sean McDermott, former defensive coordinator for the Panthers. They brought in Rick Dennison to head up the offense. Dennison was formerly of the Denver Broncos where he was OC for the last two years. So he missed out on coaching Peyton Manning, and instead had the luxury to coach Brock Osweiler and Trevor Siemian. The Broncos offense relied heavily on the defense for success. If the defense struggled, so did the Broncos. But one thing the Broncos definitely did not have, particularly in 2016, was a run game. Denver ranked 29th in rushing success last year, gaining successful runs on just 41% of their carries. That was just above those teams I mentioned earlier (Miami /Cleveland) who recorded successful runs on 40% and 41% of their runs respectively. *(cont'd - see **BUF-4**)*

2017 Rest Analysis

Avg Rest	6.47
Avg Rk	3
Team More Rest	3
Opp More Rest	1
Net Rest Edge	2
3 Days Rest	1
4 Days Rest	0
5 Days Rest	0
6 Days Rest	12
7 Days Rest	0
8 Days Rest	0
9 Days Rest	1
10 Days Rest	0
11 Days Rest	0
12 Days Rest	0
13 Days Rest	1
14 Days Rest	0

Health by Unit*

2016 Rk	25
(2015 Rk)	25
Off Rk	19
Def Rk	28
QB Rk	1
RB Rk	15
WR Rk	25
TE Rk	12
OLine Rk	18
DLine Rk	31
LB Rk	24
DB Rk	25

**Based on the great work of Scott Kacsmar from Football Outsiders*

2017 Weekly Betting Lines (wks 1-16)

1	2	3	4	5	7	8	9	10	11	12	13	14	15	16
NYJ	CAR	DEN	ATL	CIN	TB	OAK	NYJ	NO	LAC	KC	NE	IND	MIA	NE
H	A	H	A	A	H	H	A	H	A	A	H	H	H	A
-6.0	+3.5	-1.0	+7.5	+3.5	-1.5	+1.5	-1.5	-2.0	+2.0	+6.0	+7.0	-1.5	-1.5	+11.5

Avg = 1.8

Home Lines (wks 1-16)

1	3	7	8	10	13	14	15
NYJ	DEN	TB	OAK	NO	NE	IND	MIA
-6.0	-1.0	-1.5	+1.5	-2.0	+7.0	-1.5	-1.5

Avg = -0.6

Road Lines (wks 1-16)

2	4	5	9	11	12	16
CAR	ATL	CIN	NYJ	LAC	KC	NE
+3.5	+7.5	+3.5	-1.5	+2.0	+6.0	+11.5

Avg = 4.6

Buffalo Bills 2016 Play Analysis

2016 Play Tendencies

All Pass %	53%
All Pass Rk	29
All Rush %	47%
All Rush Rk	4
1 Score Pass %	50%
1 Score Pass Rk	30
2015 1 Score Pass %	49%
2015 1 Score Pass Rk	32
Pass Increase %	1%
Pass Increase Rk	13
1 Score Rush %	50%
1 Score Rush Rk	3
Up Pass %	53%
Up Pass Rk	28
Up Rush %	47%
Up Rush Rk	5
Down Pass %	53%
Down Pass Rk	29
Down Rush %	47%
Down Rush Rk	4

2016 Down & Distance Tendencies

Down	Distance	Total Plays	Pass Rate	Run Rate	Play Success %
1	Short (1-3)	6	0%	100%	67%
	Med (4-7)	16	19%	81%	50%
	Long (8-10)	288	42%	58%	54%
	XL (11+)	15	73%	27%	7%
2	Short (1-3)	38	37%	63%	58%
	Med (4-7)	82	56%	44%	49%
	Long (8-10)	74	58%	42%	49%
	XL (11+)	54	67%	33%	39%
3	Short (1-3)	52	54%	46%	58%
	Med (4-7)	48	83%	17%	52%
	Long (8-10)	22	91%	9%	36%
	XL (11+)	34	76%	24%	24%
4	Short (1-3)	6	0%	100%	83%
	XL (11+)	1	0%	100%	100%

Shotgun %:

Under Center	Shotgun
20%	80%
37% AVG	63%

Run Rate:

Under Center	Shotgun
67%	40%
68% AVG	23%

Pass Rate:

Under Center	Shotgun
33%	60%
32% AVG	77%

Short Yardage Intelligence:

2nd and Short Run

Run Freq	Run % Rk	NFL Run Freq Avg	Run 1D Rate	Run NFL 1D Avg
65%	16	65%	79%	71%

2nd and Short Pass

Pass Freq	Pass % Rk	NFL Pass Freq Avg	Pass 1D Rate	Pass NFL 1D Avg
35%	15	35%	39%	52%

Most Frequent Play

Down	Distance	Play Type	Player	Total Plays	Play Success %
1	Short (1-3)	RUSH	Tyrod Taylor	2	50%
	Med (4-7)	RUSH	LeSean McCoy	9	78%
	Long (8-10)	RUSH	LeSean McCoy	100	51%
	XL (11+)	PASS	Walt Powell	3	33%
		RUSH	LeSean McCoy	3	0%
2	Short (1-3)	RUSH	LeSean McCoy	14	57%
	Med (4-7)	RUSH	LeSean McCoy	19	63%
	Long (8-10)	RUSH	LeSean McCoy	14	36%
	XL (11+)	RUSH	LeSean McCoy	10	40%
3	Short (1-3)	RUSH	Mike Gillislee	10	80%
	Med (4-7)	PASS	Robert Woods	9	67%
	Long (8-10)	PASS	Charles Clay	5	40%
	XL (11+)	PASS	Marquise Goodwin	9	22%

Most Successful Play*

Down	Distance	Play Type	Player	Total Plays	Play Success %
1	Med (4-7)	RUSH	LeSean McCoy	9	78%
	Long (8-10)	PASS	Charles Clay	16	75%
2	Short (1-3)	RUSH	Mike Gillislee	8	100%
	Med (4-7)	PASS	Charles Clay	9	67%
	Long (8-10)	PASS	LeSean McCoy	8	50%
	XL (11+)	PASS	Robert Woods	5	80%
3	Short (1-3)	RUSH	Jerome Felton	6	83%
	Med (4-7)	PASS	Robert Woods	9	67%
	Long (8-10)	PASS	Charles Clay	5	40%
	XL (11+)	PASS	Marquise Goodwin	9	22%

*Minimum 5 plays to qualify

2016 Snap Rates

Week	Opp	Score	Charles Clay	LeSean McCoy	Marquise Goodwin	Robert Woods	Sammy Watkins	Nick O'Leary	Jerome Felton
1	BAL	L 13-7	48 (98%)	42 (86%)	11 (22%)	41 (84%)	42 (86%)	3 (6%)	
2	NYJ	L 37-31	48 (91%)	49 (92%)	29 (55%)	46 (87%)	40 (75%)	3 (6%)	5 (9%)
3	ARI	W 33-18	53 (83%)	48 (75%)	53 (83%)	61 (95%)		14 (22%)	16 (25%)
4	NE	W 16-0	71 (91%)	54 (69%)	63 (81%)	69 (88%)		27 (35%)	21 (27%)
5	LA	W 30-19	50 (91%)	44 (80%)	37 (67%)	48 (87%)		14 (25%)	21 (38%)
6	SF	W 45-16	61 (77%)	49 (62%)	50 (63%)	54 (68%)		38 (48%)	30 (38%)
7	MIA	L 28-25	54 (95%)	23 (40%)	31 (54%)			20 (35%)	13 (23%)
8	NE	L 41-25	43 (56%)			46 (60%)		43 (56%)	20 (26%)
9	SEA	L 31-25	82 (95%)	64 (74%)	48 (56%)	68 (79%)		17 (20%)	23 (27%)
11	CIN	W 16-12	60 (92%)	20 (31%)	54 (83%)	10 (15%)		14 (22%)	17 (26%)
12	JAC	W 28-21	46 (84%)	40 (73%)	43 (78%)		25 (45%)	18 (33%)	20 (36%)
13	OAK	L 38-24		45 (63%)	59 (82%)		49 (68%)	70 (97%)	28 (39%)
14	PIT	L 27-20	50 (96%)	43 (83%)	43 (83%)	27 (52%)	49 (94%)	12 (23%)	12 (23%)
15	CLE	W 33-13	60 (90%)	41 (61%)	53 (79%)	30 (45%)	42 (63%)	28 (42%)	39 (58%)
16	MIA	L 34-31	87 (95%)	70 (76%)	33 (36%)	79 (86%)	86 (93%)	28 (30%)	43 (47%)
17	NYJ	L 30-10	59 (94%)	13 (21%)	33 (52%)	56 (89%)	51 (81%)	21 (33%)	16 (25%)
Grand Total			872 (88%)	645 (66%)	640 (65%)	635 (72%)	384 (76%)	370 (33%)	324 (31%)

Personnel Groupings

Personnel	Team %	NFL Avg	Succ. %
1-1 [3WR]	48%	60%	47%
2-1 [2WR]	29%	7%	52%
1-2 [2WR]	17%	19%	47%
2-2 [1WR]	5%	3%	47%

Grouping Tendencies

Personnel	Pass Rate	Pass Succ. %	Run Succ. %
1-1 [3WR]	70%	44%	53%
2-1 [2WR]	27%	41%	56%
1-2 [2WR]	55%	42%	52%
2-2 [1WR]	9%	50%	47%

Red Zone Targets (min 3)

Receiver	All	Inside 5	6-10	11-20
Charles Clay	14	1	3	10
Robert Woods	8	2		6
Justin Hunter	7	3	2	2
LeSean McCoy	7		3	4
Marquise Goodwin	4		2	2
Sammy Watkins	4		1	3

Red Zone Rushes (min 3)

Rusher	All	Inside 5	6-10	11-20
LeSean McCoy	38	11	14	13
Mike Gillislee	18	10	1	7
Tyrod Taylor	17	8	4	5
Jonathan Williams	7	4	1	2
Jerome Felton	3	2		1
Reggie Bush	3	1	1	1

Early Down Target Rate

RB	TE	WR
21%	25%	54%
19%	20% NFL AVG	61%

Overall Target Success %

RB	TE	WR
51% #6	48% #30	48% #20

Buffalo Bills 2016 Passing Recap & 2017 Outlook

Before even digging into the passing for Taylor, let's discuss his rushing ability. He led the NFL in QB rush attempts last year, and at 6.6 yards per carry, only Colin Kaepernick averaged a higher number. Of the those considered "running quarterbacks", Taylor was the best in YAS %, which looks at his explosiveness delivered. And Taylor was 8th in success rate and 7th in missed YPA (runs which were unsuccessful but still created positive plays). McDermott is certainly familiar with a running QB from his time in Carolina, so I don't believe the frequency of Taylor's running will diminish, and it provides a nice added bump for fantasy purposes. The faster Zay Jones gets incorporated into the offense the better, so root for him to stay injury free during camp with no setbacks. Hopefully Dennison will find out how to maximize Charles Clay's effectiveness, because Taylor likes throwing to the TE but Clay's numbers haven't been impressive, particularly from a TD %. The best news for Taylor is the pass rushes he'll face this year could be weak (easiest in the league) so that should buy him time for deep shots and more rushing yardage. Denver had a high usage rate for WRs last year, but I hope Buffalo allocates considerable shares to the TE and RB.

2016 Standard Passing Table

QB	Comp	Att	Comp %	Yds	YPA	TDs	INT	Sacks	Rating	Rk
Tyrod Taylor	270	437	62%	2,997	6.9	17	6	42	89.4	24
NFL Avg			63%		7.2				90.4	

2016 Advanced Passing Table

QB	Success %	EDSR Passing Success %	20+ Yd Pass Gains	20+ Yd Pass %	30+ Yd Pass Gains	30+ Yd Pass %	Air Yds per Comp	YAC per Comp	20+ Air Yd Comp	20+ Air Yd %
Tyrod Taylor	43%	46%	32	7%	12	3%	6.8	4.3	19	4%
NFL Avg	44%	48%	27	8%	10	3%	6.4	4.8	12	4%

Tyrod Taylor Rating All Downs

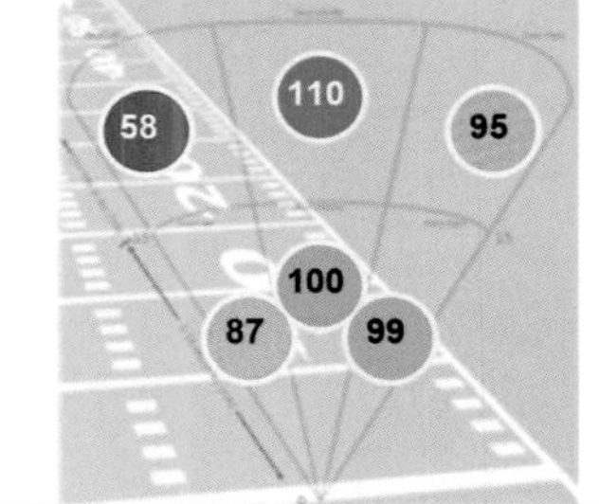

Tyrod Taylor Rating Early Downs

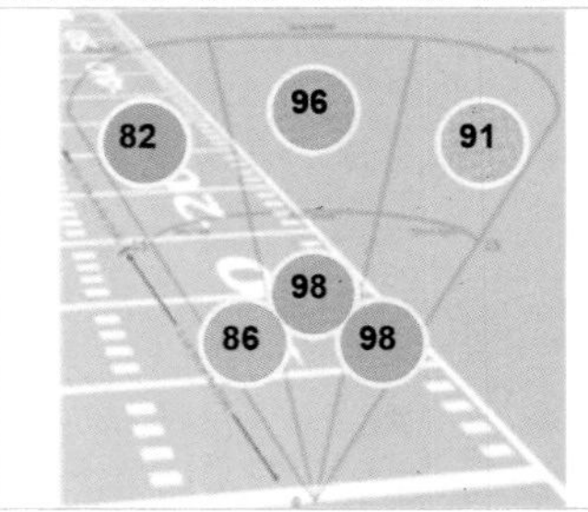

Interception Rates by Down

Yards to Go	1	2	3	4	Total
1 & 2	0.0%	0.0%	5.6%		3.1%
3, 4, 5	0.0%	3.8%	0.0%		1.6%
6 - 9	0.0%	1.9%	0.0%	0.0%	1.1%
10 - 14	1.2%	0.0%	0.0%	0.0%	0.8%
15+	0.0%	0.0%	5.9%	0.0%	2.1%
Total	1.1%	1.2%	1.5%	0.0%	1.3%

3rd Down Passing - Short of Sticks Analysis

QB	Avg Yds to Go	Air Yds (of Comps)	Avg Yds Short	Short of Sticks Rate	Rk
Tyrod Taylor	7.6	7.3	-0.3	60%	20
NFL Avg	7.6	6.8	-0.8	57%	

Air Yds vs YAC

Air Yds %	YAC %	Rk
58%	42%	18
54%	46%	

2016 Receiving Recap & 2017 Outlook

Last year Buffalo threw way less to WRs than the NFL average, and way more to their TE and RBs. It was smart to get the RBs involved, as the Bills saw a 51% success rate to RBs which was 6th best, and only a 48% success rate to WRs, which was 20th. Hopefully the Bills will find more efficiency when passing next year, which will give them more confidence to do so more often, and not be as run heavy as they were last year. They need to receive a higher success rate in the red zone. Last year their top two red zone targets (Clay & Woods) were very poor in the red zone so inside the 5, they went 18% rush/82% pass.

Player *Min 50 Targets*	Targets	Comp %	YPA	Rating	TOARS	Success %	Success Rk	Missed YPA Rk	YAS % Rk	TDs
Charles Clay	87	66%	6.3	98	4.5	47%	103	103	135	4
Robert Woods	76	67%	8.0	90	4.3	57%	33	70	97	1
Marquise Goodwin	68	43%	6.1	53	3.5	40%	133	147	79	3
LeSean McCoy	58	88%	6.1	98	4.0	53%	49	12	143	1
Sammy Watkins	52	54%	8.3	86	3.7	52%	59	53	26	2

Directional Passer Rating Delivered

Receiver	Short Left	Short Middle	Short Right	Deep Left	Deep Middle	Deep Right	Player Total
Charles Clay	87	93	83	123	110	107	98
Robert Woods	98	88	95	52	110	55	90
Marquise Goodwin	64	60	93	0	119	63	53
LeSean McCoy	92	80	110				98
Sammy Watkins	55	137	99	15	40	122	86
Team Total	84	96	97	45	106	78	87

2016 Rushing Recap & 2017 Outlook

Mike Gillislee may have been the backup, but he was great. He ranked #1 in the NFL in success rate and #2 in the NFL in Missed YPA (on unsuccessful plays, per play yardage that fell short of making the play successful). Also, Gillislee was the perfect red zone rusher. Inside the 10 yard line, Gillislee had 11 carries and a 100% success rate on those rushes. No other RB was close to that rate. Inside the red zone in general, Gillislee posted a 94% success rate on 18 attempts. Once again, no other RB was close to that efficiency. He will be missed, but Jonathan Williams will be thrust into that role. The final element is the schedule, which is much easier. Instead of the #1 most difficult schedule of run defenses, the Bills get the 18th rated schedule.

Player *Min 50 Rushes*	Rushes	YPA	Success %	Success Rk	Missed YPA Rk	YTS % Rk	YAS % Rk	Early Down Success %	Early Down Success Rk	TDs
LeSean McCoy	234	5.4	51%	20	59	47	6	51%	15	13
Mike Gillislee	101	5.7	66%	1	2	51	2	65%	1	8

Yards per Carry by Direction

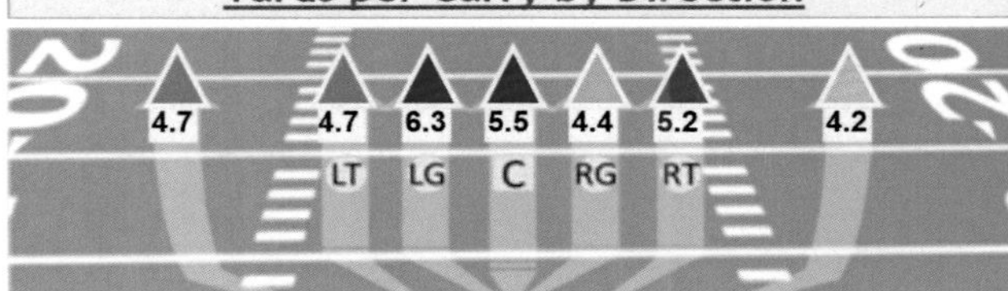

Directional Run Frequency

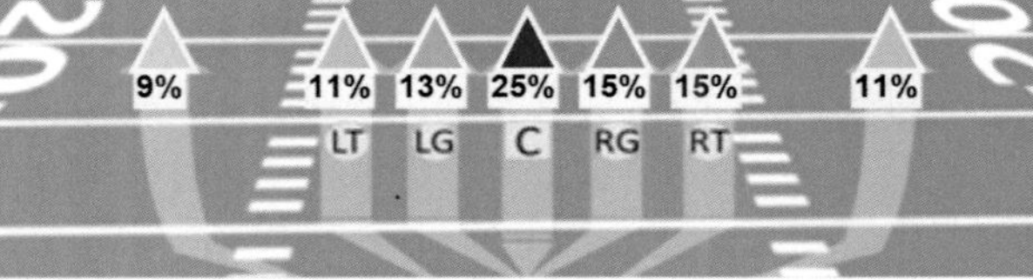

However, while Miami and Cleveland faced the #2 and #3 toughest schedule of run defenses, the Broncos faced the 6th easiest schedule of run defenses. Yet they still struggled immensely.

That shouldn't be a problem in Buffalo. The Bills don't have Mike Gillislee to back up McCoy, and Gillislee was tremendous in that role last year. They can't continue to ride McCoy as much as they did last year, so they will need Jonathan Williams to step up to assist. And of course, the passing game needs to improve by leaps and bounds.

The Bills added Zay Jones, a WR from East Carolina, in the early 2nd round. Jones broke the FBS single-season and career reception record last year. It's vital to have a productive #2 receiver on the Bills, because they haven't had one for several years. But it's also vital for Jones to not be thrust into the #1 role with another injury to Sammy Watkins. Watkins missed 8 full games last year, and cannot get healthy. Earlier this offseason, the bills declined Watkins fifth-year team option, so he will enter free agency next month. It makes perfect sense for a new staff to make Watkins earn that money by staying healthy this year and performing well. That 5th year was not a sunk cost, and just because the team made a poor decision to trade up and acquire Watkins 4th overall in 2014, this new regime is not going to let that affect their future. The Bills also brought in WR Corey Brown, a player who McDermott is familiar with from his time in Carolina.

When Watkins played, he was decent. Not great but not terrible – he averaged 8.3 yards per attempt which led the Bills, but posted just a 54% completion rate and delivered an 86 passer rating. His success rate (52%) ranked 59th in the league last year, and his best rank was his YAS %, indicative of explosive yardage. The player who needs to step up the most, however, is Charles Clay. Denver used their TEs frequently even though they didn't really have a solid option. Clay is operating on a $38M contract which extends to 2019. He was the most targeted player last year, but his rankings were terrible. His 47% success rate was 103rd, his Missed YPA rate (ranking unsuccessful plays to analyze how close they came to being successful) was also 103rd, and his YAS % was 135th. For the Bills' number 1 target offensively to post those results in a league with 32 teams was terrible. Clay has been dealing with chronic knee trouble, but if the Bills are paying him as much as they are, they certainly are not getting that return on investment.

Defensively, the loss of CB Stephon Gilmore to the Patriots was tough, but overall the unit is in a better position for future success under McDermott than it was under the Ryan brothers. Last year's defense ranked 28th in EDSR (Early Down Success Rate) and 30th against the run, and that came against the 4th easiest schedule of opposing offenses. This year they face the 6th most difficult offenses, by far the largest increase in schedule difficult for any defense. McDermott has his work cut out for him this season.

Division History: Season Wins & 2017 Projection

2013 Wins | 2014 Wins | 2015 Wins | 2016 Wins | Proj 2017 Wins

Rank of 2017 Defensive Pass Efficiency Faced by Week

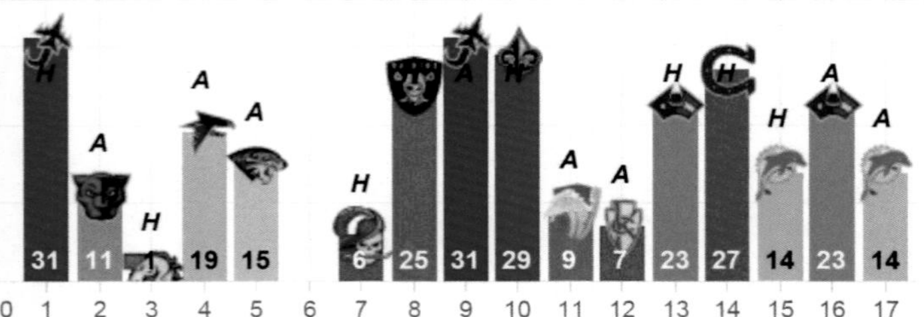

Rank of 2017 Defensive Rush Efficiency Faced by Week

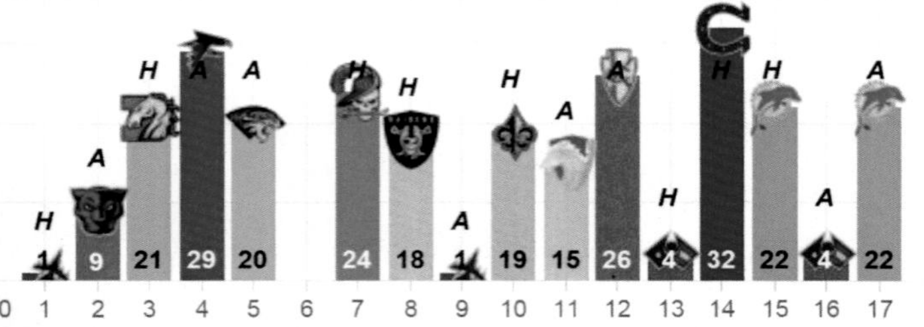

2016 Situational Usage by Player & Position

Usage Rate by Score

		Being Blown Out (14+)	Down Big (9-13)	One Score	Large Lead (9-13)	Blowout Lead (14+)	Grand Total
RUSH	LeSean McCoy	12%	15%	32%	32%	34%	28%
	Mike Gillislee	10%	11%	13%	6%	15%	12%
	Robert Woods			0%			0%
	Jonathan Williams	7%		1%		21%	3%
	Reggie Bush	2%	3%	1%		2%	1%
	Jerome Felton	1%		1%	2%		1%
	Brandon Tate			0%	2%		0%
	Percy Harvin			0%			0%
	Total	33%	30%	49%	42%	72%	46%
PASS	LeSean McCoy	13%	9%	6%	10%		7%
	Mike Gillislee	1%	6%	1%	2%		1%
	Charles Clay	12%	10%	11%	5%	6%	10%
	Robert Woods	8%	11%	8%	15%	6%	9%
	Marquise Goodwin	6%	6%	9%	15%		8%
	Sammy Watkins	11%	5%	7%		2%	6%
	Jonathan Williams			0%			0%
	Walt Powell	4%	7%	1%	6%	6%	3%
	Justin Hunter	6%	2%	2%	2%	2%	3%
	Reggie Bush	1%	3%	1%			1%
	Jerome Felton		2%	1%	2%	2%	1%
	Brandon Tate	2%	2%	1%		2%	1%
	Nick O'Leary	3%	1%	1%	3%	4%	2%
	Greg Salas		6%	0%			1%
	Percy Harvin			1%			0%
	Gerald Christian			0%			0%
	Dezmin Lewis	1%					0%
	Total	67%	70%	51%	58%	28%	54%

Positional Target Distribution vs NFL Average

		NFL Wide				Team Only			
		Left	Middle	Right	**Total**	Left	Middle	Right	**Total**
Deep	WR	1,012	576	971	**2,559**	19	5	30	**54**
	TE	151	144	158	**453**	7	3	5	**15**
	RB	25	4	40	**69**				
	All	**1,188**	**724**	**1,169**	**3,081**	**26**	**8**	**35**	**69**
Short	WR	3,025	1,756	3,127	**7,908**	68	15	59	**142**
	TE	810	862	1,118	**2,790**	26	13	33	**72**
	RB	992	609	1,091	**2,692**	23	13	22	**58**
	All	**4,827**	**3,227**	**5,336**	**13,390**	**117**	**41**	**114**	**272**
Total		**6,015**	**3,951**	**6,505**	**16,471**	**143**	**49**	**149**	**341**

Positional Success Rates vs NFL Average

		NFL Wide				Team Only			
		Left	Middle	Right	**Total**	Left	Middle	Right	**Total**
Deep	WR	37%	50%	38%	**40%**	21%	60%	37%	**33%**
	TE	44%	49%	43%	**46%**	43%	67%	40%	**47%**
	RB	32%	75%	25%	**30%**				
	All	**38%**	**50%**	**38%**	**41%**	**27%**	**63%**	**37%**	**36%**
Short	WR	52%	57%	51%	**53%**	51%	53%	61%	**56%**
	TE	50%	62%	52%	**54%**	46%	46%	48%	**47%**
	RB	47%	50%	44%	**46%**	57%	46%	55%	**53%**
	All	**51%**	**57%**	**50%**	**52%**	**51%**	**49%**	**56%**	**53%**
Total		**48%**	**56%**	**48%**	**50%**	**47%**	**51%**	**52%**	**50%**

Carolina Panthers

2017 Coaches

Head Coach:
Ron Rivera (6th yr)
Offensive Coordinator:
Mike Shula (5th yr)
Defensive Coordinator:
Sean McDermott (7th yr)

2017 Forecast

Wins	Div Rank
9	#2

Past Records

2016: 6-10
2015: 15-1
2014: 7-8-1

EASY HARD

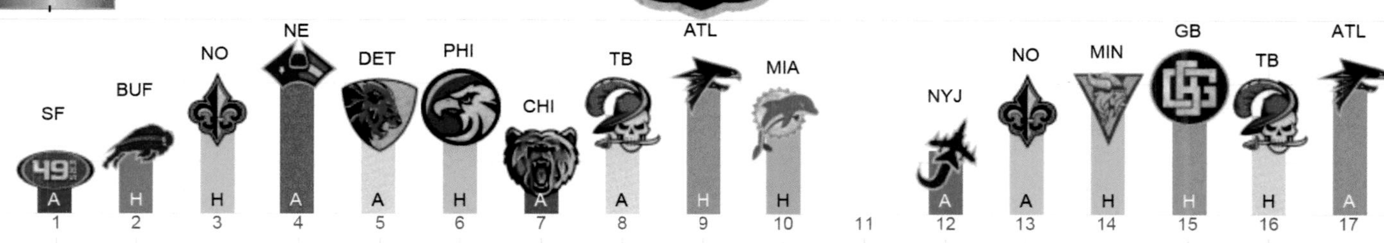

Key Players Lost

TXN	Player (POS)
Cut	Boston, Tre S
	Johnson, Devon RB
	Patmon, Tyler CB
	Rigsbee, Jordan T
	Rodgers, Jake T
	Soliai, Paul DT
	Tolbert, Mike RB
	Young, Lou CB
Declared Free Agent	Alecxih, Chas DT
	Brown, Corey WR
	Byrd, LaRon WR
	Ginn Jr., Ted WR
	Griffin, Michael S
	Johnson, Leonard CB
	Klein, A.J. LB
	Love, Kyle DT
	Remmers, Mike T
	Scott, Chris G
	Wendell, Ryan C
	Williams, Teddy CB

Average Line	# Games Favored	# Games Underdog
-0.6	9	6

Regular Season Wins: Past & Current Proj

Proj 2017 Wins  9

2016 Wins  6

Proj 2016 Wins  10.5

2015 Wins 15 

2014 Wins  7

2013 Wins  12

1 3 5 7 9 11 13 15

2017 Carolina Panthers Overview

The Super Bowl runner-up from 2015 found themselves in a slump in 2016, recording a 6-10 record and finishing in last place in the NFC South which they dominated the prior season. This came in large part to an offense which finished bottom-8 in EDSR (Early Down Success Rate) offense, offensive efficiency and pass protection efficiency vs a 1st place schedule. It was a huge difference for the front-running Panthers from 2015. In 2015 the Panthers led at halftime by 9.8 points per game on average, which was bested in the last 15 years only by the 2007 New England Patriots. In 2015, Carolina went 14-0 when leading at halftime but 3-2 when tied or trailing. They poured it on in the 3rd quarter and were able to ride a running game and predictable opposing offenses in the 2nd half to victory.

But things didn't go as smoothly last year. Despite leading at halftime in 10 games, they went just 6-4 in these games. They were unable to sustain leads in part due to their 22nd rated rushing offense (down from 6th in 2015) and their 25th rated EDSR offense (down from 2nd in 2015). And if they were behind or tied at halftime, these Panthers were unable to front-run and went 0-6, losing by over 12 points per game.

Great teams can overcome adversity and still win where other teams lose. The 2015 Panthers were that type of team. The 2016 Panthers were far from it. As an example of one key metric which showcases their slip: takeaways and giveaways. In 2015, the Panthers finished +20 in turnover margin. They went a perfect 13-0 when winning the turnover battle, but still emerged with a 4-2 record when losing it. Last year Carolina won the turnover battle in only 6 games, and went 5-1 in those 6 games. But in the 10 games they didn't win the turnover battle, Carolina went 1-9, with the lone win over the 49ers. It seems easy to suggest that the Panthers will win in 2017 if they just routinely win the turnover battle. But that is easier said than done. They threw 19 interceptions last year (just 10 in 2015) and they recorded 27 takeaways after taking 39 in 2015.

Step one is getting Cam Newton more comfortable and reducing these interceptions. Newton threw 64% of his interceptions on early downs, with over 1/3rd of his total interceptions coming on early downs with less than 10 yards to go.

(cont'd - see CAR2)

2017 Lineup & Cap Hits

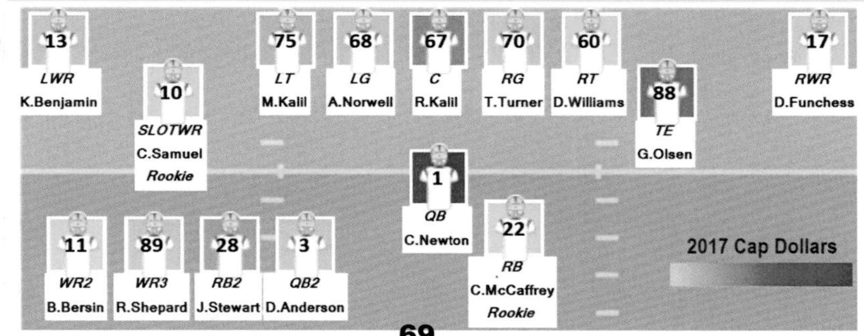

Key Free Agents/ Trades Added

Adams, Mike S
Clay, Kaelin WR
Gilbert, Garrett QB
Johnson, Charles WR
Kalil, Matt T
Moore, Zach DE
Munnerlyn, Captain CB
Peppers, Julius DE
Shepard, Russell WR

Drafted Players

Rd	Pk	Player (College)
1	8	RB - Christian McCaffrey (Stanford)
2	40	WR - Curtis Samuel (Ohio State)
	64	OT - Taylor Moton (Western Michigan)
3	77	DE - Daeshon Hall (Texas A&M)
5	152	CB - Corn Elder (Miami (FL))
6	192	DE - Alexander Armah (West Georgia)
7	233	K - Harrison Butker (Georgia Tech)

2017 Unit Spending

All DEF
All OFF

Positional Spending

	Rank	Total	2016 Rk
All OFF	7	$92.17M	9
QB	8	$22.88M	9
OL	17	$28.56M	13
RB	5	$11.78M	2
WR	29	$13.72M	27
TE	2	$15.23M	11
All DEF	15	$79.36M	32
DL	9	$36.69M	22
LB	9	$26.31M	12
CB	31	$7.34M	32
S	22	$9.02M	26

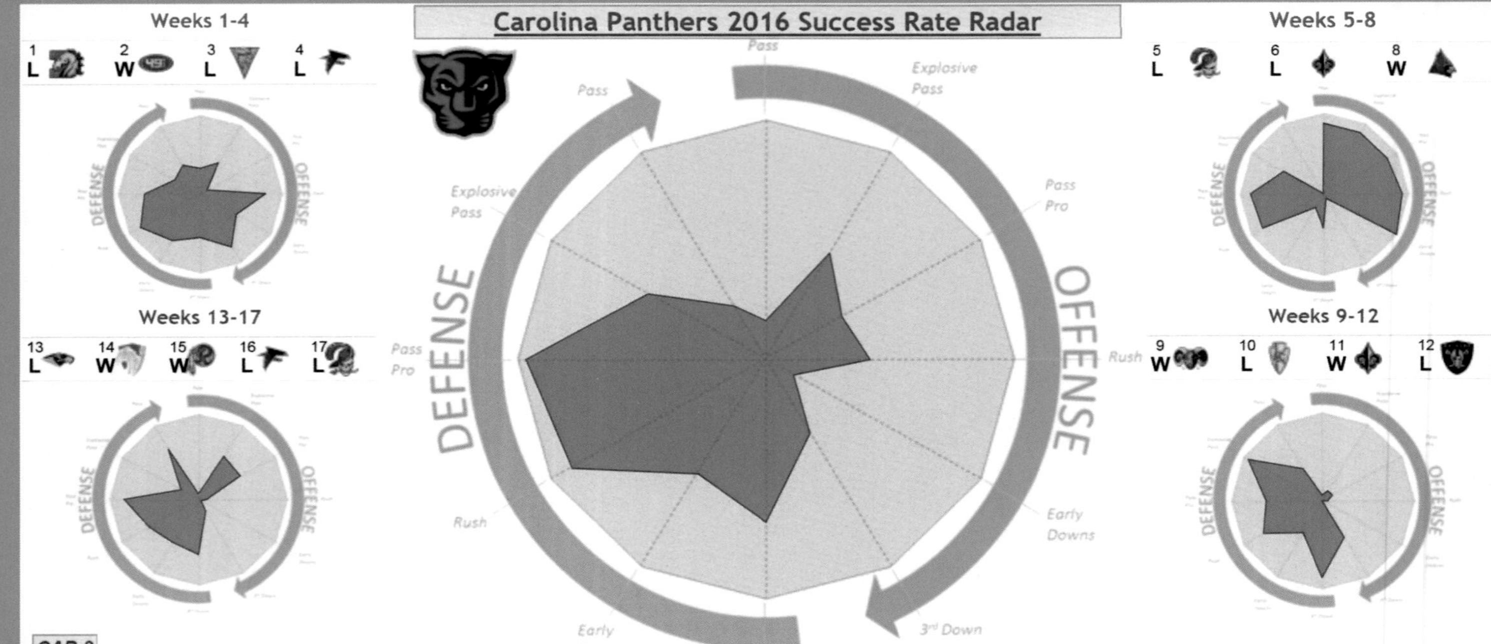

CAR-2

The phrase "live to fight another day" needs to be embraced by Newton. He cannot turn the ball over in situations where even an incompletion allows the Panthers with a very good chance to record a first down on the very next play. Carolina hopes improvements along the offensive line can assist Cam's confidence and give him more time in the pocket. They signed former Vikings LT Matt Kalil to a large $55M deal, and he will play alongside his brother at C, Ryan Kalil, who was one of the stronger points for the Panthers line last year until week 8, out of the bye, where he suffered an injury and played just one more game before going onto IR. Unfortunately he is likely to miss the entire offseason program, but the Panthers are hoping he won't have any setbacks in his recovery and will return at 100% prior to week 1. The Panthers let RT Mike Remmers leave and will roll at RT with either Michael Oher, their LT from 2016, or Daryl Williams. In either case, the line is certainly going to look different from 2016. And Cam Newton, OC Mike Shula and HC Ron Rivera hope it performs better as well.

Beyond just the new linemen, there is optimism for Panthers fans that the line may look better. It starts with the schedule. In 2016 the Panthers faced the 6th most difficult pass defenses with the 17th most difficult pass rushes. In 2017 those drop to 30th and 24th, respectively. Which should mean more time to read and react for Newton, and a better edge for his receivers in turning the attempts into completions. With Carolina facing the 3rd easiest schedule of pass defenses after facing the 6th hardest in 2016, it's the largest drop-off in pass defense for any team. And it should get off to a fast start, with its first 5 games coming against pass defenses ranking bottom-12, including #32, 29 and 28, by far the easiest pass defenses for any team through the first 5 weeks.

There is also the hope that through their draft this year, Carolina's two key early round acquisitions will allow Newton more time and better confidence simply with their presence on the field. While many look at Christian McCaffrey's 5'11", 202 pound frame and don't see a 3-down back, the reality is, they're right.

(cont'd - see CAR-3)

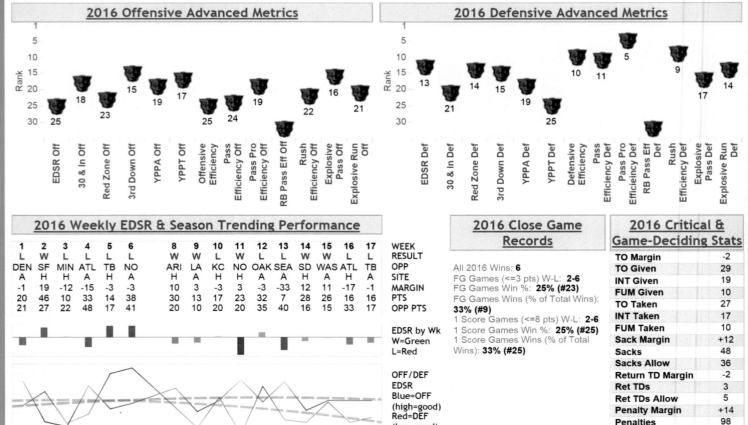

2016 Offensive Advanced Metrics

	Rank
EDSR Off	25
30 & In Off	18
Red Zone Off	23
3rd Down Off	15
YPPA Off	19
YPPT Off	17
Offensive Efficiency	25
Pass Efficiency Off	24
Pass Pro Efficiency Off	19
RB Pass Eff Off	
Rush Efficiency Off	22
Explosive Pass Off	16
Explosive Run Off	21

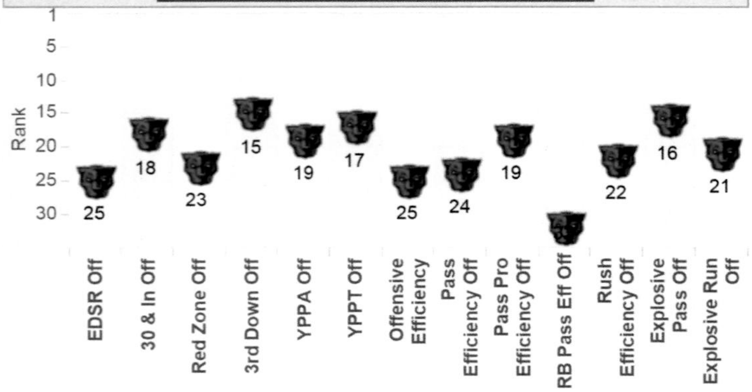

2016 Defensive Advanced Metrics

	Rank
EDSR Def	13
30 & In Def	21
Red Zone Def	14
3rd Down Def	15
YPPA Def	19
YPPT Def	25
Defensive Efficiency	10
Pass Efficiency Def	11
Pass Pro Efficiency Def	5
RB Pass Eff Def	
Rush Efficiency Def	9
Explosive Pass Def	17
Explosive Run Def	14

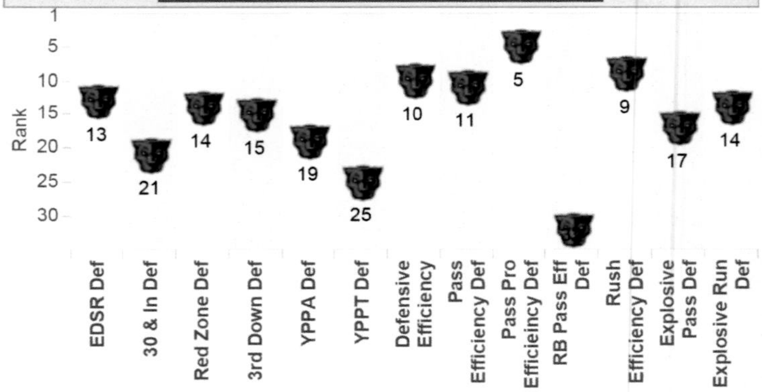

2016 Weekly EDSR & Season Trending Performance

WEEK	1	2	3	4	5	6	8	9	10	11	12	13	14	15	16	17
RESULT	L	W	L	L	L	L	W	W	L	W	L	L	W	W	L	L
OPP	DEN	SF	MIN	ATL	TB	NO	ARI	LA	KC	NO	OAK	SEA	SD	WAS	ATL	TB
SITE	A	H	H	A	H	A	H	A	H	H	A	A	H	A	H	A
MARGIN	-1	19	-12	-15	-3	-3	10	3	-3	3	-3	-33	12	11	-17	-1
PTS	20	46	10	33	14	38	30	13	17	23	32	7	28	26	16	16
OPP PTS	21	27	22	48	17	41	20	10	20	20	35	40	16	15	33	17

EDSR by Wk
W=Green
L=Red

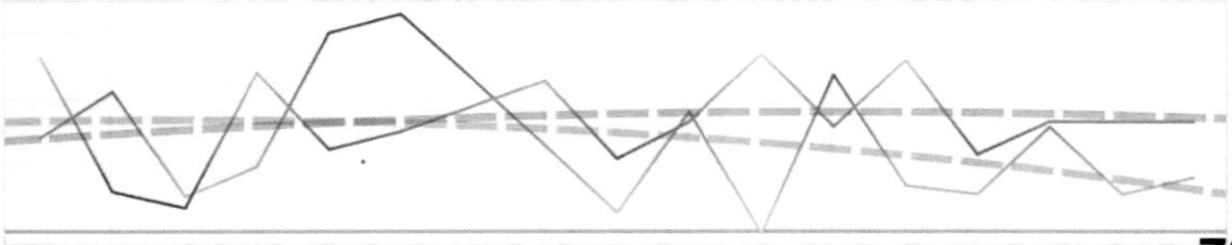

OFF/DEF EDSR
Blue=OFF (high=good)
Red=DEF (low=good)

2016 Close Game Records

All 2016 Wins: **6**
FG Games (<=3 pts) W-L: **2-6**
FG Games Win %: **25% (#23)**
FG Games Wins (% of Total Wins): **33% (#9)**
1 Score Games (<=8 pts) W-L: **2-6**
1 Score Games Win %: **25% (#25)**
1 Score Games Wins (% of Total Wins): **33% (#25)**

2016 Critical & Game-Deciding Stats

TO Margin	-2
TO Given	29
INT Given	19
FUM Given	10
TO Taken	27
INT Taken	17
FUM Taken	10
Sack Margin	+12
Sacks	48
Sacks Allow	36
Return TD Margin	-2
Ret TDs	3
Ret TDs Allow	5
Penalty Margin	+14
Penalties	98
Opponent Penalties	112

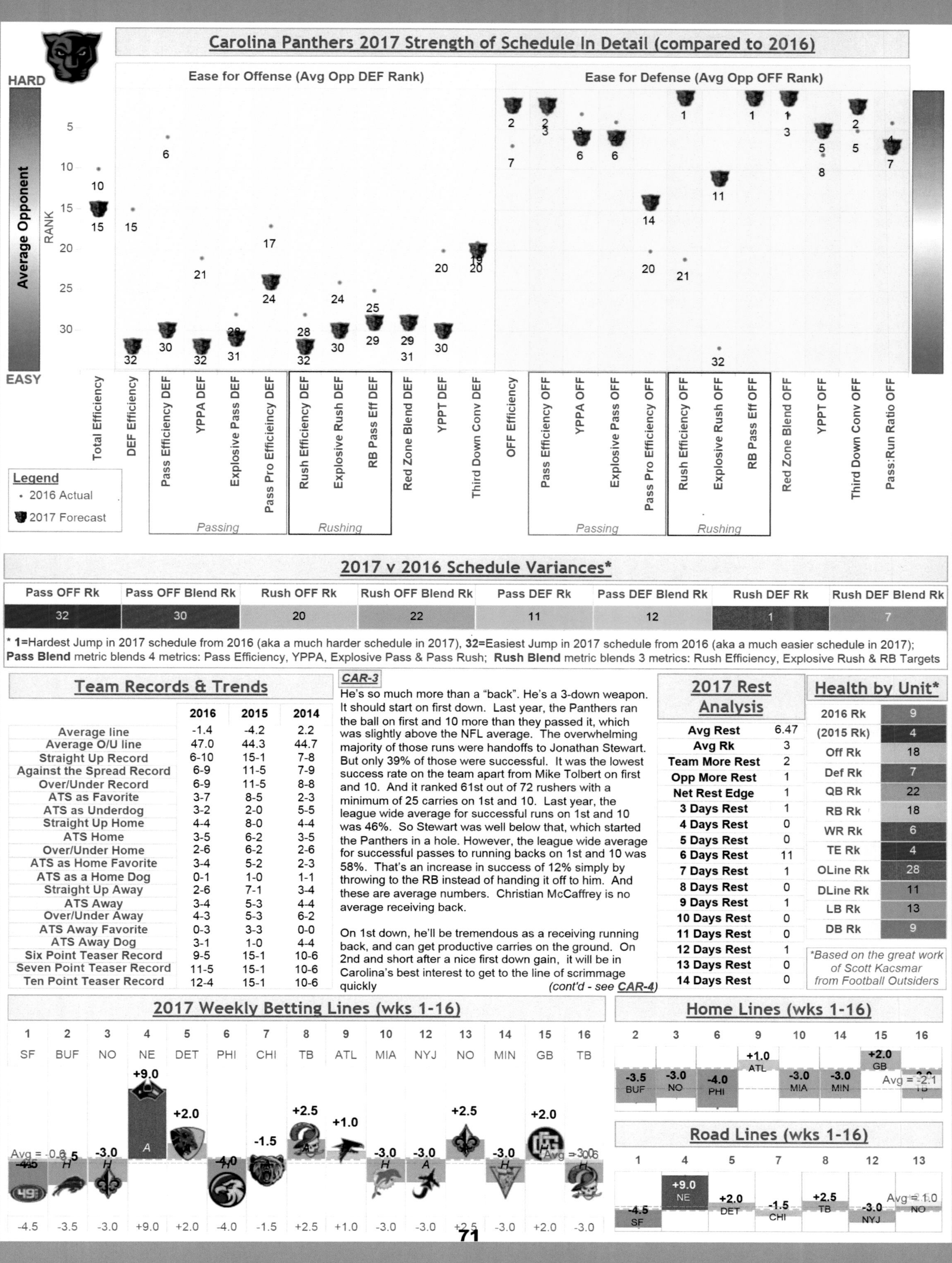

Carolina Panthers 2017 Strength of Schedule In Detail (compared to 2016)

2017 v 2016 Schedule Variances*

Pass OFF Rk	Pass OFF Blend Rk	Rush OFF Rk	Rush OFF Blend Rk	Pass DEF Rk	Pass DEF Blend Rk	Rush DEF Rk	Rush DEF Blend Rk
32	30	20	22	11	12	1	7

* **1**=Hardest Jump in 2017 schedule from 2016 (aka a much harder schedule in 2017), **32**=Easiest Jump in 2017 schedule from 2016 (aka a much easier schedule in 2017); **Pass Blend** metric blends 4 metrics: Pass Efficiency, YPPA, Explosive Pass & Pass Rush; **Rush Blend** metric blends 3 metrics: Rush Efficiency, Explosive Rush & RB Targets

Team Records & Trends

	2016	2015	2014
Average line	-1.4	-4.2	2.2
Average O/U line	47.0	44.3	44.7
Straight Up Record	6-10	15-1	7-8
Against the Spread Record	6-9	11-5	7-9
Over/Under Record	6-9	11-5	8-8
ATS as Favorite	3-7	8-5	2-3
ATS as Underdog	3-2	2-0	5-5
Straight Up Home	4-4	8-0	4-4
ATS Home	3-5	6-2	3-5
Over/Under Home	2-6	6-2	2-6
ATS as Home Favorite	3-4	5-2	2-3
ATS as a Home Dog	0-1	1-0	1-1
Straight Up Away	2-6	7-1	3-4
ATS Away	3-4	5-3	4-4
Over/Under Away	4-3	5-3	6-2
ATS Away Favorite	0-3	3-3	0-0
ATS Away Dog	3-1	1-0	4-4
Six Point Teaser Record	9-5	15-1	10-6
Seven Point Teaser Record	11-5	15-1	10-6
Ten Point Teaser Record	12-4	15-1	10-6

CAR-3

He's so much more than a "back". He's a 3-down weapon. It should start on first down. Last year, the Panthers ran the ball on first and 10 more than they passed it, which was slightly above the NFL average. The overwhelming majority of those runs were handoffs to Jonathan Stewart. But only 39% of those were successful. It was the lowest success rate on the team apart from Mike Tolbert on first and 10. And it ranked 61st out of 72 rushers with a minimum of 25 carries on 1st and 10. Last year, the league wide average for successful runs on 1st and 10 was 46%. So Stewart was well below that, which started the Panthers in a hole. However, the league wide average for successful passes to running backs on 1st and 10 was 58%. That's an increase in success of 12% simply by throwing to the RB instead of handing it off to him. And these are average numbers. Christian McCaffrey is no average receiving back.

On 1st down, he'll be tremendous as a receiving running back, and can get productive carries on the ground. On 2nd and short after a nice first down gain, it will be in Carolina's best interest to get to the line of scrimmage quickly *(cont'd - see CAR-4)*

2017 Rest Analysis

Avg Rest	6.47
Avg Rk	3
Team More Rest	2
Opp More Rest	1
Net Rest Edge	1
3 Days Rest	1
4 Days Rest	0
5 Days Rest	0
6 Days Rest	11
7 Days Rest	1
8 Days Rest	0
9 Days Rest	1
10 Days Rest	0
11 Days Rest	0
12 Days Rest	1
13 Days Rest	0
14 Days Rest	0

Health by Unit*

2016 Rk	9
(2015 Rk)	4
Off Rk	18
Def Rk	7
QB Rk	22
RB Rk	18
WR Rk	6
TE Rk	4
OLine Rk	28
DLine Rk	11
LB Rk	13
DB Rk	9

**Based on the great work of Scott Kacsmar from Football Outsiders*

2017 Weekly Betting Lines (wks 1-16)

1	2	3	4	5	6	7	8	9	10	12	13	14	15	16
SF	BUF	NO	NE	DET	PHI	CHI	TB	ATL	MIA	NYJ	NO	MIN	GB	TB
-4.5	-3.5	-3.0	+9.0	+2.0	-4.0	-1.5	+2.5	+1.0	-3.0	-3.0	+2.5	-3.0	+2.0	-3.0

Avg = -0.6

Home Lines (wks 1-16)

2	3	6	9	10	14	15	16
BUF	NO	PHI	ATL	MIA	MIN	GB	TB
-3.5	-3.0	-4.0	+1.0	-3.0	-3.0	+2.0	-3.0

Avg = -2.1

Road Lines (wks 1-16)

1	4	5	7	8	12	13
SF	NE	DET	CHI	TB	NYJ	NO
-4.5	+9.0	+2.0	-1.5	+2.5	-3.0	+2.5

Avg = 1.0

Carolina Panthers 2016 Play Analysis

2016 Play Tendencies

All Pass %	57%
All Pass Rk	24
All Rush %	43%
All Rush Rk	9
1 Score Pass %	56%
1 Score Pass Rk	21
2015 1 Score Pass %	53%
2015 1 Score Pass Rk	25
Pass Increase %	4%
Pass Increase Rk	6
1 Score Rush %	44%
1 Score Rush Rk	12
Up Pass %	57%
Up Pass Rk	17
Up Rush %	43%
Up Rush Rk	16
Down Pass %	58%
Down Pass Rk	26
Down Rush %	42%
Down Rush Rk	7

2016 Down & Distance Tendencies

Down	Distance	Total Plays	Pass Rate	Run Rate	Play Success %
1	Short (1-3)	10	20%	80%	40%
	Med (4-7)	7	29%	71%	43%
	Long (8-10)	314	49%	51%	47%
	XL (11+)	16	63%	38%	31%
2	Short (1-3)	37	35%	65%	62%
	Med (4-7)	69	46%	54%	39%
	Long (8-10)	114	59%	41%	40%
	XL (11+)	31	81%	19%	23%
3	Short (1-3)	41	51%	49%	56%
	Med (4-7)	48	90%	10%	46%
	Long (8-10)	34	94%	6%	29%
	XL (11+)	37	92%	8%	16%
4	Short (1-3)	5	0%	100%	100%
	Med (4-7)	1	100%	0%	100%
	XL (11+)	1	100%	0%	0%

Shotgun %:

Under Center	Shotgun
24%	76%
37%	*63%*

37% AVG 63%

Run Rate:

Under Center	Shotgun
75%	28%

68% AVG 23%

Pass Rate:

Under Center	Shotgun
25%	72%

32% AVG 77%

Short Yardage Intelligence:

2nd and Short Run

Run Freq	Run % Rk	NFL Run Freq Avg	Run 1D Rate	Run NFL 1D Avg
61%	22	65%	68%	71%

2nd and Short Pass

Pass Freq	Pass % Rk	NFL Pass Freq Avg	Pass 1D Rate	Pass NFL 1D Avg
39%	9	35%	43%	52%

Most Frequent Play

Down	Distance	Play Type	Player	Total Plays	Play Success %
1	Short (1-3)	RUSH	Jonathan Stewart	6	17%
	Med (4-7)	RUSH	Cam Newton	3	67%
	Long (8-10)	RUSH	Jonathan Stewart	88	43%
	XL (11+)	PASS	Greg Olsen	3	67%
		RUSH	Cameron Artis-Payne	3	0%
2	Short (1-3)	RUSH	Jonathan Stewart	12	83%
	Med (4-7)	RUSH	Jonathan Stewart	20	45%
	Long (8-10)	RUSH	Jonathan Stewart	27	30%
	XL (11+)	PASS	Ted Ginn	6	33%
3	Short (1-3)	RUSH	Cam Newton	13	77%
	Med (4-7)	PASS	Greg Olsen	10	40%
	Long (8-10)	PASS	Greg Olsen	7	57%
			Kelvin Benjamin	7	29%
	XL (11+)	PASS	Ted Ginn	8	25%

Most Successful Play*

Down	Distance	Play Type	Player	Total Plays	Play Success %
1	Short (1-3)	RUSH	Jonathan Stewart	6	17%
	Long (8-10)	RUSH	Ted Ginn	11	82%
2	Short (1-3)	RUSH	Jonathan Stewart	12	83%
	Med (4-7)	RUSH	Cam Newton	6	83%
	Long (8-10)	PASS	Greg Olsen	13	77%
	XL (11+)	PASS	Greg Olsen	5	40%
3	Short (1-3)	RUSH	Jonathan Stewart	5	100%
	Med (4-7)	PASS	Ted Ginn	6	67%
	Long (8-10)	PASS	Greg Olsen	7	57%
	XL (11+)	PASS	Ted Ginn	8	25%

**Minimum 5 plays to qualify*

2016 Snap Rates

Week	Opp	Score	Greg Olsen	Kelvin Benjamin	Ted Ginn	Corey Brown	Jonathan Stewart	Devin Funchess	Ed Dickson
1	DEN	L 21-20	73 (100%)	52 (71%)	45 (62%)	39 (53%)	42 (58%)	39 (53%)	30 (41%)
2	SF	W 46-27	76 (92%)	52 (63%)	49 (59%)	43 (52%)	7 (8%)	54 (65%)	35 (42%)
3	MIN	L 22-10	77 (100%)	61 (79%)	49 (64%)	45 (58%)		42 (55%)	24 (31%)
4	ATL	L 48-33	67 (94%)	58 (82%)	47 (66%)	54 (76%)		27 (38%)	21 (30%)
5	TB	L 17-14	54 (100%)	46 (85%)	28 (52%)	24 (44%)		21 (39%)	24 (44%)
6	NO	L 41-38	81 (100%)	60 (74%)	38 (47%)	42 (52%)	54 (67%)	45 (56%)	35 (43%)
8	ARI	W 30-20	67 (100%)	46 (69%)	35 (52%)	40 (60%)	46 (69%)	30 (45%)	26 (39%)
9	LA	W 13-10	63 (98%)	53 (83%)	43 (67%)	33 (52%)	44 (69%)	29 (45%)	23 (36%)
10	KC	L 20-17	73 (100%)	58 (79%)	53 (73%)	35 (48%)	53 (73%)	29 (40%)	33 (45%)
11	NO	W 23-20	62 (100%)	33 (53%)	35 (56%)	23 (37%)	49 (79%)	37 (60%)	35 (56%)
12	OAK	L 35-32	65 (100%)	43 (66%)	41 (63%)	27 (42%)	38 (58%)	34 (52%)	31 (48%)
13	SEA	L 40-7	58 (100%)	34 (59%)	40 (69%)	37 (64%)	42 (72%)	28 (48%)	24 (41%)
14	SD	W 28-16	69 (100%)	53 (77%)	41 (59%)	25 (36%)	57 (83%)	21 (30%)	32 (46%)
15	WAS	W 26-15	63 (86%)	43 (59%)	32 (44%)	33 (45%)	52 (71%)	44 (60%)	36 (49%)
16	ATL	L 33-16	39 (57%)	52 (75%)	56 (81%)	46 (67%)	40 (58%)	15 (22%)	36 (52%)
17	TB	L 17-16	46 (66%)	59 (84%)	54 (77%)	39 (56%)	39 (56%)		33 (47%)
	Grand Total		1,033 (93%)	803 (72%)	686 (62%)	585 (53%)	563 (63%)	495 (47%)	478 (43%)

Personnel Groupings

Personnel	Team %	NFL Avg	Succ. %
1-1 [3WR]	55%	60%	45%
1-2 [2WR]	27%	19%	41%
2-1 [2WR]	11%	7%	39%
2-2 [1WR]	7%	3%	48%

Grouping Tendencies

Personnel	Pass Rate	Pass Succ. %	Run Succ. %
1-1 [3WR]	65%	44%	47%
1-2 [2WR]	59%	39%	44%
2-1 [2WR]	32%	44%	37%
2-2 [1WR]	20%	50%	47%

Red Zone Targets (min 3)

Receiver	All	Inside 5	6-10	11-20
Greg Olsen	16	4	1	11
Kelvin Benjamin	15	3	3	9
Devin Funchess	14		3	11
Corey Brown	8	1	2	5
Mike Tolbert	4	1		3
Ed Dickson	3	2		1
Jonathan Stewart	3		1	2

Red Zone Rushes (min 3)

Rusher	All	Inside 5	6-10	11-20
Jonathan Stewart	40	16	6	18
Cam Newton	19	8	3	8
Fozzy Whittaker	7		2	5
Mike Tolbert	7	2	2	3
Cameron Artis-Pay..	3	1		2

Early Down Target Rate

	RB	TE	WR
Team	14%	28%	57%
NFL AVG	*19%*	*20%*	*61%*

Overall Target Success %

RB	TE	WR
37% #32	56% #12	43% #28

Carolina Panthers 2016 Passing Recap & 2017 Outlook

When a quarterback who is big but really doesn't love contact gets hit as much as Cam Newton, it inevitably will have an impact on his game. However, for Newton, it wasn't so much the volume (as many will argue) but the type of hit. That's because in 2015, Carolina's offensive line allowed an adjusted sack rate of 6.9%, ranking 21st in the NFL. Last year they allowed an adjusted sack rate of 6.2%, a marginal improvement, which ranked 19th on the year. The difference was Cam was taking some brutal hits in the pocket, trying to wait for things to develop further downfield or scrambling around for too long without sound protection. The way to alleviate a lot of the more brutal hits in the pocket (as well as those sustained while running) is to dump the ball off to quicker, higher percentage targets. And the Panthers just acquired two of them: McCaffrey and Samuel. Newton must focus on modifying his game some to perfect the touch on short targets and reject the instinct to just tuck the ball and run when under pressure. If he can master these techniques, not only will the offense be more productive, Newton's career will be longer. Shula must focus on higher percentage targets on early downs to increase efficiency and avoid more 3rd down attempts.

Cam Newton Rating All Downs

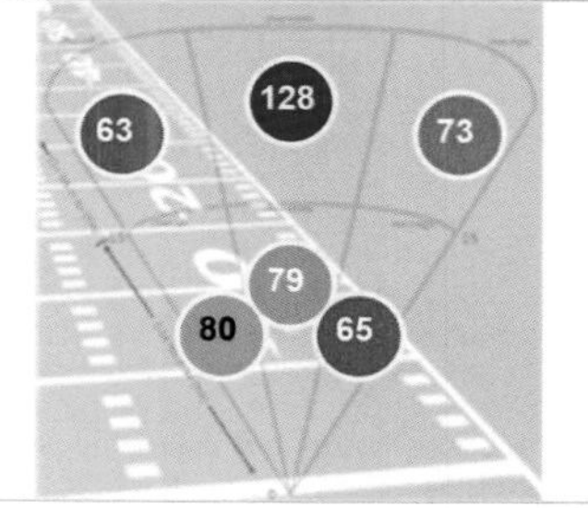

Cam Newton Rating Early Downs

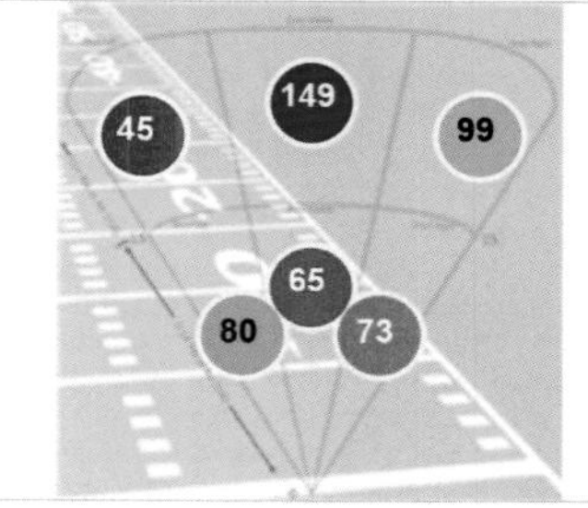

2016 Standard Passing Table

QB	Comp	Att	Comp %	Yds	YPA	TDs	INT	Sacks	Rating	Rk
Cam Newton	270	509	53%	3,504	6.9	19	14	36	76.0	43
NFL Avg			63%		7.2				90.4	

2016 Advanced Passing Table

QB	Success %	EDSR Passing Success %	20+ Yd Pass Gains	20+ Yd Pass %	30+ Yd Pass Gains	30+ Yd Pass %	Air Yds per Comp	YAC per Comp	20+ Air Yd Comp	20+ Air Yd %
Cam Newton	41%	43%	42	8%	14	3%	7.9	5.1	20	4%
NFL Avg	44%	48%	27	8%	10	3%	6.4	4.8	12	4%

Interception Rates by Down

Yards to Go	1	2	3	4	Total
1 & 2	0.0%	0.0%	0.0%	0.0%	0.0%
3, 4, 5	25.0%	4.8%	0.0%	0.0%	3.0%
6 - 9	0.0%	5.2%	1.9%		3.6%
10 - 14	2.2%	0.0%	2.3%	25.0%	2.0%
15+	0.0%	0.0%	11.1%	0.0%	5.0%
Total	2.5%	2.4%	2.4%	11.1%	2.6%

3rd Down Passing - Short of Sticks Analysis

QB	Avg Yds to Go	Air Yds (of Comps)	Avg Yds Short	Short of Sticks Rate	Rk
Cam Newton	8.6	8.5	-0.1	41%	17
NFL Avg	7.6	6.8	-0.8	57%	

Air Yds vs YAC

Air Yds %	YAC %	Rk
49%	51%	35
54%	46%	

2016 Receiving Recap & 2017 Outlook

With the new personnel, I believe Carolina needs to overhaul a lot of their personnel packages and formational decisions. They passed the ball 59% of the time when in 12 personnel, which they used 4th most in the NFL, but their success rate was terrible, and it didn't matter which position they targeted with the attempt, all were bad. With Benjamin entering OTAs overweight, Carolina's passing game will lean strongly on Olsen again. But they need either Benjamin (more likely) or Funchess (less likely) to have a big year in 2017 because deeper outside opportunity will be there given the likely frequent, shorter targets to McCaffrey and Samuel.

Player *Min 50 Targets*	Targets	Comp %	YPA	Rating	TOARS	Success %	Success Rk	Missed YPA Rk	YAS % Rk	TDs
Greg Olsen	129	62%	8.3	83	5.0	57%	29	52	51	3
Kelvin Benjamin	117	54%	8.0	90	4.9	49%	88	86	64	7
Ted Ginn	95	57%	7.9	75	4.3	42%	125	136	34	4
Devin Funchess	58	40%	6.4	78	3.6	38%	138	142	22	4
Corey Brown	53	51%	5.1	64	3.3	38%	140	139	86	1

Directional Passer Rating Delivered

Receiver	Short Left	Short Middle	Short Right	Deep Left	Deep Middle	Deep Right	Player Total
Greg Olsen	79	104	80	6	88	106	83
Kelvin Benjamin	60	116	91	115	106	82	90
Ted Ginn	87	10	45	23	158	33	75
Devin Funchess	49	67	41	129	158	111	78
Corey Brown	91	61	85	50	0	40	64
Fozzy Whittaker	99	46	66			40	81
Team Total	77	86	67	71	130	81	80

2016 Rushing Recap & 2017 Outlook

Jonathan Stewart really took a step back in 2016, after averaging 4.1 yards per attempt in 2015. Gaining just 3.8 yards per attempt and positing a 41% early down success rate, it was clear the Panthers would need to provide support at the position. Christian McCaffrey will hopefully be that player to provide a spark and generate those 2nd level yards which are vital for an offense like Carolina's, which seems to thrive emotionally on big, successful plays. Whoever takes carries in the backfield is going to enjoy facing the NFL's easiest schedule of opposing run defenses in 2017. These defenses also ranked 3rd worst in defending explosive runs. Which is what will make McCaffrey so dangerous. When he gets space to eat he scores from anywhere.

Player *Min 50 Rushes*	Rushes	YPA	Success %	Success Rk	Missed YPA Rk	YTS % Rk	YAS % Rk	Early Down Success %	Early Down Success Rk	TDs
Jonathan Stewart	218	3.8	43%	49	50	43	30	41%	54	9
Fozzy Whittaker	57	4.6	37%	64	57	67	47	38%	62	0

Yards per Carry by Direction

Directional Run Frequency

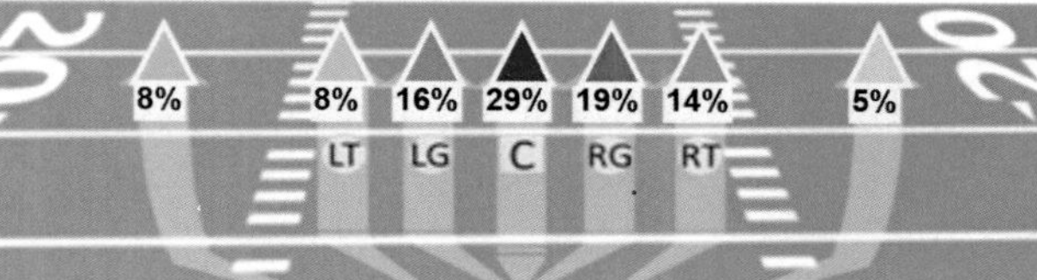

before their opponent can rotate in a short yardage package, and run McCaffrey against the base defense. On 2nd or 3rd and medium or long, McCaffrey is your prototypical "Weapon X" who can wreak havoc from any position he's lined up at. And that's one of the biggest keys for OC Mike Shula. He needs to implement McCaffrey in many different positions on the field. Every single RB position as well as line him up in the slot – he's worked with longtime reliable slot WR Brandon Stokley on releases and playing from the slot. Of course, he has the soft hands which are part of the family genes (father, WR Ed McCaffrey) and his short area quickness and acceleration make him a major threat anytime you can get him the ball in space.

Last year the Panthers targeted Greg Olsen far more than most teams target their TE. 28% of Carolina's total target allocation went to the TE position, well above average. And with a 56% success rate (12th best in the NFL) it was for good reason. Particularly when their WR targets netted only a 43% success rate, 28th in the league. WR Curtis Samuel should help out immensely here. The Panthers didn't have a reliable slot weapon last year. Olsen worked as TE, Kelvin Benjamin was their WR1 and Ted Ginn was the little speedster who they would look to hit deep. The success rate of all receivers outside of Olsen was laughable, and slot WRs typically have a solid shot at infusing a ton of success simply because of where they line up and the routes they can run. It doesn't take much to get the slot WR the ball with a bit of space such that even a minimal gain stands to be successful, and one missed tackle and another first down gain is likely. Samuel should be able to inject this type of success into the offense, and it should come on plays where Newton doesn't have to hold onto the ball as long to take those hits which rocked his 2016 season.

The ability to get highly successful targets to both McCaffrey and Samuel should be a massive boon to the offense. They can still target their taller, lankier receivers of Benjamin and Funchess out wide and in the red zone, but they should find the bulk of their success from the triumvirate of Olsen, McCaffrey and Samuel. This increased efficiency of the passing game could make the running game even more dynamic. With this core, they could seamlessly shift between 11 and 12 personnel by rotating between Ed Dickson and Devin Funchess (and I'd be inclined to use Samuel as WR2 in 12 personnel rather than Funchess).

But Cam Newton must take care of himself, as well. He will have to stop running the ball as often and instead do so in +EV situations. For example, inside the 5 yard line he's by far the best threat on the Panthers. But in the red zone between the 6-20, Newton's 36% success rate on rushes was worse than rushes by Stewart, Tolbert or passes to Olsen or Benjamin. With new weapons in the mix, Newton must preserve himself for the times when the benefits outweigh the risks.

Division History: Season Wins & 2017 Projection

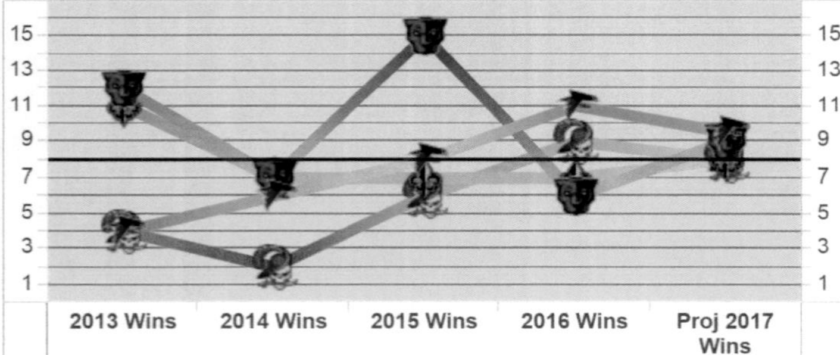

Rank of 2017 Defensive Pass Efficiency Faced by Week

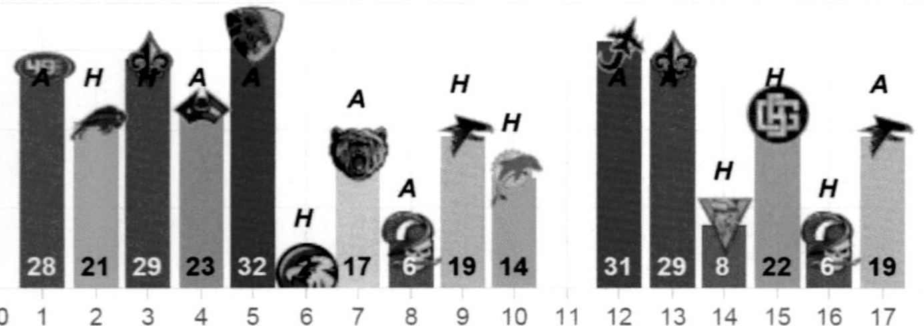

Rank of 2017 Defensive Rush Efficiency Faced by Week

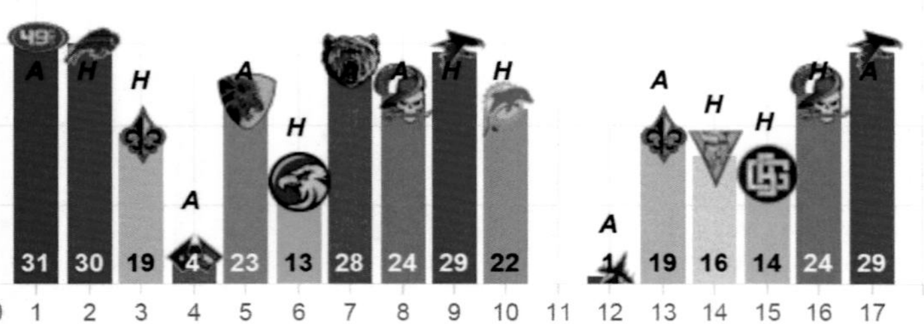

2016 Situational Usage by Player & Position

Usage Rate by Score

		Being Blown Out (14+)	Down Big (9-13)	One Score	Large Lead (9-13)	Blowout Lead (14+)	Grand Total
RUSH	Jonathan Stewart	19%	14%	23%	38%	31%	24%
	Ted Ginn	1%	4%	2%	1%		2%
	Fozzy Whittaker	5%	5%	6%	5%	9%	6%
	Corey Brown	1%		0%			0%
	Mike Tolbert	4%		4%	6%	4%	4%
	Cameron Artis-Payne	1%	4%	7%			4%
	Total	30%	27%	41%	51%	44%	40%
PASS	Jonathan Stewart	1%	4%	2%	7%	1%	2%
	Greg Olsen	16%	20%	14%	12%	13%	14%
	Kelvin Benjamin	14%	18%	13%	8%	11%	13%
	Ted Ginn	14%	9%	10%	7%	10%	10%
	Fozzy Whittaker	6%	7%	3%	1%	2%	4%
	Devin Funchess	8%	5%	6%	7%	7%	6%
	Corey Brown	6%	7%	5%	4%	9%	6%
	Mike Tolbert	1%	2%	2%	1%		2%
	Cameron Artis-Payne			0%			0%
	Ed Dickson	3%	2%	2%	1%	2%	2%
	Brenton Bersin	1%		1%			1%
	Chris Manhertz	1%					0%
	Damiere Byrd			0%			0%
	Total	70%	73%	59%	49%	56%	60%

Positional Target Distribution vs NFL Average

		NFL Wide				Team Only			
		Left	Middle	Right	**Total**	Left	Middle	Right	**Total**
Deep	WR	1,000	564	976	**2,540**	31	17	25	**73**
	TE	150	139	147	**436**	8	8	16	**32**
	RB	25	4	39	**68**			1	**1**
	All	**1,175**	**707**	**1,162**	**3,044**	**39**	**25**	**42**	**106**
Short	WR	3,006	1,731	3,063	**7,800**	87	40	123	**250**
	TE	809	851	1,105	**2,765**	27	24	46	**97**
	RB	1,001	618	1,099	**2,718**	14	4	14	**32**
	All	**4,816**	**3,200**	**5,267**	**13,283**	**128**	**68**	**183**	**379**
Total		**5,991**	**3,907**	**6,429**	**16,327**	**167**	**93**	**225**	**485**

Positional Success Rates vs NFL Average

		NFL Wide				Team Only			
		Left	Middle	Right	**Total**	Left	Middle	Right	**Total**
Deep	WR	37%	50%	38%	**40%**	35%	71%	32%	**42%**
	TE	45%	50%	44%	**46%**	25%	50%	38%	**38%**
	RB	32%	75%	26%	**31%**			0%	**0%**
	All	**38%**	**50%**	**39%**	**41%**	**33%**	**64%**	**33%**	**41%**
Short	WR	52%	57%	52%	**53%**	48%	50%	37%	**43%**
	TE	50%	61%	51%	**54%**	52%	71%	67%	**64%**
	RB	47%	50%	44%	**46%**	50%	25%	57%	**50%**
	All	**51%**	**57%**	**50%**	**52%**	**49%**	**56%**	**46%**	**49%**
Total		**48%**	**55%**	**48%**	**50%**	**46%**	**58%**	**44%**	**47%**

Chicago Bears

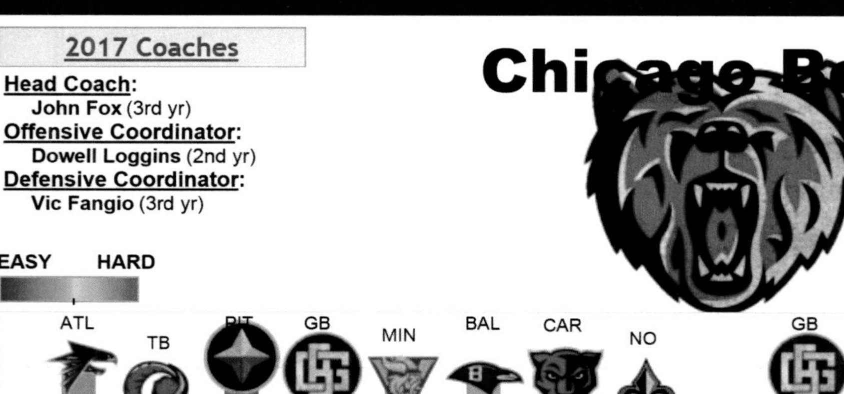

2017 Coaches

Head Coach:
John Fox (3rd yr)
Offensive Coordinator:
Dowell Loggins (2nd yr)
Defensive Coordinator:
Vic Fangio (3rd yr)

2017 Forecast

Wins	Div Rank
5.5	#4

Past Records

2016: 3-13
2015: 6-10
2014: 5-11

EASY **HARD**

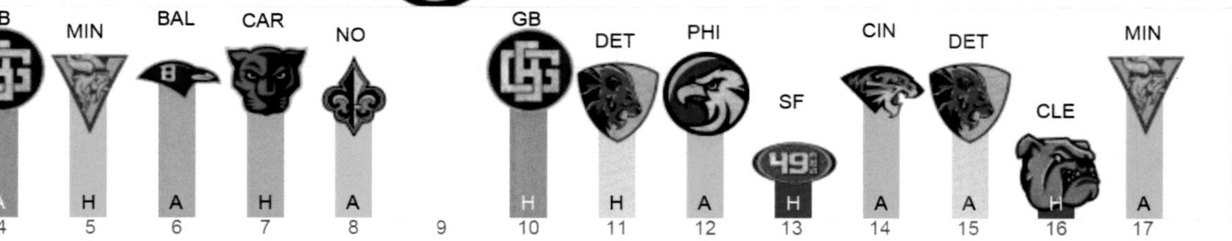

Key Players Lost

TXN	Player (POS)
Cut	Porter, Tracy CB
	Royal, Eddie WR
	Sutton, Will DT
	Whitfield, Kermit WR
Declared Free Agent	Acho, Sam LB
	Adams, Mike T
	Banks, Johnthan CB
	Barkley, Matt QB
	Boykin, Brandon CB
	Fales, David QB
	Hoyer, Brian QB
	Jeffery, Alshon WR
	Larsen, Ted C
	Paulsen, Logan TE
	Wilson, C.J. DT
	Wilson, Marquess WR

Average Line	# Games Favored	# Games Underdog
+4.1	2	13

2017 Chicago Bears Overview

Like a terrible horror movie sequel, so many questions surrounded the Bears as they entered 2016, but unfortunately, this franchise now has even more questions following the tumultuous season. The year was full of very few "ups" and mostly "downs" (both literally and figuratively) but only true optimists could see the silver linings in some of what went down in 2016.

The 2015 Bears were led by Offensive Coordinator Adam Gase employing a strategy to limit Jay Cutler's influence on the team. They shifted from the most pass heavy team in the NFL down to one of the most run heavy teams in Gase's one season. When Gase left and was replaced by Dowell Loggins, it was unclear what strategy they would employ. The team also lost their lead RB, Matt Forte, to the Jets. Many questions surrounded the Bears offense, their cap structure (with both Cutler and WR Alshon Jeffery carrying significant cap hits).

Skip past the 2016 season to present day. The team is now without both Jay Cutler and Alshon Jeffery. They bid against themselves in free agency to acquire QB Mike Glennon on a 3 year, $45M contract. They mortgaged two, third round picks and a fourth round pick to move up one spot in the draft to acquire QB Mitch Trubisky. Those two moves in conjunction are peculiar. Neither quarterback proved worthy in either arena (college or the NFL) to prove the opportunity cost was worth sacrificing. With such small sample sizes on each player, it was a total dice roll, based on projections, scouting and forecasting.

Let's assume the Bears feel confident enough in their ability to do all three (projections, scouting and forecasting) better than other teams without a franchise quarterback. Either move by itself would be understandable if you trust the Bears and their process. If they really are better at evaluation and projection than other QB needy teams, and Trubisky turns into a franchise quarterback, the ransom they paid to acquire him will be an afterthought. So why Glennon too? Why acquire Glennon at such a premium with such guaranteed money if, in all the scouting done on Trubisky, the Bears realized he was their "guy" and they coveted him and would pay to draft him?

(cont'd - see CHI2)

Key Free Agents/ Trades Added

Amukamara, Prince CB
Compton, Tom T
Cruz, Victor WR
Demps, Quintin S
Glennon, Mike QB
Howard, Jaye DT
Randle, Rueben WR
Sims, Dion TE
Wheaton, Markus WR
Wright, Kendall WR

Drafted Players

Rd	Pk	Player (College)
1	2	QB - Mitchell Trubisky (North Carolina)
2	45	TE - Adam Shaheen (Ashland)
4	112	S - Eddie Jackson (Alabama)
	119	RB - Tarik Cohen (North Carolina A&T)
5	147	G - Jordan Morgan (Kutztown)

Regular Season Wins: Past & Current Proj

Proj 2017 Wins 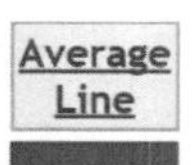 5.5

2016 Wins 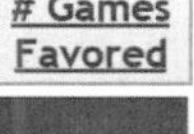 3

Proj 2016 Wins 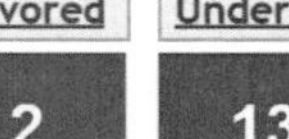 7.5

2015 Wins  6

2014 Wins  5

2013 Wins  8

1 3 5 7 9 11 13 15

2017 Lineup & Cap Hits

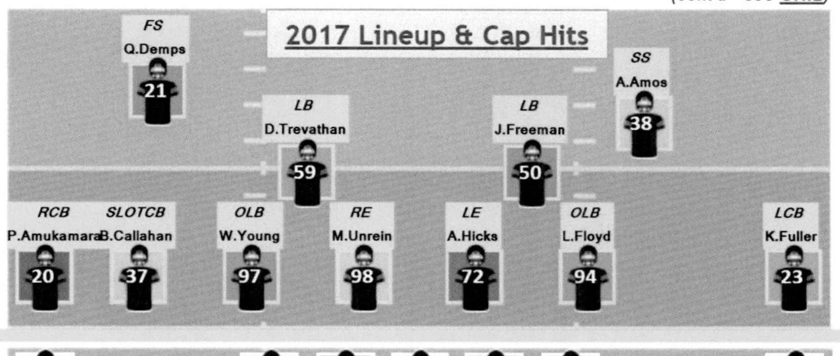

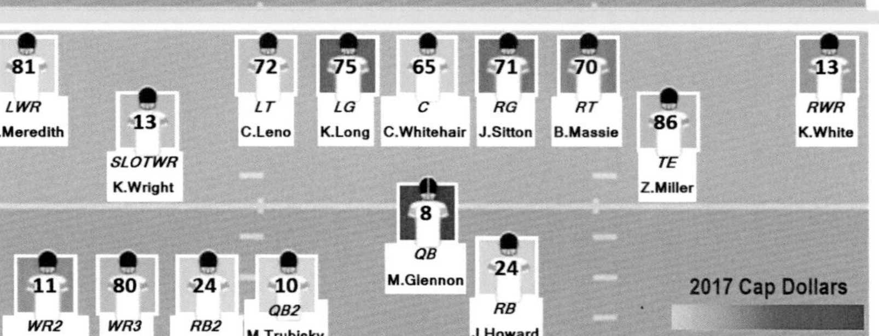

2017 Unit Spending

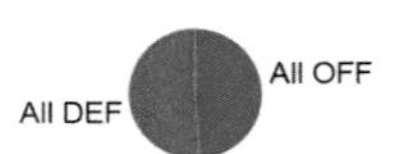

Positional Spending

	Rank	Total	2016 Rk
All OFF	20	$78.09M	8
QB	19	$16.84M	12
OL	10	$31.36M	14
RB	30	$3.94M	30
WR	21	$15.77M	3
TE	11	$10.19M	25
All DEF	12	$81.74M	23
DL	30	$13.08M	29
LB	3	$39.57M	1
CB	13	$20.98M	23
S	24	$8.10M	31

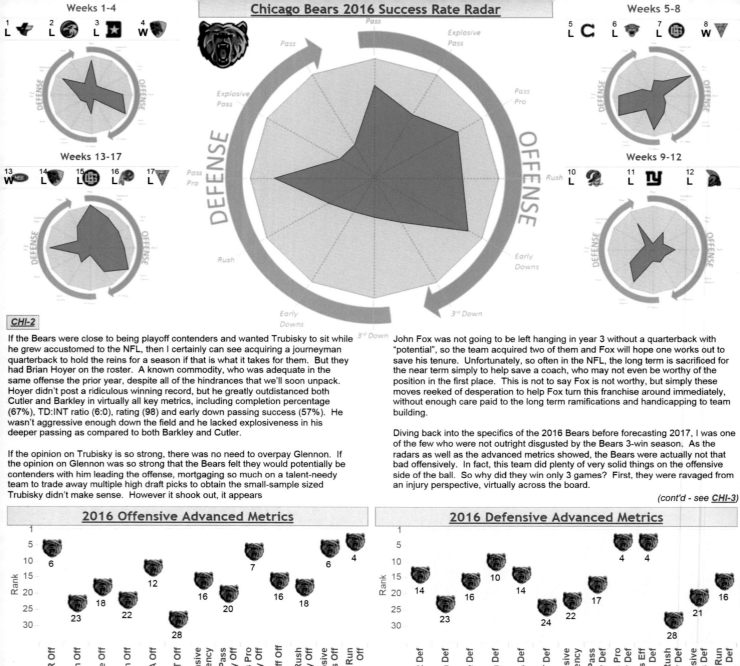

Chicago Bears 2016 Success Rate Radar

Weeks 1-4: 1 L, 2 L, 3 L, 4 W

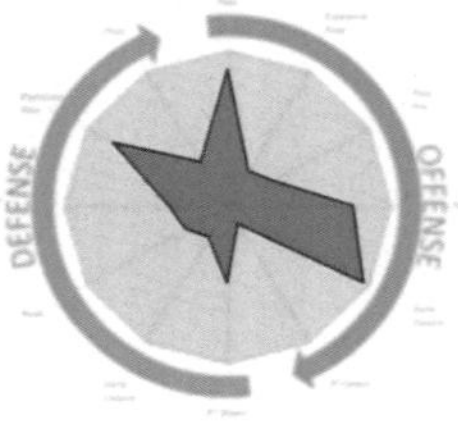

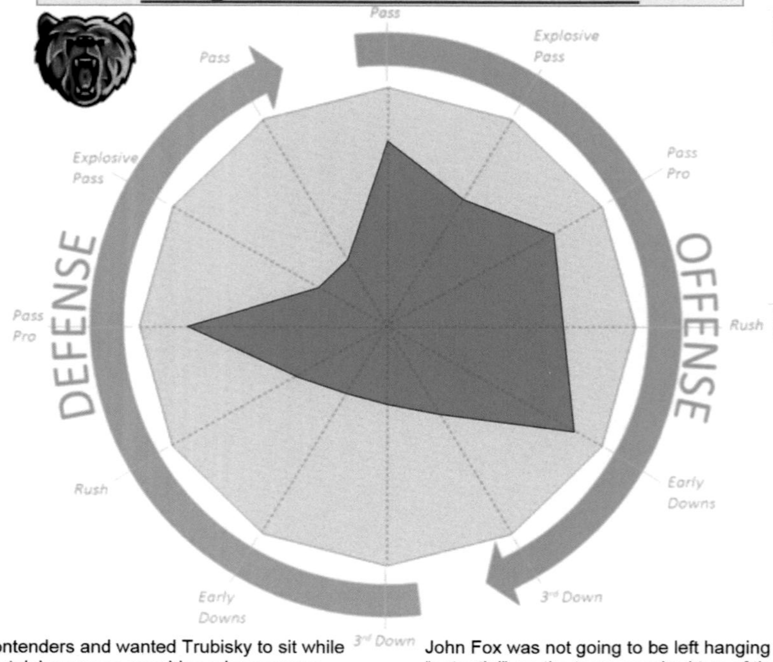

Weeks 5-8: 5 L, 6 L, 7 L, 8 W

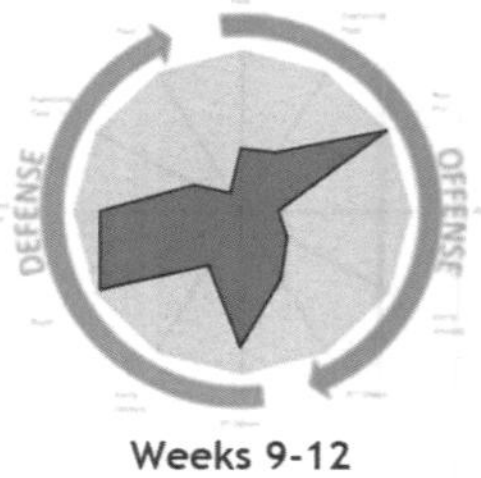

Weeks 13-17: 13 W, 14 L, 15 L, 16 L, 17 L

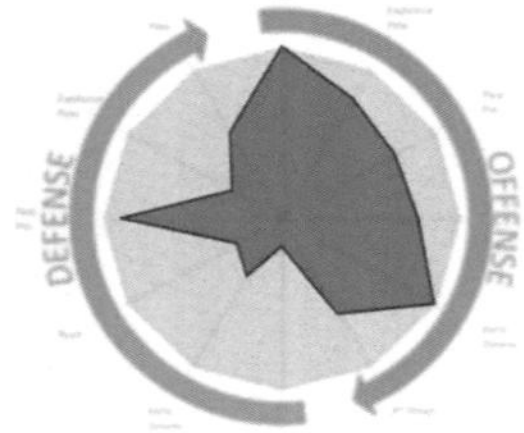

Weeks 9-12: 10 L, 11 L, 12 L

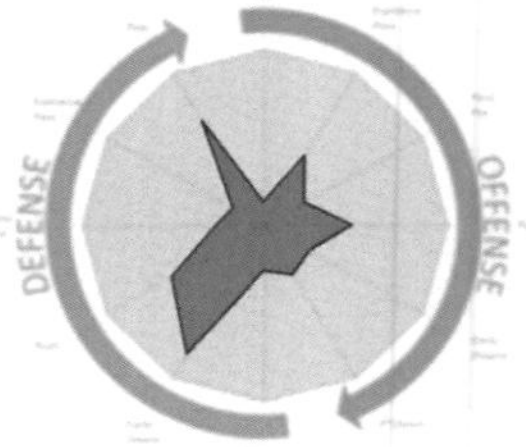

DEFENSE / OFFENSE — Pass, Explosive Pass, Pass Pro, Rush, Early Downs, 3rd Down

CHI-2

If the Bears were close to being playoff contenders and wanted Trubisky to sit while he grew accustomed to the NFL, then I certainly can see acquiring a journeyman quarterback to hold the reins for a season if that is what it takes for them. But they had Brian Hoyer on the roster. A known commodity, who was adequate in the same offense the prior year, despite all of the hindrances that we'll soon unpack. Hoyer didn't post a ridiculous winning record, but he greatly outdistanced both Cutler and Barkley in virtually all key metrics, including completion percentage (67%), TD:INT ratio (6:0), rating (98) and early down passing success (57%). He wasn't aggressive enough down the field and he lacked explosiveness in his deeper passing as compared to both Barkley and Cutler.

If the opinion on Trubisky is so strong, there was no need to overpay Glennon. If the opinion on Glennon was so strong that the Bears felt they would potentially be contenders with him leading the offense, mortgaging so much on a talent-needy team to trade away multiple high draft picks to obtain the small-sample sized Trubisky didn't make sense. However it shook out, it appears John Fox was not going to be left hanging in year 3 without a quarterback with "potential", so the team acquired two of them and Fox will hope one works out to save his tenure. Unfortunately, so often in the NFL, the long term is sacrificed for the near term simply to help save a coach, who may not even be worthy of the position in the first place. This is not to say Fox is not worthy, but simply these moves reeked of desperation to help Fox turn this franchise around immediately, without enough care paid to the long term ramifications and handicapping to team building.

Diving back into the specifics of the 2016 Bears before forecasting 2017, I was one of the few who were not outright disgusted by the Bears 3-win season. As the radars as well as the advanced metrics showed, the Bears were actually not that bad offensively. In fact, this team did plenty of very solid things on the offensive side of the ball. So why did they win only 3 games? First, they were ravaged from an injury perspective, virtually across the board.

(cont'd - see CHI-3)

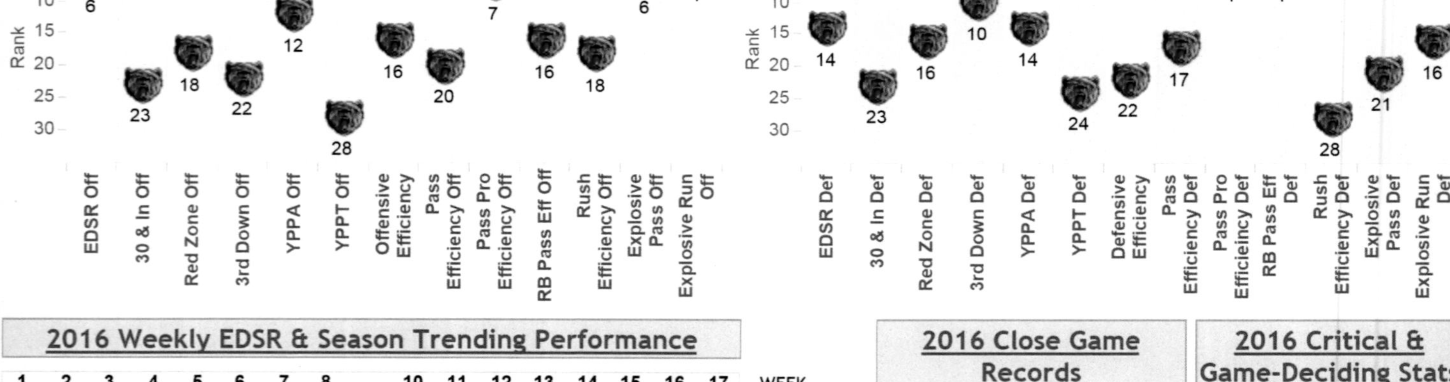

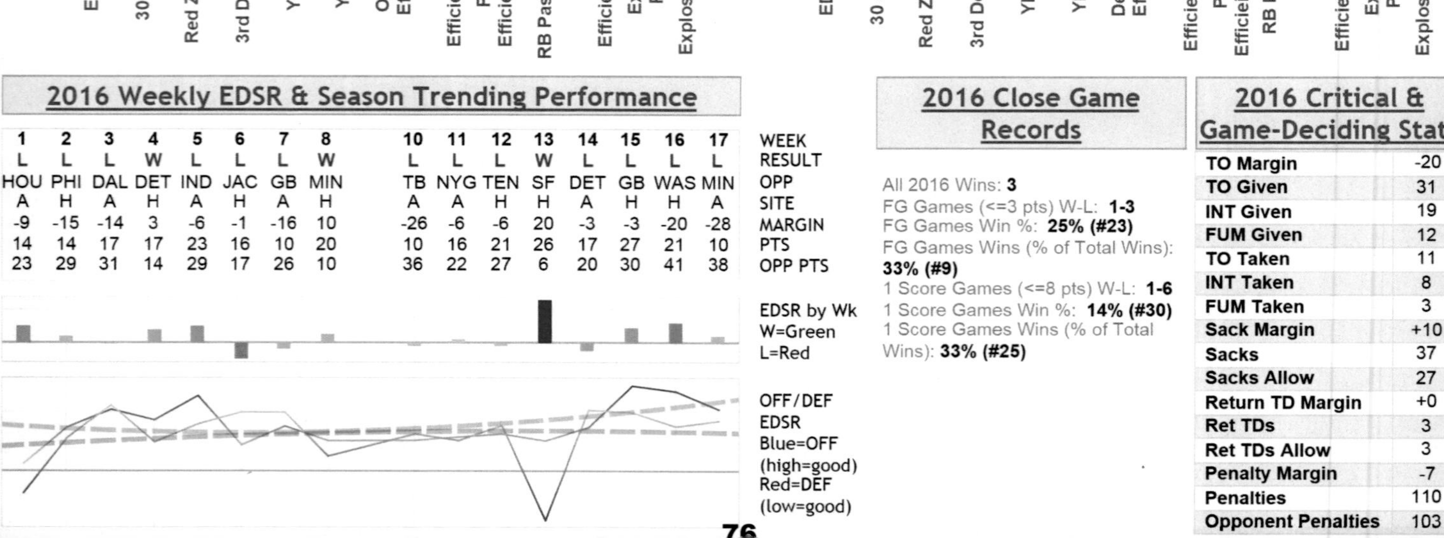

2016 Weekly EDSR & Season Trending Performance

WEEK	1	2	3	4	5	6	7	8	10	11	12	13	14	15	16	17
RESULT	L	L	L	W	L	L	L	W	L	L	L	W	L	L	L	L
OPP	HOU	PHI	DAL	DET	IND	JAC	GB	MIN	TB	NYG	TEN	SF	DET	GB	WAS	MIN
SITE	A	H	A	H	A	H	A	H	A	A	H	H	A	H	H	A
MARGIN	-9	-15	-14	3	-6	-1	-16	10	-26	-6	-6	20	-3	-3	-20	-28
PTS	14	14	17	17	23	16	10	20	10	16	21	26	17	27	21	10
OPP PTS	23	29	31	14	29	17	26	10	36	22	27	6	20	30	41	38

2016 Close Game Records

All 2016 Wins: **3**
FG Games (<=3 pts) W-L: **1-3**
FG Games Win %: **25% (#23)**
FG Games Wins (% of Total Wins): **33% (#9)**
1 Score Games (<=8 pts) W-L: **1-6**
1 Score Games Win %: **14% (#30)**
1 Score Games Wins (% of Total Wins): **33% (#25)**

2016 Critical & Game-Deciding Stats

TO Margin	-20
TO Given	31
INT Given	19
FUM Given	12
TO Taken	11
INT Taken	8
FUM Taken	3
Sack Margin	+10
Sacks	37
Sacks Allow	27
Return TD Margin	+0
Ret TDs	3
Ret TDs Allow	3
Penalty Margin	-7
Penalties	110
Opponent Penalties	103

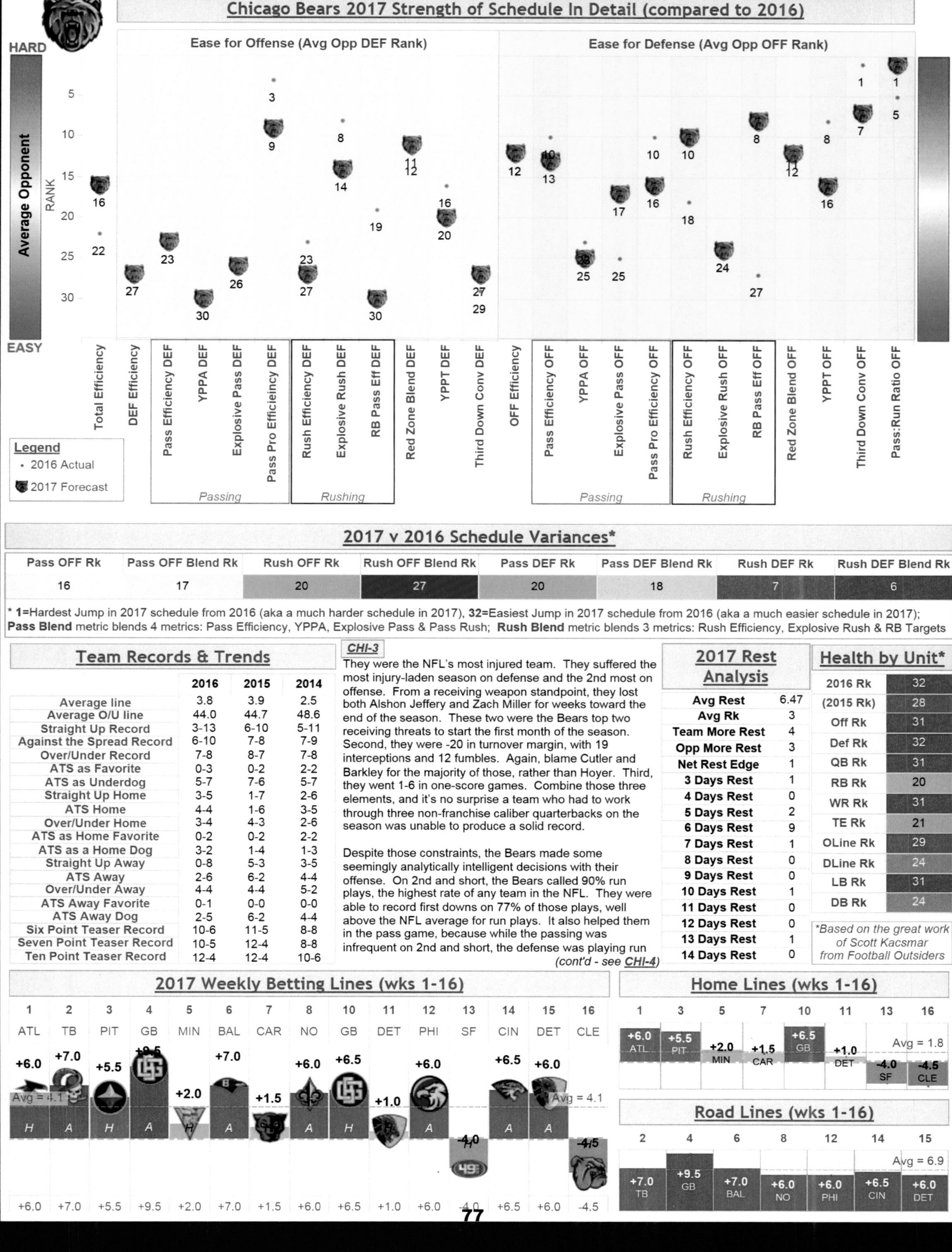

Chicago Bears 2017 Strength of Schedule In Detail (compared to 2016)

2017 v 2016 Schedule Variances*

Pass OFF Rk	Pass OFF Blend Rk	Rush OFF Rk	Rush OFF Blend Rk	Pass DEF Rk	Pass DEF Blend Rk	Rush DEF Rk	Rush DEF Blend Rk
16	17	20	27	20	18	7	6

* **1**=Hardest Jump in 2017 schedule from 2016 (aka a much harder schedule in 2017), **32**=Easiest Jump in 2017 schedule from 2016 (aka a much easier schedule in 2017); **Pass Blend** metric blends 4 metrics: Pass Efficiency, YPPA, Explosive Pass & Pass Rush; **Rush Blend** metric blends 3 metrics: Rush Efficiency, Explosive Rush & RB Targets

Team Records & Trends

	2016	2015	2014
Average line	3.8	3.9	2.5
Average O/U line	44.0	44.7	48.6
Straight Up Record	3-13	6-10	5-11
Against the Spread Record	6-10	7-8	7-9
Over/Under Record	7-8	8-7	7-8
ATS as Favorite	0-3	0-2	2-2
ATS as Underdog	5-7	7-6	5-7
Straight Up Home	3-5	1-7	2-6
ATS Home	4-4	1-6	3-5
Over/Under Home	3-4	4-3	2-6
ATS as Home Favorite	0-2	0-2	2-2
ATS as a Home Dog	3-2	1-4	1-3
Straight Up Away	0-8	5-3	3-5
ATS Away	2-6	6-2	4-4
Over/Under Away	4-4	4-4	5-2
ATS Away Favorite	0-1	0-0	0-0
ATS Away Dog	2-5	6-2	4-4
Six Point Teaser Record	10-6	11-5	8-8
Seven Point Teaser Record	10-5	12-4	8-8
Ten Point Teaser Record	12-4	12-4	10-6

CHI-3

They were the NFL's most injured team. They suffered the most injury-laden season on defense and the 2nd most on offense. From a receiving weapon standpoint, they lost both Alshon Jeffery and Zach Miller for weeks toward the end of the season. These two were the Bears top two receiving threats to start the first month of the season. Second, they were -20 in turnover margin, with 19 interceptions and 12 fumbles. Again, blame Cutler and Barkley for the majority of those, rather than Hoyer. Third, they went 1-6 in one-score games. Combine those three elements, and it's no surprise a team who had to work through three non-franchise caliber quarterbacks on the season was unable to produce a solid record.

Despite those constraints, the Bears made some seemingly analytically intelligent decisions with their offense. On 2nd and short, the Bears called 90% run plays, the highest rate of any team in the NFL. They were able to record first downs on 77% of those plays, well above the NFL average for run plays. It also helped them in the pass game, because while the passing was infrequent on 2nd and short, the defense was playing run

(cont'd - see CHI-4)

2017 Rest Analysis

Avg Rest	6.47
Avg Rk	3
Team More Rest	4
Opp More Rest	3
Net Rest Edge	1
3 Days Rest	1
4 Days Rest	0
5 Days Rest	2
6 Days Rest	9
7 Days Rest	1
8 Days Rest	0
9 Days Rest	0
10 Days Rest	1
11 Days Rest	0
12 Days Rest	0
13 Days Rest	1
14 Days Rest	0

Health by Unit*

2016 Rk	32
(2015 Rk)	28
Off Rk	31
Def Rk	32
QB Rk	31
RB Rk	20
WR Rk	31
TE Rk	21
OLine Rk	29
DLine Rk	24
LB Rk	31
DB Rk	24

**Based on the great work of Scott Kacsmar from Football Outsiders*

2017 Weekly Betting Lines (wks 1-16)

Week	1	2	3	4	5	6	7	8	10	11	12	13	14	15	16
Opp	ATL	TB	PIT	GB	MIN	BAL	CAR	NO	GB	DET	PHI	SF	CIN	DET	CLE
H/A	H	A	H	A	H	A	H	A	H	H	A	H	A	A	H
Line	+6.0	+7.0	+5.5	+9.5	+2.0	+7.0	+1.5	+6.0	+6.5	+1.0	+6.0	-4.0	+6.5	+6.0	-4.5

Home Lines (wks 1-16)

Week	1	3	5	7	10	11	13	16
Opp	ATL	PIT	MIN	CAR	GB	DET	SF	CLE
Line	+6.0	+5.5	+2.0	+1.5	+6.5	+1.0	-4.0	-4.5

Road Lines (wks 1-16)

Week	2	4	6	8	12	14	15
Opp	TB	GB	BAL	NO	PHI	CIN	DET
Line	+7.0	+9.5	+7.0	+6.0	+6.0	+6.5	+6.0

2016 Play Tendencies

All Pass %	55%
All Pass Rk	27
All Rush %	45%
All Rush Rk	6
1 Score Pass %	55%
1 Score Pass Rk	23
2015 1 Score Pass %	50%
2015 1 Score Pass Rk	31
Pass Increase %	5%
Pass Increase Rk	3
1 Score Rush %	45%
1 Score Rush Rk	10
Up Pass %	60%
Up Pass Rk	9
Up Rush %	40%
Up Rush Rk	24
Down Pass %	53%
Down Pass Rk	28
Down Rush %	47%
Down Rush Rk	5

2016 Down & Distance Tendencies

Down	Distance	Total Plays	Pass Rate	Run Rate	Play Success %
1	Short (1-3)	5	20%	80%	80%
	Med (4-7)	13	23%	77%	38%
	Long (8-10)	283	43%	57%	55%
	XL (11+)	15	73%	27%	53%
2	Short (1-3)	28	14%	86%	71%
	Med (4-7)	80	55%	45%	45%
	Long (8-10)	72	58%	42%	44%
	XL (11+)	33	79%	21%	27%
3	Short (1-3)	32	59%	41%	56%
	Med (4-7)	42	98%	2%	40%
	Long (8-10)	30	100%	0%	30%
	XL (11+)	22	86%	14%	14%
4	Short (1-3)	5	40%	60%	40%
	Med (4-7)	1	100%	0%	100%

Shotgun %:

Under Center	Shotgun
37%	63%
37%	*63%* (*AVG*)

Run Rate:

Under Center	Shotgun
69%	22%
68%	*23%* (*AVG*)

Pass Rate:

Under Center	Shotgun
31%	78%
32%	*77%* (*AVG*)

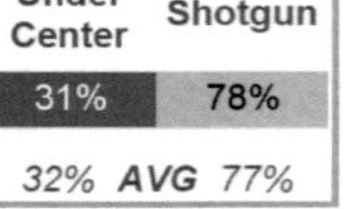

Short Yardage Intelligence:

2nd and Short Run

Run Freq	Run % Rk	NFL Run Freq Avg	Run 1D Rate	Run NFL 1D Avg
90%	1	65%	77%	71%

2nd and Short Pass

Pass Freq	Pass % Rk	NFL Pass Freq Avg	Pass 1D Rate	Pass NFL 1D Avg
10%	32	35%	67%	52%

Most Frequent Play

Down	Distance	Play Type	Player	Total Plays	Play Success %
1	Short (1-3)	RUSH	Jordan Howard	2	100%
			Jeremy Langford	2	100%
	Med (4-7)	RUSH	Jordan Howard	6	17%
	Long (8-10)	RUSH	Jordan Howard	110	49%
	XL (11+)	PASS	Cameron Meredith	3	67%
		RUSH	Jordan Howard	3	33%
2	Short (1-3)	RUSH	Jordan Howard	16	75%
	Med (4-7)	RUSH	Jordan Howard	23	43%
	Long (8-10)	RUSH	Jordan Howard	20	20%
	XL (11+)	PASS	Jordan Howard	5	20%
3	Short (1-3)	RUSH	Jordan Howard	7	86%
	Med (4-7)	PASS	Alshon Jeffery	11	27%
	Long (8-10)	PASS	Eddie Royal	7	14%
	XL (11+)	PASS	Jeremy Langford	4	0%
			Eddie Royal	4	25%

Most Successful Play*

Down	Distance	Play Type	Player	Total Plays	Play Success %
1	Med (4-7)	RUSH	Jordan Howard	6	17%
	Long (8-10)	PASS	Deonte Thompson	8	75%
2	Short (1-3)	RUSH	Jordan Howard	16	75%
	Med (4-7)	PASS	Eddie Royal	5	80%
	Long (8-10)	PASS	Alshon Jeffery	11	64%
	XL (11+)	PASS	Jordan Howard	5	20%
3	Short (1-3)	RUSH	Jordan Howard	7	86%
	Med (4-7)	PASS	Cameron Meredith	7	57%
	Long (8-10)	PASS	Eddie Royal	7	14%

**Minimum 5 plays to qualify*

2016 Snap Rates

Week	Opp	Score	Cameron Meredith	Alshon Jeffery	Jordan Howard	Zach Miller	Logan Paulsen	Deonte Thompson	Eddie Royal	Josh Bellamy
1	HOU	L 23-14		53 (95%)		43 (77%)	20 (36%)	2 (4%)	36 (64%)	
2	PHI	L 29-14		50 (96%)	11 (21%)	42 (81%)	22 (42%)	3 (6%)	38 (73%)	3 (6%)
3	DAL	L 31-17	14 (22%)	63 (97%)	48 (74%)	65 (100%)	10 (15%)		51 (78%)	
4	DET	W 17-14	26 (38%)	56 (81%)	63 (91%)	56 (81%)	46 (67%)	6 (9%)	36 (52%)	8 (12%)
5	IND	L 29-23	63 (95%)	61 (92%)	63 (95%)	57 (86%)	37 (56%)	1 (2%)	37 (56%)	7 (11%)
6	JAC	L 17-16	68 (85%)	74 (93%)	55 (69%)	64 (80%)	36 (45%)	1 (1%)	35 (44%)	30 (38%)
7	GB	L 26-10	40 (83%)	45 (94%)	22 (46%)	48 (100%)	19 (40%)	16 (33%)		16 (33%)
8	MIN	W 20-10	53 (87%)	59 (97%)	50 (82%)	60 (98%)	35 (57%)	14 (23%)		16 (26%)
10	TB	L 36-10	53 (95%)	54 (96%)	29 (52%)	49 (88%)	18 (32%)	1 (2%)	41 (73%)	1 (2%)
11	NYG	L 22-16	56 (89%)		46 (73%)	28 (44%)	32 (51%)	22 (35%)	25 (40%)	22 (35%)
12	TEN	L 27-21	69 (86%)		53 (66%)		29 (36%)	42 (53%)	12 (15%)	46 (58%)
13	SF	W 26-6	49 (78%)		53 (84%)		38 (60%)	45 (71%)		39 (62%)
14	DET	L 20-17	45 (80%)		34 (61%)		19 (34%)	49 (88%)		44 (79%)
15	GB	L 30-27	55 (83%)	61 (92%)	49 (74%)		13 (20%)	47 (71%)		17 (26%)
16	WAS	L 41-21	62 (90%)	63 (91%)	39 (57%)		9 (13%)	37 (54%)		31 (45%)
17	MIN	L 38-10	47 (78%)	49 (82%)	37 (62%)		20 (33%)	33 (55%)		25 (42%)
Grand Total			700 (78%)	688 (92%)	652 (67%)	512 (84%)	403 (40%)	319 (34%)	311 (55%)	305 (34%)

Personnel Groupings

Personnel	Team %	NFL Avg	Succ. %
1-1 [3WR]	64%	60%	48%
1-2 [2WR]	23%	19%	50%
2-1 [2WR]	7%	7%	47%
1-3 [1WR]	4%	3%	38%

Grouping Tendencies

Personnel	Pass Rate	Pass Succ. %	Run Succ. %
1-1 [3WR]	75%	47%	53%
1-2 [2WR]	40%	61%	42%
2-1 [2WR]	29%	45%	48%
1-3 [1WR]	30%	45%	35%

Red Zone Targets (min 3)

Receiver	All	Inside 5	6-10	11-20
Cameron Meredith	13	3	1	9
Alshon Jeffery	12	1	4	7
Jordan Howard	8		2	6
Zach Miller	8	2	3	3
Deonte Thompson	6	1	4	1
Eddie Royal	6	1	1	4
Daniel Brown	5	1	3	1
Kevin White	5	1		4
Josh Bellamy	3		2	1

Red Zone Rushes (min 3)

Rusher	All	Inside 5	6-10	11-20
Jordan Howard	31	10	6	15
Jeremy Langford	9	7	1	1
Ka'Deem Carey	4		1	3

Early Down Target Rate

	RB	TE	WR
	17%	16%	66%
NFL AVG	*19%*	*20%*	*61%*

Overall Target Success %

RB	TE	WR
45% #16	65% #1	50% #16

Chicago Bears 2016 Passing Recap & 2017 Outlook

The Bears are in for a completely new experience at quarterback, regardless of which one starts week 1 or week 10 out of the bye or at any other point during the season. Mitchell Trubisky started 13 games in college. Mike Glennon started 18 games in the NFL, but zero in the last two seasons. With the changes to the receiver position, it's a challenge to feel extremely confident in those projections as we don't know which receivers ultimately will win jobs, mesh with their QB and fail or succeed this season. We can start projecting the protection, which will be identical to 2016. The line was the 4th most injured unit in 2016 yet delivered the 7th best protection to a variety of QBs, so that should be a positive to build on for 2017. The line helped the Bears deliver the 6th most explosive pass offense and 4th most explosive run offense. Glennon is more likely to push the ball down the field, while Trubisky would be more conservative. The Bears coached Barkley to be more aggressive with the football last year, but that led to 8 TDs and 14 INTs. The Bears' 2017 QB needs to find that sweet spot between explosive passing plus passing beyond the sticks on 3rd down, and being too caviler with the football and losing games as a result.

Brian Hoyer Rating All Downs

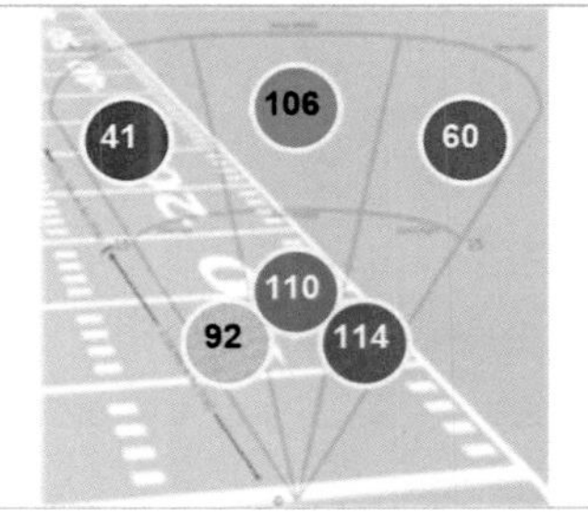

Brian Hoyer Rating Early Downs

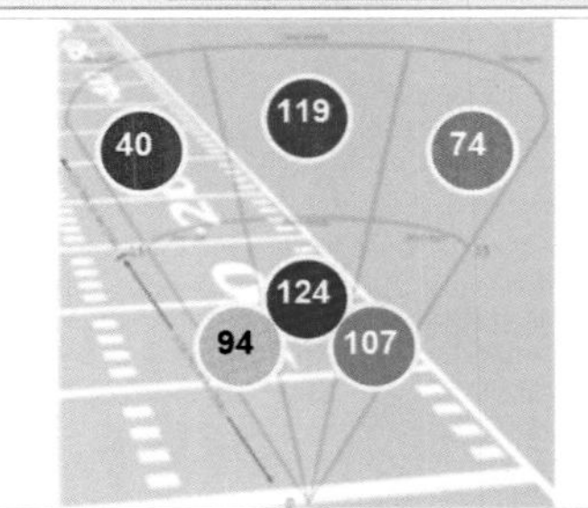

2016 Standard Passing Table

QB	Comp	Att	Comp %	Yds	YPA	TDs	INT	Sacks	Rating	Rk
Matt Barkley	129	216	60%	1,611	7.5	8	14	6	68.3	50
Brian Hoyer	134	200	67%	1,445	7.2	6	0	3	98.0	11
NFL Avg			63%		7.2				90.4	

2016 Advanced Passing Table

QB	Success %	EDSR Passing Success %	20+ Yd Pass Gains	20+ Yd Pass %	30+ Yd Pass Gains	30+ Yd Pass %	Air Yds per Comp	YAC per Comp	20+ Air Yd Comp	20+ Air Yd %
Matt Barkley	53%	55%	21	10%	6	3%	8.2	4.3	10	5%
Brian Hoyer	50%	57%	13	7%	5	3%	5.7	5.1	6	3%
NFL Avg	44%	48%	27	8%	10	3%	6.4	4.8	12	4%

Interception Rates by Down

Yards to Go	1	2	3	4	Total
1 & 2		0.0%	0.0%	0.0%	0.0%
3, 4, 5	0.0%	0.0%	0.0%		0.0%
6 - 9	0.0%	0.0%	0.0%	0.0%	0.0%
10 - 14	0.0%	0.0%	0.0%	0.0%	0.0%
15+	0.0%	0.0%	0.0%		0.0%
Total	0.0%	0.0%	0.0%	0.0%	0.0%

3rd Down Passing - Short of Sticks Analysis

QB	Avg Yds to Go	Air Yds (of Comps)	Avg Yds Short	Short of Sticks Rate	Rk
Brian Hoyer	8.7	7.8	-0.9	58%	29
NFL Avg	7.6	6.8	-0.8	57%	

Air Yds vs YAC

Air Yds %	YAC %	Rk
57%	43%	21
54%	46%	

2016 Receiving Recap & 2017 Outlook

Alshon Jeffery is gone. In 2016 when he missed 4 weeks late in the season, the target shares were dispersed in the following manner: 19% Meredith, 18% Bellamy, 14% Howard, 13% Thompson, 12% Wilson, 9% Brown and 5% Langford, with several others having less than 5 total targets. TE Miller was out the majority of games as well. Meredith becomes the clear #1 entering the season, but was completely ineffective in targets of 15 yards or less as the #1 last year, delivering only a 38 rating on a team high 18 targets. White has battled injuries, Wheaton has potential and Wright may be the most consistent of the rest, but with limited upside.

Player *Min 50 Targets	Targets	Comp %	YPA	Rating	TOARS	Success %	Success Rk	Missed YPA Rk	YAS % Rk	TDs
Cameron Meredith	97	68%	9.2	98	4.7	56%	36	51	47	4
Alshon Jeffery	94	55%	8.7	61	4.2	53%	52	57	12	2
Zach Miller	64	73%	7.6	109	4.3	63%	10	10	90	4
Jordan Howard	50	58%	6.0	74	3.4	44%	117	132	122	1

Directional Passer Rating Delivered

Receiver	Short Left	Short Middle	Short Right	Deep Left	Deep Middle	Deep Right	Player Total
Cameron Meredith	88	63	72	149	117	145	98
Alshon Jeffery	68	66	81	21	110	54	61
Zach Miller	79	94	116	40	117	149	109
Jordan Howard	90	122	63			40	84
Eddie Royal	97	103	106	40	158		117
Josh Bellamy	75	111	84	74	16	96	72
Deonte Thompson	70	82	138	63	81	68	100
Kevin White	88	88	44	40	119	44	56
Jeremy Langford	78	83	82	40			83
Daniel Brown	102	86	128		0		88
Team Total	83	86	93	39	87	103	87

2016 Rushing Recap & 2017 Outlook

When Matt Forte left, rookie Jordan Howard was thrust into the starting role and vastly exceeded expectations. His explosiveness was welcomed on the ground, and he ranked 7th in "YAS", the percentage of his total yardage which was gained after recording a successful carry. With the injuries to the line, it was more difficult for him to be consistent in his runs, and he needs to strive to consistently produce this season. He did record 50 targets in the pass game last year and that was with Jeffrey in the mix. While new receiving weapons enter the picture, look for Howard to continue significant usage in the passing game, with potentially better results as the Bears face the 3rd easiest schedule of RB-pass defenses.

Player *Min 50 Rushes	Rushes	YPA	Success %	Success Rk	Missed YPA Rk	YTS % Rk	YAS % Rk	Early Down Success %	Early Down Success Rk	TDs
Jordan Howard	251	5.2	49%	28	29	65	7	49%	29	6
Jeremy Langford	62	3.2	56%	5	25	1	53	56%	8	4

Yards per Carry by Direction

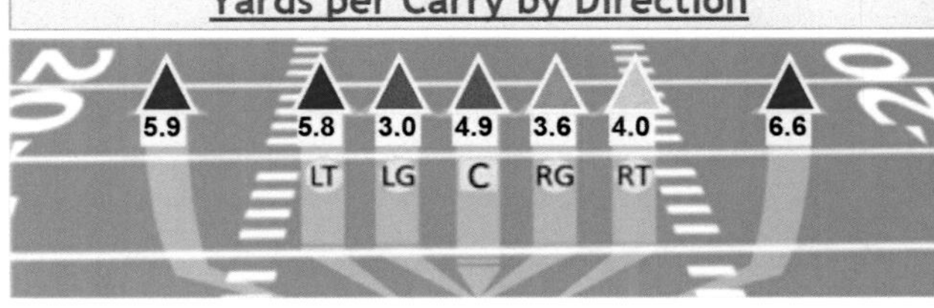

Directional Run Frequency

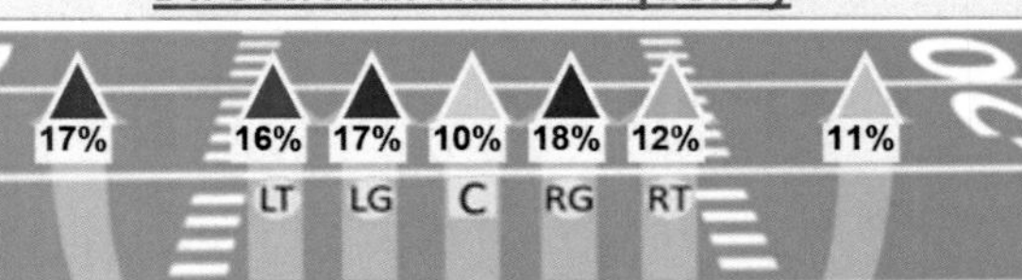

so the Bears converted on 67% of their pass attempts, well above the NFL average (52%). They were right at league averages in shotgun rate, run rate when under center and pass rate when in shotgun. They were a very run heavy team, running the ball 45% of the time, the 6th most of any team. While they likely would have liked to pass more often, the running was successful, particularly in short yardage situations.

And on 1st down and 10, they were quite balanced and quite successful: they ran the ball 57% of the time, but a whopping 52% of those runs were successful, the 3rd best rate in the NFL. When they passed the ball, 59% of those attempts were successful, the 5th best rate in the NFL. Overall, 55% of their 1st and 10 play calls were successful, which was the 3rd best in the NFL believe it or not, behind only the Falcons and Saints.

Chicago's first down success continued in the red zone as well, where they were the 3rd most successful offense in the NFL. The problem came on the other downs when in the red zone. On 2nd down, just 33% of their red zone plays were successful, 2nd worst in the NFL. On 3rd down, just 29% of their red zone plays were successful (4th worst). Combined, they dropped from a 55% success rate on 1st down plays in the red zone to 31% on 2nd and 3rd down, the 2nd worst rate in the NFL (only NYJ were worse). The Bears offense was really quite good, especially when considering all of their issues, on 1st down. But after that, it was a big problem. These are correctable issues, however, from a play calling and execution perspective.

So will they correct them in 2017? There are bigger questions than that, such as who will start for them at quarterback, and will any of these new WR targets the acquired in free agency to offset the loss of Alshon Jeffery. The Bears added Kendall Wright, Markus Wheaton and Rueben Randle in free agency, and will start Cameron Meredith and Kevin White. Needless to say, these new additions plus the new quarterbacks will take time to get accustomed to the system and to one another. And that is a problem because in their first 7 games, they play 5 pass defenses which ranked top-12 last season, and they have the 5th hardest schedule across their first 7 games. While the start will be a big challenge, it will get substantially easier. Which is why it will be interesting to see how quick John Fox could be to move from Glennon to Trubisky, because whoever is taking snaps later in the season should look much better. From weeks 8 through 16, the Bears passing offense has the easiest schedule in the NFL, facing 5 pass defenses which ranked bottom-5 in the NFL last year. A key for the Bears to develop with both quarterbacks this offseason will be the RB-pass game. They ranked 16th in efficiency of RB-passes last year against the 19th rated schedule of defenses. However, this year they face the 3rd easiest schedule, and that could be the perfect weapon for Glennon to utilize against difficult run defenses early on.

Division History: Season Wins & 2017 Projection

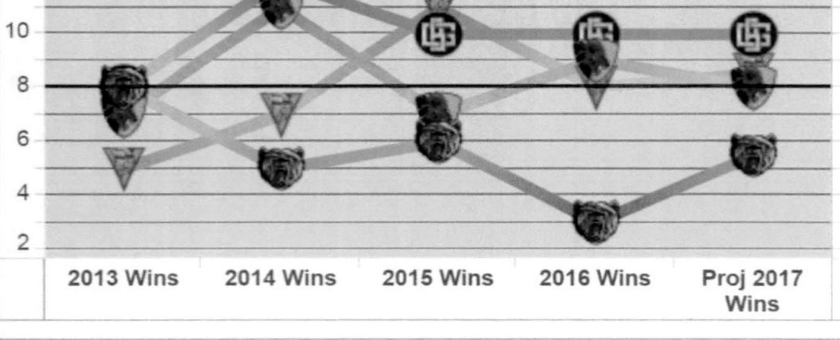

Rank of 2017 Defensive Pass Efficiency Faced by Week

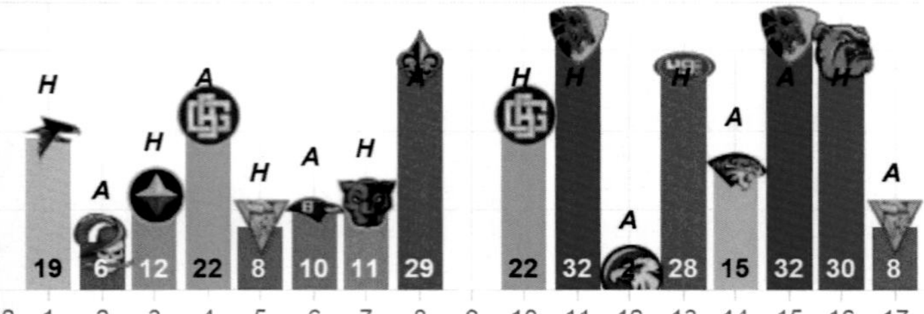

Rank of 2017 Defensive Rush Efficiency Faced by Week

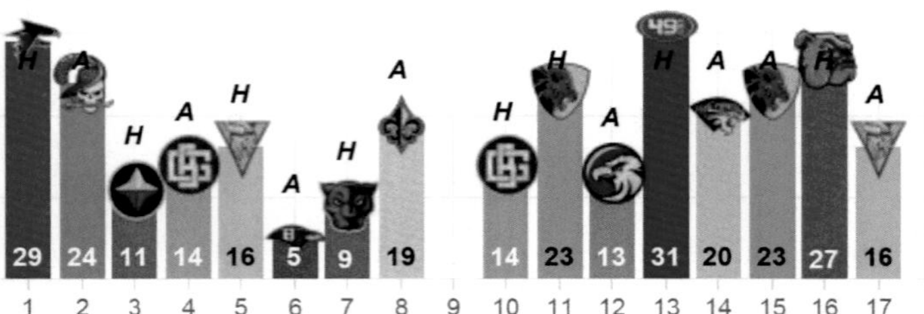

2016 Situational Usage by Player & Position

Usage Rate by Score

		Being Blown Out (14+)	Down Big (9-13)	One Score	Large Lead (9-13)	Blowout Lead (14+)	Grand Total
RUSH	Jordan Howard	23%	15%	28%	41%	67%	28%
	Cameron Meredith			0%			0%
	Jeremy Langford	8%	10%	7%			7%
	Josh Bellamy	0%		0%		3%	0%
	Ka'Deem Carey	1%	2%	4%	9%		4%
	Kevin White			0%			0%
	Paul Lasike			1%			0%
	Joique Bell			1%			0%
	Bralon Addison	0%					0%
	Total	33%	27%	41%	50%	70%	39%
PASS	Jordan Howard	5%	5%	6%		3%	6%
	Cameron Meredith	12%	12%	10%	13%	3%	11%
	Alshon Jeffery	11%	14%	10%	15%	3%	10%
	Jeremy Langford	6%	5%	2%	2%		3%
	Zach Miller	9%	5%	6%	7%	10%	7%
	Eddie Royal	2%	3%	6%	6%		5%
	Josh Bellamy	3%	10%	4%	2%	7%	4%
	Ka'Deem Carey	1%		1%	2%		1%
	Kevin White	8%	5%	3%			4%
	Deonte Thompson	3%	8%	4%			4%
	Daniel Brown	3%		2%		3%	2%
	Marquess Wilson	2%	3%	2%			2%
	Logan Paulsen			1%	4%		1%
	Ben Braunecker	1%		1%			1%
	Paul Lasike			0%			0%
	Bralon Addison			0%			0%
	Daniel Braverman		2%	0%			0%
	MyCole Pruitt	0%					0%
	Total	67%	73%	59%	50%	30%	61%

Positional Target Distribution vs NFL Average

		NFL Wide				Team Only			
		Left	Middle	Right	**Total**	Left	Middle	Right	**Total**
Deep	WR	1,001	558	961	**2,520**	30	23	40	**93**
	TE	157	142	160	**459**	1	5	3	**9**
	RB	24	4	39	**67**	1		1	**2**
	All	**1,182**	**704**	**1,160**	**3,046**	**32**	**28**	**44**	**104**
Short	WR	3,010	1,714	3,075	**7,799**	83	57	111	**251**
	TE	822	849	1,116	**2,787**	14	26	35	**75**
	RB	976	613	1,087	**2,676**	39	9	26	**74**
	All	**4,808**	**3,176**	**5,278**	**13,262**	**136**	**92**	**172**	**400**
Total		**5,990**	**3,880**	**6,438**	**16,308**	**168**	**120**	**216**	**504**

Positional Success Rates vs NFL Average

		NFL Wide				Team Only			
		Left	Middle	Right	**Total**	Left	Middle	Right	**Total**
Deep	WR	37%	50%	38%	**40%**	33%	61%	43%	**44%**
	TE	45%	49%	43%	**45%**	0%	60%	67%	**56%**
	RB	33%	75%	26%	**31%**	0%		0%	**0%**
	All	**38%**	**50%**	**38%**	**41%**	**31%**	**61%**	**43%**	**44%**
Short	WR	52%	57%	51%	**53%**	47%	56%	57%	**53%**
	TE	50%	61%	52%	**54%**	43%	73%	69%	**65%**
	RB	47%	49%	44%	**46%**	49%	67%	35%	**46%**
	All	**51%**	**56%**	**50%**	**52%**	**47%**	**62%**	**56%**	**54%**
Total		**48%**	**55%**	**48%**	**50%**	**44%**	**62%**	**53%**	**52%**

Cincinnati Bengals

2017 Coaches

Head Coach:
Marvin Lewis (15th yr)
Offensive Coordinator:
Ken Zampese (2nd yr)
Defensive Coordinator:
Paul Guenther (4th yr)

2017 Forecast

Wins	Div Rank
8.5	#3

Past Records

2016: 6-9-1
2015: 12-4
2014: 10-5-1

EASY HARD

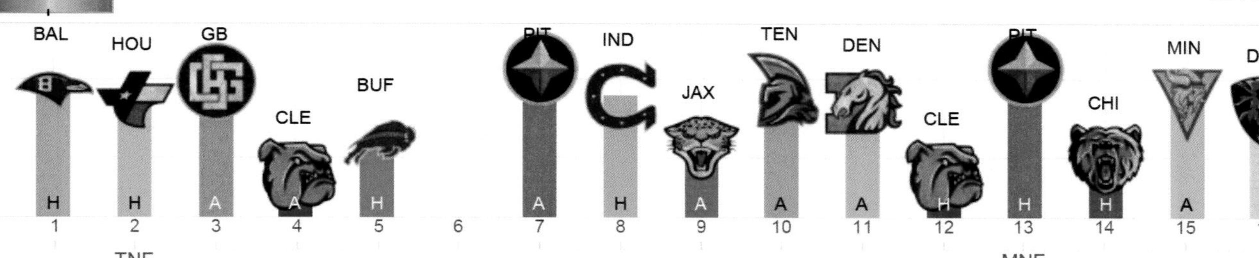

Key Players Lost

TXN	Player (POS)
Cut	Maualuga, Rey LB
	Wright, James WR
Declared Free Agent	Brown, Chykie CB
	Burkhead, Rex RB
	Dansby, Karlos LB
	Gilberry, Wallace DE
	Hunt, Margus DE
	Kirkpatrick, Dre CB
	Peerman, Cedric RB
	Peko, Domata DT
	Whitworth, Andrew T
	Winston, Eric T
	Zeitler, Kevin G
Retired	Roach, Trevor LB

Average Line	# Games Favored	# Games Underdog
-0.4	8	6

2017 Cincinnati Bengals Overview

When first year OC Ken Zampeze took over as offensive coordinator without WRs Marvin Jones and Mohamed Sanu, it wasn't expected to be easy, but the Bengals expected another trip to the postseason. The recipe was clear: rely more on AJ Green, Tyler Eifert and their top rated pass protection unit, get better production from their 7th rated run offense, and lean on a top-10 defense. The questions hinged around how different Zampeze would call the offense in 2016. But then disaster struck.

Tyler Eifert, one of the most reliable red zone tight end targets in the NFL, was injured in the offseason. By the time he was full y integrated into the offense, it was week 8 in London. The Bengals were already 3-4 on the season. They led the Redskins as the game headed to the 4th quarter, but eventually the game ended in a tie. After a bye, they once again led the Giants as the game headed to the 4th quarter, but this time lost 20-21 as the Giants came back in the 4th quarter. The very next week, after just 2 snaps, AJ Green was lost for the remainder of the season. As it turns out, it would be the last game of the year for RB Giovani Bernard, as well.

While the Bengals as a whole were an extremely healthy bunch, the 2nd healthiest defense, they ranked 27th in TE health and 21st in both RB and WR health. It was a skill unit decimated by injuries. When castoff Brandon LaFell (1,014 snaps) leads your skill position snaps by over 275 snaps, and the second most used player is a rookie (Tyler Boyd, 737 snaps), it's trouble. AJ Green saw just 554 snaps and Eifert just 427.

It forced the Bengals to rely more on the run than they perhaps should, especially considering game script. On first down, regardless of whether it was first and long, medium or short, the Bengals most frequently called play was a Jeremy Hill run. On second down, rinse and repeat: whether long, medium or short yardage to go, the Bengals simply turned and handed the ball to Jeremy hill time and time again. And time and time again, he failed to produce. Hill averaged 3.8 yards per carry on 222 rushes. He ranked 44th on early down success and 44th on overall rushing success rate. Ironically, his rushing success rate on all downs was 44%. Lots of "4s" in those stats. Which naturally led to a lot of another type of "4s": 4th downs.

(cont'd - see CIN2)

Key Free Agents/ Trades Added

- Albright, Bryson LB
- Benwikere, Bene CB
- Brown, Chris WR
- Kirkpatrick, Dre CB
- McKay, Mekale WR
- Minter, Kevin LB
- Smith, Andre T
- Smith, Chris DE

Drafted Players

Rd	Pk	Player (College)
1	9	WR - John Ross (Washington)
2	48	RB - Joe Mixon (Oklahoma)
3	73	DE - Jordan Willis (Kansas S..
4	116	DE - Carl Lawson (Auburn)
	128	WR - Josh Malone (Tenness..
4*	138	DT - Ryan Glasgow (Michiga..
5	153	K - Jake Elliott (Memphis)
5*	176	C - J. J. Dielman (Utah)
6	193	ILB - Jordan Evans (Oklaho..
	207	CB - Brandon Wilson (Houst..
7*	251	TE - Mason Schreck (Buffalo)

Regular Season Wins: Past & Current Proj

2017 Lineup & Cap Hits

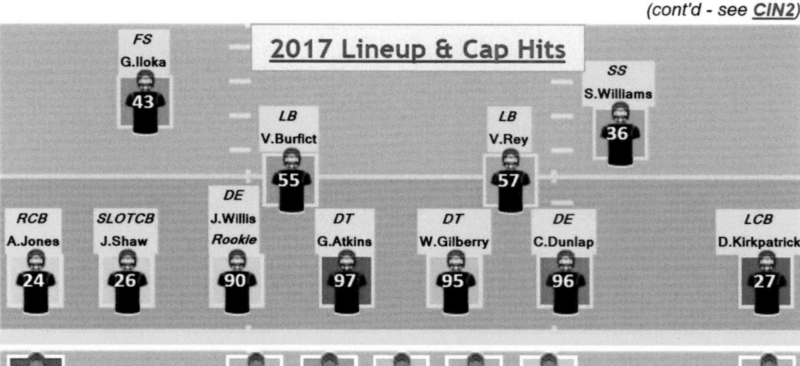

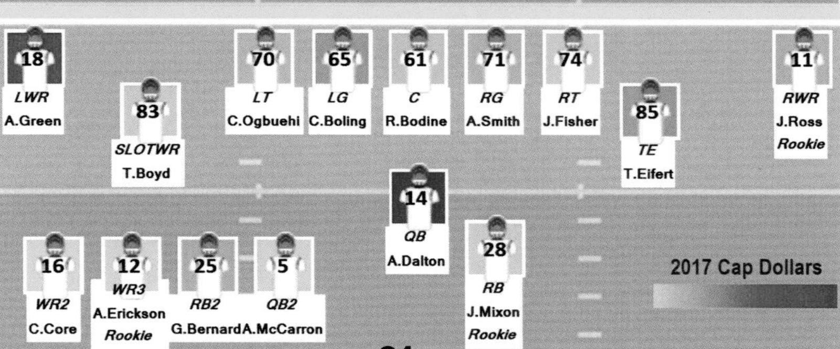

2017 Unit Spending

All DEF
All OFF

Positional Spending

	Rank	Total	2016 Rk
All OFF	18	$81.29M	11
QB	18	$16.98M	20
OL	31	$19.36M	9
RB	13	$8.84M	12
WR	6	$26.63M	12
TE	14	$9.47M	23
All DEF	8	$84.41M	1
DL	11	$32.25M	6
LB	19	$16.74M	19
CB	5	$24.78M	7
S	19	$10.63M	19

Cincinnati Bengals 2016 Success Rate Radar

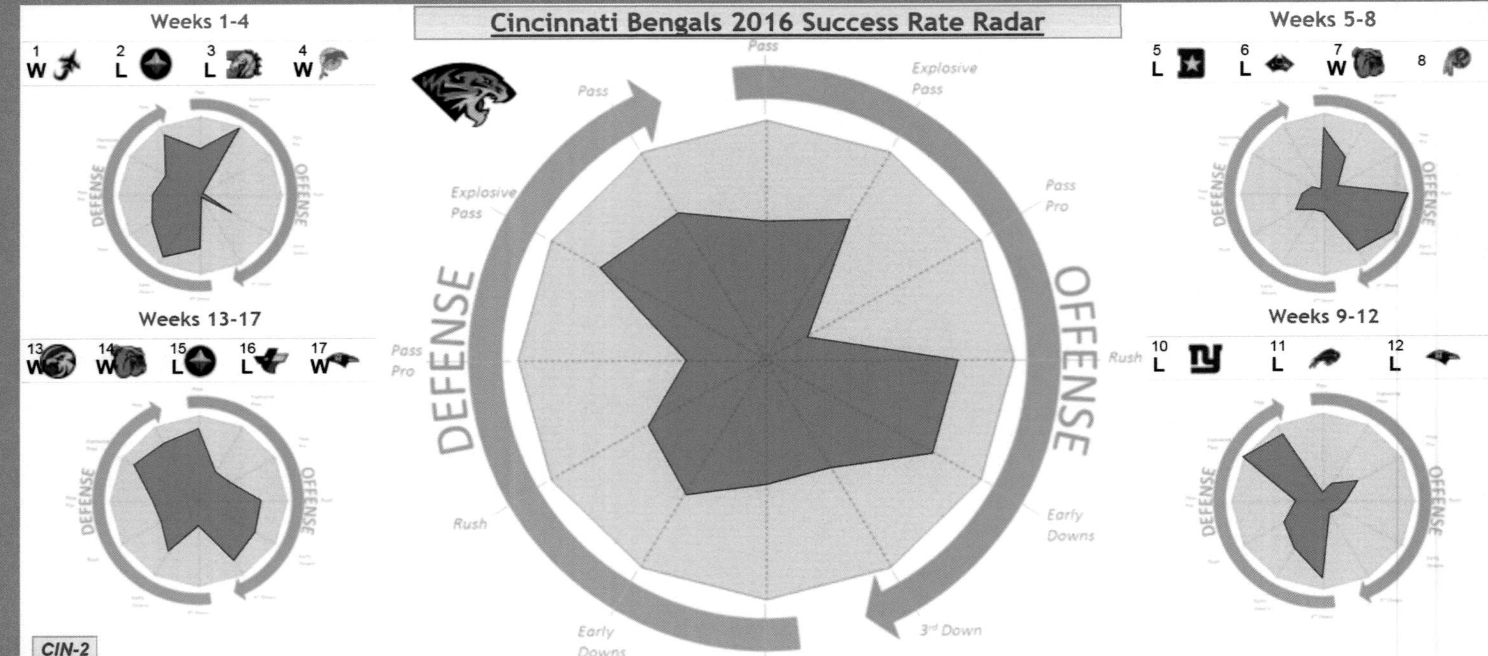

CIN-2

After consistent, double digit win seasons, the Bengals won only 6 games last year. However, with such a decimated offense, they actually played their opponents close: Of their 9 losses, 6 were by just one score or less. They were miserable in close games, posting a 14% win rate (1-6), for the 3rd worst record in the league. They didn't lose due to a terrible turnover rate: they were +3 on the season. They didn't lose because of stupid penalties: they were +17 on the season. Apart from the injuries and the tough luck in close ballgames, one of their key issues was pass protection. They ranked just 26th in pass protection efficiency, and were -8 in sack margin on the season.

Unfortunately for the Bengals, it's likely to get more challenging on that front in 2017, not easier. Apart from QB Andy Dalton and Green, the two most expensive cap hits in 2016 were LT Andrew Whitworth and RG Kevin Zeitler. They were their two best offensive linemen. And both became offseason cap casualties, who left in free agency. Their replacements are significantly worse: LT Cedric Ogbuehi recorded a 39 rating per PFF last year, and RG Andre Smith Jr. recorded a 39.3 rating. In addition, instead of playing the 24th rated schedule of pass rushes, as they did in 2016, the Bengals offensive line is scheduled to face the 5th toughest schedule of pass rushes. So where does that leave the Bengals offense this season?

It leaves them to employ a "fast-pass" style of offense. The easiest way to beat an aggressive pass rush is to welcome it and get rid of the ball quickly to players who can create in space. They added several in the draft, in the form of WR John Ross (1st round) and RB Joe Mixon (2nd round). Ross has the precise route running to open up quickly, is fast enough to be targeted in the short passing game in search of YAC, and can take the top off the defense to open up other shorter routes. Mixon is an established receiver out of the backfield. His PFF grade as a receiver out of the backfield was #1 in CFB last year per PFF. And of course the goal is to receive a healthy AJ Green and Tyler Eifert to be prime receiving targets and sensational red zone targets as well.

*(cont'd - see **CIN-3**)*

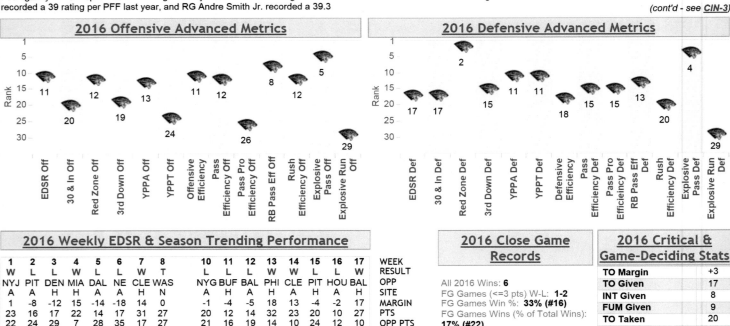

2016 Offensive Advanced Metrics

	Rank
EDSR Off	11
30 & In Off	20
Red Zone Off	12
3rd Down Off	19
YPPA Off	13
YPPT Off	24
Offensive Efficiency	11
Pass Efficiency Off	12
Pass Pro Efficiency Off	26
RB Pass Eff Off	8
Rush Efficiency Off	12
Explosive Pass Off	5
Explosive Run Off	29

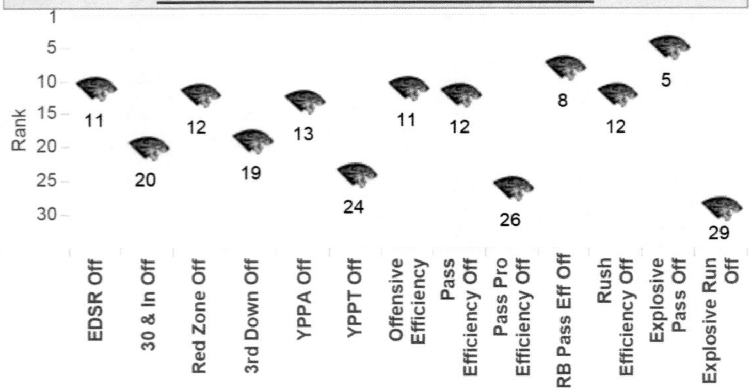

2016 Defensive Advanced Metrics

	Rank
EDSR Def	17
30 & In Def	17
Red Zone Def	2
3rd Down Def	15
YPPA Def	11
YPPT Def	11
Defensive Efficiency	18
Pass Efficiency Def	15
Pass Pro Efficieincy Def	15
RB Pass Eff Def	13
Rush Efficiency Def	20
Explosive Pass Def	4
Explosive Run Def	29

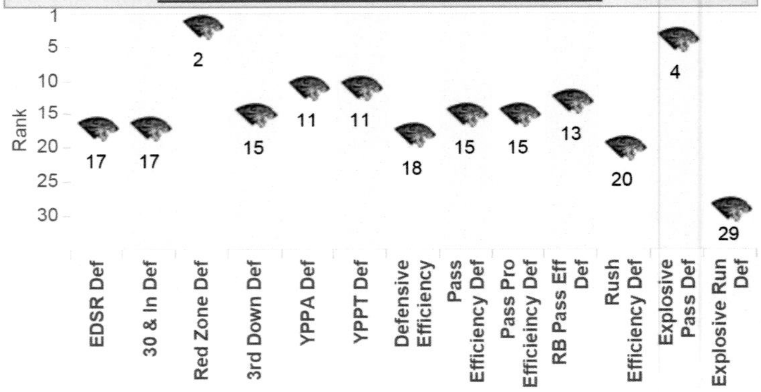

2016 Weekly EDSR & Season Trending Performance

1	2	3	4	5	6	7	8	10	11	12	13	14	15	16	17	WEEK
W	L	L	W	L	L	W	T	L	L	L	W	W	L	L	W	RESULT
NYJ	PIT	DEN	MIA	DAL	NE	CLE	WAS	NYG	BUF	BAL	PHI	CLE	PIT	HOU	BAL	OPP
A	A	H	H	A	A	H	N	A	H	A	H	A	H	A	H	SITE
1	-8	-12	15	-14	-18	14	0	-1	-4	-5	18	13	-4	-2	17	MARGIN
23	16	17	22	14	17	31	27	20	12	14	32	23	20	10	27	PTS
22	24	29	7	28	35	17	27	21	16	19	14	10	24	12	10	OPP PTS

EDSR by Wk
W=Green
L=Red

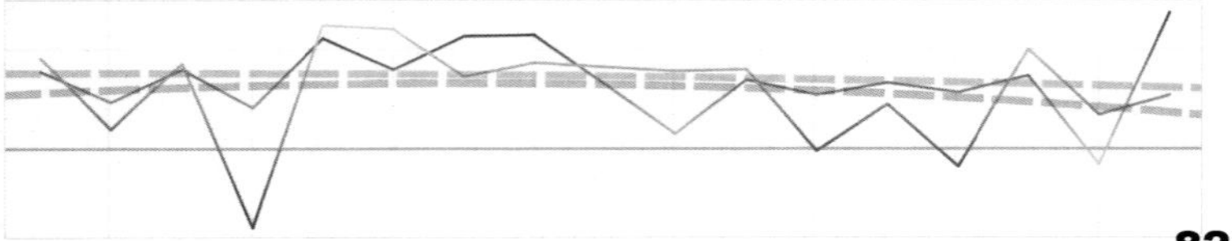

OFF/DEF EDSR
Blue=OFF (high=good)
Red=DEF (low=good)

2016 Close Game Records

All 2016 Wins: **6**
FG Games (<=3 pts) W-L: **1-2**
FG Games Win %: **33% (#16)**
FG Games Wins (% of Total Wins): **17% (#22)**
1 Score Games (<=8 pts) W-L: **1-6**
1 Score Games Win %: **14% (#30)**
1 Score Games Wins (% of Total Wins): **17% (#31)**

2016 Critical & Game-Deciding Stats

TO Margin	+3
TO Given	17
INT Given	8
FUM Given	9
TO Taken	20
INT Taken	17
FUM Taken	3
Sack Margin	-8
Sacks	33
Sacks Allow	41
Return TD Margin	+0
Ret TDs	0
Ret TDs Allow	0
Penalty Margin	+17
Penalties	88
Opponent Penalties	105

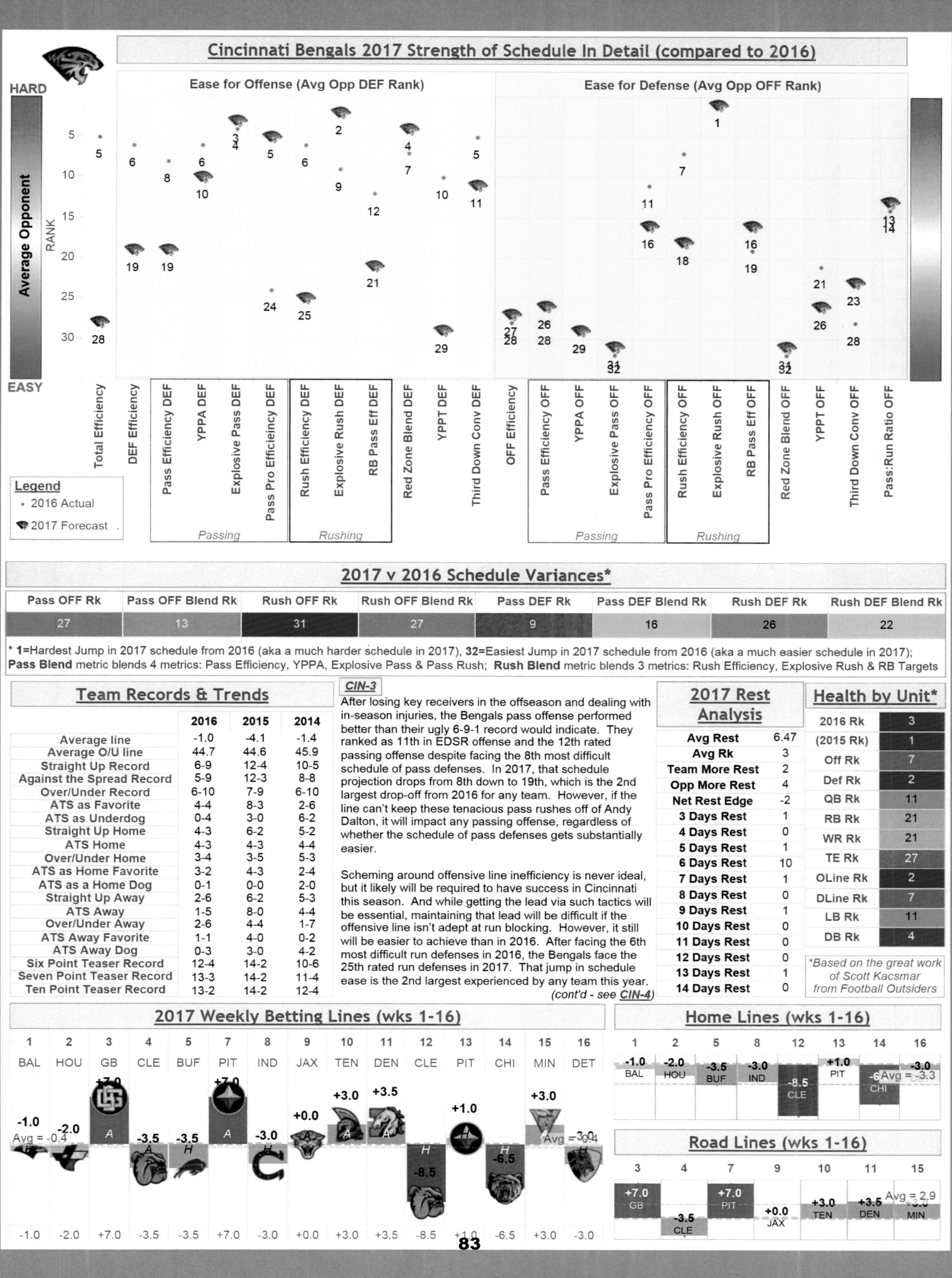

Cincinnati Bengals 2017 Strength of Schedule In Detail (compared to 2016)

2017 v 2016 Schedule Variances*

Pass OFF Rk	Pass OFF Blend Rk	Rush OFF Rk	Rush OFF Blend Rk	Pass DEF Rk	Pass DEF Blend Rk	Rush DEF Rk	Rush DEF Blend Rk
27	13	31	27	9	16	26	22

* **1=**Hardest Jump in 2017 schedule from 2016 (aka a much harder schedule in 2017), **32=**Easiest Jump in 2017 schedule from 2016 (aka a much easier schedule in 2017); **Pass Blend** metric blends 4 metrics: Pass Efficiency, YPPA, Explosive Pass & Pass Rush; **Rush Blend** metric blends 3 metrics: Rush Efficiency, Explosive Rush & RB Targets

Team Records & Trends

	2016	2015	2014
Average line	-1.0	-4.1	-1.4
Average O/U line	44.7	44.6	45.9
Straight Up Record	6-9	12-4	10-5
Against the Spread Record	5-9	12-3	8-8
Over/Under Record	6-10	7-9	6-10
ATS as Favorite	4-4	8-3	2-6
ATS as Underdog	0-4	3-0	6-2
Straight Up Home	4-3	6-2	5-2
ATS Home	4-3	4-3	4-4
Over/Under Home	3-4	3-5	5-3
ATS as Home Favorite	3-2	4-3	2-4
ATS as a Home Dog	0-1	0-0	2-0
Straight Up Away	2-6	6-2	5-3
ATS Away	1-5	8-0	4-4
Over/Under Away	2-6	4-4	1-7
ATS Away Favorite	1-1	4-0	0-2
ATS Away Dog	0-3	3-0	4-2
Six Point Teaser Record	12-4	14-2	10-6
Seven Point Teaser Record	13-3	14-2	11-4
Ten Point Teaser Record	13-2	14-2	12-4

CIN-3

After losing key receivers in the offseason and dealing with in-season injuries, the Bengals pass offense performed better than their ugly 6-9-1 record would indicate. They ranked as 11th in EDSR offense and the 12th rated passing offense despite facing the 8th most difficult schedule of pass defenses. In 2017, that schedule projection drops from 8th down to 19th, which is the 2nd largest drop-off from 2016 for any team. However, if the line can't keep these tenacious pass rushes off of Andy Dalton, it will impact any passing offense, regardless of whether the schedule of pass defenses gets substantially easier.

Scheming around offensive line inefficiency is never ideal, but it likely will be required to have success in Cincinnati this season. And while getting the lead via such tactics will be essential, maintaining that lead will be difficult if the offensive line isn't adept at run blocking. However, it still will be easier to achieve than in 2016. After facing the 6th most difficult run defenses in 2016, the Bengals face the 25th rated run defenses in 2017. That jump in schedule ease is the 2nd largest experienced by any team this year. *(cont'd - see CIN-4)*

2017 Rest Analysis

Avg Rest	6.47
Avg Rk	3
Team More Rest	2
Opp More Rest	4
Net Rest Edge	-2
3 Days Rest	1
4 Days Rest	0
5 Days Rest	1
6 Days Rest	10
7 Days Rest	1
8 Days Rest	0
9 Days Rest	1
10 Days Rest	0
11 Days Rest	0
12 Days Rest	0
13 Days Rest	1
14 Days Rest	0

Health by Unit*

2016 Rk	3
(2015 Rk)	1
Off Rk	7
Def Rk	2
QB Rk	11
RB Rk	21
WR Rk	21
TE Rk	27
OLine Rk	2
DLine Rk	7
LB Rk	11
DB Rk	4

*Based on the great work of Scott Kacsmar from Football Outsiders

2017 Weekly Betting Lines (wks 1-16)

1	2	3	4	5	7	8	9	10	11	12	13	14	15	16
BAL	HOU	GB	CLE	BUF	PIT	IND	JAX	TEN	DEN	CLE	PIT	CHI	MIN	DET
H	H	A	A	H	A	H	A	A	A	H	H	H	A	H
-1.0	-2.0	+7.0	-3.5	-3.5	+7.0	-3.0	+0.0	+3.0	+3.5	-8.5	+1.0	-6.5	+3.0	-3.0

Home Lines (wks 1-16)

1	2	5	8	12	13	14	16
BAL	HOU	BUF	IND	CLE	PIT	CHI	
-1.0	-2.0	-3.5	-3.0	-8.5	+1.0	-6	-3.0

Road Lines (wks 1-16)

3	4	7	9	10	11	15
GB	CLE	PIT	JAX	TEN	DEN	MIN
+7.0	-3.5	+7.0	+0.0	+3.0	+3.5	+3.0

Cincinnati Bengals 2016 Play Analysis

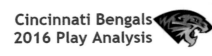

2016 Play Tendencies

All Pass %	57%
All Pass Rk	25
All Rush %	43%
All Rush Rk	8
1 Score Pass %	56%
1 Score Pass Rk	20
2015 1 Score Pass %	52%
2015 1 Score Pass Rk	26
Pass Increase %	4%
Pass Increase Rk	5
1 Score Rush %	44%
1 Score Rush Rk	13
Up Pass %	51%
Up Pass Rk	30
Up Rush %	49%
Up Rush Rk	3
Down Pass %	61%
Down Pass Rk	19
Down Rush %	39%
Down Rush Rk	14

2016 Down & Distance Tendencies

Down	Distance	Total Plays	Pass Rate	Run Rate	Play Success %
1	Short (1-3)	8	25%	75%	50%
	Med (4-7)	15	27%	73%	60%
	Long (8-10)	317	48%	52%	45%
	XL (11+)	7	86%	14%	57%
2	Short (1-3)	48	27%	73%	65%
	Med (4-7)	84	56%	44%	67%
	Long (8-10)	108	58%	42%	47%
	XL (11+)	33	85%	15%	24%
3	Short (1-3)	45	58%	42%	64%
	Med (4-7)	44	95%	5%	48%
	Long (8-10)	41	90%	10%	24%
	XL (11+)	26	88%	12%	15%
4	Short (1-3)	5	20%	80%	80%

Shotgun %:

Under Center	Shotgun
38%	62%
37%	*63%*

AVG

Run Rate:

Under Center	Shotgun
76%	21%
68%	*23%*

AVG

Pass Rate:

Under Center	Shotgun
24%	79%
32%	*77%*

AVG

Short Yardage Intelligence:

2nd and Short Run

Run Freq	Run % Rk	NFL Run Freq Avg	Run 1D Rate	Run NFL 1D Avg
66%	15	65%	66%	71%

2nd and Short Pass

Pass Freq	Pass % Rk	NFL Pass Freq Avg	Pass 1D Rate	Pass NFL 1D Avg
34%	18	35%	67%	52%

Most Frequent Play

Down	Distance	Play Type	Player	Total Plays	Play Success %
1	Short (1-3)	RUSH	Jeremy Hill	5	40%
	Med (4-7)	RUSH	Jeremy Hill	8	63%
	Long (8-10)	RUSH	Jeremy Hill	94	38%
	XL (11+)	PASS	A.J. Green	2	50%
			Tyler Boyd	2	100%
2	Short (1-3)	RUSH	Jeremy Hill	19	68%
	Med (4-7)	RUSH	Jeremy Hill	21	57%
	Long (8-10)	RUSH	Jeremy Hill	26	27%
	XL (11+)	PASS	Giovani Bernard	4	0%
3	Short (1-3)	RUSH	Jeremy Hill	8	63%
	Med (4-7)	PASS	Tyler Boyd	9	56%
	Long (8-10)	PASS	Brandon LaFell	9	22%
	XL (11+)	PASS	Tyler Boyd	5	20%

Most Successful Play*

Down	Distance	Play Type	Player	Total Plays	Play Success %
1	Short (1-3)	RUSH	Jeremy Hill	5	40%
	Med (4-7)	RUSH	Jeremy Hill	8	63%
	Long (8-10)	PASS	Tyler Eifert	11	82%
2	Short (1-3)	RUSH	Giovani Bernard	6	83%
	Med (4-7)	PASS	A.J. Green	7	86%
	Long (8-10)	PASS	Cody Core	6	83%
3	Short (1-3)	PASS	Tyler Boyd	6	100%
		RUSH	Rex Burkhead	5	100%
	Med (4-7)	PASS	A.J. Green	6	67%
	Long (8-10)	PASS	Tyler Boyd	7	29%
	XL (11+)	PASS	Tyler Boyd	5	20%

**Minimum 5 plays to qualify*

2016 Snap Rates

Week	Opp	Score	Brandon LaFell	Tyler Boyd	A.J. Green	Jeremy Hill	Tyler Eifert	C.J. Uzomah	Giovani Bernard
1	NYJ	W 23-22	55 (96%)	44 (77%)	54 (95%)	29 (51%)		52 (91%)	28 (49%)
2	PIT	L 24-16	72 (95%)	58 (76%)	72 (95%)	29 (38%)		41 (54%)	49 (64%)
3	DEN	L 29-17	60 (90%)	24 (36%)	64 (96%)	33 (49%)		39 (58%)	35 (52%)
4	MIA	W 22-7	65 (93%)	28 (40%)	59 (84%)	36 (51%)		42 (60%)	34 (49%)
5	DAL	L 28-14	66 (94%)	50 (71%)	59 (84%)	16 (23%)		54 (77%)	53 (76%)
6	NE	L 35-17	62 (91%)	55 (81%)	62 (91%)	21 (31%)		48 (71%)	45 (66%)
7	CLE	W 31-17	57 (93%)	41 (67%)	51 (84%)	21 (34%)	15 (25%)	14 (23%)	33 (54%)
8	WAS	T 27-27	86 (98%)	72 (82%)	81 (92%)	39 (44%)	74 (84%)		48 (55%)
10	NYG	L 21-20	54 (93%)	32 (55%)	50 (86%)	27 (47%)	47 (81%)	1 (2%)	31 (53%)
11	BUF	L 16-12	69 (95%)	54 (74%)	2 (3%)	29 (40%)	62 (85%)		40 (55%)
12	BAL	L 19-14	67 (89%)	55 (73%)		37 (49%)	66 (88%)		
13	PHI	W 32-14	60 (94%)	42 (66%)		37 (58%)	47 (73%)		
14	CLE	W 23-10	65 (92%)	41 (58%)		41 (58%)	58 (82%)		
15	PIT	L 24-20	52 (90%)	43 (74%)		37 (64%)	58 (100%)		
16	HOU	L 12-10	61 (97%)	48 (76%)		13 (21%)		61 (97%)	
17	BAL	W 27-10	63 (93%)	50 (74%)				59 (87%)	
Grand Total			1,014 (93%)	737 (68%)	554 (81%)	445 (44%)	427 (77%)	411 (62%)	396 (57%)

Personnel Groupings

Personnel	Team %	NFL Avg	Succ. %
1-1 [3WR]	71%	60%	50%
1-2 [2WR]	20%	19%	42%
1-3 [1WR]	6%	3%	48%

Grouping Tendencies

Personnel	Pass Rate	Pass Succ. %	Run Succ. %
1-1 [3WR]	67%	45%	50%
1-2 [2WR]	40%	40%	34%
1-3 [1WR]	16%	15%	48%

Red Zone Targets (min 3)

Receiver	All	Inside 5	6-10	11-20
Brandon LaFell	17	3	7	7
A.J. Green	12	1	4	7
Tyler Eifert	12	5	2	5
Tyler Boyd	11	2		9
Giovani Bernard	7		3	4
C.J. Uzomah	6	3	1	2
Jeremy Hill	3			3

Red Zone Rushes (min 3)

Rusher	All	Inside 5	6-10	11-20
Jeremy Hill	48	16	9	23
Rex Burkhead	14	5	3	6
Giovani Bernard	13	3	4	6
Andy Dalton	6	4		2

Early Down Target Rate

	RB	TE	WR
	19%	18%	63%
NFL AVG	*19%*	*20%*	*61%*

Overall Target Success %

RB	TE	WR
51% #7	57% #8	52% #9

Cincinnati Bengals 2016 Passing Recap & 2017 Outlook

As mediocre a QB as Andy Dalton is, his performance to start the season with literally only AJ Green intact was better than expected. It was clear the team needed a deep threat to challenge DBs to the offense's right, as Dalton's 61 rating showed, but overall Dalton's explosive passing (10%) was above league average (8%). Despite a lot of unfamiliarity and less talent than he was accustomed to, Dalton's interception rate was small, with the majority of INTs in 10+ yards to go situations. Dalton's ability to succeed in 2017 has a lot to do with his protection. But unlike cluster injuries in-season, the Bengals have months to understand how they will have to adapt their offense to succeed in spite of the offensive line. There are many aides that Dalton and the Bengals should use to help their line and put the defense on its heels before the ball is even snapped. Presnap motion can help define coverage for Dalton more clearly, and allow him to communicate protection with his line and RBs. Situational tempo can keep the defense in suboptimal packages for current down and distance. Avoiding predictable pass/rush downs also is key, by passing more on 1st down and staying out of 3rd and 4+ yards to go, where the Bengals were over 92% pass last year.

Andy Dalton Rating All Downs

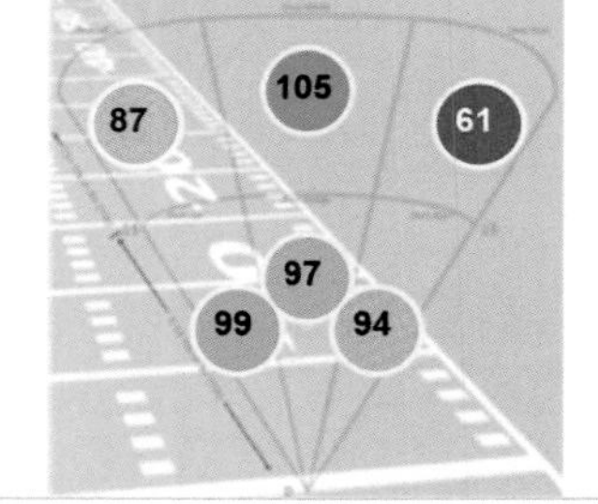

Andy Dalton Rating Early Downs

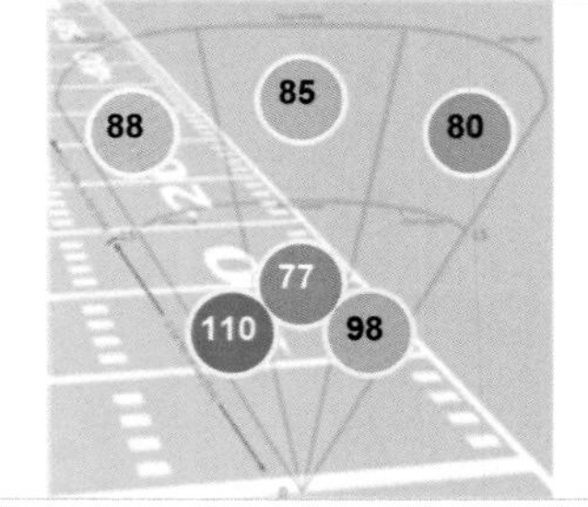

2016 Standard Passing Table

QB	Comp	Att	Comp %	Yds	YPA	TDs	INT	Sacks	Rating	Rk
Andy Dalton	363	562	65%	4,194	7.5	18	8	41	91.7	21
NFL Avg			63%		7.2				90.4	

2016 Advanced Passing Table

QB	Success %	EDSR Passing Success %	20+ Yd Pass Gains	20+ Yd Pass %	30+ Yd Pass Gains	30+ Yd Pass %	Air Yds per Comp	YAC per Comp	20+ Air Yd Comp	20+ Air Yd %
Andy Dalton	47%	52%	56	10%	17	3%	6.7	4.8	26	5%
NFL Avg	44%	48%	27	8%	10	3%	6.4	4.8	12	4%

Interception Rates by Down

Yards to Go	1	2	3	4	Total
1 & 2	0.0%	0.0%	0.0%		0.0%
3, 4, 5	0.0%	0.0%	0.0%	0.0%	0.0%
6 - 9	0.0%	1.4%	2.2%		1.6%
10 - 14	1.5%	3.0%	0.0%	0.0%	1.6%
15+	0.0%	0.0%	6.3%		2.0%
Total	1.4%	1.4%	1.2%	0.0%	1.3%

3rd Down Passing - Short of Sticks Analysis

QB	Avg Yds to Go	Air Yds (of Comps)	Avg Yds Short	Short of Sticks Rate	Rk
Andy Dalton	8.2	7.6	-0.6	56%	22
NFL Avg	7.6	6.8	-0.8	57%	

Air Yds vs YAC

Air Yds %	YAC %	Rk
55%	45%	24
54%	46%	

2016 Receiving Recap & 2017 Outlook

The receiving threats in Cincinnati are something to get excited about. When Brandon LaFell led your team in targets the prior year, it can only go up from there. Dalton's rating to all of his receivers w 50+ targets was extremely solid. But the success rates were not ideal. Doubling AJ Green leaves Ross 1-on-1, and Tyler Eifert as well as hopefully Joe Mixon out of the backfield should give plenty of threats which cannot be eliminated by the defense. I believe on a weekly basis, one of these players can go off, but there is no longer a need for Dalton to force feed Green like he had to do last year.

Player *Min 50 Targets*	Targets	Comp %	YPA	Rating	TOARS	Success %	Success Rk	Missed YPA Rk	YAS % Rk	TDs
Brandon LaFell	107	60%	8.1	100	4.9	51%	62	118	28	6
A.J. Green	100	66%	9.6	111	4.9	54%	46	85	16	4
Tyler Boyd	81	67%	7.4	77	4.2	54%	43	67	112	1
Giovani Bernard	51	76%	6.6	100	3.8	47%	105	107	132	1

Directional Passer Rating Delivered

Receiver	Short Left	Short Middle	Short Right	Deep Left	Deep Middle	Deep Right	Player Total
Brandon LaFell	106	129	88	118	119	44	100
A.J. Green	101	106	91	100	158	77	111
Tyler Boyd	92	42	96	51	104	70	77
Giovani Bernard	128	88	89			119	100
Tyler Eifert	118	95	83	48	119		106
C.J. Uzomah	60	102	108		21	96	80
Cody Core	88	96	65	119	40	40	85
Jeremy Hill	99	79	90				94
Rex Burkhead	73	108	93				97
Team Total	98	98	92	87	127	65	97

2016 Rushing Recap & 2017 Outlook

The most obvious thing about the Bengals last year was they had to rely on the run game more, and Jeremy Hill wasn't up to the task. Before we blame the situation and predictability, realize that many other RBs were forced into worse situations and produced better results, LeSean McCoy the obvious standard bearer. We all saw it, as did Cincinnati, which is why they took a risk to draft Joe Mixon after losing their most efficient RB, Rex Burkhead, in free agency to New England. If I were the Bengals I'd rather Hill be my 2nd half pounder with a lead rather than rely too much on him to get the lead. Let Mixon and Giovani Bernard share that role, and try to not be too predictable about playcalling per RB after a new one enters the game.

Player *Min 50 Rushes*	Rushes	YPA	Success %	Success Rk	Missed YPA Rk	YTS % Rk	YAS % Rk	Early Down Success %	Early Down Success Rk	TDs
Jeremy Hill	222	3.8	44%	44	32	41	29	44%	44	9
Giovani Bernard	91	3.7	49%	24	35	12	50	51%	17	2
Rex Burkhead	74	4.6	62%	2	1	10	37	59%	2	2

Yards per Carry by Direction

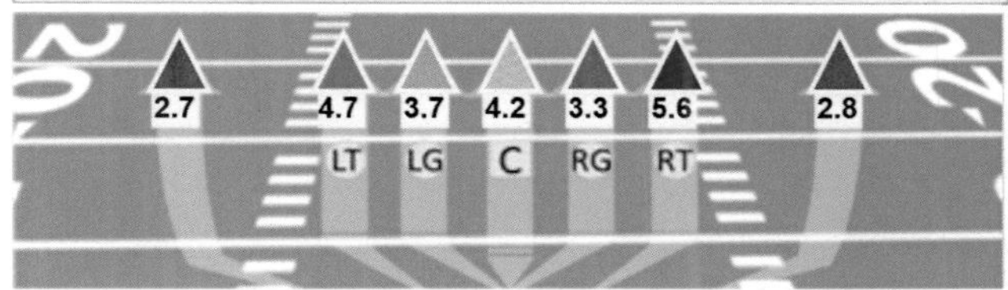

Directional Run Frequency

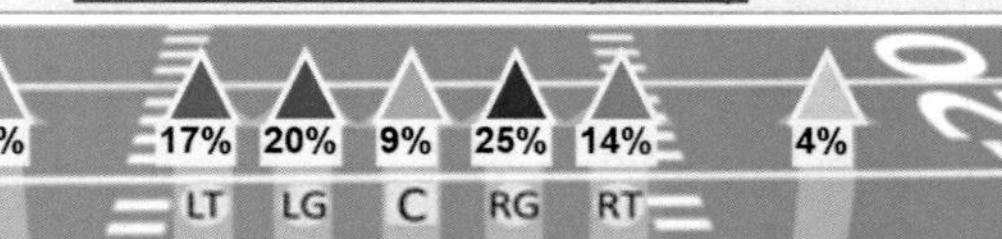

Cincinnati delivered the 12th most efficient rushing offense last season, so expectations should be higher in 2017, presuming the losses along the offensive line this offseason are capable of being replaced with a certain minimum level of performance.

Every defense is impacted by the offense, and the Bengals defense had to overcome tremendous hardships on account of the offensive performance last year. However, they were able to perform perhaps better than expected. In particular, they were a top-4 defense in red zone defense and explosive pass defense, two metrics which go a long way toward overall success. They'll be without a number of familiar faces on that side of the ball, but fortunately they play the 6th easiest schedule of opposing offenses in the NFL.

The 2017 Bengals are in a much better place than they were last year, thanks to three key elements: an easier overall schedule (from 5th toughest to 28th), the health of key receiving weapons and the infusion of their early draft picks into their struggling offense. From an odds perspective, they are favored in every game save for a battle with their nemesis the Steelers. On the road, apart from a large 7 point underdog in Pittsburgh and in Green Bay, every road game is essentially a coinflip where they underdogs of more than the standard +3 points just one other time.

From a play calling perspective, I would like to see the Bengals be a bit less predictable when under center. They ran nearly 10% more than the NFL average of 68% when lined up under center. I would also like to see more rushes on 2nd and short – they ran the ball less often than they did in 2015, and were near average in 1st down conversion rate, as opposed to well above it. Mixon should help there.

From a fantasy perspective, as mentioned earlier, the Bengals relied a ton on Jeremy Hill last year as their "most frequent play" and I expect that to change a lot this season. While the schedule gets lighter, the offensive line gets weaker and I don't see Hill having near the same success via volume as he had last year. Consider that Hill had 48 touches inside the red zone, including a massive 16 inside the 5 yard line. I expect that to plummet tremendously thanks to the other receiving options as well as the presence of Mixon, assuming he quickly earns the Bengals trust. Mixon's value, particularly early in the season, may be heavily game script influenced. He'll likely consume Rex Burkhead's touches and eat into Hill's, but Burkhead received just 6% of the Bengals total touches when the game was within one score. When the Bengals were up 9+ points, Burkhead was eating 26-28% of the team's offensive touches, a solid number. It will take time to see precisely how much involvement Ross has on a week to week basis, but if the Bengals establish him early in the season (particularly in good weather) as a legit deep threat, his mere presence on the field later in the season will cause defenses to overcompensate for him.

Division History: Season Wins & 2017 Projection

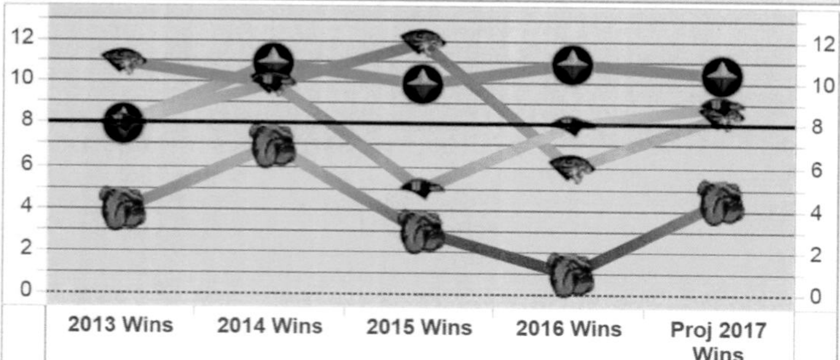

Rank of 2017 Defensive Pass Efficiency Faced by Week

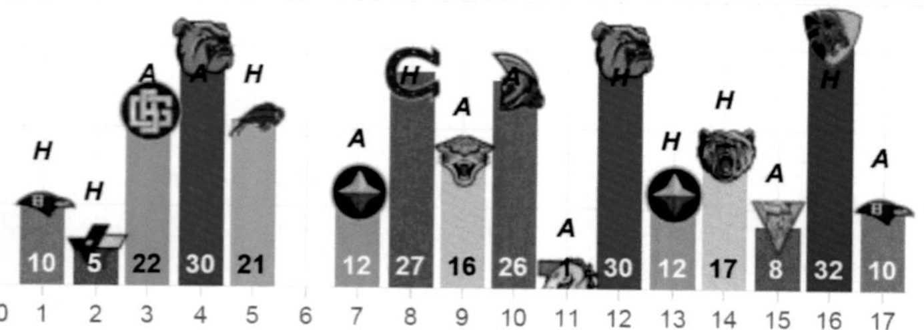

Rank of 2017 Defensive Rush Efficiency Faced by Week

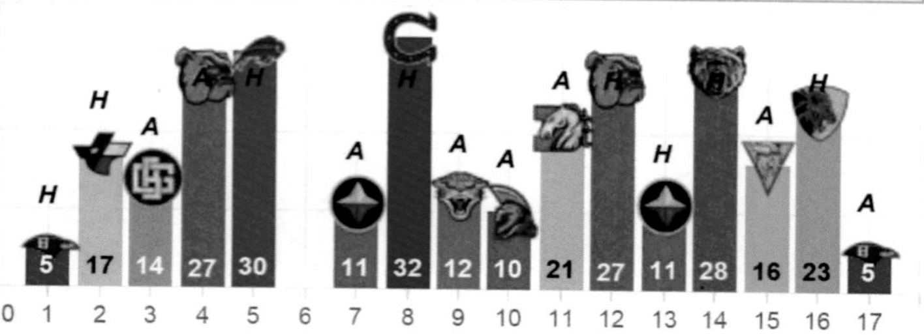

2016 Situational Usage by Player & Position

Usage Rate by Score

		Being Blown Out (14+)	Down Big (9-13)	One Score	Large Lead (9-13)	Blowout Lead (14+)	Grand Total
RUSH	Jeremy Hill	7%	15%	25%	28%	23%	24%
	Giovani Bernard	13%	5%	11%	2%	12%	10%
	Brandon LaFell			0%			0%
	Rex Burkhead	4%	1%	5%	21%	23%	8%
	Tyler Boyd			0%	1%		0%
	James Wright			0%			0%
	Cedric Peerman				3%	3%	1%
	Total	24%	22%	42%	55%	62%	43%
PASS	Jeremy Hill	2%	8%	2%	5%	2%	3%
	Giovani Bernard	16%	4%	6%	1%	1%	5%
	Brandon LaFell	18%	15%	10%	12%	11%	11%
	A.J. Green	15%	5%	13%	3%	2%	11%
	Rex Burkhead		3%	1%	5%	5%	2%
	Tyler Boyd	9%	11%	9%	7%	9%	9%
	Tyler Eifert		11%	5%	6%	1%	5%
	C.J. Uzomah	9%	5%	5%	1%		4%
	Cody Core			3%	3%	4%	3%
	James Wright	2%	8%	2%	1%		2%
	Tyler Kroft	5%	3%	1%			1%
	Alex Erickson		3%	0%	2%	1%	1%
	Cedric Peerman					1%	0%
	Ryan Hewitt		1%	0%			0%
	Total	76%	78%	58%	45%	38%	57%

Positional Target Distribution vs NFL Average

		NFL Wide				Team Only			
		Left	Middle	Right	Total	Left	Middle	Right	Total
Deep	WR	1,005	565	970	2,540	26	16	31	73
	TE	156	139	161	456	2	8	2	12
	RB	25	4	39	68			1	1
	All	1,186	708	1,170	3,064	28	24	34	86
Short	WR	2,999	1,722	3,087	7,808	94	49	99	242
	TE	811	859	1,119	2,789	25	16	32	73
	RB	989	591	1,073	2,653	26	31	40	97
	All	4,799	3,172	5,279	13,250	145	96	171	412
Total		5,985	3,880	6,449	16,314	173	120	205	498

Positional Success Rates vs NFL Average

		NFL Wide				Team Only			
		Left	Middle	Right	Total	Left	Middle	Right	Total
Deep	WR	37%	49%	38%	40%	36%	76%	30%	42%
	TE	44%	50%	43%	46%	50%	44%	50%	46%
	RB	32%	75%	23%	29%			100%	100%
	All	38%	50%	39%	41%	37%	65%	33%	43%
Short	WR	52%	57%	51%	53%	47%	44%	56%	50%
	TE	50%	61%	52%	54%	44%	69%	47%	51%
	RB	47%	49%	44%	46%	48%	58%	39%	47%
	All	51%	57%	50%	52%	47%	53%	50%	49%
Total		48%	55%	48%	50%	45%	55%	47%	48%

Cleveland Browns

2017 Coaches

Head Coach:
Hue Jackson (2nd yr)

Offensive Coordinator:
(Hue Jackson calls plays) (2nd yr)

Defensive Coordinator:
Gregg Williams (1st yr)

2017 Forecast

Wins	Div Rank
4.5	#4

Past Records

2016: 1-15
2015: 3-13
2014: 7-9

EASY HARD

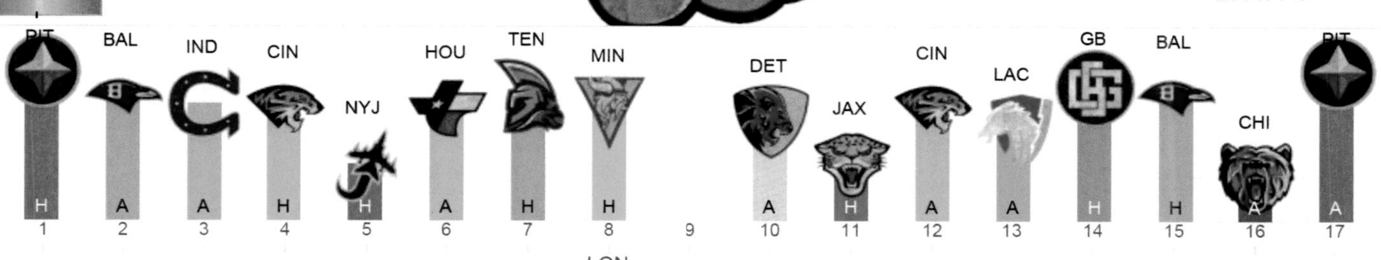

Key Players Lost

TXN	Player (POS)
Cut	Bailey, Alvin G
	Barnidge, Gary TE
	Carey, Donte S
	Elston, Trae S
	Griffin III, Robert QB
	Hawkins, Andrew WR
	Howard, Tracy S
	Lawrence-Stample, Nile DT
	McCown, Josh QB
	Powell, Tyvis S
	Williams, Tramon CB
Declared Free Agent	Neal, Rajion RB
	Paea, Stephen DT
	Parks, Dennis WR
	Pasztor, Austin T
	Poyer, Jordan CB
	Pryor Sr., Terrelle WR
	Winston, Glenn RB
	Wynn, Dylan DE
Retired	Cribbs, Josh WR

Average Line	# Games Favored	# Games Underdog
+6.5	0	14

Regular Season Wins: Past & Current Proj

Proj 2017 Wins  4.5

2016 Wins  1

Proj 2016 Wins  4.5

2015 Wins  3

2014 Wins  7

2013 Wins  4

1 3 5 7 9 11 13 15

2017 Cleveland Browns Overview

Cleveland is not yet in "win now" mode, which is a good thing, because they still lack the talent to win now. But they are progressing in a positive direction, despite the trending of their record. Surely this rebuild could be frustrating to fans, but a quick fix was never a possibility for this franchise. Additionally, what have the fans of the "Factory of Sadness" seen for the last 20+ years? Just one playoff game which resulted in a loss, 15 years ago. So it is not as if this team was on the cusp of being competitive. At least now, they are on the cusp of seeing if their rebuild plans will start to pay dividends. Not this year, but potentially in 2018 or more likely, 2019. But it takes time to get there. And in a win-now type NFL, it is actually refreshing to see a team try to take the pragmatic approach and put their best effort into staying on track with a long-term rebuild.

It was hard to picture the plan in 2015, a mere two seasons ago, saw the Browns spending $73.8M in defensive cap space, the third most in the entire NFL. It produced next to nothing. So last year the salary cap casualties began to pile up. Cleveland spend just $45M in cap space on defense in 2015, the 3rd lowest in the NFL. And their $46.5M on offense was the lowest by over $6M. So was there any surprise the Browns were the worst team in the NFL last year? It was planned to be this way.

Last year should be rock bottom, if things play true to plan. The Browns have started to spend again on positions they value. They added G Kevin Zeitler from the Bengals and C JC Tretter from the Packers. Neither were particularly cheap. Zeitler signed a 5 year, $60M deal, and Tretter signed a 3 year, $16.75M deal. Those deals represent the top paid free agency deal for a guard and the top paid free agency deal for a center. Instead of signing WR Terrelle Pryor to a long term deal, they let him walk to the Redskins for a 1 year, $6M deal. In his place, they signed WR Kenny Britt to a 4 year, $32.5M deal, making Britt the 3rd most expensive free agency signing this offseason.

Cleveland also put to use their numerous draft picks. In addition to drafting two of the top defensive prospects at their positions (DE Myles Garrett and S Jabrill Peppers) they added one to the best TE talents in David Njoku and

(cont'd - see CLE2)

Key Free Agents/ Trades Added

- Britt, Kenny WR
- Cribbs, Josh WR
- King, Deon LB
- McCants, Matt T
- McCourty, Jason CB
- Osweiler, Brock QB
- Pryor, Calvin S
- Tretter, JC C
- Zeitler, Kevin G

Drafted Players

Rd	Pk	Player (College)
	1	DE - Myles Garrett (Texas A&M)
1	25	S - Jabrill Peppers (Michigan)
	29	TE - David Njoku (Miami (FL))
2	52	QB - DeShone Kizer (Notre Dame)
3	65	DT - Larry Ogunjobi (Charlotte)
4	126	CB - Howard Wilson (Houston)
5	160	OT - Roderick Johnson (Florida State)
6	185	DT - Caleb Brantley (Florida)
7	224	K - Zane Gonzalez (Arizona State)
7*	252	RB - Matthew Dayes (NC State)

2017 Lineup & Cap Hits

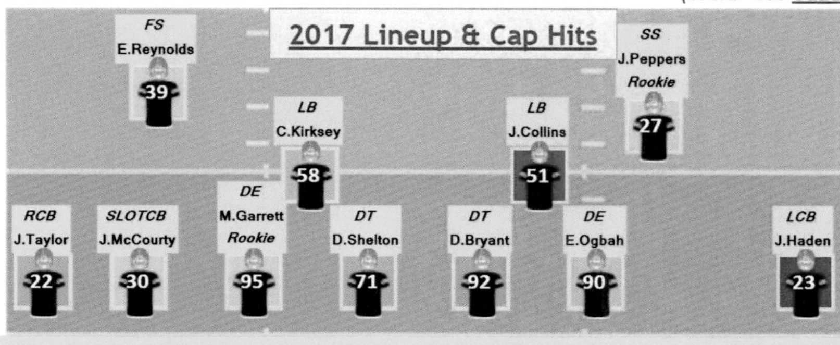

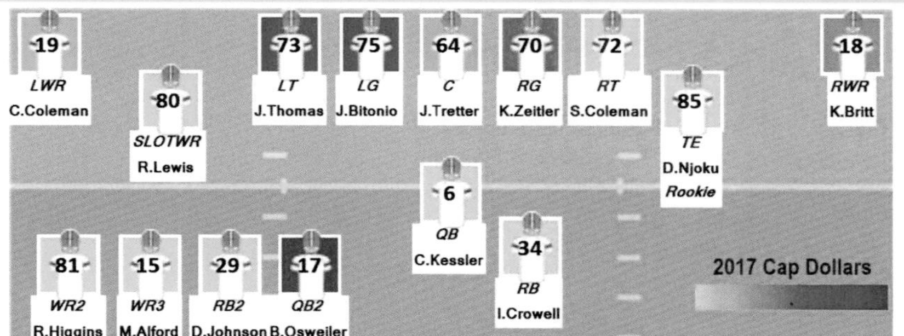

2017 Unit Spending

Positional Spending

	Rank	Total	2016 Rk
All OFF	8	$88.62M	32
QB	17	$17.78M	23
OL	1	$48.49M	19
RB	22	$5.83M	25
WR	26	$13.92M	28
TE	32	$2.60M	28
All DEF	25	$69.44M	30
DL	21	$20.08M	28
LB	15	$20.94M	31
CB	6	$23.42M	2
S	31	$5.01M	32

Cleveland Browns 2016 Success Rate Radar

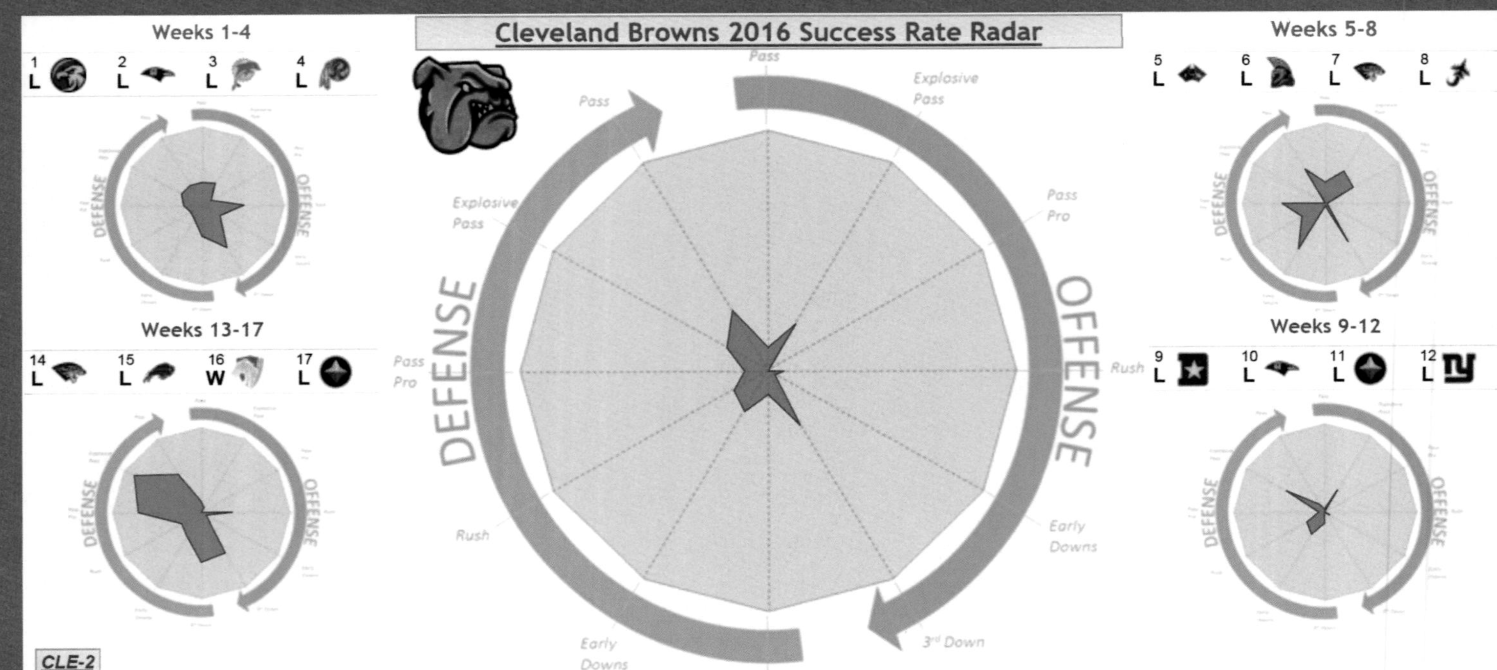

CLE-2

a QB at 52 overall (DeShone Kizer) who Hue Jackson began likening to Ben Roethlisberger. Kizer likely will need more time to develop, unlike Roethlisberger, and the team is certainly not built up enough to slip him in week 1 and see success with Kizer as a game manager, like the Steelers were able to do with Roethlisberger.

Which should mean the Browns are likely to struggle this year, as most teams do without a reasonable quarterback under center. As such, the Browns are projected to win just 4 games this season, and finish with the worst record in the NFL for a second straight season. In their 15 currently lined games, they are not favored in any of them. The Browns narrowly eluded an 0-16 season last year, but while they certainly should struggle this year, it would be surprising to see them need to wait until week 16 to notch their first victory. That said, could they land yet another top-3 pick in the 2018 draft, if not the first overall? It is certainly possible. And with the influx of solid talent thanks to another haul of draft picks next year, the team is building itself more intelligently than any Browns squad in recent memory.

I've seen more than enough from the Browns to tell that their trajectory is the proper course, and while it is impossible to judge their long term outlook at this moment, I wouldn't argue one bit with their strategy. Could they have reached to overdraft a quarterback in either of the last two drafts? Yes, they certainly could have done that. They could have drafted Paxton Lynch at 15 last year. They could have drafted Mitchell Trubisky or Patrick Mahomes at #1 overall this year. But what does that do for them near term? This digs into a far deeper rabbit hole of team building strategy. But when looking to rebuild a franchise and turn a team around, I would argue against conventional wisdom of drafting a quarterback first, and then building around him. Unless that player is a generational player, like an Andrew Luck. For the most part, what is the benefit of dumping a high draft pick quarterback behind a bad offensive line, with a terrible defense? His team is likely to be trailing most of the game

(cont'd - see CLE-3)

2016 Offensive Advanced Metrics

2016 Defensive Advanced Metrics

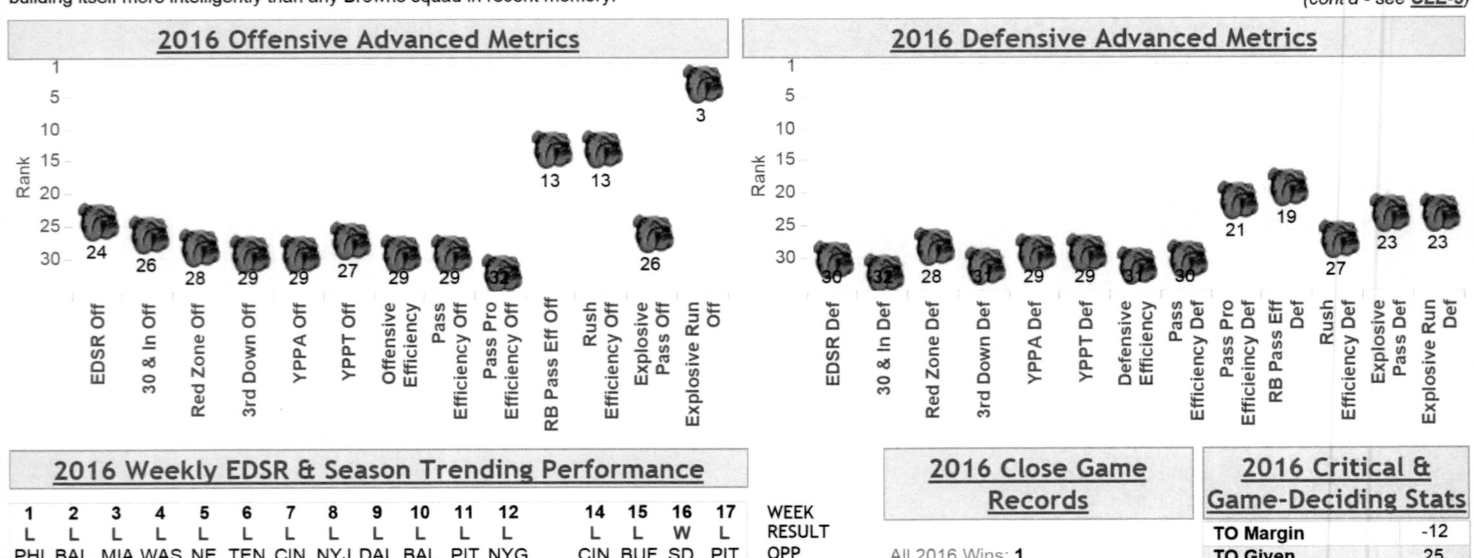

2016 Weekly EDSR & Season Trending Performance

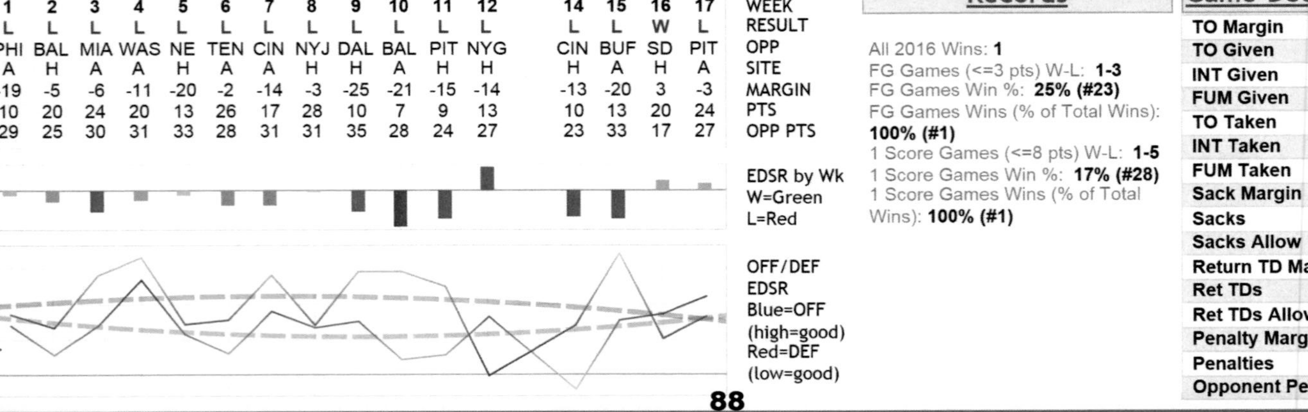

1	2	3	4	5	6	7	8	9	10	11	12	14	15	16	17	WEEK
L	L	L	L	L	L	L	L	L	L	L	L	L	L	W	L	RESULT
PHI	BAL	MIA	WAS	NE	TEN	CIN	NYJ	DAL	BAL	PIT	NYG	CIN	BUF	SD	PIT	OPP
A	H	A	A	H	A	A	H	H	A	H	H	H	A	H	A	SITE
-19	-5	-6	-11	-20	-2	-14	-3	-25	-21	-15	-14	-13	-20	3	-3	MARGIN
10	20	24	20	13	26	17	28	10	7	9	13	10	13	20	24	PTS
29	25	30	31	33	28	31	31	35	28	24	27	23	33	17	27	OPP PTS

2016 Close Game Records

All 2016 Wins: **1**
FG Games (<=3 pts) W-L: **1-3**
FG Games Win %: **25% (#23)**
FG Games Wins (% of Total Wins): **100% (#1)**
1 Score Games (<=8 pts) W-L: **1-5**
1 Score Games Win %: **17% (#28)**
1 Score Games Wins (% of Total Wins): **100% (#1)**

2016 Critical & Game-Deciding Stats

TO Margin	-12
TO Given	25
INT Given	14
FUM Given	11
TO Taken	13
INT Taken	10
FUM Taken	3
Sack Margin	-40
Sacks	26
Sacks Allow	66
Return TD Margin	-1
Ret TDs	1
Ret TDs Allow	2
Penalty Margin	+9
Penalties	95
Opponent Penalties	104

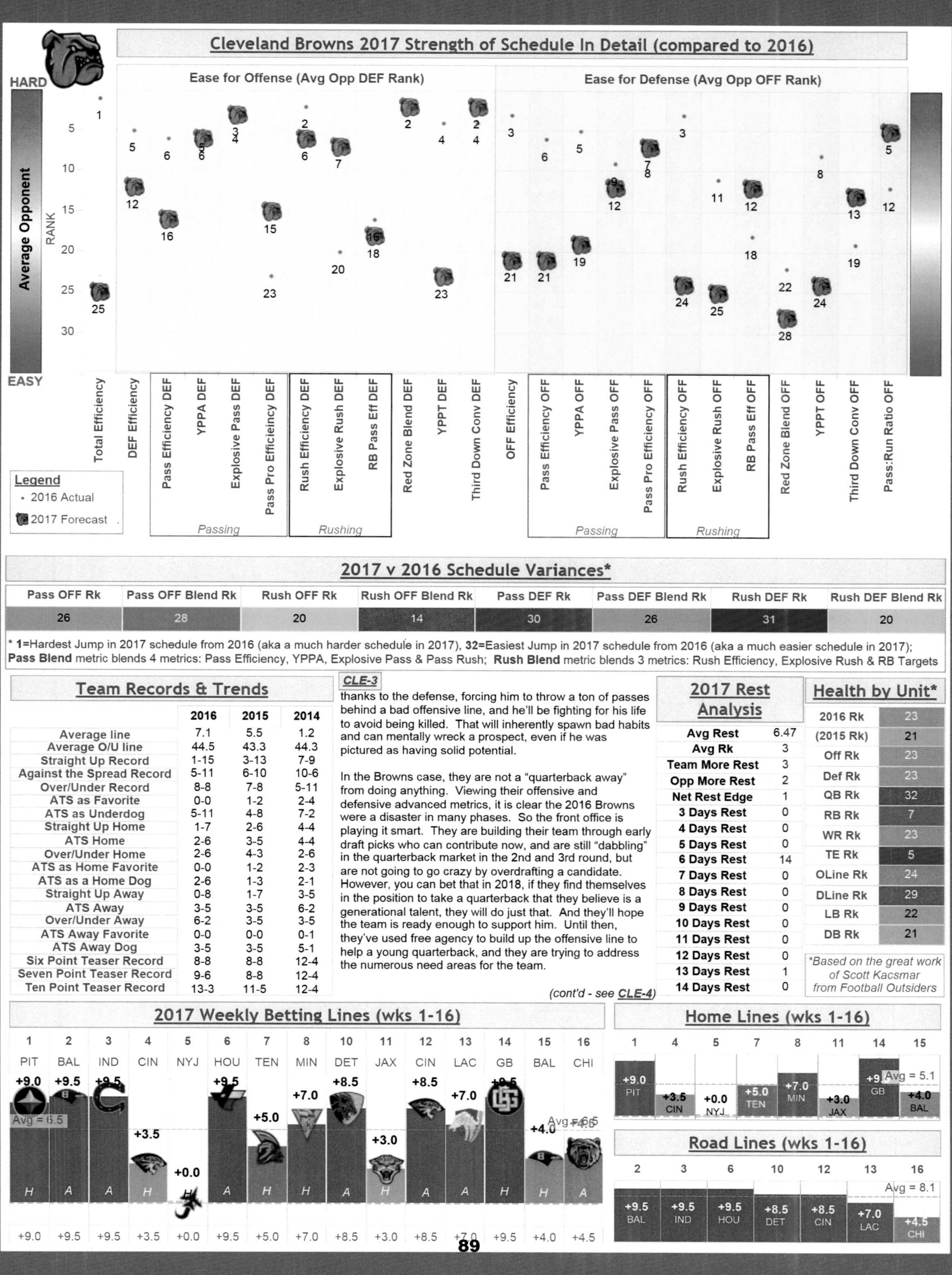

Cleveland Browns 2017 Strength of Schedule In Detail (compared to 2016)

2017 v 2016 Schedule Variances*

Pass OFF Rk	Pass OFF Blend Rk	Rush OFF Rk	Rush OFF Blend Rk	Pass DEF Rk	Pass DEF Blend Rk	Rush DEF Rk	Rush DEF Blend Rk
26	28	20	14	30	26	31	20

* **1**=Hardest Jump in 2017 schedule from 2016 (aka a much harder schedule in 2017), **32**=Easiest Jump in 2017 schedule from 2016 (aka a much easier schedule in 2017); **Pass Blend** metric blends 4 metrics: Pass Efficiency, YPPA, Explosive Pass & Pass Rush; **Rush Blend** metric blends 3 metrics: Rush Efficiency, Explosive Rush & RB Targets

Team Records & Trends

	2016	2015	2014
Average line	7.1	5.5	1.2
Average O/U line	44.5	43.3	44.3
Straight Up Record	1-15	3-13	7-9
Against the Spread Record	5-11	6-10	10-6
Over/Under Record	8-8	7-8	5-11
ATS as Favorite	0-0	1-2	2-4
ATS as Underdog	5-11	4-8	7-2
Straight Up Home	1-7	2-6	4-4
ATS Home	2-6	3-5	4-4
Over/Under Home	2-6	4-3	2-6
ATS as Home Favorite	0-0	1-2	2-3
ATS as a Home Dog	2-6	1-3	2-1
Straight Up Away	0-8	1-7	3-5
ATS Away	3-5	3-5	6-2
Over/Under Away	6-2	3-5	3-5
ATS Away Favorite	0-0	0-0	0-1
ATS Away Dog	3-5	3-5	5-1
Six Point Teaser Record	8-8	8-8	12-4
Seven Point Teaser Record	9-6	8-8	12-4
Ten Point Teaser Record	13-3	11-5	12-4

CLE-3

thanks to the defense, forcing him to throw a ton of passes behind a bad offensive line, and he'll be fighting for his life to avoid being killed. That will inherently spawn bad habits and can mentally wreck a prospect, even if he was pictured as having solid potential.

In the Browns case, they are not a "quarterback away" from doing anything. Viewing their offensive and defensive advanced metrics, it is clear the 2016 Browns were a disaster in many phases. So the front office is playing it smart. They are building their team through early draft picks who can contribute now, and are still "dabbling" in the quarterback market in the 2nd and 3rd round, but are not going to go crazy by overdrafting a candidate. However, you can bet that in 2018, if they find themselves in the position to take a quarterback that they believe is a generational talent, they will do just that. And they'll hope the team is ready enough to support him. Until then, they've used free agency to build up the offensive line to help a young quarterback, and they are trying to address the numerous need areas for the team.

(cont'd - see CLE-4)

2017 Rest Analysis

Avg Rest	6.47
Avg Rk	3
Team More Rest	3
Opp More Rest	2
Net Rest Edge	1
3 Days Rest	0
4 Days Rest	0
5 Days Rest	0
6 Days Rest	14
7 Days Rest	0
8 Days Rest	0
9 Days Rest	0
10 Days Rest	0
11 Days Rest	0
12 Days Rest	0
13 Days Rest	1
14 Days Rest	0

Health by Unit*

2016 Rk	23
(2015 Rk)	21
Off Rk	23
Def Rk	23
QB Rk	32
RB Rk	7
WR Rk	23
TE Rk	5
OLine Rk	24
DLine Rk	29
LB Rk	22
DB Rk	21

*Based on the great work of Scott Kacsmar from Football Outsiders

2017 Weekly Betting Lines (wks 1-16)

Week	1	2	3	4	5	6	7	8	10	11	12	13	14	15	16
Opponent	PIT	BAL	IND	CIN	NYJ	HOU	TEN	MIN	DET	JAX	CIN	LAC	GB	BAL	CHI
Line	+9.0	+9.5	+9.5	+3.5	+0.0	+9.5	+5.0	+7.0	+8.5	+3.0	+8.5	+7.0	+9.5	+4.0	+4.5
H/A	H	A	A	H	H	A	H	H	A	H	A	A	H	H	A

Home Lines (wks 1-16)

Week	1	4	5	7	8	11	14	15
Opponent	PIT	CIN	NYJ	TEN	MIN	JAX	GB	BAL
Line	+9.0	+3.5	+0.0	+5.0	+7.0	+3.0	+9.5	+4.0

Road Lines (wks 1-16)

Week	2	3	6	10	12	13	16
Opponent	BAL	IND	HOU	DET	CIN	LAC	CHI
Line	+9.5	+9.5	+9.5	+8.5	+8.5	+7.0	+4.5

Cleveland Browns 2016 Play Analysis

2016 Play Tendencies

All Pass %	60%
All Pass Rk	16
All Rush %	40%
All Rush Rk	17
1 Score Pass %	60%
1 Score Pass Rk	12
2015 1 Score Pass %	62%
2015 1 Score Pass Rk	7
Pass Increase %	-2%
Pass Increase Rk	20
1 Score Rush %	40%
1 Score Rush Rk	21
Up Pass %	62%
Up Pass Rk	7
Up Rush %	38%
Up Rush Rk	26
Down Pass %	59%
Down Pass Rk	25
Down Rush %	41%
Down Rush Rk	8

2016 Down & Distance Tendencies

Down	Distance	Total Plays	Pass Rate	Run Rate	Play Success %
1	Short (1-3)	6	33%	67%	50%
	Med (4-7)	9	33%	67%	56%
	Long (8-10)	290	52%	48%	44%
	XL (11+)	18	61%	39%	50%
2	Short (1-3)	23	30%	70%	61%
	Med (4-7)	62	65%	35%	45%
	Long (8-10)	97	66%	34%	37%
	XL (11+)	46	48%	52%	20%
3	Short (1-3)	28	50%	50%	64%
	Med (4-7)	43	93%	7%	49%
	Long (8-10)	45	87%	13%	29%
	XL (11+)	42	76%	24%	19%
4	Short (1-3)	3	0%	100%	100%
	Med (4-7)	2	50%	50%	50%
	Long (8-10)	1	100%	0%	100%

Shotgun %:

Under Center	Shotgun
30%	70%
37%	*63%*

37% AVG 63%

Run Rate:

Under Center	Shotgun
60%	23%

68% AVG 23%

Pass Rate:

Under Center	Shotgun
40%	77%

32% AVG 77%

Short Yardage Intelligence:

2nd and Short Run

Run Freq	Run % Rk	NFL Run Freq Avg	Run 1D Rate	Run NFL 1D Avg
52%	29	65%	75%	71%

2nd and Short Pass

Pass Freq	Pass % Rk	NFL Pass Freq Avg	Pass 1D Rate	Pass NFL 1D Avg
48%	4	35%	18%	52%

Most Frequent Play

Down	Distance	Play Type	Player	Total Plays	Play Success %
1	Short (1-3)	RUSH	Isaiah Crowell	4	75%
	Med (4-7)	RUSH	Isaiah Crowell	4	75%
	Long (8-10)	RUSH	Isaiah Crowell	86	40%
	XL (11+)	RUSH	Isaiah Crowell	5	60%
2	Short (1-3)	RUSH	Isaiah Crowell	9	89%
	Med (4-7)	RUSH	Isaiah Crowell	14	21%
	Long (8-10)	RUSH	Isaiah Crowell	20	20%
	XL (11+)	RUSH	Isaiah Crowell	17	6%
3	Short (1-3)	RUSH	Isaiah Crowell	6	67%
	Med (4-7)	PASS	Terrelle Pryor	9	67%
			Duke Johnson	9	44%
	Long (8-10)	PASS	Gary Barnidge	10	40%
	XL (11+)	PASS	Duke Johnson	11	18%

Most Successful Play*

Down	Distance	Play Type	Player	Total Plays	Play Success %
1	Long (8-10)	PASS	Duke Johnson	7	86%
	XL (11+)	RUSH	Isaiah Crowell	5	60%
2	Short (1-3)	RUSH	Isaiah Crowell	9	89%
	Med (4-7)	PASS	Terrelle Pryor	10	60%
	Long (8-10)	PASS	Duke Johnson	7	57%
	XL (11+)	RUSH	Isaiah Crowell	17	6%
3	Short (1-3)	RUSH	Isaiah Crowell	6	67%
	Med (4-7)	PASS	Terrelle Pryor	9	67%
	Long (8-10)	PASS	Gary Barnidge	10	40%
	XL (11+)	PASS	Terrelle Pryor	5	60%

**Minimum 5 plays to qualify*

2016 Snap Rates

Week	Opp	Score	Gary Barnidge	Terrelle Pryor	Andrew Hawkins	Isaiah Crowell	Corey Coleman	Duke Johnson	Ricardo Louis
1	PHI	L 29-10	51 (98%)	46 (88%)	33 (63%)	30 (58%)	47 (90%)	23 (44%)	2 (4%)
2	BAL	L 25-20	59 (95%)	56 (90%)	37 (60%)	33 (53%)	53 (85%)	31 (50%)	2 (3%)
3	MIA	L 30-24	79 (96%)	78 (95%)	60 (73%)	39 (48%)		41 (50%)	51 (62%)
4	WAS	L 31-20	72 (100%)	70 (97%)	54 (75%)	34 (47%)		40 (56%)	50 (69%)
5	NE	L 33-13	62 (98%)	63 (100%)	54 (86%)	35 (56%)		28 (44%)	41 (65%)
6	TEN	L 28-26	67 (100%)	64 (96%)	53 (79%)	38 (57%)		32 (48%)	43 (64%)
7	CIN	L 31-17	62 (97%)	31 (48%)	37 (58%)	38 (59%)		30 (47%)	50 (78%)
8	NYJ	L 31-28	69 (96%)	59 (82%)	48 (67%)	41 (57%)		31 (43%)	46 (64%)
9	DAL	L 35-10	44 (100%)	41 (93%)	29 (66%)	22 (50%)	40 (91%)	22 (50%)	0 (0%)
10	BAL	L 28-7	36 (72%)	43 (86%)	28 (56%)	30 (60%)	45 (90%)	21 (42%)	3 (6%)
11	PIT	L 24-9	60 (91%)	58 (88%)	40 (61%)	35 (53%)	57 (86%)	32 (48%)	5 (8%)
12	NYG	L 27-13	57 (76%)	65 (87%)	30 (40%)	40 (53%)	66 (88%)	35 (47%)	4 (5%)
14	CIN	L 23-10	51 (94%)	46 (85%)	29 (54%)	30 (56%)	46 (85%)	24 (44%)	1 (2%)
15	BUF	L 33-13	52 (90%)	49 (84%)	30 (52%)	29 (50%)	55 (95%)	29 (50%)	4 (7%)
16	SD	W 20-17	69 (97%)	65 (92%)	42 (59%)	38 (54%)	61 (86%)	33 (46%)	2 (3%)
17	PIT	L 27-24	71 (91%)	64 (82%)	44 (56%)	52 (67%)	63 (81%)	4 (5%)	9 (12%)
Grand Total			961 (93%)	898 (87%)	648 (63%)	564 (55%)	533 (88%)	456 (45%)	313 (28%)

Personnel Groupings

Personnel	Team %	NFL Avg	Succ. %
1-1 [3WR]	65%	60%	40%
1-2 [2WR]	16%	19%	39%
2-1 [2WR]	11%	7%	40%
2-2 [1WR]	4%	3%	55%
1-3 [1WR]	3%	3%	47%

Grouping Tendencies

Personnel	Pass Rate	Pass Succ. %	Run Succ. %
1-1 [3WR]	71%	40%	40%
1-2 [2WR]	63%	43%	32%
2-1 [2WR]	47%	45%	36%
2-2 [1WR]	32%	50%	57%
1-3 [1WR]	41%	46%	47%

Red Zone Targets (min 3)

Receiver	All	Inside 5	6-10	11-20
Terrelle Pryor	13	1	3	9
Andrew Hawkins	11	3	2	6
Duke Johnson	7	2	1	4
Isaiah Crowell	6		3	3
Gary Barnidge	5	2		3
Corey Coleman	4		1	3
Rashard Higgins	3			3
Ricardo Louis	3			3

Red Zone Rushes (min 3)

Rusher	All	Inside 5	6-10	11-20
Isaiah Crowell	28	13	5	10
Duke Johnson	7	1	4	2
Cody Kessler	3	1	1	1

Early Down Target Rate

	RB	TE	WR
	26%	15%	59%
NFL AVG	*19%*	*20%*	*61%*

Overall Target Success %

RB	TE	WR
47% #13	50% #22	45% #26

Cleveland Browns 2016 Passing Recap & 2017 Outlook

The rotation of quarterbacks included Robert Griffin III, Charlie Whitehurst and Kevin Hogan, in addition to Cody Kessler and Josh McCown shown below. Kessler was actually far better with the football than most quarterbacks. In 8 starts, he threw just 2 interceptions, far fewer than McCown's 6 in 3 starts or Griffin's 3 in 5 starts. And while Hue Jackson benched Kessler for not being aggressive enough, his rate of 20+ yard passes was actually no worse than average, but those relied on a lot of yards after the catch. Kessler had just 5 completions of 20+ air yards last season, a number well below average. However, Kessler was effective on early downs and his overall success rate was solid. The Browns now have Brock Osweiler, who will chuck the ball deep, but with a ton of inaccuracy, and they also added DeShone Kizer. At this point, it is hard to project how the ultimate depth chart will shake out, that is something likely to be firmed up in training camp, but you can expect the Browns to do their best in 2017 to evaluate exactly what they have at the position, because quarterback is likely to still be a need for the 2018 draft. I expect Hue Jackson to make internal QB evaluation one of the top priorities for 2017.

Cody Kessler Rating All Downs

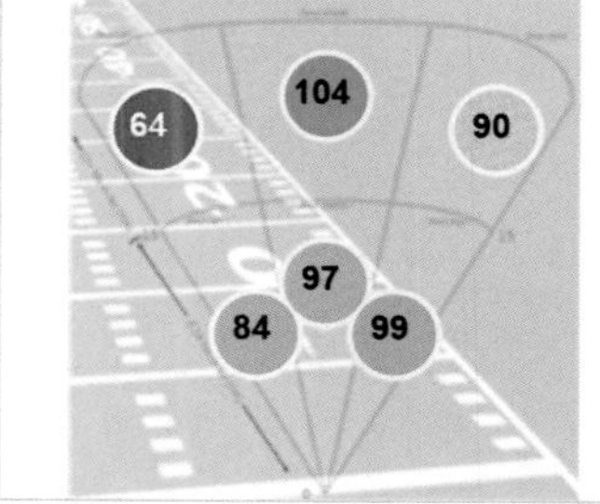

Cody Kessler Rating Early Downs

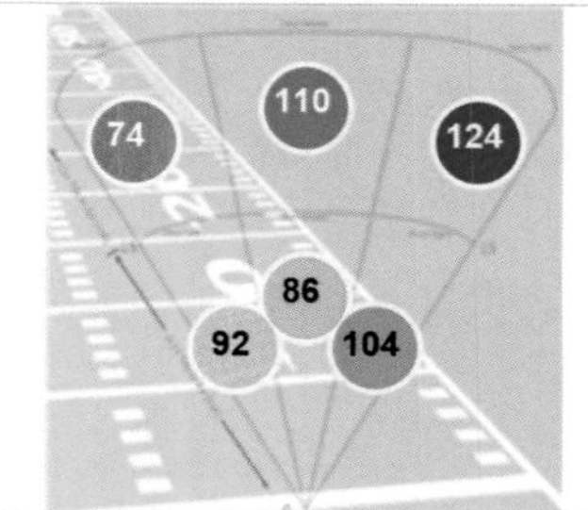

2016 Standard Passing Table

QB	Comp	Att	Comp %	Yds	YPA	TDs	INT	Sacks	Rating	Rk
Cody Kessler	128	195	66%	1,380	7.1	6	2	21	92.3	20
Josh McCown	90	165	55%	1,100	6.7	6	6	18	72.3	45
NFL Avg			63%		7.2				90.4	

2016 Advanced Passing Table

QB	Success %	EDSR Passing Success %	20+ Yd Pass Gains	20+ Yd Pass %	30+ Yd Pass Gains	30+ Yd Pass %	Air Yds per Comp	YAC per Comp	20+ Air Yd Comp	20+ Air Yd %
Cody Kessler	45%	50%	17	9%	5	3%	5.8	5.0	5	3%
Josh McCown	41%	40%	14	8%	6	4%	7.0	5.2	7	4%
NFL Avg	44%	48%	27	8%	10	3%	6.4	4.8	12	4%

Interception Rates by Down

Yards to Go	1	2	3	4	Total
1 & 2		25.0%	0.0%	0.0%	10.0%
3, 4, 5	0.0%	0.0%	0.0%	0.0%	0.0%
6 - 9		0.0%	0.0%	0.0%	0.0%
10 - 14	0.0%	0.0%	0.0%		0.0%
15+	0.0%	0.0%	16.7%		5.3%
Total	0.0%	1.4%	1.6%	0.0%	0.9%

3rd Down Passing - Short of Sticks Analysis

QB	Avg Yds to Go	Air Yds (of Comps)	Avg Yds Short	Short of Sticks Rate	Rk
Cody Kessler	8.5	4.8	-3.7	68%	41
NFL Avg	7.6	6.8	-0.8	57%	

Air Yds vs YAC

Air Yds %	YAC %	Rk
46%	54%	40
54%	46%	

2016 Receiving Recap & 2017 Outlook

Terrelle Pryor put up tremendous numbers in the short passing game. Less so in the deep game. But instead of keeping him, the Browns let him walk to the Redskins for 1 year, $6M and instead signed Kenny Britt to a 4 year, $32.5M deal. They also let second leading receiver from 2016, TE Gary Barnidge go after drafting TE David Njoku. Receivers without a capable quarterback are not going to impact the game as much as they could otherwise. The Browns will need to alleviate pressure from their quarterback by attempting a lot of fast pass offense, and sprinkling in some deeper shots. Given game script, Njoku could be a nice late round TE.

Player *Min 50 Targets*	Targets	Comp %	YPA	Rating	TOARS	Success %	Success Rk	Missed YPA Rk	YAS % Rk	TDs
Terrelle Pryor	141	55%	7.1	72	4.9	49%	86	101	74	4
Gary Barnidge	81	68%	7.6	93	4.4	53%	53	54	121	2
Duke Johnson	74	72%	6.9	79	4.0	47%	101	146	110	0
Corey Coleman	73	45%	5.7	66	3.7	37%	141	141	71	3
Andrew Hawkins	53	62%	6.1	98	3.8	47%	102	96	92	3
Isaiah Crowell	53	75%	6.0	90	3.7	49%	82	64	105	0

Directional Passer Rating Delivered

Receiver	Short Left	Short Middle	Short Right	Deep Left	Deep Middle	Deep Right	Player Total
Terrelle Pryor	76	97	106	32	67	19	70
Gary Barnidge	89	105	77	96	119	119	93
Duke Johnson	52	115	67				79
Corey Coleman	73	1	71	108	96	5	66
Andrew Hawkins	82	82	116	40	119	96	98
Isaiah Crowell	82	56	92	119	119		90
Ricardo Louis	86	99	53		0	96	56
Team Total	76	93	86	79	65	29	79

2016 Rushing Recap & 2017 Outlook

It likely could be the offensive line or the #2 hardest schedule of run defenses, but the Browns must get more out of their run game in 2017. The Browns were more of a right handed run team, going behind RG John Greco 29% of the time but averaging only 3.8 YPA. Now, RG Kevin Zeitler replaces Greco, as does C JC Tretter. Expect a more productive run game as the core element of the Browns offense as a result. Crowell was great at breaking big runs (ranked 3rd in yards above success %) but just 62nd in overall success rate. Thus, his 4.8 YPA is skewed, as many of the total yards came on much smaller number of extremely large gains. Both RBs were extremely efficient weapons out of the backfield as receivers, and I expect that to continue.

Player *Min 50 Rushes*	Rushes	YPA	Success %	Success Rk	Missed YPA Rk	YTS % Rk	YAS % Rk	Early Down Success %	Early Down Success Rk	TDs
Isaiah Crowell	197	4.8	39%	62	64	68	3	37%	63	7
Duke Johnson	74	4.9	45%	43	68	62	17	49%	26	1

Yards per Carry by Direction

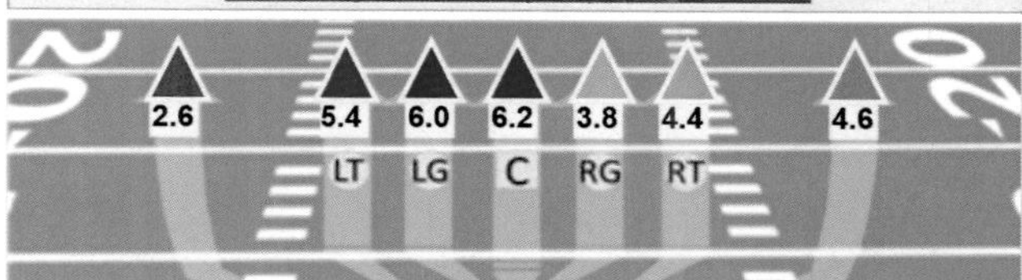

Directional Run Frequency

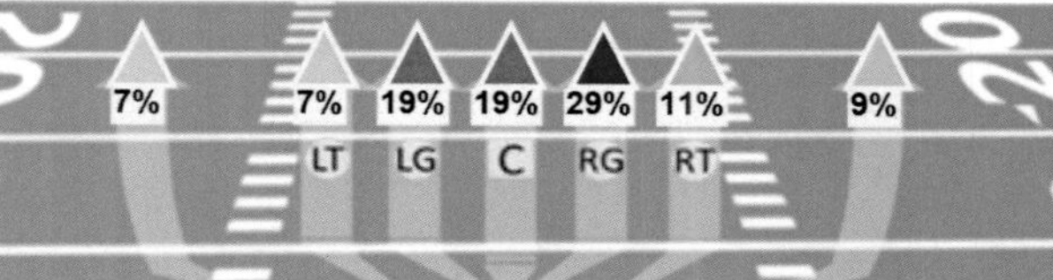

CLE-4

When we look ahead, it is more exciting to picture the 2018 or 2019 version of the Browns than the 2017 version, but what can this 2017 version deliver, despite being the least expensive team (from a cap hit perspective) in the NFL this year? As usual, we start with the 2016 version and build forward to include added pieces. While they won just one game last year, they went 1-5 in games decided by one score or less. Thanks in part to a massive 11 fumbles, the Browns were -12 in turnover margin last year. It unfortunately wasn't isolated to just a few games – they lost the turnover battle in 10 games, and lost all 10 games, generally by wide margins. The easiest way to lose games is by losing the turnover battle - teams who lose the turnover battle lose roughly 80% of the time. It's hard enough for the Browns to win a game even when winning the turnover battle: while the NFL as a whole wins 80% of the time when winning the turnover battle, the Browns are 5-10 (33%) in their last 15 games when winning the turnover battle (dating back to 2013). So they cannot afford to lose the turnover battle in 2017.

The biggest problem for this offense last year were the sacks. They allowed 66 sacks and recorded only 26. That was a -40 sack margin. Not since the Houston Texans first joined the NFL, led by David Carr, did a team record a worse sack margin. For this reason, they brought in Zeitler and Tretter. And for this reason, drafting a quarterback #1 overall, would have been inconceivable.

In Hue Jackson's first season, with a major quarterback identity crisis, the Browns faced the NFL's #1 overall most difficult schedule of opponents and won only 1 game. In 2017, the schedule lightens up tremendously, but they still face an above average difficulty of opposing offenses. For the pass game, they see a drop from the 6th most difficult schedule in 2016 to the 16th in 2017. It's an easier schedule than 2016, but at this stage in Hue Jackson's tenure, the focus should be entirely on fixing the Browns from the inside, not worrying about who they play in 2017. The run defenses the Browns face in 2017 are very similar from a schedule strength perspective to what they faced in 2016. The Browns run offense was similar to the Dolphins last year in that it was extremely explosive, but far less efficient. Large gains would be offset by more routine failures.

The Browns rarely made their way inside an opponent's 5 yard line, and when they did, it was the Isaih Crowell show, where he had 13 rushes and the team rarely passed the ball. Look for more passes to tight ends this season as well. Last year the Browns tossed just 15% of their passes to TEs, well below the NFL average of 20%. Since passing to TEs is the most successful pass, league wide and for the Browns as well, look for them to use 1st round pick David Njoku a lot, particularly as they got rid of their top 2 receivers from last year (Terrelle Pryor and Gary Barnidge).

Division History: Season Wins & 2017 Projection

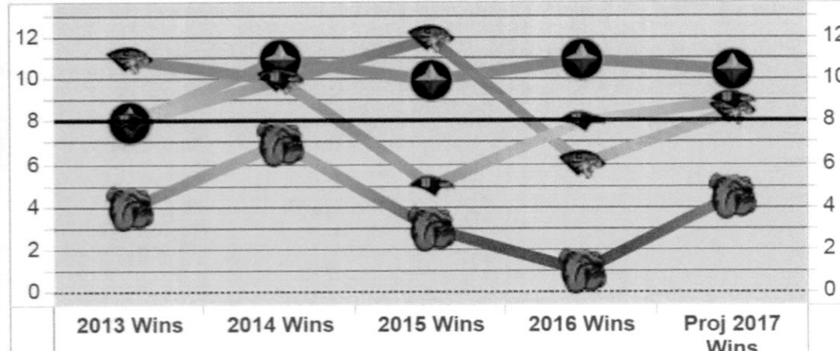

Rank of 2017 Defensive Pass Efficiency Faced by Week

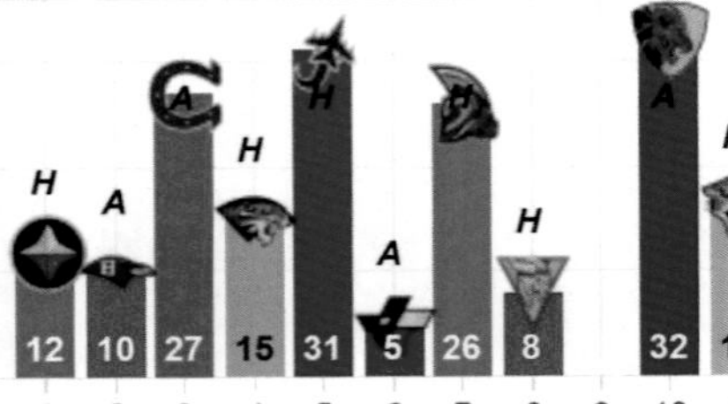

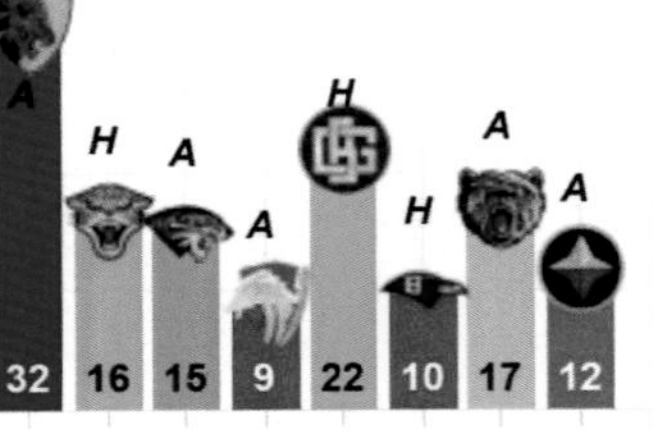

Rank of 2017 Defensive Rush Efficiency Faced by Week

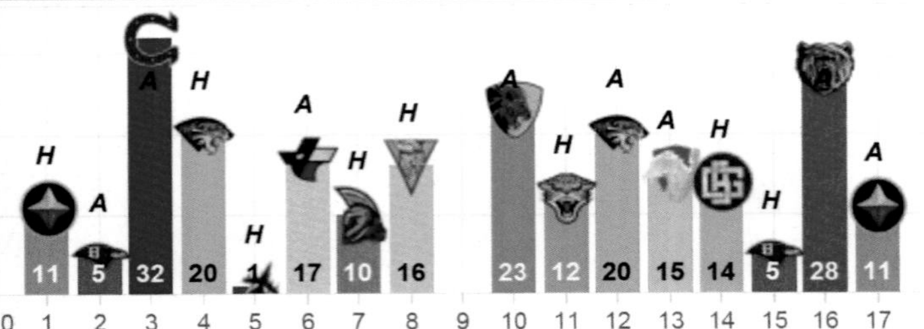

2016 Situational Usage by Player & Position

Usage Rate by Score

		Being Blown Out (14+)	Down Big (9-13)	One Score	Large Lead (9-13)	Blowout Lead (14+)	Grand Total
RUSH	Isaiah Crowell	18%	14%	27%		30%	23%
	Terrelle Pryor	1%	1%	1%			1%
	Duke Johnson	7%	10%	9%	33%	9%	9%
	Corey Coleman		1%	0%			0%
	Andrew Hawkins			0%			0%
	Malcolm Johnson			0%			0%
	George Atkinson			1%		4%	1%
	Total	26%	25%	39%	33%	43%	34%
PASS	Isaiah Crowell	8%	4%	6%		4%	6%
	Terrelle Pryor	16%	16%	17%		9%	17%
	Duke Johnson	10%	15%	7%	33%		9%
	Gary Barnidge	10%	12%	9%		13%	10%
	Corey Coleman	10%	8%	8%		13%	9%
	Andrew Hawkins	6%	8%	6%	33%	4%	6%
	Ricardo Louis	6%	5%	3%		4%	4%
	Seth DeValve	3%	2%	1%			2%
	Rashard Higgins	2%	1%	1%		9%	1%
	Malcolm Johnson	1%	2%	1%			1%
	Randall Telfer	1%	1%	1%			1%
	Dan Vitale	1%		1%			1%
	Jordan Payton		2%	0%			0%
	Connor Hamlett	1%					0%
	Total	74%	75%	61%	67%	57%	66%

Positional Target Distribution vs NFL Average

		NFL Wide				Team Only			
		Left	Middle	Right	Total	Left	Middle	Right	Total
Deep	WR	1,005	563	967	2,535	26	18	34	78
	TE	152	146	162	460	6	1	1	8
	RB	24	3	40	67	1	1		2
	All	1,181	712	1,169	3,062	33	20	35	88
Short	WR	3,012	1,734	3,080	7,826	81	37	106	224
	TE	816	853	1,120	2,789	20	22	31	73
	RB	977	592	1,056	2,625	38	30	57	125
	All	4,805	3,179	5,256	13,240	139	89	194	422
Total		5,986	3,891	6,425	16,302	172	109	229	510

Positional Success Rates vs NFL Average

		NFL Wide				Team Only			
		Left	Middle	Right	Total	Left	Middle	Right	Total
Deep	WR	37%	50%	39%	41%	23%	56%	21%	29%
	TE	44%	49%	43%	45%	50%	100%	100%	63%
	RB	29%	67%	25%	28%	100%	100%		100%
	All	38%	50%	39%	41%	30%	60%	23%	34%
Short	WR	52%	57%	51%	53%	46%	68%	46%	50%
	TE	50%	61%	52%	54%	40%	64%	52%	52%
	RB	47%	49%	44%	46%	47%	53%	44%	47%
	All	51%	56%	50%	52%	45%	62%	46%	49%
Total		48%	55%	48%	50%	42%	61%	43%	47%

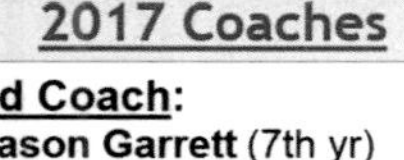

2017 Coaches

Head Coach:
Jason Garrett (7th yr)
Offensive Coordinator:
Scott Linehan (4th yr)
Defensive Coordinator:
Rod Marinelli (4th yr)

Dallas Cowboys

2017 Forecast

Wins	Div Rank
9.5	#1

Past Records

2016: 13-3
2015: 4-12
2014: 12-4

EASY HARD

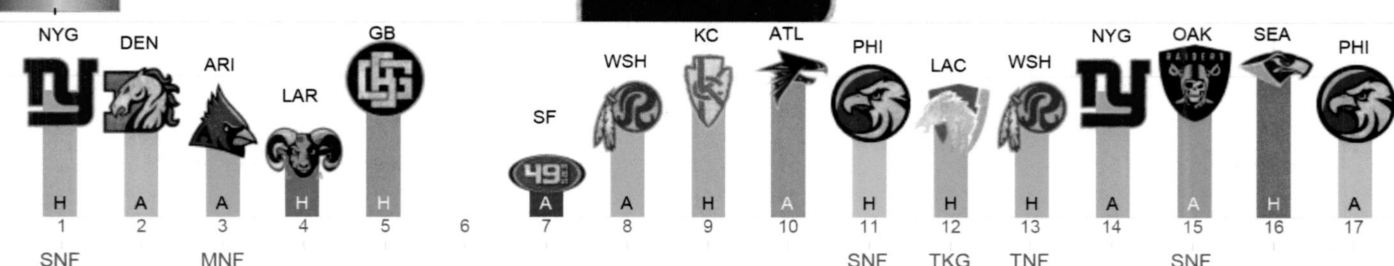

Key Players Lost

TXN	Player (POS)
Cut	Brown, Chris WR
	Romo, Tony QB
	Seymour, Ryan G
Declared Free Agent	Carr, Brandon CB
	Church, Barry S
	Claiborne, Morris CB
	Cooper, Jonathan G
	Crawford, Jack DE
	Davis, Ryan DE
	Dunbar, Lance RB
	Durant, Justin LB
	Escobar, Gavin TE
	Leary, Ronald G
	McClain, Terrell DT
	McFadden, Darren RB
	Wilcox, J.J. S
	Williams, Terrance WR
Retired	Free, Doug T

Average Line	# Games Favored	# Games Underdog
-4.5	12	1

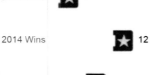

2017 Dallas Cowboys Overview

There are only a few teams more poised to win now and over the next several years than the Dallas Cowboys. Thanks to Tony Romo's injury, the Cowboys were able to start Dak Prescott in his rookie year with his $545k cap hit. And because he was a 4th round draft pick, the next 3 years his max cap hit is $816k. With the salary cap rising, it puts the Cowboys in the unique situation to build a solid, somewhat expensive corps around Dak and win now and over the next several years.

For instance, compare the edge for the Cowboys at the QB position to that of their foes in the NFC East for a moment: Kirk Cousins hits the 2017 cap for $24M on the franchise tag for the second straight year, and if the team is going to lock him down with a long-term deal, it will be costly. Eli Manning hits the cap for $19.7M this year, $22M next year and $23M in 2019. And because the Eagles acquired Carson Wentz with the #2 overall pick in 2016, he hits the cap this year for $4.9M this year and by 2019, when Prescott is hitting the cap for $816k, Wentz is hitting it for over ten times that amount ($8.5M).

This flexibility allows the Cowboys, for example, to keep an aging and declining Jason Witten on board this year even though he's an overpaid 35-year-old. But they front load his cap hit this year ($12.2M) and allowed future years' hits of $6.5M until his contract ends. Most likely he'll be cut well before that contract ends. But what he provides Dak with is a reliable early down target who is also the Cowboys #1 threat in the red zone. Last year, the most successful play for the Cowboys on 1st and 10 was a pass to Witten. Dak threw 26 of these 1st and 10 passes and a massive 77% of them graded as successful. In addition, Dak averaged a 119 passer rating on these targets and they averaged 9.6 yards per attempt. That kind of efficiency is exactly what propelled the Cowboys to the #2 team last year in EDSR (Early Down Success Rate). And no Cowboy was targeted more often in the red zone. Witten was targeted 20 times and those targets produced a 55% success rate, which was better than the #2 targeted Dez Bryant. So while Witten is surely overpaid and far from the #1 TE in the NFL, which is what he's currently hitting the cap at this year (Greg Olsen #2, Jimmy Graham #3),

(cont'd - see DAL2)

Key Free Agents/ Trades Added

- Bell, Byron G
- Blanton, Robert S
- Burbank, Ross C
- Carroll, Nolan CB
- Carter, Ruben C
- Cooper, Jonathan G
- Moore, Damontre DE
- Paea, Stephen DT
- Ware, DeMarcus LB

Drafted Players

Rd	Pk	Player (College)
1	28	DE - Taco Charlton (Michigan)
2	60	CB - Chidobe Awuzie (Colorado)
3	92	CB - Jourdan Lewis (Michigan)
4	133	WR - Ryan Switzer (North Carolina)
6	191	S - Xavier Woods (Louisiana Tech)
6*	216	CB - Marquez White (Florida State)
	228	DT - Joey Ivie (Florida)
7	239	WR - Noah Brown (Ohio State)
	246	DT - Jordan Carrell (Colorado)

Regular Season Wins: Past & Current Proj

	Wins
Proj 2017 Wins	9.5
2016 Wins	13
Proj 2016 Wins	9
2015 Wins	4
2014 Wins	12
2013 Wins	8

1 3 5 7 9 11 13 15

2017 Lineup & Cap Hits

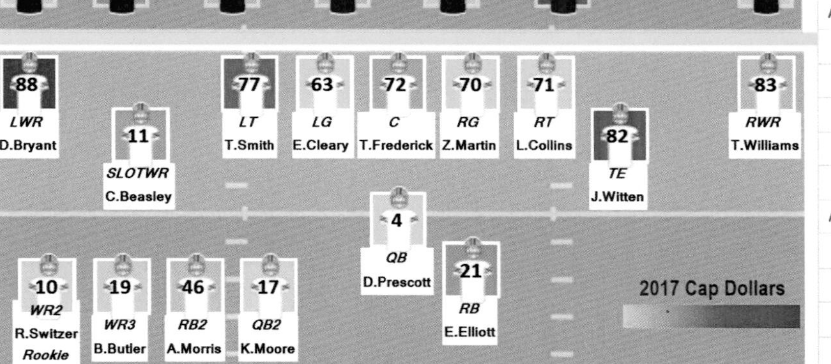

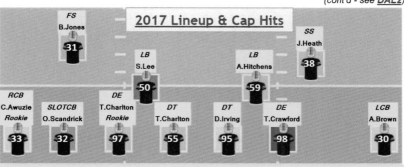

2017 Unit Spending

All DEF
All OFF

Positional Spending

	Rank	Total	2016 Rk
All OFF	17	$83.00M	1
QB	32	$2.80M	5
OL	25	$24.84M	16
RB	11	$9.58M	7
WR	3	$27.95M	8
TE	1	$17.83M	7
All DEF	30	$63.34M	20
DL	13	$29.75M	23
LB	20	$15.80M	15
CB	25	$11.76M	10
S	29	$6.03M	18

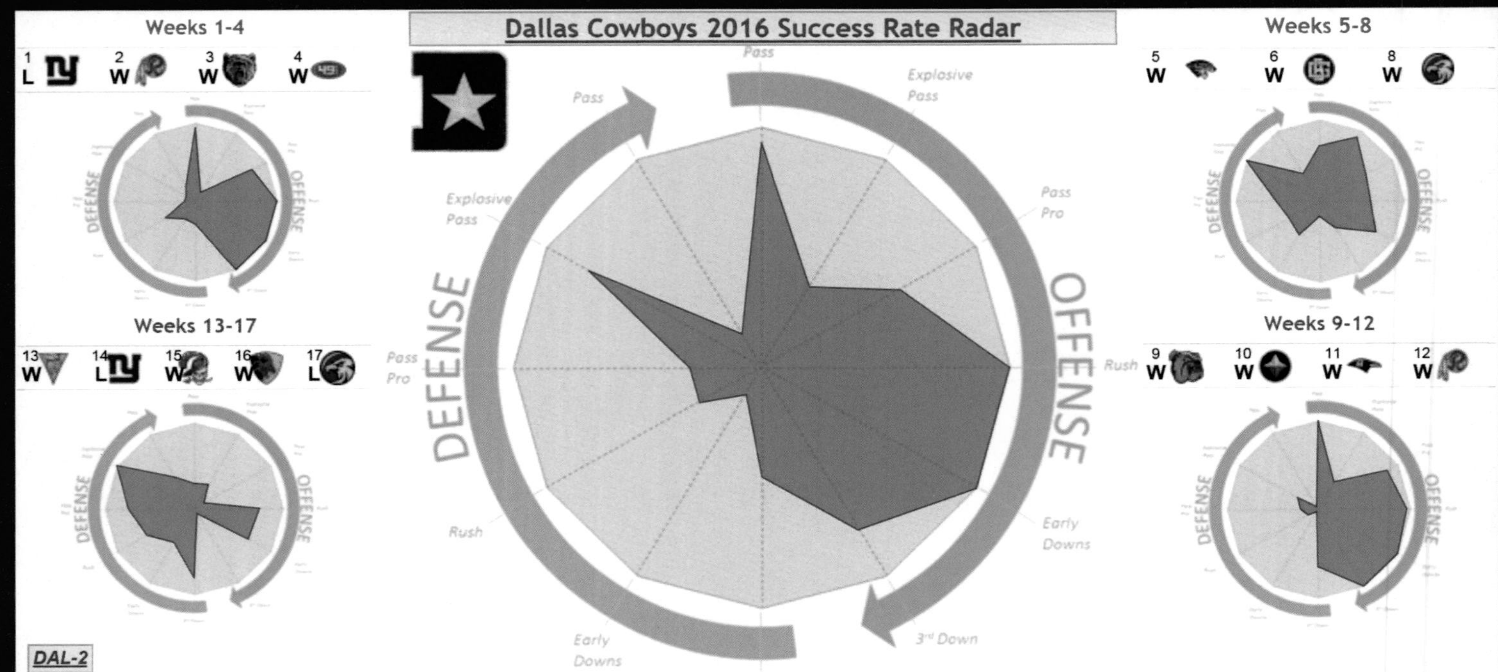

DAL-2

Witten is reliable and efficient and knows this offense inside out, which is perfect for a young QB like Prescott. And like a perfect Tinder TE, one look at the Cowboys' snap rates will show one of Witten's best abilities is his availability.

While the Cowboys have a big leg up on the competition in the NFC East and the rest of the NFL in general, with outstanding production from the QB position for such a low cap hit, they have a small window to maximize this edge. There is no telling if the Redskins will get a lot younger and cheaper at QB if Cousins leaves DC and Eli Manning's days in NY surely will be winding down sooner rather than later. And apart from getting a bit more explosiveness out of the passing offense, the Cowboys are quite stable offensively. They don't need a top-10 defense, but they must improve in a number of areas. Last year they ranked 26th in EDSR and 18th in pass efficiency. They made this a focus of their offseason moves, by acquiring defensive players in each of the first 3 rounds and going defense with 6 of their first 7 picks. They grabbed 4 players for the secondary in those selections, which were essential because they let a lot of starting veterans leave this offseason. Gone are starting SS Barry Church and starting CBs Brandon Carr and Morris Claiborne. Instead of overpaying these players in a secondary which has struggled with injuries and production the last several years, the Cowboys cut bait and are starting fresh.

There certainly will be growing pains with a less experienced and younger secondary, which is why the pass rush will be even more vital this year. Dallas used their first round draft pick on DE Taco Charlton. Several their DEs must step up, such as Demarcus Lawrence and Tyrone Crawford to apply more pressure and lessen the load on the secondary. Last year the Cowboys faced the 2nd rated schedule of opposing offensive lines, and this year they face another difficult test, going up against the 5th rated schedule. This will make it more difficult to get the sustained pass pressure. And the Cowboys face passing offenses which average more yards per attempt and are more explosive in 2017 than they faced in 2016.

*(cont'd - see **DAL-3**)*

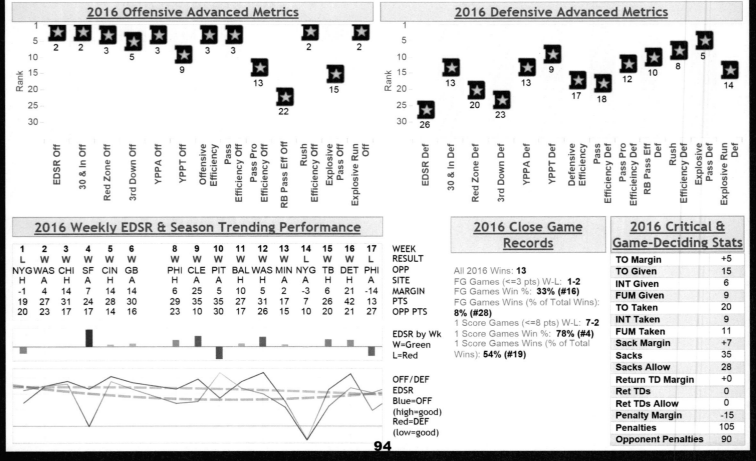

2016 Offensive Advanced Metrics

	Rank
EDSR Off	2
30 & In Off	2
Red Zone Off	3
3rd Down Off	5
YPPA Off	3
YPPT Off	9
Offensive Efficiency	3
Pass Efficiency Off	3
Pass Pro Efficiency Off	13
RB Pass Eff Off	22
Rush Efficiency Off	2
Explosive Pass Off	15
Explosive Run Off	2

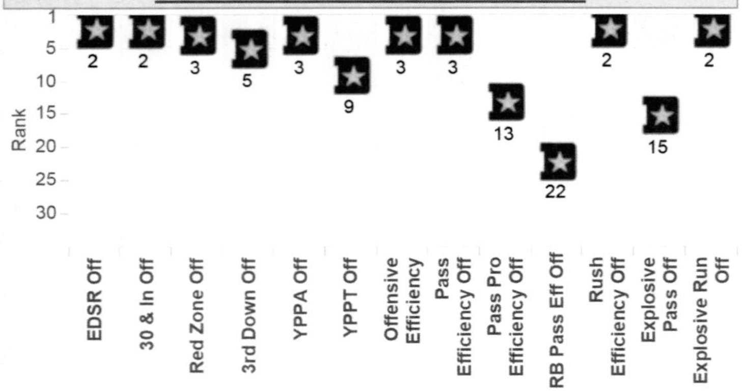

2016 Defensive Advanced Metrics

	Rank
EDSR Def	26
30 & In Def	13
Red Zone Def	20
3rd Down Def	23
YPPA Def	13
YPPT Def	9
Defensive Efficiency	17
Pass Efficiency Def	18
Pass Pro Efficiency Def	12
RB Pass Eff Def	10
Rush Efficiency Def	8
Explosive Pass Def	5
Explosive Run Def	14

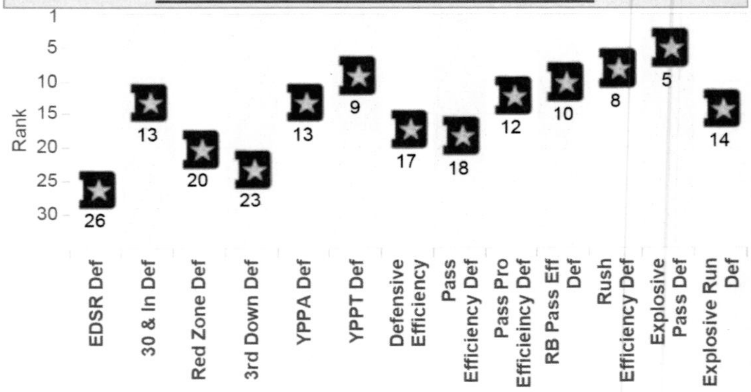

2016 Weekly EDSR & Season Trending Performance

1	2	3	4	5	6	8	9	10	11	12	13	14	15	16	17	WEEK
L	W	W	W	W	W	W	W	W	W	W	W	L	W	W	L	RESULT
NYG	WAS	CHI	SF	CIN	GB	PHI	CLE	PIT	BAL	WAS	MIN	NYG	TB	DET	PHI	OPP
H	A	H	A	H	A	H	A	A	H	H	A	A	H	H	A	SITE
-1	4	14	7	14	14	6	25	5	10	5	2	-3	6	21	-14	MARGIN
19	27	31	24	28	30	29	35	35	27	31	17	7	26	42	13	PTS
20	23	17	17	14	16	23	10	30	17	26	15	10	20	21	27	OPP PTS

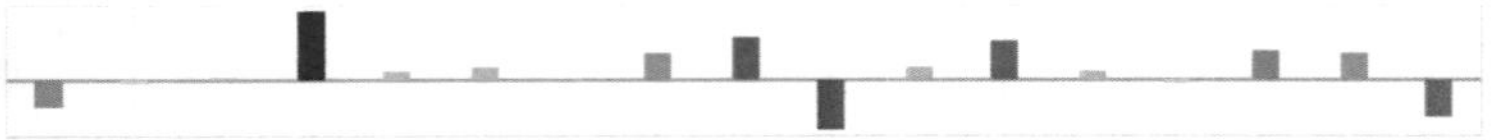

EDSR by Wk
W=Green
L=Red

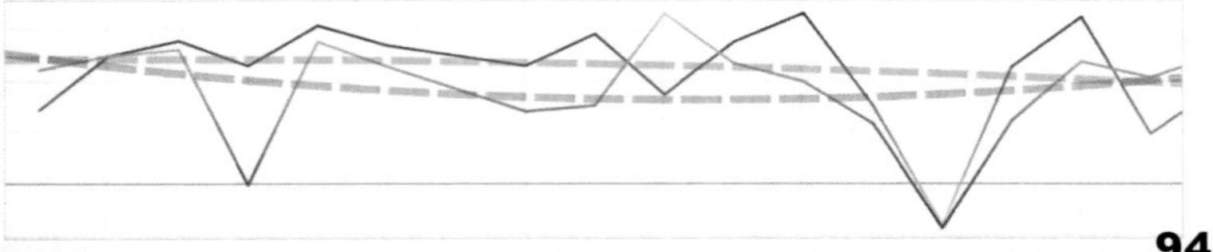

OFF/DEF
EDSR
Blue=OFF
(high=good)
Red=DEF
(low=good)

2016 Close Game Records

All 2016 Wins: **13**
FG Games (<=3 pts) W-L: **1-2**
FG Games Win %: **33% (#16)**
FG Games Wins (% of Total Wins): **8% (#28)**
1 Score Games (<=8 pts) W-L: **7-2**
1 Score Games Win %: **78% (#4)**
1 Score Games Wins (% of Total Wins): **54% (#19)**

2016 Critical & Game-Deciding Stats

TO Margin	+5
TO Given	15
INT Given	6
FUM Given	9
TO Taken	20
INT Taken	9
FUM Taken	11
Sack Margin	+7
Sacks	35
Sacks Allow	28
Return TD Margin	+0
Ret TDs	0
Ret TDs Allow	0
Penalty Margin	-15
Penalties	105
Opponent Penalties	90

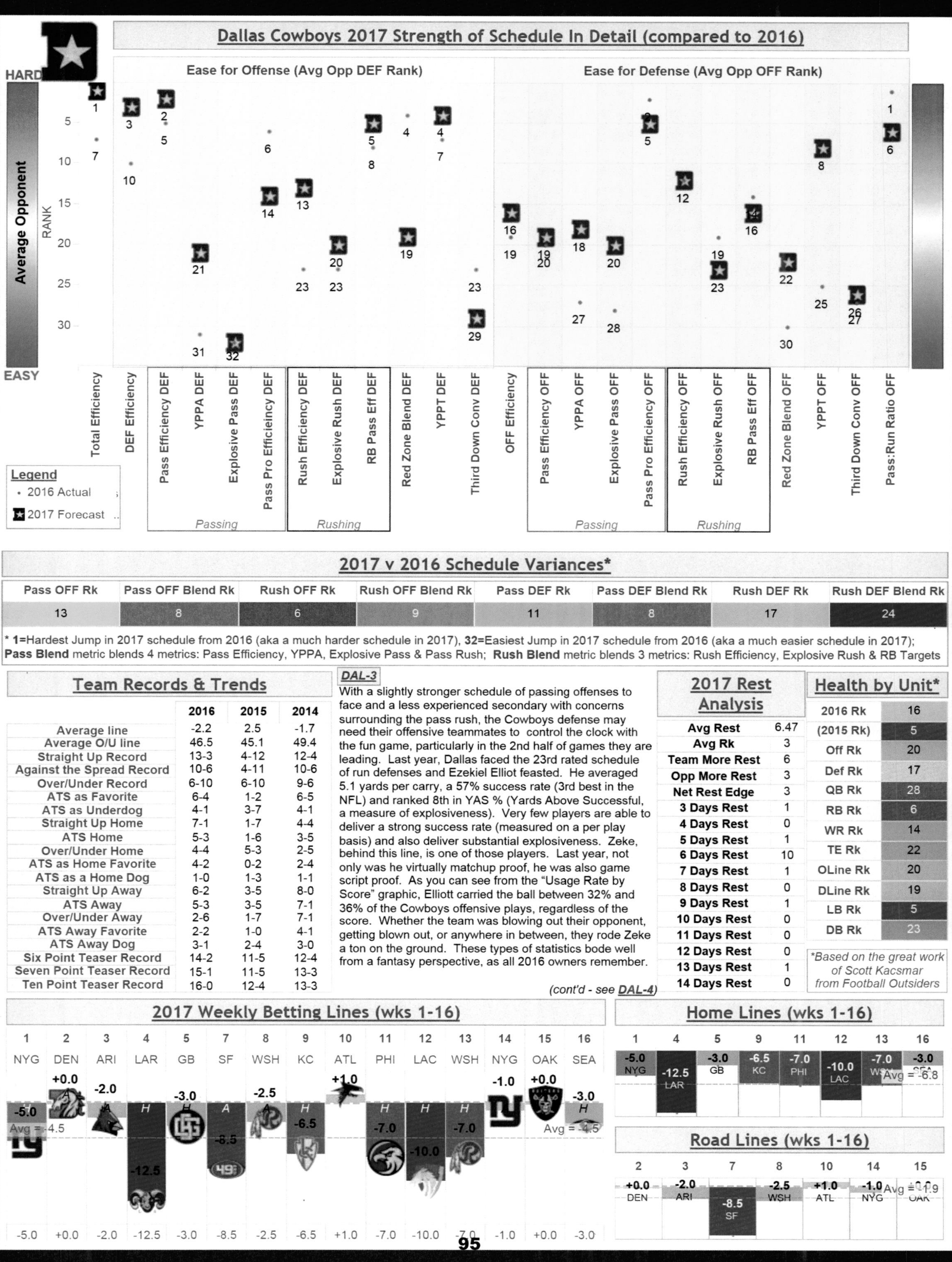

Dallas Cowboys 2017 Strength of Schedule In Detail (compared to 2016)

2017 v 2016 Schedule Variances*

Pass OFF Rk	Pass OFF Blend Rk	Rush OFF Rk	Rush OFF Blend Rk	Pass DEF Rk	Pass DEF Blend Rk	Rush DEF Rk	Rush DEF Blend Rk
13	8	6	9	11	8	17	24

* **1**=Hardest Jump in 2017 schedule from 2016 (aka a much harder schedule in 2017), **32**=Easiest Jump in 2017 schedule from 2016 (aka a much easier schedule in 2017); **Pass Blend** metric blends 4 metrics: Pass Efficiency, YPPA, Explosive Pass & Pass Rush; **Rush Blend** metric blends 3 metrics: Rush Efficiency, Explosive Rush & RB Targets

Team Records & Trends

	2016	2015	2014
Average line	-2.2	2.5	-1.7
Average O/U line	46.5	45.1	49.4
Straight Up Record	13-3	4-12	12-4
Against the Spread Record	10-6	4-11	10-6
Over/Under Record	6-10	6-10	9-6
ATS as Favorite	6-4	1-2	6-5
ATS as Underdog	4-1	3-7	4-1
Straight Up Home	7-1	1-7	4-4
ATS Home	5-3	1-6	3-5
Over/Under Home	4-4	5-3	2-5
ATS as Home Favorite	4-2	0-2	2-4
ATS as a Home Dog	1-0	1-3	1-1
Straight Up Away	6-2	3-5	8-0
ATS Away	5-3	3-5	7-1
Over/Under Away	2-6	1-7	7-1
ATS Away Favorite	2-2	1-0	4-1
ATS Away Dog	3-1	2-4	3-0
Six Point Teaser Record	14-2	11-5	12-4
Seven Point Teaser Record	15-1	11-5	13-3
Ten Point Teaser Record	16-0	12-4	13-3

DAL-3

With a slightly stronger schedule of passing offenses to face and a less experienced secondary with concerns surrounding the pass rush, the Cowboys defense may need their offensive teammates to control the clock with the fun game, particularly in the 2nd half of games they are leading. Last year, Dallas faced the 23rd rated schedule of run defenses and Ezekiel Elliot feasted. He averaged 5.1 yards per carry, a 57% success rate (3rd best in the NFL) and ranked 8th in YAS % (Yards Above Successful, a measure of explosiveness). Very few players are able to deliver a strong success rate (measured on a per play basis) and also deliver substantial explosiveness. Zeke, behind this line, is one of those players. Last year, not only was he virtually matchup proof, he was also game script proof. As you can see from the "Usage Rate by Score" graphic, Elliott carried the ball between 32% and 36% of the Cowboys offensive plays, regardless of the score. Whether the team was blowing out their opponent, getting blown out, or anywhere in between, they rode Zeke a ton on the ground. These types of statistics bode well from a fantasy perspective, as all 2016 owners remember.

(cont'd - see DAL-4)

2017 Rest Analysis

Avg Rest	6.47
Avg Rk	3
Team More Rest	6
Opp More Rest	3
Net Rest Edge	3
3 Days Rest	1
4 Days Rest	0
5 Days Rest	1
6 Days Rest	10
7 Days Rest	1
8 Days Rest	0
9 Days Rest	1
10 Days Rest	0
11 Days Rest	0
12 Days Rest	0
13 Days Rest	1
14 Days Rest	0

Health by Unit*

2016 Rk	16
(2015 Rk)	5
Off Rk	20
Def Rk	17
QB Rk	28
RB Rk	6
WR Rk	14
TE Rk	22
OLine Rk	20
DLine Rk	19
LB Rk	5
DB Rk	23

**Based on the great work of Scott Kacsmar from Football Outsiders*

2017 Weekly Betting Lines (wks 1-16)

1	2	3	4	5	7	8	9	10	11	12	13	14	15	16
NYG	DEN	ARI	LAR	GB	SF	WSH	KC	ATL	PHI	LAC	WSH	NYG	OAK	SEA
	A	A	H	H	A	A	H		H	H	H			H
-5.0	+0.0	-2.0	-12.5	-3.0	-8.5	-2.5	-6.5	+1.0	-7.0	-10.0	-7.0	-1.0	+0.0	-3.0

Avg = -4.5

Home Lines (wks 1-16)

1	4	5	9	11	12	13	16
-5.0	-12.5	-3.0	-6.5	-7.0	-10.0	-7.0	-3.0
NYG	LAR	GB	KC	PHI	LAC	WSH	SEA

Avg = -6.8

Road Lines (wks 1-16)

2	3	7	8	10	14	15
+0.0	-2.0	-8.5	-2.5	+1.0	-1.0	+0.0
DEN	ARI	SF	WSH	ATL	NYG	OAK

Avg = -1.9

Dallas Cowboys 2016 Play Analysis

2016 Play Tendencies

All Pass %	52%
All Pass Rk	30
All Rush %	48%
All Rush Rk	3
1 Score Pass %	53%
1 Score Pass Rk	28
2015 1 Score Pass %	52%
2015 1 Score Pass Rk	28
Pass Increase %	1%
Pass Increase Rk	14
1 Score Rush %	47%
1 Score Rush Rk	5
Up Pass %	54%
Up Pass Rk	25
Up Rush %	46%
Up Rush Rk	8
Down Pass %	52%
Down Pass Rk	32
Down Rush %	48%
Down Rush Rk	1

2016 Down & Distance Tendencies

Down	Distance	Total Plays	Pass Rate	Run Rate	Play Success %
1	Short (1-3)	9	22%	78%	89%
	Med (4-7)	14	36%	64%	57%
	Long (8-10)	329	42%	58%	57%
	XL (11+)	21	62%	38%	52%
2	Short (1-3)	55	27%	73%	75%
	Med (4-7)	80	55%	45%	60%
	Long (8-10)	90	60%	40%	53%
	XL (11+)	35	74%	26%	34%
3	Short (1-3)	41	49%	51%	68%
	Med (4-7)	47	91%	9%	53%
	Long (8-10)	25	100%	0%	28%
	XL (11+)	27	96%	4%	22%
4	Short (1-3)	4	25%	75%	100%
	Long (8-10)	1	0%	100%	100%

Shotgun %:

Under Center	Shotgun
51%	49%
37%	*63%*

AVG

Run Rate:

Under Center	Shotgun
78%	15%
68%	*23%*

AVG

Pass Rate:

Under Center	Shotgun
22%	85%
32%	*77%*

AVG

Short Yardage Intelligence:

2nd and Short Run

Run Freq	Run % Rk	NFL Run Freq Avg	Run 1D Rate	Run NFL 1D Avg
82%	3	65%	69%	71%

2nd and Short Pass

Pass Freq	Pass % Rk	NFL Pass Freq Avg	Pass 1D Rate	Pass NFL 1D Avg
18%	30	35%	83%	52%

Most Frequent Play

Down	Distance	Play Type	Player	Total Plays	Play Success %
1	Short (1-3)	RUSH	Ezekiel Elliott	4	100%
	Med (4-7)	RUSH	Ezekiel Elliott	5	60%
	Long (8-10)	RUSH	Ezekiel Elliott	141	59%
	XL (11+)	PASS	Cole Beasley	4	0%
		RUSH	Ezekiel Elliott	4	25%
2	Short (1-3)	RUSH	Ezekiel Elliott	27	81%
	Med (4-7)	RUSH	Ezekiel Elliott	28	61%
	Long (8-10)	RUSH	Ezekiel Elliott	20	45%
	XL (11+)	PASS	Jason Witten	8	38%
3	Short (1-3)	RUSH	Ezekiel Elliott	12	75%
	Med (4-7)	PASS	Jason Witten	8	63%
			Cole Beasley	8	88%
	Long (8-10)	PASS	Jason Witten	6	0%
	XL (11+)	PASS	Jason Witten	4	0%
			Brice Butler	4	25%
			Lance Dunbar	4	0%

Most Successful Play*

Down	Distance	Play Type	Player	Total Plays	Play Success %
1	Med (4-7)	RUSH	Ezekiel Elliott	5	60%
	Long (8-10)	PASS	Jason Witten	26	77%
2	Short (1-3)	RUSH	Ezekiel Elliott	27	81%
	Med (4-7)	PASS	Terrance Williams	7	86%
	Long (8-10)	PASS	Terrance Williams	7	86%
	XL (11+)	PASS	Jason Witten	8	38%
3	Short (1-3)	PASS	Cole Beasley	9	89%
	Med (4-7)	PASS	Cole Beasley	8	88%
	Long (8-10)	PASS	Cole Beasley	5	40%

*Minimum 5 plays to qualify

2016 Snap Rates

Week	Opp	Score	Jason Witten	Terrance Williams	Ezekiel Elliott	Dez Bryant	Cole Beasley	Brice Butler	Rob Kelley
1	NYG	L 20-19	78 (100%)	54 (69%)	48 (62%)	75 (96%)	49 (63%)	24 (31%)	
2	WAS	W 27-23	68 (100%)	42 (62%)	45 (66%)	57 (84%)	41 (60%)	26 (38%)	2 (3%)
3	CHI	W 31-17	68 (100%)	48 (71%)	51 (75%)	52 (76%)	32 (47%)	27 (40%)	
4	SF	W 24-17	76 (100%)	62 (82%)	47 (62%)		51 (67%)	62 (82%)	
5	CIN	W 28-14	57 (100%)	41 (72%)	45 (79%)		29 (51%)	46 (81%)	
6	GB	W 30-16	64 (100%)	44 (69%)	58 (91%)		30 (47%)	51 (80%)	
8	PHI	W 29-23	77 (100%)	59 (77%)	64 (83%)	68 (88%)	54 (70%)	21 (27%)	
9	CLE	W 35-10	70 (96%)	44 (60%)	44 (60%)	51 (70%)	29 (40%)	18 (25%)	
10	PIT	W 35-30	65 (100%)	45 (69%)	46 (71%)	58 (89%)	35 (54%)	16 (25%)	
11	BAL	W 27-17	67 (94%)	43 (61%)	50 (70%)	62 (87%)	44 (62%)	18 (25%)	
12	WAS	W 31-26	53 (95%)	36 (64%)	46 (82%)	43 (77%)	35 (63%)	12 (21%)	
13	MIN	W 17-15	52 (100%)	38 (73%)	43 (83%)	37 (71%)	25 (48%)	14 (27%)	
14	NYG	L 10-7	66 (100%)	52 (79%)	44 (67%)	61 (92%)	42 (64%)	16 (24%)	
15	TB	W 26-20	74 (100%)	50 (68%)	58 (78%)	63 (85%)	45 (61%)	15 (20%)	
16	DET	W 42-21	56 (98%)	38 (67%)	29 (51%)	42 (74%)	27 (47%)	21 (37%)	
17	PHI	L 27-13	22 (39%)	48 (86%)		15 (27%)	39 (70%)	42 (75%)	
Grand Total			1,013 (95%)	744 (70%)	718 (72%)	684 (78%)	607 (57%)	429 (41%)	2 (3%)

Personnel Groupings

Personnel	Team %	NFL Avg	Succ. %
1-1 [3WR]	61%	60%	53%
1-2 [2WR]	20%	19%	56%
2-1 [2WR]	7%	7%	55%
2-2 [1WR]	5%	3%	46%
0-1 [4WR]	3%	1%	55%
1-3 [1WR]	3%	3%	57%

Grouping Tendencies

Personnel	Pass Rate	Pass Succ. %	Run Succ. %
1-1 [3WR]	65%	50%	58%
1-2 [2WR]	26%	55%	57%
2-1 [2WR]	31%	50%	57%
2-2 [1WR]	7%	75%	44%
0-1 [4WR]	94%	52%	100%
1-3 [1WR]	18%	60%	57%

Red Zone Targets (min 3)

Receiver	All	Inside 5	6-10	11-20
Jason Witten	22	2	3	17
Dez Bryant	15	4	5	6
Cole Beasley	9	3	2	4
Brice Butler	7	4	2	1
Terrance Williams	6	2	2	2
Ezekiel Elliott	3	1	1	1

Red Zone Rushes (min 3)

Rusher	All	Inside 5	6-10	11-20
Ezekiel Elliott	40	13	10	17
Dak Prescott	11	4	6	1
Alfred Morris	6	2		4
Lance Dunbar	3	1	1	1

Early Down Target Rate

	RB	TE	WR
	15%	25%	61%
NFL AVG	***19%***	***20%***	***61%***

Overall Target Success %

RB	TE	WR
43%	52%	59%
#23	#16	#3

Dallas Cowboys 2016 Passing Recap & 2017 Outlook

Dak Prescott was a brilliant bright spot in the Lone Star State last year. And that came almost entirely because of his passing. But he was also tremendously successful as a rusher, even though Dallas limited that to a large extent. Prescott led the NFL with 6 QB rushing TDs and 57% of his rushes were successful, 3rd best in the NFL. For a rookie quarterback, he clearly had a number of edges that other high draft picks don't get, such as a tremendous offensive line, running back and a coaching staff capable of devising intelligent game plans to efficiently win games. What will be fascinating to watch is the Cowboys incorporation of rookie slot WR Ryan Switzer into the passing offense. That is because they already have a very similar WR in Cole Beasley. Yet they plan to use both, not just interchangeably, but operating on the field at the same time. The best plays for the Cowboys on 3rd and any yardage to go was a pass to Cole Beasley, and that is even with Ezekiel Elliott and a strong offensive line. They hit Beasley for an 89% success rate, 10.4 yards per attempt and Dak averaged a 147 passer rating when targeting Beasley in these situations. Ideally, teams are not getting to 3rd down often, which was the case for the Cowboys and their #2 EDSR offense.

Dak Prescott Rating All Downs

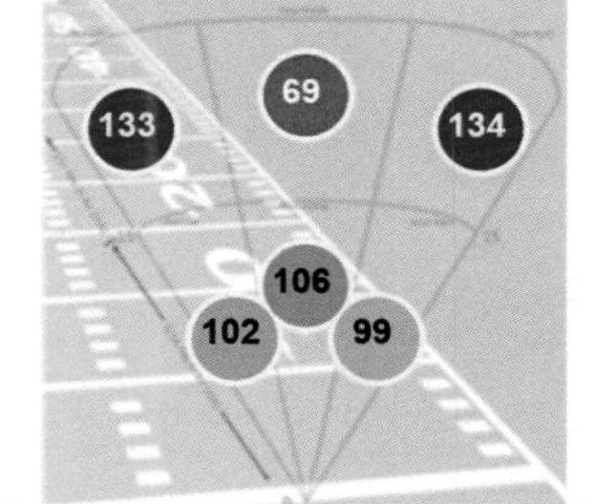

Dak Prescott Rating Early Downs

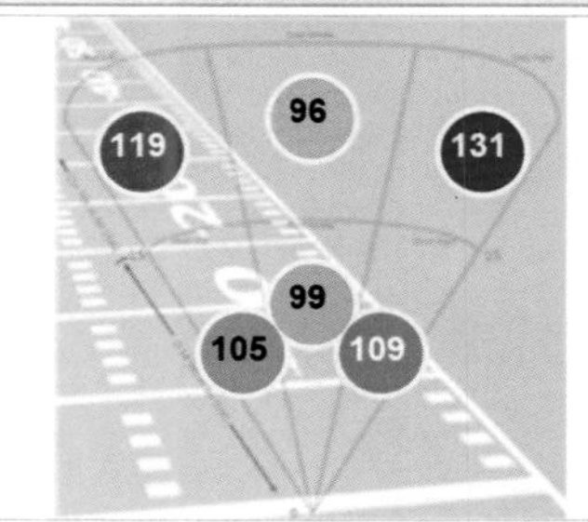

2016 Standard Passing Table

QB	Comp	Att	Comp %	Yds	YPA	TDs	INT	Sacks	Rating	Rk
Dak Prescott	335	498	67%	3,959	7.9	26	5	26	104.5	6
NFL Avg			63%		7.2				90.4	

2016 Advanced Passing Table

QB	Success %	EDSR Passing Success %	20+ Yd Pass Gains	20+ Yd Pass %	30+ Yd Pass Gains	30+ Yd Pass %	Air Yds per Comp	YAC per Comp	20+ Air Yd Comp	20+ Air Yd %
Dak Prescott	52%	57%	41	8%	14	3%	7.0	4.9	20	4%
NFL Avg	44%	48%	27	8%	10	3%	6.4	4.8	12	4%

Interception Rates by Down

Yards to Go	1	2	3	4	Total
1 & 2	0.0%	12.5%	6.7%	0.0%	8.0%
3, 4, 5	0.0%	0.0%	0.0%		0.0%
6 - 9	0.0%	1.3%	2.1%		1.5%
10 - 14	0.0%	0.0%	0.0%	0.0%	0.0%
15+	0.0%	0.0%	6.7%		2.0%
Total	0.0%	1.1%	2.1%	0.0%	1.0%

3rd Down Passing - Short of Sticks Analysis

QB	Avg Yds to Go	Air Yds (of Comps)	Avg Yds Short	Short of Sticks Rate	Rk
Dak Prescott	8.3	7.2	-1.1	61%	31
NFL Avg	7.6	6.8	-0.8	57%	

Air Yds vs YAC

Air Yds %	YAC %	Rk
57%	43%	20
54%	46%	

2016 Receiving Recap & 2017 Outlook

Dallas was an extremely balanced passing offense last year. Their top 3 targets, Bryant, Beasley and Witten, all were within 4 total targets of each other (108, 104 and 104). Beasley was the most successful target in the NFL last year. Bryant ranked 24th in explosiveness. And now with Switzer to pair with Beasley and Witten, Dallas has a number of reliable WRs who may not work deep down the field like Bryant, but can win early in a route and present a quick target for Prescott. Rather than using this shorter passing offense as an extension of the run game, they have Elliott. They use it to limit turnovers while providing a high EDSR.

Player *Min 50 Targets*	Targets	Comp %	YPA	Rating	TOARS	Success %	Success Rk	Missed YPA Rk	YAS % Rk	TDs
Dez Bryant	108	55%	8.6	107	5.0	51%	68	39	24	10
Cole Beasley	104	76%	8.4	113	5.2	69%	1	13	93	5
Jason Witten	104	72%	7.0	100	4.8	53%	54	77	130	4
Terrance Williams	67	72%	9.9	123	4.6	64%	4	3	68	4

Directional Passer Rating Delivered

Receiver	Short Left	Short Middle	Short Right	Deep Left	Deep Middle	Deep Right	Player Total
Dez Bryant	89	136	61	144	38	80	107
Jason Witten	124	94	82	40	96	149	100
Cole Beasley	95	107	126	119		110	114
Terrance Williams	128	105	109	63	114	135	123
Ezekiel Elliott	64	95	130				111
Brice Butler	130	0	53	104	40	142	83
Lance Dunbar	88	60	76				79
Team Total	104	104	101	133	69	121	107

2016 Rushing Recap & 2017 Outlook

Ezekiel Elliott was a rare specimen with his ability to deliver a high success rate and still be explosive. He ranked top 7 in success rate, YAS % and Missed YPA, the only RB to do so last year. Clearly operating in the bell cow role behind a strong line on a team that likes to run the ball, Elliott is in a great position moving forward. The only issue becomes the schedule of opposing run defenses. Last year he faced the 23rd rated schedule, and this year he faces the 13th rated schedule. It's the 6th most difficult leap from 2016 to 2017 for any team. The schedule starts off extremely tough, and will end tough as well with road games in NY, PHI and home against the Seahawks run defense. Zeke will really need to earn his success this year.

Player *Min 50 Rushes*	Rushes	YPA	Success %	Success Rk	Missed YPA Rk	YTS % Rk	YAS % Rk	Early Down Success %	Early Down Success Rk	TDs
Ezekiel Elliott	343	5.1	57%	3	10	49	8	57%	4	15
Alfred Morris	69	3.5	52%	14	12	3	62	53%	11	2

Yards per Carry by Direction

Directional Run Frequency

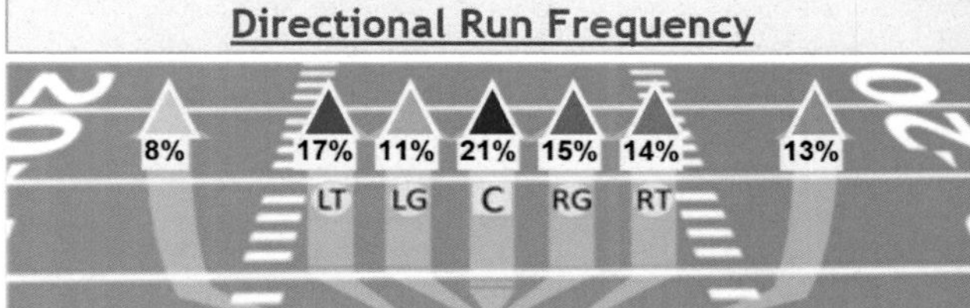

DAL-4

However, while Dallas faced an easy schedule of run defenses last year, this year the schedule gets much more difficult. Gone are the run defenses of the Browns, Lions and Bears. Enter more difficult defenses of the Cardinals Seahawks, Rams and Chargers. The team may need to rely more on the run game this year but if that run game is successful, it will be against these more difficult defenses.

When the games get tighter, the big plays matter more, and that is something Dallas needs to work on this year. Dak was great with limiting his interceptions last year, but in short yardage situation, the Cowboys can't afford to throw interceptions, particularly when the run game (as well as Dak's scramble game) is as good as it is. If the Cowboys decide to call a pass, Dak can't afford to throw the ball into a close window. On 2nd and short Dallas ran the ball 82% of the time, the 3rd most run-heavy team in the NFL, and recorded about the NFL average in success rate. But when those 2nd and short plays were handoffs to Zeke, as they were 27 times last season, he was dominant, recording a successful run 81% of the time and averaging 5.4 yards per carry. On 3rd and short, the Cowboys averaged a 63% success rate when running the ball and a 62% success rate when passing the ball, and were very balanced, calling runs 51% of the time.

In addition to not throwing interceptions on short yardage plays, the Cowboys must record more interceptions. They recorded just 9 last season, which was 5th fewest i.. INTs (Jaguars with 7, Colts, Jets and Bears with 8) all were bad teams last year, and none finished with winning records Often their opponents were running the ball late in games, as their opponents were winning these games. The Cowboys recorded 13 wins, which means they were leading late and opponents were forced to throw. Overall last year opposing offenses passed the ball on 67% of their offensive plays when facing Dallas, the highest rate in the NFL. The lack of a higher interception rate, particularly when playing with a lead, allowed opponents to stay in games. Which is why the Cowboys, despite a strong record, played in 9 games that were decided by one-score last year.

The other key element Dallas must improve upon is their explosive passing offense. While Dallas was highly efficient, they were not very explosive, which was ironic because when Prescott did pass the ball 15+ yards in the air, he recorded the NFL's best rating. While in the first half, the Cowboys connected on deep passes on 9% of their attempts (12th best), that dropped sharply to 6% in the second half, and while that may not sound like a big drop, it was 31st in the NFL. And while an argument can be made for playing conservatively with a lead, look at the teams who were the most explosive passing teams in the second half: #1 Atlanta, #2 New Orleans, #3 Washington, #4 New England, #5 Pittsburgh. Both Super Bowl teams and the AFC runner-up hit explosive pass rates in the second half of between 16% to 11%,, double that of the Dallas.

Division History: Season Wins & 2017 Projection

2013 Wins | 2014 Wins | 2015 Wins | 2016 Wins | Proj 2017 Wins

Rank of 2017 Defensive Pass Efficiency Faced by Week

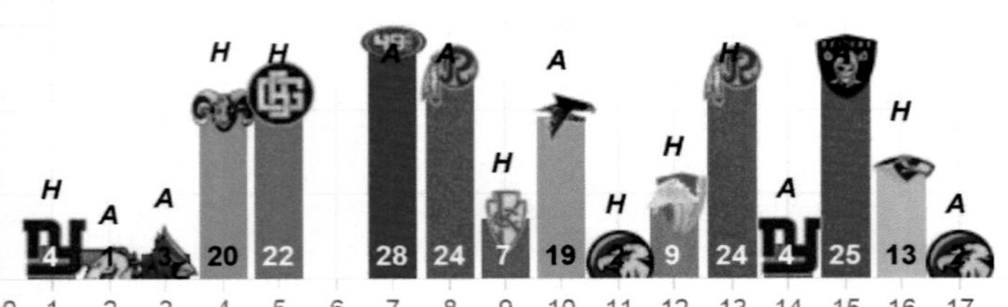

Rank of 2017 Defensive Rush Efficiency Faced by Week

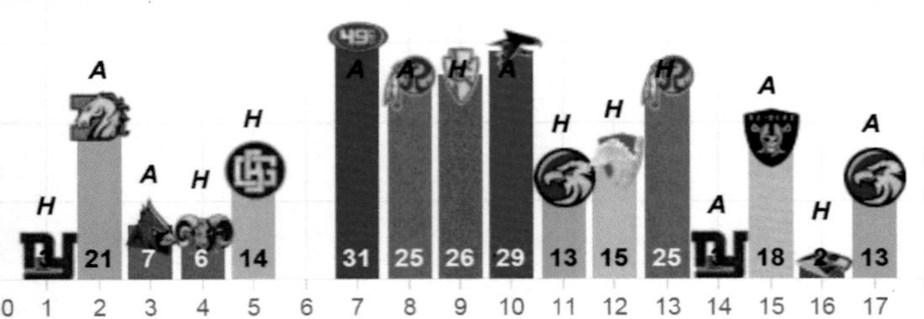

2016 Situational Usage by Player & Position

Usage Rate by Score

		Being Blown Out (14+)	Down Big (9-13)	One Score	Large Lead (9-13)	Blowout Lead (14+)	Grand Total
RUSH	Ezekiel Elliott	32%	32%	36%	36%	33%	35%
	Cole Beasley			0%			0%
	Alfred Morris	5%		6%	9%	17%	7%
	Lance Dunbar	8%		1%	2%		1%
	Darren McFadden			2%		10%	2%
	Lucky Whitehead			1%		1%	1%
	Keith Smith	3%		0%			0%
	Total	47%	32%	45%	46%	61%	47%
PASS	Ezekiel Elliott	5%	4%	4%		5%	4%
	Dez Bryant	11%	14%	12%	9%	7%	11%
	Cole Beasley	3%	14%	11%	13%	10%	11%
	Jason Witten	11%	11%	11%	20%	7%	11%
	Alfred Morris			1%	2%	1%	1%
	Terrance Williams	16%	18%	7%	5%	4%	7%
	Brice Butler	3%		4%	2%	2%	4%
	Lance Dunbar	5%		3%			2%
	Darren McFadden			1%			1%
	Lucky Whitehead			0%	2%		0%
	Geoff Swaim		4%	1%	2%	2%	1%
	Gavin Escobar			1%		1%	1%
	Keith Smith		4%	0%			0%
	Rod Smith					1%	0%
	Total	53%	68%	55%	54%	39%	53%

Positional Target Distribution vs NFL Average

		NFL Wide				Team Only			
		Left	Middle	Right	Total	Left	Middle	Right	Total
Deep	WR	997	564	973	**2,534**	34	17	28	**79**
	TE	156	145	160	**461**	2	2	3	**7**
	RB	25	4	40	**69**				
	All	**1,178**	**713**	**1,173**	**3,064**	**36**	**19**	**31**	**86**
Short	WR	3,007	1,721	3,088	**7,816**	86	50	98	**234**
	TE	812	846	1,107	**2,765**	24	29	44	**97**
	RB	993	611	1,081	**2,685**	22	11	32	**65**
	All	**4,812**	**3,178**	**5,276**	**13,266**	**132**	**90**	**174**	**396**
Total		**5,990**	**3,891**	**6,449**	**16,330**	**168**	**109**	**205**	**482**

Positional Success Rates vs NFL Average

		NFL Wide				Team Only			
		Left	Middle	Right	Total	Left	Middle	Right	Total
Deep	WR	36%	51%	38%	**40%**	50%	41%	39%	**44%**
	TE	45%	50%	43%	**46%**	0%	50%	67%	**43%**
	RB	32%	75%	25%	**30%**				
	All	**37%**	**50%**	**38%**	**41%**	**47%**	**42%**	**42%**	**44%**
Short	WR	52%	56%	51%	**52%**	64%	66%	62%	**64%**
	TE	50%	62%	52%	**54%**	58%	41%	59%	**54%**
	RB	47%	50%	44%	**46%**	41%	36%	50%	**45%**
	All	**50%**	**57%**	**50%**	**52%**	**59%**	**54%**	**59%**	**58%**
Total		**48%**	**56%**	**48%**	**50%**	**57%**	**52%**	**57%**	**56%**

Denver Broncos

2017 Coaches

Head Coach:
Vance Joseph (MIA DC) (1st yr)
Offensive Coordinator:
Mike McCoy (SD HC) (1st yr)
Defensive Coordinator:
Joe Woods (DEN DB) (0th yr)

2017 Forecast

Wins	Div Rank
8	#3

Past Records

2016: 9-7
2015: 12-4
2014: 12-4

EASY HARD

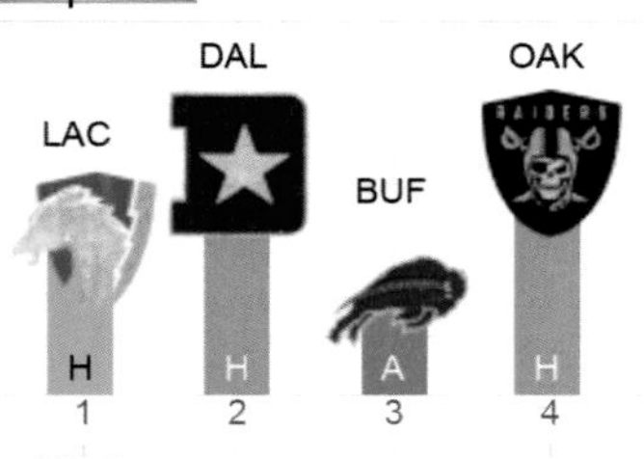

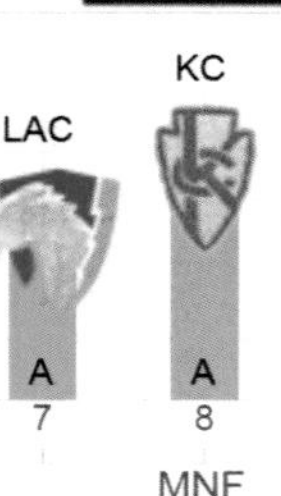
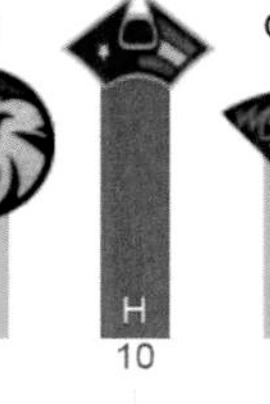
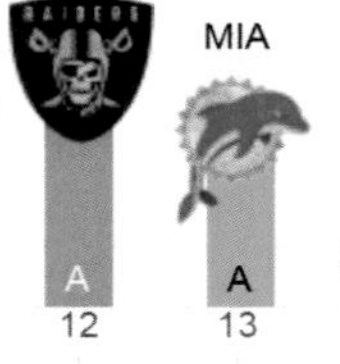

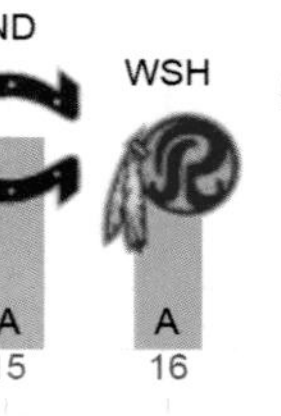

Week	1	2	3	4	5	6	7	8	9	10	11	12	13	14	15	16	17
Opponent	LAC	DAL	BUF	OAK		NYG	LAC	KC	PHI	NE	CIN	OAK	MIA	NYJ	IND	WSH	KC
H/A	H	H	A	H		H	A	A	A	H	H	A	A	H	A	A	H
Game	MNF					SNF		MNF		SNF					TNF		

Key Players Lost

TXN	Player (POS)
Cut	Austell, Erik C
	Ferentz, James C
	Iosia, Iosia DE
	McKay, Mekale WR
	Overbaugh, Jeff LB
	Raciti, Travis DT
Declared Free Agent	Brenner, Sam C
	Forsett, Justin RB
	Gafford, Thomas C
	Norwood, Jordan WR
	Okung, Russell T
	Walker, Vance DE
	Ware, DeMarcus LB
	Watson, Dekoda LB
	Webster, Kayvon CB
	Williams, Sylvester NT
	Winn, Billy DE
Retired	Brooks, Zac RB
	Forsett, Justin RB
	Ware, DeMarcus LB

Average Line	# Games Favored	# Games Underdog
-0.5	5	8

2017 Denver Broncos Overview

Low was high and high was low in Denver last season. Against the 2nd most difficult schedule of opposing offenses, the Broncos defense dominated, ranking 1st in defensive efficiency and 3rd in EDSR (Early Down Success Rate). On the other hand, against a below average schedule of opposing defenses, the Broncos offense struggled, ranking 5th worst in efficiency and 4th worst in EDSR. Of course, those played to the Broncos strengths, as their defense was the NFL's best in 2015 and the Brock Osweiler led offense was bottom-10. But it speaks to the magnitude of strengths or weaknesses of each unit, that each is absolutely dominant or terrible in spite of the hard or easy schedule of opponents.

Going 2-2 in field goal games and 3-4 in one-score games didn't skew the Broncos results. Nor did their critical and game deciding stats, where they were +2 in each of turnover margin, sack margin and return TD margin. Denver was pretty true to their weekly EDSR performance: in their 5 most dominant EDSR performances they went 4-1, with the only loss being in Tennessee in a truly bizarre game which saw Denver rack up a 330-73 passing yard edge but lost the rushing yard battle 180-18. In their 5 worst EDSR performances they went 1-4, notching a win in Jacksonville despite a miserable offensive performance, thanks to +3 turnover margin and a return touchdown.

Despite the overall strong defensive numbers, the rushing defense dropped off big time from 2015 when it ranked 4th best. They dropped all the way to 21st last year, and is something the Broncos absolutely must fix. The reason should be obvious – back when the team had Peyton Manning in his early years in Denver, the Broncos built leads such that their opponents were not able to run, particularly in the second half of games. But the 2016 Broncos did not have that kind of offensive firepower (more on that shortly). Opponents were able to be multi-dimensional most of the game thanks to the average margins and lack of Denver run game (more on that shortly) which prevented the Broncos from quickly closing out close games.

While the run defense struggled, the pass defense did not. However, where Denver struggled the most was against good passing teams. Denver ran off a record of 7-1 against passing offenses which ranked outside the top 10 last year.

(cont'd - see DEN2)

Key Free Agents/ Trades Added

Charles, Jamaal RB
Edebali, Kasim DE
Harris, Shelby DT
Lang, Cedrick TE
Leary, Ronald G
Muller, Chris G
Peko, Domata DT
Richardson, Bobby DE
Watson, Menelik T

Drafted Players

Rd	Pk	Player (College)
1	20	OT - Garett Bolles (Utah)
2	51	DE - DeMarcus Walker (Florida State)
3	82	WR - Carlos Henderson (Louisiana Tech)
3*	101	CB - Brendan Langley (Lamar)
5	145	TE - Jake Butt (Michigan)
	172	WR - Isaiah McKenzie (Georgia)
6	203	RB - De'Angelo Henderson (Coastal Carolina)
7*	253	QB - Chad Kelly (Ole Miss)

Regular Season Wins: Past & Current Proj

Proj 2017 Wins  8
2016 Wins  9
Proj 2016 Wins  9.5
2015 Wins  12
2014 Wins  12
2013 Wins  13

1 3 5 7 9 11 13 15

2017 Lineup & Cap Hits

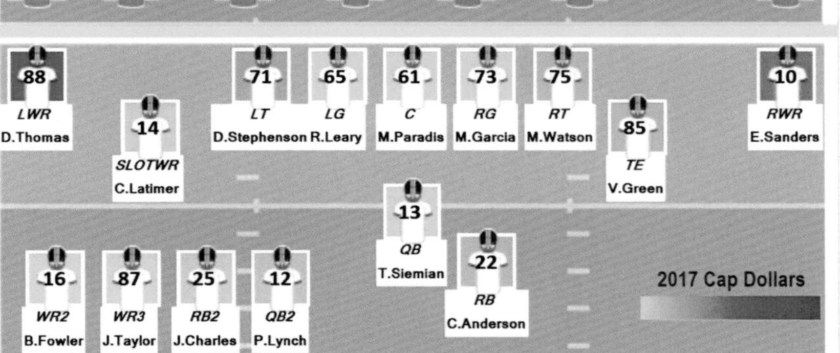

2017 Unit Spending

All OFF
All DEF

Positional Spending

	Rank	Total	2016 Rk
All OFF	29	$70.97M	31
QB	30	$3.73M	32
OL	20	$26.20M	30
RB	18	$6.68M	10
WR	4	$27.26M	1
TE	24	$7.10M	27
All DEF	1	$98.71M	2
DL	25	$19.37M	14
LB	4	$36.20M	10
CB	3	$26.85M	3
S	5	$16.29M	11

Denver Broncos 2016 Success Rate Radar

Weeks 1-4

1 W
2 W
3 W
4 W
DEFENSE
OFFENSE

Weeks 13-17

13 W
14 L
15 L
16 L
17 W
DEFENSE
OFFENSE

Pass
Explosive Pass
Pass Pro
Rush
Early Downs
3rd Down
DEFENSE
OFFENSE
Pass
Explosive Pass
Pass Pro
Rush
Early Downs
3rd Down

Weeks 5-8

5 L
6 L
7 W
8 W
DEFENSE
OFFENSE

Weeks 9-12

9 L
10 W
12 L
DEFENSE
OFFENSE

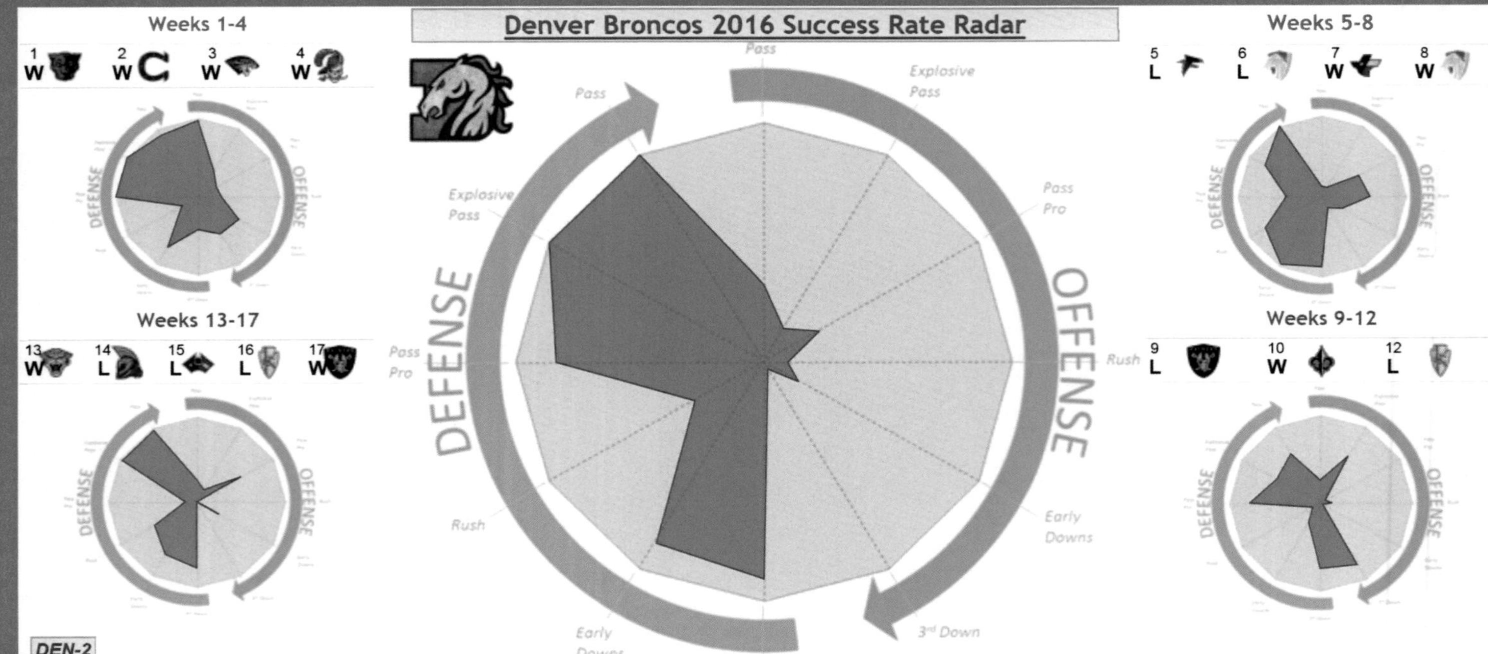

DEN-2

But against top-10 passing offenses (save for week 17 when the Raiders were without Derek Carr), the Broncos went 1-6. They allowed only 1 passing TD per game, 1.3 rushing TDs per game but a total of 24 points per game, which was too many points for an offense which put up less than 16 ppg in these 7 games.

Holding seven, top-10 passing offenses to just 1 passing touchdown per game was incredible. More than that, though, was the fact the Broncos defense held these teams to a 42% success rate on passes. The NFL average was 46%, and even a 42% season-long success rate against an entire 16-game schedule would have been the 4th best defensive mark in the NFL last year. But holding seven, top-10 passing offenses to just 42% was tremendous. Ordinarily, losing to top 10 passing offenses is not unnatural for any team. Holding them to 1 passing touchdown per game and a 42% passing success rate but still going 1-6 in these games had to be extremely frustrating for this defense. They have two things to blame for those losses: their own run defense and their offense. In these 7 games the Broncos run defense allowed 52% of opponent rushes to grade as successful.

For some perspective, the NFL average last year was 47%, and the NFL's worst run defense (Washington) allowed a 53% success rate. While their pass defense was playing lights out against the best passing offenses in the NFL, on the ground they were playing nearly equivalent to the league's worst run defense.

Denver's run defense was a clear problem in 2016, but they need to figure out a way to solve the problem quickly, because the schedule is a lot tougher in 2017. They played the 20th rated run offenses in 2016, and now face the 2nd rated run offenses in 2017. Their schedule swaps out the Jaguars, Buccaneers, Texans, Panthers and Buccaneers and adds the Bills, Cowboys, Redskins and Eagles. It's a swap out of the #29, 28, 27 and 22 run offenses from 2016 and adding in the #1, 2, 4 and 9 run offenses from last year. It's the reason the Broncos run defense experiences the 2nd largest increase in schedule difficultly from last year to this year.

*(cont'd - see **DEN-3**)*

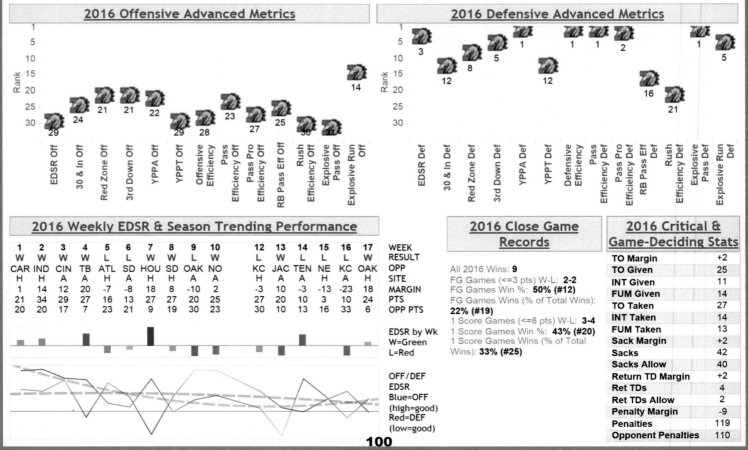

2016 Offensive Advanced Metrics

Rank
EDSR Off 29
30 & In Off 24
Red Zone Off 21
3rd Down Off 21
YPPA Off 22
YPPT Off 29
Offensive Efficiency 28
Pass Efficiency Off 23
Pass Pro Efficiency Off 27
RB Pass Eff Off 25
Rush Efficiency Off 30
Explosive Pass Off 31
Explosive Run Off 14

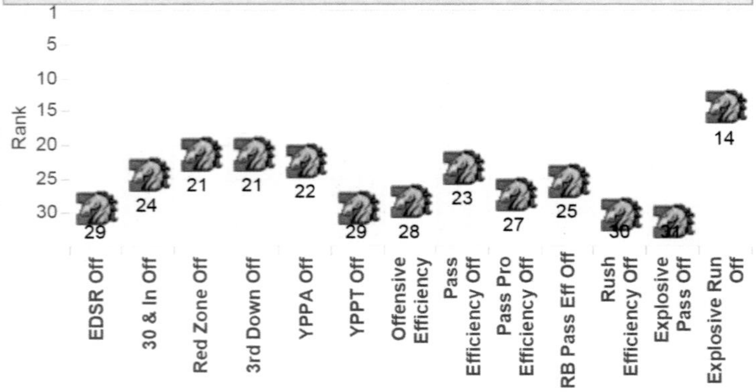

2016 Defensive Advanced Metrics

Rank
EDSR Def 3
30 & In Def 12
Red Zone Def 8
3rd Down Def 5
YPPA Def 1
YPPT Def 12
Defensive Efficiency 1
Pass Efficiency Def 1
Pass Pro Efficieincy Def 2
RB Pass Eff Def 16
Rush Efficiency Def 21
Explosive Pass Def 1
Explosive Run Def 5

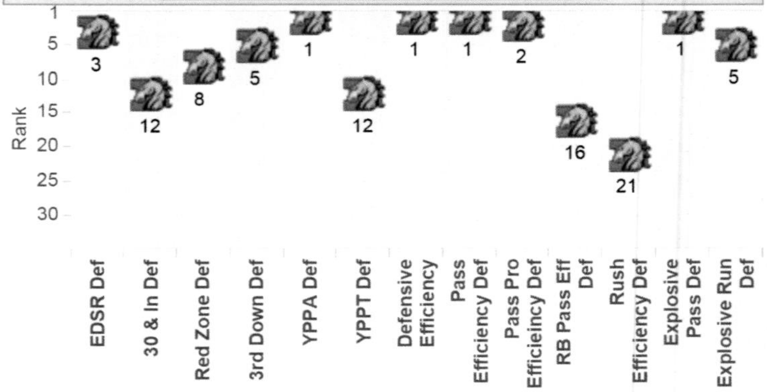

2016 Weekly EDSR & Season Trending Performance

1	2	3	4	5	6	7	8	9	10	12	13	14	15	16	17	WEEK
W	W	W	W	L	L	W	W	L	W	L	W	L	L	L	W	RESULT
CAR	IND	CIN	TB	ATL	SD	HOU	SD	OAK	NO	KC	JAC	TEN	NE	KC	OAK	OPP
H	H	A	A	H	A	H	A	A	A	H	A	A	H	A	H	SITE
1	14	12	20	-7	-8	18	8	-10	2	-3	10	-3	-13	-23	18	MARGIN
21	34	29	27	16	13	27	27	20	25	27	20	10	3	10	24	PTS
20	20	17	7	23	21	9	19	30	23	30	10	13	16	33	6	OPP PTS

EDSR by Wk
W=Green
L=Red

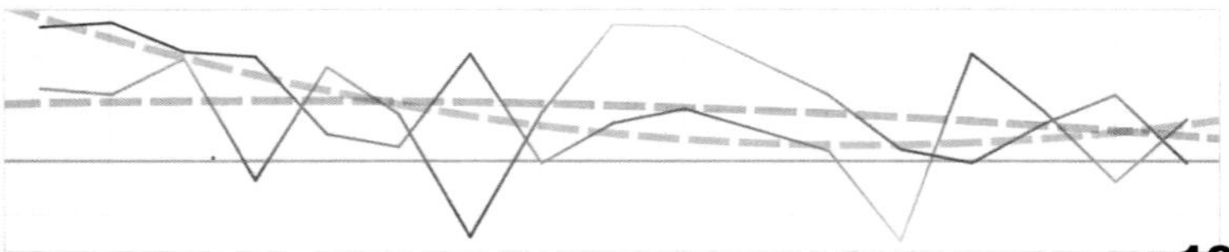

OFF/DEF
EDSR
Blue=OFF
(high=good)
Red=DEF
(low=good)

2016 Close Game Records

All 2016 Wins: **9**
FG Games (<=3 pts) W-L: **2-2**
FG Games Win %: **50% (#12)**
FG Games Wins (% of Total Wins): **22% (#19)**
1 Score Games (<=8 pts) W-L: **3-4**
1 Score Games Win %: **43% (#20)**
1 Score Games Wins (% of Total Wins): **33% (#25)**

2016 Critical & Game-Deciding Stats

TO Margin	+2
TO Given	25
INT Given	11
FUM Given	14
TO Taken	27
INT Taken	14
FUM Taken	13
Sack Margin	+2
Sacks	42
Sacks Allow	40
Return TD Margin	+2
Ret TDs	4
Ret TDs Allow	2
Penalty Margin	-9
Penalties	119
Opponent Penalties	110

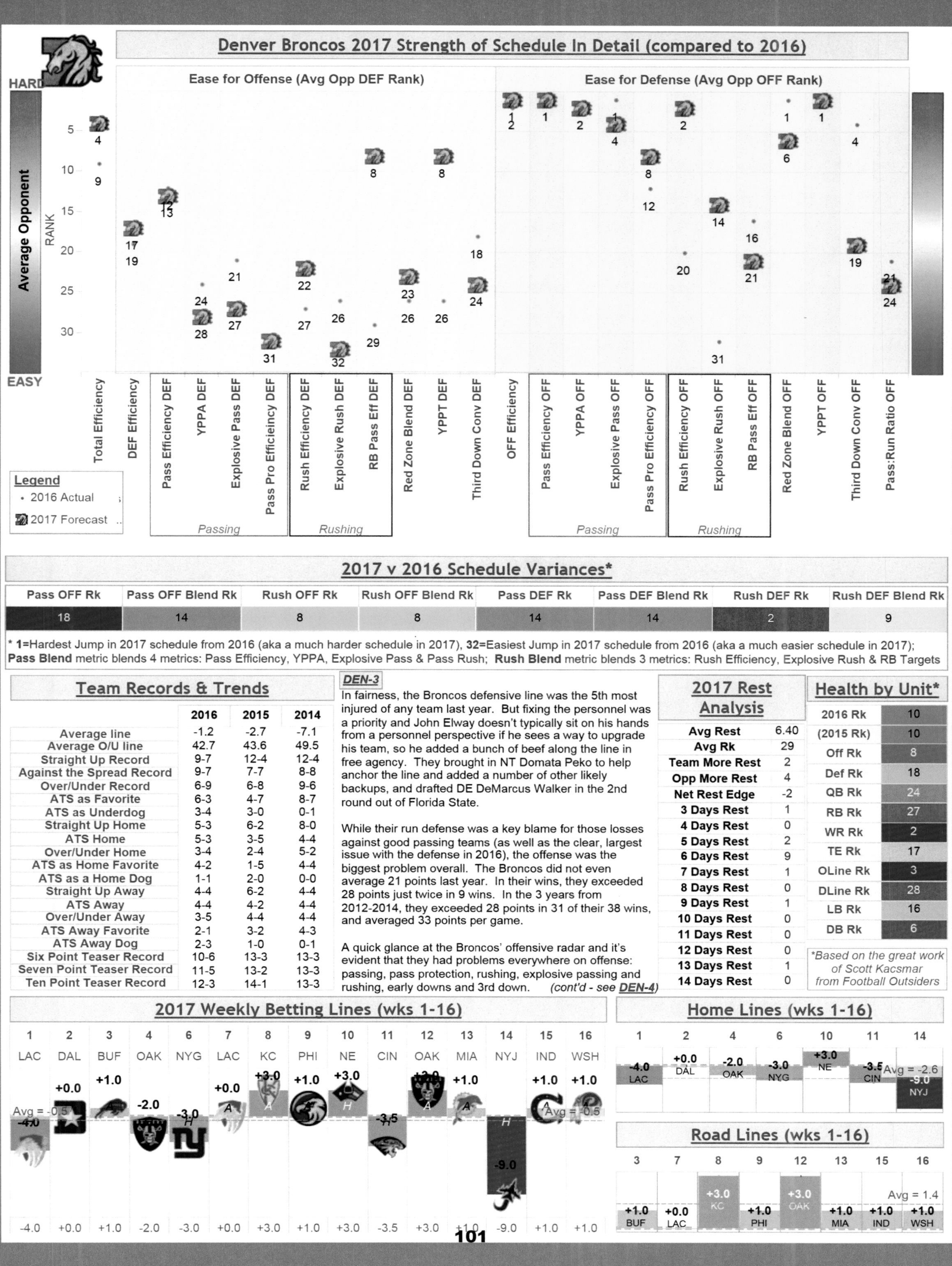

Denver Broncos 2017 Strength of Schedule In Detail (compared to 2016)

2017 v 2016 Schedule Variances*

Pass OFF Rk	Pass OFF Blend Rk	Rush OFF Rk	Rush OFF Blend Rk	Pass DEF Rk	Pass DEF Blend Rk	Rush DEF Rk	Rush DEF Blend Rk
18	14	8	8	14	14	2	9

* **1**=Hardest Jump in 2017 schedule from 2016 (aka a much harder schedule in 2017), **32**=Easiest Jump in 2017 schedule from 2016 (aka a much easier schedule in 2017); **Pass Blend** metric blends 4 metrics: Pass Efficiency, YPPA, Explosive Pass & Pass Rush; **Rush Blend** metric blends 3 metrics: Rush Efficiency, Explosive Rush & RB Targets

Team Records & Trends

	2016	2015	2014
Average line	-1.2	-2.7	-7.1
Average O/U line	42.7	43.6	49.5
Straight Up Record	9-7	12-4	12-4
Against the Spread Record	9-7	7-7	8-8
Over/Under Record	6-9	6-8	9-6
ATS as Favorite	6-3	4-7	8-7
ATS as Underdog	3-4	3-0	0-1
Straight Up Home	5-3	6-2	8-0
ATS Home	5-3	3-5	4-4
Over/Under Home	3-4	2-4	5-2
ATS as Home Favorite	4-2	1-5	4-4
ATS as a Home Dog	1-1	2-0	0-0
Straight Up Away	4-4	6-2	4-4
ATS Away	4-4	4-2	4-4
Over/Under Away	3-5	4-4	4-4
ATS Away Favorite	2-1	3-2	4-3
ATS Away Dog	2-3	1-0	0-1
Six Point Teaser Record	10-6	13-3	13-3
Seven Point Teaser Record	11-5	13-2	13-3
Ten Point Teaser Record	12-3	14-1	13-3

DEN-3

In fairness, the Broncos defensive line was the 5th most injured of any team last year. But fixing the personnel was a priority and John Elway doesn't typically sit on his hands from a personnel perspective if he sees a way to upgrade his team, so he added a bunch of beef along the line in free agency. They brought in NT Domata Peko to help anchor the line and added a number of other likely backups, and drafted DE DeMarcus Walker in the 2nd round out of Florida State.

While their run defense was a key blame for those losses against good passing teams (as well as the clear, largest issue with the defense in 2016), the offense was the biggest problem overall. The Broncos did not even average 21 points last year. In their wins, they exceeded 28 points just twice in 9 wins. In the 3 years from 2012-2014, they exceeded 28 points in 31 of their 38 wins, and averaged 33 points per game.

A quick glance at the Broncos' offensive radar and it's evident that they had problems everywhere on offense: passing, pass protection, rushing, explosive passing and rushing, early downs and 3rd down. *(cont'd - see DEN-4)*

2017 Rest Analysis

Avg Rest	6.40
Avg Rk	29
Team More Rest	2
Opp More Rest	4
Net Rest Edge	-2
3 Days Rest	1
4 Days Rest	0
5 Days Rest	2
6 Days Rest	9
7 Days Rest	1
8 Days Rest	0
9 Days Rest	1
10 Days Rest	0
11 Days Rest	0
12 Days Rest	0
13 Days Rest	1
14 Days Rest	0

Health by Unit*

2016 Rk	10
(2015 Rk)	10
Off Rk	8
Def Rk	18
QB Rk	24
RB Rk	27
WR Rk	2
TE Rk	17
OLine Rk	3
DLine Rk	28
LB Rk	16
DB Rk	6

**Based on the great work of Scott Kacsmar from Football Outsiders*

2017 Weekly Betting Lines (wks 1-16)

1	2	3	4	6	7	8	9	10	11	12	13	14	15	16
LAC	DAL	BUF	OAK	NYG	LAC	KC	PHI	NE	CIN	OAK	MIA	NYJ	IND	WSH
-4.0	+0.0	+1.0	-2.0	-3.0	+0.0	+3.0	+1.0	+3.0	-3.5	+3.0	+1.0	-9.0	+1.0	+1.0

Avg = -0.5

Home Lines (wks 1-16)

1	2	4	6	10	11	14
LAC	DAL	OAK	NYG	NE	CIN	NYJ
-4.0	+0.0	-2.0	-3.0	+3.0	-3.5	-9.0

Avg = -2.6

Road Lines (wks 1-16)

3	7	8	9	12	13	15	16
BUF	LAC	KC	PHI	OAK	MIA	IND	WSH
+1.0	+0.0	+3.0	+1.0	+3.0	+1.0	+1.0	+1.0

Avg = 1.4

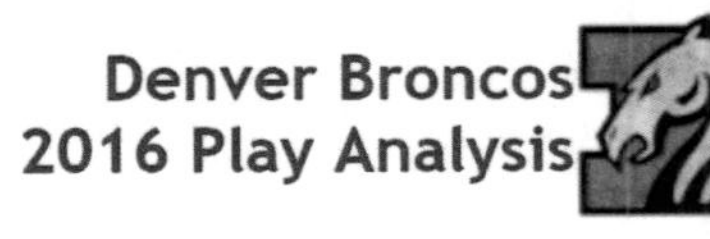

Denver Broncos 2016 Play Analysis

2016 Play Tendencies

All Pass %	61%
All Pass Rk	11
All Rush %	39%
All Rush Rk	22
1 Score Pass %	59%
1 Score Pass Rk	14
2015 1 Score Pass %	62%
2015 1 Score Pass Rk	6
Pass Increase %	-3%
Pass Increase Rk	25
1 Score Rush %	41%
1 Score Rush Rk	19
Up Pass %	54%
Up Pass Rk	23
Up Rush %	46%
Up Rush Rk	10
Down Pass %	64%
Down Pass Rk	8
Down Rush %	36%
Down Rush Rk	25

2016 Down & Distance Tendencies

Down	Distance	Total Plays	Pass Rate	Run Rate	Play Success %
1	Short (1-3)	3	0%	100%	67%
	Med (4-7)	10	50%	50%	60%
	Long (8-10)	291	54%	46%	48%
	XL (11+)	12	75%	25%	42%
2	Short (1-3)	43	28%	72%	58%
	Med (4-7)	64	55%	45%	50%
	Long (8-10)	105	66%	34%	34%
	XL (11+)	32	66%	34%	25%
3	Short (1-3)	41	54%	46%	39%
	Med (4-7)	43	95%	5%	40%
	Long (8-10)	38	100%	0%	32%
	XL (11+)	33	82%	18%	15%
4	Short (1-3)	5	20%	80%	80%
	Med (4-7)	1	100%	0%	0%
	Long (8-10)	1	0%	100%	0%

Shotgun %:

	Under Center	Shotgun
Team	58%	42%
AVG	37%	63%

Run Rate:

	Under Center	Shotgun
Team	59%	14%
AVG	68%	23%

Pass Rate:

	Under Center	Shotgun
Team	41%	86%
AVG	32%	77%

Short Yardage Intelligence:

2nd and Short Run

Run Freq	Run % Rk	NFL Run Freq Avg	Run 1D Rate	Run NFL 1D Avg
70%	9	65%	55%	71%

2nd and Short Pass

Pass Freq	Pass % Rk	NFL Pass Freq Avg	Pass 1D Rate	Pass NFL 1D Avg
30%	24	35%	50%	52%

Most Frequent Play

Down	Distance	Play Type	Player	Total Plays	Play Success %
1	Med (4-7)	PASS	Emmanuel Sanders	3	33%
		RUSH	Devontae Booker	3	67%
	Long (8-10)	RUSH	Devontae Booker	62	53%
	XL (11+)	PASS	Demaryius Thomas	3	100%
2	Short (1-3)	RUSH	Devontae Booker	17	71%
	Med (4-7)	RUSH	Devontae Booker	16	56%
	Long (8-10)	PASS	Demaryius Thomas	22	55%
	XL (11+)	PASS	Demaryius Thomas	6	17%
3	Short (1-3)	RUSH	Devontae Booker	8	25%
	Med (4-7)	PASS	Demaryius Thomas	9	33%
	Long (8-10)	PASS	Demaryius Thomas	10	40%
	XL (11+)	PASS	Demaryius Thomas	6	17%

Most Successful Play*

Down	Distance	Play Type	Player	Total Plays	Play Success %
1	Long (8-10)	PASS	Jordan Norwood	5	100%
2	Short (1-3)	RUSH	Devontae Booker	17	71%
	Med (4-7)	PASS	Demaryius Thomas	7	86%
	Long (8-10)	PASS	Demaryius Thomas	22	55%
	XL (11+)	PASS	Demaryius Thomas	6	17%
3	Short (1-3)	PASS	Demaryius Thomas	6	50%
	Med (4-7)	PASS	Jordan Taylor	5	60%
	Long (8-10)	PASS	Emmanuel Sanders	7	43%
	XL (11+)	PASS	Devontae Booker	5	20%
			Emmanuel Sanders	5	20%

*Minimum 5 plays to qualify

2016 Snap Rates

Week	Opp	Score	Demaryius Thomas	Emmanuel Sanders	Devontae Booker	Virgil Green	Jordan Norwood	C.J. Anderson
1	CAR	W 21-20	44 (76%)	50 (86%)	6 (10%)	41 (71%)	30 (52%)	48 (83%)
2	IND	W 34-20	56 (79%)	60 (85%)	14 (20%)	41 (58%)	40 (56%)	47 (66%)
3	CIN	W 29-17	57 (85%)	57 (85%)	16 (24%)		41 (61%)	48 (72%)
4	TB	W 27-7	51 (71%)	61 (85%)	18 (25%)		31 (43%)	48 (67%)
5	ATL	L 23-16	56 (80%)	68 (97%)	29 (41%)		45 (64%)	36 (51%)
6	SD	L 21-13	68 (92%)	46 (62%)	15 (20%)	57 (77%)	62 (84%)	58 (78%)
7	HOU	W 27-9	49 (77%)	52 (81%)	35 (55%)	39 (61%)	18 (28%)	29 (45%)
8	SD	W 27-19	56 (86%)	58 (89%)	54 (83%)	48 (74%)	15 (23%)	
9	OAK	L 30-20	48 (89%)	50 (93%)	45 (83%)	40 (74%)	39 (72%)	
10	NO	W 25-23	71 (86%)	75 (90%)	59 (71%)	58 (70%)	43 (52%)	
12	KC	L 30-27	75 (94%)	73 (91%)	46 (58%)	50 (63%)	17 (21%)	
13	JAC	W 20-10	46 (84%)	45 (82%)	37 (67%)	39 (71%)	22 (40%)	
14	TEN	L 13-10	62 (95%)	60 (92%)	28 (43%)	32 (49%)		
15	NE	L 16-3	57 (92%)	58 (94%)	28 (45%)	7 (11%)	47 (76%)	
16	KC	L 33-10	48 (80%)	47 (78%)	33 (55%)		18 (30%)	
17	OAK	W 24-6	38 (52%)	2 (3%)	29 (40%)	36 (49%)		
Grand Total			882 (82%)	862 (81%)	492 (46%)	488 (61%)	468 (50%)	314 (66%)

Personnel Groupings

Personnel	Team %	NFL Avg	Succ. %
1-1 [3WR]	53%	60%	44%
2-1 [2WR]	19%	7%	44%
1-0 [4WR]	11%	3%	37%
1-2 [2WR]	10%	19%	39%
0-1 [4WR]	3%	1%	42%

Grouping Tendencies

Personnel	Pass Rate	Pass Succ. %	Run Succ. %
1-1 [3WR]	66%	45%	43%
2-1 [2WR]	30%	47%	43%
1-0 [4WR]	80%	36%	39%
1-2 [2WR]	55%	43%	34%

Red Zone Targets (min 3)

Receiver	All	Inside 5	6-10	11-20
Emmanuel Sanders	22	7	4	11
Demaryius Thomas	21	8	3	10
Devontae Booker	6		1	5
Jordan Taylor	6	1	2	3
Jordan Norwood	4	3	1	
Virgil Green	4	2	1	1
Bennie Fowler	3	1		2

Red Zone Rushes (min 3)

Rusher	All	Inside 5	6-10	11-20
Devontae Booker	29	6	7	16
C.J. Anderson	23	9	3	11
Justin Forsett	4	1	1	2
Kapri Bibbs	4			4
Trevor Siemian	4		1	3

Early Down Target Rate

	RB	TE	WR
Team	18%	15%	67%
NFL AVG	19%	20%	61%

Overall Target Success %

RB	TE	WR
41% #25	51% #21	49% #17

Denver Broncos 2016 Passing Recap & 2017 Outlook

Thanks to the inefficiency of the run game as well as their own passing inefficiency, the Broncos found themselves trailing often over the second half of the season, so they became exceedingly pass heavy. This was a bad recipe for Siemian. While 10 interceptions was not a devastating number, 18 total TDs was a problem, particularly when the running game was not producing. In the red zone, Siemian produced a sub-85 passer rating, which ranked 22nd in the NFL, and just 34% of his attempts were successful, one of the worst marks in the NFL. A big problem for the Broncos passing game was options. Demaryius Thomas and Emmanuel Sanders were targeted nearly identical amounts and totaled 281 targets. The next most targeted receiver was TE Virgil Green, but he had only 37 total targets. Jordan Norwood was the next most targeted WR and he was targeted just 35 times and produced a 65 rating when targeted. Most teams don't have WR1 and WR2 the caliber of Thomas and Sanders, so there cannot be complaints there. But the WR3 or preferably the TE must be targeted more often to create more balance and challenge the defense. With TE targets being the most efficient in the NFL and McCoy's usage of the TE in San Diego, expect that to be a prio..

Trevor Siemian Rating All Downs

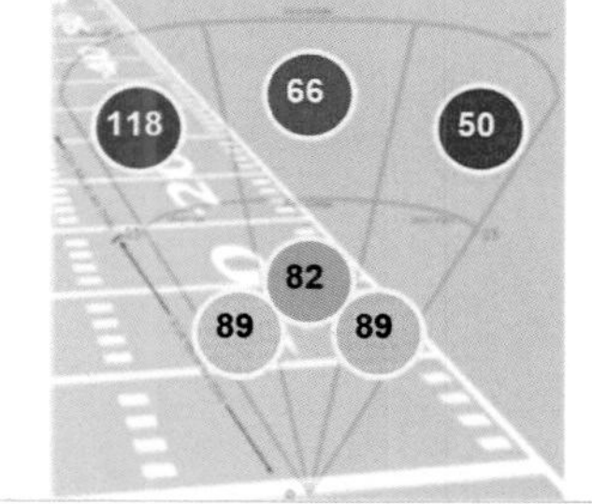

Trevor Siemian Rating Early Downs

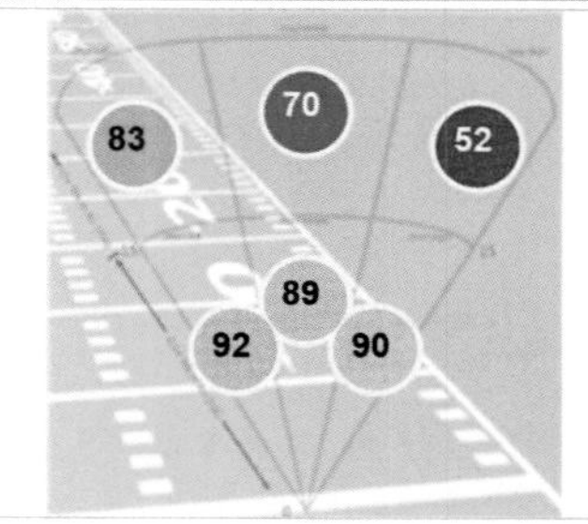

2016 Standard Passing Table

QB	Comp	Att	Comp %	Yds	YPA	TDs	INT	Sacks	Rating	Rk
Trevor Siemian	289	486	59%	3,401	7.0	18	10	31	84.6	31
Paxton Lynch	49	83	59%	497	6.0	2	1	9	79.2	36
NFL Avg			63%		7.2				90.4	

2016 Advanced Passing Table

QB	Success %	EDSR Passing Success %	20+ Yd Pass Gains	20+ Yd Pass %	30+ Yd Pass Gains	30+ Yd Pass %	Air Yds per Comp	YAC per Comp	20+ Air Yd Comp	20+ Air Yd %
Trevor Siemian	44%	48%	37	8%	16	3%	6.9	4.9	15	3%
Paxton Lynch	41%	48%	3	4%	1	1%	7.3	2.9	1	1%
NFL Avg	44%	48%	27	8%	10	3%	6.4	4.8	12	4%

Interception Rates by Down

Yards to Go	1	2	3	4	Total
1 & 2	0.0%	0.0%	0.0%	0.0%	0.0%
3, 4, 5	0.0%	0.0%	3.0%	0.0%	1.5%
6 - 9	0.0%	0.0%	4.4%	0.0%	1.9%
10 - 14	2.8%	0.0%	0.0%	100.0%	2.1%
15+	0.0%	0.0%	9.1%		2.9%
Total	2.5%	0.0%	2.8%	16.7%	1.9%

3rd Down Passing - Short of Sticks Analysis

QB	Avg Yds to Go	Air Yds (of Comps)	Avg Yds Short	Short of Sticks Rate	Rk
Trevor Siemian	7.7	8.1	0.0	60%	11
NFL Avg	7.6	6.8	-0.8	57%	

Air Yds vs YAC

Air Yds %	YAC %	Rk
59%	41%	16
54%	46%	

2016 Receiving Recap & 2017 Outlook

Demaryius Thomas and Emmanuel Sanders were both big disappointments in 2016 on account of the lack of virility of the passing offense in general. But they produced nearly identical stat lines: approx. 140 targets, 7.5 yards per target, 51-52% success rates and 5 receiving touchdowns. They also dominated in the red zone (21-22 targets each). Denver needs a third wheel to emerge, especially in the red zone, where the next most targeted TE or WR had just 3 targets. When their TE targets were more successful than their WR targets, yet they threw 67% to WRs (avg=61%) and 15% to TEs (avg=20%), better balance is needed.

Player *Min 50 Targets*	Targets	Comp %	YPA	Rating	TOARS	Success %	Success Rk	Missed YPA Rk	YAS % Rk	TDs
Demaryius Thomas	144	63%	7.5	91	5.2	52%	57	65	103	5
Emmanuel Sanders	137	58%	7.5	78	5.0	51%	66	56	33	5

Directional Passer Rating Delivered

Receiver	Short Left	Short Middle	Short Right	Deep Left	Deep Middle	Deep Right	Player Total
Demaryius Thomas	106	60	91	79	119	88	91
Emmanuel Sanders	65	107	78	142	110	21	78
Devontae Booker	128	64	80			40	89
Virgil Green	92	72	100	40	119	40	87
Jordan Norwood	44	101	64	85	0	158	65
Jordan Taylor	119	91	126	0	119	55	100
C.J. Anderson	134	71	75				94
A.J. Derby	109	69	95			119	100
Justin Forsett	65	92	79				75
Team Total	93	77	89	96	75	54	86

2016 Rushing Recap & 2017 Outlook

The big secret in Denver for 2017 could be their red zone rushing. When CJ Anderson was healthy, he took 100% of the red zone carries. When he went down, Booker took over as the #1 back and saw 100% of the touches less 4 to Kapri Bibbs. Last year, the #1 RB recorded 52 red zone touches, including 15 inside the 5 yard line, and that was on a putrid offense. Thus, if Anderson proves to be the #1 this year and the offense is even moderately improved over 2016, there could be a ton of red zone volume for him. McCoy's main focus on the ground is basic efficiency improvement across the board and if he succeeds, look for the entire offense to look substantially better than it did in 2016, which inherently will help the Denver run defense as well.

Player *Min 50 Rushes*	Rushes	YPA	Success %	Success Rk	Missed YPA Rk	YTS % Rk	YAS % Rk	Early Down Success %	Early Down Success Rk	TDs
Devontae Booker	174	3.5	45%	41	22	14	56	46%	40	4
C.J. Anderson	110	4.0	39%	60	52	52	49	40%	57	4

Yards per Carry by Direction

Directional Run Frequency

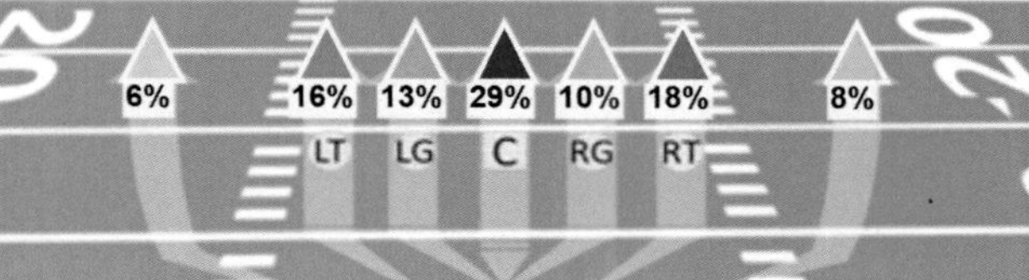

DEN-4

It was a clean sweep. It absolutely never helps when your RB1 goes out, which is what happened when CJ Anderson was done for the year in week 7. Up until he was lost, the Broncos were 5-2 on the season, 45% of their runs were successful and 47% of their passes were successful. Overall they ranked 18th in success rate but that was against the 5th easiest schedule of run defenses in the league.

Without Anderson, however, the bottom fell out. The Broncos run success rate dropped to 38%, the 2nd worst in the NFL. It impacted the pass offense, which dropped to just 41% successful (28th) and their overall success rate ranked 29th from weeks 8 onward.

The entire offense changed philosophy because they could not run the ball. Through the first 7 weeks, in one-score games outside of the 4th quarter, the Broncos passed the ball 57% of the time, just below the NFL average. From week 8 onward, they passed the ball on 61% of plays, 12th most in the NFL. They were so predictably poor on early downs that they had to passed the ball on 92% of their 3rd downs, 3rd most in the NFL. In weeks 1-7, that number was only 76%, the 6th least in the NFL.

To help with their run game, the Broncos made a few moves. They added LT Garett Bolles in the first round to replace the departed Russell Okung. They added LG Ronald Leary in free agency, and should have a completely new left side of the line.

Denver also added RB Jamaal Charles, although he's not even a lock to make the team due to his injuries and decline of play. With Booker's poor performance, the job is squarely on CJ Anderson's plate. Fortunately for Denver, they face a much easier than average schedule of run defenses. The late season schedule is the 2nd easiest close for any run offense, and fortunately, some of their toughest opponents from a run defensive perspective must play in Denver: the Giants week 6, the Patriots week 10 and the Cowboys week 2. So there is little doubt improvement in the run game is not simply hoped for, but expected by Elway and new HC Vance Joseph.

New OC, Mike McCoy, ping pongs back from the Chargers (2013-2013) to the role he held in Denver from 2009-2012. In San Diego, McCoy passed the ball more often than average, but that was with Philip Rivers. Trevor Siemian isn't on his level, and so even though McCoy knows how much more efficient passing is than rushing, he will have to be careful to stay balanced. More than anything, the Broncos need another weapon to emerge. The story is the same whether it's overall targets or red zone targets: the Broncos have 2 WRs they spoon feed and little else. No reliable WR3 or TE has emerged as a player they desire to target. For that reason, they used a 3rd round pick on WR Carlos Henderson and a 5th round pick on TE Jake Butt. McCoy will have to do his very best to find another threat in the passing game to soften up the defense.

Division History: Season Wins & 2017 Projection

2013 Wins | 2014 Wins | 2015 Wins | 2016 Wins | Proj 2017 Wins

Rank of 2017 Defensive Pass Efficiency Faced by Week

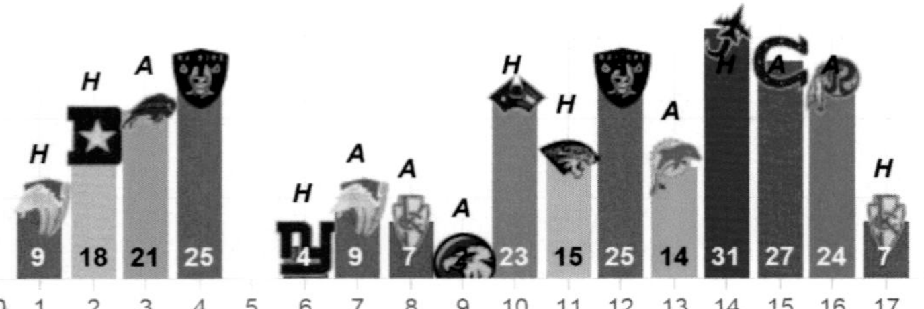

Rank of 2017 Defensive Rush Efficiency Faced by Week

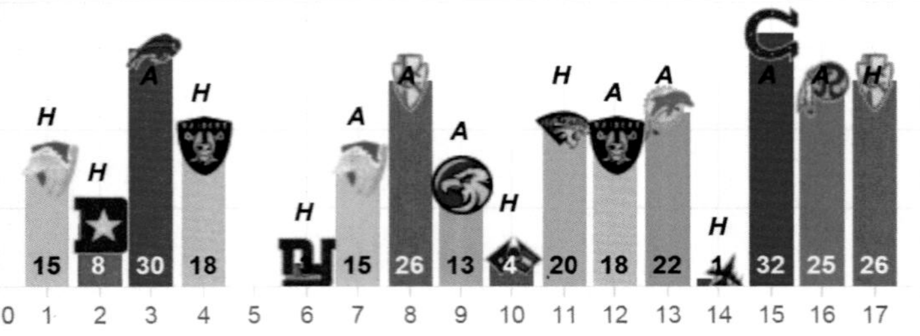

2016 Situational Usage by Player & Position

Usage Rate by Score

		Being Blown Out (14+)	Down Big (9-13)	One Score	Large Lead (9-13)	Blowout Lead (14+)	Grand Total
RUSH	Devontae Booker	7%	12%	21%	21%	32%	19%
	Emmanuel Sanders			0%			0%
	C.J. Anderson	7%	6%	13%	21%	12%	12%
	Justin Forsett	2%	4%	3%	4%	25%	5%
	Jordan Norwood			0%			0%
	Kapri Bibbs		2%	4%	6%		3%
	Andy Janovich		1%	1%			0%
	Juwan Thompson	4%		1%		4%	1%
	Total	21%	24%	43%	51%	72%	40%
PASS	Devontae Booker	13%	8%	3%	4%	4%	5%
	Demaryius Thomas	17%	19%	16%	12%	7%	16%
	Emmanuel Sanders	7%	21%	16%	15%		15%
	C.J. Anderson	9%	2%	2%	4%		3%
	Justin Forsett		2%	1%		2%	1%
	Virgil Green	2%	4%	4%	4%	4%	4%
	Jordan Norwood	7%	5%	3%	4%		4%
	Kapri Bibbs	1%	1%	0%	1%		0%
	Jordan Taylor	5%	5%	2%	3%	2%	3%
	Bennie Fowler	7%	3%	2%			3%
	A.J. Derby		4%	3%			2%
	Jeff Heuerman	5%	1%	2%		4%	2%
	Cody Latimer		2%	1%	3%	5%	2%
	Andy Janovich			1%			1%
	Juwan Thompson	1%					0%
	John Phillips	2%	1%	1%			1%
	Kalif Raymond		1%			2%	0%
	Henry Krieger-Coble	1%					0%
	Total	79%	76%	57%	49%	28%	60%

Positional Target Distribution vs NFL Average

		NFL Wide				Team Only			
		Left	Middle	Right	**Total**	Left	Middle	Right	**Total**
Deep	WR	1,000	571	969	**2,540**	31	10	32	**73**
	TE	157	145	161	**463**	1	2	2	**5**
	RB	25	4	39	**68**			1	**1**
	All	**1,182**	**720**	**1,169**	**3,071**	**32**	**12**	**35**	**79**
Short	WR	2,975	1,721	3,086	**7,782**	118	50	100	**268**
	TE	817	858	1,135	**2,810**	19	17	16	**52**
	RB	990	599	1,082	**2,671**	25	23	31	**79**
	All	**4,782**	**3,178**	**5,303**	**13,263**	**162**	**90**	**147**	**399**
Total		**5,964**	**3,898**	**6,472**	**16,334**	**194**	**102**	**182**	**478**

Positional Success Rates vs NFL Average

		NFL Wide				Team Only			
		Left	Middle	Right	**Total**	Left	Middle	Right	**Total**
Deep	WR	37%	50%	38%	**40%**	45%	60%	28%	**40%**
	TE	45%	49%	43%	**45%**	0%	100%	50%	**60%**
	RB	32%	75%	26%	**31%**			0%	**0%**
	All	**38%**	**50%**	**39%**	**41%**	**44%**	**67%**	**29%**	**41%**
Short	WR	52%	57%	51%	**53%**	55%	56%	49%	**53%**
	TE	50%	62%	52%	**54%**	53%	41%	56%	**50%**
	RB	47%	50%	44%	**46%**	40%	48%	35%	**41%**
	All	**51%**	**57%**	**50%**	**52%**	**52%**	**51%**	**47%**	**50%**
Total		**48%**	**56%**	**48%**	**50%**	**51%**	**53%**	**43%**	**49%**

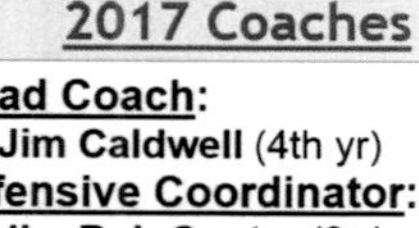

2017 Coaches

Head Coach:
Jim Caldwell (4th yr)
Offensive Coordinator:
Jim Bob Cooter (3rd yr)
Defensive Coordinator:
Teryl Austin (4th yr)

Detroit Lions

2017 Forecast

Wins	Div Rank
8	#3

Past Records

2016: 9-7
2015: 7-9
2014: 11-5

EASY HARD

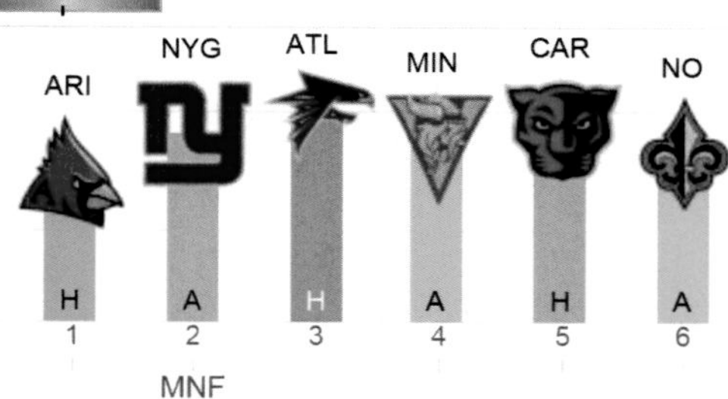

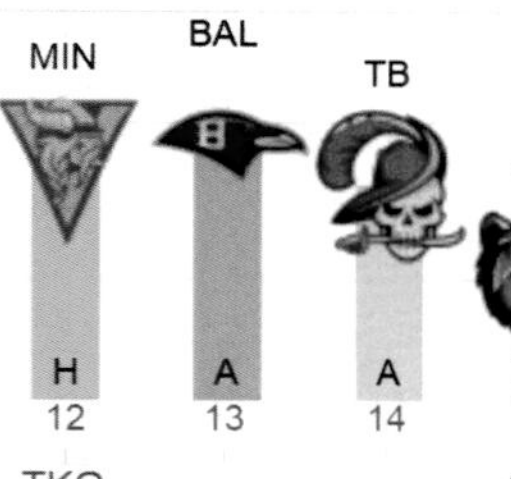

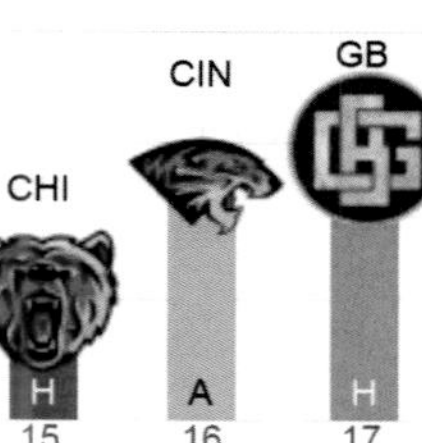

Week	Opponent	H/A	Note
1	ARI	H	
2	NYG	A	MNF
3	ATL	H	
4	MIN	A	
5	CAR	H	
6	NO	A	
7			
8	PIT	H	SNF
9	GB	A	MNF
10	CLE	H	
11	CHI	A	
12	MIN	H	TKG
13	BAL	A	
14	TB	A	
15	CHI	H	SAT
16	CIN	A	
17	GB	H	

Key Players Lost

TXN	Player (POS)
Cut	Levy, DeAndre LB
Declared Free Agent	Bell, Joique RB
	Boldin, Anquan WR
	Bostic, Jon LB
	Bush, Rafael S
	Butler, Crezdon CB
	Bynes, Josh LB
	Charles, Stefan DT
	Harbor, Clay TE
	Jackson, Asa CB
	Muhlbach, Don C
	Mulligan, Matthew TE
	Orlovsky, Dan QB
	Reiff, Riley T
	Reynolds, Garrett G
	Roberts, Andre WR
	Taylor, Devin DE
	Walker, Tyrunn DT
	Warford, Larry G
Retired	Schwartz, Geoff G

Average Line	# Games Favored	# Games Underdog
+0.3	6	9

2017 Detroit Lions Overview

Entering 2016, the biggest question surrounding the Lions is how to replace the roar from Megatron, both inside the red zone as well as in the deep game. Once Jim Bob Cooter took over in 2015, the offense turned into the most successful red zone offense based on both play success as well as TD rates. And 56% of all passes 15+ yards in the air found their way to Calvin Johnson. I felt for them to see the most success in 2016, they would absolutely need to have more success running the football. And that Ameer Abdullah would have to perform much better and become much more explosive.

As it turns out, the offense took steps backwards in all those areas. Yet somehow, despite all of that and in spite of a miserable showing from the defense, the team still won 9 games and made the playoffs. We'll address how they did it and what they must improve upon shortly, but first we need to understand the key changes to the red zone performance and deep passing without Calvin Johnson.

In the red zone, the Lions were successful on 45% of their offensive plays, which ranked 14th. Their red zone conversion rate also ranked about middle of the road, at 16th. What crippled them in the red zone was the run game. Stafford and the pass game was successful on 48% of their attempts, 6th best in the NFL. It was the run game, which ranked 30th in the NFL, that hurt this offense tremendously. The WR performance as a unit without Megatron, let the team down in the red zone, with Anquan Boldin being the most reliable target (15/23, 6 TDs, 1 INT, 99 rtg), Marvin Jones being a subpar target (6/15, 2 TDs, 88 rtg), and Golden Tate being extremely disappointing (9/17, 1 TD, 2 INTs, 39 rtg). But that was offset by Cooter designing intelligent plays to the money receivers – those with the best success rates that I've been preaching need more targets: running backs and tight ends, not wide receivers.

In the red zone when targeting backs and tight ends, Stafford completed 81% (#1) of his attempts (21/26), recorded a 7:0 TD:INT ratio and a 125 rating (#2). That is as opposed to targeting wide receivers, when Stafford completed 53% (#17) of his attempts and recorded a 79 rating (#27). Cooter figured out how to sustain red zone passing efficiency, but it wasn't by replacing Megatron with another wide receiver.

(cont'd - see DET2)

Key Free Agents/ Trades Added

- Asiata, Matt RB
- Fells, Darren TE
- Hayden, DJ CB
- Hills, Tony T
- Lang, T.J. G
- Martin, Keshawn WR
- Spence, Akeem DT
- Wagner, Rick T
- Washington, Cornelius DE
- Worrilow, Paul LB

Drafted Players

Rd	Pk	Player (College)
1	21	LB - Jarrad Davis (Florida)
2	53	CB - Teez Tabor (Florida)
3	96	WR - Kenny Golladay (Northern Illinois)
4	124	LB - Jalen Reeves-Maybin (Tennessee)
	127	TE - Michael Roberts (Toledo)
5	165	CB - Jamal Agnew (San Diego)
6	205	DE - Jeremiah Ledbetter (Arkansas)
	215	QB - Brad Kaaya (Miami (FL))
7	250	DE - Pat O'Connor (Eastern Michigan)

Regular Season Wins: Past & Current Proj

	Wins
Proj 2017 Wins	8
2016 Wins	9
Proj 2016 Wins	7
2015 Wins	7
2014 Wins	11
2013 Wins	7

1 3 5 7 9 11 13 15

2017 Lineup & Cap Hits

Defense:
- FS G.Quin 27
- SS T.Wilson 32
- LB J.Davis 40
- LB T.Whitehead 59
- RCB N.Lawson 24
- SLOTCB D.Hayden 31
- DE E.Ansah 94
- DT C.Washington 90
- DT H.Ngata 92
- DE K.Hyder 61
- LCB D.Slay 23

Offense:
- LWR T.Jones 13
- SLOTWR G.Tate 15
- LT T.Decker 68
- LG L.Tomlinson 72 (Rookie)
- C T.Swanson 64
- RG T.Lang 76
- RT R.Wagner 71
- TE E.Ebron 85
- RWR M.Jones 11
- QB M.Stafford 9
- RB A.Abdullah 21
- WR2 K.Golladay 10 (Rookie)
- WR3 J.Billingsley 16
- RB2 T.Riddick 25
- QB2 J.Rudock 14

2017 Cap Dollars

2017 Unit Spending

All DEF
All OFF

Positional Spending

	Rank	Total	2016 Rk
All OFF	15	$83.53M	16
QB	7	$23.04M	7
OL	22	$25.31M	27
RB	23	$5.79M	23
WR	12	$21.82M	13
TE	21	$7.58M	15
All DEF	13	$81.53M	27
DL	10	$33.77M	20
LB	27	$13.43M	21
CB	9	$22.54M	25
S	17	$11.79M	16

DET-2

In terms of deep passing where Megatron thrived, the Lions lost efficiency. In 2015, with Megatron, Stafford's passer rating was 100 on deep passes, and 9.0% of his deep attempts went for touchdowns. Calvin Johnson was targeted on 44 of Stafford's 78 deep attempts (56%). But in 2016 there was no Megatron. Stafford's passer rating on deep attempts dropped to 93. More importantly, his TD rate on deep attempts dropped from 9.0% down to just 5.4%. How does this impact the game? Fewer quick scores, more third down attempts and the need to convert in the red zone. Getting chunk, explosive plays is extremely valuable. Putting 7 on the scoreboard with one of them is substantially more valuable than an explosive play that moves the ball from a team's own 45 to the opponent's 30. From a comparison perspective: 19 quarterbacks had over 90 deep attempts in 2016. The only quarterbacks with fewer TDs than Stafford were Blake Bortles, Ryan Fitzpatrick and Andy Dalton.

It wasn't so much that the Lions were terrible in deep passing in 2016. They simply couldn't "hide" the WR inefficiency by using RBs and TEs, like they did in the red zone. Stafford ended up throwing more deep attempts because he wasn't hitting on as many, and the inefficiency showed.

So how can the team address both elements heading into 2017? In terms of getting more success from the WRs in the red zone, that appears unlikely. That is because their #1 red zone target, Anquan Boldin, is no longer with the team. Golden Tate, Marvin Jones and TJ Jones were all unreliable in the red zone last year. I would expect significant volume to go Eric Ebron's way yet again, but not having a reliable WR like Megatron up until 2015 and then Boldin in 2016 will certainly hurt Stafford's confidence and potentially the offense's potency. While the RBs will certainly be key targets, as they were in 2016, the re-introduction of Ameer Abdullah out of the backfield will make the RB-target picture more convoluted than it was when Theo Riddick finished #2 in total red zone team targets behind only Boldin, and scored 5 TDs on those 12 receptions.

*(cont'd - see **DET-3**)*

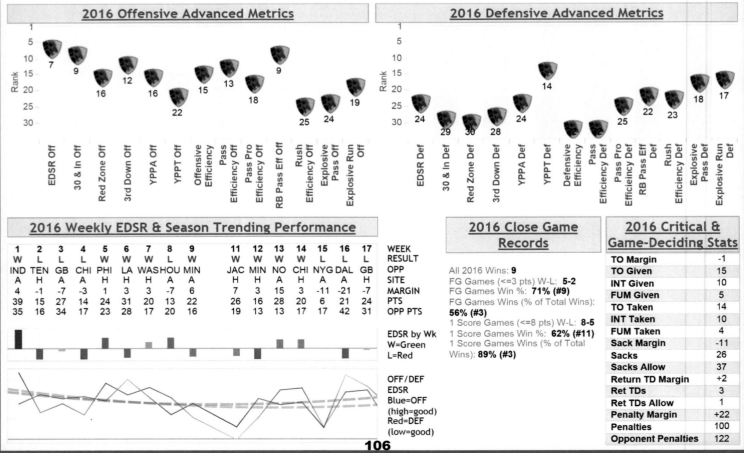

2016 Offensive Advanced Metrics

	Rank
EDSR Off	7
30 & In Off	9
Red Zone Off	16
3rd Down Off	12
YPPA Off	16
YPPT Off	22
Offensive Efficiency	15
Pass Efficiency Off	13
Pass Pro Efficiency Off	18
RB Pass Eff Off	9
Rush Efficiency Off	25
Explosive Pass Off	24
Explosive Run Off	19

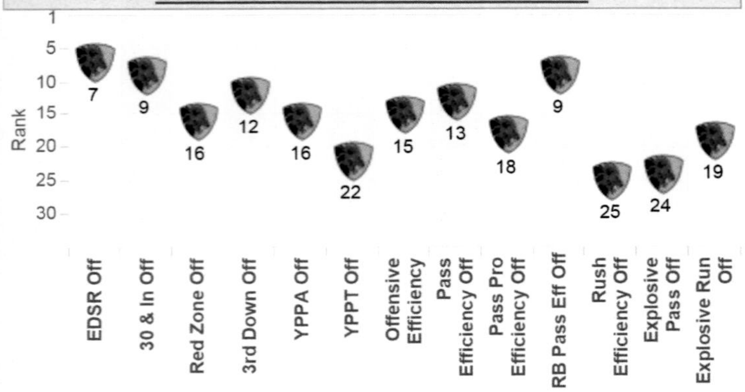

2016 Defensive Advanced Metrics

	Rank
EDSR Def	24
30 & In Def	29
Red Zone Def	30
3rd Down Def	28
YPPA Def	24
YPPT Def	14
Defensive Efficiency	32
Pass Efficiency Def	32
Pass Pro Efficieincy Def	25
RB Pass Eff Def	22
Rush Efficiency Def	23
Explosive Pass Def	18
Explosive Run Def	17

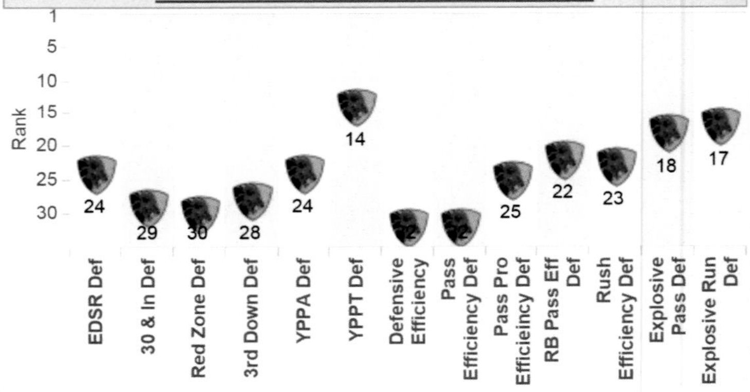

2016 Weekly EDSR & Season Trending Performance

WEEK	1	2	3	4	5	6	7	8	9	11	12	13	14	15	16	17
RESULT	W	L	L	L	W	W	W	L	W	W	W	W	W	L	L	L
OPP	IND	TEN	GB	CHI	PHI	LA	WAS	HOU	MIN	JAC	MIN	NO	CHI	NYG	DAL	GB
SITE	A	H	A	A	H	H	H	A	A	H	H	A	H	A	A	H
MARGIN	4	-1	-7	-3	1	3	3	-7	6	7	3	15	3	-11	-21	-7
PTS	39	15	27	14	24	31	20	13	22	26	16	28	20	6	21	24
OPP PTS	35	16	34	17	23	28	17	20	16	19	13	13	17	17	42	31

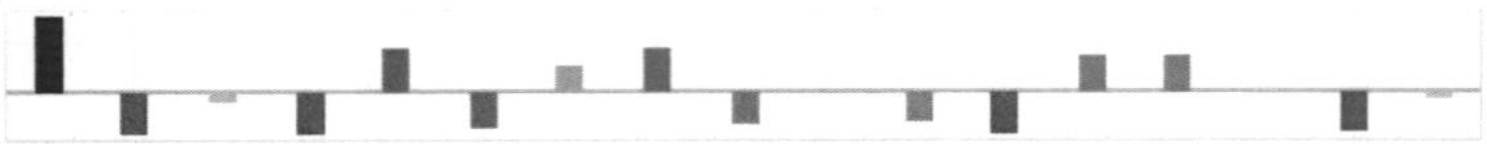

EDSR by Wk
W=Green
L=Red

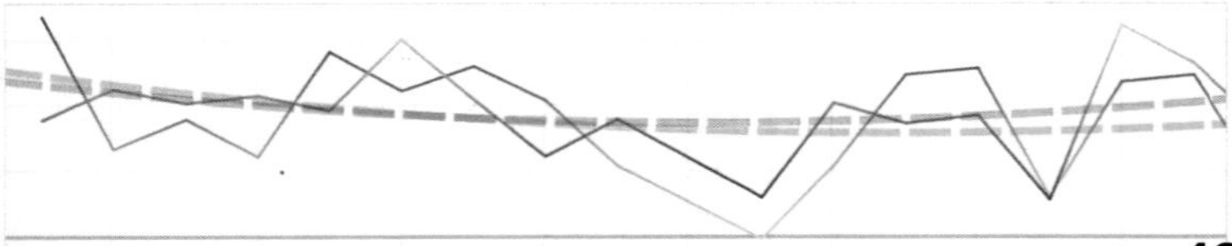

OFF/DEF EDSR
Blue=OFF (high=good)
Red=DEF (low=good)

2016 Close Game Records

All 2016 Wins: **9**
FG Games (<=3 pts) W-L: **5-2**
FG Games Win %: **71% (#9)**
FG Games Wins (% of Total Wins): **56% (#3)**
1 Score Games (<=8 pts) W-L: **8-5**
1 Score Games Win %: **62% (#11)**
1 Score Games Wins (% of Total Wins): **89% (#3)**

2016 Critical & Game-Deciding Stats

TO Margin	-1
TO Given	15
INT Given	10
FUM Given	5
TO Taken	14
INT Taken	10
FUM Taken	4
Sack Margin	-11
Sacks	26
Sacks Allow	37
Return TD Margin	+2
Ret TDs	3
Ret TDs Allow	1
Penalty Margin	+22
Penalties	100
Opponent Penalties	122

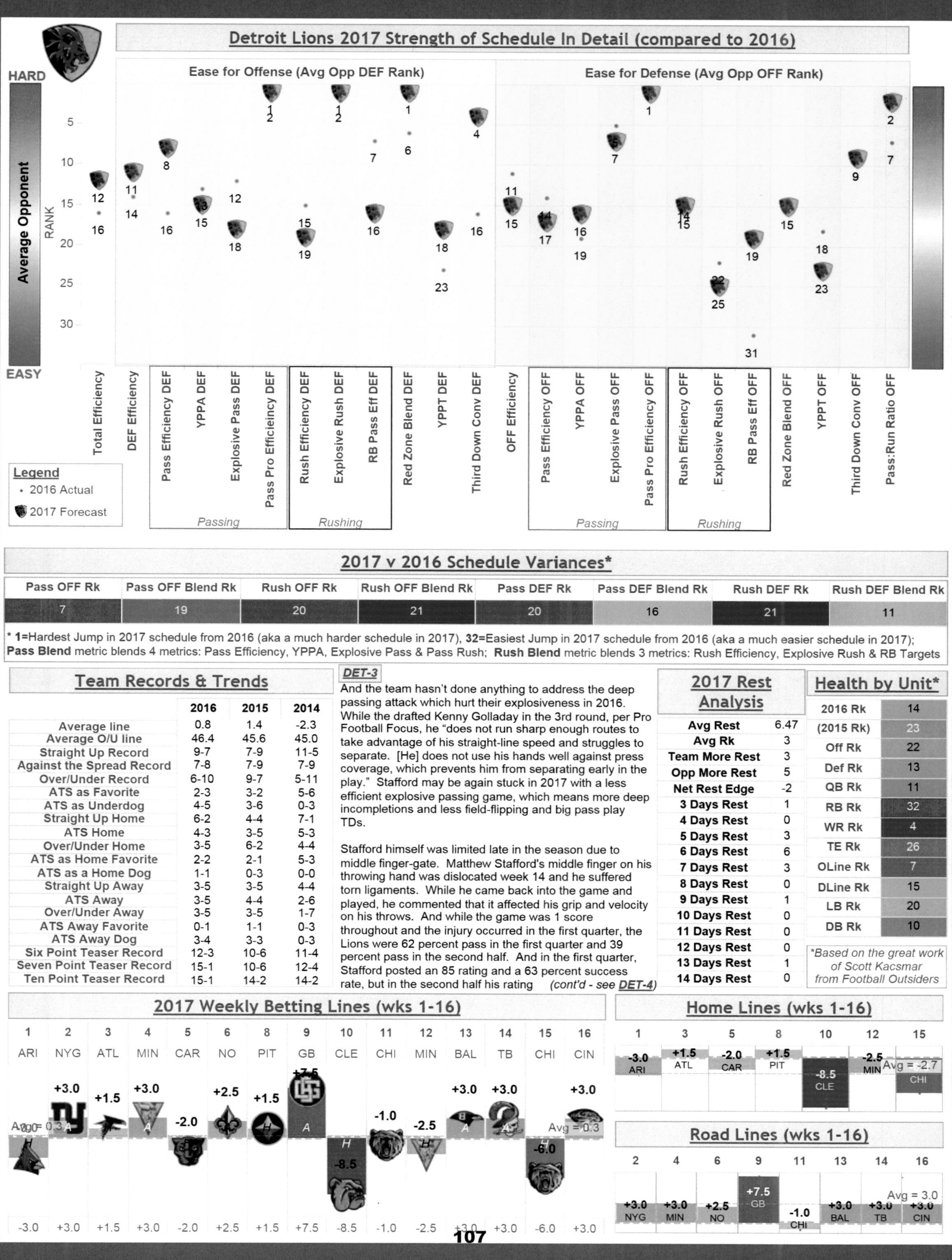

Detroit Lions 2017 Strength of Schedule In Detail (compared to 2016)

2017 v 2016 Schedule Variances*

Pass OFF Rk	Pass OFF Blend Rk	Rush OFF Rk	Rush OFF Blend Rk	Pass DEF Rk	Pass DEF Blend Rk	Rush DEF Rk	Rush DEF Blend Rk
7	19	20	21	20	16	21	11

* **1**=Hardest Jump in 2017 schedule from 2016 (aka a much harder schedule in 2017), **32**=Easiest Jump in 2017 schedule from 2016 (aka a much easier schedule in 2017); **Pass Blend** metric blends 4 metrics: Pass Efficiency, YPPA, Explosive Pass & Pass Rush; **Rush Blend** metric blends 3 metrics: Rush Efficiency, Explosive Rush & RB Targets

Team Records & Trends

	2016	2015	2014
Average line	0.8	1.4	-2.3
Average O/U line	46.4	45.6	45.0
Straight Up Record	9-7	7-9	11-5
Against the Spread Record	7-8	7-9	7-9
Over/Under Record	6-10	9-7	5-11
ATS as Favorite	2-3	3-2	5-6
ATS as Underdog	4-5	3-6	0-3
Straight Up Home	6-2	4-4	7-1
ATS Home	4-3	3-5	5-3
Over/Under Home	3-5	6-2	4-4
ATS as Home Favorite	2-2	2-1	5-3
ATS as a Home Dog	1-1	0-3	0-0
Straight Up Away	3-5	3-5	4-4
ATS Away	3-5	4-4	2-6
Over/Under Away	3-5	3-5	1-7
ATS Away Favorite	0-1	1-1	0-3
ATS Away Dog	3-4	3-3	0-3
Six Point Teaser Record	12-3	10-6	11-4
Seven Point Teaser Record	15-1	10-6	12-4
Ten Point Teaser Record	15-1	14-2	14-2

DET-3

And the team hasn't done anything to address the deep passing attack which hurt their explosiveness in 2016. While the drafted Kenny Golladay in the 3rd round, per Pro Football Focus, he "does not run sharp enough routes to take advantage of his straight-line speed and struggles to separate. [He] does not use his hands well against press coverage, which prevents him from separating early in the play." Stafford may be again stuck in 2017 with a less efficient explosive passing game, which means more deep incompletions and less field-flipping and big pass play TDs.

Stafford himself was limited late in the season due to middle finger-gate. Matthew Stafford's middle finger on his throwing hand was dislocated week 14 and he suffered torn ligaments. While he came back into the game and played, he commented that it affected his grip and velocity on his throws. And while the game was 1 score throughout and the injury occurred in the first quarter, the Lions were 62 percent pass in the first quarter and 39 percent pass in the second half. And in the first quarter, Stafford posted an 85 rating and a 63 percent success rate, but in the second half his rating *(cont'd - see DET-4)*

2017 Rest Analysis

Avg Rest	6.47
Avg Rk	3
Team More Rest	3
Opp More Rest	5
Net Rest Edge	-2
3 Days Rest	1
4 Days Rest	0
5 Days Rest	3
6 Days Rest	6
7 Days Rest	3
8 Days Rest	0
9 Days Rest	1
10 Days Rest	0
11 Days Rest	0
12 Days Rest	0
13 Days Rest	1
14 Days Rest	0

Health by Unit*

2016 Rk	14
(2015 Rk)	23
Off Rk	22
Def Rk	13
QB Rk	11
RB Rk	32
WR Rk	4
TE Rk	26
OLine Rk	7
DLine Rk	15
LB Rk	20
DB Rk	10

*Based on the great work of Scott Kacsmar from Football Outsiders

2017 Weekly Betting Lines (wks 1-16)

1	2	3	4	5	6	8	9	10	11	12	13	14	15	16
ARI	NYG	ATL	MIN	CAR	NO	PIT	GB	CLE	CHI	MIN	BAL	TB	CHI	CIN
H	A	A	A	H	A	H	A	H	H	H	A	A	H	A
-3.0	+3.0	+1.5	+3.0	-2.0	+2.5	+1.5	+7.5	-8.5	-1.0	-2.5	+3.0	+3.0	-6.0	+3.0

Avg = 0.3

Home Lines (wks 1-16)

1	3	5	8	10	12	15
ARI	ATL	CAR	PIT	CLE	MIN	CHI
-3.0	+1.5	-2.0	+1.5	-8.5	-2.5	-6.0

Avg = -2.7

Road Lines (wks 1-16)

2	4	6	9	11	13	14	16
NYG	MIN	NO	GB	CHI	BAL	TB	CIN
+3.0	+3.0	+2.5	+7.5	-1.0	+3.0	+3.0	+3.0

Avg = 3.0

Detroit Lions 2016 Play Analysis

2016 Play Tendencies

All Pass %	63%
All Pass Rk	3
All Rush %	37%
All Rush Rk	30
1 Score Pass %	62%
1 Score Pass Rk	4
2015 1 Score Pass %	62%
2015 1 Score Pass Rk	8
Pass Increase %	0%
Pass Increase Rk	16
1 Score Rush %	38%
1 Score Rush Rk	29
Up Pass %	62%
Up Pass Rk	8
Up Rush %	38%
Up Rush Rk	25
Down Pass %	66%
Down Pass Rk	6
Down Rush %	34%
Down Rush Rk	27

2016 Down & Distance Tendencies

Down	Distance	Total Plays	Pass Rate	Run Rate	Play Success %
1	Short (1-3)	10	70%	30%	50%
	Med (4-7)	8	50%	50%	100%
	Long (8-10)	307	47%	53%	48%
	XL (11+)	16	88%	13%	38%
2	Short (1-3)	46	48%	52%	57%
	Med (4-7)	73	74%	26%	55%
	Long (8-10)	103	69%	31%	43%
	XL (11+)	40	85%	15%	30%
3	Short (1-3)	44	59%	41%	55%
	Med (4-7)	38	95%	5%	47%
	Long (8-10)	40	90%	10%	30%
	XL (11+)	29	86%	14%	38%
4	Short (1-3)	7	43%	57%	71%
	Med (4-7)	1	100%	0%	0%
	Long (8-10)	1	100%	0%	0%

Shotgun %:

Under Center	Shotgun
16%	84%
37%	*63%*

37% AVG 63%

Run Rate:

Under Center	Shotgun
74%	27%

68% AVG 23%

Pass Rate:

Under Center	Shotgun
26%	73%

32% AVG 77%

Short Yardage Intelligence:

2nd and Short Run

Run Freq	Run % Rk	NFL Run Freq Avg	Run 1D Rate	Run NFL 1D Avg
47%	32	65%	62%	71%

2nd and Short Pass

Pass Freq	Pass % Rk	NFL Pass Freq Avg	Pass 1D Rate	Pass NFL 1D Avg
53%	1	35%	63%	52%

Most Frequent Play

Down	Distance	Play Type	Player	Total Plays	Play Success %
1	Short (1-3)	PASS	Anquan Boldin	3	100%
	Med (4-7)	RUSH	Zach Zenner	2	100%
	Long (8-10)	RUSH	Dwayne Washington	47	38%
	XL (11+)	PASS	Marvin Jones	4	50%
2	Short (1-3)	RUSH	Theo Riddick	8	38%
	Med (4-7)	PASS	Golden Tate	10	70%
			Marvin Jones	10	60%
			Anquan Boldin	10	60%
	Long (8-10)	PASS	Eric Ebron	15	27%
	XL (11+)	PASS	Marvin Jones	6	50%
3	Short (1-3)	PASS	Anquan Boldin	9	78%
	Med (4-7)	PASS	Anquan Boldin	10	40%
	Long (8-10)	PASS	Golden Tate	12	42%
	XL (11+)	PASS	Eric Ebron	5	80%

Most Successful Play*

Down	Distance	Play Type	Player	Total Plays	Play Success %
1	Long (8-10)	PASS	Andre Roberts	6	83%
2	Short (1-3)	RUSH	Zach Zenner	7	86%
	Med (4-7)	PASS	Eric Ebron	6	100%
	Long (8-10)	PASS	Zach Zenner	8	63%
			Theo Riddick	8	63%
	XL (11+)	PASS	Marvin Jones	6	50%
3	Short (1-3)	PASS	Anquan Boldin	9	78%
	Med (4-7)	PASS	Eric Ebron	7	100%
	Long (8-10)	PASS	Golden Tate	12	42%
	XL (11+)	PASS	Eric Ebron	5	80%

**Minimum 5 plays to qualify*

2016 Snap Rates

Week	Opp	Score	Marvin Jones	Golden Tate	Anquan Boldin	Eric Ebron	Theo Riddick	Zach Zenner
1	IND	W 39-35	61 (94%)	55 (85%)	54 (83%)	60 (92%)	25 (38%)	
2	TEN	L 16-15	73 (92%)	70 (89%)	67 (85%)	71 (90%)	52 (66%)	
3	GB	L 34-27	65 (96%)	59 (87%)	53 (78%)	58 (85%)	45 (66%)	
4	CHI	L 17-14	61 (97%)	36 (57%)	54 (86%)	53 (84%)	51 (81%)	5 (8%)
5	PHI	W 24-23	53 (87%)	49 (80%)	53 (87%)		39 (64%)	21 (34%)
6	LA	W 31-28	56 (90%)	50 (81%)	53 (85%)			48 (77%)
7	WAS	W 20-17	49 (92%)	45 (85%)	42 (79%)			32 (60%)
8	HOU	L 20-13	60 (98%)	54 (89%)	49 (80%)	49 (80%)	52 (85%)	9 (15%)
9	MIN	W 22-16	62 (94%)	53 (80%)	44 (67%)	52 (79%)	46 (70%)	
11	JAC	W 26-19	51 (89%)	47 (82%)	39 (68%)	46 (81%)	33 (58%)	
12	MIN	W 16-13	59 (97%)	51 (84%)	45 (74%)	49 (80%)	48 (79%)	1 (2%)
13	NO	W 28-13		60 (86%)	58 (83%)	54 (77%)	33 (47%)	14 (20%)
14	CHI	W 20-17	60 (83%)	63 (88%)	58 (81%)	52 (72%)		27 (38%)
15	NYG	L 17-6	51 (82%)	50 (81%)	52 (84%)	52 (84%)		18 (29%)
16	DAL	L 42-21	54 (76%)	63 (89%)	50 (70%)	60 (85%)		54 (76%)
17	GB	L 31-24	62 (94%)	62 (94%)	59 (89%)	51 (77%)		64 (97%)
Grand Total			877 (91%)	867 (83%)	830 (80%)	707 (82%)	424 (65%)	293 (41%)

Personnel Groupings

Personnel	Team %	NFL Avg	Succ. %
1-1 [3WR]	76%	60%	48%
1-2 [2WR]	9%	19%	36%
2-1 [2WR]	5%	7%	40%
1-0 [4WR]	5%	3%	43%

Grouping Tendencies

Personnel	Pass Rate	Pass Succ. %	Run Succ. %
1-1 [3WR]	72%	47%	48%
1-2 [2WR]	34%	38%	35%
2-1 [2WR]	21%	73%	31%
1-0 [4WR]	79%	43%	40%

Red Zone Targets (min 3)

Receiver	All	Inside 5	6-10	11-20
Anquan Boldin	23	9	2	12
Golden Tate	17	2	3	12
Marvin Jones	15	5	3	7
Theo Riddick	15	3	3	9
Eric Ebron	6		3	3
Andre Roberts	3	1	2	
Dwayne Washington	3		1	2

Red Zone Rushes (min 3)

Rusher	All	Inside 5	6-10	11-20
Zach Zenner	15	5	3	7
Matthew Stafford	7	2	2	3
Theo Riddick	7	2	3	2
Dwayne Washington	6	4		2
Justin Forsett	1			1

Early Down Target Rate

RB	TE	WR
23%	16%	61%
19%	*20% NFL AVG*	*61%*

Overall Target Success %

RB	TE	WR
50% #8	59% #6	51% #13

Detroit Lions 2016 Passing Recap & 2017 Outlook

Matthew Stafford has heart and guts. And he has Jim Bob Cooter, who has gotten the most out of him and this offense. What he does not have is a true #1 receiver nor a dependable deep threat. They have several adequate receivers, a solid pass catching tight end and multiple capable receiving backs. Stafford's interception rate was exceedingly good on 1st and 2nd down. It wasn't until 3rd down that he got too careless. That needs to be reined in, particularly on short yardage situations on 3rd down. Stafford had to go to the shotgun more with his injured finger, but the team used shotgun over 20% more often than the NFL average. And when they did go under center, they ran the ball well above average, making those run plays too predictable. The Lions used the 3rd most 11 personnel of any team, and when in 11 personnel, they went 72% pass (7th most pass heavy). When only 2 or fewer wide receivers were on the field, the Lions went 72% run (2nd most run heavy). It seems other teams would pick up on these traits after 1 full season of studying Cooter's offense, so he must vary things more in 2017. Stafford and the Lions must figure out how to become more explosive through the air 2017, despite facing the toughest schedule of pass rushes.

2016 Standard Passing Table

QB	Comp	Att	Comp %	Yds	YPA	TDs	INT	Sacks	Rating	Rk
Matthew Stafford	406	627	65%	4,532	7.2	24	10	39	92.3	19
NFL Avg			63%		7.2				90.4	

2016 Advanced Passing Table

QB	Success %	EDSR Passing Success %	20+ Yd Pass Gains	20+ Yd Pass %	30+ Yd Pass Gains	30+ Yd Pass %	Air Yds per Comp	YAC per Comp	20+ Air Yd Comp	20+ Air Yd %
Matthew Stafford	48%	51%	55	9%	23	4%	5.4	5.7	23	4%
NFL Avg	44%	48%	27	8%	10	3%	6.4	4.8	12	4%

Matthew Stafford Rating All Downs

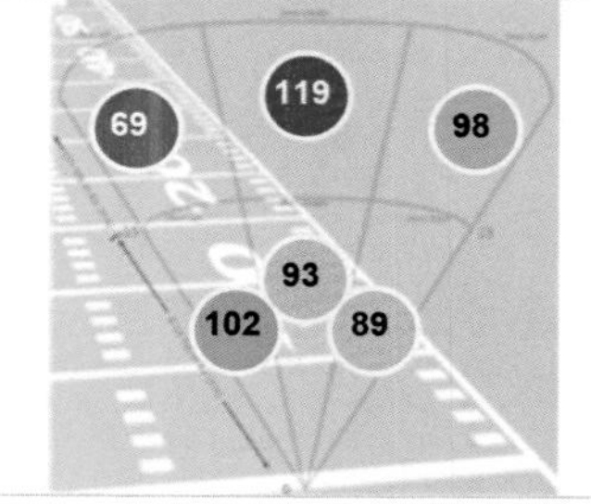

Matthew Stafford Rating Early Downs

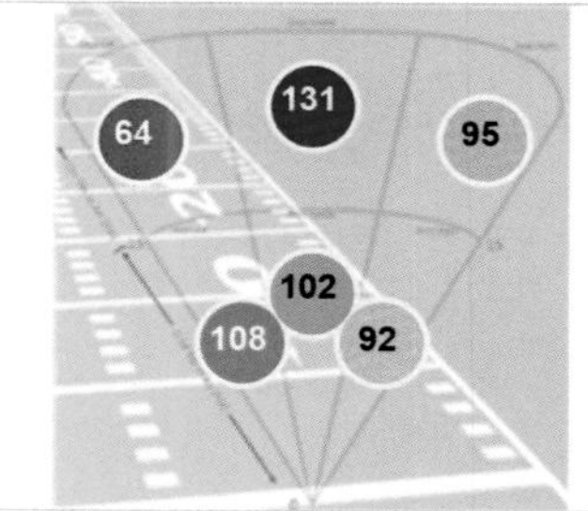

Interception Rates by Down

Yards to Go	1	2	3	4	Total
1 & 2	0.0%	0.0%	4.5%	0.0%	1.8%
3, 4, 5	0.0%	0.0%	7.0%	0.0%	3.6%
6 - 9	0.0%	1.3%	0.0%		0.7%
10 - 14	0.5%	1.3%	4.9%	0.0%	1.2%
15+	0.0%	4.3%	0.0%		2.0%
Total	0.4%	1.2%	3.4%	0.0%	1.5%

3rd Down Passing - Short of Sticks Analysis

QB	Avg Yds to Go	Air Yds (of Comps)	Avg Yds Short	Short of Sticks Rate	Rk
Matthew Stafford	7.4	7.5	0.0	50%	16
NFL Avg	7.6	6.8	-0.8	57%	

Air Yds vs YAC

Air Yds %	YAC %	Rk
40%	60%	48
54%	46%	

2016 Receiving Recap & 2017 Outlook

It will be interesting to see how the Lions replace Anquan Boldin. They will certainly miss his presence inside, and he was obviously one of Stafford's favorite targets last season. Though he only ran routes which limited his overall YPA averages, his success rate (57%) and passer rating delivered (98) was the best of any Lions receiver. His "style" of play is evident by viewing the Missed YPA and YAS stats. Boldin delivered virtually no "Yards Above Successful", but was the best receiver in Missed YPA, in that even on plays which weren't successful (he led the Lions WRs in that metric as well) he set up the Lions the best for the next down.

Player *Min 50 Targets*	Targets	Comp %	YPA	Rating	TOARS	Success %	Success Rk	Missed YPA Rk	YAS % Rk	TDs
Golden Tate	140	67%	7.9	91	5.2	50%	73	79	53	4
Marvin Jones	110	54%	9.2	97	4.8	48%	93	72	5	4
Anquan Boldin	101	68%	6.0	98	4.8	57%	27	35	128	8
Eric Ebron	91	69%	8.1	88	4.6	60%	15	32	107	1
Theo Riddick	67	79%	5.5	115	4.3	48%	96	81	140	5

Directional Passer Rating Delivered

Receiver	Short Left	Short Middle	Short Right	Deep Left	Deep Middle	Deep Right	Player Total
Golden Tate	87	81	95	96	40	113	91
Marvin Jones	97	90	80	58	117	117	97
Anquan Boldin	128	83	83	63	158	40	98
Eric Ebron	108	108	60	96	76	58	88
Theo Riddick	108	100	126	40			115
Zach Zenner	112	95	91				103
Justin Forsett	58		100				78
Team Total	104	91	89	83	122	109	97

2016 Rushing Recap & 2017 Outlook

The run game was dreadful last season. Zach Zenner led the team with 99 rushes but was the 40th rated RB in success rate, and his fellow RBs were even worse. They were no better on early down rushes, either. So it's no surprise the run game ranked 25th in total efficiency. Nor is it much of a surprise that even with a quarterback playing multiple games with a dislocated finger, the Lions still were 62% pass in one-score games, the 4th most pass heavy team in the NFL last year. The offensive line should improve in 2017, and the RBs are going to get another year in the offense. It's up to Cooter, who now knows what he's got in the backfield, to find a better way to support Stafford, the passing offense, and keep their defense off the field.

Player *Min 50 Rushes*	Rushes	YPA	Success %	Success Rk	Missed YPA Rk	YTS % Rk	YAS % Rk	Early Down Success %	Early Down Success Rk	TDs
Zach Zenner	99	3.7	45%	40	38	29	27	45%	41	4
Theo Riddick	92	3.9	42%	50	65	32	20	42%	47	1
Dwayne Washington	90	2.9	36%	66	48	16	68	35%	64	1

Yards per Carry by Direction

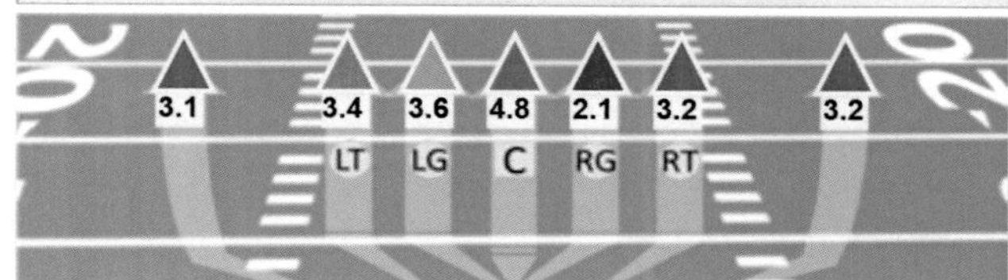

Directional Run Frequency

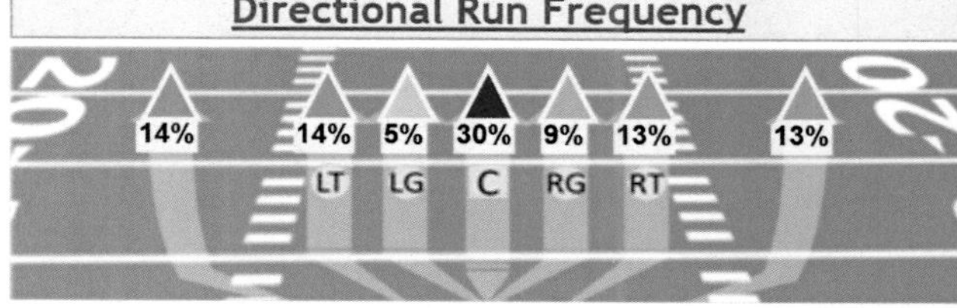

dropped to a 14, with 2 interceptions and he delivered only a 33 percent success rate. While Cooter said he didn't change calls after Stafford hurt his finger, and was simply "was encouraged" by the run game, the calls clearly changed.

From week 14 onward, Stafford's passer rating dropped to 68, he completed just 56% of his passes for 5.9 yards per attempt and recorded a 3:5 TD:INT ratio. Yet some in the media were convinced that his finger was not a big deal and didn't cause him trouble. Assuming his finger is back to 100% this season, there will be even more pressure on Stafford to get the ball deep down the field, both literally and figuratively. Detroit plays the NFL's toughest schedule of pass rushing defenses this season. They start with the 2nd toughest schedule of overall pass defenses through the first 5 weeks. And unlike last year's schedule, which kept the Lions passing offense indoors from week 5 through 17 with just one outdoor game in that span (they put up just 6 points in NY against the Giants week 15), the Lions have 5 outdoor games between weeks 9 and 16, in potentially windier environments later in the season such as Green Bay, Chicago, Baltimore, Tampa Bay and Cincinnati. It's far from a friendly schedule and the Lions passing offense must rise to the challenge.

On the ground, the Lions face the 19th most difficult schedule, a slight improvement from 15th last year. However, they ranked just 25th in rushing efficiency last season and need to see improvement in 2017. Particularly so given the number of road outdoor games the Lions have later in the season. Detroit is 5-11 in outdoor games under Caldwell, and went 0-4 last year.

With so much to touch on with this offense, both what they were and what they must improve, we haven't even touched on the defense. Which seems appropriate, because this defense rarely touched on its opponents, ranking as the NFL's worst in total defensive efficiency and pass defensive efficiency. Detroit did play stronger than average offenses in 2016, but unfortunately their strength of schedule for 2017 is quite similar. Help will be coming at LB and CB, where the Lions attempted to rob the Florida Gators defense in both the first and second round of the draft. And the Lions hope that CB Darius Slay will be healthy.

The Lions won 9 games last year, but only won one of those games by more than one score. Once again, as was the case in 2016, they simply must improve the run game. Without a solid run game, the Lions will struggle to pull away from opponents late in the game. And with a defense as bad as theirs has been, maintaining that lead effectively becomes a coin flip. A solid run game changes all of that. They've worked to improve the offensive line in the 2016 draft, added starting RG TJ Lang via free agency this offseason. If the line can perform more adequately in the run blocking game, even in a pass efficiency-driven NFL, it will go a long way toward their 2017 goals.

Division History: Season Wins & 2017 Projection

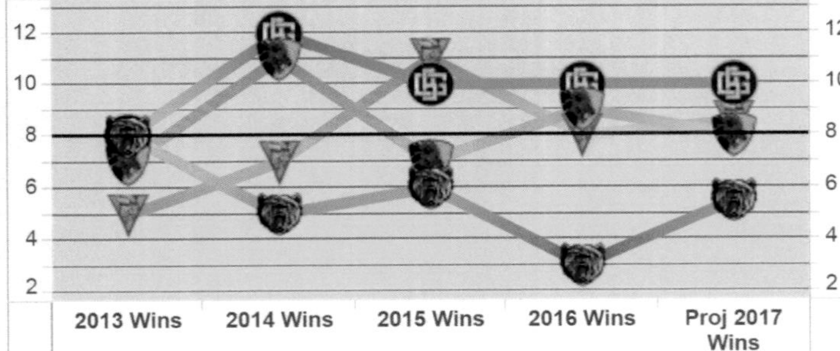

Rank of 2017 Defensive Pass Efficiency Faced by Week

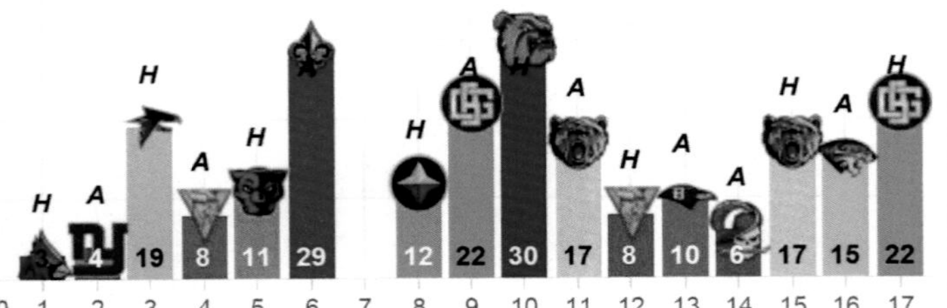

Rank of 2017 Defensive Rush Efficiency Faced by Week

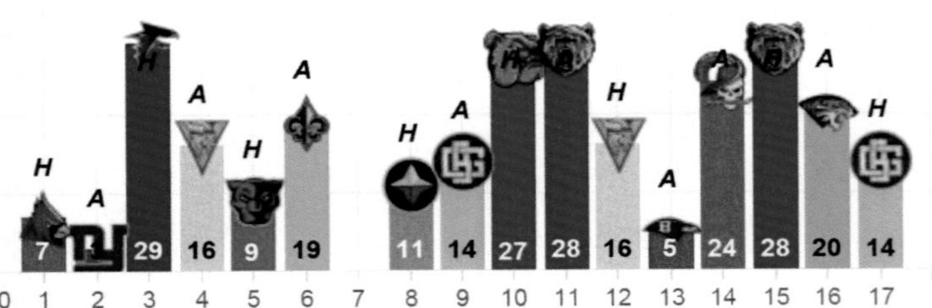

2016 Situational Usage by Player & Position

Usage Rate by Score

		Being Blown Out (14+)	Down Big (9-13)	One Score	Large Lead (9-13)	Blowout Lead (14+)	Grand Total
RUSH	Theo Riddick	6%	11%	10%	7%		10%
	Golden Tate	1%		1%			1%
	Zach Zenner	3%	2%	12%	12%	80%	11%
	Marvin Jones			0%			0%
	Dwayne Washington	13%		10%	9%		10%
	Eric Ebron			0%			0%
	Ameer Abdullah			2%	9%		2%
	Justin Forsett			2%			1%
	Total	23%	13%	37%	37%	80%	35%
PASS	Theo Riddick	11%	9%	7%	5%		7%
	Golden Tate	11%	13%	16%	9%	20%	15%
	Zach Zenner	4%	9%	3%			3%
	Marvin Jones	16%	22%	10%	14%		12%
	Dwayne Washington	3%	2%	1%			2%
	Anquan Boldin	10%	11%	11%	9%		11%
	Eric Ebron	17%	13%	8%	14%		10%
	Andre Roberts	2%	2%	2%	9%		3%
	Ameer Abdullah			1%	2%		1%
	Justin Forsett			0%			0%
	T.J. Jones	3%	7%	1%			2%
	Clay Harbor			0%			0%
	Cole Wick	1%		0%			0%
	Matthew Mulligan			0%			0%
	Joique Bell			0%			0%
	Khari Lee			0%			0%
	Mike Burton			0%			0%
	Total	77%	87%	63%	63%	20%	65%

Positional Target Distribution vs NFL Average

		NFL Wide				Team Only			
		Left	Middle	Right	Total	Left	Middle	Right	Total
Deep	WR	1,007	570	966	2,543	24	11	35	70
	TE	154	142	160	456	4	5	3	12
	RB	24	4	40	68	1			1
	All	1,185	716	1,166	3,067	29	16	38	83
Short	WR	2,982	1,704	3,083	7,769	111	67	103	281
	TE	810	857	1,116	2,783	26	18	35	79
	RB	972	602	1,078	2,652	43	20	35	98
	All	4,764	3,163	5,277	13,204	180	105	173	458
Total		5,949	3,879	6,443	16,271	209	121	211	541

Positional Success Rates vs NFL Average

		NFL Wide				Team Only			
		Left	Middle	Right	Total	Left	Middle	Right	Total
Deep	WR	37%	50%	38%	40%	38%	64%	34%	40%
	TE	44%	50%	43%	46%	50%	40%	33%	42%
	RB	33%	75%	25%	31%	0%			0%
	All	38%	50%	39%	41%	38%	56%	34%	40%
Short	WR	52%	57%	51%	53%	57%	60%	49%	54%
	TE	50%	61%	52%	54%	62%	78%	57%	63%
	RB	47%	49%	44%	46%	47%	70%	49%	52%
	All	50%	56%	50%	52%	55%	65%	50%	55%
Total		48%	55%	48%	50%	53%	64%	47%	53%

Green Bay Packers

2017 Coaches

Head Coach:
Mike McCarthy (12th yr)
Offensive Coordinator:
Tom Clements (6th yr)
Defensive Coordinator:
Dom Capers (9th yr)

EASY HARD

2017 Forecast

Wins	Div Rank
10	#1

Past Records

2016: 10-6
2015: 10-6
2014: 12-4

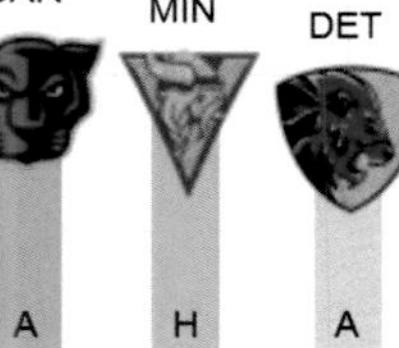
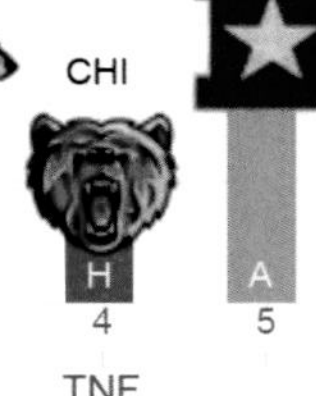
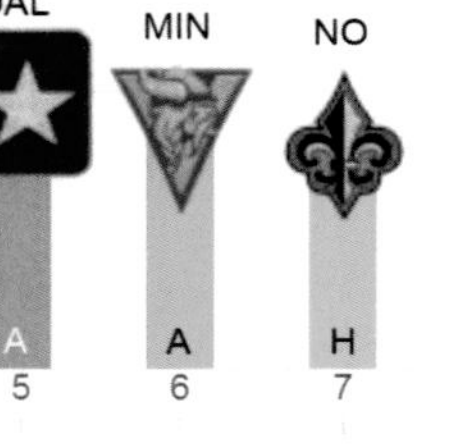
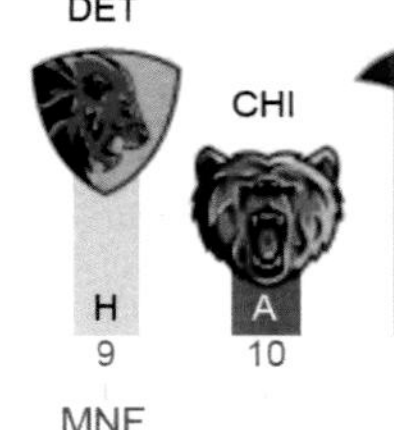
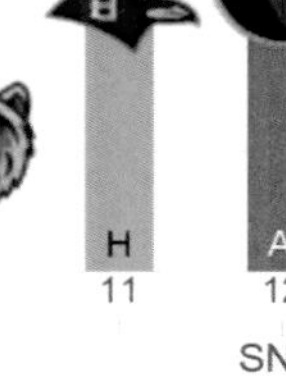
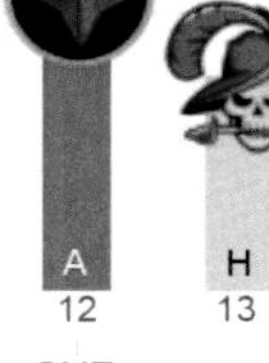
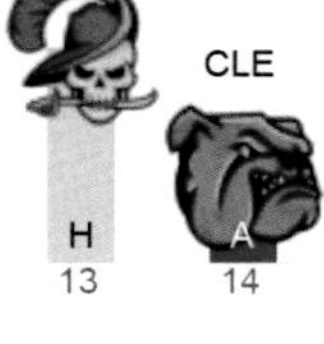
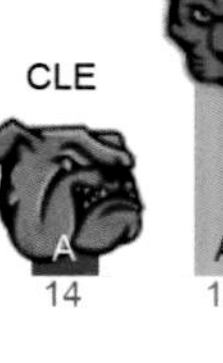
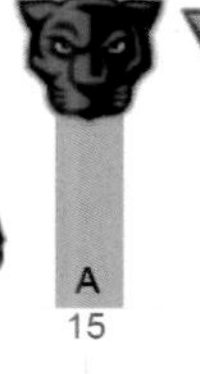

Week	Opponent	H/A	Note
1	SEA	H	
2	ATL	A	SNF
3	CIN	H	
4	CHI	H	TNF
5	DAL	A	
6	MIN	A	
7	NO	H	
8			
9	DET	H	MNF
10	CHI	A	
11	BAL	H	
12	PIT	A	SNF
13	TB	H	
14	CLE	A	
15	CAR	A	
16	MIN	H	SAT
17	DET	A	

Key Players Lost

TXN	Player (POS)
Cut	Dorleant, Makinton CB
	Ferguson, Ego DT
	Michael, Christine RB
	Pennel, Mike DT
	Shields, Sam CB
	Starks, James RB
Declared Free Agent	Barclay, Don T
	Cook, Jared TE
	Crockett, John RB
	Elliott, Jayrone LB
	Goode, Brett C
	Hyde, Micah S
	Jones, Datone DE
	Lacy, Eddie RB
	Lang, T.J. G
	Michael, Christine RB
	Peppers, Julius DE
	Perry, Nick LB
	Tretter, JC C
	Tripp, Jordan LB

Average Line	# Games Favored	# Games Underdog
-4.4	12	3

2017 Green Bay Packers Overview

The Packers 2017 season was complicated. And we'll rehash it all in great detail, diving into analytics and personnel and much more. But there was also a very simple explanation for their successes and struggles in 2016, and it can be represented by one statistic. The explanation is the defense was a huge liability and cost them in their losses. The statistic to depict this:

Against offenses ranking 15th or worse in efficiency the 2016 Packers went 11-1, but against offenses ranking 14th or better, the 2016 Packers went 1-6.

In a nutshell, it was that straightforward. Overall, the Packers played the 13th rated schedule of opposing offenses, so it was not a particularly hard nor easy gauntlet for their defense to run as a whole. But when you ignore the averages and segregate out the average to below average offensive opponents, the picture becomes more clear.

The Packers offense averaged 28.9 ppg against the bad offenses and 25.4 ppg against the good offenses. While that is a mild drop, it still is well above the league average and would not explain flipping a 11-1 record to 1-6. The key is their defense held the offenses ranking 15th or worse to only 18.3 ppg but against the good offenses their defense allowed a whopping 37 ppg. The Packers defense did not hold even one of those 7 opponents below 30 points, while in the 12 games against the bad offenses, no opponent ever exceeded 27 points.

As great as Aaron Rodgers is, expecting him to outscore the 37 ppg average that was put up against his defense was a tall order. They narrowly squeaked by the Cowboys in the playoffs, 34-31, in a game the Cowboys likely could have and should have won. But the Falcons steamrolled 45 points on them in the Conference Championship round and the Packers offense, without a healthy Davante Adams and Jordy Nelson, couldn't muster enough to pull off the upset.

So let's start with the defense, which is what Ted Thompson started with in the draft. Injuries certainly helped to start their decline. Specifically, injuries to the defensive backs, as they ranked as the 5th most injured DB unit last season. They did rank as the 2nd healthiest defensive line which helped to translate into the 6th best pass rush defense.

(cont'd - see GB2)

Key Free Agents/ Trades Added

- Bennett, Martellus TE
- Evans, Jahri G
- Ferguson, Ego DT
- House, Davon CB
- Jean Francois, Ricky DE
- Kendricks, Lance TE
- Leff, Robert G
- McCray, Justin G

Drafted Players

Rd	Pk	Player (College)
2	33	CB - Kevin King (Washington)
	61	S - Josh Jones (NC State)
3	93	DT - Montravius Adams (Auburn)
4	108	LB - Vince Biegel (Wisconsin)
	134	RB - Jamaal Williams (BYU)
5	175	WR - DeAngelo Yancey (Purdue)
5*	182	RB - Aaron Jones (UTEP)
6	212	OT - Kofi Amichia (South Florida)
7	238	RB - Devante Mays (Utah State)
	247	WR - Malachi Dupre (LSU)

Regular Season Wins: Past & Current Proj

	Wins
Proj 2017 Wins	10
2016 Wins	10
Proj 2016 Wins	11
2015 Wins	10
2014 Wins	12
2013 Wins	8

1 3 5 7 9 11 13 15

2017 Lineup & Cap Hits

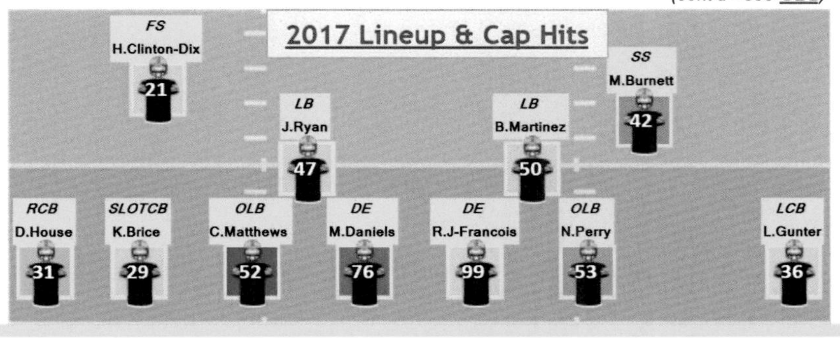

2017 Unit Spending

Positional Spending

	Rank	Total	2016 Rk
All OFF	6	$92.74M	15
QB	11	$21.98M	14
OL	18	$27.88M	20
RB	32	$3.32M	22
WR	1	$31.09M	6
TE	19	$8.48M	29
All DEF	22	$74.04M	6
DL	20	$20.79M	26
LB	6	$29.37M	2
CB	26	$11.47M	17
S	13	$12.41M	14

Green Bay Packers 2016 Success Rate Radar

Weeks 1-4

1 W · 2 L · 3 W

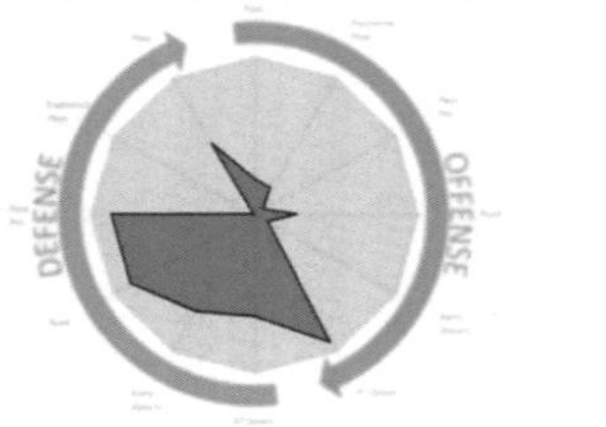

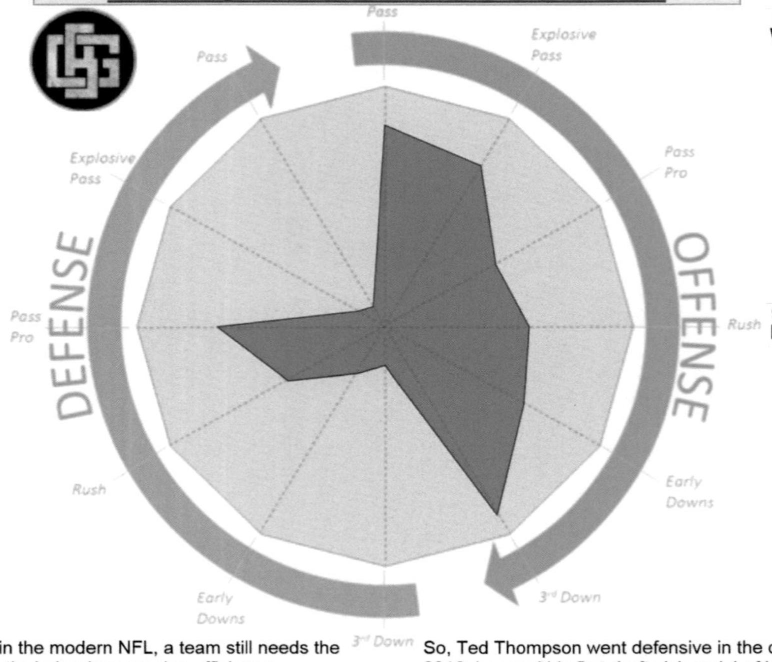

Weeks 5-8

5 W · 6 L · 7 W · 8 L

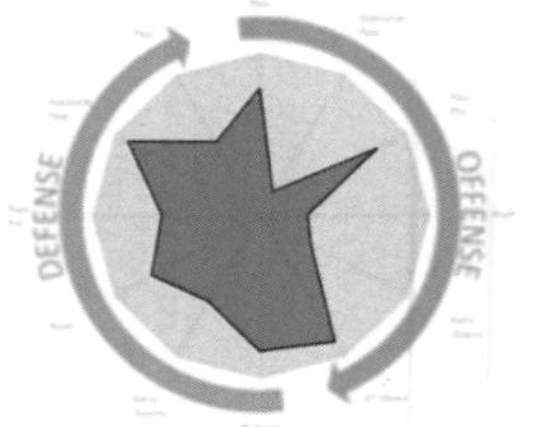

Weeks 13-17

13 W · 14 W · 15 W · 16 W · 17 W

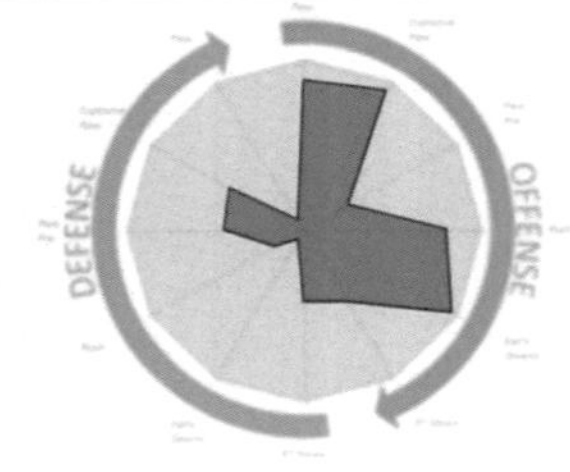

Weeks 9-12

9 L · 10 L · 11 L · 12 W

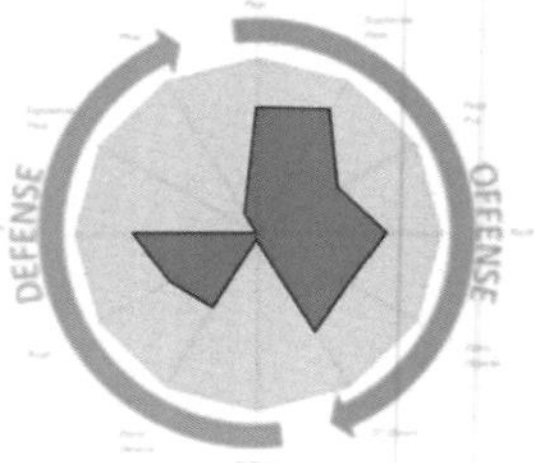

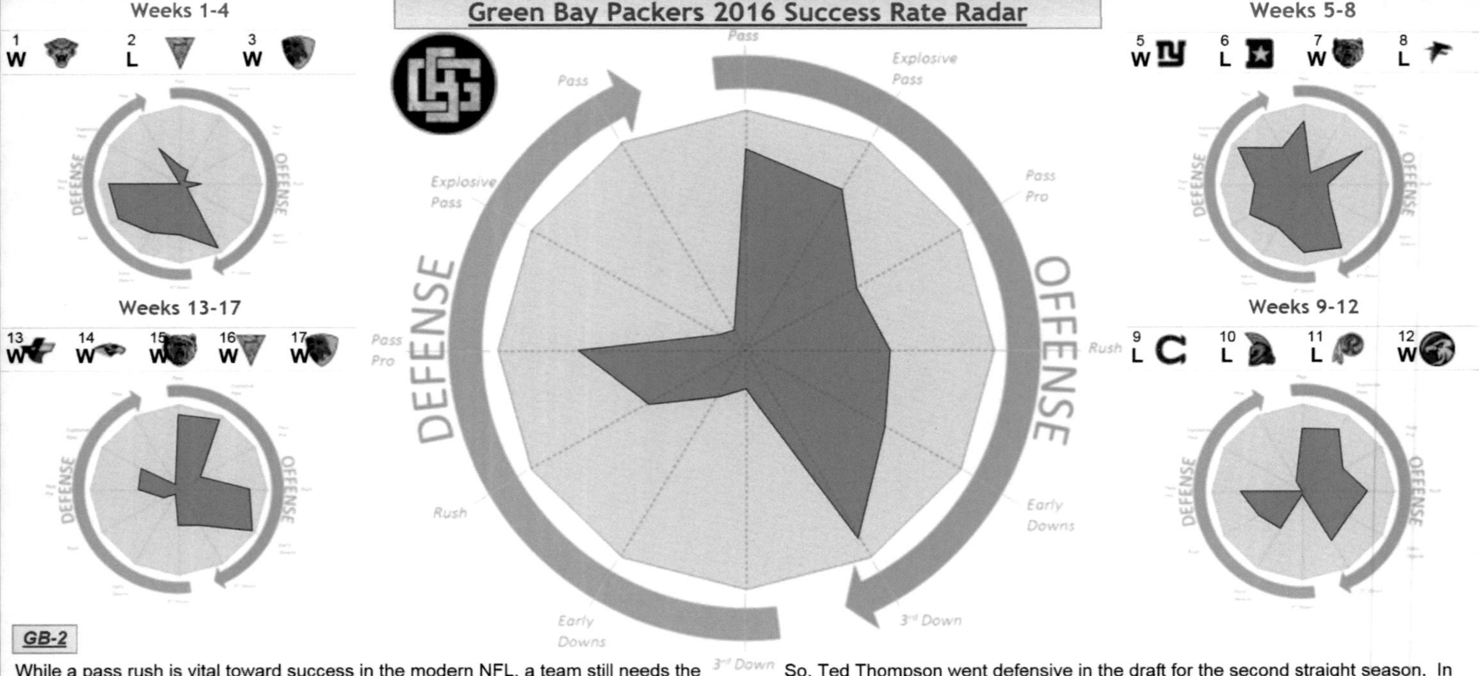

GB-2

While a pass rush is vital toward success in the modern NFL, a team still needs the back end to compliment the front end. Particularly when passing efficiency contributes over 4 times more to winning games. As the injuries piled up in the secondary, their pass defense dropped to the worst in the NFL. From week 10 onward, they allowed 52% of all passes to grade as successful, the worst rate in the NFL.

On the ground, while the Packers ranked 14th in run defensive efficiency, those numbers were deceiving to the extent they faced the 7th easiest schedule of run offenses, and posted an average rating against these teams. As the run offenses became tougher and the secondary began to fall apart, the Packers run defense struggled more as well. From week 10 onward, the Packers run defense allowed 50% of opponent rushes to grade as successful, 8th worst in the NFL and well below average. With the defense struggling to defend the pass inside their own red zone, the run defense was knifed through with ease – they allowed 61% of rushes in their red zone to grade as successful, 4th worst in the NFL.

So, Ted Thompson went defensive in the draft for the second straight season. In 2016, he used his first draft pick and 4 of his first 5 picks on defense. This year, he used his first four picks on defense, focusing specifically on that brutal secondary with two second round draft picks. They used a tremendously underrated cap move from Thompson on CB Davon House. After his rookie deal expired in 2014, the Packers couldn't envision paying over $6M per year to House after paying him just $585K over his first four year. So they let Jacksonville overpay in free agency, and the Jaguars signed him to a $24.5M deal over 4 years. Like many overpaid free agency deals go, the Jaguars cut him 2 years into a 4 year deal, paying him a total of $12.5M the last two years while rarely even playing him. With his reputation in question, the Packers signed House to a 1 year, $2.8M "prove it" deal with only $850K guaranteed this season. Thompson also added DE Ricky Jean Francois to the mix (in addition to some offensive pieces such as TE Martellus Bennett), being a bit more active in free agency than is expected.

(cont'd - see GB-3)

2016 Offensive Advanced Metrics

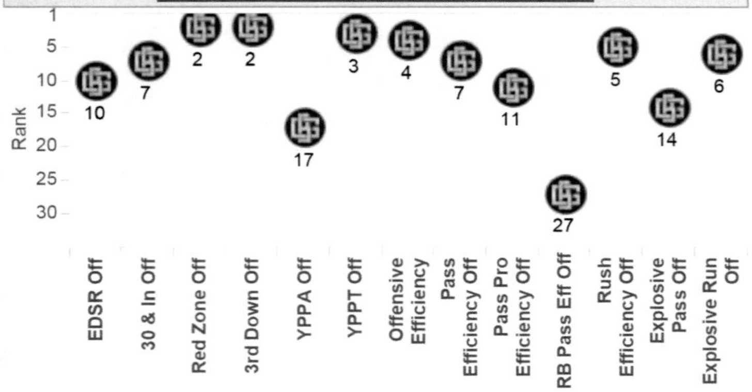

2016 Defensive Advanced Metrics

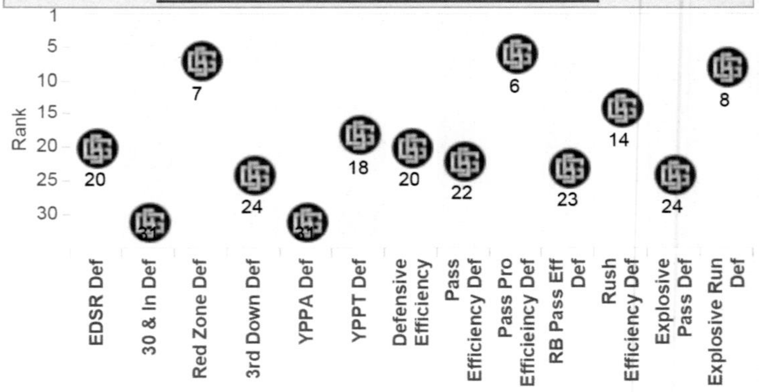

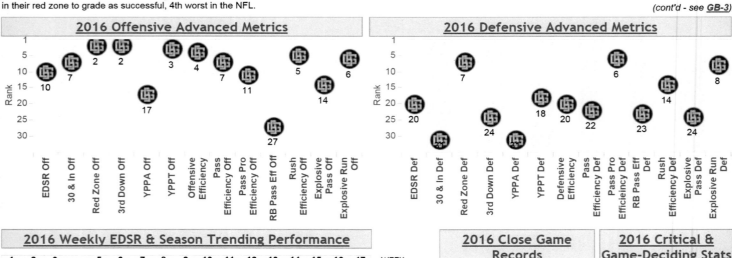

2016 Weekly EDSR & Season Trending Performance

WEEK	1	2	3	5	6	7	8	9	10	11	12	13	14	15	16	17
RESULT	W	L	W	W	L	W	L	L	L	L	W	W	W	W	W	W
OPP	JAC	MIN	DET	NYG	DAL	CHI	ATL	IND	TEN	WAS	PHI	HOU	SEA	CHI	MIN	DET
SITE	A	A	H	H	H	H	A	H	A	A	A	H	H	A	H	A
MARGIN	4	-3	7	7	-14	16	-1	-5	-22	-18	14	8	28	3	13	7
PTS	27	14	34	23	16	26	32	26	25	24	27	21	38	30	38	31
OPP PTS	23	17	27	16	30	10	33	31	47	42	13	13	10	27	25	24

EDSR by Wk
W=Green
L=Red

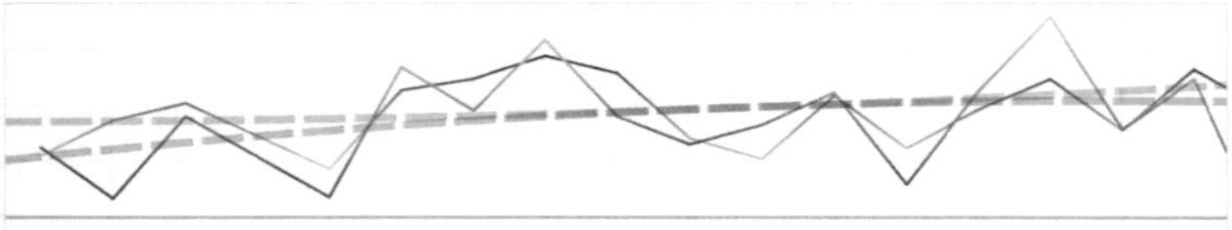

OFF/DEF EDSR
Blue=OFF (high=good)
Red=DEF (low=good)

2016 Close Game Records

All 2016 Wins: **10**
FG Games (<=3 pts) W-L: **1-2**
FG Games Win %: **33% (#16)**
FG Games Wins (% of Total Wins): **10% (#25)**
1 Score Games (<=8 pts) W-L: **6-3**
1 Score Games Win %: **67% (#8)**
1 Score Games Wins (% of Total Wins): **60% (#17)**

2016 Critical & Game-Deciding Stats

TO Margin	+8
TO Given	17
INT Given	8
FUM Given	9
TO Taken	25
INT Taken	17
FUM Taken	8
Sack Margin	+6
Sacks	41
Sacks Allow	35
Return TD Margin	-2
Ret TDs	0
Ret TDs Allow	2
Penalty Margin	+9
Penalties	100
Opponent Penalties	109

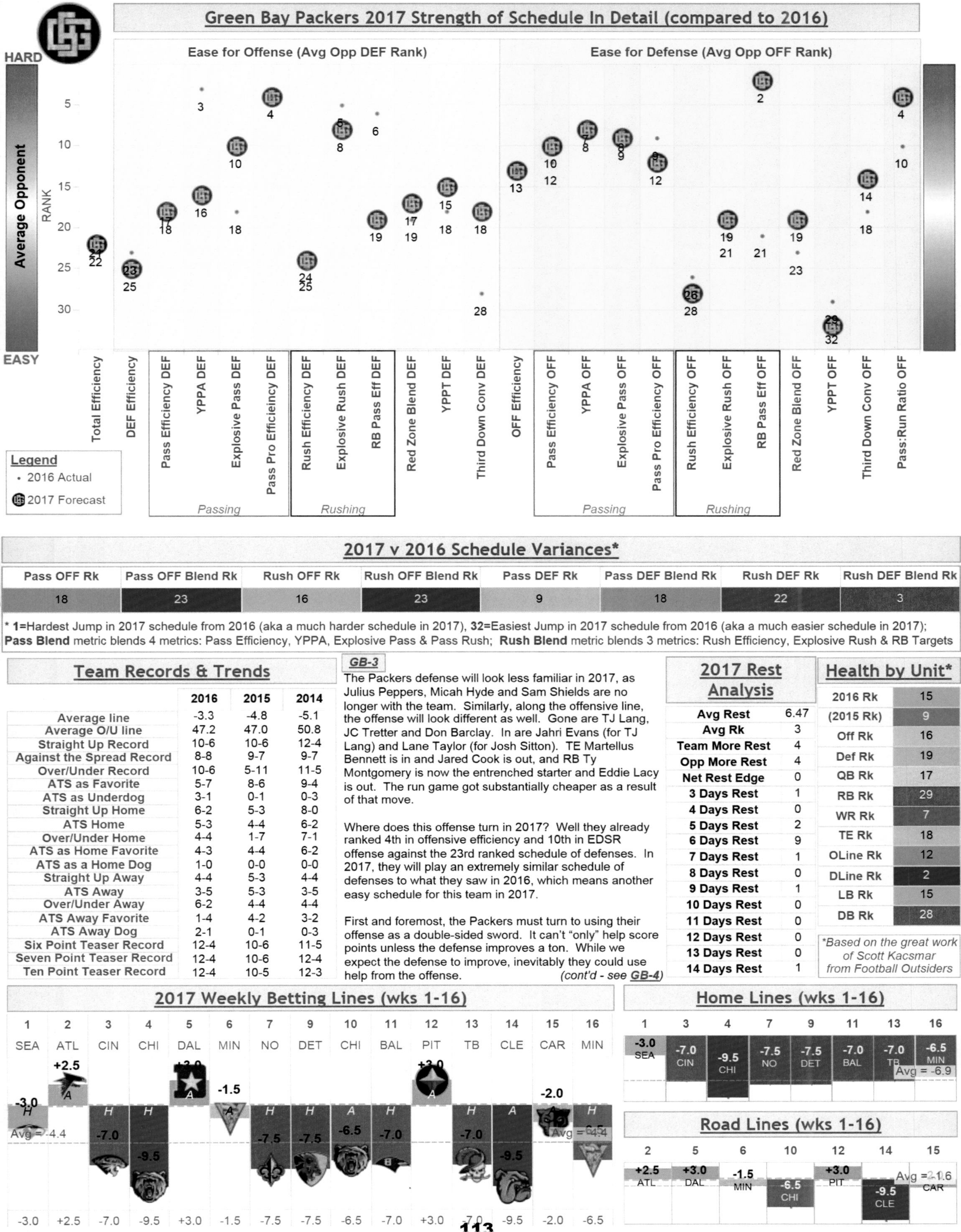

Green Bay Packers 2017 Strength of Schedule In Detail (compared to 2016)

2017 v 2016 Schedule Variances*

Pass OFF Rk	Pass OFF Blend Rk	Rush OFF Rk	Rush OFF Blend Rk	Pass DEF Rk	Pass DEF Blend Rk	Rush DEF Rk	Rush DEF Blend Rk
18	23	16	23	9	18	22	3

* **1**=Hardest Jump in 2017 schedule from 2016 (aka a much harder schedule in 2017), **32**=Easiest Jump in 2017 schedule from 2016 (aka a much easier schedule in 2017); **Pass Blend** metric blends 4 metrics: Pass Efficiency, YPPA, Explosive Pass & Pass Rush; **Rush Blend** metric blends 3 metrics: Rush Efficiency, Explosive Rush & RB Targets

Team Records & Trends

	2016	2015	2014
Average line	-3.3	-4.8	-5.1
Average O/U line	47.2	47.0	50.8
Straight Up Record	10-6	10-6	12-4
Against the Spread Record	8-8	9-7	9-7
Over/Under Record	10-6	5-11	11-5
ATS as Favorite	5-7	8-6	9-4
ATS as Underdog	3-1	0-1	0-3
Straight Up Home	6-2	5-3	8-0
ATS Home	5-3	4-4	6-2
Over/Under Home	4-4	1-7	7-1
ATS as Home Favorite	4-3	4-4	6-2
ATS as a Home Dog	1-0	0-0	0-0
Straight Up Away	4-4	5-3	4-4
ATS Away	3-5	5-3	3-5
Over/Under Away	6-2	4-4	4-4
ATS Away Favorite	1-4	4-2	3-2
ATS Away Dog	2-1	0-1	0-3
Six Point Teaser Record	12-4	10-6	11-5
Seven Point Teaser Record	12-4	10-6	12-4
Ten Point Teaser Record	12-4	10-5	12-3

GB-3

The Packers defense will look less familiar in 2017, as Julius Peppers, Micah Hyde and Sam Shields are no longer with the team. Similarly, along the offensive line, the offense will look different as well. Gone are TJ Lang, JC Tretter and Don Barclay. In are Jahri Evans (for TJ Lang) and Lane Taylor (for Josh Sitton). TE Martellus Bennett is in and Jared Cook is out, and RB Ty Montgomery is now the entrenched starter and Eddie Lacy is out. The run game got substantially cheaper as a result of that move.

Where does this offense turn in 2017? Well they already ranked 4th in offensive efficiency and 10th in EDSR offense against the 23rd ranked schedule of defenses. In 2017, they will play an extremely similar schedule of defenses to what they saw in 2016, which means another easy schedule for this team in 2017.

First and foremost, the Packers must turn to using their offense as a double-sided sword. It can't "only" help score points unless the defense improves a ton. While we expect the defense to improve, inevitably they could use help from the offense. *(cont'd - see GB-4)*

2017 Rest Analysis

Avg Rest	6.47
Avg Rk	3
Team More Rest	4
Opp More Rest	4
Net Rest Edge	0
3 Days Rest	1
4 Days Rest	0
5 Days Rest	2
6 Days Rest	9
7 Days Rest	1
8 Days Rest	0
9 Days Rest	1
10 Days Rest	0
11 Days Rest	0
12 Days Rest	0
13 Days Rest	0
14 Days Rest	1

Health by Unit*

2016 Rk	15
(2015 Rk)	9
Off Rk	16
Def Rk	19
QB Rk	17
RB Rk	29
WR Rk	7
TE Rk	18
OLine Rk	12
DLine Rk	2
LB Rk	15
DB Rk	28

**Based on the great work of Scott Kacsmar from Football Outsiders*

2017 Weekly Betting Lines (wks 1-16)

Week	1	2	3	4	5	6	7	9	10	11	12	13	14	15	16
Opponent	SEA	ATL	CIN	CHI	DAL	MIN	NO	DET	CHI	BAL	PIT	TB	CLE	CAR	MIN
H/A	H	A	H	H	A	A	H	H	A	H	A	H	A	A	H
Line	-3.0	+2.5	-7.0	-9.5	+3.0	-1.5	-7.5	-7.5	-6.5	-7.0	+3.0	-7.0	-9.5	-2.0	-6.5

Avg = -4.4

Home Lines (wks 1-16)

Week	1	3	4	7	9	11	13	16
Opponent	SEA	CIN	CHI	NO	DET	BAL	TB	MIN
Line	-3.0	-7.0	-9.5	-7.5	-7.5	-7.0	-7.0	-6.5

Avg = -6.9

Road Lines (wks 1-16)

Week	2	5	6	10	12	14	15
Opponent	ATL	DAL	MIN	CHI	PIT	CLE	CAR
Line	+2.5	+3.0	-1.5	-6.5	+3.0	-9.5	

Avg = -1.6

Green Bay Packers 2016 Play Analysis

2016 Play Tendencies

All Pass %	66%
All Pass Rk	2
All Rush %	34%
All Rush Rk	31
1 Score Pass %	66%
1 Score Pass Rk	1
2015 1 Score Pass %	58%
2015 1 Score Pass Rk	18
Pass Increase %	8%
Pass Increase Rk	2
1 Score Rush %	34%
1 Score Rush Rk	32
Up Pass %	64%
Up Pass Rk	3
Up Rush %	36%
Up Rush Rk	30
Down Pass %	71%
Down Pass Rk	2
Down Rush %	29%
Down Rush Rk	31

2016 Down & Distance Tendencies

Down	Distance	Total Plays	Pass Rate	Run Rate	Play Success %
1	Short (1-3)	12	67%	33%	58%
	Med (4-7)	13	46%	54%	23%
	Long (8-10)	373	57%	43%	51%
	XL (11+)	15	67%	33%	60%
2	Short (1-3)	45	56%	44%	64%
	Med (4-7)	98	70%	30%	60%
	Long (8-10)	127	73%	27%	43%
	XL (11+)	28	79%	21%	25%
3	Short (1-3)	55	67%	33%	62%
	Med (4-7)	57	98%	2%	53%
	Long (8-10)	43	91%	9%	28%
	XL (11+)	25	96%	4%	16%
4	Short (1-3)	11	18%	82%	55%
	Med (4-7)	3	100%	0%	67%

Shotgun %:

Under Center	Shotgun
25%	75%
37%	*63%*

37% AVG 63%

Run Rate:

Under Center	Shotgun
62%	23%

68% AVG 23%

Pass Rate:

Under Center	Shotgun
38%	77%

32% AVG 77%

Short Yardage Intelligence:

2nd and Short Run

Run Freq	Run % Rk	NFL Run Freq Avg	Run 1D Rate	Run NFL 1D Avg
50%	30	65%	81%	71%

2nd and Short Pass

Pass Freq	Pass % Rk	NFL Pass Freq Avg	Pass 1D Rate	Pass NFL 1D Avg
50%	2	35%	53%	52%

Most Frequent Play

Down	Distance	Play Type	Player	Total Plays	Play Success %
1	Short (1-3)	PASS	Jordy Nelson	3	100%
	Med (4-7)	RUSH	Eddie Lacy	3	67%
	Long (8-10)	PASS	Jordy Nelson	53	58%
	XL (11+)	PASS	Davante Adams	3	33%
2	Short (1-3)	RUSH	Ty Montgomery	8	88%
	Med (4-7)	PASS	Jordy Nelson	16	56%
	Long (8-10)	PASS	Jordy Nelson	19	47%
	XL (11+)	PASS	Jordy Nelson	5	60%
			Davante Adams	5	40%
3	Short (1-3)	PASS	Davante Adams	7	86%
			Randall Cobb	7	86%
	Med (4-7)	PASS	Jordy Nelson	13	54%
	Long (8-10)	PASS	Davante Adams	8	25%
	XL (11+)	PASS	Jordy Nelson	5	20%

Most Successful Play*

Down	Distance	Play Type	Player	Total Plays	Play Success %
1	Long (8-10)	RUSH	Christine Michael	11	64%
2	Short (1-3)	RUSH	Ty Montgomery	8	88%
	Med (4-7)	RUSH	Aaron Rodgers	6	100%
			Christine Michael	5	100%
	Long (8-10)	PASS	Ty Montgomery	9	67%
	XL (11+)	PASS	Jordy Nelson	5	60%
3	Short (1-3)	PASS	Davante Adams	7	86%
			Randall Cobb	7	86%
	Med (4-7)	PASS	Jared Cook	7	86%
	Long (8-10)	PASS	Randall Cobb	6	33%
	XL (11+)	PASS	Jordy Nelson	5	20%

**Minimum 5 plays to qualify*

2016 Snap Rates

Week	Opp	Score	Jordy Nelson	Davante Adams	Randall Cobb	Richard Rodgers	Ty Montgomery	Jared Cook	Aaron Ripkowski
1	JAC	W 27-23	54 (84%)	57 (89%)	62 (97%)	25 (39%)	11 (17%)	33 (52%)	8 (13%)
2	MIN	L 17-14	68 (96%)	54 (76%)	70 (99%)	34 (48%)		46 (65%)	2 (3%)
3	DET	W 34-27	49 (91%)	24 (44%)	42 (78%)	43 (80%)	3 (6%)	14 (26%)	11 (20%)
5	NYG	W 23-16	72 (90%)	60 (75%)	55 (69%)	73 (91%)	2 (3%)		25 (31%)
6	DAL	L 30-16	64 (91%)	31 (44%)	50 (71%)	47 (67%)	35 (50%)		18 (26%)
7	CHI	W 26-10	84 (97%)	70 (80%)	78 (90%)	48 (55%)	60 (69%)		22 (25%)
8	ATL	L 33-32	59 (95%)	58 (94%)		26 (42%)			32 (52%)
9	IND	L 31-26	63 (91%)	66 (96%)	23 (33%)	46 (67%)	31 (45%)		22 (32%)
10	TEN	L 47-25	73 (94%)	74 (95%)	54 (69%)	65 (83%)	22 (28%)		
11	WAS	L 42-24	68 (100%)	65 (96%)	58 (85%)	21 (31%)	27 (40%)	42 (62%)	14 (21%)
12	PHI	W 27-13	64 (90%)	64 (90%)	56 (79%)	26 (37%)	16 (23%)	33 (46%)	25 (35%)
13	HOU	W 21-13	55 (95%)	49 (84%)	44 (76%)	27 (47%)	29 (50%)	29 (50%)	24 (41%)
14	SEA	W 38-10	55 (93%)	53 (90%)	32 (54%)	34 (58%)	30 (51%)	16 (27%)	24 (41%)
15	CHI	W 30-27	60 (98%)	60 (98%)	51 (84%)	20 (33%)	51 (84%)	40 (66%)	11 (18%)
16	MIN	W 38-26	56 (95%)	55 (93%)		28 (47%)	37 (63%)	35 (59%)	15 (25%)
17	DET	W 31-24	70 (93%)	70 (93%)		35 (47%)	35 (47%)	40 (53%)	36 (48%)
Grand Total			1,014 (93%)	910 (84%)	675 (76%)	598 (54%)	389 (41%)	328 (51%)	289 (29%)

Personnel Groupings

Personnel	Team %	NFL Avg	Succ. %
1-1 [3WR]	52%	60%	49%
0-1 [4WR]	18%	1%	53%
1-2 [2WR]	7%	19%	36%
2-0 [3WR]	6%	1%	53%
2-1 [2WR]	6%	7%	40%
0-0 [5WR]	5%	1%	46%
1-0 [4WR]	4%	3%	51%

Grouping Tendencies

Personnel	Pass Rate	Pass Succ. %	Run Succ. %
1-1 [3WR]	70%	49%	51%
0-1 [4WR]	80%	50%	63%
1-2 [2WR]	44%	34%	37%
2-0 [3WR]	36%	65%	47%
2-1 [2WR]	41%	36%	43%
0-0 [5WR]	82%	46%	50%
1-0 [4WR]	60%	56%	44%

Red Zone Targets (min 3)

Receiver	All	Inside 5	6-10	11-20
Jordy Nelson	34	10	7	17
Davante Adams	27	8	4	15
Randall Cobb	19	2	7	10
Jared Cook	15	4	3	8
Ty Montgomery	13	3	2	8
Geronimo Allison	7	1	2	4
Richard Rodgers	6	2	1	3
Aaron Ripkowski	5	1	2	2
James Starks	3			3
Jeff Janis	3	1	1	1

Red Zone Rushes (min 3)

Rusher	All	Inside 5	6-10	11-20
Ty Montgomery	18	8	3	7
Aaron Rodgers	15	2	6	7
Aaron Ripkowski	11	4	2	5
Eddie Lacy	11	3	3	5
James Starks	7	2	2	3
Christine Michael	3			3
Knile Davis	1			1

Early Down Target Rate

	RB	TE	WR
	8%	18%	73%
NFL AVG	*19%*	*20%*	*61%*

Overall Target Success %

RB	TE	WR
40%	51%	54%
#27	#19	#6

Green Bay Packers 2016 Passing Recap & 2017 Outlook

Aaron Rodgers was a marksman on short passes last season. He was 2nd in the NFL in passer rating on passes within 15 yards of the line of scrimmage, had the most TDs (37) and completed 73% of his attempts. But more impressive in these numbers was the fact that Rodgers rarely threw to his backs and TEs, which typically are higher percentage throws. It was the deeper throws which were problematic for Rodgers to start the season. Through 10 weeks, on passes 15+ yards in the air, he was 24/70 (34%), 4:3 TD:INT and a 72.9 rating, which ranked 25th in the NFL. Davante Adams led the team with a 106 rating and caught 48% of his passes, but all other targets combined to be significantly worse. The Packers were 4-6 through 11 weeks, and from that point onward, Rodgers went 38/85 (45%), 8:2 TD:INT and a 113 rating on deep passes as the Packers reeled off 8 straight wins. Rodgers deep passing was a key turnaround to that performance. But the design was a team effort. Randall Cobb's efficiency on deep passes increased to a perfect 158.3 rating, and all other key receivers who struggled in the first 10 games performed drastically better over the final 9. Rodgers and the Packers needs this deep passing attack to pick up where they left off in 2017.

Aaron Rodgers Rating All Downs

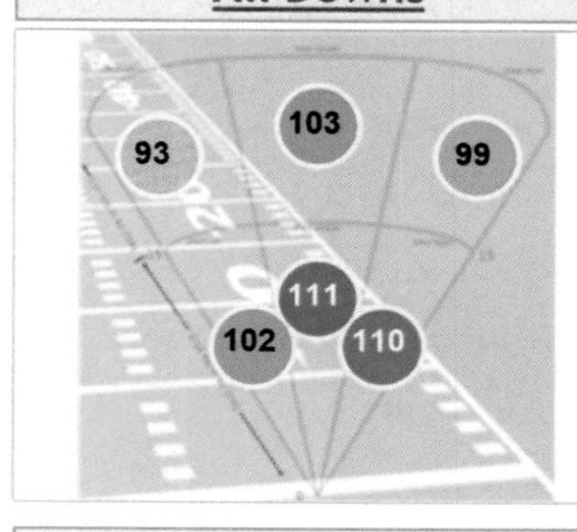

Aaron Rodgers Rating Early Downs

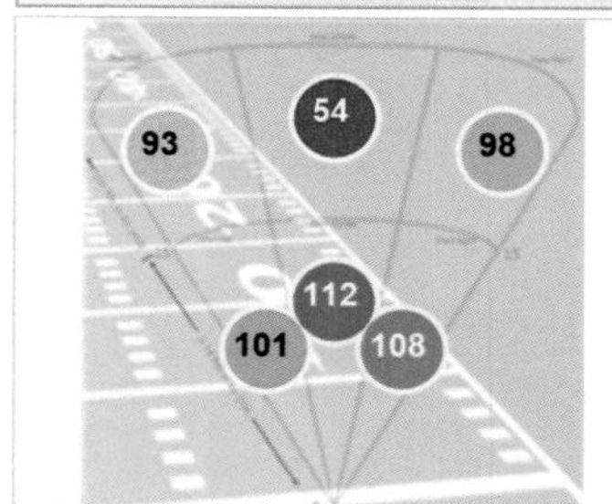

2016 Standard Passing Table

QB	Comp	Att	Comp %	Yds	YPA	TDs	INT	Sacks	Rating	Rk
Aaron Rodgers	481	738	65%	5,433	7.4	49	9	45	104.1	7
NFL Avg			63%		7.2				90.4	

2016 Advanced Passing Table

QB	Success %	EDSR Passing Success %	20+ Yd Pass Gains	20+ Yd Pass %	30+ Yd Pass Gains	30+ Yd Pass %	Air Yds per Comp	YAC per Comp	20+ Air Yd Comp	20+ Air Yd %
Aaron Rodgers	49%	50%	74	10%	31	4%	6.4	4.9	39	5%
NFL Avg	44%	48%	27	8%	10	3%	6.4	4.8	12	4%

Interception Rates by Down

Yards to Go	1	2	3	4	Total
1 & 2	0.0%	0.0%	0.0%	0.0%	0.0%
3, 4, 5	0.0%	1.9%	0.0%	0.0%	0.8%
6 - 9	0.0%	1.1%	5.7%	0.0%	2.6%
10 - 14	0.0%	0.0%	4.2%		0.5%
15+	0.0%	0.0%	14.3%	0.0%	5.3%
Total	0.0%	0.7%	3.5%	0.0%	1.1%

3rd Down Passing - Short of Sticks Analysis

QB	Avg Yds to Go	Air Yds (of Comps)	Avg Yds Short	Short of Sticks Rate	Rk
Aaron Rodgers	7.0	9.4	0.0	44%	2
NFL Avg	7.6	6.8	-0.8	57%	

Air Yds vs YAC

Air Yds %	YAC %	Rk
52%	48%	30
54%	46%	

2016 Receiving Recap & 2017 Outlook

In years past, when Jordy Nelson was a strong deep threat, he absolutely was not in his return to the Packers after missing 2015. He caught just 18 of 50 deep targets and delivered a mere 82.5 rating. A tremendous week 3 against a terrible Lions defense saw him deliver a 149 rating. But from that point onward, in the remaining 16 games, he delivered a 71.9 rating on deep targets & the lowest completion percentage of any receiver. If his explosiveness doesn't return in 2017, the Packers must rely even more on Davante Adams deep. The Packers absolutely must get better production from the RBs and TEs in the receiving game.

Player *Min 50 Targets*	Targets	Comp %	YPA	Rating	TOARS	Success %	Success Rk	Missed YPA Rk	YAS % Rk	TDs
Jordy Nelson	164	63%	8.2	114	5.8	59%	22	25	41	15
Davante Adams	146	62%	8.3	106	5.4	50%	73	66	15	14
Randall Cobb	108	72%	8.1	114	5.1	57%	28	33	39	7
Jared Cook	83	58%	7.3	93	4.4	48%	92	43	75	3
Ty Montgomery	70	77%	6.1	86	4.0	50%	73	37	131	0

Directional Passer Rating Delivered

Receiver	Short Left	Short Middle	Short Right	Deep Left	Deep Middle	Deep Right	Player Total
Jordy Nelson	126	116	118	96	47	86	114
Davante Adams	94	120	115	75	87	115	106
Randall Cobb	91	97	114	68	149	96	114
Jared Cook	104	97	101	72	40	96	93
Ty Montgomery	95	61	86		119		86
Richard Rodgers	82	104	95	144	40	0	93
Geronimo Allison	88	107	113	119		90	109
James Starks	113	86	134				114
Christine Michael	79		44				65
Team Total	104	101	112	93	104	99	105

2016 Rushing Recap & 2017 Outlook

While the Patriots used free agency to load up on running backs, the Packers used the middle rounds of the draft to do the same. In rounds 4, 5 and 7, they drafted Jamaal Williams, Aaron Jones and Devante Mays. They needed bodies, to say the least, as they rid themselves of the remaining backs on their roster apart from Ty Montgomery. Montgomery was tremendous last season as a RB and should only improve with more reps. And the best part about Mongtomery from a fantasy perspective is he's game script proof. In close games, he grabbed 17% of the total GB volume. When up big, he was still always in the 14-16% range thanks to the run volume. When down big, he remained in the 14-16% range thanks to the pass volume.

Player *Min 50 Rushes*	Rushes	YPA	Success %	Success Rk	Missed YPA Rk	YTS % Rk	YAS % Rk	Early Down Success %	Early Down Success Rk	TDs
Ty Montgomery	102	5.4	52%	16	9	64	4	53%	11	5
Eddie Lacy	71	5.1	49%	26	14	60	13	48%	34	0
James Starks	63	2.3	32%	68	66	17	57	32%	66	0

Yards per Carry by Direction

Directional Run Frequency

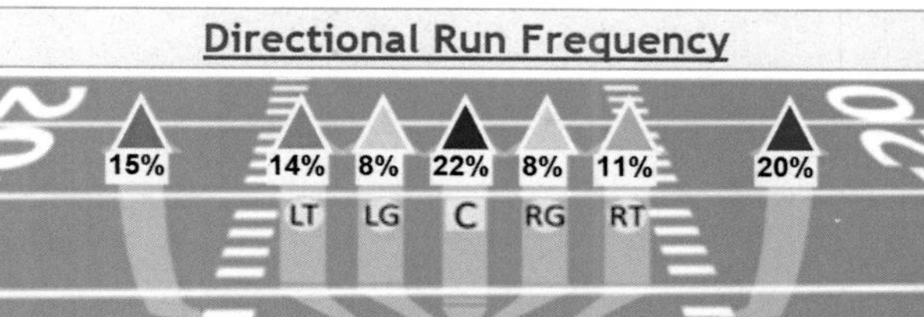

And that's the other side of the sword, the offense must keep the defense off the field. And it can accomplish both by mastering two things: running the ball more effectively and gaining more first downs. The Packers were the NFL's most pass heavy team in one-score games in 2016, passing the ball 66% of the time. That was an 8% increase over 2015 when they were just 58% pass in one-score games. They passed more because the run game wasn't as reliable. Or at least that is what they thought.

The Packers run game ranked 5th in overall efficiency. And it should have been used more often in medium and short yardage situations. As an example: when passing the ball with 4-7 yards to go, the Packers were successful on 51% of plays (13th in the NFL) and averaged 5.6 yards per play. But when running the ball, they were successful on 67% of plays (#2 in the NFL) and averaged a whopping 5.6 yards per play. Yet the Packers called 152 passes and only 52 runs. That was nearly 10% above the NFL average, and the Packers could have called far more runs considering how successful they were when running. This plays into the second thing that the Packers must master: gaining more first downs. And we'll lead with another example. The most effective time to pick up a first down is on 2nd and short. Teams convert nearly 20% more 2nd and short plays into first downs when running than when passing. For the Packers, they converted 53% of their 2nd and short passes into first downs, about NFL average. But when they ran the ball, they converted 81% of those rushes into first downs, 10% above NFL average. Yet the Packers went 50/50 run/pass.

The NFL average was 65/35 run/pass, and despite recording first downs almost 30% more frequently when running, the Packers were the 2nd most pass heavy team in 2nd and short situations.

So even with an offense that is incredibly good, there was a ton of inefficiency. This is what separates a Patriots team from a Packers team. Bill Belichick and his staff would find each and every efficiency leak possible in the offseason and try to squeeze the most out of it the next season. Whereas other teams with good to great offenses simply are satisfied to "do what we do" over and over again. Even though they never are winning Super Bowls, and should be thirsty for new ways to improve their own offensive efficiency wherever possible.

Another example: targeting TEs and RBs in the passing game. I realize the Packers did not have a healthy, solid TE so that is likely the reason they didn't target them as much. But they were highly unsuccessful in targeting these two positions, which likely resulted in them choosing to target them 13% less than average. With new pieces and more solidified roles in 2017, the Packers must target these positions more often, because they are matchup nightmares for defenses. TE targets are more efficient than WR targets, and better situational use of RBs in the pass game has proven to be more advantageous than targeting WRs on those same plays.

Division History: Season Wins & 2017 Projection

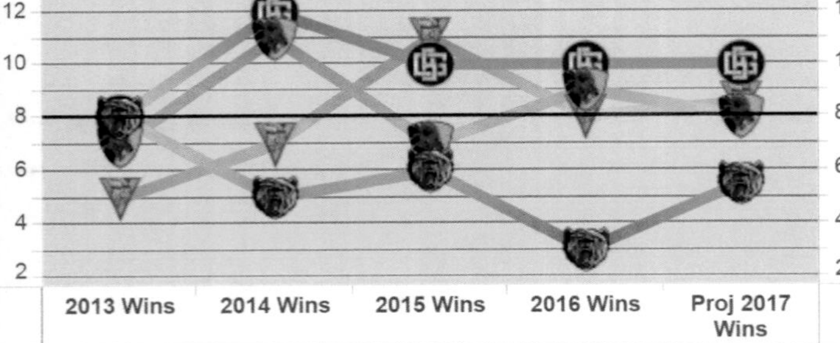

Rank of 2017 Defensive Pass Efficiency Faced by Week

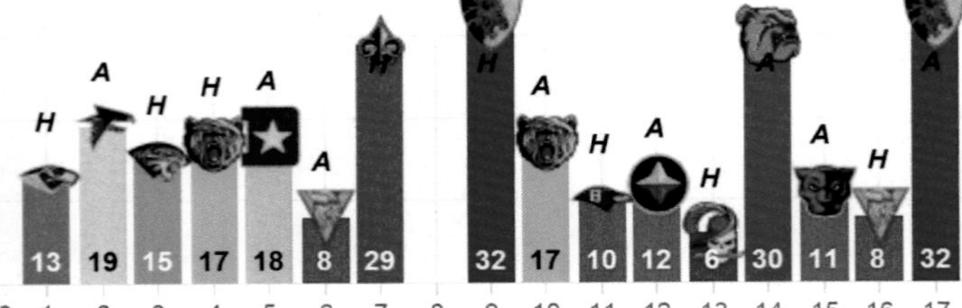

Rank of 2017 Defensive Rush Efficiency Faced by Week

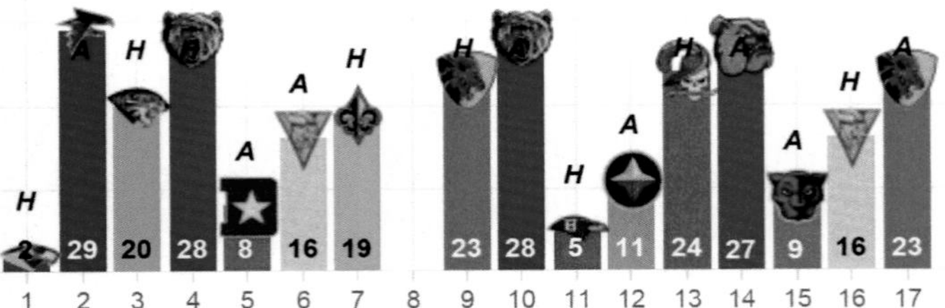

2016 Situational Usage by Player & Position

Usage Rate by Score

		Being Blown Out (14+)	Down Big (9-13)	One Score	Large Lead (9-13)	Blowout Lead (14+)	Grand Total
RUSH	Ty Montgomery	5%	3%	11%	10%	9%	9%
	Randall Cobb			1%	4%		1%
	James Starks	3%	13%	5%	16%	2%	6%
	Eddie Lacy	3%	8%	7%	1%	10%	6%
	Aaron Ripkowski	1%	3%	4%	9%	4%	4%
	Christine Michael	4%		4%	1%	15%	4%
	Jeff Janis			0%		1%	0%
	Don Jackson	1%	3%	1%			1%
	Knile Davis			0%		2%	0%
	Joe Kerridge					1%	0%
	Total	18%	32%	33%	42%	45%	32%
PASS	Ty Montgomery	9%	12%	6%	4%	7%	6%
	Jordy Nelson	21%	12%	15%	15%	11%	15%
	Davante Adams	11%	5%	15%	14%	10%	13%
	Randall Cobb	12%	10%	10%	11%	3%	10%
	James Starks	3%	5%	2%		2%	2%
	Jared Cook	7%	10%	8%	1%	5%	8%
	Eddie Lacy			1%	1%	1%	1%
	Aaron Ripkowski	2%	3%	1%	3%	2%	1%
	Christine Michael	1%	2%	0%			0%
	Richard Rodgers	7%	8%	4%	4%	4%	4%
	Geronimo Allison	3%		2%	5%	5%	3%
	Jeff Janis	5%		2%		1%	2%
	Don Jackson			0%			0%
	Knile Davis			0%			0%
	Trevor Davis	1%		1%		1%	1%
	Justin Perillo	1%	2%	0%		1%	0%
	Jared Abbrederis			0%			0%
	Total	82%	68%	67%	58%	55%	68%

Positional Target Distribution vs NFL Average

		NFL Wide				Team Only			
		Left	Middle	Right	**Total**	Left	Middle	Right	**Total**
Deep	WR	983	551	952	**2,486**	48	30	49	**127**
	TE	141	142	154	**437**	17	5	9	**31**
	RB	25	4	40	**69**				
	All	**1,149**	**697**	**1,146**	**2,992**	**65**	**35**	**58**	**158**
Short	WR	2,936	1,693	3,030	**7,659**	157	78	156	**391**
	TE	804	849	1,108	**2,761**	32	26	43	**101**
	RB	1,003	614	1,103	**2,720**	12	8	10	**30**
	All	**4,743**	**3,156**	**5,241**	**13,140**	**201**	**112**	**209**	**522**
Total		**5,892**	**3,853**	**6,387**	**16,132**	**266**	**147**	**267**	**680**

Positional Success Rates vs NFL Average

		NFL Wide				Team Only			
		Left	Middle	Right	**Total**	Left	Middle	Right	**Total**
Deep	WR	37%	50%	38%	**40%**	38%	47%	43%	**42%**
	TE	45%	51%	43%	**46%**	41%	0%	44%	**35%**
	RB	32%	75%	25%	**30%**				
	All	**38%**	**51%**	**38%**	**41%**	**38%**	**40%**	**43%**	**41%**
Short	WR	52%	57%	51%	**52%**	52%	55%	67%	**59%**
	TE	50%	61%	52%	**54%**	50%	65%	53%	**55%**
	RB	47%	49%	44%	**46%**	17%	50%	40%	**33%**
	All	**51%**	**57%**	**49%**	**52%**	**50%**	**57%**	**63%**	**57%**
Total		**48%**	**56%**	**47%**	**50%**	**47%**	**53%**	**58%**	**53%**

2017 Coaches

Head Coach:
Bill O'Brien (4th yr)
Offensive Coordinator:
(O'Brien calls plays) (4th yr)
Defensive Coordinator:
Romeo Crennel (4th yr)

Houston Texans

2017 Forecast

Wins	Div Rank
8.5	#3

Past Records

2016: 9-7
2015: 9-7
2014: 9-7

EASY — HARD

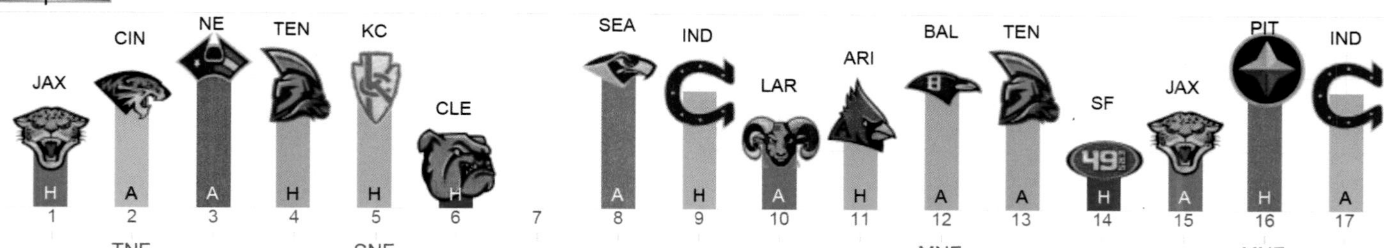

Key Players Lost

TXN	Player (POS)
Cut	Bergstrom, Tony C
	Camiel, Dimitric T
	Mumphery, Keith WR
	Mutcherson, T.J. S
	Rivers, Gerald LB
Declared Free Agent	Aboushi, Oday G
	Bouye, A.J. CB
	Demps, Quintin S
	Dent, Akeem LB
	Griffin, Ryan TE
	Grimes, Jonathan RB
	Jones, Don S
	Lechler, Shane P
	Novak, Nick K
	Simon, John LB
	Smith, Antonio DE
	Still, Devon DE
	Wilfork, Vince NT
Retired	Johnson, Andre WR

Average Line	# Games Favored	# Games Underdog
-0.8	9	6

2017 Houston Texans Overview

If you wanted to see a division where all 4 teams have young quarterbacks but some were among the worst in the NFL while others are clearly star caliber, the AFC South is your division. At the conclusion of the 2015 season, all 4 quarterbacks were still on their rookie contract. Brock Osweiler signed to quarterback the Texans while Andrew Luck signed to stay on board with the Colts. Marcus Mariota and Blake Bortles are still in their rookie deals. Andrew Luck and Marcus Mariota have shown tremendous ability in their NFL careers thus far and certainly are the next generation of star quarterbacks. Brock Osweiler and Blake Bortles are on the opposite end of the spectrum. One look at Osweiler's passing cones and you'll see the entire screen filled with shades of red. There was literally nothing good from his arm last season except for sparks or flashes of a good throw here or a proper read there. Being that they were few and far between, it's even possible to believe those were lucky plays or fortunate occurrences. Most of us have never thrown a pass in the NFL or even college. But most of us probably have played basketball at some point and have shot a ball that felt rushed or offline as it left our fingertips, only to see it find its way into the basket. So many things happen on a football field that from an outsider's perspective, it's difficult to know if a deep completion was 100% planned and intentional, or if there was luck involved with either the read or the throw or the coverage.

One of the biggest problems with the Texans last year was one of the things the team thought could be a positive heading into the season: deep passing. But the only quarterback worse than Blake Bortles on deep passes last year was Brock Osweiler. Brock posted a 31 passer rating and a 24% success rate, averaging only 6.9 yards per attempt with a 4:9 TD:INT ratio on 98 deep passes. Heading into the season, the Texans moved on from Brian Hoyer. Hoyer is a very accurate underneath passer. He, too, struggles throwing deep. He prefers the shorter reads and simply is not a very aggressive passer, at least he has not been to this stage in his career. In Houston in 2015, Hoyer attempted 67 deep passes, recorded a 5:4 TD:INT ratio and a 79 rating. Compared to Osweiler's numbers just mentioned, these seem like All-Pro numbers but the reality is they are not. And they were a huge drop in what Hoyer was able to do with the Texans on short passes, which was 300 attempts, a 14:3 TD:INT ratio and a 95 rating.

(cont'd - see HOU2)

Key Free Agents/ Trades Added

Anderson, Dres WR
Austell, Erik C
Giacomini, Breno T
Johnson, Andre WR
Moore, Sio LB
Roberson, Marcus CB

Drafted Players

Rd	Pk	Player (College)
1	12	QB - Deshaun Watson (Clemson)
2	57	LB - Zach Cunningham (Vanderbilt)
3	89	RB - D'Onta Foreman (Texas)
4	130	OT - Julién Davenport (Bucknell)
4*	142	DT - Carlos Watkins (Clemson)
5	169	CB - Treston Decoud (Oregon State)
7	243	C - Kyle Fuller (Baylor)

Regular Season Wins: Past & Current Proj

Proj 2017 Wins  8.5

2016 Wins  9

Proj 2016 Wins  8.5

2015 Wins  9

2014 Wins  9

2013 Wins  2

1 3 5 7 9 11 13 15

2017 Lineup & Cap Hits

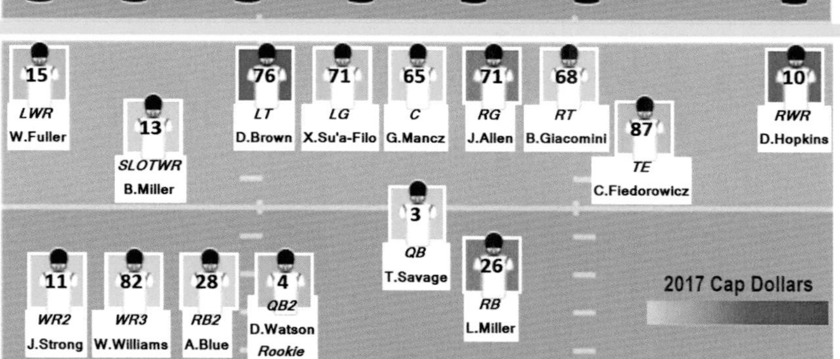

2017 Unit Spending

Positional Spending

	Rank	Total	2016 Rk
All OFF	31	$66.95M	23
QB	29	$4.91M	19
OL	12	$29.99M	4
RB	12	$9.44M	9
WR	24	$15.17M	29
TE	23	$7.44M	32
All DEF	17	$77.53M	4
DL	15	$26.59M	8
LB	13	$23.10M	8
CB	12	$21.54M	9
S	28	$6.30M	27

Houston Texans 2016 Success Rate Radar

Weeks 1-4: 1 W, 2 W, 3 L, 4 W

Weeks 5-8: 5 L, 6 W, 7 L, 8 W

Weeks 9-12: 10 W, 11 L, 12 L

Weeks 13-17: 13 L, 14 W, 15 W, 16 W, 17 L

HOU-2

There should be absolutely no reason why a QB with those numbers on short passes would be released. He was only planning to hit the cap for $4.8M in 2016, and when the Texans cut him the Bears picked him up for a very team friendly 1 year, $2M deal. But the Texans must have looked at his limitations and desired more. So they added Brock Osweiler. I warned at the time that this was a bad idea. A few highlights included: his passer rating decreased on every down and in every quarter. His best plays were in the 1st quarter on 1st down, which were plays heavily scripted by Gary Kubiak. On later downs, playing situationally rather than scripted, he suffered. On 3rd/4th down in the 4th quarter (crunch time) he completed 40% of his passes, averaged 4.2 yards per attempt and a 61 rating. And what should have stood out the most to the Texans: he went 14/48 (29%) on deep passes (15+ yards in the air), with a 1:3 TD:INT rate and a 40.6 rating, which was the worst rating in the NFL in 2015. That didn't deter Bill O'Brien, who either hasn't had much luck with quarterbacks through no talent evaluation fault of his own, or is one of the worst QB talent evaluators in football.

Since becoming head coach, Tom Brady's former QB coach and acclaimed "QB Whisperer" has made the following moves in his 4 years with the Texans: 2014: signed Ryan Fitzpatrick, drafted Tom Savage, traded away TJ Yates, traded for Ryan Mallett, waived Case Keenum, signed Thaddeus Lewis, signed Keenum. 2015: signed Mallett to a new contract, cut Lewis, traded away Keenum, traded away Fitzpatrick, signed Brian Hoyer, signed Kevin Rodgers, released Mallett, signed Yates, claimed Brandon Weeden, Claimed BJ Daniels. 2016: waived Yates, signed Brock Osweiler, signed Weeden, cut Hoyer, waived Daniels. 2017: traded away Osweiler, drafted Deshaun Watson. If that looks like a mess of poor quarterbacks, who were added, released, and re-added in some cases, then you're reading it correctly.

Heading into last season, despite knowing Brock Osweiler wouldn't work in Houston, I still took the Texans to win the AFC South at +200 because I knew the schedule that this offense would face should allow

(cont'd - see HOU-3)

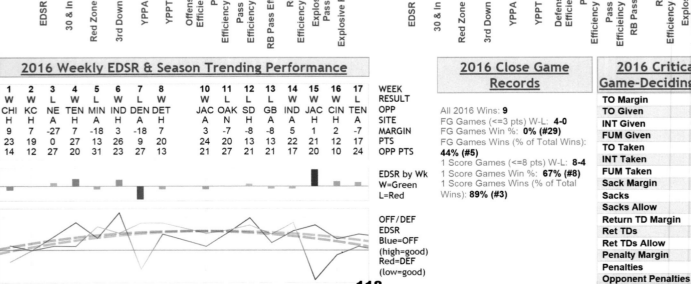

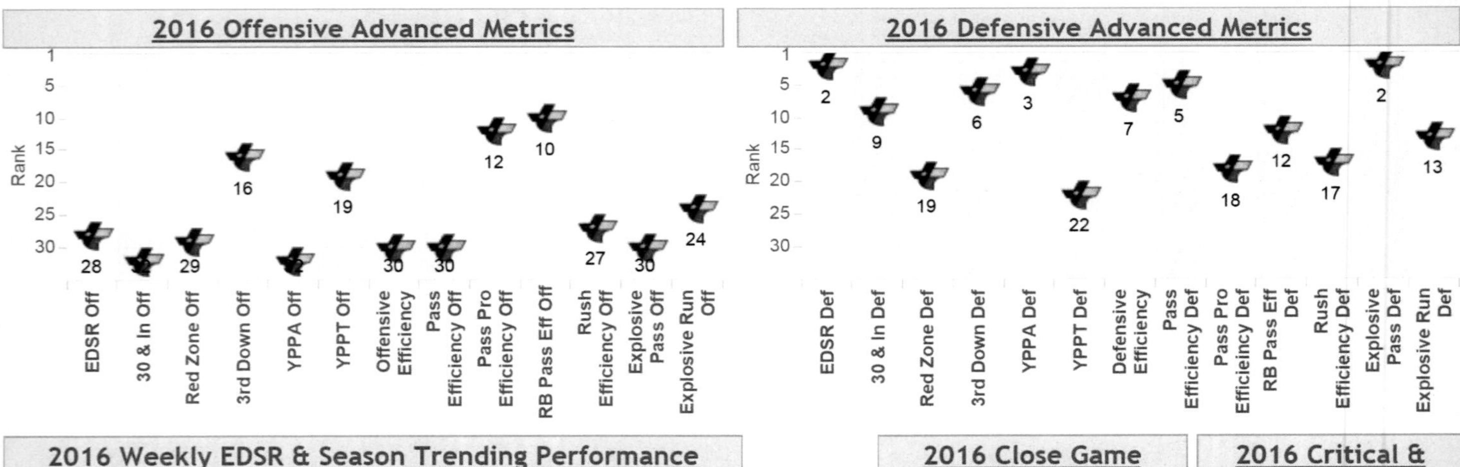

2016 Weekly EDSR & Season Trending Performance

WEEK	1	2	3	4	5	6	7	8	10	11	12	13	14	15	16	17
RESULT	W	W	L	W	L	W	L	W	W	L	L	L	W	W	W	L
OPP	CHI	KC	NE	TEN	MIN	IND	DEN	DET	JAC	OAK	SD	GB	IND	JAC	CIN	TEN
SITE	H	H	A	H	A	H	A	H	A	N	H	A	A	H	H	A
MARGIN	9	7	-27	7	-18	3	-18	7	3	-7	-8	-8	5	1	2	-7
PTS	23	19	0	27	13	26	9	20	24	20	13	13	22	21	12	17
OPP PTS	14	12	27	20	31	23	27	13	21	27	21	21	17	20	10	24

EDSR by Wk W=Green L=Red

OFF/DEF EDSR Blue=OFF (high=good) Red=DEF (low=good)

2016 Close Game Records

All 2016 Wins: **9**
FG Games (<=3 pts) W-L: **4-0**
FG Games Win %: **0% (#29)**
FG Games Wins (% of Total Wins): **44% (#5)**
1 Score Games (<=8 pts) W-L: **8-4**
1 Score Games Win %: **67% (#8)**
1 Score Games Wins (% of Total Wins): **89% (#3)**

2016 Critical & Game-Deciding Stats

TO Margin	-7
TO Given	24
INT Given	16
FUM Given	8
TO Taken	17
INT Taken	11
FUM Taken	6
Sack Margin	-1
Sacks	31
Sacks Allow	32
Return TD Margin	-1
Ret TDs	2
Ret TDs Allow	3
Penalty Margin	+27
Penalties	87
Opponent Penalties	114

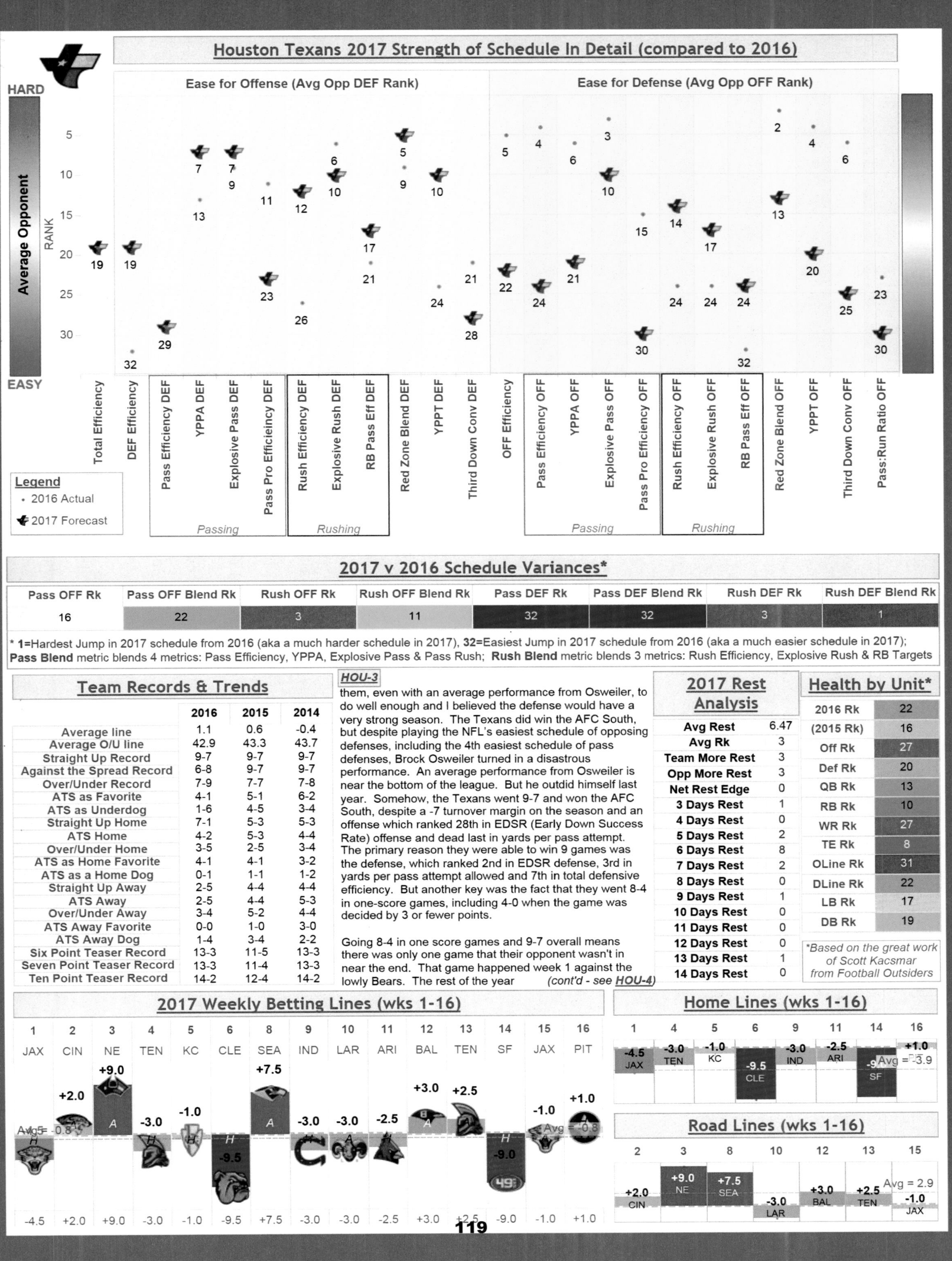

Houston Texans 2017 Strength of Schedule In Detail (compared to 2016)

2017 v 2016 Schedule Variances*

Pass OFF Rk	Pass OFF Blend Rk	Rush OFF Rk	Rush OFF Blend Rk	Pass DEF Rk	Pass DEF Blend Rk	Rush DEF Rk	Rush DEF Blend Rk
16	22	3	11	32	32	3	1

* **1**=Hardest Jump in 2017 schedule from 2016 (aka a much harder schedule in 2017), **32**=Easiest Jump in 2017 schedule from 2016 (aka a much easier schedule in 2017); **Pass Blend** metric blends 4 metrics: Pass Efficiency, YPPA, Explosive Pass & Pass Rush; **Rush Blend** metric blends 3 metrics: Rush Efficiency, Explosive Rush & RB Targets

Team Records & Trends

	2016	2015	2014
Average line	1.1	0.6	-0.4
Average O/U line	42.9	43.3	43.7
Straight Up Record	9-7	9-7	9-7
Against the Spread Record	6-8	9-7	9-7
Over/Under Record	7-9	7-7	7-8
ATS as Favorite	4-1	5-1	6-2
ATS as Underdog	1-6	4-5	3-4
Straight Up Home	7-1	5-3	5-3
ATS Home	4-2	5-3	4-4
Over/Under Home	3-5	2-5	3-4
ATS as Home Favorite	4-1	4-1	3-2
ATS as a Home Dog	0-1	1-1	1-2
Straight Up Away	2-5	4-4	4-4
ATS Away	2-5	4-4	5-3
Over/Under Away	3-4	5-2	4-4
ATS Away Favorite	0-0	1-0	3-0
ATS Away Dog	1-4	3-4	2-2
Six Point Teaser Record	13-3	11-5	13-3
Seven Point Teaser Record	13-3	11-4	13-3
Ten Point Teaser Record	14-2	12-4	14-2

HOU-3

them, even with an average performance from Osweiler, to do well enough and I believed the defense would have a very strong season. The Texans did win the AFC South, but despite playing the NFL's easiest schedule of opposing defenses, including the 4th easiest schedule of pass defenses, Brock Osweiler turned in a disastrous performance. An average performance from Osweiler is near the bottom of the league. But he outdid himself last year. Somehow, the Texans went 9-7 and won the AFC South, despite a -7 turnover margin on the season and an offense which ranked 28th in EDSR (Early Down Success Rate) offense and dead last in yards per pass attempt. The primary reason they were able to win 9 games was the defense, which ranked 2nd in EDSR defense, 3rd in yards per pass attempt allowed and 7th in total defensive efficiency. But another key was the fact that they went 8-4 in one-score games, including 4-0 when the game was decided by 3 or fewer points.

Going 8-4 in one score games and 9-7 overall means there was only one game that their opponent wasn't in near the end. That game happened week 1 against the lowly Bears. The rest of the year *(cont'd - see HOU-4)*

2017 Rest Analysis

Avg Rest	6.47
Avg Rk	3
Team More Rest	3
Opp More Rest	3
Net Rest Edge	0
3 Days Rest	1
4 Days Rest	0
5 Days Rest	2
6 Days Rest	8
7 Days Rest	2
8 Days Rest	0
9 Days Rest	1
10 Days Rest	0
11 Days Rest	0
12 Days Rest	0
13 Days Rest	1
14 Days Rest	0

Health by Unit*

2016 Rk	22
(2015 Rk)	16
Off Rk	27
Def Rk	20
QB Rk	13
RB Rk	10
WR Rk	27
TE Rk	8
OLine Rk	31
DLine Rk	22
LB Rk	17
DB Rk	19

**Based on the great work of Scott Kacsmar from Football Outsiders*

2017 Weekly Betting Lines (wks 1-16)

1	2	3	4	5	6	8	9	10	11	12	13	14	15	16
JAX	CIN	NE	TEN	KC	CLE	SEA	IND	LAR	ARI	BAL	TEN	SF	JAX	PIT
H	A	A	H	H	H	A	H	A	H	A	A	H	A	H
-4.5	+2.0	+9.0	-3.0	-1.0	-9.5	+7.5	-3.0	-3.0	-2.5	+3.0	+2.5	-9.0	-1.0	+1.0

Avg = -0.8

Home Lines (wks 1-16)

1	4	5	6	9	11	14	16
JAX	TEN	KC	CLE	IND	ARI	SF	PIT
-4.5	-3.0	-1.0	-9.5	-3.0	-2.5	-9.0	+1.0

Avg = -3.9

Road Lines (wks 1-16)

2	3	8	10	12	13	15
CIN	NE	SEA	LAR	BAL	TEN	JAX
+2.0	+9.0	+7.5	-3.0	+3.0	+2.5	-1.0

Avg = 2.9

Houston Texans 2016 Play Analysis

2016 Play Tendencies

All Pass %	57%
All Pass Rk	21
All Rush %	43%
All Rush Rk	12
1 Score Pass %	55%
1 Score Pass Rk	24
2015 1 Score Pass %	57%
2015 1 Score Pass Rk	21
Pass Increase %	-2%
Pass Increase Rk	21
1 Score Rush %	45%
1 Score Rush Rk	9
Up Pass %	63%
Up Pass Rk	4
Up Rush %	37%
Up Rush Rk	29
Down Pass %	62%
Down Pass Rk	14
Down Rush %	38%
Down Rush Rk	19

2016 Down & Distance Tendencies

Down	Distance	Total Plays	Pass Rate	Run Rate	Play Success %
1	Short (1-3)	10	20%	80%	50%
	Med (4-7)	10	10%	90%	60%
	Long (8-10)	337	52%	48%	46%
	XL (11+)	15	67%	33%	7%
2	Short (1-3)	49	37%	63%	76%
	Med (4-7)	78	53%	47%	42%
	Long (8-10)	121	46%	54%	25%
	XL (11+)	40	75%	25%	20%
3	Short (1-3)	35	57%	43%	49%
	Med (4-7)	82	83%	17%	44%
	Long (8-10)	47	91%	9%	21%
	XL (11+)	28	71%	29%	11%
4	Short (1-3)	7	43%	57%	71%
	Med (4-7)	2	100%	0%	50%
	Long (8-10)	1	100%	0%	0%
	XL (11+)	1	100%	0%	0%

Shotgun %:

Under Center	Shotgun
35%	65%
37%	*63%*

AVG

Run Rate:

Under Center	Shotgun
69%	29%
68%	*23%*

AVG

Pass Rate:

Under Center	Shotgun
31%	71%
32%	*77%*

AVG

Short Yardage Intelligence:

2nd and Short Run

Run Freq	Run % Rk	NFL Run Freq Avg	Run 1D Rate	Run NFL 1D Avg
62%	21	65%	92%	71%

2nd and Short Pass

Pass Freq	Pass % Rk	NFL Pass Freq Avg	Pass 1D Rate	Pass NFL 1D Avg
38%	12	35%	80%	52%

Most Frequent Play

Down	Distance	Play Type	Player	Total Plays	Play Success %
1	Short (1-3)	RUSH	Lamar Miller	6	83%
	Med (4-7)	RUSH	Lamar Miller	6	50%
	Long (8-10)	RUSH	Lamar Miller	116	40%
	XL (11+)	PASS	DeAndre Hopkins	4	0%
		RUSH	Lamar Miller	4	0%
2	Short (1-3)	RUSH	Lamar Miller	21	76%
	Med (4-7)	RUSH	Lamar Miller	26	38%
	Long (8-10)	RUSH	Lamar Miller	42	14%
	XL (11+)	PASS	Will Fuller	7	14%
3	Short (1-3)	PASS	DeAndre Hopkins	8	38%
		RUSH	Lamar Miller	8	63%
	Med (4-7)	PASS	DeAndre Hopkins	16	50%
	Long (8-10)	PASS	DeAndre Hopkins	8	25%
	XL (11+)	PASS	Will Fuller	5	0%

Most Successful Play*

Down	Distance	Play Type	Player	Total Plays	Play Success %
1	Short (1-3)	RUSH	Lamar Miller	6	83%
	Med (4-7)	RUSH	Lamar Miller	6	50%
	Long (8-10)	RUSH	Akeem Hunt	6	83%
2	Short (1-3)	PASS	C.J. Fiedorowicz	5	80%
	Med (4-7)	PASS	Lamar Miller	6	67%
	Long (8-10)	PASS	C.J. Fiedorowicz	6	50%
	XL (11+)	PASS	DeAndre Hopkins	6	33%
			C.J. Fiedorowicz	6	33%
3	Short (1-3)	RUSH	Lamar Miller	8	63%
	Med (4-7)	RUSH	Brock Osweiler	5	100%
	Long (8-10)	PASS	C.J. Fiedorowicz	5	40%
			Will Fuller	5	40%
	XL (11+)	PASS	Will Fuller	5	0%

**Minimum 5 plays to qualify*

2016 Snap Rates

Week	Opp	Score	DeAndre Hopkins	Will Fuller	C.J. Fiedorowicz	Lamar Miller	Ryan Griffin	Braxton Miller	Jaelen Strong
1	CHI	W 23-14	73 (97%)	54 (72%)	38 (51%)	60 (80%)	35 (47%)	52 (69%)	12 (16%)
2	KC	W 19-12	72 (100%)	65 (90%)	41 (57%)	53 (74%)	27 (38%)	20 (28%)	42 (58%)
3	NE	L 27-0	69 (97%)	71 (100%)	25 (35%)	54 (76%)	47 (66%)		53 (75%)
4	TEN	W 27-20	61 (95%)	56 (88%)	47 (73%)	52 (81%)	32 (50%)		33 (52%)
5	MIN	L 31-13	64 (100%)	64 (100%)	42 (66%)	42 (66%)	18 (28%)	14 (22%)	46 (72%)
6	IND	W 26-23	70 (99%)		44 (62%)	59 (83%)	22 (31%)	56 (79%)	69 (97%)
7	DEN	L 27-9	70 (100%)	66 (94%)	51 (73%)	31 (44%)	21 (30%)	5 (7%)	32 (46%)
8	DET	W 20-13	66 (99%)	47 (70%)	48 (72%)	33 (49%)	30 (45%)	31 (46%)	13 (19%)
10	JAC	W 24-21	61 (97%)		55 (87%)	24 (38%)	34 (54%)	47 (75%)	
11	OAK	L 27-20	74 (97%)	42 (55%)	56 (74%)	57 (75%)	35 (46%)	66 (87%)	
12	SD	L 21-13	67 (97%)	53 (77%)	45 (65%)	48 (70%)	27 (39%)	61 (88%)	
13	GB	L 21-13	66 (100%)	52 (79%)	46 (70%)	31 (47%)	17 (26%)	27 (41%)	
14	IND	W 22-17	71 (99%)	58 (81%)	56 (78%)	33 (46%)	21 (29%)		
15	JAC	W 21-20	82 (98%)	68 (81%)		48 (57%)	66 (79%)		
16	CIN	W 12-10	64 (100%)	61 (95%)	43 (67%)		19 (30%)		
17	TEN	L 24-17	55 (74%)	74 (100%)	39 (53%)		54 (73%)		
Grand Total			1,085 (97%)	831 (84%)	676 (65%)	625 (63%)	505 (44%)	379 (54%)	300 (54%)

Personnel Groupings

Personnel	Team %	NFL Avg	Succ. %
1-1 [3WR]	63%	60%	44%
1-2 [2WR]	17%	19%	42%
2-1 [2WR]	8%	7%	38%
2-2 [1WR]	6%	3%	33%
2-0 [3WR]	3%	1%	41%

Grouping Tendencies

Personnel	Pass Rate	Pass Succ. %	Run Succ. %
1-1 [3WR]	67%	44%	45%
1-2 [2WR]	48%	43%	41%
2-1 [2WR]	32%	27%	44%
2-2 [1WR]	7%	60%	31%
2-0 [3WR]	35%	42%	41%

Red Zone Targets (min 3)

Receiver	All	Inside 5	6-10	11-20
C.J. Fiedorowicz	14	3	5	6
DeAndre Hopkins	12	6	1	5
Braxton Miller	11	1	3	7
Will Fuller	10	1	4	5
Ryan Griffin	8	1	2	5
Lamar Miller	6		2	4
Stephen Anderson	4	1	1	2
Jonathan Grimes	3	1		2
Keith Mumphery	3	2		1

Red Zone Rushes (min 3)

Rusher	All	Inside 5	6-10	11-20
Lamar Miller	39	11	7	21
Alfred Blue	16	4	7	5
Brock Osweiler	7	3		4
Akeem Hunt	5	1	1	3

Early Down Target Rate

	RB	TE	WR
	17%	32%	52%
NFL AVG	*19%*	*20%*	*61%*

Overall Target Success %

RB	TE	WR
49% #9	49% #25	41% #31

Houston Texans 2016 Passing Recap & 2017 Outlook

The efficiency gain that the Texans can experience this year with a quarterback who is actually competent will be noticeable. Defenses need to be stretched, and with Osweiler the threat of the deep pass was never believable. Be it Tom Savage or Deshaun Watson, the deep passes will be more accurate and more impactful. That will help to open up the run game. Three of the most useful, successful targets for an inexperienced quarterback are the TE, RB and slot WR. Last year passes to their TE and RB were successful 49% of the time, while passes to their WRs were successful only 41% (31st in NFL). While both Savage and Watson are very different quarterbacks with different skill sets, there are upsides to both which could legitimately allow the Texans to have a successful season if channeled correctly. My word of advice to Bill O'Brien and the Texans is if you roll with Savage and he's in several situations where he must come from behind to win the game in the 4th quarter, odds are it's because the run game isn't firing. And for the Texans to make noise in the playoffs, the run game needs to be firing (regardless of the QB). With an efficient run game and this defense, the Texans can win with either QB.

Brock Osweiler Rating All Downs

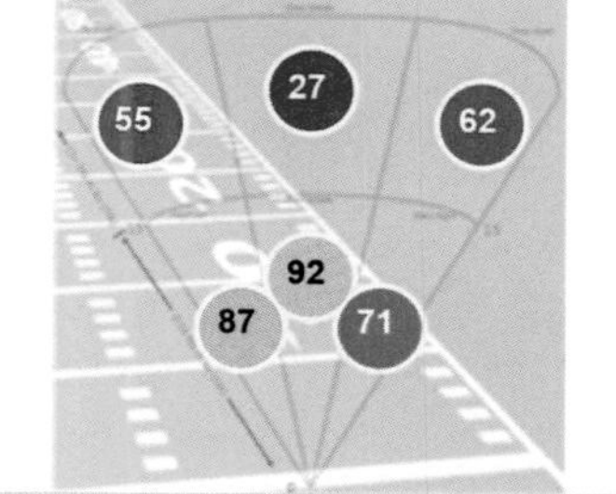

Brock Osweiler Rating Early Downs

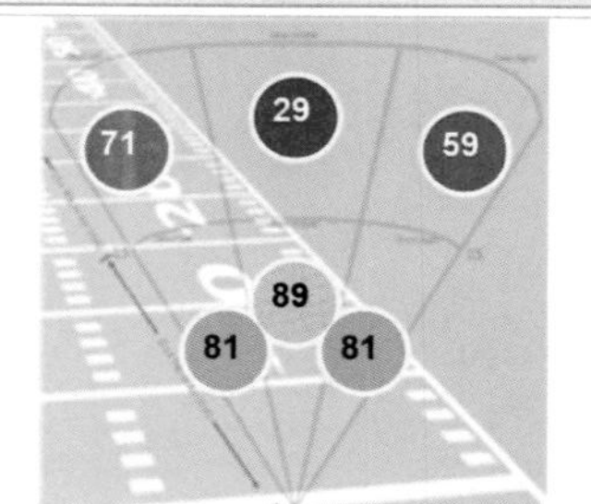

2016 Standard Passing Table

QB	Comp	Att	Comp %	Yds	YPA	TDs	INT	Sacks	Rating	Rk
Brock Osweiler	338	576	59%	3,323	5.8	17	19	29	71.1	46
Tom Savage	46	73	63%	461	6.3	0	0	5	80.9	35
NFL Avg			63%		7.2				90.4	

2016 Advanced Passing Table

QB	Success %	EDSR Passing Success %	20+ Yd Pass Gains	20+ Yd Pass %	30+ Yd Pass Gains	30+ Yd Pass %	Air Yds per Comp	YAC per Comp	20+ Air Yd Comp	20+ Air Yd %
Brock Osweiler	42%	46%	30	5%	9	2%	5.9	3.9	13	2%
Tom Savage	45%	52%	5	7%	1	1%	6.6	3.4	2	3%
NFL Avg	44%	48%	27	8%	10	3%	6.4	4.8	12	4%

Interception Rates by Down

Yards to Go	1	2	3	4	Total
1 & 2	0.0%	0.0%	11.8%	0.0%	5.6%
3, 4, 5	0.0%	2.6%	1.8%	0.0%	2.0%
6 - 9	0.0%	1.7%	2.9%	0.0%	2.3%
10 - 14	3.7%	5.9%	0.0%	0.0%	3.7%
15+	8.3%	0.0%	0.0%	0.0%	2.5%
Total	**3.8%**	**2.8%**	**2.8%**	**0.0%**	**3.1%**

3rd Down Passing - Short of Sticks Analysis

QB	Avg Yds to Go	Air Yds (of Comps)	Avg Yds Short	Short of Sticks Rate	Rk
Brock Osweiler	6.7	6.1	-0.7	63%	23
NFL Avg	7.6	6.8	-0.8	57%	

Air Yds vs YAC

Air Yds %	YAC %	Rk
65%	35%	7
54%	46%	

2016 Receiving Recap & 2017 Outlook

The Texans make extremely efficient use of their TEs, which is a huge boon to the passing game and a nice comfort for any developing QB. That success should continue in 2017. Last year, Braxton Miller struggled a ton in 11 personnel packages but was significantly better in limited exposure to 12 personnel. They need more out of their slot WR. Hopkins was targeted far too often last year (169 targets), making for predictable plays from defenders. While he's "worth" many targets, he was force fed and it backfired. They need to spread the load this season and get more out of Fuller and B. Miller. If Watson becomes QB, look for RB targets to dip.

Player *Min 50 Targets*	Targets	Comp %	YPA	Rating	TOARS	Success %	Success Rk	Missed YPA Rk	YAS % Rk	TDs
DeAndre Hopkins	169	53%	6.3	55	4.9	46%	107	76	84	5
Will Fuller	103	52%	6.6	76	4.4	38%	139	133	29	2
C.J. Fiedorowicz	98	60%	6.4	88	4.6	49%	85	49	100	5
Ryan Griffin	81	65%	5.8	79	4.2	49%	79	58	127	2

Directional Passer Rating Delivered

Receiver	Short Left	Short Middle	Short Right	Deep Left	Deep Middle	Deep Right	Player Total
DeAndre Hopkins	79	76	25	34	51	73	55
Will Fuller	116	92	93	52	24	52	76
C.J. Fiedorowicz	83	93	92	40	96		88
Ryan Griffin	67	83	109	96	11	86	79
Lamar Miller	96	129	70				90
Braxton Miller	52	112	36		0	40	44
Jonathan Grimes	97	104	69				92
Team Total	85	94	70	47	41	62	72

2016 Rushing Recap & 2017 Outlook

Against the 7th easiest schedule of opposing run defenses, Lamar Miller was a disappointment and showed little signs of the explosiveness that he flashed in Miami. He ranked 50th in early down rushing & 53rd in overall rushing success. On 1st and 10 rushes, Miller averaged 3.8 yards per carry and a 45% success rate, which ranked 38th last year. Miller was best in short yardage situations, needing 3 yards or less for a first down, Miller's 78% success rate was 4th best in the NFL. Which is why it was surprising that the Texans did not run the ball more often on 2nd and short. They converted a 92% success rate on rushes, but called pass plays above average. Miller needs more success in the red zone but was at his best inside the 5.

Player *Min 50 Rushes*	Rushes	YPA	Success %	Success Rk	Missed YPA Rk	YTS % Rk	YAS % Rk	Early Down Success %	Early Down Success Rk	TDs
Lamar Miller	318	3.8	42%	53	44	53	48	42%	50	6
Alfred Blue	103	4.1	43%	48	23	50	42	42%	52	1

Yards per Carry by Direction

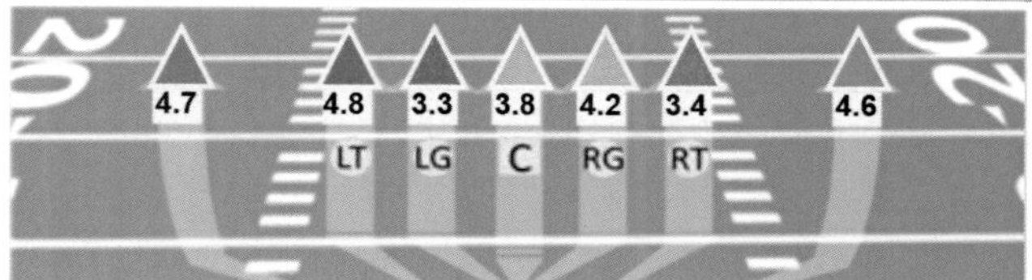

Directional Run Frequency

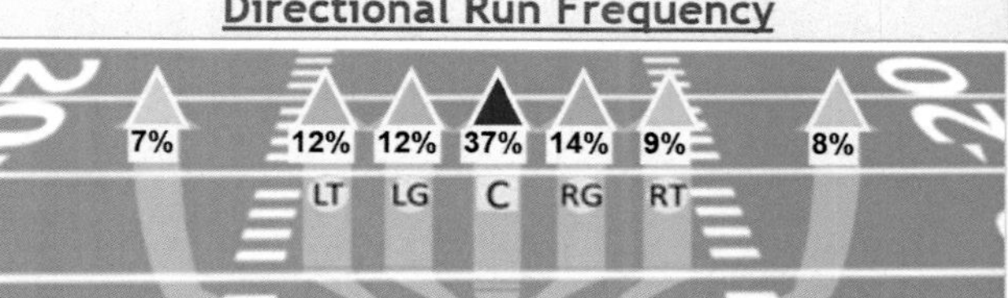

their wins were by 7, 7, 3, 7, 3, 5, 1 and 2 points. They trailed entering the 4th quarter 9 times, and in 3 of those games, they put up double digit points in the 4th quarter to win the game. After going 0-5 in 2015 when losing the turnover battle, they won 3 of 8 games in 2016. The Texans season was highly volatile, and they easily could have been much worse. In fact, their Pythagorean wins for the 2016 season was only 6.5 wins instead of the 9 they won.

With all of that in mind, what about this year's Texans squad? The first question is who is their quarterback. It likely will be a 2 man battle between Tom Savage and rookie Deshaun Watson from Clemson. Comparing Savage's numbers to Osweiler's last year (see the player metrics page) Savage posted better standard stats, a better success rate and early down success rate and better explosive passing numbers. Last year the Texans thought with Will Fuller's speed, Brock Osweiler would be more successful on deep passes, but he was not. Perhaps he would be better with Savage under center.

But here is the other issue. The run game was not strong last year, and Lamar Miller didn't make the impact he was projected, as the offense ranked 6th worst in rushing efficiency despite playing the 7th easiest schedule of run defenses. Part of that had to do with the offensive line, which was the 2nd most injured of any in the NFL last year. Hopefully they will be healthier this year, but the run defenses will not be easier.

The Texans are projected to face the 12th most difficult schedule of run defenses this year, the 3rd largest increase in difficulty felt by any team as compared to 2016. Lamar Miller gained just 3.8 yards per carry on his 318 total rushes. His 42% success rate ranked 53rd in the NFL. He ranked 44th in Missed YPA (how close he came to grading as successful on runs which were unsuccessful) and 48th in YAS %. Even inside the red zone, he was successful on just 44% of his 39 total carries. Many times, run games are sparked by mobile quarterbacks. There is an inherent efficiency gained by the defense having to play for the possibility of a QB run call. This is why we see solid rushing numbers for OK running backs when playing with mobile quarterbacks. Think Alfred Morris when playing with Robert Griffin III. With Griffin in 2012 and 2013, Morris averaged 4.7 yards per attempt and scored 20 rushing TDs. His last 2 years in Washington (without Griffin for most games), Morris averaged just 3.9 yards per attempt and only 3.5 in Dallas last year.

The Texans must take a holistic approach to their quarterback decision for 2017. They can have a solid season because the defense should still be stout with a healthy JJ Watt alongside Jadeveon Clowney and Whitney Mercilus up front and they face a much easier schedule (5th hardest last year, 11th easiest this year) as well. Houston doesn't need their QB to be proficient on 35 attempts. They need a strong running game and 22 attempts, without interceptions and several timely throws.

Division History: Season Wins & 2017 Projection

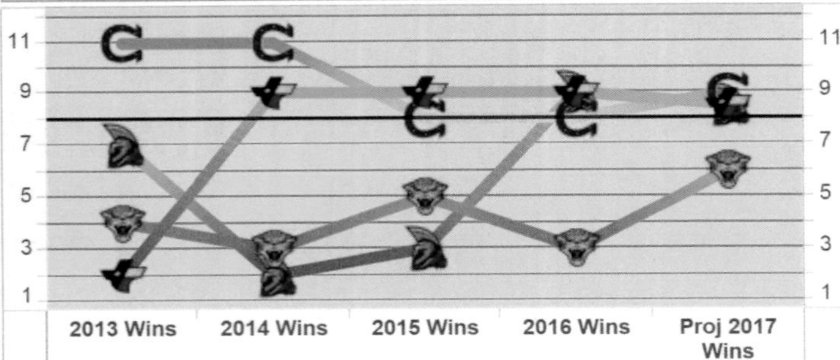

Rank of 2017 Defensive Pass Efficiency Faced by Week

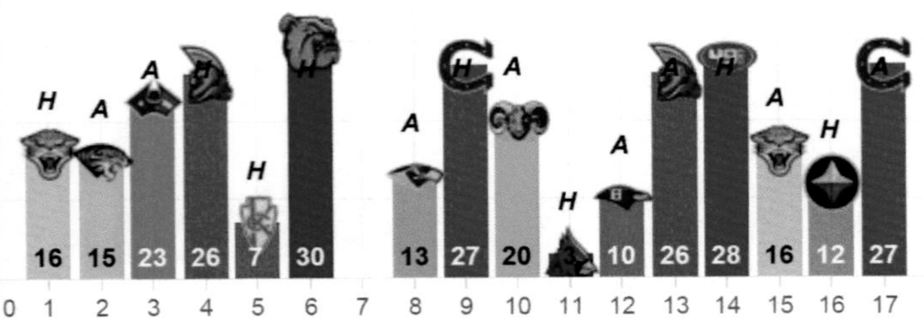

Rank of 2017 Defensive Rush Efficiency Faced by Week

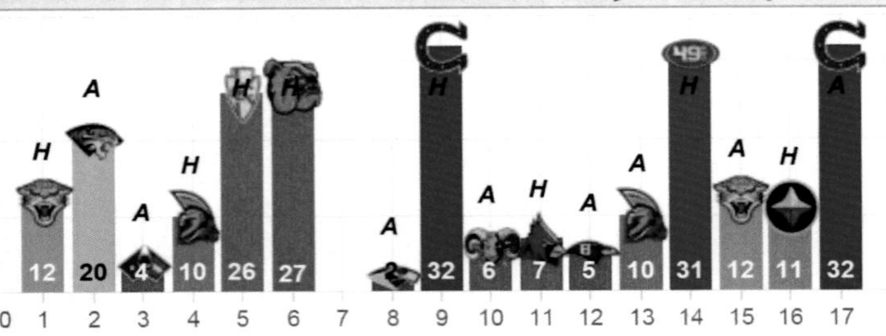

2016 Situational Usage by Player & Position

Usage Rate by Score

		Being Blown Out (14+)	Down Big (9-13)	One Score	Large Lead (9-13)	Blowout Lead (14+)	Grand Total
RUSH	Lamar Miller	10%	31%	30%	48%		28%
	Alfred Blue	9%	2%	11%		11%	9%
	Will Fuller		1%				0%
	Jonathan Grimes	3%	1%	2%	7%		3%
	Braxton Miller			0%			0%
	Akeem Hunt		1%	2%			2%
	Jay Prosch			1%	1%		0%
	Tyler Ervin			0%			0%
	Total	22%	36%	48%	56%	11%	43%
PASS	Lamar Miller	5%	9%	3%	4%		4%
	DeAndre Hopkins	16%	20%	14%	10%	22%	15%
	Alfred Blue	1%	1%	2%			1%
	Will Fuller	9%	9%	9%	14%	22%	9%
	C.J. Fiedorowicz	11%	6%	9%	7%	33%	9%
	Ryan Griffin	13%	12%	6%	1%		7%
	Jonathan Grimes	7%	1%	1%	1%		2%
	Braxton Miller	2%	3%	3%	1%	11%	2%
	Akeem Hunt		1%	1%	1%		1%
	Jaelen Strong	8%		1%			2%
	Stephen Anderson	1%		2%	3%		2%
	Keith Mumphery	2%	1%	1%	1%		1%
	Wendall Williams	2%	1%	0%			1%
	Jay Prosch			0%			0%
	Tyler Ervin		1%	0%			0%
	Total	78%	64%	52%	44%	89%	57%

Positional Target Distribution vs NFL Average

		NFL Wide				Team Only			
		Left	Middle	Right	Total	Left	Middle	Right	Total
Deep	WR	1,004	563	963	**2,530**	27	18	38	**83**
	TE	152	141	159	**452**	6	6	4	**16**
	RB	25	4	40	**69**				
	All	**1,181**	**708**	**1,162**	**3,051**	**33**	**24**	**42**	**99**
Short	WR	3,005	1,722	3,106	**7,833**	88	49	80	**217**
	TE	788	831	1,080	**2,699**	48	44	71	**163**
	RB	995	608	1,078	**2,681**	20	14	35	**69**
	All	**4,788**	**3,161**	**5,264**	**13,213**	**156**	**107**	**186**	**449**
Total		**5,969**	**3,869**	**6,426**	**16,264**	**189**	**131**	**228**	**548**

Positional Success Rates vs NFL Average

		NFL Wide				Team Only			
		Left	Middle	Right	Total	Left	Middle	Right	Total
Deep	WR	37%	51%	39%	**41%**	19%	33%	21%	**23%**
	TE	45%	50%	43%	**46%**	33%	33%	50%	**38%**
	RB	32%	75%	25%	**30%**				
	All	**38%**	**51%**	**39%**	**41%**	**21%**	**33%**	**24%**	**25%**
Short	WR	52%	57%	52%	**53%**	53%	51%	41%	**48%**
	TE	51%	62%	52%	**55%**	40%	55%	55%	**50%**
	RB	47%	49%	44%	**46%**	65%	79%	40%	**55%**
	All	**51%**	**57%**	**50%**	**52%**	**51%**	**56%**	**46%**	**50%**
Total		**48%**	**56%**	**48%**	**50%**	**46%**	**52%**	**42%**	**46%**

Indianapolis Colts

2017 Coaches

Head Coach:
Chuck Pagano (6th yr)
Offensive Coordinator:
Rob Chudzinski (3rd yr)
Defensive Coordinator:
Ted Monachino (3rd yr)

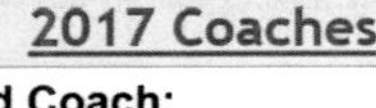

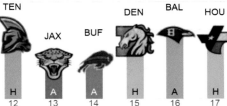

2017 Forecast

Wins	Div Rank
9	#2

Past Records

2016: 8-8
2015: 8-8
2014: 11-5

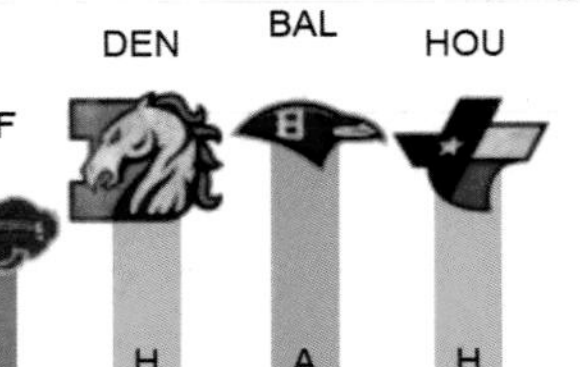

EASY HARD

Week	1	2	3	4	5	6	7	8	9	10	11	12	13	14	15	16	17
Opponent	LAR	ARI	CLE	SEA	SF	TEN	JAX	CIN	HOU	PIT		TEN	JAX	BUF	DEN	BAL	HOU
H/A	A	H	H	A	H	A	H	A	A	H		H	A	A	H	A	H
Note				SNF		MNF									TNF	SAT	

Key Players Lost

TXN	Player (POS)
Cut	Jackson, D'Qwell LB
	Jones, Arthur DT
	Overton, Matt LB
	Porter, Reggie CB
	Robinson, Patrick CB
	Street, Devin WR
Declared Free Agent	Adams, Mike S
	Butler, Darius CB
	Carter, Chris LB
	Cole, Trent LB
	Harrison, Jonotthan C
	Kerr, Zach NT
	Mathis, Robert LB
	McNary, Josh LB
	Thornton, Hugh G
	Todman, Jordan RB
	Turbin, Robert RB
	Walden, Erik LB
Retired	McAfee, Pat P
	Reitz, Joe T

Average Line	# Games Favored	# Games Underdog
-1.0	8	7

2017 Indianapolis Colts Overview

The trajectory of the Indianapolis Colts in Andrew Luck's 2nd contract changed immediately the moment GM Ryan Grigson was fired and GM Chris Ballard was hired. Expect to see the impact this very season. For years, Grigson believed in building his offense through the draft and his defense through free agency. The Colts fielded the NFL's most expensive defense in 2015, and from 2013 through 2015, it was the 2nd most expensive defense based on cap dollar allocation. The problem with that strategy is obvious. Since the 2011 CBA, slotted contracts and 5th year options have allowed the smartest teams to stockpile draft picks and often let free agents walk for compensatory selections. As the salary cap started to grow considerably the last couple of years, some of the smartest teams have signed a few, targeted free agents from other teams, but they still build through the draft.

Looking at the defensive advanced metrics, it is clear Ballard made a strong statement to address the Colts needs on defense by drafting two players for the secondary (S Malik Hooker, CB Quincy Wilson) in the first two rounds and adding DE Tarell Basham in the 3rd round. Last year the Colts faced the NFL's 3rd easiest schedule of opposing offenses. They played 7 games against offenses which ranked bottom-6 in the NFL. And yet their defense ranked dead last in EDSR (Early Down Success Rate) and 29th in total defensive efficiency. They badly lost the EDSR battle in 5 of their first 6 games, and lost to the Lions, Broncos, Jaguars and Texans in the process. For years the Colts had been "good enough" to get to the playoffs but not good enough to beat a "complete" opponent.

The defense will look much different this season with a lot of new faces. Penciling in both rookies in the secondary as starters, along with free agent acquisitions NT Johnathan Hankins, LB Jabaal Sheard, LB John Simon and ILB Sean Spence, there is the potential for 6 new starters on the field defensively. The defense will be fortunate in that it is forecast to face the NFL's easiest schedule of opposing offenses. In addition to their division rivals whose offenses have struggled for years, such as the Jaguars and Texans, the Colts also get to face the offenses of the Rams, Browns, 49ers, Ravens and Broncos. Listed there are over half (9) of their 16 opponents whose offenses are legitimately works in progress, to put it kindly. Importantly, none of those offenses have quarterbacks of Andrew Luck's caliber. So this defense gets a nice

(cont'd - see IND2)

Key Free Agents/ Trades Added

Aiken, Kamar WR
Boyd, Josh DT
Hankins, Johnathan DT
Hunt, Margus DE
Michael, Christine RB
Mingo, Barkevious LB
Sheard, Jabaal DE
Simon, John LB
Spence, Sean LB
Woods, Al NT

Drafted Players

Rd	Pk	Player (College)
1	15	S - Malik Hooker (Ohio State)
2	46	CB - Quincy Wilson (Florida)
3	80	DE - Tarell Basham (Ohio)
4	137	G - Zach Banner (USC)
4*	143	RB - Marlon Mack (South Florida)
	144	DT - Grover Stewart (Albany State)
5	158	CB - Nate Hairston (Temple)
	161	LB - Anthony Walker Jr. (Northwestern)

Regular Season Wins: Past & Current Proj

Proj 2017 Wins	9
2016 Wins	8
Proj 2016 Wins	9
2015 Wins	8
2014 Wins	11
2013 Wins	11

1 3 5 7 9 11 13 15

2017 Lineup & Cap Hits

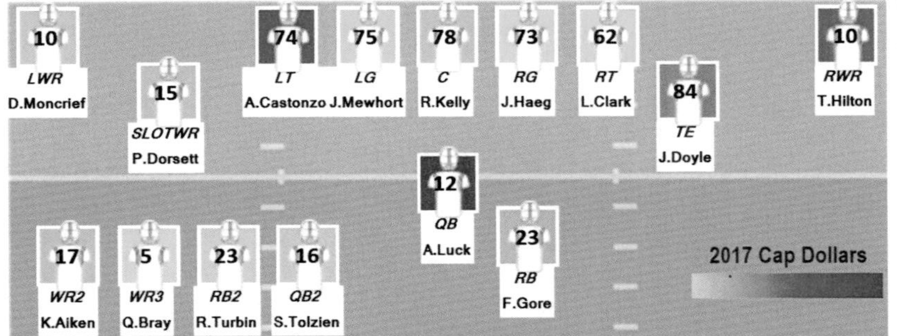

2017 Unit Spending

All DEF All OFF

Positional Spending

	Rank	Total	2016 Rk
All OFF	13	$84.87M	10
QB	10	$22.41M	13
OL	26	$23.52M	18
RB	16	$7.07M	15
WR	14	$20.77M	21
TE	9	$11.10M	4
All DEF	18	$77.01M	25
DL	18	$24.92M	30
LB	7	$27.43M	7
CB	18	$18.19M	14
S	26	$6.46M	29

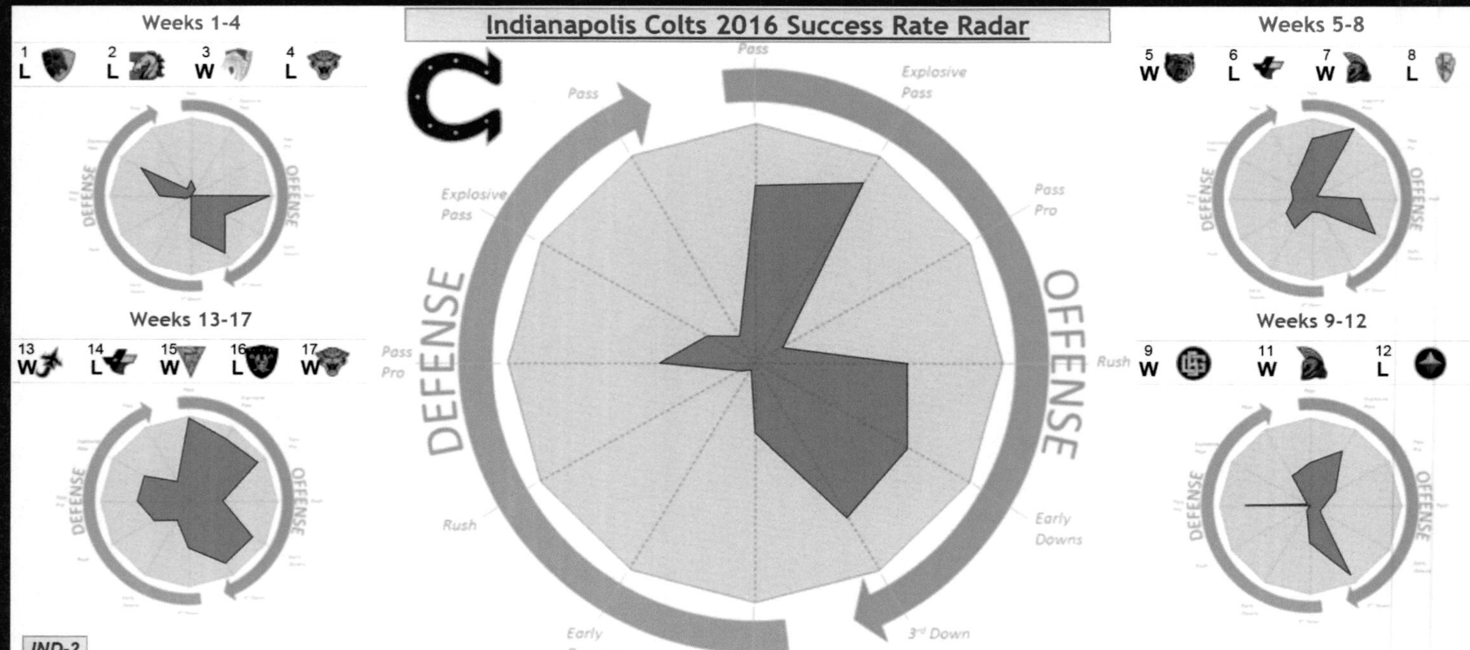

IND-2

head start thanks to the schedule, but it has a lot of ground to make up with a lot of new pieces.

Offensively, the Colts were tremendous last season despite constant injuries to their most vital player. Andrew Luck was listed on the injury report as a "full" participant in half of the Colts regular season practices. He sustained injuries to his right shoulder, elbow and thumb, his left ankle as well as a concussion. His injured shoulder was so bad that he decided to undergo shoulder surgery in January. Luck said hits he took during the course of the season continued to bother his shoulder. There are no assurances he'll be ready for the start of training camp, but there have not been any setbacks and even if he misses some of camp, there is no indication at all that he won't be ready for week 1. Andrew Luck has his offensive line, in large part, to thank for his injury. He was the NFL's most pressured quarterback last year. But despite all of those things, and learning a new offensive system, Luck was actually great last year. It gets overlooked because of the team's 8-8 record, but let's examine what Luck was able to do with this offense las..

Against the 11th most difficult schedule of opposing pass defenses last year. Luck posted a career best 63.5% completion rate while simultaneously posting a career best 7.8 yards per attempt. Those two metrics are inherently diametrically opposed. It might not be surprising to see a quarterback post a career best completion rate if he started throwing the ball much closer to the line of scrimmage. Or a quarterback could be coached to start attacking deeper, which might increase his yards per attempt while decreasing his completion rate. Luck increased both metrics together, to career bests. This was despite a sack rate of 7%, a career high, after recording 4.9% and 4.2% the prior two seasons.

Luck recorded a 48% success rate (+4% vs NFL avg) and a 52% EDSR success rate (+4% vs NFL avg). He recorded a better deep passing attack than average, with 6% of his yardage coming on 20+ air yard passes (+2% vs NFL avg). And as his passing cone clearly visualizes, his deep passing was tremendous:

*(cont'd - see **IND-3**)*

2016 Offensive Advanced Metrics

	Rank
EDSR Off	3
30 & In Off	10
Red Zone Off	5
3rd Down Off	10
YPPA Off	7
YPPT Off	10
Offensive Efficiency	12
Pass Efficiency Off	15
Pass Pro Efficiency Off	28
RB Pass Eff Off	15
Rush Efficiency Off	10
Explosive Pass Off	8
Explosive Run Off	28

2016 Defensive Advanced Metrics

	Rank
EDSR Def	32
30 & In Def	26
Red Zone Def	6
3rd Down Def	25
YPPA Def	23
YPPT Def	17
Defensive Efficiency	29
Pass Efficiency Def	27
Pass Pro Efficiency Def	13
RB Pass Eff Def	31
Rush Efficiency Def	32
Explosive Pass Def	20
Explosive Run Def	30

2016 Weekly EDSR & Season Trending Performance

WEEK	1	2	3	4	5	6	7	8	9	11	12	13	14	15	16	17
RESULT	L	L	W	L	W	L	W	L	W	W	L	W	L	W	L	W
OPP	DET	DEN	SD	JAC	CHI	HOU	TEN	KC	GB	TEN	PIT	NYJ	HOU	MIN	OAK	JAC
SITE	H	A	H	N	H	A	A	H	A	H	H	A	H	A	A	H
MARGIN	-4	-14	4	-3	6	-3	8	-16	5	7	-21	31	-5	28	-8	4
PTS	35	20	26	27	29	23	34	14	31	24	7	41	17	34	25	24
OPP PTS	39	34	22	30	23	26	26	30	26	17	28	10	22	6	33	20

EDSR by Wk
W=Green
L=Red

OFF/DEF EDSR
Blue=OFF (high=good)
Red=DEF (low=good)

2016 Close Game Records

All 2016 Wins: **8**
FG Games (<=3 pts) W-L: **0-2**
FG Games Win %: **0% (#29)**
FG Games Wins (% of Total Wins): **0% (#30)**
1 Score Games (<=8 pts) W-L: **6-5**
1 Score Games Win %: **55% (#14)**
1 Score Games Wins (% of Total Wins): **75% (#8)**

2016 Critical & Game-Deciding Stats

TO Margin	-5
TO Given	22
INT Given	15
FUM Given	7
TO Taken	17
INT Taken	8
FUM Taken	9
Sack Margin	-11
Sacks	33
Sacks Allow	44
Return TD Margin	-1
Ret TDs	2
Ret TDs Allow	3
Penalty Margin	+23
Penalties	102
Opponent Penalties	125

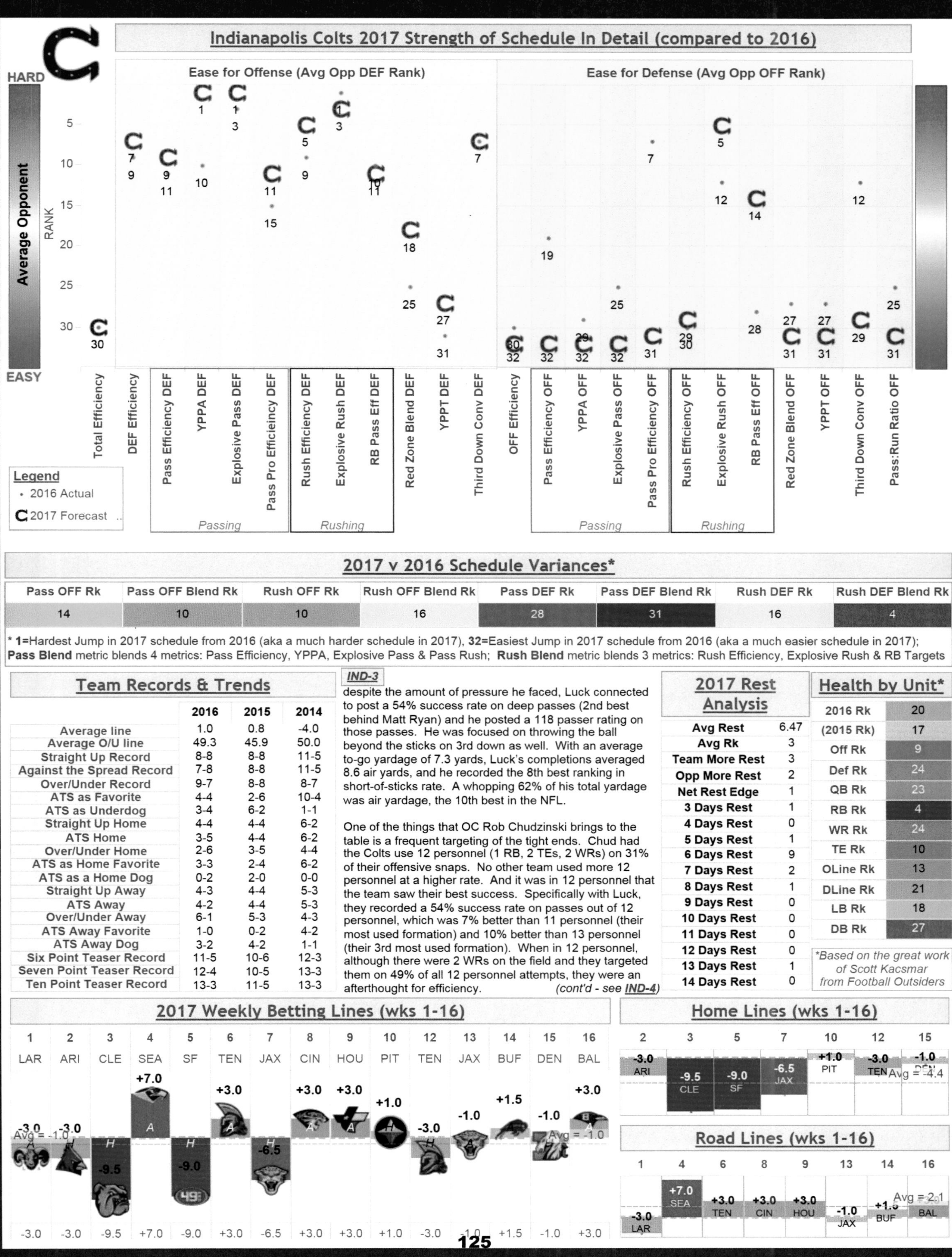

Indianapolis Colts 2017 Strength of Schedule In Detail (compared to 2016)

2017 v 2016 Schedule Variances*

Pass OFF Rk	Pass OFF Blend Rk	Rush OFF Rk	Rush OFF Blend Rk	Pass DEF Rk	Pass DEF Blend Rk	Rush DEF Rk	Rush DEF Blend Rk
14	10	10	16	28	31	16	4

* **1**=Hardest Jump in 2017 schedule from 2016 (aka a much harder schedule in 2017), **32**=Easiest Jump in 2017 schedule from 2016 (aka a much easier schedule in 2017); **Pass Blend** metric blends 4 metrics: Pass Efficiency, YPPA, Explosive Pass & Pass Rush; **Rush Blend** metric blends 3 metrics: Rush Efficiency, Explosive Rush & RB Targets

Team Records & Trends

	2016	2015	2014
Average line	1.0	0.8	-4.0
Average O/U line	49.3	45.9	50.0
Straight Up Record	8-8	8-8	11-5
Against the Spread Record	7-8	8-8	11-5
Over/Under Record	9-7	8-8	8-7
ATS as Favorite	4-4	2-6	10-4
ATS as Underdog	3-4	6-2	1-1
Straight Up Home	4-4	4-4	6-2
ATS Home	3-5	4-4	6-2
Over/Under Home	2-6	3-5	4-4
ATS as Home Favorite	3-3	2-4	6-2
ATS as a Home Dog	0-2	2-0	0-0
Straight Up Away	4-3	4-4	5-3
ATS Away	4-2	4-4	5-3
Over/Under Away	6-1	5-3	4-3
ATS Away Favorite	1-0	0-2	4-2
ATS Away Dog	3-2	4-2	1-1
Six Point Teaser Record	11-5	10-6	12-3
Seven Point Teaser Record	12-4	10-5	13-3
Ten Point Teaser Record	13-3	11-5	13-3

IND-3

despite the amount of pressure he faced, Luck connected to post a 54% success rate on deep passes (2nd best behind Matt Ryan) and he posted a 118 passer rating on those passes. He was focused on throwing the ball beyond the sticks on 3rd down as well. With an average to-go yardage of 7.3 yards, Luck's completions averaged 8.6 air yards, and he recorded the 8th best ranking in short-of-sticks rate. A whopping 62% of his total yardage was air yardage, the 10th best in the NFL.

One of the things that OC Rob Chudzinski brings to the table is a frequent targeting of the tight ends. Chud had the Colts use 12 personnel (1 RB, 2 TEs, 2 WRs) on 31% of their offensive snaps. No other team used more 12 personnel at a higher rate. And it was in 12 personnel that the team saw their best success. Specifically with Luck, they recorded a 54% success rate on passes out of 12 personnel, which was 7% better than 11 personnel (their most used formation) and 10% better than 13 personnel (their 3rd most used formation). When in 12 personnel, although there were 2 WRs on the field and they targeted them on 49% of all 12 personnel attempts, they were an afterthought for efficiency. *(cont'd - see **IND-4**)*

2017 Rest Analysis

Avg Rest	6.47
Avg Rk	3
Team More Rest	3
Opp More Rest	2
Net Rest Edge	1
3 Days Rest	1
4 Days Rest	0
5 Days Rest	1
6 Days Rest	9
7 Days Rest	2
8 Days Rest	1
9 Days Rest	0
10 Days Rest	0
11 Days Rest	0
12 Days Rest	0
13 Days Rest	1
14 Days Rest	0

Health by Unit*

2016 Rk	20
(2015 Rk)	17
Off Rk	9
Def Rk	24
QB Rk	23
RB Rk	4
WR Rk	24
TE Rk	10
OLine Rk	13
DLine Rk	21
LB Rk	18
DB Rk	27

**Based on the great work of Scott Kacsmar from Football Outsiders*

2017 Weekly Betting Lines (wks 1-16)

1	2	3	4	5	6	7	8	9	10	12	13	14	15	16
LAR	ARI	CLE	SEA	SF	TEN	JAX	CIN	HOU	PIT	TEN	JAX	BUF	DEN	BAL
H	H	H	A	H	A	H	A	A	H	A	A	A	H	A
-3.0	-3.0	-9.5	+7.0	-9.0	+3.0	-6.5	+3.0	+3.0	+1.0	-3.0	-1.0	+1.5	-1.0	+3.0

Avg = -1.0

Home Lines (wks 1-16)

2	3	5	7	10	12	15
ARI	CLE	SF	JAX	PIT	TEN	DEN
-3.0	-9.5	-9.0	-6.5	+1.0	-3.0	-1.0

Avg = -4.4

Road Lines (wks 1-16)

1	4	6	8	9	13	14	16
LAR	SEA	TEN	CIN	HOU	JAX	BUF	BAL
-3.0	+7.0	+3.0	+3.0	+3.0	-1.0	+1.5	+3.0

Avg = 2.1

Indianapolis Colts 2016 Play Analysis

2016 Play Tendencies

All Pass %	58%
All Pass Rk	19
All Rush %	42%
All Rush Rk	14
1 Score Pass %	59%
1 Score Pass Rk	15
2015 1 Score Pass %	59%
2015 1 Score Pass Rk	13
Pass Increase %	-1%
Pass Increase Rk	17
1 Score Rush %	41%
1 Score Rush Rk	18
Up Pass %	57%
Up Pass Rk	16
Up Rush %	43%
Up Rush Rk	17
Down Pass %	60%
Down Pass Rk	23
Down Rush %	40%
Down Rush Rk	10

2016 Down & Distance Tendencies

Down	Distance	Total Plays	Pass Rate	Run Rate	Play Success %
1	Short (1-3)	7	43%	57%	29%
	Med (4-7)	19	32%	68%	58%
	Long (8-10)	313	50%	50%	50%
	XL (11+)	11	91%	9%	18%
2	Short (1-3)	48	35%	65%	58%
	Med (4-7)	76	49%	51%	68%
	Long (8-10)	103	70%	30%	45%
	XL (11+)	29	86%	14%	31%
3	Short (1-3)	60	63%	37%	55%
	Med (4-7)	37	84%	16%	41%
	Long (8-10)	25	84%	16%	36%
	XL (11+)	21	86%	14%	33%
4	Short (1-3)	5	80%	20%	60%
	Med (4-7)	3	67%	33%	67%

Shotgun %:

Under Center	Shotgun
43%	57%
37%	*63%*

AVG

Run Rate:

Under Center	Shotgun
66%	15%
68%	*23%*

AVG

Pass Rate:

Under Center	Shotgun
34%	85%
32%	*77%*

AVG

Short Yardage Intelligence:

2nd and Short Run

Run Freq	Run % Rk	NFL Run Freq Avg	Run 1D Rate	Run NFL 1D Avg
61%	22	65%	64%	71%

2nd and Short Pass

Pass Freq	Pass % Rk	NFL Pass Freq Avg	Pass 1D Rate	Pass NFL 1D Avg
39%	9	35%	64%	52%

Most Frequent Play

Down	Distance	Play Type	Player	Total Plays	Play Success %
1	Short (1-3)	RUSH	Frank Gore	3	0%
	Med (4-7)	RUSH	Robert Turbin	7	71%
	Long (8-10)	RUSH	Frank Gore	130	44%
	XL (11+)	PASS	Ty Hilton	3	33%
2	Short (1-3)	RUSH	Frank Gore	24	58%
	Med (4-7)	RUSH	Frank Gore	29	66%
	Long (8-10)	RUSH	Frank Gore	22	27%
	XL (11+)	PASS	Ty Hilton	10	40%
3	Short (1-3)	RUSH	Robert Turbin	8	100%
	Med (4-7)	PASS	Ty Hilton	6	67%
			Dwayne Allen	6	67%
		RUSH	Andrew Luck	6	50%
	Long (8-10)	PASS	Ty Hilton	6	33%
	XL (11+)	PASS	Ty Hilton	5	60%

Most Successful Play*

Down	Distance	Play Type	Player	Total Plays	Play Success %
1	Med (4-7)	RUSH	Robert Turbin	7	71%
	Long (8-10)	PASS	Jack Doyle	25	72%
2	Short (1-3)	RUSH	Robert Turbin	5	80%
	Med (4-7)	PASS	Frank Gore	5	80%
			Dwayne Allen	5	80%
	Long (8-10)	PASS	Dwayne Allen	9	67%
	XL (11+)	PASS	Ty Hilton	10	40%
3	Short (1-3)	RUSH	Robert Turbin	8	100%
	Med (4-7)	PASS	Ty Hilton	6	67%
			Dwayne Allen	6	67%
	Long (8-10)	PASS	Ty Hilton	6	33%
	XL (11+)	PASS	Ty Hilton	5	60%

**Minimum 5 plays to qualify*

2016 Snap Rates

Week	Opp	Score	Ty Hilton	Phillip Dorsett	Jack Doyle	Frank Gore	Dwayne Allen	Donte Moncrief	Chester Rogers
1	DET	L 39-35	67 (96%)	51 (73%)	39 (56%)	48 (69%)	49 (70%)	68 (97%)	
2	DEN	L 34-20	64 (88%)	61 (84%)	45 (62%)	35 (48%)	62 (85%)	9 (12%)	23 (32%)
3	SD	W 26-22	62 (87%)	62 (87%)	53 (75%)	43 (61%)	59 (83%)		31 (44%)
4	JAC	L 30-27	75 (96%)	71 (91%)	40 (51%)	34 (44%)	62 (79%)		51 (65%)
5	CHI	W 29-23	61 (90%)	64 (94%)	28 (41%)	54 (79%)	48 (71%)		54 (79%)
6	HOU	L 26-23	73 (99%)	55 (74%)	66 (89%)	47 (64%)	6 (8%)		53 (72%)
7	TEN	W 34-26	68 (97%)		66 (94%)	57 (81%)			57 (81%)
8	KC	L 30-14	54 (82%)	56 (85%)	50 (76%)	32 (48%)		59 (89%)	
9	GB	W 31-26	59 (87%)	42 (62%)	50 (74%)	47 (69%)	44 (65%)	66 (97%)	1 (1%)
11	TEN	W 24-17	52 (87%)	34 (57%)	39 (65%)	44 (73%)	49 (82%)	56 (93%)	1 (2%)
12	PIT	L 28-7	25 (40%)	47 (75%)	38 (60%)	35 (56%)	40 (63%)	62 (98%)	27 (43%)
13	NYJ	W 41-10	46 (63%)	40 (55%)	51 (70%)	45 (62%)	45 (62%)	64 (88%)	18 (25%)
14	HOU	L 22-17	63 (95%)	53 (80%)	42 (64%)	33 (50%)	38 (58%)	47 (71%)	18 (27%)
15	MIN	W 34-6	60 (86%)	57 (81%)	51 (73%)	38 (54%)	36 (51%)		42 (60%)
16	OAK	L 33-25	50 (91%)	38 (69%)	35 (64%)	26 (47%)	35 (64%)	36 (65%)	18 (33%)
17	JAC	W 24-20	69 (97%)	61 (86%)	58 (82%)	32 (45%)	41 (58%)		41 (58%)
Grand Total			948 (86%)	792 (77%)	751 (68%)	650 (59%)	614 (64%)	467 (79%)	435 (44%)

Personnel Groupings

Personnel	Team %	NFL Avg	Succ. %
1-1 [3WR]	60%	60%	48%
1-2 [2WR]	31%	19%	52%
1-3 [1WR]	7%	3%	34%

Grouping Tendencies

Personnel	Pass Rate	Pass Succ. %	Run Succ. %
1-1 [3WR]	71%	47%	51%
1-2 [2WR]	51%	54%	50%
1-3 [1WR]	24%	44%	30%

Red Zone Targets (min 3)

Receiver	All	Inside 5	6-10	11-20
Ty Hilton	14	5	3	6
Jack Doyle	13	2	4	7
Donte Moncrief	10	5	1	4
Dwayne Allen	9	3	2	4
Phillip Dorsett	7	2	2	3
Frank Gore	6	2	2	2
Chester Rogers	5	3	1	1
Robert Turbin	5	3		2

Red Zone Rushes (min 3)

Rusher	All	Inside 5	6-10	11-20
Frank Gore	30	10	9	11
Robert Turbin	19	10	5	4
Josh Ferguson	8			8
Andrew Luck	7		1	6
Jordan Todman	3			3

Early Down Target Rate

RB	TE	WR
20%	27%	53%
19%	*20%* NFL AVG	*61%*

Overall Target Success %

RB	TE	WR
45% #15	64% #2	50% #15

Indianapolis Colts 2016 Passing Recap & 2017 Outlook

Andrew Luck was a huge pleasure to watch in this offense, except for watching him try to evade pressure and take hits, which happened far too often. The fact he hit career highs in completion rate and yards per attempt while posting the second best deep passing success rates was more than impressive. This year, the test is projected to get slightly harder because of the schedule. Luck must face the 9th rated pass defenses which allowed the NFL's lowest yards per pass attempt last year, and also ranked best in defending explosive passes. Fortunately, the start of the season is much easier than the end from that respect, so Luck should get off to a nice start through week 6. Luck's success rate to the deep right was better than to the deep left, particularly to TEs: when targeted 15+ yards downfield, targets to TEs were successful 71% of the time, which was +29% vs the NFL average. Luck could use more efficiency out of RB targets this year, particularly if they are going to target them above league average. Perhaps rookie Marlon Mack will provide explosiveness as a backfield target. Hopefully Erik Swoope is adequate to pair with Doyle to form a strong 2TE set, as the Colts love to use 12 personnel.

Andrew Luck Rating All Downs

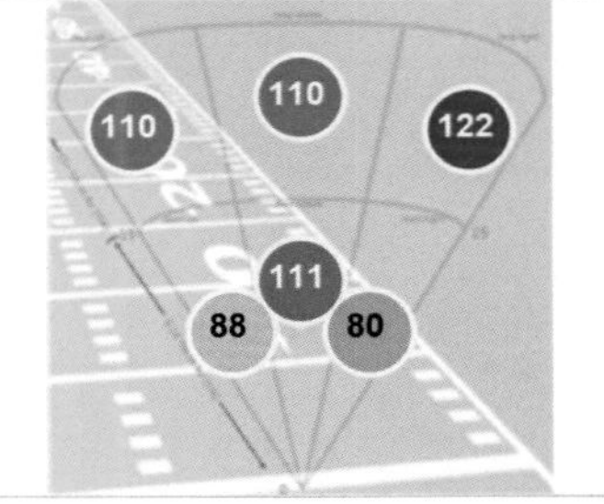

2016 Standard Passing Table

QB	Comp	Att	Comp %	Yds	YPA	TDs	INT	Sacks	Rating	Rk
Andrew Luck	346	545	63%	4,243	7.8	31	13	41	96.4	13
NFL Avg			63%		7.2				90.4	

Andrew Luck Rating Early Downs

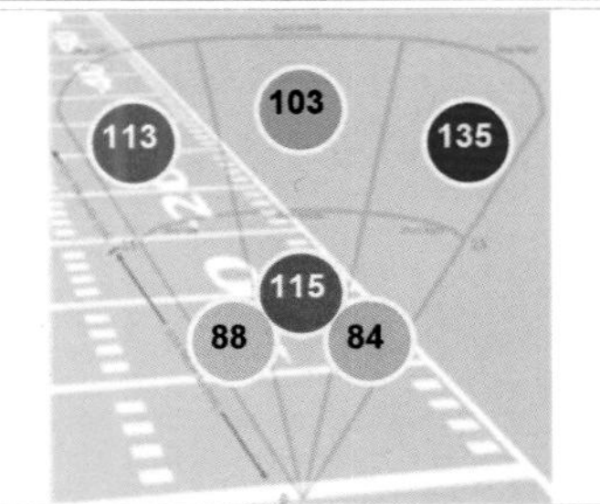

2016 Advanced Passing Table

QB	Success %	EDSR Passing Success %	20+ Yd Pass Gains	20+ Yd Pass %	30+ Yd Pass Gains	30+ Yd Pass %	Air Yds per Comp	YAC per Comp	20+ Air Yd Comp	20+ Air Yd %
Andrew Luck	48%	52%	61	11%	26	5%	7.5	4.7	32	6%
NFL Avg	44%	48%	27	8%	10	3%	6.4	4.8	12	4%

Interception Rates by Down

Yards to Go	1	2	3	4	Total
1 & 2	0.0%	0.0%	3.6%	0.0%	2.0%
3, 4, 5	0.0%	3.6%	2.8%		2.7%
6 - 9	0.0%	0.0%	2.5%	0.0%	0.9%
10 - 14	3.3%	1.4%	0.0%	0.0%	2.6%
15+	0.0%	0.0%	8.3%	0.0%	2.3%
Total	**2.8%**	**1.1%**	**2.8%**	**0.0%**	**2.2%**

3rd Down Passing - Short of Sticks Analysis

QB	Avg Yds to Go	Air Yds (of Comps)	Avg Yds Short	Short of Sticks Rate	Rk
Andrew Luck	7.3	8.6	0.0	43%	8
NFL Avg	7.6	6.8	-0.8	57%	

Air Yds vs YAC

	Air Yds %	YAC %	Rk
Andrew Luck	62%	38%	10
NFL Avg	54%	46%	

2016 Receiving Recap & 2017 Outlook

If Moncrief can post a healthy season, the Colts receiving corps will be deep and skilled. Moncrief has struggled to stay healthy and posted a very low 5.5 yards per attempt last year. But Moncrief is a lethal weapon in the red zone. 70% of his red zone targets were successful, including all 5 targets inside the 5. Not only was his success rate 100%, his TD rate was also 100%, scoring TDs on all 5 targets. Luck's success to TEs within 15 yards of the line of scrimmage was tremendous. 66% of those targets were successful (+12% vs NFL average). The rest of their targets to WRs and TEs within 15 yards were equal to the NFL average.

Player *Min 50 Targets*	Targets	Comp %	YPA	Rating	TOARS	Success %	Success Rk	Missed YPA Rk	YAS % Rk	TDs
Ty Hilton	155	59%	9.3	89	5.3	54%	45	71	18	6
Jack Doyle	75	79%	7.8	110	4.6	64%	5	8	118	5
Phillip Dorsett	59	56%	8.9	76	3.6	44%	116	109	20	2
Donte Moncrief	56	54%	5.5	94	3.8	48%	91	60	55	7
Dwayne Allen	52	67%	7.8	121	4.2	63%	6	6	69	6

Directional Passer Rating Delivered

Receiver	Short Left	Short Middle	Short Right	Deep Left	Deep Middle	Deep Right	Player Total
Ty Hilton	74	112	65	59	120	96	89
Jack Doyle	87	126	93	0	158	149	110
Phillip Dorsett	95	40	58	144	40	98	76
Donte Moncrief	82	103	75	104	83	35	94
Dwayne Allen	80	116	110	158	40	149	121
Frank Gore	104	128	113				120
Robert Turbin	102	95	73				95
Chester Rogers	72	56	20	119	84	110	70
Josh Ferguson	90	51	89				88
Erik Swoope	119	75	95	144	96	119	126
Team Total	93	112	80	107	109	103	98

2016 Rushing Recap & 2017 Outlook

Frank Gore is one of the toughest RBs in the NFL. He doesn't get the credit he deserves, because he's in the twilight of his career and no longer averages strong yards per attempt. But the fact that he always seems to drive forward and get close to what is required (#6 in Missed YPA) is extremely valuable to an offense. That said, the Colts are smart to rotate in Turbin near the goal line, because whether it was Gore getting used up elsewhere on the field or simply poor sample size, Turbin's success rate (90%) dwarfed Gore's (20%). If Mack can be rotated in for his explosiveness, this ground game can be very balanced. The key, however, will be to not slow down the tempo and pace of the offense to rotate in RBs in too predictable of roles.

Player *Min 50 Rushes*	Rushes	YPA	Success %	Success Rk	Missed YPA Rk	YTS % Rk	YAS % Rk	Early Down Success %	Early Down Success Rk	TDs
Frank Gore	263	3.9	48%	33	6	21	61	48%	34	4

Yards per Carry by Direction

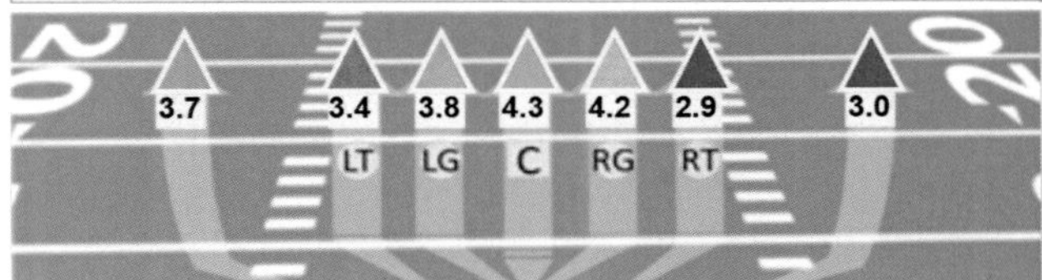

Directional Run Frequency

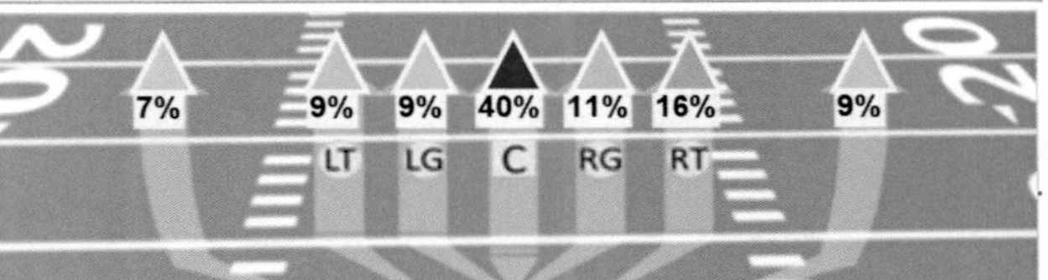

WRs in 12 personnel posted a 53% success rate and an 83 passer rating. Passes targeting TEs and RBs hit a 59% success rate and a 130 passer rating. Due to the amount of time the Colts also spent in 11 personnel, TEs were also targeted often there, and they excelled, posting a 60% success rate, a 119 rating and a 7:1 TD:INT ratio.

Thanks to Chud's principles, the Colts targeted tight ends on 27% of their attempts, 3rd most in the NFL. And even with those tendencies on tape, the Colts still recorded a 64% success rate to their tight ends, the 2nd best mark in the NFL. That rating was substantially better than targeting WRs (50% success rate, 15th) or RBs (45% success rate, 15th). The Colts lost TE Dwayne Allen to the New England Patriots this offseason, as he was brought in to replace Martellus Bennett. This move thrusts Jack Doyle firmly into the TE1 role. As you can visualize by looking at the 2016 Snap Rates, when Allen was injured against the Texans and then missed the next two games, Doyle played 66, 66 and 50 snaps in the 3 games without Allen.

Against the Texans, Doyle delivered a 100% success rate and a perfect 158.3 passer rating, catching all 4 targets while averaging 13.3 yards per attempt and scoring 1 TD. All of those were team highs for the Colts. On the road against the Titans the following week, Doyle beasted. He was targeted 10 times, he caught 9 for 78 yards, a 60% success rate and a 133 rating. And inside the red zone, the Colts had 6 targets. Doyle was targeted on 5 of the 6, catching 4 for 1 TD and a 120 rating. In the last game before Allen returned, the Colts only targeted Allen 3 times. They lost 30-14 at home against the Chiefs.

There is no doubt Doyle should produce solid numbers offensively this year. TE Erik Swoope will take over the TE2 role, which shouldn't be too much of a dropoff if he can deliver similar results to last year with less exposure. When targeted, Swoope recorded a 68% success rate and a 126 passer rating. If Moncrief can stay healthy (he missed 7 games last year) I have no doubt this receiving corps will deliver for Luck and Chud. Between the efficieincy of the TE position as well as the talent of T.Y. Hilton, Moncrief and Phillip Dorsett, this passing game will be just fine.

The run game is more of a question mark thanks to Frank Gore's age, but he held up last year for 263 carries. While fantasy owners won't like to hear this, the Colts should consider limiting Gore's rushes inside the 5, where he delivered only a 20% success rate on 10 carries, while RB Robert Turbin delivered a 90% success rate on the same number of carries. But Gore's best asset is his availability and his consistency, and he ranked 6th in the NFL for Missed YPA, so on the plays he didn't record a successful run, he came extremely close. That set up the Colts with more manageable situations on the next play, which was a huge benefit.

Division History: Season Wins & 2017 Projection

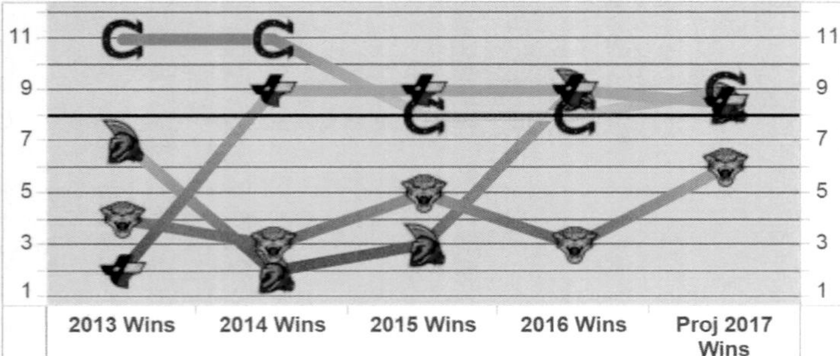

Rank of 2017 Defensive Pass Efficiency Faced by Week

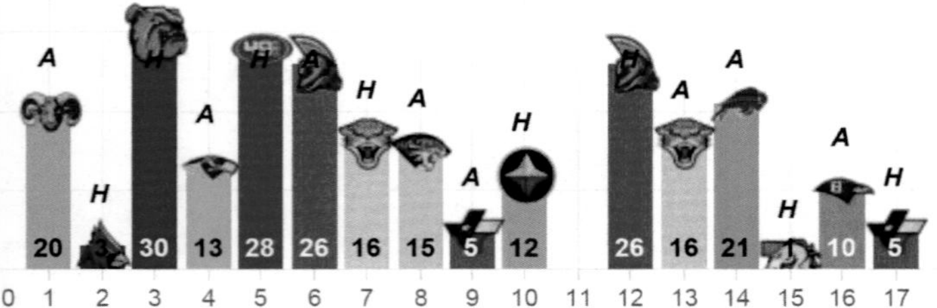

Rank of 2017 Defensive Rush Efficiency Faced by Week

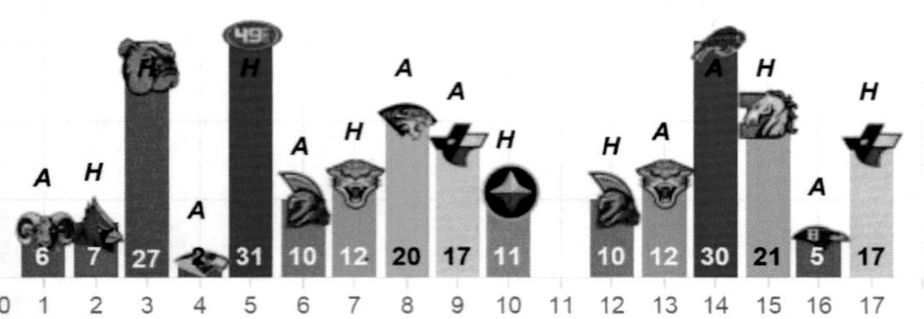

2016 Situational Usage by Player & Position

Usage Rate by Score

		Being Blown Out (14+)	Down Big (9-13)	One Score	Large Lead (9-13)	Blowout Lead (14+)	Grand Total
RUSH	Frank Gore	20%	21%	30%	38%	35%	29%
	Robert Turbin	4%	3%	5%	3%	10%	5%
	Phillip Dorsett			0%			0%
	Donte Moncrief	1%					0%
	Josh Ferguson	2%	1%	1%		7%	2%
	Jordan Todman	2%		0%		5%	1%
	Quan Bray			0%			0%
	Total	29%	26%	37%	42%	56%	37%
PASS	Frank Gore	5%	10%	5%	5%	4%	5%
	Ty Hilton	12%	23%	19%	10%	12%	17%
	Robert Turbin	7%	3%	3%	8%	2%	4%
	Jack Doyle	5%	12%	9%	8%	7%	8%
	Phillip Dorsett	9%	8%	7%	7%	2%	6%
	Donte Moncrief	12%	3%	5%	2%	9%	6%
	Dwayne Allen	11%	3%	6%		4%	6%
	Josh Ferguson	3%	6%	3%			3%
	Chester Rogers	2%	3%	4%	7%	2%	4%
	Erik Swoope	3%	2%	1%	12%	2%	2%
	Jordan Todman					1%	0%
	Devin Street	2%		1%			1%
	Quan Bray			1%			0%
	Total	71%	74%	63%	58%	44%	63%

Positional Target Distribution vs NFL Average

		NFL Wide				Team Only			
		Left	Middle	Right	Total	Left	Middle	Right	Total
Deep	WR	998	553	967	2,518	33	28	34	95
	TE	150	140	156	446	8	7	7	22
	RB	25	4	40	69				
	All	1,173	697	1,163	3,033	41	35	41	117
Short	WR	3,030	1,709	3,102	7,841	63	62	84	209
	TE	804	820	1,111	2,735	32	55	40	127
	RB	961	601	1,080	2,642	54	21	33	108
	All	4,795	3,130	5,293	13,218	149	138	157	444
Total		5,968	3,827	6,456	16,251	190	173	198	561

Positional Success Rates vs NFL Average

		NFL Wide				Team Only			
		Left	Middle	Right	Total	Left	Middle	Right	Total
Deep	WR	37%	50%	37%	40%	48%	46%	56%	51%
	TE	44%	50%	42%	45%	50%	43%	71%	55%
	RB	32%	75%	25%	30%				
	All	37%	50%	38%	41%	49%	46%	59%	51%
Short	WR	52%	57%	52%	53%	62%	52%	42%	51%
	TE	50%	61%	51%	54%	53%	71%	70%	66%
	RB	47%	50%	44%	46%	43%	43%	52%	45%
	All	51%	57%	50%	52%	53%	58%	51%	54%
Total		48%	55%	48%	50%	52%	55%	53%	53%

Jacksonville Jaguars

2017 Coaches

Head Coach:
Doug Marrone (JAC AHC) (1st yr)
Offensive Coordinator:
Nathaniel Hackett (Wk 7 2016) (2nd yr)
Defensive Coordinator:
Todd Wash (2nd yr)

2017 Forecast

Wins	Div Rank
6	#4

Past Records

2016: 3-13
2015: 5-11
2014: 3-13

EASY HARD

Week	1	2	3	4	5	6	7	8	9	10	11	12	13	14	15	16	17
Opponent	HOU	TEN	BAL (LON)	NYJ	PIT	LAR	IND		CIN	LAC	CLE	ARI	IND	SEA	HOU	SF	TEN
H/A	A	H	H	A	A	H	A		H	H	A	A	H	H	H	A	A

Key Players Lost

TXN	Player (POS)
Cut	House, Davon CB
	Marks, Sen'Derrick DT
	Miller III, Roy DT
	Odrick, Jared DT
	Porter, Sean LB
	Richardson, Daryl RB
	Skuta, Dan LB
	Van Roten, Greg G
	Walters, Bryan WR
Declared Free Agent	Alualu, Tyson DE
	Amukamara, Prince CB
	Banyard, Joe RB
	Beachum, Kelvin T
	Cyprien, Johnathan S
	Hill, Jordan DT
	Joeckel, Luke T
	Omameh, Patrick G
	Robinson, Denard RB
	Walters, Bryan WR
Retired	Scobee, Josh K

Average Line	# Games Favored	# Games Underdog
+1.7	4	10

Regular Season Wins: Past & Current Proj

	Wins
Proj 2017 Wins	6
2016 Wins	3
Proj 2016 Wins	7
2015 Wins	5
2014 Wins	3
2013 Wins	4

1 3 5 7 9 11 13 15

2017 Jacksonville Jaguars Overview

One would expect Tom Coughlin would bring more discipline to the front office. After spending the most in free agency in 2016 ($230M), the second most in 2015 ($176M) and the most in 2014 ($160M), the Jaguars posted 3-13, 5-11 and 3-13 records. Clearly not a team looking to learn from its mistakes, the Jaguars pulled out their best Uncle Rico impression, wishing they could go back in time and do it all over again, except even better. If they outspent everyone in free agency yet again, maybe, just maybe, they could take state. So the Jaguars spent $173M in free agency, the most of any team this offseason. While the Patriots spent more than typical in free agency this year, there is a big difference between handing out 1 out of every 6 deals as a market deal while making other guys sign for less to play for a Super Bowl contender, and what happens in Jacksonville, which is guys getting market deals, tax-free, to live in the sunshine state.

It's not that every single move was bad, but collectively they continue to be concerning. For example, after just one year of Toby Gerhart (signed as a free agent in 2014), the Jaguars drafted T.J. Yeldon 36th overall in the 2015 draft. That year, the Jaguars ranked 5th worst in rushing efficiency. Yeldon led the team in rushing with 182 carries. So in the 2016 offseason, the Jaguars decided to offer Chris Ivory a 5 year, $32M contract. It was the richest RB contract of the offseason; an offseason which saw a grand total of 26 free agent RBs signed for $61.6M. Chris Ivory's deal in Jacksonville was over half the total for all 26 RBs. Last year, despite the bounty paid to Ivory, T.J. Yeldon still led the team in rushing with 130 carries. Yeldon averaged only 3.6 yards per carry. On Ivory's 117 carries, he only averaged only 3.8 yards per carry, and battled injuries. And the Jaguars ranked 4th worst in rushing efficiency, even worse than the 5th worst they ranked in 2015. So the Jaguars went out this year and used their 4th overall pick on Leonard Fournette. That is a ridiculous amount of capital and draft pick value invested in the position of running back in the modern era of football. In terms of yearly average contract value, the Jaguars now have the #5 most expensive RB (Fournette at $6.8M annually) and the #7 most expensive RB (Ivory at $6.4M annually).

Ivory was effective in certain situations, such as inside the red zone. But even the Jaguars have to admit that using the 4th overall draft pick on a RB after signing the most expensive RB in free

(cont'd - see JAC2)

2017 Lineup & Cap Hits

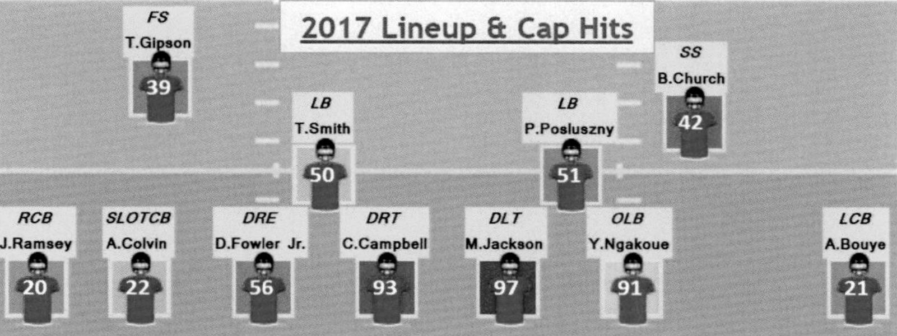

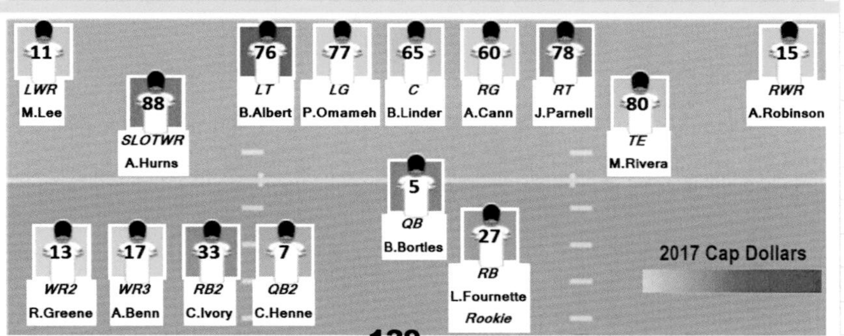

Key Free Agents/ Trades Added

Albert, Branden T
Bouye, A.J. CB
Campbell, Calais DE
Charles, Stefan DT
Church, Barry S
Cole, Audie LB
McCray, Lerentee LB
McNary, Josh LB
Rivera, Mychal TE
Watford, Earl G

Drafted Players

Rd	Pk	Player (College)
1	4	RB - Leonard Fournette (LSU)
2	34	OT - Cam Robinson (Alabama)
3	68	DE - Dawuane Smoot (Illinois)
4	110	WR - Dede Westbrook (Oklahoma)
5	148	LB - Blair Brown (Ohio)
7	222	CB - Jalen Myrick (Minnesota)
	240	FB - Marquez Williams (Miami (FL))

2017 Unit Spending

Positional Spending

	Rank	Total	2016 Rk
All OFF	26	$74.98M	20
QB	22	$10.64M	24
OL	19	$27.21M	15
RB	2	$14.10M	16
WR	22	$15.49M	20
TE	22	$7.55M	3
All DEF	5	$93.03M	5
DL	4	$43.50M	2
LB	24	$14.82M	27
CB	20	$16.95M	13
S	3	$17.75M	22

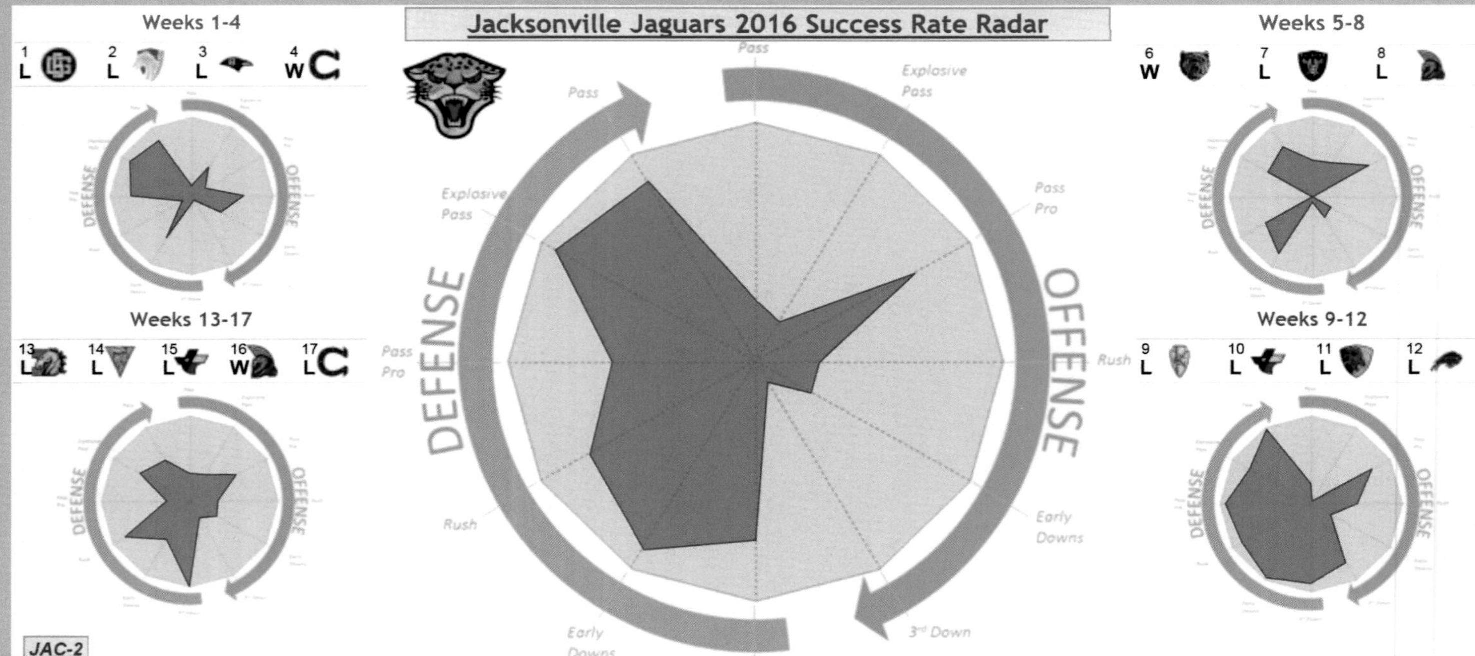

JAC-2

agency the year before is a sign of admitting to a mistake. Then comes the amount of spending and where it is being spent. Last year the Jaguars made a tremendous turnaround defensively. After ranking 26th in EDSR (Early Down Success Rate) defense and 26th in total defensive efficiency in 2015 (against the 2nd easiest schedule of opposing offenses), the Jaguars ranked 4th in EDSR defense and 13th in total defensive efficiency last season (against the 15th hardest schedule of opposing offenses). The defense was tremendous at times. Over their last 9 games they allowed 17 offensive touchdowns (1.9 per game) and that doesn't account for short fields caused by their struggling offense.

But the Jaguars wanted to add a ton more on defense in free agency and move players around, via their McDuck-style money bin. This is the perfect time to mention a player they just cut, CB Davon House, who they signed in 2015 free agency to a 4 year, $24.5M contract. House, who made just one-tenth of that over his rookie deal (4 year, $2.3M) wasn't re-signed by a Packers team who needed help at the CB position.

Apparently, that didn't set off any red flags for the Jaguars, however. House was a complete liability in 2015, frequently getting burned, and lasted only 4 games before he was benched last season, as he continued to struggle. House earned $12.5M over the last two years then was cut, just another example of free agent signings that didn't work out.

This year the Jaguars appear (yet again) to have improved defensively. The first two days of free agency, the Jaguars signed 5 players, and 4 of them were defensive players, with top deals going to SS Barry Church (4 yrs, $26M), CB AJ Bouye (5 yrs, $68M) and DE Calias Campbell (4 years, $60M). They proceeded to add two more LBs, a DT and a DE. There is zero doubt this team should have one of the best metric defenses in the NFL. The only question as to whether or not it will be a good scoring defense hinges on whether their own offense sets them up in bad field position, or not. Not only are they extremely talented, but they will be playing a very easy schedule.

(cont'd - see JAC-3)

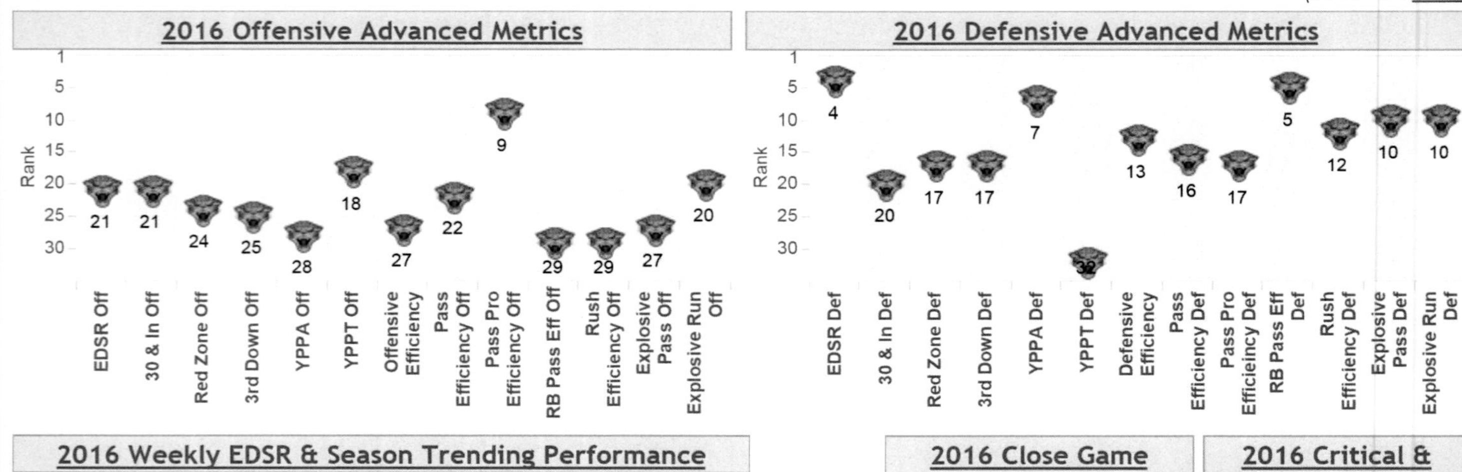

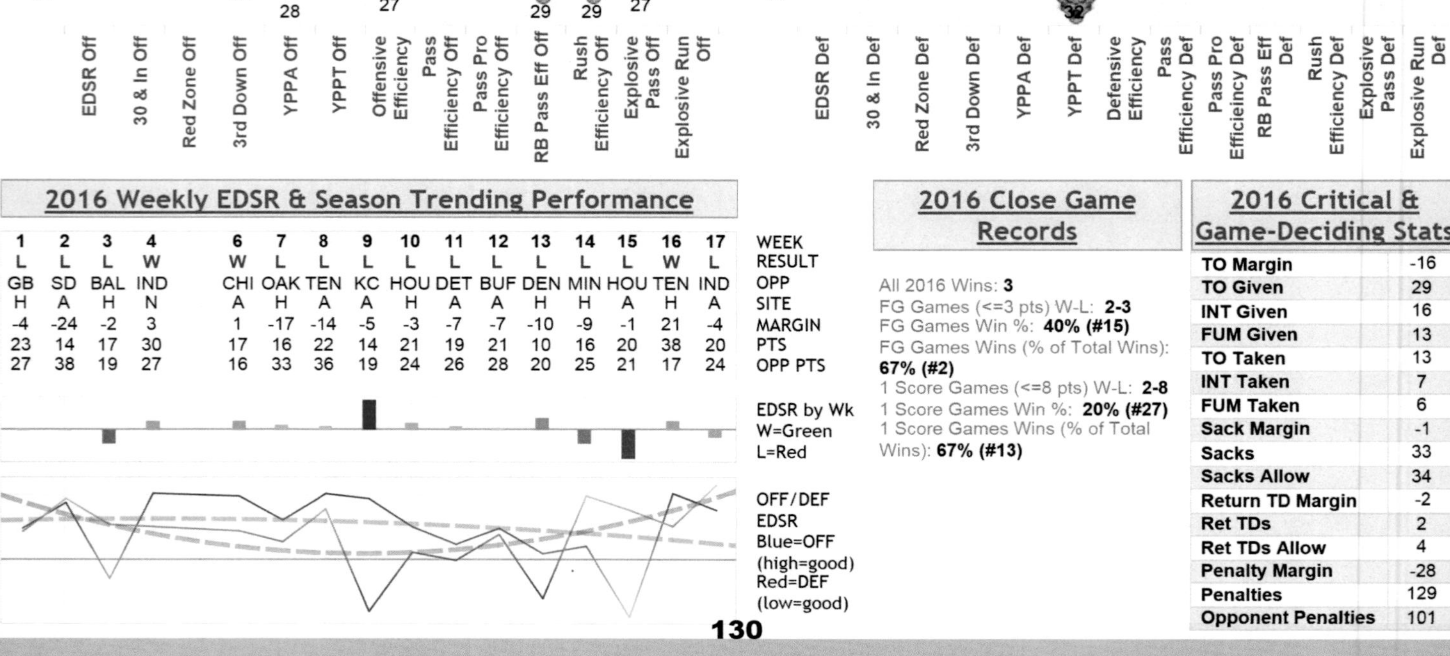

2016 Weekly EDSR & Season Trending Performance

WEEK	1	2	3	4	6	7	8	9	10	11	12	13	14	15	16	17
RESULT	L	L	L	W	W	L	L	L	L	L	L	L	L	L	W	L
OPP	GB	SD	BAL	IND	CHI	OAK	TEN	KC	HOU	DET	BUF	DEN	MIN	HOU	TEN	IND
SITE	H	A	H	N	A	H	A	A	H	A	A	H	H	A	H	A
MARGIN	-4	-24	-2	3	1	-17	-14	-5	-3	-7	-7	-10	-9	-1	21	-4
PTS	23	14	17	30	17	16	22	14	21	19	21	10	16	20	38	20
OPP PTS	27	38	19	27	16	33	36	19	24	26	28	20	25	21	17	24

2016 Close Game Records

All 2016 Wins: **3**
FG Games (<=3 pts) W-L: **2-3**
FG Games Win %: **40% (#15)**
FG Games Wins (% of Total Wins): **67% (#2)**
1 Score Games (<=8 pts) W-L: **2-8**
1 Score Games Win %: **20% (#27)**
1 Score Games Wins (% of Total Wins): **67% (#13)**

2016 Critical & Game-Deciding Stats

TO Margin	-16
TO Given	29
INT Given	16
FUM Given	13
TO Taken	13
INT Taken	7
FUM Taken	6
Sack Margin	-1
Sacks	33
Sacks Allow	34
Return TD Margin	-2
Ret TDs	2
Ret TDs Allow	4
Penalty Margin	-28
Penalties	129
Opponent Penalties	101

Jacksonville Jaguars 2017 Strength of Schedule In Detail (compared to 2016)

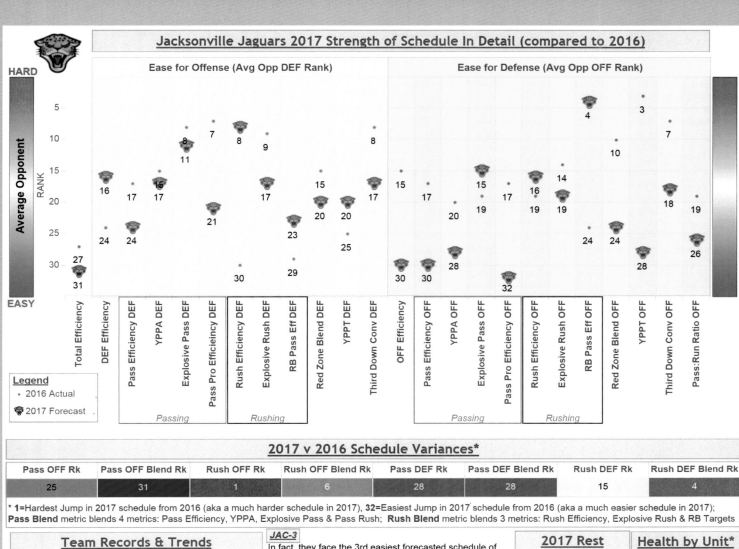

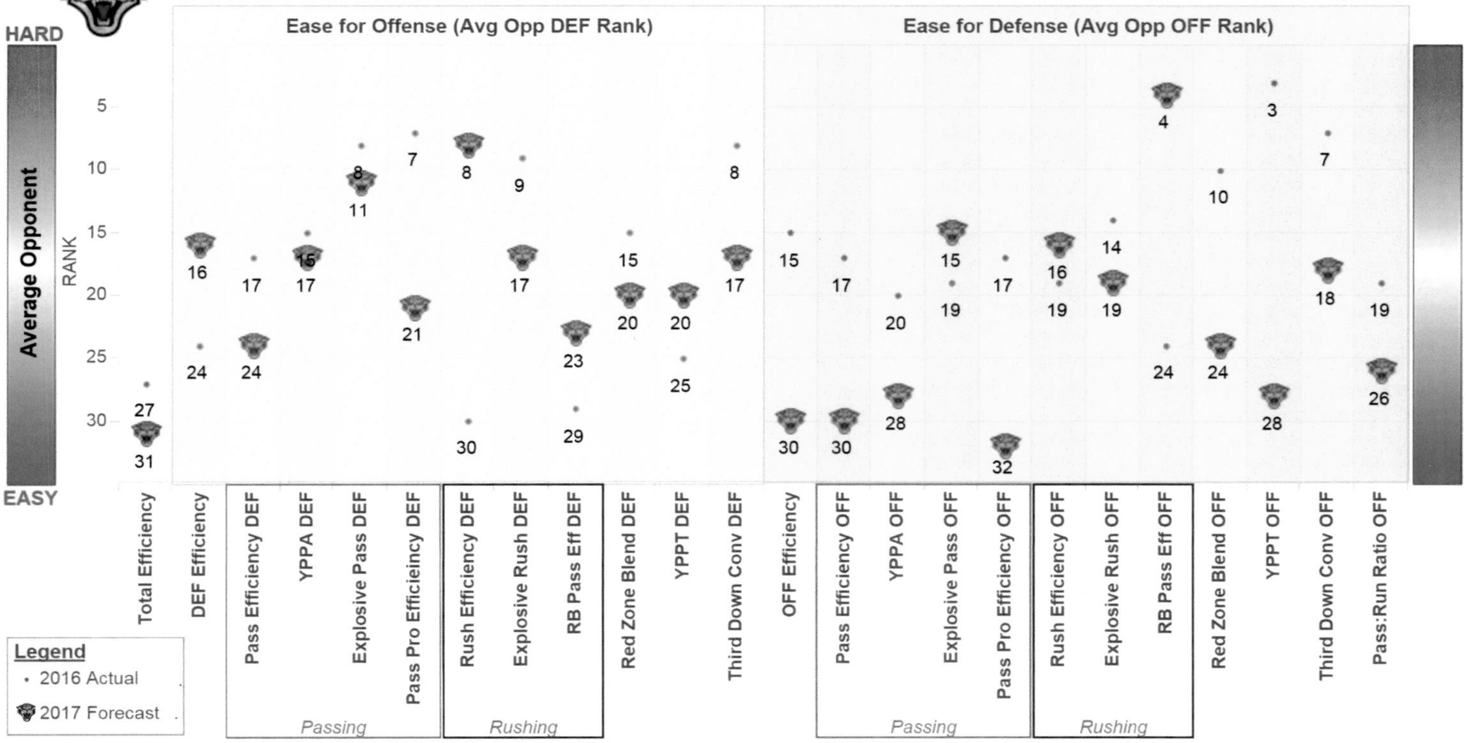

HARD / EASY — Average Opponent RANK

Ease for Offense (Avg Opp DEF Rank)

Metric	Group	2016 Actual	2017 Forecast
Total Efficiency		27	31
DEF Efficiency		24	16
Pass Efficiency DEF	Passing	17	24
YPPA DEF	Passing	15	17
Explosive Pass DEF	Passing	8	11
Pass Pro Efficieincy DEF	Passing	7	21
Rush Efficiency DEF	Rushing	30	8
Explosive Rush DEF	Rushing	9	17
RB Pass Eff DEF	Rushing	29	23
Red Zone Blend DEF		15	20
YPPT DEF		25	20
Third Down Conv DEF		8	17

Ease for Defense (Avg Opp OFF Rank)

Metric	Group	2016 Actual	2017 Forecast
OFF Efficiency		15	30
Pass Efficiency OFF	Passing	17	30
YPPA OFF	Passing	20	28
Explosive Pass OFF	Passing	19	15
Pass Pro Efficiency OFF	Passing	17	32
Rush Efficiency OFF	Rushing	19	16
Explosive Rush OFF	Rushing	14	19
RB Pass Eff OFF	Rushing	24	4
Red Zone Blend OFF		10	24
YPPT OFF		3	28
Third Down Conv OFF		7	18
Pass:Run Ratio OFF		19	26

Legend
- 2016 Actual
- 2017 Forecast

2017 v 2016 Schedule Variances*

Pass OFF Rk	Pass OFF Blend Rk	Rush OFF Rk	Rush OFF Blend Rk	Pass DEF Rk	Pass DEF Blend Rk	Rush DEF Rk	Rush DEF Blend Rk
25	31	1	6	28	28	15	4

* **1**=Hardest Jump in 2017 schedule from 2016 (aka a much harder schedule in 2017), **32**=Easiest Jump in 2017 schedule from 2016 (aka a much easier schedule in 2017); **Pass Blend** metric blends 4 metrics: Pass Efficiency, YPPA, Explosive Pass & Pass Rush; **Rush Blend** metric blends 3 metrics: Rush Efficiency, Explosive Rush & RB Targets

Team Records & Trends

	2016	2015	2014
Average line	3.4	2.6	7.2
Average O/U line	44.7	44.9	44.1
Straight Up Record	3-13	5-11	3-13
Against the Spread Record	8-8	7-9	7-9
Over/Under Record	10-6	10-6	7-8
ATS as Favorite	0-1	2-3	1-0
ATS as Underdog	8-6	5-6	6-9
Straight Up Home	1-6	4-4	3-5
ATS Home	2-5	4-4	3-5
Over/Under Home	5-2	5-3	3-5
ATS as Home Favorite	0-1	2-3	1-0
ATS as a Home Dog	2-3	2-1	2-5
Straight Up Away	1-7	1-7	0-8
ATS Away	5-3	3-5	4-4
Over/Under Away	4-4	5-3	4-3
ATS Away Favorite	0-0	0-0	0-0
ATS Away Dog	5-3	3-5	4-4
Six Point Teaser Record	12-3	9-7	8-6
Seven Point Teaser Record	13-3	9-7	10-4
Ten Point Teaser Record	13-3	12-4	14-2

JAC-3

In fact, they face the 3rd easiest forecasted schedule of opposing offenses, which just so happen to sport the worst pass protection in the NFL. And if the defense can get pressure and disrupt the passing game, it could become a high scoring fantasy defense is well, via sacks, turnovers and potential return TDs.

I assume if the Jaguars felt they could have improved further along their own offensive line, they would have. But this was a weak offseason for offensive line pieces to be found. One early thought I had was the Jaguars were trying to build a team based on defense and the run game, and hope they could get their QB to do just enough to make a run to the Super Bowl while still on his rookie deal. That is exactly what the Seahawks did with Russell Wilson, although it's clear Wilson is vastly superior to Blake Bortles. But here is the problem with that idea: this is year 4 of Bortles. This is the final year that he's cheap. The Jaguars already committed to his 5th round option, and so his cap hit moves from $6.6M this year to $19.1M next. Right now, that is slated to be QB16, although it's highly likely that Tom Brady's deal gets re-done to lower his cap hit to well below (cont'd - see *JAC-4*)

2017 Rest Analysis

Avg Rest	6.47
Avg Rk	3
Team More Rest	2
Opp More Rest	1
Net Rest Edge	1
3 Days Rest	0
4 Days Rest	0
5 Days Rest	0
6 Days Rest	14
7 Days Rest	0
8 Days Rest	0
9 Days Rest	0
10 Days Rest	0
11 Days Rest	0
12 Days Rest	0
13 Days Rest	1
14 Days Rest	0

Health by Unit*

2016 Rk	17
(2015 Rk)	20
Off Rk	26
Def Rk	10
QB Rk	15
RB Rk	19
WR Rk	19
TE Rk	30
OLine Rk	25
DLine Rk	30
LB Rk	2
DB Rk	7

*Based on the great work of Scott Kacsmar from Football Outsiders

2017 Weekly Betting Lines (wks 1-16)

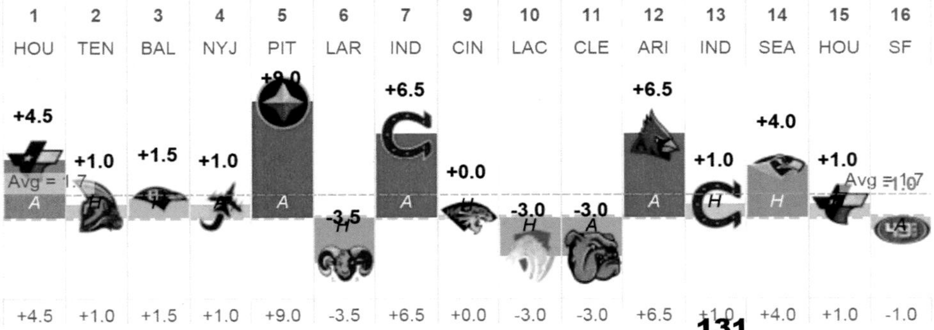

Week	Opponent	H/A	Line
1	HOU	A	+4.5
2	TEN	H	+1.0
3	BAL	H	+1.5
4	NYJ	A	+1.0
5	PIT	A	+9.0
6	LAR	H	-3.5
7	IND	A	+6.5
9	CIN	H	+0.0
10	LAC	H	-3.0
11	CLE	A	-3.0
12	ARI	A	+6.5
13	IND	H	+1.0
14	SEA	H	+4.0
15	HOU	H	+1.0
16	SF	A	-1.0

Avg = 1.7

Home Lines (wks 1-16)

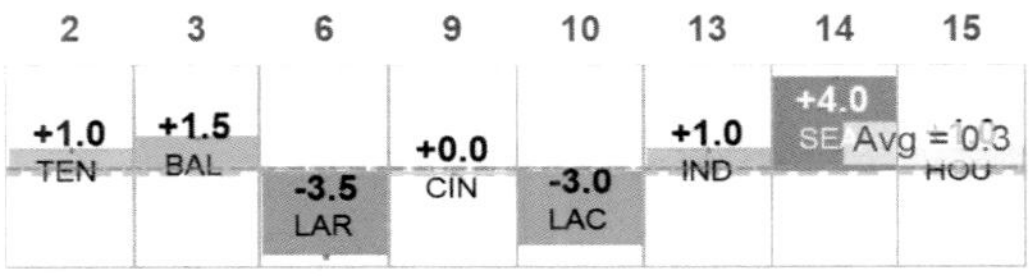

Week	2	3	6	9	10	13	14	15
Opponent	TEN	BAL	LAR	CIN	LAC	IND	SEA	HOU
Line	+1.0	+1.5	-3.5	+0.0	-3.0	+1.0	+4.0	

Avg = 0.3

Road Lines (wks 1-16)

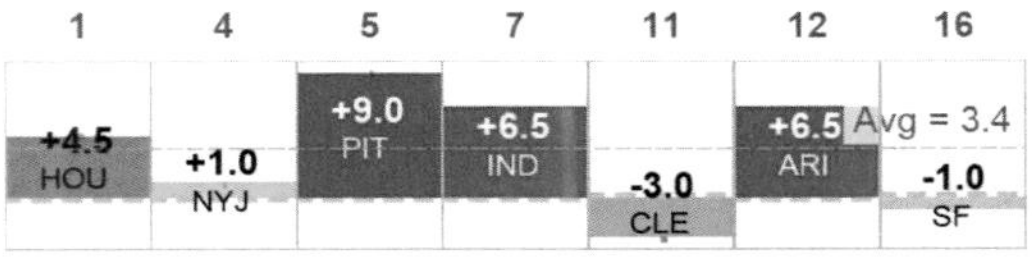

Week	1	4	5	7	11	12	16
Opponent	HOU	NYJ	PIT	IND	CLE	ARI	SF
Line	+4.5	+1.0	+9.0	+6.5	-3.0	+6.5	-1.0

Avg = 3.4

Jacksonville Jaguars 2016 Play Analysis

2016 Play Tendencies

All Pass %	58%
All Pass Rk	20
All Rush %	42%
All Rush Rk	13
1 Score Pass %	53%
1 Score Pass Rk	27
2015 1 Score Pass %	60%
2015 1 Score Pass Rk	11
Pass Increase %	-7%
Pass Increase Rk	30
1 Score Rush %	47%
1 Score Rush Rk	6
Up Pass %	59%
Up Pass Rk	10
Up Rush %	41%
Up Rush Rk	23
Down Pass %	61%
Down Pass Rk	17
Down Rush %	39%
Down Rush Rk	16

2016 Down & Distance Tendencies

Down	Distance	Total Plays	Pass Rate	Run Rate	Play Success %
1	Short (1-3)	7	43%	57%	71%
	Med (4-7)	5	20%	80%	80%
	Long (8-10)	316	45%	55%	46%
	XL (11+)	9	44%	56%	22%
2	Short (1-3)	40	48%	53%	60%
	Med (4-7)	81	49%	51%	40%
	Long (8-10)	101	55%	45%	43%
	XL (11+)	36	83%	17%	31%
3	Short (1-3)	41	78%	22%	59%
	Med (4-7)	67	93%	7%	48%
	Long (8-10)	32	88%	13%	38%
	XL (11+)	30	83%	17%	0%
4	Short (1-3)	4	75%	25%	50%
	Med (4-7)	1	100%	0%	100%

Shotgun %:

Under Center	Shotgun
27%	73%
37% AVG	*63%*

Run Rate:

Under Center	Shotgun
65%	24%
68% AVG	*23%*

Pass Rate:

Under Center	Shotgun
35%	76%
32% AVG	*77%*

Short Yardage Intelligence:

2nd and Short Run

Run Freq	Run % Rk	NFL Run Freq Avg	Run 1D Rate	Run NFL 1D Avg
50%	30	65%	53%	71%

2nd and Short Pass

Pass Freq	Pass % Rk	NFL Pass Freq Avg	Pass 1D Rate	Pass NFL 1D Avg
50%	2	35%	47%	52%

Most Frequent Play

Down	Distance	Play Type	Player	Total Plays	Play Success %
1	Short (1-3)	PASS	Allen Robinson	3	67%
		RUSH	Chris Ivory	3	100%
	Med (4-7)	RUSH	Chris Ivory	3	67%
	Long (8-10)	RUSH	Chris Ivory	63	49%
	XL (11+)	PASS	Allen Robinson	2	50%
		RUSH	T.J. Yeldon	2	0%
			Chris Ivory	2	0%
2	Short (1-3)	RUSH	T.J. Yeldon	8	38%
	Med (4-7)	RUSH	T.J. Yeldon	13	62%
			Chris Ivory	13	31%
	Long (8-10)	RUSH	T.J. Yeldon	21	33%
	XL (11+)	PASS	Allen Robinson	7	43%
3	Short (1-3)	PASS	Allen Robinson	13	62%
	Med (4-7)	PASS	Allen Robinson	20	40%
	Long (8-10)	PASS	Allen Robinson	6	17%
			Marqise Lee	6	17%
	XL (11+)	PASS	T.J. Yeldon	7	0%

Most Successful Play*

Down	Distance	Play Type	Player	Total Plays	Play Success %
1	Long (8-10)	PASS	Bryan Walters	8	75%
2	Short (1-3)	RUSH	Chris Ivory	6	50%
	Med (4-7)	RUSH	T.J. Yeldon	13	62%
	Long (8-10)	PASS	T.J. Yeldon	6	67%
	XL (11+)	PASS	Marqise Lee	5	60%
3	Short (1-3)	PASS	Marqise Lee	5	80%
	Med (4-7)	PASS	Bryan Walters	7	86%
	Long (8-10)	PASS	Allen Robinson	6	17%
			Marqise Lee	6	17%
	XL (11+)	PASS	T.J. Yeldon	7	0%
			Allen Robinson	5	0%

**Minimum 5 plays to qualify*

2016 Snap Rates

Week	Opp	Score	Allen Robinson	Marqise Lee	Allen Hurns	T.J. Yeldon	Julius Thomas	Ben Koyack	Chris Ivory
1	GB	L 27-23	69 (96%)	39 (54%)	62 (86%)	63 (88%)	56 (78%)	6 (8%)	
2	SD	L 38-14	58 (88%)	42 (64%)	58 (88%)	44 (67%)	61 (92%)	1 (2%)	
3	BAL	L 19-17	64 (97%)	42 (64%)	58 (88%)	33 (50%)	57 (86%)		32 (48%)
4	IND	W 30-27	70 (97%)	51 (71%)	64 (89%)	54 (75%)			18 (25%)
6	CHI	W 17-16	57 (95%)	44 (73%)	49 (82%)	37 (62%)	50 (83%)	0 (0%)	24 (40%)
7	OAK	L 33-16	65 (96%)	48 (71%)	57 (84%)	39 (57%)	55 (81%)	4 (6%)	27 (40%)
8	TEN	L 36-22	68 (94%)	58 (81%)	61 (85%)	41 (57%)	34 (47%)	10 (14%)	29 (40%)
9	KC	L 19-14	73 (95%)	62 (81%)	42 (55%)	43 (56%)	42 (55%)	12 (16%)	34 (44%)
10	HOU	L 24-21	70 (90%)	54 (69%)	72 (92%)	41 (53%)	41 (53%)	24 (31%)	37 (47%)
11	DET	L 26-19	62 (94%)	44 (67%)	59 (89%)	11 (17%)	54 (82%)	36 (55%)	39 (59%)
12	BUF	L 28-21	66 (97%)	51 (75%)	54 (79%)	23 (34%)		40 (59%)	15 (22%)
13	DEN	L 20-10	83 (99%)	79 (94%)		53 (63%)		53 (63%)	
14	MIN	L 25-16	62 (94%)	48 (73%)		53 (80%)		40 (61%)	
15	HOU	L 21-20	51 (96%)	50 (94%)		39 (74%)		33 (62%)	14 (26%)
16	TEN	W 38-17	62 (86%)	61 (85%)		3 (4%)		52 (72%)	42 (58%)
17	IND	L 24-20	70 (96%)	47 (64%)				50 (68%)	
Grand Total			1,050 (94%)	820 (74%)	636 (83%)	577 (56%)	450 (73%)	361 (37%)	311 (41%)

Personnel Groupings

Personnel	Team %	NFL Avg	Succ. %
1-1 [3WR]	76%	60%	46%
1-2 [2WR]	20%	19%	39%

Grouping Tendencies

Personnel	Pass Rate	Pass Succ. %	Run Succ. %
1-1 [3WR]	69%	44%	49%
1-2 [2WR]	45%	39%	38%

Red Zone Targets (min 3)

Receiver	All	Inside 5	6-10	11-20
Allen Robinson	19	6	5	8
Allen Hurns	13	2	1	10
Marqise Lee	9	1	1	7
T.J. Yeldon	8		2	6
Julius Thomas	7	1	3	3
Bryan Walters	4		1	3
Marcedes Lewis	4	2	1	1

Red Zone Rushes (min 3)

Rusher	All	Inside 5	6-10	11-20
Chris Ivory	13	9	2	2
T.J. Yeldon	10	2		8
Blake Bortles	6	3	1	2

Early Down Target Rate

RB	TE	WR
19%	22%	59%
19%	*20% NFL AVG*	*61%*

Overall Target Success %

RB	TE	WR
39% #29	49% #27	46% #23

Jacksonville Jaguars 2016 Passing Recap & 2017 Outlook

Jacksonville seemingly has the defense and potentially has the run game (at least they've spent so much they should have the run game) to produce this year. What they need is Bortles to live up to his expectations. There is no doubt that Allen Robinson, Allen Hurns and Marquise Lee aren't a strong enough receiving corps. Truth be told, those 3 WRs are arguably better than what is out there in half the NFL. So there is really no excuse for Bortles' passing cone to look like what it does on the right. There is no excuse for Bortles to hit only 6.2 yards per attempt and post a 78.5 passer rating. Bortles absolutely must improve what he's doing on 3rd down. His completions on 3rd down fall an average of 2.1 yards short of the sticks (yards to gain). That ranked 36th in the NFL. It's hard to depend continually on receivers running after the catch for required yardage on 3rd downs, so Bortles must do a better job of putting the ball to or past the sticks. His passing is similarly not nearly as explosive as is required, as referenced by the poor deep passing rating. His deep passer rating on passes 15+ yards in the air was 39.3, averaging just 7 yards per attempt, 3:7 TD:INT and completing only 29% of his attempts.

Blake Bortles Rating All Downs

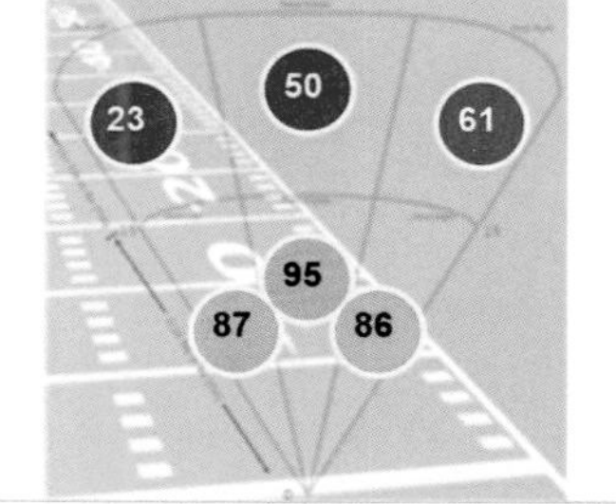

Blake Bortles Rating Early Downs

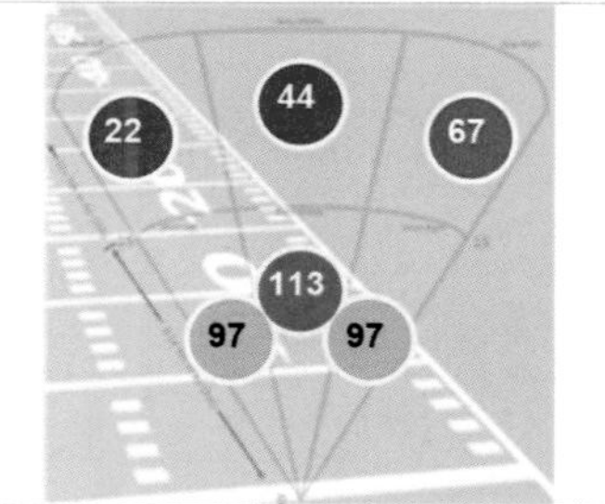

2016 Standard Passing Table

QB	Comp	Att	Comp %	Yds	YPA	TDs	INT	Sacks	Rating	Rk
Blake Bortles	368	627	59%	3,894	6.2	23	16	32	78.5	39
NFL Avg			63%		7.2				90.4	

2016 Advanced Passing Table

QB	Success %	EDSR Passing Success %	20+ Yd Pass Gains	20+ Yd Pass %	30+ Yd Pass Gains	30+ Yd Pass %	Air Yds per Comp	YAC per Comp	20+ Air Yd Comp	20+ Air Yd %
Blake Bortles	43%	47%	43	7%	15	2%	5.4	5.2	15	2%
NFL Avg	44%	48%	27	8%	10	3%	6.4	4.8	12	4%

Interception Rates by Down

Yards to Go	1	2	3	4	Total
1 & 2	0.0%	0.0%	0.0%	0.0%	0.0%
3, 4, 5	0.0%	3.4%	3.8%	0.0%	3.2%
6 - 9	0.0%	0.0%	8.5%	0.0%	3.9%
10 - 14	1.3%	2.3%	7.1%		2.1%
15+	0.0%	0.0%	4.5%	0.0%	2.1%
Total	1.2%	1.4%	5.3%	0.0%	2.4%

3rd Down Passing - Short of Sticks Analysis

QB	Avg Yds to Go	Air Yds (of Comps)	Avg Yds Short	Short of Sticks Rate	Rk
Blake Bortles	7.4	5.3	-2.1	57%	36
NFL Avg	7.6	6.8	-0.8	57%	

Air Yds vs YAC

Air Yds %	YAC %	Rk
50%	50%	32
54%	46%	

2016 Receiving Recap & 2017 Outlook

Jacksonville seemingly has the talent, but isn't getting them on the same page at the same time with Bortles. The only WR with over a 50% completion rate was Marquise Lee, who averaged 8.1 yards per attempt and a 60% completion rate. But his rating was only a 76 on account of interceptions. Hurns (46% completions) and Robinson (49% completions) both simply must figure out how to be where Bortles needs them to be. No doubt Bortles has issues, but Hurns posted a 50 PFF grade and Robinson a 73.9 last year. It's difficult to imagine a slot receiver catching only 46% of his targets. Apart from Lee the other top receivers ranked 127th at best.

Player *Min 50 Targets*	Targets	Comp %	YPA	Rating	TOARS	Success %	Success Rk	Missed YPA Rk	YAS % Rk	TDs
Allen Robinson	150	49%	5.9	64	4.8	42%	127	108	67	6
Marqise Lee	105	60%	8.1	76	4.6	54%	44	75	31	3
Allen Hurns	76	46%	6.3	69	3.9	39%	135	115	14	3
T.J. Yeldon	68	74%	4.6	81	3.8	38%	137	144	147	1
Julius Thomas	51	59%	5.5	100	3.7	41%	130	47	88	4

Directional Passer Rating Delivered

Receiver	Short Left	Short Middle	Short Right	Deep Left	Deep Middle	Deep Right	Player Total
Allen Robinson	91	73	96	5	34	51	64
Marqise Lee	98	75	53	80	138	32	76
Allen Hurns	63	71	97	80	11	82	69
T.J. Yeldon	86	63	89				81
Julius Thomas	75	125	63	40	40	158	100
Bryan Walters	86	136	107			119	109
Marcedes Lewis	90	132	61	79	40		92
Chris Ivory	102	72	92				89
Ben Koyack	85	138	94			40	109
Team Total	88	95	83	30	43	65	79

2016 Rushing Recap & 2017 Outlook

Ivory outperformed Yeldon last year, but he still wasn't great except in the red zone. His success rate was 46th in the league and he ranked 41st in Missed YPA. He was more of a boom or bust, and was more bust than boom with a 3.8 yards per carry average. With Fournette, hopefully the Yeldon experiment will ends unless the team has visions of cutting Ivory next season. Inside the red zone, Ivory's 62% success rate dwarfed Yeldon's 40% rate. Passes targeting Yeldon (8 of them) recorded a 13% success rate. Lee was the Jags only reliable red zone receiver (56% success rate), the others such as Robinson & Hurns, averaged 37% and 31% respectively. Those targets need to go to Fournette or Ivory until the defense shows they can stop them.

Player *Min 50 Rushes*	Rushes	YPA	Success %	Success Rk	Missed YPA Rk	YTS % Rk	YAS % Rk	Early Down Success %	Early Down Success Rk	TDs
T.J. Yeldon	130	3.6	38%	63	51	15	65	38%	61	1
Chris Ivory	117	3.8	44%	46	41	25	18	43%	45	3

Yards per Carry by Direction

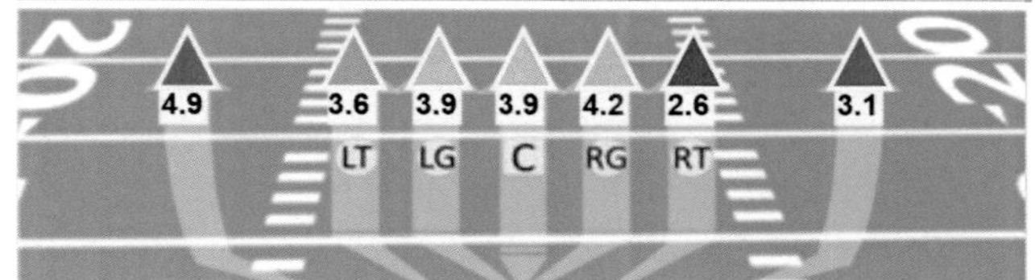

Directional Run Frequency

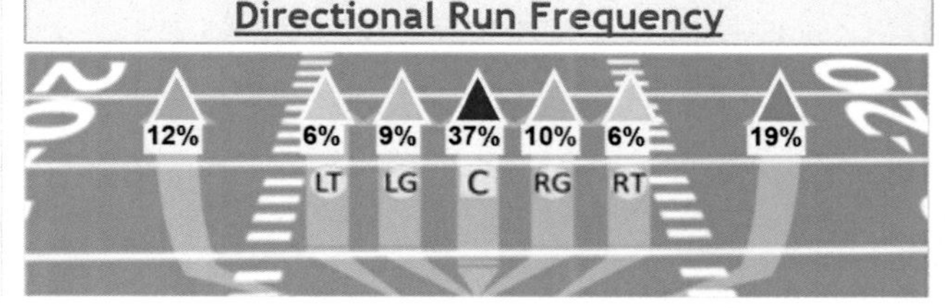

JAC-4

Bortles (Brady has annually hit the cap for $14M or less for years). So that shot has come and will go this January at the end of the season. Unless Bortles pulls off one of the most incredible runs we've ever witnessed (Jacksonville is currently +15473 to win the Super Bowl, so $100 bet nets $15,473), the Jaguars will be trying to win one while paying a QB market rate outside of rookie deal savings.

The play calling was beyond bad in terms of predictability and likely cost the Jaguars several wins. Thanks to the advanced personnel grouping information at Sharp Football Stats, we have the following: When winning in the second half, the Jaguars either had 3 WRs on the field and were in 11 personnel, or they were in some variation of 1 or 2 receivers such as 12 or 21 or 22. Here is the tell: if the Jaguars did not have 3 WRs on the field, they were running. They ran 89% of the time if leading in the 2nd half in those groupings, and not surprisingly, only 13% of their rushes were successful, as the defense knew exactly what they were doing. If the Jaguars had 3 WRs on the field, which they did 84% of the time (NFL average was 48% in that situation), they were passes 65% of the time. On 2nd or 3rd down with 3 WRs, they were passing 77% of the time (10% above average), and with the defense playing the percentages, only 23% of these passes were successful.

This truly was sad, because the Jaguars actually led at halftime in 5 games and lost 3 of them. Regardless of halftime score, there were 5 games the Jaguars lost which they led at some point in the second half, but were outscored thereafter and lost the game. To recap the play calling predictability: less than 3 WRs, 89% run with a 13% success rate. 3 WRs, 65% pass and if 2nd or 3rd down, 77% pass with a 23% success rate.

Their 2017 OC is Nathaniel Hackett, who took over in week 7 of 2016. I would like to say things got better once he took over from this predictability perspective, but they actually were worse. In weeks 11, 12, 13, 15 and 17, the Jaguars led at some point in the second half but lost every single game. If less than 3 WRs on any play, they went 100% run, with a 29% run success rate. If 3 WRs on any play, 65% pass including 78% pass after first down, with a 29% pass success rate. How did this parlay into more conventional stats? The Jags passed 57% of the time. Bortles averaged 4.7 yards per att with a 61 passer rating and on the ground they averaged 2.8 yards per rush.

The Jaguars are set up to have a great season defensively. And they face the 3rd easiest schedule of opposing offenses. Particularly in the first quarter of the season, the defense should give the Jags the opportunity to win each game. The issue this year, as it was last year, is Bortles. If the Jags have less predictable 2nd half play calling when leading and Bortles improves his game, particularly on his deeper passes, the Jaguars should be able to balance out that one-score game record which saw them lose 8 of 10 last year.

Division History: Season Wins & 2017 Projection

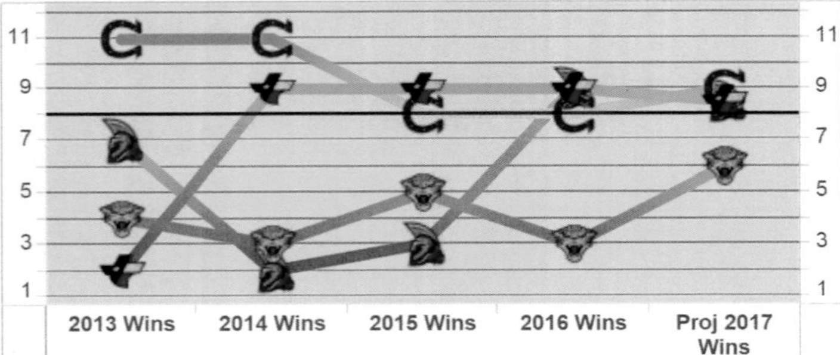

Rank of 2017 Defensive Pass Efficiency Faced by Week

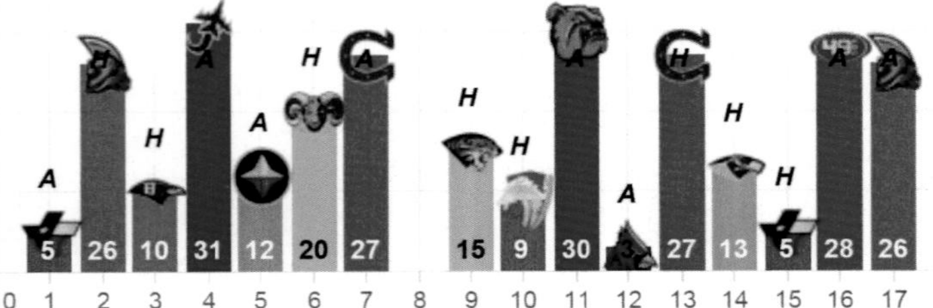

Rank of 2017 Defensive Rush Efficiency Faced by Week

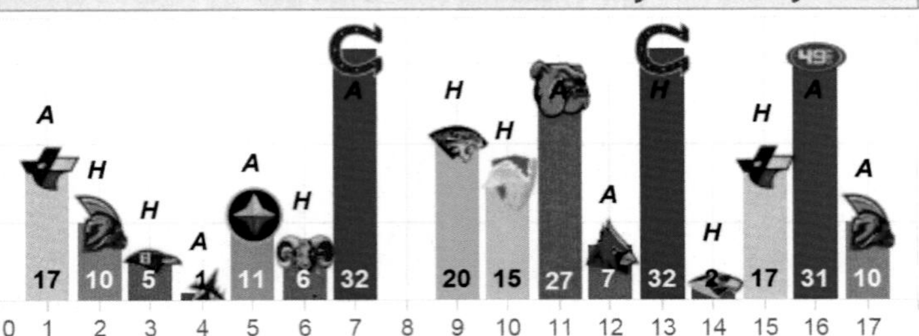

2016 Situational Usage by Player & Position

Usage Rate by Score

		Being Blown Out (14+)	Down Big (9-13)	One Score	Large Lead (9-13)	Blowout Lead (14+)	Grand Total
RUSH	T.J. Yeldon	7%	10%	17%	9%	6%	14%
	Chris Ivory	1%	17%	14%	13%	15%	12%
	Marqise Lee	1%	1%	1%			1%
	Denard Robinson	1%		6%		6%	4%
	Corey Grant			4%	4%	18%	3%
	Bryan Walters				1%		0%
	Shane Wynn	1%					0%
	Bronson Hill				3%		0%
	Joe Banyard			0%			0%
	Total	12%	28%	42%	31%	45%	35%
PASS	T.J. Yeldon	11%	6%	7%	4%	3%	7%
	Allen Robinson	15%	16%	16%	16%	18%	16%
	Chris Ivory	4%	2%	3%	4%		3%
	Marqise Lee	11%	16%	10%	10%	15%	11%
	Allen Hurns	18%	14%	5%	3%		8%
	Julius Thomas	8%	8%	5%			5%
	Denard Robinson	1%		0%	1%		1%
	Corey Grant	1%		0%	6%		1%
	Bryan Walters	3%	1%	3%	9%	9%	4%
	Marcedes Lewis	7%	3%	3%			3%
	Ben Koyack	4%	1%	2%	6%	9%	3%
	Neal Sterling		2%	2%	1%		2%
	Arrelious Benn	4%	2%	0%	1%		1%
	Rashad Greene	3%		1%	1%		1%
	Shane Wynn		2%	0%			0%
	Alex Ellis			1%	1%		0%
	Bronson Hill				1%		0%
	Tony Washington				1%		0%
	Total	88%	72%	58%	69%	55%	65%

Positional Target Distribution vs NFL Average

		NFL Wide				Team Only			
		Left	Middle	Right	Total	Left	Middle	Right	Total
Deep	WR	987	554	973	**2,514**	44	27	28	**99**
	TE	155	145	161	**461**	3	2	2	**7**
	RB	25	4	40	**69**				
	All	**1,167**	**703**	**1,174**	**3,044**	**47**	**29**	**30**	**106**
Short	WR	2,986	1,705	3,093	**7,784**	107	66	93	**266**
	TE	805	840	1,119	**2,764**	31	35	32	**98**
	RB	984	589	1,081	**2,654**	31	33	32	**96**
	All	**4,775**	**3,134**	**5,293**	**13,202**	**169**	**134**	**157**	**460**
Total		**5,942**	**3,837**	**6,467**	**16,246**	**216**	**163**	**187**	**566**

Positional Success Rates vs NFL Average

		NFL Wide				Team Only			
		Left	Middle	Right	Total	Left	Middle	Right	Total
Deep	WR	38%	51%	38%	**41%**	23%	37%	32%	**29%**
	TE	45%	50%	43%	**46%**	33%	0%	50%	**29%**
	RB	32%	75%	25%	**30%**				
	All	**38%**	**51%**	**39%**	**41%**	**23%**	**34%**	**33%**	**29%**
Short	WR	52%	57%	51%	**53%**	51%	55%	55%	**53%**
	TE	50%	61%	52%	**54%**	42%	69%	38%	**50%**
	RB	47%	49%	44%	**46%**	39%	48%	31%	**40%**
	All	**51%**	**57%**	**50%**	**52%**	**47%**	**57%**	**46%**	**50%**
Total		**48%**	**56%**	**48%**	**50%**	**42%**	**53%**	**44%**	**46%**

Kansas City Chiefs

2017 Coaches

Head Coach:
Andy Reid (5th yr)
Offensive Coordinator:
Brad Childress (2nd yr)
Defensive Coordinator:
Bob Sutton (5th yr)

2017 Forecast

Wins	Div Rank
9	#2

Past Records

2016: 12-4
2015: 11-5
2014: 9-7

EASY HARD

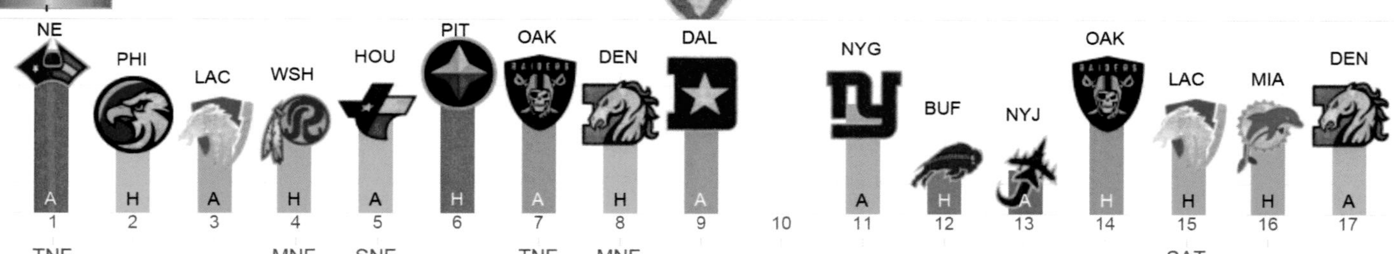

Key Players Lost

TXN	Player (POS)
Cut	Charles, Jamaal RB
	Greene, Khaseem LB
	Harris, Vernon CB
	Hasic, Anas WR
	Houston, Wyatt TE
	Howard, Jaye DT
	Johnson, Cory DT
	Maclin, Jeremy WR
	Reaves, Darrin RB
	Williams, Tourek LB
	Wilson, Julian CB
Declared Free Agent	Cook, Kenny WR
	Davis, Knile RB
	Foles, Nick QB
	Jenkins, Jarvis DE
	Mauga, Josh LB
	Millard, Trey RB
	Person, Mike G
	Poe, Dontari DT
	Reyes, Kendall DE

Average Line	# Games Favored	# Games Underdog
-1.3	10	5

2017 Kansas City Chiefs Overview

You can't judge a book by its cover, and you can't judge the Chiefs by their record. The days of Bill Parcells and "you are what your record says you are" are dead. We can look much deeper than the surface to uncover the composition and measure of a team. For a 12-win team that played a slightly easier than average schedule in 2016, the Chiefs sure don't have the metrics to match that record, with one huge exception that we'll discuss momentarily. Flip the page to the radar charts on the second page of this chapter, where a "full" radar indicates strength and an "empty" radar indicates weakness, and you'll see the full season radar certainly lacks that "fullness" which most often would accompany a great team. Look down the page to the offensive and defensive advanced metrics. You'll find essentially an average team. A team that excelled in certain areas, had severe shortcomings in others, but as a whole was no worse than average, but wasn't much better than it, either.

My key custom metric, EDSR (Early Down Success Rate) showed the Chiefs to rank 22nd on offense and 15th on defense. The first metric I mention is EDSR, because it's the single best metric which correlates to wins and losses and which is predictive in nature. There is a better metric than EDSR to correlate to wins and losses, but it's difficult to model it predictively, and that is turnover ratio. The team that wins the turnover margin wins over 79% of the time. Obviously the larger the margin, the more likely the win. Last year, turnover margin correlated exceedingly well to wins for the Chiefs. Which was a good thing for them, because they dominated in turnover margin.

They won the turnover margin in 10 games last year. No team performed better. And the Chiefs won 9 of those 10 games. Their sole loss was to the Titans when they led 17-7 heading into the 4th quarter and gave up 12 unanswered to lose 19-17. The Chiefs tied the turnover margin in one game last year. And that game nearly finished in a tie. It was a win in Atlanta, by a final score of 29-28. The Chiefs lost the turnover margin in 4 games last year, and went 2-3 in these games, squeaking out one-score wins in home games against the Chargers and Raiders (on a short week).

Overall the Chiefs were +16 in turnover margin. They had tremendous fumble luck

(cont'd - see KC2)

Key Free Agents/ Trades Added

Charles, Orson TE
Escobar, Gavin TE
Huff, Marqueston S
Hughes, Montori DT
James, Josh T
Jean-Baptiste, Stanley CB
Logan, Bennie DT
Spiller, C.J. RB
Thomas, Cam DT
Williams, Tourek LB

Drafted Players

Rd	Pk	Player (College)
1	10	QB - Patrick Mahomes II (Texas Tech)
2	59	DE - Tanoh Kpassagnon (Villanova)
3	86	RB - Kareem Hunt (Toledo)
4*	139	WR - Jehu Chesson (Michigan)
5*	183	OLB - Ukeme Eligwe (Georgia Southern)
6*	218	S - Leon McQuay III (USC)

Regular Season Wins: Past & Current Proj

2017 Lineup & Cap Hits

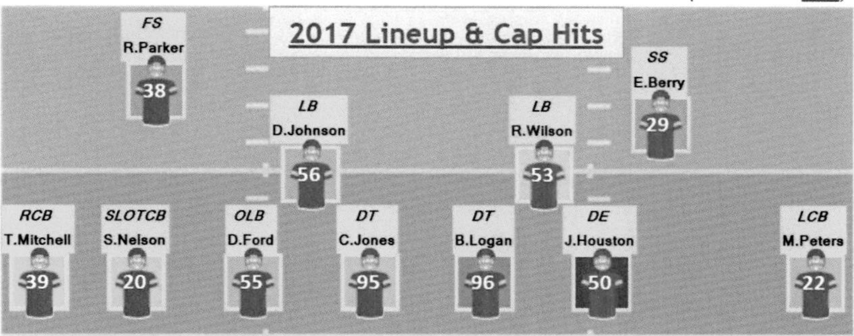

2017 Unit Spending

Positional Spending

	Rank	Total	2016 Rk
All OFF	28	$71.92M	22
QB	16	$19.15M	11
OL	9	$31.42M	29
RB	26	$5.06M	8
WR	32	$7.41M	18
TE	17	$8.89M	22
All DEF	6	$86.44M	15
DL	22	$19.99M	19
LB	1	$42.60M	4
CB	27	$8.69M	29
S	6	$15.16M	4

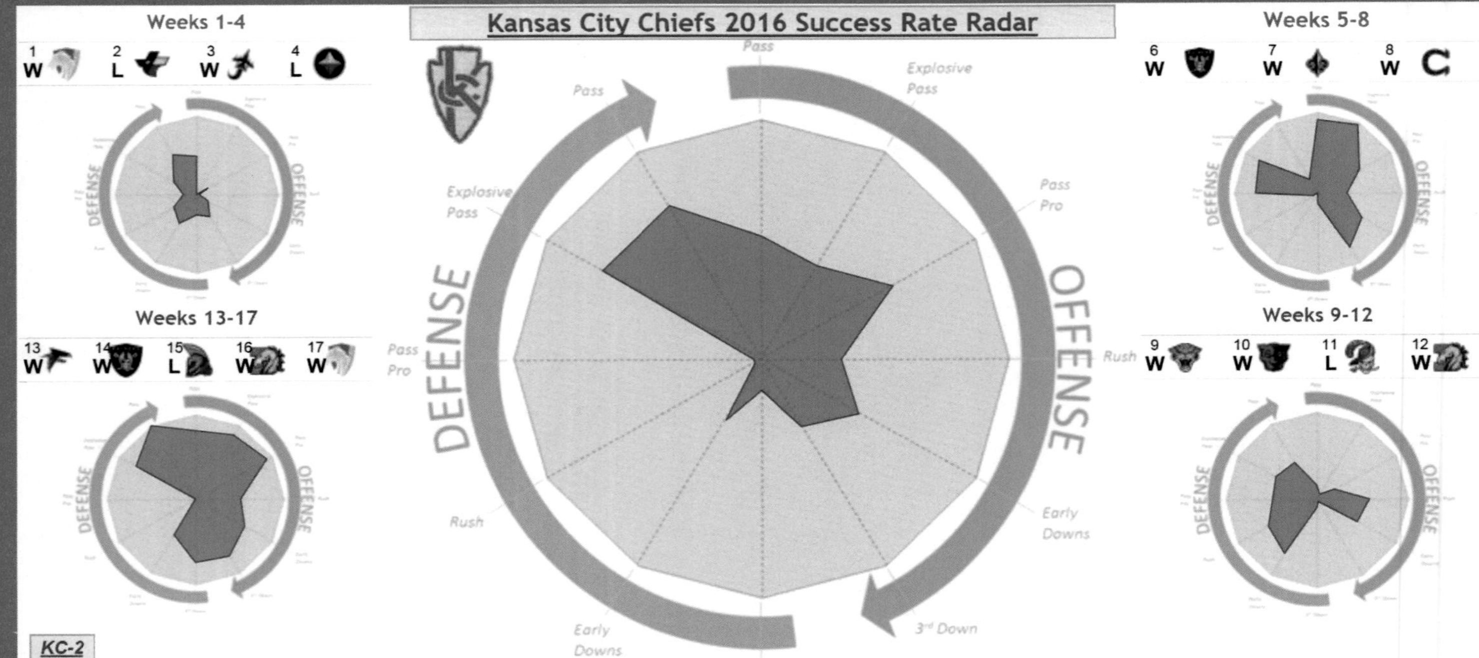

KC-2

recovering 15 fumbles while losing only 9. And thanks to their more conservative passing game and the game scripting forcing opponents to get more aggressive in games, the Chiefs threw only 8 interceptions but took away 18 from opposing quarterbacks. Such margins will erase a lot of average football, and can turn a tossup game into solid win, and a likely loss into a narrow win. Look no further than their week 9 home win over the Jaguars for evidence of a likely loss being turned into a narrow win, thanks to a +4 turnover margin including a Jaguars fumble into the Chiefs end zone giving away a 4th quarter TD. The Jaguars offense and defense completely dominated that game, recording a 25-10 first down edge, a 48%-30% play success edge and a 6.5-4.5 yards per early down edge. But the turnover margin allowed the Chiefs to pull out the 19-14 win.

There exists another sneaky metric which is nearly as correlated to wins as turnovers but is nearly impossible to model predictively, and that is return TDs. Whether they are from punts, kickoffs or turnovers, if a team has an edge in non-offensive touchdowns (return TDs), they win the game 75% of the time.

No team won the return TD margin in 2016 as often as the Chiefs, who finished +7 in return TD margin on the season, and in 6 separate games, walked away with more return TDs than their opponent. To no surprise, they won all 6 of these games.

After going two straight years (2011 and 2012) with just one game total which featured more return TDs than their opponent, the last 4 seasons, no team has more games with return TDs than the Chiefs, and it's not even close. The Chiefs have scored more return TDs than their opponents in 24 games (they are 22-2 in these games). The #2 team (PHI) is 18 games, and the NFL average is 10 games. The Chiefs have lost the return TD margin in just 2 games over the last 4 seasons, the best mark in the NFL. These 4 seasons coincided with the start of Andy Reid and Bob Sutton's stewardship. Return TDs are clearly massive to a team's chances in a particular game. They always occur when the offense

(cont'd - see KC-3)

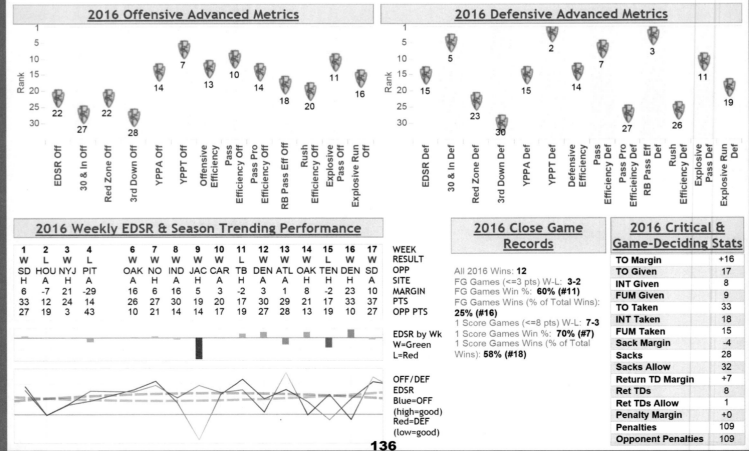

2016 Offensive Advanced Metrics

Metric	Rank
EDSR Off	22
30 & In Off	27
Red Zone Off	22
3rd Down Off	28
YPPA Off	14
YPPT Off	7
Offensive Efficiency	13
Pass Efficiency Off	10
Pass Pro Efficiency Off	14
RB Pass Eff Off	18
Rush Efficiency Off	20
Explosive Pass Off	11
Explosive Run Off	16

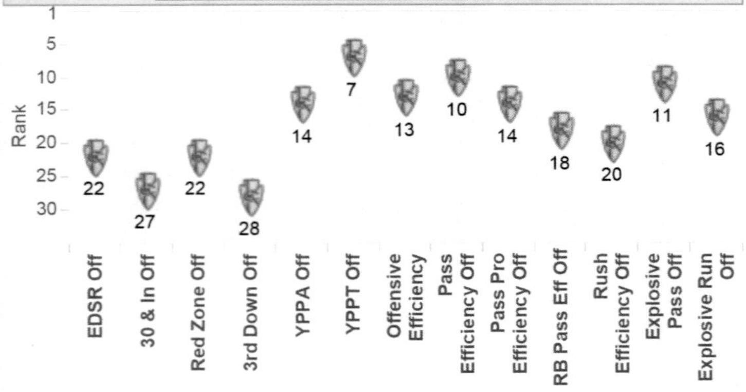

2016 Defensive Advanced Metrics

Metric	Rank
EDSR Def	15
30 & In Def	5
Red Zone Def	23
3rd Down Def	30
YPPA Def	15
YPPT Def	2
Defensive Efficiency	14
Pass Efficiency Def	7
Pass Pro Efficiency Def	27
RB Pass Eff Def	3
Rush Efficiency Def	26
Explosive Pass Def	11
Explosive Run Def	19

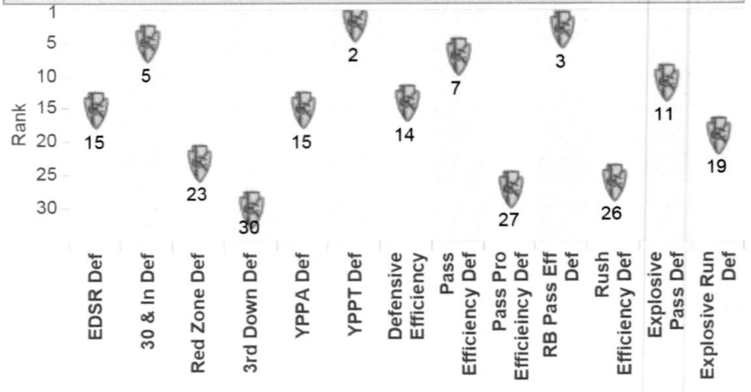

2016 Weekly EDSR & Season Trending Performance

WEEK	1	2	3	4	6	7	8	9	10	11	12	13	14	15	16	17
RESULT	W	L	W	L	W	W	W	W	W	L	W	W	W	L	W	W
OPP	SD	HOU	NYJ	PIT	OAK	NO	IND	JAC	CAR	TB	DEN	ATL	OAK	TEN	DEN	SD
SITE	H	A	H	A	A	H	A	H	A	H	A	A	H	H	H	A
MARGIN	6	-7	21	-29	16	6	16	5	3	-2	3	1	8	-2	23	10
PTS	33	12	24	14	26	27	30	19	20	17	30	29	21	17	33	37
OPP PTS	27	19	3	43	10	21	14	14	17	19	27	28	13	19	10	27

EDSR by Wk
W=Green
L=Red

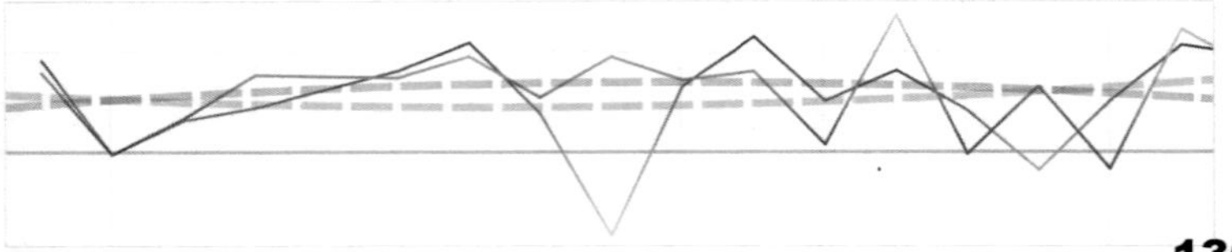

OFF/DEF
EDSR
Blue=OFF
(high=good)
Red=DEF
(low=good)

2016 Close Game Records

All 2016 Wins: **12**
FG Games (<=3 pts) W-L: **3-2**
FG Games Win %: **60% (#11)**
FG Games Wins (% of Total Wins): **25% (#16)**
1 Score Games (<=8 pts) W-L: **7-3**
1 Score Games Win %: **70% (#7)**
1 Score Games Wins (% of Total Wins): **58% (#18)**

2016 Critical & Game-Deciding Stats

TO Margin	+16
TO Given	17
INT Given	8
FUM Given	9
TO Taken	33
INT Taken	18
FUM Taken	15
Sack Margin	-4
Sacks	28
Sacks Allow	32
Return TD Margin	+7
Ret TDs	8
Ret TDs Allow	1
Penalty Margin	+0
Penalties	109
Opponent Penalties	109

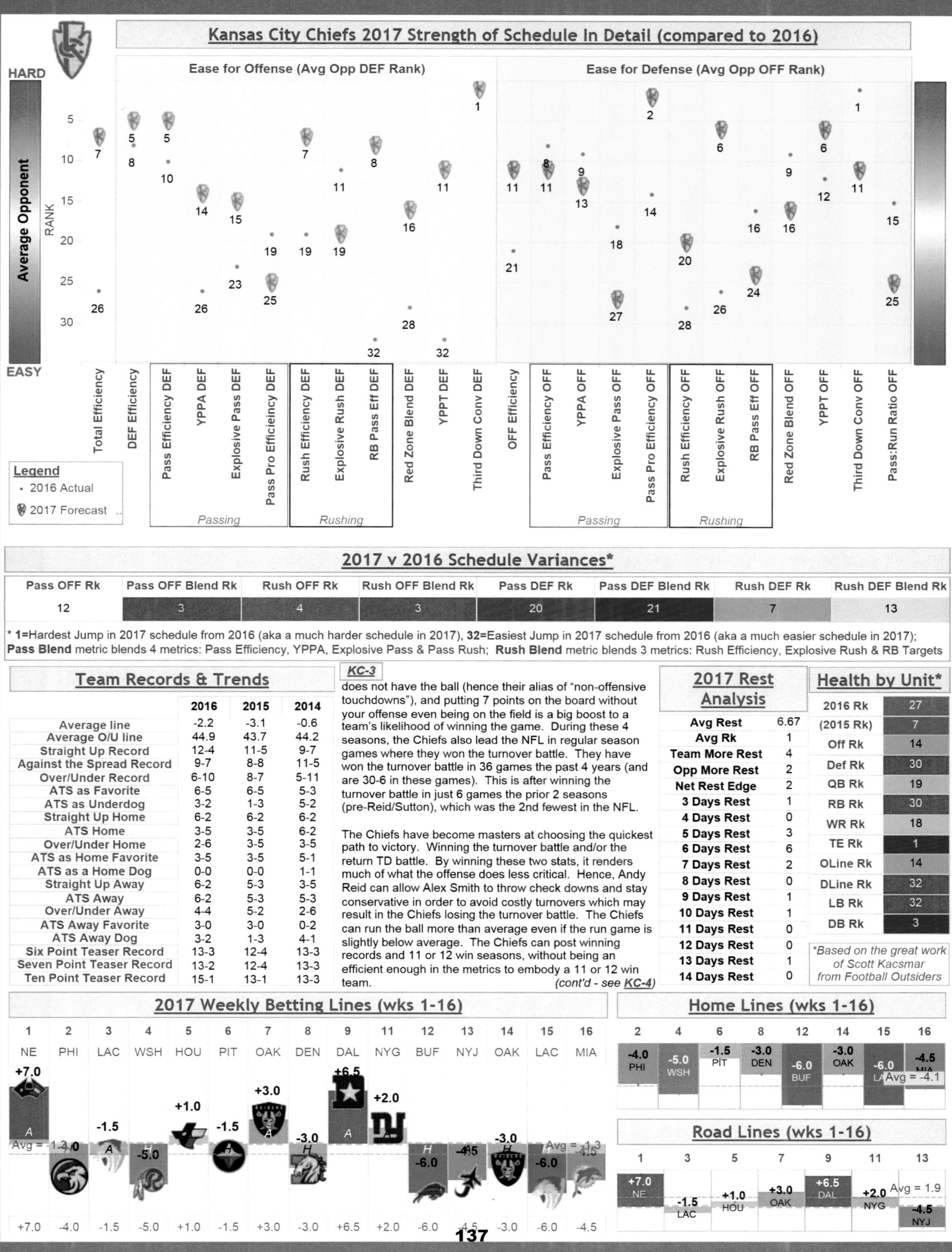

Kansas City Chiefs 2017 Strength of Schedule In Detail (compared to 2016)

2017 v 2016 Schedule Variances*

Pass OFF Rk	Pass OFF Blend Rk	Rush OFF Rk	Rush OFF Blend Rk	Pass DEF Rk	Pass DEF Blend Rk	Rush DEF Rk	Rush DEF Blend Rk
12	3	4	3	20	21	7	13

* **1**=Hardest Jump in 2017 schedule from 2016 (aka a much harder schedule in 2017), **32**=Easiest Jump in 2017 schedule from 2016 (aka a much easier schedule in 2017); **Pass Blend** metric blends 4 metrics: Pass Efficiency, YPPA, Explosive Pass & Pass Rush; **Rush Blend** metric blends 3 metrics: Rush Efficiency, Explosive Rush & RB Targets

Team Records & Trends

	2016	2015	2014
Average line	-2.2	-3.1	-0.6
Average O/U line	44.9	43.7	44.2
Straight Up Record	12-4	11-5	9-7
Against the Spread Record	9-7	8-8	11-5
Over/Under Record	6-10	8-7	5-11
ATS as Favorite	6-5	6-5	5-3
ATS as Underdog	3-2	1-3	5-2
Straight Up Home	6-2	6-2	6-2
ATS Home	3-5	3-5	6-2
Over/Under Home	2-6	3-5	3-5
ATS as Home Favorite	3-5	3-5	5-1
ATS as a Home Dog	0-0	0-0	1-1
Straight Up Away	6-2	5-3	3-5
ATS Away	6-2	5-3	5-3
Over/Under Away	4-4	5-2	2-6
ATS Away Favorite	3-0	3-0	0-2
ATS Away Dog	3-2	1-3	4-1
Six Point Teaser Record	13-3	12-4	13-3
Seven Point Teaser Record	13-2	12-4	13-3
Ten Point Teaser Record	15-1	13-1	13-3

KC-3

does not have the ball (hence their alias of "non-offensive touchdowns"), and putting 7 points on the board without your offense even being on the field is a big boost to a team's likelihood of winning the game. During these 4 seasons, the Chiefs also lead the NFL in regular season games where they won the turnover battle. They have won the turnover battle in 36 games the past 4 years (and are 30-6 in these games). This is after winning the turnover battle in just 6 games the prior 2 seasons (pre-Reid/Sutton), which was the 2nd fewest in the NFL.

The Chiefs have become masters at choosing the quickest path to victory. Winning the turnover battle and/or the return TD battle. By winning these two stats, it renders much of what the offense does less critical. Hence, Andy Reid can allow Alex Smith to throw check downs and stay conservative in order to avoid costly turnovers which may result in the Chiefs losing the turnover battle. The Chiefs can run the ball more than average even if the run game is slightly below average. The Chiefs can post winning records and 11 or 12 win seasons, without being an efficient enough in the metrics to embody a 11 or 12 win team. (cont'd - see KC-4)

2017 Rest Analysis

Avg Rest	6.67
Avg Rk	1
Team More Rest	4
Opp More Rest	2
Net Rest Edge	2
3 Days Rest	1
4 Days Rest	0
5 Days Rest	3
6 Days Rest	6
7 Days Rest	2
8 Days Rest	0
9 Days Rest	1
10 Days Rest	1
11 Days Rest	0
12 Days Rest	0
13 Days Rest	1
14 Days Rest	0

Health by Unit*

2016 Rk	27
(2015 Rk)	7
Off Rk	14
Def Rk	30
QB Rk	19
RB Rk	30
WR Rk	18
TE Rk	1
OLine Rk	14
DLine Rk	32
LB Rk	32
DB Rk	3

**Based on the great work of Scott Kacsmar from Football Outsiders*

2017 Weekly Betting Lines (wks 1-16)

1	2	3	4	5	6	7	8	9	11	12	13	14	15	16
NE	PHI	LAC	WSH	HOU	PIT	OAK	DEN	DAL	NYG	BUF	NYJ	OAK	LAC	MIA
A	H	A	H	A	H	A	H	A	A	H	H	H	H	
+7.0	-4.0	-1.5	-5.0	+1.0	-1.5	+3.0	-3.0	+6.5	+2.0	-6.0	-4.5	-3.0	-6.0	-4.5

Home Lines (wks 1-16)

2	4	6	8	12	14	15	16
PHI	WSH	PIT	DEN	BUF	OAK	LAC	MIA
-4.0	-5.0	-1.5	-3.0	-6.0	-3.0	-6.0	-4.5

Road Lines (wks 1-16)

1	3	5	7	9	11	13
NE	LAC	HOU	OAK	DAL	NYG	NYJ
+7.0	-1.5	+1.0	+3.0	+6.5	+2.0	-4.5

Kansas City Chiefs 2016 Play Analysis

2016 Play Tendencies

All Pass %	60%
All Pass Rk	14
All Rush %	40%
All Rush Rk	19
1 Score Pass %	57%
1 Score Pass Rk	18
2015 1 Score Pass %	55%
2015 1 Score Pass Rk	23
Pass Increase %	3%
Pass Increase Rk	9
1 Score Rush %	43%
1 Score Rush Rk	15
Up Pass %	59%
Up Pass Rk	11
Up Rush %	41%
Up Rush Rk	22
Down Pass %	63%
Down Pass Rk	10
Down Rush %	37%
Down Rush Rk	23

2016 Down & Distance Tendencies

Down	Distance	Total Plays	Pass Rate	Run Rate	Play Success %
1	Short (1-3)	5	60%	40%	40%
	Med (4-7)	15	47%	53%	53%
	Long (8-10)	306	51%	49%	50%
	XL (11+)	12	92%	8%	8%
2	Short (1-3)	30	43%	57%	63%
	Med (4-7)	79	54%	46%	53%
	Long (8-10)	90	64%	36%	49%
	XL (11+)	45	73%	27%	20%
3	Short (1-3)	46	48%	52%	61%
	Med (4-7)	47	91%	9%	40%
	Long (8-10)	32	97%	3%	25%
	XL (11+)	34	88%	12%	15%
4	Short (1-3)	8	38%	63%	63%
	Med (4-7)	2	100%	0%	100%

Shotgun %:

Under Center	Shotgun
33%	67%
37%	*63%*

AVG

Run Rate:

Under Center	Shotgun
71%	24%
68%	*23%*

AVG

Pass Rate:

Under Center	Shotgun
29%	76%
32%	*77%*

AVG

Short Yardage Intelligence:

2nd and Short Run

Run Freq	Run % Rk	NFL Run Freq Avg	Run 1D Rate	Run NFL 1D Avg
55%	28	65%	50%	71%

2nd and Short Pass

Pass Freq	Pass % Rk	NFL Pass Freq Avg	Pass 1D Rate	Pass NFL 1D Avg
45%	5	35%	30%	52%

Most Frequent Play

Down	Distance	Play Type	Player	Total Plays	Play Success %
1	Short (1-3)	RUSH	Spencer Ware	2	100%
	Med (4-7)	RUSH	Spencer Ware	4	25%
	Long (8-10)	RUSH	Spencer Ware	84	49%
	XL (11+)	PASS	Tyreek Hill	2	0%
			Jeremy Maclin	2	0%
2	Short (1-3)	RUSH	Spencer Ware	5	80%
			Charcandrick West	5	80%
	Med (4-7)	RUSH	Spencer Ware	22	64%
	Long (8-10)	RUSH	Spencer Ware	16	56%
	XL (11+)	PASS	Travis Kelce	7	71%
3	Short (1-3)	RUSH	Spencer Ware	15	67%
	Med (4-7)	PASS	Travis Kelce	11	82%
	Long (8-10)	PASS	Chris Conley	7	43%
	XL (11+)	PASS	Albert Wilson	7	14%

Most Successful Play*

Down	Distance	Play Type	Player	Total Plays	Play Success %
1	Long (8-10)	PASS	Chris Conley	13	77%
2	Short (1-3)	RUSH	Spencer Ware	5	80%
			Charcandrick West	5	80%
	Med (4-7)	PASS	Chris Conley	6	67%
	Long (8-10)	PASS	Chris Conley	7	71%
	XL (11+)	PASS	Travis Kelce	7	71%
3	Short (1-3)	RUSH	Spencer Ware	15	67%
	Med (4-7)	PASS	Travis Kelce	11	82%
	Long (8-10)	PASS	Chris Conley	7	43%
	XL (11+)	PASS	Jeremy Maclin	5	40%

**Minimum 5 plays to qualify*

2016 Snap Rates

Week	Opp	Score	Travis Kelce	Chris Conley	Jeremy Maclin	Spencer Ware	Albert Wilson	Demetrius Harris	Tyreek Hill	Ch. West
1	SD	W 33-27	62 (87%)	61 (86%)	65 (92%)	34 (48%)	49 (69%)	28 (39%)	11 (15%)	35 (49%)
2	HOU	L 19-12	52 (81%)	54 (84%)	63 (98%)	33 (52%)	41 (64%)	19 (30%)	7 (11%)	24 (38%)
3	NYJ	W 24-3	58 (92%)	51 (81%)	60 (95%)	45 (71%)	21 (33%)	31 (49%)	12 (19%)	14 (22%)
4	PIT	L 43-14	71 (95%)	71 (95%)	73 (97%)	55 (73%)	51 (68%)	15 (20%)	18 (24%)	
6	OAK	W 26-10	55 (86%)	38 (59%)	51 (80%)	40 (63%)	9 (14%)	36 (56%)	18 (28%)	8 (13%)
7	NO	W 27-21	47 (90%)	30 (58%)	43 (83%)	36 (69%)	11 (21%)	28 (54%)	18 (35%)	14 (27%)
8	IND	W 30-14	67 (91%)	54 (73%)	65 (88%)	26 (35%)	20 (27%)	36 (49%)	21 (28%)	42 (57%)
9	JAC	W 19-14	43 (74%)	51 (88%)	2 (3%)		41 (71%)	30 (52%)	34 (59%)	45 (78%)
10	CAR	W 20-17	61 (95%)	54 (84%)		41 (64%)	46 (72%)	22 (34%)	39 (61%)	20 (31%)
11	TB	L 19-17	44 (83%)	51 (96%)		41 (77%)	40 (75%)	20 (38%)	36 (68%)	10 (19%)
12	DEN	W 30-27	77 (91%)	85 (100%)		41 (48%)	58 (68%)	31 (36%)	57 (67%)	32 (38%)
13	ATL	W 29-28	39 (80%)	42 (86%)		38 (78%)	33 (67%)	31 (63%)	25 (51%)	11 (22%)
14	OAK	W 21-13	41 (75%)	36 (65%)	42 (76%)	40 (73%)	11 (20%)	33 (60%)	25 (45%)	13 (24%)
15	TEN	L 19-17	49 (84%)	44 (76%)	49 (84%)	36 (62%)	8 (14%)	20 (34%)	30 (52%)	21 (36%)
16	DEN	W 33-10	69 (91%)	54 (71%)	65 (86%)	37 (49%)	17 (22%)	50 (66%)	28 (37%)	29 (38%)
17	SD	W 37-27	47 (77%)	40 (66%)	49 (80%)		10 (16%)	31 (51%)	38 (62%)	38 (62%)
Grand Total			882 (86%)	816 (79%)	627 (80%)	543 (62%)	466 (45%)	461 (46%)	417 (41%)	356 (37%)

Personnel Groupings

Personnel	Team %	NFL Avg	Succ. %
1-1 [3WR]	51%	60%	45%
1-2 [2WR]	20%	19%	50%
2-1 [2WR]	10%	7%	47%
1-3 [1WR]	10%	3%	44%
2-2 [1WR]	5%	3%	29%

Grouping Tendencies

Personnel	Pass Rate	Pass Succ. %	Run Succ. %
1-1 [3WR]	69%	44%	47%
1-2 [2WR]	59%	51%	48%
2-1 [2WR]	51%	41%	53%
1-3 [1WR]	39%	56%	35%
2-2 [1WR]	2%	0%	30%

Red Zone Targets (min 3)

Receiver	All	Inside 5	6-10	11-20
Travis Kelce	19	3	5	11
Tyreek Hill	16	2	5	9
Chris Conley	14	1	3	10
Jeremy Maclin	12		1	11
Albert Wilson	8	3	2	3
Charcandrick West	7	3		4
Demetrius Harris	5	2	1	2
Spencer Ware	3	2		1

Red Zone Rushes (min 3)

Rusher	All	Inside 5	6-10	11-20
Spencer Ware	28	12	9	7
Charcandrick West	15	4	7	4
Alex Smith	12	3	5	4
Jamaal Charles	4	2	1	1
Tyreek Hill	4	1		3
Knile Davis	2			2

Early Down Target Rate

RB	TE	WR
17%	29%	54%
19%	*20% NFL AVG*	*61%*

Overall Target Success %

RB	TE	WR
44% #18	57% #9	48% #21

Kansas City Chiefs 2016 Passing Recap & 2017 Outlook

We know Alex Smith operates a conservative Chiefs gameplan. Andy Reid did a great job last year of designing shorter passes which produce large, chunk gains. As such, while Alex Smith averaged just 4.9 air yards per completion (NFL avg = 6.4) he still achieved an 8% rate of 20+ yard gains in the passing game thanks to the YAC. It is somewhat amazing that on 523 pass attempts a starting quarterback on a 12-win team records just 16 touchdown passes, but such was the Chiefs offense last year. Smith struggles in targeting players beyond the sticks on 3rd down. 76% of his 3rd down completions were short of the sticks, which ranked 37th out of 40 quarterbacks. To Reid's credit, they were able to design these plays such that 58% of the plays thrown short were converted into first downs, one of the best rates in the NFL. The receiving corps still lacks talent outside the top couple of threats, so play design becomes even more of a factor and fortunately Reid excels there. The Chiefs either need to run more often on 3rd and short or they need to improve the pass offense. While their play frequency was similar, the Chiefs were above average (68%) in rushing success rate but below average in pass success rate (52%).

Alex Smith Rating All Downs

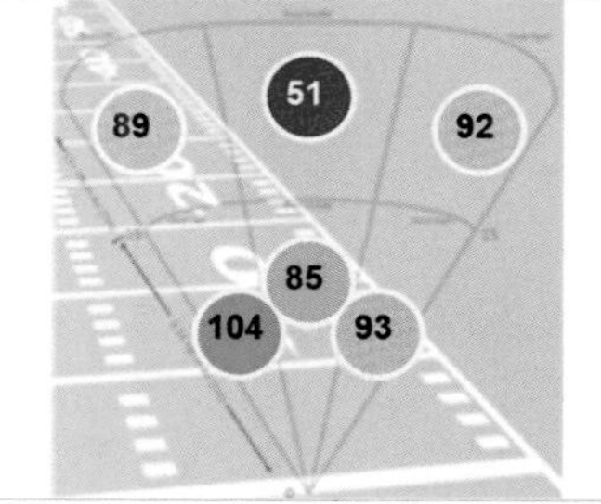

Alex Smith Rating Early Downs

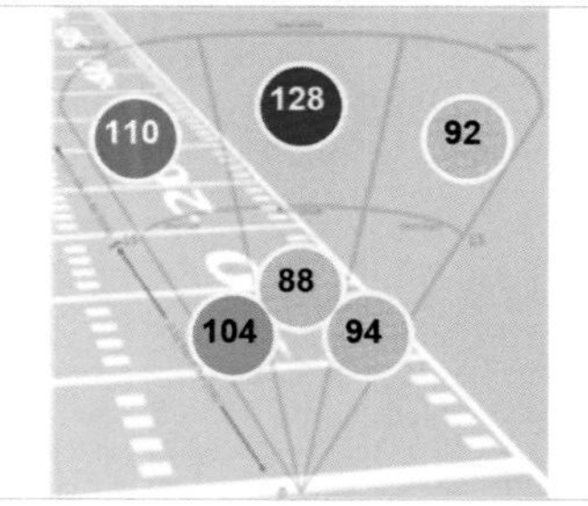

2016 Standard Passing Table

QB	Comp	Att	Comp %	Yds	YPA	TDs	INT	Sacks	Rating	Rk
Alex Smith	348	523	67%	3,685	7.0	16	9	29	89.9	23
NFL Avg			63%		7.2				90.4	

2016 Advanced Passing Table

QB	Success %	EDSR Passing Success %	20+ Yd Pass Gains	20+ Yd Pass %	30+ Yd Pass Gains	30+ Yd Pass %	Air Yds per Comp	YAC per Comp	20+ Air Yd Comp	20+ Air Yd %
Alex Smith	48%	52%	42	8%	17	3%	4.9	5.7	16	3%
NFL Avg	44%	48%	27	8%	10	3%	6.4	4.8	12	4%

Interception Rates by Down

Yards to Go	1	2	3	4	Total
1 & 2	0.0%	0.0%	0.0%	0.0%	0.0%
3, 4, 5	0.0%	6.5%	0.0%	0.0%	2.7%
6 - 9	0.0%	1.9%	6.0%	0.0%	3.7%
10 - 14	1.5%	0.0%	0.0%	0.0%	1.0%
15+	0.0%	0.0%	0.0%		0.0%
Total	1.4%	1.7%	2.0%	0.0%	1.6%

3rd Down Passing - Short of Sticks Analysis

QB	Avg Yds to Go	Air Yds (of Comps)	Avg Yds Short	Short of Sticks Rate	Rk
Alex Smith	7.7	5.5	-2.2	76%	37
NFL Avg	7.6	6.8	-0.8	57%	

Air Yds vs YAC

Air Yds %	YAC %	Rk
40%	60%	49
54%	46%	

2016 Receiving Recap & 2017 Outlook

The receiving corps from 2016 is largely what we'll see in 2017, with the exception of 4th round pick Jehu Chesson from Michigan. Travis Kelce obviously is the alpha dog in this passing attack, and his success rate and missed YPA are top 10 in the NFL. It is a bit surprising that Tyreek Hill's YAS % isn't higher considering his explosiveness. But the fact is he scored 3 of his 9 offensive TDs when rushing the ball and averaged 10.6 yds/carry vs 7.0 yds/reception. Expect more Hill in 2017. Also, the Chiefs may want to implement more 12 personnel and less 11, as their success rates with 2 WRs are much better than 3.

Player *Min 50 Targets*	Targets	Comp %	YPA	Rating	TOARS	Success %	Success Rk	Missed YPA Rk	YAS % Rk	TDs
Travis Kelce	124	73%	9.7	114	5.4	63%	8	5	30	4
Tyreek Hill	89	73%	7.0	105	4.7	51%	71	88	77	6
Jeremy Maclin	80	58%	7.1	72	4.0	48%	98	97	72	2
Chris Conley	72	64%	7.6	81	4.1	57%	32	41	108	0
Albert Wilson	54	61%	5.2	93	3.6	35%	144	137	123	3

Directional Passer Rating Delivered

Receiver	Short Left	Short Middle	Short Right	Deep Left	Deep Middle	Deep Right	Player Total
Travis Kelce	126	112	106	104	77	95	114
Tyreek Hill	113	110	86	119	96	87	105
Jeremy Maclin	34	71	81	99	45	106	72
Chris Conley	99	51	89	96	40	69	81
Albert Wilson	95	70	100	131	88	54	93
Spencer Ware	145	74	93	40	119	96	112
Charcandrick West	101	78	118			40	109
Demetrius Harris	83	49	65	40	40		60
Team Total	105	87	96	116	52	89	96

2016 Rushing Recap & 2017 Outlook

While Ware saw massive usage all game long, West's usage was only evident in large to blowout leads. Interestingly, this increased usage (8% on the ground in one-score games vs 22% on the ground in blowout games) did not hurt Ware, as Ware actually saw a higher usage rate when West was up at 22% (Ware received 27% of offensive plays). Ware was the vastly superior rusher in almost every situation, and deserves a higher rate of the team's red zone rushes, specifically inside the 10, where West was successful on just 36% of carries, while Ware was successful on 53%. On short yardage in general, KC was not strong running in short yardage: with 1-2 yards to go, only 61% of their plays were successful, 26th in the NFL.

Player *Min 50 Rushes*	Rushes	YPA	Success %	Success Rk	Missed YPA Rk	YTS % Rk	YAS % Rk	Early Down Success %	Early Down Success Rk	TDs
Spencer Ware	222	4.3	52%	13	4	20	41	52%	14	4
Charcandrick West	89	3.3	36%	65	62	40	60	34%	65	1

Yards per Carry by Direction

Directional Run Frequency

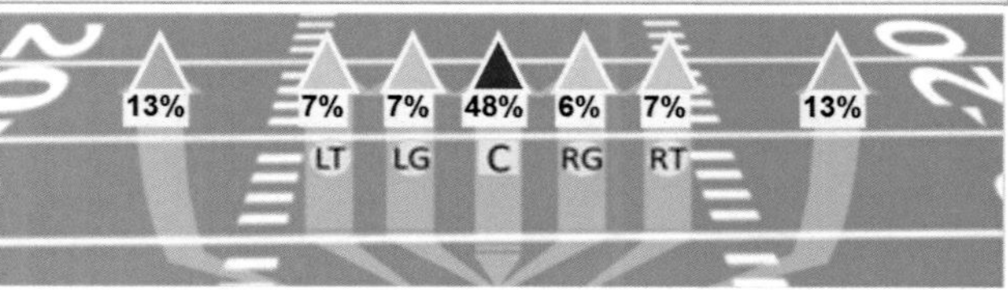

KC-4

So the big question becomes can the Chiefs replicate this success in 2017? Undoubtedly the answer is they are favorites to do just that. They return a roster nearly identical to 2016. Offensively, their skill positions are identical and while WR Tyreek Hill should receive more usage, his ability to target him in low risk / high upside positions thanks to his speed keeps Alex Smith's comfort rate high. Hill is also a freak in the return game, and the defense should not take a step back thanks to continuity of personnel and coaching. That side of the ball will face a similar schedule to last year with two key exceptions: better pass protection from opposing offensive lines and slightly more efficient and explosive rushing offenses. In a competitive AFC West, they are favored in 10 of their first 15 games and are projected to win 9 games.

There is a very good chance that many of those wins occur by the Chiefs continuing to have Alex Smith err on the side of caution with the football, allow Tyreek Hill to stay explosive in the return game and let Bob Sutton's defense play an aggressive style to maximize turnovers and/or return TDs. However, like in years past, while this formula has proven to be reproduced it always falls short in the postseason because other good playoff teams aren't prone to be turnover machines, for example. And when the Chiefs can't win that battle, their offense has lacked the potency to ward off playoff competition

The Chiefs made the first move toward understanding of this issue by trading up to acquire QB Patrick Mahomes. Mahomes in many ways is the anti-Alex Smith. It will be interesting to see how and when they work Mahomes into the offense, but I can imagine a rollercoaster of emotions presented (highs and lows) to Andy Reid during the course of the game that Alex Smith didn't provide. The Chiefs can do other things to build a more efficient offense in 2017 which don't require new personnel.

First they have to be much more efficient on 2nd and short. They need to run the ball more (they ran it 5th least often) and more efficiently (they were below average in first down conversion rate at 50% vs the avg of 71%). Though they passed it often, they were 22% below average in conversion rate (30% vs avg of 52%). Thus, their rushing was 20% more likely to convert a first down than their passing. The Chiefs must get more run heavy and perhaps better use of tempo and scheme on these 2nd and short plays is the recipe.

Another would be a more efficient use of the run game inside the opponent's 5 yard line. Excluding a random Travis Kelce run, the Chiefs passed 19 times and ran 24 times. But their passing was successful just 42% of the time, whereas their rushing was successful 54% of the time. Minimizing Alex Smith runs outside the 5 (where other rushers are more efficient) but using more designed Smith runs inside the 5 (where Smith is more efficient) is advised, as is cease targeting Chris Conley and maximizing Tyreek Hill targets in the red zone.

Division History: Season Wins & 2017 Projection

2013 Wins | 2014 Wins | 2015 Wins | 2016 Wins | Proj 2017 Wins

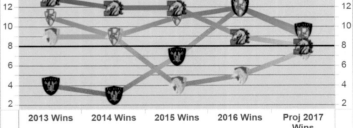

Rank of 2017 Defensive Pass Efficiency Faced by Week

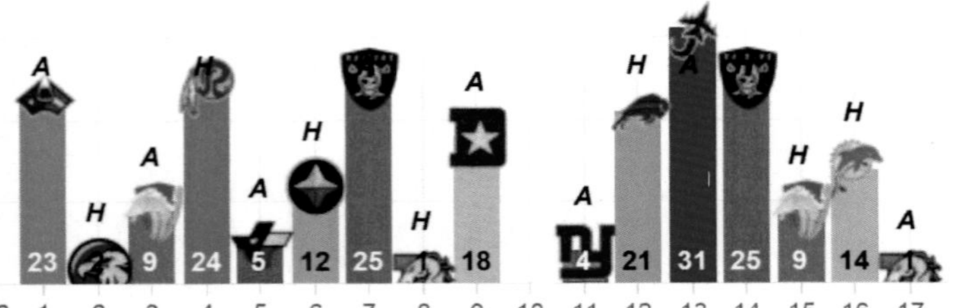

Rank of 2017 Defensive Rush Efficiency Faced by Week

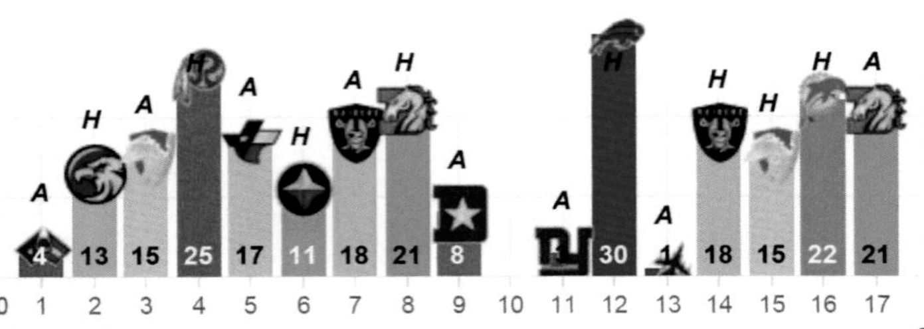

2016 Situational Usage by Player & Position

Usage Rate by Score

		Being Blown Out (14+)	Down Big (9-13)	One Score	Large Lead (9-13)	Blowout Lead (14+)	Grand Total
RUSH	Spencer Ware	15%	17%	26%	23%	27%	24%
	Charcandrick West	3%	8%	8%	16%	22%	9%
	Travis Kelce			0%			0%
	Tyreek Hill	1%	2%	4%	3%	1%	3%
	Jeremy Maclin	1%					0%
	Albert Wilson			0%			0%
	Knile Davis	1%		1%	3%	3%	1%
	Jamaal Charles	1%		2%	1%		1%
	De'Anthony Thomas			0%	1%		0%
	Total	22%	27%	41%	48%	53%	40%
PASS	Spencer Ware	6%	10%	4%	3%	5%	5%
	Charcandrick West	5%	8%	3%	5%	4%	4%
	Travis Kelce	13%	10%	16%	10%	6%	13%
	Tyreek Hill	13%	3%	10%	8%	6%	9%
	Jeremy Maclin	9%	15%	8%	7%	10%	9%
	Chris Conley	12%	13%	7%	6%	5%	8%
	Albert Wilson	14%	10%	5%	3%		6%
	Demetrius Harris	3%	2%	3%	5%	8%	3%
	Knile Davis	3%		0%	1%		1%
	Jamaal Charles			0%	1%		0%
	De'Anthony Thomas			1%	1%		1%
	Anthony Sherman			1%		1%	1%
	Ross Travis	2%	2%	1%			1%
	James O'Shaughnes..			0%	1%	1%	0%
	Total	78%	73%	59%	52%	47%	60%

Positional Target Distribution vs NFL Average

		NFL Wide				Team Only			
		Left	Middle	Right	Total	Left	Middle	Right	Total
Deep	WR	1,013	567	978	**2,558**	18	14	23	**55**
	TE	151	143	155	**449**	7	4	8	**19**
	RB	24	3	37	**64**	1	1	3	**5**
	All	**1,188**	**713**	**1,170**	**3,071**	**26**	**19**	**34**	**79**
Short	WR	3,007	1,721	3,082	**7,810**	86	50	104	**240**
	TE	796	832	1,097	**2,725**	40	43	54	**137**
	RB	991	609	1,073	**2,673**	24	13	40	**77**
	All	**4,794**	**3,162**	**5,252**	**13,208**	**150**	**106**	**198**	**454**
Total		**5,982**	**3,875**	**6,422**	**16,279**	**176**	**125**	**232**	**533**

Positional Success Rates vs NFL Average

		NFL Wide				Team Only			
		Left	Middle	Right	Total	Left	Middle	Right	Total
Deep	WR	37%	51%	38%	**40%**	39%	29%	43%	**38%**
	TE	44%	50%	43%	**46%**	43%	25%	50%	**42%**
	RB	33%	67%	24%	**30%**	0%	100%	33%	**40%**
	All	**38%**	**51%**	**38%**	**41%**	**38%**	**32%**	**44%**	**39%**
Short	WR	52%	57%	51%	**53%**	50%	54%	50%	**51%**
	TE	49%	62%	52%	**54%**	70%	60%	56%	**61%**
	RB	47%	49%	44%	**46%**	54%	62%	43%	**49%**
	All	**50%**	**57%**	**50%**	**52%**	**56%**	**58%**	**50%**	**54%**
Total		**48%**	**56%**	**48%**	**50%**	**53%**	**54%**	**49%**	**52%**

Los Angeles Chargers

2017 Coaches

Head Coach:
Anthony Lynn (BUF OC) (1st yr)
Offensive Coordinator:
Ken Whisenhunt (2nd yr)
Defensive Coordinator:
Gus Bradley (SD HC) (1st yr)

2017 Forecast

Wins	Div Rank
7.5	#4

Past Records

2016: 5-11
2015: 4-12
2014: 9-7

EASY HARD

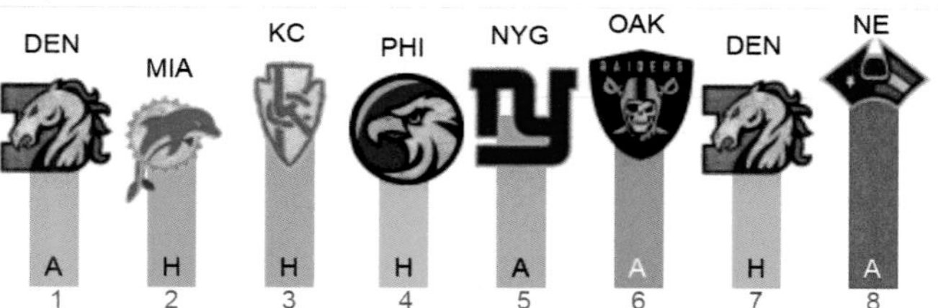

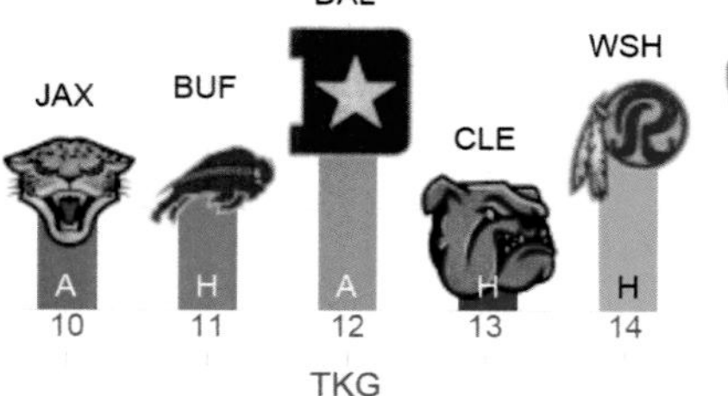

MNF TKG TNF

Key Players Lost

TXN	Player (POS)
Cut	Dunlap, King T
	Fields, Carlos LB
	Flowers, Brandon CB
	Fluker, D.J. G
	Franklin, Orlando G
	Hekking, Brock LB
	Johnson, Stevie WR
	Lee, Mike CB
	McGee, Jake TE
Declared Free Agent	Addae, Jahleel S
	Cumberland, Jeff TE
	Hillman, Ronnie RB
	McClain, Robert CB
	McCluster, Dexter RB
	Oliver, Branden RB
	Square, Damion DT
	Te'o, Manti LB
	Williams, Tourek LB
	Woodhead, Danny RB
Retired	Dunlap, King T

Average Line	# Games Favored	# Games Underdog
+2.6	5	8

Regular Season Wins: Past & Current Proj

Proj 2017 Wins  7.5

2016 Wins  5

Proj 2016 Wins  6.5

2015 Wins  4

2014 Wins  9

2013 Wins  9

1 3 5 7 9 11 13 15

2017 Los Angeles Chargers Overview

The Chargers would rather trade the water in San Diego for the smog of Los Angeles given their injury history the last couple of years. They were the 4th most injured team in 2015 and became the 2nd most injured team last year. Unlike in 2015, when it was their offensive line leading the way, this year the offensive line and quarterback position was relatively healthy. But a season many experts including myself could have exceeded expectations got off to a brutal start as WR Keenan Allen went down in week 1 and the hits kept coming from there. By the end of the season, the Chargers WRs were the most injured in football, the RBs were the 2nd most injured, the defensive backs were the 3rd most injured and the linebackers were the 7th most injured.

While these injuries really hurt the Chargers, absent them the Chargers still had deficiencies which would have prevented them from making too much noise into the postseason. And as we sit ready for 2017, the Chargers and Philip Rivers are not really built to run the distance this year either. They are forecast to finish with a losing record in from oddsmakers, but they sure as hell should be fun to watch this year.

In 2016 the Chargers faced the 9th most difficult passing offenses and had tons of injuries to their receivers and their primary receiving running back, yet still delivered the 14th rated passing offense which recorded the 8th best EDSR (Early Down Success Rate) and likewise was 8th in 3rd down efficiency. Heading into the season, Keenan Allen and Travis Benjamin were forecast as their top threats, with Stevie Johnson being forecast in the slot. None of those players even ranked top 5 on the Chargers for skill position snaps in 2016. Instead, the team was led by Dontrelle Inman and Tyrell Williams as the 2 players recording the most snaps. It truly was a remarkable year in San Diego.

Those snap rates were unintentional, and the result of injuries. But they intentionally chose to become more inefficient by playing Antonio Gates so much more than the rookie Hunter Henry. They wanted Gates to break the TD record, and he's a legend in San Diego, and the Chargers obviously were doing nothing with their season, so there were sentimental reasons why they let it happen. But when you look at virtually any advanced metric (or even basic metrics)

(cont'd - see LAC2)

2017 Lineup & Cap Hits

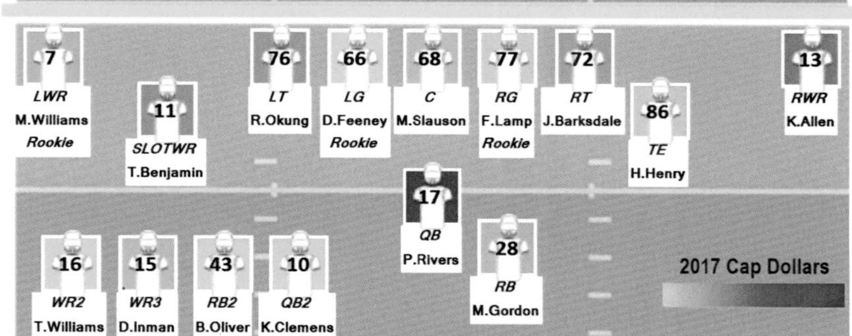

Key Free Agents/ Trades Added

Barner, Kenjon RB

Boston, Tre S

Brown, Da'Ron WR

Okung, Russell T

Drafted Players

Rd	Pk	Player (College)
1	7	WR - Mike Williams (Clemson)
2	38	G - Forrest Lamp (Western Kentucky)
3	71	G - Dan Feeney (Indiana)
4	113	S - Rayshawn Jenkins (Miami (FL))
5	151	CB - Desmond King (Iowa)
6	190	OT - Sam Tevi (Utah)
7	225	DE - Isaac Rochell (Notre Dame)

2017 Unit Spending

Positional Spending

	Rank	Total	2016 Rk
All OFF	12	$85.30M	5
QB	12	$21.63M	17
OL	29	$22.07M	12
RB	20	$6.21M	13
WR	7	$26.12M	11
TE	15	$9.27M	10
All DEF	21	$74.54M	18
DL	17	$25.01M	12
LB	12	$24.10M	18
CB	23	$11.80M	11
S	10	$13.63M	24

Los Angeles Chargers 2016 Success Rate Radar

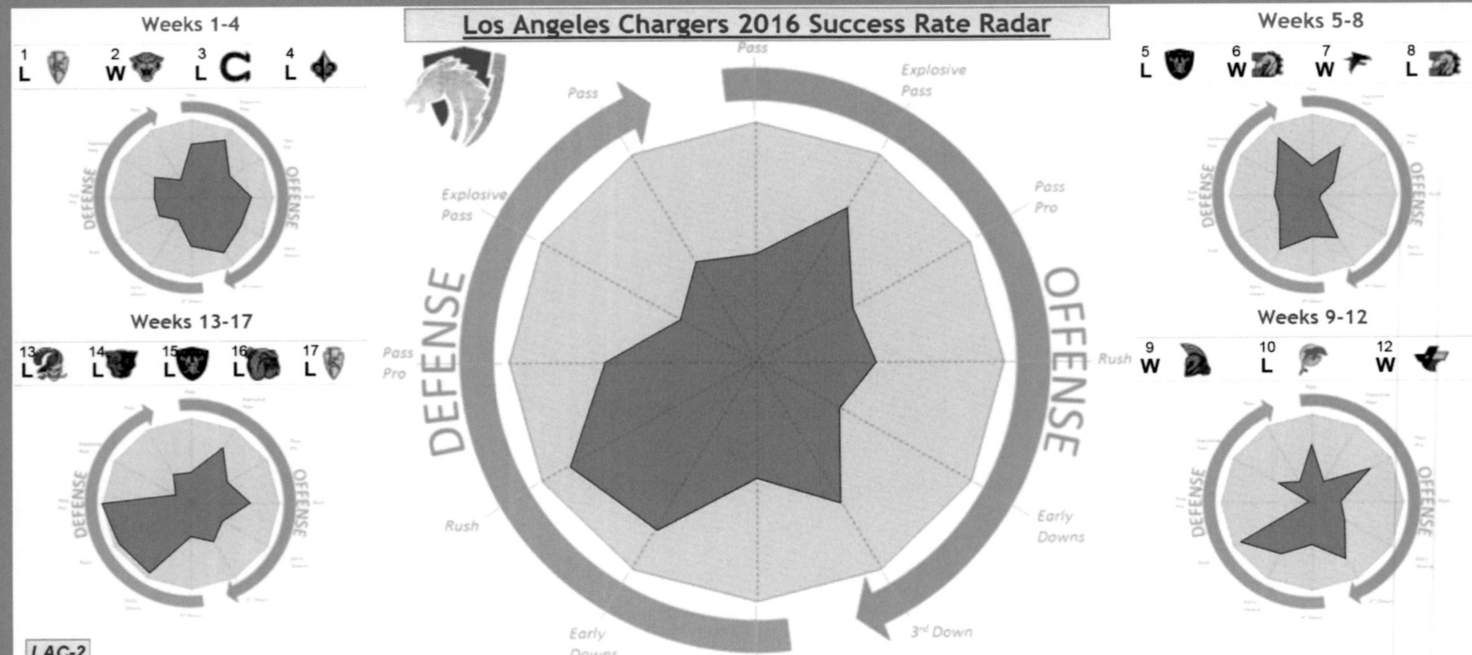

LAC-2

it wasn't close. Henry averaged 9.1 yards per attempt (best on the team) while Gates averaged just 5.9. Henry delivered a 136 rating (best on the team) while Gates delivered an 86 rating. In terms of advanced metrics, Henry ranked #1 in the entire NFL for missed YPA (yards per attempt), a metric which measures how close to successful a player was on unsuccessful plays. Gates was 46th in this metric. Henry was also 16th in overall success rate while Gates was 60th. Clearly, targeting Gates 93 times to only 53 targets for Henry was not an efficient usage of these players. While Gates is back in 2017 and looking for the TD record, Henry has the ability to emerge early in the season, overtake Gates rather quickly, and become their dominant TE. Gates will still see usage in an effort to get him the TD record (he has 111 receiving TDs, tied with Tony Gonzalez for most all time).

While the wide receiver inefficiency was prompted by injury and the tight end inefficiency was prompted by usage, the running back inefficiency was prompted by injury and inefficiency despite an easy schedule. Pass catching specialist Danny Woodhead was lost due to injury and that left Melvin Gordon as the benefactor of a heavy workload. He saw 254 rushes, the #2 (Kenneth Farrow) seeing just 60 carries and every other back carrying 23 or fewer times. Heading into 2016, I was concerned with the Chargers running game. They ranked as the 2nd worst run team in 2015. Gordon's metrics were bad virtually across the board. Couple that with offseason microfracture surgery and he needed a big bounce back in 2016.

Gordon was great on 3rd down, but poor in many other situations. On 3rd and short, Gordon converted 75% of his 16 carries into first down, tied for 6th best in the NFL. But he struggled tremendously on all other downs. While he was solid on short yardage on 3rd down, such was not the case on other downs. On 2nd and short, Gordon converted just 61% into first downs, which was the 4th best (and worst) on his team, and ranked 3rd worst in the NFL (min 15 attempts). He averaged just 1.5 yards per carry on these runs, the worst mark in the NFL. Zooming back

(cont'd - see LAC-3)

2016 Offensive Advanced Metrics

Metric	Rank
EDSR Off	8
30 & In Off	8
Red Zone Off	15
3rd Down Off	8
YPPA Off	7
YPPT Off	4
Offensive Efficiency	19
Pass Efficiency Off	14
Pass Pro Efficiency Off	24
RB Pass Eff Off	19
Rush Efficiency Off	24
Explosive Pass Off	10
Explosive Run Off	25

2016 Defensive Advanced Metrics

Metric	Rank
EDSR Def	21
30 & In Def	17
Red Zone Def	22
3rd Down Def	14
YPPA Def	17
YPPT Def	27
Defensive Efficiency	8
Pass Efficiency Def	9
Pass Pro Efficiency Def	16
RB Pass Eff Def	11
Rush Efficiency Def	15
Explosive Pass Def	25
Explosive Run Def	22

2016 Weekly EDSR & Season Trending Performance

WEEK	1	2	3	4	5	6	7	8	9	10	12	13	14	15	16	17
RESULT	L	W	L	L	L	W	W	L	W	L	W	L	L	L	L	L
OPP	KC	JAC	IND	NO	OAK	DEN	ATL	DEN	TEN	MIA	HOU	TB	CAR	OAK	CLE	KC
SITE	A	H	A	H	A	H	A	A	H	H	A	H	A	H	A	H
MARGIN	-6	24	-4	-1	-3	8	3	-8	8	-7	8	-7	-12	-3	-3	-10
PTS	27	38	22	34	31	21	33	19	43	24	21	21	16	16	17	27
OPP PTS	33	14	26	35	34	13	30	27	35	31	13	28	28	19	20	37

EDSR by Wk
W=Green
L=Red

OFF/DEF
EDSR
Blue=OFF
(high=good)
Red=DEF
(low=good)

2016 Close Game Records

All 2016 Wins: **5**
FG Games (<=3 pts) W-L: **1-4**
FG Games Win %: **20% (#28)**
FG Games Wins (% of Total Wins): **20% (#20)**
1 Score Games (<=8 pts) W-L: **4-9**
1 Score Games Win %: **31% (#24)**
1 Score Games Wins (% of Total Wins): **80% (#5)**

2016 Critical & Game-Deciding Stats

TO Margin	-7
TO Given	35
INT Given	21
FUM Given	14
TO Taken	28
INT Taken	18
FUM Taken	10
Sack Margin	-1
Sacks	35
Sacks Allow	36
Return TD Margin	+0
Ret TDs	5
Ret TDs Allow	5
Penalty Margin	+11
Penalties	107
Opponent Penalties	118

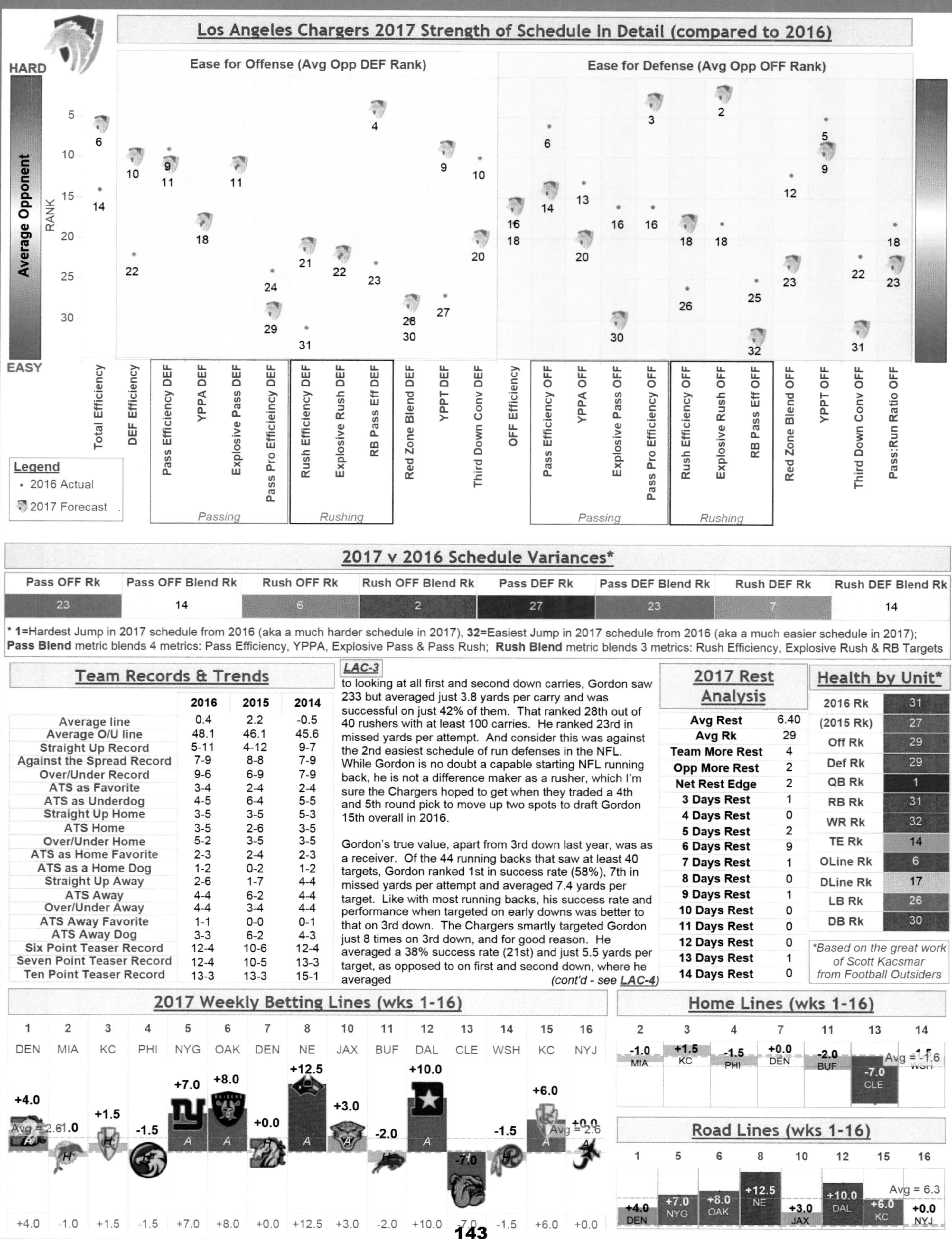

Los Angeles Chargers 2017 Strength of Schedule In Detail (compared to 2016)

2017 v 2016 Schedule Variances*

Pass OFF Rk	Pass OFF Blend Rk	Rush OFF Rk	Rush OFF Blend Rk	Pass DEF Rk	Pass DEF Blend Rk	Rush DEF Rk	Rush DEF Blend Rk
23	14	6	2	27	23	7	14

* **1**=Hardest Jump in 2017 schedule from 2016 (aka a much harder schedule in 2017), **32**=Easiest Jump in 2017 schedule from 2016 (aka a much easier schedule in 2017); **Pass Blend** metric blends 4 metrics: Pass Efficiency, YPPA, Explosive Pass & Pass Rush; **Rush Blend** metric blends 3 metrics: Rush Efficiency, Explosive Rush & RB Targets

Team Records & Trends

	2016	2015	2014
Average line	0.4	2.2	-0.5
Average O/U line	48.1	46.1	45.6
Straight Up Record	5-11	4-12	9-7
Against the Spread Record	7-9	8-8	7-9
Over/Under Record	9-6	6-9	7-9
ATS as Favorite	3-4	2-4	2-4
ATS as Underdog	4-5	6-4	5-5
Straight Up Home	3-5	3-5	5-3
ATS Home	3-5	2-6	3-5
Over/Under Home	5-2	3-5	3-5
ATS as Home Favorite	2-3	2-4	2-3
ATS as a Home Dog	1-2	0-2	1-2
Straight Up Away	2-6	1-7	4-4
ATS Away	4-4	6-2	4-4
Over/Under Away	4-4	3-4	4-4
ATS Away Favorite	1-1	0-0	0-1
ATS Away Dog	3-3	6-2	4-3
Six Point Teaser Record	12-4	10-6	12-4
Seven Point Teaser Record	12-4	10-5	13-3
Ten Point Teaser Record	13-3	13-3	15-1

LAC-3

to looking at all first and second down carries, Gordon saw 233 but averaged just 3.8 yards per carry and was successful on just 42% of them. That ranked 28th out of 40 rushers with at least 100 carries. He ranked 23rd in missed yards per attempt. And consider this was against the 2nd easiest schedule of run defenses in the NFL. While Gordon is no doubt a capable starting NFL running back, he is not a difference maker as a rusher, which I'm sure the Chargers hoped to get when they traded a 4th and 5th round pick to move up two spots to draft Gordon 15th overall in 2016.

Gordon's true value, apart from 3rd down last year, was as a receiver. Of the 44 running backs that saw at least 40 targets, Gordon ranked 1st in success rate (58%), 7th in missed yards per attempt and averaged 7.4 yards per target. Like with most running backs, his success rate and performance when targeted on early downs was better to that on 3rd down. The Chargers smartly targeted Gordon just 8 times on 3rd down, and for good reason. He averaged a 38% success rate (21st) and just 5.5 yards per target, as opposed to on first and second down, where he averaged *(cont'd - see **LAC-4**)*

2017 Rest Analysis

Avg Rest	6.40
Avg Rk	29
Team More Rest	4
Opp More Rest	2
Net Rest Edge	2
3 Days Rest	1
4 Days Rest	0
5 Days Rest	2
6 Days Rest	9
7 Days Rest	1
8 Days Rest	0
9 Days Rest	1
10 Days Rest	0
11 Days Rest	0
12 Days Rest	0
13 Days Rest	1
14 Days Rest	0

Health by Unit*

2016 Rk	31
(2015 Rk)	27
Off Rk	29
Def Rk	29
QB Rk	1
RB Rk	31
WR Rk	32
TE Rk	14
OLine Rk	6
DLine Rk	17
LB Rk	26
DB Rk	30

**Based on the great work of Scott Kacsmar from Football Outsiders*

2017 Weekly Betting Lines (wks 1-16)

Week	1	2	3	4	5	6	7	8	10	11	12	13	14	15	16
Opponent	DEN	MIA	KC	PHI	NYG	OAK	DEN	NE	JAX	BUF	DAL	CLE	WSH	KC	NYJ
Line	+4.0	-1.0	+1.5	-1.5	+7.0	+8.0	+0.0	+12.5	+3.0	-2.0	+10.0	-7.0	-1.5	+6.0	+0.0

Avg = 2.6

Home Lines (wks 1-16)

Week	2	3	4	7	11	13	14
Opponent	MIA	KC	PHI	DEN	BUF	CLE	WSH
Line	-1.0	+1.5	-1.5	+0.0	-2.0	-7.0	-1.5

Avg = -1.6

Road Lines (wks 1-16)

Week	1	5	6	8	10	12	15	16
Opponent	DEN	NYG	OAK	NE	JAX	DAL	KC	NYJ
Line	+4.0	+7.0	+8.0	+12.5	+3.0	+10.0	+6.0	+0.0

Avg = 6.3

Los Angeles Chargers 2016 Play Analysis

2016 Play Tendencies

All Pass %	60%
All Pass Rk	12
All Rush %	40%
All Rush Rk	21
1 Score Pass %	60%
1 Score Pass Rk	8
2015 1 Score Pass %	63%
2015 1 Score Pass Rk	3
Pass Increase %	-3%
Pass Increase Rk	24
1 Score Rush %	40%
1 Score Rush Rk	25
Up Pass %	62%
Up Pass Rk	6
Up Rush %	38%
Up Rush Rk	27
Down Pass %	62%
Down Pass Rk	15
Down Rush %	38%
Down Rush Rk	18

2016 Down & Distance Tendencies

Down	Distance	Total Plays	Pass Rate	Run Rate	Play Success %
1	Short (1-3)	14	29%	71%	79%
	Med (4-7)	13	54%	46%	54%
	Long (8-10)	299	44%	56%	46%
	XL (11+)	13	62%	38%	31%
2	Short (1-3)	34	18%	82%	59%
	Med (4-7)	73	64%	36%	52%
	Long (8-10)	96	78%	22%	46%
	XL (11+)	40	80%	20%	30%
3	Short (1-3)	38	68%	32%	63%
	Med (4-7)	51	98%	2%	51%
	Long (8-10)	33	100%	0%	39%
	XL (11+)	22	95%	5%	23%
4	Short (1-3)	3	0%	100%	100%

Shotgun %:

Under Center	Shotgun
39%	61%
37% AVG	*63%*

Run Rate:

Under Center	Shotgun
74%	19%
68% AVG	*23%*

Pass Rate:

Under Center	Shotgun
26%	81%
32% AVG	*77%*

Short Yardage Intelligence:

2nd and Short Run

Run Freq	Run % Rk	NFL Run Freq Avg	Run 1D Rate	Run NFL 1D Avg
71%	6	65%	67%	71%

2nd and Short Pass

Pass Freq	Pass % Rk	NFL Pass Freq Avg	Pass 1D Rate	Pass NFL 1D Avg
29%	25	35%	9%	52%

Most Frequent Play

Down	Distance	Play Type	Player	Total Plays	Play Success %
1	Short (1-3)	RUSH	Melvin Gordon	9	78%
	Med (4-7)	RUSH	Melvin Gordon	4	25%
	Long (8-10)	RUSH	Melvin Gordon	110	39%
	XL (11+)	RUSH	Melvin Gordon	4	25%
2	Short (1-3)	RUSH	Melvin Gordon	18	61%
	Med (4-7)	RUSH	Melvin Gordon	15	40%
	Long (8-10)	PASS	Tyrell Williams	15	53%
	XL (11+)	PASS	Melvin Gordon	7	43%
3	Short (1-3)	RUSH	Melvin Gordon	9	89%
	Med (4-7)	PASS	Tyrell Williams	13	46%
	Long (8-10)	PASS	Tyrell Williams	8	38%
	XL (11+)	PASS	Melvin Gordon	3	67%
			Tyrell Williams	3	33%
			Dontrelle Inman	3	33%

Most Successful Play*

Down	Distance	Play Type	Player	Total Plays	Play Success %
1	Short (1-3)	RUSH	Melvin Gordon	9	78%
	Long (8-10)	PASS	Melvin Gordon	12	67%
		RUSH	Danny Woodhead	6	67%
2	Short (1-3)	RUSH	Kenneth Farrow	7	86%
	Med (4-7)	PASS	Hunter Henry	8	88%
	Long (8-10)	PASS	Travis Benjamin	7	86%
	XL (11+)	PASS	Hunter Henry	5	60%
3	Short (1-3)	RUSH	Melvin Gordon	9	89%
	Med (4-7)	PASS	Antonio Gates	8	75%
	Long (8-10)	PASS	Antonio Gates	7	71%

**Minimum 5 plays to qualify*

2016 Snap Rates

Week	Opp	Score	Dontrelle Inman	Tyrell Williams	Melvin Gordon	Antonio Gates	Hunter Henry	Travis Benjamin
1	KC	L 33-27	58 (79%)	44 (60%)	23 (32%)	48 (66%)	30 (41%)	55 (75%)
2	JAC	W 38-14	59 (87%)	50 (74%)	51 (75%)	36 (53%)	40 (59%)	44 (65%)
3	IND	L 26-22	53 (90%)	51 (86%)	51 (86%)		59 (100%)	45 (76%)
4	NO	L 35-34	68 (97%)	67 (96%)	62 (89%)		68 (97%)	54 (77%)
5	OAK	L 34-31	44 (86%)	34 (67%)	46 (90%)	18 (35%)	42 (82%)	31 (61%)
6	DEN	W 21-13	60 (91%)	48 (73%)	54 (82%)	31 (47%)	45 (68%)	25 (38%)
7	ATL	W 33-30	66 (88%)	66 (88%)	65 (87%)	38 (51%)	45 (60%)	46 (61%)
8	DEN	L 27-19	79 (98%)	59 (73%)	65 (80%)	55 (68%)	45 (56%)	38 (47%)
9	TEN	W 43-35	76 (95%)	66 (83%)	65 (81%)	66 (83%)		7 (9%)
10	MIA	L 31-24	69 (90%)	73 (95%)	70 (91%)	58 (75%)	26 (34%)	
12	HOU	W 21-13	53 (95%)	47 (84%)	51 (91%)	35 (63%)	28 (50%)	37 (66%)
13	TB	L 28-21	53 (96%)	53 (96%)	49 (89%)	33 (60%)	24 (44%)	43 (78%)
14	CAR	L 28-16	61 (94%)	61 (94%)	8 (12%)	37 (57%)	35 (54%)	44 (68%)
15	OAK	L 19-16	47 (85%)	52 (95%)		35 (64%)	29 (53%)	29 (53%)
16	CLE	L 20-17	56 (82%)	56 (82%)		57 (84%)	19 (28%)	49 (72%)
17	KC	L 37-27	53 (80%)	62 (94%)		38 (58%)	36 (55%)	
Grand Total			955 (90%)	889 (84%)	660 (76%)	585 (62%)	571 (59%)	547 (60%)

Personnel Groupings

Personnel	Team %	NFL Avg	Succ. %
1-1 [3WR]	63%	60%	45%
1-2 [2WR]	18%	19%	46%
2-2 [1WR]	6%	3%	51%
1-3 [1WR]	5%	3%	57%
2-1 [2WR]	5%	7%	40%

Grouping Tendencies

Personnel	Pass Rate	Pass Succ. %	Run Succ. %
1-1 [3WR]	74%	46%	43%
1-2 [2WR]	41%	45%	47%
2-2 [1WR]	17%	45%	52%
1-3 [1WR]	37%	44%	65%
2-1 [2WR]	40%	53%	31%

Red Zone Targets (min 3)

Receiver	All	Inside 5	6-10	11-20
Antonio Gates	22	5	2	15
Hunter Henry	17	3	5	9
Tyrell Williams	17	6	4	7
Melvin Gordon	8	2		6
Dexter McCluster	7		1	6
Dontrelle Inman	7	1	1	5
Travis Benjamin	7		1	6

Red Zone Rushes (min 3)

Rusher	All	Inside 5	6-10	11-20
Melvin Gordon	52	20	9	23
Kenneth Farrow	8	2	1	5
Danny Woodhead	3			3
Philip Rivers	3	1		2
Ronnie Hillman	3	1		2

Early Down Target Rate

RB	TE	WR
21%	25%	54%
19%	*20% NFL AVG*	*61%*

Overall Target Success %

RB	TE	WR
48% #12	55% #14	48% #19

Los Angeles Chargers 2016 Passing Recap & 2017 Outlook

Facing the 4th easiest ranked schedule of opposing pass rushes, the arrow is up in a major way for the Chargers passing game and Philip Rivers. That obviously presumes two rookie guards can play well enough to protect Rivers against this far worse than average pass rush, but assuming they can, look out. This is one of the deeper receiving corps in the NFL. I am extremely big on Hunter Henry and hope the Chargers allow him to dominate the targets instead of Gates this year. Between Keenan Allen, Rookie Mike Williams, Travis Benjamin, Tyrelle Williams and Dontrelle Inman, Rivers has tons of targets at receiver with unique skill sets capable of exploiting opponent weaknesses. While in theory Allen should receive the larger target share, the Chargers primary receiving package is 11 personnel which means 5 capable targets because in addition to the 3 wide outs and Henry at tight end, Melvin Gordon proved to be a very capable target out of the backfield. The mismatches the Chargers can create should be fun to watch. It will be fun to watch OC Ken Whisenhunt scheme some of these players open, but ultimately it comes down to Rivers, who has been doing more audibling and directing at the line of scrimmage the last few years.

Philip Rivers Rating All Downs

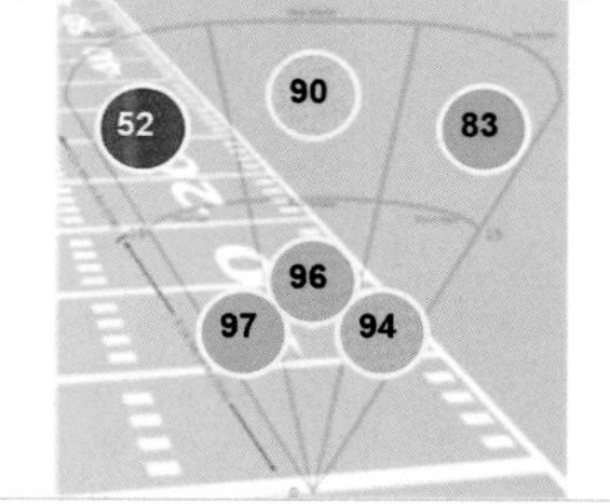

Philip Rivers Rating Early Downs

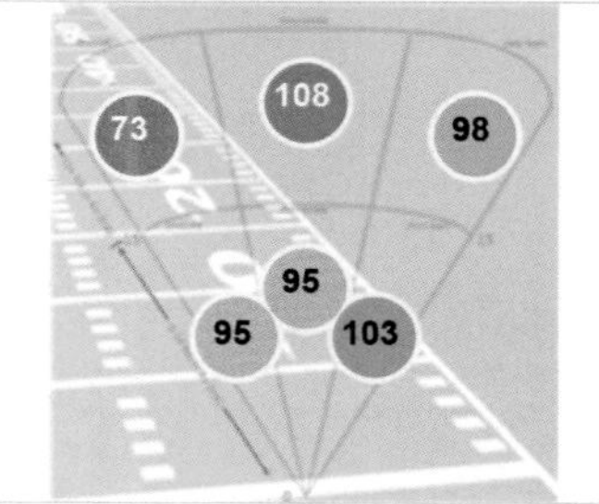

2016 Standard Passing Table

QB	Comp	Att	Comp %	Yds	YPA	TDs	INT	Sacks	Rating	Rk
Philip Rivers	349	578	60%	4,390	7.6	33	21	36	87.9	25
NFL Avg			63%		7.2				90.4	

2016 Advanced Passing Table

QB	Success %	EDSR Passing Success %	20+ Yd Pass Gains	20+ Yd Pass %	30+ Yd Pass Gains	30+ Yd Pass %	Air Yds per Comp	YAC per Comp	20+ Air Yd Comp	20+ Air Yd %
Philip Rivers	46%	49%	57	10%	24	4%	6.7	5.8	22	4%
NFL Avg	44%	48%	27	8%	10	3%	6.4	4.8	12	4%

Interception Rates by Down

Yards to Go	1	2	3	4	Total
1 & 2	0.0%	18.2%	0.0%	0.0%	4.9%
3, 4, 5	0.0%	0.0%	2.3%		1.4%
6 - 9	0.0%	2.3%	3.7%	0.0%	2.7%
10 - 14	3.2%	2.3%	2.4%	50.0%	3.1%
15+	10.0%	0.0%	10.0%	100.0%	10.5%
Total	3.3%	2.7%	2.9%	37.5%	3.4%

3rd Down Passing - Short of Sticks Analysis

QB	Avg Yds to Go	Air Yds (of Comps)	Avg Yds Short	Short of Sticks Rate	Rk
Philip Rivers	7.2	5.9	-1.3	62%	33
NFL Avg	7.6	6.8	-0.8	57%	

Air Yds vs YAC

Air Yds %	YAC %	Rk
52%	48%	28
54%	46%	

2016 Receiving Recap & 2017 Outlook

With only one football it will be hard to provide enough targets to players who surely will find mismatches on each snap. One key for production this season will be how the red zone shares that went to Antonio Gates are divided up. In the red zone, Rivers clearly favored size. His top 3 targets were 6'5" (Hunter Henry, 17 targets), 6'4" (Antonio Gates, 20 targets) and 6'4" (Tyrell Williams, 17 targets). No other receiver saw more than 6 targets. Rookie Mike Williams is 6'4", tips the scale at 218 lbs and is the biggest WR on the roster. I hope Henry's targets ratchet up and expect Mike Williams to be the lesser benefactor of fewer snaps for Gates.

Player *Min 50 Targets*	Targets	Comp %	YPA	Rating	TOARS	Success %	Success Rk	Missed YPA Rk	YAS % Rk	TDs
Tyrell Williams	119	58%	8.9	76	4.7	49%	87	90	11	7
Dontrelle Inman	97	60%	8.4	83	4.5	47%	99	99	40	4
Antonio Gates	93	57%	5.9	86	4.5	52%	60	46	138	7
Travis Benjamin	75	63%	9.0	99	4.3	51%	69	55	35	4
Melvin Gordon	57	72%	7.4	104	4.1	58%	25	29	125	2
Hunter Henry	53	68%	9.1	136	4.4	60%	16	1	57	8

Directional Passer Rating Delivered

Receiver	Short Left	Short Middle	Short Right	Deep Left	Deep Middle	Deep Right	Player Total
Tyrell Williams	54	87	109	77	110	56	76
Dontrelle Inman	96	88	63	88	46	103	83
Antonio Gates	97	105	79	1	40	7	86
Travis Benjamin	133	81	73	40	0	144	99
Melvin Gordon	126	105	83				104
Hunter Henry	98	156	148	81	158	50	136
Team Total	102	107	90	58	90	91	93

2016 Rushing Recap & 2017 Outlook

Melvin Gordon will be a fantasy stud simply from the target share he should receive. The depth behind Gordon is muddy, with a recovering Branden Oliver having a wide skill set and Kenneth Farrow proving last year to be nothing more than a backup. The simple fact that the Chargers will have to run some in the red zone and Gordon is their go-to player there makes him valueable. He had 52 carries and #2 on the team was Farrow with just 5. Inside the 10, Gordon saw all 29 rushes from the Chargers last year. Factor in his usage as a receiver out of the backfield, and the better situations he should face thanks to the expected passing game efficiency, and while I'm tepid on Gordon is a solid rusher he has big fantasy upside.

Player *Min 50 Rushes*	Rushes	YPA	Success %	Success Rk	Missed YPA Rk	YTS % Rk	YAS % Rk	Early Down Success %	Early Down Success Rk	TDs
Melvin Gordon	254	3.9	44%	45	33	48	15	42%	48	10
Kenneth Farrow	60	3.2	52%	18	13	2	67	51%	19	0

Yards per Carry by Direction

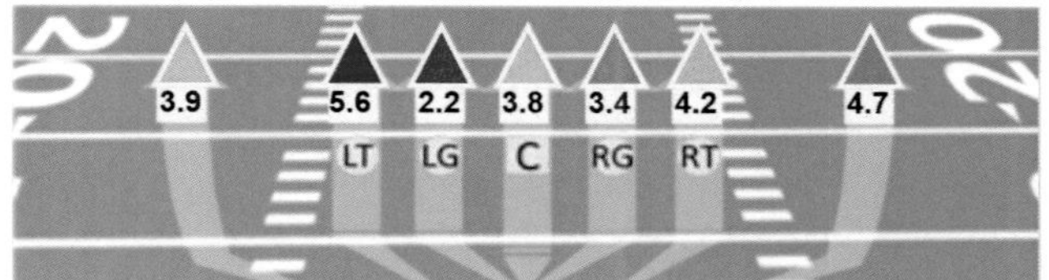

Directional Run Frequency

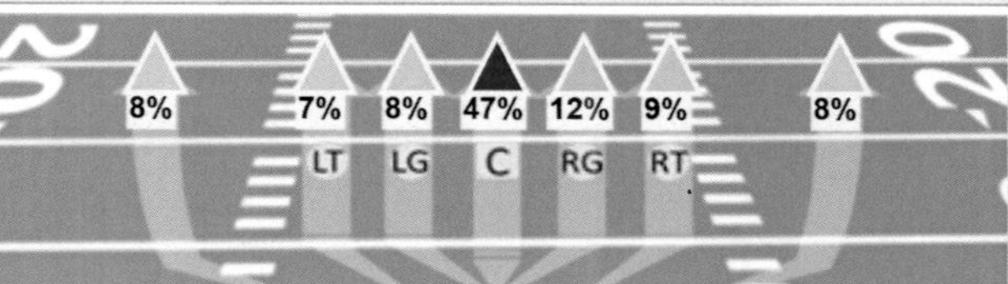

a 63% success rate (2nd) and 7.8 yards per target.

The Chargers will help the infusion of inexpensive youth along the offensive line can help take the running game to that next level. Gone are King Dunlap, DJ Fluker and Orlando Franklin. In 2017 they drafted two guards (Forrest Lamp and Dan Feeney). Both appear set to be week one starters atop the depth chart. Theoretically, their additions to the receiving position should make the run game that much more difficult to defend. A healthy Keenan Allen to pair with the rookie Mike Williams, and Travis Benjamin in the slot are a solid corps. Particularly given Hunter Henry will be roaming inside. And of course, they still have youngsters and massive contributors last year such as Tyrell Williams and Dontrelle Inman.

While the expectations are high for this passing offense, the Chargers schedule is brutal to start the season. Weeks 1 through 5, they face four top-7 pass defenses. The schedule is far and away the most difficult in the NFL, projecting 192% worse than average and 61% worse than the 2nd most difficult schedule. If the Chargers passing offense can weather the storm, they should sail through the second half of the schedule. Following their week 9 bye, they face the 2nd easiest schedule of pass defenses in the NFL. From week 13 onward it's the easiest in the NFL, highlighted by 4 out of 5 games coming against bottom-10 pass defenses.

One key the team simply must improve upon is their turnover margin. The last two years, the only two teams to have lost the turnover battle more than the Chargers are the Browns and Bears. Turnovers are the biggest difference maker in the NFL and the Chargers have a difficult enough time winning games when they win the turnover battle. They are 5-4 when winning the turnover battle, well below average, but are 3-15 when losing it, also well below average. Rivers last year was careless and erratic with his passing and that turned into 21 interceptions. He threw 7 interceptions alone on 1st and 10+ yards to go. More ridiculous, 18% of his passes on 2nd and short were intercepted. This is just one of several reasons I am such an advocate of running on 2nd and short. The Chargers passed the ball on 29% of their 2nd and short play calls, and gained a first down on just 9% of these plays, substantially worse than the NFL average of 52%. And two of these failures were intercepted. The Chargers should limit Rivers in these situations and focus on rushing to convert first downs and move the chains.

Given the difficult pass defenses the Chargers faced last year and the numerous injuries they sustained yet still produced efficient numbers, particularly when passing, I am extremely optimistic about their passing offense in 2017. I am less excited about their rushing outlook although there are plenty of reasons to embrace Gordon in a fantasy role thanks to his massive usage, particularly in the red zone, and his receiving volume. Their defense got better as the season went onward last year as the radar charts beautifully show.

Division History: Season Wins & 2017 Projection

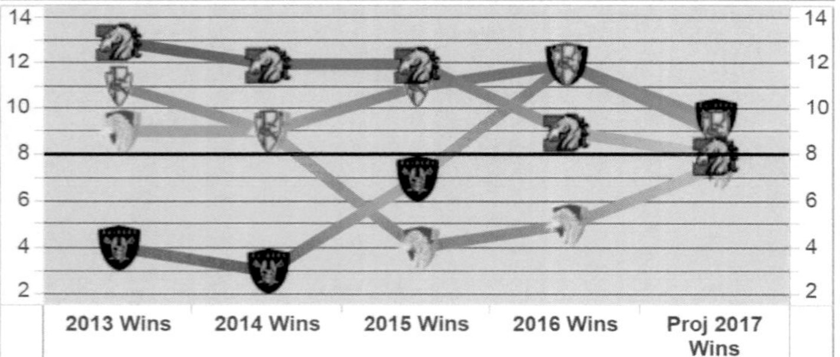

Rank of 2017 Defensive Pass Efficiency Faced by Week

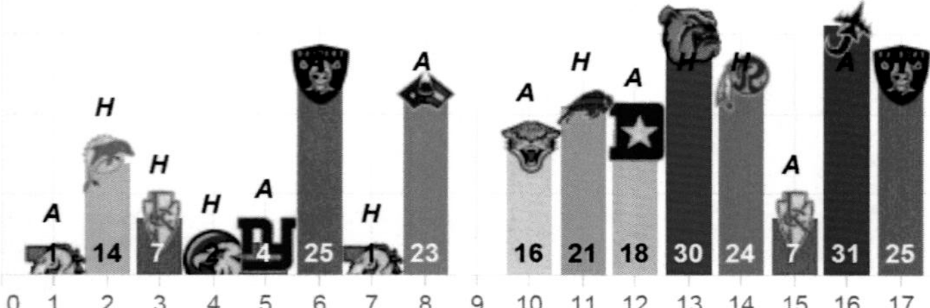

Rank of 2017 Defensive Rush Efficiency Faced by Week

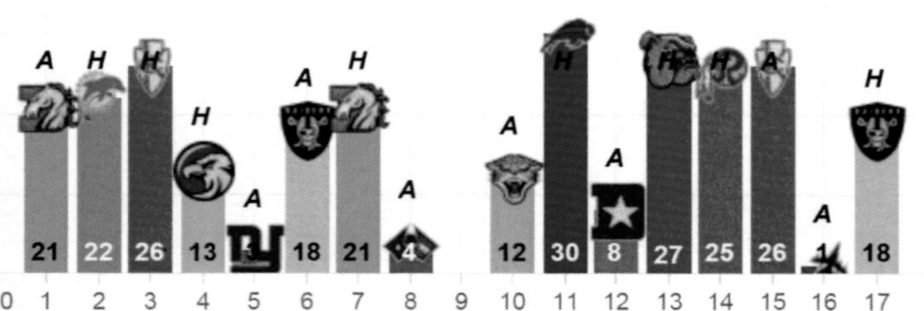

2016 Situational Usage by Player & Position

Usage Rate by Score

		Being Blown Out (14+)	Down Big (9-13)	One Score	Large Lead (9-13)	Blowout Lead (14+)	Grand Total
RUSH	Melvin Gordon	5%	21%	27%	44%	38%	27%
	Travis Benjamin	2%				1%	0%
	Kenneth Farrow	18%	7%	5%	3%	8%	6%
	Ronnie Hillman		6%	3%			2%
	Danny Woodhead			1%	5%	9%	2%
	Andre Williams	10%	1%	2%			2%
	Dexter McCluster			0%			0%
	Derek Watt		1%	0%			0%
	Total	35%	36%	38%	52%	56%	40%
PASS	Melvin Gordon		7%	7%	3%	4%	6%
	Tyrell Williams	13%	10%	13%	13%	12%	13%
	Dontrelle Inman	10%	14%	11%	5%	5%	10%
	Antonio Gates	15%	13%	10%	8%	6%	10%
	Travis Benjamin	3%	7%	9%	2%	9%	8%
	Kenneth Farrow	7%	2%	1%	2%	1%	2%
	Hunter Henry	8%	4%	6%	7%		6%
	Ronnie Hillman	3%	1%	1%			1%
	Danny Woodhead			0%	3%	4%	1%
	Andre Williams	2%		0%			0%
	Dexter McCluster			2%	2%		1%
	Keenan Allen			1%	2%	3%	1%
	Derek Watt			1%			0%
	Griff Whalen		2%	0%			0%
	Isaiah Burse	2%	1%	0%			0%
	Geremy Davis	2%	1%				0%
	Jeremy Butler			0%	2%		0%
	Sean McGrath		1%	0%			0%
	Total	65%	64%	62%	48%	44%	60%

Positional Target Distribution vs NFL Average

		NFL Wide				Team Only			
		Left	Middle	Right	**Total**	Left	Middle	Right	**Total**
Deep	WR	998	569	964	**2,531**	33	12	37	**82**
	TE	150	144	153	**447**	8	3	10	**21**
	RB	25	4	40	**69**				
	All	**1,173**	**717**	**1,157**	**3,047**	**41**	**15**	**47**	**103**
Short	WR	3,006	1,730	3,105	**7,841**	87	41	81	**209**
	TE	795	823	1,119	**2,737**	41	52	32	**125**
	RB	992	614	1,087	**2,693**	23	8	26	**57**
	All	**4,793**	**3,167**	**5,311**	**13,271**	**151**	**101**	**139**	**391**
Total		**5,966**	**3,884**	**6,468**	**16,318**	**192**	**116**	**186**	**494**

Positional Success Rates vs NFL Average

		NFL Wide				Team Only			
		Left	Middle	Right	**Total**	Left	Middle	Right	**Total**
Deep	WR	37%	50%	38%	**40%**	36%	42%	49%	**43%**
	TE	45%	49%	45%	**46%**	25%	67%	20%	**29%**
	RB	32%	75%	25%	**30%**				
	All	**38%**	**50%**	**38%**	**41%**	**34%**	**47%**	**43%**	**40%**
Short	WR	52%	57%	51%	**53%**	56%	51%	46%	**51%**
	TE	50%	61%	52%	**54%**	46%	65%	66%	**59%**
	RB	47%	49%	44%	**46%**	57%	75%	54%	**58%**
	All	**51%**	**57%**	**50%**	**52%**	**54%**	**60%**	**52%**	**55%**
Total		**48%**	**55%**	**48%**	**50%**	**49%**	**59%**	**49%**	**52%**

Los Angeles Rams

2017 Coaches

Head Coach:
Sean McVay (WAS OC) (1st yr)
Offensive Coordinator:
(McVay calls plays) (1st yr)
Defensive Coordinator:
Wade Phillips (DEN DC) (1st yr)

EASY HARD

2017 Forecast

Wins	Div Rank
6	#3

Past Records

2016: 4-12
2015: 7-9
2014: 6-10

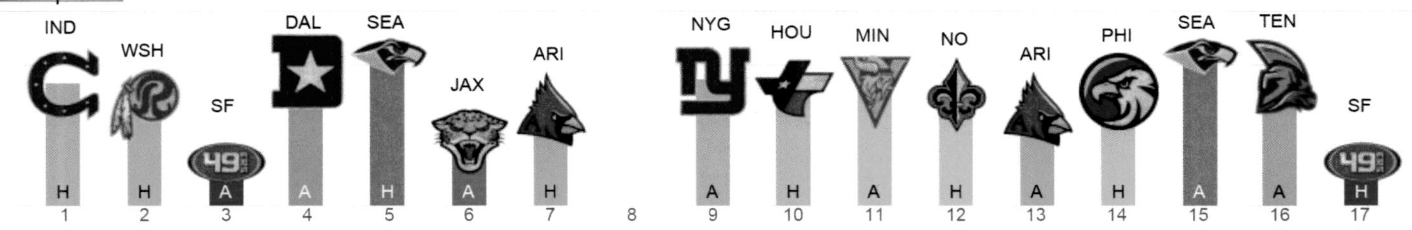

Key Players Lost

TXN	Player (POS)
Cut	Arkin, David G
	Bailey, Stedman WR
	Barnes, Tim C
	Couplin, Jerome S
	East, Andrew LB
	Jackson, Tre' G
	Kendricks, Lance TE
	Mason, Tre RB
	Short, Kevin CB
	Sims, Eugene DE
	Watts, Trey RB
	Williams, Bryce TE
Declared Free Agent	Britt, Kenny WR
	Cunningham, Benny RB
	Keenum, Case QB
	McDonald, T.J. S
	Quick, Brian WR
	Reynolds, Chase RB
	Thomas, Cam DE
	Zuerlein, Greg K

Average Line	# Games Favored	# Games Underdog
+5.5	0	15

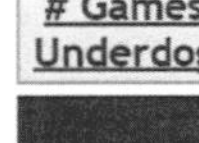

2017 Los Angeles Rams Overview

The coaching staff is new, Jared Goff is the full-time starter and the Rams drafted multiple new offensive starters they will in 11 personnel, yet the expectations are lower in 2017 than they were heading into 2016. Entering 2016 the Rams were projected to win 7 games. This year that number has shrunk to 5.5 games. I don't know what new HC Sean McVay will bring to the team as a head coach, but offensively we can envision what he would like given his time with the Redskins. But I don't consider him a downgrade over what Jeff Fisher was getting out of this team. Similarly, on defense the new coordinator is Wade Phillips (from Denver) and there is no defensive coordinator in the league that I would consider Phillips to be a downgrade over if replaced by Phillips. So the bottom line is the Rams should be in a better place from a coaching perspective in 2017.

So why the pessimism? Why is this season viewed as being worse than last season? It starts by perhaps too much emphasis on what this team did last season. But the results were pretty terrible, especially when taken in context, so the concerns are justifiable. First and foremost, this wasn't a Rams team steamrolled by injuries and spiraling out of control. This was a team, after being the 9th most injured unit in 2015, was the #1 healthiest unit last season. Their offense was the healthiest in the NFL. Their defense was 8th healthiest. Not a single position group finished in the bottom half of the NFL. So, the 2017 Rams won't suddenly be infused by talent which was sitting on the IR last year.

The metrics the Rams offense posted were indeed dreadful. One look at their Advanced Metrics on the following page and you can see across the board, they ranked bottom 3 in virtually every metric. It was a horrendous offense, one which failed to break 10 points in 7 of its last 10 games. And many of these metrics got substantially worse when Jared Goff took over in week 11. For instance, the lone metric I capture in which the Rams did not rank bottom 5 was explosive passing offense. These are percentage of pass plays which make 20+ yard gains. However, in weeks 1-10 (pre-Goff) the Rams recorded explosive pass gains on 10% of their attempts, ranking 6th in the NFL. With Goff in weeks 11 onward, the Rams recorded just a 6% explosive passing rate, good for 27th in the NFL to close out the season.

(cont'd - see LA2)

Key Free Agents/ Trades Added

Barwin, Connor LB
Dunbar, Lance RB
Jackson, Tre' G
Murray, Aaron QB
Robey-Coleman, Nickell CB
Sullivan, John C
Walker, Tyrunn DT
Webster, Kayvon CB
Whitworth, Andrew T
Woods, Robert WR

Drafted Players

Rd	Pk	Player (College)
2	44	TE - Gerald Everett (South Alabama)
3	69	WR - Cooper Kupp (Eastern Washington)
	91	S - John Johnson (Boston College)
4	117	WR - Josh Reynolds (Texas A&M)
	125	LB - Samson Ebukam (Eastern Washington)
6	189	DT - Tanzel Smart (Tulane)
	206	FB - Sam Rogers (Virginia Tech)
7	234	OLB - Ejuan Price (Pittsburgh)

Regular Season Wins: Past & Current Proj

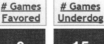

Proj 2017 Wins  6

2016 Wins  4

Proj 2016 Wins  7

2015 Wins  7

2014 Wins  6

2013 Wins 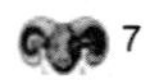 7

1 3 5 7 9 11 13 15

2017 Lineup & Cap Hits

FS L.Joyner 20
SS M.Alexander 31
LB M.Barron 26
LB A.Ogletree 52
RCB T.Johnson 22
SLOTCB N.R-Coleman 23
DL R.Quinn 94
DT D.Easley 99
DT A.Donald 99
DL C.Barwin 98
LCB E.Gaines 33

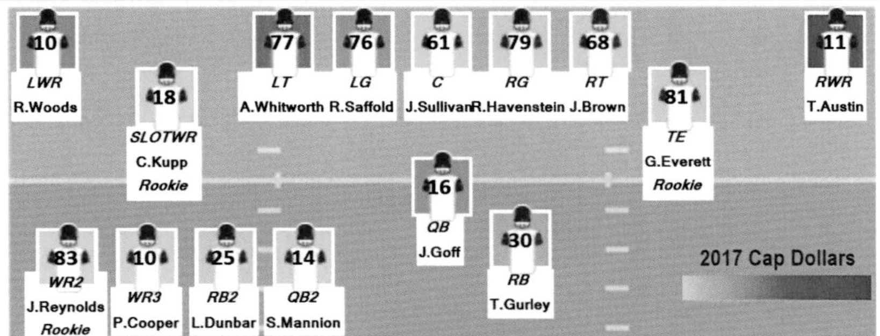

2017 Unit Spending

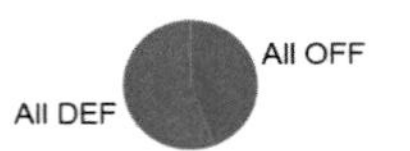

Positional Spending

	Rank	Total	2016 Rk
All OFF	22	$76.38M	28
QB	28	$7.78M	28
OL	15	$28.91M	25
RB	15	$7.65M	14
WR	5	$26.95M	14
TE	28	$5.09M	14
All DEF	2	$96.25M	16
DL	23	$19.73M	3
LB	2	$41.65M	32
CB	2	$28.91M	15
S	30	$5.96M	15

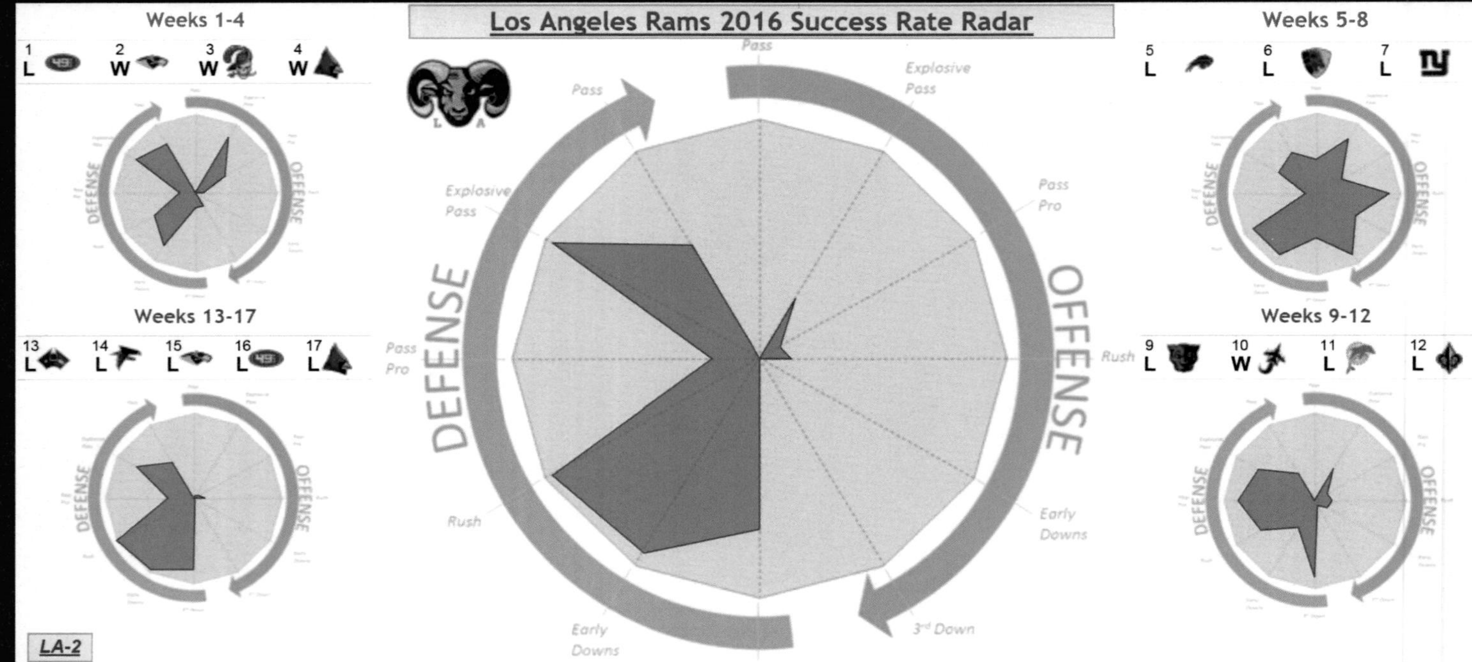

LA-2

The EDSR (Early Down Success Rate) battle was similar. On a weekly basis before Goff took over, the Rams were 5-4 in winning this battle, and won 3 of these 9 games. But with Goff as QB, the Rams lost every single EDSR battle. So as we view the season long stats, consider that these were all worse (and at times much worse) with Goff starting.

One look at the schedule and it is clear that the Rams really didn't get Goff incorporated at the right time. Instead of letting him play in week 9, fresh out of the bye, and getting to face the struggling Panthers in LA and then take on the lowly Jets, the Rams held him out until week 11. At which point in his first 5 starts, Goff played 4 playoff teams (Dolphins, Patriots, Falcons and Seahawks) plus one of the best offense in the NFL (Saints). His final two games came against the 49ers and Cardinals. The Rams had the 49ers beat, and led 21-7 with 5 minutes left in the game. But two touchdowns, including the final one with 31 seconds left, followed by a 2-point conversion to win the game 22-21, saw the Rams lose in dramatic fashion.

Defensively the team was far better than what they deserved. Despite being stuck on the field so often thanks to the NFL's worst 3rd down offense, the Rams were valiant in a number of metrics. They were 9th best in EDSR defense and 15th in total defensive efficiency. They ranked 4th in 3rd down defense and 6th in run defense efficiency. Their biggest struggles were indicative of a tired unit, being left on the field far too often: they ranked 21st in explosive run defense, 29th in pass rush efficiency and 27th in the red zone. While the pass rush does need improvement, the number of times this defense was forced to enter the game after 3-and-outs or a turnover inevitably cause fatigue in getting to the QB. Similarly, as games went on and the run defense (6th best) fatigued a bit, opposing RBs found lanes open up more and bigger holes to exploit to record explosive gains.

Wade Phillips has work to do to improve this pass rush and also help cover in the secondary better, but the defense is not a 4-12 defense.

(cont'd - see LA-3)

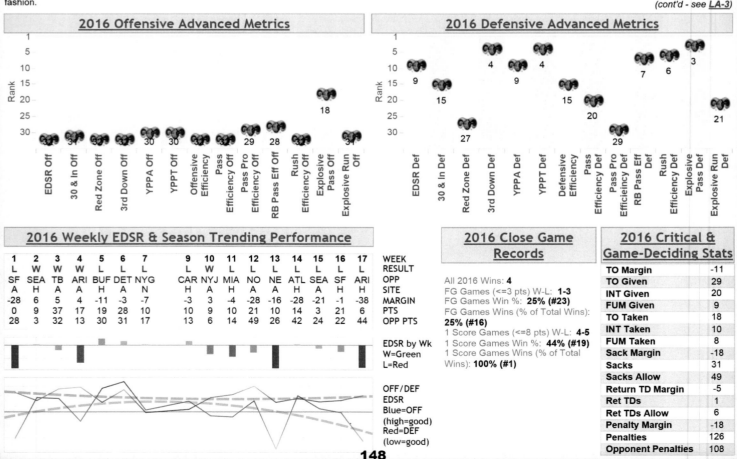

2016 Offensive Advanced Metrics

Metric	Rank
EDSR Off	32
30 & In Off	31
Red Zone Off	32
3rd Down Off	32
YPPA Off	30
YPPT Off	30
Offensive Efficiency	32
Pass Efficiency Off	32
Pass Pro Efficiency Off	29
RB Pass Eff Off	28
Rush Efficiency Off	32
Explosive Pass Off	18
Explosive Run Off	31

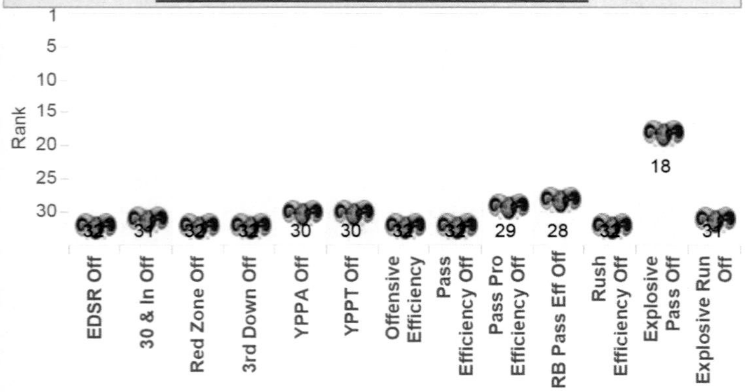

2016 Defensive Advanced Metrics

Metric	Rank
EDSR Def	9
30 & In Def	15
Red Zone Def	27
3rd Down Def	4
YPPA Def	9
YPPT Def	4
Defensive Efficiency	15
Pass Efficiency Def	20
Pass Pro Efficieincy Def	29
RB Pass Eff Def	7
Rush Efficiency Def	6
Explosive Pass Def	3
Explosive Run Def	21

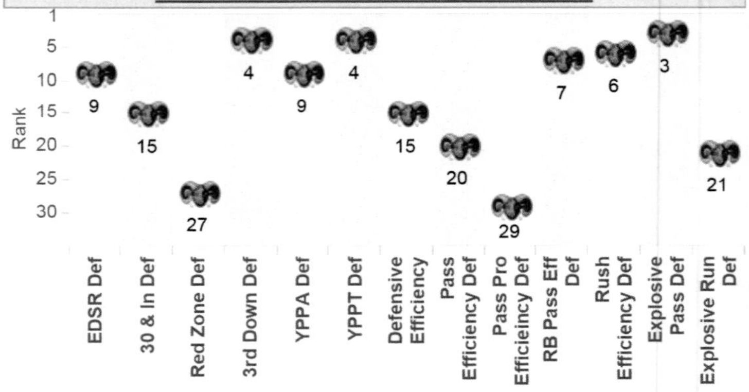

2016 Weekly EDSR & Season Trending Performance

WEEK	1	2	3	4	5	6	7	9	10	11	12	13	14	15	16	17
RESULT	L	W	W	W	L	L	L	L	W	L	L	L	L	L	L	L
OPP	SF	SEA	TB	ARI	BUF	DET	NYG	CAR	NYJ	MIA	NO	NE	ATL	SEA	SF	ARI
SITE	A	H	A	A	H	A	N	H	A	H	A	A	H	A	H	H
MARGIN	-28	6	5	4	-11	-3	-7	-3	3	-4	-28	-16	-28	-21	-1	-38
PTS	0	9	37	17	19	28	10	10	9	10	21	10	14	3	21	6
OPP PTS	28	3	32	13	30	31	17	13	6	14	49	26	42	24	22	44

EDSR by Wk
W=Green
L=Red

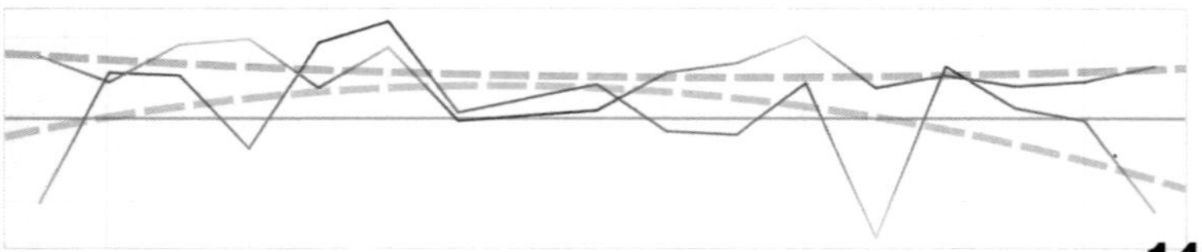

OFF/DEF EDSR
Blue=OFF (high=good)
Red=DEF (low=good)

2016 Close Game Records

All 2016 Wins: **4**
FG Games (<=3 pts) W-L: **1-3**
FG Games Win %: **25% (#23)**
FG Games Wins (% of Total Wins): **25% (#16)**
1 Score Games (<=8 pts) W-L: **4-5**
1 Score Games Win %: **44% (#19)**
1 Score Games Wins (% of Total Wins): **100% (#1)**

2016 Critical & Game-Deciding Stats

TO Margin	-11
TO Given	29
INT Given	20
FUM Given	9
TO Taken	18
INT Taken	10
FUM Taken	8
Sack Margin	-18
Sacks	31
Sacks Allow	49
Return TD Margin	-5
Ret TDs	1
Ret TDs Allow	6
Penalty Margin	-18
Penalties	126
Opponent Penalties	108

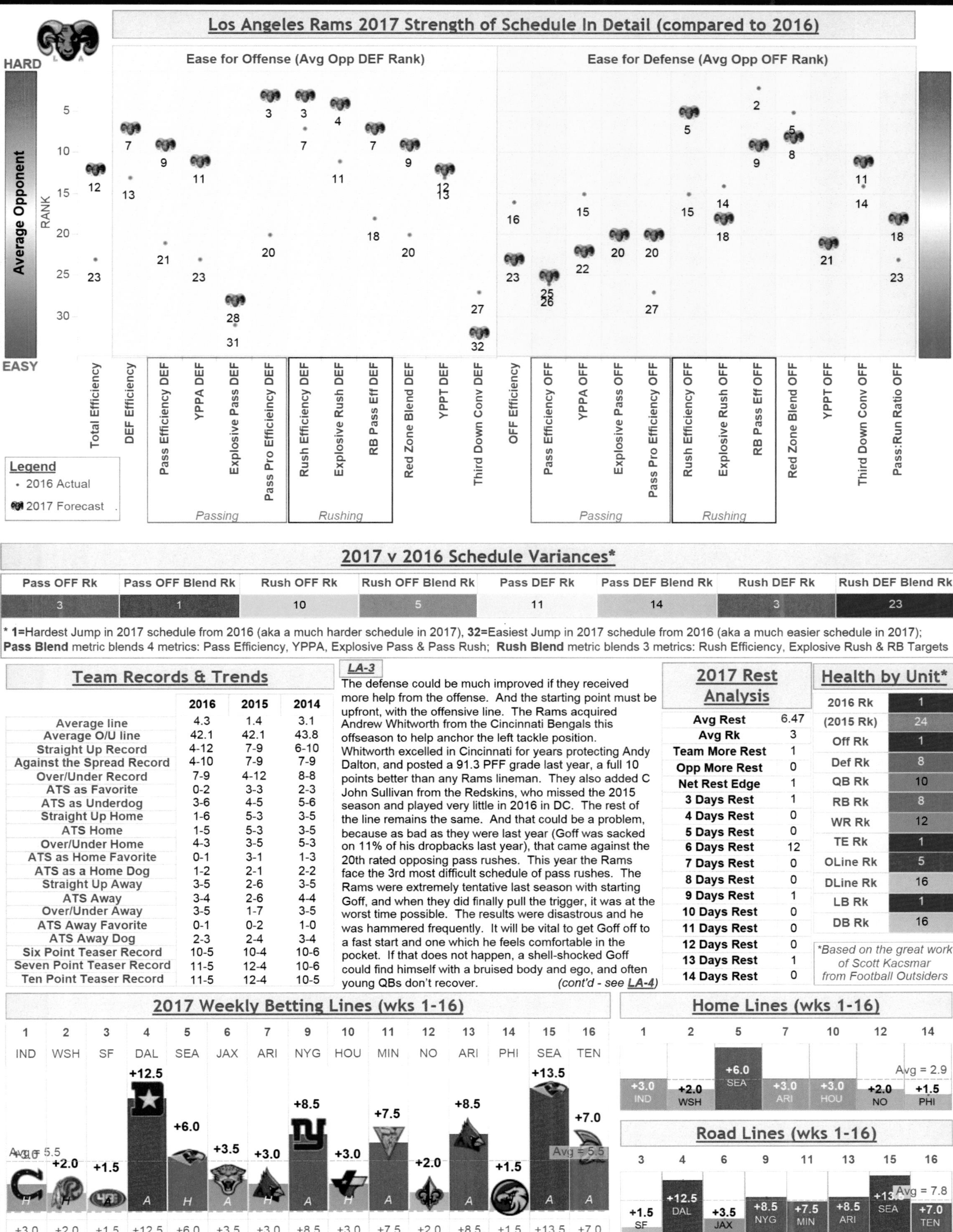

Los Angeles Rams 2017 Strength of Schedule In Detail (compared to 2016)

Metric	2016 Actual	2017 Forecast
Total Efficiency	23	12
DEF Efficiency	13	7
Pass Efficiency DEF	21	9
YPPA DEF	23	11
Explosive Pass DEF	31	28
Pass Pro Efficiency DEF	20	3
Rush Efficiency DEF	7	3
Explosive Rush DEF	11	4
RB Pass Eff DEF	18	7
Red Zone Blend DEF	20	9
YPPT DEF	13	12
Third Down Conv DEF	27	32
OFF Efficiency	16	23
Pass Efficiency OFF	26	25
YPPA OFF	15	22
Explosive Pass OFF	20	20
Pass Pro Efficiency OFF	27	20
Rush Efficiency OFF	15	5
Explosive Rush OFF	14	18
RB Pass Eff OFF	2	9
Red Zone Blend OFF	5	8
YPPT OFF	21	21
Third Down Conv OFF	14	11
Pass:Run Ratio OFF	23	18

2017 v 2016 Schedule Variances*

Pass OFF Rk	Pass OFF Blend Rk	Rush OFF Rk	Rush OFF Blend Rk	Pass DEF Rk	Pass DEF Blend Rk	Rush DEF Rk	Rush DEF Blend Rk
3	1	10	5	11	14	3	23

* **1**=Hardest Jump in 2017 schedule from 2016 (aka a much harder schedule in 2017), **32**=Easiest Jump in 2017 schedule from 2016 (aka a much easier schedule in 2017); **Pass Blend** metric blends 4 metrics: Pass Efficiency, YPPA, Explosive Pass & Pass Rush; **Rush Blend** metric blends 3 metrics: Rush Efficiency, Explosive Rush & RB Targets

Team Records & Trends

	2016	2015	2014
Average line	4.3	1.4	3.1
Average O/U line	42.1	42.1	43.8
Straight Up Record	4-12	7-9	6-10
Against the Spread Record	4-10	7-9	7-9
Over/Under Record	7-9	4-12	8-8
ATS as Favorite	0-2	3-3	2-3
ATS as Underdog	3-6	4-5	5-6
Straight Up Home	1-6	5-3	3-5
ATS Home	1-5	5-3	3-5
Over/Under Home	4-3	3-5	5-3
ATS as Home Favorite	0-1	3-1	1-3
ATS as a Home Dog	1-2	2-1	2-2
Straight Up Away	3-5	2-6	3-5
ATS Away	3-4	2-6	4-4
Over/Under Away	3-5	1-7	3-5
ATS Away Favorite	0-1	0-2	1-0
ATS Away Dog	2-3	2-4	3-4
Six Point Teaser Record	10-5	10-4	10-6
Seven Point Teaser Record	11-5	12-4	10-6
Ten Point Teaser Record	11-5	12-4	10-5

LA-3

The defense could be much improved if they received more help from the offense. And the starting point must be upfront, with the offensive line. The Rams acquired Andrew Whitworth from the Cincinnati Bengals this offseason to help anchor the left tackle position. Whitworth excelled in Cincinnati for years protecting Andy Dalton, and posted a 91.3 PFF grade last year, a full 10 points better than any Rams lineman. They also added C John Sullivan from the Redskins, who missed the 2015 season and played very little in 2016 in DC. The rest of the line remains the same. And that could be a problem, because as bad as they were last year (Goff was sacked on 11% of his dropbacks last year), that came against the 20th rated opposing pass rushes. This year the Rams face the 3rd most difficult schedule of pass rushes. The Rams were extremely tentative last season with starting Goff, and when they did finally pull the trigger, it was at the worst time possible. The results were disastrous and he was hammered frequently. It will be vital to get Goff off to a fast start and one which he feels comfortable in the pocket. If that does not happen, a shell-shocked Goff could find himself with a bruised body and ego, and often young QBs don't recover. *(cont'd - see LA-4)*

2017 Rest Analysis

Avg Rest	6.47
Avg Rk	3
Team More Rest	1
Opp More Rest	0
Net Rest Edge	1
3 Days Rest	1
4 Days Rest	0
5 Days Rest	0
6 Days Rest	12
7 Days Rest	0
8 Days Rest	0
9 Days Rest	1
10 Days Rest	0
11 Days Rest	0
12 Days Rest	0
13 Days Rest	1
14 Days Rest	0

Health by Unit*

2016 Rk	1
(2015 Rk)	24
Off Rk	1
Def Rk	8
QB Rk	10
RB Rk	8
WR Rk	12
TE Rk	1
OLine Rk	5
DLine Rk	16
LB Rk	1
DB Rk	16

**Based on the great work of Scott Kacsmar from Football Outsiders*

2017 Weekly Betting Lines (wks 1-16)

Week	1	2	3	4	5	6	7	9	10	11	12	13	14	15	16
Opp	IND	WSH	SF	DAL	SEA	JAX	ARI	NYG	HOU	MIN	NO	ARI	PHI	SEA	TEN
Site	H	H	A	A	H	A	H	A	H	A	A	A	H	A	A
Line	+3.0	+2.0	+1.5	+12.5	+6.0	+3.5	+3.0	+8.5	+3.0	+7.5	+2.0	+8.5	+1.5	+13.5	+7.0

Avg = 5.5

Home Lines (wks 1-16)

Week	1	2	5	7	10	12	14
Opp	IND	WSH	SEA	ARI	HOU	NO	PHI
Line	+3.0	+2.0	+6.0	+3.0	+3.0	+2.0	+1.5

Avg = 2.9

Road Lines (wks 1-16)

Week	3	4	6	9	11	13	15	16
Opp	SF	DAL	JAX	NYG	MIN	ARI	SEA	TEN
Line	+1.5	+12.5	+3.5	+8.5	+7.5	+8.5	+13.5	+7.0

Avg = 7.8

Los Angeles Rams 2016 Play Analysis

2016 Play Tendencies

All Pass %	59%
All Pass Rk	17
All Rush %	41%
All Rush Rk	16
1 Score Pass %	44%
1 Score Pass Rk	32
2015 1 Score Pass %	54%
2015 1 Score Pass Rk	24
Pass Increase %	-10%
Pass Increase Rk	32
1 Score Rush %	56%
1 Score Rush Rk	1
Up Pass %	54%
Up Pass Rk	24
Up Rush %	46%
Up Rush Rk	9
Down Pass %	60%
Down Pass Rk	20
Down Rush %	40%
Down Rush Rk	13

2016 Down & Distance Tendencies

Down	Distance	Total Plays	Pass Rate	Run Rate	Play Success %
1	Short (1-3)	6	17%	83%	50%
	Med (4-7)	5	20%	80%	60%
	Long (8-10)	277	43%	57%	42%
	XL (11+)	14	57%	43%	21%
2	Short (1-3)	30	40%	60%	57%
	Med (4-7)	71	59%	41%	44%
	Long (8-10)	86	65%	35%	36%
	XL (11+)	44	77%	23%	30%
3	Short (1-3)	38	61%	39%	55%
	Med (4-7)	54	100%	0%	31%
	Long (8-10)	33	97%	3%	12%
	XL (11+)	27	93%	7%	11%
4	Short (1-3)	6	33%	67%	50%
	Long (8-10)	1	100%	0%	0%

Shotgun %:

Under Center	Shotgun
42%	58%
37%	*63%*

AVG

Run Rate:

Under Center	Shotgun
70%	18%
68%	*23%*

AVG

Pass Rate:

Under Center	Shotgun
30%	82%
32%	*77%*

AVG

Short Yardage Intelligence:

2nd and Short Run

Run Freq	Run % Rk	NFL Run Freq Avg	Run 1D Rate	Run NFL 1D Avg
60%	25	65%	67%	71%

2nd and Short Pass

Pass Freq	Pass % Rk	NFL Pass Freq Avg	Pass 1D Rate	Pass NFL 1D Avg
40%	7	35%	43%	52%

Most Frequent Play

Down	Distance	Play Type	Player	Total Plays	Play Success %
1	Short (1-3)	RUSH	Todd Gurley	3	67%
	Med (4-7)	RUSH	Todd Gurley	3	33%
	Long (8-10)	RUSH	Todd Gurley	124	40%
	XL (11+)	RUSH	Todd Gurley	6	33%
2	Short (1-3)	RUSH	Todd Gurley	13	69%
	Med (4-7)	RUSH	Todd Gurley	18	50%
	Long (8-10)	RUSH	Todd Gurley	25	12%
	XL (11+)	PASS	Lance Kendricks	9	33%
3	Short (1-3)	RUSH	Todd Gurley	12	67%
	Med (4-7)	PASS	Kenny Britt	15	40%
	Long (8-10)	PASS	Brian Quick	7	0%
	XL (11+)	PASS	Tavon Austin	6	17%

Most Successful Play*

Down	Distance	Play Type	Player	Total Plays	Play Success %
1	Long (8-10)	RUSH	Tavon Austin	15	73%
	XL (11+)	RUSH	Todd Gurley	6	33%
2	Short (1-3)	RUSH	Todd Gurley	13	69%
	Med (4-7)	PASS	Kenny Britt	8	75%
	Long (8-10)	PASS	Brian Quick	5	100%
	XL (11+)	PASS	Lance Kendricks	9	33%
3	Short (1-3)	RUSH	Todd Gurley	12	67%
	Med (4-7)	PASS	Brian Quick	10	50%
	Long (8-10)	PASS	Tavon Austin	6	17%
			Lance Kendricks	6	17%
	XL (11+)	PASS	Tavon Austin	6	17%

**Minimum 5 plays to qualify*

2016 Snap Rates

Week	Opp	Score	Lance Kendricks	Kenny Britt	Todd Gurley	Tavon Austin	Brian Quick	Tyler Higbee
1	SF	L 28-0	58 (95%)	59 (97%)	37 (61%)	57 (93%)	31 (51%)	21 (34%)
2	SEA	W 9-3	58 (94%)	49 (79%)	44 (71%)	45 (73%)	38 (61%)	26 (42%)
3	TB	W 37-32	60 (92%)	56 (86%)	52 (80%)	50 (77%)	36 (55%)	21 (32%)
4	ARI	W 17-13	56 (95%)	46 (78%)	51 (86%)	47 (80%)	36 (61%)	18 (31%)
5	BUF	L 30-19	59 (89%)	52 (79%)	57 (86%)	44 (67%)	43 (65%)	32 (48%)
6	DET	L 31-28	56 (97%)	47 (81%)	42 (72%)	49 (84%)	40 (69%)	19 (33%)
7	NYG	L 17-10	66 (85%)	70 (90%)	49 (63%)	61 (78%)	56 (72%)	29 (37%)
9	CAR	L 13-10	54 (79%)	60 (88%)	43 (63%)	53 (78%)	50 (74%)	31 (46%)
10	NYJ	W 9-6	56 (81%)	58 (84%)	42 (61%)	47 (68%)	43 (62%)	25 (36%)
11	MIA	L 14-10	52 (84%)	60 (97%)	43 (69%)	51 (82%)	38 (61%)	24 (39%)
12	NO	L 49-21	36 (68%)	47 (89%)	34 (64%)	40 (75%)	41 (77%)	23 (43%)
13	NE	L 26-10	33 (65%)	48 (94%)	35 (69%)		48 (94%)	28 (55%)
14	ATL	L 42-14	36 (50%)	58 (81%)	64 (89%)	48 (67%)	51 (71%)	38 (53%)
15	SEA	L 24-3	44 (73%)	43 (72%)	51 (85%)	43 (72%)	46 (77%)	26 (43%)
16	SF	L 22-21	52 (88%)	31 (53%)	50 (85%)	48 (81%)	36 (61%)	29 (49%)
17	ARI	L 44-6	52 (87%)		50 (83%)	47 (78%)	59 (98%)	12 (20%)
Grand Total			828 (83%)	784 (83%)	744 (74%)	730 (77%)	692 (69%)	402 (40%)

Personnel Groupings

Personnel	Team %	NFL Avg	Succ. %
1-1 [3WR]	66%	60%	36%
1-2 [2WR]	26%	19%	44%
1-3 [1WR]	4%	3%	40%

Grouping Tendencies

Personnel	Pass Rate	Pass Succ. %	Run Succ. %
1-1 [3WR]	71%	33%	43%
1-2 [2WR]	40%	46%	43%
1-3 [1WR]	18%	57%	36%

Red Zone Targets (min 3)

Receiver	All	Inside 5	6-10	11-20
Kenny Britt	12	3	6	3
Tavon Austin	10		3	7
Todd Gurley	10			10
Brian Quick	8	2	2	4
Lance Kendricks	6	2	2	2
Tyler Higbee	4	1	1	2
Benny Cunningham	3	1		2
Michael Thomas	1			1

Red Zone Rushes (min 3)

Rusher	All	Inside 5	6-10	11-20
Todd Gurley	35	10	10	15
Tavon Austin	4		2	2
Benny Cunningham	3	2		1

Early Down Target Rate

	RB	TE	WR
	16%	24%	60%
NFL AVG	***19%***	***20%***	***61%***

Overall Target Success %

RB	TE	WR
43% #19	34% #32	40% #32

Los Angeles Rams 2016 Passing Recap & 2017 Outlook

You could look at Jared Goff's 2016 stats and really rush to a pretty tempered judgment that he's not a good quarterback. Given the competition he was thrown up against (faced playoff teams in 4 of first 5 games), the caliber of his line, his run game and the coaching strategy, I'm more inclined to give him a pass. He had a terrible rookie season, that is a fact. Bill Barnwell noted out of 53 first round rookie QBs since 1970 with 200 attempts, Goff ranked dead last in yards per attempt, 2nd worst in passer rating and 5th worst in completion percentage. However, consider he finished 2nd worst in sack percentage, and it would be foolish to think his terrible performance was solely his fault. But I intentionally left Case Keenum on the below tables to show his performance behind the same exact line. It was much better than Goff (though still poor). McVay needs to pass more on 1st and 10 to create balance and easier throws for Goff. On 1st and 10 in the first half, the Rams ran the ball 60% of the time (3rd most, avg = 51%). Goff also must look to improve deeper down the field, and do a better job of targeting players beyond the sticks on 3rd down, as his completions fell an average of 1.2 yards short of the sticks.

2016 Standard Passing Table

QB	Comp	Att	Comp %	Yds	YPA	TDs	INT	Sacks	Rating	Rk
Case Keenum	196	322	61%	2,201	6.8	9	11	23	76.4	41
Jared Goff	112	205	55%	1,089	5.3	5	7	26	63.6	53
NFL Avg			63%		7.2				90.4	

2016 Advanced Passing Table

QB	Success %	EDSR Passing Success %	20+ Yd Pass Gains	20+ Yd Pass %	30+ Yd Pass Gains	30+ Yd Pass %	Air Yds per Comp	YAC per Comp	20+ Air Yd Comp	20+ Air Yd %
Case Keenum	40%	44%	31	10%	15	5%	5.9	5.3	13	4%
Jared Goff	29%	33%	12	6%	2	1%	4.8	4.9	4	2%
NFL Avg	44%	48%	27	8%	10	3%	6.4	4.8	12	4%

Jared Goff Rating All Downs

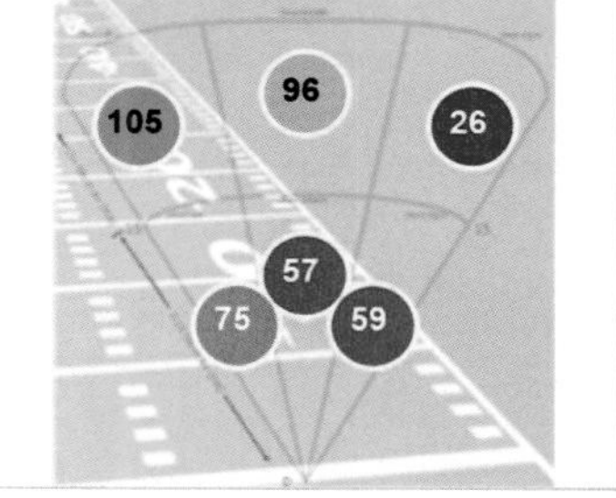

Jared Goff Rating Early Downs

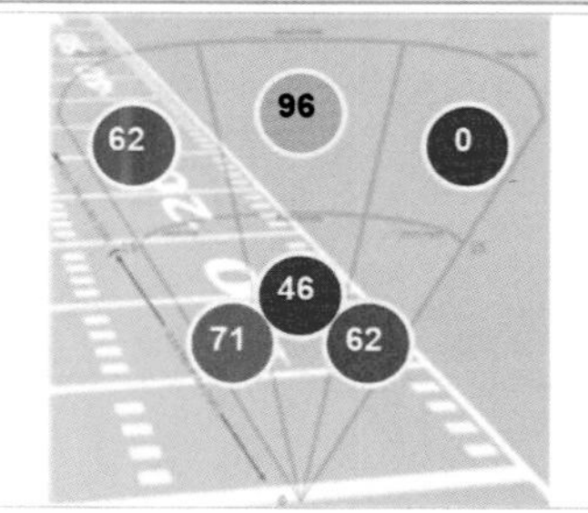

Interception Rates by Down

Yards to Go	1	2	3	4	Total
1 & 2	0.0%	0.0%	0.0%	0.0%	0.0%
3, 4, 5	0.0%	0.0%	7.7%	0.0%	4.8%
6 - 9	0.0%	0.0%	4.2%		2.0%
10 - 14	3.1%	7.7%	0.0%	0.0%	3.5%
15+	16.7%	0.0%	0.0%		3.4%
Total	4.1%	2.6%	2.6%	0.0%	3.0%

3rd Down Passing - Short of Sticks Analysis

QB	Avg Yds to Go	Air Yds (of Comps)	Avg Yds Short	Short of Sticks Rate	Rk
Jared Goff	7.2	6.1	-1.2	80%	32
NFL Avg	7.6	6.8	-0.8	57%	

Air Yds vs YAC

Air Yds %	YAC %	Rk
60%	40%	15
54%	46%	

2016 Receiving Recap & 2017 Outlook

McVay wants to use Tavon Austin more like DeSean Jackson this year. I certainly won't argue that such usage would be detrimental to the team. If they can make it work, kudos to them. But Austin struggled on deep routes his entire career. But last year he was terrible on short routes as well, so might as well use his small frame and speed to stretch the field. Assuming McVay gets his wish, Austin won't be catching many passes this year. So the role of leading receiver would probably fall to Robert Woods, fresh in from 4 years in Buffalo. Woods was infrequently targeted deep or across the middle; 65% of his receptions were short left or right.

Player *Min 50 Targets*	Targets	Comp %	YPA	Rating	TOARS	Success %	Success Rk	Missed YPA Rk	YAS % Rk	TDs
Kenny Britt	111	61%	9.0	95	4.8	50%	72	34	59	5
Tavon Austin	106	55%	4.8	57	4.1	34%	146	140	119	3
Lance Kendricks	87	57%	5.7	62	4.0	41%	129	100	126	2
Brian Quick	77	53%	7.3	79	4.0	40%	132	94	48	3
Todd Gurley	58	74%	5.6	73	3.5	40%	134	125	89	0

Directional Passer Rating Delivered

Receiver	Short Left	Short Middle	Short Right	Deep Left	Deep Middle	Deep Right	Player Total
Kenny Britt	83	92	87	108	73	85	95
Tavon Austin	71	60	48	149	0	40	57
Lance Kendricks	93	60	59	96	56	40	62
Brian Quick	74	87	100	1	158	26	79
Todd Gurley	93	15	99			0	73
Benny Cunningham	67	85	83				84
Michael Thomas	52	40	66	40			47
Team Total	82	60	76	104	74	28	74

2016 Rushing Recap & 2017 Outlook

The Rams don't just have a problem with their quarterback, they have a problem with the run game. Todd Gurley was quite bad last year, but he was also used less than efficiently. The Rams ran from too much 11 on 1st and 10 and they ran too often in general on 1st and 10. Gurley had to face too many stacked boxes with 3 WRs on the field. The Rams have to figure out a way to get Gurley more space to operate out of with fewer defenders for the line to block. That comes from being less predictable with run calls. I feel confident McVay can diagnose these issues. The key is getting the Rams to stop playing behind in the chains and forcing too many runs on 1st or 2nd down and obvious pass situations on 3rd down.

Player *Min 50 Rushes*	Rushes	YPA	Success %	Success Rk	Missed YPA Rk	YTS % Rk	YAS % Rk	Early Down Success %	Early Down Success Rk	TDs
Todd Gurley	278	3.2	41%	57	46	11	54	40%	58	6

Yards per Carry by Direction

Directional Run Frequency

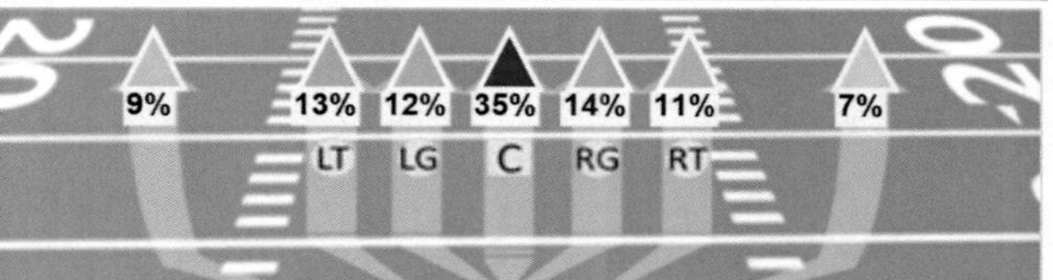

LA-4

Having protection for Goff is key, especially when the offense faces such a jump in competition of opposing pass defenses. When blending together 4 key passing metrics: pass efficiency, yards per pass allowed, explosive passing and pass rush, the Rams face the biggest increase in difficult for any team this year as compared to 2016. It's not just the pass rushes that get stronger in 2017, it's also the overall pass defenses, which ranked 21st last year and a projected 9th this year.

The best way to help a young QB is with a run game. And that will be another problem due to the schedule, which is the 3rd most difficult slate of opposing run defenses. Last year, to help protect their quarterbacks, the Rams were the most run heavy team in one-score games. They ran the ball 56% of the time. It was an increase of 10% as compared to 2015. The problem was predictability. The most common play for the Rams on any of 4 "to go" distance ranges on 1st down and on 2nd down was a Todd Gurley handoff. On 1st or 2nd and 10, he was successful on just 38% of his runs and gained just 3.7 yards per carry, which ranked 28th in the NFL.

One thing McVay will immediately look to do is to figure out how to get Gurley going on early downs. The Redskins offense was actually similar from a personnel grouping frequency as the Rams last year. The Rams used 11 personnel 66% of snaps, 12 personnel 26% and 13 personnel 4%.

The Redskins used 11 personnel 73% of snaps, 12 personnel 19% and 13 personnel 7%. So I would expect similar usage as 2016 from that perspective. On 1st and 10 last year with Goff as QB, Gurley posted a 2.6 yards per carry and a 35% success rate from 11 personnel but 4.1 yards per carry and a 36% success rate from 12 personnel. The results were similar on all early down situations with a to-go distance of 10 or less: Gurley was slightly more efficient and definitely more explosive when running out of 12 personnel.

Last year the Rams were so bad on early downs, particularly under Goff, that on their 90 third down attempts, they called passes 90% of the time because of the yardage to-go required. It was the highest pass rate in the NFL. Certainly that is not ideal for a rookie QB. And it won't be ideal next season either. McVay must figure out how to get production from Gurley on the ground in the early downs. The next step is making Goff comfortable with efficient targets which don't require much time in the pocket. Washington was one of 3 teams to rank top-10 in success rate on passes to each of the 3 position groups (WR, TE, RB). The Rams ranked 19th in success rate to RBs, but dead last when throwing to TEs and WRs. Passes to TE are, on average, the most efficient pass in today's game. With Lance Kendricks cut, the job is either Tyler Higbee's or 2nd rounder Gerald Everett's to take. McVay must get some high efficiency targets out of that position group for Goff's comfort and overall success.

Division History: Season Wins & 2017 Projection

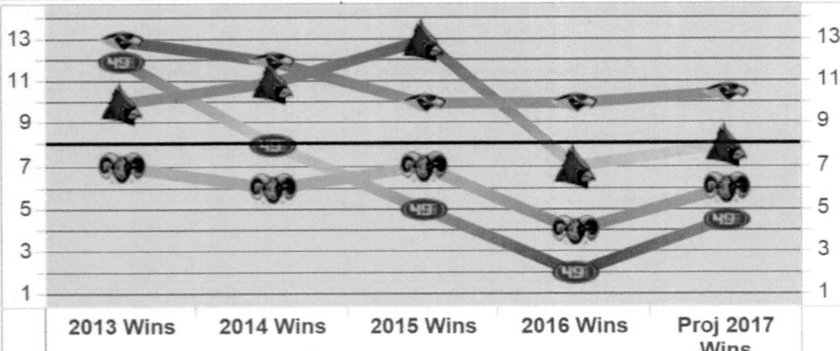

Rank of 2017 Defensive Pass Efficiency Faced by Week

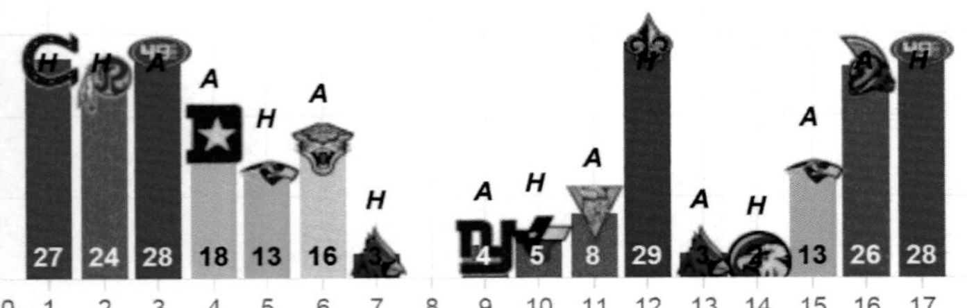

Rank of 2017 Defensive Rush Efficiency Faced by Week

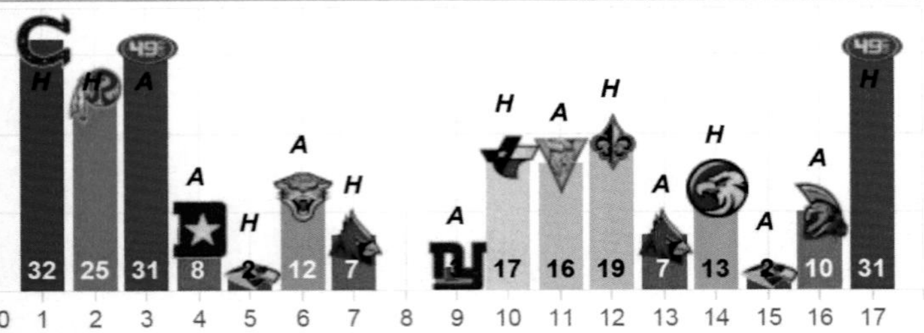

2016 Situational Usage by Player & Position

Usage Rate by Score

		Being Blown Out (14+)	Down Big (9-13)	One Score	Large Lead (9-13)	Grand Total
RUSH	Todd Gurley	23%	29%	35%	40%	32%
	Tavon Austin	2%	6%	4%		3%
	Benny Cunningham	1%		3%		2%
	Malcolm Brown	6%		1%		2%
	Bradley Marquez			0%		0%
	Total	32%	35%	42%	40%	39%
PASS	Todd Gurley	6%	7%	7%	13%	7%
	Tavon Austin	13%	7%	13%	7%	12%
	Kenny Britt	13%	12%	13%	13%	13%
	Lance Kendricks	8%	13%	10%	13%	10%
	Brian Quick	10%	10%	8%		9%
	Benny Cunningham	1%	6%	2%	7%	2%
	Tyler Higbee	5%	6%	2%	7%	3%
	Malcolm Brown	1%		0%		0%
	Pharoh Cooper	7%	1%	1%		2%
	Michael Thomas	2%	1%	1%		1%
	Bradley Marquez	1%		1%		1%
	Chase Reynolds	1%				0%
	Paul McRoberts			0%		0%
	Total	68%	65%	58%	60%	61%

Positional Target Distribution vs NFL Average

		NFL Wide				Team Only			
		Left	Middle	Right	Total	Left	Middle	Right	Total
Deep	WR	1,003	569	979	2,551	28	12	22	62
	TE	154	145	162	461	4	2	1	7
	RB	25	4	37	66			3	3
	All	1,182	718	1,178	3,078	32	14	26	72
Short	WR	2,997	1,734	3,078	7,809	96	37	108	241
	TE	812	853	1,117	2,782	24	22	34	80
	RB	977	606	1,091	2,674	38	16	22	76
	All	4,786	3,193	5,286	13,265	158	75	164	397
Total		5,968	3,911	6,464	16,343	190	89	190	469

Positional Success Rates vs NFL Average

		NFL Wide				Team Only			
		Left	Middle	Right	Total	Left	Middle	Right	Total
Deep	WR	37%	50%	38%	40%	50%	42%	27%	40%
	TE	44%	50%	44%	46%	50%	50%	0%	43%
	RB	32%	75%	27%	32%			0%	0%
	All	37%	50%	39%	41%	50%	43%	23%	39%
Short	WR	52%	57%	52%	53%	44%	41%	41%	42%
	TE	50%	62%	53%	55%	46%	55%	29%	41%
	RB	47%	50%	44%	46%	42%	25%	55%	42%
	All	51%	57%	50%	52%	44%	41%	40%	42%
Total		48%	56%	48%	50%	45%	42%	38%	41%

2017 Coaches

Head Coach:
Adam Gase (2nd yr)
Offensive Coordinator:
Clyde Christensen (2nd yr)
Defensive Coordinator:
Matt Burke (MIA LB) (1st yr)

EASY HARD

2017 Forecast

Wins	Div Rank
7.5	#2

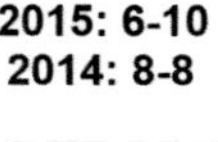

Past Records

2016: 10-6
2015: 6-10
2014: 8-8

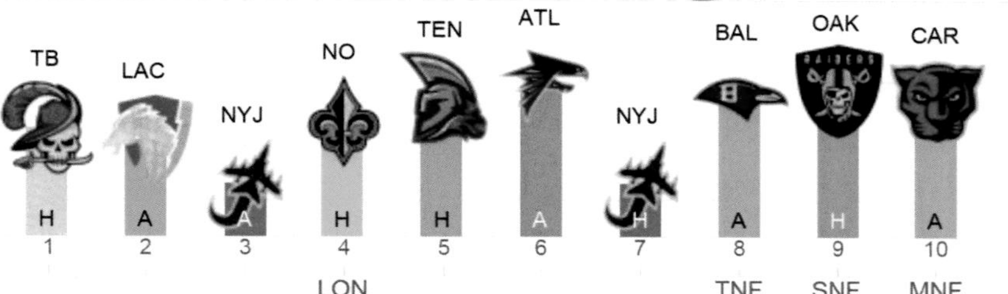

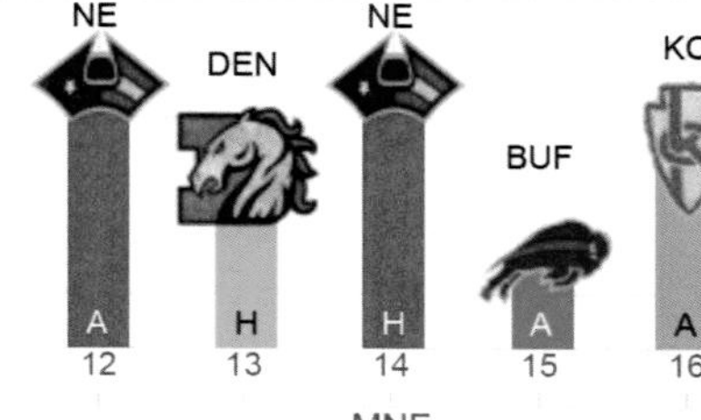

Key Players Lost

TXN	Player (POS)
Cut	Abdul-Quddus, Isa S
	Ekpre-Olomu, Ifo CB
	Jones, Jason DE
	Jordan, Dion DE
	Mitchell, Earl DT
	Williams, Mario DE
Declared Free Agent	Branch, Andre DE
	Bushrod, Jermon G
	Butler, Donald LB
	Cameron, Jordan TE
	Chekwa, Chimdi CB
	Denney, John DE
	Jenkins, Jelani LB
	Jones, Dominique TE
	Paysinger, Spencer LB
	Rambo, Bacarri S
	Sims, Dion TE
	Stills, Kenny WR
	Yates, T.J. QB
Retired	Cameron, Jordan TE

Average Line	# Games Favored	# Games Underdog
+0.8	7	8

Regular Season Wins: Past & Current Proj

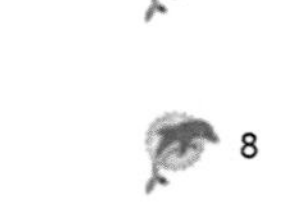

2017 Miami Dolphins Overview

By all accounts the Dolphins exceeded expectations in year 1 of Adam Gase. Gase is one of the innovative, young coaches I respect for their willingness to be inventive and creative. Gase saw a lot of success in Denver with Peyton Manning and was able to make Jay Cutler look competent thanks to the game plan and strategy he employed in Chicago. In his first season in Miami, he faced some uphill challenges. Yet he was able to get enough out of this team to win 10 games and make the playoffs, despite the team being favored in only 4 games by oddsmakers before the season started.

The first challenge he faced was health. The 2016 Dolphins were the 7th most injured team in the NFL. Ryan Tannehill was lost 13 games into the season, yet the team still went 2-1 in their final 3 games (losing only to the Patriots) to secure a trip to the playoffs. While the D-Line was healthy, the LB and DB groups each ranked in the 7 most injured units last year. The TE corps was the most injured in the NFL. So there was a struggle for consistency last season. When the offensive line was intact, the team was nearly unbeatable. But players were hurt and rotated around and such disruptions impact all aspects of the offense, which filters over to the defense as a result.

The second challenge he faced was youth and inexperience. His leading running back, a focal point for an Adam Gase led team if the quarterback is not Peyton Manning, was a 23-year-old, 2nd year player who averaged 3.8 yards per attempt his rookie season. The 2nd leading RB was a 24-year-old, 3rd year player who averaged a career 3.5 yards per carry his prior two seasons. His 2nd most targeted receiver was also a 23-year-old, 2nd year player who caught just 52% of his targets in his rookie season. His top receiver was a 24-year-old slot receiver, skilled but who never seemed to get his production to match expectations.

And then there was Ryan Tannehill with a 29-35 record, a 61.9% completion rate, a 6.9 yards per attempt avg and a lifetime 85 passer rating. Gase had faced challenging projects in the past, but turning this team (off of 6-10, 8-8 and 8-8 seasons)) was going to be a task. Despite facing the 3rd most difficult schedule of run defenses, Gase implemented a run first strategy. On first downs in the first half, they ran the ball on 57% of their plays, 3rd most often in the NFL.

(cont'd - see MIA2)

2017 Lineup & Cap Hits

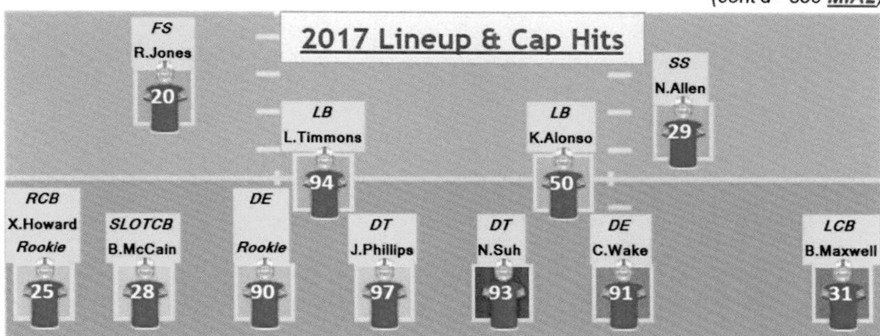

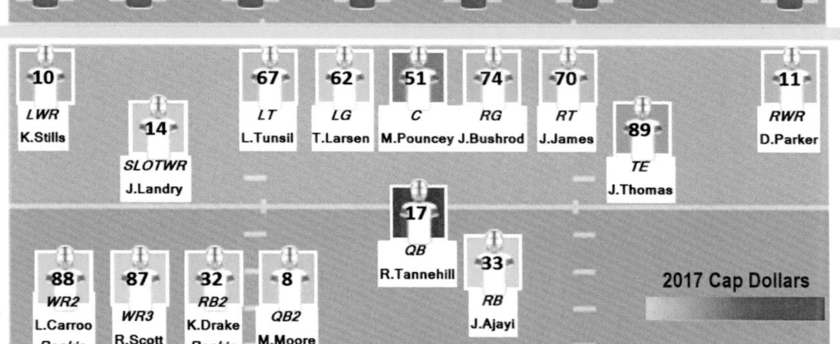

Key Free Agents/ Trades Added

Allen, Nate S
Fasano, Anthony TE
Hayes, William DE
Lacey, Deon LB
McDonald, T.J. S
Miley, Arthur DE
Okoye, Lawrence DE
Pantale, Chris TE
Thomas, Julius TE
Timmons, Lawrence LB

Drafted Players

Rd	Pk	Player (College)
1	22	DE - Charles Harris (Missouri)
2	54	LB - Raekwon McMillan (Ohio State)
3*	97	DB - Cordrea Tankersley (Clemson)
5	164	G - Isaac Asiata (Utah)
5*	178	DT - Davon Godchaux (LSU)
6	194	DT - Vincent Taylor (Oklahoma State)
7	237	WR - Isaiah Ford (Virginia Tech)

2017 Unit Spending

All DEF
All OFF

Positional Spending

	Rank	Total	2016 Rk
All OFF	24	$75.28M	27
QB	5	$23.61M	21
OL	24	$24.87M	5
RB	27	$4.81M	31
WR	30	$12.48M	30
TE	12	$9.51M	6
All DEF	7	$84.46M	7
DL	1	$45.20M	1
LB	28	$13.33M	30
CB	22	$13.92M	21
S	15	$12.01M	8

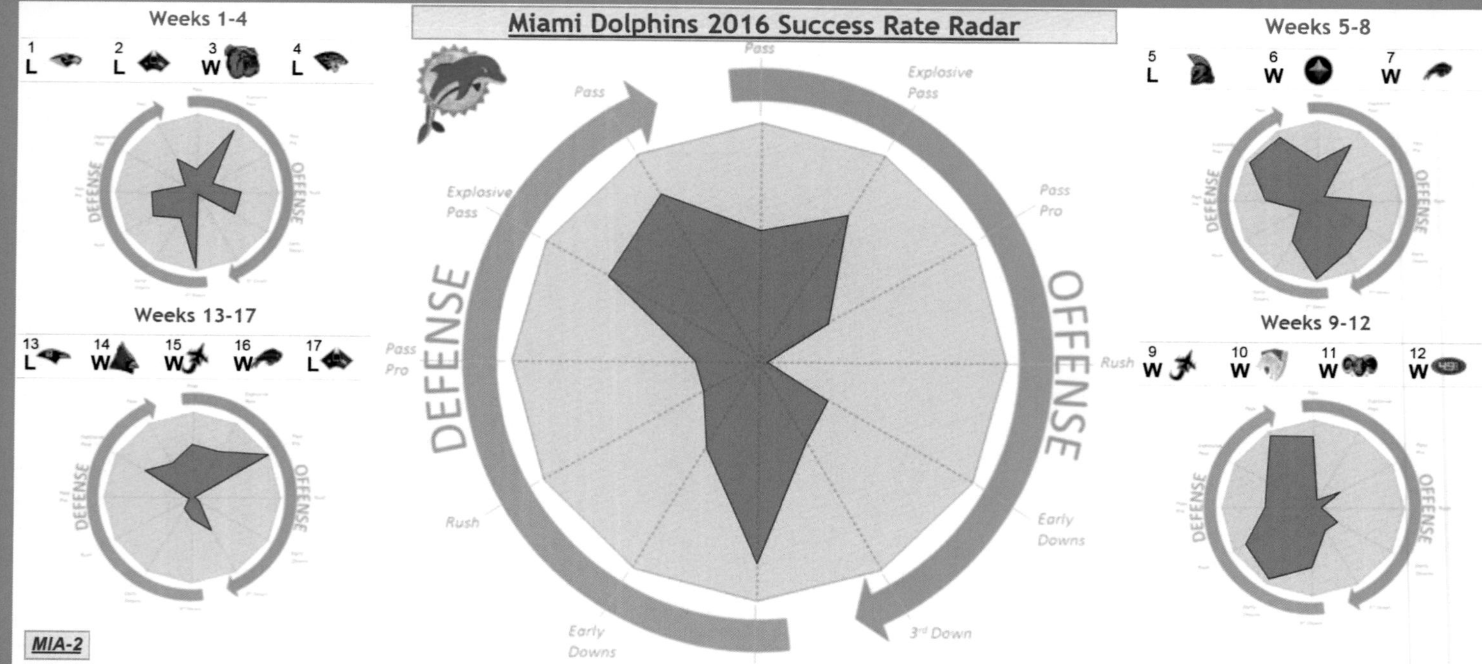

MIA-2

But the season didn't get off to a great start, nor did it start off very run heavy. The schedule opened with a brutal two-game road stretch, in Seattle and in New England. RB Jay Ajayi did not play week one, and Arian Foster took the starting role. In the first half of these two games, the team went 63% pass to 38% rush, a higher than average pass rate. It didn't turn out well. Tannehill didn't throw a first half touchdown in either game, and posted first half ratings of 64 and 52. Over their first 5 games, which saw a 1-4 record posted (the only win over the Browns), Jay Ajayi saw 5, 7, 6 and 13 total carries in his 4 games played. Gase re-evaluated some things and made a point to feed the ground game from that point onward.

Week 6 over the Steelers, Ajayi received 25 carries, recorded 204 total yards (8.2 yards per attempt) and ignoring the 4th quarter when they were running the air out of the clock, the Dolphins went 61% run on first down and 47% run overall. And over the course of the next 5 weeks, the Dolphins became the most run heavy team in football, calling run plays 50% of the time (9% above average) in the first 3 quarters of games, and on 61% of their first downs.

They won every single game. And as the run game excelled, so did Tannehill. In those 4 games (1 bye week) he recorded a 99 rating, tossed 4 TDs to 0 INTs and completed 65% of his passes.

From week 6 until Tannehill's final game last year, on early downs the Dolphins called run plays 56% of the time (again, ignoring the 4th quarter where they led in most games), the 3rd highest rate in the NFL behind only Tennessee and San Francisco. Overall last season, the Dolphins ran the ball on 46% of their plays, the 5th highest run rate in the NFL. This was not surprising at all. I predicted they would turn to the ground in last year's preview, because I saw what Gase did in Chicago. And it produced even better results in Miami. And keep in mind, this was against the 3rd most difficult schedule of run defenses last year.

Given the impediments and the challenges he faced, 10 wins and a trip to the playoffs was a big deal for Gase and the Dolphins. But there are multiple things

(cont'd - see MIA-3)

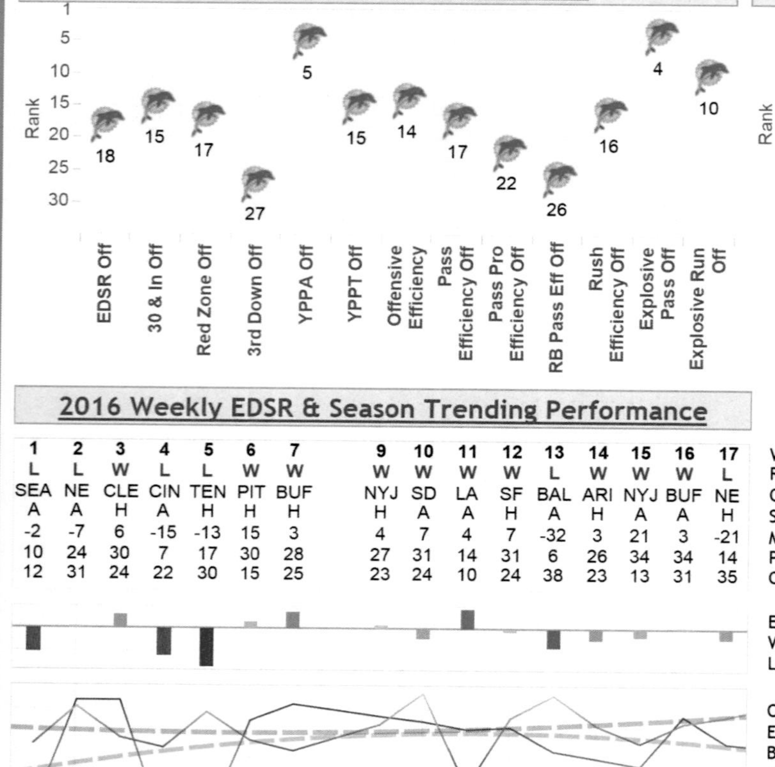

2016 Defensive Advanced Metrics

Metric	Rank
EDSR Def	25
30 & In Def	11
Red Zone Def	18
3rd Down Def	2
YPPA Def	7
YPPT Def	14
Defensive Efficiency	19
Pass Efficiency Def	14
Pass Pro Efficiency Def	31
RB Pass Eff Def	14
Rush Efficiency Def	22
Explosive Pass Def	7
Explosive Run Def	31

2016 Weekly EDSR & Season Trending Performance

WEEK	1	2	3	4	5	6	7	9	10	11	12	13	14	15	16	17
RESULT	L	L	W	L	L	W	W	W	W	W	W	L	W	W	W	L
OPP	SEA	NE	CLE	CIN	TEN	PIT	BUF	NYJ	SD	LA	SF	BAL	ARI	NYJ	BUF	NE
SITE	A	A	H	A	H	H	H	H	A	A	H	A	H	A	A	H
MARGIN	-2	-7	6	-15	-13	15	3	4	7	4	7	-32	3	21	3	-21
PTS	10	24	30	7	17	30	28	27	31	14	31	6	26	34	34	14
OPP PTS	12	31	24	22	30	15	25	23	24	10	24	38	23	13	31	35

2016 Close Game Records

All 2016 Wins: **10**
FG Games (<=3 pts) W-L: **3-1**
FG Games Win %: **75% (#7)**
FG Games Wins (% of Total Wins): **30% (#12)**
1 Score Games (<=8 pts) W-L: **8-2**
1 Score Games Win %: **80% (#2)**
1 Score Games Wins (% of Total Wins): **80% (#5)**

2016 Critical & Game-Deciding Stats

TO Margin	+2
TO Given	23
INT Given	15
FUM Given	8
TO Taken	25
INT Taken	16
FUM Taken	9
Sack Margin	+3
Sacks	33
Sacks Allow	30
Return TD Margin	+3
Ret TDs	4
Ret TDs Allow	1
Penalty Margin	-16
Penalties	125
Opponent Penalties	109

Miami Dolphins 2017 Strength of Schedule In Detail (compared to 2016)

HARD / EASY — Average Opponent RANK

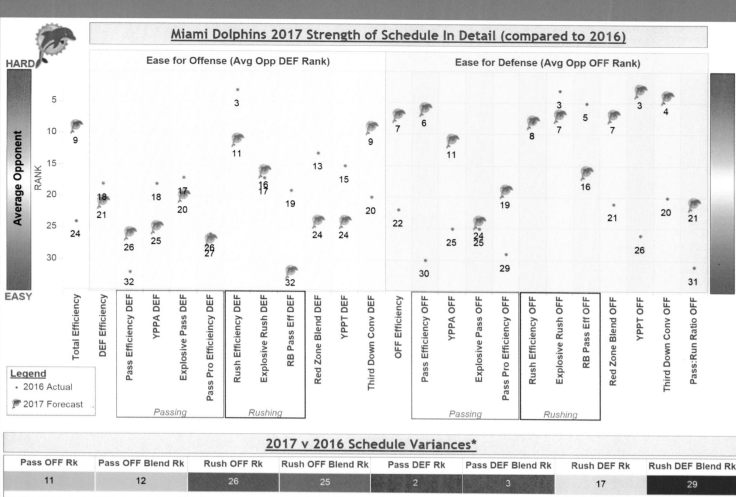

Ease for Offense (Avg Opp DEF Rank)

Metric	Group	2016 Actual	2017 Forecast
Total Efficiency		24	9
DEF Efficiency		18	21
Pass Efficiency DEF	Passing	32	26
YPPA DEF	Passing	18	25
Explosive Pass DEF	Passing	17	20
Pass Pro Efficiency DEF	Passing	27	26
Rush Efficiency DEF	Rushing	3	11
Explosive Rush DEF	Rushing	17	16
RB Pass Eff DEF	Rushing	19	32
Red Zone Blend DEF		13	24
YPPT DEF		15	24
Third Down Conv DEF		20	9

Ease for Defense (Avg Opp OFF Rank)

Metric	Group	2016 Actual	2017 Forecast
OFF Efficiency		22	7
Pass Efficiency OFF	Passing	30	6
YPPA OFF	Passing	25	11
Explosive Pass OFF	Passing	25	24
Pass Pro Efficiency OFF	Passing	29	19
Rush Efficiency OFF	Rushing		8
Explosive Rush OFF	Rushing	3	7
RB Pass Eff OFF	Rushing	5	16
Red Zone Blend OFF		21	7
YPPT OFF		26	3
Third Down Conv OFF		20	4
Pass:Run Ratio OFF		31	21

Legend
- • 2016 Actual
- 2017 Forecast

2017 v 2016 Schedule Variances*

Pass OFF Rk	Pass OFF Blend Rk	Rush OFF Rk	Rush OFF Blend Rk	Pass DEF Rk	Pass DEF Blend Rk	Rush DEF Rk	Rush DEF Blend Rk
11	12	26	25	2	3	17	29

* **1**=Hardest Jump in 2017 schedule from 2016 (aka a much harder schedule in 2017), **32**=Easiest Jump in 2017 schedule from 2016 (aka a much easier schedule in 2017); **Pass Blend** metric blends 4 metrics: Pass Efficiency, YPPA, Explosive Pass & Pass Rush; **Rush Blend** metric blends 3 metrics: Rush Efficiency, Explosive Rush & RB Targets

Team Records & Trends

	2016	2015	2014
Average line	1.8	1.2	-0.7
Average O/U line	44.2	44.9	44.3
Straight Up Record	10-6	6-10	8-8
Against the Spread Record	9-7	5-11	7-9
Over/Under Record	12-4	7-9	8-8
ATS as Favorite	2-3	2-4	4-5
ATS as Underdog	6-4	3-6	3-4
Straight Up Home	6-2	3-5	4-4
ATS Home	4-4	2-6	3-5
Over/Under Home	7-1	3-5	5-3
ATS as Home Favorite	1-3	1-3	2-4
ATS as a Home Dog	3-1	1-2	1-1
Straight Up Away	4-4	3-5	4-4
ATS Away	5-3	3-5	4-4
Over/Under Away	5-3	4-4	3-5
ATS Away Favorite	1-0	1-1	2-1
ATS Away Dog	3-3	2-4	2-3
Six Point Teaser Record	12-4	6-10	11-5
Seven Point Teaser Record	12-4	6-9	11-5
Ten Point Teaser Record	13-3	10-6	11-5

MIA-3

he and the team need to do better in 2017. Ironically, it starts with where they were at their best last year: the run game. Jay Ajayi totaled 1,272 rushing yards (4th most) despite missing one game, and averaged 4.9 yards per rush, 7th best in the NFL. On the surface, these numbers are great. But when you dig into the analytics, they show problems. There are three key rushing analytics I like to use: Success Rate, Missed YPA and YAS %. Success Rate is the frequency which a player generates the required yardage (per play, based on down and distance-to-go) to grade as successful. Missed YPA measures yardage on unsuccessful plays which fell short of the required distance-to-go to grade as successful. And YAS % (Yards Above Successful) isolates only the yardage on successful plays which was in excess of required, aka measuring explosive yardage. These are three key metrics that evaluate runs that come up short, just enough, or more than required. And they are more valuable than total or average yardage because those numbers lie. Take an example: A RB is used only on 1st down and has 10 rushes in a game. 9 of those 10 rushes gain exactly 2 yards.

*(cont'd - see **MIA-4**)*

2017 Rest Analysis

Avg Rest	6.47
Avg Rk	3
Team More Rest	3
Opp More Rest	3
Net Rest Edge	0
3 Days Rest	1
4 Days Rest	0
5 Days Rest	1
6 Days Rest	9
7 Days Rest	2
8 Days Rest	0
9 Days Rest	1
10 Days Rest	0
11 Days Rest	0
12 Days Rest	1
13 Days Rest	0
14 Days Rest	0

Health by Unit*

2016 Rk	26
(2015 Rk)	15
Off Rk	24
Def Rk	25
QB Rk	26
RB Rk	17
WR Rk	15
TE Rk	32
OLine Rk	22
DLine Rk	8
LB Rk	27
DB Rk	26

*Based on the great work of Scott Kacsmar from Football Outsiders

2017 Weekly Betting Lines (wks 1-16)

1	2	3	4	5	6	7	8	9	10	12	13	14	15	16
TB	LAC	NYJ	NO	TEN	ATL	NYJ	BAL	OAK	CAR	NE	DEN	NE	BUF	KC
H	A	A	H	H	A	H	A	H	A	A	H	H	A	A
-1.5	+1.0	-2.0	-3.0	-3.0	+6.5	-8.5	+3.0	-1.0	+3.0	+9.0	-1.0	+4.0	+1.5	+4.5

Home Lines (wks 1-16)

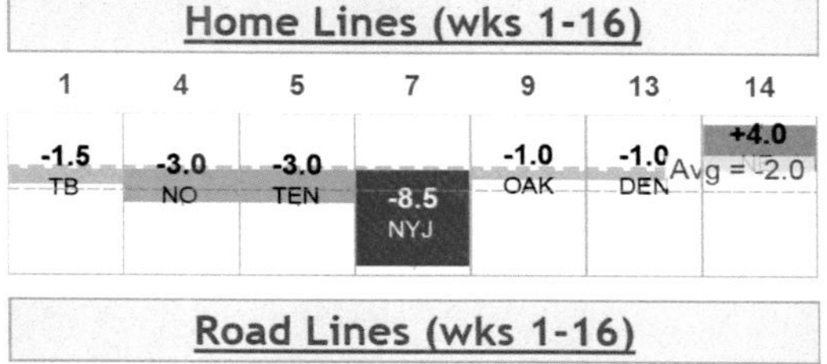

1	4	5	7	9	13	14
TB	NO	TEN	NYJ	OAK	DEN	NE
-1.5	-3.0	-3.0	-8.5	-1.0	-1.0	+4.0

Road Lines (wks 1-16)

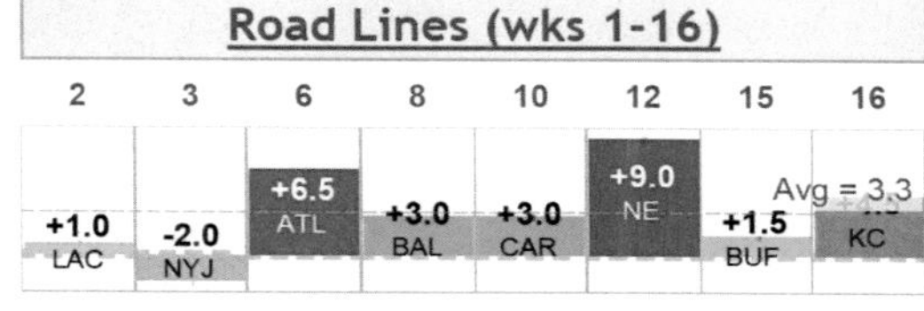

2	3	6	8	10	12	15	16
LAC	NYJ	ATL	BAL	CAR	NE	BUF	KC
+1.0	-2.0	+6.5	+3.0	+3.0	+9.0	+1.5	

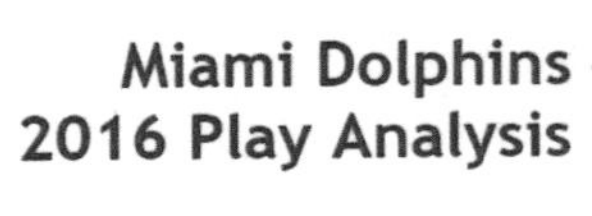

Miami Dolphins 2016 Play Analysis

2016 Play Tendencies

All Pass %	54%
All Pass Rk	28
All Rush %	46%
All Rush Rk	5
1 Score Pass %	58%
1 Score Pass Rk	17
2015 1 Score Pass %	60%
2015 1 Score Pass Rk	12
Pass Increase %	-2%
Pass Increase Rk	19
1 Score Rush %	42%
1 Score Rush Rk	16
Up Pass %	50%
Up Pass Rk	31
Up Rush %	50%
Up Rush Rk	2
Down Pass %	57%
Down Pass Rk	27
Down Rush %	43%
Down Rush Rk	6

2016 Down & Distance Tendencies

Down	Distance	Total Plays	Pass Rate	Run Rate	Play Success %
1	Short (1-3)	5	0%	100%	60%
	Med (4-7)	10	20%	80%	60%
	Long (8-10)	301	43%	57%	50%
	XL (11+)	11	55%	45%	18%
2	Short (1-3)	39	36%	64%	59%
	Med (4-7)	72	43%	57%	49%
	Long (8-10)	87	53%	47%	33%
	XL (11+)	42	69%	31%	36%
3	Short (1-3)	31	71%	29%	65%
	Med (4-7)	67	94%	6%	43%
	Long (8-10)	17	100%	0%	29%
	XL (11+)	34	85%	15%	15%
4	Short (1-3)	2	0%	100%	50%
	Med (4-7)	1	0%	100%	0%

Shotgun %:

Under Center	Shotgun
40%	60%
37%	*63%*

37% AVG 63%

Run Rate:

Under Center	Shotgun
71%	25%

68% AVG 23%

Pass Rate:

Under Center	Shotgun
29%	75%

32% AVG 77%

Short Yardage Intelligence:

2nd and Short Run

Run Freq	Run % Rk	NFL Run Freq Avg	Run 1D Rate	Run NFL 1D Avg
69%	10	65%	65%	71%

2nd and Short Pass

Pass Freq	Pass % Rk	NFL Pass Freq Avg	Pass 1D Rate	Pass NFL 1D Avg
31%	22	35%	78%	52%

Most Frequent Play

Down	Distance	Play Type	Player	Total Plays	Play Success %
1	Short (1-3)	RUSH	Damien Williams	3	33%
	Med (4-7)	RUSH	Jay Ajayi	7	57%
	Long (8-10)	RUSH	Jay Ajayi	126	43%
	XL (11+)	RUSH	Jay Ajayi	3	33%
2	Short (1-3)	RUSH	Jay Ajayi	19	47%
	Med (4-7)	RUSH	Jay Ajayi	33	48%
	Long (8-10)	RUSH	Jay Ajayi	21	19%
	XL (11+)	RUSH	Jay Ajayi	10	20%
3	Short (1-3)	PASS	Damien Williams	5	60%
	Med (4-7)	PASS	DeVante Parker	12	42%
			Kenny Stills	12	42%
	Long (8-10)	PASS	Jarvis Landry	6	17%
	XL (11+)	PASS	Jarvis Landry	8	13%

Most Successful Play*

Down	Distance	Play Type	Player	Total Plays	Play Success %
1	Med (4-7)	RUSH	Jay Ajayi	7	57%
	Long (8-10)	PASS	MarQueis Gray	10	80%
2	Short (1-3)	RUSH	Jay Ajayi	19	47%
	Med (4-7)	PASS	Jarvis Landry	8	50%
	Long (8-10)	PASS	Jarvis Landry	13	69%
	XL (11+)	PASS	Kenny Stills	9	44%
3	Short (1-3)	PASS	Damien Williams	5	60%
	Med (4-7)	PASS	Dion Sims	7	57%
	Long (8-10)	PASS	Jarvis Landry	6	17%
	XL (11+)	PASS	Kenny Stills	5	60%

**Minimum 5 plays to qualify*

2016 Snap Rates

Week	Opp	Score	Jarvis Landry	Kenny Stills	DeVante Parker	Dion Sims	Jay Ajayi
1	SEA	L 12-10	51 (96%)	53 (100%)		13 (25%)	
2	NE	L 31-24	60 (94%)	63 (98%)	59 (92%)	33 (52%)	37 (58%)
3	CLE	W 30-24	66 (99%)	65 (97%)	58 (87%)	60 (90%)	18 (27%)
4	CIN	L 22-7	43 (96%)	45 (100%)	40 (89%)	45 (100%)	14 (31%)
5	TEN	L 30-17	42 (95%)	35 (80%)	35 (80%)	43 (98%)	30 (68%)
6	PIT	W 30-15	63 (90%)	54 (77%)	60 (86%)	47 (67%)	48 (69%)
7	BUF	W 28-25	68 (93%)	68 (93%)	49 (67%)		47 (64%)
9	NYJ	W 27-23	60 (95%)	15 (24%)	57 (90%)		43 (68%)
10	SD	W 31-24	49 (96%)	36 (71%)	41 (80%)	49 (96%)	38 (75%)
11	LA	W 14-10	55 (92%)	50 (83%)	53 (88%)	60 (100%)	47 (78%)
12	SF	W 31-24	55 (93%)	51 (86%)	37 (63%)	59 (100%)	47 (80%)
13	BAL	L 38-6	61 (98%)	62 (100%)	49 (79%)	60 (97%)	40 (65%)
14	ARI	W 26-23	58 (97%)	57 (95%)	58 (97%)	60 (100%)	42 (70%)
15	NYJ	W 35-13	36 (75%)	26 (54%)	28 (58%)	45 (94%)	41 (85%)
16	BUF	W 34-31	66 (96%)	59 (86%)	53 (77%)	69 (100%)	52 (75%)
17	NE	L 35-14	58 (98%)	55 (93%)	57 (97%)	58 (98%)	34 (58%)
Grand Total			891 (94%)	794 (84%)	734 (82%)	701 (87%)	578 (65%)

Personnel Groupings

Personnel	Team %	NFL Avg	Succ. %
1-1 [3WR]	74%	60%	44%
1-2 [2WR]	16%	19%	43%
0-1 [4WR]	3%	1%	39%
1-0 [4WR]	3%	3%	48%

Grouping Tendencies

Personnel	Pass Rate	Pass Succ. %	Run Succ. %
1-1 [3WR]	60%	46%	41%
1-2 [2WR]	37%	51%	39%
0-1 [4WR]	93%	38%	50%
1-0 [4WR]	74%	45%	57%

Red Zone Targets (min 3)

Receiver	All	Inside 5	6-10	11-20
DeVante Parker	10		5	5
Jarvis Landry	10		4	6
Damien Williams	8	2	2	4
Dion Sims	8	3	3	2
Kenny Stills	6		2	4
Jay Ajayi	5		1	4
MarQueis Gray	4			4

Red Zone Rushes (min 3)

Rusher	All	Inside 5	6-10	11-20
Jay Ajayi	32	8	9	15
Damien Williams	11	7		4
Ryan Tannehill	9	3	1	5
Arian Foster	3	2		1
Kenyan Drake	3		2	1

Early Down Target Rate

	RB	TE	WR
	15%	16%	69%
NFL AVG	*19%*	*20%*	*61%*

Overall Target Success %

RB	TE	WR
40% #28	62% #3	51% #11

Miami Dolphins 2016 Passing Recap & 2017 Outlook

There is no doubt Tannehill can use more work, but there is also no doubt he will likely see his best pro years thus far under the tutelage of Adam Gase. Tannehill's completion rate, yards per attempt and rating were just above the league average last year. As were his advanced stats almost across the board. Tannehill did a good job of limiting his interceptions to long yardage or 3rd down situations, except for on 2nd and short, which is just one more reason to hand the ball off for an efficient first down in those situations. Tannehill even did an adequate job of throwing the ball beyond the sticks on 3rd down, averaging more air yards per completion than the average to-go yardage. Given the strong rate of completions to his TEs and the 62% success rate, I'm extremely interested to see how TE Julius Thomas gets involved in this offense. Additionally, Gase and Tannehill simply must do a better job of finding ways to get the ball to Ajayi in the passing game. He's a dangerous weapon if he can catch the ball in space, already thundering downhill. Unless something changes early, Tannehill should stop targeting DeVante Parker so much in the red zone (30% success rate) and target Landry more (70% success rate).

Ryan Tannehill Rating All Downs

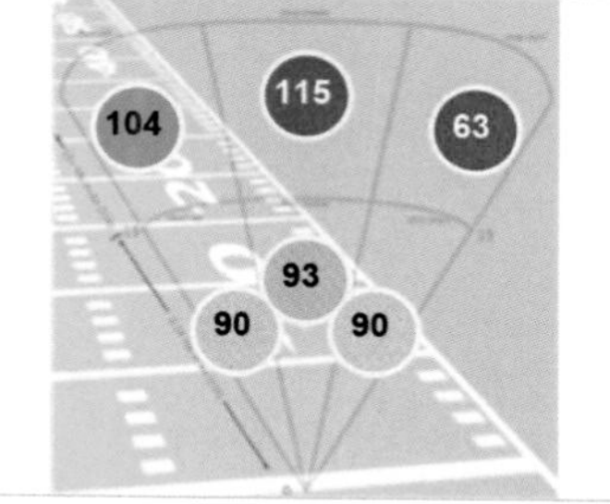

Ryan Tannehill Rating Early Downs

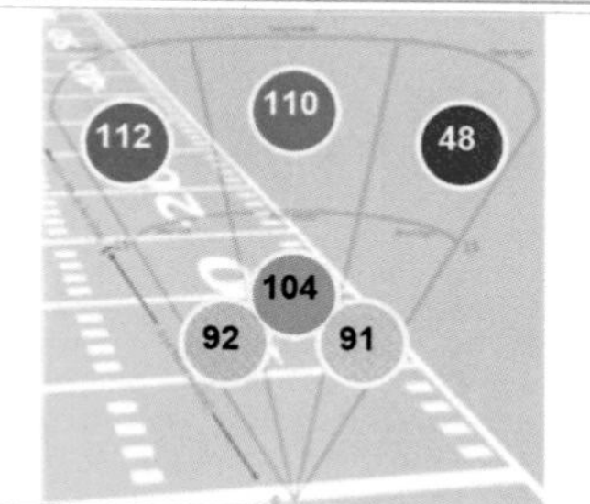

2016 Standard Passing Table

QB	Comp	Att	Comp %	Yds	YPA	TDs	INT	Sacks	Rating	Rk
Ryan Tannehill	261	390	67%	2,986	7.7	19	12	27	93.2	17
NFL Avg			63%		7.2				90.4	

2016 Advanced Passing Table

QB	Success %	EDSR Passing Success %	20+ Yd Pass Gains	20+ Yd Pass %	30+ Yd Pass Gains	30+ Yd Pass %	Air Yds per Comp	YAC per Comp	20+ Air Yd Comp	20+ Air Yd %
Ryan Tannehill	46%	52%	37	9%	15	4%	6.0	5.4	17	4%
NFL Avg	44%	48%	27	8%	10	3%	6.4	4.8	12	4%

Interception Rates by Down

Yards to Go	1	2	3	4	Total
1 & 2	0.0%	11.1%	0.0%		4.2%
3, 4, 5	0.0%	0.0%	5.7%	50.0%	5.5%
6 - 9	0.0%	0.0%	0.0%		0.0%
10 - 14	2.1%	3.9%	7.7%		3.2%
15+	20.0%	0.0%	0.0%		4.0%
Total	2.6%	2.2%	3.1%	50.0%	2.9%

3rd Down Passing - Short of Sticks Analysis

QB	Avg Yds to Go	Air Yds (of Comps)	Avg Yds Short	Short of Sticks Rate	Rk
Ryan Tannehill	7.7	7.9	0.0	66%	14
NFL Avg	7.6	6.8	-0.8	57%	

Air Yds vs YAC

Air Yds %	YAC %	Rk
49%	51%	36
54%	46%	

2016 Receiving Recap & 2017 Outlook

While Jarvis Landry delivered a very solid 72% completion rate, his success rate was only 54%, a full 18% lower. This was because many of Landry's targets came close to the line of scrimmage and required YAC to achieve the required yardage to meet the standards of a successful play, yet fell short. But even then, they fell quite short, as his Missed YPA ranked 91st among receivers. There is absolutely no doubt the Dolphins need to target the TE more often, and with a former Gase TE in Julius Thomas in the fold, Tannehill could find success assuming Thomas can regain some of his form from those years in Denver.

Player *Min 50 Targets*	Targets	Comp %	YPA	Rating	TOARS	Success %	Success Rk	Missed YPA Rk	YAS % Rk	TDs
Jarvis Landry	145	72%	8.6	99	5.3	54%	41	91	46	4
DeVante Parker	94	64%	8.5	83	4.5	51%	67	63	25	4
Kenny Stills	86	55%	9.4	93	4.4	48%	97	114	7	9

Directional Passer Rating Delivered

Receiver	Short Left	Short Middle	Short Right	Deep Left	Deep Middle	Deep Right	Player Total
Jarvis Landry	98	108	81	147	26	96	99
DeVante Parker	120	89	86	28	158	62	83
Kenny Stills	30	61	57	132	116	79	93
Dion Sims	97	158	121	56	40		120
Jay Ajayi	89	85	81			40	85
Damien Williams	119	74	125	158		40	134
Team Total	95	99	91	94	108	57	98

2016 Rushing Recap & 2017 Outlook

I'm not sure when the Dolphins plan to stop the Damien Williams experiment but it has not performed well. He's averaged 3.4 yards per carry in his 3 years in Miami, and while he saw only 35 seemingly insignificant carries total last season, 11 of them came in the red zone. And only 27% of those were successful. Red zone touches are incredibly important. When Ajayi is recording successful runs on 53% of his red zone carries, including 75% of his carries inside the 5, why would Gase give Williams nearly the same number (7) of carries as Ajayi (8) when his success rate inside the 5 was only 29%? Last year's rookie 3rd round pick Kenyan Drake performed better (5.4 yards per carry) and the less Williams receives red zone touches the mor..

Player *Min 50 Rushes*	Rushes	YPA	Success %	Success Rk	Missed YPA Rk	YTS % Rk	YAS % Rk	Early Down Success %	Early Down Success Rk	TDs
Jay Ajayi	276	4.7	42%	51	56	63	5	42%	49	8

Yards per Carry by Direction

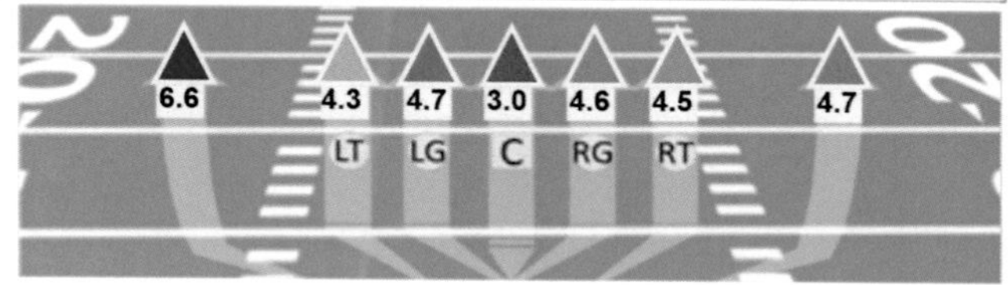

Directional Run Frequency

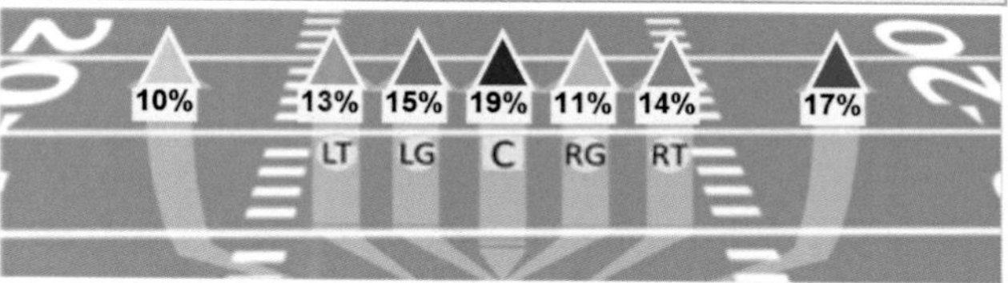

MIA-4

But on one play, the LB fills the wrong hole, a lineman gets to the second level and creates an even larger alley, and the RB breaks one tackle and then bulldozes a CB as he runs 82 yards for a TD. The RB totals 100 yards on the game. He averages 10 yards per carry. Sounds like a great game. But the reality was, his 2 yard gains on those other 1st downs set up 2nd and long each time, and his team was at a major disadvantage. Success rate knows that on 1st and 10, a play needs at least 4 yards to grade as successful. Therefore, only 1 of his 10 carries was successful. His missed YPA was 2.0, as on each unsuccessful run which needed 4 yards, he fell 2 yards short. And his YAS % is going to be substantial, as his lone successful play saw 82 yards gained: 4 of which were required and 78 of which were "above successful".

Jay Ajayi was not to that extreme, not by far. But while he ranked 7th best in yards per attempt and 4th best in total yards, he ranked 43rd in success rate and 49th in Missed YPA. However, his YAS % was 5th best. Much like the example above, a lot of Ajayi's yardage came on big, explosive runs. But he was bottled up an awful lot on other occasions: 23% of his total production for the entire season came on just 2.5% (7 runs) of his total runs. 57% (157 runs) of Ajayi's rushes gained 3 or fewer yards. Ajayi's success rate was not consistently bad. Without Mike Pouncey and Brandon Albert, Ajayi's success rate was 38% (on 180 carries). With both in the lineup, his success rate was 49% (on 96 carries).

Gase and the Dolphins will certainly hope for health along the offensive line, and while they did play a difficult schedule or run defenses, they have to work to improve Ajayi's consistency, which is partly on Ajayi and partly on the line.

Another thing that Gase probably studied which needs improvement relates to formations. Despite the injuries to their TE corps, targets to TEs were successful 62% of the time for the Dolphins, which was the 3rd best rate in the NFL and much better than WR targets (51%) or RB targets (40%). But the Dolphins targeted the TE on only 16% of their attempts, well below the NFL average. Gase loved 11 personnel (used it 74% of the time, well above the 60% avg). But when targeting WRs out of 11 personnel, the Dolphins were successful just 51% of the time, with a 88 rating and a 12:13 TD:INT ratio. When targeting TEs out of 11, the Dolphins were successful 60% of the time with a 112 rating and a 2:0 TD:INT ratio. The best time for the Dolphins to target their WRs was out of zero-back sets, where they recorded a 55% success rate, a 142 rating and a 4:0 TD:INT ratio. Additionally, Miami must improve their targeting of RBs. When targeted on 1st down, they are successful 59% of the time. But 45% of their targets come on 3rd down, and the success rate was only 35%.

This year opposing offenses will give this Dolphins defense a huge test. Going 8-2 in one-score games last year gave Miami a big boost. They'll be better this year but the record may not be as strong.

Division History: Season Wins & 2017 Projection

2013 Wins | 2014 Wins | 2015 Wins | 2016 Wins | Proj 2017 Wins

Rank of 2017 Defensive Pass Efficiency Faced by Week

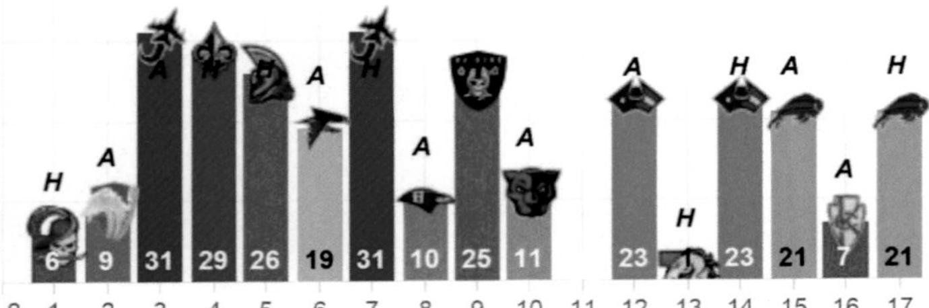

Rank of 2017 Defensive Rush Efficiency Faced by Week

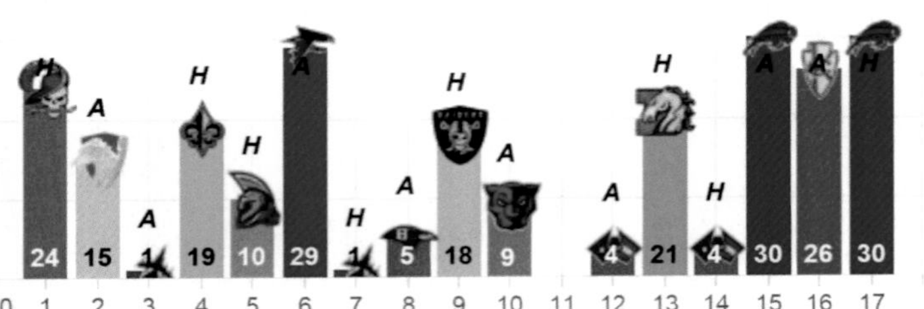

2016 Situational Usage by Player & Position

Usage Rate by Score

		Being Blown Out (14+)	Down Big (9-13)	One Score	Large Lead (9-13)	Blowout Lead (14+)	Grand Total
RUSH	Jay Ajayi	19%	27%	35%	41%	40%	31%
	Jarvis Landry	1%		1%			1%
	Damien Williams	3%	1%	5%	5%	13%	4%
	Kenyan Drake	4%	3%	3%		17%	4%
	Arian Foster	1%	1%	3%			2%
	Isaiah Pead		1%	1%			1%
	Jakeem Grant	1%					0%
	Total	29%	33%	48%	45%	70%	43%
PASS	Jay Ajayi	9%	5%	3%			4%
	Jarvis Landry	25%	21%	13%	14%	13%	16%
	DeVante Parker	13%	19%	9%	9%	3%	11%
	Kenny Stills	9%	12%	10%	5%	3%	10%
	Damien Williams	3%	4%	4%	5%		4%
	Kenyan Drake	2%		1%			1%
	Dion Sims	6%	4%	4%	18%		5%
	Arian Foster			2%		3%	1%
	MarQueis Gray			3%		7%	2%
	Jordan Cameron	3%		1%			1%
	Dominique Jones	1%	1%	1%			1%
	Isaiah Pead		1%				0%
	Leonte Carroo	1%		1%	5%		1%
	Jakeem Grant			0%			0%
	Total	71%	67%	52%	55%	30%	57%

Positional Target Distribution vs NFL Average

		NFL Wide				Team Only			
		Left	Middle	Right	Total	Left	Middle	Right	Total
Deep	WR	1,000	562	983	**2,545**	31	19	18	**68**
	TE	156	146	163	**465**	2	1		**3**
	RB	24	4	36	**64**	1		4	**5**
	All	**1,180**	**712**	**1,182**	**3,074**	**34**	**20**	**22**	**76**
Short	WR	3,011	1,705	3,077	**7,793**	82	66	109	**257**
	TE	826	868	1,131	**2,825**	10	7	20	**37**
	RB	996	604	1,084	**2,684**	19	18	29	**66**
	All	**4,833**	**3,177**	**5,292**	**13,302**	**111**	**91**	**158**	**360**
Total		**6,013**	**3,889**	**6,474**	**16,376**	**145**	**111**	**180**	**436**

Positional Success Rates vs NFL Average

		NFL Wide				Team Only			
		Left	Middle	Right	Total	Left	Middle	Right	Total
Deep	WR	37%	50%	38%	**40%**	42%	68%	44%	**50%**
	TE	44%	50%	43%	**46%**	50%	0%		**33%**
	RB	29%	75%	28%	**31%**	100%		0%	**20%**
	All	**38%**	**50%**	**38%**	**41%**	**44%**	**65%**	**36%**	**47%**
Short	WR	52%	57%	51%	**53%**	56%	55%	48%	**52%**
	TE	50%	61%	52%	**54%**	50%	71%	65%	**62%**
	RB	47%	50%	44%	**46%**	42%	39%	41%	**41%**
	All	**51%**	**57%**	**50%**	**52%**	**53%**	**53%**	**49%**	**51%**
Total		**48%**	**55%**	**48%**	**50%**	**51%**	**55%**	**47%**	**50%**

Minnesota Vikings

2017 Coaches

Head Coach:
Mike Zimmer (4th yr)
Offensive Coordinator:
Pat Shurmur (wk 9 2016) (2nd yr)
Defensive Coordinator:
George Edwards (4th yr)

2017 Forecast

Wins	Div Rank
8.5	#2

Past Records

2016: 8-8
2015: 11-5
2014: 7-9

EASY HARD

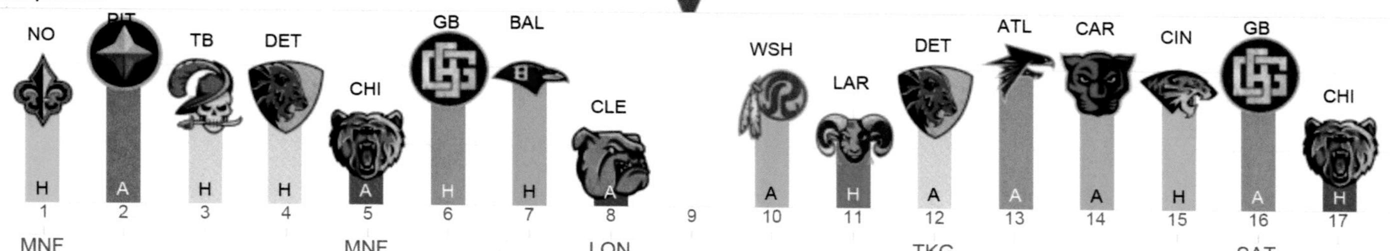

Key Players Lost

TXN	Player (POS)
Cut	Crichton, Scott DE
	Fusco, Brandon G
	Harris, Mike G
Declared Free Agent	Asiata, Matt RB
	Cole, Audie LB
	Ellison, Rhett TE
	Hill, Shaun QB
	Johnson, Charles WR
	Kalil, Matt T
	Line, Zach RB
	Locke, Jeff P
	Long, Jake T
	Munnerlyn, Captain CB
	Newman, Terence CB
	Patterson, Cordarrelle WR
	Peterson, Adrian RB
	Smith, Andre T
	Trattou, Justin DE
Retired	Greenway, Chad LB
	Long, Jake T

Average Line	# Games Favored	# Games Underdog
-0.4	8	7

2017 Minnesota Vikings Overview

It's difficult to win without a quarterback in the modern NFL. Since the rules changes during the 2010 season which led to steep fines and suspensions for helmet-to-helmet hits, passing efficiency contributes over four times more toward winning games than rushing efficiency. So when a team's franchise quarterback goes down before the start of the season, it's typically a crippling, season altering problem.

Off a 11-win season in 2015, the Vikings did not want to let their season end before it started. So they obtained QB Sam Bradford just weeks before the start of the season to replace Teddy Bridgewater. When passing is so much more important that rushing, the pass protection of an offensive line is vital. The Vikings made a concisions attempt to build a strong offensive line for QB Teddy Bridgewater, and in 2016, boasted the 3rd most expensive offensive line in the NFL. Unfortunately, the line was ravaged by injuries. They were the most injured offensive line in the NFL. Bradford didn't even have a chance to get familiar with his line over the offseason, due to the timeframe of when he was brought on. And before he could get comfortable, the line began dropping like flies. Making matters worse, the Vikings faced the #1 most difficult schedule of opposing pass rushes in 2016.

With a new quarterback and a beat up offensive line trying to protect him, most teams would probably lean more on the NFL's highest paid ground game. There were two problems with that: Adrian Peterson went down in the 2nd game of the season and was (for all intents and purposes) lost for the remainder of the season, and due to the offensive line's injuries, the Vikings run game ranked 2nd worst in run efficiency.

One of the most insane storylines of 2016 was the start of the Minnesota Vikings despite those above hindrances. Minnesota started out 5-0 heading into their bye. They didn't beat a bunch of trash teams, either. They went 4-0 against 4 teams that posted winning records in 2016, three of which made the postseason: Green Bay, NY Giants, Houston and Tennessee. They also beat the Panthers, who had a down 2016. The winning masked the problems of offensive inefficiency. The defense was incredible, holding every single opponent to less than 17 points. They scored multiple non-offensive touchdowns en route to this hot start.

(cont'd - see MIN2)

Key Free Agents/ Trades Added

Floyd, Michael WR
Jones, Datone DE
Keenum, Case QB
Mathews, Mitch WR
Murray, Latavius RB
Quigley, Ryan P
Reiff, Riley T
Remmers, Mike T
Sutton, Will DT
Truesdell, Nick TE

Drafted Players

Rd	Pk	Player (College)
2	41	RB - Dalvin Cook (Florida St..
3	70	OL - Pat Elflein (Ohio State)
4	109	DT - Jaleel Johnson (Iowa)
	120	LB - Ben Gedeon (Michigan)
5	170	WR - Rodney Adams (South ..
5*	180	G - Danny Isidora (Miami (FL))
6	201	TE - Bucky Hodges (Virginia ..
	219	WR - Stacy Coley (Miami (FL))
7	220	DE - Ifeadi Odenigbo (North..
	232	OLB - Elijah Lee (Kansas Sta..
	245	CB - Jack Tocho (NC State)

Regular Season Wins: Past & Current Proj

Proj 2017 Wins  8.5

2016 Wins  8

Proj 2016 Wins  9

2015 Wins  11

2014 Wins  7

2013 Wins 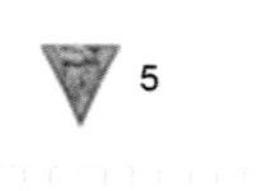 5

1 3 5 7 9 11 13 15

2017 Lineup & Cap Hits

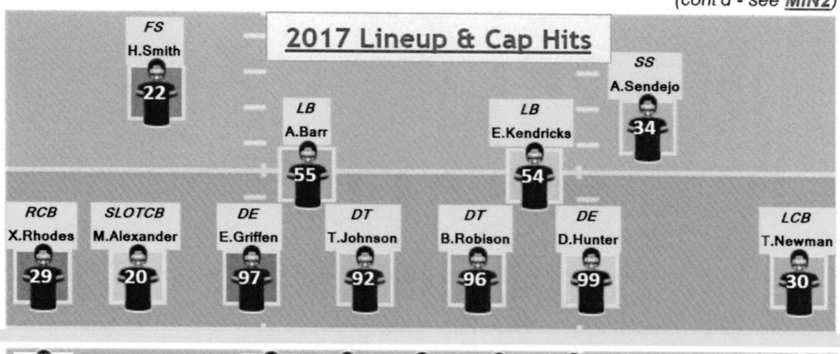

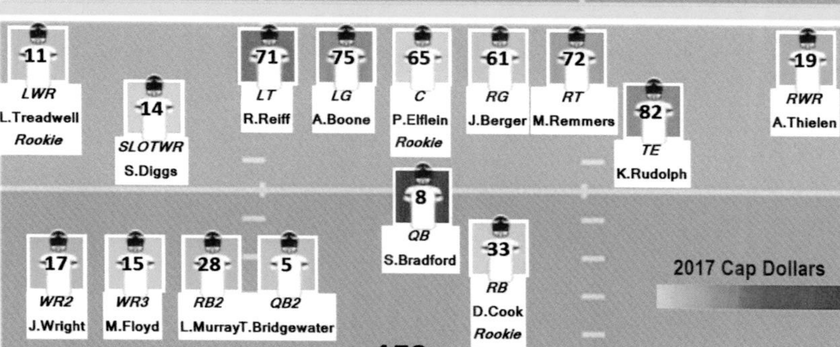

2017 Unit Spending

Positional Spending

	Rank	Total	2016 Rk
All OFF	16	$83.25M	7
QB	6	$23.17M	22
OL	13	$29.69M	3
RB	19	$6.56M	1
WR	25	$15.02M	26
TE	18	$8.81M	13
All DEF	9	$84.27M	12
DL	6	$39.70M	9
LB	29	$11.48M	24
CB	14	$20.96M	12
S	14	$12.14M	9

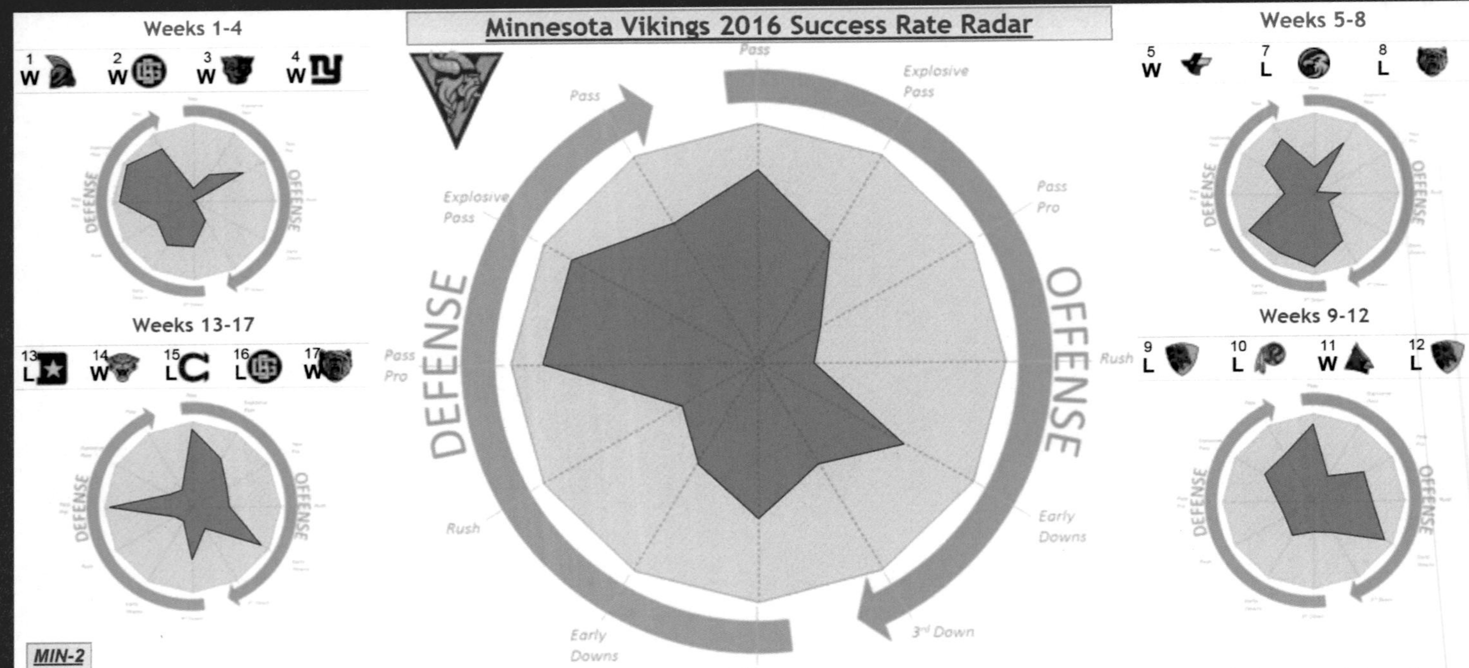

MIN-2

They lost the EDSR battle in their first 4 games (typically correlates with losses) and won it in their blowout over the Texans week 5. But they returned from their bye and promptly lost 4 consecutive games, and 8 of their next 10. After coming out of the bye and scoring 10 points in their first two losses, OC Norv Turner "resigned" and was replaced by former TE coach Pat Shurmur. The season also featured the loss of Mike Zimmer for a time due to a detached retina and numerous surgeries to address it.

If that sounds like a ton of "off the field" distractions, issues and obstacles, it certainly is. No team faced a tougher road of injuries to key positions, coaches and resignations last season. The question is, what did the team become last season and will they be able to right the ship in 2017? They were a team who wanted to run the ball, but they couldn't run enough because of the scoreboard. In one-score games, the Vikings ran the ball 50% of the time, 4th most in the NFL. But because they were trailing so often, they ended up being one of the most pass heavy teams in the NFL (62% pass). The Vikings don't want to be forced into that situation and with a defense as strong as they have, they would like to stay balanced on offense. It's impossible to be balanced with the NFL's 2nd worst run attack, so that is where the Vikings started in the offseason.

They signed running back Latavius Murray as the highest paid free agent RB, used their first draft pick on RB Dalvin Cook from Florida State and used their second pick on OL Pat Elflein from Ohio State (a much better run blocker than pass blocker). Even with those moves, the Vikings are a much different offense than they were in 2016. The team completely retooled their offensive cap structure.

This 2016 offense was the 7th most expensive in the NFL, led by the most expensive RB corps and the 3rd most expensive offensive line. In 2017, they become the 18th most expensive offense. They trimmed a lot of money along the offensive line, with Matt Kalil and Brandon Fusco starters who are no longer with the team. They added Mike Remmers and Riley Reiff in

(cont'd - see MIN-3)

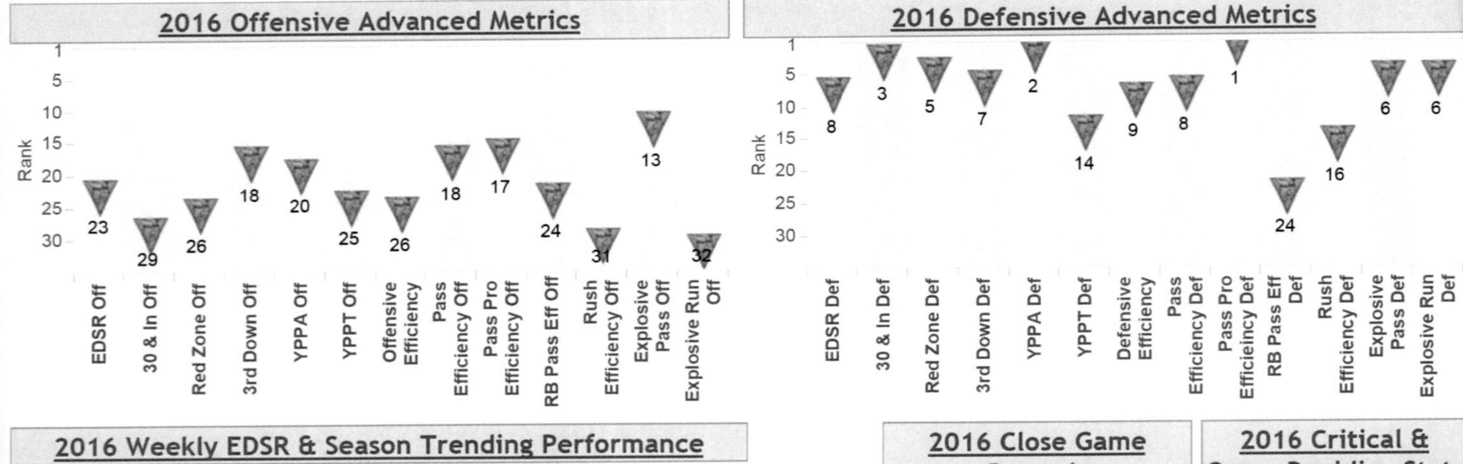

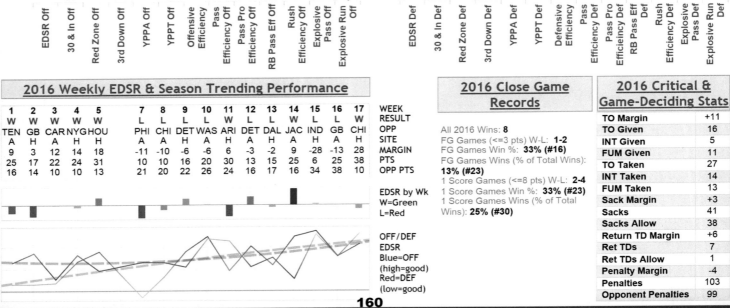

2016 Weekly EDSR & Season Trending Performance

1	2	3	4	5	7	8	9	10	11	12	13	14	15	16	17	WEEK
W	W	W	W	W	L	L	L	L	W	L	L	W	L	L	W	RESULT
TEN	GB	CAR	NYG	HOU	PHI	CHI	DET	WAS	ARI	DET	DAL	JAC	IND	GB	CHI	OPP
A	H	A	H	H	A	A	H	A	H	A	H	A	H	A	H	SITE
9	3	12	14	18	-11	-10	-6	-6	6	-3	-2	9	-28	-13	28	MARGIN
25	17	22	24	31	10	10	16	20	30	13	15	25	6	25	38	PTS
16	14	10	10	13	21	20	22	26	24	16	17	16	34	38	10	OPP PTS

EDSR by Wk
W=Green
L=Red

OFF/DEF
EDSR
Blue=OFF
(high=good)
Red=DEF
(low=good)

2016 Close Game Records

All 2016 Wins: **8**
FG Games (<=3 pts) W-L: **1-2**
FG Games Win %: **33% (#16)**
FG Games Wins (% of Total Wins): **13% (#23)**
1 Score Games (<=8 pts) W-L: **2-4**
1 Score Games Win %: **33% (#23)**
1 Score Games Wins (% of Total Wins): **25% (#30)**

2016 Critical & Game-Deciding Stats

TO Margin	+11
TO Given	16
INT Given	5
FUM Given	11
TO Taken	27
INT Taken	14
FUM Taken	13
Sack Margin	+3
Sacks	41
Sacks Allow	38
Return TD Margin	+6
Ret TDs	7
Ret TDs Allow	1
Penalty Margin	-4
Penalties	103
Opponent Penalties	99

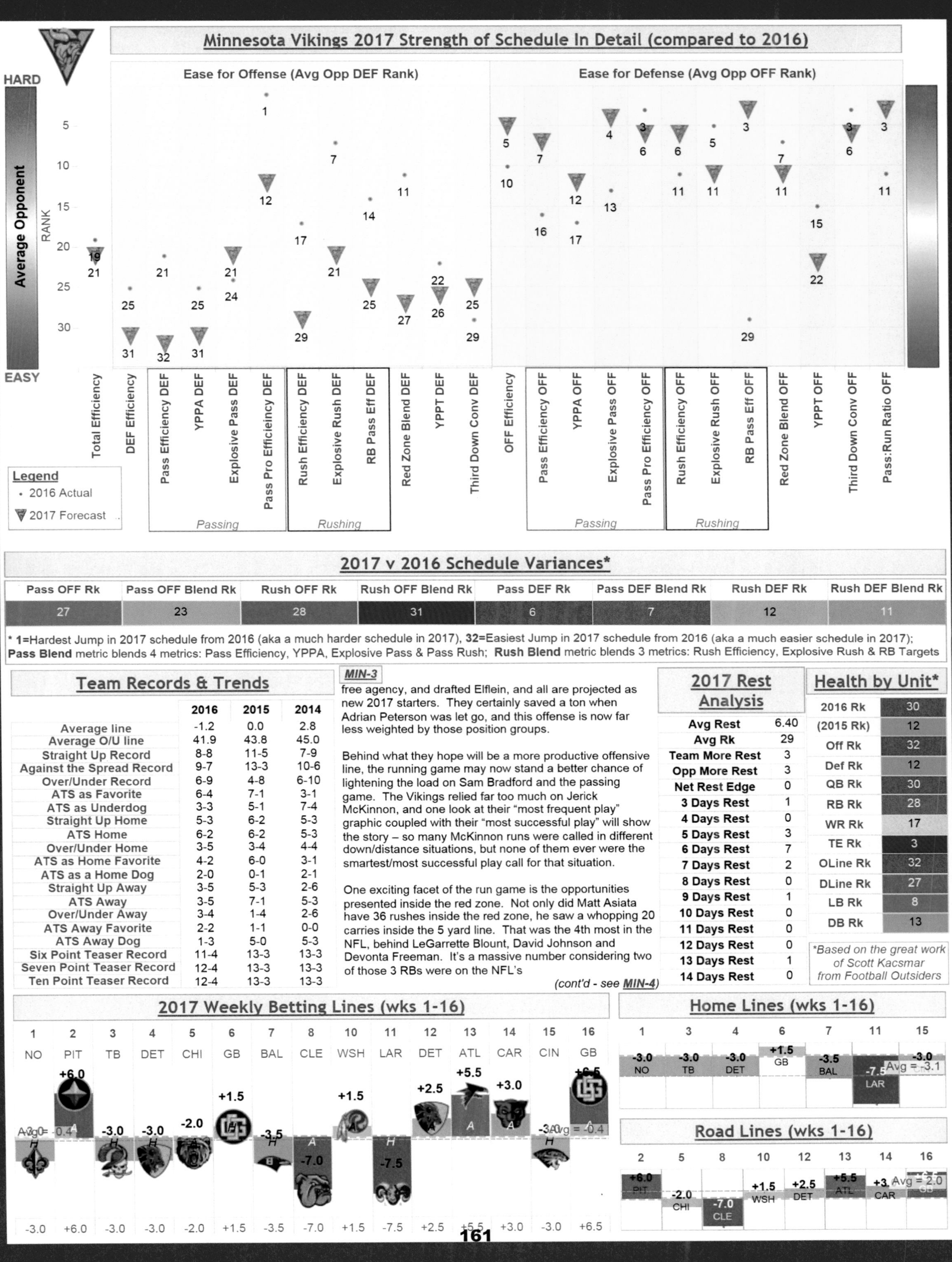

2017 v 2016 Schedule Variances*

Pass OFF Rk	Pass OFF Blend Rk	Rush OFF Rk	Rush OFF Blend Rk	Pass DEF Rk	Pass DEF Blend Rk	Rush DEF Rk	Rush DEF Blend Rk
27	23	28	31	6	7	12	11

* **1**=Hardest Jump in 2017 schedule from 2016 (aka a much harder schedule in 2017), **32**=Easiest Jump in 2017 schedule from 2016 (aka a much easier schedule in 2017); **Pass Blend** metric blends 4 metrics: Pass Efficiency, YPPA, Explosive Pass & Pass Rush; **Rush Blend** metric blends 3 metrics: Rush Efficiency, Explosive Rush & RB Targets

Team Records & Trends

	2016	2015	2014
Average line	-1.2	0.0	2.8
Average O/U line	41.9	43.8	45.0
Straight Up Record	8-8	11-5	7-9
Against the Spread Record	9-7	13-3	10-6
Over/Under Record	6-9	4-8	6-10
ATS as Favorite	6-4	7-1	3-1
ATS as Underdog	3-3	5-1	7-4
Straight Up Home	5-3	6-2	5-3
ATS Home	6-2	6-2	5-3
Over/Under Home	3-5	3-4	4-4
ATS as Home Favorite	4-2	6-0	3-1
ATS as a Home Dog	2-0	0-1	2-1
Straight Up Away	3-5	5-3	2-6
ATS Away	3-5	7-1	5-3
Over/Under Away	3-4	1-4	2-6
ATS Away Favorite	2-2	1-1	0-0
ATS Away Dog	1-3	5-0	5-3
Six Point Teaser Record	11-4	13-3	13-3
Seven Point Teaser Record	12-4	13-3	13-3
Ten Point Teaser Record	12-4	13-3	13-3

MIN-3

free agency, and drafted Elflein, and all are projected as new 2017 starters. They certainly saved a ton when Adrian Peterson was let go, and this offense is now far less weighted by those position groups.

Behind what they hope will be a more productive offensive line, the running game may now stand a better chance of lightening the load on Sam Bradford and the passing game. The Vikings relied far too much on Jerick McKinnon, and one look at their "most frequent play" graphic coupled with their "most successful play" will show the story – so many McKinnon runs were called in different down/distance situations, but none of them ever were the smartest/most successful play call for that situation.

One exciting facet of the run game is the opportunities presented inside the red zone. Not only did Matt Asiata have 36 rushes inside the red zone, he saw a whopping 20 carries inside the 5 yard line. That was the 4th most in the NFL, behind LeGarrette Blount, David Johnson and Devonta Freeman. It's a massive number considering two of those 3 RBs were on the NFL's

(cont'd - see MIN-4)

2017 Rest Analysis

Avg Rest	6.40
Avg Rk	29
Team More Rest	3
Opp More Rest	3
Net Rest Edge	0
3 Days Rest	1
4 Days Rest	0
5 Days Rest	3
6 Days Rest	7
7 Days Rest	2
8 Days Rest	0
9 Days Rest	1
10 Days Rest	0
11 Days Rest	0
12 Days Rest	0
13 Days Rest	1
14 Days Rest	0

Health by Unit*

2016 Rk	30
(2015 Rk)	12
Off Rk	32
Def Rk	12
QB Rk	30
RB Rk	28
WR Rk	17
TE Rk	3
OLine Rk	32
DLine Rk	27
LB Rk	8
DB Rk	13

**Based on the great work of Scott Kacsmar from Football Outsiders*

2017 Weekly Betting Lines (wks 1-16)

1	2	3	4	5	6	7	8	10	11	12	13	14	15	16
NO	PIT	TB	DET	CHI	GB	BAL	CLE	WSH	LAR	DET	ATL	CAR	CIN	GB
H	A	H	H	A	H	H	A	A	H	A	A	A	H	A
-3.0	+6.0	-3.0	-3.0	-2.0	+1.5	-3.5	-7.0	+1.5	-7.5	+2.5	+5.5	+3.0	-3.0	+6.5

Avg = -0.4

Home Lines (wks 1-16)

1	3	4	6	7	11	15
NO	TB	DET	GB	BAL	LAR	CIN
-3.0	-3.0	-3.0	+1.5	-3.5	-7.5	-3.0

Avg = -3.1

Road Lines (wks 1-16)

2	5	8	10	12	13	14	16
PIT	CHI	CLE	WSH	DET	ATL	CAR	GB
+6.0	-2.0	-7.0	+1.5	+2.5	+5.5	+3.0	

Avg = 2.0

Minnesota Vikings 2016 Play Analysis

2016 Play Tendencies

All Pass %	62%
All Pass Rk	7
All Rush %	38%
All Rush Rk	26
1 Score Pass %	50%
1 Score Pass Rk	29
2015 1 Score Pass %	52%
2015 1 Score Pass Rk	29
Pass Increase %	-1%
Pass Increase Rk	18
1 Score Rush %	50%
1 Score Rush Rk	4
Up Pass %	57%
Up Pass Rk	15
Up Rush %	43%
Up Rush Rk	18
Down Pass %	64%
Down Pass Rk	9
Down Rush %	36%
Down Rush Rk	24

2016 Down & Distance Tendencies

Down	Distance	Total Plays	Pass Rate	Run Rate	Play Success %
1	Short (1-3)	8	25%	75%	50%
	Med (4-7)	6	0%	100%	67%
	Long (8-10)	294	51%	49%	51%
	XL (11+)	7	43%	57%	0%
2	Short (1-3)	37	30%	70%	57%
	Med (4-7)	71	61%	39%	58%
	Long (8-10)	93	70%	30%	34%
	XL (11+)	36	67%	33%	33%
3	Short (1-3)	37	68%	32%	73%
	Med (4-7)	45	98%	2%	44%
	Long (8-10)	38	100%	0%	32%
	XL (11+)	31	84%	16%	10%
4	Short (1-3)	4	75%	25%	25%

Shotgun %:

Under Center	Shotgun
36%	64%
37%	*AVG 63%*

Run Rate:

Under Center	Shotgun
72%	19%
68%	*AVG 23%*

Pass Rate:

Under Center	Shotgun
28%	81%
32%	*AVG 77%*

Short Yardage Intelligence:

2nd and Short Run

Run Freq	Run % Rk	NFL Run Freq Avg	Run 1D Rate	Run NFL 1D Avg
71%	6	65%	67%	71%

2nd and Short Pass

Pass Freq	Pass % Rk	NFL Pass Freq Avg	Pass 1D Rate	Pass NFL 1D Avg
29%	25	35%	50%	52%

Most Frequent Play

Down	Distance	Play Type	Player	Total Plays	Play Success %
1	Short (1-3)	RUSH	Matt Asiata	5	60%
	Med (4-7)	RUSH	Jerick McKinnon	4	50%
	Long (8-10)	RUSH	Jerick McKinnon	63	48%
	XL (11+)	RUSH	Jerick McKinnon	2	0%
2	Short (1-3)	RUSH	Matt Asiata	11	64%
	Med (4-7)	RUSH	Jerick McKinnon	15	47%
	Long (8-10)	PASS	Kyle Rudolph	14	43%
		RUSH	Jerick McKinnon	14	7%
	XL (11+)	RUSH	Jerick McKinnon	9	22%
3	Short (1-3)	PASS	Kyle Rudolph	9	89%
		RUSH	Matt Asiata	9	56%
	Med (4-7)	PASS	Kyle Rudolph	10	50%
	Long (8-10)	PASS	Kyle Rudolph	9	22%
			Adam Thielen	9	33%
	XL (11+)	PASS	Kyle Rudolph	6	0%

Most Successful Play*

Down	Distance	Play Type	Player	Total Plays	Play Success %
1	Short (1-3)	RUSH	Matt Asiata	5	60%
	Long (8-10)	PASS	Matt Asiata	5	80%
			Rhett Ellison	5	80%
2	Short (1-3)	RUSH	Matt Asiata	11	64%
	Med (4-7)	PASS	Adam Thielen	8	88%
	Long (8-10)	PASS	Adam Thielen	11	73%
	XL (11+)	PASS	Adam Thielen	6	67%
3	Short (1-3)	PASS	Kyle Rudolph	9	89%
	Med (4-7)	PASS	Cordarrelle Patterson	5	60%
	Long (8-10)	PASS	Adam Thielen	9	33%
	XL (11+)	PASS	Stefon Diggs	5	20%
			Adam Thielen	5	20%

**Minimum 5 plays to qualify*

2016 Snap Rates

Week	Opp	Score	Kyle Rudolph	Adam Thielen	Stefon Diggs	Cordarrelle Patterson	Jerick McKinnon	Charles Johnson	Matt Asiata
1	TEN	W 25-16	58 (92%)	35 (56%)	56 (89%)	5 (8%)	16 (25%)	49 (78%)	9 (14%)
2	GB	W 17-14	56 (97%)	39 (67%)	51 (88%)	3 (5%)	12 (21%)	40 (69%)	12 (21%)
3	CAR	W 22-10	53 (96%)	33 (60%)	49 (89%)	5 (9%)	36 (65%)	39 (71%)	19 (35%)
4	NYG	W 24-10	72 (97%)	39 (53%)	69 (93%)	36 (49%)	46 (62%)	22 (30%)	29 (39%)
5	HOU	W 31-13	68 (92%)	68 (92%)		45 (61%)	41 (55%)	12 (16%)	34 (46%)
7	PHI	L 20-10	71 (93%)	67 (88%)	61 (80%)	51 (67%)	16 (21%)	18 (24%)	57 (75%)
8	CHI	L 20-10	57 (93%)	54 (89%)	57 (93%)	41 (67%)		19 (31%)	43 (70%)
9	DET	L 22-16	64 (93%)	35 (51%)	57 (83%)	40 (58%)	26 (38%)	22 (32%)	27 (39%)
10	WAS	L 26-20	57 (85%)	57 (85%)	51 (76%)	44 (66%)	32 (48%)	13 (19%)	23 (34%)
11	ARI	W 30-24	55 (95%)	44 (76%)	43 (74%)	35 (60%)	31 (53%)	13 (22%)	20 (34%)
12	DET	L 16-13	51 (88%)	55 (95%)		34 (59%)	36 (62%)	21 (36%)	23 (40%)
13	DAL	L 17-15	63 (85%)	63 (85%)	58 (78%)	47 (64%)	51 (69%)	26 (35%)	21 (28%)
14	JAC	W 25-16	64 (97%)	45 (68%)	38 (58%)	32 (48%)	40 (61%)	15 (23%)	25 (38%)
15	IND	L 34-6	56 (97%)	18 (31%)	49 (84%)	44 (76%)	34 (59%)	39 (67%)	12 (21%)
16	GB	L 38-26	75 (96%)	75 (96%)	58 (74%)	45 (58%)	54 (69%)	29 (37%)	25 (32%)
17	CHI	W 38-10	48 (76%)	61 (97%)		24 (38%)	40 (63%)	29 (46%)	25 (40%)
Grand Total			968 (92%)	788 (74%)	697 (82%)	531 (50%)	511 (51%)	406 (40%)	404 (38%)

Personnel Groupings

Personnel	Team %	NFL Avg	Succ. %
1-1 [3WR]	62%	60%	47%
1-2 [2WR]	14%	19%	53%
2-1 [2WR]	10%	7%	34%
2-2 [1WR]	8%	3%	43%
2-0 [3WR]	2%	1%	64%
1-3 [1WR]	2%	3%	52%

Grouping Tendencies

Personnel	Pass Rate	Pass Succ. %	Run Succ. %
1-1 [3WR]	75%	47%	46%
1-2 [2WR]	65%	55%	51%
2-1 [2WR]	36%	47%	27%
2-2 [1WR]	16%	54%	41%
2-0 [3WR]	18%	50%	67%
1-3 [1WR]	19%	75%	47%

Red Zone Targets (min 3)

Receiver	All	Inside 5	6-10	11-20
Kyle Rudolph	25	8	4	13
Stefon Diggs	12	2	1	9
Adam Thielen	10	2	3	5
Cordarrelle Patterson	8	1	2	5
Jerick McKinnon	6	1	1	4
Rhett Ellison	4	1	1	2
Matt Asiata	3		1	2
Zach Line	3	2	1	

Red Zone Rushes (min 3)

Rusher	All	Inside 5	6-10	11-20
Matt Asiata	36	20	9	7
Jerick McKinnon	23	3	10	10
Adrian Peterson	3			3
Ronnie Hillman	1			1

Early Down Target Rate

RB	TE	WR
19%	25%	56%
19%	*20% NFL AVG*	*61%*

Overall Target Success %

RB	TE	WR
40% #26	49% #28	57% #4

Minnesota Vikings 2016 Passing Recap & 2017 Outlook

Sam Bradford posted a 99.3 rating last season, the 6th best in the NFL (min 100 att). Those 5 quarterbacks ahead of him were Matt Ryan, Tom Brady, Kak Prescott, Aaron Rodgers and Drew Brees. It was extremely remarkable considering all of the obstacles and impediments that challenged this offense in 2016. Which is why the potential exists for 2017 to be even better. The offensive line should be better and it should be healthier. The schedule of pass rushes should be easier. The run game should be more supportive. And Bradford won't have to deal with Norv Turner for most of the season, nor a mid-season coordinator change. Another element which should help will be the RB pass usage. Last season, Bradford was ranked 26th in success rate targeting RBs, and they targeted them about the league average. Their two new RBs should allow more opportunities for targeting and the success rate should be higher as well, which will inevitably help Bradford's ceiling to be higher than it was in 2016. While the offensive style, run frequency and inevitable balance we should see won't make Bradford a volume based fantasy target, the potential efficiency and defense he's playing with should help the Vikings deliver a respectable 2017 season.

2016 Standard Passing Table

QB	Comp	Att	Comp %	Yds	YPA	TDs	INT	Sacks	Rating	Rk
Sam Bradford	395	552	72%	3,877	7.0	20	5	37	99.3	10
NFL Avg			63%		7.2				90.4	

2016 Advanced Passing Table

QB	Success %	EDSR Passing Success %	20+ Yd Pass Gains	20+ Yd Pass %	30+ Yd Pass Gains	30+ Yd Pass %	Air Yds per Comp	YAC per Comp	20+ Air Yd Comp	20+ Air Yd %
Sam Bradford	49%	54%	49	9%	17	3%	4.8	5.1	21	4%
NFL Avg	44%	48%	27	8%	10	3%	6.4	4.8	12	4%

Sam Bradford Rating All Downs

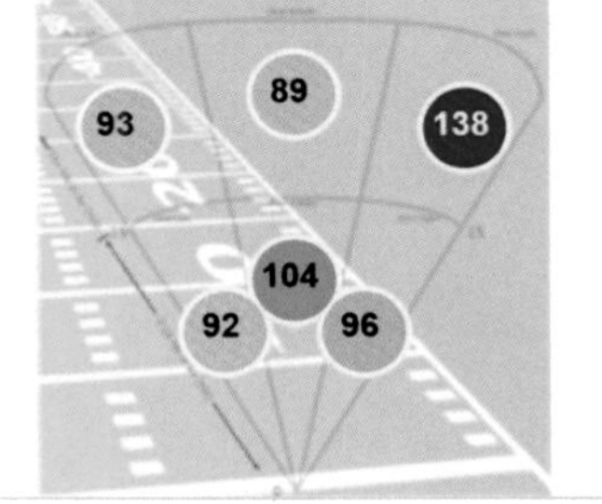

Sam Bradford Rating Early Downs

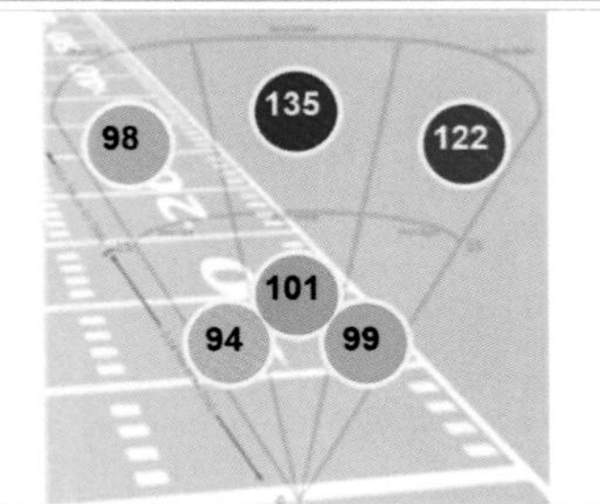

Interception Rates by Down

Yards to Go	1	2	3	4	Total
1 & 2	0.0%	0.0%	0.0%	0.0%	0.0%
3, 4, 5	0.0%	0.0%	0.0%	0.0%	0.0%
6 - 9	0.0%	0.0%	3.6%	0.0%	1.4%
10 - 14	0.5%	1.8%	2.6%	0.0%	1.0%
15+	0.0%	0.0%	0.0%	0.0%	0.0%
Total	0.5%	0.5%	1.8%	0.0%	0.8%

3rd Down Passing - Short of Sticks Analysis

QB	Avg Yds to Go	Air Yds (of Comps)	Avg Yds Short	Short of Sticks Rate	Rk
Sam Bradford	8.0	4.1	-3.9	68%	42
NFL Avg	7.6	6.8	-0.8	57%	

Air Yds vs YAC

Air Yds %	YAC %	Rk
45%	55%	42
54%	46%	

2016 Receiving Recap & 2017 Outlook

Kyle Rudolph put together a very underrated season last year, and that was when despite the terrible offensive line. Even though the Vikings trotted out an above average usage of 11 personnel (1 RB, 1 TE, 3 WRs), Rudolph wasn't helping block very often. He was out running routes, and led the team in targets and receiving TDs. He was the one target that was consistently used regardless of game script, good or bad. Meanwhile, Adam Thielen was just 1 of 3 players with 100+ receiving yards vs the strong Jags pass D, 1 of 3 players with 125+ vs the strong Texans pass D, and against top-15 pass defenses, he posted 23/30 (77%) with 13 ypa.

Player *Min 50 Targets*	Targets	Comp %	YPA	Rating	TOARS	Success %	Success Rk	Missed YPA Rk	YAS % Rk	TDs
Kyle Rudolph	132	63%	6.4	99	5.2	50%	73	84	87	7
Stefon Diggs	112	75%	8.1	103	5.1	63%	7	15	81	3
Adam Thielen	92	75%	10.5	113	4.9	61%	12	30	85	5
Cordarrelle Patterson	70	74%	6.5	95	4.2	51%	61	116	137	2
Jerick McKinnon	53	81%	4.8	99	3.8	43%	119	62	109	2

Directional Passer Rating Delivered

Receiver	Short Left	Short Middle	Short Right	Deep Left	Deep Middle	Deep Right	Player Total
Kyle Rudolph	93	111	92	110	119	90	99
Stefon Diggs	90	95	88	96	127	146	103
Adam Thielen	62	95	98	114	88	154	113
Cordarrelle Patterson	93	102	108	40	0	68	95
Jerick McKinnon	105	91	99				99
Charles Johnson	89	102	80	56		53	73
Matt Asiata	101	93	90				96
Team Total	92	105	96	94	92	138	100

2016 Rushing Recap & 2017 Outlook

Predicting exactly who will take over for the Vikings with a high degree of certainty at this point in the offseason is difficult. There is no doubt the ceiling on Cook is higher than Murray. Murray had a down season behind a great line in Oakland last year. But for a slightly more conservative coach like Zimmer, he may view Murray as a more proven veteran who has excelled near the goal line and in short yardage. They would not have paid him what they did in free agency if they were not planning on giving him the reigns early in the season, and make it his job to lose. That said, it's unlikely he will receive overwhelming volume with a potential young stud like Cook in the wings. It's a messy situation at this point in the offseason.

Player *Min 50 Rushes*	Rushes	YPA	Success %	Success Rk	Missed YPA Rk	YTS % Rk	YAS % Rk	Early Down Success %	Early Down Success Rk	TDs
Jerick McKinnon	159	3.4	42%	56	61	13	51	42%	46	2
Matt Asiata	121	3.3	50%	22	17	8	59	51%	18	6

Yards per Carry by Direction

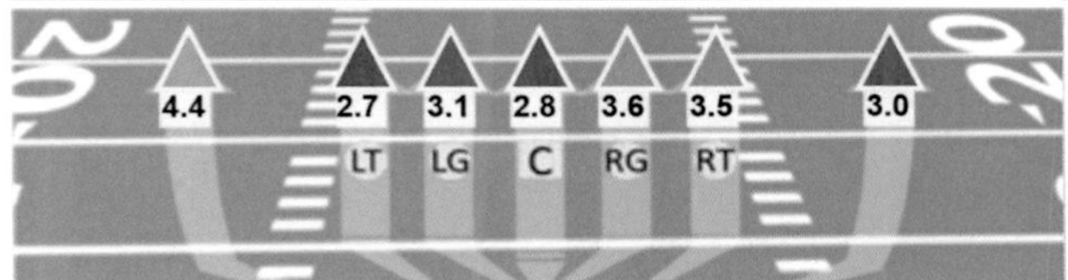

Directional Run Frequency

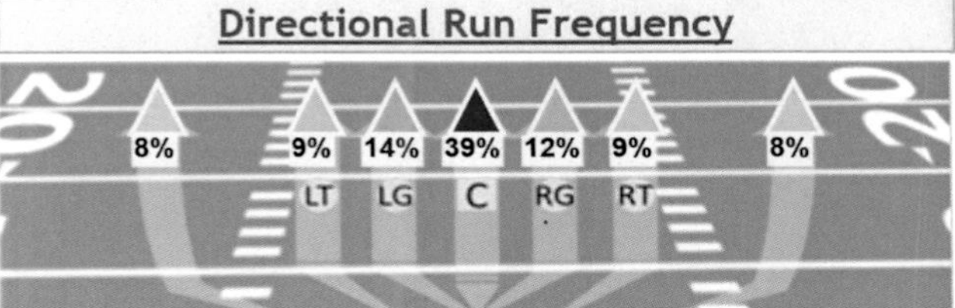

best teams last year, thus they had plenty of +EV opportunities, and the other was the #1 fantasy RB drafted last year. With the increased volume predicted thanks to a better offensive line producing fewer 3rd and 4th downs, the only problem is the mouths to feed. Asiata is gone. Even when McKinnon was the #1 RB, Asiata took the lion share of touches inside the 5 (20 to 3). But the Vikings drafted Dalvin Cook and gained Murray in free agency. Trusting a rookie inside the 5 sometimes isn't easy, and last year Murray turned 18 carries inside the 5 into 10 TDs.

With the Vikings not picking up the 5th year option on recovering QB Teddy Bridgewater, they are all in for another season of Sam Bradford. Bradford campaigned for Shurmur, and the hope is they pick up on a solid note. The receiving positions are almost entirely unchanged, and count me in as a big Adam Thielen fan in 2017. Bradford showed a lot of promise in this offense, and given the unenviable position he was placed in to start the season, the line and the mid-year coordinator change, the fact he posted a 99 rating (10th best last year) with 72% completions was extremely underrated.

The play calling was perplexing to say the least. It's a big reason Turner was gone mid-season. However, Shurmur continued the pattern of questionable play calls to start his tenure. Despite no run game last year, on 1st downs in the 1st half, the Vikings were 54% run through 11 weeks of the season. After Peterson went down (week 3 onward), they were 58% run (NFL avg = 50%) including a staggering 63% in the 1st quarter, the 5th most run heavy team. Yet they averaged just 3 yards per carry on these plays, the worst in the NFL. Why would they run so predictably despite the terrible results? That's the question, as they were consistently facing 2nd and long and obvious passing situations after failed 1st down runs.

Fortunately, Shurmur started to correct that by week 12, and they ran just 49% (below average) on 1st downs in the 1st half and averaged better per carry averages when rushing on 1st down (4.1 ypa) and passing. In fact, the Vikings averaged a whopping 11.6 yards per attempt on 1st down passes in the first half, by far the best in the NFL (avg = 7.0 ypa) and 72% of their attempts graded as successful, tied for the best in the NFL with the Falcons. Leading that attack was Adam Thielen, who caught 7 of 8 targets for 16 ypa and posted a 119 rating (Diggs was targeted just 3 times and averaged only 2.3 ypa).

In 2017 Minnesota faces the easiest pass defenses of any team in the NFL and the 4th easiest run defenses. It's the 5th easiest jump for the run game as compared to their 2016 schedule, and the 6th easiest jump for the pass game. While the Vikings formula under Zimmer has been apparent, the offense could provide better balance and stability in 2017.

Division History: Season Wins & 2017 Projection

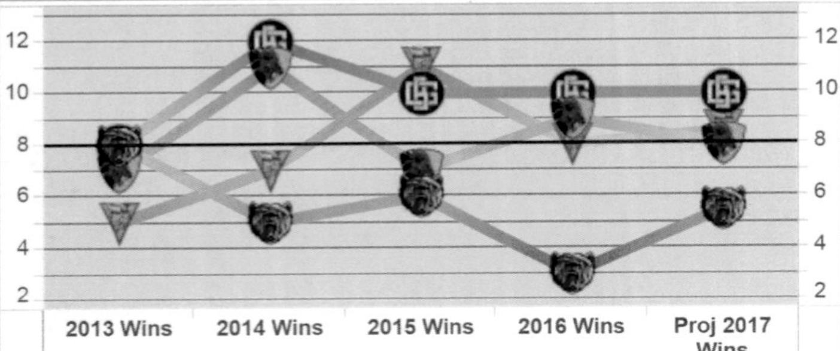

Rank of 2017 Defensive Pass Efficiency Faced by Week

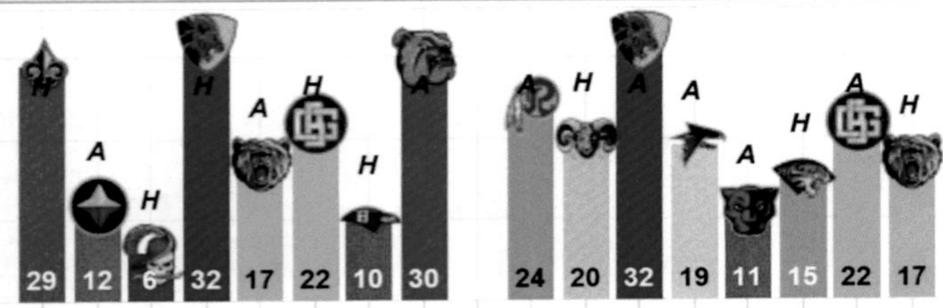

Rank of 2017 Defensive Rush Efficiency Faced by Week

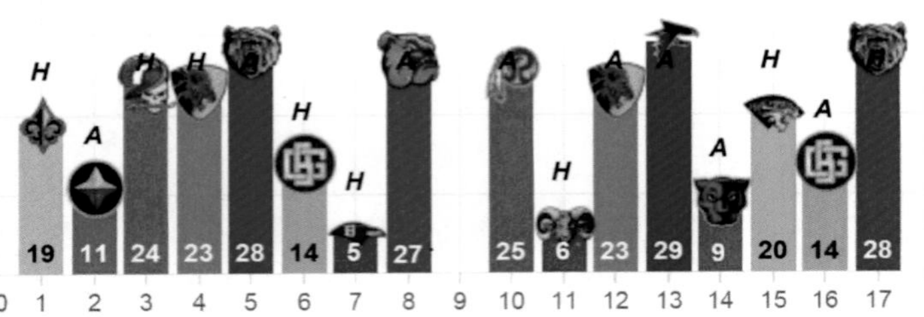

2016 Situational Usage by Player & Position

Usage Rate by Score

		Being Blown Out (14+)	Down Big (9-13)	One Score	Large Lead (9-13)	Blowout Lead (14+)	Grand Total
RUSH	Jerick McKinnon	11%	6%	16%	24%	32%	17%
	Matt Asiata	8%	13%	13%	14%	19%	13%
	Stefon Diggs			0%	3%		0%
	Adam Thielen	1%	2%				0%
	Cordarrelle Patterson			1%		1%	1%
	Adrian Peterson	2%	6%	5%	3%		4%
	Ronnie Hillman	3%		2%	1%		2%
	Rhett Ellison			0%			0%
	Zach Line	1%		1%		1%	1%
	Total	26%	27%	38%	45%	53%	38%
PASS	Jerick McKinnon	9%	8%	5%	3%	6%	6%
	Matt Asiata	9%	2%	3%	3%	3%	4%
	Kyle Rudolph	15%	21%	13%	15%	13%	14%
	Stefon Diggs	12%	13%	14%	9%	3%	12%
	Adam Thielen	8%	10%	12%	4%	5%	10%
	Cordarrelle Patterson	11%	4%	6%	11%	6%	7%
	Adrian Peterson			1%			1%
	Charles Johnson	5%	10%	4%	3%	2%	4%
	Ronnie Hillman	3%	2%	0%			1%
	Rhett Ellison	1%	2%	2%	3%		1%
	Jarius Wright	1%		1%	4%	6%	1%
	Zach Line			0%		1%	0%
	Laquon Treadwell			1%			0%
	David Morgan	1%					0%
	Isaac Fruechte				1%		0%
	MyCole Pruitt					1%	0%
	Total	74%	73%	62%	55%	47%	62%

Positional Target Distribution vs NFL Average

		NFL Wide				Team Only			
		Left	Middle	Right	Total	Left	Middle	Right	Total
Deep	WR	998	573	974	**2,545**	33	8	27	**68**
	TE	155	144	156	**455**	3	3	7	**13**
	RB	25	4	40	**69**				
	All	**1,178**	**721**	**1,170**	**3,069**	**36**	**11**	**34**	**81**
Short	WR	3,000	1,721	3,086	**7,807**	93	50	100	**243**
	TE	806	847	1,090	**2,743**	30	28	61	**119**
	RB	987	603	1,072	**2,662**	28	19	41	**88**
	All	**4,793**	**3,171**	**5,248**	**13,212**	**151**	**97**	**202**	**450**
Total		**5,971**	**3,892**	**6,418**	**16,281**	**187**	**108**	**236**	**531**

Positional Success Rates vs NFL Average

		NFL Wide				Team Only			
		Left	Middle	Right	Total	Left	Middle	Right	Total
Deep	WR	37%	51%	38%	**40%**	45%	25%	56%	**47%**
	TE	44%	49%	43%	**45%**	67%	100%	43%	**62%**
	RB	32%	75%	25%	**30%**				
	All	**37%**	**50%**	**38%**	**41%**	**47%**	**45%**	**53%**	**49%**
Short	WR	52%	56%	51%	**53%**	49%	74%	64%	**60%**
	TE	50%	62%	52%	**55%**	47%	54%	48%	**49%**
	RB	47%	50%	44%	**46%**	43%	47%	46%	**45%**
	All	**51%**	**56%**	**50%**	**52%**	**48%**	**63%**	**55%**	**54%**
Total		**48%**	**55%**	**48%**	**50%**	**48%**	**61%**	**55%**	**54%**

New England Patriots

2017 Coaches

Head Coach:
Bill Belichick (18th yr)
Offensive Coordinator:
Josh McDaniels (6th yr)
Defensive Coordinator:
Matt Patrica (6th yr)

2017 Forecast

Wins	Div Rank
12	#1

Past Records

2016: 14-2
2015: 12-4
2014: 12-4

EASY HARD

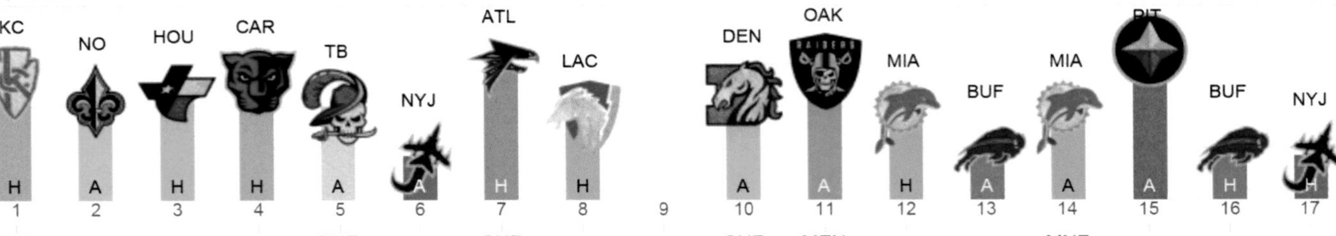

Key Players Lost

TXN	Player (POS)
Cut	Housler, Rob TE
	Jackson, Tre' G
	Street, Devin WR
	Williams, Michael TE
Declared Free Agent	Bennett, Martellus TE
	Blount, LeGarrette RB
	Bolden, Brandon RB
	Branch, Alan DT
	Floyd, Michael WR
	Harmon, Duron S
	Hightower, Dont'a LB
	Long, Chris DE
	Mingo, Barkevious LB
	Ryan, Logan CB
	Scruggs, Greg TE
	Sheard, Jabaal DE
	Williams, Michael TE
Retired	Knighton, Terrance DT
	Stork, Bryan C
	Vollmer, Sebastian T

Average Line	# Games Favored	# Games Underdog
-6.6	15	

2017 New England Patriots Overview

I don't love the Patriots nor do I love Bill Belichick. I don't love or hate any team or coach. I take a completely cold, robotic and dispassionate approach toward those elements of the league. Instead I live in the world of ideas, strategies, innovations and efficiencies. Because I love efficient football and digging in dark corners to find real edges that most of the league ignores, I inevitably get drawn to the Patriots like a black hole. Many of my concepts and ideas get incorporated into their strategy that at times it becomes difficult to recall whether I came up with the concept first or if I saw them use it first. I won't belabor all of the elements that I think are valuable to modern NFL in this team chapter, and plan to put that into a separate article fo inclusion in this book. But before we tackle who the Patriots were and what they'll become this year, let's examine structurally what they are.

They are what they are because Tom Brady is willing to take much less than he deserves. He's happy to do this because it helps the Patriots build a much better team in the salary cap era. He's able to do this thanks to two other streams of income (apart from sponsors which many other players have as well). His wife has a net worth of $360M. And he receives an alternate stream of revenue directly from the Patriots to his nutrition company, because his company has a deal with the team to provide countless services to players (which the team pays for) ranging from expensive treatment services such as massages and adjustments, to nutritional advice. Thus, while Joe Flacco is hitting the salary cap for $24.55M and Carson Palmer hits it for $24.125M, Tom Brady hits it for only $14M in 2017, which is the exact same as Mike Glennon. It is less than Andy Dalton, Brock Osweiler, and a total of 19 other quarterbacks this year. Many players are primarily paid on past performances with future expectations in mind. Whatever the ratio of those would be for Brady, there is no real discussion that he shouldn't be the top paid quarterback in the NFL. But fortunately, the Patriots don't have to let him hit the cap for anything more than $14M.

With the Patriots spending just less than most teams at quarterback, they can allocate the remainder of the cap in other places they value. So it is interesting to see where they've allocated it. Offensively, they rank as the 20th most expensive QBs, 21st most expensive offensive line and 19th most expensive WRs.

(cont'd - see NE2)

Key Free Agents/ Trades Added

Allen, Dwayne TE
Burkhead, Rex RB
Cooks, Brandin WR
Ealy, Kony DE
Gillislee, Mike RB
Gilmore, Stephon CB
Guy, Lawrence DE
Hawkins, Andrew WR
O'Shaughnessy, James TE
Street, Devin WR

Drafted Players

Rd	Pk	Player (College)
3	83	DE - Derek Rivers (Youngstown State)
	85	OT - Antonio Garcia (Troy)
4	131	DE - Deatrich Wise Jr. (Arkansas)
6	211	OT - Conor McDermott (UCLA)

Regular Season Wins: Past & Current Proj

	Wins
Proj 2017 Wins	12
2016 Wins	14
Proj 2016 Wins	10.5
2015 Wins	12
2014 Wins	12
2013 Wins	12

1 3 5 7 9 11 13 15

2017 Lineup & Cap Hits

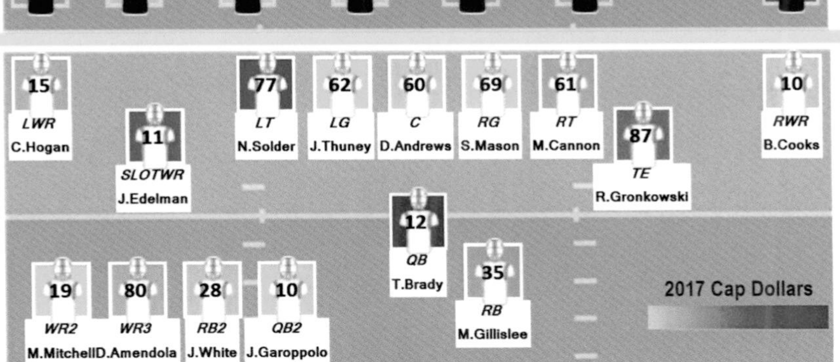

2017 Unit Spending

All DEF
All OFF

Positional Spending

	Rank	Total	2016 Rk
All OFF	11	$86.28M	4
QB	20	$15.88M	18
OL	21	$25.50M	10
RB	3	$13.47M	19
WR	18	$17.64M	15
TE	5	$13.78M	1
All DEF	23	$72.41M	26
DL	27	$18.48M	17
LB	26	$13.49M	23
CB	19	$17.29M	31
S	1	$23.16M	6

New England Patriots 2016 Success Rate Radar

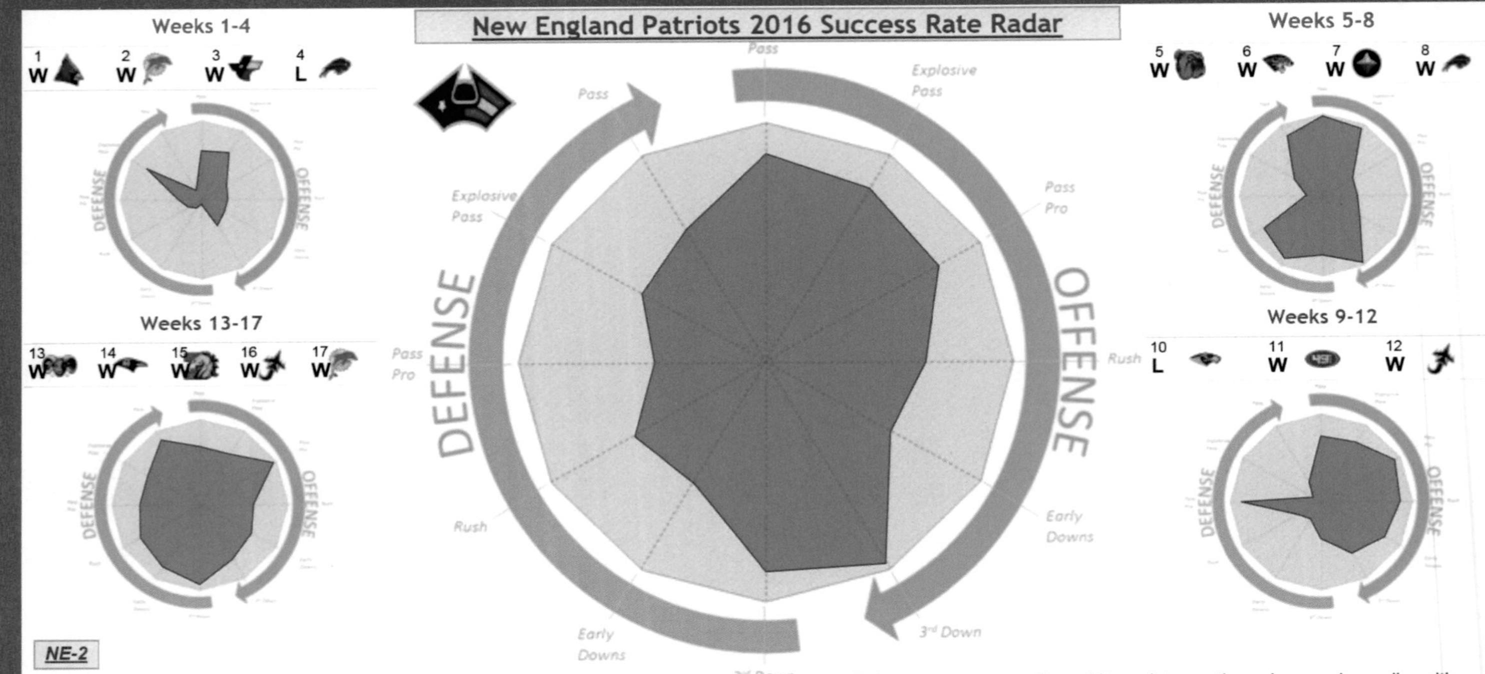

NE-2

They rank much higher at two interesting positions: RBs and TEs. They have the 3rd most expensive RBs and the 5th most expensive TEs. Naturally with Rob Gronkowski, the assumption is he takes up the majority of that amount. But in reality, he's less than half the team's total allocation. That is because they signed TE Dwayne Allen who is hitting the 2017 cap for $4.9M, just below Gronkowski's $6.75M, and they have 4 other TEs on the roster. At the RB position, they released LeGarrette Blount but added both Mike Gillislee and Rex Burkhead in free agency, and both hit the cap for between $3 and $4M. But the team also kept James White, Dion Lewis and Brandon Bolden on the roster.

The reason why I say they interestingly are spending a lot more at RB and TE is because my metrics show passes which target RBs and WRs are highly efficient and also extremely squandered by NFL teams. Starting with the TE, league wide passes to TEs are more successful than passes to WRs. Yet passes are thrown to WRs over 3 times more often than to TEs. For every single down, passing to the TE is more successful than to the WR. And as you shift into opponent's territory, that efficiency gap grows until you hit a point near the red zone where all position group rates congeal.

As for RB targets, most NFL teams use passing backs in the complete opposite manner for efficiency purposes. Targets on 1st down to RBs have a 56% success rate, even higher than that of WRs. On 2nd down, that success rate drops to 43% and on 3rd down it's 32%. Targeting RBs on 1st down is 24% more successful than on 3rd down. But teams constantly bring in "3rd down backs" aka scat backs to catch these targets. And on average, even if they catch a pass, it won't convert the first down. This isn't a "garbage time" accounting either. Even if you look only at first half passing, RB targets on 1st down (54% success) are 24% more successful than RB targets on 3rd down (30% success). In a league where the rules are slanted toward passing and the game is as much about finding and exploiting mismatches as it ever has been, getting RBs out of the backfield matched up with LBs or a S is an exploitable matchup, and comes

(cont'd - see NE-3)

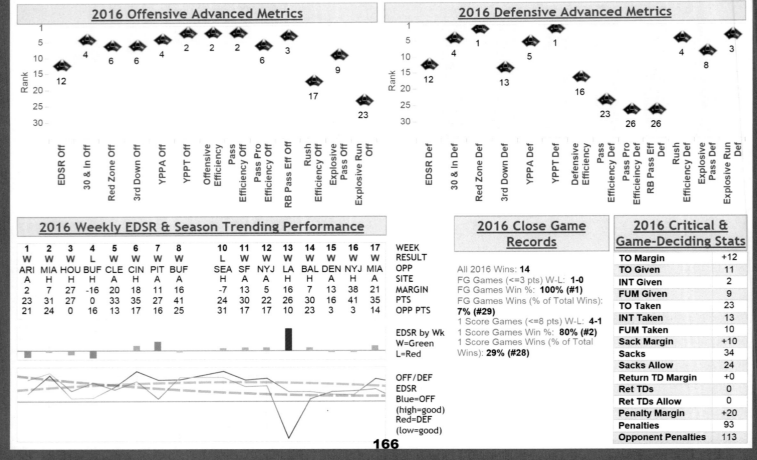

2016 Offensive Advanced Metrics

Metric	Rank
EDSR Off	12
30 & In Off	4
Red Zone Off	6
3rd Down Off	6
YPPA Off	4
YPPT Off	2
Offensive Efficiency	2
Pass Efficiency Off	2
Pass Pro Efficiency Off	6
RB Pass Eff Off	3
Rush Efficiency Off	17
Explosive Pass Off	9
Explosive Run Off	23

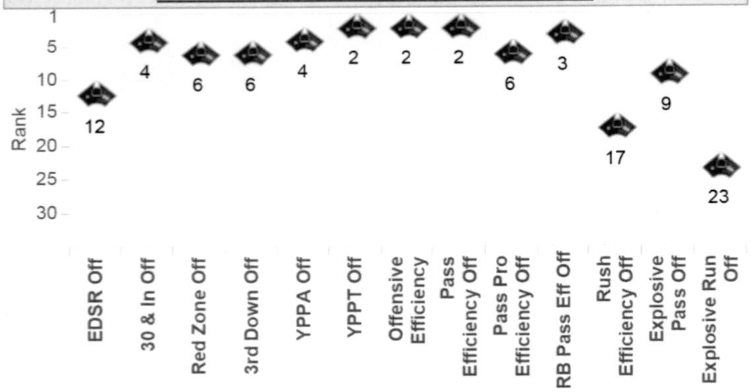

2016 Defensive Advanced Metrics

Metric	Rank
EDSR Def	12
30 & In Def	4
Red Zone Def	1
3rd Down Def	13
YPPA Def	5
YPPT Def	1
Defensive Efficiency	16
Pass Efficiency Def	23
Pass Pro Efficiency Def	26
RB Pass Eff Def	26
Rush Efficiency Def	4
Explosive Pass Def	8
Explosive Run Def	3

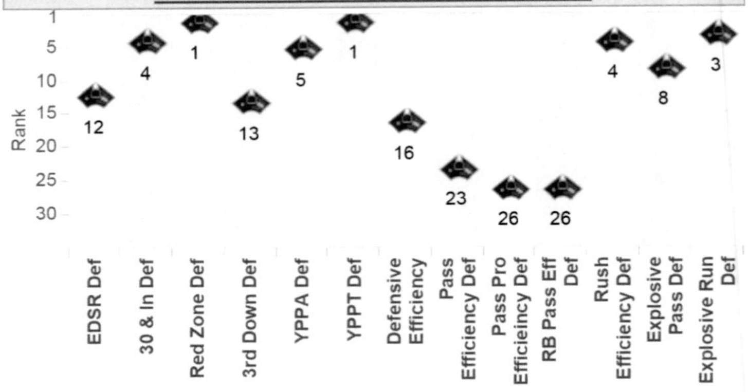

2016 Weekly EDSR & Season Trending Performance

WEEK	1	2	3	4	5	6	7	8	10	11	12	13	14	15	16	17
RESULT	W	W	W	L	W	W	W	W	L	W	W	W	W	W	W	W
OPP	ARI	MIA	HOU	BUF	CLE	CIN	PIT	BUF	SEA	SF	NYJ	LA	BAL	DEN	NYJ	MIA
SITE	A	H	H	H	A	H	A	A	H	A	A	H	H	A	H	A
MARGIN	2	7	27	-16	20	18	11	16	-7	13	5	16	7	13	38	21
PTS	23	31	27	0	33	35	27	41	24	30	22	26	30	16	41	35
OPP PTS	21	24	0	16	13	17	16	25	31	17	17	10	23	3	3	14

EDSR by Wk
W=Green
L=Red

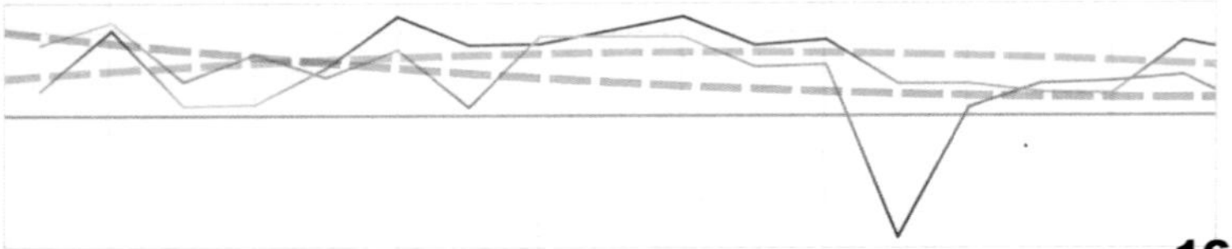

OFF/DEF
EDSR
Blue=OFF
(high=good)
Red=DEF
(low=good)

2016 Close Game Records

All 2016 Wins: **14**
FG Games (<=3 pts) W-L: **1-0**
FG Games Win %: **100% (#1)**
FG Games Wins (% of Total Wins): **7% (#29)**
1 Score Games (<=8 pts) W-L: **4-1**
1 Score Games Win %: **80% (#2)**
1 Score Games Wins (% of Total Wins): **29% (#28)**

2016 Critical & Game-Deciding Stats

TO Margin	+12
TO Given	11
INT Given	2
FUM Given	9
TO Taken	23
INT Taken	13
FUM Taken	10
Sack Margin	+10
Sacks	34
Sacks Allow	24
Return TD Margin	+0
Ret TDs	0
Ret TDs Allow	0
Penalty Margin	+20
Penalties	93
Opponent Penalties	113

New England Patriots 2017 Strength of Schedule In Detail (compared to 2016)

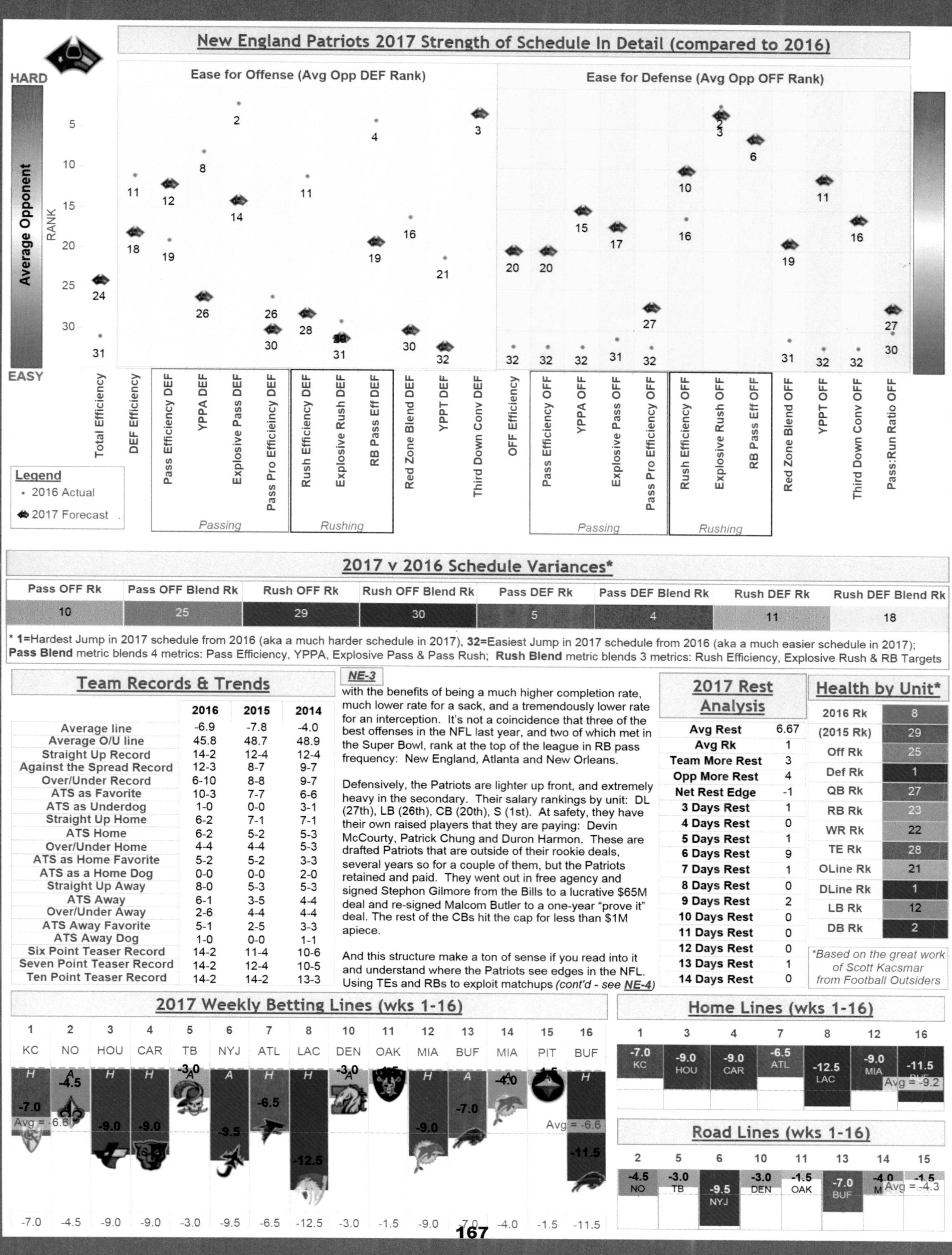

2017 v 2016 Schedule Variances*

Pass OFF Rk	Pass OFF Blend Rk	Rush OFF Rk	Rush OFF Blend Rk	Pass DEF Rk	Pass DEF Blend Rk	Rush DEF Rk	Rush DEF Blend Rk
10	25	29	30	5	4	11	18

* **1**=Hardest Jump in 2017 schedule from 2016 (aka a much harder schedule in 2017), **32**=Easiest Jump in 2017 schedule from 2016 (aka a much easier schedule in 2017); **Pass Blend** metric blends 4 metrics: Pass Efficiency, YPPA, Explosive Pass & Pass Rush; **Rush Blend** metric blends 3 metrics: Rush Efficiency, Explosive Rush & RB Targets

Team Records & Trends

	2016	2015	2014
Average line	-6.9	-7.8	-4.0
Average O/U line	45.8	48.7	48.9
Straight Up Record	14-2	12-4	12-4
Against the Spread Record	12-3	8-7	9-7
Over/Under Record	6-10	8-8	9-7
ATS as Favorite	10-3	7-7	6-6
ATS as Underdog	1-0	0-0	3-1
Straight Up Home	6-2	7-1	7-1
ATS Home	6-2	5-2	5-3
Over/Under Home	4-4	4-4	5-3
ATS as Home Favorite	5-2	5-2	3-3
ATS as a Home Dog	0-0	0-0	2-0
Straight Up Away	8-0	5-3	5-3
ATS Away	6-1	3-5	4-4
Over/Under Away	2-6	4-4	4-4
ATS Away Favorite	5-1	2-5	3-3
ATS Away Dog	1-0	0-0	1-1
Six Point Teaser Record	14-2	11-4	10-6
Seven Point Teaser Record	14-2	12-4	10-5
Ten Point Teaser Record	14-2	14-2	13-3

NE-3

with the benefits of being a much higher completion rate, much lower rate for a sack, and a tremendously lower rate for an interception. It's not a coincidence that three of the best offenses in the NFL last year, and two of which met in the Super Bowl, rank at the top of the league in RB pass frequency: New England, Atlanta and New Orleans.

Defensively, the Patriots are lighter up front, and extremely heavy in the secondary. Their salary rankings by unit: DL (27th), LB (26th), CB (20th), S (1st). At safety, they have their own raised players that they are paying: Devin McCourty, Patrick Chung and Duron Harmon. These are drafted Patriots that are outside of their rookie deals, several years so for a couple of them, but the Patriots retained and paid. They went out in free agency and signed Stephon Gilmore from the Bills to a lucrative $65M deal and re-signed Malcom Butler to a one-year "prove it" deal. The rest of the CBs hit the cap for less than $1M apiece.

And this structure make a ton of sense if you read into it and understand where the Patriots see edges in the NFL. Using TEs and RBs to exploit matchups *(cont'd - see NE-4)*

2017 Rest Analysis

Avg Rest	6.67
Avg Rk	1
Team More Rest	3
Opp More Rest	4
Net Rest Edge	-1
3 Days Rest	1
4 Days Rest	0
5 Days Rest	1
6 Days Rest	9
7 Days Rest	1
8 Days Rest	0
9 Days Rest	2
10 Days Rest	0
11 Days Rest	0
12 Days Rest	0
13 Days Rest	1
14 Days Rest	0

Health by Unit*

2016 Rk	8
(2015 Rk)	29
Off Rk	25
Def Rk	1
QB Rk	27
RB Rk	23
WR Rk	22
TE Rk	28
OLine Rk	21
DLine Rk	1
LB Rk	12
DB Rk	2

**Based on the great work of Scott Kacsmar from Football Outsiders*

2017 Weekly Betting Lines (wks 1-16)

1	2	3	4	5	6	7	8	10	11	12	13	14	15	16
KC	NO	HOU	CAR	TB	NYJ	ATL	LAC	DEN	OAK	MIA	BUF	MIA	PIT	BUF
H	A	H	H	A	A	H	H	A	A	H	A	A	A	H
-7.0	-4.5	-9.0	-9.0	-3.0	-9.5	-6.5	-12.5	-3.0	-1.5	-9.0	-7.0	-4.0	-1.5	-11.5

Avg = -6.6

Home Lines (wks 1-16)

1	3	4	7	8	12	16
-7.0 KC	-9.0 HOU	-9.0 CAR	-6.5 ATL	-12.5 LAC	-9.0 MIA	-11.5 BUF

Avg = -9.2

Road Lines (wks 1-16)

2	5	6	10	11	13	14	15
-4.5 NO	-3.0 TB	-9.5 NYJ	-3.0 DEN	-1.5 OAK	-7.0 BUF	-4.0 MIA	-1.5 PIT

Avg = -4.3

2016 Play Tendencies

All Pass %	57%
All Pass Rk	23
All Rush %	43%
All Rush Rk	10
1 Score Pass %	61%
1 Score Pass Rk	6
2015 1 Score Pass %	65%
2015 1 Score Pass Rk	1
Pass Increase %	-4%
Pass Increase Rk	27
1 Score Rush %	39%
1 Score Rush Rk	27
Up Pass %	57%
Up Pass Rk	19
Up Rush %	43%
Up Rush Rk	14
Down Pass %	63%
Down Pass Rk	11
Down Rush %	37%
Down Rush Rk	22

2016 Down & Distance Tendencies

Down	Distance	Total Plays	Pass Rate	Run Rate	Play Success %
1	Short (1-3)	15	13%	87%	67%
	Med (4-7)	15	40%	60%	40%
	Long (8-10)	386	53%	47%	51%
	XL (11+)	17	53%	47%	47%
2	Short (1-3)	50	28%	72%	68%
	Med (4-7)	101	54%	46%	48%
	Long (8-10)	120	64%	36%	41%
	XL (11+)	43	72%	28%	28%
3	Short (1-3)	55	62%	38%	71%
	Med (4-7)	69	90%	10%	55%
	Long (8-10)	46	93%	7%	48%
	XL (11+)	31	81%	19%	16%
4	Short (1-3)	6	50%	50%	83%

Shotgun %:

Under Center	Shotgun
46%	54%
37%	*63%*

AVG

Run Rate:

Under Center	Shotgun
70%	18%
68%	*23%*

AVG

Pass Rate:

Under Center	Shotgun
30%	82%
32%	*77%*

AVG

New England Patriots 2016 Play Analysis

Short Yardage Intelligence:

2nd and Short Run

Run Freq	Run % Rk	NFL Run Freq Avg	Run 1D Rate	Run NFL 1D Avg
76%	4	65%	71%	71%

2nd and Short Pass

Pass Freq	Pass % Rk	NFL Pass Freq Avg	Pass 1D Rate	Pass NFL 1D Avg
24%	28	35%	63%	52%

Most Frequent Play

Down	Distance	Play Type	Player	Total Plays	Play Success %
1	Short (1-3)	RUSH	LeGarrette Blount	10	70%
	Med (4-7)	RUSH	LeGarrette Blount	6	33%
	Long (8-10)	RUSH	LeGarrette Blount	129	40%
	XL (11+)	PASS	Julian Edelman	4	75%
2	Short (1-3)	RUSH	LeGarrette Blount	21	71%
	Med (4-7)	RUSH	LeGarrette Blount	29	34%
	Long (8-10)	PASS	Julian Edelman	23	48%
	XL (11+)	PASS	Julian Edelman	10	60%
3	Short (1-3)	PASS	Julian Edelman	11	73%
		RUSH	LeGarrette Blount	11	55%
	Med (4-7)	PASS	Julian Edelman	22	55%
	Long (8-10)	PASS	Julian Edelman	8	75%
			James White	8	13%
	XL (11+)	PASS	Julian Edelman	6	33%

Most Successful Play*

Down	Distance	Play Type	Player	Total Plays	Play Success %
1	Short (1-3)	RUSH	LeGarrette Blount	10	70%
	Med (4-7)	RUSH	LeGarrette Blount	6	33%
	Long (8-10)	PASS	Chris Hogan	27	70%
2	Short (1-3)	RUSH	LeGarrette Blount	21	71%
	Med (4-7)	PASS	Chris Hogan	9	56%
	Long (8-10)	PASS	Danny Amendola	6	67%
	XL (11+)	PASS	Julian Edelman	10	60%
3	Short (1-3)	PASS	James White	7	100%
		RUSH	Tom Brady	5	100%
	Med (4-7)	PASS	Danny Amendola	5	80%
	Long (8-10)	PASS	Rob Gronkowski	5	100%
	XL (11+)	PASS	Danny Amendola	5	40%

**Minimum 5 plays to qualify*

2016 Snap Rates

Week	Opp	Score	Julian Edelman	Martellus Bennett	Chris Hogan	Malcolm Mitchell	LeGarrette Blount	James White	Rob Gronkowski	James Develin	Danny Amendola
1	ARI	W 23-21	62 (87%)	69 (97%)	55 (77%)	39 (55%)	40 (56%)	24 (34%)		18 (25%)	19 (27%)
2	MIA	W 31-24	63 (79%)	80 (100%)	63 (79%)	31 (39%)	51 (64%)	28 (35%)		24 (30%)	19 (24%)
3	HOU	W 27-0	46 (74%)	61 (98%)	55 (89%)	16 (26%)	44 (71%)	16 (26%)	14 (23%)	23 (37%)	13 (21%)
4	BUF	L 16-0	50 (89%)	44 (79%)	52 (93%)	20 (36%)	30 (54%)	21 (38%)	39 (70%)	5 (9%)	14 (25%)
5	CLE	W 33-13	59 (74%)	55 (69%)	49 (61%)	25 (31%)	31 (39%)	38 (48%)	65 (81%)	22 (28%)	21 (26%)
6	CIN	W 35-17	58 (91%)	36 (56%)	56 (88%)	11 (17%)	22 (34%)	39 (61%)	57 (89%)	8 (13%)	26 (41%)
7	PIT	W 27-16	51 (89%)	30 (53%)	33 (58%)	31 (54%)	31 (54%)	25 (44%)	52 (91%)	11 (19%)	19 (33%)
8	BUF	W 41-25	60 (88%)	41 (60%)	63 (93%)		35 (51%)	33 (49%)	62 (91%)	7 (10%)	32 (47%)
10	SEA	L 31-24	52 (79%)	43 (65%)	30 (45%)	20 (30%)	37 (56%)	29 (44%)	59 (89%)	22 (33%)	26 (39%)
11	SF	W 30-17	66 (87%)	73 (96%)		65 (86%)	34 (45%)	24 (32%)		34 (45%)	42 (55%)
12	NYJ	W 22-17	66 (90%)	58 (79%)	67 (92%)	34 (47%)	27 (37%)	26 (36%)	7 (10%)	25 (34%)	17 (23%)
13	LA	W 26-10	54 (68%)	54 (68%)	68 (86%)	67 (85%)	36 (46%)	29 (37%)		26 (33%)	19 (24%)
14	BAL	W 30-23	47 (69%)	56 (82%)	57 (84%)	54 (79%)	30 (44%)	29 (43%)		25 (37%)	
15	DEN	W 16-3	44 (59%)	67 (89%)	52 (69%)	67 (89%)	23 (31%)	24 (32%)		43 (57%)	
16	NYJ	W 41-3	36 (48%)	47 (63%)	62 (83%)	58 (77%)	30 (40%)	19 (25%)		41 (55%)	
17	MIA	W 35-14	60 (90%)	52 (78%)	64 (96%)		22 (33%)	21 (31%)		17 (25%)	
Grand Total			874 (79%)	866 (77%)	826 (79%)	538 (54%)	523 (47%)	425 (38%)	355 (68%)	351 (31%)	267 (32%)

Personnel Groupings

Personnel	Team %	NFL Avg	Succ. %
1-1 [3WR]	53%	60%	49%
2-1 [2WR]	16%	7%	48%
1-2 [2WR]	15%	19%	51%
2-2 [1WR]	10%	3%	39%
2-3 [0WR]	3%	1%	46%
2-0 [3WR]	2%	1%	56%

Grouping Tendencies

Personnel	Pass Rate	Pass Succ. %	Run Succ. %
1-1 [3WR]	73%	48%	52%
2-1 [2WR]	34%	54%	45%
1-2 [2WR]	58%	50%	51%
2-2 [1WR]	12%	53%	37%
2-3 [0WR]	11%	0%	52%
2-0 [3WR]	74%	55%	57%

Red Zone Targets (min 3)

Receiver	All	Inside 5	6-10	11-20
Julian Edelman	17	5	5	7
Martellus Bennett	15	5	2	8
Chris Hogan	14	4	5	5
James White	14	2	4	8
Malcolm Mitchell	13	2	2	9
Danny Amendola	11	1	3	7
Rob Gronkowski	6	2	2	2
Dion Lewis	4		1	3
James Develin	4	2		2

Red Zone Rushes (min 3)

Rusher	All	Inside 5	6-10	11-20
LeGarrette Blount	81	32	15	34
Dion Lewis	18	3	6	9
Tom Brady	11	7	2	2
James White	7	4	3	

Early Down Target Rate

RB	TE	WR
25%	20%	55%
19%	*20%*	*61%*

NFL AVG

Overall Target Success %

RB	TE	WR
43%	57%	55%
#22	#10	#5

New England Patriots 2016 Passing Recap & 2017 Outlook

One of the things the Patriots definitely put an emphasis on last season was deeper passing. Interestingly, the team didn't even attempt to target Rob Gronkowski once over 15 yards downfield until Tom Brady came back. Gronk was blocking and not going deep. As soon as Brady returned, they unleashed him. In Brady's first 4 games back, Gronk had 10 deep targets, and all other players combined had 10 total. 70% of the targets to Gronk were successful, for a 152 rating with 2 TDs. He was the Patriots best deep threat. Then he went down in week 8 and was lost for the season. For the rest of the playoff run, Julian Edelman was the most targeted player, but those were poor targets. Of the 33 attempts, only 36% were successful and he delivered a 63 rating. The Patriots were fortunate they snagged Chris Hogan prior to the season, because he was their deep savior. He delivered a 149 rating on 21 targets (no one else had more than 10) and a 67% success rate. Hopefully the Patriots will continue throwing deep this year, primarily to Gronk and Hogan, but leave Edelman out of that mix, particularly when it's at the rate they targeted him last year. With Cooks and Allen and multiple pass catching RBs, this offense can be as diverse as it wants.

Tom Brady Rating All Downs

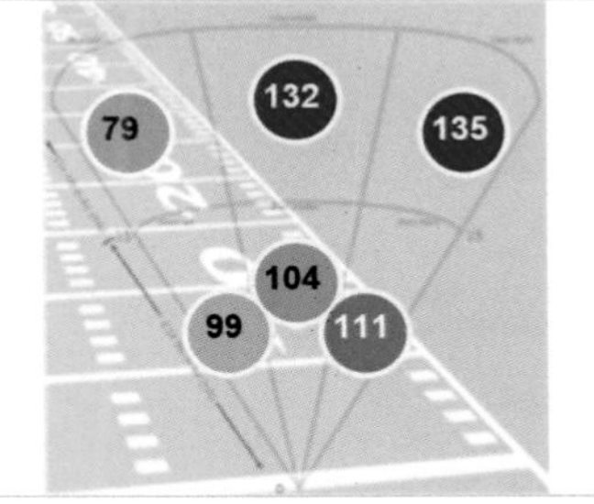

Tom Brady Rating Early Downs

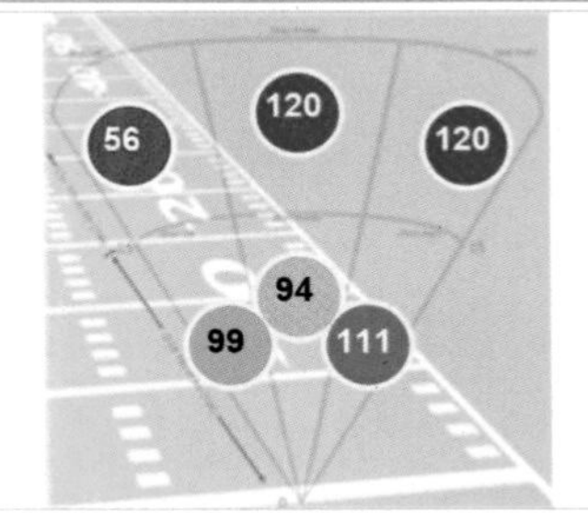

2016 Standard Passing Table

QB	Comp	Att	Comp %	Yds	YPA	TDs	INT	Sacks	Rating	Rk
Tom Brady	384	574	67%	4,691	8.2	35	5	24	108.6	4
Jimmy Garoppolo	43	64	67%	504	7.9	4	0	3	111.7	3
NFL Avg			63%		7.2				90.4	

2016 Advanced Passing Table

QB	Success %	EDSR Passing Success %	20+ Yd Pass Gains	20+ Yd Pass %	30+ Yd Pass Gains	30+ Yd Pass %	Air Yds per Comp	YAC per Comp	20+ Air Yd Comp	20+ Air Yd %
Tom Brady	50%	50%	62	11%	31	5%	7.0	5.3	31	5%
Jimmy Garoppolo	51%	48%	7	11%	2	3%	6.9	4.8	4	6%
NFL Avg	44%	48%	27	8%	10	3%	6.4	4.8	12	4%

Interception Rates by Down

Yards to Go	1	2	3	4	Total
1 & 2	0.0%	0.0%	5.6%	0.0%	3.1%
3, 4, 5	0.0%	0.0%	0.0%	0.0%	0.0%
6 - 9	0.0%	0.0%	1.9%		0.8%
10 - 14	0.9%	1.4%	0.0%		0.9%
15+	0.0%	0.0%	0.0%		0.0%
Total	0.9%	0.5%	1.2%	0.0%	0.8%

3rd Down Passing - Short of Sticks Analysis

QB	Avg Yds to Go	Air Yds (of Comps)	Avg Yds Short	Short of Sticks Rate	Rk
Tom Brady	7.5	10.4	0.0	39%	1
NFL Avg	7.6	6.8	-0.8	57%	

Air Yds vs YAC

Air Yds %	YAC %	Rk
55%	45%	26
54%	46%	

2016 Receiving Recap & 2017 Outlook

The Patriots used 3+ WR formations the 5th least of any team. While 11 personnel was still used most, the team used a variety of groupings to catch defenses off guard and play to their advantage. The trouble with predicting this attack is determining where the shares go now that Gronk is healthy. In Gronk's 4 healthy games last year with Brady, the shares went: Edelman 26%, Gronk 20%, White 18%, Bennett 15%, Hogan 9%. Only 1 WR in the top 4 most targeted players. And with Hogan and Cooks competing for outside targets with Edelman in the slot, it will be tough to see enough volume, especially with frequent 2nd half leads.

Player *Min 50 Targets*	Targets	Comp %	YPA	Rating	TOARS	Success %	Success Rk	Missed YPA Rk	YAS % Rk	TDs
Julian Edelman	196	61%	7.4	88	5.6	52%	58	61	83	4
James White	107	73%	6.4	111	5.0	46%	109	110	98	7
Martellus Bennett	88	75%	9.1	129	5.0	53%	50	17	32	7
Chris Hogan	81	68%	12.5	130	4.9	59%	19	14	3	6
Malcolm Mitchell	59	66%	8.1	106	4.2	59%	18	42	44	4

Directional Passer Rating Delivered

Receiver	Short Left	Short Middle	Short Right	Deep Left	Deep Middle	Deep Right	Player Total
Julian Edelman	101	84	105	56	45	74	88
James White	113	76	108	40		158	112
Martellus Bennett	95	131	114	40	158	158	129
Chris Hogan	93	119	80	130	158	156	130
Malcolm Mitchell	96	137	143	28	109	127	106
Danny Amendola	91	143	118	96	40	85	125
Rob Gronkowski	86	119	135	119	144	67	135
Dion Lewis	110	56	80	40		40	77
Michael Floyd	69	92	104	40			69
Team Total	100	110	108	78	129	135	109

2016 Rushing Recap & 2017 Outlook

While LeGarrette Blount underperformed last year from an efficiency perspective, he dominated the metrics from a volume perspective. Blount had 81 red zone carries, including 32 inside the 5 yard line. Overall he was successful on 54% of them. The Patriots just acquired the #1 RB inside the red zone last year in Mike Gillislee. Gillislee posted a whopping 94% success rate inside the red zone, and a 100% success rate inside the 10 yard line. The Patriots also have Rex Burkhead as well, in addition to their #1 most successful red zone back last season: Dion Lewis. Lewis posted a 72% success rate on his red zone rushes last season. With such balance and possibly higher efficiency this year, the Patriots could be deadly inside the red zone.

Player *Min 50 Rushes*	Rushes	YPA	Success %	Success Rk	Missed YPA Rk	YTS % Rk	YAS % Rk	Early Down Success %	Early Down Success Rk	TDs
LeGarrette Blount	334	3.8	45%	42	37	45	24	44%	43	19
Dion Lewis	89	4.1	57%	4	16	4	66	58%	3	1

Yards per Carry by Direction

Directional Run Frequency

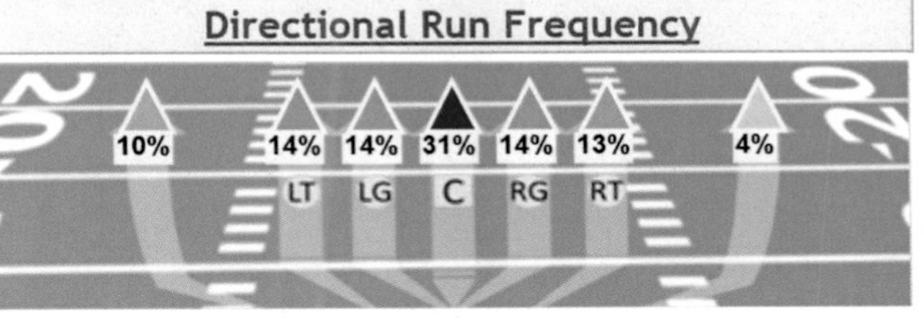

becomes ideal, so having safeties who can drop into one-on-one matchups with TEs is a luxury most teams don't have.

Now that we know how they are built and perhaps why they've chosen to build that way, we can better understand what they are looking to become. Last year this was a team that was tactically advantaged with a willingness to attack opponent weakness.

Before last year's Super Bowl, I was on top of what would happen in the game fairly accurately. And I said "running back passes will destroy both defenses". Atlanta ranked 30th defending RB passes, the easiest opponent for New England all year. And I mentioned "in the red zone, the Falcons allowed a 126 rating and a 82% completion rate on the year." And James White led all receivers with 16 targets, 14 catches, 110 yards and 3 total TDs. This is just an example of what the Patriots were capable of doing, if they simply needed to pull out the tricks to win. They don't always unleash their full bag of tricks or call their best plays in every situation (the Seattle loss was a prime example of predictable and inefficient play calling) but they are the best in the NFL at doing what it takes, when it takes it from a decision making perspective to beat their opponent.

Their 2016 offense was great, ranking top 6 in almost all of my advanced metrics except for run efficiency, and that's the full body of work, not just the Tom Brady games after week 4. Their offense will be even better this year.

They still have offensive line coach Dante Scarnecchia and Tom Brady, so their base is solid. But the additions of both Mike Gillislee and Rex Burkhead, the #1 and #2 RBs last year in both success rate and Missed YPA, will make this backfield much more dangerous and multiple. They added multiple TEs including Dwayne Allen. This offense will face an even easier time next year based on their schedule, especially the run game. The issue last year was their defense.

The biggest fallacy entering the Super Bowl was the Patriots "#1 Scoring Defense". I burned that argument to the ground, fueled by efficiency ratings and strength of schedule faced. And we saw Atlanta (finally a very good offense) was able to score. One of their biggest weaknesses last year was that on early downs in the first half, the Patriots defense ranked 32nd in success rate against passes and 24th in success rate against runs inside their own 40 yard line. Overall they ranked 31st, allowing successful plays to be executed 56% of the time, which came against the easiest schedule of opposing offenses. This defense needed a ton of improvement, and they received it via new personnel: DE Kony Ealy, CB Stephon Gilmore, in free agency and they drafted DE Derek Rivers in the 3rd round. As opposed to facing the NFL's easiest schedule of opposing offenses, the schedule will be slightly tougher this year but still manageable for the Patriots defense. With the returning and new pieces, it's hard to not envision another tremendous season in New England.

Division History: Season Wins & 2017 Projection

	2013 Wins	2014 Wins	2015 Wins	2016 Wins	Proj 2017 Wins

Rank of 2017 Defensive Pass Efficiency Faced by Week

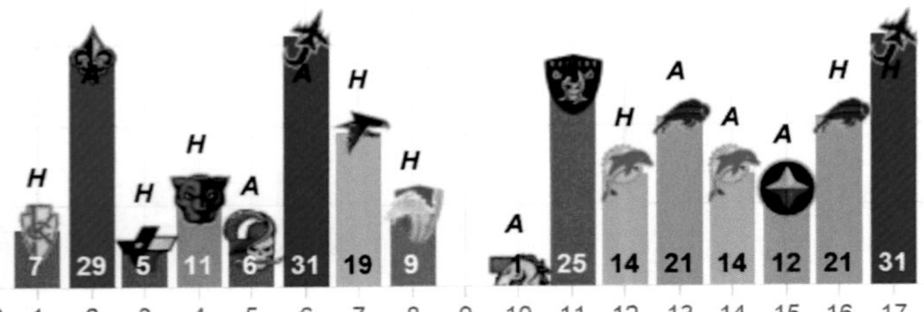

Rank of 2017 Defensive Rush Efficiency Faced by Week

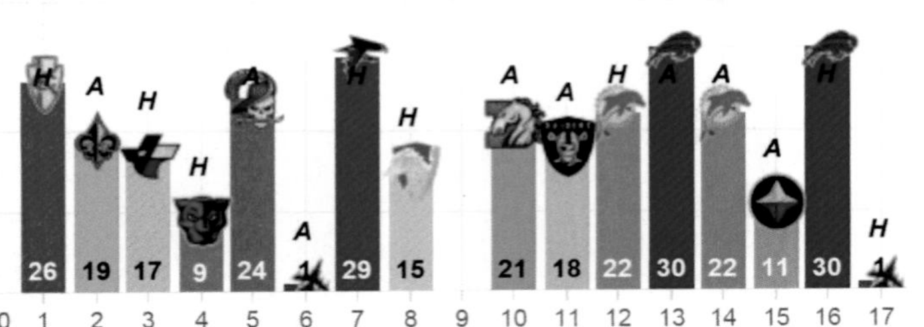

2016 Situational Usage by Player & Position

Usage Rate by Score

		Being Blown Out (14+)	Down Big (9-13)	One Score	Large Lead (9-13)	Blowout Lead (14+)	Grand Total
RUSH	LeGarrette Blount	13%	27%	27%	34%	30%	28%
	Julian Edelman			1%	2%	1%	1%
	James White	7%	3%	3%	5%	5%	4%
	Dion Lewis	6%	3%	8%	8%	7%	8%
	Martellus Bennett			0%	1%		0%
	Chris Hogan			0%		0%	0%
	Danny Amendola					0%	0%
	D.J. Foster					2%	1%
	Brandon Bolden			0%			0%
	Matthew Slater					0%	0%
	Total	26%	33%	40%	49%	48%	42%
PASS	LeGarrette Blount	3%	3%	1%			1%
	Julian Edelman	12%	10%	17%	16%	17%	17%
	James White	16%	10%	10%	6%	6%	9%
	Dion Lewis	4%		4%	2%	1%	3%
	Martellus Bennett	9%	23%	7%	6%	6%	7%
	Chris Hogan	7%	3%	7%	6%	7%	7%
	Malcolm Mitchell	6%	3%	4%	6%	6%	5%
	Danny Amendola	12%	7%	3%	3%	4%	4%
	Rob Gronkowski	3%		4%	1%	2%	3%
	D.J. Foster			0%		0%	0%
	James Develin			1%	1%	0%	1%
	Michael Floyd			0%	2%	1%	1%
	Brandon Bolden	1%	7%	0%			0%
	Matt Lengel			0%	1%	0%	0%
	Matthew Slater					0%	0%
	Total	74%	67%	60%	51%	52%	58%

Positional Target Distribution vs NFL Average

		NFL Wide				Team Only			
		Left	Middle	Right	Total	Left	Middle	Right	Total
Deep	WR	988	562	970	2,520	43	19	31	93
	TE	152	140	153	445	6	7	10	23
	RB	21	4	34	59	4		6	10
	All	1,161	706	1,157	3,024	53	26	47	126
Short	WR	2,965	1,691	3,098	7,754	128	80	88	296
	TE	801	848	1,110	2,759	35	27	41	103
	RB	954	605	1,059	2,618	61	17	54	132
	All	4,720	3,144	5,267	13,131	224	124	183	531
Total		5,881	3,850	6,424	16,155	277	150	230	657

Positional Success Rates vs NFL Average

		NFL Wide				Team Only			
		Left	Middle	Right	Total	Left	Middle	Right	Total
Deep	WR	37%	50%	38%	40%	33%	58%	48%	43%
	TE	43%	49%	42%	45%	67%	71%	60%	65%
	RB	38%	75%	24%	32%	0%		33%	20%
	All	38%	50%	38%	41%	34%	62%	49%	45%
Short	WR	52%	56%	51%	53%	59%	64%	56%	59%
	TE	50%	61%	52%	54%	46%	67%	54%	54%
	RB	47%	50%	44%	46%	48%	29%	48%	45%
	All	50%	57%	50%	52%	54%	60%	53%	55%
Total		48%	55%	48%	50%	50%	60%	52%	53%

New Orleans Saints

2017 Coaches

Head Coach:
Sean Payton (12th yr)
Offensive Coordinator:
Pete Carmichael (9th yr)
Defensive Coordinator:
Dennis Allen (3rd yr)

2017 Forecast

Wins	Div Rank
8	#3

Past Records

2016: 7-9
2015: 7-9
2014: 7-9

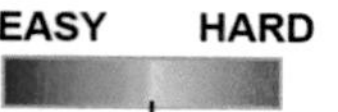

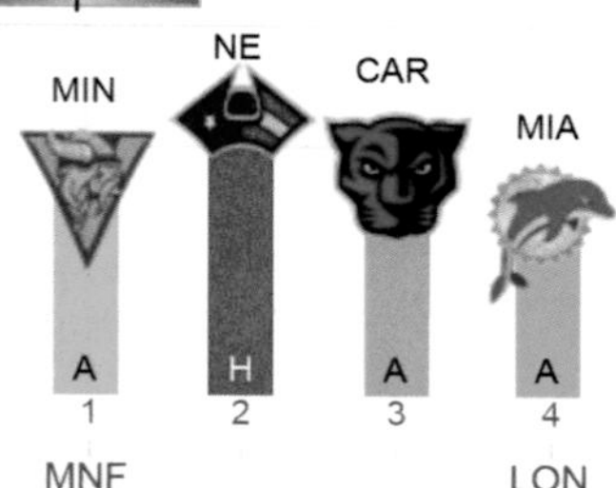

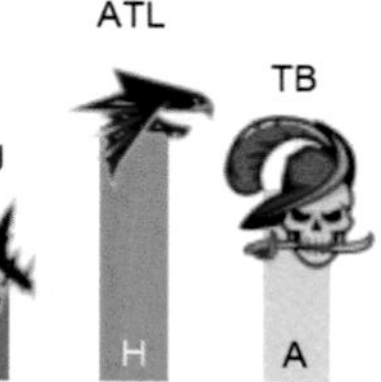

Key Players Lost

TXN	Player (POS)
Cut	Barnes, Khalif T
	Byrd, Jairus S
	Keo, Shiloh S
	Young, Avery T
Declared Free Agent	Cadet, Travaris RB
	Drescher, Justin C
	Evans, Jahri G
	Fairley, Nick DT
	Harper, Roman S
	Hightower, Tim RB
	Hills, Tony T
	Kruger, Paul DE
	Moore, Sterling CB
	Phillips, John TE
	Sanford, Jamarca S
	Tapp, Darryl DE
	Trusnik, Jason LB
	Wilson, Kyle CB
Retired	Laurinaitis, James LB
	Moore, Lance WR

Average Line	# Games Favored	# Games Underdog
+0.4	7	7

Regular Season Wins: Past & Current Proj

	Wins
Proj 2017 Wins	8
2016 Wins	7
Proj 2016 Wins	7
2015 Wins	7
2014 Wins	7
2013 Wins	11

1 3 5 7 9 11 13 15

2017 New Orleans Saints Overview

It is difficult to write about the 2017 New Orleans Saints without getting slightly sentimental over the 38-year-old Drew Brees. Just before he was scheduled to hit the cap for $30M in 2016, he agreed to a deal with the Saints which included a no trade clause and a no franchise tag clause as well. It's hard to imagine that Brees entered the league back in 2001, the second quarterback drafted (behind Michael Vick). There is no doubt that the diminutive quarterback wants to end his career in New Orleans, took this new deal because it was in the Saints best interest, and is on pace to break Peyton Manning's all-time records in passing yards and touchdowns.

One look through the graphics-laden pages of this Saints chapter and it is evident how phenomenal Brees is playing, even at this stage in his career. The offensive numbers are so outrageous they make the defensive metrics look downright pathetic. And that is where we get to the disappointment of Brees and the city of New Orleans, as well as the rest of us who want to see more opportunities to watch Brees duel with other legendary quarterbacks in the postseason. It's hard to build a balanced roster when allocating so much money to the quarterback position. You can build a good roster overall, which is capable of winning 7 or 8 games on the shoulders of a great quarterback, but to get to the playoffs and beyond, you need more out of your defense. And for 3 consecutive years, the Saints have posted a 7-9 record in large part because the defense is terrible. And this is also why, in the last 5 seasons, the Saints made the playoffs just one time.

Even if the defense wasn't as terrible as it has been, it would be difficult for the Saints unless they excelled in the regular season to win a #1 or #2 seed for the playoffs. Since Brees came to New Orleans, he and the Saints have never lost a non-away playoff game. They went 5-0, winning 4 at home (one in 2006, two in 2009 and one in 2011) and the Super Bowl at a neutral site to end the 2009 season. But in road playoff games the Saints went 1-4, with their lone win coming via a last-minute field goal over the Chip Kelly and Nick Foles-led Eagles in 2013. The problem in most of these road losses came because the defense allowed an average of 35 points per game across the 4 losses. It's hard enough for the dome-developed Saints offense to win on the road, but they valiantly put up over 31 points in multiple road playoff losses.

(cont'd - see NO2)

Key Free Agents/ Trades Added

Bush, Rafael S
Ginn Jr., Ted WR
Harbor, Clay TE
Klein, A.J. LB
LeRibeus, Josh G
Okafor, Alex LB
Peterson, Adrian RB
Te'o, Manti LB
Warford, Larry G

Drafted Players

Rd	Pk	Player (College)
1	11	CB - Marshon Lattimore (Ohio State)
	32	OT - Ryan Ramczyk (Wisconsin)
2	42	S - Marcus Williams (Utah)
3	67	RB - Alvin Kamara (Tennessee)
	76	LB - Alex Anzalone (Florida)
3*	103	OLB - Trey Hendrickson (Florida Atlantic)
6	196	DE - Al-Quadin Muhammad (Miami (FL))

2017 Lineup & Cap Hits

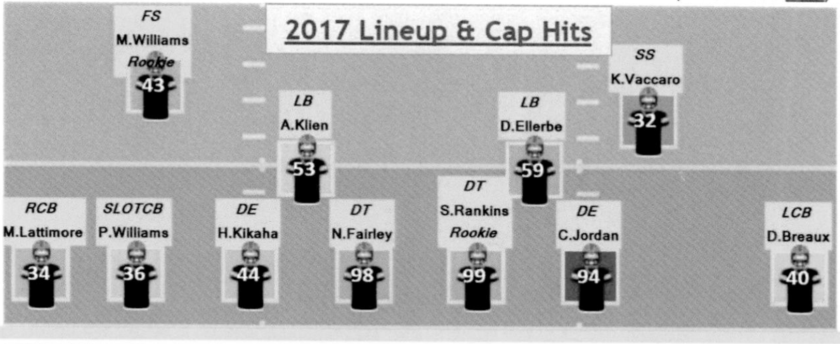

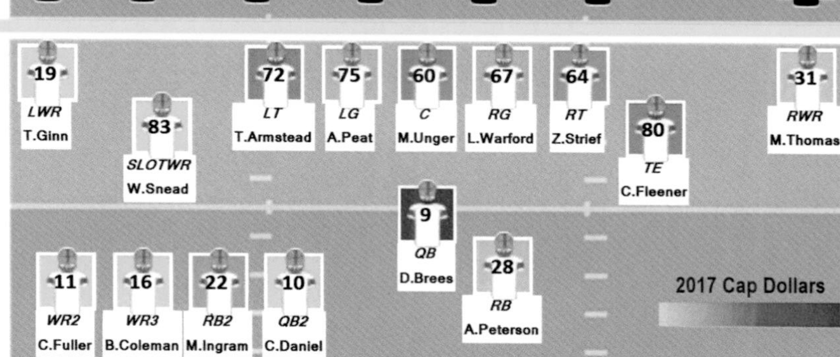

2017 Unit Spending

All DEF
All OFF

Positional Spending

	Rank	Total	2016 Rk
All OFF	9	$88.46M	30
QB	14	$20.44M	16
OL	7	$34.44M	24
RB	9	$10.19M	20
WR	31	$9.03M	31
TE	3	$14.36M	18
All DEF	31	$61.27M	29
DL	16	$25.12M	24
LB	18	$17.16M	29
CB	29	$8.37M	30
S	20	$10.61M	3

New Orleans Saints 2016 Success Rate Radar

Weeks 1-4
1 L
2 L
3 L
4 W
Weeks 5-8
6 W
7 L
8 W
Weeks 9-12
9 W
10 L
11 L
12 W
Weeks 13-17
13 L
14 L
15 W
16 W
17 L
Pass
Explosive Pass
Pass Pro
Rush
Early Downs
3rd Down
DEFENSE
OFFENSE

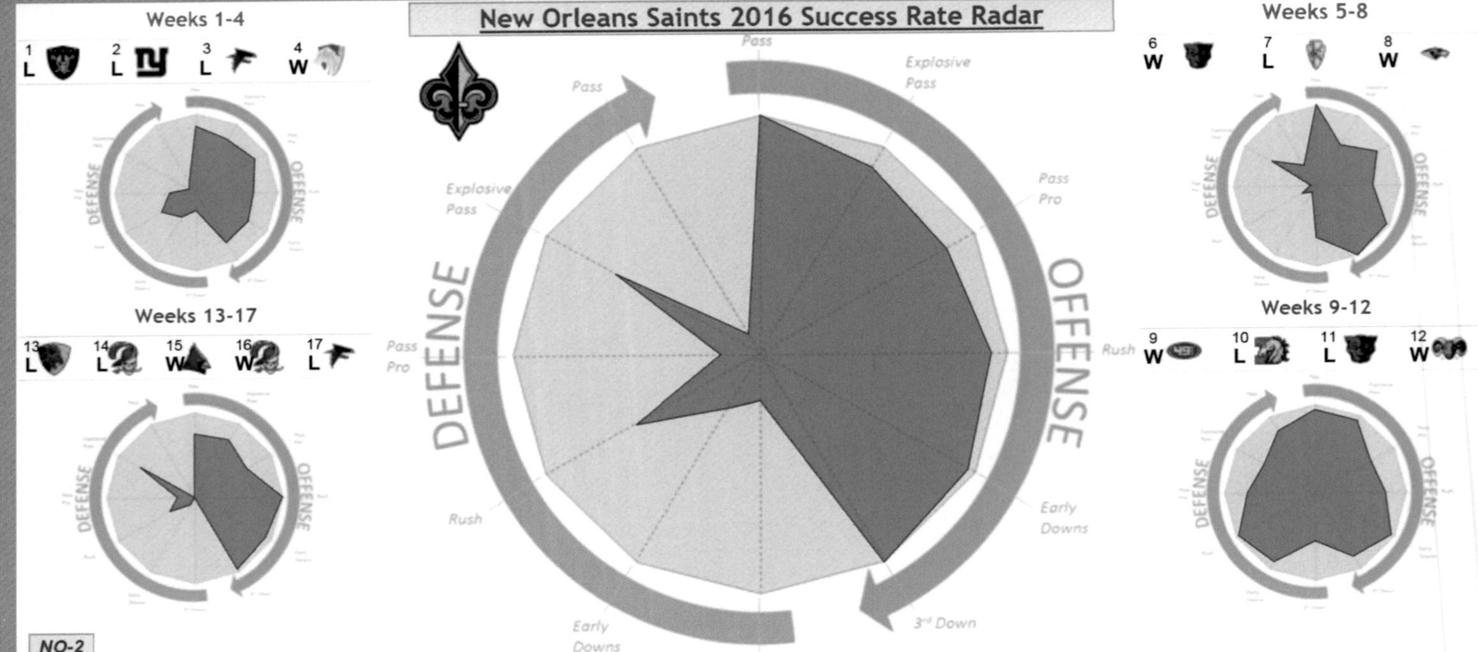

NO-2

Thanks to their offense last season, the Saints only lost 2 games by more than 1 score: against the Falcons and the Lions. All their other games were either wins or close losses. They lost 7 games last year by less than 7 points. With so many games which could have come down to a single critical play (such as the blocked extra point returned for two points which lost the Saints the game against the Broncos), what do the Saints need to do better in 2017?

For starters, the Saints need better performance out of the defense, and they also need better luck with injuries to that unit. Their DBs were the 4th most injured unit last year and their LBs were the 5th most injured unit. The defense, and in particular the pass defense, was not something that went South overnight. Bad decisions came via free agency and the NFL draft, with free agents such as Jarius Byrd and Brandon Browner failing badly, as well as high draft picks such as Stanley Jean-Baptiste and P.J. Williams. So the Saints need three more high draft picks from this class to step up, and do so quickly, to help this secondary. New Orleans drafted CB Marshon Lattimore in the 1st round and Marcus Williams in the 2nd round. Young players typically take time to work into the secondary, but New Orleans will need Dennis Allen to find a way to get the most out of the secondary. They also added LBs A.J. Klien, Alex Okafor and Manti Te'o in free agency, as well as SS Rafael Bush. But the problem for the Saints will be their defense's 2017 schedule is substantially more difficult than was their 2016 schedule. Instead of facing the 27th rated offenses, as they did last year, they must face the 9th rated schedule this year. The New Orleans pass defense sees the 7th largest increase in schedule difficult from 2016 to 2017. Instead of facing the struggling offenses of the 49ers, Giants and Broncos from 2016, the Saints must deal with the Packers, Patriots and Redskins offenses.

When the defense struggles, as it is likely to do, the pressure will once again fall on Brees and the offense, a familiar refrain for the Saints. Fortunately, while the schedule is unkind to their defense, the schedule is extremely kind to the Saints offense.

(cont'd - see NO-3)

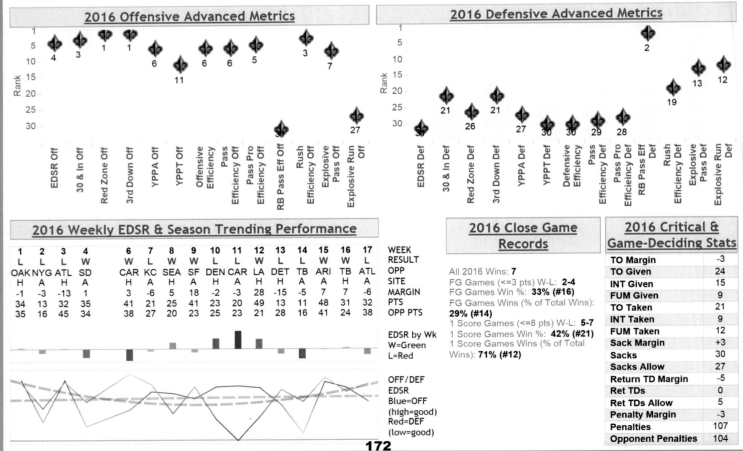

2016 Offensive Advanced Metrics

Rank
EDSR Off 4
30 & In Off 3
Red Zone Off 1
3rd Down Off 1
YPPA Off 6
YPPT Off 11
Offensive Efficiency 6
Pass Efficiency Off 6
Pass Pro Efficiency Off 5
RB Pass Eff Off
Rush Efficiency Off 3
Explosive Pass Off 7
Explosive Run Off 27

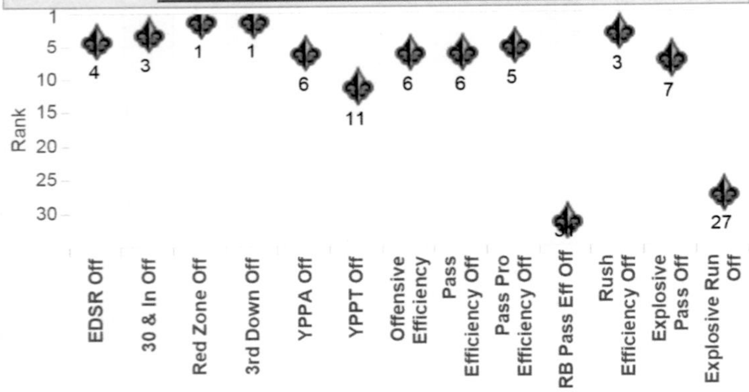

2016 Defensive Advanced Metrics

Rank
EDSR Def
30 & In Def 21
Red Zone Def 26
3rd Down Def 21
YPPA Def 27
YPPT Def 30
Defensive Efficiency 30
Pass Efficiency Def 29
Pass Pro Efficiency Def 28
RB Pass Eff Def 2
Rush Efficiency Def 19
Explosive Pass Def 13
Explosive Run Def 12

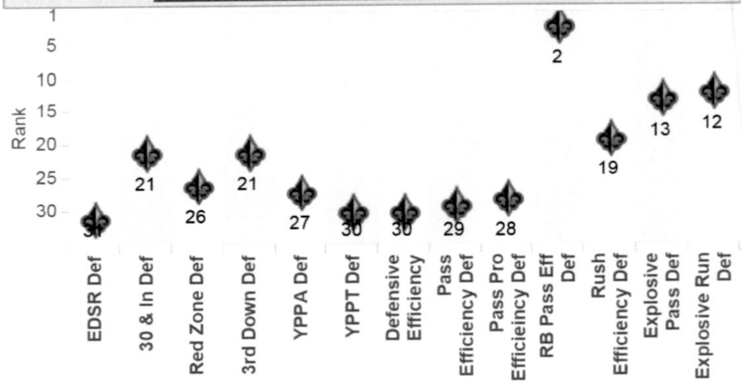

2016 Weekly EDSR & Season Trending Performance

1	2	3	4	6	7	8	9	10	11	12	13	14	15	16	17	WEEK
L	L	L	W	W	L	W	W	L	L	W	L	L	W	W	L	RESULT
OAK	NYG	ATL	SD	CAR	KC	SEA	SF	DEN	CAR	LA	DET	TB	ARI	TB	ATL	OPP
H	A	H	A	H	A	H	A	H	A	H	H	A	A	H	A	SITE
-1	-3	-13	1	3	-6	5	18	-2	-3	28	-15	-5	7	7	-6	MARGIN
34	13	32	35	41	21	25	41	23	20	49	13	11	48	31	32	PTS
35	16	45	34	38	27	20	23	25	23	21	28	16	41	24	38	OPP PTS

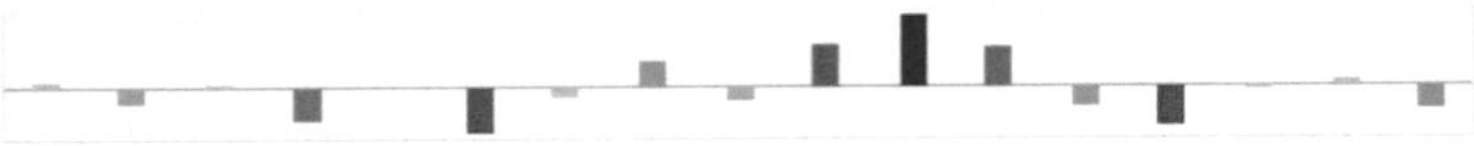

EDSR by Wk
W=Green
L=Red

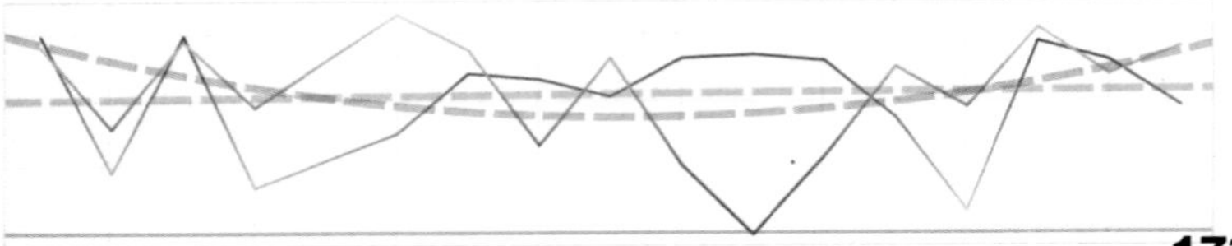

OFF/DEF
EDSR
Blue=OFF
(high=good)
Red=DEF
(low=good)

2016 Close Game Records

All 2016 Wins: **7**
FG Games (<=3 pts) W-L: **2-4**
FG Games Win %: **33% (#16)**
FG Games Wins (% of Total Wins): **29% (#14)**
1 Score Games (<=8 pts) W-L: **5-7**
1 Score Games Win %: **42% (#21)**
1 Score Games Wins (% of Total Wins): **71% (#12)**

2016 Critical & Game-Deciding Stats

TO Margin	-3
TO Given	24
INT Given	15
FUM Given	9
TO Taken	21
INT Taken	9
FUM Taken	12
Sack Margin	+3
Sacks	30
Sacks Allow	27
Return TD Margin	-5
Ret TDs	0
Ret TDs Allow	5
Penalty Margin	-3
Penalties	107
Opponent Penalties	104

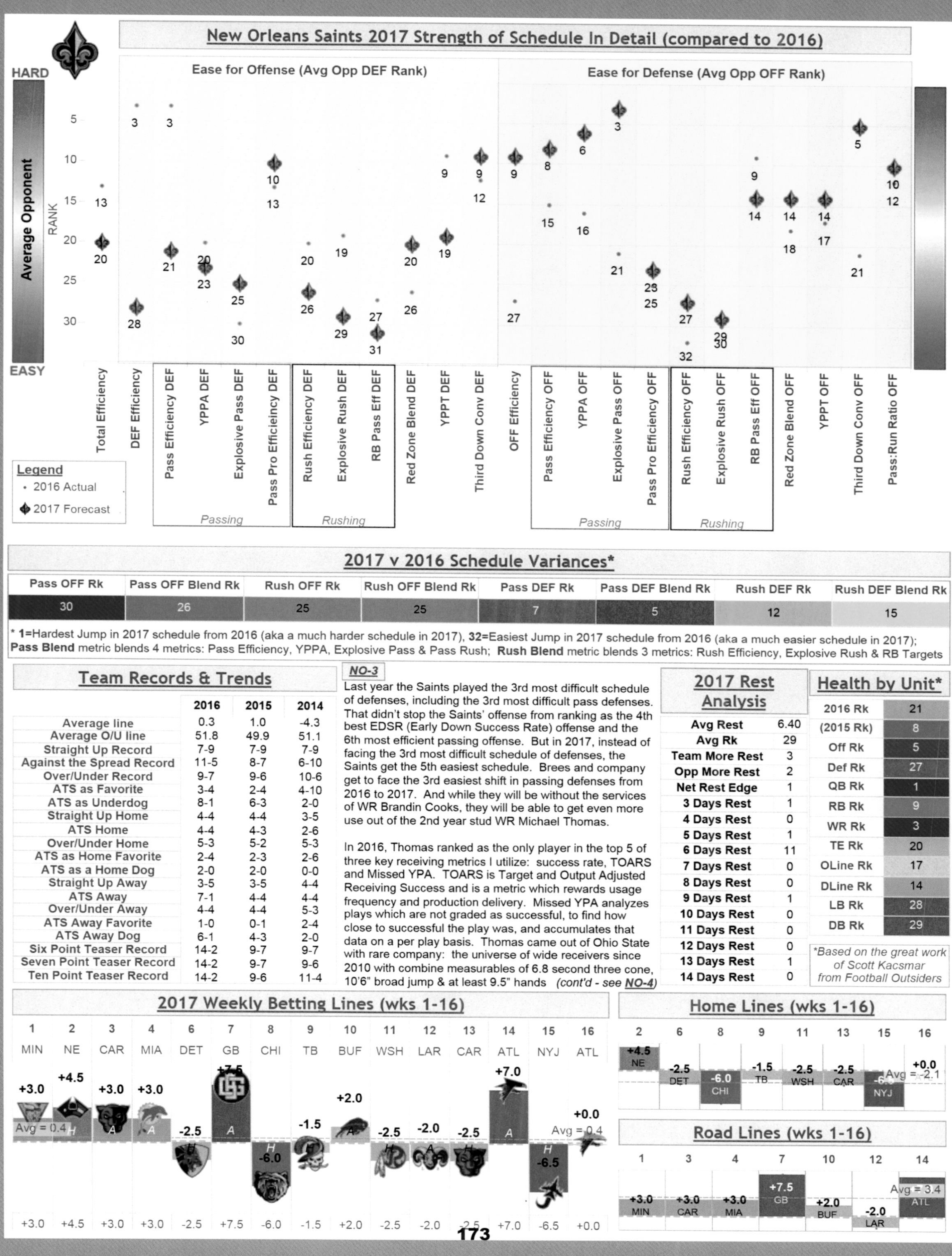

New Orleans Saints 2017 Strength of Schedule In Detail (compared to 2016)

2017 v 2016 Schedule Variances*

Pass OFF Rk	Pass OFF Blend Rk	Rush OFF Rk	Rush OFF Blend Rk	Pass DEF Rk	Pass DEF Blend Rk	Rush DEF Rk	Rush DEF Blend Rk
30	26	25	25	7	5	12	15

* **1**=Hardest Jump in 2017 schedule from 2016 (aka a much harder schedule in 2017), **32**=Easiest Jump in 2017 schedule from 2016 (aka a much easier schedule in 2017); **Pass Blend** metric blends 4 metrics: Pass Efficiency, YPPA, Explosive Pass & Pass Rush; **Rush Blend** metric blends 3 metrics: Rush Efficiency, Explosive Rush & RB Targets

Team Records & Trends

	2016	2015	2014
Average line	0.3	1.0	-4.3
Average O/U line	51.8	49.9	51.1
Straight Up Record	7-9	7-9	7-9
Against the Spread Record	11-5	8-7	6-10
Over/Under Record	9-7	9-6	10-6
ATS as Favorite	3-4	2-4	4-10
ATS as Underdog	8-1	6-3	2-0
Straight Up Home	4-4	4-4	3-5
ATS Home	4-4	4-3	2-6
Over/Under Home	5-3	5-2	5-3
ATS as Home Favorite	2-4	2-3	2-6
ATS as a Home Dog	2-0	2-0	0-0
Straight Up Away	3-5	3-5	4-4
ATS Away	7-1	4-4	4-4
Over/Under Away	4-4	4-4	5-3
ATS Away Favorite	1-0	0-1	2-4
ATS Away Dog	6-1	4-3	2-0
Six Point Teaser Record	14-2	9-7	9-7
Seven Point Teaser Record	14-2	9-7	9-6
Ten Point Teaser Record	14-2	9-6	11-4

NO-3

Last year the Saints played the 3rd most difficult schedule of defenses, including the 3rd most difficult pass defenses. That didn't stop the Saints' offense from ranking as the 4th best EDSR (Early Down Success Rate) offense and the 6th most efficient passing offense. But in 2017, instead of facing the 3rd most difficult schedule of defenses, the Saints get the 5th easiest schedule. Brees and company get to face the 3rd easiest shift in passing defenses from 2016 to 2017. And while they will be without the services of WR Brandin Cooks, they will be able to get even more use out of the 2nd year stud WR Michael Thomas.

In 2016, Thomas ranked as the only player in the top 5 of three key receiving metrics I utilize: success rate, TOARS and Missed YPA. TOARS is Target and Output Adjusted Receiving Success and is a metric which rewards usage frequency and production delivery. Missed YPA analyzes plays which are not graded as successful, to find how close to successful the play was, and accumulates that data on a per play basis. Thomas came out of Ohio State with rare company: the universe of wide receivers since 2010 with combine measurables of 6.8 second three cone, 10'6" broad jump & at least 9.5" hands *(cont'd - see NO-4)*

2017 Rest Analysis

Avg Rest	6.40
Avg Rk	29
Team More Rest	3
Opp More Rest	2
Net Rest Edge	1
3 Days Rest	1
4 Days Rest	0
5 Days Rest	1
6 Days Rest	11
7 Days Rest	0
8 Days Rest	0
9 Days Rest	1
10 Days Rest	0
11 Days Rest	0
12 Days Rest	0
13 Days Rest	1
14 Days Rest	0

Health by Unit*

2016 Rk	21
(2015 Rk)	8
Off Rk	5
Def Rk	27
QB Rk	1
RB Rk	9
WR Rk	3
TE Rk	20
OLine Rk	17
DLine Rk	14
LB Rk	28
DB Rk	29

**Based on the great work of Scott Kacsmar from Football Outsiders*

2017 Weekly Betting Lines (wks 1-16)

Week	1	2	3	4	6	7	8	9	10	11	12	13	14	15	16
Opp	MIN	NE	CAR	MIA	DET	GB	CHI	TB	BUF	WSH	LAR	CAR	ATL	NYJ	ATL
H/A		H	A	A	H	A	H			H	A	H	A	H	
Line	+3.0	+4.5	+3.0	+3.0	-2.5	+7.5	-6.0	-1.5	+2.0	-2.5	-2.0	-2.5	+7.0	-6.5	+0.0

Avg = 0.4

Home Lines (wks 1-16)

Week	2	6	8	9	11	13	15	16
Opp	NE	DET	CHI	TB	WSH	CAR	NYJ	
Line	+4.5	-2.5	-6.0	-1.5	-2.5	-2.5	-6.5	+0.0

Avg = -2.1

Road Lines (wks 1-16)

Week	1	3	4	7	10	12	14
Opp	MIN	CAR	MIA	GB	BUF	LAR	ATL
Line	+3.0	+3.0	+3.0	+7.5	+2.0	-2.0	

Avg = 3.4

New Orleans Saints 2016 Play Analysis

2016 Play Tendencies

All Pass %	62%
All Pass Rk	6
All Rush %	38%
All Rush Rk	27
1 Score Pass %	60%
1 Score Pass Rk	7
2015 1 Score Pass %	64%
2015 1 Score Pass Rk	2
Pass Increase %	-3%
Pass Increase Rk	23
1 Score Rush %	40%
1 Score Rush Rk	26
Up Pass %	67%
Up Pass Rk	1
Up Rush %	33%
Up Rush Rk	32
Down Pass %	61%
Down Pass Rk	18
Down Rush %	39%
Down Rush Rk	15

2016 Down & Distance Tendencies

Down	Distance	Total Plays	Pass Rate	Run Rate	Play Success %
1	Short (1-3)	8	50%	50%	50%
	Med (4-7)	10	30%	70%	60%
	Long (8-10)	327	53%	47%	56%
	XL (11+)	11	82%	18%	18%
2	Short (1-3)	41	27%	73%	83%
	Med (4-7)	102	66%	34%	56%
	Long (8-10)	85	72%	28%	48%
	XL (11+)	33	94%	6%	27%
3	Short (1-3)	58	45%	55%	67%
	Med (4-7)	44	95%	5%	50%
	Long (8-10)	32	100%	0%	34%
	XL (11+)	27	85%	15%	15%
4	Short (1-3)	8	38%	63%	100%
	Med (4-7)	1	100%	0%	100%

Shotgun %:

Under Center	Shotgun
46%	54%
37% AVG	*63%*

Run Rate:

Under Center	Shotgun
65%	13%
68% AVG	*23%*

Pass Rate:

Under Center	Shotgun
35%	87%
32% AVG	*77%*

Short Yardage Intelligence:

2nd and Short Run

Run Freq	Run % Rk	NFL Run Freq Avg	Run 1D Rate	Run NFL 1D Avg
61%	22	65%	87%	71%

2nd and Short Pass

Pass Freq	Pass % Rk	NFL Pass Freq Avg	Pass 1D Rate	Pass NFL 1D Avg
39%	9	35%	40%	52%

Most Frequent Play

Down	Distance	Play Type	Player	Total Plays	Play Success %
1	Short (1-3)	PASS	Michael Thomas	2	50%
		RUSH	Tim Hightower	2	0%
	Med (4-7)	RUSH	Mark Ingram	4	50%
	Long (8-10)	RUSH	Mark Ingram	84	55%
	XL (11+)	PASS	Brandin Cooks	2	50%
			Willie Snead	2	50%
			Coby Fleener	2	0%
		RUSH	Mark Ingram	2	0%
2	Short (1-3)	RUSH	Mark Ingram	16	88%
	Med (4-7)	RUSH	Tim Hightower	16	56%
	Long (8-10)	PASS	Brandin Cooks	15	67%
		RUSH	Mark Ingram	15	33%
	XL (11+)	PASS	Mark Ingram	7	29%
3	Short (1-3)	RUSH	Mark Ingram	12	58%
	Med (4-7)	PASS	Brandin Cooks	8	50%
	Long (8-10)	PASS	Willie Snead	9	44%
	XL (11+)	PASS	Willie Snead	6	0%

Most Successful Play*

Down	Distance	Play Type	Player	Total Plays	Play Success %
1	Long (8-10)	PASS	Tim Hightower	7	86%
2	Short (1-3)	RUSH	Tim Hightower	11	91%
	Med (4-7)	PASS	Michael Thomas	8	88%
	Long (8-10)	PASS	Michael Thomas	6	100%
	XL (11+)	PASS	Mark Ingram	7	29%
3	Short (1-3)	PASS	Willie Snead	5	80%
	Med (4-7)	PASS	Willie Snead	7	86%
	Long (8-10)	PASS	Willie Snead	9	44%
	XL (11+)	PASS	Willie Snead	6	0%

**Minimum 5 plays to qualify*

2016 Snap Rates

Week	Opp	Score	Brandin Cooks	Michael Thomas	Willie Snead	Coby Fleener	Mark Ingram	Brandon Coleman	Josh Hill
1	OAK	L 35-34	62 (90%)	54 (78%)	52 (75%)	56 (81%)	29 (42%)	5 (7%)	13 (19%)
2	NYG	L 16-13	53 (85%)	37 (60%)	54 (87%)	48 (77%)	36 (58%)	21 (34%)	
3	ATL	L 45-32	78 (96%)	72 (89%)		63 (78%)	40 (49%)	69 (85%)	
4	SD	W 35-34	50 (68%)	56 (77%)	49 (67%)	47 (64%)	48 (66%)	17 (23%)	
6	CAR	W 41-38	56 (77%)	52 (71%)	51 (70%)	41 (56%)	39 (53%)	15 (21%)	46 (63%)
7	KC	L 27-21	67 (89%)	63 (84%)	63 (84%)	43 (57%)	38 (51%)	17 (23%)	42 (56%)
8	SEA	W 25-20	38 (50%)	61 (80%)	56 (74%)	26 (34%)	6 (8%)	28 (37%)	61 (80%)
9	SF	W 41-23	57 (66%)	72 (84%)	52 (60%)	29 (34%)	33 (38%)	24 (28%)	63 (73%)
10	DEN	L 25-23	38 (75%)	44 (86%)	30 (59%)	32 (63%)	22 (43%)	15 (29%)	26 (51%)
11	CAR	L 23-20	65 (86%)	60 (79%)	50 (66%)	42 (55%)	26 (34%)	13 (17%)	43 (57%)
12	LA	W 49-21	45 (61%)	50 (68%)	41 (55%)	18 (24%)	42 (57%)	27 (36%)	58 (78%)
13	DET	L 28-13	52 (84%)	53 (85%)	49 (79%)	41 (66%)	21 (34%)	7 (11%)	10 (16%)
14	TB	L 16-11	52 (85%)		48 (79%)	42 (69%)	18 (30%)	51 (84%)	
15	ARI	W 48-41	66 (77%)	70 (81%)	75 (87%)	53 (62%)	41 (48%)	15 (17%)	
16	TB	W 31-24	48 (68%)	58 (82%)	40 (56%)	30 (42%)	48 (68%)	7 (10%)	
17	ATL	L 38-32	55 (71%)	66 (86%)	37 (48%)	54 (70%)	45 (58%)	32 (42%)	
Grand Total			882 (77%)	868 (79%)	747 (70%)	665 (58%)	532 (46%)	363 (32%)	362 (55%)

Personnel Groupings

Personnel	Team %	NFL Avg	Succ. %
1-1 [3WR]	62%	60%	54%
1-2 [2WR]	12%	19%	49%
2-1 [2WR]	12%	7%	62%
1-0 [4WR]	4%	3%	51%
2-2 [1WR]	4%	3%	36%
2-0 [3WR]	3%	1%	64%

Grouping Tendencies

Personnel	Pass Rate	Pass Succ. %	Run Succ. %
1-1 [3WR]	68%	52%	57%
1-2 [2WR]	55%	52%	44%
2-1 [2WR]	54%	66%	58%
1-0 [4WR]	65%	57%	40%
2-2 [1WR]	28%	27%	39%
2-0 [3WR]	53%	74%	53%

Red Zone Targets (min 3)

Receiver	All	Inside 5	6-10	11-20
Michael Thomas	19	7	4	8
Coby Fleener	18	4	3	11
Willie Snead	12	4	4	4
Brandin Cooks	11	3	3	5
Mark Ingram	11	4		7
Travaris Cadet	10	3	5	2
Brandon Coleman	9	1	5	3
John Kuhn	6	2		4
Tim Hightower	6	2	2	2
Josh Hill	3		2	1

Red Zone Rushes (min 3)

Rusher	All	Inside 5	6-10	11-20
Mark Ingram	37	9	13	15
Tim Hightower	26	12	4	10
Drew Brees	9	2	3	4
John Kuhn	7	4		3
Brandin Cooks	3		1	2
Daniel Lasco	3	1		2

Early Down Target Rate

RB	TE	WR
26%	17%	57%
19%	*20% NFL AVG*	*61%*

Overall Target Success %

RB	TE	WR
52% #3	54% #15	60% #2

New Orleans Saints 2016 Passing Recap & 2017 Outlook

Drew Brees remains an NFL legend who likely won't be remembered as well as he should solely because of the lack of playoff success. This year, assuming Max Unger is healthy, could be extremely special for Brees. This offense truly is loaded, and while Cooks is gone, Ted Ginn can surely open things up in this offense with his speed on the fast track. Fleener can't possibly have a worse year than 2016, and with Thomas and Snead having another year to develop with Payton and Brees, it is unlikely this offense won't look even better than 2016. And last year's version was top 6 in virtually every key offensive metric. They also get to face a much easier schedule of defenses than they had last year, particularly for Brees, whose schedule difficulty drops from 3rd hardest down to 21st hardest. One look at the Directional Passer Rating Delivered table below and it is easy to see how dominant Brees was in two key areas: virtually anything short, as well as the deep middle of the field. On all short attempts, Brees' passer rating was bested only by Matt Ryan and Aaron Rodgers, and Brees posted the NFL's best passer rating to the deep middle. Look for even more passing yards to come in 2017 thanks to short Kamara receptions and deep Ginn targets.

Drew Brees Rating All Downs

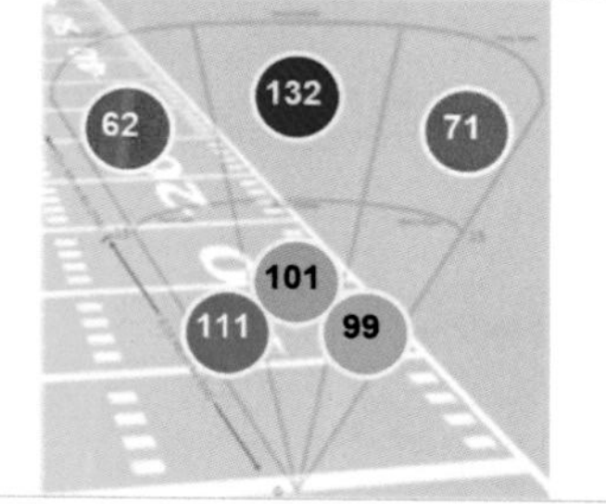

Drew Brees Rating Early Downs

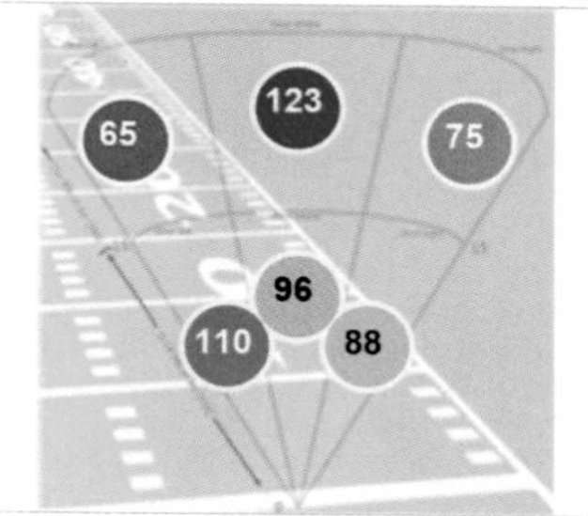

2016 Standard Passing Table

QB	Comp	Att	Comp %	Yds	YPA	TDs	INT	Sacks	Rating	Rk
Drew Brees	470	672	70%	5,208	7.8	37	15	27	101.7	9
NFL Avg			63%		7.2				90.4	

2016 Advanced Passing Table

QB	Success %	EDSR Passing Success %	20+ Yd Pass Gains	20+ Yd Pass %	30+ Yd Pass Gains	30+ Yd Pass %	Air Yds per Comp	YAC per Comp	20+ Air Yd Comp	20+ Air Yd %
Drew Brees	54%	56%	70	10%	26	4%	6.1	5.0	30	4%
NFL Avg	44%	48%	27	8%	10	3%	6.4	4.8	12	4%

Interception Rates by Down

Yards to Go	1	2	3	4	Total
1 & 2	0.0%	0.0%	7.7%	20.0%	6.3%
3, 4, 5	0.0%	0.0%	0.0%	0.0%	0.0%
6 - 9	11.1%	2.2%	2.0%		2.7%
10 - 14	2.4%	0.0%	2.6%		2.0%
15+	0.0%	0.0%	11.1%		2.5%
Total	2.5%	0.8%	2.9%	14.3%	2.1%

3rd Down Passing - Short of Sticks Analysis

QB	Avg Yds to Go	Air Yds (of Comps)	Avg Yds Short	Short of Sticks Rate	Rk
Drew Brees	6.4	5.7	-0.7	60%	25
NFL Avg	7.6	6.8	-0.8	57%	

Air Yds vs YAC

	Air Yds %	YAC %	Rk
Drew Brees	61%	39%	13
NFL Avg	54%	46%	

2016 Receiving Recap & 2017 Outlook

Michael Thomas is one of the most underrated receivers in the NFL, and will likely prove himself further this year now the shadow of Brandin Cooks has disappeared. In addition to being lethal on short passes, Thomas delivered a 67% success rate on deep passes, which was the best rate in the NFL last year. Ginn's speed will open even more up for Fleener and Snead, and RB passes to Kamara and Ingram should be even more effective in 2016 thanks to Ginn's on-field presence. Even with a bad season from Newton last year, Ginn's success rate, yards per attempt and total TDs were the best for any Panthers player.

Player **Min 50 Targets*	Targets	Comp %	YPA	Rating	TOARS	Success %	Success Rk	Missed YPA Rk	YAS % Rk	TDs
Michael Thomas	130	73%	9.0	111	5.4	67%	2	4	36	9
Brandin Cooks	117	67%	10.0	115	5.2	52%	56	38	8	8
Willie Snead	104	69%	8.6	96	4.9	61%	13	40	52	4
Coby Fleener	82	61%	7.7	82	4.3	56%	34	31	45	3
Mark Ingram	57	79%	5.6	113	4.1	54%	42	69	141	4
Travaris Cadet	54	74%	5.2	102	3.9	54%	48	24	144	4

Directional Passer Rating Delivered

Receiver	Short Left	Short Middle	Short Right	Deep Left	Deep Middle	Deep Right	Player Total
Michael Thomas	121	135	95	46	110	158	116
Brandin Cooks	114	121	106	75	144	82	115
Willie Snead	84	81	107	104	149	70	96
Coby Fleener	89	85	76	119	116	17	82
Mark Ingram	118	90	131	40			113
Travaris Cadet	127	94	103	119		0	102
Brandon Coleman	122	141	77	3	119	96	94
Tim Hightower	92	81	92			158	112
Josh Hill	135	56	95	119	40		107
John Kuhn	78	72	120				98
Team Total	111	102	102	70	132	80	105

2016 Rushing Recap & 2017 Outlook

I'm a big fan of Mark Ingram, but unfortunately Sean Payton apparently is not. However, that doesn't limit what Ingram does when inserted, but does govern his playing time and upside this season. Last year, Ingram received 37 red zone carries and was successful on 62% of them. Payton allowed Hightower to out-carry Ingram inside the 5, even though Hightower's success rate in the red zone (38%) was well worse than Ingram's, and inside the 5 Ingram bested him again, with a 67% success rate vs Hightower's 58% rate. Peterson will likely assume the Hightower role and could eat even more into Ingram's production so it will be messy attempting to predict roles until we see it play out more in the preseason.

Player **Min 50 Rushes*	Rushes	YPA	Success %	Success Rk	Missed YPA Rk	YTS % Rk	YAS % Rk	Early Down Success %	Early Down Success Rk	TDs
Mark Ingram	205	5.1	55%	10	11	55	14	55%	10	6
Tim Hightower	133	4.1	52%	17	3	23	39	51%	20	4

Yards per Carry by Direction

	LT	LG	C	RG	RT	
5.0	3.7	3.0	3.6	5.5	6.7	4.1

Directional Run Frequency

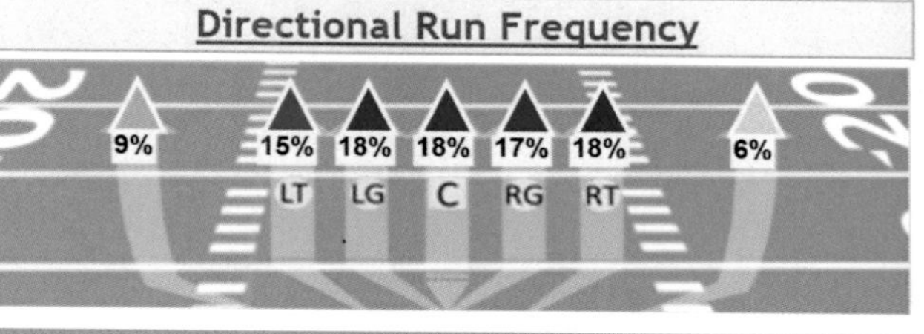

consists of two players. Julio Jones and Michael Thomas. Sean Payton built a large percentage of the Saints offense around Thomas. He led the team in targets, and saw sustained usage regardless of the scoreboard.

The Saints intelligently targeted their RBs in the passing game the 2nd most often of any team last year. Their success rate when targeting RBs was 3rd best. And they delivered the 2nd best success rate in the NFL when targeting WRs. But their rank dipped when Brees targeted his TEs. Coby Fleener was a massive disappointment in 2016. Brees had season lows in completion rate, TD:INT ratio and passer rating when targeting Fleener. All of those numbers were slightly better when targeting the backup Josh Hill, but Hill was targeted just 21 times and recorded only a 43% success rate, one which was worse than even Fleener's. The team needs significant improvement from Fleener, especially in the red zone, where Fleener's success rate was at least 14% worse than any other receiver with at least 10 targets. If the Saints want to improve their success to Fleener, they could try using more 12 personnel. Considering Fleener's overall success rate was 56% and passer rating delivered was 82, he was able to deliver a 67% success rate and a 123 rating when targeted out of 12 personnel. When the sole TE on the field in 11 personnel, Fleener delivered just a 56% success rate and a 77 rating.

On the ground, the Saints are more productive than many think, including Sean Payton. While so much talk surrounds Mark Ingram being in the dog house, getting benched, and having to earn his role, Ingram took the NFL by storm last year. His 55% success ranked him 10th out of 68 RB with at least 50 rushes. He also ranked 14th in YAS % (Yards Above Successful), which was indicative of his ability to break away for larger gains. The Saints added Adrian Peterson to the mix and time will tell as to whether this will become a true time share of if one of these two workhorses would emerge with a majority share of the carries. They operate much more from under center (46%) than average (37%) which will help Peterson, who has struggled in his career running from shotgun. The Saints absolutely must run the ball more often in 2nd and short, regardless of the back in the game: they pass it in these situations 9th most of any team, yet are successful on just 40% of those passes. Yet when they run the ball, 87% of those rushes are successful, well above the 71% average. Incorporating newly drafted RB Alvin Kamara should be easy, particularly in passing situations, as he should see a ton of success given the Saints are playing the 2nd easiest schedule of RB pass defenses this year.

They must get C Max Unger back at 100% before the season starts to maximize their potential this year. But even with Brees taking the team friendly contract and freeing up cap space, I struggle to see how the team overcomes the defense enough to land home field, and without it, even a playoff trip may end quickly.

Division History: Season Wins & 2017 Projection

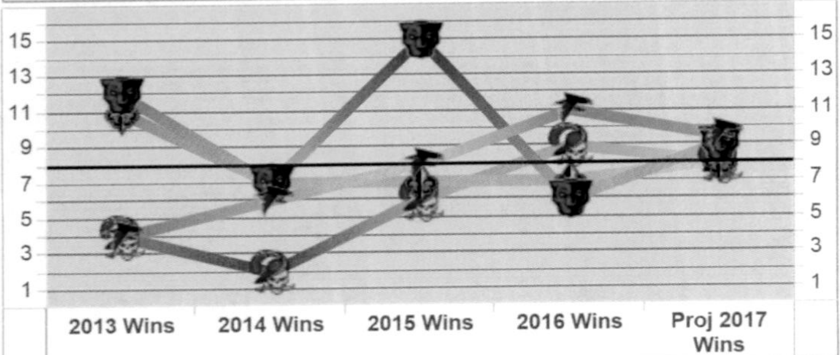

Rank of 2017 Defensive Pass Efficiency Faced by Week

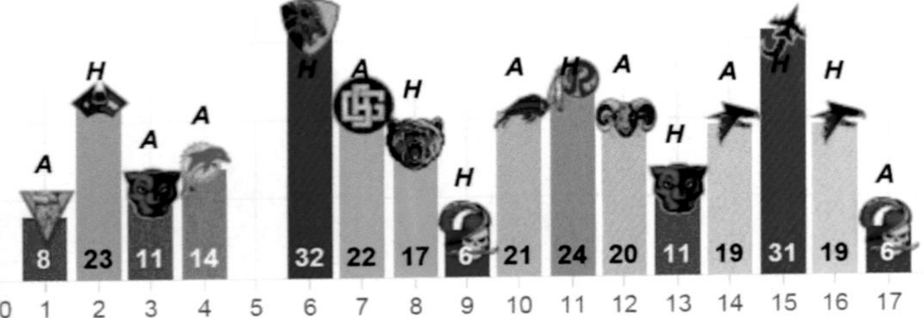

Rank of 2017 Defensive Rush Efficiency Faced by Week

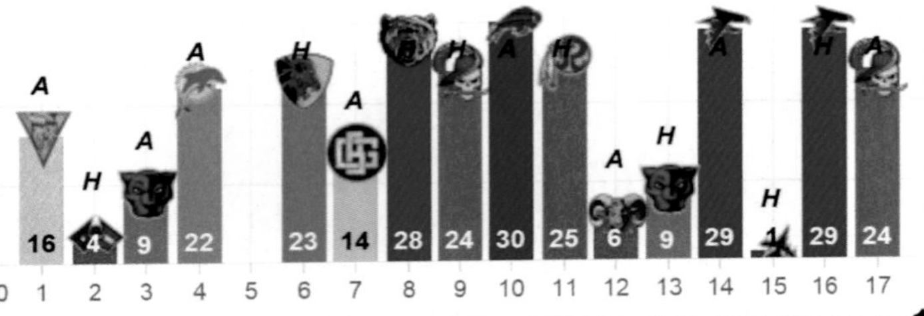

2016 Situational Usage by Player & Position

Usage Rate by Score

		Being Blown Out (14+)	Down Big (9-13)	One Score	Large Lead (9-13)	Blowout Lead (14+)	Grand Total
RUSH	Mark Ingram	21%	13%	21%	12%	28%	20%
	Tim Hightower	6%	10%	13%	21%	18%	13%
	Brandin Cooks	1%	1%	0%	3%	1%	1%
	Coby Fleener			0%			0%
	Travaris Cadet			1%			0%
	John Kuhn	3%	2%	2%	3%	1%	2%
	Daniel Lasco		2%	1%		3%	1%
	Tommylee Lewis		1%	0%		1%	0%
	Total	31%	28%	38%	38%	54%	36%
PASS	Mark Ingram	6%	9%	5%	6%	1%	5%
	Tim Hightower	3%	3%	2%	6%	3%	2%
	Brandin Cooks	11%	10%	12%	9%	4%	11%
	Michael Thomas	16%	15%	10%	18%	13%	12%
	Willie Snead	8%	9%	11%	6%	6%	10%
	Coby Fleener	12%	7%	8%	12%		8%
	Travaris Cadet	6%	8%	5%	3%	1%	5%
	Brandon Coleman	4%	4%	4%		1%	4%
	John Kuhn		1%	3%		1%	2%
	Josh Hill	1%	3%	2%	3%	6%	2%
	Daniel Lasco			0%		3%	0%
	Tommylee Lewis	1%	1%	1%		4%	1%
	John Phillips		1%	1%			1%
	Marcus Murphy	1%					0%
	Total	69%	72%	62%	62%	46%	64%

Positional Target Distribution vs NFL Average

		NFL Wide				Team Only			
		Left	Middle	Right	**Total**	Left	Middle	Right	**Total**
Deep	WR	997	566	975	**2,538**	34	15	26	**75**
	TE	152	136	155	**443**	6	11	8	**25**
	RB	23	4	36	**63**	2		4	**6**
	All	**1,172**	**706**	**1,166**	**3,044**	**42**	**26**	**38**	**106**
Short	WR	2,952	1,716	3,077	**7,745**	141	55	109	**305**
	TE	807	858	1,119	**2,784**	29	17	32	**78**
	RB	950	594	1,055	**2,599**	65	28	58	**151**
	All	**4,709**	**3,168**	**5,251**	**13,128**	**235**	**100**	**199**	**534**
Total		**5,881**	**3,874**	**6,417**	**16,172**	**277**	**126**	**237**	**640**

Positional Success Rates vs NFL Average

		NFL Wide				Team Only			
		Left	Middle	Right	**Total**	Left	Middle	Right	**Total**
Deep	WR	37%	50%	38%	**40%**	38%	67%	58%	**51%**
	TE	43%	49%	44%	**45%**	83%	64%	25%	**56%**
	RB	30%	75%	25%	**30%**	50%		25%	**33%**
	All	**38%**	**50%**	**38%**	**41%**	**45%**	**65%**	**47%**	**51%**
Short	WR	52%	57%	51%	**52%**	62%	62%	63%	**62%**
	TE	50%	62%	52%	**54%**	52%	53%	53%	**53%**
	RB	47%	49%	43%	**46%**	52%	64%	50%	**54%**
	All	**50%**	**57%**	**50%**	**52%**	**58%**	**61%**	**58%**	**58%**
Total		**48%**	**55%**	**48%**	**49%**	**56%**	**62%**	**56%**	**57%**

New York Giants

2017 Coaches

Head Coach:
Ben McAdoo (2nd yr)
Offensive Coordinator:
Mike Sullivan (2nd yr)
Defensive Coordinator:
Steve Spagnuolo (3rd yr)

2017 Forecast

Wins	Div Rank
8.5	#2

Past Records

2016: 11-5
2015: 6-10
2014: 6-10

EASY HARD

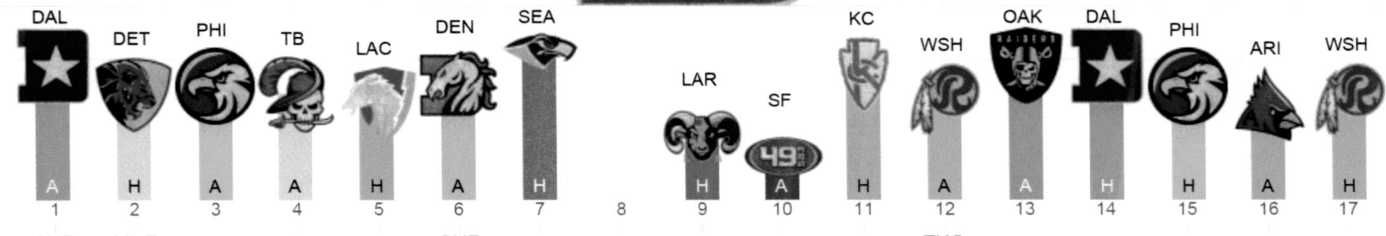

Key Players Lost

TXN	Player (POS)
Cut	Cruz, Victor WR
	Holmes, Khaled C
	Jennings, Rashad RB
	Johnson, Will RB
	Moore, Rahim S
Declared Free Agent	Beatty, Will T
	Darkwa, Orleans RB
	Donnell, Larry TE
	Hall, Leon CB
	Hankins, Johnathan DT
	Herzlich, Mark LB
	Jerry, John G
	Johnson, Josh QB
	Newhouse, Marshall T
	Rainey, Bobby RB
	Robinson, Keenan LB
	Sensabaugh, Coty CB
	Sheppard, Kelvin LB
	Whitlock, Nikita RB

Average Line	# Games Favored	# Games Underdog
-0.7	6	8

2017 New York Giants Overview

With the edges the offenses have in today's game, it's pretty bad when the best thing you can say about an offense is the quarterback released the ball quickly so he didn't take many sacks. Ordinarily you wouldn't expect such a team to make the playoffs. The Giants were able to still make the postseason thanks to two key elements: a ridiculously strong defensive turnaround and an unbelievable record in close games.

Their defensive turnaround was thanks to an infusion of new personnel via free agency and the draft. Starters Damon Harrison, Oliver Vernon, Janoris Jenkins and Eli Apple were all added in free agency. Jason Pierre-Paul, who missed the start of the 2015 season thanks to a fireworks accident and played shorthanded in the second half of the season, was at full strength to start 2017. According to Pro Football Focus, those 5 players earned the following grades last year: 85.8, 85.4, 88.4, 55.9 and 86.2. The influence of such players made a measurable difference for the defense, which actually played the 4th most difficult schedule of opposing offenses last year.

And it was the defense which allowed the Giants to post a 4-1 record in field goal games and a 8-3 record in one-score games. When the game was within one score, the Giants defense held opposing offenses to a 33% success rate, which was the 2nd best in the NFL, and well below the NFL average of 44%. The offense, on the other hand, recorded just a 43% success rate, 19th best in the NFL. In these situations (one-score game in the 4th quarter) Eli Manning posted a miserable 69.5 rating, with 5 TDs and a massive 8 interceptions. Only one other quarterback threw more than half (4) the interceptions that Eli threw (8), and it is almost unforgivable to throw interceptions in the 4th quarter of a one-score game. The run offense was clearly no help last season, and it didn't show up late in one score games either. Whether the goal was to run out the clock or run the ball to get into scoring position to overcome a deficit in a close game, the Giants were terrible. Only 35% of their rushes were successful, which was 4th worst in the NFL and they averaged just 3.3 yards per carry.

Pivoting to the offense in general, it was and is in sore need of a lot of improvement. First and foremost, the offense ran 11 personnel (1 running back,

(cont'd - see NYG2)

Key Free Agents/ Trades Added

Blake, Valentino CB
Edwards, SaQwan CB
Ellison, Rhett TE
Fluker, D.J. G
Holmes, Khaled C
Ihenacho, Duke S
Lane, Jerome WR
Marshall, Brandon WR
Moore, Rahim S
Taylor, Devin DE

Drafted Players

Rd	Pk	Player (College)
1	23	TE - Evan Engram (Ole Miss)
2	55	DT - Dalvin Tomlinson (Alabama)
3	87	QB - Davis Webb (California)
4	140	RB - Wayne Gallman (Clemson)
5	167	DE - Avery Moss (Youngstown State)
6	200	G - Adam Bisnowaty (Pittsburgh)

Regular Season Wins: Past & Current Proj

	Wins
Proj 2017 Wins	8.5
2016 Wins	11
Proj 2016 Wins	8
2015 Wins	6
2014 Wins	6
2013 Wins	7

1 3 5 7 9 11 13 15

2017 Lineup & Cap Hits

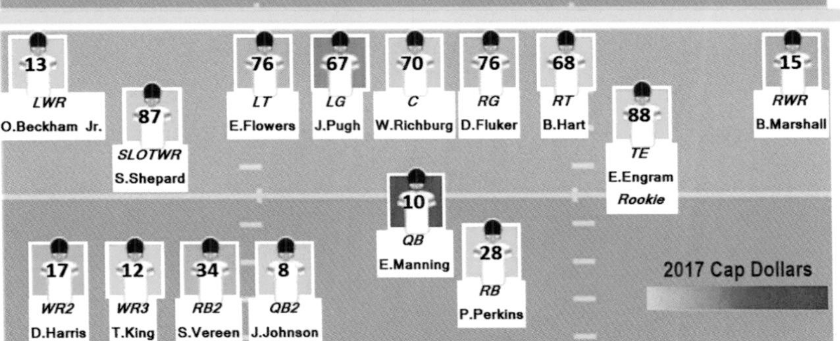

2017 Unit Spending

Positional Spending

	Rank	Total	2016 Rk
All OFF	23	$75.93M	17
QB	9	$22.46M	2
OL	27	$23.51M	31
RB	14	$8.52M	6
WR	19	$16.61M	17
TE	29	$4.84M	30
All DEF	3	$95.75M	9
DL	3	$43.80M	4
LB	21	$15.43M	25
CB	1	$30.07M	4
S	27	$6.45M	30

New York Giants 2016 Success Rate Radar

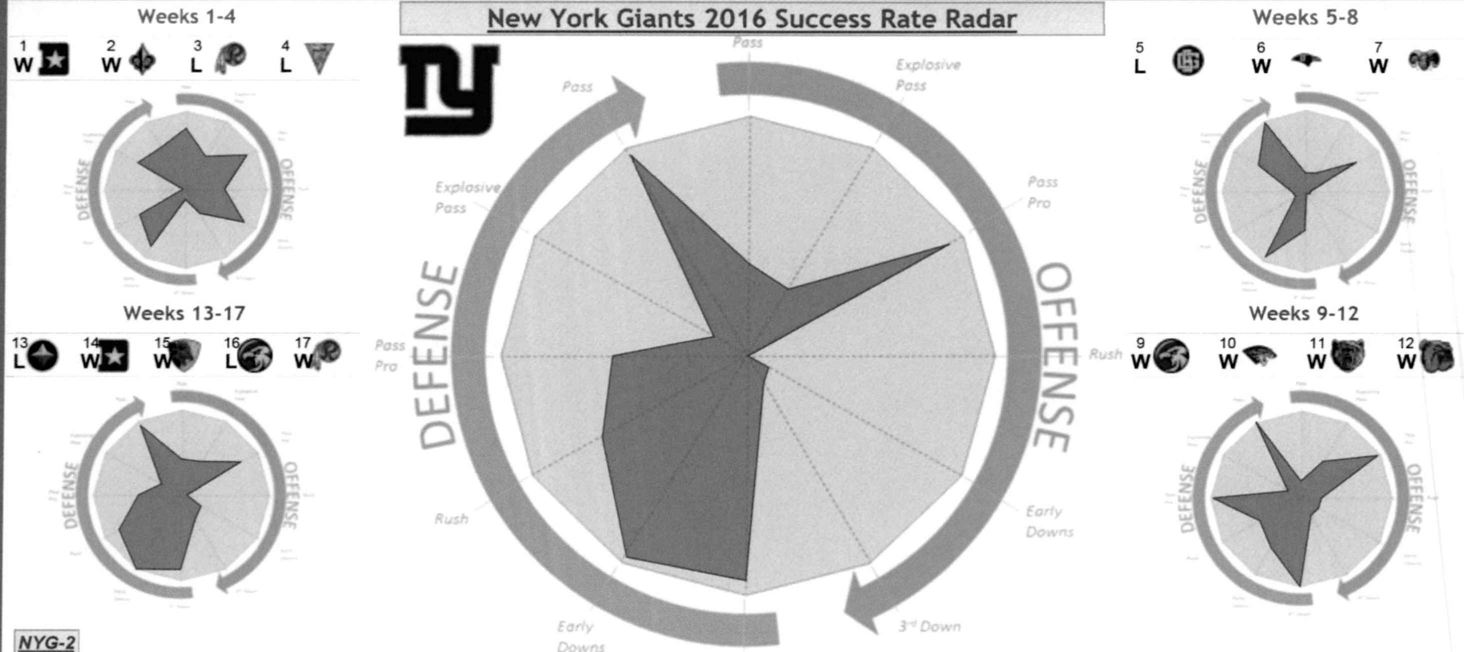

NYG-2

1 tight end and 3 wide receivers) 92% of the time, the most of any team in the NFL. Ordinarily you would think that if a team was having a ton of success, they could get carried away and go to it a lot. But in the Giants case, in 11 personnel their passes were only successful 39% of the time. The NFL average was a 45% success rate in 11 personnel, which teams use on an average of 60% of offensive snaps. The Giants second most used grouping, 12 personnel, saw a big increase to a 53% success rate for passes, well above the NFL average of 48%. Yet the Giants went to 12 personnel only 5% of the time, even though they improved from a 39% success rate on passes to a 53% success rate.

The problem wasn't just with their personnel grouping usage, it was that the Giants simply were not explosive in their passing game nor could they run the ball effectively. Relying on efficient, short passes absent those other two factors won't allow you to consistently make trips to the red zone. Only 40 of the Giants drives made it into the opponent's red zone, which was the 3rd fewest in the NFL. Exploring the deep passing game issues, we find that Eli Manning simply wasn't getting it done. Manning posted a 56 rating on the 100 passes he attempted more than 15 yards in the air. The handful of QBs below that 56 rating included Joe Flacco, Blake Bortles and Brock Osweiler. As Eli's passing cones show, he was well below average to all sides of the field when throwing deep, particularly to the deep left.

Specifically to his #1 receiver, Eli had very little chemistry when throwing deep. Targeting Odell Beckham Jr. over 15 yards downfield resulted in 14/44, 1 TD, 1 INT and a 65.7 rating. That is completely dwarfed by what this connection did within 15 yards of the line of scrimmage, where Eli hit Beckham Jr on 67% of his targets, 9 TDs, 1 INT and a 107 rating. The only way for the Giants to be explosive was to hit Beckham Jr on these short slants and let him use his speed and elusiveness to take that the distance or deliver a huge chunk play. But when a team has one route (literally and figuratively) to recording an explosive gain in the passing game,

(cont'd - see NYG-3)

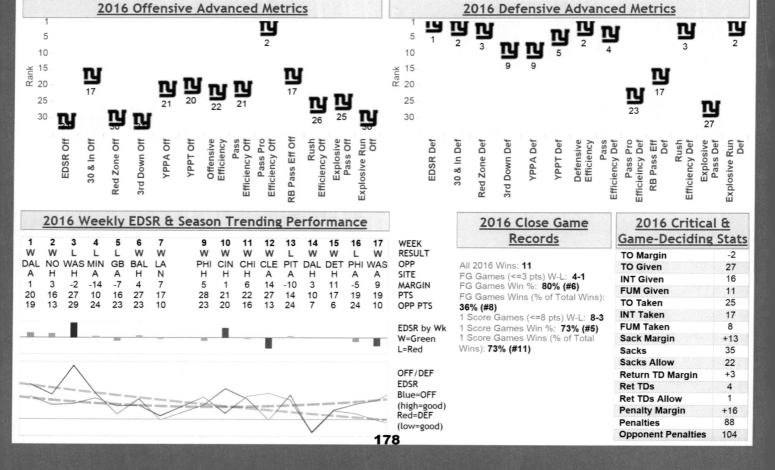

2016 Offensive Advanced Metrics

Metric	Rank
EDSR Off	[illegible]
30 & In Off	17
Red Zone Off	30
3rd Down Off	[illegible]
YPPA Off	21
YPPT Off	20
Offensive Efficiency	22
Pass Efficiency Off	21
Pass Pro Efficiency Off	2
RB Pass Eff Off	17
Rush Efficiency Off	26
Explosive Pass Off	25
Explosive Run Off	30

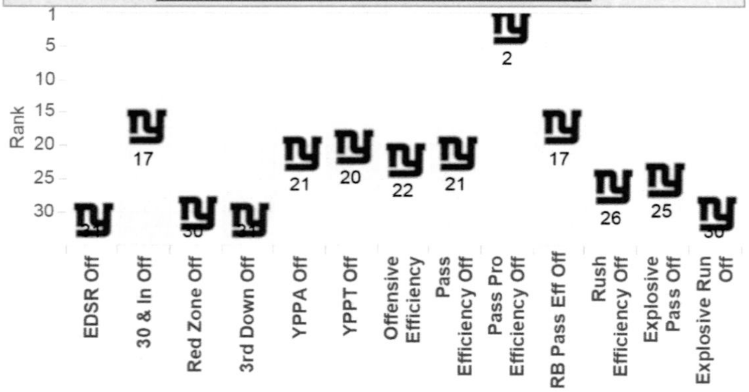

2016 Defensive Advanced Metrics

Metric	Rank
EDSR Def	1
30 & In Def	2
Red Zone Def	3
3rd Down Def	9
YPPA Def	9
YPPT Def	5
Defensive Efficiency	2
Pass Efficiency Def	4
Pass Pro Efficiency Def	23
RB Pass Eff Def	17
Rush Efficiency Def	3
Explosive Pass Def	27
Explosive Run Def	2

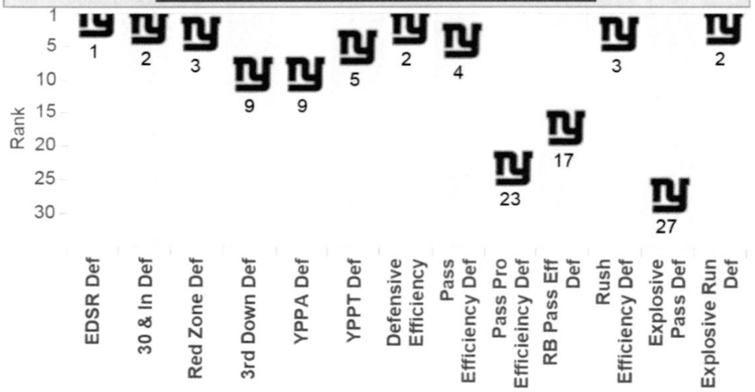

2016 Weekly EDSR & Season Trending Performance

WEEK	1	2	3	4	5	6	7	9	10	11	12	13	14	15	16	17
RESULT	W	W	L	L	L	W	W	W	W	W	W	L	W	W	L	W
OPP	DAL	NO	WAS	MIN	GB	BAL	LA	PHI	CIN	CHI	CLE	PIT	DAL	DET	PHI	WAS
SITE	A	H	H	A	A	H	N	H	H	H	A	A	H	H	A	A
MARGIN	1	3	-2	-14	-7	4	7	5	1	6	14	-10	3	11	-5	9
PTS	20	16	27	10	16	27	17	28	21	22	27	14	10	17	19	19
OPP PTS	19	13	29	24	23	23	10	23	20	16	13	24	7	6	24	10

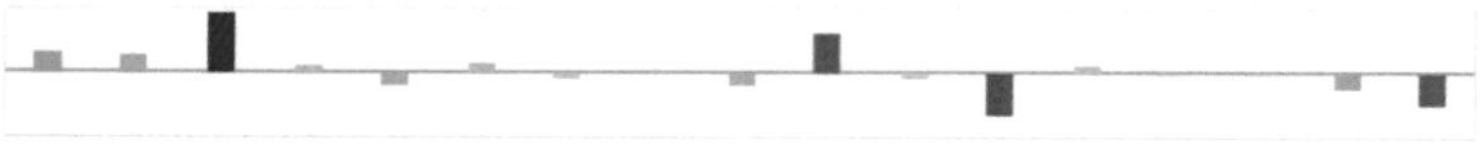

EDSR by Wk
W=Green
L=Red

OFF/DEF
EDSR
Blue=OFF
(high=good)
Red=DEF
(low=good)

2016 Close Game Records

All 2016 Wins: **11**
FG Games (<=3 pts) W-L: **4-1**
FG Games Win %: **80% (#6)**
FG Games Wins (% of Total Wins): **36% (#8)**
1 Score Games (<=8 pts) W-L: **8-3**
1 Score Games Win %: **73% (#5)**
1 Score Games Wins (% of Total Wins): **73% (#11)**

2016 Critical & Game-Deciding Stats

TO Margin	-2
TO Given	27
INT Given	16
FUM Given	11
TO Taken	25
INT Taken	17
FUM Taken	8
Sack Margin	+13
Sacks	35
Sacks Allow	22
Return TD Margin	+3
Ret TDs	4
Ret TDs Allow	1
Penalty Margin	+16
Penalties	88
Opponent Penalties	104

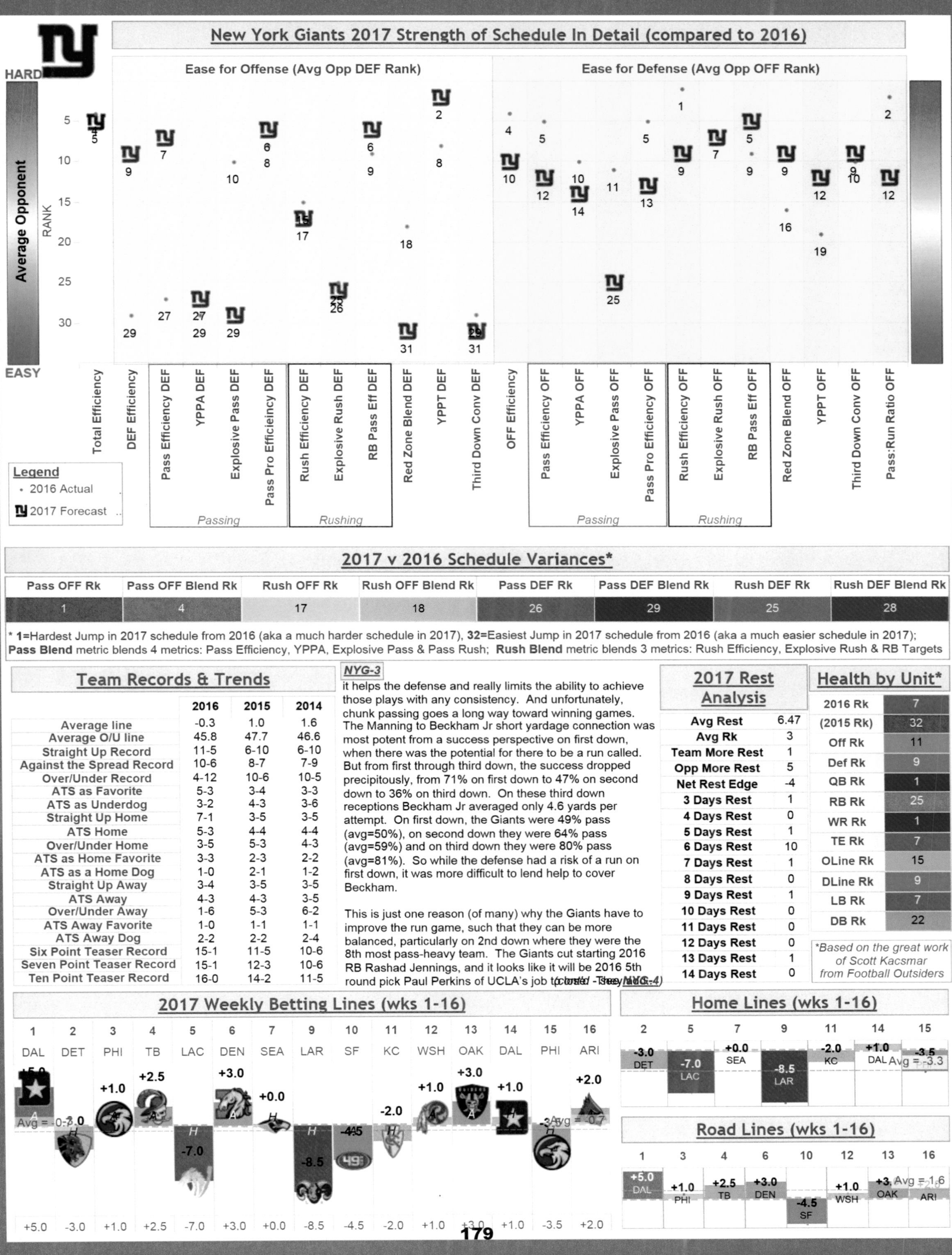

New York Giants 2017 Strength of Schedule In Detail (compared to 2016)

2017 v 2016 Schedule Variances*

Pass OFF Rk	Pass OFF Blend Rk	Rush OFF Rk	Rush OFF Blend Rk	Pass DEF Rk	Pass DEF Blend Rk	Rush DEF Rk	Rush DEF Blend Rk
1	4	17	18	26	29	25	28

* **1**=Hardest Jump in 2017 schedule from 2016 (aka a much harder schedule in 2017), **32**=Easiest Jump in 2017 schedule from 2016 (aka a much easier schedule in 2017); **Pass Blend** metric blends 4 metrics: Pass Efficiency, YPPA, Explosive Pass & Pass Rush; **Rush Blend** metric blends 3 metrics: Rush Efficiency, Explosive Rush & RB Targets

Team Records & Trends

	2016	2015	2014
Average line	-0.3	1.0	1.6
Average O/U line	45.8	47.7	46.6
Straight Up Record	11-5	6-10	6-10
Against the Spread Record	10-6	8-7	7-9
Over/Under Record	4-12	10-6	10-5
ATS as Favorite	5-3	3-4	3-3
ATS as Underdog	3-2	4-3	3-6
Straight Up Home	7-1	3-5	3-5
ATS Home	5-3	4-4	4-4
Over/Under Home	3-5	5-3	4-3
ATS as Home Favorite	3-3	2-3	2-2
ATS as a Home Dog	1-0	2-1	1-2
Straight Up Away	3-4	3-5	3-5
ATS Away	4-3	4-3	3-5
Over/Under Away	1-6	5-3	6-2
ATS Away Favorite	1-0	1-1	1-1
ATS Away Dog	2-2	2-2	2-4
Six Point Teaser Record	15-1	11-5	10-6
Seven Point Teaser Record	15-1	12-3	10-6
Ten Point Teaser Record	16-0	14-2	11-5

NYG-3

it helps the defense and really limits the ability to achieve those plays with any consistency. And unfortunately, chunk passing goes a long way toward winning games. The Manning to Beckham Jr short yardage connection was most potent from a success perspective on first down, when there was the potential for there to be a run called. But from first through third down, the success dropped precipitously, from 71% on first down to 47% on second down to 36% on third down. On these third down receptions Beckham Jr averaged only 4.6 yards per attempt. On first down, the Giants were 49% pass (avg=50%), on second down they were 64% pass (avg=59%) and on third down they were 80% pass (avg=81%). So while the defense had a risk of a run on first down, it was more difficult to lend help to cover Beckham.

This is just one reason (of many) why the Giants have to improve the run game, such that they can be more balanced, particularly on 2nd down where they were the 8th most pass-heavy team. The Giants cut starting 2016 RB Rashad Jennings, and it looks like it will be 2016 5th round pick Paul Perkins of UCLA's job to lose. (cont'd - see NYG-4)

2017 Rest Analysis

Avg Rest	6.47
Avg Rk	3
Team More Rest	1
Opp More Rest	5
Net Rest Edge	-4
3 Days Rest	1
4 Days Rest	0
5 Days Rest	1
6 Days Rest	10
7 Days Rest	1
8 Days Rest	0
9 Days Rest	1
10 Days Rest	0
11 Days Rest	0
12 Days Rest	0
13 Days Rest	1
14 Days Rest	0

Health by Unit*

2016 Rk	7
(2015 Rk)	32
Off Rk	11
Def Rk	9
QB Rk	1
RB Rk	25
WR Rk	1
TE Rk	7
OLine Rk	15
DLine Rk	9
LB Rk	7
DB Rk	22

**Based on the great work of Scott Kacsmar from Football Outsiders*

2017 Weekly Betting Lines (wks 1-16)

1	2	3	4	5	6	7	9	10	11	12	13	14	15	16
DAL	DET	PHI	TB	LAC	DEN	SEA	LAR	SF	KC	WSH	OAK	DAL	PHI	ARI
A	H	A	A	H	A	H	H	A	H	A	A	H	H	A
+5.0	-3.0	+1.0	+2.5	-7.0	+3.0	+0.0	-8.5	-4.5	-2.0	+1.0	+3.0	+1.0	-3.5	+2.0

Avg = -0.7

Home Lines (wks 1-16)

2	5	7	9	11	14	15
DET	LAC	SEA	LAR	KC	DAL	PHI
-3.0	-7.0	+0.0	-8.5	-2.0	+1.0	-3.5

Avg = -3.3

Road Lines (wks 1-16)

1	3	4	6	10	12	13	16
DAL	PHI	TB	DEN	SF	WSH	OAK	ARI
+5.0	+1.0	+2.5	+3.0	-4.5	+1.0	+3.0	+2.0

Avg = 1.6

New York Giants 2016 Play Analysis

2016 Play Tendencies

All Pass %	62%
All Pass Rk	5
All Rush %	38%
All Rush Rk	28
1 Score Pass %	57%
1 Score Pass Rk	19
2015 1 Score Pass %	61%
2015 1 Score Pass Rk	9
Pass Increase %	-4%
Pass Increase Rk	26
1 Score Rush %	43%
1 Score Rush Rk	14
Up Pass %	53%
Up Pass Rk	27
Up Rush %	47%
Up Rush Rk	6
Down Pass %	68%
Down Pass Rk	3
Down Rush %	32%
Down Rush Rk	30

2016 Down & Distance Tendencies

Down	Distance	Total Plays	Pass Rate	Run Rate	Play Success %
1	Short (1-3)	5	0%	100%	80%
	Med (4-7)	4	50%	50%	75%
	Long (8-10)	315	49%	51%	44%
	XL (11+)	14	43%	57%	21%
2	Short (1-3)	27	48%	52%	56%
	Med (4-7)	84	61%	39%	56%
	Long (8-10)	104	72%	28%	47%
	XL (11+)	44	77%	23%	18%
3	Short (1-3)	48	60%	40%	56%
	Med (4-7)	59	90%	10%	39%
	Long (8-10)	33	97%	3%	24%
	XL (11+)	29	79%	21%	7%
4	Short (1-3)	10	100%	0%	50%
	Med (4-7)	1	100%	0%	100%

Shotgun %:

Under Center	Shotgun
27%	73%
37%	*63%*

AVG

Run Rate:

Under Center	Shotgun
73%	25%
68%	*23%*

AVG

Pass Rate:

Under Center	Shotgun
27%	75%
32%	*77%*

AVG

Short Yardage Intelligence:

2nd and Short Run

Run Freq	Run % Rk	NFL Run Freq Avg	Run 1D Rate	Run NFL 1D Avg
65%	16	65%	80%	71%

2nd and Short Pass

Pass Freq	Pass % Rk	NFL Pass Freq Avg	Pass 1D Rate	Pass NFL 1D Avg
35%	15	35%	75%	52%

Most Frequent Play

Down	Distance	Play Type	Player	Total Plays	Play Success %
1	Short (1-3)	RUSH	Rashad Jennings	3	67%
	Long (8-10)	RUSH	Rashad Jennings	78	33%
	XL (11+)	RUSH	Rashad Jennings	3	0%
			Orleans Darkwa	3	0%
2	Short (1-3)	RUSH	Rashad Jennings	6	67%
	Med (4-7)	RUSH	Rashad Jennings	19	63%
	Long (8-10)	PASS	Odell Beckham Jr.	15	53%
	XL (11+)	PASS	Odell Beckham Jr.	9	22%
3	Short (1-3)	PASS	Sterling Shepard	10	80%
	Med (4-7)	PASS	Odell Beckham Jr.	16	50%
	Long (8-10)	PASS	Odell Beckham Jr.	10	10%
	XL (11+)	PASS	Odell Beckham Jr.	6	17%

Most Successful Play*

Down	Distance	Play Type	Player	Total Plays	Play Success %
1	Long (8-10)	PASS	Jerell Adams	7	86%
2	Short (1-3)	RUSH	Paul Perkins	5	80%
	Med (4-7)	PASS	Will Tye	7	86%
	Long (8-10)	PASS	Will Tye	9	67%
	XL (11+)	PASS	Will Tye	5	60%
3	Short (1-3)	PASS	Sterling Shepard	10	80%
	Med (4-7)	PASS	Odell Beckham Jr.	16	50%
	Long (8-10)	PASS	Sterling Shepard	8	25%
	XL (11+)	PASS	Odell Beckham Jr.	6	17%

**Minimum 5 plays to qualify*

2016 Snap Rates

Week	Opp	Score	Sterling Shepard	Odell Beckham Jr.	Victor Cruz	Will Tye	Rashad Jennings	Paul Perkins
1	DAL	W 20-19	53 (95%)	56 (100%)	50 (89%)	25 (45%)	31 (55%)	
2	NO	W 16-13	75 (95%)	78 (99%)	74 (94%)	41 (52%)	34 (43%)	
3	WAS	L 29-27	66 (99%)	67 (100%)	66 (99%)	26 (39%)		
4	MIN	L 24-10	60 (91%)	66 (100%)	66 (100%)	52 (79%)		15 (23%)
5	GB	L 23-16	56 (100%)	56 (100%)	56 (100%)	37 (66%)		14 (25%)
6	BAL	W 27-23	64 (96%)	54 (81%)	67 (100%)	23 (34%)	32 (48%)	9 (13%)
7	LA	W 17-10	53 (95%)	54 (96%)	41 (73%)	25 (45%)	28 (50%)	15 (27%)
9	PHI	W 28-23	59 (92%)	62 (97%)	15 (23%)	46 (72%)	37 (58%)	22 (34%)
10	CIN	W 21-20	70 (93%)	75 (100%)		62 (83%)	45 (60%)	30 (40%)
11	CHI	W 22-16	63 (94%)	67 (100%)	60 (90%)	52 (78%)	47 (70%)	20 (30%)
12	CLE	W 27-13	51 (91%)	44 (79%)	42 (75%)	49 (88%)	28 (50%)	22 (39%)
13	PIT	L 24-14	60 (100%)	59 (98%)	26 (43%)	47 (78%)	30 (50%)	22 (37%)
14	DAL	W 10-7	61 (91%)	67 (100%)	49 (73%)	51 (76%)	36 (54%)	25 (37%)
15	DET	W 17-6	61 (95%)	60 (94%)	41 (64%)	42 (66%)	25 (39%)	25 (39%)
16	PHI	L 24-19	88 (99%)	85 (96%)	53 (60%)	60 (67%)	41 (46%)	34 (38%)
17	WAS	W 19-10	62 (86%)	48 (67%)	61 (85%)	47 (65%)	28 (39%)	36 (50%)
Grand Total			1,002 (94%)	998 (94%)	767 (78%)	685 (64%)	442 (51%)	289 (33%)

Personnel Groupings

Personnel	Team %	NFL Avg	Succ. %
1-1 [3WR]	92%	60%	43%
1-2 [2WR]	5%	19%	36%
1-0 [4WR]	2%	3%	36%

Grouping Tendencies

Personnel	Pass Rate	Pass Succ. %	Run Succ. %
1-1 [3WR]	64%	39%	37%
1-2 [2WR]	29%	53%	26%
1-0 [4WR]	52%	27%	21%

Red Zone Targets (min 3)

Receiver	All	Inside 5	6-10	11-20
Odell Beckham Jr.	24	7	4	13
Sterling Shepard	17	3	5	9
Victor Cruz	8	2		6
Will Tye	8	1	3	4
Rashad Jennings	4			4
Larry Donnell	3	1	1	1
Shane Vereen	3			3

Red Zone Rushes (min 3)

Rusher	All	Inside 5	6-10	11-20
Rashad Jennings	16	7	3	6
Paul Perkins	9	1	1	7
Shane Vereen	7	3	2	2
Eli Manning	5	4		1
Orleans Darkwa	5	3		2

Early Down Target Rate

RB	TE	WR
21%	20%	58%
19%	*20% NFL AVG*	*61%*

Overall Target Success %

RB	TE	WR
37% #31	52% #18	47% #22

New York Giants 2016 Passing Recap & 2017 Outlook

One of two things, or both, must happen for Eli Manning and the Giants passing offense to get back to a more efficient, productive and contributing asset to this team: either better pass protection or a better run game. I could get more restrictive and ask for a more efficient use of personnel packages and play calling, but that could be reaching. If the Giants can get better protection and Eli can hold onto the ball to let deeper routes develop, it will be a big aide. Eli's explosive pass rates are about the NFL average, but his deep air yardage rate and his air yardage per completion are both below average. This signifies a team designing shorter passes to make equivalent chunk gains in lieu of deeper passes. While this seems like it could be lower risk and higher reward, such gains typically come as a result of poor coverage and/or broken tackles. They are not as reliable or repeatable as simply executing a deep pass completion when given proper quarterback protection. Manning struggled particularly to his deep left, and he also must figure out a way to eliminate interceptions on short yardage passes. This speaks somewhat to the inefficiency of the run game, but when 5% of 3rd and 1-5 yard plays are interceptions, it needs work.

Eli Manning Rating All Downs

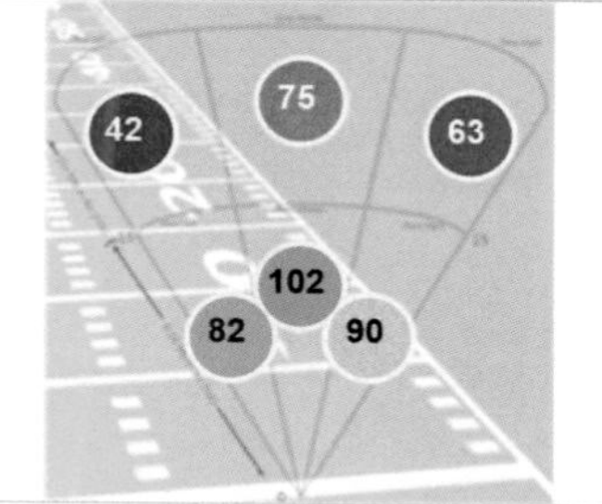

Eli Manning Rating Early Downs

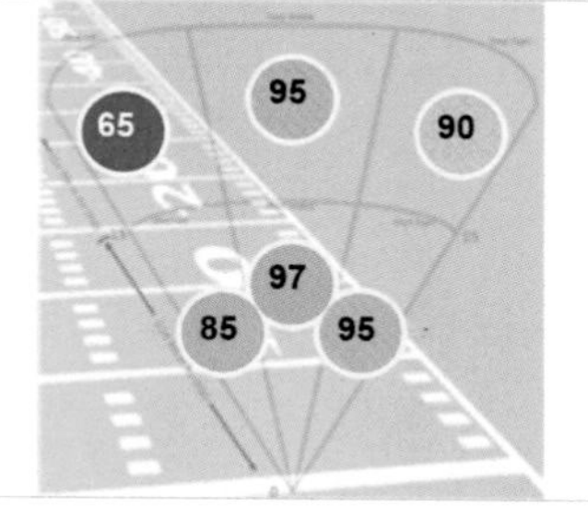

2016 Standard Passing Table

QB	Comp	Att	Comp %	Yds	YPA	TDs	INT	Sacks	Rating	Rk
Eli Manning	400	643	62%	4,319	6.7	27	17	22	84.9	30
NFL Avg			63%		7.2				90.4	

2016 Advanced Passing Table

QB	Success %	EDSR Passing Success %	20+ Yd Pass Gains	20+ Yd Pass %	30+ Yd Pass Gains	30+ Yd Pass %	Air Yds per Comp	YAC per Comp	20+ Air Yd Comp	20+ Air Yd %
Eli Manning	45%	49%	51	8%	23	4%	5.6	5.3	22	3%
NFL Avg	44%	48%	27	8%	10	3%	6.4	4.8	12	4%

Interception Rates by Down

Yards to Go	1	2	3	4	Total
1 & 2	0.0%	0.0%	5.3%	0.0%	2.9%
3, 4, 5	0.0%	2.9%	4.9%	0.0%	3.7%
6 - 9	0.0%	3.1%	1.6%	0.0%	2.4%
10 - 14	1.8%	2.8%	3.1%	100.0%	2.5%
15+	0.0%	0.0%	0.0%		0.0%
Total	1.7%	2.6%	3.2%	5.0%	2.6%

3rd Down Passing - Short of Sticks Analysis

QB	Avg Yds to Go	Air Yds (of Comps)	Avg Yds Short	Short of Sticks Rate	Rk
Eli Manning	6.8	7.7	0.0	52%	10
NFL Avg	7.6	6.8	-0.8	57%	

Air Yds vs YAC

Air Yds %	YAC %	Rk
55%	45%	25
54%	46%	

2016 Receiving Recap & 2017 Outlook

With Brandon Marshall in the mix, the Giants have another reliable threat. But truthfully what the Giants need is more frequent usage from their TE and better efficiency out of RB passes. They targeted the TE 20% of attempts and saw a better success rate than even their WRs. Despite Will Tye having the best success rate for any WR, he wasn't targeted inside the 10. On 1st and 10 RB passes league-wide have a better success rate than WR-passes, yet the Giants rarely use them. In the red zone for the NYG, the success rates by position on 1st and 10: TE 75%, RB 33% and WR 29%. Yet the target rates of WRs is over 3x more than either RB or TE.

Player *Min 50 Targets*	Targets	Comp %	YPA	Rating	TOARS	Success %	Success Rk	Missed YPA Rk	YAS % Rk	TDs
Odell Beckham Jr.	180	58%	7.8	97	5.6	48%	95	95	19	10
Sterling Shepard	114	61%	6.5	81	4.7	49%	81	93	70	8
Will Tye	77	68%	6.0	66	4.0	53%	51	48	136	1
Victor Cruz	76	55%	8.1	81	4.1	47%	100	22	78	1

Directional Passer Rating Delivered

Receiver	Short Left	Short Middle	Short Right	Deep Left	Deep Middle	Deep Right	Player Total
Odell Beckham Jr.	72	137	119	74	42	76	97
Sterling Shepard	65	126	107	0	53	69	81
Will Tye	83	40	85	119	88	0	66
Victor Cruz	68	138	72	40	119	104	82
Rashad Jennings	81	98	105				94
Paul Perkins	67	65	113				81
Bobby Rainey	107	84	83				92
Larry Donnell	96	98	41		40		73
Jerell Adams	139	89	89	40			106
Team Total	80	107	95	38	57	60	87

2016 Rushing Recap & 2017 Outlook

Last year, Paul Perkins delivered a better yards per attempt, success rate, early down success rate and missed yards per attempt than Rashad Jennings. As such, the team felt no desire to resign the far more expensive Jennings. Hopefully they finally will let Perkins see how he can perform when carrying the load. Far too often over the last several years it appeared the Giants were content with a very frequent running back rotation. Which might be conceivable given similar body types, but the problem is all of them were far less successful than Jennings. The team would rotate in Orleans Darkwa, Bobby Rainey and others with little success, and the run game lacked rhythm, personality and virility.

Player *Min 50 Rushes*	Rushes	YPA	Success %	Success Rk	Missed YPA Rk	YTS % Rk	YAS % Rk	Early Down Success %	Early Down Success Rk	TDs
Rashad Jennings	186	3.3	39%	61	47	28	64	39%	60	3
Paul Perkins	122	4.0	42%	54	40	54	55	41%	56	0

Yards per Carry by Direction

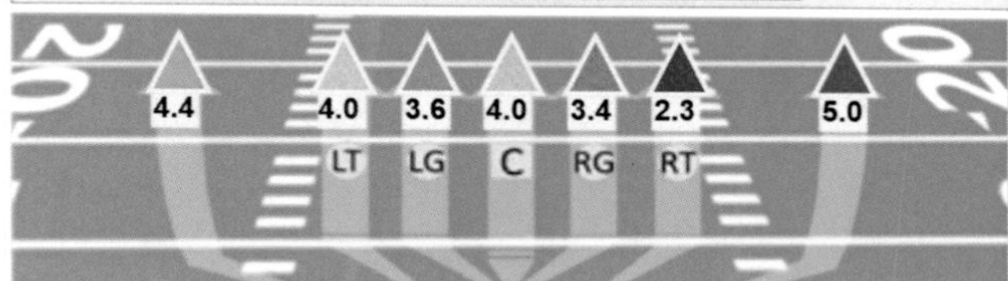

Directional Run Frequency

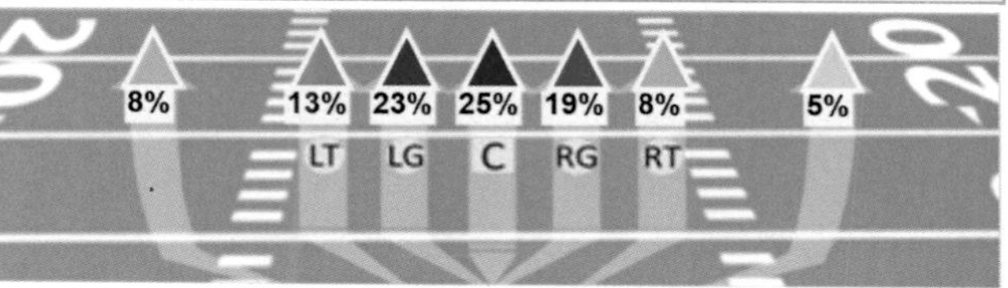

in the 4th round this year to help out, with Shane Vereen being the typical change of pace / receiving back.

The biggest problem for the Giants run game turned into one of the biggest problems for the offense. The Giants were very balanced on first down, calling 237 runs and 230 passes on the season. Typically, this would be a good thing. The problem is, that while they ran the ball more often than average, they were horrible when doing so. The first down run offense was successful on just 33% of plays, dead last in the NFL. Meanwhile, the passing game (as Beckham Jr's stats indicate) was one of the best in the NFL, finding success on 56% of first down attempts, 7th best in the league.

Much like the personnel grouping issues, the Giants have to figure out a way in which to look into the analytics to find the solutions that exist, because they are there. The Giants must figure out a way to get more success out of the run game, particularly on first down, but they also cannot be so afraid to pass more often on first down if their play design and execution is superior to the run design.

Assuming the infusion of younger, fresher talent at the RB position improves efficiency on the ground, the Giants offensive line must do a better job protecting Eli Manning.

On the surface, it appeared as though the Giants were tremendous at protecting for Eli, but reality was one reason Eli was not as strong throwing deep was the protection would not hold up well. LT Ereck Flowers received a terrible 48.4 grade from PFF and ranked 57th at his position. Protection up the middle was OK, but the right side was less than ideal. As such, the Giants signed RG DJ Fluker to take his role in the starting lineup in 2017. And they let RT Marshall Newhouse walk in free agency. The line must do a better job of sustaining blocks and giving Eli a pocket in order to hit on some of the explosive pass plays this offense so desperately needs. New WR Brandon Marshall should provide an additional reliable WR target who could hopefully keep Manning more comfortable in the pocket for a longer period of time.

Defensively, there is only one thing the unit needs to fix and that is the pass rush. The Giants defensive pass rush ranked 23rd in sack rate and that led to their rank of 27th on explosive pass defense. It was the reverse of the offense, which had to throw the ball quickly due to poor protection and didn't gain explosive plays. The defense couldn't get pressure, and opposing quarterbacks could hold the ball a bit longer to let the downfield routes develop, ultimately causing their undoing against the Packers. The schedule should help slightly in this respect – last year the Giants defense faced the 5th rated pass protection units and the 11th rated explosive passing offenses. This year they face the 13th rated pass protection units and 25th rated explosive passing offenses. They face the 4th largest decrease in "pass blend" offense from 2016 to 2017.

Division History: Season Wins & 2017 Projection

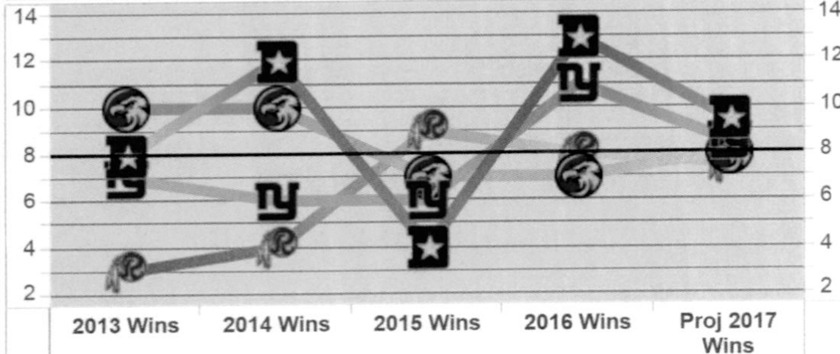

Rank of 2017 Defensive Pass Efficiency Faced by Week

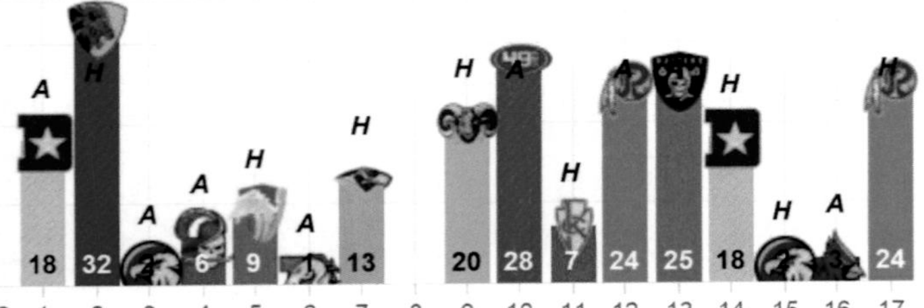

Rank of 2017 Defensive Rush Efficiency Faced by Week

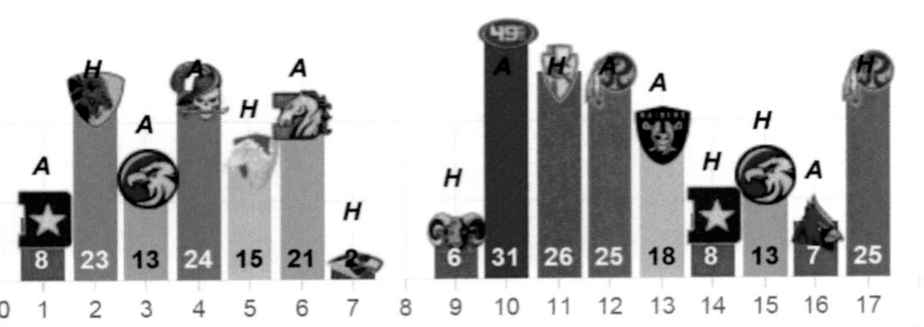

2016 Situational Usage by Player & Position

Usage Rate by Score

		Being Blown Out (14+)	Down Big (9-13)	One Score	Large Lead (9-13)	Blowout Lead (14+)	Grand Total
RUSH	Rashad Jennings	4%	11%	20%	32%		18%
	Odell Beckham Jr.			0%			0%
	Paul Perkins	12%	7%	11%	21%	100%	12%
	Sterling Shepard			0%			0%
	Shane Vereen			4%			3%
	Bobby Rainey	3%	9%	1%			2%
	Orleans Darkwa	3%	4%	3%			3%
	Total	22%	31%	40%	53%	100%	38%
PASS	Rashad Jennings	3%	7%	4%	2%		4%
	Odell Beckham Jr.	22%	17%	17%	17%		17%
	Paul Perkins	6%	2%	2%	4%		3%
	Sterling Shepard	14%	15%	11%	4%		11%
	Will Tye	8%	4%	8%	9%		7%
	Victor Cruz	10%	13%	7%	4%		7%
	Shane Vereen			2%			2%
	Bobby Rainey	8%	4%	2%	2%		3%
	Orleans Darkwa			1%			0%
	Larry Donnell		2%	3%			2%
	Jerell Adams	3%		2%	4%		2%
	Roger Lewis	1%	4%	2%	2%		2%
	Tavarres King	3%		1%			1%
	Dwayne Harris			0%			0%
	Total	78%	69%	60%	47%		62%

Positional Target Distribution vs NFL Average

		NFL Wide				Team Only			
		Left	Middle	Right	Total	Left	Middle	Right	Total
Deep	WR	998	567	965	**2,530**	33	14	36	**83**
	TE	155	141	161	**457**	3	6	2	**11**
	RB	25	4	40	**69**				
	All	**1,178**	**712**	**1,166**	**3,056**	**36**	**20**	**38**	**94**
Short	WR	2,982	1,684	3,098	**7,764**	111	87	88	**286**
	TE	809	837	1,107	**2,753**	27	38	44	**109**
	RB	980	594	1,078	**2,652**	35	28	35	**98**
	All	**4,771**	**3,115**	**5,283**	**13,169**	**173**	**153**	**167**	**493**
Total		**5,949**	**3,827**	**6,449**	**16,225**	**209**	**173**	**205**	**587**

Positional Success Rates vs NFL Average

		NFL Wide				Team Only			
		Left	Middle	Right	Total	Left	Middle	Right	Total
Deep	WR	37%	51%	38%	**41%**	26%	20%	32%	**28%**
	TE	45%	51%	44%	**46%**	33%	14%	0%	**17%**
	RB	32%	75%	25%	**30%**				
	All	**38%**	**51%**	**39%**	**41%**	**27%**	**18%**	**31%**	**27%**
Short	WR	53%	57%	51%	**53%**	38%	59%	47%	**47%**
	TE	50%	62%	53%	**55%**	45%	51%	39%	**45%**
	RB	47%	50%	44%	**47%**	33%	45%	28%	**35%**
	All	**51%**	**57%**	**50%**	**52%**	**38%**	**54%**	**41%**	**44%**
Total		**49%**	**56%**	**48%**	**50%**	**36%**	**50%**	**39%**	**41%**

2017 Coaches

Head Coach:
Todd Bowles (3rd yr)

Offensive Coordinator:
John Morton (NO WR) (1st yr)

Defensive Coordinator:
Kacy Rodgers (3rd yr)

New York Jets

2017 Forecast

Wins	Div Rank
5	#4

Past Records

2016: 5-11
2015: 10-6
2014: 4-12

EASY HARD

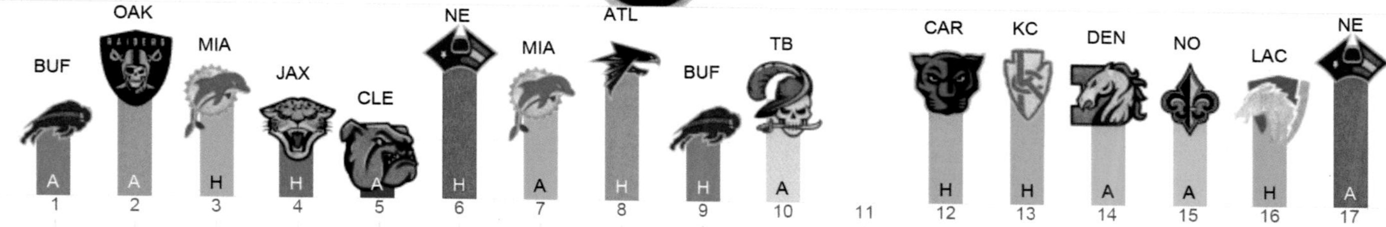

Key Players Lost

TXN	Player (POS)
Cut	Decker, Eric WR
	Folk, Nick K
	Giacomini, Breno T
	Gilchrist, Marcus S
	Harris, David LB
	Mangold, Nick C
	Marshall, Brandon WR
	Revis, Darrelle CB
	Robinson, Khiry RB
	Smith, Devin WR
Declared Free Agent	Allen, Antonio S
	Bostick, Brandon TE
	Carter, Bruce LB
	Clady, Ryan T
	Davis, Kellen TE
	Fitzpatrick, Ryan QB
	Henderson, Erin LB
	Ijalana, Ben T
	Smith, Geno QB

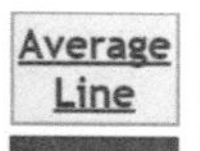

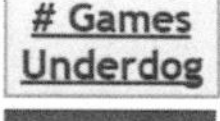

Average Line	# Games Favored	# Games Underdog
+4.9	1	12

Regular Season Wins: Past & Current Proj

2017 New York Jets Overview

In last year's preview, even though the Jets were projected to win as many games as the Bills and more games than the Dolphins, I projected the Dolphins (thought to be last) to finish 2nd in the division and the Bills 3rd, leaving the Jets for last in the AFC East. Coming off of 10 win in 2015, that seemed to many like an odd projection. But I projected them to face a brutal 2016 schedule, and after finishing +6 in turnover margin and +17 in sack margin in 2015, I did not think either would repeat, and based on my other analytics I projected a step back. So how did those predictions turn out?

The Jets won only 5 games in 2016 and finished in last place in the AFC East. They finished -20 in turnover margin, -9 in sack margin and played the overall 12th hardest schedule of opposing teams. In one-score games they went 4-4, meaning they won only 1 game convincingly, and it was week 17 of the season at home against the Bills. Since they lost 11 games, it also means they were blown out in a number of games. From weeks 3-6 they lost every game by double digits. And after a narrow loss to rival New England out of the bye, they dropped 3 of their next 4 games, all by at least 21 points. A number of factors helped to cause their problems.

The first place to look, as usual, is lack of quarterback performance. Ryan Fitzpatrick was a disaster. His passing tree is shades of red. His directional passer rating is likewise shades of red. His 4% interception rate was a disaster. He completed only 57% of his attempts (-6% vs NFL avg) and posted a 70.5 rating (-20 vs NFL avg), ranking 48th. The Jets ranked 31st in passing efficiency, 26th in EDSR (Early Down Success Rate) offense and 31st in total offensive efficiency.

Another key factor was injuries. After being the 13th healthiest team in 2015, the Jets were the 4th most injured team in 2016. The worst hit was the offense. Specifically, the offensive line, which was the 2nd most injured. In the offseason, LT D'Brickashaw Ferguson announced his retirement, so the Jets traded for Ryan Clady. Clady is a walking spot on the injury report, and the move completely backfired. The projected starting 5 did not play a single snap together last season. Clady played the first 8 weeks before landing on IR with a shoulder injury. Breno Giacomini suffered a back strain lifting weights last June,

(cont'd - see NYJ2)

2017 Lineup & Cap Hits

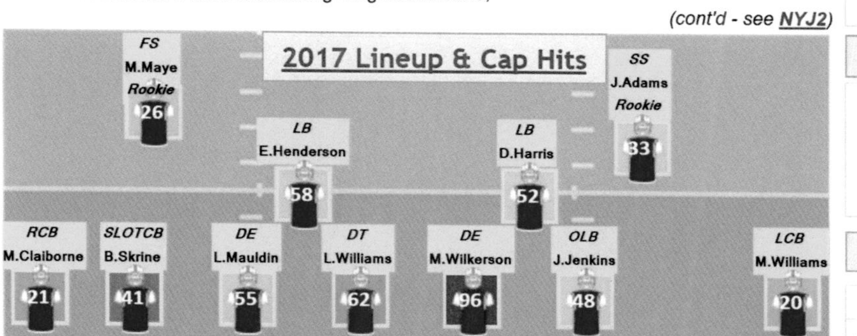

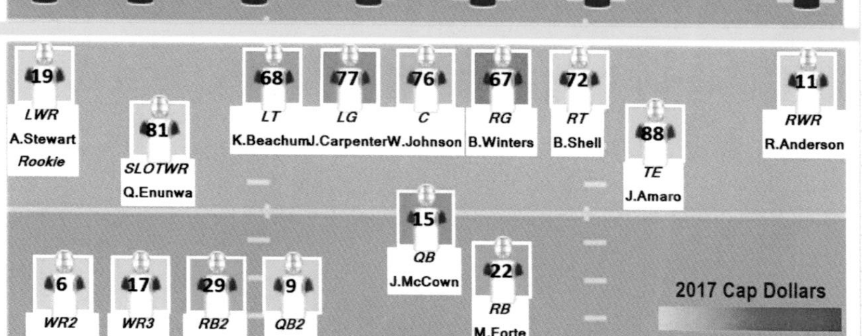

Key Free Agents/ Trades Added

Adams, Jeff T
Balducci, Alex G
Beachum, Kelvin T
Claiborne, Morris CB
Davis, Demario LB
Lemonier, Corey LB
Martin, Josh LB
McCown, Josh QB
Pennel, Mike DT
Thomas, Shamarko S

Drafted Players

Rd	Pk	Player (College)
1	6	S - Jamal Adams (LSU)
2	39	S - Marcus Maye (Florida)
3	79	WR - ArDarius Stewart (Alabama)
4*	141	WR - Chad Hansen (California)
5	150	TE - Jordan Leggett (Clemson)
5*	181	DE - Dylan Donahue (West Georgia)
	188	RB - Elijah McGuire (Louisiana-Lafayette)
6	197	CB - Jeremy Clark (Michigan)
	204	CB - Derrick Jones (Ole Miss)

2017 Unit Spending

Positional Spending

	Rank	Total	2016 Rk
All OFF	27	$73.57M	19
QB	25	$8.31M	26
OL	8	$32.64M	8
RB	7	$11.15M	17
WR	16	$18.25M	5
TE	31	$3.22M	31
All DEF	16	$78.33M	14
DL	7	$39.57M	16
LB	23	$14.91M	22
CB	15	$19.81M	1
S	32	$4.04M	20

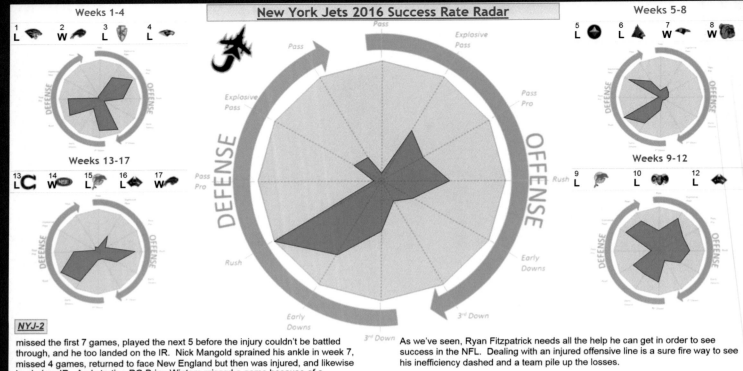

New York Jets 2016 Success Rate Radar

Weeks 1-4: 1 L, 2 W, 3 L, 4 L

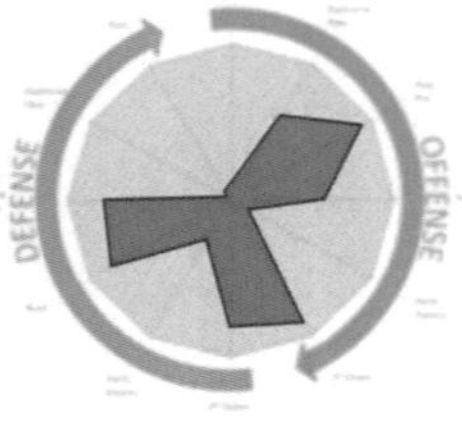

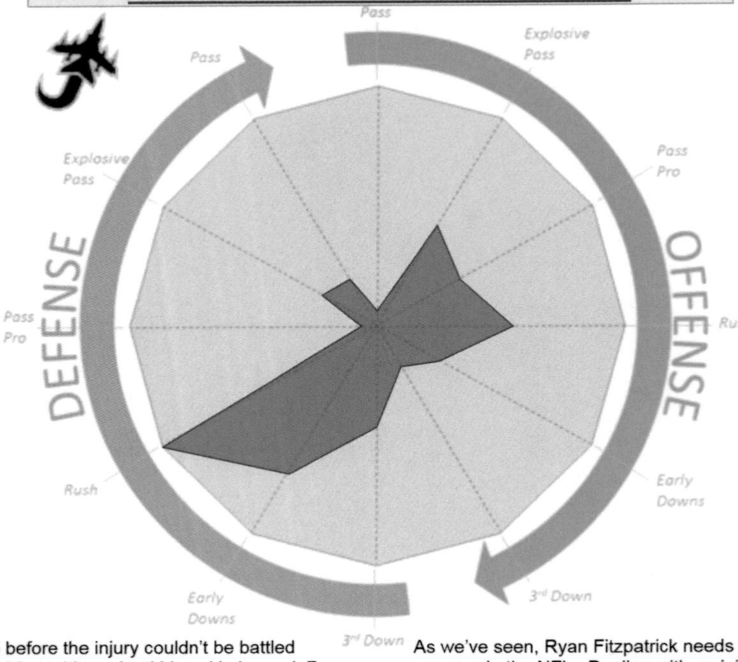

Weeks 5-8: 5 L, 6 L, 7 W, 8 W

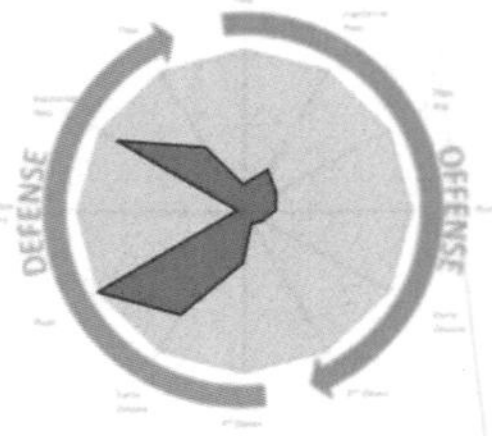

Weeks 9-12: 9 L, 10 L, 12 L

Weeks 13-17: 13 L, 14 W, 15 L, 16 L, 17 W

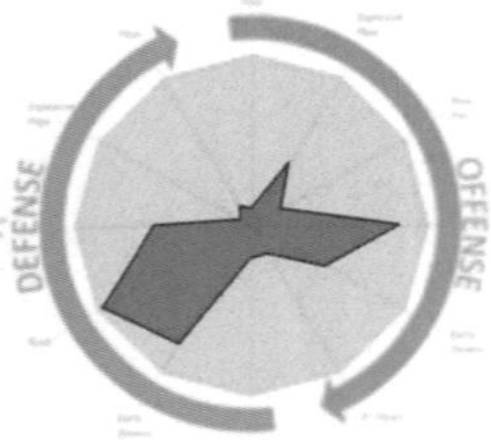

Pass | Explosive Pass | Pass Pro | Rush | Early Downs | 3rd Down | Early Downs | Rush | Pass Pro | Explosive Pass | Pass

DEFENSE | OFFENSE

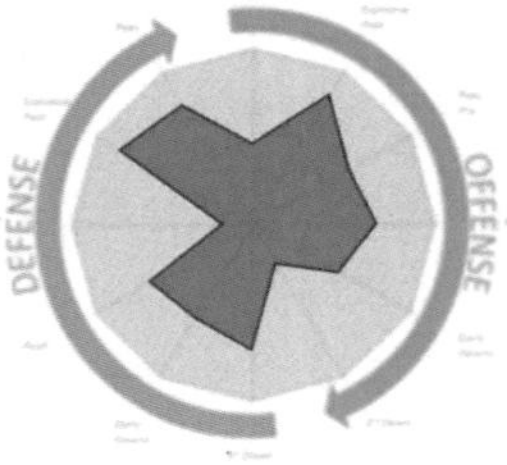

NYJ-2

missed the first 7 games, played the next 5 before the injury couldn't be battled through, and he too landed on the IR. Nick Mangold sprained his ankle in week 7, missed 4 games, returned to face New England but then was injured, and likewise landed on IR. And starting RG Brian Winters missed a game because of a concussion. In the offseason, the projected starting lineup was to be Clady, James Carpenter, Mangold, Winters and Giacomini. As you can see from the above injury dissertation, the health of their line was a disaster. They were starting undrafted free agents and backups who would not start on any other team, if they even made rosters elsewhere.

The impact on a passing game with such a injury-plagued offensive line is massive. In a given game, the team who wins the sack battle wins 71% of their games. The reason being is sacks correlate to pressure rate. And with passing being such a driver toward wins and losses (as compared to rushing), disrupting an opponent's passing game has a major impact on game results. And that assumes that the Jets would have an adequate passing game even without the pressure.

As we've seen, Ryan Fitzpatrick needs all the help he can get in order to see success in the NFL. Dealing with an injured offensive line is a sure fire way to see his inefficiency dashed and a team pile up the losses.

But the offensive line was not the only unit on offense to suffer injuries. While Brandon Marshall lasted until week 16, starting WR Eric Decker played in only 3 games and caught only 9 passes last season before landing on the IR. WR Devin Smith tore his ACL in April and missed the entirety of his 3rd NFL season. He was the 37th overall pick in the 2015 draft, yet played in only 14 of 48 possible games for the Jets. With those types of injuries to penciled-in contributors, defenses were able to line up and focus on taking away Brandon Marshall. And they did a solid job. Only 47% of passes targeting Marshall were completed. He averaged only 6.1 yards per attempt and posed a 51 passer rating on his targets. His 41% success rate ranked 131 and his Missed YPA ranked 113th. Clearly the passing game did not work last year. At all.

(cont'd - see NYJ-3)

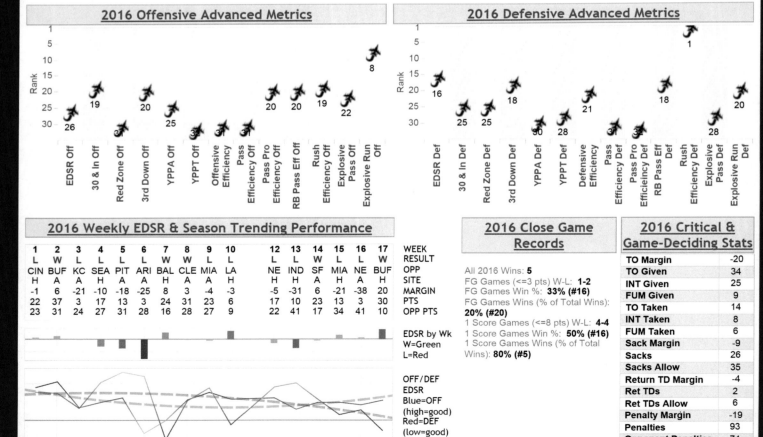

2016 Offensive Advanced Metrics

Metric	Rank
EDSR Off	26
30 & In Off	19
Red Zone Off	31
3rd Down Off	20
YPPA Off	25
YPPT Off	32
Offensive Efficiency	31
Pass Efficiency Off	31
Pass Pro Efficiency Off	20
RB Pass Eff Off	20
Rush Efficiency Off	19
Explosive Pass Off	22
Explosive Run Off	8

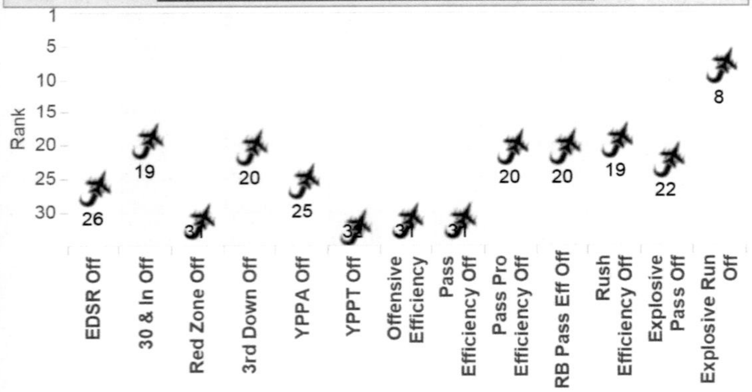

2016 Defensive Advanced Metrics

Metric	Rank
EDSR Def	16
30 & In Def	25
Red Zone Def	25
3rd Down Def	18
YPPA Def	30
YPPT Def	28
Defensive Efficiency	21
Pass Efficiency Def	31
Pass Pro Effieicny Def	32
RB Pass Eff Def	18
Rush Efficiency Def	1
Explosive Pass Def	28
Explosive Run Def	20

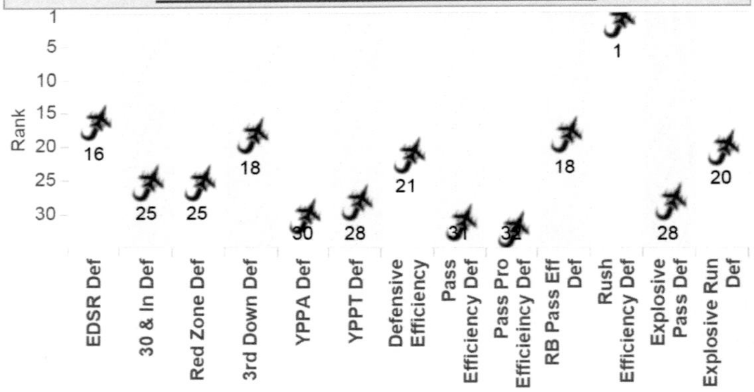

2016 Weekly EDSR & Season Trending Performance

WEEK	1	2	3	4	5	6	7	8	9	10	12	13	14	15	16	17
RESULT	L	W	L	L	L	L	W	W	L	L	L	L	W	L	L	W
OPP	CIN	BUF	KC	SEA	PIT	ARI	BAL	CLE	MIA	LA	NE	IND	SF	MIA	NE	BUF
SITE	H	A	A	H	A	A	H	A	A	H	H	H	A	H	A	H
MARGIN	-1	6	-21	-10	-18	-25	8	3	-4	-3	-5	-31	6	-21	-38	20
PTS	22	37	3	17	13	3	24	31	23	6	17	10	23	13	3	30
OPP PTS	23	31	24	27	31	28	16	28	27	9	22	41	17	34	41	10

EDSR by Wk
W=Green
L=Red

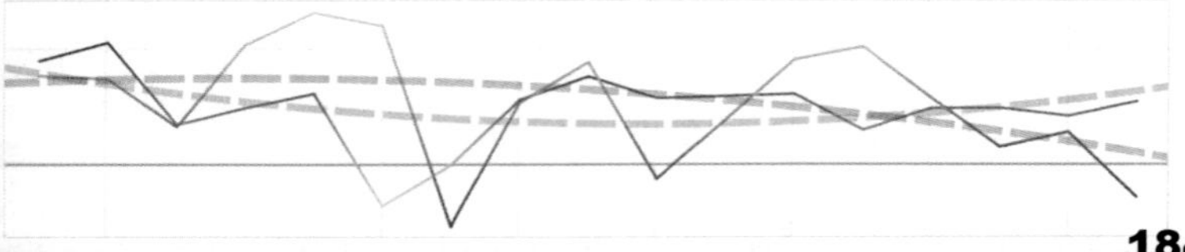

OFF/DEF EDSR
Blue=OFF (high=good)
Red=DEF (low=good)

2016 Close Game Records

All 2016 Wins: **5**
FG Games (<=3 pts) W-L: **1-2**
FG Games Win %: **33% (#16)**
FG Games Wins (% of Total Wins): **20% (#20)**
1 Score Games (<=8 pts) W-L: **4-4**
1 Score Games Win %: **50% (#16)**
1 Score Games Wins (% of Total Wins): **80% (#5)**

2016 Critical & Game-Deciding Stats

TO Margin	-20
TO Given	34
INT Given	25
FUM Given	9
TO Taken	14
INT Taken	8
FUM Taken	6
Sack Margin	-9
Sacks	26
Sacks Allow	35
Return TD Margin	-4
Ret TDs	2
Ret TDs Allow	6
Penalty Margin	-19
Penalties	93
Opponent Penalties	74

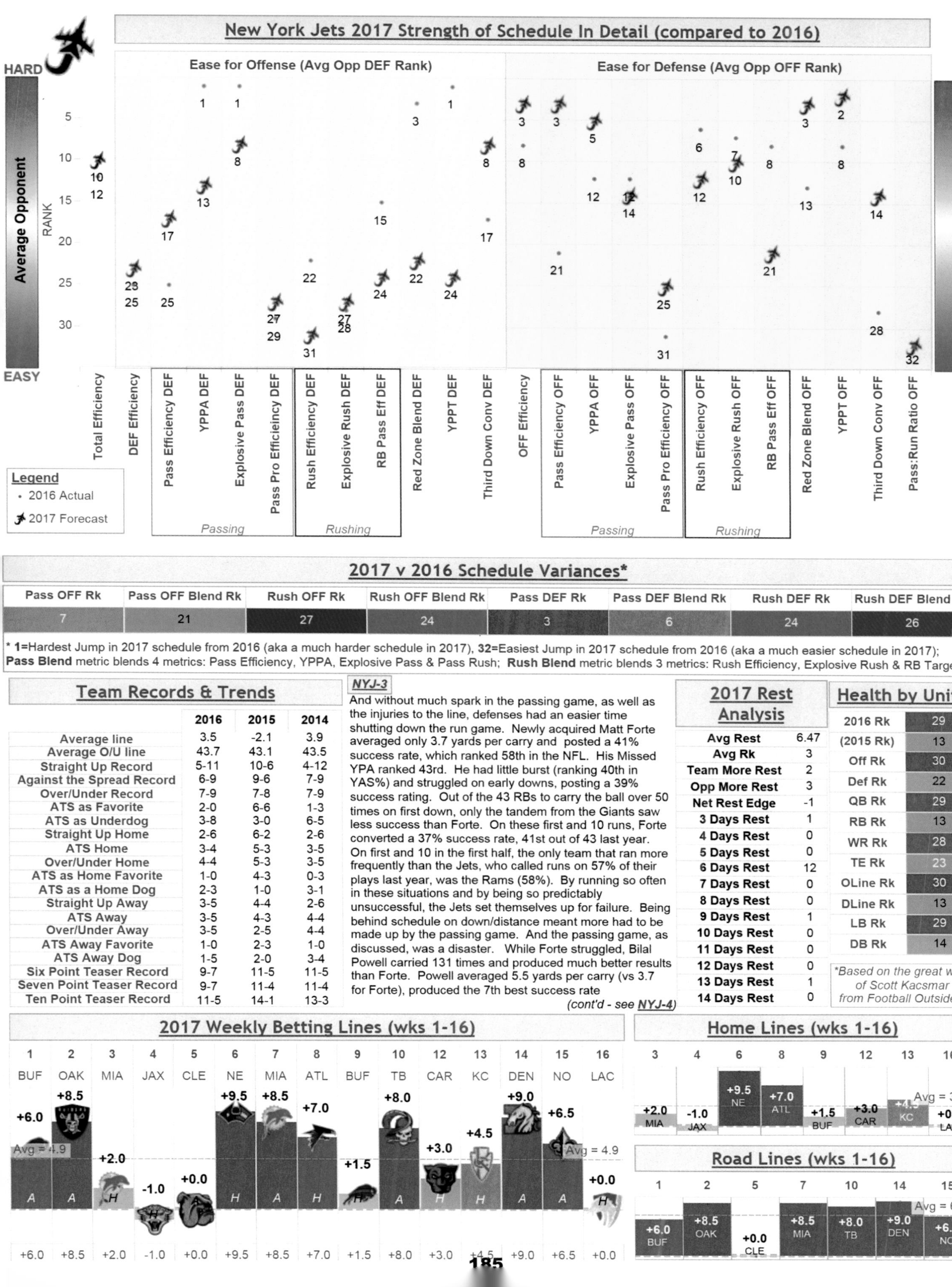

New York Jets 2017 Strength of Schedule In Detail (compared to 2016)

2017 v 2016 Schedule Variances*

Pass OFF Rk	Pass OFF Blend Rk	Rush OFF Rk	Rush OFF Blend Rk	Pass DEF Rk	Pass DEF Blend Rk	Rush DEF Rk	Rush DEF Blend
7	21	27	24	3	6	24	26

* **1**=Hardest Jump in 2017 schedule from 2016 (aka a much harder schedule in 2017), **32**=Easiest Jump in 2017 schedule from 2016 (aka a much easier schedule in 2017); **Pass Blend** metric blends 4 metrics: Pass Efficiency, YPPA, Explosive Pass & Pass Rush; **Rush Blend** metric blends 3 metrics: Rush Efficiency, Explosive Rush & RB Targe

Team Records & Trends

	2016	2015	2014
Average line	3.5	-2.1	3.9
Average O/U line	43.7	43.1	43.5
Straight Up Record	5-11	10-6	4-12
Against the Spread Record	6-9	9-6	7-9
Over/Under Record	7-9	7-8	7-9
ATS as Favorite	2-0	6-6	1-3
ATS as Underdog	3-8	3-0	6-5
Straight Up Home	2-6	6-2	2-6
ATS Home	3-4	5-3	3-5
Over/Under Home	4-4	5-3	3-5
ATS as Home Favorite	1-0	4-3	0-3
ATS as a Home Dog	2-3	1-0	3-1
Straight Up Away	3-5	4-4	2-6
ATS Away	3-5	4-3	4-4
Over/Under Away	3-5	2-5	4-4
ATS Away Favorite	1-0	2-3	1-0
ATS Away Dog	1-5	2-0	3-4
Six Point Teaser Record	9-7	11-5	11-5
Seven Point Teaser Record	9-7	11-4	11-4
Ten Point Teaser Record	11-5	14-1	13-3

NYJ-3

And without much spark in the passing game, as well as the injuries to the line, defenses had an easier time shutting down the run game. Newly acquired Matt Forte averaged only 3.7 yards per carry and posted a 41% success rate, which ranked 58th in the NFL. His Missed YPA ranked 43rd. He had little burst (ranking 40th in YAS%) and struggled on early downs, posting a 39% success rating. Out of the 43 RBs to carry the ball over 50 times on first down, only the tandem from the Giants saw less success than Forte. On these first and 10 runs, Forte converted a 37% success rate, 41st out of 43 last year. On first and 10 in the first half, the only team that ran more frequently than the Jets, who called runs on 57% of their plays last year, was the Rams (58%). By running so often in these situations and by being so predictably unsuccessful, the Jets set themselves up for failure. Being behind schedule on down/distance meant more had to be made up by the passing game. And the passing game, as discussed, was a disaster. While Forte struggled, Bilal Powell carried 131 times and produced much better results than Forte. Powell averaged 5.5 yards per carry (vs 3.7 for Forte), produced the 7th best success rate

(cont'd - see NYJ-4)

2017 Rest Analysis

Avg Rest	6.47
Avg Rk	3
Team More Rest	2
Opp More Rest	3
Net Rest Edge	-1
3 Days Rest	1
4 Days Rest	0
5 Days Rest	0
6 Days Rest	12
7 Days Rest	0
8 Days Rest	0
9 Days Rest	1
10 Days Rest	0
11 Days Rest	0
12 Days Rest	0
13 Days Rest	1
14 Days Rest	0

Health by Unit*

2016 Rk	29
(2015 Rk)	13
Off Rk	30
Def Rk	22
QB Rk	29
RB Rk	13
WR Rk	28
TE Rk	23
OLine Rk	30
DLine Rk	13
LB Rk	29
DB Rk	14

*Based on the great w of Scott Kacsmar from Football Outside

2017 Weekly Betting Lines (wks 1-16)

1	2	3	4	5	6	7	8	9	10	12	13	14	15	16
BUF	OAK	MIA	JAX	CLE	NE	MIA	ATL	BUF	TB	CAR	KC	DEN	NO	LAC
A	A	H	H	H	H	A	H	H	A	H	H	A	A	H
+6.0	+8.5	+2.0	-1.0	+0.0	+9.5	+8.5	+7.0	+1.5	+8.0	+3.0	+4.5	+9.0	+6.5	+0.0

Avg = 4.9

Home Lines (wks 1-16)

3	4	6	8	9	12	13	16
MIA	JAX	NE	ATL	BUF	CAR	KC	LAC
+2.0	-1.0	+9.5	+7.0	+1.5	+3.0	+4.5	+0.

Avg = 3

Road Lines (wks 1-16)

1	2	5	7	10	14	15
BUF	OAK	CLE	MIA	TB	DEN	NO
+6.0	+8.5	+0.0	+8.5	+8.0	+9.0	+6.

Avg = 6

2016 Play Tendencies

ll Pass %	57%
ll Pass Rk	22
ll Rush %	43%
ll Rush Rk	11
Score Pass %	60%
Score Pass Rk	11
015 1 Score Pass %	58%
015 1 Score Pass Rk	17
ass Increase %	2%
ass Increase Rk	10
Score Rush %	40%
Score Rush Rk	22
p Pass %	57%
p Pass Rk	20
p Rush %	43%
p Rush Rk	13
own Pass %	60%
own Pass Rk	22
own Rush %	40%
own Rush Rk	11

2016 Down & Distance Tendencies

Down	Distance	Total Plays	Pass Rate	Run Rate	Play Success %
1	Short (1-3)	4	25%	75%	50%
	Med (4-7)	12	58%	42%	33%
	Long (8-10)	293	44%	56%	47%
	XL (11+)	15	67%	33%	47%
2	Short (1-3)	32	34%	66%	72%
	Med (4-7)	82	54%	46%	46%
	Long (8-10)	95	60%	40%	39%
	XL (11+)	40	88%	13%	35%
3	Short (1-3)	32	50%	50%	66%
	Med (4-7)	51	90%	10%	35%
	Long (8-10)	39	87%	13%	36%
	XL (11+)	32	91%	9%	19%
4	Short (1-3)	5	20%	80%	40%
	Med (4-7)	1	0%	100%	0%

Shotgun %:

Under Center	Shotgun
34%	66%
37%	*63%*

AVG

Run Rate:

Under Center	Shotgun
68%	27%
68%	*23%*

AVG

Pass Rate:

Under Center	Shotgun
32%	73%
32%	*77%*

AVG

New York Jets 2016 Play Analysis

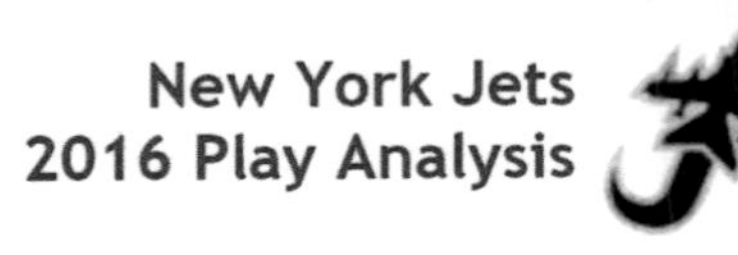

Short Yardage Intelligence:

2nd and Short Run

Run Freq	Run % Rk	NFL Run Freq Avg	Run 1D Rate	Run NFL 1D Avg
71%	6	65%	64%	71%

2nd and Short Pass

Pass Freq	Pass % Rk	NFL Pass Freq Avg	Pass 1D Rate	Pass NFL 1D Avg
29%	25	35%	60%	52%

Most Frequent Play

own	Distance	Play Type	Player	Total Plays	Play Success %
1	Short (1-3)	RUSH	Matt Forte	2	50%
	Med (4-7)	PASS	Brandon Marshall	4	25%
		RUSH	Matt Forte	4	25%
	Long (8-10)	RUSH	Matt Forte	95	37%
	XL (11+)	PASS	Brandon Marshall	3	67%
2	Short (1-3)	RUSH	Bilal Powell	9	89%
	Med (4-7)	RUSH	Matt Forte	20	50%
	Long (8-10)	RUSH	Matt Forte	26	35%
	XL (11+)	PASS	Brandon Marshall	8	38%
3	Short (1-3)	PASS	Brandon Marshall	7	43%
		RUSH	Matt Forte	7	86%
	Med (4-7)	PASS	Brandon Marshall	10	60%
			Quincy Enunwa	10	20%
	Long (8-10)	PASS	Brandon Marshall	8	38%
	XL (11+)	PASS	Bilal Powell	11	9%

Most Successful Play*

Down	Distance	Play Type	Player	Total Plays	Play Success %
1	Long (8-10)	PASS	Matt Forte	14	79%
2	Short (1-3)	RUSH	Bilal Powell	9	89%
	Med (4-7)	PASS	Bilal Powell	7	71%
	Long (8-10)	PASS	Matt Forte	5	60%
	XL (11+)	PASS	Quincy Enunwa	7	57%
3	Short (1-3)	RUSH	Bilal Powell	6	100%
	Med (4-7)	PASS	Brandon Marshall	10	60%
	Long (8-10)	PASS	Quincy Enunwa	6	67%
	XL (11+)	PASS	Robby Anderson	6	33%

**Minimum 5 plays to qualify*

016 Snap Rates

eek	Opp	Score	Brandon Marshall	Quincy Enunwa	Robby Anderson	Bilal Powell	Matt Forte	Charone Peake
1	CIN	L 23-22	67 (94%)	63 (89%)	4 (6%)	17 (24%)	54 (76%)	
2	BUF	W 37-31	68 (92%)	46 (62%)	6 (8%)	17 (23%)	60 (81%)	
3	KC	L 24-3	66 (97%)	56 (82%)	11 (16%)	28 (41%)	41 (60%)	4 (6%)
4	SEA	L 27-17	63 (89%)	67 (94%)	62 (87%)	37 (52%)	34 (48%)	44 (62%)
5	PIT	L 31-13	56 (97%)	45 (78%)	52 (90%)	27 (47%)	36 (62%)	21 (36%)
6	ARI	L 28-3	53 (98%)	50 (93%)	54 (100%)	39 (72%)	21 (39%)	29 (54%)
7	BAL	W 24-16	65 (96%)	44 (65%)	50 (74%)	9 (13%)	57 (84%)	15 (22%)
8	CLE	W 31-28	67 (93%)	58 (81%)	62 (86%)	30 (42%)	45 (63%)	29 (40%)
9	MIA	L 27-23	54 (93%)	44 (76%)	55 (95%)	26 (45%)	32 (55%)	20 (34%)
10	LA	L 9-6	57 (95%)	60 (100%)	53 (88%)	32 (53%)	34 (57%)	16 (27%)
12	NE	L 22-17	54 (95%)	46 (81%)	44 (77%)	28 (49%)	29 (51%)	
13	IND	L 41-10	48 (92%)	48 (92%)	42 (81%)	28 (54%)	24 (46%)	17 (33%)
14	SF	W 23-17	78 (93%)	75 (89%)	64 (76%)	73 (87%)	6 (7%)	35 (42%)
15	MIA	L 35-13	73 (96%)	67 (88%)	71 (93%)	64 (84%)	13 (17%)	24 (32%)
16	NE	L 41-3	29 (52%)	54 (96%)	43 (77%)	32 (57%)		28 (50%)
17	BUF	W 30-10		45 (73%)	44 (71%)	43 (69%)		40 (65%)
Grand Total			898 (91%)	868 (84%)	717 (70%)	530 (51%)	486 (53%)	322 (39%)

Personnel Groupings

Personnel	Team %	NFL Avg	Succ. %
1-1 [3WR]	42%	60%	46%
1-0 [4WR]	33%	3%	38%
1-2 [2WR]	17%	19%	49%
2-0 [3WR]	5%	1%	44%

Grouping Tendencies

Personnel	Pass Rate	Pass Succ. %	Run Succ. %
1-1 [3WR]	53%	44%	48%
1-0 [4WR]	79%	36%	46%
1-2 [2WR]	33%	55%	46%
2-0 [3WR]	70%	40%	53%

Red Zone Targets (min 3)

Receiver	All	Inside 5	6-10	11-20
Brandon Marshall	21	6	2	13
Quincy Enunwa	15	5	5	5
Bilal Powell	13	3	1	9
Robby Anderson	5			5
Eric Decker	4	3		1
Jalin Marshall	4		1	3
Matt Forte	4	1		3
Charone Peake	3		1	2

Red Zone Rushes (min 3)

Rusher	All	Inside 5	6-10	11-20
Matt Forte	33	12	4	17
Bilal Powell	21	3	6	12
Ryan Fitzpatrick	6	1	1	4

Early Down Target Rate

RB	TE	WR
23%	7%	70%
19%	*20%*	*61%*

NFL AVG

Overall Target Success %

RB	TE	WR
44%	50%	43%
#17	#22	#30

New York Jets 2016 Passing Recap & 2017 Outlook

With Josh McCown under center, it's hard to project which receivers will deliver best for him, considering looking to last year's numbers look terrible across the board with the lone exception of Quincy Enunwa on deep passes, where he delivered a 117 rating deep left, 110 rating deep middle and 141 rating deep right. In 2015 with Cleveland, McCown posted a very respectable 93 passer rating, and was solid hitting deep routes, particularly to Gary Barnidge and even to Travis Benjamin for the most part. But last year in Cleveland, he struggled immensely when going deep. He ranked 34th out of 35 QBs in rating (39) when throwing 15+ yards in the air; only Brock Osweiler was worse. McCown was successful on only 29% of his deep targets, ranking 34th out of 35. On passes closer to the line of scrimmage, he was much better comparatively, but still bad against the rest of the NFL. His rating was 82.5, 30th out of 40 qualifying QBs. New OC John Morton needs to emphasize groupings, routes and concepts that McCown is most comfortable with. When Hue Jackson yanked Cody Kessler for being too conservative downfield, McCown came in and threw 2 bad interceptions in relief, trying to go deep just to go deep.

2016 Standard Passing Table

QB	Comp	Att	Comp %	Yds	YPA	TDs	INT	Sacks	Rating	Rk
Ryan Fitzpatrick	229	404	57%	2,709	6.7	13	17	19	70.5	48
Bryce Petty	75	133	56%	799	6.0	3	7	13	59.7	55
NFL Avg			63%		7.2				90.4	

2016 Advanced Passing Table

QB	Success %	EDSR Passing Success %	20+ Yd Pass Gains	20+ Yd Pass %	30+ Yd Pass Gains	30+ Yd Pass %	Air Yds per Comp	YAC per Comp	20+ Air Yd Comp	20+ Air Yd %
Ryan Fitzpatrick	42%	47%	38	9%	13	3%	7.1	4.8	21	5%
Bryce Petty	38%	40%	9	7%	4	3%	5.9	4.7	7	5%
NFL Avg	44%	48%	27	8%	10	3%	6.4	4.8	12	4%

Ryan Fitzpatrick Rating All Downs

35 96 70
66
82 67

Ryan Fitzpatrick Rating Early Downs

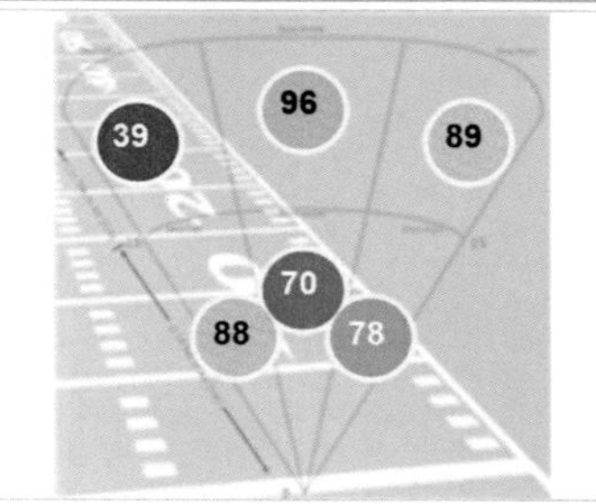

Interception Rates by Down

Yards to Go	1	2	3	4	Total
1 & 2		12.5%	0.0%	0.0%	3.8%
3, 4, 5	0.0%	3.8%	0.0%	0.0%	1.7%
6 - 9	0.0%	5.5%	7.3%	50.0%	7.1%
10 - 14	3.7%	2.0%	3.0%	50.0%	3.7%
15+	0.0%	0.0%	0.0%		0.0%
Total	3.4%	4.0%	3.4%	25.0%	4.0%

3rd Down Passing - Short of Sticks Analysis

QB	Avg Yds to Go	Air Yds (of Comps)	Avg Yds Short	Short of Sticks Rate	Rk
Ryan Fitzpatrick	7.4	6.5	-0.9	64%	28
NFL Avg	7.6	6.8	-0.8	57%	

Air Yds vs YAC

	Air Yds %	YAC %	Rk
Ryan Fitzpatrick	54%	46%	27
NFL Avg	54%	46%	

2016 Receiving Recap & 2017 Outlook

Jets WRs 1 and 2 (Decker and Enunwa) are not a terrible top 2. Decker is better suited as a #2, but Enunwa showed a lot of potential last season, as his 8.2 yards per attempt showed. He actually ranked 10th in YAS%, meaning he showed a lot of explosiveness, and was adept on deeper routes. The issue comes after them. The #3 is a mystery, and at this point in the offseason, so is the TE. The Jets targeted their TEs just 5% overall (7% on early downs), which is terrible given the efficiency gain from that position. The Jets absolutely must find a TE who can be baseline reliable, and target that position 20% of the time (NFL avg).

Player *Min 50 Targets*	Targets	Comp %	YPA	Rating	TOARS	Success %	Success Rk	Missed YPA Rk	YAS % Rk	TDs
Brandon Marshall	129	47%	6.1	51	4.4	41%	131	113	56	4
Quincy Enunwa	105	55%	8.2	79	4.5	45%	112	82	10	4
Robby Anderson	78	54%	7.5	55	3.7	42%	124	105	96	2
Bilal Powell	75	77%	5.1	87	4.1	43%	122	138	146	1

Directional Passer Rating Delivered

Receiver	Short Left	Short Middle	Short Right	Deep Left	Deep Middle	Deep Right	Player Total
Brandon Marshall	76	71	56	27	24	27	51
Quincy Enunwa	81	55	52	117	110	141	79
Robby Anderson	68	61	57	27	96	20	55
Bilal Powell	88	39	106				87
Matt Forte	83	114	62				83
Charone Peake	70	83	41	38	40	40	46
Team Total	81	65	66	35	85	48	66

2016 Rushing Recap & 2017 Outlook

Complain as he might given his reduced role, Bilal Powell outperformed Matt Forte in virtually every metric possible. Except for one key area (the red zone) where Powell was successful on just 29% of his runs and 38% of his passing targets. The numbers below clearly demonstrate the efficiency comparison. After playing the 11th most difficult schedule of run defenses last year, the Jets are projected to face the 2nd easiest schedule this year. Theoretically it should allow them to rely more on the run and less on McCown, presuming their defense can stand up to the 3rd rated schedule of opposing offenses. Considering projected game script, the Jets could be tempted to rely too much on McCown, but for obvious reasons that would be a mistake.

Player *Min 50 Rushes*	Rushes	YPA	Success %	Success Rk	Missed YPA Rk	YTS % Rk	YAS % Rk	Early Down Success %	Early Down Success Rk	TDs
Matt Forte	218	3.7	41%	58	43	39	40	39%	59	7
Bilal Powell	131	5.5	56%	7	8	58	16	55%	9	3

Yards per Carry by Direction

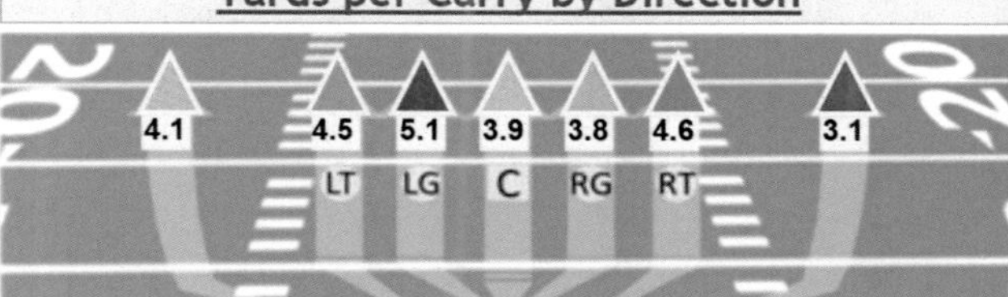

Directional Run Frequency

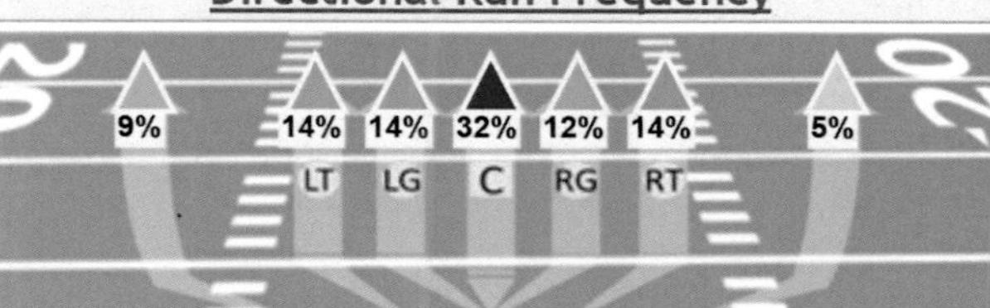

on his runs (56%, vs 41% for Forte), the 8th best ranking on Missed YPA (vs 43rd for Forte) and ranked 16th in YAS % (vs 40th for Forte). Forte complained about the RB rotation, and said that former OC Chan Gailey pulled him off the field too much on 3rd downs. What Gailey should have done was to pull Forte off the field more on early downs, as Powell ranked 9th and Forte ranked 59th. On first and 10 in the first half, Powell recorded a 55% success rate and averaged 5.2 yards per attempt. That was 6th best in the NFL. As mentioned earlier, Forte's success rate on such runs was 20% lower (35%), which ranked 38th in the NFL.

While all of those above metrics explain why the offense struggled, they ordinarily wouldn't be such a massive issue if the defense was #1 in EDSR and #5 in total defense, as they were in 2015. But in 2016, the defense fell off in a major way. This unit ranked 16th in EDSR and 21st in total defense. Their biggest problem was against the pass, as Darelle Revis saw first hand. They ranked 31st in defensive pass efficiency. The main problem was they couldn't rush the quarterback, ranking dead last in pressure rate. As we discussed above, line pressure is a major contributor toward wins and losses. With the Jets offensive line beat up and the Jets featuring the 2nd worst rated passing offense while the Jets defensive line unable to get solid pressure and ranked 2nd worst against the pass, the season was over before it began.

So the Jets decided to rebuild, cutting Marshall, Revis, Mangold & Clady.

They worked to recoup that 5th round pick they lost in the futile obtainment of Clady by trading down in the draft. They focused first on providing pieces necessary to improve the league's 2nd worst pass defense, and drafted two safeties in the first two rounds. They acquired two WRs and a TE over their next 3 draft picks, to try to provide a spark to the passing game which still has Decker and Quincy Enunwa, but little else. And they tried to supplant the offensive line by adding Kelvin Beachum in free agency. The most notable move was to acquire QB Josh McCown. McCown, last seen in Cleveland where he struggled in 2016 after a respectable 2015, is by far their best option at QB, with Bryce Petty and Christian Hackenberg behind him. But clearly the QB position is still one of need. McCown is 37 and was average to below average over his career when younger. The Jets may be poised to take a QB atop the 2018 draft.

The outlook for the 2017 Jets is grim. Step one is get the offensive line to perform better and stay healthier. They are utterly doomed if that unit doesn't improve. Step two should be to fill the efficiency void at TE. They targeted this position a league low 7% (-13% vs avg), but the TE is the most successful of all positions to target in the NFL. Step three is to improve the first down rushing efficiency, and if Forte is incapable they need to be faster to insert Powell and find a rotation which works. With those elements in place, the team still won't be good, but they will be functional.

Division History: Season Wins & 2017 Projection

2013 Wins | 2014 Wins | 2015 Wins | 2016 Wins | Proj 2017 Wins

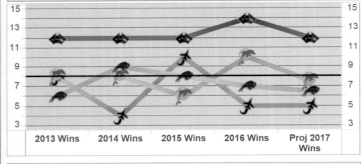

Rank of 2017 Defensive Pass Efficiency Faced by Week

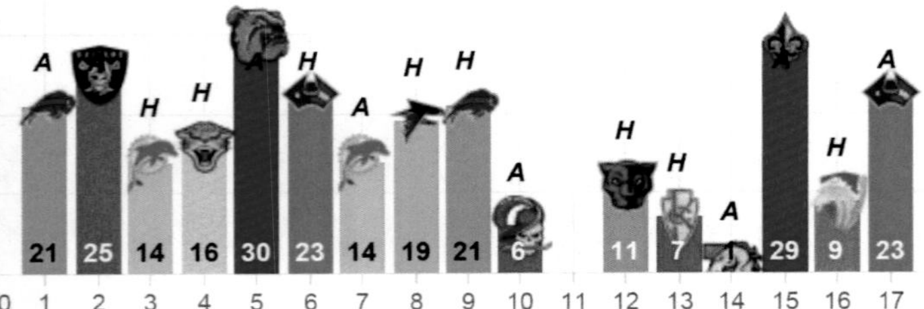

Rank of 2017 Defensive Rush Efficiency Faced by Week

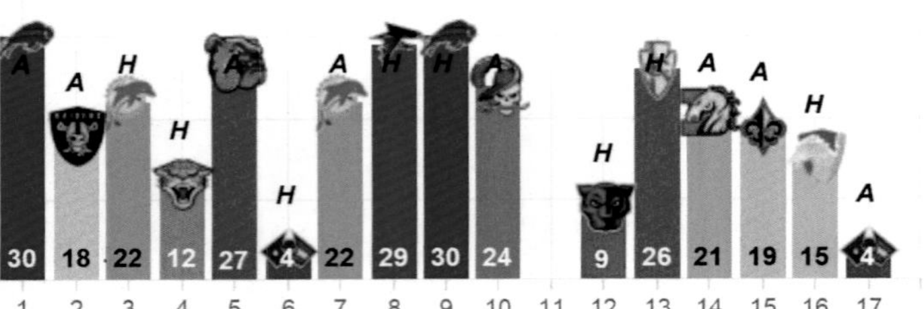

2016 Situational Usage by Player & Position

Usage Rate by Score

		Being Blown Out (14+)	Down Big (9-13)	One Score	Blowout Lead (14+)	Grand Total
RUSH	Matt Forte	9%	14%	31%		24%
	Bilal Powell	14%	20%	13%	25%	14%
	Quincy Enunwa	0%				0%
	Robby Anderson	0%	1%	0%		0%
	Brandon Wilds	2%		1%		1%
	Khiry Robinson	2%	3%			1%
	C.J. Spiller	1%		0%		0%
	Brandon Burks				17%	0%
	Troymaine Pope			0%		0%
	Total	30%	38%	45%	42%	41%
PASS	Matt Forte	5%	2%	5%		5%
	Bilal Powell	8%	13%	8%		8%
	Brandon Marshall	12%	18%	15%		14%
	Quincy Enunwa	14%	13%	10%	25%	11%
	Robby Anderson	13%	7%	7%		8%
	Charone Peake	6%	6%	2%	8%	4%
	Jalin Marshall	3%		3%		2%
	Eric Decker	2%		3%		2%
	Austin Seferian-Jenki..	3%	3%	1%		2%
	Brandon Wilds				17%	0%
	Brandon Bostick	2%	1%	1%	8%	1%
	C.J. Spiller	1%		0%		0%
	Devin Smith	1%				0%
	Braedon Bowman			0%		0%
	Kellen Davis			0%		0%
	Total	70%	63%	55%	58%	59%

Positional Target Distribution vs NFL Average

		NFL Wide				Team Only			
		Left	Middle	Right	Total	Left	Middle	Right	Total
Deep	WR	988	554	963	**2,505**	43	27	38	**108**
	TE	158	147	163	**468**				
	RB	25	4	40	**69**				
	All	**1,171**	**705**	**1,166**	**3,042**	**43**	**27**	**38**	**108**
Short	WR	3,006	1,712	3,093	**7,811**	87	59	93	**239**
	TE	836	875	1,151	**2,862**				
	RB	968	595	1,071	**2,634**	47	27	42	**116**
	All	**4,810**	**3,182**	**5,315**	**13,307**	**134**	**86**	**135**	**355**
Total		**5,981**	**3,887**	**6,481**	**16,349**	**177**	**113**	**173**	**463**

Positional Success Rates vs NFL Average

		NFL Wide				Team Only			
		Left	Middle	Right	Total	Left	Middle	Right	Total
Deep	WR	37%	51%	38%	**41%**	35%	44%	32%	**36%**
	TE	44%	50%	43%	**46%**				
	RB	32%	75%	25%	**30%**				
	All	**38%**	**50%**	**39%**	**41%**	**35%**	**44%**	**32%**	**36%**
Short	WR	52%	57%	52%	**53%**	48%	46%	43%	**46%**
	TE	50%	62%	52%	**54%**				
	RB	47%	50%	44%	**46%**	51%	30%	50%	**46%**
	All	**51%**	**57%**	**50%**	**52%**	**49%**	**41%**	**45%**	**46%**
Total		**48%**	**56%**	**48%**	**50%**	**46%**	**42%**	**42%**	**43%**

Oakland Raiders

2017 Coaches

Head Coach:
Jack Del Rio (3rd yr)
Offensive Coordinator:
Todd Downing (OAK QB) (1st yr)
Defensive Coordinator:
Ken Norton Jr. (3rd yr)

EASY HARD

2017 Forecast

Wins	Div Rank
9.5	#1

Past Records

2016: 12-4
2015: 7-9
2014: 3-13

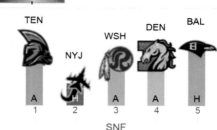

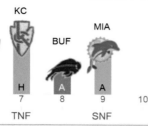

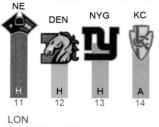

Week	1	2	3	4	5	6	7	8	9	10	11	12	13	14	15	16	17
Opponent	TEN	NYJ	WSH	DEN	BAL	LAC	KC	BUF	MIA		NE	DEN	NYG	KC	DAL	PHI	LAC
Site	A	H	A	A	H	H	H	A	A		H	H	H	A	H	A	A
Game			SNF				TNF		SNF		LON				SNF	MNF	

Key Players Lost

TXN	Player (POS)
Cut	Cherry, Demetrius DE
	Norman, Dwayne LB
	Thomas, Ahmad S
	Wade, Jordan DT
	Williams, Dan DT
Declared Free Agent	Allen, Nate S
	Bates, Daren LB
	Condo, Jon LB
	Edwards, SaQwan CB
	Hayden, DJ CB
	Holmes, Andre WR
	McGee, Stacy DT
	McGloin, Matt QB
	Murray, Latavius RB
	Riley Jr., Perry LB
	Rivera, Mychal TE
	Smith, Malcolm LB
	Trawick, Brynden S
	Watson, Menelik T

Average Line	# Games Favored	# Games Underdog
-1.8	10	4

2017 Oakland Raiders Overview

Last year I believed the Raiders were in a position to make great strides compared to the 7 wins the earned in 2015. A huge part of that reason was Carr's rookie contract, which saw him hit the cap for only $1.45M and the Raiders allocating the 2nd least of any team to the most important position in football. If Carr was able to play well, and the more expensive pieces surrounding him did their job, the Raiders should have outperformed those 7 wins from 2015. And they did, winning 12 games in 2016.

Before we unpack this tremendous win improvement and the manner in which the current 2017 Raiders are built to take the next step, let's first touch on some remarkable metrics from 2016. First, EDSR (Early Down Success Rate). The Raiders were able to turn EDSR on its head for much of the season. As it stands, the team that wins the EDSR battle is likely to win the game. There are several instances in blowout wins where the winner has a worse EDSR by the end of the game thanks to their turtled up 3rd and particularly 4th quarter as the opponent continues to pick on the prevent defense in full comeback mode. But absent those situations, there is only one thing that can foil EDSR most frequently and its turnovers.

The Raiders actually lost the EDSR battle in their first 7 games. That's 0-7. In other words, their opponent was more efficient offensively at avoiding 3rd downs while converting new first downs on first or second down, and their opponent was more efficient defensively at forcing the Raiders into 3rd down. Yet the Raiders went 5-2 in these games, posting winning margins of 1 point (twice) over the Saints and Ravens, 3 points over the Chargers, 7 points over the Titans and 17 points over the Jaguars. In these 5 wins, they went +0, +1, +2, +3 and +3 in the turnover battle. In other words, they used the turnovers to offset the fact they were less efficient in EDSR.

The Raiders only won the EDSR battle in 5 games out of 16 last year. They won all 5 of these games. That means of their other 7 wins, they lost the EDSR battle yet won the game. We mentioned the first 5 games in the prior paragraph. The other two came against the Panthers (won by 3, were +0 in turnover margin) and the Colts (won by 8, were +3 in turnover margin). If it looks like the Raiders were really strong in turnover margin last year, they were:

(cont'd - see OAK2)

Key Free Agents/ Trades Added

Cook, Jared TE
Jenkins, Jelani LB
Lynch, Marshawn RB
Manuel, EJ QB
Mulumba, Andy LB
Newhouse, Marshall T
Norman, Dwayne LB
Patterson, Cordarrelle WR

Drafted Players

Rd	Pk	Player (College)
1	24	CB - Gareon Conley (Ohio State)
2	56	S - Obi Melifonwu (Connecticut)
3	88	DT - Eddie Vanderdoes (UCLA)
4	129	OT - David Sharpe (Florida)
5	168	LB - Marquel Lee (Wake Forest)
7	221	S - Shalom Luani (Washington State)
	231	OT - Jaylen Ware (Alabama State)
	242	RB - Elijah Hood (North Carolina)
	244	DT - Treyvon Hester (Toledo)

Regular Season Wins: Past & Current Proj

	Wins
Proj 2017 Wins	9.5
2016 Wins	12
Proj 2016 Wins	8
2015 Wins	7
2014 Wins	3
2013 Wins	4

1 3 5 7 9 11 13 15

2017 Lineup & Cap Hits

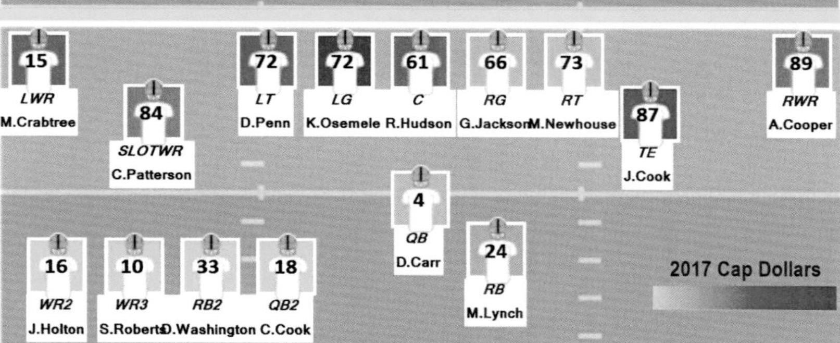

2017 Unit Spending

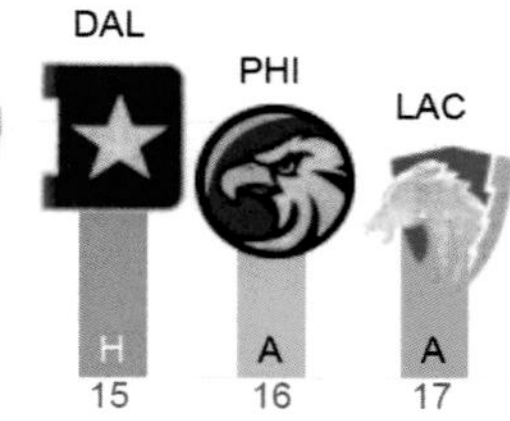

Positional Spending

	Rank	Total	2016 Rk
All OFF	14	$84.37M	14
QB	31	$3.04M	31
OL	3	$42.41M	1
RB	25	$5.28M	26
WR	11	$22.26M	10
TE	8	$11.37M	17
All DEF	27	$66.43M	10
DL	28	$17.48M	18
LB	25	$14.25M	11
CB	8	$22.84M	6
S	16	$11.85M	7

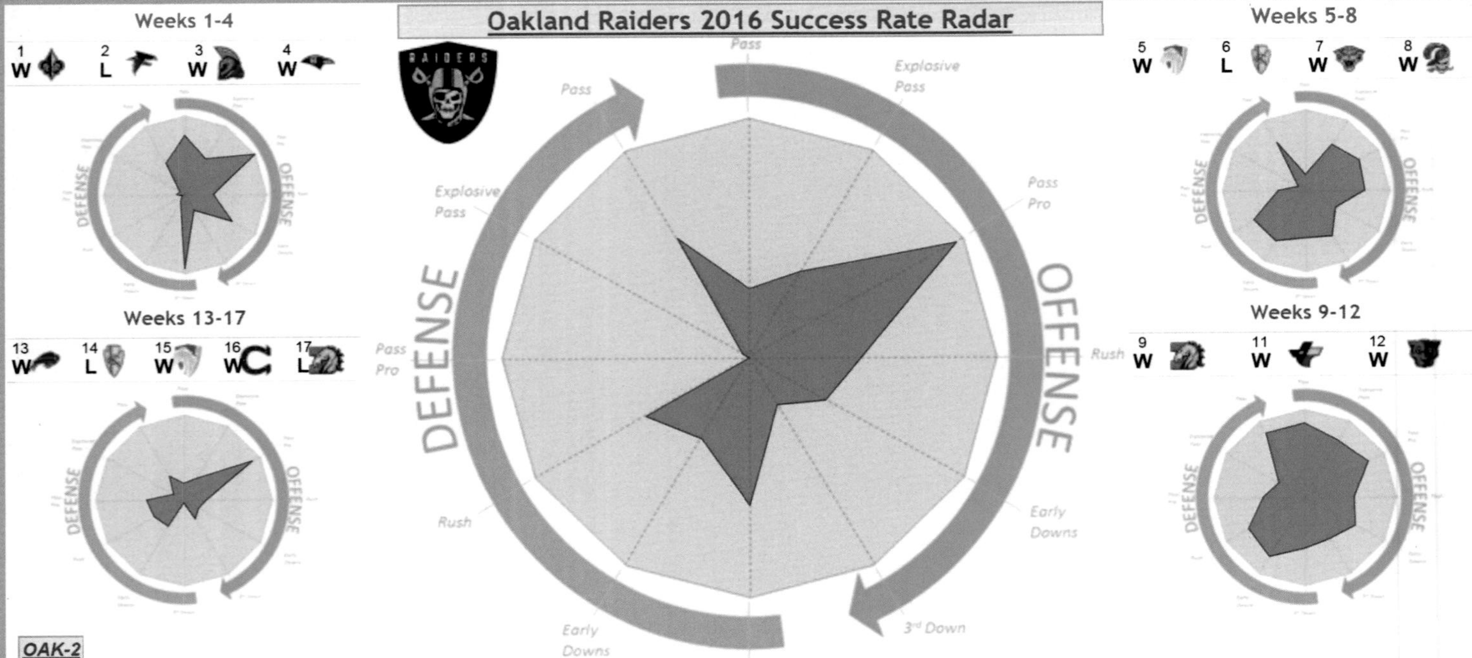

OAK-2

The Raiders went +16 in turnover margin, thanks to a +9 mark in interceptions and a +7 mark in fumbles. They lost the turnover battle in 4 games and went 1-3 in those 4 games (including their playoff loss). But went 11-2 when winning or pushing the turnover battle. These types of performances in turnover margin go a long way toward producing a 12-4 record.

But the other thing that goes far was their ability to play clutch and win close games. They played in 5 games decided by 3 or fewer points and went 5-0. They played in 11 games decided by one-score or less and went 9-2. A lot of that had to do with the performance of Derek Carr. In the 4th quarter of games which were tied or the Raiders trailed by up to 7 points, Carr averaged over 10 yards per attempt, posted a 8:0 TD:INT ratio and delivered a 132 passer rating, the second best in the NFL. But the 8 TDs were by far the most of any quarterback. Many quarterbacks with more attempts recorded half that number of passing TDs or less. In back and forth games, where the Raiders led at the half and saw their opponent take a lead into the 4th quarter, Carr never let the Raiders lose. They went 3-0 in these games (after never winning a game like this in his prior 2 seasons combined).

Carr posted a very solid 27:6 TD:INT ratio and was a big factor in the strength of the turnover margin edge enjoyed by the Raiders. His overall interception rate was 1%, and he threw one total interception in 230 attempts with between 1 and 9 yards-to-go on all downs combined. The most remarkable thing about the Raiders passing offense last year was the caliber of competition they did it against.

After 3 subpar defenses to start the season (Saints, Falcons and Titans) the Raiders began the gauntlet which saw them face a schedule of pass defenses which was substantially the most difficult in the NFL. They played 11 of their final 14 games against pass defenses which ranked top-11 in the NFL. And yet Carr and the passing offense still delivered.

(cont'd - see OAK-3)

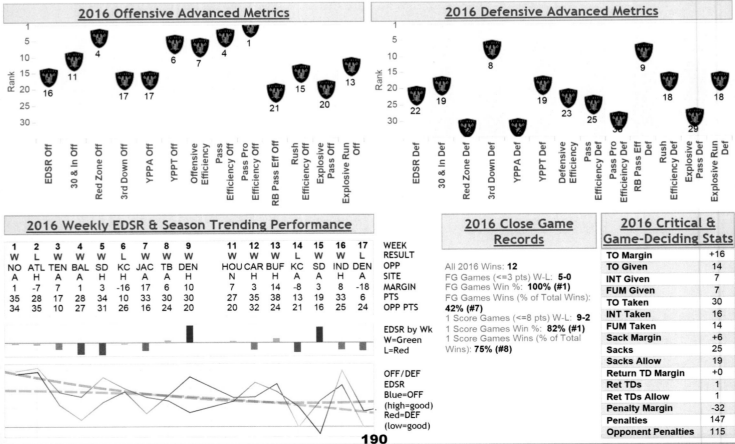

2016 Offensive Advanced Metrics

Metric	Rank
EDSR Off	16
30 & In Off	11
Red Zone Off	4
3rd Down Off	17
YPPA Off	17
YPPT Off	6
Offensive Efficiency	7
Pass Efficiency Off	4
Pass Pro Efficiency Off	1
RB Pass Eff Off	21
Rush Efficiency Off	15
Explosive Pass Off	20
Explosive Run Off	13

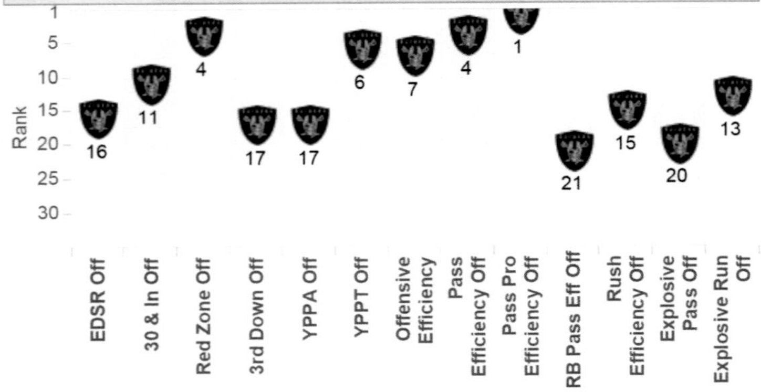

2016 Defensive Advanced Metrics

Metric	Rank
EDSR Def	22
30 & In Def	19
Red Zone Def	[illegible]
3rd Down Def	8
YPPA Def	[illegible]
YPPT Def	19
Defensive Efficiency	23
Pass Efficiency Def	25
Pass Pro Efficieincy Def	30
RB Pass Eff Def	9
Rush Efficiency Def	18
Explosive Pass Def	29
Explosive Run Def	18

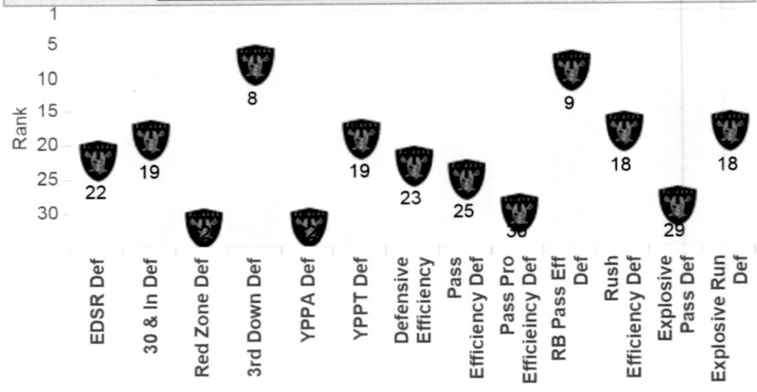

2016 Weekly EDSR & Season Trending Performance

WEEK	1	2	3	4	5	6	7	8	9	11	12	13	14	15	16	17
RESULT	W	L	W	W	W	L	W	W	W	W	W	W	L	W	W	L
OPP	NO	ATL	TEN	BAL	SD	KC	JAC	TB	DEN	HOU	CAR	BUF	KC	SD	IND	DEN
SITE	A	H	A	A	H	H	A	A	H	N	H	H	A	A	H	A
MARGIN	1	-7	7	1	3	-16	17	6	10	7	3	14	-8	3	8	-18
PTS	35	28	17	28	34	10	33	30	30	27	35	38	13	19	33	6
OPP PTS	34	35	10	27	31	26	16	24	20	20	32	24	21	16	25	24

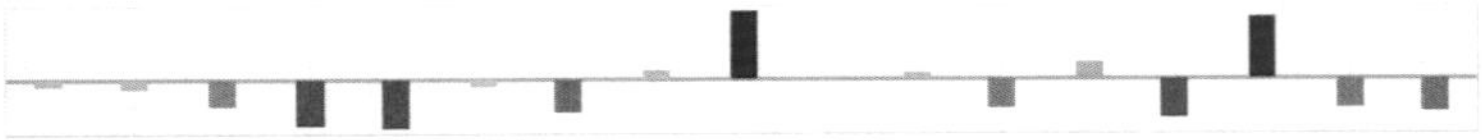

EDSR by Wk
W=Green
L=Red

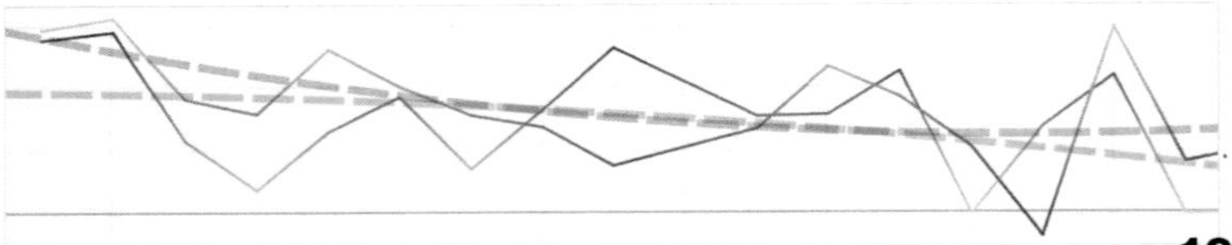

OFF/DEF EDSR
Blue=OFF (high=good)
Red=DEF (low=good)

2016 Close Game Records

All 2016 Wins: **12**
FG Games (<=3 pts) W-L: **5-0**
FG Games Win %: **100% (#1)**
FG Games Wins (% of Total Wins): **42% (#7)**
1 Score Games (<=8 pts) W-L: **9-2**
1 Score Games Win %: **82% (#1)**
1 Score Games Wins (% of Total Wins): **75% (#8)**

2016 Critical & Game-Deciding Stats

TO Margin	+16
TO Given	14
INT Given	7
FUM Given	7
TO Taken	30
INT Taken	16
FUM Taken	14
Sack Margin	+6
Sacks	25
Sacks Allow	19
Return TD Margin	+0
Ret TDs	1
Ret TDs Allow	1
Penalty Margin	-32
Penalties	147
Opponent Penalties	115

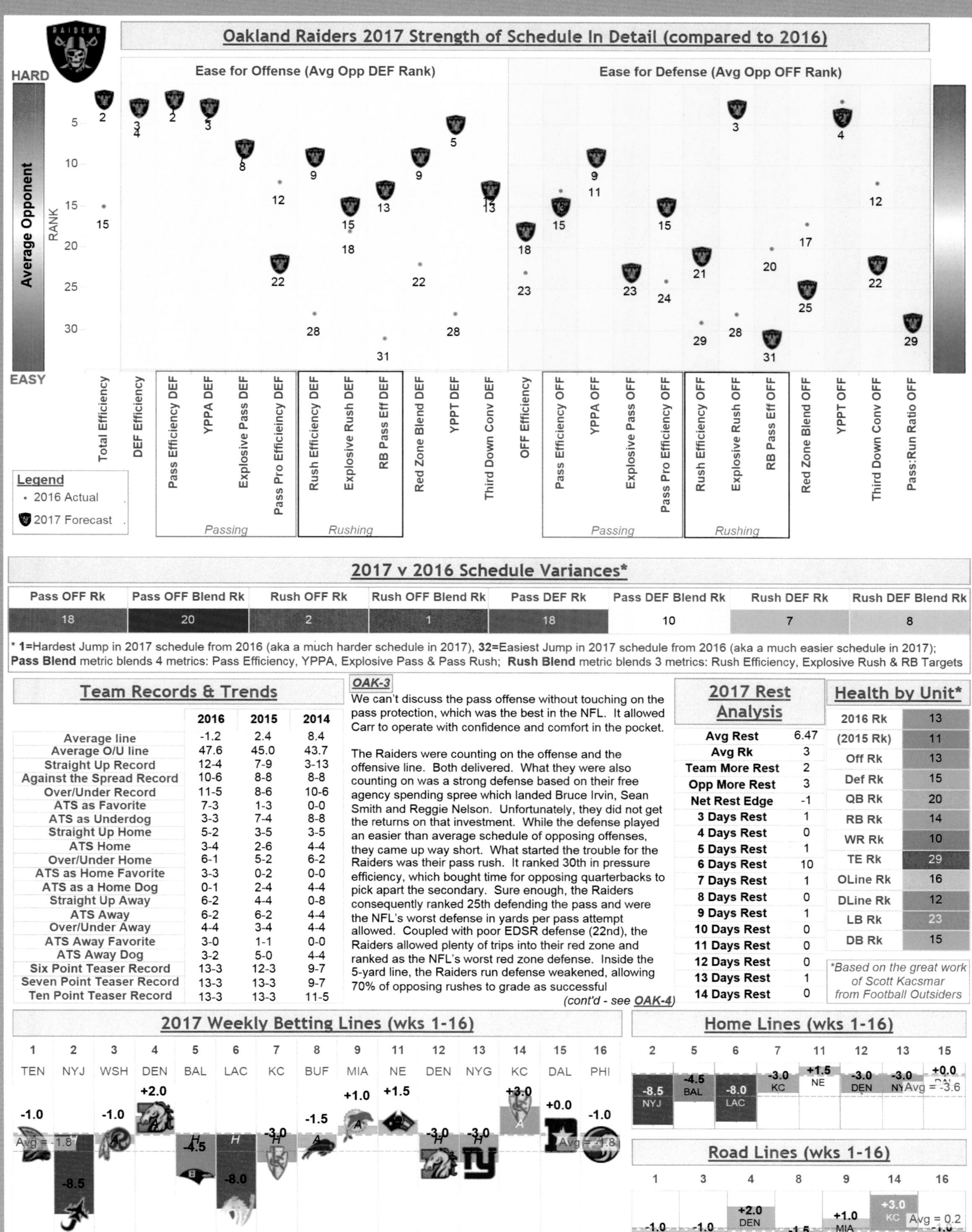

Oakland Raiders 2017 Strength of Schedule In Detail (compared to 2016)

2017 v 2016 Schedule Variances*

Pass OFF Rk	Pass OFF Blend Rk	Rush OFF Rk	Rush OFF Blend Rk	Pass DEF Rk	Pass DEF Blend Rk	Rush DEF Rk	Rush DEF Blend Rk
18	20	2	1	18	10	7	8

* **1**=Hardest Jump in 2017 schedule from 2016 (aka a much harder schedule in 2017), **32**=Easiest Jump in 2017 schedule from 2016 (aka a much easier schedule in 2017); **Pass Blend** metric blends 4 metrics: Pass Efficiency, YPPA, Explosive Pass & Pass Rush; **Rush Blend** metric blends 3 metrics: Rush Efficiency, Explosive Rush & RB Targets

Team Records & Trends

	2016	2015	2014
Average line	-1.2	2.4	8.4
Average O/U line	47.6	45.0	43.7
Straight Up Record	12-4	7-9	3-13
Against the Spread Record	10-6	8-8	8-8
Over/Under Record	11-5	8-6	10-6
ATS as Favorite	7-3	1-3	0-0
ATS as Underdog	3-3	7-4	8-8
Straight Up Home	5-2	3-5	3-5
ATS Home	3-4	2-6	4-4
Over/Under Home	6-1	5-2	6-2
ATS as Home Favorite	3-3	0-2	0-0
ATS as a Home Dog	0-1	2-4	4-4
Straight Up Away	6-2	4-4	0-8
ATS Away	6-2	6-2	4-4
Over/Under Away	4-4	3-4	4-4
ATS Away Favorite	3-0	1-1	0-0
ATS Away Dog	3-2	5-0	4-4
Six Point Teaser Record	13-3	12-3	9-7
Seven Point Teaser Record	13-3	13-3	9-7
Ten Point Teaser Record	13-3	13-3	11-5

OAK-3

We can't discuss the pass offense without touching on the pass protection, which was the best in the NFL. It allowed Carr to operate with confidence and comfort in the pocket.

The Raiders were counting on the offense and the offensive line. Both delivered. What they were also counting on was a strong defense based on their free agency spending spree which landed Bruce Irvin, Sean Smith and Reggie Nelson. Unfortunately, they did not get the returns on that investment. While the defense played an easier than average schedule of opposing offenses, they came up way short. What started the trouble for the Raiders was their pass rush. It ranked 30th in pressure efficiency, which bought time for opposing quarterbacks to pick apart the secondary. Sure enough, the Raiders consequently ranked 25th defending the pass and were the NFL's worst defense in yards per pass attempt allowed. Coupled with poor EDSR defense (22nd), the Raiders allowed plenty of trips into their red zone and ranked as the NFL's worst red zone defense. Inside the 5-yard line, the Raiders run defense weakened, allowing 70% of opposing rushes to grade as successful

(cont'd - see OAK-4)

2017 Rest Analysis

Avg Rest	6.47
Avg Rk	3
Team More Rest	2
Opp More Rest	3
Net Rest Edge	-1
3 Days Rest	1
4 Days Rest	0
5 Days Rest	1
6 Days Rest	10
7 Days Rest	1
8 Days Rest	0
9 Days Rest	1
10 Days Rest	0
11 Days Rest	0
12 Days Rest	0
13 Days Rest	1
14 Days Rest	0

Health by Unit*

2016 Rk	13
(2015 Rk)	11
Off Rk	13
Def Rk	15
QB Rk	20
RB Rk	14
WR Rk	10
TE Rk	29
OLine Rk	16
DLine Rk	12
LB Rk	23
DB Rk	15

*Based on the great work of Scott Kacsmar from Football Outsiders

2017 Weekly Betting Lines (wks 1-16)

1	2	3	4	5	6	7	8	9	11	12	13	14	15	16
TEN	NYJ	WSH	DEN	BAL	LAC	KC	BUF	MIA	NE	DEN	NYG	KC	DAL	PHI
-1.0	-8.5	-1.0	+2.0	-4.5	-8.0	-3.0	-1.5	+1.0	+1.5	-3.0	-3.0	+3.0	+0.0	-1.0

Avg = -1.8

Home Lines (wks 1-16)

2	5	6	7	11	12	13	15
NYJ	BAL	LAC	KC	NE	DEN	NYG	DAL
-8.5	-4.5	-8.0	-3.0	+1.5	-3.0	-3.0	+0.0

Avg = -3.6

Road Lines (wks 1-16)

1	3	4	8	9	14	16
TEN	WSH	DEN	BUF	MIA	KC	PHI
-1.0	-1.0	+2.0	-1.5	+1.0	+3.0	-1.0

Avg = 0.2

2016 Play Tendencies

All Pass %	61%
All Pass Rk	8
All Rush %	39%
All Rush Rk	25
1 Score Pass %	55%
1 Score Pass Rk	22
2015 1 Score Pass %	60%
2015 1 Score Pass Rk	10
Pass Increase %	-5%
Pass Increase Rk	29
1 Score Rush %	45%
1 Score Rush Rk	11
Up Pass %	56%
Up Pass Rk	21
Up Rush %	44%
Up Rush Rk	12
Down Pass %	62%
Down Pass Rk	13
Down Rush %	38%
Down Rush Rk	20

2016 Down & Distance Tendencies

Down	Distance	Total Plays	Pass Rate	Run Rate	Play Success %
1	Short (1-3)	9	22%	78%	56%
	Med (4-7)	16	31%	69%	69%
	Long (8-10)	310	53%	47%	50%
	XL (11+)	19	63%	37%	32%
2	Short (1-3)	41	34%	66%	59%
	Med (4-7)	79	48%	52%	54%
	Long (8-10)	107	64%	36%	39%
	XL (11+)	40	78%	23%	15%
3	Short (1-3)	45	58%	42%	51%
	Med (4-7)	59	92%	8%	49%
	Long (8-10)	35	97%	3%	31%
	XL (11+)	38	92%	8%	5%
4	Short (1-3)	3	100%	0%	67%
	Med (4-7)	1	100%	0%	0%
	XL (11+)	1	0%	100%	0%

Shotgun %:

Under Center	Shotgun
32%	68%
37%	*63%*

AVG

Run Rate:

Under Center	Shotgun
66%	27%
68%	*23%*

AVG

Pass Rate:

Under Center	Shotgun
34%	73%
32%	*77%*

AVG

Short Yardage Intelligence:

2nd and Short Run

Run Freq	Run % Rk	NFL Run Freq Avg	Run 1D Rate	Run NFL 1D Avg
63%	20	65%	68%	71%

2nd and Short Pass

Pass Freq	Pass % Rk	NFL Pass Freq Avg	Pass 1D Rate	Pass NFL 1D Avg
37%	13	35%	43%	52%

Most Frequent Play

Down	Distance	Play Type	Player	Total Plays	Play Success %
1	Short (1-3)	RUSH	Latavius Murray	6	67%
	Med (4-7)	RUSH	Latavius Murray	6	67%
	Long (8-10)	RUSH	Latavius Murray	72	39%
	XL (11+)	RUSH	Jalen Richard	3	0%
2	Short (1-3)	RUSH	Latavius Murray	15	80%
	Med (4-7)	RUSH	Latavius Murray	22	45%
	Long (8-10)	PASS	Amari Cooper	18	56%
	XL (11+)	PASS	Michael Crabtree	7	29%
			Jalen Richard	7	29%
3	Short (1-3)	RUSH	Latavius Murray	12	67%
	Med (4-7)	PASS	Michael Crabtree	19	47%
	Long (8-10)	PASS	Amari Cooper	11	36%
	XL (11+)	PASS	Michael Crabtree	8	0%

Most Successful Play*

Down	Distance	Play Type	Player	Total Plays	Play Success %
1	Short (1-3)	RUSH	Latavius Murray	6	67%
	Med (4-7)	RUSH	Latavius Murray	6	67%
	Long (8-10)	PASS	DeAndre Washington	8	75%
2	Short (1-3)	RUSH	Latavius Murray	15	80%
	Med (4-7)	PASS	Seth Roberts	5	60%
		RUSH	Jalen Richard	5	60%
	Long (8-10)	PASS	Amari Cooper	18	56%
	XL (11+)	PASS	Michael Crabtree	7	29%
			Jalen Richard	7	29%
3	Short (1-3)	PASS	Michael Crabtree	8	75%
	Med (4-7)	PASS	Clive Walford	6	67%
	Long (8-10)	PASS	Amari Cooper	11	36%
	XL (11+)	PASS	Amari Cooper	5	40%

*Minimum 5 plays to qualify

2016 Snap Rates

Week	Opp	Score	Amari Cooper	Michael Crabtree	Seth Roberts	Clive Walford	Latavius Murray	Mychal Rivera
1	NO	W 35-34	72 (99%)	68 (93%)	60 (82%)	37 (51%)	45 (62%)	
2	ATL	L 35-28	69 (92%)	57 (76%)	51 (68%)	47 (63%)	36 (48%)	
3	TEN	W 17-10	52 (80%)	49 (75%)	40 (62%)	44 (68%)	31 (48%)	
4	BAL	W 28-27	55 (92%)	46 (77%)	41 (68%)	44 (73%)	34 (57%)	16 (27%)
5	SD	W 34-31	65 (90%)	53 (74%)	51 (71%)			47 (65%)
6	KC	L 26-10	55 (100%)	45 (82%)	48 (87%)	29 (53%)		11 (20%)
7	JAC	W 33-16	68 (94%)	50 (69%)	47 (65%)	49 (68%)	42 (58%)	17 (24%)
8	TB	W 30-24	90 (96%)	72 (77%)	62 (66%)	59 (63%)	36 (38%)	21 (22%)
9	DEN	W 30-20	64 (75%)	48 (56%)	26 (31%)	72 (85%)	43 (51%)	48 (56%)
11	HOU	W 27-20	42 (79%)	39 (74%)	22 (42%)	37 (70%)	32 (60%)	25 (47%)
12	CAR	W 35-32	71 (96%)	65 (88%)	55 (74%)	43 (58%)	49 (66%)	22 (30%)
13	BUF	W 38-24	63 (89%)	57 (80%)	55 (77%)	45 (63%)	50 (70%)	20 (28%)
14	KC	L 21-13	74 (99%)	64 (85%)	71 (95%)	44 (59%)	52 (69%)	23 (31%)
15	SD	W 19-16	50 (81%)	45 (73%)	33 (53%)	45 (73%)	31 (50%)	21 (34%)
16	IND	W 33-25	61 (80%)	39 (51%)	51 (67%)	64 (84%)	31 (41%)	15 (20%)
17	DEN	L 24-6	42 (78%)	35 (65%)	32 (59%)	41 (76%)	16 (30%)	27 (50%)
Grand Total			993 (89%)	832 (75%)	745 (67%)	700 (67%)	528 (53%)	313 (35%)

Personnel Groupings

Personnel	Team %	NFL Avg	Succ. %
1-1 [3WR]	28%	60%	43%
1-0 [4WR]	22%	3%	39%
1-2 [2WR]	19%	19%	47%
0-0 [5WR]	9%	1%	53%
1-3 [1WR]	6%	3%	56%
2-0 [3WR]	4%	1%	44%
2-2 [1WR]	4%	3%	45%
2-1 [2WR]	3%	7%	38%

Grouping Tendencies

Personnel	Pass Rate	Pass Succ. %	Run Succ. %
1-1 [3WR]	54%	41%	46%
1-0 [4WR]	84%	38%	42%
1-2 [2WR]	46%	48%	47%
0-0 [5WR]	99%	52%	100%
1-3 [1WR]	15%	56%	57%
2-0 [3WR]	81%	41%	56%
2-2 [1WR]	20%	56%	43%
2-1 [2WR]	38%	55%	28%

Red Zone Targets (min 3)

Receiver	All	Inside 5	6-10	11-20
Michael Crabtree	22	6	2	14
Seth Roberts	20	4	5	11
Amari Cooper	13	6	1	6
Clive Walford	10	4	2	4
Andre Holmes	9	5	2	2
Jalen Richard	5	1		4
Latavius Murray	5		2	3
Mychal Rivera	4	1	2	1
Jamize Olawale	3		1	2

Red Zone Rushes (min 3)

Rusher	All	Inside 5	6-10	11-20
Latavius Murray	43	18	10	15
Derek Carr	6			6
Jalen Richard	5			5
Jamize Olawale	5	4		1
DeAndre Washingt..	4	2	1	1

Early Down Target Rate

RB	TE	WR
23%	16%	61%
19%	*20%*	*61%*

NFL AVG

Overall Target Success %

RB	TE	WR
43%	49%	45%
#20	#26	#25

Oakland Raiders 2016 Passing Recap & 2017 Outlook

Derek Carr's season should start off strong in the pass game, as the Raiders first 3 opponents ranked bottom-10 in pass defense last season. They have the easiest first-3 games in the NFL. But it's all downhill from there. The Raiders face the most difficult schedule of pass defenses from week 4 onward, in large part due to the strength of the AFC West, but it doesn't help playing top-10 pass defenses of the Ravens, Giants and Eagles in 2017. That said, they played the most difficult pass defenses in 2016 and were still able to deliver. Behind this strong offensive line, Derek Carr needs to improve on two key items from 2016: get the ball to Jared Cook and create more explosive pass plays. With TE targets being better for the Raiders in 2016 and a better receiving TE now on the roster, it absolutely needs to be a priority to incorporate Cook quickly. Of their 3 most used personnel packages, the Raiders were the most successful with at least 1 TE on the field, so I hope they decide to dial back the 10 personnel groupings with Cook in the mix. They went to 10 personnel (1 RB/0 TE/4 WRs) 22% of the time whereas the NFL average was just 3%. Adding Cook as the TE should open up more opportunities for efficiency.

Derek Carr Rating All Downs

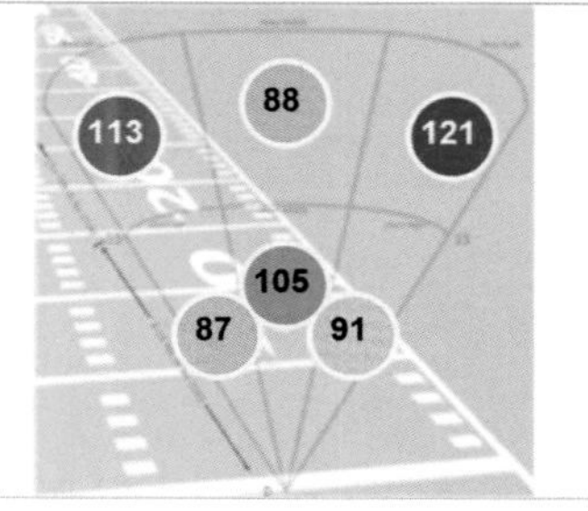

Derek Carr Rating Early Downs

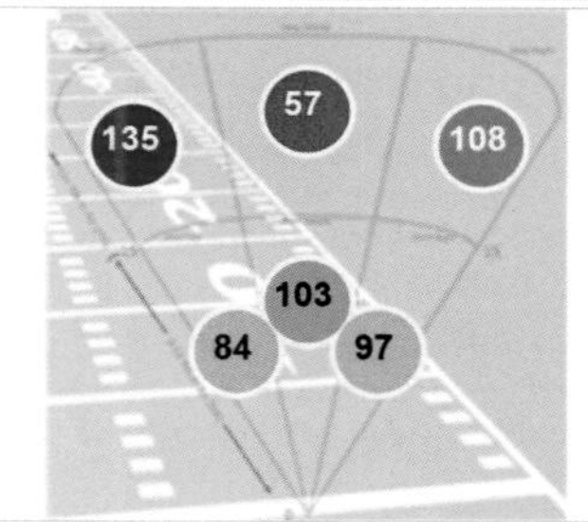

2016 Standard Passing Table

QB	Comp	Att	Comp %	Yds	YPA	TDs	INT	Sacks	Rating	Rk
Derek Carr	355	558	64%	3,933	7.0	27	6	17	96.1	14
Connor Cook	32	66	48%	311	4.7	2	4	5	47.0	57
NFL Avg			63%		7.2				90.4	

2016 Advanced Passing Table

QB	Success %	EDSR Passing Success %	20+ Yd Pass Gains	20+ Yd Pass %	30+ Yd Pass Gains	30+ Yd Pass %	Air Yds per Comp	YAC per Comp	20+ Air Yd Comp	20+ Air Yd %
Derek Carr	45%	49%	50	9%	21	4%	5.9	5.2	24	4%
Connor Cook	34%	43%	2	3%	1	2%	5.7	4.1	2	3%
NFL Avg	44%	48%	27	8%	10	3%	6.4	4.8	12	4%

Interception Rates by Down

Yards to Go	1	2	3	4	Total
1 & 2	0.0%	0.0%	0.0%	0.0%	0.0%
3, 4, 5	0.0%	0.0%	0.0%	0.0%	0.0%
6 - 9	0.0%	0.0%	1.9%	0.0%	0.8%
10 - 14	1.0%	4.8%	0.0%	0.0%	1.7%
15+	0.0%	0.0%	0.0%		0.0%
Total	0.9%	1.7%	0.6%	0.0%	1.0%

3rd Down Passing - Short of Sticks Analysis

QB	Avg Yds to Go	Air Yds (of Comps)	Avg Yds Short	Short of Sticks Rate	Rk
Derek Carr	8.0	8.1	0.0	56%	15
NFL Avg	7.6	6.8	-0.8	57%	

Air Yds vs YAC

Air Yds %	YAC %	Rk
45%	55%	43
54%	46%	

2016 Receiving Recap & 2017 Outlook

While Cooper's big play ability should serve Oakland well in 2017, Crabtree was more reliable from a success rate perspective. I'd like to see more 12 personnel passes in 2017. The Raiders threw a ton of passes inside the 5 yard line, but should plan these better over the offseason to maximize efficiency. Crabtree's targets were by far the highest hit rate (4 TDs on 6 targets and a 67% success rate) but Roberts, Cooper and Holmes were very inefficient on these short range passes (20% success rate on 15 targets). They would have been much better served running the ball more (58% success rate) and feeding Crabtree (67% success rate).

Player *Min 50 Targets*	Targets	Comp %	YPA	Rating	TOARS	Success %	Success Rk	Missed YPA Rk	YAS % Rk	TDs
Michael Crabtree	152	60%	6.8	92	5.3	51%	65	123	65	8
Amari Cooper	141	60%	8.2	89	5.1	44%	118	87	37	5
Seth Roberts	84	46%	4.7	75	4.0	35%	145	145	42	5
Clive Walford	54	65%	6.9	104	3.9	44%	114	68	58	3

Directional Passer Rating Delivered

Receiver	Short Left	Short Middle	Short Right	Deep Left	Deep Middle	Deep Right	Player Total
Michael Crabtree	75	107	95	57	106	88	92
Amari Cooper	87	70	67	138	56	135	89
Seth Roberts	88	75	69	40	59	49	70
Clive Walford	70	126	94	135	79	79	104
Latavius Murray	56	92	83				78
Jalen Richard	108	132	74			96	102
Andre Holmes	49	113	101	40	119		102
Mychal Rivera	94	123	95	40	56	110	91
DeAndre Washington	34	62	90				64
Team Total	78	103	86	112	63	105	89

2016 Rushing Recap & 2017 Outlook

With Latavius Murray now in Minnesota, it will be on Marshawn Lynch to try to stay injury free and produce. The best part is, he is running behind one of the best lines he's ever run behind. So the yardage before contact should be far superior to what he saw in Seattle. In addition, with Seattle being more run heavy with him in the mix, he was the key focus for defenses. In Oakland, the team is extremely balanced. On more standard down/distances, such as 1st and 10, 2nd and medium and 3rd and short, the Raiders are (respectively), 53% pass, 48% pass and 58% pass. There are ample run opportunities without being too run heavy and inefficient. It could be a perfect marriage assuming his health holds up.

Player *Min 50 Rushes*	Rushes	YPA	Success %	Success Rk	Missed YPA Rk	YTS % Rk	YAS % Rk	Early Down Success %	Early Down Success Rk	TDs
Latavius Murray	207	4.0	48%	34	19	56	34	47%	37	13
DeAndre Washington	90	5.4	47%	38	49	66	10	46%	39	2
Jalen Richard	87	5.7	47%	37	58	61	21	49%	24	1

Yards per Carry by Direction

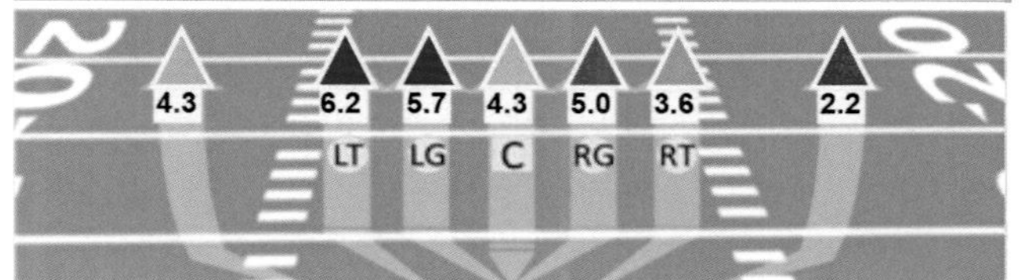

Directional Run Frequency

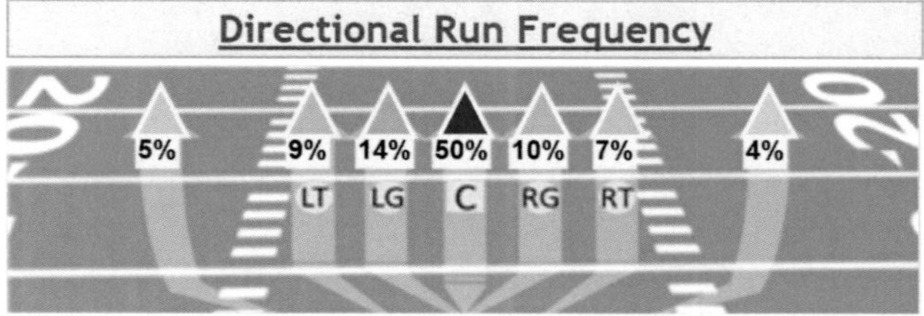

one of the worst marks in the NFL. To help protect that defense, the Raiders went to a more possession oriented offense. In one-score games, they ran the ball 5% more often in 2016 than 2015, which was the 4th largest shift to the run of any team in the NFL.

So for 2017, it was clearly a prime objective to help improve the defense. The Raiders used their first 3 draft picks plus 5 of their first 6 overall to draft defensive players. Oakland will hope these pieces will help the defense and the other element which would help is a stronger running game. They (intelligently) turned down pursuing another contract for Latavius Murray and instead let him walk to Minnesota. Instead, they brought back Marshawn Lynch, formerly of the Seahawks. It will be an interesting season for the run game.

I am of the belief that Latavius Murray did not produce well enough as a bell cow back last season. Particularly behind this offensive line. He had his spots of performance, such as in short yardage and near the goal line. For example, on 2nd through 4th down and short, Murray produced successful runs 74% of the time, which ranked 9th best in the NFL out of 32 rushers. The issue becomes, however, that behind this offensive line, DeAndre Washington produced successful runs 78% of the time, but had too small of a sample size to qualify. In the red zone, Murray was solid. He had the 6th most touches in the NFL inside the 5 yard line and among those above him, only David Johnson had a better success rate on those touches. Murray scored 10 TDs on 18 carries with 61% of those touches grading as successful. And of his touches between the 6-10 yard line, 70% graded as successful, a better number than any RB with more than 7 touches. But with such small sample sizes, it is impossible to accurately compare to other Raiders RBs. What we should find out in 2017 is how much of that production was the line itself, rather than Murray himself?

From the passing perspective, not much changes from 2016 from a personnel perspective with one exception: TE Jared Cook. Even though league-wide, passes to TEs are the most efficient pass a quarterback can throw, the Raiders severely underutilized their TEs last year. They targeted them 4% less than average. These targets resulted in a 49% success rate. While ranking 26th in the NFL, it was the most successful target on the Raiders, as targets to WRs were successful just 45% of the time and RBs just 43%. Not only were these targets more successful than others, they also saw better yards per attempt, which is not always the case. The Raiders must develop more opportunities to dial up plays specifically for Cook. If they can do that, it could open a lot of opportunities for the other receivers and potentially add a bit of mustard to the explosive passing game which took a step back in 2016.

Division History: Season Wins & 2017 Projection

2013 Wins | 2014 Wins | 2015 Wins | 2016 Wins | Proj 2017 Wins

Rank of 2017 Defensive Pass Efficiency Faced by Week

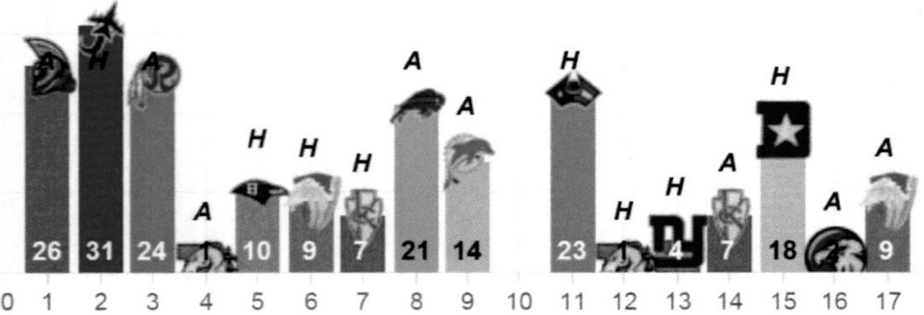

Rank of 2017 Defensive Rush Efficiency Faced by Week

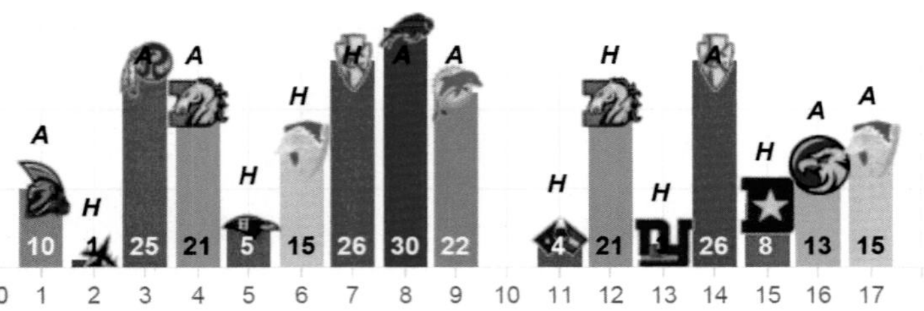

2016 Situational Usage by Player & Position

Usage Rate by Score

		Being Blown Out (14+)	Down Big (9-13)	One Score	Large Lead (9-13)	Blowout Lead (14+)	Grand Total
RUSH	Latavius Murray	16%	16%	18%	35%	41%	20%
	Amari Cooper		1%	0%			0%
	Jalen Richard	2%	6%	9%	10%	5%	8%
	DeAndre Washington	6%	8%	8%	14%	16%	9%
	Jamize Olawale	1%	1%	2%	1%	3%	2%
	Johnny Holton	1%		1%	1%		1%
	Taiwan Jones			0%			0%
	Total	26%	32%	38%	62%	65%	39%
PASS	Latavius Murray	5%	6%	5%		5%	5%
	Michael Crabtree	11%	13%	15%	12%	14%	15%
	Amari Cooper	14%	16%	14%	4%	11%	14%
	Jalen Richard	3%	6%	4%		3%	4%
	DeAndre Washington	2%	3%	2%	3%		2%
	Seth Roberts	11%	9%	8%	6%	3%	8%
	Clive Walford	8%	3%	6%	1%		5%
	Jamize Olawale	3%	3%	1%	1%		1%
	Andre Holmes	6%	3%	2%	7%		3%
	Mychal Rivera	7%	5%	2%	3%		3%
	Johnny Holton	2%	1%	0%			0%
	Lee Smith			1%			1%
	Taiwan Jones	1%		0%			0%
	Total	74%	68%	62%	38%	35%	61%

Positional Target Distribution vs NFL Average

		NFL Wide				Team Only			
		Left	Middle	Right	**Total**	Left	Middle	Right	**Total**
Deep	WR	1,004	561	969	**2,534**	27	20	32	**79**
	TE	155	143	158	**456**	3	4	5	**12**
	RB	25	4	38	**67**			2	**2**
	All	**1,184**	**708**	**1,165**	**3,057**	**30**	**24**	**39**	**93**
Short	WR	2,967	1,705	3,051	**7,723**	126	66	135	**327**
	TE	821	852	1,117	**2,790**	15	23	34	**72**
	RB	980	590	1,070	**2,640**	35	32	43	**110**
	All	**4,768**	**3,147**	**5,238**	**13,153**	**176**	**121**	**212**	**509**
Total		**5,952**	**3,855**	**6,403**	**16,210**	**206**	**145**	**251**	**602**

Positional Success Rates vs NFL Average

		NFL Wide				Team Only			
		Left	Middle	Right	**Total**	Left	Middle	Right	**Total**
Deep	WR	37%	50%	38%	**40%**	33%	60%	38%	**42%**
	TE	45%	50%	43%	**46%**	33%	50%	60%	**50%**
	RB	32%	75%	24%	**30%**			50%	**50%**
	All	**38%**	**50%**	**38%**	**41%**	**33%**	**58%**	**41%**	**43%**
Short	WR	52%	57%	52%	**53%**	44%	55%	44%	**46%**
	TE	50%	62%	52%	**54%**	33%	61%	47%	**49%**
	RB	47%	50%	44%	**47%**	43%	34%	40%	**39%**
	All	**51%**	**57%**	**50%**	**52%**	**43%**	**50%**	**43%**	**45%**
Total		**48%**	**56%**	**48%**	**50%**	**42%**	**52%**	**43%**	**45%**

Philadelphia Eagles

2017 Coaches

Head Coach:
Doug Pederson (2nd yr)
Offensive Coordinator:
Frank Reich (2nd yr)
Defensive Coordinator:
Jim Schwartz (2nd yr)

EASY HARD

2017 Forecast

Wins	Div Rank
8	#3

Past Records

2016: 7-9
2015: 7-9
2014: 10-6

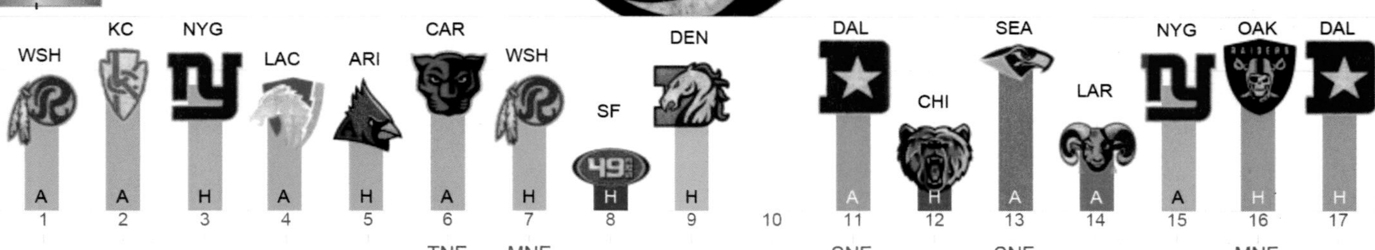

Key Players Lost

TXN	Player (POS)
Cut	Bailey, Rasheed WR
	Barwin, Connor LB
	Daniel, Chase QB
	Daniels, Steven LB
	Evans, Jerod QB
	LeRibeus, Josh G
	McKelvin, Leodis CB
	Oliver, Marcus LB
	Shittu, Aziz DT
	Walker, Charles DT
	Williams, Dom WR
	Wujciak, Connor DT
Declared Free Agent	Barner, Kenjon RB
	Braman, Bryan DE
	Carroll, Nolan CB
	Logan, Bennie DT
	Tulloch, Stephen LB
	Wisniewski, Stefen C
Retired	Tulloch, Stephen LB

Average Line	# Games Favored	# Games Underdog
+0.6	7	8

2017 Philadelphia Eagles Overview

Last spring, the Eagles traded up to draft QB Carson Wentz, who was projected to learn behind QB Sam Bradford. Then Teddy Bridgewater went down and Wentz was immediately thrust into a starting role. And the Eagles thrived to start the season, winning 3 straight games and scoring no less than 29 points in any game, winning by solid margins in each game. And Wentz did well in each game, posting over a 100 passer rating twice (averaged a 104 rating), throwing a total of 5 TDs and 0 Ints while taking no more than 2 sacks in any game, and 4 total sacks over his first 3 games.

Then the Eagles entered their bye week (week 4) and the season wasn't the same. Key offensive lineman Lane Johnson saw his 10-game suspension, which was on appeal, upheld by the league. Week 4 was his last game and he would not return until week 15. Ironically, with Johnson in the lineup, the Eagles were 5-1 last year. Without him anchoring the line at right tackle, the team was 2-8. The Eagles could not stay healthy at the right tackle position and it was a virtual revolving door of players trying to stay healthy enough to fill that role.

The other element making it so difficult to overcome injuries along the line is to witness the lower right graphic to see the Eagles positional spending. In 2016 the Eagles spent the 2nd most of any team on the offensive line. The team was inexpensively built last year, spending the most on the offensive line and running back. But when you're trying to protect a young quarterback, it's nice to have a system built to keep him upright and comfortable, and the Eagles thought they had that covered but injuries derailed it. Remarkably, however, the Eagles still ranked 10th in pass protection efficiency. But that was, in large reason, because of the number of passes they (intelligently) threw to RBs and TEs, which are typically more efficient and can be released quicker. Wentz targeted his TEs and RBs each over the NFL average, and while the RB success rate was subpar apart from Sproles, the TE success rate was the 5th best in the NFL.

Speaking of the TE, the Eagles loved using 12 personnel (1 RB, 2 TE). They used it more than any other team in the NFL, and when they lined up in 12 personnel, they passed the ball almost as much as they did when in 11 personnel.

(cont'd - see PHI2)

Key Free Agents/ Trades Added

Blount, LeGarrette RB
Daniels, Steven LB
Foles, Nick QB
Jeffery, Alshon WR
Jernigan, Timmy DT
Long, Chris DE
Robinson, Patrick CB
Smith, Torrey WR
Thomas, Dallas G
Warmack, Chance G

Drafted Players

Rd	Pk	Player (College)
1	14	DE - Derek Barnett (Tennessee)
2	43	CB - Sidney Jones (Washington)
3*	99	CB - Rasul Douglas (West Virginia)
4	118	WR - Mack Hollins (North Carolina)
	132	RB - Donnel Pumphrey (San Diego State)
5	166	WR - Shelton Gibson (West Virginia)
5*	184	S - Nathan Gerry (Nebraska)
6	214	DT - Elijah Qualls (Washington)

Regular Season Wins: Past & Current Proj

Proj 2017 Wins	8
2016 Wins	7
Proj 2016 Wins	7
2015 Wins	7
2014 Wins	10
2013 Wins	10

1 3 5 7 9 11 13 15

2017 Lineup & Cap Hits

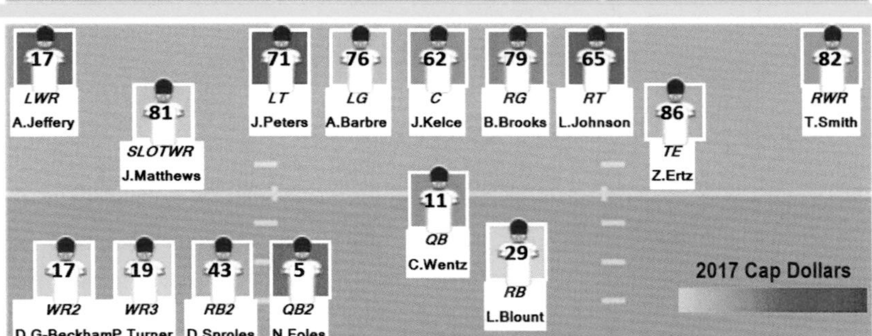

2017 Unit Spending

All DEF
All OFF

Positional Spending

	Rank	Total	2016 Rk
All OFF	2	$99.27M	21
QB	26	$8.30M	27
OL	2	$45.35M	2
RB	6	$11.22M	3
WR	9	$23.55M	32
TE	10	$10.85M	16
All DEF	20	$75.80M	21
DL	8	$39.21M	7
LB	22	$15.02M	26
CB	30	$7.53M	26
S	9	$14.04M	12

Philadelphia Eagles 2016 Success Rate Radar

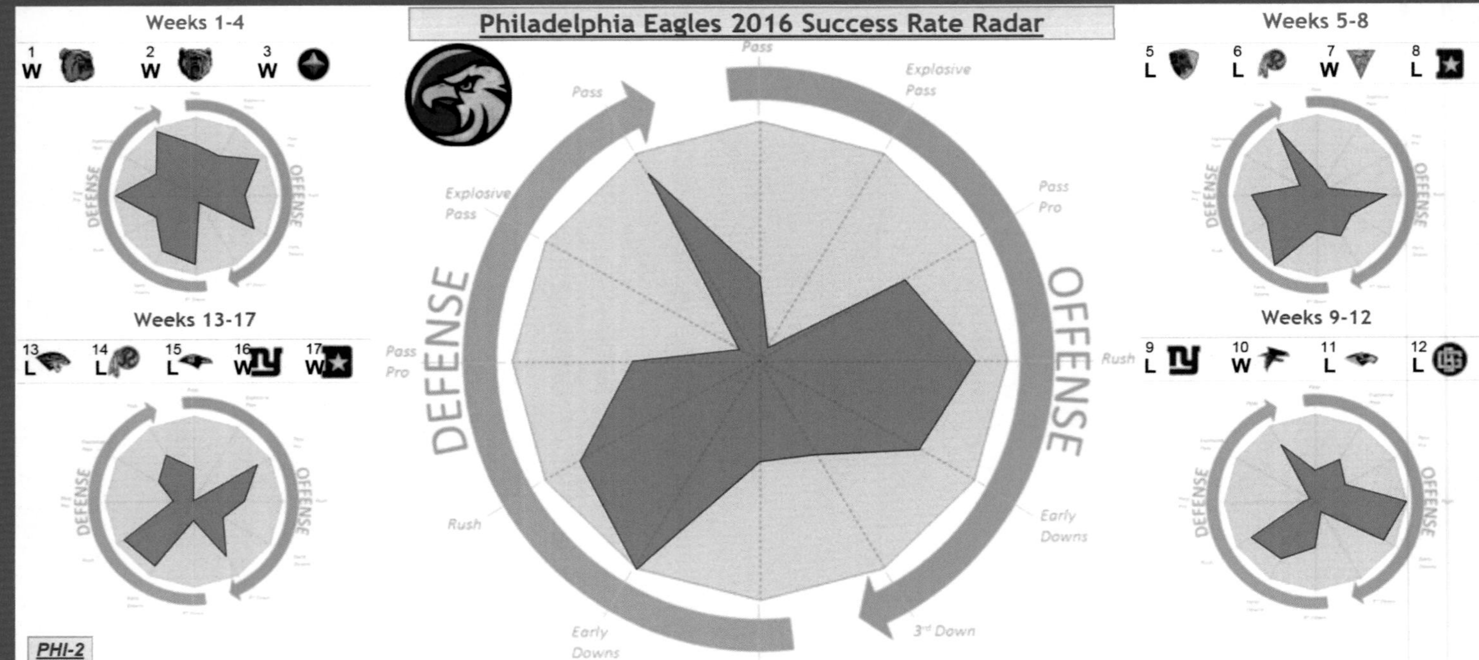

PHI-2

The problem in 12 personnel came when targeting their WRs instead of TEs. When targeting WRs in 12 personnel, the Eagles were successful on just 36% of their passes, with a 58 rating from Wentz (compare that to in 11 personnel, when the success rate was 48%). But when targeting the TEs in 12 personnel (as there are 2 on the field), the Eagles were successful on 64% of their plays (with a 98 rating from Wentz). So clearly the Eagles were great when targeting their TEs in 12 personnel, and they ran 12 personnel more often than any other team in the NFL. But they targeted WRs on 70% of their non-RB passes in 12 personnel, while targeting the TEs on only 30% of those attempts.

This positional usage was extremely odd because it was far and away the most in the NFL. While the average targeting of WRs came from 12 personnel on just 13% of plays, the Eagles were using 12 personnel on 31% of their WR targets. Most teams averaged about 45 targets to WRs when in 12 personnel. The Eagles targeted them 115 times. And the target quality was, as mentioned, 36% success rate and 58 passer rating. Hopefully Doug Peterson sees these numbers and modifies his targets and play calls when in 12 personnel to focus more on the TE. Because that was the best time to use the TEs – in 11 personnel, the success rate for the Eagles as well as Wentz's passer rating were not nearly as strong as they were when in 12 personnel.

There are some other areas the Eagles could clean up their play calling to improve efficiency. I won't tackle them all here. One lesser area would be to run the ball more often on 2nd and short. It wasn't as egregious as other play calling inefficiencies, but they were 25% more successful at converting first downs when running than passing (larger than the NFL average) but they still ran it only as often as the NFL average. This is a smaller issue, but the larger issue is this:

It is very difficult for most sophomore quarterbacks in the NFL. Opponents have a full season of tape on them. They've seen their best and their worst. Defensive coordinators have a lot of ammunition to throw at the young signal callers.

(cont'd - see PHI-3)

2016 Offensive Advanced Metrics

Metric	Rank
EDSR Off	20
30 & In Off	24
Red Zone Off	25
3rd Down Off	26
YPPA Off	27
YPPT Off	8
Offensive Efficiency	20
Pass Efficiency Off	25
Pass Pro Efficiency Off	10
RB Pass Eff Off	1
Rush Efficiency Off	9
Explosive Pass Off	28
Explosive Run Off	7

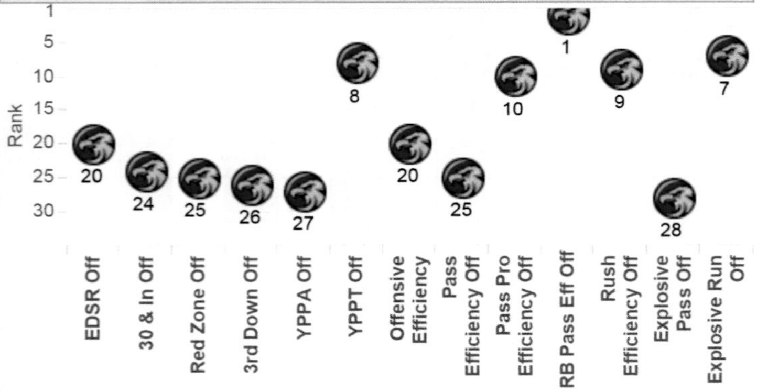

2016 Defensive Advanced Metrics

Metric	Rank
EDSR Def	7
30 & In Def	16
Red Zone Def	12
3rd Down Def	19
YPPA Def	25
YPPT Def	6
Defensive Efficiency	4
Pass Efficiency Def	2
Pass Pro Efficiency Def	11
RB Pass Eff Def	6
Rush Efficiency Def	13
Explosive Pass Def	30
Explosive Run Def	28

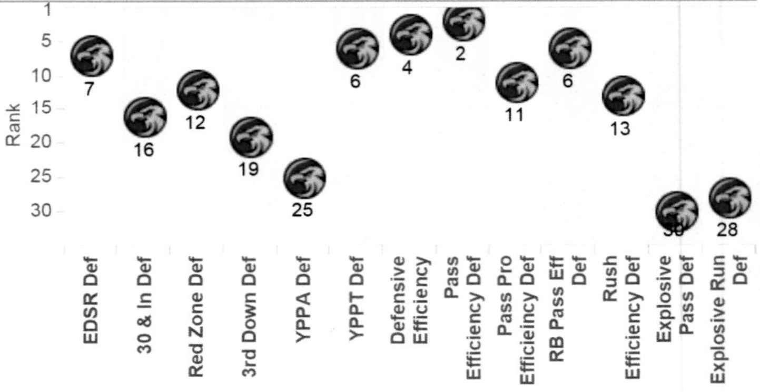

2016 Weekly EDSR & Season Trending Performance

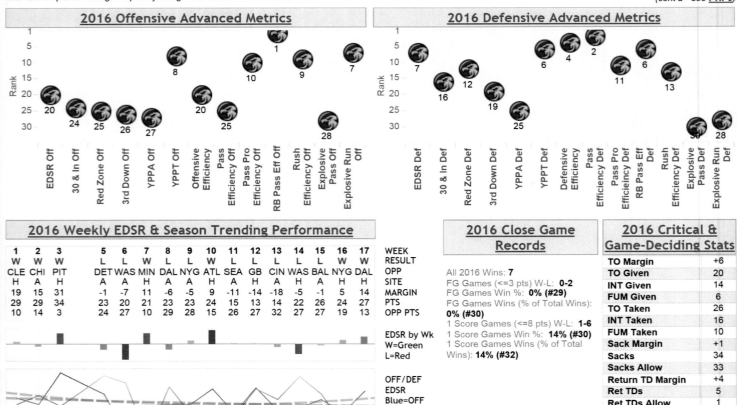

WEEK	1	2	3	5	6	7	8	9	10	11	12	13	14	15	16	17
RESULT	W	W	W	L	L	W	L	L	W	L	L	L	L	L	W	W
OPP	CLE	CHI	PIT	DET	WAS	MIN	DAL	NYG	ATL	SEA	GB	CIN	WAS	BAL	NYG	DAL
SITE	H	A	H	A	A	H	A	A	H	A	H	A	H	A	H	H
MARGIN	19	15	31	-1	-7	11	-6	-5	9	-11	-14	-18	-5	-1	5	14
PTS	29	29	34	23	20	21	23	23	24	15	13	14	22	26	24	27
OPP PTS	10	14	3	24	27	10	29	28	15	26	27	32	27	27	19	13

EDSR by Wk
W=Green
L=Red

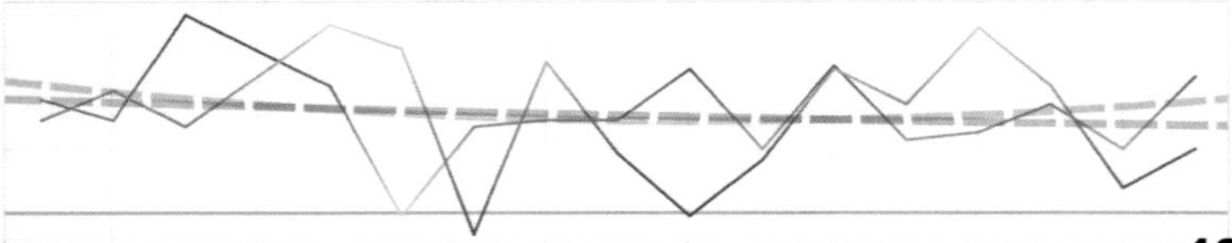

OFF/DEF EDSR
Blue=OFF (high=good)
Red=DEF (low=good)

2016 Close Game Records

All 2016 Wins: **7**
FG Games (<=3 pts) W-L: **0-2**
FG Games Win %: **0% (#29)**
FG Games Wins (% of Total Wins): **0% (#30)**
1 Score Games (<=8 pts) W-L: **1-6**
1 Score Games Win %: **14% (#30)**
1 Score Games Wins (% of Total Wins): **14% (#32)**

2016 Critical & Game-Deciding Stats

TO Margin	+6
TO Given	20
INT Given	14
FUM Given	6
TO Taken	26
INT Taken	16
FUM Taken	10
Sack Margin	+1
Sacks	34
Sacks Allow	33
Return TD Margin	+4
Ret TDs	5
Ret TDs Allow	1
Penalty Margin	-14
Penalties	113
Opponent Penalties	99

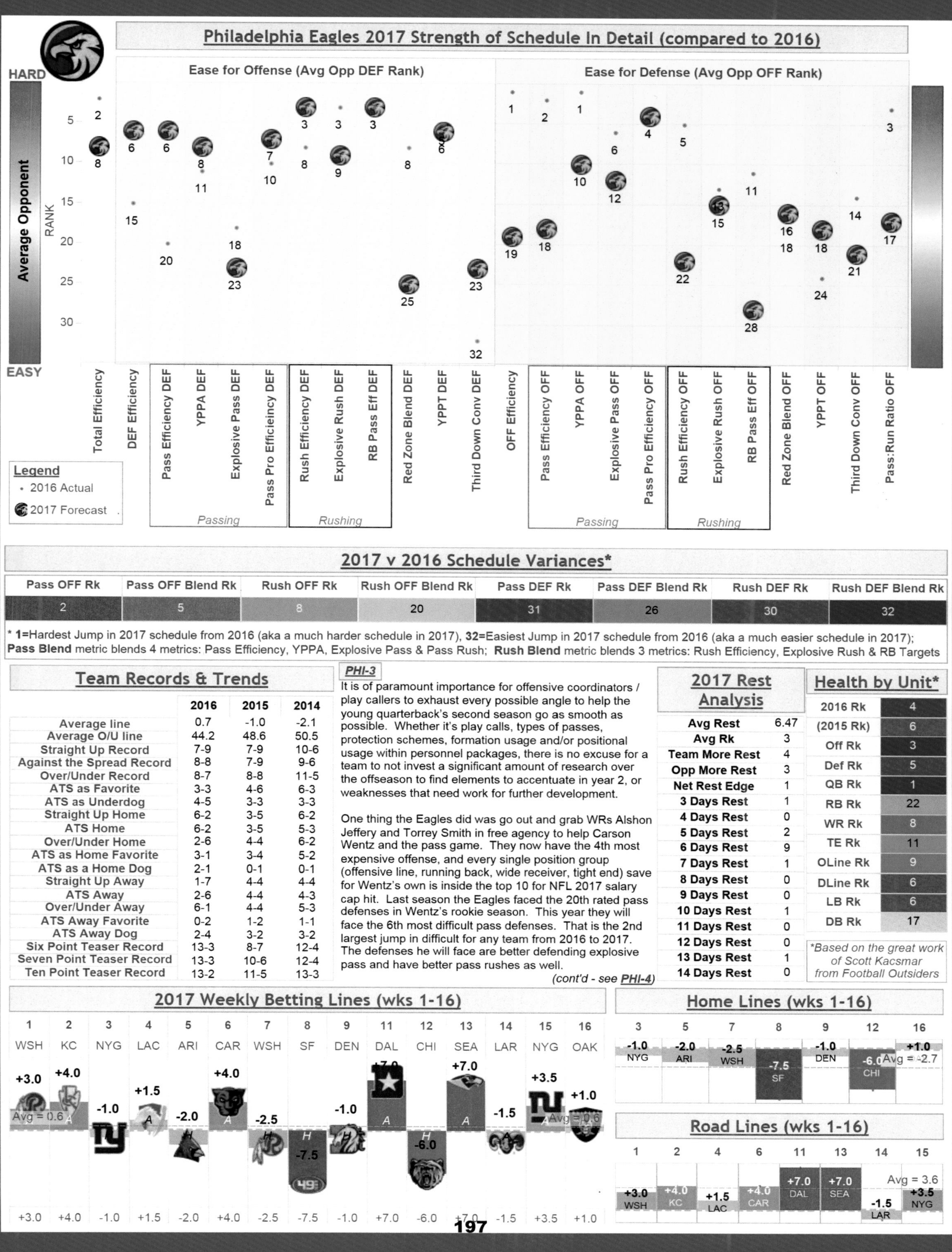

Philadelphia Eagles 2017 Strength of Schedule In Detail (compared to 2016)

2017 v 2016 Schedule Variances*

Pass OFF Rk	Pass OFF Blend Rk	Rush OFF Rk	Rush OFF Blend Rk	Pass DEF Rk	Pass DEF Blend Rk	Rush DEF Rk	Rush DEF Blend Rk
2	5	8	20	31	26	30	32

* **1**=Hardest Jump in 2017 schedule from 2016 (aka a much harder schedule in 2017), **32**=Easiest Jump in 2017 schedule from 2016 (aka a much easier schedule in 2017); **Pass Blend** metric blends 4 metrics: Pass Efficiency, YPPA, Explosive Pass & Pass Rush; **Rush Blend** metric blends 3 metrics: Rush Efficiency, Explosive Rush & RB Targets

Team Records & Trends

	2016	2015	2014
Average line	0.7	-1.0	-2.1
Average O/U line	44.2	48.6	50.5
Straight Up Record	7-9	7-9	10-6
Against the Spread Record	8-8	7-9	9-6
Over/Under Record	8-7	8-8	11-5
ATS as Favorite	3-3	4-6	6-3
ATS as Underdog	4-5	3-3	3-3
Straight Up Home	6-2	3-5	6-2
ATS Home	6-2	3-5	5-3
Over/Under Home	2-6	4-4	6-2
ATS as Home Favorite	3-1	3-4	5-2
ATS as a Home Dog	2-1	0-1	0-1
Straight Up Away	1-7	4-4	4-4
ATS Away	2-6	4-4	4-3
Over/Under Away	6-1	4-4	5-3
ATS Away Favorite	0-2	1-2	1-1
ATS Away Dog	2-4	3-2	3-2
Six Point Teaser Record	13-3	8-7	12-4
Seven Point Teaser Record	13-3	10-6	12-4
Ten Point Teaser Record	13-2	11-5	13-3

PHI-3

It is of paramount importance for offensive coordinators / play callers to exhaust every possible angle to help the young quarterback's second season go as smooth as possible. Whether it's play calls, types of passes, protection schemes, formation usage and/or positional usage within personnel packages, there is no excuse for a team to not invest a significant amount of research over the offseason to find elements to accentuate in year 2, or weaknesses that need work for further development.

One thing the Eagles did was go out and grab WRs Alshon Jeffery and Torrey Smith in free agency to help Carson Wentz and the pass game. They now have the 4th most expensive offense, and every single position group (offensive line, running back, wide receiver, tight end) save for Wentz's own is inside the top 10 for NFL 2017 salary cap hit. Last season the Eagles faced the 20th rated pass defenses in Wentz's rookie season. This year they will face the 6th most difficult pass defenses. That is the 2nd largest jump in difficult for any team from 2016 to 2017. The defenses he will face are better defending explosive pass and have better pass rushes as well.

(cont'd - see ***PHI-4***)

2017 Rest Analysis

Avg Rest	6.47
Avg Rk	3
Team More Rest	4
Opp More Rest	3
Net Rest Edge	1
3 Days Rest	1
4 Days Rest	0
5 Days Rest	2
6 Days Rest	9
7 Days Rest	1
8 Days Rest	0
9 Days Rest	0
10 Days Rest	1
11 Days Rest	0
12 Days Rest	0
13 Days Rest	1
14 Days Rest	0

Health by Unit*

2016 Rk	4
(2015 Rk)	6
Off Rk	3
Def Rk	5
QB Rk	1
RB Rk	22
WR Rk	8
TE Rk	11
OLine Rk	9
DLine Rk	6
LB Rk	6
DB Rk	17

**Based on the great work of Scott Kacsmar from Football Outsiders*

2017 Weekly Betting Lines (wks 1-16)

1	2	3	4	5	6	7	8	9	11	12	13	14	15	16
WSH	KC	NYG	LAC	ARI	CAR	WSH	SF	DEN	DAL	CHI	SEA	LAR	NYG	OAK
+3.0	+4.0	-1.0	+1.5	-2.0	+4.0	-2.5	-7.5	-1.0	+7.0	-6.0	+7.0	-1.5	+3.5	+1.0

Home Lines (wks 1-16)

3	5	7	8	9	12	16
-1.0	-2.0	-2.5	-7.5	-1.0	-6.0	+1.0
NYG	ARI	WSH	SF	DEN	CHI	

Road Lines (wks 1-16)

1	2	4	6	11	13	14	15
+3.0	+4.0	+1.5	+4.0	+7.0	+7.0	-1.5	+3.5
WSH	KC	LAC	CAR	DAL	SEA	LAR	NYG

Philadelphia Eagles 2016 Play Analysis

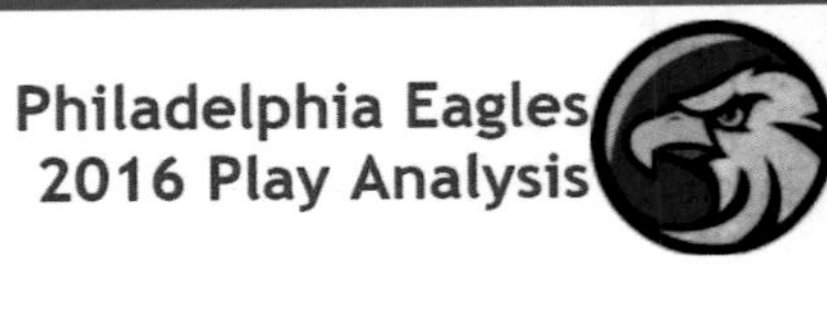

2016 Play Tendencies

All Pass %	58%
All Pass Rk	18
All Rush %	42%
All Rush Rk	15
1 Score Pass %	63%
1 Score Pass Rk	3
2015 1 Score Pass %	59%
2015 1 Score Pass Rk	15
Pass Increase %	4%
Pass Increase Rk	4
1 Score Rush %	37%
1 Score Rush Rk	30
Up Pass %	57%
Up Pass Rk	18
Up Rush %	43%
Up Rush Rk	15
Down Pass %	59%
Down Pass Rk	24
Down Rush %	41%
Down Rush Rk	9

2016 Down & Distance Tendencies

Down	Distance	Total Plays	Pass Rate	Run Rate	Play Success %
1	Short (1-3)	7	29%	71%	86%
	Med (4-7)	10	20%	80%	70%
	Long (8-10)	318	50%	50%	53%
	XL (11+)	8	88%	13%	38%
2	Short (1-3)	42	33%	67%	74%
	Med (4-7)	71	49%	51%	56%
	Long (8-10)	95	68%	32%	35%
	XL (11+)	46	74%	26%	37%
3	Short (1-3)	37	49%	51%	65%
	Med (4-7)	42	88%	12%	50%
	Long (8-10)	44	91%	9%	32%
	XL (11+)	27	81%	19%	11%
4	Short (1-3)	9	56%	44%	44%
	Med (4-7)	2	100%	0%	100%
	Long (8-10)	1	100%	0%	0%
	XL (11+)	1	0%	100%	0%

Shotgun %:

Under Center	Shotgun
34%	66%
37% AVG	*63%*

Run Rate:

Under Center	Shotgun
70%	23%
68% AVG	*23%*

Pass Rate:

Under Center	Shotgun
30%	77%
32% AVG	*77%*

Short Yardage Intelligence:

2nd and Short Run

Run Freq	Run % Rk	NFL Run Freq Avg	Run 1D Rate	Run NFL 1D Avg
65%	16	65%	79%	71%

2nd and Short Pass

Pass Freq	Pass % Rk	NFL Pass Freq Avg	Pass 1D Rate	Pass NFL 1D Avg
35%	15	35%	54%	52%

Most Frequent Play

Down	Distance	Play Type	Player	Total Plays	Play Success %
1	Short (1-3)	RUSH	Ryan Mathews	2	100%
	Med (4-7)	RUSH	Ryan Mathews	5	80%
	Long (8-10)	RUSH	Ryan Mathews	65	55%
2	Short (1-3)	RUSH	Ryan Mathews	9	78%
	Med (4-7)	RUSH	Ryan Mathews	15	40%
	Long (8-10)	PASS	Jordan Matthews	17	35%
	XL (11+)	PASS	Zach Ertz	7	29%
3	Short (1-3)	PASS	Zach Ertz	5	60%
		RUSH	Ryan Mathews	5	60%
			Darren Sproles	5	80%
	Med (4-7)	PASS	Jordan Matthews	9	67%
	Long (8-10)	PASS	Dorial Green-Beckha..	8	25%
	XL (11+)	PASS	Nelson Agholor	6	0%

Most Successful Play*

Down	Distance	Play Type	Player	Total Plays	Play Success %
1	Med (4-7)	RUSH	Ryan Mathews	5	80%
	Long (8-10)	PASS	Brent Celek	6	83%
2	Short (1-3)	RUSH	Darren Sproles	6	83%
	Med (4-7)	PASS	Zach Ertz	10	80%
			Nelson Agholor	5	80%
	Long (8-10)	PASS	Brent Celek	6	67%
		RUSH	Wendell Smallwood	6	67%
	XL (11+)	PASS	Zach Ertz	7	29%
3	Short (1-3)	RUSH	Darren Sproles	5	80%
	Med (4-7)	PASS	Jordan Matthews	9	67%
			Dorial Green-Beckham	6	67%
	Long (8-10)	PASS	Trey Burton	5	80%
	XL (11+)	PASS	Nelson Agholor	6	0%

**Minimum 5 plays to qualify*

2016 Snap Rates

Week	Opp	Score	Nelson Agholor	Zach Ertz	Jordan Matthews	Dorial Green-Beckham	Darren Sproles	Brent Celek	Trey Burton
1	CLE	W 29-10	67 (87%)	59 (77%)	74 (96%)	25 (32%)	38 (49%)	38 (49%)	
2	CHI	W 29-14	56 (78%)		71 (99%)	33 (46%)	38 (53%)	53 (74%)	31 (43%)
3	PIT	W 34-3	52 (80%)		55 (85%)	29 (45%)	24 (37%)	45 (69%)	33 (51%)
5	DET	L 24-23	48 (79%)	52 (85%)	57 (93%)	32 (52%)	34 (56%)	23 (38%)	11 (18%)
6	WAS	L 27-20	44 (85%)	46 (88%)	48 (92%)	42 (81%)	23 (44%)	13 (25%)	6 (12%)
7	MIN	W 20-10	40 (69%)	48 (83%)	45 (78%)	28 (48%)	26 (45%)	28 (48%)	16 (28%)
8	DAL	L 29-23	69 (91%)	61 (80%)	68 (89%)	49 (64%)	61 (80%)	23 (30%)	12 (16%)
9	NYG	L 28-23	69 (92%)	62 (83%)	65 (87%)	49 (65%)	60 (80%)	21 (28%)	17 (23%)
10	ATL	W 24-15	72 (91%)	59 (75%)	75 (95%)	44 (56%)	31 (39%)	29 (37%)	9 (11%)
11	SEA	L 26-15	70 (88%)	70 (88%)	73 (91%)	64 (80%)	10 (13%)	19 (24%)	7 (9%)
12	GB	L 27-13		55 (93%)	24 (41%)	48 (81%)	31 (53%)	23 (39%)	19 (32%)
13	CIN	L 32-14	80 (100%)	69 (86%)		50 (63%)	44 (55%)	19 (24%)	52 (65%)
14	WAS	L 27-22	68 (87%)	67 (86%)	76 (97%)		30 (38%)	30 (38%)	37 (47%)
15	BAL	L 27-26	85 (98%)	81 (93%)	76 (87%)	55 (63%)		26 (30%)	22 (25%)
16	NYG	W 24-19	56 (100%)	48 (86%)	39 (70%)	27 (48%)	27 (48%)	30 (54%)	16 (29%)
17	DAL	W 27-13	6 (8%)	70 (92%)		64 (84%)	29 (38%)	23 (30%)	42 (55%)
Grand Total			882 (82%)	847 (85%)	846 (86%)	639 (61%)	506 (49%)	443 (40%)	330 (31%)

Personnel Groupings

Personnel	Team %	NFL Avg	Succ. %
1-1 [3WR]	58%	60%	48%
1-2 [2WR]	31%	19%	44%
1-3 [1WR]	8%	3%	50%

Grouping Tendencies

Personnel	Pass Rate	Pass Succ. %	Run Succ. %
1-1 [3WR]	62%	45%	53%
1-2 [2WR]	59%	42%	47%
1-3 [1WR]	40%	52%	49%

Red Zone Targets (min 3)

Receiver	All	Inside 5	6-10	11-20
Zach Ertz	17	3	3	11
Nelson Agholor	14		3	11
Darren Sproles	13	1	1	11
Dorial Green-Beckham	12	2		10
Jordan Matthews	12	3	1	8
Trey Burton	8	2	1	5
Josh Huff	4	1		3
Brent Celek	3			3
Byron Marshall	3		1	2
Ryan Mathews	3	1	1	1

Red Zone Rushes (min 3)

Rusher	All	Inside 5	6-10	11-20
Ryan Mathews	37	17	8	12
Darren Sproles	18	3	5	10
Carson Wentz	8	3		5
Wendell Smallwood	7	2	1	4
Kenjon Barner	5	1	3	1
Byron Marshall	3		1	2
Terrell Watson	3	2	1	

Early Down Target Rate

RB	TE	WR
20%	22%	58%
19%	*20% NFL AVG*	*61%*

Overall Target Success %

RB	TE	WR
43% #21	59% #5	44% #27

Philadelphia Eagles 2016 Passing Recap & 2017 Outlook

Carson Wentz is being given the pieces to have a successful 2017 campaign. All of his support positions are top 10 most expensive in the NFL this year: a healthy offensive line (suspension & injuries last year), with multiple new receivers and a new running back. Clearly one look at the visual passing cone to the right and you'll see Wentz needs a lot of work. Wentz needs to work on his deep passing offense and explosive passing offense. He threw a below average rate of 20+ air yard completions (deep passing) and the offense generated a below average rate of 20+ or 30+ yard pass play gains (explosive passing). His overall yards per attempt is low, but that's not because his YAC per completion was low – in fact it was the NFL average. But his air yardage per completion was well over 1 yard below the NFL average, and his air yards vs YAC were the inverse of the NFL average. Related is the fact Wentz must pass the ball beyond the sticks on 3rd down more often. On average, his completions were 2.25 yards short of the sticks, which resulted in just a 36% conversion rate on 3rd down when passing, and a 60 passer rating. His new WR weapons should increase the efficiency of those targets, but the Eagles still need to focus on more TE target..

Carson Wentz Rating All Downs

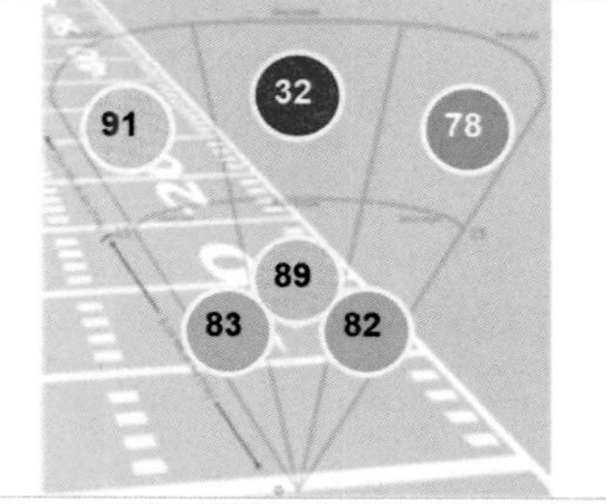

Carson Wentz Rating Early Downs

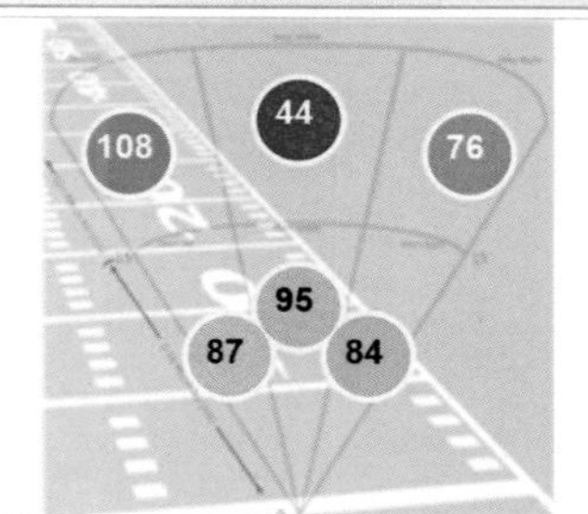

2016 Standard Passing Table

QB	Comp	Att	Comp %	Yds	YPA	TDs	INT	Sacks	Rating	Rk
Carson Wentz	379	608	62%	3,782	6.2	16	14	33	79.1	37
NFL Avg			63%		7.2				90.4	

2016 Advanced Passing Table

QB	Success %	EDSR Passing Success %	20+ Yd Pass Gains	20+ Yd Pass %	30+ Yd Pass Gains	30+ Yd Pass %	Air Yds per Comp	YAC per Comp	20+ Air Yd Comp	20+ Air Yd %
Carson Wentz	44%	47%	39	6%	11	2%	5.1	4.8	20	3%
NFL Avg	44%	48%	27	8%	10	3%	6.4	4.8	12	4%

Interception Rates by Down

Yards to Go	1	2	3	4	Total
1 & 2	0.0%	0.0%	0.0%	0.0%	0.0%
3, 4, 5	0.0%	3.1%	4.1%	12.5%	4.3%
6 - 9	0.0%	1.5%	3.8%	0.0%	2.4%
10 - 14	1.3%	3.8%	2.7%	0.0%	2.0%
15+	0.0%	0.0%	0.0%	0.0%	0.0%
Total	**1.2%**	**2.5%**	**3.0%**	**5.3%**	**2.2%**

3rd Down Passing - Short of Sticks Analysis

QB	Avg Yds to Go	Air Yds (of Comps)	Avg Yds Short	Short of Sticks Rate	Rk
Carson Wentz	7.4	5.1	-2.2	56%	38
NFL Avg	7.6	6.8	-0.8	57%	

Air Yds vs YAC

	Air Yds %	YAC %	Rk
Carson Wentz	46%	54%	41
NFL Avg	54%	46%	

2016 Receiving Recap & 2017 Outlook

Inserting Alshon Jeffery and Torrey Smith should have the intended impact of getting more explosiveness out of the passing offense. Of course, the line has to stay healthy to provide protection and Wentz has to be accurate to hit them. Apart from Jordan Matthews and Zach Ertz, the Eagles were completely ineffective on any pass thrown 15+ yards in the air, particularly those targets to Dorial Green-Beckham and Nelson Agholor. Last year the Eagles rarely threw the ball inside the 10, instead they ran much more and were extremely successful when running. The most successful plays on 1st & 10 and 2nd & medium or long were all passes to TEs.

Player *Min 50 Targets*	Targets	Comp %	YPA	Rating	TOARS	Success %	Success Rk	Missed YPA Rk	YAS % Rk	TDs
Jordan Matthews	116	63%	6.9	92	4.9	49%	80	83	82	3
Zach Ertz	106	74%	7.7	92	4.8	58%	26	27	99	4
Dorial Green-Beckham	74	49%	5.3	62	3.8	45%	113	124	104	2
Darren Sproles	71	73%	6.0	98	4.2	45%	111	131	129	2
Nelson Agholor	69	52%	5.3	59	3.6	39%	136	120	113	2
Trey Burton	60	62%	5.5	75	3.6	43%	120	50	124	1

Directional Passer Rating Delivered

Receiver	Short Left	Short Middle	Short Right	Deep Left	Deep Middle	Deep Right	Player Total
Jordan Matthews	72	138	78	101	70	96	92
Zach Ertz	91	106	88	158	24	92	92
Dorial Green-Beckham	70	52	93	44	65	40	63
Darren Sproles	95	81	84			158	98
Nelson Agholor	91	74	37	122	42	49	59
Trey Burton	80	66	108	40	40	74	76
Josh Huff	93	40	119				103
Team Total	84	94	81	103	33	92	83

2016 Rushing Recap & 2017 Outlook

With LeGarrette Blount as the clear #1 back, the team may look to deal Ryan Mathews. But keep in mind the Eagles face the 3rd most difficult schedule of run defenses this year, up from 8th most difficult in 2016. Mathews was used in 16% of the Eagles overall plays, but the offense became extremely run-heavy when up by more than one-score, and Mathews was the prime benefactor. Which would inherently bode well for Blount. But the Eagles have to gain the lead to get there, and Wentz will need support on the ground when the game is within one-score. He had that support in 2016, as the Eagles ranked 8th in success rate on 1st down runs, including 5th when in opponent's territory, recording a 57% success rate.

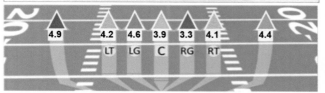

Player *Min 50 Rushes*	Rushes	YPA	Success %	Success Rk	Missed YPA Rk	YTS % Rk	YAS % Rk	Early Down Success %	Early Down Success Rk	TDs
Ryan Mathews	155	4.3	52%	12	20	19	25	52%	13	8
Darren Sproles	94	4.7	52%	15	60	30	33	56%	6	2
Wendell Smallwood	77	4.1	49%	25	30	7	45	49%	25	1

Yards per Carry by Direction

4.9 | 4.2 | 4.6 | 3.9 | 3.3 | 4.1 | 4.4

LT | LG | C | RG | RT

Directional Run Frequency

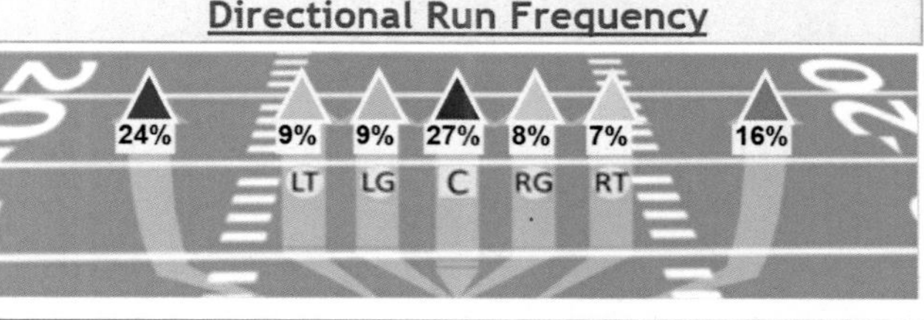

Despite the 10th best pass protection last year, Wentz led the Eagles to a 25th ranking in passing efficiency. After a week one battle in DC against the Redskins, the schedule immediately will challenge the young Wentz. From weeks 2 through 6, the Eagles will face the most difficult schedule of pass defenses in the NFL, by a long way.

And at the running back position, they added LeGarrette Blount, who was off of a down season in New England despite volume driven success. Blount's averages and efficiency metrics were poor, but thanks to the success of the Patriots offense, he received a ton of usage as well as opportunities in the red zone. If the Eagles release Ryan Mathews once he passes his physical, as is rumored, there is no doubt Blount should see a fair amount of usage. The Eagles most frequent play on first down and any distance as well as second and any distance less than 8 yards to go was a Ryan Mathews run. And inside the 5 yard line, Mathews dominated the offensive opportunities, racking up 17 carries while the rest of the team had fewer than 7 combined rushes and 7 combined passes. Blount should be successful there, but he will have to improve over 2016 because this offense is not the Patriots, and he won't have as many chances to rack up those numbers.

The Eagles play the 3rd most difficult schedule of run efficiency defense, 9th most difficult for explosive rushes and 3rd most difficult for RB-targets in the pass game. They faced a difficult schedule in 2016 as well, but this is actually slightly more difficult. And unlike the second half of the schedule for the passing offenses, it's a brutal close to the season for the Eagles run offense. They face five top-8 run defenses in the 7 weeks after their bye, and 4 of those 5 games come on the road. A struggling run game on the road means more reliance upon Wentz's arm. The 2017 season will prove whether the Eagles found their franchise QB or if they should have concerns about Wentz moving forward.

Defensively the Eagles faced a brutal schedule of opposing offenses last year – it was the toughest in the NFL. This year it gets much easier. It's the #2 easiest shift in pass offenses faced from 2016 to 2017, and the #1 easiest shift in rush offense "blend" from 2016 to 2017. That's what happens when you swap out the Steelers, Falcons, Packers and Lions and instead insert the Rams, 49ers, Chiefs and Panthers. It's not an easy schedule but it's much easier than the Eagles faced in 2016.

An improved defense and a stronger offensive line would allow Wentz to efficiently progress in his sophomore campaign. But Doug Pederson and Frank Reich must help Wentz as much as possible. Flashy new WRs to pair with Jordan Matthews may look great, but the efficiency that Wentz enjoyed when passing to his TEs last year cannot be forgotten. And there are a number of basic yet simple things the Eagles can do offensively to clean up some efficiency leaks to keep the Wentz Wagon moving in the right direction.

Division History: Season Wins & 2017 Projection

2013 Wins | 2014 Wins | 2015 Wins | 2016 Wins | Proj 2017 Wins

Rank of 2017 Defensive Pass Efficiency Faced by Week

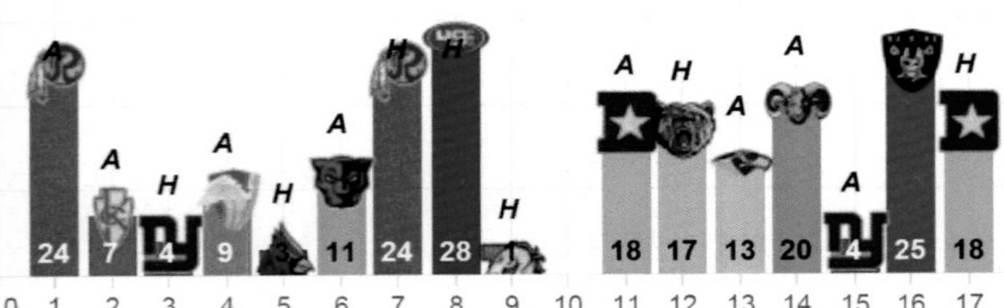

Rank of 2017 Defensive Rush Efficiency Faced by Week

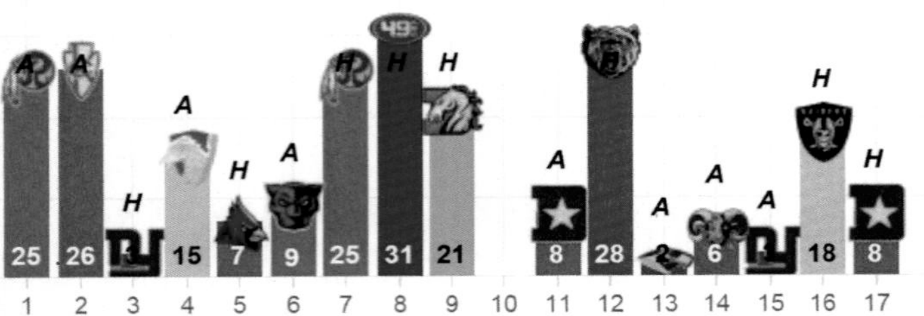

2016 Situational Usage by Player & Position

Usage Rate by Score

		Being Blown Out (14+)	Down Big (9-13)	One Score	Large Lead (9-13)	Blowout Lead (14+)	Grand Total
RUSH	Ryan Mathews	1%	12%	18%	33%	15%	16%
	Darren Sproles	9%	12%	8%	8%	20%	9%
	Wendell Smallwood	7%	7%	7%	6%	28%	8%
	Nelson Agholor	1%	1%	0%			1%
	Kenjon Barner	1%	3%	2%	3%	11%	3%
	Byron Marshall		2%	3%			2%
	Josh Huff		1%	0%			0%
	Bryce Treggs			0%			0%
	Terrell Watson			1%			1%
	Total	19%	37%	39%	50%	74%	39%
PASS	Ryan Mathews	2%	2%	1%			1%
	Darren Sproles	12%	4%	7%	8%	4%	7%
	Jordan Matthews	7%	10%	13%	14%	6%	12%
	Zach Ertz	19%	14%	10%	6%		11%
	Wendell Smallwood	4%	5%	0%			1%
	Dorial Green-Beckha..	11%	11%	7%			7%
	Nelson Agholor	5%	5%	8%	3%	9%	7%
	Trey Burton	9%	6%	6%	11%	2%	6%
	Kenjon Barner	1%	2%	1%			1%
	Byron Marshall		1%	1%			1%
	Josh Huff		2%	2%	3%	4%	2%
	Brent Celek			3%	3%	2%	2%
	Bryce Treggs	1%	3%	1%	3%		1%
	Paul Turner	8%		1%			1%
	Terrell Watson			0%			0%
	Total	81%	63%	61%	50%	26%	61%

Positional Target Distribution vs NFL Average

		NFL Wide				Team Only			
		Left	Middle	Right	**Total**	Left	Middle	Right	**Total**
Deep	WR	1,006	565	974	**2,545**	25	16	27	**68**
	TE	153	141	159	**453**	5	6	4	**15**
	RB	25	4	39	**68**			1	**1**
	All	**1,184**	**710**	**1,172**	**3,066**	**30**	**22**	**32**	**84**
Short	WR	2,992	1,715	3,077	**7,784**	101	56	109	**266**
	TE	806	844	1,121	**2,771**	30	31	30	**91**
	RB	983	614	1,083	**2,680**	32	8	30	**70**
	All	**4,781**	**3,173**	**5,281**	**13,235**	**163**	**95**	**169**	**427**
Total		**5,965**	**3,883**	**6,453**	**16,301**	**193**	**117**	**201**	**511**

Positional Success Rates vs NFL Average

		NFL Wide				Team Only			
		Left	Middle	Right	**Total**	Left	Middle	Right	**Total**
Deep	WR	37%	50%	38%	**41%**	28%	44%	33%	**34%**
	TE	44%	50%	43%	**46%**	60%	33%	50%	**47%**
	RB	32%	75%	23%	**29%**			100%	**100%**
	All	**38%**	**51%**	**38%**	**41%**	**33%**	**41%**	**38%**	**37%**
Short	WR	52%	57%	52%	**53%**	50%	57%	41%	**48%**
	TE	50%	61%	52%	**54%**	57%	77%	43%	**59%**
	RB	47%	49%	44%	**46%**	50%	50%	37%	**44%**
	All	**51%**	**56%**	**50%**	**52%**	**51%**	**63%**	**41%**	**50%**
Total		**48%**	**55%**	**48%**	**50%**	**48%**	**59%**	**40%**	**48%**

2017 Coaches

Head Coach:
Mike Tomlin (11th yr)
Offensive Coordinator:
Todd Haley (6th yr)
Defensive Coordinator:
Keith Butler (3rd yr)

EASY HARD

2017 Forecast

Wins	Div Rank
10.5	#1

Past Records

2016: 11-5
2015: 10-6
2014: 11-5

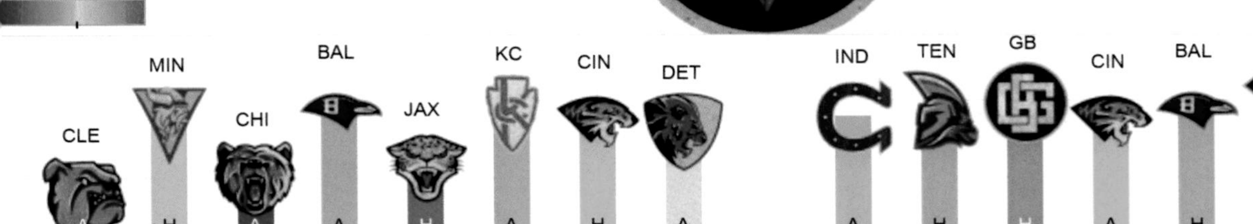

Key Players Lost

TXN	Player (POS)
Cut	Fanaika, Jason LB
	Gilbert, Justin CB
	Green, Ladarius TE
	Warren, Greg C
	Williams, Karlos RB
Declared Free Agent	Anderson, Kevin LB
	Johnson, David TE
	Jones, Jarvis LB
	Jones, Landry QB
	Manhart, Cole G
	Mathews, Ricardo DE
	Thomas, Shamarko S
	Timmons, Lawrence LB
	Ume-Ezeoke, Valerian C
	Wallace, Cody C
	Wheaton, Markus WR
	Williams, DeAngelo RB
Retired	Harris, Ryan T

Average Line	# Games Favored	# Games Underdog
-3.7	13	2

2017 Pittsburgh Steelers Overview

Only four teams have recorded double digit wins each of the last 3 seasons: the Patriots, Packers, Seahawks and Steelers. The Patriots have won two Super Bowls in that 3 year span. The Seahawks have been to one. The Packers have been to two Conference Championship games but lost them both. And the Steelers are slowly making their way, from the Wild Card round in 2014 to the Divisional Round in 2015 to the Conference Championship in 2016. Is 2017 the year they can make that jump? Ultimately, it will be up to the offense to propel the team, as a result of their build. But to win in the postseason, they will need an inexperienced secondary to take that next step, which they were unable to do last season.

The Steelers roster boasts the most expensive offense in the NFL, and the second least expensive defense. This is becoming an increasingly consistent trend with a number of the best offenses in the NFL. The Steelers are spending 64% of their salary cap on the offensive side of the ball, the most in the NFL. Other teams in the top 10 include the Cowboys, Packers, Patriots, Falcons, Raiders and Redskins. In offensive efficiency last year, these teams ranked 1st (ATL), 2nd (NE), 3rd (DAL), 4th (GB), 5th (WAS), 7th (OAK) and 8th (PIT). Those are strong numbers. Teams paid for strong offenses and those offenses delivered based on their price.

Ordinarily, so many teams would not be able to succeed unless they had reasonable defense. Of these 7 teams, only the Steelers had an above average defense based on efficiency. The other 6 defenses ranged from average (NE and DAL) to 20th-27th (GB, OAK, WAS and ATL). Yet it didn't seem to matter. Offenses carried the day in 2016. These teams were able to "work around" their bad defenses by scoring at obscene rates on offense as well as possessing the football in clock draining strategy, when the situation warranted it. In terms of success, these teams delivered. The Patriots beat the Falcons in the Super Bowl, and every one of those 7 teams made the playoffs except the Redskins, who still finished with a winning record.

The question becomes, was this an ushering in of a new era in NFL efficiency or was it just a magical year for elite offenses? Well if the draft was any indication, none of those teams were

(cont'd - see PIT2)

Key Free Agents/ Trades Added

- Alualu, Tyson DE
- Davis, Knile RB
- Hunter, Justin WR
- Rodgers, Jake T
- Sensabaugh, Coty CB
- Stafford, Daimion S
- Watson, Terrell RB

Drafted Players

Rd	Pk	Player (College)
1	30	OLB - T. J. Watt (Wisconsin)
2	62	WR - Juju Smith-Schuster (USC)
3	94	DB - Cameron Sutton (Tennessee)
3*	105	RB - James Conner (Pittsburgh)
4	135	QB - Joshua Dobbs (Tennessee)
5	173	CB - Brian Allen (Utah)
6	213	LS - Colin Holba (Louisville)
7	248	DE - Keion Adams (Western Michigan)

Regular Season Wins: Past & Current Proj

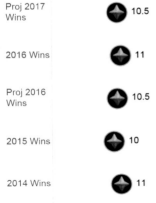

	Wins
Proj 2017 Wins	10.5
2016 Wins	11
Proj 2016 Wins	10.5
2015 Wins	10
2014 Wins	11
2013 Wins	8

1 3 5 7 9 11 13 15

2017 Lineup & Cap Hits

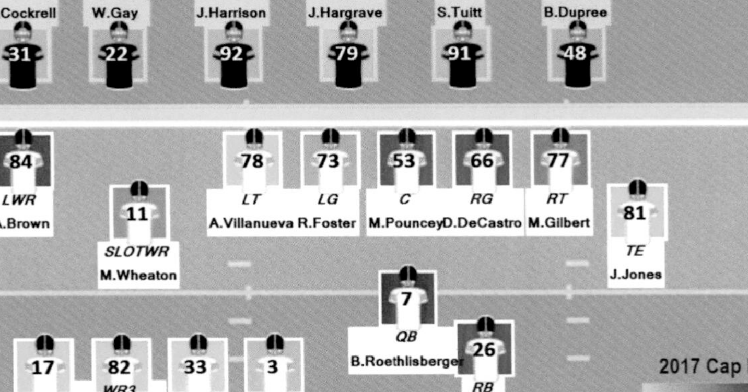

2017 Unit Spending

All DEF
All OFF

Positional Spending

	Rank	Total	2016 Rk
All OFF	1	$101.23M	3
QB	13	$21.48M	3
OL	4	$39.42M	6
RB	1	$16.15M	21
WR	15	$20.48M	16
TE	30	$3.69M	26
All DEF	32	$61.14M	24
DL	26	$19.12M	25
LB	17	$17.70M	3
CB	24	$11.76M	27
S	12	$12.57M	23

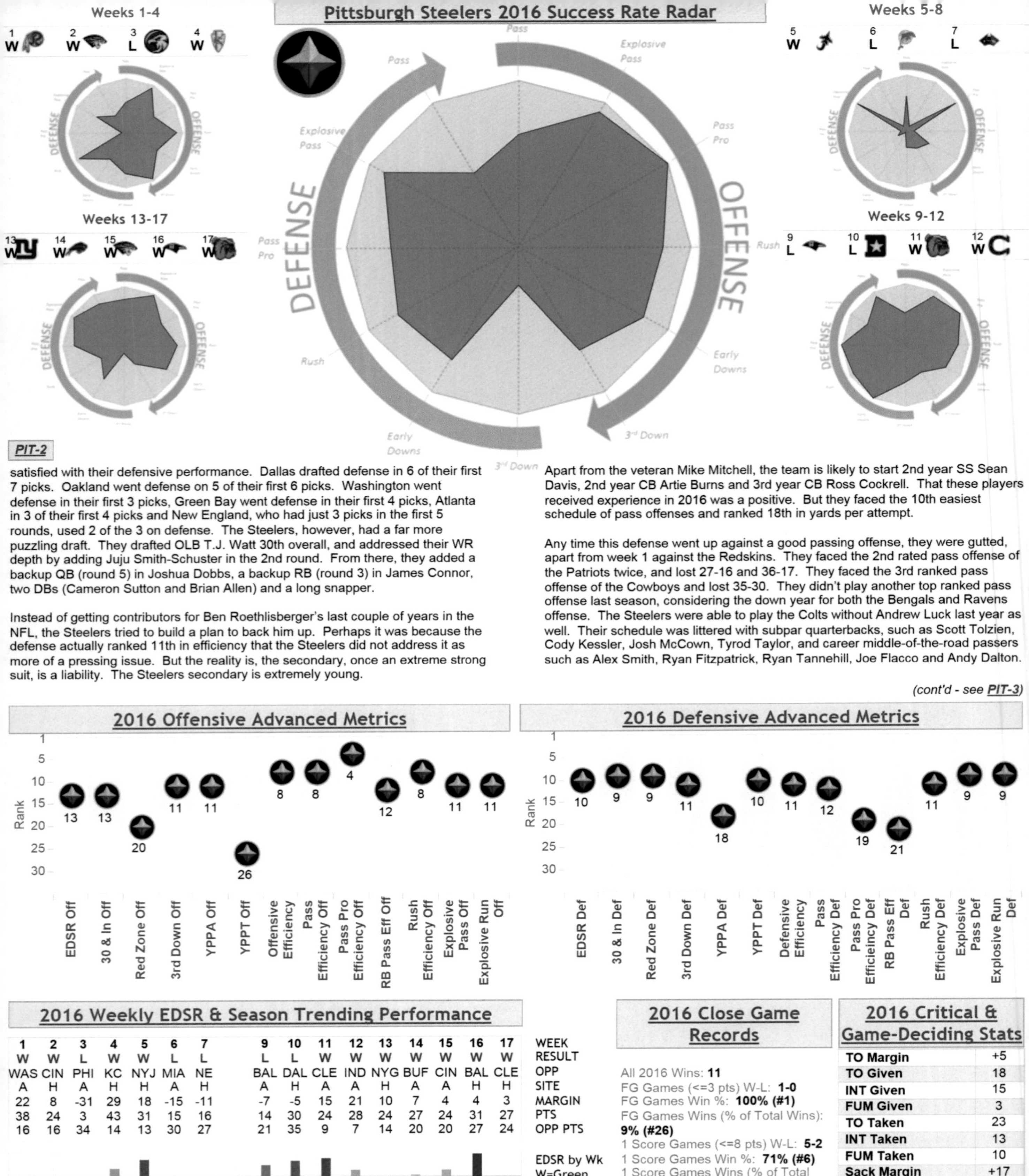

satisfied with their defensive performance. Dallas drafted defense in 6 of their first 7 picks. Oakland went defense on 5 of their first 6 picks. Washington went defense in their first 3 picks, Green Bay went defense in their first 4 picks, Atlanta in 3 of their first 4 picks and New England, who had just 3 picks in the first 5 rounds, used 2 of the 3 on defense. The Steelers, however, had a far more puzzling draft. They drafted OLB T.J. Watt 30th overall, and addressed their WR depth by adding Juju Smith-Schuster in the 2nd round. From there, they added a backup QB (round 5) in Joshua Dobbs, a backup RB (round 3) in James Connor, two DBs (Cameron Sutton and Brian Allen) and a long snapper.

Instead of getting contributors for Ben Roethlisberger's last couple of years in the NFL, the Steelers tried to build a plan to back him up. Perhaps it was because the defense actually ranked 11th in efficiency that the Steelers did not address it as more of a pressing issue. But the reality is, the secondary, once an extreme strong suit, is a liability. The Steelers secondary is extremely young.

Apart from the veteran Mike Mitchell, the team is likely to start 2nd year SS Sean Davis, 2nd year CB Artie Burns and 3rd year CB Ross Cockrell. That these players received experience in 2016 was a positive. But they faced the 10th easiest schedule of pass offenses and ranked 18th in yards per attempt.

Any time this defense went up against a good passing offense, they were gutted, apart from week 1 against the Redskins. They faced the 2nd rated pass offense of the Patriots twice, and lost 27-16 and 36-17. They faced the 3rd ranked pass offense of the Cowboys and lost 35-30. They didn't play another top ranked pass offense last season, considering the down year for both the Bengals and Ravens offense. The Steelers were able to play the Colts without Andrew Luck last year as well. Their schedule was littered with subpar quarterbacks, such as Scott Tolzien, Cody Kessler, Josh McCown, Tyrod Taylor, and career middle-of-the-road passers such as Alex Smith, Ryan Fitzpatrick, Ryan Tannehill, Joe Flacco and Andy Dalton.

*(cont'd - see **PIT-3**)*

2016 Weekly EDSR & Season Trending Performance

WEEK	1	2	3	4	5	6	7	9	10	11	12	13	14	15	16	17
RESULT	W	W	L	W	W	L	L	L	L	W	W	W	W	W	W	W
OPP	WAS	CIN	PHI	KC	NYJ	MIA	NE	BAL	DAL	CLE	IND	NYG	BUF	CIN	BAL	CLE
SITE	A	H	A	H	H	A	H	A	H	A	A	H	A	A	H	H
MARGIN	22	8	-31	29	18	-15	-11	-7	-5	15	21	10	7	4	4	3
PTS	38	24	3	43	31	15	16	14	30	24	28	24	27	24	31	27
OPP PTS	16	16	34	14	13	30	27	21	35	9	7	14	20	20	27	24

EDSR by Wk
W=Green
L=Red

OFF/DEF
EDSR
Blue=OFF
(high=good)
Red=DEF
(low=good)

2016 Close Game Records

All 2016 Wins: **11**
FG Games (<=3 pts) W-L: **1-0**
FG Games Win %: **100% (#1)**
FG Games Wins (% of Total Wins): **9% (#26)**
1 Score Games (<=8 pts) W-L: **5-2**
1 Score Games Win %: **71% (#6)**
1 Score Games Wins (% of Total Wins): **45% (#22)**

2016 Critical & Game-Deciding Stats

TO Margin	+5
TO Given	18
INT Given	15
FUM Given	3
TO Taken	23
INT Taken	13
FUM Taken	10
Sack Margin	+17
Sacks	38
Sacks Allow	21
Return TD Margin	+0
Ret TDs	1
Ret TDs Allow	1
Penalty Margin	-3
Penalties	112
Opponent Penalties	109

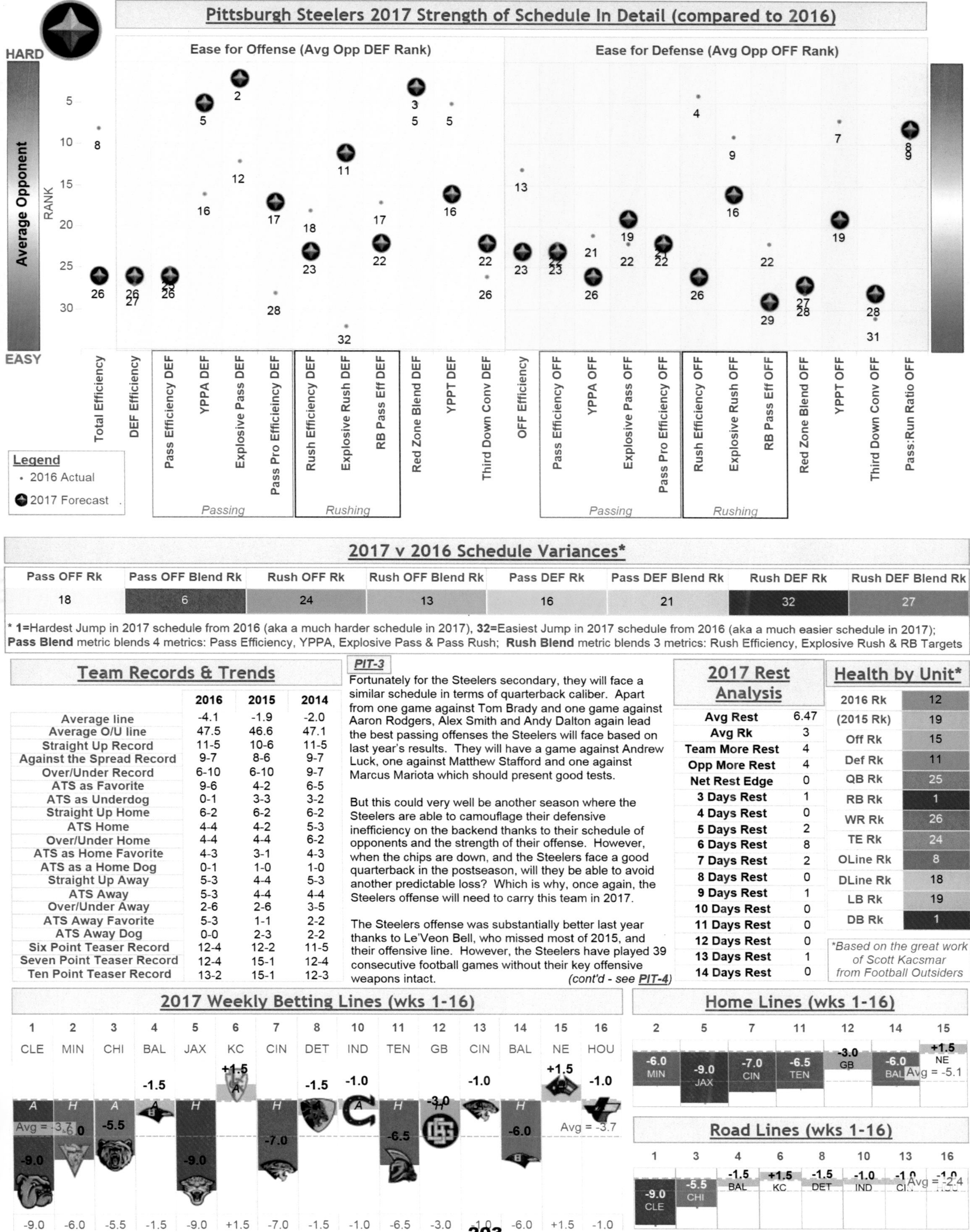

Pittsburgh Steelers 2017 Strength of Schedule In Detail (compared to 2016)

2017 v 2016 Schedule Variances*

Pass OFF Rk	Pass OFF Blend Rk	Rush OFF Rk	Rush OFF Blend Rk	Pass DEF Rk	Pass DEF Blend Rk	Rush DEF Rk	Rush DEF Blend Rk
18	6	24	13	16	21	32	27

* **1**=Hardest Jump in 2017 schedule from 2016 (aka a much harder schedule in 2017), **32**=Easiest Jump in 2017 schedule from 2016 (aka a much easier schedule in 2017); **Pass Blend** metric blends 4 metrics: Pass Efficiency, YPPA, Explosive Pass & Pass Rush; **Rush Blend** metric blends 3 metrics: Rush Efficiency, Explosive Rush & RB Targets

Team Records & Trends

	2016	2015	2014
Average line	-4.1	-1.9	-2.0
Average O/U line	47.5	46.6	47.1
Straight Up Record	11-5	10-6	11-5
Against the Spread Record	9-7	8-6	9-7
Over/Under Record	6-10	6-10	9-7
ATS as Favorite	9-6	4-2	6-5
ATS as Underdog	0-1	3-3	3-2
Straight Up Home	6-2	6-2	6-2
ATS Home	4-4	4-2	5-3
Over/Under Home	4-4	4-4	6-2
ATS as Home Favorite	4-3	3-1	4-3
ATS as a Home Dog	0-1	1-0	1-0
Straight Up Away	5-3	4-4	5-3
ATS Away	5-3	4-4	4-4
Over/Under Away	2-6	2-6	3-5
ATS Away Favorite	5-3	1-1	2-2
ATS Away Dog	0-0	2-3	2-2
Six Point Teaser Record	12-4	12-2	11-5
Seven Point Teaser Record	12-4	15-1	12-4
Ten Point Teaser Record	13-2	15-1	12-3

PIT-3

Fortunately for the Steelers secondary, they will face a similar schedule in terms of quarterback caliber. Apart from one game against Tom Brady and one game against Aaron Rodgers, Alex Smith and Andy Dalton again lead the best passing offenses the Steelers will face based on last year's results. They will have a game against Andrew Luck, one against Matthew Stafford and one against Marcus Mariota which should present good tests.

But this could very well be another season where the Steelers are able to camouflage their defensive inefficiency on the backend thanks to their schedule of opponents and the strength of their offense. However, when the chips are down, and the Steelers face a good quarterback in the postseason, will they be able to avoid another predictable loss? Which is why, once again, the Steelers offense will need to carry this team in 2017.

The Steelers offense was substantially better last year thanks to Le'Veon Bell, who missed most of 2015, and their offensive line. However, the Steelers have played 39 consecutive football games without their key offensive weapons intact. *(cont'd - see PIT-4)*

2017 Rest Analysis

Avg Rest	6.47
Avg Rk	3
Team More Rest	4
Opp More Rest	4
Net Rest Edge	0
3 Days Rest	1
4 Days Rest	0
5 Days Rest	2
6 Days Rest	8
7 Days Rest	2
8 Days Rest	0
9 Days Rest	1
10 Days Rest	0
11 Days Rest	0
12 Days Rest	0
13 Days Rest	1
14 Days Rest	0

Health by Unit*

2016 Rk	12
(2015 Rk)	19
Off Rk	15
Def Rk	11
QB Rk	25
RB Rk	1
WR Rk	26
TE Rk	24
OLine Rk	8
DLine Rk	18
LB Rk	19
DB Rk	1

**Based on the great work of Scott Kacsmar from Football Outsiders*

2017 Weekly Betting Lines (wks 1-16)

1	2	3	4	5	6	7	8	10	11	12	13	14	15	16
CLE	MIN	CHI	BAL	JAX	KC	CIN	DET	IND	TEN	GB	CIN	BAL	NE	HOU
A	H	A	A	H	A	H	A	A	H	H	A	H	H	A
-9.0	-6.0	-5.5	-1.5	-9.0	+1.5	-7.0	-1.5	-1.0	-6.5	-3.0	-1.0	-6.0	+1.5	-1.0

Avg = -3.7

Home Lines (wks 1-16)

2	5	7	11	12	14	15
MIN	JAX	CIN	TEN	GB	BAL	NE
-6.0	-9.0	-7.0	-6.5	-3.0	-6.0	+1.5

Avg = -5.1

Road Lines (wks 1-16)

1	3	4	6	8	10	13	16
CLE	CHI	BAL	KC	DET	IND	CIN	HOU
-9.0	-5.5	-1.5	+1.5	-1.5	-1.0	-1.0	-1.0

Avg = -2.4

Pittsburgh Steelers 2016 Play Analysis

2016 Play Tendencies

All Pass %	61%
All Pass Rk	10
All Rush %	39%
All Rush Rk	23
1 Score Pass %	58%
1 Score Pass Rk	16
2015 1 Score Pass %	63%
2015 1 Score Pass Rk	4
Pass Increase %	-4%
Pass Increase Rk	28
1 Score Rush %	42%
1 Score Rush Rk	17
Up Pass %	58%
Up Pass Rk	14
Up Rush %	42%
Up Rush Rk	19
Down Pass %	66%
Down Pass Rk	5
Down Rush %	34%
Down Rush Rk	28

2016 Down & Distance Tendencies

Down	Distance	Total Plays	Pass Rate	Run Rate	Play Success %
1	Short (1-3)	6	50%	50%	33%
	Med (4-7)	8	63%	38%	50%
	Long (8-10)	371	49%	51%	51%
	XL (11+)	13	62%	38%	38%
2	Short (1-3)	49	41%	59%	61%
	Med (4-7)	101	49%	51%	58%
	Long (8-10)	117	64%	36%	44%
	XL (11+)	31	74%	26%	26%
3	Short (1-3)	54	67%	33%	63%
	Med (4-7)	55	95%	5%	44%
	Long (8-10)	36	94%	6%	47%
	XL (11+)	33	82%	18%	9%
4	Short (1-3)	7	71%	29%	86%
	Med (4-7)	2	100%	0%	0%

Shotgun %:

Under Center	Shotgun
34%	66%
37%	*63%*

AVG

Run Rate:

Under Center	Shotgun
73%	24%
68%	*23%*

AVG

Pass Rate:

Under Center	Shotgun
27%	76%
32%	*77%*

AVG

Short Yardage Intelligence:

2nd and Short Run

Run Freq	Run % Rk	NFL Run Freq Avg	Run 1D Rate	Run NFL 1D Avg
67%	13	65%	83%	71%

2nd and Short Pass

Pass Freq	Pass % Rk	NFL Pass Freq Avg	Pass 1D Rate	Pass NFL 1D Avg
33%	19	35%	47%	52%

Most Frequent Play

Down	Distance	Play Type	Player	Total Plays	Play Success %
1	Short (1-3)	RUSH	Le'Veon Bell	2	50%
	Med (4-7)	PASS	Antonio Brown	4	25%
	Long (8-10)	RUSH	Le'Veon Bell	132	55%
	XL (11+)	RUSH	Le'Veon Bell	4	75%
2	Short (1-3)	RUSH	Le'Veon Bell	18	89%
	Med (4-7)	RUSH	Le'Veon Bell	41	63%
	Long (8-10)	PASS	Antonio Brown	27	48%
		RUSH	Le'Veon Bell	27	30%
	XL (11+)	PASS	Le'Veon Bell	6	33%
		RUSH	Le'Veon Bell	6	33%
3	Short (1-3)	RUSH	Le'Veon Bell	13	69%
	Med (4-7)	PASS	Eli Rogers	10	30%
	Long (8-10)	PASS	Antonio Brown	7	43%
			Eli Rogers	7	71%
	XL (11+)	PASS	Antonio Brown	7	0%

Most Successful Play*

Down	Distance	Play Type	Player	Total Plays	Play Success %
1	Long (8-10)	PASS	Eli Rogers	13	77%
2	Short (1-3)	RUSH	Le'Veon Bell	18	89%
	Med (4-7)	PASS	Eli Rogers	5	80%
	Long (8-10)	PASS	Eli Rogers	11	55%
	XL (11+)	PASS	Antonio Brown	5	60%
3	Short (1-3)	PASS	Le'Veon Bell	5	80%
			Eli Rogers	5	80%
	Med (4-7)	PASS	Cobi Hamilton	5	80%
	Long (8-10)	PASS	Eli Rogers	7	71%
	XL (11+)	PASS	Ladarius Green	5	40%

**Minimum 5 plays to qualify*

2016 Snap Rates

Week	Opp	Score	Antonio Brown	Jesse James	Le'Veon Bell	Eli Rogers	Cobi Hamilton	Sammie Coates	DeAngelo Williams	David Johnson
1	WAS	W 38-16	66 (97%)	68 (100%)		47 (69%)		44 (65%)	56 (82%)	17 (25%)
2	CIN	W 24-16	74 (100%)	74 (100%)		41 (55%)		35 (47%)	66 (89%)	26 (35%)
3	PHI	L 34-3	60 (100%)	58 (97%)		21 (35%)		40 (67%)	52 (87%)	7 (12%)
4	KC	W 43-14	52 (88%)	50 (85%)	52 (88%)			33 (56%)	17 (29%)	24 (41%)
5	NYJ	W 31-13	74 (97%)	72 (95%)	73 (96%)			44 (58%)	12 (16%)	11 (14%)
6	MIA	L 30-15	55 (100%)	52 (95%)	53 (96%)	32 (58%)	12 (22%)	17 (31%)	7 (13%)	7 (13%)
7	NE	L 27-16	59 (81%)	54 (74%)	72 (99%)		49 (67%)	7 (10%)		17 (23%)
9	BAL	L 21-14	69 (100%)	31 (45%)	65 (94%)	46 (67%)	18 (26%)	47 (68%)	4 (6%)	17 (25%)
10	DAL	L 35-30	72 (97%)	52 (70%)	74 (100%)	64 (86%)	67 (91%)	2 (3%)		10 (14%)
11	CLE	W 24-9	69 (100%)	68 (99%)	69 (100%)	45 (65%)	43 (62%)	1 (1%)		23 (33%)
12	IND	W 28-7	49 (91%)	41 (76%)	47 (87%)	27 (50%)	31 (57%)	8 (15%)		12 (22%)
13	NYG	W 24-14	72 (99%)	45 (62%)	72 (99%)	45 (62%)	40 (55%)	4 (5%)		21 (29%)
14	BUF	W 27-20	75 (100%)	50 (67%)	72 (96%)	35 (47%)	34 (45%)	1 (1%)		22 (29%)
15	CIN	W 24-20	75 (100%)	29 (39%)	75 (100%)	48 (64%)	18 (24%)	30 (40%)		15 (20%)
16	BAL	W 31-27	54 (93%)	49 (84%)	57 (98%)	44 (76%)	29 (50%)		1 (2%)	10 (17%)
17	CLE	W 27-24		61 (86%)		55 (77%)	45 (63%)		56 (79%)	19 (27%)
Grand Total			975 (96%)	854 (79%)	781 (96%)	550 (62%)	386 (51%)	313 (33%)	271 (45%)	258 (24%)

Personnel Groupings

Personnel	Team %	NFL Avg	Succ. %
1-1 [3WR]	64%	60%	51%
1-2 [2WR]	18%	19%	47%
2-1 [2WR]	9%	7%	53%
1-3 [1WR]	5%	3%	49%

Grouping Tendencies

Personnel	Pass Rate	Pass Succ. %	Run Succ. %
1-1 [3WR]	72%	49%	54%
1-2 [2WR]	46%	43%	50%
2-1 [2WR]	21%	43%	56%
1-3 [1WR]	30%	59%	45%

Red Zone Targets (min 3)

Receiver	All	Inside 5	6-10	11-20
Antonio Brown	19	6	3	10
Jesse James	15	1	7	7
Le'Veon Bell	10	3	2	5
Eli Rogers	9	4	1	4
Cobi Hamilton	7	3		4
Ladarius Green	6	1		5
Sammie Coates	5	2		3
DeAngelo Williams	3	1		2
Xavier Grimble	3	1		2
David Johnson	1		1	

Red Zone Rushes (min 3)

Rusher	All	Inside 5	6-10	11-20
Le'Veon Bell	42	9	9	24
DeAngelo Williams	16	7	2	7
Ben Roethlisberger	5	2	2	1

Early Down Target Rate

RB	TE	WR
24%	21%	55%
19%	*20% NFL AVG*	*61%*

Overall Target Success %

RB	TE	WR
54% #1	51% #20	49% #18

Pittsburgh Steelers 2016 Passing Recap & 2017 Outlook

The AFC North has competent quarterback play, while perhaps not as "elite" as billed in certain circles. But Ben Roethlisberger is as complete a quarterback as exists in the division. League-wide, he's likely underrated. He may not be the QB to load it all onto his shoulders, like Aaron Rodgers, but he has been more than responsible for many of the solid results this team has had while their defense transitioned from the Steel Curtain V2 in the mid 2000s to a downright dreadful unit a few years back, to this slightly above average unit we see today. Roethlisberger certainly was hoping Ladarius Green would pay off in Pittsburgh after Heath Miller retired, but Green didn't even see substantial playing time. It hurts going from Antonio Brown, Martavius Bryant and Heath Miller in 2015 to being led at receiver by Brown, Jesse James and Eli Rodgers. But such was the 2016 Steelers passing game. The Steelers passing game overall was extremely effective and Ben ranked 6th in 3rd down passes past the line to gain. He needs to clean up his massive interception rate on short-medium (3, 4, 5 yds to go) passing. Even without a deep threat apart from Brown, Ben completed 39 passes which traveled 20+ yards in the air, a solid number.

Ben Roethlisberger Rating All Downs

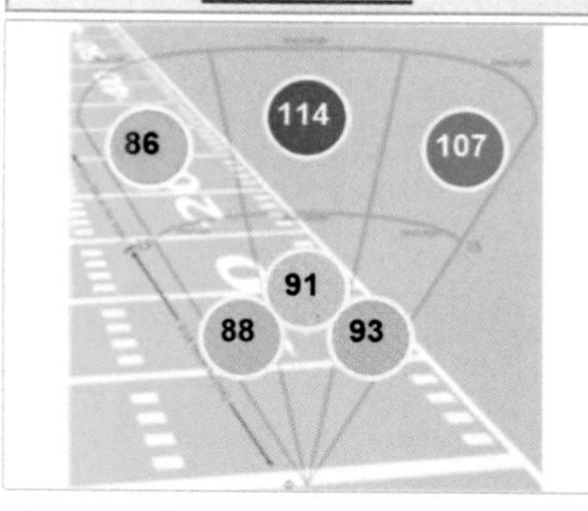

Ben Roethlisberger Rating Early Downs

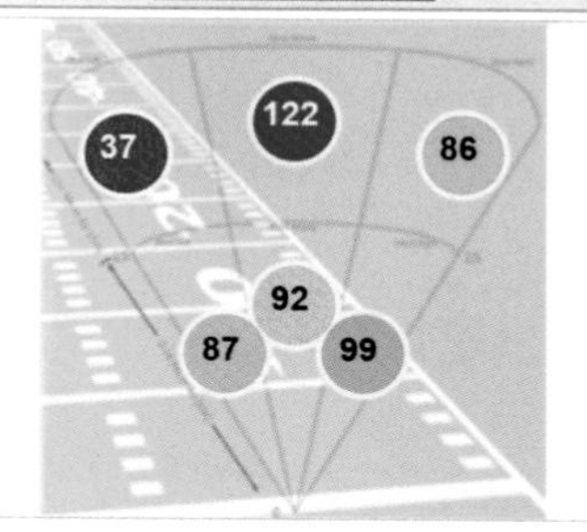

2016 Standard Passing Table

QB	Comp	Att	Comp %	Yds	YPA	TDs	INT	Sacks	Rating	Rk
Ben Roethlisberger	392	605	65%	4,554	7.5	32	17	19	93.4	16
Landry Jones	53	86	62%	558	6.5	4	2	4	86.3	27
NFL Avg			63%		7.2				90.4	

2016 Advanced Passing Table

QB	Success %	EDSR Passing Success %	20+ Yd Pass Gains	20+ Yd Pass %	30+ Yd Pass Gains	30+ Yd Pass %	Air Yds per Comp	YAC per Comp	20+ Air Yd Comp	20+ Air Yd %
Ben Roethlisberger	50%	51%	68	11%	28	5%	6.5	5.1	39	6%
Landry Jones	39%	45%	5	6%	2	2%	6.5	4.1	4	5%
NFL Avg	44%	48%	27	8%	10	3%	6.4	4.8	12	4%

Interception Rates by Down

Yards to Go	1	2	3	4	Total
1 & 2	0.0%	0.0%	0.0%	0.0%	0.0%
3, 4, 5	16.7%	2.9%	1.9%	20.0%	4.1%
6 - 9	0.0%	1.4%	2.1%	0.0%	1.6%
10 - 14	2.3%	6.3%	3.2%	0.0%	3.2%
15+	0.0%	6.3%	0.0%	0.0%	2.6%
Total	2.5%	3.5%	1.8%	8.3%	2.7%

3rd Down Passing - Short of Sticks Analysis

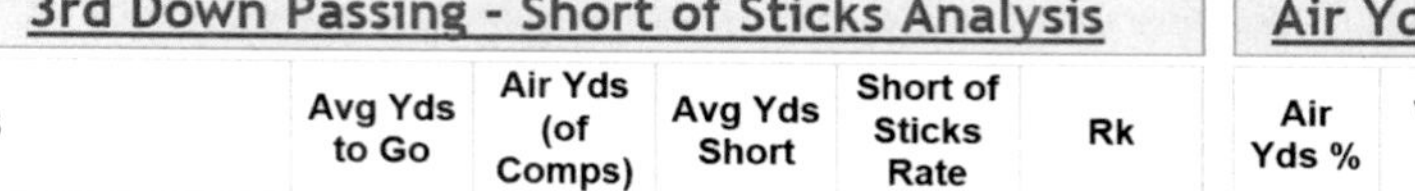

QB	Avg Yds to Go	Air Yds (of Comps)	Avg Yds Short	Short of Sticks Rate	Rk
Ben Roethlisberger	6.8	8.5	0.0	53%	6
NFL Avg	7.6	6.8	-0.8	57%	

Air Yds vs YAC

Air Yds %	YAC %	Rk
43%	57%	45
54%	46%	

2016 Receiving Recap & 2017 Outlook

The Steelers really maxed out their production given the talent they had beyond Antonio Brown at the receiver position last year. Targeting RB Le'Veon Bell was successful 78% of the time and averaged over 6 yards per attempt. The Steelers need to continue this high volume usage of Bell in the pass game due to its efficiency. The Steelers pass attack is extremely score dependent. While 59% pass in one-score games, that quickly drops 20% to 39% when another 6 points are added to the scoreboard. If possible, target receivers on Ben's right side, as the frequency and success are much better than when he throws left, especially deep.

Player *Min 50 Targets	Targets	Comp %	YPA	Rating	TOARS	Success %	Success Rk	Missed YPA Rk	YAS % Rk	TDs
Antonio Brown	183	68%	8.7	109	5.8	51%	64	73	17	14
Le'Veon Bell	101	78%	6.1	99	4.8	55%	37	18	134	2
Eli Rogers	84	73%	8.4	100	4.6	57%	30	59	111	3
Jesse James	75	67%	6.3	75	4.1	56%	35	11	117	3
Sammie Coates	54	43%	8.7	63	3.2	33%	147	127	1	2

Directional Passer Rating Delivered

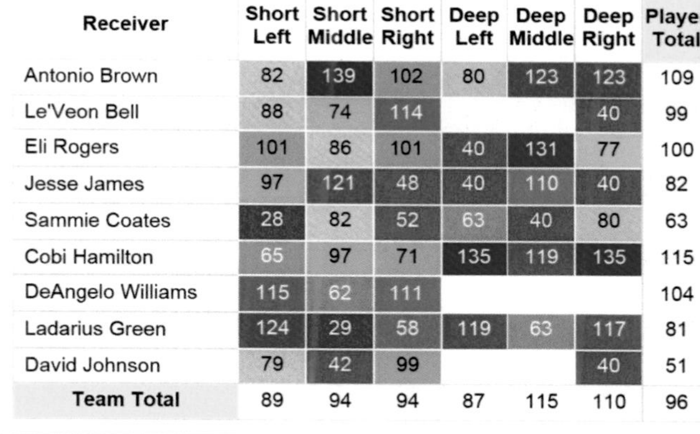

Receiver	Short Left	Short Middle	Short Right	Deep Left	Deep Middle	Deep Right	Player Total
Antonio Brown	82	139	102	80	123	123	109
Le'Veon Bell	88	74	114			40	99
Eli Rogers	101	86	101	40	131	77	100
Jesse James	97	121	48	40	110	40	82
Sammie Coates	28	82	52	63	40	80	63
Cobi Hamilton	65	97	71	135	119	135	115
DeAngelo Williams	115	62	111				104
Ladarius Green	124	29	58	119	63	117	81
David Johnson	79	42	99			40	51
Team Total	89	94	94	87	115	110	96

2016 Rushing Recap & 2017 Outlook

Le'Veon Bell is everything you would want in a feature back. He's adept at just about every single feature a back in today's game should be. He's especially tremendous out of the backfield as a receiver, where he ranked as the 3rd most successful receiving RB and 3rd in missed yards per attempt. Look for even more success for the Steelers when targeting Bell out of the backfield in 2017. I wasn't thrilled about the Steelers decision to draft RB James Connor, as I felt they were better suited to go defense and simply keep a very productive DeAngelo Williams. But Connor should see an immediate opportunity to contribute as a backup RB, potentially vulturing away a few TDs from Bell, as last year Williams did last year (25% of red zone TDs).

Player *Min 50 Rushes	Rushes	YPA	Success %	Success Rk	Missed YPA Rk	YTS % Rk	YAS % Rk	Early Down Success %	Early Down Success Rk	TDs
Le'Veon Bell	326	5.0	56%	6	7	33	35	57%	5	9
DeAngelo Williams	114	3.3	43%	47	53	9	43	41%	55	5

Yards per Carry by Direction

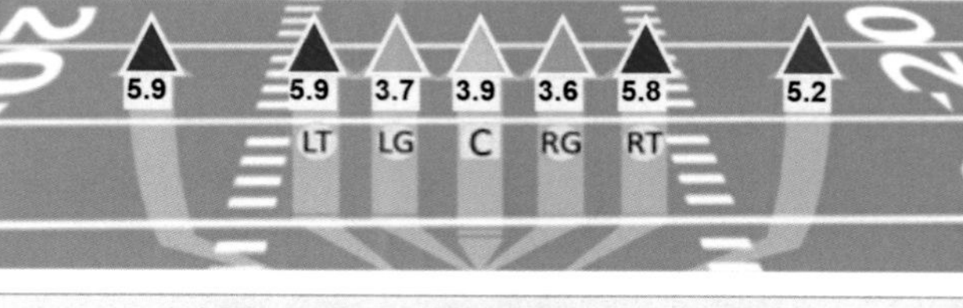

Directional Run Frequency

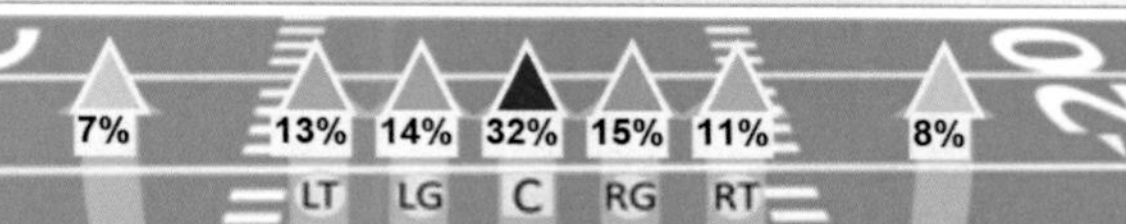

In 2014, the Steelers drafted Clemson WR Martavius Bryant, a year after letting WR Mike Wallace walk in free agency and instead, signing Antonio Brown. And that started what has been referred to as the "Killer Bs": Big Ben, Bell, Brown and Bryant. These 4 key players have been on the Steelers for the last 3 full seasons, when the team recorded three consecutive double-digit win seasons. But you would have to go back to December of 2014 to find the last game they all played together.

In 2014 as a rookie, Bryant didn't work his way into games until mid-October. The Steelers went 7-2 in 2014 with the Killer Bs intact. Then Le'Veon Bell was injured to close the 2014 season, and they lost in the playoffs. To start 2015, both Bell and Bryant were suspended and Big Ben got injured. In Ben's first game back, Bell was injured and missed the remainder of the 2016 season. And last season, Bryant was suspended for the entire season. It's too early to suggest this season will be the first that the Killer Bs will play together, especially given their injury and suspension history. But behind what has become an extremely solid offensive line, having the Killer Bs back and working in concert would be tremendous to watch. And for their sake, they should hope Bryant comes out hot and Smith-Schuster gets acclimated quickly, because this passing game, particularly late, was bad.

'The Steelers offensive line did an unheralded job of keeping Ben Rothelisberger upright, ranking 4th in pass protection efficiency last year.

But that came against the 5th easiest schedule, and this year they have the 17th rated schedule of pass rush defenses. From weeks 2-7, the Steelers schedule of pass defenses is brutal: every single defense ranks top-10 in pass "blend" defense except for a road game against the Chiefs. However, the dark clouds lift week 8, and the Steelers pass offense will face the 4th easiest schedule of pass defenses to close the season. On the ground, last year the Steelers faced the NFL's easiest schedule of explosive run defenses. This year, they face the 11th hardest schedule. And, while the Steelers pass offense faces a very tough stretch of pass defenses, look for Le'Veon Bell to see a ton of action in the pass game. Pittsburgh ranked #1 in RB-pass efficiency against the #17 rated schedule. That schedule becomes easier (22nd) in 2017. Against a stronger pass rush, Roethlisberger may look for Bell in the pass game even more often in 2017.

While Pittsburgh is certainly built to make the playoffs and noise when there, they are errily reminiscent of a more jazzed-up, visually-appealing version of the Chiefs. They may do well in the regular season if healthy, but can they go into Foxboro and defeat the Patriots in January? They'll need a healthy Killer Bs on offense to stand a chance, but they'll need growth and development from the young secondary to pull it off.

Division History: Season Wins & 2017 Projection

2013 Wins | 2014 Wins | 2015 Wins | 2016 Wins | Proj 2017 Wins

Rank of 2017 Defensive Pass Efficiency Faced by Week

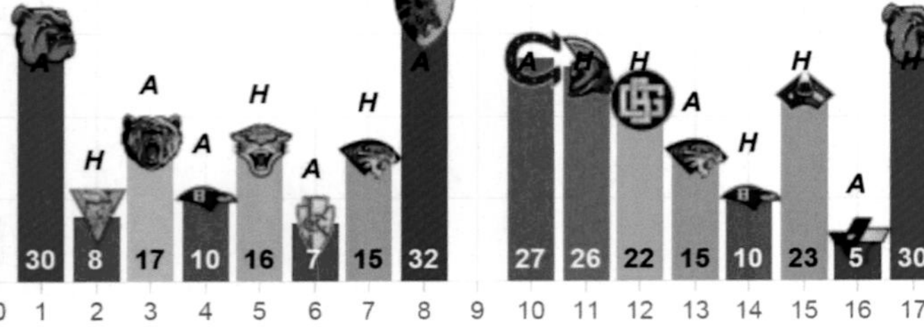

Rank of 2017 Defensive Rush Efficiency Faced by Week

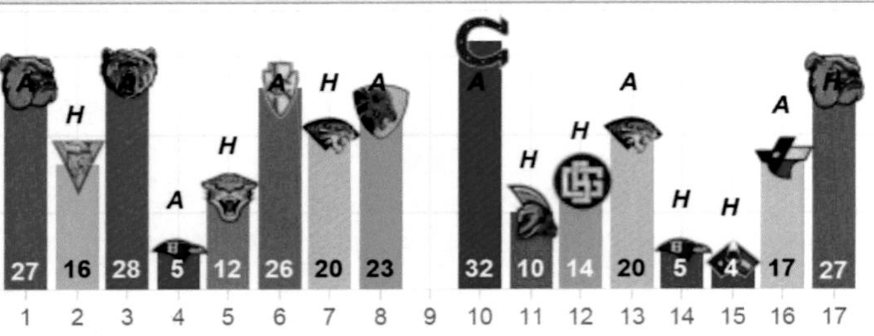

2016 Situational Usage by Player & Position

Usage Rate by Score

		Being Blown Out (14+)	Down Big (9-13)	One Score	Large Lead (9-13)	Blowout Lead (14+)	Grand Total
RUSH	Le'Veon Bell	7%	15%	27%	52%	50%	28%
	Antonio Brown			0%			0%
	DeAngelo Williams	7%	16%	11%		8%	10%
	Eli Rogers			0%			0%
	Sammie Coates		1%	0%			0%
	Darrius Heyward-Bey			0%			0%
	Demarcus Ayers	1%		0%			0%
	Fitzgerald Toussaint			1%		3%	1%
	Daryl Richardson		1%	0%			0%
	Total	14%	33%	41%	52%	61%	41%
PASS	Le'Veon Bell	9%	8%	10%	10%	4%	9%
	Antonio Brown	22%	18%	16%	12%	11%	16%
	DeAngelo Williams	7%	4%	3%	3%	1%	3%
	Eli Rogers	15%	9%	8%	1%	1%	7%
	Jesse James	5%	10%	7%	4%	5%	7%
	Sammie Coates	10%	4%	3%	6%	7%	5%
	Cobi Hamilton	6%	3%	3%	1%	3%	3%
	Ladarius Green	1%	1%	3%	6%	5%	3%
	Darrius Heyward-Bey	5%	6%	1%			2%
	Xavier Grimble	2%	2%	2%		1%	2%
	Demarcus Ayers	2%		2%		1%	1%
	Fitzgerald Toussaint			0%			0%
	David Johnson			1%	1%	1%	1%
	Markus Wheaton	2%		1%	1%	1%	1%
	Roosevelt Nix		1%	0%			0%
	Total	86%	67%	59%	48%	39%	59%

Positional Target Distribution vs NFL Average

		NFL Wide				Team Only			
		Left	Middle	Right	Total	Left	Middle	Right	Total
Deep	WR	987	552	962	2,501	44	29	39	112
	TE	155	137	157	449	3	10	6	19
	RB	25	4	38	67			2	2
	All	1,167	693	1,157	3,017	47	39	47	133
Short	WR	3,007	1,716	3,083	7,806	86	55	103	244
	TE	814	837	1,110	2,761	22	38	41	101
	RB	970	593	1,054	2,617	45	29	59	133
	All	4,791	3,146	5,247	13,184	153	122	203	478
Total		5,958	3,839	6,404	16,201	200	161	250	611

Positional Success Rates vs NFL Average

		NFL Wide				Team Only			
		Left	Middle	Right	Total	Left	Middle	Right	Total
Deep	WR	37%	50%	37%	40%	39%	48%	54%	46%
	TE	45%	50%	43%	46%	33%	40%	50%	42%
	RB	32%	75%	26%	31%			0%	0%
	All	38%	51%	38%	41%	38%	46%	51%	45%
Short	WR	52%	57%	51%	53%	48%	51%	55%	52%
	TE	49%	62%	52%	54%	68%	53%	51%	55%
	RB	47%	50%	43%	46%	53%	45%	61%	55%
	All	51%	57%	50%	52%	52%	50%	56%	53%
Total		48%	56%	48%	50%	49%	49%	55%	52%

2017 Coaches

Head Coach:
Kyle Shanahan (1st yr)
Offensive Coordinator:
(Shanahan will call plays) (1st yr)
Defensive Coordinator:
Robert Saleh (JAC LB) (1st yr)

San Francisco 49ers

2017 Forecast

Wins	Div Rank
4.5	#4

Past Records

2016: 2-14
2015: 5-11
2014: 8-8

EASY HARD

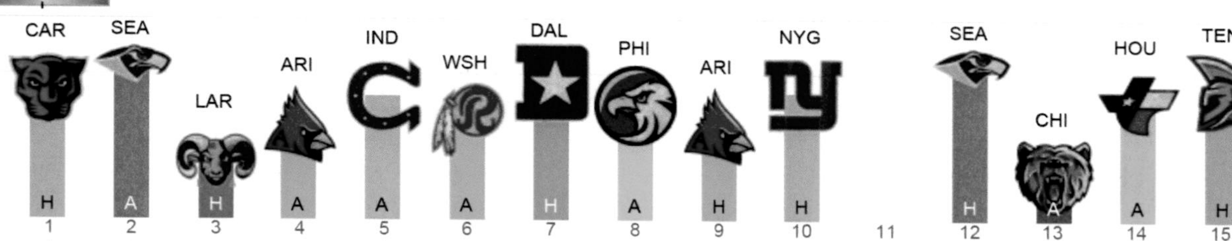

Key Players Lost

TXN	Player (POS)
Cut	Bethea, Antoine S
	Brock, Tramaine CB
	Golden, Malik S
	Harris, DuJuan RB
	Martin, Marcus C
	Ross, Rashad WR
	Skov, Shayne LB
	Smith, Torrey WR
Declared Free Agent	Bellore, Nick LB
	Cromartie, Marcus CB
	Dawson, Phil K
	Dorsey, Glenn DT
	Draughn, Shaun RB
	Gabbert, Blaine QB
	Harris, DuJuan RB
	Hodges Jr., Gerald LB
	Kaepernick, Colin QB
	Kerley, Jeremy WR
	Patton, Quinton WR
	Streater, Rod WR

2017 San Francisco 49ers Overview

The "O" in San Francisco is at the end, which is exactly where their own "O" finished in 2016, marking two straight years where they finished at or near the bottom in many key offensive categories. They ranked 30th in EDSR (Early Down Success Rate) offense and were 31st in yards per attempt. It was a bad season for a bad offense, bad defense and poor talent.

This was predictable, however. In this very page in the 2016 Football Preview, I remarked about Chip Kelly and the fact that his "magic dust" isn't real. The turnaround he achieved in Philadelphia back in 2013, moving from 4 wins to 10, was entirely related to team talent, receiving back injured players who missed the prior year, and a solid draft class of immediate contributors. The 49ers were entirely devoid of this talent, and I had absolutely no belief that a new scheme from Kelly would suddenly produce talent on the football field. The fact that Kelly's only 2 wins came against the Rams says more about the Rams than the 49ers. Yes, some games were more competitive for the 49ers, but these generally came against bad teams in 2016, such as a 2 point loss to the Seahawks or a 3 point loss to the Cardinals or a 6 point loss to the Jets.

In search of new direction, the team fired GM Trent Baalke and brought in John Lynch, and fired Kelly and brought in Kyle Shanahan, giving each of them six-year deals. Shanahan certainly didn't want to start out his tenure with a bad quarterback, not after making his mark with Matt Ryan last year in Atlanta. So they signed two QBs from Chicago in free agency: Brian Hoyer and Matt Barkley. They also added C.J. Beathard in the draft, and those are the lone 3 quarterbacks on the roster.

Hoyer played incredibly well in Chicago last season. He posted a 98 passer rating, completed 67% of his passes and averaged 7.2 yards per attempt. All of these were at or above the NFL average. In terms of advanced stats, his 57% success rate on early down passing was nearly 10% above the NFL average. That rating was actually tied for first place in the NFL with Kyle Shanahan's former QB, Matt Ryan. However, one knock on Hoyer was he was not explosive in his passing. His % of completions which traveled 20+ air yards was below average, as was his average air yards per completion.

(cont'd - see SF2)

Key Free Agents/ Trades Added

Barkley, Matt QB
Dumervil, Elvis LB
Garcon, Pierre WR
Goodwin, Marquise WR
Hightower, Tim RB
Hoyer, Brian QB
Juszczyk, Kyle RB
Robinson, Aldrick WR
Smith, Malcolm LB
Zuttah, Jeremy G

Drafted Players

Rd	Pk	Player (College)
1	3	DE - Solomon Thomas (Stanford)
	31	LB - Reuben Foster (Alabama)
3	66	CB - Ahkello Witherspoon (Colorado)
3*	104	QB - C. J. Beathard (Iowa)
4	121	RB - Joe Williams (Utah)
5	146	TE - George Kittle (Iowa)
5*	177	WR - Trent Taylor (Louisiana Tech)
6	198	DT - D. J. Jones (Ole Miss)
	202	DE - Pita Taumoepenu (Utah)
7	229	CB - Adrian Colbert (Miami (FL))

Average Line	# Games Favored	# Games Underdog
 +6.0	 1	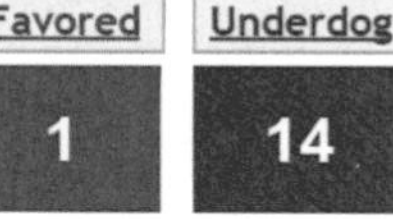 14

Regular Season Wins: Past & Current Proj

Proj 2017 Wins 4.5
2016 Wins 2

Proj 2016 Wins 6

2015 Wins 5

2014 Wins 8

2013 Wins 12

1 3 5 7 9 11 13 15

2017 Lineup & Cap Hits

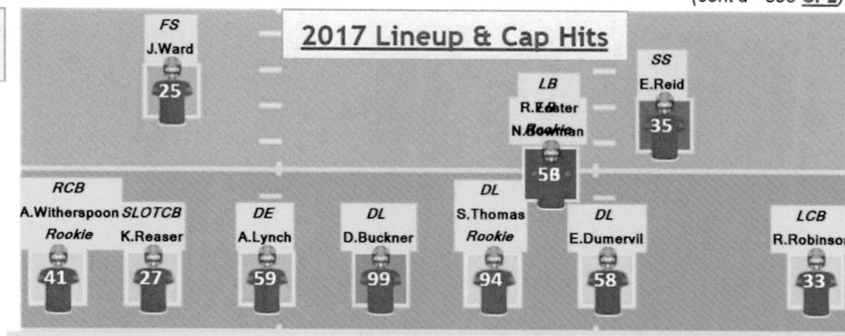

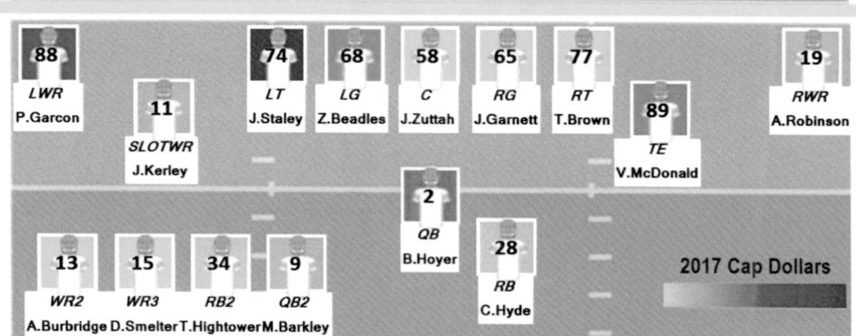

2017 Unit Spending

Positional Spending

	Rank	Total	2016 Rk
All OFF	30	$68.50M	26
QB	27	$8.12M	6
OL	16	$28.59M	28
RB	29	$4.60M	24
WR	17	$17.71M	25
TE	13	$9.49M	19
All DEF	29	$64.75M	22
DL	24	$19.49M	27
LB	10	$25.66M	5
CB	28	$8.68M	24
S	18	$10.92M	10

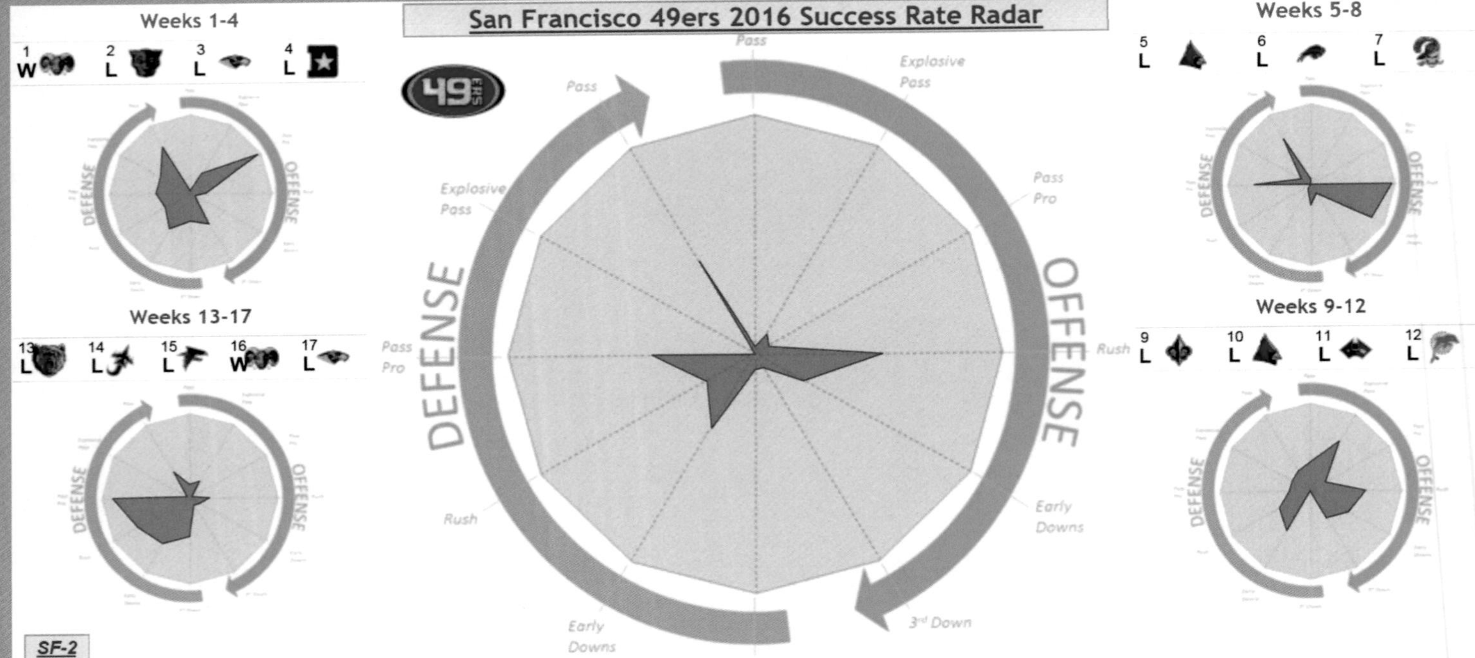

SF-2

He also ranked 29th in percentage of throws which went short of the sticks on 3rd down. Hoyer's strengths were accuracy on short and intermediate passes and sound decision making. He didn't throw a single interception last year in 200 attempts. But the lack of aggressiveness and lack of success when throwing the ball downfield was a concern.

The 49ers cleaned house on wide receivers as well. They signed a foundational piece of the future passing game in Pierre Garcon from the Redskins. Garcon produced NFL ranks of 8th in success rate, 6th in Missed YPA (how close did plays come to being successful even when they fell short) and 19th in YAS % (Yards Above Success, an explosiveness factor). He was reliable and dependable, particularly on short passes, which is what Hoyer will be throwing. Garcon delivered a 76% completion rate, 7.9 yards per attempt and a 64% success rate on passes within 15 yards of the line of scrimmage. The only WRs with similar success on short passes were Jordy Nelson, Mohamed Sanu, Michael Thomas and Cole Beasley. These types of WRs make life much easier on a quarterback.

San Francisco also added speedster from Buffalo Marquise Goodwin and a player Shanahan is quite familiar with, Aldrick Robinson from Atlanta. While the deep passes may not hit home as much as Shanahan saw in Atlanta, the threat of speed on the field can open some things up, and now it's on Hoyer to work with Goodwin, understand his speed, and allow Shanahan to design some plays which will play to their strengths while still being explosive in nature.

On the ground, the 49ers will still ride with Carlos Hyde. Last year was tough on the run game for the 49ers. They faced the 3rd most difficult schedule of run defenses in the NFL. Despite winning only 2 games and trailing most of the time against a very difficult schedule of run defenses, the 49ers still went run-heavy, rushing the ball on 52% of their offensive plays, the most in the NFL. And remarkably, Hyde was fairly productive. He averaged 4.6 yards per attempt, but all of his advanced rankings were subpar, as to be expected. He ranked 35th in success rate,

(cont'd - see SF-3)

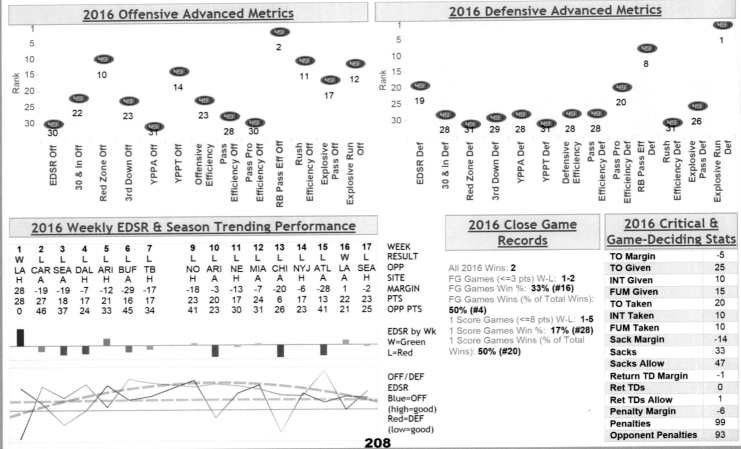

2016 Offensive Advanced Metrics

Metric	Rank
EDSR Off	30
30 & In Off	22
Red Zone Off	10
3rd Down Off	23
YPPA Off	31
YPPT Off	14
Offensive Efficiency	23
Pass Efficiency Off	28
Pass Pro Efficiency Off	30
RB Pass Eff Off	2
Rush Efficiency Off	11
Explosive Pass Off	17
Explosive Run Off	12

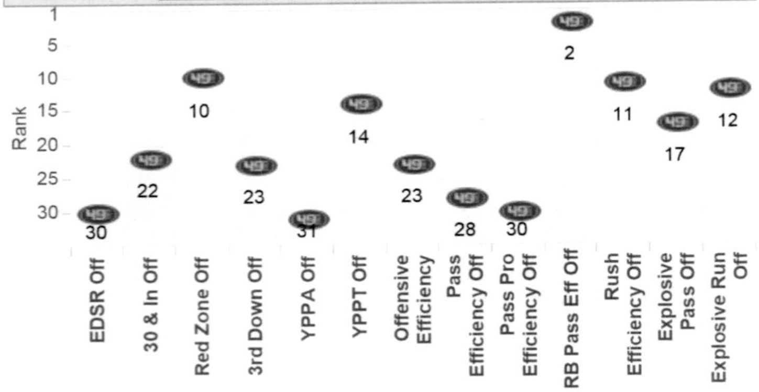

2016 Defensive Advanced Metrics

Metric	Rank
EDSR Def	19
30 & In Def	28
Red Zone Def	31
3rd Down Def	29
YPPA Def	28
YPPT Def	31
Defensive Efficiency	28
Pass Efficiency Def	28
Pass Pro Efficieincy Def	20
RB Pass Eff Def	8
Rush Efficiency Def	31
Explosive Pass Def	26
Explosive Run Def	1

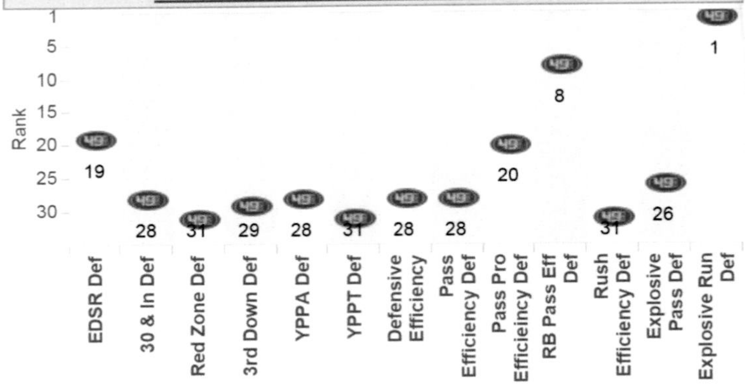

2016 Weekly EDSR & Season Trending Performance

WEEK	1	2	3	4	5	6	7	9	10	11	12	13	14	15	16	17
RESULT	W	L	L	L	L	L	L	L	L	L	L	L	L	L	W	L
OPP	LA	CAR	SEA	DAL	ARI	BUF	TB	NO	ARI	NE	MIA	CHI	NYJ	ATL	LA	SEA
SITE	H	A	A	H	H	A	H	H	A	H	A	A	H	A	A	H
MARGIN	28	-19	-19	-7	-12	-29	-17	-18	-3	-13	-7	-20	-6	-28	1	-2
PTS	28	27	18	17	21	16	17	23	20	17	24	6	17	13	22	23
OPP PTS	0	46	37	24	33	45	34	41	23	30	31	26	23	41	21	25

EDSR by Wk
W=Green
L=Red

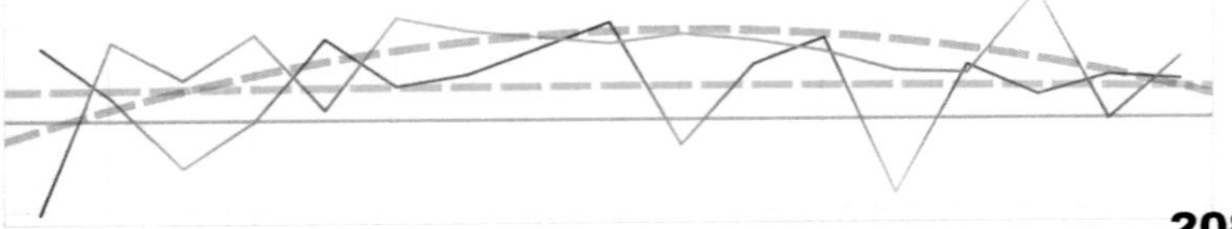

OFF/DEF EDSR
Blue=OFF (high=good)
Red=DEF (low=good)

2016 Close Game Records

All 2016 Wins: **2**
FG Games (<=3 pts) W-L: **1-2**
FG Games Win %: **33% (#16)**
FG Games Wins (% of Total Wins): **50% (#4)**
1 Score Games (<=8 pts) W-L: **1-5**
1 Score Games Win %: **17% (#28)**
1 Score Games Wins (% of Total Wins): **50% (#20)**

2016 Critical & Game-Deciding Stats

TO Margin	-5
TO Given	25
INT Given	10
FUM Given	15
TO Taken	20
INT Taken	10
FUM Taken	10
Sack Margin	-14
Sacks	33
Sacks Allow	47
Return TD Margin	-1
Ret TDs	0
Ret TDs Allow	1
Penalty Margin	-6
Penalties	99
Opponent Penalties	93

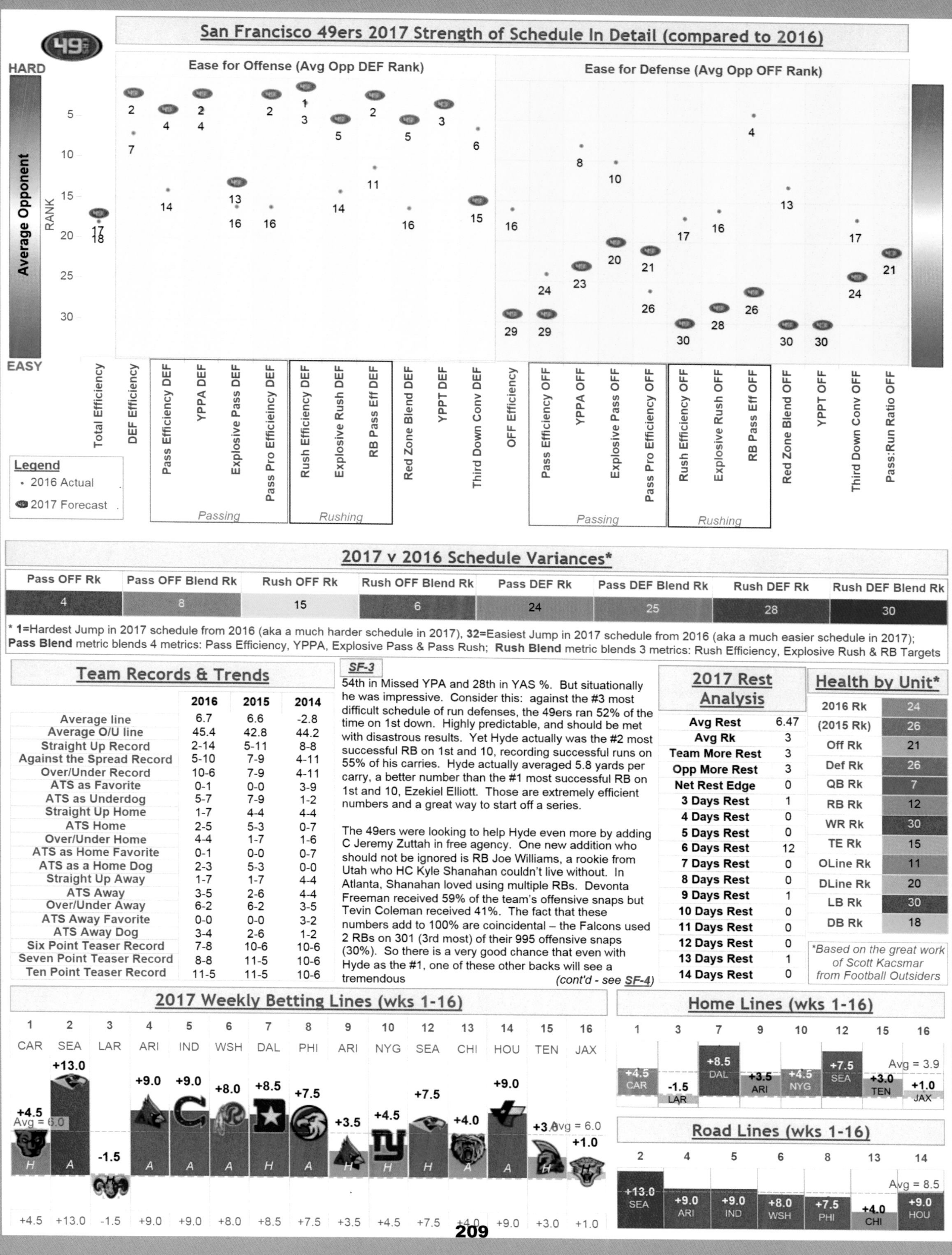

San Francisco 49ers 2017 Strength of Schedule In Detail (compared to 2016)

Metric	2016 Actual	2017 Forecast
Total Efficiency	18	17
DEF Efficiency	7	2
Pass Efficiency DEF	14	4
YPPA DEF	4	2
Explosive Pass DEF	16	13
Pass Pro Efficieincy DEF	16	2
Rush Efficiency DEF	3	1
Explosive Rush DEF	14	5
RB Pass Eff DEF	11	2
Red Zone Blend DEF	16	5
YPPT DEF		3
Third Down Conv DEF	6	15
OFF Efficiency	16	29
Pass Efficiency OFF	24	29
YPPA OFF	8	23
Explosive Pass OFF	10	20
Pass Pro Efficiency OFF	26	21
Rush Efficiency OFF	17	30
Explosive Rush OFF	16	28
RB Pass Eff OFF	4	26
Red Zone Blend OFF	13	30
YPPT OFF		30
Third Down Conv OFF	17	24
Pass:Run Ratio OFF		21

2017 v 2016 Schedule Variances*

Pass OFF Rk	Pass OFF Blend Rk	Rush OFF Rk	Rush OFF Blend Rk	Pass DEF Rk	Pass DEF Blend Rk	Rush DEF Rk	Rush DEF Blend Rk
4	8	15	6	24	25	28	30

* **1**=Hardest Jump in 2017 schedule from 2016 (aka a much harder schedule in 2017), **32**=Easiest Jump in 2017 schedule from 2016 (aka a much easier schedule in 2017); **Pass Blend** metric blends 4 metrics: Pass Efficiency, YPPA, Explosive Pass & Pass Rush; **Rush Blend** metric blends 3 metrics: Rush Efficiency, Explosive Rush & RB Targets

Team Records & Trends

	2016	2015	2014
Average line	6.7	6.6	-2.8
Average O/U line	45.4	42.8	44.2
Straight Up Record	2-14	5-11	8-8
Against the Spread Record	5-10	7-9	4-11
Over/Under Record	10-6	7-9	4-11
ATS as Favorite	0-1	0-0	3-9
ATS as Underdog	5-7	7-9	1-2
Straight Up Home	1-7	4-4	4-4
ATS Home	2-5	5-3	0-7
Over/Under Home	4-4	1-7	1-6
ATS as Home Favorite	0-1	0-0	0-7
ATS as a Home Dog	2-3	5-3	0-0
Straight Up Away	1-7	1-7	4-4
ATS Away	3-5	2-6	4-4
Over/Under Away	6-2	6-2	3-5
ATS Away Favorite	0-0	0-0	3-2
ATS Away Dog	3-4	2-6	1-2
Six Point Teaser Record	7-8	10-6	10-6
Seven Point Teaser Record	8-8	11-5	10-6
Ten Point Teaser Record	11-5	11-5	10-6

SF-3

54th in Missed YPA and 28th in YAS %. But situationally he was impressive. Consider this: against the #3 most difficult schedule of run defenses, the 49ers ran 52% of the time on 1st down. Highly predictable, and should be met with disastrous results. Yet Hyde actually was the #2 most successful RB on 1st and 10, recording successful runs on 55% of his carries. Hyde actually averaged 5.8 yards per carry, a better number than the #1 most successful RB on 1st and 10, Ezekiel Elliott. Those are extremely efficient numbers and a great way to start off a series.

The 49ers were looking to help Hyde even more by adding C Jeremy Zuttah in free agency. One new addition who should not be ignored is RB Joe Williams, a rookie from Utah who HC Kyle Shanahan couldn't live without. In Atlanta, Shanahan loved using multiple RBs. Devonta Freeman received 59% of the team's offensive snaps but Tevin Coleman received 41%. The fact that these numbers add to 100% are coincidental – the Falcons used 2 RBs on 301 (3rd most) of their 995 offensive snaps (30%). So there is a very good chance that even with Hyde as the #1, one of these other backs will see a tremendous *(cont'd - see SF-4)*

2017 Rest Analysis

Avg Rest	6.47
Avg Rk	3
Team More Rest	3
Opp More Rest	3
Net Rest Edge	0
3 Days Rest	1
4 Days Rest	0
5 Days Rest	0
6 Days Rest	12
7 Days Rest	0
8 Days Rest	0
9 Days Rest	1
10 Days Rest	0
11 Days Rest	0
12 Days Rest	0
13 Days Rest	1
14 Days Rest	0

Health by Unit*

2016 Rk	24
(2015 Rk)	26
Off Rk	21
Def Rk	26
QB Rk	7
RB Rk	12
WR Rk	30
TE Rk	15
OLine Rk	11
DLine Rk	20
LB Rk	30
DB Rk	18

*Based on the great work of Scott Kacsmar from Football Outsiders

2017 Weekly Betting Lines (wks 1-16)

Week	1	2	3	4	5	6	7	8	9	10	12	13	14	15	16
Opp	CAR	SEA	LAR	ARI	IND	WSH	DAL	PHI	ARI	NYG	SEA	CHI	HOU	TEN	JAX
Line	+4.5	+13.0	-1.5	+9.0	+9.0	+8.0	+8.5	+7.5	+3.5	+4.5	+7.5	+4.0	+9.0	+3.0	+1.0
H/A	H	A		A	A	A	H	A	H	H	H	A	A	H	

Avg = 6.0

Home Lines (wks 1-16)

Week	1	3	7	9	10	12	15	16
Opp	CAR	LAR	DAL	ARI	NYG	SEA	TEN	JAX
Line	+4.5	-1.5	+8.5	+3.5	+4.5	+7.5	+3.0	+1.0

Avg = 3.9

Road Lines (wks 1-16)

Week	2	4	5	6	8	13	14
Opp	SEA	ARI	IND	WSH	PHI	CHI	HOU
Line	+13.0	+9.0	+9.0	+8.0	+7.5	+4.0	+9.0

Avg = 8.5

San Francisco 49ers 2016 Play Analysis

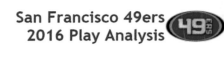

2016 Play Tendencies

All Pass %	48%
All Pass Rk	32
All Rush %	52%
All Rush Rk	1
1 Score Pass %	60%
1 Score Pass Rk	13
2015 1 Score Pass %	56%
2015 1 Score Pass Rk	22
Pass Increase %	3%
Pass Increase Rk	7
1 Score Rush %	40%
1 Score Rush Rk	20
Up Pass %	42%
Up Pass Rk	32
Up Rush %	58%
Up Rush Rk	1
Down Pass %	53%
Down Pass Rk	31
Down Rush %	47%
Down Rush Rk	2

2016 Down & Distance Tendencies

Down	Distance	Total Plays	Pass Rate	Run Rate	Play Success %
1	Short (1-3)	4	0%	100%	75%
	Med (4-7)	5	20%	80%	100%
	Long (8-10)	302	45%	55%	53%
	XL (11+)	9	11%	89%	22%
2	Short (1-3)	28	32%	68%	68%
	Med (4-7)	80	35%	65%	49%
	Long (8-10)	90	40%	60%	30%
	XL (11+)	35	49%	51%	26%
3	Short (1-3)	38	37%	63%	55%
	Med (4-7)	50	86%	14%	28%
	Long (8-10)	42	86%	14%	24%
	XL (11+)	33	88%	12%	21%
4	Short (1-3)	8	25%	75%	38%
	Med (4-7)	1	100%	0%	100%

Shotgun %:

Under Center	Shotgun
2%	98%

37% AVG 63%

Run Rate:

Under Center	Shotgun
44%	42%

68% AVG 23%

Pass Rate:

Under Center	Shotgun
56%	58%

32% AVG 77%

Short Yardage Intelligence:

2nd and Short Run

Run Freq	Run % Rk	NFL Run Freq Avg	Run 1D Rate	Run NFL 1D Avg
68%	12	65%	59%	71%

2nd and Short Pass

Pass Freq	Pass % Rk	NFL Pass Freq Avg	Pass 1D Rate	Pass NFL 1D Avg
32%	21	35%	38%	52%

Most Frequent Play

Down	Distance	Play Type	Player	Total Plays	Play Success %
1	Short (1-3)	RUSH	Carlos Hyde	2	50%
	Med (4-7)	RUSH	Mike Davis	2	100%
	Long (8-10)	RUSH	Carlos Hyde	89	58%
	XL (11+)	RUSH	Carlos Hyde	5	40%
2	Short (1-3)	RUSH	Carlos Hyde	12	67%
	Med (4-7)	RUSH	Carlos Hyde	23	43%
	Long (8-10)	RUSH	Carlos Hyde	29	21%
	XL (11+)	PASS	Jeremy Kerley	9	22%
		RUSH	Carlos Hyde	9	22%
3	Short (1-3)	RUSH	Carlos Hyde	9	67%
	Med (4-7)	PASS	Jeremy Kerley	18	28%
	Long (8-10)	PASS	Jeremy Kerley	5	0%
	XL (11+)	PASS	Aaron Burbridge	5	20%

Most Successful Play*

Down	Distance	Play Type	Player	Total Plays	Play Success %
1	Long (8-10)	RUSH	Colin Kaepernick	21	71%
	XL (11+)	RUSH	Carlos Hyde	5	40%
2	Short (1-3)	RUSH	Carlos Hyde	12	67%
	Med (4-7)	RUSH	Colin Kaepernick	9	67%
	Long (8-10)	PASS	Quinton Patton	7	43%
	XL (11+)	PASS	Jeremy Kerley	9	22%
		RUSH	Carlos Hyde	9	22%
3	Short (1-3)	RUSH	Blaine Gabbert	5	80%
	Med (4-7)	PASS	Jeremy Kerley	18	28%
	Long (8-10)	PASS	Jeremy Kerley	5	0%
	XL (11+)	PASS	Aaron Burbridge	5	20%

*Minimum 5 plays to qualify

2016 Snap Rates

Week	Opp	Score	Jeremy Kerley	Quinton Patton	Torrey Smith	Garrett Celek	Carlos Hyde	Vance McDonald	Shaun Draughn
1	LA	W 28-0	54 (67%)	71 (88%)	78 (96%)	45 (56%)	57 (70%)	51 (63%)	22 (27%)
2	CAR	L 46-27	47 (72%)	57 (88%)	55 (85%)	32 (49%)	39 (60%)	38 (58%)	22 (34%)
3	SEA	L 37-18	42 (72%)	51 (88%)	44 (76%)	39 (67%)	41 (71%)	10 (17%)	17 (29%)
4	DAL	L 24-17	47 (89%)	51 (96%)	51 (96%)	39 (74%)	45 (85%)		15 (28%)
5	ARI	L 33-21	78 (100%)	70 (90%)	73 (94%)	61 (78%)	64 (82%)		9 (12%)
6	BUF	L 45-16	57 (93%)	55 (90%)	51 (84%)	27 (44%)	32 (52%)	30 (49%)	5 (8%)
7	TB	L 34-17	41 (59%)	63 (90%)	56 (80%)	41 (59%)		54 (77%)	23 (33%)
9	NO	L 41-23	45 (75%)	55 (92%)	45 (75%)	30 (50%)		42 (70%)	
10	ARI	L 23-20	51 (81%)	53 (84%)	57 (90%)	20 (32%)	42 (67%)	44 (70%)	
11	NE	L 30-17	42 (68%)	54 (87%)		33 (53%)	40 (65%)	46 (74%)	9 (15%)
12	MIA	L 31-24	48 (62%)	28 (36%)	66 (85%)	33 (42%)	49 (63%)	57 (73%)	24 (31%)
13	CHI	L 26-6	37 (64%)	39 (67%)	38 (66%)	22 (38%)	33 (57%)	53 (91%)	25 (43%)
14	NYJ	L 23-17	40 (70%)	51 (89%)	30 (53%)	44 (77%)	30 (53%)	19 (33%)	27 (47%)
15	ATL	L 41-13	52 (95%)	10 (18%)		29 (53%)	34 (62%)		21 (38%)
16	LA	W 22-21	58 (77%)			59 (79%)	31 (41%)		42 (56%)
17	SEA	L 25-23	50 (82%)			48 (79%)			52 (85%)
Grand Total			789 (77%)	708 (79%)	644 (82%)	602 (58%)	537 (64%)	444 (62%)	313 (35%)

Personnel Groupings

Personnel	Team %	NFL Avg	Succ. %
1-1 [3WR]	76%	60%	43%
1-2 [2WR]	20%	19%	44%

Grouping Tendencies

Personnel	Pass Rate	Pass Succ. %	Run Succ. %
1-1 [3WR]	59%	35%	42%
1-2 [2WR]	33%	46%	39%

Red Zone Targets (min 3)

Receiver	All	Inside 5	6-10	11-20
Jeremy Kerley	7		2	5
Carlos Hyde	6		2	4
Garrett Celek	6	1	2	3
Vance McDonald	6		2	4
Torrey Smith	5	1	3	1
Quinton Patton	4		3	1
Shaun Draughn	4		1	3
Rod Streater	3	1	1	1

Red Zone Rushes (min 3)

Rusher	All	Inside 5	6-10	11-20
Carlos Hyde	33	6	8	19
Shaun Draughn	10	5	2	3
Colin Kaepernick	7	1	2	4
DuJuan Harris	7	3	2	2
Blaine Gabbert	6	2		4

Early Down Target Rate

	RB	TE	WR
	20%	25%	55%
NFL AVG	*19%*	*20%*	*61%*

Overall Target Success %

RB	TE	WR
49%	47%	43%
#11	#31	#29

San Francisco 49ers 2016 Passing Recap & 2017 Outlook

Brian Hoyer is about to find the good and the bad of playing QB for Kyle Shanahan. The good is he's got one of the brightest, creative and advanced-thought coaches in the NFL. The bad is this offense typically isn't an easy one to grasp, and takes time to pick it up all the way, particularly the nuances. And against a brutal schedule of pass defenses (4th hardest schedule) it won't be any easier for Hoyer. In Chicago, Hoyer targeted TE Zach Miller more than any other receiver, and saw a 125 rating when targeting him, connecting on 3 of his 6 TDs. His 2nd most successful target was RB Jordan Howard. This could likely be a similar situation, where TE Vance McDonald was the best 49ers receiver last year, and in Atlanta, Shanahan targeted the RBs 6th most often of any team. In Atlanta, the Falcons really didn't have a great TE, and not that McDonald is a great TE, but there is a great chance he could be in the top 2 most frequently targeted this year. This is because Hoyer hasn't shown aptitude to push the ball downfield. He needs to improve in this area, but how much will Shanahan push him to do what he's incapable of doing, rather than play to his strengths? And if Shanahan somehow pulls a deep passing threat out of Hoyer, kudos Shanahan.

Colin Kaepernick Rating All Downs

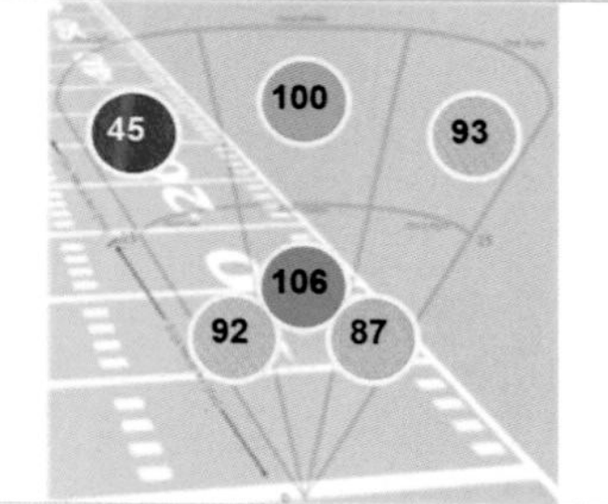

Colin Kaepernick Rating Early Downs

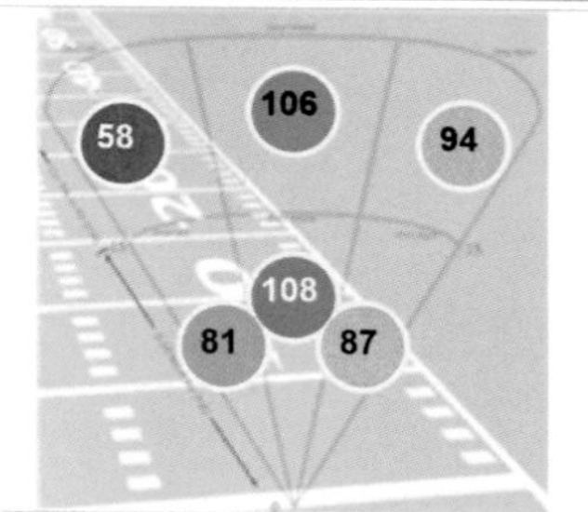

2016 Standard Passing Table

QB	Comp	Att	Comp %	Yds	YPA	TDs	INT	Sacks	Rating	Rk
Colin Kaepernick	196	332	59%	2,241	6.8	16	4	36	90.4	22
Blaine Gabbert	91	160	57%	925	5.8	5	6	11	68.4	49
NFL Avg			63%		7.2				90.4	

2016 Advanced Passing Table

QB	Success %	EDSR Passing Success %	20+ Yd Pass Gains	20+ Yd Pass %	30+ Yd Pass Gains	30+ Yd Pass %	Air Yds per Comp	YAC per Comp	20+ Air Yd Comp	20+ Air Yd %
Colin Kaepernick	41%	46%	30	9%	10	3%	5.8	5.7	11	3%
Blaine Gabbert	40%	48%	10	6%	3	2%	6.3	3.9	2	1%
NFL Avg	44%	48%	27	8%	10	3%	6.4	4.8	12	4%

Interception Rates by Down

Yards to Go	1	2	3	4	Total
1 & 2		0.0%	0.0%	0.0%	0.0%
3, 4, 5		0.0%	0.0%		0.0%
6 - 9	0.0%	0.0%	0.0%	0.0%	0.0%
10 - 14	2.0%	2.6%	0.0%	0.0%	1.8%
15+	0.0%	0.0%	0.0%	0.0%	0.0%
Total	1.9%	1.0%	0.0%	0.0%	1.1%

3rd Down Passing - Short of Sticks Analysis

QB	Avg Yds to Go	Air Yds (of Comps)	Avg Yds Short	Short of Sticks Rate	Rk
Colin Kaepernick	9.1	3.9	-5.1	82%	44
NFL Avg	7.6	6.8	-0.8	57%	

Air Yds vs YAC

Air Yds %	YAC %	Rk
44%	56%	44
54%	46%	

2016 Receiving Recap & 2017 Outlook

Last year in Atlanta, Julio Jones received 24% of the targets (and a 45% share of deep targets), Mohamed Sanu saw 15% and RB Devonta Freeman saw 12%. Speedster Taylor Gabriel saw 10% and the 2nd largest share of deep targets. So the question is who gets what in this offense? Garcon is their best WR, but he's more the Mohamed Sanu receiver type. When he was with the Redskins in his last 2 yrs as OC, Shanahan saw Garcon targeted 249 times, which was over 100 more than Santana Moss (#2 most targeted) and Leonard Hankerson (#3). I'll venture the top 3 most targeted are Garson, McDonald and whichever RB emerges.

Player *Min 50 Targets*	Targets	Comp %	YPA	Rating	TOARS	Success %	Success Rk	Missed YPA Rk	YAS % Rk	TDs
Jeremy Kerley	115	56%	5.8	70	4.5	43%	123	112	95	3
Quinton Patton	63	59%	6.5	71	3.7	46%	108	135	50	0
Garrett Celek	51	57%	6.9	81	3.5	49%	83	9	62	3

Directional Passer Rating Delivered

Receiver	Short Left	Short Middle	Short Right	Deep Left	Deep Middle	Deep Right	Player Total
Jeremy Kerley	50	49	79	116	94	99	70
Quinton Patton	80	53	97	40	110	40	73
Garrett Celek	123	75	87	40		20	81
Torrey Smith	96	77	34	110	0	75	54
Vance McDonald	158	75	87	0	110	95	103
Shaun Draughn	92	113	98	93		119	109
Carlos Hyde	87	141	123	40			118
Rod Streater	128	108	97		40		112
Team Total	95	81	83	65	46	79	84

2016 Rushing Recap & 2017 Outlook

As mentioned elsewhere in this chapter, Carlos Hyde was a beast in predictable 49ers run situations last year, like in 1st and 10. But he struggled in many other areas. And there have been early questions in OTAs that Hyde has been tentative and could lack the vision to succeed in Shanahan's outside-zone system. Hyde is the best back on the 49ers, but as Shanahan gets familiar with Hyde, Hightower and Williams, he may find that Hyde isn't the best back for the system. In any case, whoever is RB2 will get a ton of work in, and Shanahan uses his RBs as targets out of the backfield a ton. Last year Hyde dominated the overall target share inside the red zone, pass or rush. He had 39 total opportunities, and the #2 player (Draughn) saw only 10.

Player *Min 50 Rushes*	Rushes	YPA	Success %	Success Rk	Missed YPA Rk	YTS % Rk	YAS % Rk	Early Down Success %	Early Down Success Rk	TDs
Carlos Hyde	217	4.6	47%	35	54	38	28	46%	38	6
Shaun Draughn	74	2.6	32%	67	67	44	52	29%	67	4

Yards per Carry by Direction

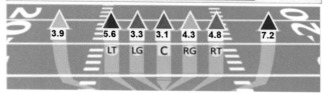

	LT	LG	C	RG	RT	
3.9	5.6	3.3	3.1	4.3	4.8	7.2

Directional Run Frequency

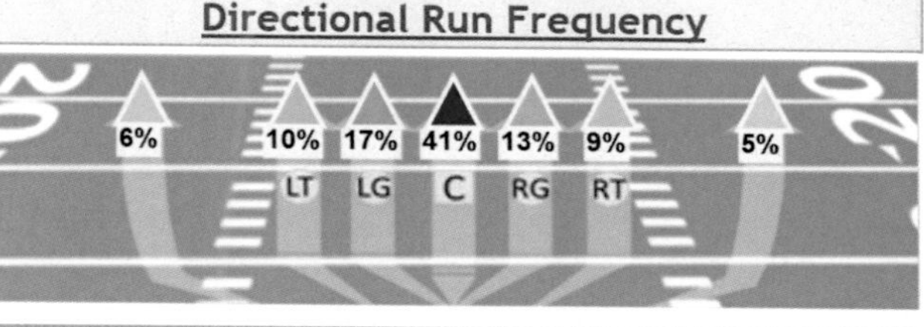

workload (assuming the offense has the snaps required). The 49ers also added Tim Hightower, formerly of the Saints, to the RB rotation and while he's likely slated for a fair number of those RB2 snaps, Joe Williams certainly will get more opportunity to shine than a lot of other backup rookie RBs in the league. What he does with those early opportunities will dictate how many more he will get.

The problem for the run game, and the pass game for that matter, is that as brutal a schedule that the 49ers' offense had last year, it's even worse this year. The 49ers run offense faces the #1 most difficult schedule of run defenses this year. The schedule starts off with a brutal 4 week stretch of top-10 run defenses from 2016: the Panthers, Seahawks, Rams and Cardinals. This schedule won't provide the cushion for Shanahan to rely on the run game while his new starting QB eases into the saddle in San Francisco. This run schedule is so difficult, of their 16 games, the 49ers play just 3 teams that ranked below average in run defense efficiency last year: the Colts, Bears and Redskins. Every single other opponent ranked average or better. They play 10 games against run defenses which ranked top-10 in run defense last season.

Much will be different on offense with Kyle Shanahan instead of Chip Kelly. One thing will be very obvious to fans and that will be more formations and personnel groupings. Chip Kelly used 11 personnel 76% of the time and 12 personnel 20% of the time. Right there were 96% of their offensive snaps with just two personnel groupings. The NFL average for 11 personnel is 60% of offensive snaps. Whereas Chip Kelly used it 2nd most in the NFL, the Falcons used 11 personnel 4th least often, just 44% of the time. While the 49ers last year used just 2 personnel groupings on over 2% of their snaps, the Falcons used 5 groupings over 2% of the time. In addition to the 11 personnel, they used: 21 (26%), 12 (17%), 13 (8%) and 22 (3%). Another team with a pretty efficient offense used similar percentages last year to the Falcons, and that was the team who beat them in the Super Bowl – the Patriots. So if the 49ers start incorporating more personnel groupings akin to the Falcons and Patriots, it will be a great thing for the team.

The only good news, schedule wise, for the 49ers is the schedule of opposing offenses. Things should be easier now that they don't have to face the Falcons, Patriots and Saints next season. However, they will still have to tangle with the Redskins, Colts and Titans.

We should expect the 49ers to be noticeably better & win more games. However I think they'll be more dangerous in the first half of games. I question their ability late in games to sustain leads if they can't run well, and I question their late-game pass defense if ahead. If behind, I don't know that Hoyer has the explosiveness to score often quickly. But much like the Falcons, Shanahan could get the 49ers off to faster starts. They'll be better, but let's not rush to judge them on their final W-L record alone.

Division History: Season Wins & 2017 Projection

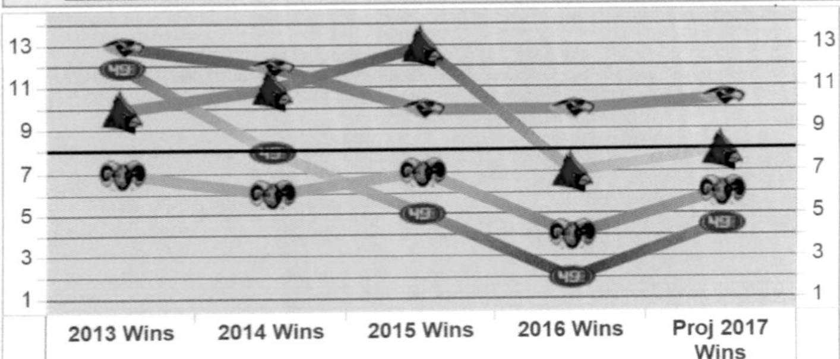

Rank of 2017 Defensive Pass Efficiency Faced by Week

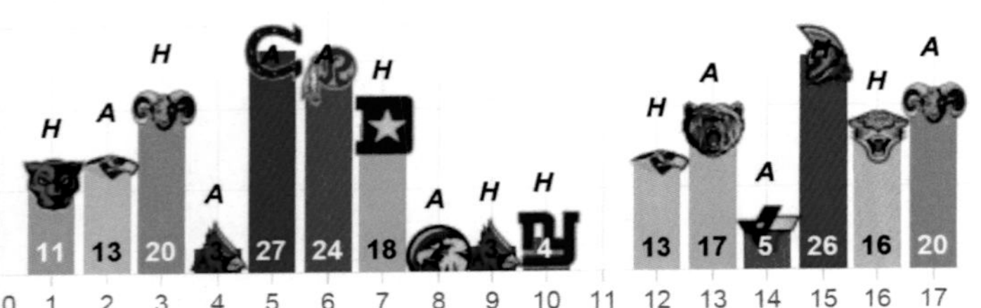

Rank of 2017 Defensive Rush Efficiency Faced by Week

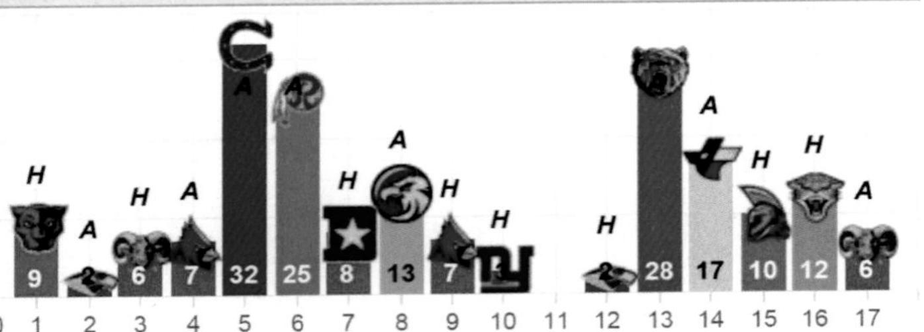

2016 Situational Usage by Player & Position

Usage Rate by Score

		Being Blown Out (14+)	Down Big (9-13)	One Score	Large Lead (9-13)	Blowout Lead (14+)	Grand Total
RUSH	Carlos Hyde	20%	16%	29%	42%	35%	26%
	Shaun Draughn	6%	4%	12%	17%	8%	9%
	DuJuan Harris	1%	14%	5%			5%
	Mike Davis	1%	3%	2%		5%	2%
	Raheem Mostert		1%				0%
	Total	29%	38%	48%	58%	48%	42%
PASS	Carlos Hyde	5%	1%	4%		2%	4%
	Jeremy Kerley	13%	10%	14%	33%	17%	14%
	Shaun Draughn	5%	4%	5%		3%	5%
	Quinton Patton	10%	9%	6%		11%	8%
	Garrett Celek	8%	10%	5%		3%	6%
	Torrey Smith	6%	6%	6%	8%	5%	6%
	DuJuan Harris	2%	2%	0%			1%
	Vance McDonald	6%	10%	4%		5%	5%
	Rod Streater	4%	4%	3%		2%	3%
	Mike Davis	2%	1%				1%
	Chris Harper	3%	3%	2%		3%	3%
	Aaron Burbridge	2%	2%	2%			2%
	Blake Bell	3%	1%			3%	1%
	Je'Ron Hamm	2%					0%
	DeAndre Smelter			0%			0%
	Total	71%	62%	52%	42%	52%	58%

Positional Target Distribution vs NFL Average

		NFL Wide				Team Only			
		Left	Middle	Right	Total	Left	Middle	Right	Total
Deep	WR	1,009	570	980	2,559	22	11	21	54
	TE	155	144	153	452	3	3	10	16
	RB	21	4	39	64	4		1	5
	All	1,185	718	1,172	3,075	29	14	32	75
Short	WR	3,018	1,728	3,105	7,851	75	43	81	199
	TE	813	848	1,121	2,782	23	27	30	80
	RB	988	611	1,084	2,683	27	11	29	67
	All	4,819	3,187	5,310	13,316	125	81	140	346
Total		6,004	3,905	6,482	16,391	154	95	172	421

Positional Success Rates vs NFL Average

		NFL Wide				Team Only			
		Left	Middle	Right	Total	Left	Middle	Right	Total
Deep	WR	37%	51%	38%	41%	29%	27%	33%	30%
	TE	45%	49%	44%	46%	0%	67%	30%	31%
	RB	33%	75%	23%	30%	25%		100%	40%
	All	38%	51%	38%	41%	26%	36%	34%	31%
Short	WR	52%	57%	52%	53%	44%	49%	39%	43%
	TE	49%	62%	52%	54%	65%	46%	40%	49%
	RB	47%	50%	44%	46%	38%	38%	35%	37%
	All	51%	57%	50%	52%	46%	46%	38%	43%
Total		48%	56%	48%	50%	42%	45%	38%	41%

2017 Coaches

Head Coach:
Pete Carroll (8th yr)
Offensive Coordinator:
Darrell Bevell (7th yr)
Defensive Coordinator:
Kris Richard (3rd yr)

Seattle Seahawks

2017 Forecast

Wins	Div Rank
10.5	#1

Past Records

2016: 10-5-1
2015: 10-6
2014: 12-4

EASY HARD

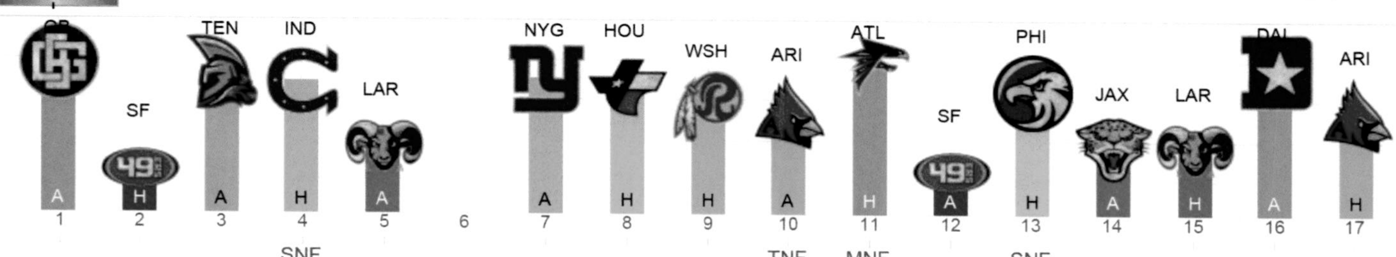

Key Players Lost

TXN	Player (POS)
Cut	Cox, Perrish CB
	Powell, Tyvis S
Declared Free Agent	Barnes, Tavaris DE
	Cottom, Brandon TE
	Hauschka, Steven K
	Hester, Devin WR
	Jean-Baptiste, Stanley CB
	Jenkins, John DT
	Johnson, Jeron S
	McCray, Kelcie S
	McDaniel, Tony DT
	Moore, Damontre DE
	Morgan, Mike LB
	Reece, Marcel RB
	Shead, Deshawn CB
	Slavin, Tyler WR
	Sommers, Joe TE
	Sowell, Bradley T
	Thorpe, Neiko CB
	Tukuafu, Will RB
	Willson, Luke TE

Average Line	# Games Favored	# Games Underdog
-4.9	12	2

Regular Season Wins: Past & Current Proj

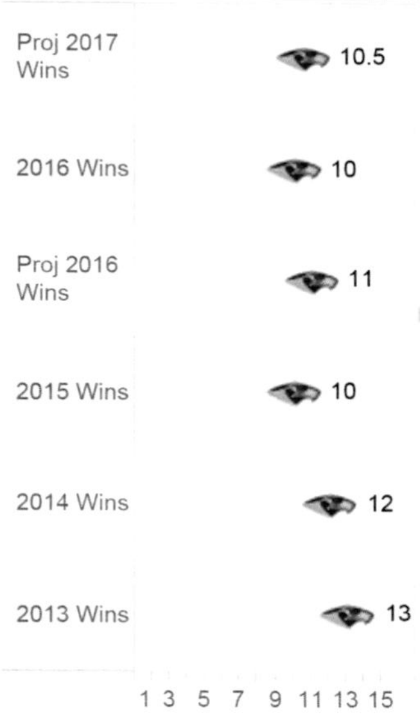

	Wins
Proj 2017 Wins	10.5
2016 Wins	10
Proj 2016 Wins	11
2015 Wins	10
2014 Wins	12
2013 Wins	13

1 3 5 7 9 11 13 15

2017 Seattle Seahawks Overview

Seattle's 2016 season was one of the more bizarre seasons you'll find. Seattle defeated both Super Bowl participants and yet against the Rams, Buccaneers and Cardinals, put up 3, 5 and 6 total points. A team historically willing to win via defense and a ground attack, was the 5th most pass heavy team in one-score games, even though the offensive line was one of the least talented in the NFL. Seattle chose to pass the ball 10% more in one score games than they did in 2015, the largest shift to the pass of any team last year. Seattle's only wins on the road were over the Jets, 49ers and of course, the Patriots, and their only loss at home was to the Cardinals in a game which featured 41 points scored in the 4th quarter. Out of the 13 metrics I published on the Advanced Metrics graphics, the Seattle's offense ranked anywhere from 7th best to 2nd worst, and their defense ranked anywhere from 2nd best to 6th worst. And of course, their season ended for all intents and purposes in a 40-7 win over the Panthers week 13 which pushed their record to 8-3-1 at the time.

Would it have been possible for the 2016 Seahawks to march into Atlanta with Earl Thomas and beat the Falcons in the playoffs? It's unlikely, but not outside of the realm of possibility. But without Thomas, they really didn't stand much of a chance, and the numbers bear that out perfectly. The following come via the visualizations at Sharp Football Stats: Seattle moved from 3rd best to 5th worst in deep passer rating, shifting from a 55.5 rating allowed with Thomas to a 100.2 without Thomas. In particular, prior to Thomas' injury, Seattle's pass defense was allowing a passer rating of 9 (that's "nine") down the deep middle of the field. After Thomas' injury, that rating rose to 135. Seattle also allowed 5% more pass plays to make explosive gains (regardless of aerial pass yards) without Thomas, which shifted Seattle from 8th best to the NFL's worst explosive pass defense. And to put it further into perspective: Seattle played the 7th easiest schedule of explosive pass offenses without Thomas, yet ranked dead last in explosive gains. But with Thomas, even though they played the 10th hardest schedule of explosive pass offenses, they ranked 8th best in preventing them.

Perhaps if the Seahawks faced multiple teams in the postseason featuring quarterbacks with 4 functioning fingers on their throwing hand (Detroit and Matthew Stafford) the loss of Thomas wouldn't be noticed. But Aaron Rodgers sure knew how to dissect them in a 38-10 victory in

(cont'd - see SEA2)

Key Free Agents/ Trades Added

Aboushi, Oday G
Brown, Arthur LB
Davis, Mike RB
Garvin, Terence LB
Joeckel, Luke T
Jordan, Dion DE
Lacy, Eddie RB
Lunsford, John K
McDougald, Bradley S
Wilhoite, Michael LB

Drafted Players

Rd	Pk	Player (College)
2	35	DT - Malik McDowell (Michig..
	58	C - Ethan Pocic (LSU)
3	90	CB - Shaquill Griffin (UCF)
	95	S - Delano Hill (Michigan)
3*	102	DT - Nazair Jones (North Car..
	106	WR - Amara Darboh (Michig..
4	111	S - Tedric Thompson (Colora..
6	187	S - Michael Tyson (Cincinnati)
	210	OT - Justin Senior (Mississip..
7	226	WR - David Moore (East Cen..
	249	RB - Christopher Carson (Okl..

2017 Lineup & Cap Hits

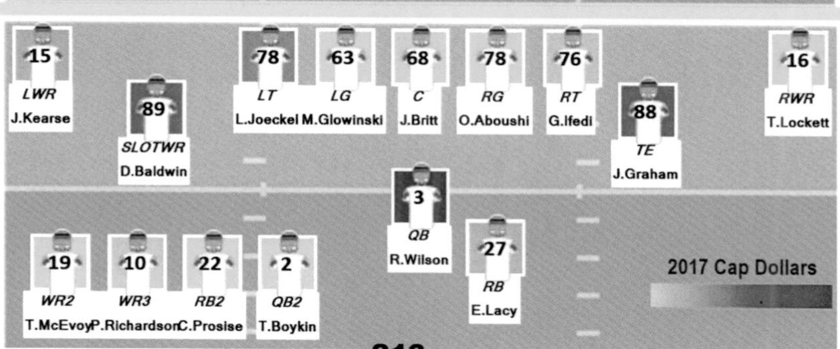

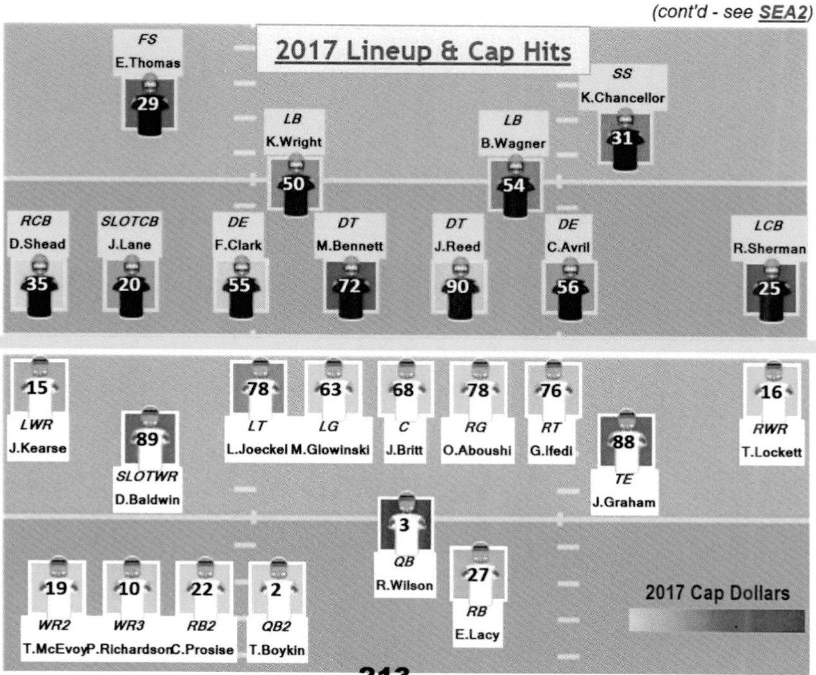

2017 Unit Spending

Positional Spending

	Rank	Total	2016 Rk
All OFF	21	$77.67M	29
QB	15	$19.35M	15
OL	32	$15.96M	32
RB	17	$7.07M	27
WR	13	$21.22M	22
TE	4	$14.07M	2
All DEF	4	$95.54M	3
DL	14	$28.25M	15
LB	14	$21.55M	16
CB	7	$23.38M	8
S	2	$22.36M	2

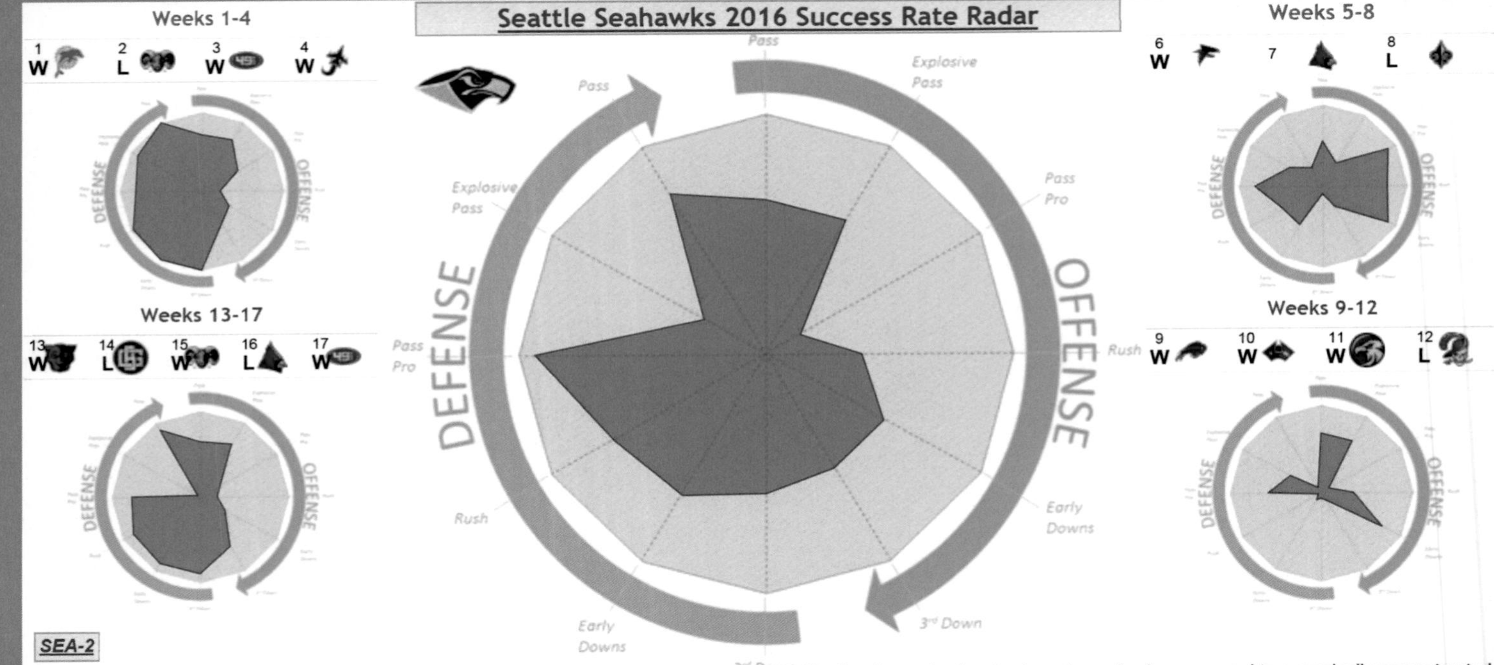

SEA-2

the regular season. The #2 ranked deep passer last year, Matt Ryan, rolled to a 36-20 victory in the postseason. And if by some chance Seattle pulled that upset, you can bet Dallas and Dak Prescott (the #1 ranked deep passer last year) would have been ready to attack the weakness. And if somehow Seattle pulled out that upset, they would have faced Tom Brady in a Super Bowl rematch, who just so happened to be the #3 ranked deep passer last year. It was an unfortunate situation for Seattle, and on account of that injury, they stood literally no chance to run that gauntlet of explosive passing offenses without Thomas.

The good news for Seattle is that Thomas will be back this season. At first Thomas lamented the injury and pondered retirement, perhaps because of the long road to recovery and the fact he hasn't been injured much in the past. But the reality was it was a broken fibula. Speaking from personal experience as someone who broke his tibia (shin bone) in half playing sports and also required three knee surgeries, also from playing sports, I'd much rather break my leg again than tear up my knee. Soft tissue injuries are much more difficult to recover from and the rehab is a pain. Healing from a broken leg is a piece of cake compared to a surgically reconstructed knee. And a fibula is even easier to come back from than the tibia.

With Thomas on schedule to be ready before the start of the season, Seattle will have it's big 3 in the secondary back intact, as will the majority of their defensive starters. Seattle has the 2nd most expensive defense in the NFL, and will certainly look to lean on it for success. While the offenses of the NFC West are not particularly intimidating, the Seahawks must take on the Falcons, Packers, Cowboys, Redskins, Colts and Titans offenses this year. While those offenses aren't the Patriots or Saints, it will be a more difficult schedule than they faced last year.

Two areas where the Seattle defense needs to show improvement should actually be the responsibility of their own offense. And if the offense fixes its issues, things should fall in line for the defense.

(cont'd - see SEA-3)

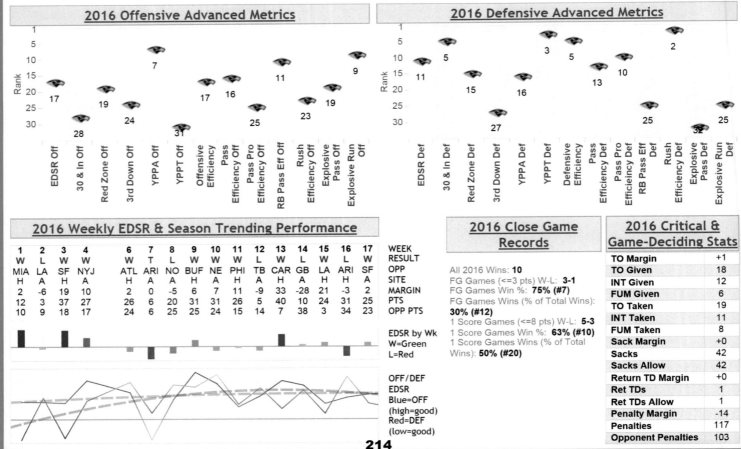

2016 Offensive Advanced Metrics

Metric	Rank
EDSR Off	17
30 & In Off	28
Red Zone Off	19
3rd Down Off	24
YPPA Off	7
YPPT Off	31
Offensive Efficiency	17
Pass Efficiency Off	16
Pass Pro Efficiency Off	25
RB Pass Eff Off	11
Rush Efficiency Off	23
Explosive Pass Off	19
Explosive Run Off	9

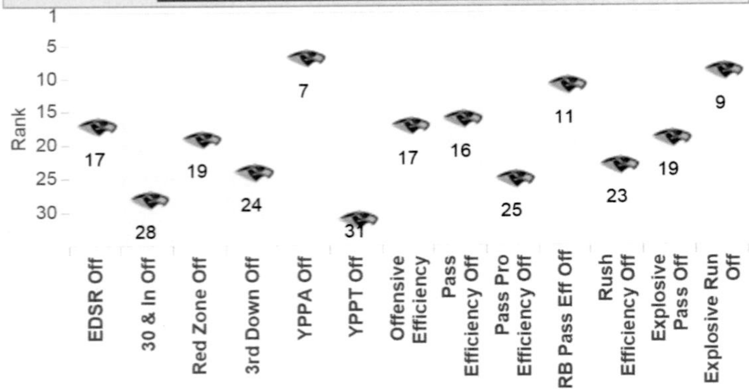

2016 Defensive Advanced Metrics

Metric	Rank
EDSR Def	11
30 & In Def	5
Red Zone Def	15
3rd Down Def	27
YPPA Def	16
YPPT Def	3
Defensive Efficiency	5
Pass Efficiency Def	13
Pass Pro Efficiency Def	10
RB Pass Eff Def	25
Rush Efficiency Def	2
Explosive Pass Def	32
Explosive Run Def	25

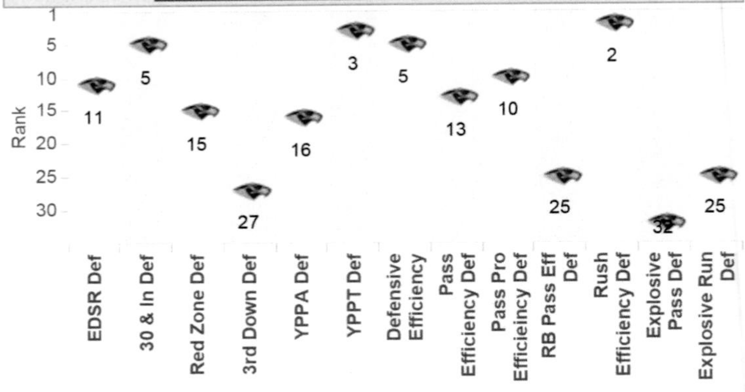

2016 Weekly EDSR & Season Trending Performance

WEEK	1	2	3	4	6	7	8	9	10	11	12	13	14	15	16	17
RESULT	W	L	W	W	W	T	L	W	W	W	L	W	L	W	L	W
OPP	MIA	LA	SF	NYJ	ATL	ARI	NO	BUF	NE	PHI	TB	CAR	GB	LA	ARI	SF
SITE	H	A	H	A	H	A	A	H	A	H	A	H	A	H	H	A
MARGIN	2	-6	19	10	2	0	-5	6	7	11	-9	33	-28	21	-3	2
PTS	12	3	37	27	26	6	20	31	31	26	5	40	10	24	31	25
OPP PTS	10	9	18	17	24	6	25	25	24	15	14	7	38	3	34	23

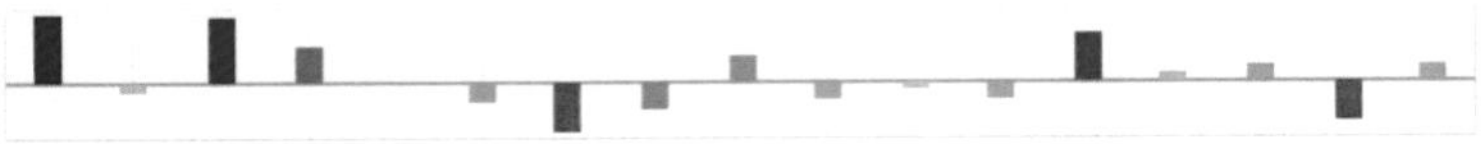

EDSR by Wk W=Green L=Red

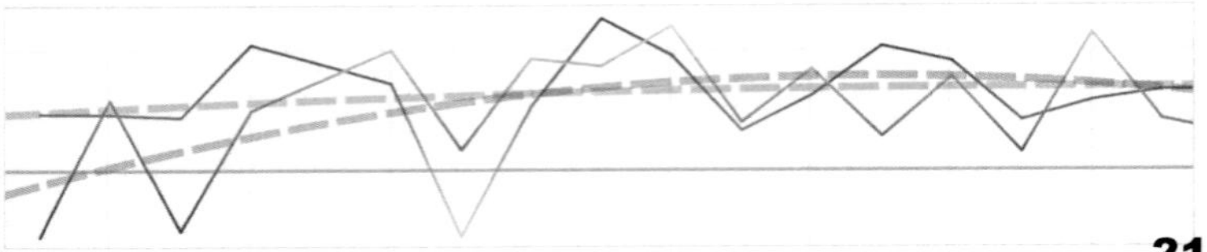

OFF/DEF EDSR Blue=OFF (high=good) Red=DEF (low=good)

2016 Close Game Records

All 2016 Wins: **10**
FG Games (<=3 pts) W-L: **3-1**
FG Games Win %: **75% (#7)**
FG Games Wins (% of Total Wins): **30% (#12)**
1 Score Games (<=8 pts) W-L: **5-3**
1 Score Games Win %: **63% (#10)**
1 Score Games Wins (% of Total Wins): **50% (#20)**

2016 Critical & Game-Deciding Stats

TO Margin	+1
TO Given	18
INT Given	12
FUM Given	6
TO Taken	19
INT Taken	11
FUM Taken	8
Sack Margin	+0
Sacks	42
Sacks Allow	42
Return TD Margin	+0
Ret TDs	1
Ret TDs Allow	1
Penalty Margin	-14
Penalties	117
Opponent Penalties	103

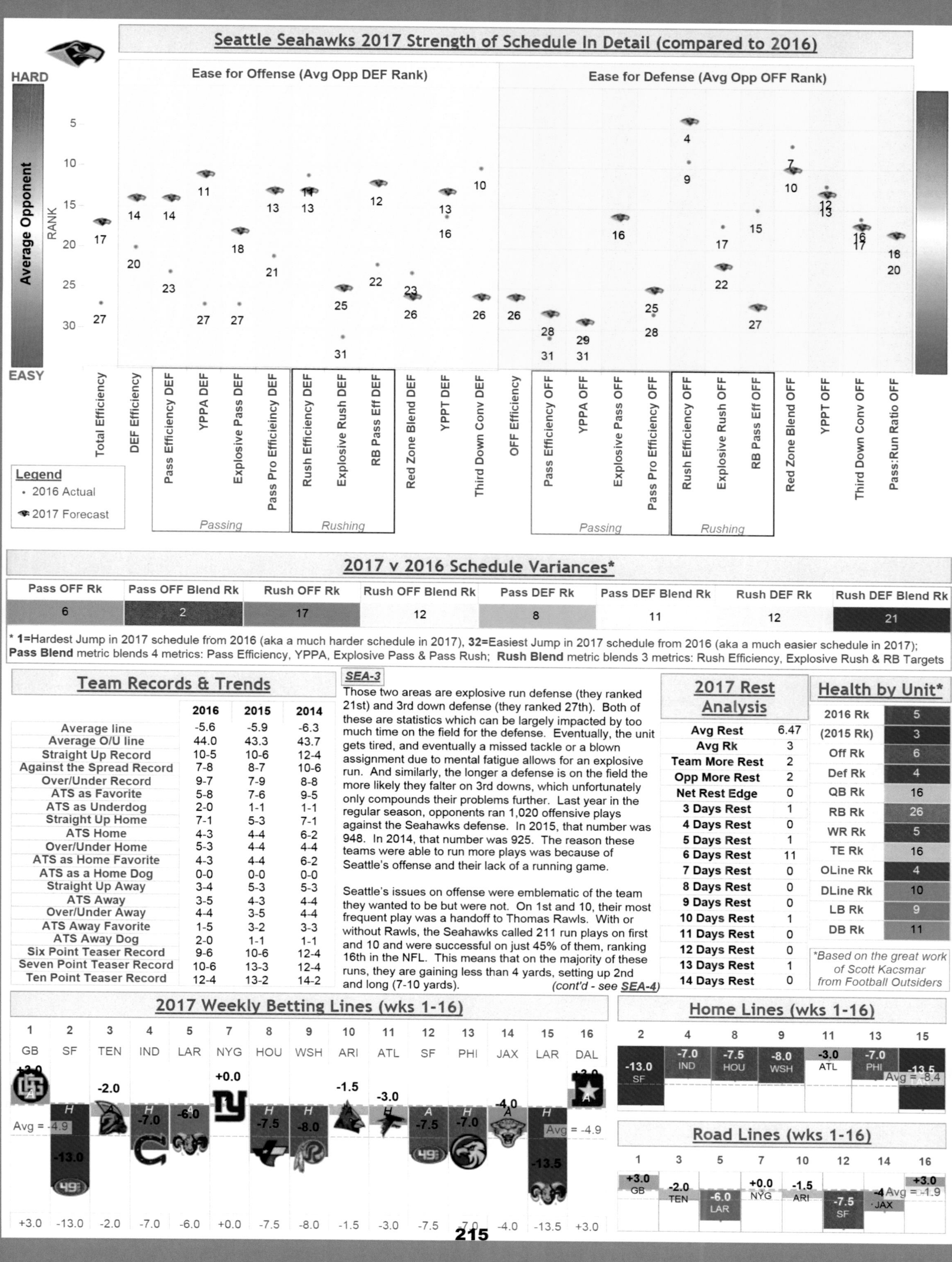

Seattle Seahawks 2017 Strength of Schedule In Detail (compared to 2016)

2017 v 2016 Schedule Variances*

Pass OFF Rk	Pass OFF Blend Rk	Rush OFF Rk	Rush OFF Blend Rk	Pass DEF Rk	Pass DEF Blend Rk	Rush DEF Rk	Rush DEF Blend Rk
6	2	17	12	8	11	12	21

* **1**=Hardest Jump in 2017 schedule from 2016 (aka a much harder schedule in 2017), **32**=Easiest Jump in 2017 schedule from 2016 (aka a much easier schedule in 2017); **Pass Blend** metric blends 4 metrics: Pass Efficiency, YPPA, Explosive Pass & Pass Rush; **Rush Blend** metric blends 3 metrics: Rush Efficiency, Explosive Rush & RB Targets

Team Records & Trends

	2016	2015	2014
Average line	-5.6	-5.9	-6.3
Average O/U line	44.0	43.3	43.7
Straight Up Record	10-5	10-6	12-4
Against the Spread Record	7-8	8-7	10-6
Over/Under Record	9-7	7-9	8-8
ATS as Favorite	5-8	7-6	9-5
ATS as Underdog	2-0	1-1	1-1
Straight Up Home	7-1	5-3	7-1
ATS Home	4-3	4-4	6-2
Over/Under Home	5-3	4-4	4-4
ATS as Home Favorite	4-3	4-4	6-2
ATS as a Home Dog	0-0	0-0	0-0
Straight Up Away	3-4	5-3	5-3
ATS Away	3-5	4-3	4-4
Over/Under Away	4-4	3-5	4-4
ATS Away Favorite	1-5	3-2	3-3
ATS Away Dog	2-0	1-1	1-1
Six Point Teaser Record	9-6	10-6	12-4
Seven Point Teaser Record	10-6	13-3	12-4
Ten Point Teaser Record	12-4	13-2	14-2

SEA-3

Those two areas are explosive run defense (they ranked 21st) and 3rd down defense (they ranked 27th). Both of these are statistics which can be largely impacted by too much time on the field for the defense. Eventually, the unit gets tired, and eventually a missed tackle or a blown assignment due to mental fatigue allows for an explosive run. And similarly, the longer a defense is on the field the more likely they falter on 3rd downs, which unfortunately only compounds their problems further. Last year in the regular season, opponents ran 1,020 offensive plays against the Seahawks defense. In 2015, that number was 948. In 2014, that number was 925. The reason these teams were able to run more plays was because of Seattle's offense and their lack of a running game.

Seattle's issues on offense were emblematic of the team they wanted to be but were not. On 1st and 10, their most frequent play was a handoff to Thomas Rawls. With or without Rawls, the Seahawks called 211 run plays on first and 10 and were successful on just 45% of them, ranking 16th in the NFL. This means that on the majority of these runs, they are gaining less than 4 yards, setting up 2nd and long (7-10 yards). *(cont'd - see SEA-4)*

2017 Rest Analysis

Avg Rest	6.47
Avg Rk	3
Team More Rest	2
Opp More Rest	2
Net Rest Edge	0
3 Days Rest	1
4 Days Rest	0
5 Days Rest	1
6 Days Rest	11
7 Days Rest	0
8 Days Rest	0
9 Days Rest	0
10 Days Rest	1
11 Days Rest	0
12 Days Rest	0
13 Days Rest	1
14 Days Rest	0

Health by Unit*

2016 Rk	5
(2015 Rk)	3
Off Rk	6
Def Rk	4
QB Rk	16
RB Rk	26
WR Rk	5
TE Rk	16
OLine Rk	4
DLine Rk	10
LB Rk	9
DB Rk	11

**Based on the great work of Scott Kacsmar from Football Outsiders*

2017 Weekly Betting Lines (wks 1-16)

1	2	3	4	5	7	8	9	10	11	12	13	14	15	16
GB	SF	TEN	IND	LAR	NYG	HOU	WSH	ARI	ATL	SF	PHI	JAX	LAR	DAL
A	H	A	H	A		H	H		H	A	H	A	H	A
+3.0	-13.0	-2.0	-7.0	-6.0	+0.0	-7.5	-8.0	-1.5	-3.0	-7.5	-7.0	-4.0	-13.5	+3.0

Avg = -4.9

Home Lines (wks 1-16)

2	4	8	9	11	13	15
SF	IND	HOU	WSH	ATL	PHI	LAR
-13.0	-7.0	-7.5	-8.0	-3.0	-7.0	-13.5

Avg = -8.4

Road Lines (wks 1-16)

1	3	5	7	10	12	14	16
GB	TEN	LAR	NYG	ARI	SF	JAX	
+3.0	-2.0	-6.0	+0.0	-1.5	-7.5	-4	+3.0

Avg = -1.9

Seattle Seahawks 2016 Play Analysis

2016 Play Tendencies

All Pass %	60%
All Pass Rk	15
All Rush %	40%
All Rush Rk	18
1 Score Pass %	62%
1 Score Pass Rk	5
2015 1 Score Pass %	51%
2015 1 Score Pass Rk	30
Pass Increase %	10%
Pass Increase Rk	1
1 Score Rush %	38%
1 Score Rush Rk	28
Up Pass %	58%
Up Pass Rk	12
Up Rush %	42%
Up Rush Rk	21
Down Pass %	60%
Down Pass Rk	21
Down Rush %	40%
Down Rush Rk	12

2016 Down & Distance Tendencies

Down	Distance	Total Plays	Pass Rate	Run Rate	Play Success %
1	Short (1-3)	8	13%	88%	63%
	Med (4-7)	7	43%	57%	43%
	Long (8-10)	332	52%	48%	54%
	XL (11+)	19	53%	47%	32%
2	Short (1-3)	49	41%	59%	61%
	Med (4-7)	77	48%	52%	45%
	Long (8-10)	92	61%	39%	40%
	XL (11+)	45	82%	18%	31%
3	Short (1-3)	53	53%	47%	53%
	Med (4-7)	48	90%	10%	38%
	Long (8-10)	31	97%	3%	35%
	XL (11+)	34	88%	12%	18%
4	Short (1-3)	4	75%	25%	50%
	Med (4-7)	1	100%	0%	0%
	Long (8-10)	1	0%	100%	0%

Shotgun %:

Under Center	Shotgun
33%	67%
37%	*63%*

37% AVG 63%

Run Rate:

Under Center	Shotgun
67%	24%

68% AVG 23%

Pass Rate:

Under Center	Shotgun
33%	76%

32% AVG 77%

Short Yardage Intelligence:

2nd and Short Run

Run Freq	Run % Rk	NFL Run Freq Avg	Run 1D Rate	Run NFL 1D Avg
64%	19	65%	69%	71%

2nd and Short Pass

Pass Freq	Pass % Rk	NFL Pass Freq Avg	Pass 1D Rate	Pass NFL 1D Avg
36%	14	35%	50%	52%

Most Frequent Play

Down	Distance	Play Type	Player	Total Plays	Play Success %
1	Short (1-3)	RUSH	Thomas Rawls	3	33%
	Med (4-7)	RUSH	Christine Michael	2	50%
	Long (8-10)	RUSH	Thomas Rawls	70	47%
	XL (11+)	PASS	Doug Baldwin	3	33%
			Jermaine Kearse	3	33%
		RUSH	Russell Wilson	3	0%
			C.J. Prosise	3	67%
2	Short (1-3)	RUSH	Thomas Rawls	11	64%
	Med (4-7)	RUSH	Thomas Rawls	13	31%
	Long (8-10)	RUSH	Thomas Rawls	17	41%
	XL (11+)	PASS	Jimmy Graham	7	43%
3	Short (1-3)	RUSH	Thomas Rawls	9	67%
			Christine Michael	9	44%
	Med (4-7)	PASS	Doug Baldwin	12	50%
	Long (8-10)	PASS	Tyler Lockett	5	60%
	XL (11+)	PASS	Jimmy Graham	6	50%

Most Successful Play*

Down	Distance	Play Type	Player	Total Plays	Play Success %
1	Long (8-10)	PASS	Doug Baldwin	31	68%
2	Short (1-3)	RUSH	Christine Michael	10	70%
	Med (4-7)	PASS	Doug Baldwin	11	55%
	Long (8-10)	PASS	Doug Baldwin	15	47%
	XL (11+)	PASS	Jimmy Graham	7	43%
3	Short (1-3)	PASS	Jimmy Graham	5	80%
		RUSH	Russell Wilson	5	80%
	Med (4-7)	RUSH	Russell Wilson	5	80%
	Long (8-10)	PASS	Tyler Lockett	5	60%
	XL (11+)	PASS	Jimmy Graham	6	50%

**Minimum 5 plays to qualify*

2016 Snap Rates

Week	Opp	Score	Doug Baldwin	Jermaine Kearse	Jimmy Graham	Tyler Lockett	Luke Willson	Paul Richardson	Thomas Rawls
1	MIA	W 12-10	70 (85%)	70 (85%)	17 (21%)	62 (76%)	62 (76%)	17 (21%)	22 (27%)
2	LA	L 9-3	58 (87%)	55 (82%)	55 (82%)	27 (40%)	16 (24%)	45 (67%)	15 (22%)
3	SF	W 37-18	55 (79%)	54 (77%)	47 (67%)	21 (30%)	48 (69%)	27 (39%)	
4	NYJ	W 27-17	45 (75%)	44 (73%)	40 (67%)	14 (23%)	40 (67%)	39 (65%)	
6	ATL	W 26-24	56 (85%)	53 (80%)	64 (97%)	42 (64%)	19 (29%)	10 (15%)	
7	ARI	T 6-6	62 (98%)	56 (89%)	61 (97%)	49 (78%)		10 (16%)	
8	NO	L 25-20	47 (87%)	47 (87%)	50 (93%)	34 (63%)		14 (26%)	
9	BUF	W 31-25	40 (85%)	40 (85%)	42 (89%)	28 (60%)		8 (17%)	
10	NE	W 31-24	63 (90%)	56 (80%)	68 (97%)	42 (60%)		20 (29%)	
11	PHI	W 26-15	56 (84%)	47 (70%)	50 (75%)	35 (52%)	34 (51%)	20 (30%)	39 (58%)
12	TB	L 14-5	58 (92%)	50 (79%)	63 (100%)	52 (83%)	2 (3%)	15 (24%)	37 (59%)
13	CAR	W 40-7	61 (86%)	64 (90%)	53 (75%)	44 (62%)			39 (55%)
14	GB	L 38-10	60 (85%)	53 (75%)	41 (58%)	43 (61%)	28 (39%)	12 (17%)	37 (52%)
15	LA	W 24-3	43 (70%)	37 (61%)	37 (61%)	38 (62%)	38 (62%)	11 (18%)	57 (93%)
16	ARI	L 34-31	77 (93%)	66 (80%)	68 (82%)	26 (31%)	27 (33%)	49 (59%)	36 (43%)
17	SF	W 25-23	45 (70%)	37 (58%)	37 (58%)		35 (55%)	43 (67%)	20 (31%)
Grand Total			896 (84%)	829 (78%)	793 (76%)	557 (56%)	349 (46%)	340 (34%)	302 (49%)

Personnel Groupings

Personnel	Team %	NFL Avg	Succ. %
1-1 [3WR]	63%	60%	46%
1-2 [2WR]	19%	19%	50%
2-1 [2WR]	6%	7%	50%
1-3 [1WR]	4%	3%	55%
2-2 [1WR]	2%	3%	26%
0-1 [4WR]	2%	1%	52%

Grouping Tendencies

Personnel	Pass Rate	Pass Succ. %	Run Succ. %
1-1 [3WR]	68%	42%	44%
1-2 [2WR]	49%	52%	40%
2-1 [2WR]	36%	38%	38%
1-3 [1WR]	40%	47%	48%
2-2 [1WR]	11%	33%	23%
0-1 [4WR]	92%	32%	100%

Red Zone Targets (min 3)

Receiver	All	Inside 5	6-10	11-20
Jimmy Graham	25	2	2	21
Doug Baldwin	22	3	7	12
Jermaine Kearse	18	5	6	7
Paul Richardson	6	3	1	2
Tyler Lockett	5	1	1	3
Luke Willson	4		1	3
C.J. Spiller	3		2	1
Christine Michael	3		2	1
Thomas Rawls	3	1		2

Red Zone Rushes (min 3)

Rusher	All	Inside 5	6-10	11-20
Thomas Rawls	25	6	6	13
Christine Michael	21	9	3	9
Alex Collins	8	2		6
C.J. Prosise	8	2	3	3
Russell Wilson	6	2	2	2

Early Down Target Rate

RB	TE	WR
17%	23%	61%
19%	*20% NFL AVG*	*61%*

Overall Target Success %

RB	TE	WR
53% #2	58% #7	53% #7

Seattle Seahawks 2016 Passing Recap & 2017 Outlook

Russell Wilson's 2016 season will be remembered as a down year, and it certainly was, but in spite of all the issues he faced, his overall numbers were not bad. His standard metrics, like completion rate, yards per attempt, TD:INT ratio and passer rating were all above average. His more advanced metrics like success rate and EDSR passing were above average as well. And impressively, his air yardage numbers were actually solid even though he was passing behind a turnstile offensive line. There were situations beyond his control that hurt his efficiency, such as the decision to pass the ball 53% of the time in short yardage situations despite the team recording a 63% success rate when rushing and only a 51% success rate when passing. And Wilson's interception rates on these short yardage plays were very bad: on 1st/2nd and less than 5, Wilson threw 3 interceptions in 56 attempts. Playing with an injured knee, Wilson didn't run the ball often, which held him and the offense back a bit. Inside the opponent's 7 yard line, of the 25 Seattle rushes, only two were Wilson runs. Wilson's deep targeting of Jimmy Graham last year was impressive and I hope the Seahawks incorporate more of it in 2017.

Russell Wilson Rating All Downs

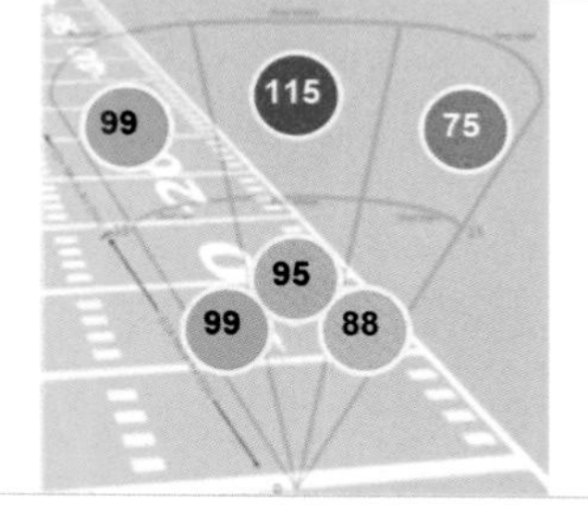

Russell Wilson Rating Early Downs

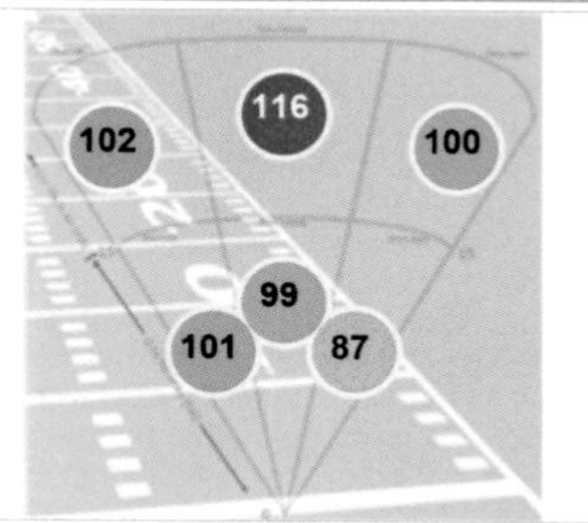

2016 Standard Passing Table

QB	Comp	Att	Comp %	Yds	YPA	TDs	INT	Sacks	Rating	Rk
Russell Wilson	393	606	65%	4,662	7.7	25	13	46	93.0	18
NFL Avg			63%		7.2				90.4	

2016 Advanced Passing Table

QB	Success %	EDSR Passing Success %	20+ Yd Pass Gains	20+ Yd Pass %	30+ Yd Pass Gains	30+ Yd Pass %	Air Yds per Comp	YAC per Comp	20+ Air Yd Comp	20+ Air Yd %
Russell Wilson	48%	52%	60	10%	31	5%	7.1	4.8	38	6%
NFL Avg	44%	48%	27	8%	10	3%	6.4	4.8	12	4%

Interception Rates by Down

Yards to Go	1	2	3	4	Total
1 & 2	0.0%	6.3%	0.0%	0.0%	2.2%
3, 4, 5	25.0%	2.9%	2.1%	0.0%	3.4%
6 - 9	0.0%	1.8%	0.0%		0.9%
10 - 14	1.3%	1.4%	0.0%	0.0%	1.2%
15+	7.7%	0.0%	13.6%		6.5%
Total	1.9%	2.0%	2.2%	0.0%	2.0%

3rd Down Passing - Short of Sticks Analysis

QB	Avg Yds to Go	Air Yds (of Comps)	Avg Yds Short	Short of Sticks Rate	Rk
Russell Wilson	7.8	6.9	-0.9	53%	27
NFL Avg	7.6	6.8	-0.8	57%	

Air Yds vs YAC

Air Yds %	YAC %	Rk
50%	50%	33
54%	46%	

2016 Receiving Recap & 2017 Outlook

Seattle desperately needs a 2nd WR to step up apart from Doug Baldwin. Paul Richardson outperformed Jermaine Kearse and Tyler Locket, but he was only targeted on 45 attempts last year. While most of Seattle's WRs posted an extremely solid 9 yards per attempt, Kearse was all the way down at 5.6 yards per attempt, catching just 46% of his targets and delivering a 50 passer rating. Jimmy Graham posted an impressive comeback season last year, but was not targeted enough in the red zone. In fact, of the 71 offensive plays Seattle ran inside the 10 yard line, Graham was targeted on only 4 of them.

Player **Min 50 Targets*	Targets	Comp %	YPA	Rating	TOARS	Success %	Success Rk	Missed YPA Rk	YAS % Rk	TDs
Doug Baldwin	146	75%	9.0	117	5.6	59%	20	19	43	9
Jimmy Graham	102	70%	9.6	119	5.1	59%	21	36	49	7
Jermaine Kearse	95	46%	5.6	50	4.0	42%	125	128	66	1
Tyler Lockett	66	62%	9.0	90	4.0	50%	73	89	38	1

Directional Passer Rating Delivered

Receiver	Short Left	Short Middle	Short Right	Deep Left	Deep Middle	Deep Right	Player Total
Doug Baldwin	130	126	90	102	61	135	117
Jimmy Graham	114	112	75	135	158	144	119
Jermaine Kearse	70	1	91	68	77	5	50
Tyler Lockett	104	79	72	96	40	104	90
Paul Richardson	83	92	112	74	119	119	98
Christine Michael	91	80	103	40			94
Luke Willson	93	100	119	40		0	77
C.J. Prosise	93	109	72	119		119	112
Team Total	104	91	90	94	118	79	98

2016 Rushing Recap & 2017 Outlook

The weak link last year was the run offense, and it was in part due to the offensive line, the running backs themselves and the play calling. Seattle ran the ball too often in long yardage situations. On early downs with 7-10 yards to go, Seattle ran the ball slightly above NFL average but recorded a 42% success rate (18th) while they recorded a 56% success rate (4th) when passing. And on short yardage situations they were far more efficient running than passing (by 12%) but passed more often. If Seattle gets a healthy Eddie Lacy to churn out yardage and they call plays more to their strengths, Seattle's run efficiency can improve substantially which will help all aspects of the team including their defense & allow them fewer on-field snaps in 2017.

Player **Min 50 Rushes*	Rushes	YPA	Success %	Success Rk	Missed YPA Rk	YTS % Rk	YAS % Rk	Early Down Success %	Early Down Success Rk	TDs
Thomas Rawls	147	3.7	46%	39	55	24	9	45%	42	4
Christine Michael	164	4.0	49%	30	21	22	31	49%	27	7

Yards per Carry by Direction

Directional Run Frequency

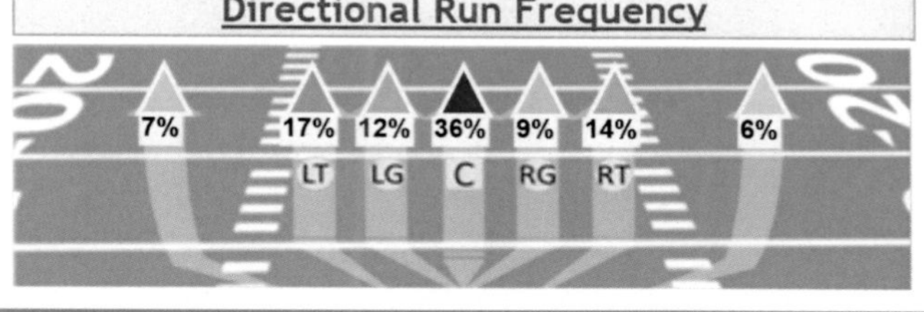

SEA-4

Seattle was very run-dominant in these situations, running the ball 8% more than the NFL average (6th most often). But their success was even worse, with only 32% of these runs resulting in successful gains (20th in the NFL). Seattle would have loved to establish an identity on offense and smash people on the ground, but they simply weren't capable of executing efficiently enough. Rawls finished the season averaging just 3.6 yards per attempt, and ranked 39th in success rate, 42nd in early down success rate and 55th in missed YPA (a metric which examines only unsuccessful runs to see how close the RB was to making the run successful) on a per-play basis. As a result of this inefficient ground attack, Seattle was forced to turn to the air.

Seattle's offense ranked 17th in EDSR (Early Down Success Rate) and 16th in passing efficiency, and to be honest they could have gone even more pass heavy to maximize efficiency. While they were close to an even split on play usage on 1st and 10 (52% pass), they were the 4th best team in the NFL in success rate on 1st and 10 passing, recording successful passes 59% of the time. That was 14% better than when they ran on 1st and 10 (45%). Doug Baldwin led the way, recording successful gains when targeted 68% of the time.

Once again, Seattle needed to shift more to the pass but were stuck on an idea of who they had been and wanted to be, as opposed to who they were. For example: inside the red zone on 1st and 10, Seattle chose to run on 56% of their opportunities. But only 25% of those runs graded as successful, the 4th worst mark in the NFL. When they passed, they recorded successful gains over twice as often, at a 56% clip (8th best). The NFL average in the red zone on 1st and 10 was a 42% success rate when rushing and a 45% success rate when passing. So you can see how terrible Seattle was when running and how incredible they were when passing. But they were stuck in their old ways of pounding the football down there and it cost them. That early down inefficiency caught up with them. On 3rd down in the red zone, based on yards to go and lack of confidence in the run game, Seattle went 89% pass (40 att), 11% run (5 rushes) and unsurprisingly saw a 25% success rate regardless of the play call.

Seattle's offensive line is receiving a slight makeover, though not as bold as many hoped, as they acquired Luke Joeckel in free agency and drafted Ethan Pocic in the 2nd round. Once again they have the least expensive line in the NFL. To help the ground game, they acquired RB Eddie Lacy to allow Rawls to return to the change of pace back. They absolutely must be more efficient on the ground, but Seattle can't be hung up on an image of a team they want to be if they aren't that team. They don't need to pass "more", as they already were passing 5th most often in one-score games. But they need to reexamine when they are passing and should run much more often in short yardage situations, but pass more often on early downs, particularly in the red zone.

Division History: Season Wins & 2017 Projection

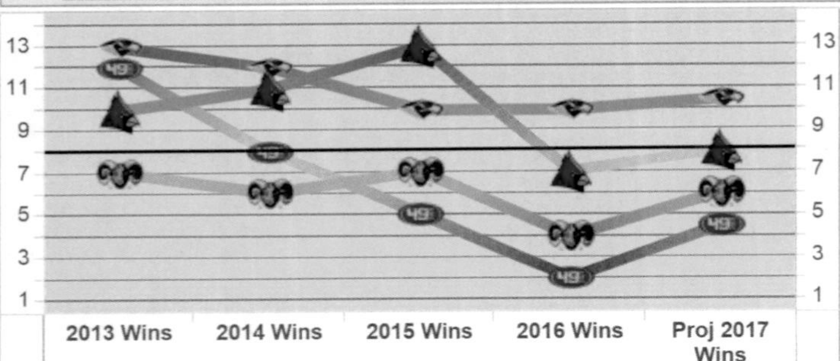

Rank of 2017 Defensive Pass Efficiency Faced by Week

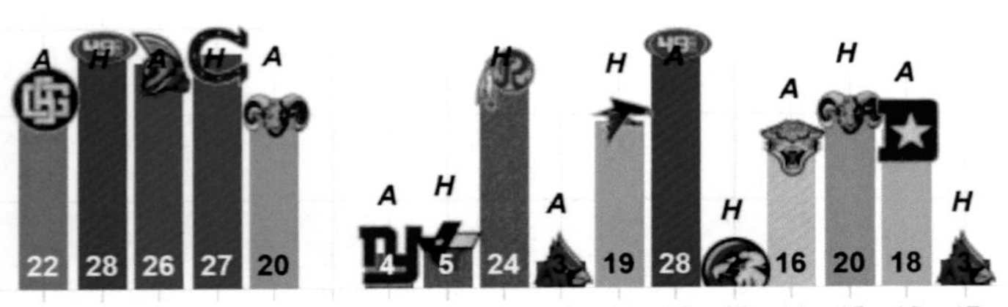

Rank of 2017 Defensive Rush Efficiency Faced by Week

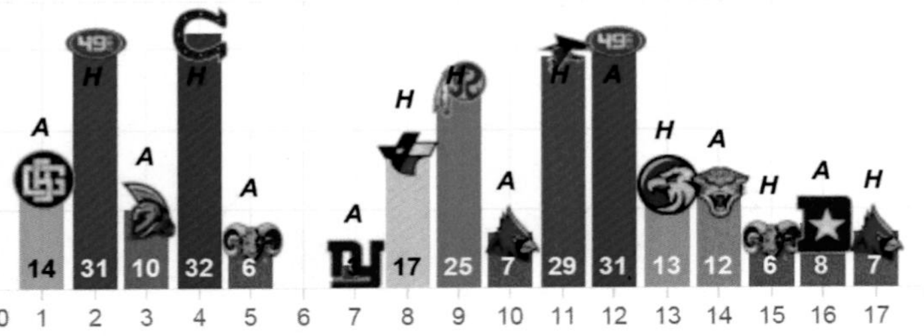

2016 Situational Usage by Player & Position

Usage Rate by Score

		Being Blown Out (14+)	Down Big (9-13)	One Score	Large Lead (9-13)	Blowout Lead (14+)	Grand Total
RUSH	Thomas Rawls	15%	14%	15%	14%	17%	15%
	Doug Baldwin		1%	0%	2%		1%
	Christine Michael			15%	7%	16%	12%
	Jimmy Graham			0%			0%
	Tyler Lockett	2%		0%		1%	1%
	Alex Collins	9%	11%	2%	3%	6%	4%
	C.J. Prosise			4%	2%		3%
	Paul Richardson			0%			0%
	Troymaine Pope	1%			7%	6%	1%
	C.J. Spiller			0%	2%	1%	0%
	Marcel Reece			0%			0%
	J.D. McKissic			0%			0%
	George Farmer					1%	0%
	Terrence Magee					3%	0%
	Total	27%	26%	39%	36%	50%	38%
PASS	Thomas Rawls	2%	1%	2%	5%	2%	2%
	Doug Baldwin	21%	18%	14%	12%	16%	15%
	Christine Michael			4%		2%	3%
	Jimmy Graham	5%	10%	11%	12%	11%	10%
	Jermaine Kearse	11%	18%	10%	8%	6%	10%
	Tyler Lockett	10%	7%	6%	7%	6%	7%
	Alex Collins	9%	6%	1%		1%	2%
	C.J. Prosise			3%	3%		2%
	Paul Richardson	4%	10%	5%	3%	2%	5%
	Luke Willson	4%		2%	3%	2%	2%
	Tanner McEvoy	5%		1%	2%	2%	1%
	Troymaine Pope	1%			2%		0%
	C.J. Spiller			1%	2%		1%
	Marcel Reece	2%	1%	1%			1%
	J.D. McKissic			1%			0%
	George Farmer		3%		2%		0%
	Nick Vannett			0%	2%	1%	0%
	Brandon Williams			0%	2%		0%
	Kasen Williams			0%			0%
	Total	73%	74%	61%	64%	50%	62%

Positional Target Distribution vs NFL Average

		NFL Wide				Team Only			
		Left	Middle	Right	**Total**	Left	Middle	Right	**Total**
Deep	WR	982	567	978	**2,527**	49	14	23	**86**
	TE	151	140	156	**447**	7	7	7	**21**
	RB	23	4	39	**66**	2		1	**3**
	All	**1,156**	**711**	**1,173**	**3,040**	**58**	**21**	**31**	**110**
Short	WR	2,976	1,727	3,081	**7,784**	117	44	105	**266**
	TE	805	840	1,113	**2,758**	31	35	38	**104**
	RB	1,002	612	1,094	**2,708**	13	10	19	**42**
	All	**4,783**	**3,179**	**5,288**	**13,250**	**161**	**89**	**162**	**412**
Total		**5,939**	**3,890**	**6,461**	**16,290**	**219**	**110**	**193**	**522**

Positional Success Rates vs NFL Average

		NFL Wide				Team Only			
		Left	Middle	Right	**Total**	Left	Middle	Right	**Total**
Deep	WR	37%	50%	38%	**40%**	43%	50%	33%	**42%**
	TE	44%	48%	44%	**45%**	43%	86%	25%	**50%**
	RB	30%	75%	23%	**29%**	50%		100%	**67%**
	All	**37%**	**50%**	**39%**	**41%**	**44%**	**62%**	**33%**	**44%**
Short	WR	52%	57%	51%	**53%**	52%	44%	52%	**51%**
	TE	50%	61%	53%	**55%**	42%	77%	31%	**49%**
	RB	47%	49%	44%	**46%**	62%	50%	37%	**48%**
	All	**51%**	**57%**	**50%**	**52%**	**51%**	**58%**	**45%**	**50%**
Total		**48%**	**55%**	**48%**	**50%**	**49%**	**59%**	**43%**	**49%**

Tampa Bay Buccaneers

2017 Coaches

Head Coach:
Dirk Koetter (2nd yr)
Offensive Coordinator:
Todd Monken (2nd yr)
Defensive Coordinator:
Mike Smith (2nd yr)

2017 Forecast

Wins	Div Rank
8	#4

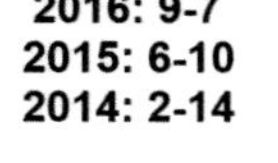

Past Records

2016: 9-7
2015: 6-10
2014: 2-14

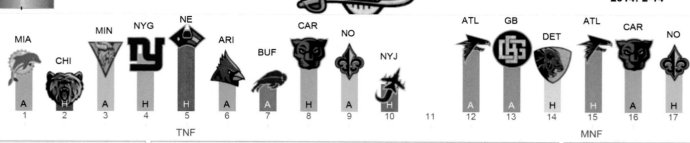

EASY HARD

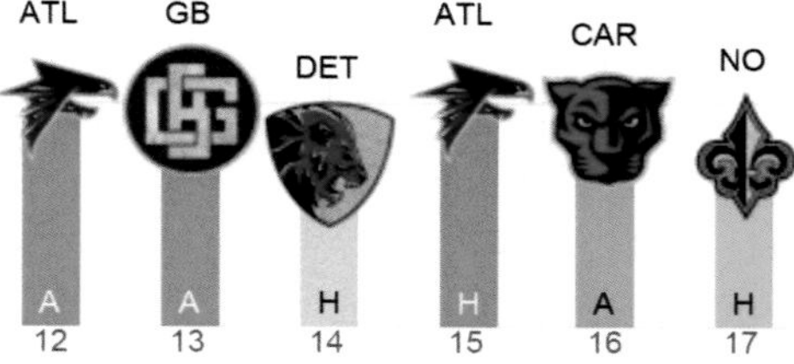

Week	Opponent	H/A	Note
1	MIA	A	
2	CHI	H	
3	MIN	A	
4	NYG	H	
5	NE	H	TNF
6	ARI	A	
7	BUF	A	
8	CAR	H	
9	NO	A	
10	NYJ	H	
11			
12	ATL	A	
13	GB	A	
14	DET	H	
15	ATL	H	MNF
16	CAR	A	
17	NO	H	

Key Players Lost

TXN	Player (POS)
Cut	Gottschalk, Ben C
	Mabin, Greg CB
	Verner, Alterraun CB
Declared Free Agent	Cherilus, Gosder T
	Conte, Chris S
	DePaola, Andrew TE
	Glennon, Mike QB
	Hawley, Joe C
	Hughes III, John DT
	Jackson, Vincent WR
	Jones, Howard DE
	McDougald, Bradley S
	Myers, Brandon TE
	Robinson, Josh CB
	Rodgers, Jacquizz RB
	Shepard, Russell WR
	Shorts III, Cecil WR
	Siliga, Sealver DT
	Smith, Antone RB
	Smith, Daryl LB
	Spence, Akeem DT

Average Line	# Games Favored	# Games Underdog
+0.6	5	10

Regular Season Wins: Past & Current Proj

Proj 2017 Wins  8

2016 Wins  9

Proj 2016 Wins 7

2015 Wins  6

2014 Wins  2

2013 Wins  4

1 3 5 7 9 11 13 15

2017 Tampa Bay Buccaneers Overview

The fact the 2016 Buccaneers were able to win 9 games last season was impressive because their body of work and impediments they had to overcome were tremendous. Particularly with a young quarterback and an offense which disintegrated around him. It started with the run game. After an impressive week 1 victory over the Super Bowl runner up Falcons in Atlanta, Doug Margin played 13 snaps in week 2 before leaving with an injury. While he returned in week 10, he was a shell of himself the remainder of the season. Martin recoded fewer than 3 yards per carry in 5 of his remaining 6 games. While Jaquizz Rodgers did his best in reserve, the bulk of his 2016 production came in just 2 games against poor run defenses (49ers, Raiders), and then he too was injured. When both Martin and Rodgers was out, the team had to turn to Peyton Barber, but in his lone start he averaged only 2.8 yards per carry.

Overall, the run game clocked in as the 5th least efficient in the NFL and the sophomore quarterback didn't have any run game to rely on. As a result, the Bucs likely would have shifted more to the passing game. However, the receivers were even more injured than the RBs. While the RBs for the Bucs were the 9th most injured in the NFL, the WRs were the 4th most injured. Vincent Jackson was the most notable, when he went out after week 5, but the team lost many more games to injured WRs. As a measure of how much the receiving corps was beat up, even though the Buccaneers passed the ball on 56% of their offensive plays, only 3 receivers (Mike Evans, Adam Humphries and Cameron Brate) were targeted at least 50 times, whereas 4 RBs had 50+ carries.

With limited receiving threats and a non-existent running game, everything gets more difficult for an offense. Mike Evans was routinely doubled, and while Winston recorded 11 yards per attempt and a 45% completion rate on deep passes in 2015, those both declined last year to 9 yards per attempt and a 39.5% completion rate, and his passer rating dropped by over 10 points. Adam Humphries was extremely reliable to the short left or right, but his rating and reliability plummeted across the middle. Whether it was the severe hits he took at points in his career or not, Humphries has a very narrow role on an NFL offense and it appears receiving across the middle is something both he and the team should avoid.

(cont'd - see TB2)

Key Free Agents/ Trades Added

- Bailey, Sterling DE
- Baker, Chris DE
- Barnes, Tavaris DE
- Fitzpatrick, Ryan QB
- Harrison, Jarvis G
- Jackson, DeSean WR
- McClain, Robert CB
- Walker, Derel WR
- Wilcox, J.J. S

Drafted Players

Rd	Pk	Player (College)
1	19	TE - O. J. Howard (Alabama)
2	50	S - Justin Evans (Texas A&M)
3	84	WR - Chris Godwin (Penn State)
3*	107	LB - Kendell Beckwith (LSU)
5	162	RB - Jeremy McNichols (Boise State)
7	223	DT - Stevie Tu'ikolovatu (USC)

2017 Unit Spending

2017 Lineup & Cap Hits

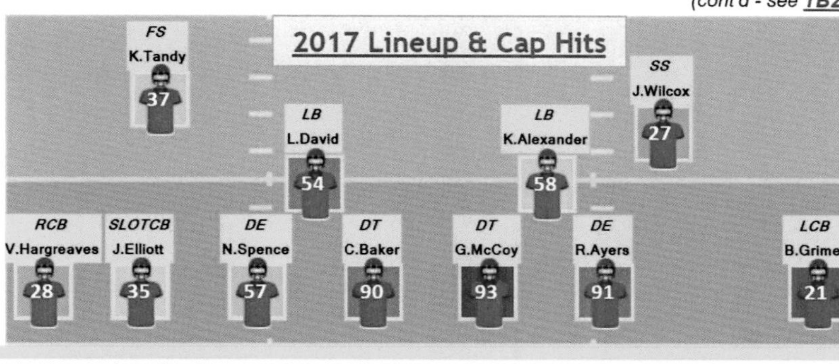

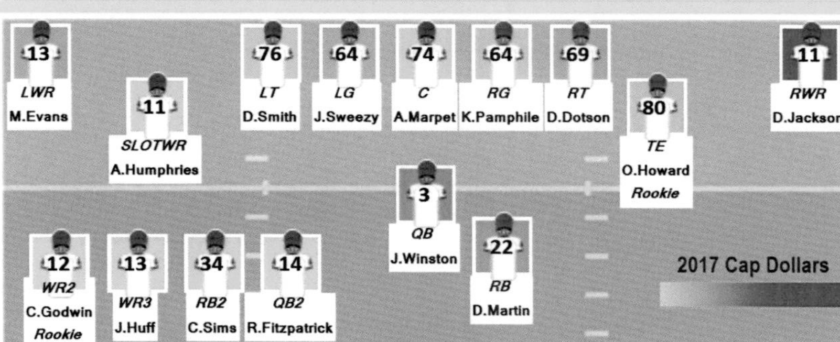

Positional Spending

	Rank	Total	2016 Rk
All OFF	25	$75.01M	12
QB	24	$9.18M	29
OL	23	$24.90M	7
RB	4	$13.27M	5
WR	10	$22.33M	7
TE	26	$5.34M	24
All DEF	11	$82.49M	8
DL	2	$45.07M	5
LB	31	$10.57M	20
CB	17	$18.50M	5
S	23	$8.35M	25

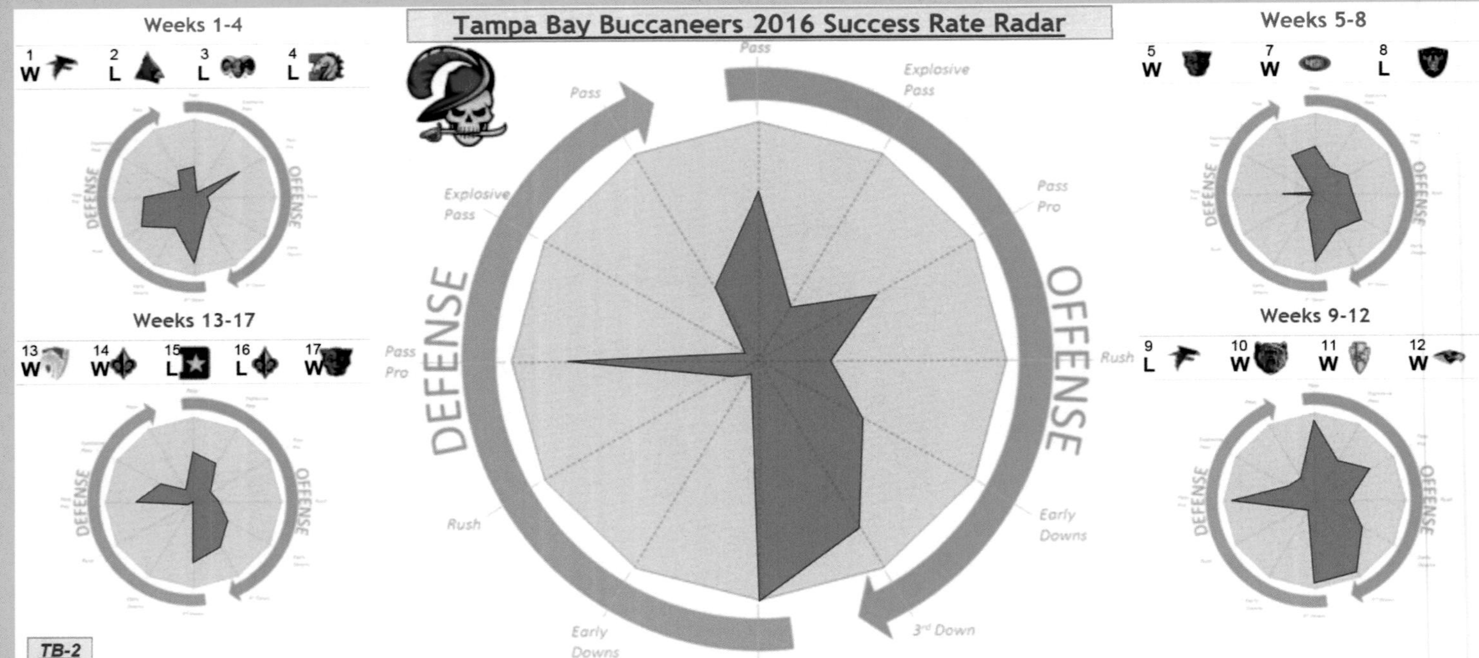

TB-2

By far the most reliable receiver on the Bucs last year was Cameron Brate, whose 70% completion rate, 8 yards per reception and 60% success rate was by far the best on the team.

What became clear was the Buccaneers needed more offensive threats. And they addressed that need in a major way heading into Winston's 3rd season. The first major difference maker was WR DeSean Jackson, who was signed in free agency from the Redskins. An extreme deep threat, Jackson's speed opens up an entire offense. He once was largely responsible for sending Nick Foles to the Pro Bowl when Jackson was with the Eagles. Last year with the Redskins, Jackson delivered the second best passer rating on early down deep targets, and averaged the NFL's best 19.2 yards per attempt. This is exactly where Winston struggled last year, as he averaged just a 88 rating and only 9.9 yards per attempt, one of the worst marks in the league. And in terms of adding precise value, Jackson will certainly add it to the deep right side of the field. As great as Kirk Cousins was throwing deep, he struggled big going deep right to anyone apart from DeSean Ja.. But to Jackson, he recorded a 125 passer rating. Like Cousins, Winston struggled tremendously to the deep right, recording a 72 rating with only 8.4 yards per attempt to the deep right. Eliminating 3rd or 4th and long desperation tosses, Winston posted a 102 rating with 11.5 yards per attempt deep left. With Jackson in the lineup, Winston's efficiency to the deep right will be evident.

The other element that Jackson provides anytime he is on the field is to force the defense to adjust to his speed. It won't be possible to double both Mike Evans and DeSean Jackson, and playing single coverage on either is a recipe for disaster over time. It will also open up running lanes to improve the efficiency of the run game, which certainly is necessary given their results last season.

Tampa Bay also added a key receiving weapon in the first round of the draft: Alabama's tight end O.J. Howard. Howard's receiving skills are tremendous and he has the size and speed to present major mismatches for any defense.

(cont'd - see TB-3)

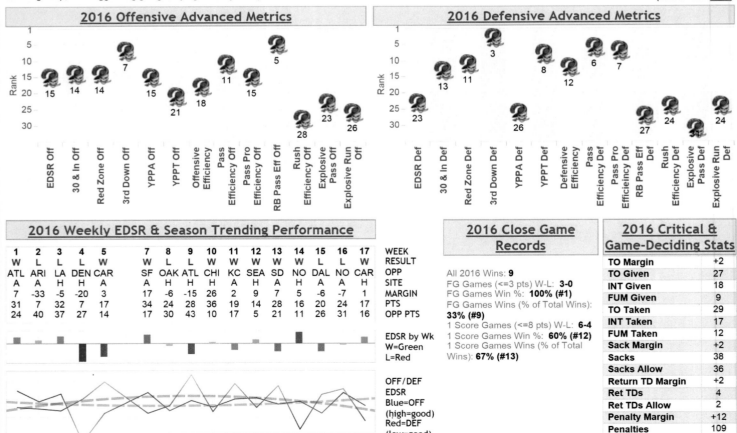

2016 Offensive Advanced Metrics

Metric	Rank
EDSR Off	15
30 & In Off	14
Red Zone Off	14
3rd Down Off	7
YPPA Off	15
YPPT Off	21
Offensive Efficiency	18
Pass Efficiency Off	11
Pass Pro Efficiency Off	15
RB Pass Eff Off	5
Rush Efficiency Off	28
Explosive Pass Off	23
Explosive Run Off	26

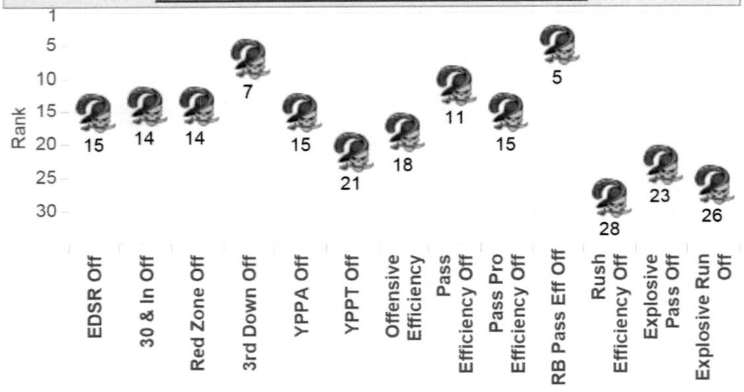

2016 Defensive Advanced Metrics

Metric	Rank
EDSR Def	23
30 & In Def	13
Red Zone Def	11
3rd Down Def	3
YPPA Def	26
YPPT Def	8
Defensive Efficiency	12
Pass Efficiency Def	6
Pass Pro Efficieincy Def	7
RB Pass Eff Def	27
Rush Efficiency Def	24
Explosive Pass Def	31
Explosive Run Def	24

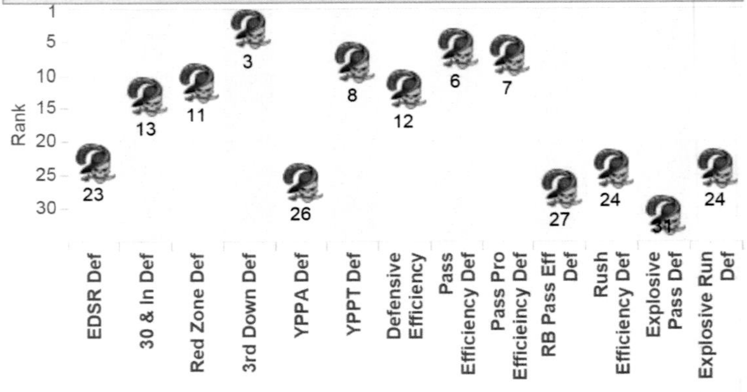

2016 Weekly EDSR & Season Trending Performance

1	2	3	4	5	7	8	9	10	11	12	13	14	15	16	17	WEEK
W	L	L	L	W	W	L	L	W	W	W	W	W	L	L	W	RESULT
ATL	ARI	LA	DEN	CAR	SF	OAK	ATL	CHI	KC	SEA	SD	NO	DAL	NO	CAR	OPP
A	A	H	H	A	A	H	H	H	A	H	A	H	A	A	H	SITE
7	-33	-5	-20	3	17	-6	-15	26	2	9	7	5	-6	-7	1	MARGIN
31	7	32	7	17	34	24	28	36	19	14	28	16	20	24	17	PTS
24	40	37	27	14	17	30	43	10	17	5	21	11	26	31	16	OPP PTS

EDSR by Wk
W=Green
L=Red

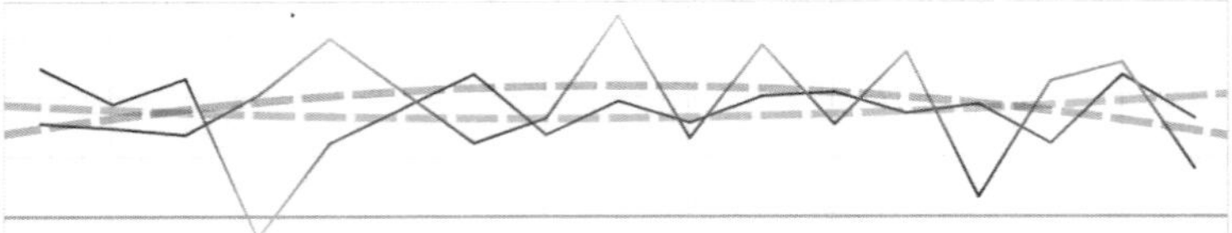

OFF/DEF
EDSR
Blue=OFF
(high=good)
Red=DEF
(low=good)

2016 Close Game Records

All 2016 Wins: **9**
FG Games (<=3 pts) W-L: **3-0**
FG Games Win %: **100% (#1)**
FG Games Wins (% of Total Wins): **33% (#9)**
1 Score Games (<=8 pts) W-L: **6-4**
1 Score Games Win %: **60% (#12)**
1 Score Games Wins (% of Total Wins): **67% (#13)**

2016 Critical & Game-Deciding Stats

TO Margin	+2
TO Given	27
INT Given	18
FUM Given	9
TO Taken	29
INT Taken	17
FUM Taken	12
Sack Margin	+2
Sacks	38
Sacks Allow	36
Return TD Margin	+2
Ret TDs	4
Ret TDs Allow	2
Penalty Margin	+12
Penalties	109
Opponent Penalties	121

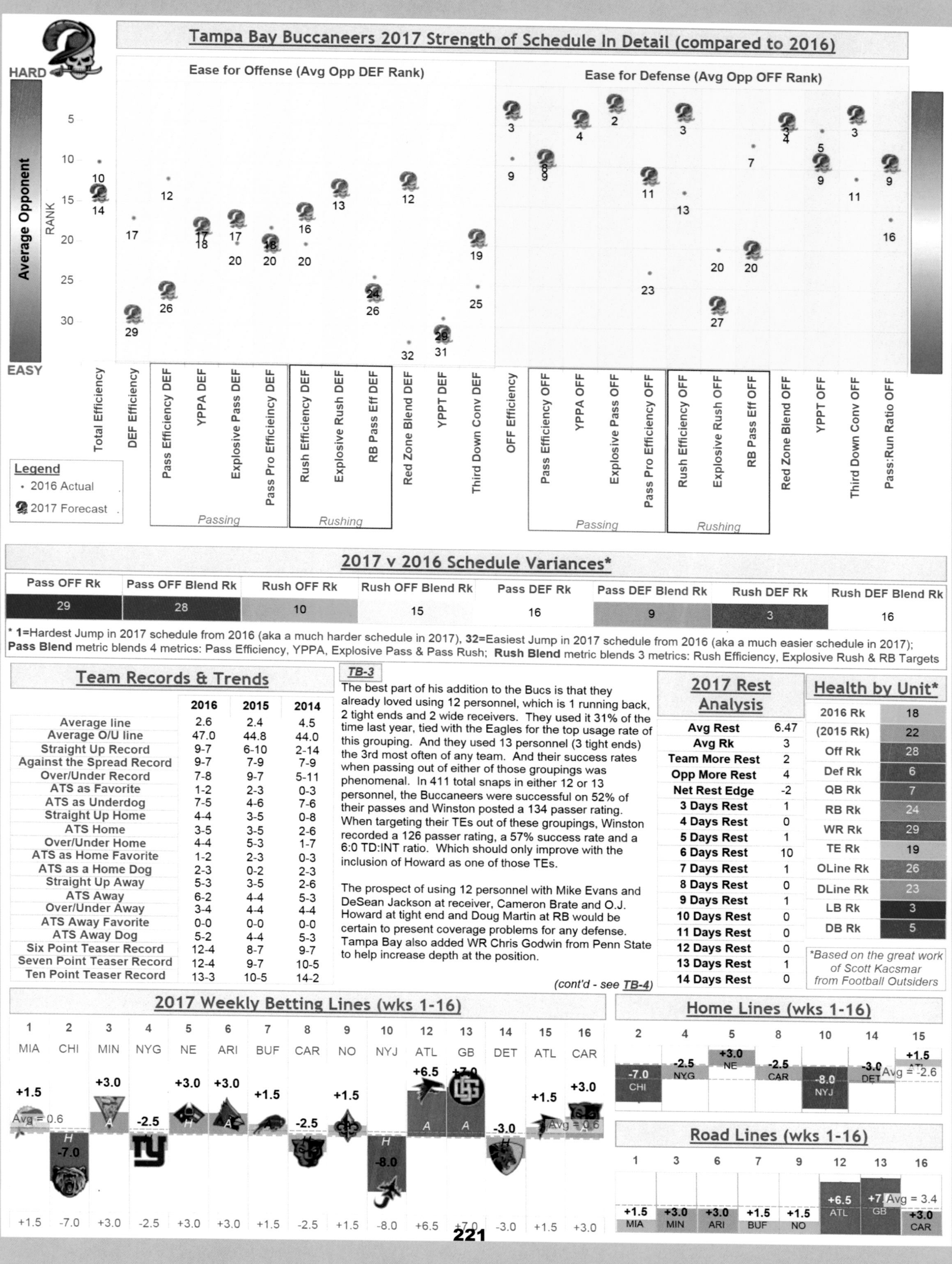

Tampa Bay Buccaneers 2017 Strength of Schedule In Detail (compared to 2016)

2017 v 2016 Schedule Variances*

Pass OFF Rk	Pass OFF Blend Rk	Rush OFF Rk	Rush OFF Blend Rk	Pass DEF Rk	Pass DEF Blend Rk	Rush DEF Rk	Rush DEF Blend Rk
29	28	10	15	16	9	3	16

* **1**=Hardest Jump in 2017 schedule from 2016 (aka a much harder schedule in 2017), **32**=Easiest Jump in 2017 schedule from 2016 (aka a much easier schedule in 2017); **Pass Blend** metric blends 4 metrics: Pass Efficiency, YPPA, Explosive Pass & Pass Rush; **Rush Blend** metric blends 3 metrics: Rush Efficiency, Explosive Rush & RB Targets

Team Records & Trends

	2016	2015	2014
Average line	2.6	2.4	4.5
Average O/U line	47.0	44.8	44.0
Straight Up Record	9-7	6-10	2-14
Against the Spread Record	9-7	7-9	7-9
Over/Under Record	7-8	9-7	5-11
ATS as Favorite	1-2	2-3	0-3
ATS as Underdog	7-5	4-6	7-6
Straight Up Home	4-4	3-5	0-8
ATS Home	3-5	3-5	2-6
Over/Under Home	4-4	5-3	1-7
ATS as Home Favorite	1-2	2-3	0-3
ATS as a Home Dog	2-3	0-2	2-3
Straight Up Away	5-3	3-5	2-6
ATS Away	6-2	4-4	5-3
Over/Under Away	3-4	4-4	4-4
ATS Away Favorite	0-0	0-0	0-0
ATS Away Dog	5-2	4-4	5-3
Six Point Teaser Record	12-4	8-7	9-7
Seven Point Teaser Record	12-4	9-7	10-5
Ten Point Teaser Record	13-3	10-5	14-2

TB-3

The best part of his addition to the Bucs is that they already loved using 12 personnel, which is 1 running back, 2 tight ends and 2 wide receivers. They used it 31% of the time last year, tied with the Eagles for the top usage rate of this grouping. And they used 13 personnel (3 tight ends) the 3rd most often of any team. And their success rates when passing out of either of those groupings was phenomenal. In 411 total snaps in either 12 or 13 personnel, the Buccaneers were successful on 52% of their passes and Winston posted a 134 passer rating. When targeting their TEs out of these groupings, Winston recorded a 126 passer rating, a 57% success rate and a 6:0 TD:INT ratio. Which should only improve with the inclusion of Howard as one of those TEs.

The prospect of using 12 personnel with Mike Evans and DeSean Jackson at receiver, Cameron Brate and O.J. Howard at tight end and Doug Martin at RB would be certain to present coverage problems for any defense. Tampa Bay also added WR Chris Godwin from Penn State to help increase depth at the position.

(cont'd - see TB-4)

2017 Rest Analysis

Avg Rest	6.47
Avg Rk	3
Team More Rest	2
Opp More Rest	4
Net Rest Edge	-2
3 Days Rest	1
4 Days Rest	0
5 Days Rest	1
6 Days Rest	10
7 Days Rest	1
8 Days Rest	0
9 Days Rest	1
10 Days Rest	0
11 Days Rest	0
12 Days Rest	0
13 Days Rest	1
14 Days Rest	0

Health by Unit*

2016 Rk	18
(2015 Rk)	22
Off Rk	28
Def Rk	6
QB Rk	7
RB Rk	24
WR Rk	29
TE Rk	19
OLine Rk	26
DLine Rk	23
LB Rk	3
DB Rk	5

*Based on the great work of Scott Kacsmar from Football Outsiders

2017 Weekly Betting Lines (wks 1-16)

1	2	3	4	5	6	7	8	9	10	12	13	14	15	16
MIA	CHI	MIN	NYG	NE	ARI	BUF	CAR	NO	NYJ	ATL	GB	DET	ATL	CAR
+1.5	-7.0	+3.0	-2.5	+3.0	+3.0	+1.5	-2.5	+1.5	-8.0	+6.5	+7.0	-3.0	+1.5	+3.0

Avg = 0.6

Home Lines (wks 1-16)

2	4	5	8	10	14	15
CHI	NYG	NE	CAR	NYJ	DET	ATL
-7.0	-2.5	+3.0	-2.5	-8.0	-3.0	+1.5

Avg = -2.6

Road Lines (wks 1-16)

1	3	6	7	9	12	13	16
MIA	MIN	ARI	BUF	NO	ATL	GB	CAR
+1.5	+3.0	+3.0	+1.5	+1.5	+6.5	+7.0	+3.0

Avg = 3.4

Tampa Bay Buccaneers 2016 Play Analysis

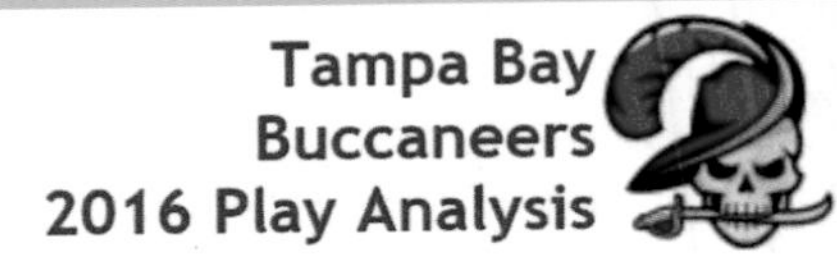

2016 Play Tendencies

All Pass %	56%
All Pass Rk	26
All Rush %	44%
All Rush Rk	7
1 Score Pass %	55%
1 Score Pass Rk	25
2015 1 Score Pass %	52%
2015 1 Score Pass Rk	27
Pass Increase %	3%
Pass Increase Rk	8
1 Score Rush %	45%
1 Score Rush Rk	8
Up Pass %	53%
Up Pass Rk	26
Up Rush %	47%
Up Rush Rk	7
Down Pass %	61%
Down Pass Rk	16
Down Rush %	39%
Down Rush Rk	17

2016 Down & Distance Tendencies

Down	Distance	Total Plays	Pass Rate	Run Rate	Play Success %
1	Short (1-3)	5	20%	80%	60%
	Med (4-7)	6	33%	67%	0%
	Long (8-10)	325	42%	58%	46%
	XL (11+)	20	50%	50%	30%
2	Short (1-3)	37	27%	73%	70%
	Med (4-7)	75	45%	55%	48%
	Long (8-10)	104	71%	29%	51%
	XL (11+)	56	80%	20%	45%
3	Short (1-3)	47	62%	38%	55%
	Med (4-7)	52	90%	10%	46%
	Long (8-10)	32	91%	9%	53%
	XL (11+)	26	88%	12%	15%
4	Short (1-3)	3	33%	67%	67%

Shotgun %:

Under Center	Shotgun
52%	48%
37%	*63%*

37% AVG 63%

Run Rate:

Under Center	Shotgun
69%	11%

68% AVG 23%

Pass Rate:

Under Center	Shotgun
31%	89%

32% AVG 77%

Short Yardage Intelligence:

2nd and Short Run

Run Freq	Run % Rk	NFL Run Freq Avg	Run 1D Rate	Run NFL 1D Avg
76%	4	65%	64%	71%

2nd and Short Pass

Pass Freq	Pass % Rk	NFL Pass Freq Avg	Pass 1D Rate	Pass NFL 1D Avg
24%	28	35%	50%	52%

Most Frequent Play

Down	Distance	Play Type	Player	Total Plays	Play Success %
1	Short (1-3)	RUSH	Doug Martin	3	33%
	Med (4-7)	RUSH	Doug Martin	2	0%
			Jacquizz Rodgers	2	0%
	Long (8-10)	RUSH	Doug Martin	68	35%
	XL (11+)	RUSH	Doug Martin	3	33%
			Peyton Barber	3	0%
2	Short (1-3)	RUSH	Jacquizz Rodgers	11	64%
	Med (4-7)	RUSH	Jacquizz Rodgers	15	53%
	Long (8-10)	PASS	Mike Evans	19	63%
	XL (11+)	PASS	Mike Evans	11	82%
3	Short (1-3)	PASS	Mike Evans	12	67%
	Med (4-7)	PASS	Adam Humphries	12	42%
	Long (8-10)	PASS	Mike Evans	10	50%
	XL (11+)	PASS	Mike Evans	4	75%

Most Successful Play*

Down	Distance	Play Type	Player	Total Plays	Play Success %
1	Long (8-10)	PASS	Doug Martin	5	100%
2	Short (1-3)	RUSH	Doug Martin	9	67%
	Med (4-7)	RUSH	Doug Martin	12	58%
	Long (8-10)	PASS	Cameron Brate	12	83%
	XL (11+)	PASS	Mike Evans	11	82%
3	Short (1-3)	PASS	Cameron Brate	5	80%
	Med (4-7)	PASS	Cameron Brate	11	64%
	Long (8-10)	PASS	Mike Evans	10	50%

**Minimum 5 plays to qualify*

2016 Snap Rates

Week	Opp	Score	Mike Evans	Cameron Brate	Adam Humphries	Russell Shepard	Brandon Myers	Jacquizz Rodgers	Doug Martin	Luke Stocker	Vincent Jackson
1	ATL	W 31-24	55 (86%)	25 (39%)	49 (77%)	6 (9%)	13 (20%)		44 (69%)	37 (58%)	51 (80%)
2	ARI	L 40-7	69 (87%)	33 (42%)	58 (73%)	14 (18%)	22 (28%)	14 (18%)	13 (16%)	9 (11%)	68 (86%)
3	LA	L 37-32	78 (87%)	70 (78%)	58 (64%)	11 (12%)	43 (48%)	21 (23%)			77 (86%)
4	DEN	L 27-7	62 (87%)	62 (87%)	39 (55%)	8 (11%)	21 (30%)	30 (42%)			67 (94%)
5	CAR	W 17-14	64 (88%)	54 (74%)	31 (42%)	14 (19%)	48 (66%)	68 (93%)			53 (73%)
7	SF	W 34-17	57 (76%)	45 (60%)	38 (51%)	27 (36%)	28 (37%)	51 (68%)		41 (55%)	
8	OAK	L 30-24	60 (88%)	38 (56%)	46 (68%)	24 (35%)	14 (21%)	43 (63%)		37 (54%)	
9	ATL	L 43-28	50 (63%)	53 (66%)	73 (91%)		14 (18%)			23 (29%)	
10	CHI	W 36-10	64 (85%)	48 (64%)	50 (67%)		12 (16%)		31 (41%)	38 (51%)	
11	KC	W 19-17	64 (83%)	62 (81%)	42 (55%)	35 (45%)	22 (29%)		60 (78%)	21 (27%)	
12	SEA	W 14-5	55 (82%)	41 (61%)	39 (58%)	32 (48%)	15 (22%)		53 (79%)	38 (57%)	
13	SD	W 28-21	56 (86%)	40 (62%)	14 (22%)	50 (77%)	39 (60%)	22 (34%)	36 (55%)	1 (2%)	
14	NO	W 16-11	51 (77%)	56 (85%)		45 (68%)	40 (61%)	7 (11%)	44 (67%)		
15	DAL	L 26-20	52 (87%)	51 (85%)	41 (68%)	56 (93%)	3 (5%)		40 (67%)	15 (25%)	
16	NO	L 31-24	55 (90%)	32 (52%)	33 (54%)	52 (85%)	26 (43%)	37 (61%)		25 (41%)	
17	CAR	W 17-16	54 (86%)		37 (59%)	58 (92%)	36 (57%)	43 (68%)		34 (54%)	
Grand Total			946 (84%)	710 (66%)	648 (60%)	432 (46%)	396 (35%)	336 (48%)	321 (59%)	319 (39%)	316 (84%)

Personnel Groupings

Personnel	Team %	NFL Avg	Succ. %
1-1 [3WR]	58%	60%	47%
1-2 [2WR]	31%	19%	46%
1-3 [1WR]	8%	3%	50%

Grouping Tendencies

Personnel	Pass Rate	Pass Succ. %	Run Succ. %
1-1 [3WR]	69%	48%	44%
1-2 [2WR]	41%	50%	43%
1-3 [1WR]	24%	60%	47%

Red Zone Targets (min 3)

Receiver	All	Inside 5	6-10	11-20
Mike Evans	19	6	3	10
Cameron Brate	17	4	5	8
Adam Humphries	10	1	1	8
Russell Shepard	7	1	2	4
Brandon Myers	5	1		4
Vincent Jackson	4			4
Peyton Barber	3		1	2

Red Zone Rushes (min 3)

Rusher	All	Inside 5	6-10	11-20
Doug Martin	23	9	3	11
Jacquizz Rodgers	15	4	1	10
Peyton Barber	8		3	5
Charles Sims	6	3	1	.2
Jameis Winston	5		3	2

Early Down Target Rate

RB	TE	WR
16%	21%	63%
19%	*20% NFL AVG*	*61%*

Overall Target Success %

RB	TE	WR
49% #10	56% #11	51% #10

Tampa Bay Buccaneers 2016 Passing Recap & 2017 Outlook

There aren't many quarterbacks more thankful for the what happened in the offseason than Jameis Winston. He received the speedy DeSean Jackson, a young, skilled rookie TE O.J. Howard and the 4th easiest schedule of opposing defenses next season. Winston's success rate last year was top-11 to each of his position groups (WR, TE, RB). Only 3 other offenses can say the same (CIN, SEA and WAS). And this was despite the significant injuries to all 3 of those position groups in 2016. The upside for Winston this season is substantial. It's also impossible to ignore the fact that when the Bucs get into the red zone, they will have to rely on Winston's passing. That is because last year, their "top" RBs (Doug Martin, Jacquizz Rodgers) each produced a very poor 43% success rate in the red zone. Todd Monken needs to design better red zone passing offense, because apart from Cameron Brate's 59% success rate, the other receivers really struggled. And inside the red zone is the one place that Jackson loses a ton of value because his speed won't soften up defenses, nor does it command double teams. Tampa should avoid 11 personnel in the red zone and pass out of 2+ TE sets, where Winston hit a 60% success rate and a 123 rating with 12 TDs & 0 INTs.

Jameis Winston Rating All Downs

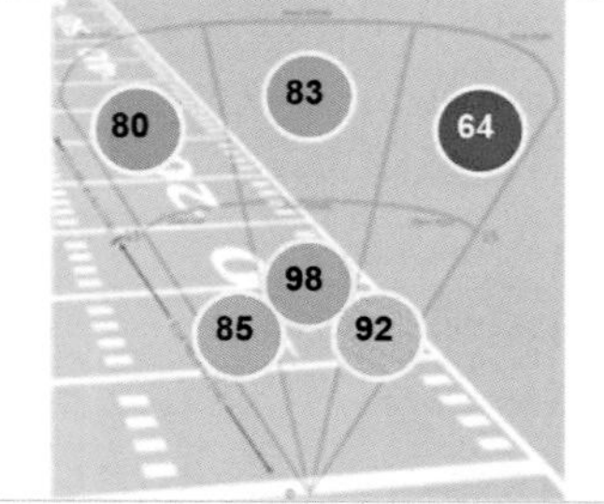

Jameis Winston Rating Early Downs

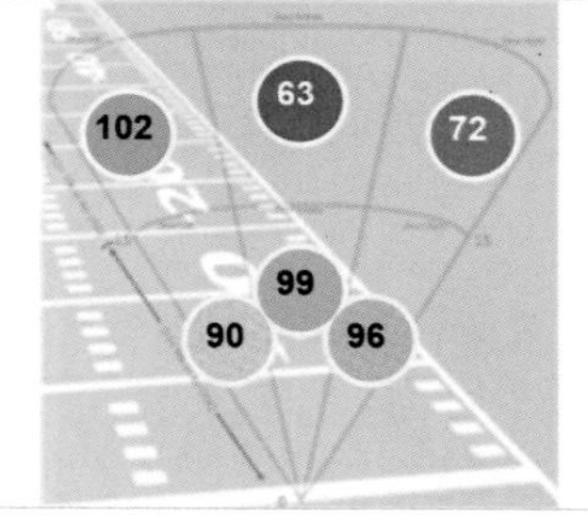

2016 Standard Passing Table

QB	Comp	Att	Comp %	Yds	YPA	TDs	INT	Sacks	Rating	Rk
Jameis Winston	345	570	61%	4,082	7.2	28	18	34	85.6	28
NFL Avg			63%		7.2				90.4	

2016 Advanced Passing Table

QB	Success %	EDSR Passing Success %	20+ Yd Pass Gains	20+ Yd Pass %	30+ Yd Pass Gains	30+ Yd Pass %	Air Yds per Comp	YAC per Comp	20+ Air Yd Comp	20+ Air Yd %
Jameis Winston	48%	50%	43	8%	14	2%	8.0	3.8	21	4%
NFL Avg	44%	48%	27	8%	10	3%	6.4	4.8	12	4%

Interception Rates by Down

Yards to Go	1	2	3	4	Total
1 & 2		0.0%	0.0%	0.0%	0.0%
3, 4, 5	0.0%	0.0%	1.9%		1.3%
6 - 9	0.0%	2.7%	2.2%		2.4%
10 - 14	2.1%	1.1%	7.5%	50.0%	2.8%
15+	8.3%	8.3%	5.3%	33.3%	8.6%
Total	2.4%	2.3%	3.4%	33.3%	3.0%

3rd Down Passing - Short of Sticks Analysis

QB	Avg Yds to Go	Air Yds (of Comps)	Avg Yds Short	Short of Sticks Rate	Rk
Jameis Winston	7.6	9.6	0.0	35%	4
NFL Avg	7.6	6.8	-0.8	57%	

Air Yds vs YAC

Air Yds %	YAC %	Rk
59%	41%	17
54%	46%	

2016 Receiving Recap & 2017 Outlook

With the inclusion of DeSean Jackson and O.J. Howard, it is extremely unlikely Mike Evans sees 171 targets again this season. However, the quality should improve and Evans get more opportunities in the red zone if the offense produces more trips. Instead of just 3 players with at least 50 receiving targets, we likely should see 5 and could see 6. Last year everything on 2nd and 3rd and long seemed destined for Mike Evans, when Winston should be targeting Brate and/or Howard. It will be interesting to see the impact of Jackson's presence on Tampa's 11 personnel, because last year it was their most used but least efficient grouping to pass from.

Player *Min 50 Targets*	Targets	Comp %	YPA	Rating	TOARS	Success %	Success Rk	Missed YPA Rk	YAS % Rk	TDs
Mike Evans	171	56%	7.7	87	5.4	54%	47	102	54	12
Adam Humphries	83	66%	7.5	82	4.3	51%	70	104	116	2
Cameron Brate	82	70%	8.0	126	4.9	60%	17	45	91	8

Directional Passer Rating Delivered

Receiver	Short Left	Short Middle	Short Right	Deep Left	Deep Middle	Deep Right	Player Total
Mike Evans	99	119	67	72	64	56	87
Adam Humphries	87	29	95	17	156	40	82
Cameron Brate	134	125	118	117	106	82	126
Russell Shepard	53	104	78	99	119	78	81
Charles Sims	38	91	122	40		40	74
Vincent Jackson	78	51	90	44	15	0	38
Josh Huff	69		117	40	79		72
Team Total	87	105	93	78	92	49	88

2016 Rushing Recap & 2017 Outlook

Tampa Bay needs a ton of help here and I have a low level of confidence the run game will be significantly better. They were the 5th worst run offense against the 20th rated schedule last year, and their schedule gets more difficult this year. Particularly on first down, the Bucs absolutely have dial up something more efficient. 68 times last year on 1st and long, the Bucs handed the ball off to Doug Martin. And only 38% of those runs were successful. It was one of the worst rates in the NFL. Thus, on average the Bucs were voluntarily agreeing to 2nd and long when handing off to Martin. Whether it is Martin or Jacquizz Rodgers, the Bucs absolutely need to be more successful on early down runs, particularly on first down.

Player *Min 50 Rushes*	Rushes	YPA	Success %	Success Rk	Missed YPA Rk	YTS % Rk	YAS % Rk	Early Down Success %	Early Down Success Rk	TDs
Doug Martin	144	2.9	42%	55	39	5	63	42%	51	3
Jacquizz Rodgers	129	4.3	49%	29	31	26	26	48%	33	2
Peyton Barber	55	4.1	47%	36	18	35	58	50%	22	1
Charles Sims	51	2.9	39%	59	63	6	44	38%	61	1

Yards per Carry by Direction

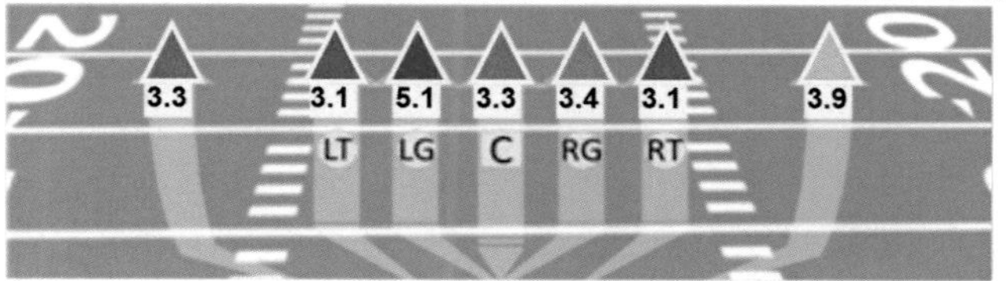

Directional Run Frequency

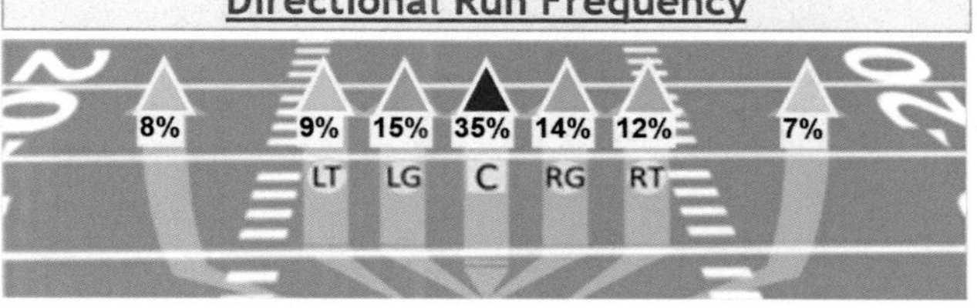

TB-4

One key area of concern the Buccaneers didn't address in free agency but did in the draft was at running back. It's a big area of concern not just because of the depth and injuries, but also because the team was so inefficient last year. Tampa Bay drafted RB Jeremy McNichols out of Boise State in the 5th round. McNichols should start at the bottom of the depth chart and I'm not overly excited about his prospects in the NFL. But there are two things that will certainly help the Bucs this season when it comes to the run game:

The first is J.R. Sweezy along the offensive line. Sweezy was signed last year in free agency from Seattle, but missed the entire season on account of a back injury. His presence will help solidify a stronger line. And then there is the addition of DeSean Jackson. As mentioned above, anytime he lines up on the field it will inherently assist with rushing efficiency. Just ask the mediocre RBs used by the Redskins who were able to produce solid success rates and yards per attempt.

Offensively the Buccaneers should be in a good place so long as they stay healthy. They will be aided by better personnel and an easier schedule. the Buccaneers face the 6th weakest explosive pass defenses from 2016. And overall, the Buccaneers strength of pass defense faced drops from 12th in 2016 to 26th in 2017, the 4th largest drop-off for any team. Under a developing Jameis Winston with limited passing weapons, the Buccaneers pass offense ranked 11th in the NFL last year. With an easier schedule and more weapons, it should create more excitement in 2017.

And this offense better be ready to perform, because the Bucs defense faces the 3rd most difficult schedule of opposing offenses in 2017. Their division foes have predictably tough offenses (Atlanta, New Orleans and Carolina) but they add games against Green Bay, Detroit and New England as well. Which means the Tampa Bay offense will have the need to continue to produce for all 4 quarters, potentially leading to a better fantasy season for this passing offense.

Defensively last season, the Bucs were quite strong against the pass, despite facing the 8th rated schedule of passing offenses. But they were very poor against the run. And that could cause trouble again this season. That is because they play the 3rd most difficult schedule of rushing offenses in 2017, and against the 13th most difficult schedule last year they ranked 24th in run defense efficiency. When you struggle to run the ball, as the Bucs did last year, and you can't stop the run, as the Bucs couldn't last year, it creates big problems from a game script perspective. Tampa Bay will hope the addition of Chris Baker will help in that respect. Baker's 2016 PFF run defense grade was better than any Bucs player in 2016.

If Jameis continues to develop, their new weaponry allows them to run the ball better and their run defense improves, it could signal playoffs in Tampa.

Division History: Season Wins & 2017 Projection

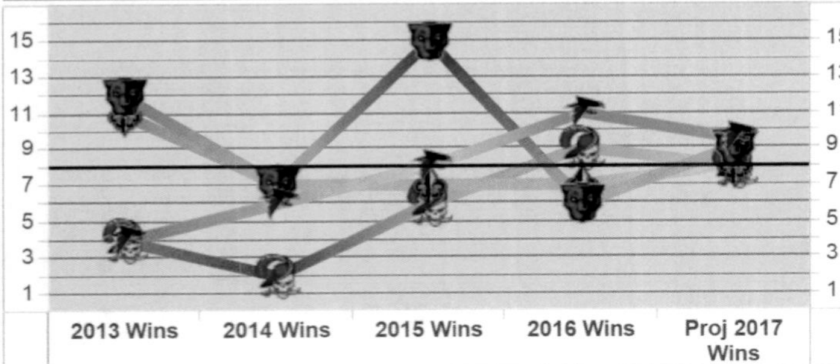

Rank of 2017 Defensive Pass Efficiency Faced by Week

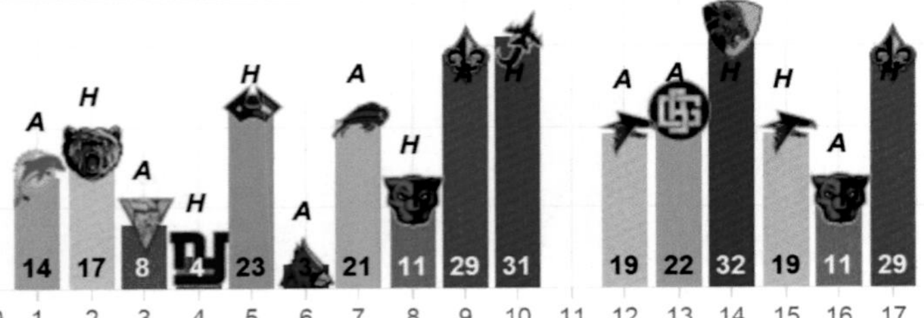

Rank of 2017 Defensive Rush Efficiency Faced by Week

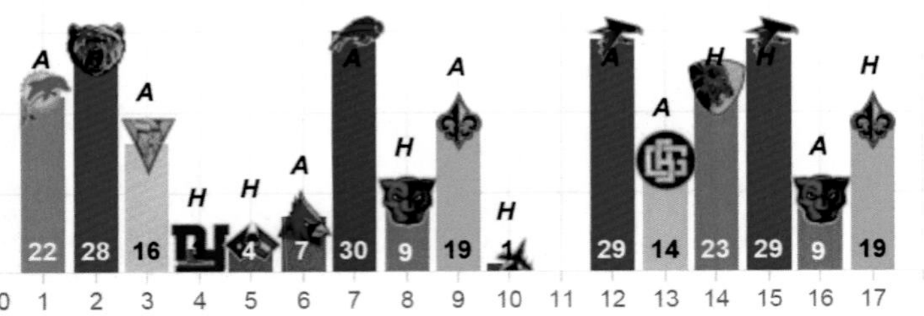

2016 Situational Usage by Player & Position

Usage Rate by Score

		Being Blown Out (14+)	Down Big (9-13)	One Score	Large Lead (9-13)	Blowout Lead (14+)	Grand Total
RUSH	Doug Martin	4%	4%	16%	27%	17%	15%
	Jacquizz Rodgers	6%	8%	16%	9%		13%
	Adam Humphries	1%		0%	2%		1%
	Charles Sims	6%	11%	5%	5%		5%
	Peyton Barber	4%		5%	3%	47%	6%
	Russell Shepard				1%		0%
	Antone Smith		1%	1%			1%
	Mike James			0%	1%	3%	0%
	Josh Huff			0%			0%
	Total	20%	25%	44%	49%	67%	41%
PASS	Mike Evans	27%	17%	16%	22%	11%	18%
	Doug Martin			2%	1%	3%	2%
	Jacquizz Rodgers	2%	1%	2%	1%		2%
	Adam Humphries	12%	11%	8%	6%	8%	9%
	Charles Sims	5%	11%	3%	1%		3%
	Cameron Brate	9%	10%	9%	7%	3%	8%
	Peyton Barber	5%		0%			1%
	Russell Shepard	2%	8%	4%	6%		4%
	Vincent Jackson	5%	3%	4%	1%		3%
	Cecil Shorts	4%	1%	3%	5%	3%	3%
	Antone Smith	3%		1%			1%
	Brandon Myers	3%	6%	1%			1%
	Freddie Martino	2%		1%			1%
	Alan Cross		3%	1%	1%		1%
	Luke Stocker			1%	1%	6%	1%
	Mike James	2%		0%			0%
	Josh Huff	1%	1%	1%			1%
	Austin Seferian-Jenki..	1%	1%	0%			0%
	Total	80%	75%	56%	51%	33%	59%

Positional Target Distribution vs NFL Average

		NFL Wide				Team Only			
		Left	Middle	Right	Total	Left	Middle	Right	Total
Deep	WR	989	562	965	2,516	42	19	36	97
	TE	154	141	160	455	4	6	3	13
	RB	24	4	39	67	1		1	2
	All	1,167	707	1,164	3,038	47	25	40	112
Short	WR	3,000	1,725	3,090	7,815	93	46	96	235
	TE	816	855	1,122	2,793	20	20	29	69
	RB	1,007	616	1,097	2,720	8	6	16	30
	All	4,823	3,196	5,309	13,328	121	72	141	334
Total		5,990	3,903	6,473	16,366	168	97	181	446

Positional Success Rates vs NFL Average

		NFL Wide				Team Only			
		Left	Middle	Right	Total	Left	Middle	Right	Total
Deep	WR	37%	50%	38%	40%	36%	47%	36%	38%
	TE	44%	49%	43%	45%	75%	67%	33%	62%
	RB	33%	75%	26%	31%	0%		0%	0%
	All	38%	50%	38%	41%	38%	52%	35%	40%
Short	WR	52%	57%	51%	53%	58%	57%	59%	58%
	TE	49%	62%	52%	54%	75%	60%	48%	59%
	RB	47%	49%	44%	46%	13%	83%	50%	47%
	All	50%	57%	50%	52%	58%	60%	56%	57%
Total		48%	55%	48%	50%	52%	58%	51%	53%

Tennessee Titans

2017 Coaches

Head Coach:
Mike Mularkey (2nd yr)
Offensive Coordinator:
Terry Robiskie (2nd yr)
Defensive Coordinator:
Dick LeBeau (2nd yr)

2017 Forecast

Wins	Div Rank
8.5	#1

Past Records

2016: 9-7
2015: 3-13
2014: 2-14

EASY HARD

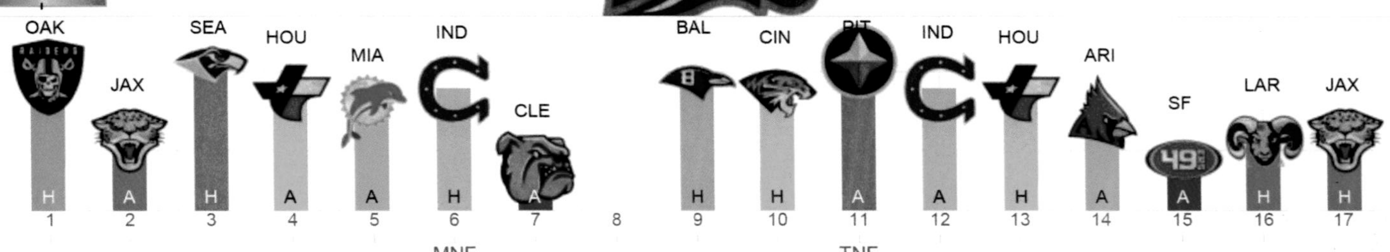

Key Players Lost

TXN	Player (POS)
Cut	Cliett, Reshard LB
	McCourty, Jason CB
	Woods, Al NT
Declared Free Agent	Andrews, Antonio RB
	Bass, David LB
	Bell, Byron G
	Blake, Valentino CB
	Cassel, Matt QB
	Fasano, Anthony TE
	Johnson, Rashad S
	Klug, Karl DT
	Mariani, Marc WR
	Palmer, Nate LB
	Schwenke, Brian C
	Spence, Sean LB
	Stafford, Daimion S
	Supernaw, Phillip TE
	Warmack, Chance G
	Wright, Kendall WR
Retired	Okotcha, Bennett CB

Average Line	# Games Favored	# Games Underdog
-0.4	8	7

2017 Tennessee Titans Overview

The Titans offense improved leaps and bounds in 2016 from what it was in 2015. That was the driver in what propelled them to 9 wins. But as always, we must keep context with performance in the NFL. The Titans were the 2nd most run heavy team in the NFL last year, passing on just 49% of offensive plays in one-score games and 50% overall. The reason they ran so frequently was because they played the easiest schedule of run defenses, facing no team ranking 10th or better, while playing 6 games against team ranking in the bottom 10 in run defense.

While the Titans ran off 9 wins last season vs a projected 5.5 headed into the season, here are the rankings of the run defenses they beat with Marcus Mariota starting at quarterback: 21, 22, 23, 26, 27, 28, *12, **14. *12 Jaguars, led by Blake Bortles, **14 Packers, whose run offense was not nearly as good as 14, as I often discussed throughout the season and in the Packers chapter of this book.

In addition to playing the NFL's easiest run defenses, the Titans played the 2nd easiest schedule of opposing offenses. They played Blake Bortles twice, Brock Osweiler twice, Matt Barkley, Trevor Siemian and Cody Kessler. They were able to call 298 plays when leading by 7+ points, the 8th most in the NFL. And they ran the ball on 55% of these plays (NFL average was 51% run when leading by 7+ points).

It's amazing when looking at the Titans most frequent play calls (see the 4th page of this chapter) that based on 4 different distances "to go" for each down, it's not until 3rd and medium that the Titans called a play more often than a DeMarco Murray run. For all four distances "to go" on 1st down and all four distances "to go" on 2nd down and on 3rd and short, the Titans most frequent play was a DeMarco Murray run. Murray was a massive force who also was not just the most utilized red zone rusher on the Titans by a landslide margin, he was also the most utilized red zone receiver as well. Combined, Murray saw a whopping 36 touches/targets inside the 10 yard line – no other Titan saw more than 11.

If this usage of the run game occurred for some other quarterbacks, and those quarterbacks numbers were poor and inefficient, I would argue the team was intentionally trying to hide their

(cont'd - see TEN2)

Key Free Agents/ Trades Added

Bates, Daren LB
Cyprien, Johnathan S
Gay, Jordan K
Hartfield, Trevon CB
Hurst, Demontre CB
Lelito, Tim G
Ryan, Logan CB
Trawick, Brynden S
Weems, Eric WR
Williams, Sylvester NT

Drafted Players

Rd	Pk	Player (College)
1	5	WR - Corey Davis (Western Michigan)
	18	CB - Adoree' Jackson (USC)
3	72	WR - Taywan Taylor (Western Kentucky)
3*	100	TE - Jonnu Smith (Florida International)
5	155	LB - Jayon Brown (UCLA)
6*	217	G - Corey Levin (Chattanooga)
	227	OLB - Josh Carraway (TCU)
7	236	OT - Brad Seaton (Villanova)
	241	RB - Khalfani Muhammad (California)

Regular Season Wins: Past & Current Proj

Proj 2017 Wins  8.5

2016 Wins  9

Proj 2016 Wins  5.5

  3

 2

  7

1 3 5 7 9 11 13 15

2017 Lineup & Cap Hits

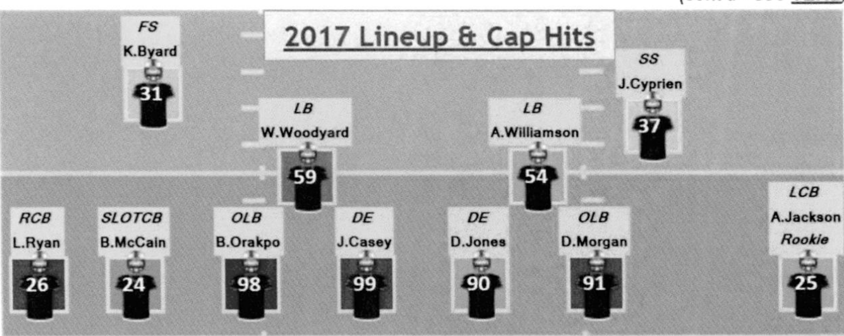

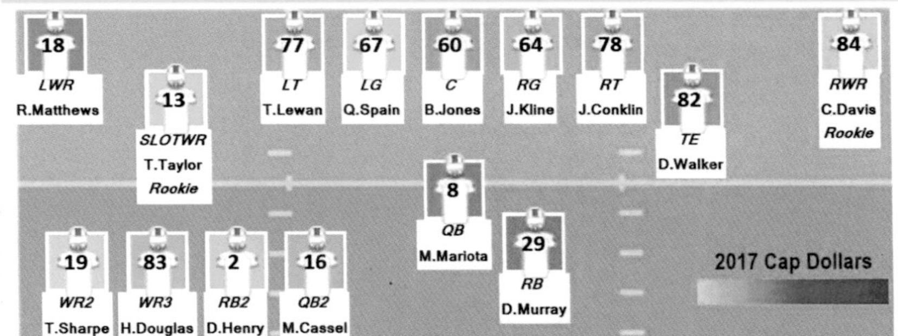

2017 Unit Spending

Positional Spending

	Rank	Total	2016 Rk
All OFF	32	$64.86M	24
QB	23	$10.36M	30
OL	30	$20.42M	21
RB	10	$9.67M	11
WR	23	$15.25M	19
TE	16	$9.17M	5
All DEF	10	$83.85M	17
DL	19	$22.08M	21
LB	5	$30.72M	6
CB	21	$16.77M	19
S	8	$14.29M	17

Tennessee Titans 2016 Success Rate Radar

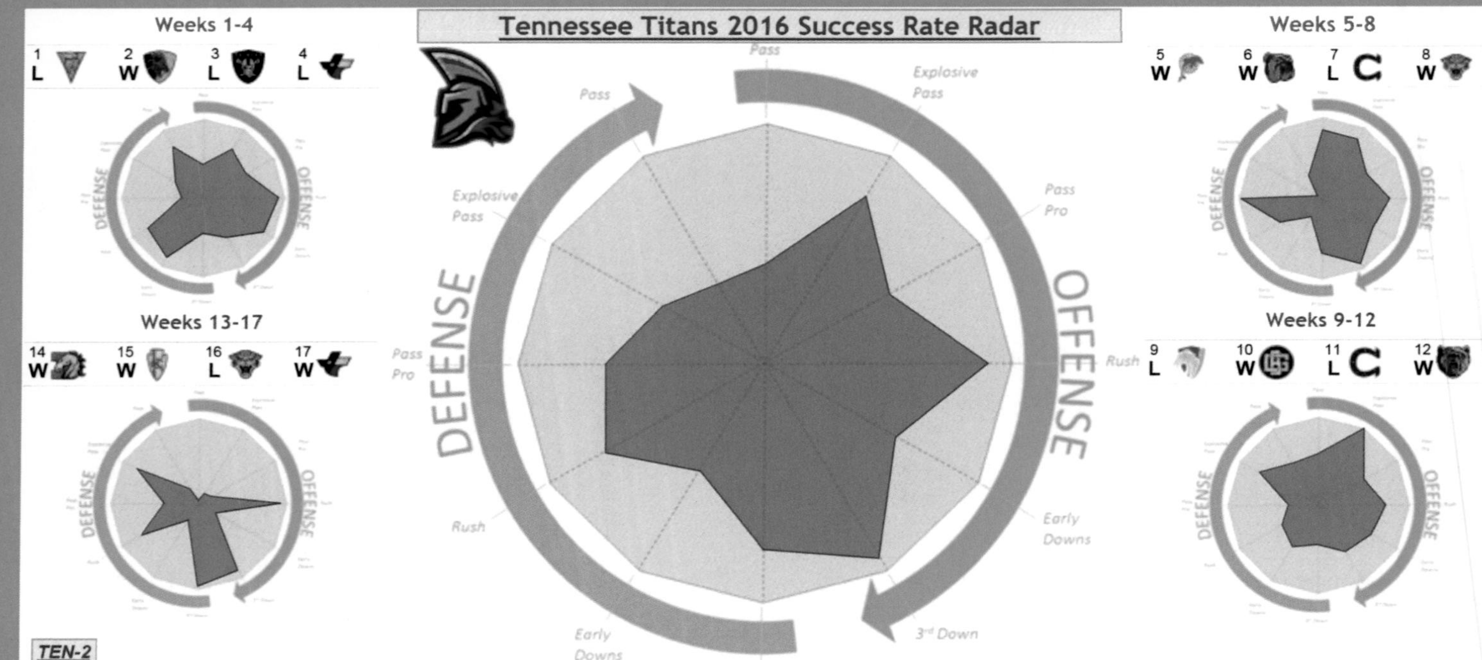

TEN-2

quarterback due to his struggles. But such was not the case for the Titans. They simply were using the most efficient path to victory. They played defenses weak against the run and ran the ball. A lot. It was smart. They were smart in other decisions to run the ball, which again was smart, as opposed to hiding the pass game. For instance, on second and short, the Titans ran the ball on 85% of their play calls. That was 2nd most in the NFL, with the average being 65%. They ended up gaining first downs on 82% of those runs, nearly 11% above the NLF average. And because they were so run heavy, they had a slight edge in the pass game due to tendencies. So when they passed the ball on second and short, they converted 60% of the time, still above the 52% league average. Clearly, their 82% success rate when rushing dwarfed the 60% conversion rate when passing, but you can't run the ball much more often in a given down/distance than 85% of the time.

To further support the fact that the Titans were simply playing the most +EV strategy, rather than hiding their passing game, Marcus Mariota was extremely sol.. of his receivers and the average pass protection he got from his offensive line. While absorbing 24 sacks, Mariota posted a 95 rating (NFL average = 90), a 25:9 TD:INT ratio and 7.6 yards per attempt (NFL average = 7.2). In addition, his completions averaged 8.1 air yards (NFL average of 6.4) and he threw just 51% of his 3rd down completions short of the sticks (13th best in the NFL). And that was with a lack of receiving talent in Tennessee, and against the 14th ranked schedule of opposing defenses.

But that's not to say Mariota was didn't make his share of mistakes and can't improve on his efficiency to give a massive boost to the Titans. On early downs in the first quarter, due in part to play scripting, Mariota recorded a 100 passer rating, averaged 8.2 yards per attempt and completed 69% of his passes. However, after the first quarter, his early down passer rating dropped to 81 (25th in the NFL), he averaged just 6.3 yards per attempt and completed just 57% of his passes.

(cont'd - see TEN-3)

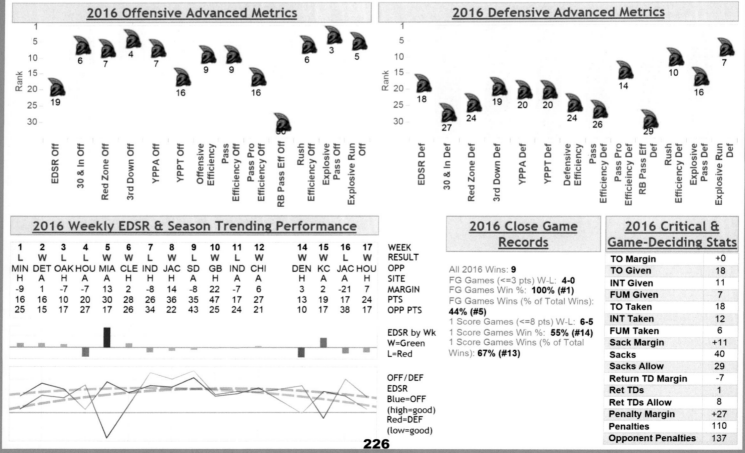

2016 Offensive Advanced Metrics

Metric	Rank
EDSR Off	19
30 & In Off	6
Red Zone Off	7
3rd Down Off	4
YPPA Off	7
YPPT Off	16
Offensive Efficiency	9
Pass Efficiency Off	9
Pass Pro Efficiency Off	16
RB Pass Eff Off	30
Rush Efficiency Off	6
Explosive Pass Off	3
Explosive Run Off	5

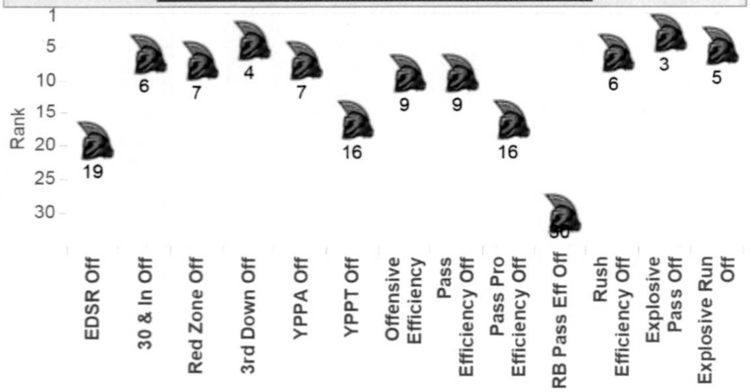

2016 Defensive Advanced Metrics

Metric	Rank
EDSR Def	18
30 & In Def	27
Red Zone Def	24
3rd Down Def	19
YPPA Def	20
YPPT Def	20
Defensive Efficiency	24
Pass Efficiency Def	26
Pass Pro Efficiency Def	14
RB Pass Eff Def	29
Rush Efficiency Def	10
Explosive Pass Def	16
Explosive Run Def	7

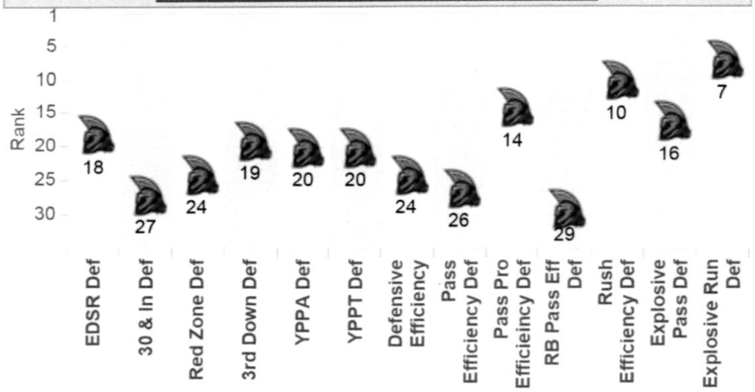

2016 Weekly EDSR & Season Trending Performance

1	2	3	4	5	6	7	8	9	10	11	12		14	15	16	17	WEEK
L	W	L	L	W	W	L	W	L	W	L	W		W	W	L	W	RESULT
MIN	DET	OAK	HOU	MIA	CLE	IND	JAC	SD	GB	IND	CHI		DEN	KC	JAC	HOU	OPP
H	A	H	A	A	H	H	H	A	H	A	A		H	A	A	H	SITE
-9	1	-7	-7	13	2	-8	14	-8	22	-7	6		3	2	-21	7	MARGIN
16	16	10	20	30	28	26	36	35	47	17	27		13	19	17	24	PTS
25	15	17	27	17	26	34	22	43	25	24	21		10	17	38	17	OPP PTS

EDSR by Wk
W=Green
L=Red

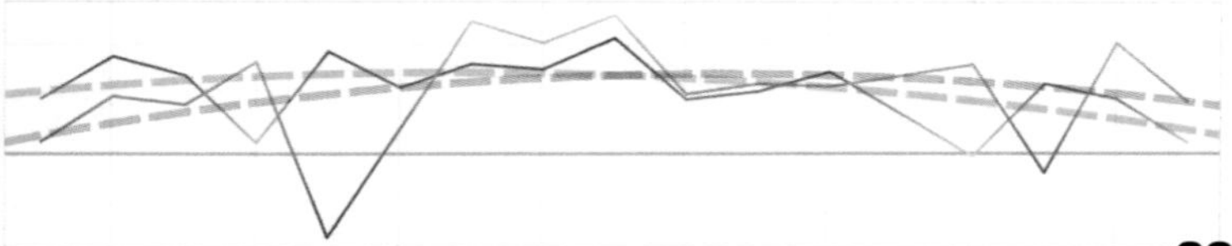

OFF/DEF EDSR
Blue=OFF (high=good)
Red=DEF (low=good)

2016 Close Game Records

All 2016 Wins: **9**
FG Games (<=3 pts) W-L: **4-0**
FG Games Win %: **100% (#1)**
FG Games Wins (% of Total Wins): **44% (#5)**
1 Score Games (<=8 pts) W-L: **6-5**
1 Score Games Win %: **55% (#14)**
1 Score Games Wins (% of Total Wins): **67% (#13)**

2016 Critical & Game-Deciding Stats

TO Margin	+0
TO Given	18
INT Given	11
FUM Given	7
TO Taken	18
INT Taken	12
FUM Taken	6
Sack Margin	+11
Sacks	40
Sacks Allow	29
Return TD Margin	-7
Ret TDs	1
Ret TDs Allow	8
Penalty Margin	+27
Penalties	110
Opponent Penalties	137

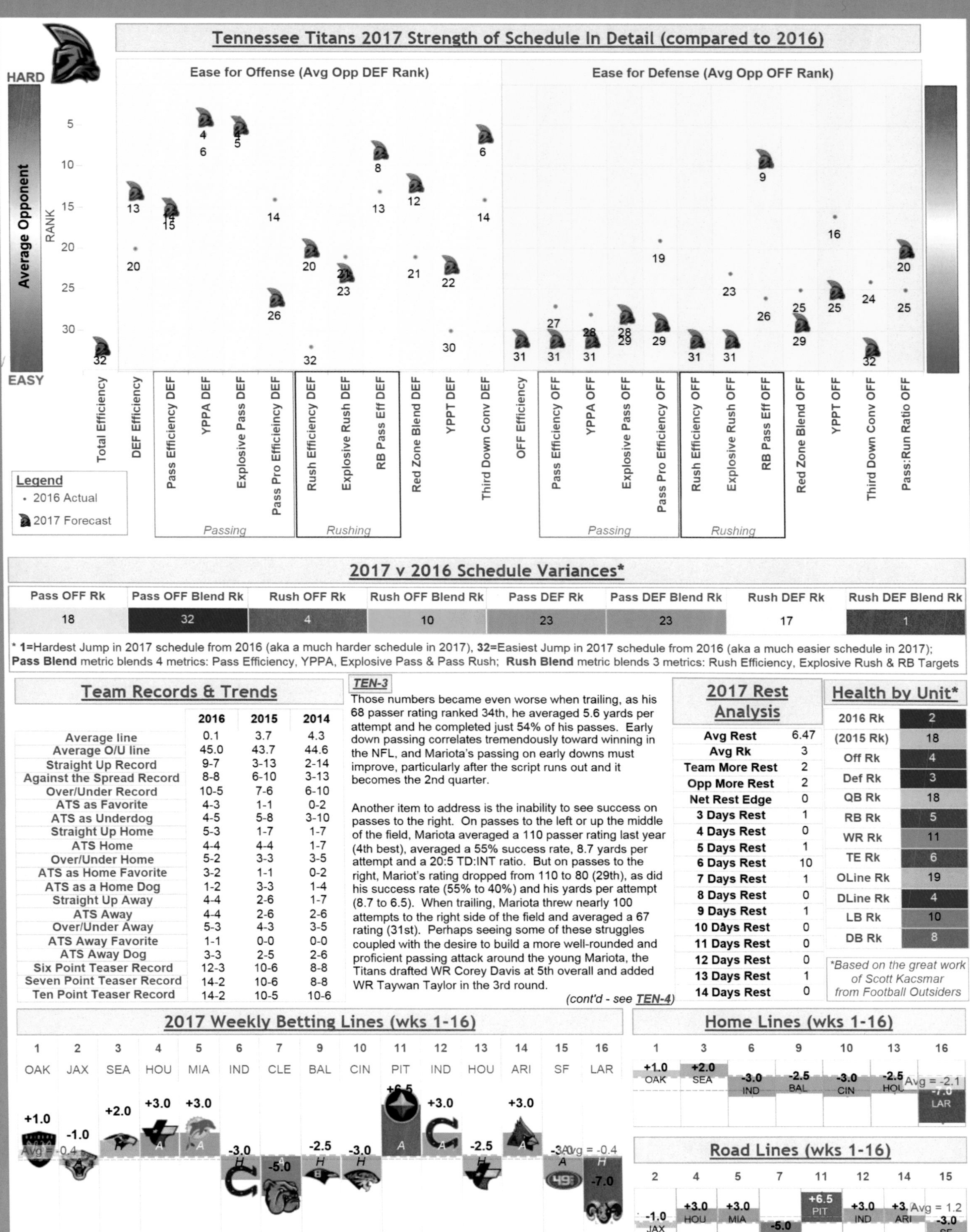

Tennessee Titans 2017 Strength of Schedule In Detail (compared to 2016)

2017 v 2016 Schedule Variances*

Pass OFF Rk	Pass OFF Blend Rk	Rush OFF Rk	Rush OFF Blend Rk	Pass DEF Rk	Pass DEF Blend Rk	Rush DEF Rk	Rush DEF Blend Rk
18	32	4	10	23	23	17	1

* **1**=Hardest Jump in 2017 schedule from 2016 (aka a much harder schedule in 2017), **32**=Easiest Jump in 2017 schedule from 2016 (aka a much easier schedule in 2017); **Pass Blend** metric blends 4 metrics: Pass Efficiency, YPPA, Explosive Pass & Pass Rush; **Rush Blend** metric blends 3 metrics: Rush Efficiency, Explosive Rush & RB Targets

Team Records & Trends

	2016	2015	2014
Average line	0.1	3.7	4.3
Average O/U line	45.0	43.7	44.6
Straight Up Record	9-7	3-13	2-14
Against the Spread Record	8-8	6-10	3-13
Over/Under Record	10-5	7-6	6-10
ATS as Favorite	4-3	1-1	0-2
ATS as Underdog	4-5	5-8	3-10
Straight Up Home	5-3	1-7	1-7
ATS Home	4-4	4-4	1-7
Over/Under Home	5-2	3-3	3-5
ATS as Home Favorite	3-2	1-1	0-2
ATS as a Home Dog	1-2	3-3	1-4
Straight Up Away	4-4	2-6	1-7
ATS Away	4-4	2-6	2-6
Over/Under Away	5-3	4-3	3-5
ATS Away Favorite	1-1	0-0	0-0
ATS Away Dog	3-3	2-5	2-6
Six Point Teaser Record	12-3	10-6	8-8
Seven Point Teaser Record	14-2	10-6	8-8
Ten Point Teaser Record	14-2	10-5	10-6

TEN-3

Those numbers became even worse when trailing, as his 68 passer rating ranked 34th, he averaged 5.6 yards per attempt and he completed just 54% of his passes. Early down passing correlates tremendously toward winning in the NFL, and Mariota's passing on early downs must improve, particularly after the script runs out and it becomes the 2nd quarter.

Another item to address is the inability to see success on passes to the right. On passes to the left or up the middle of the field, Mariota averaged a 110 passer rating last year (4th best), averaged a 55% success rate, 8.7 yards per attempt and a 20:5 TD:INT ratio. But on passes to the right, Mariot's rating dropped from 110 to 80 (29th), as did his success rate (55% to 40%) and his yards per attempt (8.7 to 6.5). When trailing, Mariota threw nearly 100 attempts to the right side of the field and averaged a 67 rating (31st). Perhaps seeing some of these struggles coupled with the desire to build a more well-rounded and proficient passing attack around the young Mariota, the Titans drafted WR Corey Davis at 5th overall and added WR Taywan Taylor in the 3rd round.

(cont'd - see *TEN-4*)

2017 Rest Analysis

Avg Rest	6.47
Avg Rk	3
Team More Rest	2
Opp More Rest	2
Net Rest Edge	0
3 Days Rest	1
4 Days Rest	0
5 Days Rest	1
6 Days Rest	10
7 Days Rest	1
8 Days Rest	0
9 Days Rest	1
10 Days Rest	0
11 Days Rest	0
12 Days Rest	0
13 Days Rest	1
14 Days Rest	0

Health by Unit*

2016 Rk	2
(2015 Rk)	18
Off Rk	4
Def Rk	3
QB Rk	18
RB Rk	5
WR Rk	11
TE Rk	6
OLine Rk	19
DLine Rk	4
LB Rk	10
DB Rk	8

**Based on the great work of Scott Kacsmar from Football Outsiders*

2017 Weekly Betting Lines (wks 1-16)

1	2	3	4	5	6	7	9	10	11	12	13	14	15	16
OAK	JAX	SEA	HOU	MIA	IND	CLE	BAL	CIN	PIT	IND	HOU	ARI	SF	LAR
			A	A	H	A	H	H	A	A	H	A	A	H
+1.0	-1.0	+2.0	+3.0	+3.0	-3.0	-5.0	-2.5	-3.0	+6.5	+3.0	-2.5	+3.0	-3.0	-7.0

Avg = -0.4

Home Lines (wks 1-16)

1	3	6	9	10	13	16
OAK	SEA	IND	BAL	CIN	HOU	LAR
+1.0	+2.0	-3.0	-2.5	-3.0	-2.5	-7.0

Avg = -2.1

Road Lines (wks 1-16)

2	4	5	7	11	12	14	15
JAX	HOU	MIA	CLE	PIT	IND	ARI	SF
-1.0	+3.0	+3.0	-5.0	+6.5	+3.0	+3.0	-3.0

Avg = 1.2

Tennessee Titans 2016 Play Analysis

2016 Play Tendencies

All Pass %	50%
All Pass Rk	31
All Rush %	50%
All Rush Rk	2
1 Score Pass %	49%
1 Score Pass Rk	31
2015 1 Score Pass %	58%
2015 1 Score Pass Rk	19
Pass Increase %	-8%
Pass Increase Rk	31
1 Score Rush %	51%
1 Score Rush Rk	2
Up Pass %	51%
Up Pass Rk	29
Up Rush %	49%
Up Rush Rk	4
Down Pass %	53%
Down Pass Rk	30
Down Rush %	47%
Down Rush Rk	3

2016 Down & Distance Tendencies

Down	Distance	Total Plays	Pass Rate	Run Rate	Play Success %
1	Short (1-3)	5	40%	60%	40%
	Med (4-7)	17	29%	71%	59%
	Long (8-10)	287	45%	55%	52%
	XL (11+)	16	50%	50%	13%
2	Short (1-3)	46	24%	76%	74%
	Med (4-7)	75	37%	63%	67%
	Long (8-10)	84	43%	57%	50%
	XL (11+)	39	62%	38%	23%
3	Short (1-3)	55	51%	49%	58%
	Med (4-7)	46	93%	7%	54%
	Long (8-10)	18	100%	0%	33%
	XL (11+)	30	83%	17%	23%
4	Short (1-3)	2	0%	100%	50%
	Med (4-7)	2	100%	0%	0%

Shotgun %:

Under Center	Shotgun
47%	53%
37%	*63%*

37% AVG 63%

Run Rate:

Under Center	Shotgun
77%	18%

68% AVG 23%

Pass Rate:

Under Center	Shotgun
23%	82%

32% AVG 77%

Short Yardage Intelligence:

2nd and Short Run

Run Freq	Run % Rk	NFL Run Freq Avg	Run 1D Rate	Run NFL 1D Avg
85%	2	65%	82%	71%

2nd and Short Pass

Pass Freq	Pass % Rk	NFL Pass Freq Avg	Pass 1D Rate	Pass NFL 1D Avg
15%	31	35%	60%	52%

Most Frequent Play

Down	Distance	Play Type	Player	Total Plays	Play Success %
1	Short (1-3)	RUSH	DeMarco Murray	3	67%
	Med (4-7)	RUSH	DeMarco Murray	10	60%
	Long (8-10)	RUSH	DeMarco Murray	103	49%
	XL (11+)	RUSH	DeMarco Murray	7	0%
2	Short (1-3)	RUSH	DeMarco Murray	22	77%
	Med (4-7)	RUSH	DeMarco Murray	32	66%
	Long (8-10)	RUSH	DeMarco Murray	22	27%
	XL (11+)	RUSH	DeMarco Murray	8	0%
3	Short (1-3)	RUSH	DeMarco Murray	16	56%
	Med (4-7)	PASS	Delanie Walker	15	53%
	Long (8-10)	PASS	Rishard Matthews	6	50%
	XL (11+)	PASS	Delanie Walker	5	0%
			Tajae Sharpe	5	60%

Most Successful Play*

Down	Distance	Play Type	Player	Total Plays	Play Success %
1	Med (4-7)	RUSH	DeMarco Murray	10	60%
	Long (8-10)	RUSH	Marcus Mariota	16	75%
	XL (11+)	RUSH	DeMarco Murray	7	0%
2	Short (1-3)	RUSH	Derrick Henry	11	82%
	Med (4-7)	PASS	Tajae Sharpe	5	80%
	Long (8-10)	RUSH	Marcus Mariota	7	100%
	XL (11+)	RUSH	DeMarco Murray	8	0%
3	Short (1-3)	RUSH	Marcus Mariota	5	100%
	Med (4-7)	PASS	DeMarco Murray	6	67%
	Long (8-10)	PASS	Rishard Matthews	6	50%
	XL (11+)	PASS	Tajae Sharpe	5	60%

**Minimum 5 plays to qualify*

2016 Snap Rates

Week	Opp	Score	DeMarco Murray	Tajae Sharpe	Rishard Matthews	Delanie Walker	Anthony Fasano	Kendall Wright	Phillip Supernaw
1	MIN	L 25-16	50 (75%)	61 (91%)	35 (52%)	54 (81%)	25 (37%)		13 (19%)
2	DET	W 16-15	41 (61%)	67 (100%)	36 (54%)	50 (75%)	46 (69%)		18 (27%)
3	OAK	L 17-10	51 (75%)	51 (75%)	43 (63%)		38 (56%)		30 (44%)
4	HOU	L 27-20	64 (96%)	59 (88%)	25 (37%)	36 (54%)	31 (46%)	25 (37%)	32 (48%)
5	MIA	W 30-17	60 (81%)	59 (80%)	41 (55%)	43 (58%)	38 (51%)	22 (30%)	33 (45%)
6	CLE	W 28-26	59 (95%)	48 (77%)	25 (40%)	42 (68%)	33 (53%)	22 (35%)	26 (42%)
7	IND	L 34-26	70 (96%)	61 (84%)	49 (67%)	54 (74%)	23 (32%)	37 (51%)	19 (26%)
8	JAC	W 36-22	39 (58%)	37 (55%)	59 (88%)	43 (64%)	40 (60%)	26 (39%)	33 (49%)
9	SD	L 43-35	62 (95%)	54 (83%)	58 (89%)	52 (80%)	26 (40%)	44 (68%)	6 (9%)
10	GB	W 47-25	46 (77%)	36 (60%)	49 (82%)	49 (82%)	33 (55%)	26 (43%)	17 (28%)
11	IND	L 24-17	70 (99%)	61 (86%)	66 (93%)	53 (75%)	28 (39%)	38 (54%)	11 (15%)
12	CHI	W 27-21	51 (88%)	41 (71%)	51 (88%)	47 (81%)	27 (47%)	16 (28%)	
14	DEN	W 13-10	54 (81%)	46 (69%)	62 (93%)	46 (69%)	42 (63%)		21 (31%)
15	KC	W 19-17	52 (79%)	52 (79%)	63 (95%)	45 (68%)	33 (50%)	27 (41%)	7 (11%)
16	JAC	L 38-17	60 (85%)	35 (49%)	67 (94%)	58 (82%)	31 (44%)	27 (38%)	17 (24%)
17	HOU	W 24-17	33 (54%)	17 (28%)	55 (90%)	34 (56%)	43 (70%)		17 (28%)
Grand Total			862 (81%)	785 (73%)	784 (74%)	706 (71%)	537 (51%)	310 (42%)	300 (30%)

Personnel Groupings

Personnel	Team %	NFL Avg	Succ. %
1-1 [3WR]	42%	60%	50%
1-2 [2WR]	21%	19%	51%
2-1 [2WR]	14%	7%	35%
2-2 [1WR]	9%	3%	48%
1-3 [1WR]	9%	3%	46%

Grouping Tendencies

Personnel	Pass Rate	Pass Succ. %	Run Succ. %
1-1 [3WR]	74%	46%	62%
1-2 [2WR]	43%	42%	57%
2-1 [2WR]	45%	35%	36%
2-2 [1WR]	13%	25%	52%
1-3 [1WR]	30%	54%	43%

Red Zone Targets (min 3)

Receiver	All	Inside 5	6-10	11-20
DeMarco Murray	18	3	4	11
Delanie Walker	17	2	5	10
Rishard Matthews	15	5	2	8
Tajae Sharpe	5		2	3
Andre Johnson	3	1	1	1
Derrick Henry	3			3
Harry Douglas	3	1		2
Kendall Wright	3	1	1	1

Red Zone Rushes (min 3)

Rusher	All	Inside 5	6-10	11-20
DeMarco Murray	44	15	14	15
Derrick Henry	22	4	7	11
Marcus Mariota	9	1	2	6

Early Down Target Rate

	RB	TE	WR
	17%	26%	57%
NFL AVG	*19%*	*20%*	*61%*

Overall Target Success %

RB	TE	WR
38% #30	50% #24	51% #12

Tennessee Titans 2016 Passing Recap & 2017 Outlook

Mariota's 2016 was better in some cases than expected, worse in others. The chapter analysis broke him down in detail. The real question is his development ahead for 2017, because he is still making mistakes a lot of young quarterbacks make. For example, over half (5) of his interceptions came on first and 10 last year. And after those scripted first quarter plays are over, it becomes even worse. On first down, Mariota didn't throw a single first quarter interception last year, but threw 5 on first down in quarters 2-4. If Mariota can clean up his play after the first quarter and can improve on his passing to the right side of the field, this offense will get dangerous, quickly. Mariota and the Titans also need to improve on their targeting of the running backs in the pass game. They target the RB 2% less than average, but only 38% of the time were those targets successful, ranking 30th in the NFL. One benefit for the Titans offense is the flexibility to run so many different formations offensively. No one formation was particularly dominant over the other, although they saw their best passing success when passing from a run heavy 13 personnel set, followed by the more traditional 11 personnel set.

Marcus Mariota Rating All Downs

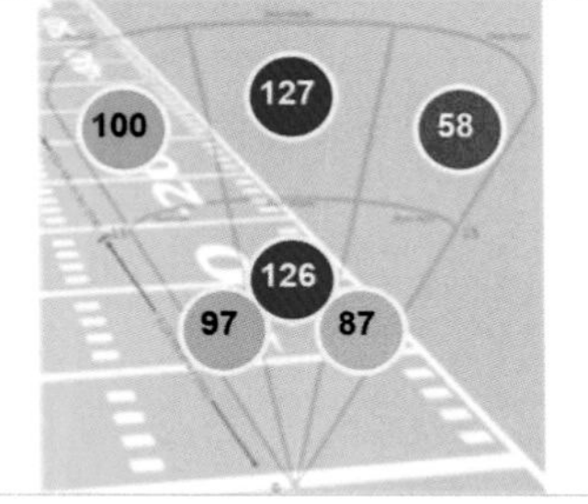

Marcus Mariota Rating Early Downs

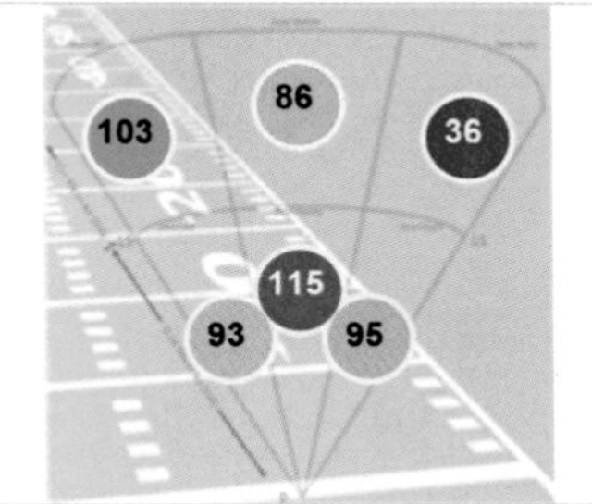

2016 Standard Passing Table

QB	Comp	Att	Comp %	Yds	YPA	TDs	INT	Sacks	Rating	Rk
Marcus Mariota	275	450	61%	3,416	7.6	25	9	24	94.8	15
NFL Avg			63%		7.2				90.4	

2016 Advanced Passing Table

QB	Success %	EDSR Passing Success %	20+ Yd Pass Gains	20+ Yd Pass %	30+ Yd Pass Gains	30+ Yd Pass %	Air Yds per Comp	YAC per Comp	20+ Air Yd Comp	20+ Air Yd %
Marcus Mariota	45%	47%	50	11%	19	4%	8.1	4.3	26	6%
NFL Avg	44%	48%	27	8%	10	3%	6.4	4.8	12	4%

Interception Rates by Down

Yards to Go	1	2	3	4	Total
1 & 2	0.0%	0.0%	6.3%	0.0%	4.5%
3, 4, 5	0.0%	4.3%	2.0%	0.0%	2.5%
6 - 9	0.0%	0.0%	2.3%	0.0%	1.2%
10 - 14	2.9%	0.0%	0.0%		2.0%
15+	0.0%	0.0%	0.0%		0.0%
Total	2.6%	0.8%	2.0%	0.0%	1.9%

3rd Down Passing - Short of Sticks Analysis

QB	Avg Yds to Go	Air Yds (of Comps)	Avg Yds Short	Short of Sticks Rate	Rk
Marcus Mariota	7.9	8.1	0.0	51%	13
NFL Avg	7.6	6.8	-0.8	57%	

Air Yds vs YAC

Air Yds %	YAC %	Rk
63%	37%	8
54%	46%	

2016 Receiving Recap & 2017 Outlook

The draft acquisitions of Corey Davis and Taywan Taylor should give the Titans even more flexibility offensively than they had in 2016. With Rishard Matthews and Davis outside and Taylor operating from the slot, the Titans could go to more 11 personnel than they did in 2016, which was tied for 2nd least often in the NFL. They far more 22 and 21 personnel than average, having more comfort in their running backs, TEs as opposed to their WR3 last year. But to make more of an impact, they need to play strongly enough to convince the OC to pass more often in the red zone, as there were not enough red zone targets for the WRs.

Player *Min 50 Targets*	Targets	Comp %	YPA	Rating	TOARS	Success %	Success Rk	Missed YPA Rk	YAS % Rk	TDs
Rishard Matthews	108	60%	8.8	101	4.9	55%	40	20	76	9
Delanie Walker	102	64%	7.8	98	4.8	49%	83	121	73	7
Tajae Sharpe	83	49%	6.3	72	4.1	46%	110	130	80	2
DeMarco Murray	67	79%	5.6	105	4.1	36%	143	117	139	3

Directional Passer Rating Delivered

Receiver	Short Left	Short Middle	Short Right	Deep Left	Deep Middle	Deep Right	Player Total
Rishard Matthews	124	112	85	138	141	50	106
Delanie Walker	89	147	90	98	87	50	98
Tajae Sharpe	65	69	64	74	118	84	72
DeMarco Murray	100	128	91				105
Kendall Wright	71	87	83	158		104	102
Harry Douglas	36		93	96	119	88	80
Team Total	88	128	85	102	130	64	96

2016 Rushing Recap & 2017 Outlook

When the Titans line up in 21 personnel (2 RBs, 1 TE, 2 WRs) they are fairly balanced in their play selection. But they may want to use this formation less often. They use it twice as often as the NFL average but it is by far their least successful formation. Similarly, when they go full jumbo package with 22 personnel, they should always run it, as their success rate when passing is terrible out of that formation. I expect Henry, who exhibited a better success rate, especially on early downs, to get more work. He did not have the burst or explosiveness last year that Murray did, as referenced by their ranking in YAS (yards above successful). The key question is how much does Henry eat in the red zone this year?

Player *Min 50 Rushes*	Rushes	YPA	Success %	Success Rk	Missed YPA Rk	YTS % Rk	YAS % Rk	Early Down Success %	Early Down Success Rk	TDs
DeMarco Murray	293	4.4	51%	21	26	46	19	49%	30	9
Derrick Henry	110	4.5	55%	9	24	18	38	56%	7	5

Yards per Carry by Direction

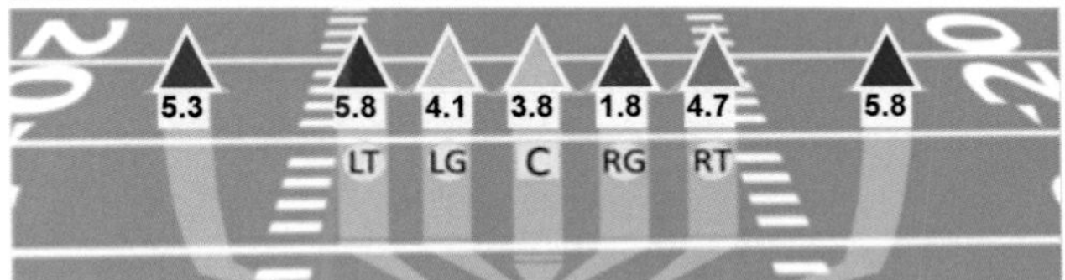

Directional Run Frequency

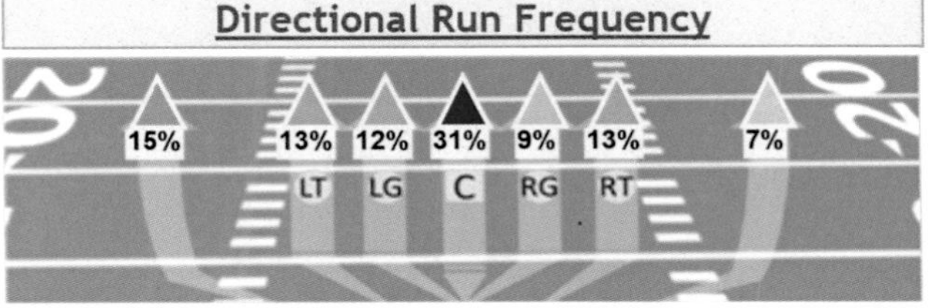

TEN-4

Assuming he's healthy, Davis appears to be well suited for the #1 receiver role, but he will have to earn it because WR Rishard Matthews, in his first season in Tennessee, built a great comrade with Mariota and delivered a very solid stat line.

What are some positives from the passing game in 2017? Unlike 2016, where the Titans played the 14th rated pass rushing defenses, which helped parlay into the 4th best defenses preventing explosive passes, it's much easier this year. The Titans play the 26th rated pass rushing defenses and likely as a result, these defenses allow the 2nd highest rate of explosive passes. In Nashville, that's literally music to the ears of Mariota, Matthews and Davis. Matthews was the most dominant deep threat for the Titans last year, and delivered a 138 rating deep left and a 141 rating deep middle. [Likely on account of Mariota's struggles deep right, discussed earlier, Matthews rating to the deep right was only 50, the same as Delanie Walker's.]

So where does all of this leave the Titans in 2017? It's impossible for the run schedule for their offense to get easier than 2016, when it was the "easiest in the NFL". It still is easier than average, but should be more difficult and challenging than last year. However, given the opportunity to face the NFL's 2nd easiest schedule of opposing offenses should allow the Titans to continue to run the ball thanks to game script.

The passing schedule should be able to provide the punch the offense was looking for. Even against the 4th toughest explosive pass defenses from 2016, the Titans passing offense actually ranked 3rd in explosive pass offense. Now they added multiple talented WRs through the draft and face far worse pass rushes and the 2nd easiest schedule of explosive pass defenses. Thus, the setup is perfect for the Titans if they want to pass early to gain a lead, and run late. Or, in the case of them falling behind, these explosive pass defenses with mediocre pass rushes should allow Mariota to will his team back into the game.

But that assumes, as we all believe, Marcus Mariota takes that next step, particularly when trailing. And as mentioned earlier, Mariota's performance when trailing after the first quarter was particularly troubling in 2016. Count me as a believer in his ability to take that next step. However, with Mariota fracturing his fibula in their week 16 game last year he is on the mend. They hope to use Mariota in a lot of 7-on-7 drills so at least he can get familiar with his new receiving weapons but there is no doubt that incorporating new targets & fixing problem areas with such limitations isn't ideal.

The trouble with Tennessee for 2017 is the AFC South is more competitive than ever With the new GM in Indianapolis, the new quarterback in Houston and the new philosophy in Jacksonville, it won't be easy to post a winning record in 2017, let alone exceed last year's 9 wins.

Division History: Season Wins & 2017 Projection

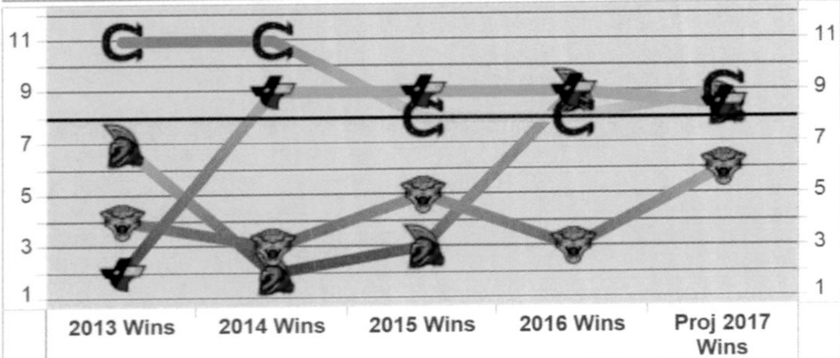

Rank of 2017 Defensive Pass Efficiency Faced by Week

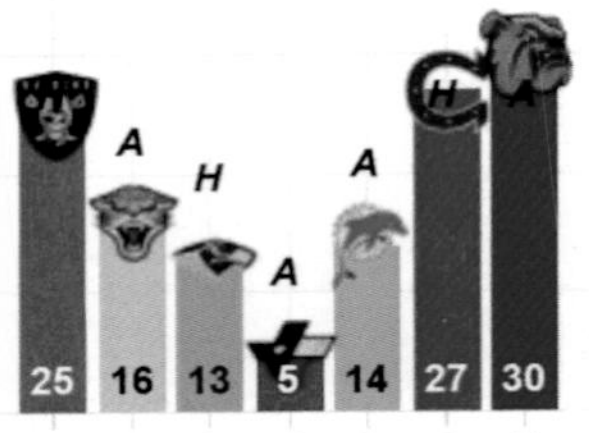

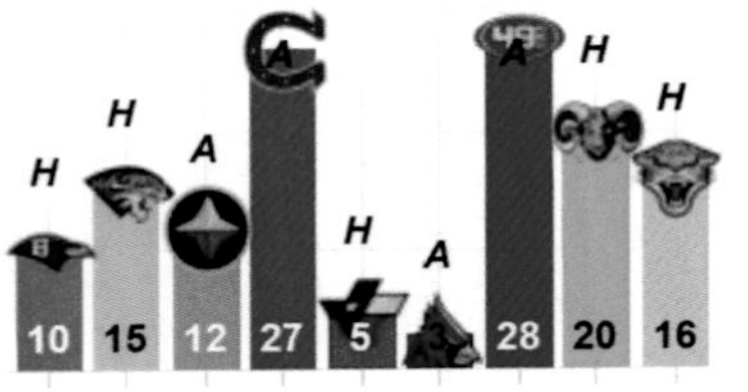

0 1 2 3 4 5 6 7 8 9 10 11 12 13 14 15 16 17

Rank of 2017 Defensive Rush Efficiency Faced by Week

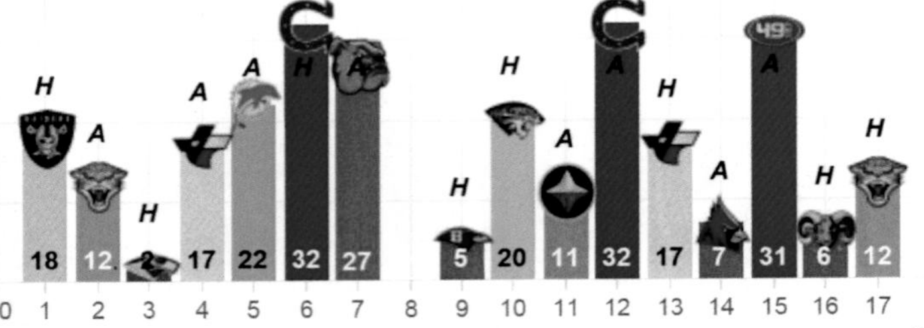

2016 Situational Usage by Player & Position

Usage Rate by Score

		Being Blown Out (14+)	Down Big (9-13)	One Score	Large Lead (9-13)	Blowout Lead (14+)	Grand Total
RUSH	DeMarco Murray	22%	29%	34%	44%	33%	33%
	Derrick Henry	6%	9%	11%	21%	22%	12%
	Delanie Walker					1%	0%
	Tajae Sharpe			0%			0%
	Kendall Wright					1%	0%
	Jalston Fowler			0%			0%
	Antonio Andrews	1%	1%				0%
	Marc Mariani			0%			0%
	Total	29%	38%	46%	65%	57%	46%
PASS	DeMarco Murray	7%	6%	9%	5%	3%	7%
	Derrick Henry	2%	2%	1%	2%	3%	2%
	Rishard Matthews	17%	15%	11%	8%	11%	12%
	Delanie Walker	16%	13%	10%	6%	14%	11%
	Tajae Sharpe	13%	13%	9%	5%	3%	9%
	Kendall Wright	4%	7%	4%	3%	6%	5%
	Andre Johnson	3%	3%	3%			3%
	Harry Douglas	5%	2%	2%	3%	1%	2%
	Anthony Fasano	2%	2%	1%	3%	1%	2%
	Phillip Supernaw			1%		1%	1%
	Jace Amaro	1%		1%			0%
	Jalston Fowler	1%			2%		0%
	Total	71%	62%	54%	35%	43%	54%

Positional Target Distribution vs NFL Average

		NFL Wide				Team Only			
		Left	Middle	Right	Total	Left	Middle	Right	Total
Deep	WR	1,000	566	972	2,538	31	15	29	75
	TE	149	140	156	445	9	7	7	23
	RB	25	4	40	69				
	All	1,174	710	1,168	3,052	40	22	36	98
Short	WR	3,015	1,740	3,115	7,870	78	31	71	180
	TE	805	860	1,118	2,783	31	15	33	79
	RB	992	608	1,083	2,683	23	14	30	67
	All	4,812	3,208	5,316	13,336	132	60	134	326
Total		5,986	3,918	6,484	16,388	172	82	170	424

Positional Success Rates vs NFL Average

		NFL Wide				Team Only			
		Left	Middle	Right	Total	Left	Middle	Right	Total
Deep	WR	36%	50%	39%	40%	52%	60%	24%	43%
	TE	44%	50%	43%	46%	56%	43%	43%	48%
	RB	32%	75%	25%	30%				
	All	37%	50%	39%	41%	53%	55%	28%	44%
Short	WR	52%	57%	51%	53%	62%	55%	52%	57%
	TE	50%	61%	52%	54%	45%	80%	39%	49%
	RB	47%	50%	44%	46%	52%	36%	23%	36%
	All	50%	57%	50%	52%	56%	57%	43%	51%
Total		48%	55%	48%	50%	55%	56%	39%	49%

Washington Redskins

2017 Coaches

Head Coach:
Jay Gruden (4th yr)
Offensive Coordinator:
(Gruden calls plays) (1st yr)
Defensive Coordinator:
Greg Manusky (WAS OLC) (1st yr)

2017 Forecast

Wins	Div Rank
7.5	#4

Past Records

2016: 8-7-1
2015: 9-7
2014: 4-12

EASY HARD

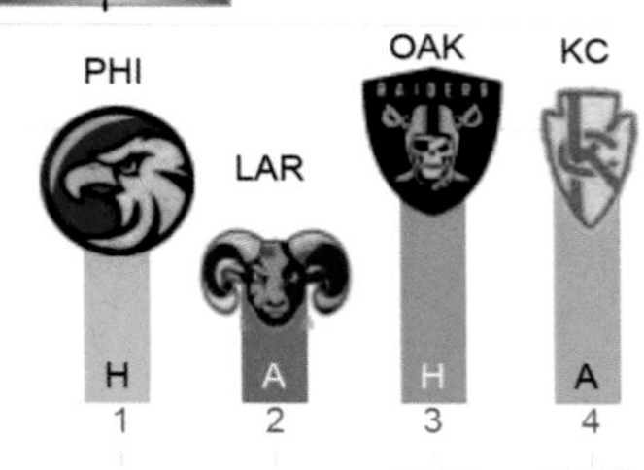

Week	1	2	3	4	5	6	7	8	9	10	11	12	13	14	15	16	17
Opponent	PHI	LAR	OAK	KC		SF	PHI	DAL	SEA	MIN	NO	NYG	DAL	LAC	ARI	DEN	NYG
Site	H	A	H	A		H	A	H	A	H	A	H	A	A	H	H	A
			SNF	MNF			MNF					TKG	TNF				

Key Players Lost

TXN	Player (POS)
Cut	Daniels, Steven LB
	Diggs, Reggie WR
	Fortt, Khairi LB
	Jean Francois, Ricky DE
	Johnson, Rufus LB
	Randolph, Shak CB
	Schooley, Quinton C
	Simon, Tharold CB
Declared Free Agent	Baker, Chris DE
	Garcon, Pierre WR
	Garvin, Terence LB
	Golston, Kedric NT
	Hood, Ziggy DE
	Ihenacho, Duke S
	Jackson, DeSean WR
	Jenkins, Cullen DT
	Sullivan, John C
	Toler, Greg CB
	Whitner, Donte S
Retired	Lichtensteiger, Kory C

Average Line	# Games Favored	# Games Underdog
+0.8	7	8

2017 Washington Redskins Overview

Improvement despite worse results. Such was the Redskins' 2017 season. Heading into 2016, the knock on the Redskins 9-7 record from the previous year was that it came against a cakewalk schedule. The defense was a disaster, the rush offense literally was the worst in the NFL and the team relied entirely on the passing offense (playing bad pass defenses) to score enough to win games. The Redskins franchised Kirk Cousins and made 2016 into a "prove it" season. I forecast the Redskins to have a downright brutal schedule, and it would be up to Cousins to deliver despite the challenges.

Indeed, the Redskins schedule last year was brutal. They faced the toughest schedule of opposing defenses, and it was the toughest by far. Yet they delivered. In a massive way. Looking at their radars on the next page, or simply their offensive advanced metrics, it is extremely impressive to see what this offense produced against a brutally difficult schedule of defenses. The team ranked 5th in EDSR offense (Early Down Success Rate), 5th in passing efficiency and 4th in rushing efficiency. While I'm a massive proponent of EDSR, the most impressive of those three rankings was the rushing efficiency, and that is because of the lack of talent at the position.

Looking purely at RB success rate, the Redskins were successful on 50% of their runs, 7th best in the NFL. Their 4.7 yards per carry was tied with the best rushing success team in the NFL, the Dallas Cowboys. Matt Jones, the incumbent, started off the season as the lead back. And he was serviceable, averaging 4.6 yards per carry and delivered the best success rate for all Redskins' RBs on the entire season. But he fumbled three times in 3 games, including a 3-point loss to the Lions (20-17) which saw Jones fumble into the endzone and nullify a Washington touchdown. So in came Rob Kelley, nicknamed "Fat Rob", and he delivered 4.2 yards per carry, a 48% success rate and most importantly, didn't fumble the ball. This quality was most important, because his overall success rate, his explosiveness and his early down success rate were worse than Matt Jones. But the one thing Kelley did was finish his runs.

I recently invented a metric called "Missed YPA". This is the companion metric to success rate.

(cont'd - see WAS2)

Key Free Agents/ Trades Added

Brown, Zach RB
Carter, Chris LB
Kling, John T
McClain, Terrell DT
McGee, Stacy DT
Pryor Sr., Terrelle WR
Quick, Brian WR
Swearinger, D.J. S

Drafted Players

Rd	Pk	Player (College)
1	17	DE - Jonathan Allen (Alabama)
2	49	OLB - Ryan Anderson (Alabama)
3	81	CB - Fabian Moreau (UCLA)
4	114	RB - Samaje Perine (Oklahoma)
	123	S - Montae Nicholson (Michigan State)
5	154	TE - Jeremy Sprinkle (Arkansas)
6	199	C - Chase Roullier (Wyoming)
	209	WR - Robert Davis (Georgia State)
7	230	S - Josh Harvey-Clemons (Louisville)
	235	CB - Joshua Holsey (Auburn)

Regular Season Wins: Past & Current Proj

	Wins
Proj 2017 Wins	7.5
2016 Wins	8
Proj 2016 Wins	7
2015 Wins	9
2014 Wins	4
2013 Wins	3

1 3 5 7 9 11 13 15

2017 Lineup & Cap Hits

FS D.Swearinger 36
SS S.Cravens 30
LB M.Foster 54
LB Z.Brown 55
RCB B.Breeland 26
SLOTCB K.Fuller 29
OLB P.Smith 94
DL J.Allen Rookie 95
DL S.McGee 92
OLB R.Kerrigan 91
LCB J.Norman 24

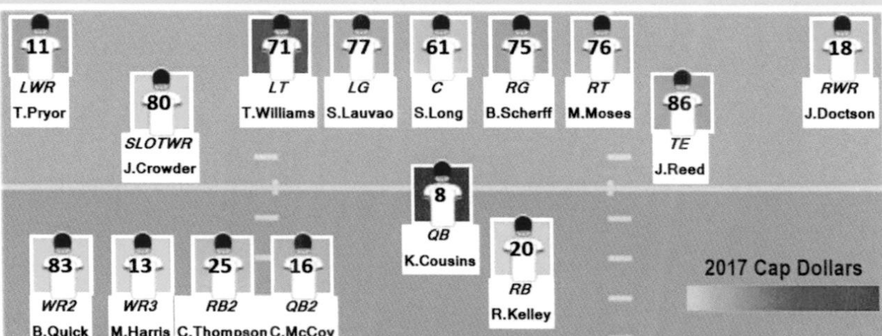

2017 Unit Spending

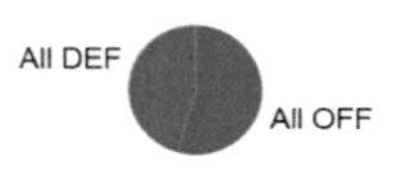

Positional Spending

	Rank	Total	2016 Rk
All OFF	4	$97.90M	2
QB	3	$28.12M	8
OL	6	$36.84M	11
RB	24	$5.73M	29
WR	27	$13.91M	2
TE	6	$13.30M	9
All DEF	14	$81.02M	31
DL	29	$14.58M	31
LB	8	$27.35M	14
CB	4	$26.05M	22
S	11	$13.05M	21

Washington Redskins 2016 Success Rate Radar

Weeks 1-4

1 L, 2 L, 3 W, 4 W

DEFENSE
OFFENSE

Pass
Explosive Pass
Pass
Pass Pro
Rush
Early Downs
3rd Down
Rush
Early Downs
3rd Down
Pass Pro
Explosive Pass
DEFENSE
OFFENSE

Weeks 5-8

5 W, 6 W, 7 L, 8

DEFENSE
OFFENSE

Weeks 13-17

13 L, 14 W, 15 L, 16 W, 17 L

DEFENSE
OFFENSE

Weeks 9-12

10 W, 11 W, 12 L

DEFENSE
OFFENSE

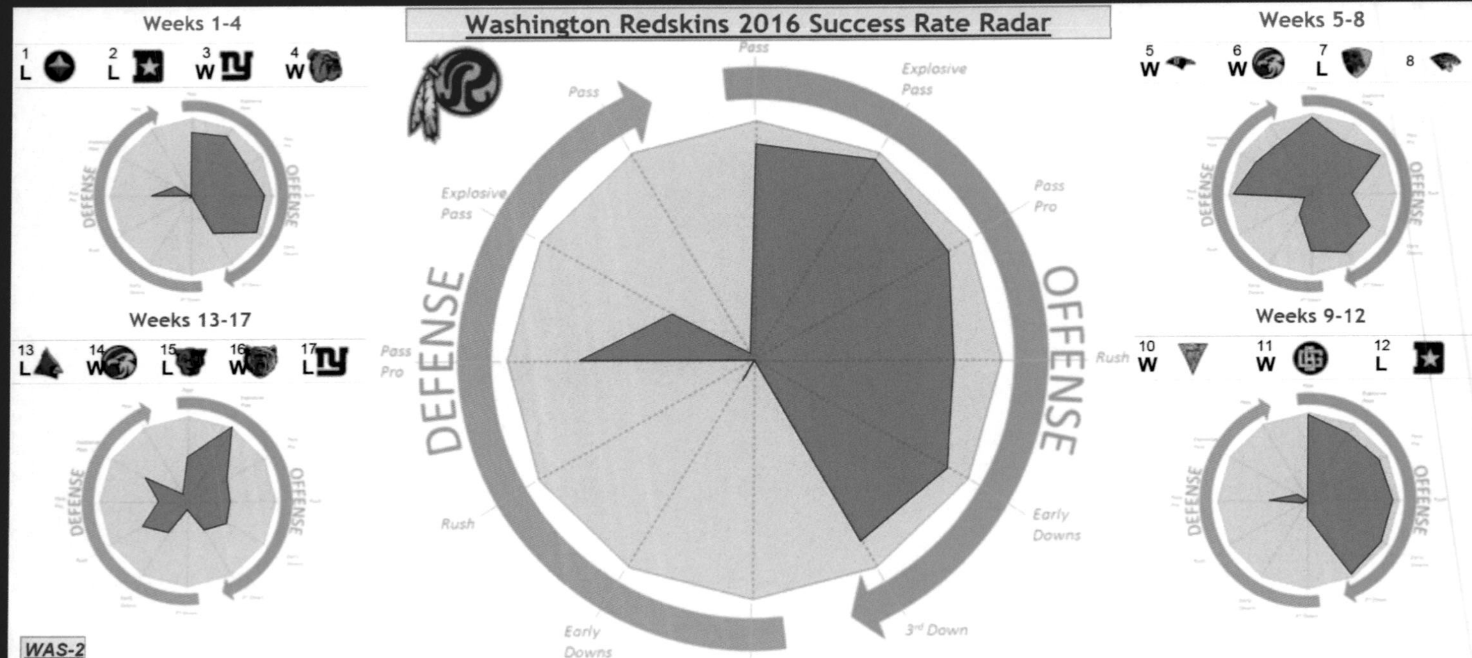

WAS-2

Success rate is an accumulation of successful plays divided by the entire sample of plays, and successful plays are a binomial – a 1 or a 0. So 45 successful plays in a 100 play sample and the player's success rate was 45%, which is a metric generally more important to efficiency than average yardage. However, what about the other 55 plays which were unsuccessful? Do we just dump them as unimportant? That is where "Missed YPA" comes in. It measures the yardage on an unsuccessful play that was missed. For example: on 1st and 10, needing 4 yards to grade as successful, the running back gains only 1 yard. He "missed" being successful by 3 yards. The lower your "Missed YPA", the better the player did on unsuccessful plays at trying to obtain the required yardage. It's an important metric. And Rob Kelley ranked 5th last year among RBs.

So how did a RB that the Redskins no longer want (Matt Jones) and an undrafted free agent rookie RB from Tulane launch the Redskins run game to the 4th most efficient in the NFL despite facing the 5th most difficult schedule of run defenses, particularly after the team posted the NFL's worst marks from 2016?

A lot of it had to do with coaching and personnel. Linemen that fired GM Scot McCloughan drafted. Coupled with year 2 of one of the best line coaches in the NFL (Bill Callahan) who was also responsible for the Cowboys tremendous line from 2012-2014. And then the offensive philosophy of Jay Gruden, which was successful in Cincinnati with a young Andy Dalton and translated even better in Washington with Kirk Cousins.

For these reasons, I'm exceedingly high on 4th round RB Samaje Perine this season. The offensive line was actually the 10th most injured last season and far less talented RBs, like Jones and Fat Rob, were able to produce tremendous results. There are numerous reasons why this success could carry over to Perine. The Redskins actually only passed the ball on 55% of plays when the game was within one score, which was the 7th fewest in the NFL. The Redskins use shotgun far less than most teams (55% vs the NFL average of 63%) and thus are more equipped to run more often.

(cont'd - see WAS-3)

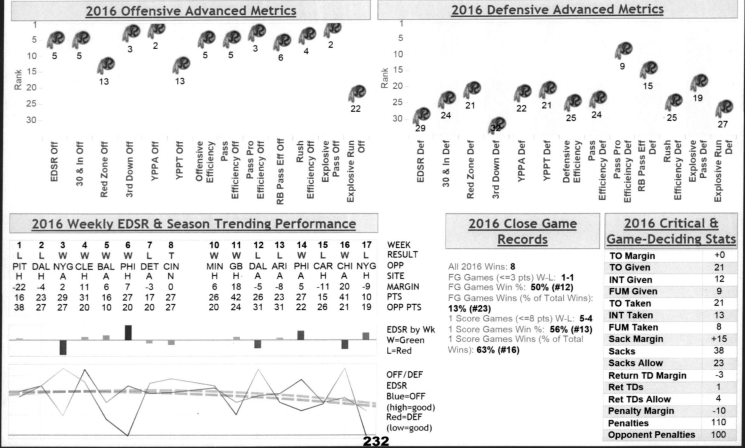

2016 Offensive Advanced Metrics

Rank
1
5
10
15
20
25
30
EDSR Off 5
30 & In Off 5
Red Zone Off 13
3rd Down Off 3
YPPA Off 2
YPPT Off 13
Offensive Efficiency 5
Pass Efficiency Off 5
Pass Pro Efficiency Off 3
RB Pass Eff Off 6
Rush Efficiency Off 4
Explosive Pass Off 2
Explosive Run Off 22

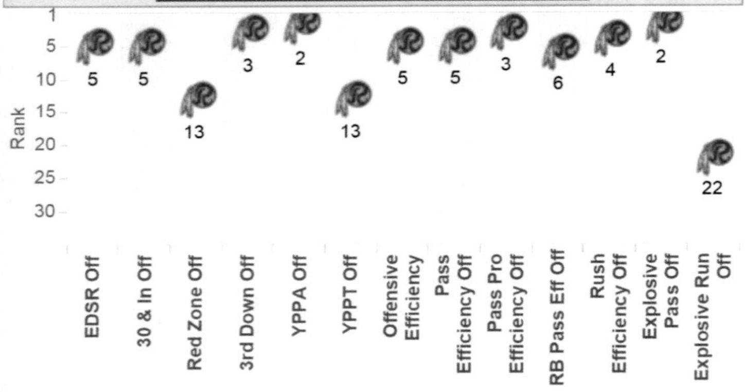

2016 Defensive Advanced Metrics

Rank
1
5
10
15
20
25
30
EDSR Def 29
30 & In Def 24
Red Zone Def 21
3rd Down Def 32
YPPA Def 22
YPPT Def 21
Defensive Efficiency 25
Pass Efficiency Def 24
Pass Pro Efficieincy Def 9
RB Pass Eff Def 15
Rush Efficiency Def 25
Explosive Pass Def 19
Explosive Run Def 27

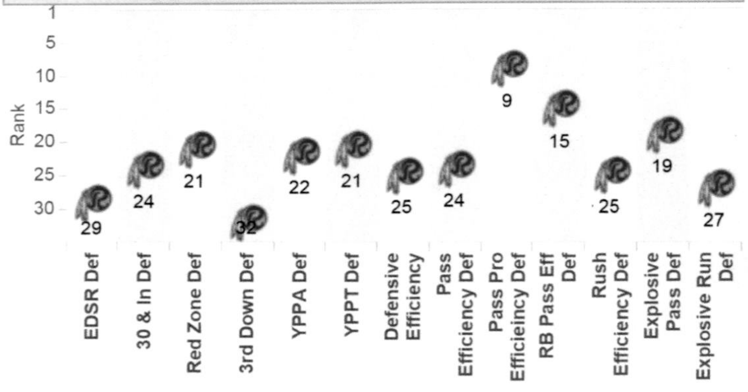

2016 Weekly EDSR & Season Trending Performance

WEEK	1	2	3	4	5	6	7	8	10	11	12	13	14	15	16	17
RESULT	L	L	W	W	W	W	L	T	W	W	L	L	W	L	W	L
OPP	PIT	DAL	NYG	CLE	BAL	PHI	DET	CIN	MIN	GB	DAL	ARI	PHI	CAR	CHI	NYG
SITE	H	H	A	A	A	H	A	N	H	H	A	A	A	H	A	H
MARGIN	-22	-4	2	11	6	7	-3	0	6	18	-5	-8	5	-11	20	-9
PTS	16	23	29	31	16	27	17	27	26	42	26	23	27	15	41	10
OPP PTS	38	27	27	20	10	20	20	27	20	24	31	31	22	26	21	19

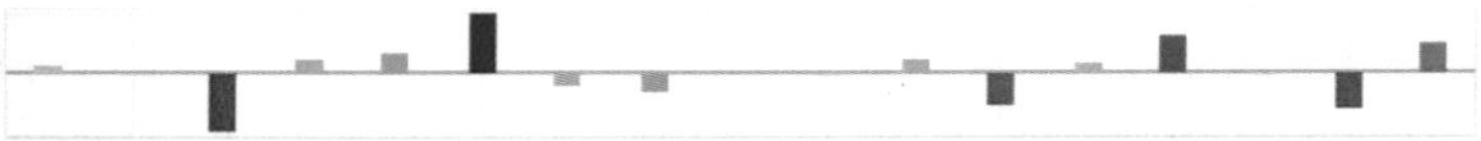

EDSR by Wk
W=Green
L=Red

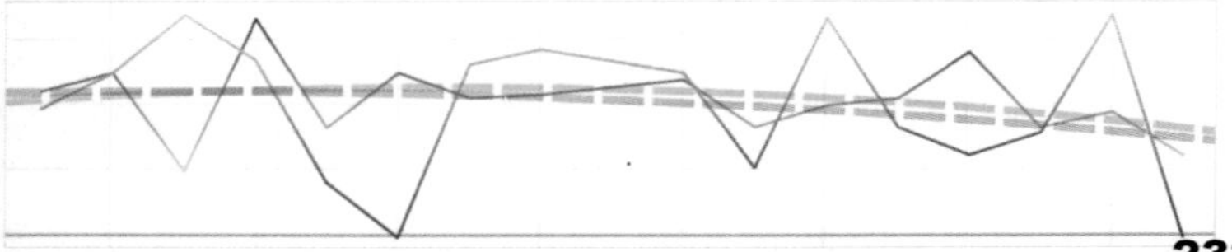

OFF/DEF EDSR
Blue=OFF (high=good)
Red=DEF (low=good)

2016 Close Game Records

All 2016 Wins: **8**
FG Games (<=3 pts) W-L: **1-1**
FG Games Win %: **50% (#12)**
FG Games Wins (% of Total Wins): **13% (#23)**
1 Score Games (<=8 pts) W-L: **5-4**
1 Score Games Win %: **56% (#13)**
1 Score Games Wins (% of Total Wins): **63% (#16)**

2016 Critical & Game-Deciding Stats

TO Margin	+0
TO Given	21
INT Given	12
FUM Given	9
TO Taken	21
INT Taken	13
FUM Taken	8
Sack Margin	+15
Sacks	38
Sacks Allow	23
Return TD Margin	-3
Ret TDs	1
Ret TDs Allow	4
Penalty Margin	-10
Penalties	110
Opponent Penalties	100

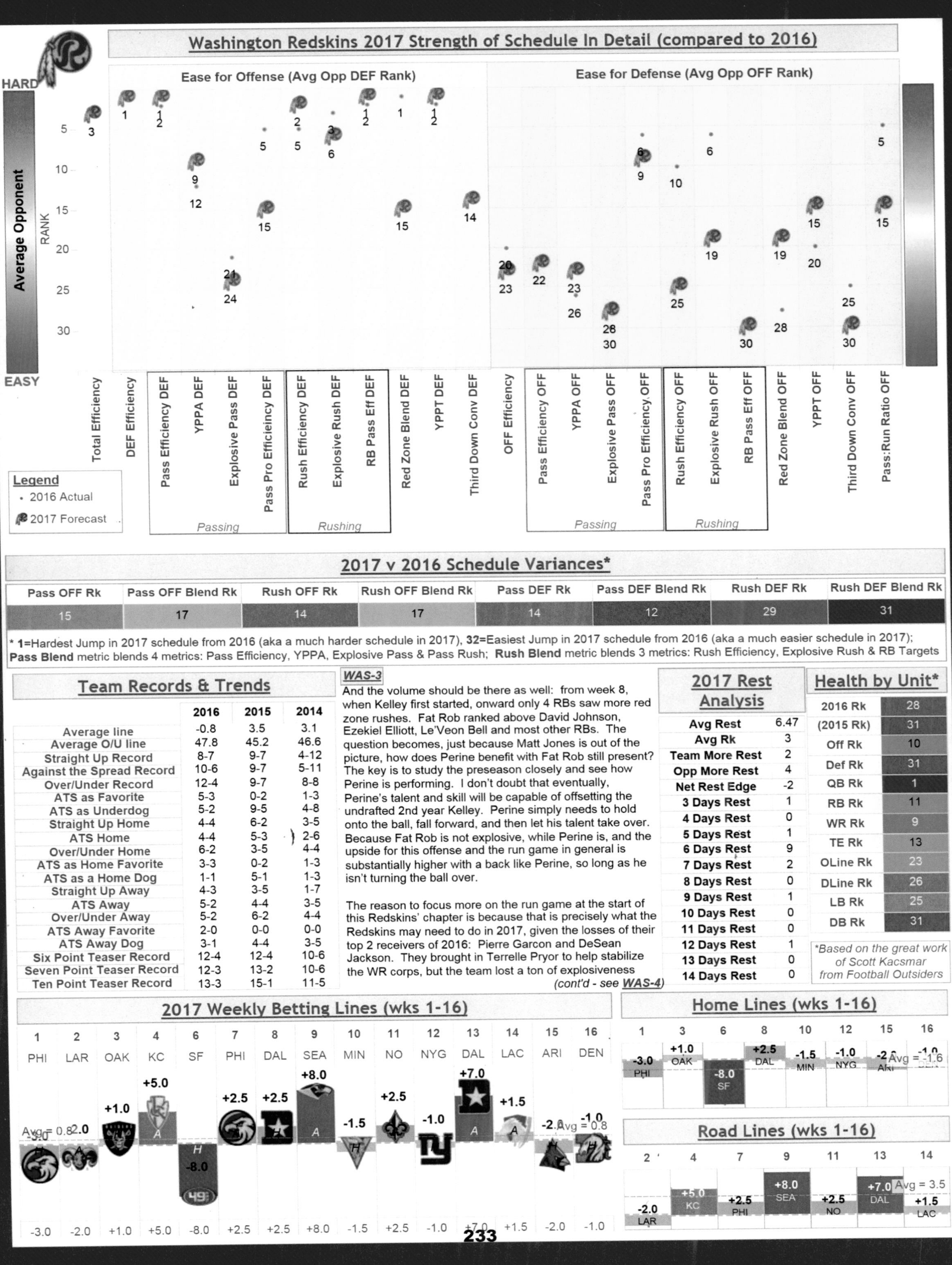

Washington Redskins 2017 Strength of Schedule In Detail (compared to 2016)

2017 v 2016 Schedule Variances*

Pass OFF Rk	Pass OFF Blend Rk	Rush OFF Rk	Rush OFF Blend Rk	Pass DEF Rk	Pass DEF Blend Rk	Rush DEF Rk	Rush DEF Blend Rk
15	17	14	17	14	12	29	31

* **1**=Hardest Jump in 2017 schedule from 2016 (aka a much harder schedule in 2017), **32**=Easiest Jump in 2017 schedule from 2016 (aka a much easier schedule in 2017); **Pass Blend** metric blends 4 metrics: Pass Efficiency, YPPA, Explosive Pass & Pass Rush; **Rush Blend** metric blends 3 metrics: Rush Efficiency, Explosive Rush & RB Targets

Team Records & Trends

	2016	2015	2014
Average line	-0.8	3.5	3.1
Average O/U line	47.8	45.2	46.6
Straight Up Record	8-7	9-7	4-12
Against the Spread Record	10-6	9-7	5-11
Over/Under Record	12-4	9-7	8-8
ATS as Favorite	5-3	0-2	1-3
ATS as Underdog	5-2	9-5	4-8
Straight Up Home	4-4	6-2	3-5
ATS Home	4-4	5-3	2-6
Over/Under Home	6-2	3-5	4-4
ATS as Home Favorite	3-3	0-2	1-3
ATS as a Home Dog	1-1	5-1	1-3
Straight Up Away	4-3	3-5	1-7
ATS Away	5-2	4-4	3-5
Over/Under Away	5-2	6-2	4-4
ATS Away Favorite	2-0	0-0	0-0
ATS Away Dog	3-1	4-4	3-5
Six Point Teaser Record	12-4	12-4	10-6
Seven Point Teaser Record	12-3	13-2	10-6
Ten Point Teaser Record	13-3	15-1	11-5

WAS-3

And the volume should be there as well: from week 8, when Kelley first started, onward only 4 RBs saw more red zone rushes. Fat Rob ranked above David Johnson, Ezekiel Elliott, Le'Veon Bell and most other RBs. The question becomes, just because Matt Jones is out of the picture, how does Perine benefit with Fat Rob still present? The key is to study the preseason closely and see how Perine is performing. I don't doubt that eventually, Perine's talent and skill will be capable of offsetting the undrafted 2nd year Kelley. Perine simply needs to hold onto the ball, fall forward, and then let his talent take over. Because Fat Rob is not explosive, while Perine is, and the upside for this offense and the run game in general is substantially higher with a back like Perine, so long as he isn't turning the ball over.

The reason to focus more on the run game at the start of this Redskins' chapter is because that is precisely what the Redskins may need to do in 2017, given the losses of their top 2 receivers of 2016: Pierre Garcon and DeSean Jackson. They brought in Terrelle Pryor to help stabilize the WR corps, but the team lost a ton of explosiveness

(cont'd - see *WAS-4*)

2017 Rest Analysis

Avg Rest	6.47
Avg Rk	3
Team More Rest	2
Opp More Rest	4
Net Rest Edge	-2
3 Days Rest	1
4 Days Rest	0
5 Days Rest	1
6 Days Rest	9
7 Days Rest	2
8 Days Rest	0
9 Days Rest	1
10 Days Rest	0
11 Days Rest	0
12 Days Rest	1
13 Days Rest	0
14 Days Rest	0

Health by Unit*

2016 Rk	28
(2015 Rk)	31
Off Rk	10
Def Rk	31
QB Rk	1
RB Rk	11
WR Rk	9
TE Rk	13
OLine Rk	23
DLine Rk	26
LB Rk	25
DB Rk	31

*Based on the great work of Scott Kacsmar from Football Outsiders

2017 Weekly Betting Lines (wks 1-16)

1	2	3	4	6	7	8	9	10	11	12	13	14	15	16
PHI	LAR	OAK	KC	SF	PHI	DAL	SEA	MIN	NO	NYG	DAL	LAC	ARI	DEN
H	A	H	A	H	A	H	A	H	A	H	A	A	H	H
-3.0	-2.0	+1.0	+5.0	-8.0	+2.5	+2.5	+8.0	-1.5	+2.5	-1.0	+7.0	+1.5	-2.0	-1.0

Avg = 0.8

Home Lines (wks 1-16)

1	3	6	8	10	12	15	16
PHI	OAK	SF	DAL	MIN	NYG	ARI	DEN
-3.0	+1.0	-8.0	+2.5	-1.5	-1.0	-2.0	-1.0

Avg = -1.6

Road Lines (wks 1-16)

2	4	7	9	11	13	14
LAR	KC	PHI	SEA	NO	DAL	LAC
-2.0	+5.0	+2.5	+8.0	+2.5	+7.0	+1.5

Avg = 3.5

2016 Play Tendencies

All Pass %	63%
All Pass Rk	4
All Rush %	37%
All Rush Rk	29
1 Score Pass %	55%
1 Score Pass Rk	26
2015 1 Score Pass %	58%
2015 1 Score Pass Rk	20
Pass Increase %	-3%
Pass Increase Rk	22
1 Score Rush %	45%
1 Score Rush Rk	7
Up Pass %	55%
Up Pass Rk	22
Up Rush %	45%
Up Rush Rk	11
Down Pass %	67%
Down Pass Rk	4
Down Rush %	33%
Down Rush Rk	29

2016 Down & Distance Tendencies

Down	Distance	Total Plays	Pass Rate	Run Rate	Play Success %
1	Short (1-3)	3	33%	67%	33%
	Med (4-7)	14	50%	50%	43%
	Long (8-10)	298	51%	49%	51%
	XL (11+)	20	55%	45%	30%
2	Short (1-3)	25	44%	56%	56%
	Med (4-7)	90	57%	43%	57%
	Long (8-10)	96	75%	25%	52%
	XL (11+)	37	73%	27%	30%
3	Short (1-3)	45	58%	42%	62%
	Med (4-7)	56	95%	5%	55%
	Long (8-10)	28	100%	0%	39%
	XL (11+)	22	100%	0%	9%
4	Short (1-3)	6	50%	50%	50%
	Med (4-7)	1	100%	0%	0%
	XL (11+)	2	100%	0%	50%

Shotgun %:

Under Center	Shotgun
45%	55%
37%	*63%*

AVG

Run Rate:

Under Center	Shotgun
61%	17%
68%	*23%*

AVG

Pass Rate:

Under Center	Shotgun
39%	83%
32%	*77%*

AVG

Washington Redskins 2016 Play Analysis

Short Yardage Intelligence:

2nd and Short Run

Run Freq	Run % Rk	NFL Run Freq Avg	Run 1D Rate	Run NFL 1D Avg
56%	27	65%	64%	71%

2nd and Short Pass

Pass Freq	Pass % Rk	NFL Pass Freq Avg	Pass 1D Rate	Pass NFL 1D Avg
44%	6	35%	64%	52%

Most Frequent Play

Down	Distance	Play Type	Player	Total Plays	Play Success %
1	Short (1-3)	RUSH	Rob Kelley	2	50%
	Med (4-7)	RUSH	Rob Kelley	4	50%
	Long (8-10)	RUSH	Rob Kelley	86	43%
	XL (11+)	RUSH	Chris Thompson	5	20%
2	Short (1-3)	RUSH	Rob Kelley	7	29%
	Med (4-7)	RUSH	Rob Kelley	20	55%
	Long (8-10)	RUSH	Chris Thompson	15	47%
	XL (11+)	RUSH	Chris Thompson	8	38%
3	Short (1-3)	PASS	Pierre Garcon	7	71%
		RUSH	Rob Kelley	7	71%
	Med (4-7)	PASS	Jamison Crowder	12	42%
	Long (8-10)	PASS	Jordan Reed	5	60%
			Jamison Crowder	5	40%
	XL (11+)	PASS	Jamison Crowder	6	33%

Most Successful Play*

Down	Distance	Play Type	Player	Total Plays	Play Success %
1	Long (8-10)	PASS	Matt Jones	6	100%
	XL (11+)	RUSH	Chris Thompson	5	20%
2	Short (1-3)	RUSH	Rob Kelley	7	29%
	Med (4-7)	RUSH	Chris Thompson	8	75%
	Long (8-10)	PASS	Vernon Davis	7	71%
	XL (11+)	PASS	Pierre Garcon	7	57%
3	Short (1-3)	RUSH	Matt Jones	6	100%
	Med (4-7)	PASS	Jordan Reed	11	82%
	Long (8-10)	PASS	Jordan Reed	5	60%
	XL (11+)	PASS	Jamison Crowder	6	33%

**Minimum 5 plays to qualify*

2016 Snap Rates

Week	Opp	Score	Pierre Garcon	Jamison Crowder	DeSean Jackson	Vernon Davis	Jordan Reed	Chris Thompson	Rob Kelley
1	PIT	L 38-16	40 (69%)	47 (81%)	48 (83%)	19 (33%)	50 (86%)	39 (67%)	
2	DAL	L 27-23	46 (69%)	49 (73%)	51 (76%)	27 (40%)	58 (87%)	29 (43%)	
3	NYG	W 29-27	55 (77%)	44 (62%)	51 (72%)	35 (49%)	64 (90%)	34 (48%)	4 (6%)
4	CLE	W 31-20	44 (71%)	34 (55%)	48 (77%)	34 (55%)	57 (92%)	20 (32%)	1 (2%)
5	BAL	W 16-10	49 (74%)	37 (56%)	51 (77%)	33 (50%)	59 (89%)	21 (32%)	8 (12%)
6	PHI	W 27-20	60 (81%)	56 (76%)	50 (68%)	72 (97%)		36 (49%)	9 (12%)
7	DET	L 20-17	57 (78%)	55 (75%)	54 (74%)	71 (97%)		43 (59%)	10 (14%)
8	CIN	T 27-27	78 (86%)	64 (70%)	32 (35%)	39 (43%)	72 (79%)	48 (53%)	43 (47%)
10	MIN	W 26-20	51 (81%)	48 (76%)		34 (54%)	50 (79%)	21 (33%)	42 (67%)
11	GB	W 42-24	50 (76%)	39 (59%)	47 (71%)	37 (56%)	57 (86%)	23 (35%)	41 (62%)
12	DAL	L 31-26	52 (69%)	60 (80%)	56 (75%)	45 (60%)	37 (49%)	43 (57%)	32 (43%)
13	ARI	L 31-23	48 (80%)	50 (83%)	45 (75%)	59 (98%)		26 (43%)	34 (57%)
14	PHI	W 27-22	40 (83%)	41 (85%)	42 (88%)	38 (79%)	10 (21%)	17 (35%)	31 (65%)
15	CAR	L 26-15	45 (70%)	56 (88%)	58 (91%)	44 (69%)	19 (30%)	35 (55%)	29 (45%)
16	CHI	W 41-21	44 (66%)	56 (84%)	30 (45%)	64 (96%)		22 (33%)	34 (51%)
17	NYG	L 19-10	45 (82%)	48 (87%)	42 (76%)	21 (38%)	36 (65%)	31 (56%)	24 (44%)
Grand Total			804 (76%)	784 (74%)	705 (72%)	672 (63%)	569 (71%)	488 (46%)	342 (37%)

Personnel Groupings

Personnel	Team %	NFL Avg	Succ. %
1-1 [3WR]	73%	60%	49%
1-2 [2WR]	19%	19%	55%
1-3 [1WR]	7%	3%	56%

Grouping Tendencies

Personnel	Pass Rate	Pass Succ. %	Run Succ. %
1-1 [3WR]	70%	49%	48%
1-2 [2WR]	47%	64%	47%
1-3 [1WR]	24%	50%	58%

Red Zone Targets (min 3)

Receiver	All	Inside 5	6-10	11-20
Jamison Crowder	17	5	2	10
Jordan Reed	14	3	5	6
Pierre Garcon	14	3	4	7
DeSean Jackson	11	3	2	6
Chris Thompson	8	2		6
Vernon Davis	7	1	3	3
Ryan Grant	5			5
Josh Doctson	3	1	1	1

Red Zone Rushes (min 3)

Rusher	All	Inside 5	6-10	11-20
Rob Kelley	34	10	7	17
Matt Jones	18	3	3	12
Chris Thompson	7	2	2	3
Kirk Cousins	7	3	1	3

Early Down Target Rate

RB	TE	WR
15%	27%	58%
19%	*20% NFL AVG*	*61%*

Overall Target Success %

RB	TE	WR
51% #5	61% #4	52% #8

Washington Redskins 2016 Passing Recap & 2017 Outlook

Against the second most difficult schedule of opposing defenses, Kirk Cousins came through in a major way for the Redskins in 2016. In all the standard metrics, he was well above the NFL average. In the more advanced metrics, such as success rate and EDSR (Early Down Success Rate), explosive passing, air yards and deep passing, nothing changed – Cousins was well above the NFL average. Cousins could look to improve his passing on 3rd down, where he threw short of the sticks too often, but overall the Redskins were still an efficient 3rd down passing offense. One area that Cousins needs to improve upon is red zone passing. The Redskins had the 4th overall ranked offense from a success rate perspective, with a 51% success rate, but inside the red zone that plummeted to 32%, ranking 29th. In all other areas of the field the Redskins were successful on 54% of their passes. Targeting WRs in the red zone was a disaster. Only 32% of those passes were successful, yet they used 62% of their attempts on the WRs. It didn't matter which WR, Crowder, Garcon and Jackson were all subpar. RB passes were even worse (30% success rate). The only passes with avg success were TE passes, and then it was only those to Reed (57% success, Davis saw only 33%).

Kirk Cousins Rating All Downs

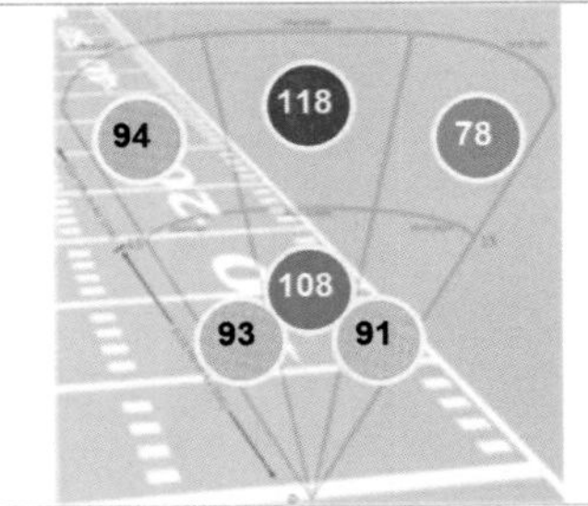

Kirk Cousins Rating Early Downs

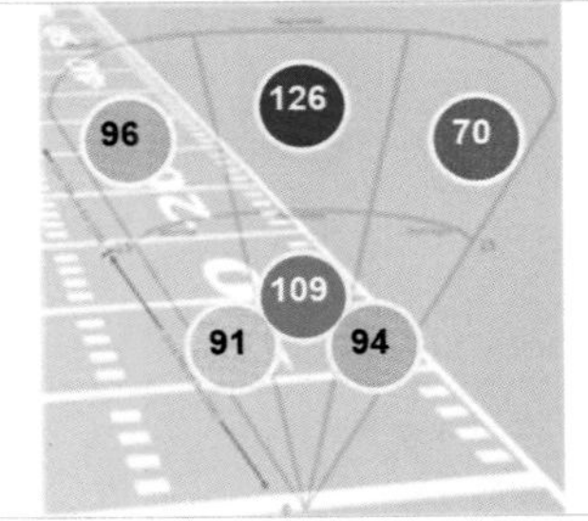

2016 Standard Passing Table

QB	Comp	Att	Comp %	Yds	YPA	TDs	INT	Sacks	Rating	Rk
Kirk Cousins	406	606	67%	4,915	8.1	25	12	23	97.2	12
NFL Avg			63%		7.2				90.4	

2016 Advanced Passing Table

QB	Success %	EDSR Passing Success %	20+ Yd Pass Gains	20+ Yd Pass %	30+ Yd Pass Gains	30+ Yd Pass %	Air Yds per Comp	YAC per Comp	20+ Air Yd Comp	20+ Air Yd %
Kirk Cousins	51%	55%	69	11%	27	4%	7.3	4.8	38	6%
NFL Avg	44%	48%	27	8%	10	3%	6.4	4.8	12	4%

Interception Rates by Down

Yards to Go	1	2	3	4	Total
1 & 2	0.0%	0.0%	0.0%	0.0%	0.0%
3, 4, 5	0.0%	0.0%	4.9%		2.3%
6 - 9	0.0%	2.3%	2.1%	0.0%	2.1%
10 - 14	2.8%	0.0%	3.3%	0.0%	2.3%
15+	0.0%	0.0%	0.0%		0.0%
Total	2.5%	0.9%	2.4%	0.0%	1.9%

3rd Down Passing - Short of Sticks Analysis

QB	Avg Yds to Go	Air Yds (of Comps)	Avg Yds Short	Short of Sticks Rate	Rk
Kirk Cousins	7.3	6.7	-0.6	49%	21
NFL Avg	7.6	6.8	-0.8	57%	

Air Yds vs YAC

Air Yds %	YAC %	Rk
56%	44%	22
54%	46%	

2016 Receiving Recap & 2017 Outlook

The receiving corps will look much different this year. The number one element the team needs to attempt to replace is an explosive threat. The team must make defenses adjust to that speed. Doctson ran a 4.5 sec 40, so he's not the guy to replace DeSean Jackson's 4.35 sec 40. However, Terrelle Pryor ran a 4.38 sec 40 and while he's much bigger (6'4", 223 lbs) than Jackson (5'10", 175 lbs), that speed is even more impressive considering the frame. Additionally, Pryor's receptions in 2016 contained 818 air yards, the 7th best in the NFL for all receivers, which is extremely impressive considering the quarterbacks in Cleveland last year.

Player *Min 50 Targets*	Targets	Comp %	YPA	Rating	TOARS	Success %	Success Rk	Missed YPA Rk	YAS % Rk	TDs
Pierre Garcon	114	69%	9.1	99	5.1	61%	14	16	27	3
DeSean Jackson	100	56%	10.1	96	4.7	48%	94	80	2	4
Jamison Crowder	99	68%	8.6	105	4.8	49%	78	74	101	7
Jordan Reed	89	74%	7.7	109	4.8	58%	23	21	106	6
Chris Thompson	62	79%	5.6	101	4.0	47%	106	129	145	2
Vernon Davis	59	75%	9.8	102	4.1	63%	9	2	9	2

Directional Passer Rating Delivered

Receiver	Short Left	Short Middle	Short Right	Deep Left	Deep Middle	Deep Right	Player Total
Pierre Garcon	105	97	86	119	104	79	99
DeSean Jackson	68	153	60	79	104	125	96
Jamison Crowder	110	99	82	141	158	0	105
Jordan Reed	124	98	125	24	104	96	109
Chris Thompson	91	101	102				101
Vernon Davis	48	141	91	104		96	102
Team Total	97	110	90	107	116	84	102

2016 Rushing Recap & 2017 Outlook

Samaje Perine has a chance to unseat Rob Kelley, but to do so, he absolutely must have tremendous ball security, which is a key selling point for Fat Rob. The issue is can either emerge with enough touches to be truly fantasy relevant? One impediment for significant volume for either back is the "3rd down" back – Chris Thompson, who HC Gruden called one of the best "3rd down" backs in the NFL. Here's the problem with that: his success rate on 20, 3rd down targets was only 30%, which was the worst of any Redskins WR, RB or TE last year. However, on early downs, his success rate was 55%, which was better than any non-TE except for Garcon. Gruden must focus 3rd down targets more on WRs and TEs, and let Thompson get..

Player *Min 50 Rushes*	Rushes	YPA	Success %	Success Rk	Missed YPA Rk	YTS % Rk	YAS % Rk	Early Down Success %	Early Down Success Rk	TDs
Rob Kelley	168	4.2	48%	32	5	27	36	47%	36	6
Matt Jones	99	4.6	53%	11	15	57	11	49%	23	3
Chris Thompson	68	5.2	51%	19	36	37	46	51%	21	3

Yards per Carry by Direction

Directional Run Frequency

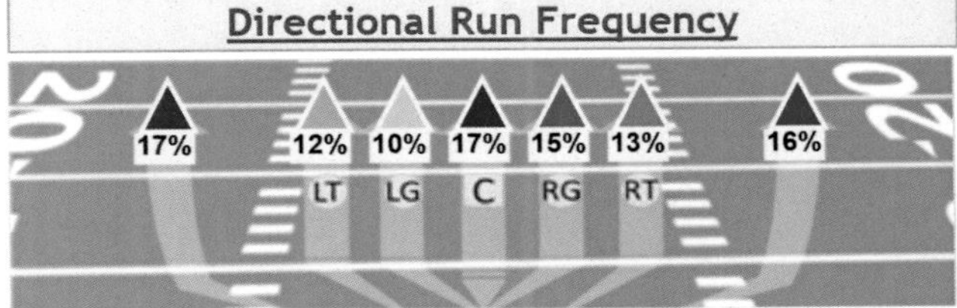

WAS-4

in Jackson and consistency in Garcon. However, what it enabled the Redskins to do was reduce the WR salary hit a ton. They move from the 2nd most expensive WR corps in 2016 to the 25th most expensive this year. But both players will be difficult to replace. You can't find the speed and talent of DeSean Jackson often. He ranked 2nd in Yards Above Successful (YAS%) last year. (YAS is a metric which isolates only the yardage on a successful play which was more than what was required.) Meanwhile, Garcon caught 69% of targets while still recording a 9.1 yards per target. In the last 10 years, only 8 other WRs delivered 9+ yards per target while catching at least 69% of their targets. So to suggest replacing that efficiency will be easy is unlikely.

The Redskins still have slot WR Jamison Crowder, who led their receivers in red zone targets and targets inside the 5, and of course they have the stellar TE Jordan Reed, who was in and out of the lineup last year due to injuries. With the addition of Pryor as their WR #1, the Redskins are hopeful WR Josh Doctson, who they drafted in the first round of 2016's draft, will be ready to assume the role opposite Pryor when they go 3-wide. They used a 5th round pick on TE Jeremy Sprinkle out of Arkansas, and still have TEs Vernon Davis and Niles Paul on the roster. If Doctson has a setback, I can envision the Redskins using more 12 personnel which they used on 19% of their plays last year. However, when using 12 personnel instead of the more frequent (73%) 11 personnel, their passing success rate increased to 64% from 49% in 11 personnel, and Cousins' passer rating jumped to 118 from 104.

And in fact, when the Redskins deployed at least 2 TEs in any grouping (12, 13, 22) they were virtually unstoppable: 62% of their passes were successful and Cousins averaged a 141 passer rating and a 12:2 TD:INT ratio. They also averaged a 51% success rate on run plays. While their numbers in 11 personnel were still very good, the Redskins were successful on passes (and runs) at just a 49% rate, a definite drop from the 62% when 2+ TEs were deployed, and Cousins passer rating and TD:INT ratio were also superior. The Redskins used 11 personnel well above the NFL average and even if Doctson is healthy, they may want to consider using 12 personnel more than they did in 2016.

Defensively, the line is much less expensive than average, much like 2016. But they will be able to incorporate what could be a tremendous draft pick in DE Jonathan Allen (Alabama) and the unit as a whole was extremely injured. The Redskins' defense was the 5th most injured of 2016, with every single position group falling between 2nd most injured (DBs) to 8th most injured (LBs). The opposing offensive schedule gets slightly easier in 2017 compared to 2016, which could be a big factor in their overall success considering the difficulty of the schedule for the offense this year. Looking at the radars, it is clear the defense needs more than just health. New DC Greg Manusky has his work cut out on that side of the ball.

Division History: Season Wins & 2017 Projection

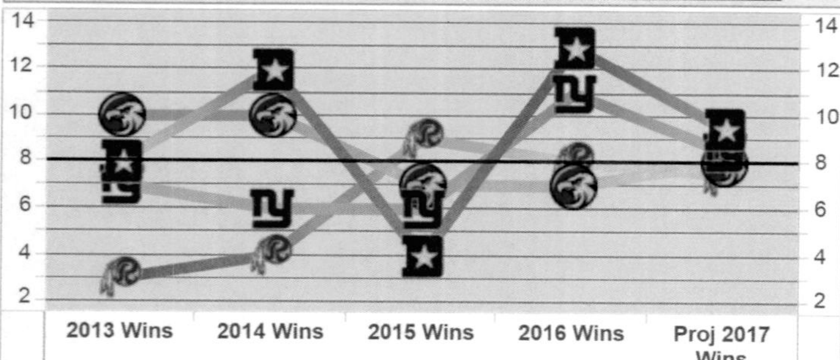

Rank of 2017 Defensive Pass Efficiency Faced by Week

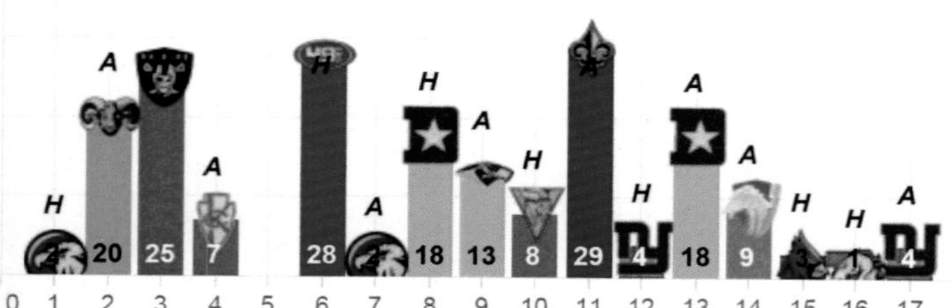

Rank of 2017 Defensive Rush Efficiency Faced by Week

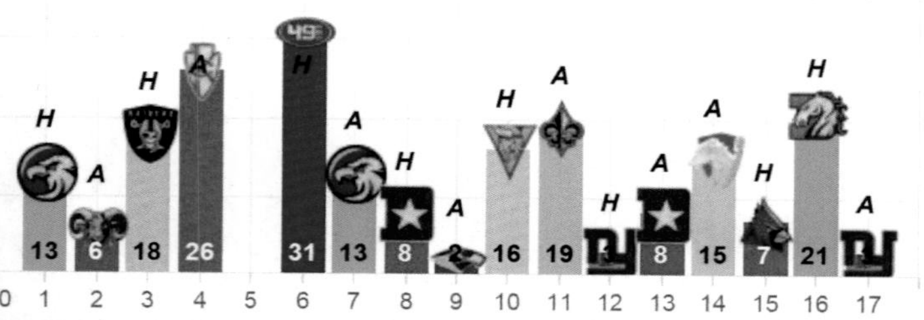

2016 Situational Usage by Player & Position

Usage Rate by Score

		Being Blown Out (14+)	Down Big (9-13)	One Score	Large Lead (9-13)	Blowout Lead (14+)	Grand Total
RUSH	Rob Kelley	4%	18%	18%	42%	14%	18%
	Chris Thompson	4%	4%	8%	3%	5%	7%
	Matt Jones	2%	5%	12%	13%		11%
	Jamison Crowder			0%			0%
	Mack Brown				10%	24%	1%
	Total	11%	27%	39%	68%	43%	37%
PASS	Rob Kelley	2%	2%	2%	3%		2%
	Chris Thompson	6%	12%	6%	3%		7%
	Pierre Garcon	17%	9%	12%	10%	14%	12%
	Matt Jones	2%	1%	1%			1%
	Jamison Crowder	19%	10%	11%		10%	11%
	DeSean Jackson	19%	13%	10%	10%	5%	11%
	Jordan Reed	11%	15%	9%			9%
	Vernon Davis	9%	8%	6%	3%	5%	6%
	Ryan Grant		2%	2%		19%	2%
	Maurice Harris	2%	1%	1%		5%	1%
	Mack Brown				3%		0%
	Josh Doctson	2%		1%			1%
	Derek Carrier		1%	0%			0%
	Niles Paul			0%			0%
	Rashad Ross			0%			0%
	Total	89%	73%	61%	32%	57%	63%

Positional Target Distribution vs NFL Average

		NFL Wide				Team Only			
		Left	Middle	Right	Total	Left	Middle	Right	Total
Deep	WR	1,003	560	973	2,536	28	21	28	77
	TE	150	142	153	445	8	5	10	23
	RB	25	4	40	69				
	All	1,178	706	1,166	3,050	36	26	38	100
Short	WR	3,007	1,725	3,082	7,814	86	46	104	236
	TE	807	836	1,094	2,737	29	39	57	125
	RB	996	600	1,092	2,688	19	22	21	62
	All	4,810	3,161	5,268	13,239	134	107	182	423
Total		5,988	3,867	6,434	16,289	170	133	220	523

Positional Success Rates vs NFL Average

		NFL Wide				Team Only			
		Left	Middle	Right	Total	Left	Middle	Right	Total
Deep	WR	37%	50%	38%	40%	46%	67%	36%	48%
	TE	44%	49%	43%	45%	50%	60%	50%	52%
	RB	32%	75%	25%	30%				
	All	37%	50%	38%	41%	47%	65%	39%	49%
Short	WR	52%	56%	51%	53%	51%	70%	51%	55%
	TE	50%	61%	51%	54%	48%	69%	63%	62%
	RB	47%	49%	44%	46%	53%	59%	29%	47%
	All	51%	56%	50%	52%	51%	67%	52%	56%
Total		48%	55%	48%	50%	50%	67%	50%	54%